The Relevance of Social Research

Social Research Methods

Qualitative and Quantitative Approaches

SEVENTH EDITION

W. Lawrence Neuman
University of Wisconsin at Whitewater

Allyn & Bacon

Boston   Columbus   Indianapolis   New York   San Francisco   Upper Saddle River
Amsterdam   Cape Town   Dubai   London   Madrid   Milan   Munich   Paris   Montreal   Toronto
Delhi   Mexico City   Sao Paulo   Sydney   Hong Kong   Seoul   Singapore   Taipei   Tokyo

Editor-in-Chief: Dickson Musslewhite
Associate Editor: Lauren Macey
Editorial Assistant: Brittany Diego
Executive Marketing Manager: Kelly May
Marketing Assistant: Janeli Bitor
Production Project Manager: Claudine Bellanton
Manufacturing Buyer: Debbie Rossi
Cover Designer/Administrator: Kristina Mose-Libon
Editorial Production and Composition Service: TexTech International

Library of Congress Cataloging-in-Publication Data

Neuman, William Lawrence.
  Social research methods : qualitative and quantitative approaches / W. Lawrence Neuman.
— 7th ed.
    p. cm.
  Includes bibliographical references and indexes.
  ISBN-13: 978-0-205-61596-4
  ISBN-10: 0-205-61596-1
  1. Sociology—Research—Methodology.   2. Social sciences—Research—Methodology.
I. Title.
  HM571.N48 2011
  301.072—dc22

                                                    2010039467

10   9   8   7   6   5   4   3   2   1   V013   14   13   12   11   10

Allyn & Bacon
is an imprint of

www.pearsonhighered.com

ISBN 10: 0-205-61596-1
ISBN 13: 978-0-205-61596-4

Preface

With the current edition, this text enters its second decade of publication. I continue to update and make minor changes with each edition—changes I trust the text's large, loyal following welcomes. I continue to strive to make this a comprehensive, authoritative introduction to social science research that students new to social research will find highly accessible.

The book is about research methodology more than research methods. *Methods* are the techniques of research design, measurement, data collection, and data analysis. *Methodology* includes methods and more. Its emphasis is to understand the entire research process. Compared with research methods, methodology focuses more on the core principles for conducting quality research and learning to make sound judgments about method. Methodology includes an awareness of the social-political context within which social research is embedded, the place of social research in the broader scientific community and the enterprise of science, and assumptions about social reality and knowledge creation on which social research rests. The purpose of a book on methodology is to move beyond preparing the student to become a research technician and to help him or her develop into a reflective social scientist.

Since its origin two decades ago, this text has been distinctive in several ways. First, I fully embrace both qualitative and quantitative approaches to social research. Both are valuable ways to conduct social scientific studies that can advance knowledge and understanding. Second, I discuss the epistemological concerns that underlie several approaches to social research. By understanding the fundamental assumptions that support the various approaches, I believe students and members of the research community can see how each approach can be a basis for creating significant social scientific knowledge. These often unstated, implicit assumptions also enable us to see why each approach operates as it does and how the diverse approaches can complement one another. Third, I provide numerous examples from the recent research literature to illustrate methodological concepts or techniques. I believe that methodology comes alive in the substance of particular studies. Students can best learn methodology by seeing how active social scientists engaged in the practice of knowledge creation are applying it in specific studies. Lastly, the statistics and quantitative data analysis chapter remains basic and is more conceptual than computational. I believe that students who plan to conduct quantitative studies need to complete coursework devoted to statistics, so this text provides only a foundation on statistical analysis.

In addition to updating examples and incorporating advances in specific techniques or methodological debates, I have made a few other changes since the sixth edition that attempt to improve the clarity of presentation and increase student engagement. I rewrote several chapters, including those on theory and research design. Example studies appear at the beginning of several chapters. I added the example studies to make abstract methodological ideas more concrete and relevant. I also altered the voice in the text. I now speak more of what we, as members of the social scientific research community, do and situate the student-reader as someone who will soon be making methodological decisions and planning/conducting a study.

The textbook includes the following supplements: Instructor's Manual with Test Items, MyTest Test Bank, Lecture Outline PowerPoint Presentation, Student SPSS software (packaged with the text on request at a special price), and MyResearchKit, which offers book-specific learning objectives, chapter summaries, flashcards, and practice tests, as well as video clips and activities to aid student learning and comprehension.

This edition continues my commitment to show students that social research is an exciting, vital process. Real people conduct research studies in the "real world" to advance what we know. Social research is a living, breathing process of discovery and knowledge creation. It is a process that most students can master or at least understand with modest effort and study. Professional researchers have a high level of dedication and commitment, but they are only human and live in a real social, political, and historical world.

As a final note, the text continues to speak to a global audience. As researchers, we need to be aware of how cultural assumptions, beliefs, and values influence social research activities. Because we conduct social research to examine concerns occurring in real human societies, we must be sensitive to how ethnocentric or nationalist pressures within those societies might limit the full potential of social research to advance understanding.

ACKNOWLEDGMENTS

I would like to thank the reviewers of this edition of *Social Research Methods*: Chardie L. Baird, Kansas State University; Samuel L. Gilmore, University of California, Irvine; Bryan Robinson, The Sage Colleges; and Margaret E. Stiffler, North Carolina State University.

PART FOUR
Qualitative Data Collection and Analysis

PART FIVE
Communicating with Others

Contents

PART TWO
Planning and Preparation

PART THREE
Quantitative Data Collection and Analysis

Why Do Research?

> *The sociologist, then, is someone concerned with understanding society in a disciplined way. The nature of this discipline is scientific. This means that what the sociologist finds and says about the social phenomena he studies occurs within a certain rather strictly defined frame of reference.*
> —Peter Berger, *An Invitation to Sociology*, p. 16

I wrote this book to help you learn about how social scientists do research and so you can conduct your own studies. I consider two main issues in this chapter: why you should learn about doing social research and the basics of what social science research is all about. In subsequent chapters, I delve into the various approaches to social research and examine the principles and techniques you use when conducting a study.

Social science research is pervasive, and it affects your daily life as well as that of your family, friends, neighbors, and co-workers. Findings from social science studies appear on broadcast news programs, in magazines and newspapers, and on many Web sites and blogs. They cover dozens of topics and fields: law and public safety, schooling, health care, personal and family relations, political issues, and business activities as well as international and social trends. We use the knowledge and principles of social science research, directly or indirectly, as we engage in relationships with family, friends, and co-workers, participate in community life or public policy, and make daily decisions in business, professional life, and health care. Social research is not just for college classrooms and professors; high

school teachers, parents, business owners, advertisers, managers, administrators, officials, service providers, health care professionals, and others use its findings and principles. They use them to raise children, reduce crime, manage health concerns, sell products or services, digest news events, and so forth. There is little doubt about the importance and centrality of social science research. Despite scattered criticism to the contrary, research is highly relevant for understanding social life generally and to the decisions you make each day.

To see the practical relevance of social research, let us consider a couple raising a three-year-old child. One study (Wrigley and Derby, 2005) found that paid child care is quite safe but also discovered striking differences in fatality rates across various types of care. Center-based care is far safer than care provided in private homes. Another study (Bridges et al., 2007) showed that center-based care significantly raises a child's reading and math scores, but it has a negative effect on socio-behavioral measures (e.g., the child exhibits less cooperation, more aggression). Children who start at ages two to three get the largest benefit rather than younger or older children. Active parental involvement with a child lessens any negative be- havioral consequences from child care. Another study (Love et al., 2003) showed that child care centers vary widely in quality. Quality of care makes a bigger difference than amount of time in care or whether parents or a care center is provid- ing the care. Another study (Sosinsky, Lord, and Zigler, 2007) learned that care center quality was generally higher in nonprofit, nonreligiously affil- iated centers than other types. Based on these find- ings, a couple may decide to look for a specific type of child care center, devote time to checking into the quality of care it offers, and make special ef- forts to encourage their child's social skill devel- opment. The studies are not only relevant for specific parents but also have implications for pub- lic policy and how a community addresses child care issues.

Social science research yields valuable infor- mation and expands our understanding, but it is not 100 percent foolproof. It does not guarantee per- fect results every time or offer "absolute truth." This may be why some people distrust research- based knowledge or why some people, including a few media commentators, even ridicule profes- sional researchers and study results. Despite some derision, in a head-to-head comparison with the al- ternative ways we can learn about the world and make decisions, research readily wins hands-down. This is why professionals, educated people, and responsible leaders consistently turn to the methods, principles, and findings of social research when they want to learn more or make important decisions.

This book considers both the methodology and methods of social science research. The terms may seem to be synonyms, but methodology is broader and envelops methods. *Methodology* means under- standing the entire research process—including its social-organizational context, philosophical as- sumptions, ethical principles, and the political im- pact of new knowledge from the research enterprise. *Methods* refer to the collection of specific tech- niques we use in a study to select cases, measure and observe social life, gather and refine data, ana- lyze data, and report on results. The two are closely linked and interdependent.

Reading and doing social research can be ex- citing: It is a process of discovery in which we learn many new things. Doing social science research re- quires persistence, personal integrity, tolerance for ambiguity, interaction with others, and pride in doing top-quality work. It also requires logical thinking, carefully following rules, and repeating steps over and again. In the research process, we join theories or ideas with facts in a systematic way. We also use our creativity. To conduct a study, we must organize and plan. We need to select research methods appropriate to a specific question. We must always treat the study participants in an ethical or moral way. In addition, we need to communicate to others how we conducted a study and what we learned from it.

In this chapter, we consider some alternatives to social science research and why research is pre- ferred. We next examine how the enterprise of sci- entific research works, including the steps in doing a research study and types of social science studies.

ALTERNATIVES TO SOCIAL SCIENCE RESEARCH

In this section, we look at four commonly used alternatives to social science research that many people rely on to acquire knowledge and make decisions:

- Personal experience and common sense
- Experts and authorities
- Popular and media messages
- Ideological beliefs and values

Knowledge from Personal Experience and Common Sense

If something happens to us, if we personally see it or experience it, we probably accept it as true. Per- sonal experience or "seeing is believing" is a pow- erful type of knowledge. Unfortunately, it can also lead us astray. Something similar to an optical illu- sion or mirage can occur. What appears to be true actually is due to an illusion, yet the power of im- mediacy and direct personal contact is so strong that we easily fall for illusions without even realizing it.

This is why many people insist on believing what they personally experience rather than what they learn by reading a carefully conducted research study that was designed to avoid the errors of personal experience. This is especially true when research studies contradict what personal experience or common sense tell us. Moreover, errors of personal experience reinforce each other. A few people even purposely use the distortions of personal experience to mislead others through propaganda, cons or fraud, magic tricks, political manipulation, and advertising gimmicks.

Entire subfields of research are devoted to uncovering the ways we misjudge, over- or underestimate, and make mistakes. Here is an example: Women tend to stick with skin creams that do not work. Moreover, the less effective a beauty product or treatment, the more likely they will keep using it. These are the findings of a study of 300 women, ages 27 to 65, who were trying to achieve a more youthful appearance by using creams, vitamins, and other beauty treatments. The findings were not what we might expect: The women were most loyal to products and treatments when they didn't work! Among women who felt that the treatments were not working, 27 percent stopped using them. Among women who felt the treatments were successful, 55 percent stopped using them. The researchers think the women keep doing something that did not work because when people don't feel good about themselves, fear is a more powerful motivator than success. Fear about looking older spurred the women to keep trying even when products don't work.[1]

While studies that uncover our tendency to misjudge are fun to read, they point to a general principle: Everyday reasoning and perceptions are imperfect and subject to error. More significantly, we rarely notice or catch such errors right away if at all.

Knowledge from personal experience, common sense "facts," and reasoning might be correct, but they can lead us astray (see Expansion Box 1.1, What We Think We Will Do and What We Actually Do). For example, common sense says that distributing free condoms in high schools will encourage teens to engage in sexual activity or that imposing harsh punishment, such as the death penalty,

What We Think We Will Do and What We Actually Do

Social scientists note a paradox: Most people strongly condemn overt racism, yet acts of blatant racism still occur. To examine this, Kawakami and associates (2009) conducted an experiment. They thought perhaps people inaccurately estimate what they would feel and do if they were to witness racism. To examine this, they asked non-Black students how they would feel and what they thought they would do if a racist act occurred. Most predicted that they would be very upset. However, when the researchers staged a racist act in front of them, most of the students showed little distress. Most said they would avoid a person who made a crude racist comment, but again what people said did not match their actual behavior. Study results suggest that one reason racism continues is that many people who believe they would feel upset or take action actually respond with indifference when an act of racism actually occurs. Apparently, we are not good at predicting how we will act in real situations when they happen.

decreases violent crimes—yet numerous studies suggest that both of these beliefs are false. Most people think an eyewitness account of a crime is ideal, but studies show they are highly inaccurate. Many of us worry about tragic accidents and horrific events, such as a plane crash or a school shooting. However, we tend to worry about the "wrong" things because our estimates of something happening are far from actual probabilities based on careful studies. Likewise, we can be misled by surface appearances. Many people purchased a large, powerful-looking SUV for its safety at a time when crash tests and accident records showed SUVs to be less safe than many meeker looking cars.[2]

Erroneous "common sense" misperceptions have real consequences. Moreover, the media often repeat and spread the misperceptions, schools or businesses make decisions based on them, and lawmakers and politicians advance new laws or policies founded on them. We often make the following five errors in our everyday decisions, but the research process tries to reduce such errors.

- Overgeneralization
- Selective observation
- Premature closure
- Halo effect
- False consensus

1. Overgeneralization occurs when we have some believable evidence and then assume that it applies to many other situations as well. Note the word "over." Generalization can be appropriate but it is limited. We can generalize a small amount of evidence to a broader situation but only if we do so with great care. Unfortunately, many of us tend to generalize far beyond what is acceptable with limited evidence. We often generalize from what we know to unknown areas. For example, over the years, I have personally known five people who are blind. All of them were very outgoing and friendly. Can I conclude that all people who are blind are friendly? Do the five people with whom I had personal experience fully represent all people on the planet who are blind?

2. Selective observation is slightly different than overgeneralization. It occurs when we take special notice of certain people or events and then generalize from them. Most often we focus on particular cases or situations, especially when they fit preconceived ideas. We also tend to seek out evidence that confirms what we already believe. At the same time, most of us tend to overlook the entire range of cases. We often dismiss contradictory information as being an exception we can ignore. For example, I believe people who are overweight are more outgoing and friendly than thin people. My belief comes from stereotypes learned from my parents and media sources. I observe people who are overweight and, without being aware, pay more attention to their smiling, laughing, and so on. I notice thin people more when they are looking serious, distracted, or angry. Without realizing it, I notice people and situations that reinforce my preconceived way of thinking. Studies also document our tendency to "seek out" and distort memories to make them more consistent with what we already think.

3. Premature closure operates with and inforces the first two errors. It occurs when we feel we have the answer and no longer need to listen, seek information, or raise questions. For practical purposes, at some point, we need to stop gathering information and come to a decision. Unfortunately, most of us are a little lazy or get a little sloppy. We gather a small amount of evidence or look at events for a short time and then think we have it figured out. We look for evidence to confirm or reject an idea and stop after getting a small amount of evidence and jump to conclusions.

4. The **halo effect** occurs when we overgeneralize from what we believe to be highly positive or prestigious. We give a halo to, or a positive reputation to, things or people we respect. This halo "rubs off" on other things or people about which we know little. Thus, I pick up a report by a person from a prestigious university, say, Harvard or Cambridge University. I assume that the author is smart and talented, and I expect the report to be excellent. I do not make the same assumption about a report written by someone from Unknown University. I form an opinion in advance, and I do not approach each report on its own merits alone. Perhaps a celebrity or person I trust endorses a product or political candidate about which I know little. I use my positive feelings as a substitute for doing the work of finding out for myself or as a shortcut when making decisions.

Overgeneralization   Statement that goes far beyond what can be justified based on the data or empirical observations that one has.

Selective observation   Process of examination in a way that reinforces preexisting thinking rather than in a neutral and balanced manner.

Premature closure   Act of making a judgment or reaching a decision and ending an investigation before gathering the amount or depth of evidence required by scientific standards.

Halo effect   Occurrence that allows the prior reputation of persons, places, or things to color one's evaluations rather than evaluating all in a neutral, equal manner.

5. False consensus is a psychological effect documented by dozens of studies (Marks and Miller, 1987). It suggests that we are not good at distinguishing between what we personally think and what we think most other people believe. In short, we tend to see the views of most other people as being similar to our own views. This is not a matter of purposely conforming to and copying a crowd perspective. Rather, most of us feel that our own views are "normal" or "ordinary" in comparison with others. While this might be true, we greatly overestimate how much our views match those of other people. In terms of social events and issues, studies suggest that most of us are not very good at judging the thoughts of people around us.

Social research helps address the errors of personal experience. Research standards, rules, and principles are designed to reduce the misjudgment, bias, and distorted thinking that frequently occurs with personal experience.

Knowledge from Experts and Authorities

Most of what we know probably comes from our parents, teachers, and experts as well as from books, film, television, the Internet, and other media. Often we accept something as being true because someone with expertise or in a position of authority says it is so or because it appears in an authoritative, trusted source. This is using authority as a basis of knowledge. In many ways, relying on the wisdom of experts and authorities is a quick, simple, and inexpensive way to learn something. An expert may spend a great amount of time to learn something, and we can benefit from that person's experience and efforts.

Relying on experts has limitations, and it is easy to overestimate someone's expertise. Authorities may speak on fields they know little about; they can be plain wrong. Someone with expertise in one area may extend his or her real authority to an unrelated area. Using the halo effect, an expert on one area may illegitimately act as an authority in a different area. Have you ever seen commercials in which a movie star or football hero tries to convince you to buy a product?

Who decides who is or is not a genuine expert or authority? A person might become a "senior fellow" or "adjunct scholar" in a private "think tank"

> **False consensus** A tendency to project one's way of thinking onto other people. In other words, the person assumes that everyone else thinks like he or she does.

with an impressive name, such as the Center for the Scientific Study of X. Some think tanks are legitimate research centers, but many are fronts for wealthy special-interest groups who want to engage in advocacy politics. No regulations control the titles of think tanks, and anyone can become a "scholar" in the group. Think tanks enable an "expert" to make authoritative statements to the mass media, giving the impression of being neutral and knowledgeable. Such people may lack real expertise and make statements based on opinion or ideology, not on research.[3] Later in this chapter, you will read about how the scientific community operates and how it determines who is a genuine expert.

Even if we locate legitimate experts in a specific field, they may disagree. Perhaps you have heard the dozens of contradictory and confusing research-based recommendations about health and diet. You might ask what is so great about research if there is so much disagreement. This situation happens because much of what fills the mass media using the words "research" or "scientific" does not involve scientific research. Unfortunately, the media often use "research" when technically no real research backs a statement. Nonetheless, scientists or experts do not agree 100 percent of the time. In many areas—the best diet, health practice, public policy, or climate change—there is some disagreement. Later in this chapter, you will read about the principles of science and the operation of the scientific community and see how disagreement arises and is resolved as part of the process of scientific research.

More than finding an expert, it is important for us to learn how to think independently and evaluate research on our own. Always relying on experts and authorities is not consistent with the principles of a free, democratic society. Experts might promote ideas that strengthen their power and position. We lose the ability to decide for ourselves if we follow only the authorities. This is a reason to learn about research and acquire the skills so we can evaluate strong from weak studies.

Knowledge Based on Popular and Media Messages

Beyond relying on common sense, personal experience, and experts, we may try to extend our knowledge by talking to others and picking up what we can from the media. This is a good idea, but it has serious limitations. Talking to others may be helpful, but studies have found that most people are weak with regard to scientific literacy, geographic knowledge, and clear, logical thinking. This is true even in a rich, advanced, and educated country like the United States in the twenty-first century. (See Expansion 1.2, Scientific Literacy Discussion later in this chapter.) Our ability to use advanced technology (an iPhone, geographic positioning system, or car with advanced equipment) does not mean we generally think in a rational, scientific way. A 2006 survey of young men and women ages 18–24 found about half could not locate the states of New York or Ohio on a U.S. map (50% and 43%, respectively) and a majority (63%) could not find Iraq on a map of the Middle East despite nearly constant news coverage since the U.S. invasion in March 2003. Large proportions of the U.S. population believe in phenomena that science rejects, such as UFOs (34%), horoscopes and astrology (31%), ghosts and goblins (51%), witches (34%), or a devil (61%).[4]

Average levels of formal schooling have risen, but many people lack factual knowledge, rely on inaccurate information, or cling to nonlogical thinking. Some people go through schooling but learned little or do not continue to apply the knowledge, skills, or thinking they acquired in their school years later in their daily life or in job decisions. Also, many people "follow the herd," or rely on mass opinion. The mass media often echoes mass opinion without serious evaluation. As you know well, just because most people believe something is true does not make it true. However, many of us just follow "what most other people think" even thought it might be wrong.

Many of us rely on the mass media (i.e., film, television, newspapers, magazines, and Internet sources) for information. Unfortunately, the media tend to jumble together different types of statements—ones that are based on sound research and ones without real backing. In addition, the media can distort social issues. The media tend to perpetuate the cultural myths or create "hype" that a serious social problem exists when it may not. We may hear of a terrible problem in the mass media, but with closer inspection and a little research, we may learn that it was seriously overstated.

Road Rage Example

Americans hear a lot about road rage. *Newsweek* magazine, *Time* magazine, and newspapers in most major cities have carried headlines about it. Leading national political officials have held public hearings on it, and the federal government gives millions of dollars in grants to law enforcement and transportation departments to reduce it. A California psychologist now specializes in this disorder and has appeared on several major television programs to discuss it.

The term "road rage" first appeared in 1988, and by 1997, the print media were carrying more than 4,000 articles per year on it. Despite media attention about "aggressive driving" and "anger behind the wheel," there is no scientific evidence concerning road rage. The term is not precisely defined and can refer to anything from gunshots from cars, use of hand gestures, running bicyclists off the road, tailgating, and even anger over auto repair bills! All of the data on crashes and accidents show declines during the period when road rage reached an epidemic.

What instead happened was that media reports fueled perceptions of road rage. After hearing or reading about road rage and having a label for the behavior, people started to notice rude driving behavior and engaged in selective observation. We will not know for sure until it is properly studied, but the amount of such behavior appears not to have changed. It may turn out that the national epidemic of road rage is a widely held myth stimulated by reports in the mass media.

Holiday Havoc Example

Newspapers and television reports are filled with dire warnings about the many traffic accidents that occur on holidays. Thus, the Fourth of July weekend holiday in the United States is presented as very deadly with an average of 161 people killed each year, yet the holiday period may be no more dangerous than other times and may even be a bit safer! How can this be? After a careful comparison with other weekends and accounting for the extra amount of driving, the holiday's accident rate is not very different. Safety advocates publicize and distort statistical information in the media to encourage people to drive more safely.

Lesson

Road rage and holiday havoc are hardly unique situations; misrepresentation happens with many social issues. "Problem promoters," especially in the broadcast media, highlight dramatic cases or selectively use statistical information to generate attention and agitate the public about a social problem. The media reports are not so much wrong as they are misleading. They are more effective for public persuasion than is giving a carefully documented presentation of the entire picture. If we rely on mass media reports to learn about the social world, major trends, or serious problems, we can easily be misled (Best, 2001; Fumento, 1998; and Wald, 2004).

Studies have documented poverty, crime, and many other concerns shown in film, on television, and in magazines do not accurately represent social reality. The writers who create or "adapt" real life for television shows and movie scripts often distort reality. This is rarely done intentionally; rather, they repeat misinformation they have picked up, and their primary goal is to entertain. For example, about only 5 of 400 films that portray psychiatric treatment do so accurately. Likewise, media reports on the size of the Muslim population in the United States are two to three times more than scientifically based estimates suggest. African Americans were 62 percent of all poor people shown in newsmagazine photos and 65 percent on television news, yet in the true racial mix of poor people, only 29 percent are African Americans. What we see on television or visually in photos strongly shapes our views on social issues. Media distortions mean that if we rely on the media for knowledge of the social world, we will often have inaccurate knowledge.[5]

In addition to informing and entertaining us, the media provide a forum in which competing interests try to win over public support. Those for or against a cause will mount public relations campaigns and use the media to shape public thinking. As mentioned earlier, advocacy think tanks sometimes have false "experts" to discuss topics in the media. Also, in recent years, the number of video news releases (VNR), also called "fake TV news," has grown dramatically. A VNR is the result of a major company or advocacy group that pays to create sophisticated video that looks just like an independently produced news report. In a VNR, an actor or actress plays an independent reporter. The "reporter" presents what appears to be neutral information or news. In reality, it is a public relations or a promotional statement. Most TV stations show the VNRs without informing viewers about the source. A news report on television might be a type of sophisticated propaganda designed to influence our views on a topic or product. We need to be careful before accepting the mass media as an authority.[6]

Many earnest science writers and serious journalists try to deliver accurate research-based information. However, they can be overshadowed by the volume and prominence of other media messages. As you will see later in this chapter, the mass media are not the best sources to learn about research studies. Instead, rely on the scientific community's communication system that is available at no cost to anyone with some knowledge of research and who devotes the time to explore it.

Knowledge Subordinated to Ideological Beliefs and Values

Despite the strength and availability of social science research, some managers and decision makers consciously reject it and instead promote and defend actions based on their political, religious, or ideological beliefs. For example, in 2001, the U.S. federal government began to fund "faith-based" social programs. Studies questioned the effectiveness of such programs, yet they replaced programs that were supported by research. At the same time, knowledgeable scientists serving in government

TABLE 1.1   Alternative Explanations to Social Research

EXAMPLE ISSUE: WOMEN ARE MORE LIKELY THAN MEN TO DO LAUNDRY.

Personal experience and common sense: In my experience, men just are not as concerned about clothing or appearance as much as women are, so it makes sense that women do the laundry. When my friends and I were growing up, my mother and their mothers did the laundry, and female friends did it for their boyfriends but never did the men do it.

Experts and authority: Experts say that as children, females are taught to make, select, mend, and clean clothing as part of a female focus on physical appearance and on caring for children or others in a family. Women do the laundry based on their childhood preparation.

Popular and media messages: Movies and television commercials show women often doing laundry and enjoying it, but men hate it and mess it up. So, women must be doing laundry because they enjoy it and are skilled at it. It is what we see everywhere and what everyone says.

Ideological beliefs: The proper, natural place division of labor is for women to take charge of the home, caring for children and overseeing household duties, including cooking, cleaning, and doing the laundry.

agencies were replaced by political appointees, persons committed to certain ideologies. Respected research findings that contradicted ideological views were removed from official health or environmental public information.[7]

At one time, leading U.S. government officials promoted antiscience beliefs. One top aide to President George W. Bush claimed to reject "the reality-based community," defined as people who "believe that solutions emerge from your judicious study of discernible reality" (Suskind, 2004). You will look at the issue of ideology again in Chapter 3 when you examine social theory.

For an example of how the alternatives would explain an aspect of social life, see Table 1.1.

WHAT RESEARCH INVOLVES: A SCIENTIFIC APPROACH

Social science research is central in a "reality-based community." It relies on people carefully studying experiences, events, and facts in social reality. While social research helps us answer questions about the social world, it also raises new questions and may change how we look at the world as well. It relies on the process and evidence of science as such, and it can differ from casual observation, common sense reasoning, and other ways to evaluate evidence, including pure logical-rational reasoning (mathematical or

philosophical proof) or legal-judicial procedure. We next examine *science* in the context of doing social science research.

Science

When most people hear the word "science," the first image that comes to mind is likely to be a lab with test tubes, electronic equipment and microscopes, exotic space ships, and people in white lab coats. These outward trappings are a part of science. The physical and biological sciences—biology, chemistry, physics, and zoology—deal with the physical and material world (e.g., rocks, plants, chemical compounds, stars, muscles, blood, electricity). These natural sciences are at the forefront of new technology and receive a great deal of publicity. Most people first think of them when they hear the word "science."

The social-cultural sciences (such as anthropology, economics, human geography, psychology, political science, and sociology) involve the study of human social-cultural life: beliefs, behaviors, relationships, interactions, institutions, and so forth. Just as we apply knowledge from the physical and biological sciences in related, more pragmatic fields (such as agriculture, aviation, engineering, medicine, and pharmacology), we apply social science knowledge to practical concerns in related applied areas (such as counseling, criminal justice, education, management, marketing, public administration, public health, social work, and urban planning).

Some people call social sciences "soft sciences." This is not because the fields lack rigor but because their subject matter—human social life—is highly fluid, formidable to observe, and difficult to measure precisely. The subject matter of a science (e.g., human attitudes, protoplasm, or galaxies) shapes the techniques and instruments (e.g., surveys, microscopes, or telescopes) it uses. We consider the relationship between the physical and social sciences in Chapter 4.

Science is a human invention. Today's science emerged out of a major shift in thinking nearly 400 years ago. It began with the Age of Reason or Enlightenment period in western European history (1600s–1700s). The Enlightenment Era ushered in new thinking that included logical reasoning, careful observations of the material world, a belief in human progress, and a questioning of traditional religious and political doctrines. It built on past knowledge and started by studying the natural world. Later it spread to the study of the social world. A dramatic societal transformation, the Industrial Revolution, spread scientific thinking. The advancement of science and related applied fields did not just happen on its own—it was punctuated by the triumphs and struggles of individual researchers. It was also influenced by significant social events, such as war, economic depression, government policies, and shifts in public support.

Before scientific reasoning grew and became widespread, people relied on nonscientific methods. These included the alternatives discussed previously as well as other methods less accepted today (e.g., oracles, mysticism, magic, astrology, and spirits). Such systems continue to exist, but science is now generally accepted. We still use nonscientific methods to study topics defined as outside the scope of science (e.g., religion, art, literary forms, and philosophy).

Science refers to both a system for producing knowledge and the knowledge that results from that system. Science evolved over centuries and continues to slowly evolve. It combines assumptions about the world; accumulated understandings; an orientation toward knowledge; and many specific procedures, techniques, and instruments. The system of science is most tangible and visible as a social institution, the scientific community (see discussion of it later in this section).

The knowledge that science yields is organized into theories and grounded in empirical data. Let us examine three key terms: *theory, data,* and *empirical.* Many people confuse theory with opinion, unfounded belief, or wild guess. "Whereas a scientist understands theory to be a well-grounded opinion . . . the general public understands it as 'just a theory,' no more valid than any other opinion on the matter" (Yankelovich, 2003:8). For now, we can define **social theory** as a coherent system of logically consistent and interconnected ideas used to condense and organize knowledge. You will read about types of social theory in Chapter 3. You can think of theory as a map that helps us better visualize the complexity in the world, see connections, and explain why things happen. We use data to determine whether a theory is true and we should retain it or is false and needs adjustments or can be discarded. **Data** are the forms of empirical evidence or information carefully collected according to the rules or procedures of science. **Empirical** refers to evidence or observations grounded in human sensory experience: touch, sight, hearing, smell, and taste. Scientific researchers cannot use their senses to observe directly some aspects of the world (e.g., intelligence, attitudes, opinions, emotions, power, authority, quarks, black holes of space, force fields, gravity). However, they have created specialized instruments

Social theory   A system of interconnected ideas that condenses and organizes the knowledge about the social world and explains how it works.

Data   Numerical (quantitative) and non-numerical (qualitative) information and evidence that have been carefully gathered according to rules or established procedures.

Empirical   Description of what we can observe and experience directly through human senses (e.g., touch, sight, hearing, smell, taste) or indirectly using techniques that extend the senses.

and techniques to observe and measure such aspects indirectly.

Data or empirical observations can be *quantitative* (i.e., expressed precisely as numbers) or *qualitative* (i.e., expressed as words, images, or objects). Later in this book, you will see how we can measure aspects of the social world to produce quantitative or qualitative data.

Pseudoscience, Junk Science, and "Real" Science

Across the centuries, science achieved broad respect and acceptance around the globe; however, many people still lack scientific literacy (See Expansion Box 1.2, Scientific Literacy) or confuse real science with **pseudoscience**. The prefix *pseudo* is Greek for false or counterfeit. We face a barrage of pseudoscience through television, magazines, film, newspapers, highly advertised special seminars or workshops, and the like. Some individuals weave the outward trappings of science (e.g., technical jargon, fancy-looking machines, complex formulas and statistics, and white lab coats) with a few scientific facts and myths, fantasy, or hopes to claim a "miracle cure," "new wonder treatment," "revolutionary learning program," "evidence of alien visitors," or "new age spiritual energy." Experts in pseudoscience might hold an advanced academic degree, but often it is in unrelated academic fields or from a very weak, marginal school.

In addition to experts, magazines or books offer popularized or "pop" social science. Some of these are accurate popularizations written by legitimate social researchers to communicate to a wide public audience. Others look like legitimate social science

to a nonspecialist but actually present a distorted picture or a misuse of social science. These authors write the books to promote a particular political or social position in the guise of social science, but they do not meet the standards of scientific community. For example, the famous Hite Report on female sexuality was a seriously flawed study conducted by a nonscientist who seriously distorted actual social relations. Despite its weaknesses, the book became a best seller that was widely discussed on television talk shows and in newspapers. The same is true of the book *The Bell Curve* that made claims of African American intellectual inferiority.[8] Unfortunately, books advertised on television or radio, cited in newspaper articles, or sold at a local bookstore can be filled with opinion, personal beliefs, or seriously flawed research. It is easy for an unwary consumer to be misled and confuse such inaccurate or highly opinionated books with legitimate social science.

Perhaps you have heard the term **junk science**. Public relations firms created this term in the 1980s as a strategy to denigrate actual scientific evidence. They used the term to attack research findings that were presented in courts to document injury or abuses caused by powerful, large corporations. In press releases and public statements, such firms manipulated language to contrast *junk* with *sound* science (i.e., studies that supported their own position). *Sound* and *junk* are rhetorical and imprecise terms. More important, the quality, methodology, or precision of the research for each may not differ in quality. Publicists applied the term "junk science" to any research study, no matter how accurate or rigorous, that they opposed and "sound science" to any research study, no matter how flawed, that they used to challenge opponents. For example, the tobacco industry used junk science as a tactic to criticize research on secondhand smoke and spent millions of dollars to deny the harmful health effects of smoking.[9] The goal was to confuse juries and the public and to create an impression that the scientists lacked consistent research evidence. In contrast to pseudo- or junk science, authentic science comes from the outlook, operations, and products of the scientific community (see the next section).

Pseudoscience A body of ideas or information clothed in the jargon and outward appearance of science that seeks to win acceptance but that was not created with the systematic rigor or standards required of the scientific method.

Junk science A public relations term used to criticize scientific research even if it is conducted properly that produces findings that an advocacy group opposes.

EXPANSION BOX **1.2**

Scientific Literacy

For more than 50 years, leading educators, business leaders, and policy makers stressed the need for quantitative and scientific literacy to perform professional work and make good everyday decisions in a complex world. *Quantitative literacy, or numeracy,* is the ability to reason with numbers and other mathematical concepts. A person with quantitative literacy can think in quantitative-spatial terms and apply such thinking to solve problems. They understand how data are gathered by counting and measuring and presented in graphs, diagrams, charts, and tables. A lack of quantitative literacy is called **innumeracy** (Paulson, 1990). **Scientific literacy** is the capacity to understand scientific knowledge; apply scientific concepts, principles, and theories; use scientific processes to solve problems and make decisions; and interact in a way that reflects core scientific values (Laugksch, 2000:76). The Programme for International Student Assessment (PISA) of the Organisation for Economic Co-operation and Development (OECD) carries out international studies of how much students know about science and defines scientific literacy as the following (PISA, 2006:23):

- Scientific knowledge and use of that knowledge to identify questions, acquire new knowledge, explain scientific phenomena, and draw evidence-based conclusions about science-related issues
- Understanding of the characteristic features of science as a form of human knowledge and enquiry
- Awareness of how science and technology shape our material, intellectual, and cultural environments
- Willingness as a reflective citizen to engage in science-related issues and with the ideas of science

People who lack quantitative and scientific literacy easily accept pseudoscience and make judgment errors. Innumeracy also leads journalists to report inaccurate news and to readers/viewers lacking sufficient skepticism to evaluate the reports. Innumerate people make poor financial investment decisions and often lose money on gambling and related activities because they do not understand basic math concepts. People who lack these types of literacy are poor at assessing risk. Their prospects for a career as a technical-managerial professional, the fast growing, high-income part of the labor market, are poor.

You may think that those people are not like you, in a technologically advanced, ultra-modern society.

However, people can use modern technology (computers, cell phones, iPods, airplanes, and the like) and retain prescientific thinking or rely on magic or supernatural beliefs to explain events make decisions. An ability to use advanced technology does not mean a person thinks in a rational, scientific way.

Only 25–28 percent of American adults qualify as scientifically literate. Overall, adults in other advanced countries are at about the same general scientific literacy. However, international math and science tests for high school students regularly show that United States ranks about twentieth among other nations. A cross-national study of the United States and nine European nations in 2002–2003 confirmed that American adults are near the bottom in endorsing the theory of evolution compared to other all other advanced nations: only 32 percent in 2009. A June 2007 *USA Today*/Gallup Poll found that 37 percent of Americans rejected the scientific theory of evolution and 56 percent favored a religious explanation instead. A March 2007 poll found that 39 percent said something completely opposite from the opinion of the world scientific community: that scientific evidence does not support evolution. A Pew Research Center for the People poll in 2006 found more than one-half of Americans said schools should teach religious views on scientific issues in public schools and that it should be nationally mandated. A Gallup Poll in 2006 found that over one-half believed that humans did not evolve (Polling Report, 2007). Scientists generally agree on global warming, and 84 percent say the earth is getting warmer because of human activity such as burning fossil fuels, but only 49 percent of the public agrees. Well over 90 percent of scientists favor the use of animals in research and stem cell research compared with slightly

Innumeracy The lack of quantitative literacy; not having an ability to reason with numbers and other mathematical concepts.

Scientific literacy The capacity to understand and apply scientific knowledge, concepts, principles, and theories to solve problems and make decisions based on scientific reasoning and to interact in a way that reflects the core values of the scientific community.

(continued)

over half of the public (Pew Research Center for the People and the Press, 2009).

While evolution has been extremely politicized in the United States with some elected officials attempting to impose religious beliefs as science in public schools, Americans also do poorly in terms of general scientific-quantitative thinking and other scientific concepts. Despite getting X-rays, only about 10 percent of the U.S. public knows what radiation is and about 20 percent think the sun revolves around the earth—an idea science abandoned in the seventeenth century ("Scientific Savvy? In U.S., Not Much," Dean, *New York Times,* August 30, 2005). You may think college students know better. Studies found that many college students used illogical "magic" rather than science-based thinking. Large numbers of college students accepted voodoo magical power as a cause of someone becoming ill, and college sports fans believed their thoughts could influence the outcome of a basketball game as they watched it on television (Pronin, Wegner, McCarthy, and Rodriguez, 2006).

The Scientific Community

The scientific community brings science to life; it sustains the assumptions, attitudes, and techniques of science. The **scientific community** is a social institution of people, organizations, and roles as well as a set of norms, behaviors, and attitudes that all operate together. It is not a geographic community existing in one physical location nor does everyone know everyone else within it, although its members communicate and interact with one another frequently. Rather, it is a loose collection of professionals who share training, ethical principles, values, techniques, and career paths.[10]

The community is organized like a series of concentric circles. Its rings or layers are based on the productivity and engagement of researchers. At the core are a small number of highly productive, very creative, and intense scientific leaders. They slowly move into and out of the core over time based on career stage and contributions to knowledge. At the fringe or outer ring are millions of practitioners, clinicians, and technicians. They regularly use and apply the knowledge, principles, and techniques first developed and refined by those within the core. Professionals who toil on the outer rings develop a level of expertise in and regularly use various scientific research principles and techniques; however,

Scientific community A collection of people who share a system of attitudes, beliefs, and rules that sustains the production and advance of scientific knowledge.

their knowledge of science may not be as deep as those in the middle or core of the scientific community. Also, those on the outer rings are usually less engaged in advancing the overall enterprise of science (i.e., to generate significant new knowledge). Nonetheless, everyone who uses scientific methods and results of science, whether at the core, middle layer, or outer fringe, can benefit from an understanding of how the scientific community operates and its key principles.

The boundaries and membership of the scientific community are fuzzy and defined loosely. There is no membership card or master roster. In some respects, a doctorate of philosophy (Ph.D.) degree in a scientific field is an informal "membership ticket." The Ph.D. is an advanced graduate degree beyond the master's degree that prepares people to conduct independent research. A few members of the scientific community lack a Ph.D. and many people who earn Ph.D.s enter occupations in which they do not conduct research studies. They focus exclusively on teaching, administration, consulting, clinical practice, advising, or sharing knowledge with the wider public. In fact, about one-half of the people who receive scientific Ph.D.s do not follow careers as active researchers.

The core of the scientific community is made up of researchers who conduct studies on a full-time or regular basis, usually with the help of assistants, many of whom are graduate students. Working as a research assistant, more or less as an apprentice, is the best way to learn the details of scientific research. Most core members work at colleges, universities, or research institutes. Some work for the government, nonprofit organizations, or private industry in organizations such as the Bureau of Labor Statistics, the National Opinion Research Center, and the Rand Corporation. The majority are at approximately 200 major research universities or institutes in about a dozen advanced industrialized countries. The scientific community is scattered geographically, but its members usually work together in small clusters and communicate with one another regularly. The community is widely accepting, and anyone in it can contribute to it. A key principle is to share one's research findings and techniques (i.e., new knowledge) with others in the community. Over time, the community develops a consensus about the significance or worth of the new knowledge based on an unbiased evaluation of it. The process of producing and evaluating new knowledge is highly dynamic with new knowledge being generated on nearly a daily basis.

We do not really know the exact size of the scientific community. As of 2006, roughly 3 percent of the total U.S. workforce was employed in a science or engineering field (U.S. Census, 2008: Table 790). The basic unit in the larger scientific community is an academic field or discipline (e.g., sociology, biology, psychology). Academic fields overlap somewhat, but this gives us a better idea of size. The United States has about 11,000 anthropologists, 16,000 sociologists, and 15,000 political scientists, most with doctoral degrees. These are small numbers compared to practitioners in related technical-professional areas: about 180,000 architects, 950,000 lawyers, and 820,000 medical doctors. Each year, about 600 people receive a Ph.D. in sociology, 15,000 receive medical degrees, and 38,000 receive law degrees.

Recall that only about one-half of people who earn an advanced degree in a scientific field become lifelong, active researchers. During a career, an active researcher may complete only two to ten studies. A small handful of researchers is highly productive and conducts numerous studies, particularly highly influential and widely read ones. At any one time, perhaps one hundred researchers are actively conducting studies on a specific topic within a discipline (e.g., study of divorce or of the death penalty) around the world.[11] New knowledge from their studies could influence the lives of

millions of people around the globe for generations to come. This knowledge creation process makes being an active participant in the scientific community or the consumer of new research findings both personally rewarding and exciting.

The Scientific Community's Norms and Values

Social norms regulate behavior in all human communities. During their many years of schooling and regular interactions with one another, researchers learn and internalize professional norms and values. The norms and values are mutually reinforcing and contribute to the unique role of a social scientist. Professional norms express ideals of proper conduct, yet ideals do not always work perfectly in practice. Researchers are real human beings with prejudices, egos, ambitions, and personal lives. Such factors may influence a few researchers to violate the community's norms.[12]

The scientific community does not operate in a vacuum isolated from the "real world." It is affected by social, political, and economic forces (see Chapters 3 and 16 for a discussion of these issues). Nonetheless, the norms and values teach us how the scientific community and the larger research enterprise operate. They also provide a guide for the proper way to conduct a research study and provide the principles of good research practice.

The five basic **norms of the scientific community** (see Summary Review Box 1.1, Norms of the Scientific Community on page 14) differ from those in other social institutions (e.g., business, government, law) and tend to set professional researchers apart. For example, consistent with the norm of *universalism,* scientists tend to admire a brilliant, creative researcher even if the person has strange personal habits or a disheveled appearance. Scientists may argue intensely with one another and "tear apart" a carefully prepared research report as part of the norm of *organized skepticism.* Scientists are usually very

---

Norms of the scientific community   Informal rules, principles, and values that govern the way scientists conduct their research.

SUMMARY REVIEW BOX **1.1**

Norms of the Scientific Community

1. **Universalism.** Regardless of who conducts research (e.g., old or young, male or female) and of where it was conducted (e.g., United States, France, Harvard, or Unknown University), the research is to be judged only on the basis of scientific merit.
2. **Organized skepticism.** Scientists should not accept new ideas or evidence in a carefree, uncritical manner. They should challenge and question all evidence and subject each study to intense scrutiny. The purpose of their criticism is not to attack the individual but to ensure that the methods used in research can stand up to close, careful examination.
3. **Disinterestedness.** Scientists must be neutral, impartial, receptive, and open to unexpected observations and new ideas. They should not be rigidly wedded to a particular idea or point of view. They should accept, even look for, evidence that runs against their positions and should honestly accept all findings based on high-quality research.
4. **Communalism.** Scientific knowledge must be shared with others; it belongs to everyone. Creating scientific knowledge is a public act, and the findings are public property, available for all to use. The way in which the research is conducted must be described in detail. New knowledge is not formally accepted until other researchers have reviewed it and it has been made publicly available in a special form and style.
5. **Honesty.** This is a general cultural norm, but it is especially strong in scientific research. Scientists demand honesty in all research; dishonesty or cheating in scientific research is a major taboo.

---

open and willing to listen to new ideas, no matter how odd they might appear at first. Following *disinterestedness,* scientists tend to be somewhat detached. They see study results, including those from their own research, as being tentative and subject to external evaluation and criticism. They want other social scientists to read and react to their research. A deep belief in openness has led many social scientists to oppose all forms of censorship. This is consistent with the norm of *communalism* or sharing new knowledge without personal ownership, which is like adding an ingredient into a shared soup that we all

eat together. However, this does not always work, especially when communalism conflicts with the profit motive. For example, the publication of research findings by scientists in the tobacco, pharmaceutical, and computer chip industries often were suppressed or seriously delayed by corporate officials for whom the profit motive overrode the scientific norm of commumalism.[13] Scientists expect strict *honesty* in the conduct and reporting of research. They become morally outraged if anyone cheats in research.

Scientific Method, Attitude, or Orientation

You have probably heard of the scientific method, and you may be wondering how it fits into this discussion. The scientific method is not one thing; it is a collection of ideas, rules, techniques, and approaches used by the scientific community. It grows out of a consensus formed within the community. It is important to grasp the orientation or attitude of science instead of a "scientific method." The scientific community values craftsmanship, pride in creativity, high-quality standards, and plain hard work. As Grinnell (1987:125) stated:

> Most people learn about the "scientific method" rather than about the scientific attitude. While the "scientific method" is an ideal construct, the scientific attitude is the way people have of looking at the world. Doing science includes many methods; what makes them scientific is their acceptance by the scientific collective.

The scientific orientation tends simultaneously to be precise and logical, adopt a long-term view, be flexible and open ended, and be willing to share information widely (see Yankelovich, 2003). By contrast, nonscientific thinking is impatient with pursuing great accuracy or rigor, wants definite immediate answers to particular issues that are current now, and tends to be rather possessive and apprehensive about freely sharing everything.

Journal Articles in Science

Perhaps you have seen an article from an academic or scholarly journal. When the scientific community creates new knowledge, the new information appears in scholarly journals or academic books (called *research monographs*). You can read more about scholarly journals in Chapter 5. Most new research findings often first appear as **scholarly journal articles.** These articles are the way that scientists formally communicate with one another and disseminate the research results. The articles are also part of the much discussed "explosion of knowledge." An academic discipline or field may have 50–300 such journals. Each may publish an issue every one or two months, with five to twenty-five articles in each issue. For example, a leader among the sociology journals, the *American Sociological Review,* publishes about 65 articles each year. The scholarly journal article is critical to the research process and the scientific community, but it is not always well understood.[14]

Let us consider what happens once a social scientist completes a research study. First, the scientist writes a description of the study and the results as a research report in a special format. Often he or she gives a 20-minute oral presentation of the report at the meeting of a professional association, such as the American Sociological Association or Society for the Study of Social Problems. He or she gives an oral summary of the research to dozens of social scientists and students and answers questions from the audience. He or she may send a copy of the report to a few other researchers for comments and suggestions. Finally, the researcher sends copies to the editor of a scholarly journal, such as the *Social Forces* or the *Social Science Quarterly.* Each editor, a respected researcher who has been chosen by other scientists to oversee the journal, removes the title page, which is the only place the author's name appears and then sends the report to several referees for a **blind review.** The referees are social scientists who have conducted research in the same topic area. The review is called "blind" because the referees do not know who conducted the research and the author does not know who the referees are. This reinforces the norm of universalism because referees judge the study on its merits alone. They evaluate the research based on its clarity, adherence to high standards of research methodology, and original contribution to knowledge. The referees return their evaluations to the editor, who decides to reject the

Scholarly journal article An article in a specialized publication that has members of the scientific community as its primary audience; a means to disseminate new ideas and findings within the scientific community.

Blind review A process of judging the merits of a research report in which the peer researchers do not know the identity of the researcher, and the researcher does not know the identity of the evaluators in advance.

report, ask the author for revisions, or accept it for publication.

Almost all academic fields use peer referees for publication, but not all use a blind review process. Fields such as sociology, psychology, and political science use blind reviews for almost all scholarly journals, often having three or more referees. By contrast, fields such as biology, history, and economics use a mix of review processes; sometimes referees know the author's identity and only one or two review the study. Blind reviews with many referees slow the process and lower acceptance rates.[15] The blind review is a very cautious way to ensure quality control. Its purpose is to advance the norm of organized skepticism and universalism in the scientific community.

Some scholarly journals are widely read and highly respected and receive many more reports than they can publish. For example, major social science journals, such as *American Economic Review, American Sociological Review, American Political Science Review,* and *Social Problems,* accept only 10 to 15 percent of submitted manuscripts. Even less esteemed journals regularly reject half of their submissions. Publication represents tentative acceptance by the scientific community. Publishing a book involves a somewhat different review process that also includes cost and sales considerations, but the acceptance rate is often lower than for journals.[16]

Unlike popular magazines that you see at newsstands that pay authors for their writing, scholarly journals do not pay authors for publishing. In fact, to have their manuscript considered, an author often is required to pay a small fee to help defray administrative costs. Social scientists want to make their research available to informed peers (i.e., other scientists and researchers) through scholarly journals. Likewise, referees are not paid for reviewing papers. They accept the work as a responsibility of membership in the scientific community. Members of the scientific community impart great respect to researchers who are able to publish many articles in the foremost scholarly journals. The articles confirm that they are highly skilled and leaders in advancing the primary goal of the scientific community: to contribute to the accumulation of scientific knowledge.

Publication of research is the primary way a social scientist gains respect from peers, achieves honor within the scientific community, and builds a reputation as an accomplished researcher. More respect from peers (i.e., knowledgeable social scientists) enables a scientist to move toward the center of the scientific community. Publications and the resulting respect from peers also help a social scientist obtain grant money for further research, fellowships, a following of top students, improved working conditions, lucrative jobs offers, and salary increases.[17]

Even if you never publish a scholarly journal article, you will likely read some of them. They are a vital part of the system of scientific research. Most new scientific knowledge first appears in scholarly journals. Active social scientists and college teachers regularly read the journals to learn about new knowledge being produced and the research methods used.

Science as a Transformative Process

In the research process, social scientists apply various scientific methods to transform ideas, hunches, and questions, sometimes called *hypotheses,* into new knowledge (we will discuss hypotheses in Chapter 5). Thus, the social scientific research process essentially transforms our ideas, theories, guesses, or questions into a "finished product" with real value: new knowledge. The new knowledge can improve our understanding of the social world and its operation. It might be used to help solve problems or to expand future knowledge and understanding.

Many newcomers to social research feel overwhelmed and that doing a study is beyond them. Doing so requires analytic reasoning, complex technical skills, intensive concentration, and a significant time commitment. Yet with time, practice, and education, most college students find they can master the fundamentals of doing a research study. Learning to do social research is no different from learning many other activities. You want to begin small and simple, practice over and again, and learn from your experiences and missteps. Gradually, you will see improvements and be able advance to bigger and more complex endeavors. In addition to assimilating a scientific attitude, you will need to learn how and when to apply specific research techniques. After studying this book, you should grasp both the method and methodology of social science research and be able to conduct research studies.

VARIETIES OF SOCIAL RESEARCH

You may think social scientific research means conducting a survey or an experiment and perhaps using advanced statistics with charts, tables, and graphs. Or you may think it involves carefully observing people as they carry out their everyday affairs in some natural setting such as a café, family reunion, or classroom. Both are partially true. Some social scientific research involves quantitative data, (i.e., data in the form of numbers), but other research uses qualitative data (i.e., non-numerical) without statistics.

After the first several chapters of this text, you will see that we examine both quantitative and qualitative data and associated approaches to conducting social science research. Both approaches use multiple research techniques (e.g., survey, interview, ethnography) to gather and analyze empirical data. Despite some real differences between quantitative and qualitative research, they overlap a great deal. Unfortunately, advocates of one approach do not always understand or appreciate the other approach. Some social scientists treat the differences in the approaches as being at war with one another. Levine (1993:xii) called the quantitative approach "real social science" and claimed it "won the battle" against qualitative studies. On the other hand, Denzin and Lincoln (2005:ix) argued that "the extent to

TABLE 1.2   Quantitative versus Qualitative Approaches

QUANTITATIVE APPROACH	QUALITATIVE APPROACH
Measure objective facts	Construct social reality, cultural meaning
Focus on variables	Focus on interactive processes, events
Reliability the key factor	Authenticity the key factor
Value free	Values present and explicit
Separate theory and data	Theory and data fused
Independent of context	Situationally constrained
Many cases, subjects	Few cases, subjects
Statistical analysis	Thematic analysis
Researcher detached	Researcher involved

Sources: Crewsell (1994), Denzin and Lincoln (2003a), Guba and Lincoln (1994), Marvasti (2004), Mostyn (1985), and Tashakkori and Teddlie (1998).

which a qualitative revolution is taking over the social sciences and related professional fields is nothing short of amazing."

Both approaches share core scientific principles, but they also differ in significant ways (see Table 1.2). Each approach has its strengths and limitations. There are topics or issues where it excel, and classic studies that provide remarkable insights into social life. Social scientists who do quantitative or qualitative research try to avoid both the misjudgments and errors discussed earlier. All social scientists gather data systematically, make careful comparisons, and use critical thinking. By understanding both approaches, you can best understand the full range of social scientific research and use them in complementary ways.

Ragin (1994a:92) explained how the approaches complement each other as data condensers or enhancers:

> *The key features common to all qualitative methods can be seen when they are contrasted with quantitative methods. Most quantitative data techniques are data condensers. They condense data in order to see the big picture. . . . Qualitative methods, by contrast, are best understood as data enhancers. When data are enhanced, it is possible to see key aspects of cases more clearly.*

The ideal is to conduct a multimethod study that draws on the strengths of both the quantitative

and qualitative approaches, but this rarely happens for several reasons. Mixing approaches is more time consuming. Few researchers have expertise in more than one approach. Also, each approach uses a distinct logic for guiding the research process, and blending the distinct logics in one study adds significant complexity.

STEPS IN THE RESEARCH PROCESS

The Steps

To conduct a study, we follow a sequence of steps; however, the exact sequence and specific steps vary according to whether we follow a quantitative or qualitative approach and the type of social research study we are conducting (Chapters 2 and 4 discuss types of research). Later you will see that the steps outlined here may be somewhat simplified and idealized from the actual process, but they are still a useful starting point.

Quantitative Approach to Social Research

1. *Select a topic.* This may be a general area of study or an issue of professional or personal interest. Topics are broad, such as the effects of divorce, reasons for delinquency, impact of homelessness, or how elites use the media.

2. *Focus the question.* A topic is too broad for actually conducting a study. This makes the next step crucial: We must narrow the topic to focus on a specific research question that a study can address. Often this requires reviewing the research literature (discussed in Chapter 5) and developing hypotheses (discussed in Chapter 6) that often come from social theory (discussed in Chapter 3). For example, a broad topic—reasons for delinquency—becomes the focused research question: Are teenage East Asian immigrant males with strong ties to their home culture and who have not assimilated into the new society more likely to engage in delinquent acts than those with weaker home culture ties and who have assimilated? Notice how the initial broad topic, reasons for delinquency, becomes focused. We focus on a specific reason for delinquency (i.e., degree of assimilation) and look at a specific group of people (i.e., teenaged immigrant males from East Asia).

3. *Design the study.* Once we settle on a research question, we need to design the study (discussed in Chapters 6–11). Designing a study requires making many decisions about the type of case or sample to select, how to measure relevant factors, and what research technique (e.g., questionnaire, experiment) to employ. At this stage as well, decision making is informed by theory.

4. *Collect data.* After we design a study in detail, we must carefully record and verify information typically in the form of numbers. Next we must transfer numerical data into a computer-readable format if it is not already in that format.

5. *Analyze the data.* This step usually requires the use of computer software to manipulate the numerical data to create many charts, tables, graphs, and statistical measures (see Chapter 12). These computer-generated documents provide a condensed picture of the data.

6. *Interpret the data.* After we produce charts, tables, and statistics, we must determine what they mean. We examine the analyzed data, use knowledge of the research topic, and draw on theory to answer our research question. We

consider alternative interpretations of the data, compare our results with those of past studies, and draw out wider implications of what we have learned.

7. *Inform others.* At this stage, we write a report about the study in a specific format (described in Chapter 16) and present a description of both the study and its results (see Figure 1.1).

We next consider three examples of the quantitative approach to social research. Each is a type of quantitative research that will be the focus of a chapter later in this book: the experiment (Chapter 9), sample survey (Chapter 10), and existing statistics (Chapter 11).

Authors and title of the study: Lowery and colleagues (2007) "Long-Term Effects of Subliminal Priming on Academic Performance"

1. *Select a topic.* Priming and academic performance

2. *Focus the question.* Do undergraduate college students who are "primed" subliminally with intelligence-related words improve their performance on a test? *Subliminally* means to present something in a way so that the receiver is not consciously aware of it. *Priming* occurs when a word, image, or information alerts, prepares or "sets up" a person for a subsquent behavior.

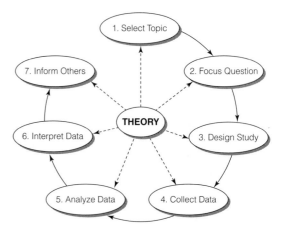

FIGURE 1.1   Steps in the Quantitative Research Process

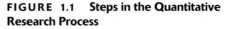

3. *Design the study.* The authors conducted two similar experiments. The first was with seventy students in a beginning undergraduate statistics class. The second was with seventy-eight students in an introduction to social psychology class. In both experiments, the authors showed students words on different sides of a computer screen. They told students that the study was about their ability to locate the words (this was not true). One random half of students saw words related to intelligence (e.g., sharp, bright, genius, educated). The other random half saw unrelated words. Students in both experiments took a practice exam. A few days later, they took the exam in their course.

4. *Collect the data.* Data for this study were test results for both the practice and actual exam in both the statistics and introduction to social psychology classes.

5. *Analyze the data.* The authors looked at various tables and conducted statistical tests.

6. *Interpret the data.* The results showed that the students in both classes who had been exposed or "primed" with intelligence-related words scored much higher on both tests.

7. *Inform others.* A description of the study with its results appeared in the scholarly journal *Basic and Applied Social Psychology*.

How does theory fit in? The authors retested a theory of subliminal priming. They looked at whether effects can continue for several days after a priming event.

Authors and title of the study: Penny Edgell and Eric Tranby (2007) "Religious Influences on Understandings of Racial Inequality in the United States"

1. *Select a topic.* Religion and racial attitudes

2. *Focus the question.* Does a white evangelical Christian subculture and belief system encourage or discourage an individualist, nonsupportive stance toward inequality and toward African Americans?

3. *Design the study.* The authors prepared a large-scale national survey in 2003 involving 2,081 randomly selected adults in the United States.

4. *Collect the data.* The randomly selected adults answered many questions on social backgrounds, religious practice and belief, explanations of racial inequality, and beliefs about African Americans in a 30-minute telephone interview.

5. *Analyze the data.* The authors looked at numerous tables with percentages and statistical tests.

6. *Interpret the data.* The authors found that survey respondents with strong conservative Protestant Christian beliefs and who were most involved in religious activities favored individualistic explanations of Black inequality (i.e., personal failings, lack of motivation) over structural explanations (i.e., racial discrimination). In addition, among conservative Christians, the views of women differed from men, and the educated from the less educated.

7. *Inform others.* The authors prepared a description of the study with its results that they submitted to the scholarly journal *Social Problems*.

How does theory fit in? The authors examined a theory suggesting that a white evanglical subculture fosters particular attitudes about social and political issues; it deemphasizes structural explanations (discrimination, government help) and emphasizes individualist, self-help explanations.

Authors and title of the study: Rory McVeigh and Julian Sobolewski (2007) "Red Counties, Blue Counties, and Occupational Segregation by Sex and Race"

1. *Select a topic.* Social inequality and voting

2. *Focus the question.* Did occupational segregation by gender and race—a major source of social inequality—influence how people voted in the 2004 U.S. presidential election? *Occupational segregation* occurs when one group (e.g., one gender, one race) almost exclusively holds a type of job.

3. *Design the study.* The authors identified specific factors for which the government collects data at the county level: choice of presidential

candidate and occupational segregation by race and gender. They also considered features of the labor market in a county (e.g., racial mix of the county, educational credentials of women and non-Whites, degree of mobility into a county) that might threaten or weaken the degree of occupational segregation.

4. *Collect the data.* Data came from the U.S. census on occupations, demographics, and voting.

5. *Analyze the data.* The authors examined numerous correlations, charts, and statistical tests.

6. *Interpret the data.* The authors found that both occupational and sex segregation in county-level labor markets to be related to election outcomes. In counties that had equal or integrated labor markets, the Democratic party candidate received more votes. In counties with highly segegrated labor markets, especially with other conditions that threatened to undermine the segegration, the Republican party candidate received more votes.

7. *Inform others.* The authors submitted a description of the study with its results to the scholarly journal *American Journal of Sociology*.

How does theory fit in? The authors used ethnic competition theory and split labor market theory to explain how county-level inequality influence the local political climate and voting behavior.

Qualitative Approach to Social Research. Many social scientists who adopt a qualitative approach follow a slightly different set of steps than they use in quantitative studies. These steps also vary according to the specific qualitative research methods used. In addition, this approach is more fluid and less linear, or step by step (see Chapter 5).

1. *Acknowledge self and context.* Social scientists also start with a topic as with quantitative research, but the start is simultaneous with performing a self-assessment and situating the topic in a socio-historical context. Many qualitative researchers rely on personal beliefs,

biography, or specific current issues to identify a topic of interest or importance.

2. *Adopt a perspective.* Qualitative researchers may ponder the theoretical-philosophical *paradigm* (discussed in Chapter 4) or place their inquiry in the context of ongoing discussions with other researchers. Rather than narrowing down a topic, this means choosing a direction that may contain many potential questions.

3–6. *Design a study and collect, analyze, and interpret data.* As with quantitative research, a qualitative researcher will *design a study* (Chapter 6), *collect data* (Chapters 13–14), *analyze data* (see Chapter 15), and *interpret data.* More so than the quantitative researcher, a qualitative researcher is likely to collect, analyze, and interpret data simultaneously. This is a fluid process with much going back and forth among the steps multiple times. Often the researcher not only uses or tests a past theory, but also builds new theory. At the *interpret data* stage, the qualitative researcher creates new concepts and theoretical interpretations.

7. *Inform others.* This is similar for both approaches, but here again, the style of a report varies according to the approach used (see Chapter 16). (See Figure 1.2.)

Next we consider examples of two qualitative studies. Each illustrates a type of study that is the focus of a chapter, field research-ethnography (Chapter 14), and historical-comparative research (Chapter 15).

Author and title of the study: Sudhir Venkatesh (2008) "Gang Leader for a Day"

1. *Acknowledge self and context.* This author describes his personal interest and background and explains how an interest in inner-city poverty shifted to gangs in an urban housing project.

2. *Socio-cultural context.* The physical-social setting was an urban housing project in South Chicago located near the University of Chicago where the author was a graduate student. Drug-dealing gangs operated in the projects that had

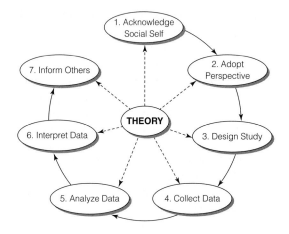

FIGURE 1.2   Steps in the Qualitative Research Process

very high rates of poverty and that were overwhelming occupied by African Americans.

3–6. *Design, collect, analyze, and interpret.* The author initially tried to conduct a quantitative survey but dropped this technique. Instead, he observed and talked with gang members and people in the housing project several days a week over eight years between 1990 and 1998 and took very detailed notes every day on what he saw, heard, participated in, and thought.

7. *Inform others.* Results appeared in a semiacademic book *Gang Leader for a Day* about 10 years after the original research study ended, although the author had written several studies and books related to the same general research in the meantime.

How does theory fit in: As with many ethnographies, the study is largely descriptive with little theory. The author provides a little theory on how a gang provides social organization and services to a local community, the economics of drug dealing, and how local poor people must negotiate with a range of others for their day-to-day survival.

Authors and title of the study: Holly McCammon and six colleagues (2008) "Becoming Full Citizens:

The U.S. Women's Jury Rights Campaign, The Pace of Reform, and Strategic Adaptation"

1. *Select a topic.* Women gaining full citizenship rights
2. *Socio-cultural context.* U.S. women did not get the right to serve on juries after they won the national right to vote in 1920. The right was not upheld by the Supreme Court until 1975. Women gained the right at dramatically different times in different states (also sometimes losing and regaining the right). Advocated by women's groups, the issue was hotly contested for many decades.
3. *Design, collect, analyze, and interpret.* The seven authors devoted the most part of two years to gathering data on jury-rights movements in fifteen states between the 1910s and the late 1960s. They visited twenty-two archives (specialized libraries with historical records) in the various states. They examined the records of movement organizations, consulted local newspapers and relevant magazines, and read all relevant legal and political documents (i.e., court decisions, legislative hearings, and statutes) in each of the fifteen states. In addition to analyzing details of each state and movement organization, they looked at the length of time required to enact jury rights for women in each state and classified specific features of each organization and its activities. The major finding was that in states where jury rights were won most quickly, organizations had engaged in strategic actions. They had continuously adjusted their demands, sought a range of political allies, and changed the way they phrased their arguments. In states where progress was very slow, movement groups were sporadic, inconsistent, or inflexible and failed to take advantage of changing conditions.
4. *Inform others.* A description of the study and the results were published in a scholarly journal, *American Journal of Sociology*

How does theory fit in: The authors wanted to explain why some social-political movements achieve their political goals rapidly while others do so slowly. They built on past social movement theory and advanced the new idea of "strategic adapation" by a movement.

The seven-step process shown in Figures 1.1 and 1.2 are oversimplified. In practice, we rarely complete step 1, then leave it entirely to move to step 2, and so on. Research is more of an interactive process, and the steps blend into each other. A later step may stimulate the reconsideration of an earlier one. The process is not strictly linear; it may flow in several directions before reaching an end. Research does not abruptly end at step 7. This is an ongoing process, and the end of one study often stimulates new thinking and fresh research questions.

The seven-step cycle is for a single research study. Each study builds on prior research and contributes to a larger body of knowledge. The broader process of conducting scientific research and accumulating new knowledge requires many researchers conducting numerous studies. A single researcher may work on multiple studies at once, or several researchers may collaborate on one study. Likewise, one study may result in one or several scholarly articles, and sometimes one article will report on several smaller studies.

WHY LEARN HOW TO CONDUCT SOCIAL RESEARCH?

Professional social scientists working in universities, research centers, and government agencies, often with assistants and technicians, conduct research. Results of their studies typically appear in specialized scholarly journals or college textbooks. Their studies expand our understanding of the social world and have an indirect impact on broad public knowledge. One reason you may want to learn how to conduct social science research is to advance knowledge of the social world in ways that avoid the many failings of alternative, nonscientific ways that people create knowledge.

People who work for newspapers, television networks, market research firms, schools, hospitals, social service agencies, political parties, consulting firms, government agencies, personnel departments, public interest organizations, insurance companies, and law firms also conduct social research. They do so as part of their jobs and use the same social science research techniques. They use the results of their studies internally and do not widely share or publish them, yet research-based findings yield better informed, less biased decisions than the guessing, hunches, intuition, and personal experience that were previously used (see Summary Review Box 1.2, The Practitioner and Social Science). Beyond expanding knowledge, a second reason you may want to learn how to conduct social research is for a practical reason: to improve decision making.

Unfortunately, a few people and organizations misuse or abuse social research: use sloppy research techniques, misinterpret findings, manipulate stud-

SUMMARY REVIEW BOX **1.2**
The Practitioner and Social Science

Science does not and cannot provide people with fixed, absolute "Truth." This is so because science is a slow, incomplete process of reducing untruth. It is a quest for the best possible answers carried out by a collection of devoted people who labor strenuously in a careful, systematic, and open-minded manner. Many people are uneasy with the painstaking pace, hesitating progress, and incertitude of science. They demand immediate, absolute answers. Many turn to religious fanatics or political demagogues who offer final, conclusive truths in abundance. What does this mean for diligent practitioners (e.g., human service workers, health care professionals, criminal justice officers, journalists, or policy analysts) who have to make prompt decisions in their daily work? Must they abandon scientific thinking and rely only on common sense, personal conviction, or political doctrine? No, they, too, can use social scientific thinking. Their task is difficult but possible. They must conscientiously try to locate the best knowledge currently available; use careful, independent reasoning; avoid known errors or fallacies; and be wary of any doctrine offering complete, final answers. Practitioners must always be open to new ideas, use multiple information sources, and constantly question the evidence offered to support a course of action.

ies to find previously decided results, and so on (we will look more at this in Chapter 3). In addition, some people believe that they are being overly studied or overloaded by research studies. For example, people have refused exit poll studies during elections, and rates of answering surveys have declined. Negative reactions against the misuse of social research can produce negative views toward research in general. A third reason you may want to learn how to conduct research studies is to distinguish legitimate, valuable research from bogus or poorly conducted studies, pseudoscience, and misused research.

CONCLUSION

This chapter presented what social science research is, how the research process operates, and who conducts research. It also described alternatives to social research: ways to get fast, easy, and practical knowledge that often contains error, misinformation, and false reasoning. It showed you how the scientific community works, how social research fits into the scientific enterprise, and how the norms of science and journal articles are crucial to the scientific community. The chapter also outlined the steps of research.

Social science research is for, about, and conducted by *people.* Despite the attention to the principles, rules, or procedures, social research is a human activity. Social researchers are people not unlike you. They developed a desire to create and discover knowledge and now find doing social research to be fun and exciting. They conduct research to discover new knowledge and to understand the social world. Whether you become a professional social researcher, someone who applies a research technique as part of a job, or just someone who uses the results of research, you will benefit from learning about the research process. You will be enriched if you can begin to create a personal link between yourself and the research process.

Mills (1959:196) offered the valuable advice in his *Sociological Imagination*:

> You must learn to use your life experiences in your intellectual work: continually to examine and interpret it. In this sense craftsmanship is the center of yourself and you are personally involved in every intellectual product upon which you may work.

KEY TERMS

blind review	junk science	scholarly journal article
data	norms of the scientific	scientific community
empirical	community	scientific literacy
false consensus	overgeneralization	selective observation
halo effect	premature closure	social theory
innumeracy	pseudoscience	

REVIEW QUESTIONS

1. What sources of knowledge are alternatives to social research?
2. Why is social research usually better than the alternatives?
3. Is social research always right? Can it answer any question? Explain.
4. How did science and oracles serve similar purposes in different eras?
5. What is the scientific community? What is its role?
6. What are the norms of the scientific community? What are their effects?

7. What is the process to have a study published in a scholarly social science journal?

8. What steps are involved in conducting a research project?

9. What does it mean to say that research steps are not rigidly fixed?

10. What types of people do social research? For what reasons?

NOTES

1. See Parker-Pope (2007) on the face cream study and related research.

2. On the limits to self-knowledge, see Wilson and Dunn (2004); on inaccurate eyewitness accounts, Wells and Olson (2003); on inaccurate risk evaluation, Gowda and Fox (2002) and Paulos (2001); on condoms in schools (Kirby et al., 1999); on SUVs, Bradsher (2002).

3. From Rampton and Stauber (2001:274–277, 305–306).

4. Results on geographic information are from *National Geographic* (2006). Results on UFOs, devils, and so forth is from Harris Poll (2003, 2005).

5. On media inaccuracy on psychiatric treatment, see Goode (2002), on the Muslim population, see Smith (2002), and on African Americans in poverty, see Gilens (1996).

6. Video News Reports are described by the Center for Media and Democracy http://www.prwatch.org/fakenews3/summary and Consumer Product Safety Commission http://www.cpsc.gov/businfo/vnrprod.html. Also see Barstow and Stein (2005, March 13), "Under Bush, a New Age of Prepackaged TV News," *New York Times*; Aiello and Profitt (2008).

7. On "faith-based" programs, see Goodstein, "Church-Based Projects Lack Data on Results," *New York Times* (April 24, 2001); Crary, "Faith Based Prisons Multiply," *USA Today* (October 14, 2007); Ferguson et al. (2007); and Reingold et al. (2007). On restrictions of science in government, see Mooney (2005) and Union of Concerned Scientists (2004).

8. See Herrnstein and Murray (1994) and a critique in Fischer et al. (1996).

9. "Junk science" is discussed in Rampton and Stauber (2001:223).

10. For more on the scientific community, see Cole (1983), Cole, Cole, and Simon (1981), Collins (1983), Collins and Restivo (1983), Hagstrom (1965), Merton (1973), Stoner (1966), and Ziman (1968).

11. See Cappell and Guterbock (1992) and Ennis (1992) for studies of sociological specialties.

12. For more on the social role of the scientist, see Ben-David (1971), Camic (1980), and Tuma and Grimes (1981). Hagstrom (1965), Merton (1973), and Stoner (1966) discuss norms of science, and Blume (1974) and Mitroff (1974) talk about norm violation.

13. See Altman, "Drug Firm, Relenting, Allows Unflattering Study to Appear," *New York Times* (April 16, 1997); Markoff, "Dispute over Unauthorized Reviews Leaves Intel Embarrassed," *New York Times* (March 12, 1997); and Barry Meier, "Philip Morris Censored Data about Addiction," *New York Times* (May 7, 1998).

14. Science's communication and publication system is described in Bakanic and colleagues (1987), Blau (1978), Cole (1983), Crane (1967), Gusfield (1976), Hargens (1988), Mullins (1973), Singer (1989), and Ziman (1968).

15. See Clemens and Powell (1995:446).

16. See Clemens and Powell (1995:444).

17. For more on the system of reward and stratification in science, see Cole and Cole (1973), Cole (1978), Fuchs and Turner (1986), Gaston (1978), Gustin (1973), Long (1978), Meadows (1974), and Reskin (1977).

CHAPTER 2

What Are the Major Types of Social Research?

Use and Audience of Research
Purpose of Research
Within or across Cases

Single or Multiple Points in Time
Data Collection Techniques
Conclusion

The objective of academic research, whether by sociologists, political scientists, or anthropologists, is to try to find answers to theoretical questions within their respective fields. In contrast, the objective of applied social research is to use data so that decisions can be made.

—Herbert J. Rubin, *Applied Social Research*, pp. 6–7

Three years after they graduated from college, Tim and Sharon met for lunch. Tim asked Sharon, "So, how is your new job as a researcher for Social Data, Inc.? What are you doing?" Sharon answered. "Right now I'm working on a cross-sectional survey of teachers as part of an applied research project on six day care centers to provide descriptive data that we can use in an evaluation study being prepared for a nonprofit foundation." Sharon's description of her research project on the topic of day care touches on dimensions of social science research. In this chapter, you will learn about the dimensions and get a "road map" of the types of social research.

Chapter 1 gave you a simplified picture of social science research. Social research comes in many shapes and sizes. We can organize research in several ways: experimental versus nonexperimental, case study versus cross-case research, or qualitative versus quantitative.[1] We can organize the many kinds of studies along five dimensions (see Chart 2.1 on page 26). The dimensions include how we use a study's findings and its primary audience;

why we conduct a study; the number of cases and how we examine them; how we incorporate time; and decide which techniques we deploy to gather data. You can position a single research study on each of the dimensions of social research.

You will find learning the dimensions and their interrelationships to one another useful. First, they make it easier to understand research reports that you hear about or read in scholarly journals. After you recognize a study's dimensions, you can quickly grasp what a study says and how it was conducted. Second, when you conduct your own study, you must make many decisions. You can think of the dimensions as decision points you will encounter as you develop a specific research plan. To make good decisions, you should be aware of trade-offs and the strengths and weaknesses at each decision point. Additionally, the dimensions are interrelated. Some dimensions tend to go together (e.g., study goal and a data collection technique). As you learn about the dimensions, you can begin to see how best to combine dimensions to address specific research questions of interest.

CHART 2.1   Dimensions and Major Types of Social Research

USE AND AUDIENCE OF RESEARCH

▓ Basic
▓ Applied
   • Evaluation
   • Action
   • Social Impact

PURPOSE OF RESEARCH

▓ Explore
▓ Describe
▓ Explain

WITHIN OR ACROSS CASES

▓ Case Study Research
▓ Across Case Research

SINGLE OR MULTIPLE POINTS IN TIME

▓ Cross-Sectional
▓ Longitudinal
   • Time series
   • Panel
   • Cohort
▓ Case Study

DATA COLLECTION TECHNIQUES

▓ Quantitative Data
   • Experiment
   • Survey
   • Nonreactive (content analysis, secondary analysis, existing statistics)
▓ Qualitative Data
   • Field (ethnography, participant observation)
   • Historical-comparitive

USE AND AUDIENCE OF RESEARCH

Social research has two wings or orientations. There is a somewhat detached "scientific" or "academic" orientation and a more activist, practical, and action-

---

Basic research   Research designed to advance fundamental knowledge about how the world works and build/test theoretical explanations by focusing on the "why" question. The scientific community is its primary audience.

---

oriented orientation. This is not a rigid separation. Many researchers work in both, or they move from one to the other at different career stages. The orientations differ in how to use findings and who the primary audience is.

Basic Research

Also called *academic research* or *pure research,* **basic research** advances fundamental knowledge about the social world. It is the source of most new scientific ideas and ways to think about social events. The scientific community is its primary audience. Researchers use basic research to support or refute theories about how the social world operates and changes, what makes things happen, and why social relations or events are a certain way.

Some people criticize the basic research orientation and ask, "What good is it?" They consider basic research to be a waste of time and money because they cannot see an immediate use for it or resolve a pressing issue with it. While many practitioners want answers to questions that they can implement within the next week, month, or year, a basic researcher might devote years to painstakingly seeking answers to questions that could reshape thinking for many decades to come. Much basic research lacks practical applications in the short term, but it builds a foundation for knowledge and broad understanding that has an impact on many issues, policy areas, or areas of study. Basic research is also the main source of the tools—methods, theories, and ideas—that all researchers use. Almost all of the major breakthroughs and significant advances in knowledge originated in basic research. It lays a foundation for core understandings and may have implications for issues that do not even exist when a study is conducted.

Basic researchers may examine issues that appear impractical because applications for the resulting knowledge may not appear for many years or decades. Often we can see only the practical applications after diverse basic knowledge advances have accumulated over a long time. For example, in 1984 Alec Jeffreys, a geneticist at the University of Leicester in the United Kingdom, was engaged in basic research studying the evolution of genes. As an indirect accidental side effect of a new technique he developed, he learned how to produce human DNA "fingerprints" or unique markings of the DNA of individuals. This was not his intent. Jeffreys even said he would never have thought of the technique if creating DNA fingerprints had been his goal. By the mid-1990s, applied uses of the technique had been developed. Today, DNA analysis is widely use in criminal investigations and other areas. Dozens of major practical breakthroughs and innovations had similar origins in initially unrelated basic research.

Few practitioners (e.g., police officers, counselors of youthful offenders) see relevance to a basic research question such as "Why does deviant behavior occur?" Nevertheless, answering such foundational questions stimulates new ways of thinking. The answers might revolutionize and dramatically improve what practitioners do. Public policies and social services can be ineffective and misguided without an understanding of core causes of events or behaviors. Applied research, too, builds new knowledge. Nonetheless, basic research is essential to expand knowledge. Researchers working close to the center of the scientific community conduct most basic research.

Applied Research

When we do **applied research** we address a specific concern. We may offer solutions to a question raised by an employer, a local community, or a social cause.[2] Only rarely in applied research do we try to build, test, or make connections to theory. Most applied research studies are short term and small scale. They offer practical results that we can use within a year or less. For example, the student government of University X wants to reduce alcohol abuse. It wants, therefore, to find out whether the number of University X students arrested for driving while intoxicated would decline if the student government were to sponsor alcohol-free parties next year. An applied research study would be most applicable for this situation.

Businesses, government offices, health care facilities, social service agencies, political organizations, and educational institutions conduct applied studies and make decisions based on findings.

Applied research findings shape many decisions. They might trigger the decision to begin a program that will reduce the wait time before a client receives benefits. Findings may help police decide whether to adopt a new police response to reduce spousal abuse. Applied research findings may help a firm decide to market product A to mature adults instead of teenagers.

Active practitioners (e.g., teachers, doctors and nurses, sales representatives, counselors and caseworkers, judges, managers, supervisors, and city managers) are the audience for applied findings. Many in this large diverse audience lack a background in research or a strong scientific perspective. This can create complications. For example, a court proceeding obtains the results from a research study such as a survey. However, nonscientists (judges, jurors, lawyers) evaluate the survey's methodology and findings on a nonscientific basis.[3] As a result, they can misinterpret the results and use evaluation standards that diverge from those of the scientific community. They may accept findings from a study that does not meet basic scientific criteria but reject findings from a study with the highest standards of scientific rigor. Applied researchers must translate scientific-technical findings into the language of lay decision makers. The researchers need to highlight strengths and limitations of a study's design or findings.

A researcher might conduct an applied research study for a decision maker who is uninterested in details of how it was conducted and who wants only a brief summary of key findings. Nonetheless, the researcher should also prepare a complete, detailed research report. Others who have the time and ability to evaluate the quality of the research may be interested, or disputes might arise later. One constraint regarding applied research is that it is less likely to appear in a peer-reviewed publication, if at all. Many times, findings have only limited distribution and are available only to a few decision makers or the practitioners in one organization.

Because we put applied research into practice, it can generate controversy. This is not new. For

---

Applied research Research designed to offer practical solutions to a concrete problem or address the immediate and specific needs of clinicians or practitioners.

example, in 1903, Ellwood conducted an applied study of the jails and poorhouses and documented serious deficiencies. His research report generated great public indignation. However, he was accused of slandering the state government that had given him employment.[4] William Whyte (1984) encountered conflict over applied studies of a factory in Oklahoma and of restaurants in Chicago. In the first case, the management was more interested in defeating a union than in learning about employment relations. In the other case, the restaurant owners wanted to make the industry look good rather than let anyone learn about the practical details of its operations. Some business organizations have a mind-set that differs from a research-oriented inquiry. Learning to negotiate and communicate across mind-sets is an important skill to develop (Reingold, 1999). A related issue is that sometimes officials call for an applied study on a policy controversy as a delaying tactic. They want only to deflect criticism or postpone a decision until after the political heat dies down and have no real interest in the study or its results.

Applied and basic research orientations weigh research methodology differently (see Table 2.1). In applied research, researchers must make more trade-offs or compromise scientific rigor to obtain fast, usable results. Compromise is no excuse for sloppy research, however. Applied researchers learn to how to squeeze research into the constraints of an applied setting and balance rigor against practical needs. Such balancing requires an in-depth knowledge of research and an awareness of the consequences of compromising standards.

Three Types of Applied Research. Applied social research comes in about a dozen forms. Here you will learn about three major types: evaluation, action oriented, and social impact assessment.

1. Evaluation research is the most widely used type of applied research.[5] Large bureaucratic

---

Evaluation research Applied research in which one tries to determine how well a program or policy is working or reaching its goals and objectives.

TABLE 2.1   Basic and Applied Research Compared

ASPECT	BASIC	APPLIED
Primary audiences	Scientific community (other researchers)	Practitioners, participants, or supervisors (nonresearchers)
Evaluators	Research peers	Practitioners, supervisors
Autonomy of researcher	High	Low-moderate
Research rigor	Very high	Varies, moderate
Highest priority	Verified truth	Relevance
Purpose	Create new knowledge	Resolve a practical problem
Success indicated by	Publication and impact on knowledge/ scientists	Direct application to address a specific concern/problem

organizations (e.g., businesses, schools, hospitals, governments, large nonprofit agencies) frequently use it to learn whether a program, a new way of doing something, a marketing campaign, a policy, and so forth is effective—in other words, "Does it work?" There is even a scholarly journal devoted to advancing the field of evaluation research, *Evaluation Review*.

Evaluation research greatly expanded in the 1960s in the United States when the federal government created many new social programs. Most researchers adopted a positivist approach (see Chapter 4) and used cost-benefit analysis (we will examine this later in this chapter). By the 1970s, most government social programs required evaluation research studies to determine their effectiveness.

Evaluation research questions could include these: Does a law enforcement program of mandatory arrest reduce spousal abuse? Will a rape awareness program reduce college men's coercive sex with women? Will a flextime program increase employee productivity? In an evaluation research study, we measure the effectiveness of a program, policy, or way of doing something. In evaluation research, we can use several techniques (e.g., survey and ethnographic field research), but if the experiment can be used, the result is most effective.

Some practitioners conduct their own evaluation research studies. More often, however, outside managers or decision makers request a study. Outsiders sometimes place boundaries on what a study can include. They might specify one specific outcome of interest. For example, education officials may request a study on improvements in math skills between the second and fifth grades but tell the researcher to ignore other subjects, other aspects of learning, and changes in cognitive-social development in the children.

Ethical and political tensions often arise in evaluation research. This happens because people develop strong interests in specific findings. The findings can affect who is hired, who builds political popularity, or which program is advanced. If someone is displeased with the study findings, they may criticize the researcher or call the study sloppy, biased, or inadequate. Some evaluation researchers have experienced pressures to rig a study, especially one about controversial issues or programs. The possibility of controversy makes it especially important for the applied researcher to be honest and open, and to carefully adhere to proper research procedures.

Despite their value, evaluation research studies have limitations. Few go through a rigorous peer review process, and their raw data are rarely publicly available for scrutiny or replication. In addition, policy makers can selectively use or ignore evaluation reports (See Example Box 2.1, Evaluation Research). Many studies adopt a very narrow focus, looking at select inputs and outputs more than the entire process or ramifications of a program. For example, in 1996, U.S. social welfare programs were dramatically changed or "reformed." Evaluation research studies of the new welfare programs focused on whether they reduced welfare caseloads and the costs of administering new programs. Few studies considered the impact of new programs on unfulfilled family obligations or rising distress among children. To justify the new programs, policy

EXAMPLE BOX 2.1
Evaluation Research

Wysong, Aniskiewicz, and Wright (1994) evaluated the effectiveness of the Drug Abuse Resistance Education (D.A.R.E.) program found in 10,000 schools in the United States and 42 other countries. The program is widely used, well funded, and very popular with police departments, school officials, parent groups, and others. By having police officers deliver talks in early grades, D.A.R.E. tries to reduce illicit drug use among teens by increasing their knowledge of drugs, developing antidrug coping skills, and raising self-esteem. The authors examined two groups of students who were seniors in a high school in Indiana. One group had participated in the D.A.R.E. program in seventh grade and the other group had not. Consistent with many past studies, the authors found no lasting differences among the groups regarding age of first drug use, frequency of drug use, or self-esteem. The authors suggest that the program's popularity may be due to its political symbolic impact. The program may be effective for latent goals (i.e., helping politicians, school officials, and others feel morally good and involved in antidrug actions) but ineffective for official goals (i.e., reducing illegal drug use by teenagers).

makers and politicians used the evidence selectively and boasted of its positive benefits.[6]

Two types of evaluation research are formative and summative. *Formative evaluation* has built-in monitoring or continuous feedback on a program used for program management. *Summative evaluation* reviews final program outcomes. Both are usually necessary.

Many organizations (e.g., schools, government agencies, businesses) have made evaluation research part of their ongoing operations. One example is the *Planning, Programming, and Budgeting System (PPBS),* first used by the U.S. Department of Defense in the 1960s. The PPBS rests on the idea that researchers can evaluate a program by measuring its accomplishments against stated goals and objectives. The evaluator divides a program into components and analyzes each component with regard to its costs (staff, supplies, etc.)

and accomplishments relative to explicit program objectives. For example, a women's health center offers pregnancy education. It has four program components: outreach, education, counseling, and referrals. The program has four main objectives: reach out to and offer emotional support to women who believe they are pregnant, provide current information about pregnancy, counsel women about their health risks and concerns, and refer pregnant women to health care providers or family planning agencies. An evaluation researcher might examine the cost of each component and measure how well the program has met each of its four objectives. For example, the researcher asks (1) how much staff time and how many supplies have been devoted to outreach activities in the last year, (2) how many calls or inquiries can be traced to such efforts, and (3) how many of women from targeted groups contacted or came to the center for counseling.[7]

2. Action research treats knowledge as a form of power. It blends acquiring new knowledge with using the knowledge to achieve a specific purpose. In action research, we do not remain detached. We close the gap between studying an issue and engaging in social-political action to influence the issue. Various types of action research are inspired

> *by different philosophical stances, in the main driven by varying core assumptions about epistemology and ontology, which normatively inform their practitioners in terms of aims and requirements. Yet the impact of such philosophical variation usually remains unnoticed in published accounts thereby fuelling ambiguity and controversy . . . (Cassell and Johnson 2006:785–786)*

Action research Applied research in which the primary goal is to facilitate social change or bring about a value-oriented political-social goal.

Participatory action research Action research in which the research participants actively help design and conduct the research study. It emphasizes democratizing knowledge-creation and engaging in collective action, and it assumes that political knowledge emerges from participating in research.

In Chapter 4, we will consider such philosophical differences. Most action research shares five characteristics:

- The people who are studied are active participants in the research process.
- The study incorporates the popular knowledge and concerns of ordinary people.
- The study examines power relations and documents social inequality or injustice.
- Study findings are shared to raise the awareness and empower ordinary people.
- The research is tied directly to social-political action and achieving social goals.

Action research tries to equalize the power relations between research participants and researchers. We avoid having control, status, and authority over the people we study. Instead, we encourage equality and direct involvement by research participants. We want to raise awareness among participants and the public, so published articles are secondary goals. Instead, the emphasis is on sharing the findings with research participants and the public. This takes the form of general reports and pamphlets, press releases for the mass media, or public meetings.

Action research often attracts researchers with impassioned views on an issue (e.g., environmental, egalitarian, feminist). A deeply committed feminist action researcher may see a study as both advancing knowledge and creating social change to transform gender relations.[8] If the researcher studies sexual harassment, the outcome might be making policy changes to reduce its occurences and working with potential victims so they can better defend their rights. Action researchers worked to preserve a town that was about to be destroyed by a dam project. They collaborated with union officials and management to redesign work to prevent layoffs. In developing nations, action researchers often work among illiterate, impoverished peasants to teach literacy, spread an awareness of problems, and improve living conditions.[9]

Participatory action research, a subtype of action research, emphasizes democratizing the knowledge-creation process, revealing injustices, highlighting social inequality and conflict, and engaging in collective action to improve conditions.

A key belief in participatory action research is that knowledge grows out of directly experiencing social-political activism. As the research participants engage in direct action, they become more informed and empowered. They learn and are more likely to succeed.

In a participatory action study, research participants take an active role in formulating, designing, and carrying out the research. They cogenerate findings with professional researchers in a collaborative process. Research participants are involved in problem definition and study implementation. Because most participants are unfamiliar with professional social research, the trained researcher acts as a consultant or collaborator who assists and provides expertise in study design, data gathering, and data analysis/interpretation.

An action researcher balances professional standards with the practical limits of adapting to local conditions and specific participant concerns. Involvement and control by local participants means joint ownership of the findings. The researcher who wants to publish study results in a professional outlet might find that the participants feel the researcher is only trying to advance his or her career. This makes getting the permission and cooperation of participants critical before releasing findings in a professional setting or outlet.[10]

Organizations or people with value/advocacy views who are opposed to the interests of study participants may challenge visible and successful action-research. For this reason, an action researcher needs to have an in-depth knowledge of proper research procedures and very carefully document study methods (see Example Box 2.2, Action Research).

3. Social impact assessment research estimates the likely social consequences in advance of a planned change.[11] Often social impact assessment (SIA) research is part of a larger environmental impact statement required by government agencies. In the United States, the 1969 National Environmental Policy Act (NEPA) requires an Environmental Impact Statement (EIS) before a federal government agency may take "actions significantly affecting the quality of the human environment" (NEPA, section 102). Preparing SIA for an EIS requires social science research, and it assesses both positive and negative impacts.

> **Social impact assessment** Applied research that documents the likely consequences for various areas of social life if a major new change is introduced into a community.

An EIS is required for locating and building schools, hospitals, prisons, housing developments, shopping centers, factories, landfills, highways, airports, reservoirs, parks, recreation areas, and power plants. If SIA is part of the EIS, it evaluates the consequences of such action including the availability and quality of housing, population characteristics (such as age structure, racial-ethnic diversity, income and education levels), and the distribution of power-authority. It may examine attitudes or perceptions, family bonds, and friendship networks. The SIA part of the EIS can consider impacts on community resources such as health, police, fire, and sanitation services, employment, school and recreational opportunities, and the vitality of nonprofit organizations. The SIA also considers impacts on the survival or continuity of distinct communities of people who have established local historical and cultural roots.[12]

Researchers conducting social impact assessments often work in an interdisciplinary research team to measure areas of impact (see Example Box 2.3, Social Impact Research). Social impact researchers have a professional organization, the International Association for Impact Assessment, with a scholarly journal, *Impact Assessment and Project Appraisal*.

After decades of development, the tools and effectiveness of social impact assessment research are well established; however, this type of applied research is seriously underutilized. This is due to several factors. First, most EISs do not require a SIA. Legislators, policy officials, or decision makers rarely ask for a SIA before they approve a major project. Except for a very few large-scale programs, most decision makers choose to change zoning regulations, develop a new business park, create a housing development, alter transportation routes, and so forth without systematically considering the social impact. These issues are decided based on

EXAMPLE BOX **2.2**

Action Research

Williams and associates (2007) used a participatory action approach to study quality of life in Saskatoon, Canada. They gathered quantitative and qualitative data from three areas of the city (low, middle, and high income) in 2001 and again in 2004. They focused on three themes: (1) a growing income gap, (2) social knowledge translation strategies that would include low socioeconomic populations, and (3) how to bring about a positive change in local quality of life. The researchers developed a "hybrid" research organization. It was both university based and local community based and had coleaders (one from the university and one from the community). Community leaders concerned about quality of life issues in Saskatoon were active throughout the study. They incorporated four knowledge-translation strategies: regularly engage the local media (newspaper and television), conduct several community forums, create a Saskatoon Quality of Life Steering Committee with several community organizations, and employ an action researcher who would be a policy entrepreneur (advocate for starting new policies). Community members participated in research design, data collection, and data analysis-interpretation. The authors treated research findings as learning tool for the community that could raise awareness and stimulate action. They used several methods to communicate results: published short briefing papers, created posters, and distributed research summaries at community forums for discussion. Discussing findings was not an endpoint; rather, it was a stage toward creating new policies, programs, or actions based on community reactions to the findings.

Another action research study, this one by Quach and associates (2008), involved an applied action research study of Vietnamese nail salon workers in one county in California "to collect preliminary descriptive information" (p. 340). The authors noted that California has 35,000 nail salons with 300,000

nail technicians who work for long periods with nail products that have toxic and hazardous ingredients. In California, 59–80 percent of licensed manicurists are of Vietnamese descent, and 95 percent are female. Between 1987 and 2002, the proportion of Vietnamese nail workers grew tenfold, but almost nothing was known about their health situation. Researchers designed the study to raise awareness of health issues and encourage participation by workers by creating a Community Advisory Committee to oversee the study. An important feature was that targeted population were immigrants, many with limited English language ability (99 percent had been born in Vietnam and over one-half had lived in the United States ten years or longer). Led by the outreach staff of a local health center, the committee was comprised of ten Vietnamese community members (including nail salon workers), patients at the health center, cosmetology instructors, breast cancer survivors, and mental health counselors from Alameda County (San Francisco Bay area). The study included 201 nail salon workers at 74 salons in the county. Researchers used a 10-minute Vietnamese language questionnaire, focus groups, and observations of salon conditions (e.g., number of doors and windows, ventilators). The study documented numerous health issues. More than one-half of salon workers reported acute health problems (e.g., eye irritation, headaches, breathing difficulties) that started after they began working in the industry. A large majority of nail salon workers reported concerns over exposure to workplace chemicals, but less than one-half of the salons had exhaust ventilation to reduce chemical exposure. Local community members were actively involved at several research stages. Study authors used the findings to educate a range of people in the local community and developed strategies to help reduce exposure to hazardous occupational conditions.

---

political and economic interests. Second, a social impact assessment study requires time and money. Officials resist spending funds and object to slowing the decision-making process. Because they work in a short time frame, they do not require

studies, even if one could produce a more informed decision that saves money and anguish in the long-term. Third, in many places, the political-cultural climate is wary of planning and distrustful of "expert" advice. Such distrust combines with

EXAMPLE BOX **2.3**

Social Impact Research

Many forms of gambling, or "gaming," have expanded in the United States over the past 30 years. In 1980, gambling was legal in only a few states and yielded less than $10 billion in profits. Today, it is legal in 48 states, and profits exceed $50 billion a year. Lawmakers sought new sources of revenue without raising taxes and wanted to promote economic development. The gambling industry promised new jobs, economic revitalization, and a "cut" of the flow of money from gambling. This allowed lawmakers to create jobs, strengthen the local economy, and obtain more revenue—all without raising taxes. Legal rulings have recognized the treaty rights of AmerIndian people, meaning that gaming laws did not apply to AmeriIndian lands. When a new casino was proposed for downtown Rochester, New York, Kent (2004) was commissioned to conduct a social impact study. Like most reports of social impact studies, it was not published in a scholarly journal. The report estimated that the proposed casino would add 1,300 new jobs to the city. New York state could earn an additional $23 million per year, and the city of Rochester about $11 million in tax revenues from casino operations. To estimate the impact, one part of the study compared data from several gambling versus nongambling cities and considered past studies on gambling addiction behavior. This part considered both the economic benefits and added social costs (e.g., crime rates, prostitution, illegal drug use, compulsive gamblers) that appeared in cities with casinos. The report stated that pathological gambling increases with proximity to casino gambling and has costs for individuals and families (with increased divorce and child abuse). The report estimated the dollar value of social costs could reach $10 million annually.

limited knowledge of social science research. As a result, people cling to traditional decision-making methods. They use guesswork rather than research-based knowledge about social impacts of decisions. Fourth, the promoters or investors in new projects often oppose conducting a social impact assessment study. They fear that its findings will create delays, force costly alterations, or derail their plans by

identifying social concerns. Lastly, in cases of social impact studies, officials often ignore their results because of overriding political concerns and the influence of entrenched political-economic interests.

Two Tools in Applied Research. Many applied researchers use two tools as part of their research studies: needs assessment and cost-benefit analysis.

A **needs assessment** involves collecting data to determine major social needs and their severity. It is often a preliminary step before a government agency or charity decides on a strategy to help people or conduct further study. Needs assessments often become tangled in complex community relations, and when doing one, we may encounter several issues (see Summary Review Box 2.1, Dilemmas in Needs Assessment on page 34).

A first issue is to prioritize serious needs or problems. Perhaps a community has a dozen issues or concerns, such as women subject to violent domestic abuse, preteens abusing drugs, people who are homeless sleeping in a park, working people losing large amounts of money betting at a racetrack, or executives drinking too much at the country club and then driving. Which issue receives the needs assessment? The most visible need may not be the most serious one or one that mobilizes a great public outcry.

A second issue is to identify information sources for the needs assessment. For example, when deciding to conduct a needs assessment for a program to aid people who are homeless, who is in a best position to provide information? Should we talk about the needs of people who are homeless with the business owners who complain about homeless people living on their street? Should we ask the current service providers to the homeless population (e.g., social workers, health care centers, schools, homeless shelters, food pantries, and soup kitchens)? Should we rely on law enforcement (e.g., police, jailers, court officials)? Should we ask friends, family members, and nonprofessional

Needs assessment An applied research tool that gathers descriptive information about a need, issue, or concern, including its magnitude, scope, and severity.

advocates of people living on the street? Should we ask the people themselves? Ideally, we would include all sources, but identifying the full range may not be easy or make take too much time.

A third issue is that explicit, immediate needs may not include the full range of less visible issues or link them to long-term solutions. For example, we learn that people who are homeless say they need housing. After examining the situation, however, we determine that housing would be available if these people had jobs. The housing problem is caused by a need for jobs, which, in turn, may be caused by a need for skills, a "living wage," and certain types of businesses. Thus, to address the housing need, it is necessary to attract specific types of businesses, enact a new minimum wage, and provide job training. Often the surface, apparent needs are rooted in deeper conditions and causes about which many people are unaware. For example, drinking polluted water, having a poor diet, and lacking exercise may cause an increased need for health care. Does this indicate a need for more health care or for better water treatment and a public health education program?

A fourth issue is that the needs assessment may generate political controversy. It may suggest solutions beyond local control or without a realistic chance of implementation. Powerful groups may not want some of the social needs documented or publicized. We may learn that a city has much unreported crime; however, publicizing the situation may tarnish the image of a safe, well-run city that the Chamber of Commerce and the city government are promoting. Often one group's needs, such as the people who bet too much money at the racetrack, are linked to the actions of others who benefit by creating that need, such as the racetrack's owners and employees. By documenting needs and offering

Cost-benefit analysis An applied research tool economists developed in which a monetary value is assigned to the inputs and outcomes of a process and then the researcher examines the balance between them.

SUMMARY REVIEW BOX **2.1**

Dilemmas in Needs Assessment

1. Who defines what is the most serious issue for which needs should be assessed?
2. Whom should you ask to learn about the needs of a group of people?
3. Should you consider both conscious, visible needs and unspoken, hidden needs?
4. When many areas of needs coexist, which ones should you include in an assessment?
5. Should you limit remedies/solutions for needs to what can be realistically accomplished within the limits set by established powerholders or consider all possibilities even if they may be disruptive?

a resolution, we may be caught between opposing groups.

Economists developed the second tool, **cost-benefit analysis**. It involves estimating the future costs and benefits of a proposed action and assigning them monetary values. We start by identifying all consequences including tangibles, such as job creation, business formation, or graduation rates and intangibles, such as clean air, political freedom, scenic beauty, or low stress levels of a program or action. Next, we assign each consequence a monetary value; some (such as costs) may be negative, some (e.g., benefits) positive, and some neutral. We then calculate a probability or likelihood for each consequence. Lastly, we compare all costs to benefits and decide whether they balance.

Cost-benefit analysis appears to be a nonpolitical, rational, and technical decision-making strategy; however, it is often controversial. As with needs assessment, people disagree about the activities considered relevant or important. Thus, some people will say that the top concerns are business stability and profitability, lower taxes, and new job creation. Others say the top priorities are a healthy and clean environment, open green space, and increased artistic expression and free speech. People may disagree on whether a given consequence is positive or negative. For example, I see widening a road as a benefit. It will allow me to travel to work much more rapidly and reduce congestion. However, a homeowner who lives along the road sees it as a cost. Building the road will require removing some of his or her front yard, increase noise and pollution, and lower the house's market value. In the social impact study on opening a new casino in Rochester, New York (Example Box 2.3), the report weighed economic benefits (profits, jobs, tax revenues) against social costs (crime, gambling addition, family breakup, illegal drug use). It stated that benefits outweighed costs, yet the people receiving the economic benefits (i.e., local business owners and taxpayers, people who get casino jobs) were not the same ones who pay the social costs associated with the casino (i.e., families that break up because of compulsive gambling, people with worse health due to increased drug use, or women who become prostitutes).

We assign monetary values to costs and benefits in two ways. *Contingency evaluation* asks people how much something is worth to them: for example, a town considering whether to allow a polluting factory to locate there. We would want to estimate the cost of air pollution on the average person's health. We might ask people "How much is it worth to you not to cough a lot and miss work 10 days a year because you are sick with asthma?" If the average value people assign is $150 in a town of 20,000, we estimate the contingency evaluation or subjective benefit of health to be $150 x 20,000 people per year, or $3 million. We balance this cost against higher profits for a company and new jobs created by allowing pollution. One problem with estimates is that few people give accurate ones. In addition, different people often assign very different cost values. To an impoverished person, coughing and missing work may be worth $150. For a wealthy person, it may be $150,000. Broader consequences exist as well. In this example, polluting companies will move to towns with many low-income people who assign lower costs. This will worsen living conditions in lower income areas and increase the gap in life quality between rich and poor.

Using the same example, *actual cost evaluation* estimates the actual medical and job loss costs. We estimate the health impact and then add up likely medical bills and costs for employers to replace sick or disabled workers. Let us say that medical treatment averages $150 per person and a replacement worker costs an extra $300 per lost day of work. The cost of treating 10,000 people each year would be $150 x 10,000 people = $1,500,000. The cost of hiring 1,000 replacement workers for 2 days would be $600 x 1,000 workers = $600,000, for a total estimate of $2.1 million. This method ignores pain and suffering, inconvenience, and indirect costs (e.g., a parent stays home with a sick child or a child cannot play sports because of asthma). To balance the costs with benefits by this method, the polluting factory would need to earn an extra $2.1 million in profits.

Cost-benefit analysis rests on the assumption that we can attach a monetary value to everything (e.g., a child's learning, health, love, happiness, human dignity, chastity) and that people assign similar valuations. We might question these assumptions. Cost-benefit analysis can also raise moral and political concerns. The people paying the cost may not be the ones getting the benefits. In addition, cost-benefit calculations tend to favor wealthy, high-income people over poor, low-income people. A high-income person's time is worth more, so she or he places a higher value on saving 15 minutes in a commute to work than a low-income person would. A high-income person thinks saving 15 minutes is worth $50, but to a low-income person, it is worth $5. Cost-benefit analysis often finds inconveniencing or disrupting the lives of low-income people is more "cost effective."

Cost-benefit analysis tends to conceal the moral-political dimension of decisions. For instance, should we "pull the plug" on a life-support machine for a seriously ill elderly person or keep the person alive for another 6 months. We compare the benefits to the costs. Maybe it costs $200,000 in medical expenses to extend the person's life by 6 months. Is the benefit of 6 months of life for a nonproductive member of society worth $200,000 in costs? In addition to its economic aspect, the cost-benefit balance decision has a moral dimension, yet that dimension in decisions is most visible when it involves a single identifiable person (your grandmother) with whom you have a personal, emotional attachment. The moral dimension is less visible when make it for someone identified as an individual, (i.e., lost among a group of 1,000 hospital patients) and for whom decision makers (e.g., health insurance officials in a distant city) lack direct, personal contact. Although obscured, the moral dimension of the decision remains.

Moving Beyond the Basic–Applied Dichotomy. The basic versus applied research dichotomy is overly simplistic. Three related issues elaborate on this distinction to build additional types of research beyond the dichotomy:

1. The form of knowledge a study creates
2. The range of audiences that can use research findings
3. Who initiates, designs, and controls a study— an independent researcher or others

Forms of Knowledge. Social researchers produce two forms of knowledge, instrumental and reflexive. Although they overlap, the forms mirror a distinction between neutral, impartial, and task-oriented actions and principled, value-based, engaged behavior. Most studies published in scholarly journals and applied studies by practitioners build and expand **instrumental knowledge**. It is a means–ends or task-oriented knowledge. We use it to accomplish something: a practical task or advancement of what we know about how the world works. We create such knowledge as we extend old or invent new research techniques and gather, verify, connect, and accumulate new information. Instrumental knowledge advances the frontiers of understanding. As we create instrumental

knowledge, we can avoid direct engagement in moral or value-directed concerns.

By contrast, **reflexive knowledge** is self-aware, value-oriented knowledge. It is principled and oriented toward an ultimate value or end in itself. We create reflexive knowledge to build on specific moral commitments, consciously reflect on the context and processes of knowledge creation, and emphasize the implications of knowledge. When we create reflexive knowledge, we ask questions such as: Why and how are we creating this knowledge? What is the relevance or importance of this knowledge, and for whom? What are its implications for other knowledge and for moral principles such as justice, truth, fairness, freedom, or equality?

Audiences for Research Findings. As noted earlier, the primary audience of basic research is other professional researchers in the scientific community. Practitioner nonresearchers are the primary audience for applied research. We can expand the practitioner audiences into four types: the public, activists, general practitioners, and narrow practitioners. Each has a different interest. Most of the *public* have only a general interest. They learn about research results in schooling or from the mass media outlets. *Activists,* community advocates, and research participants in action research have a direct, immediate interest in results that are very relevant to their immediate concerns. The *general practitioner,* a high-level decision maker or policy specialist in government or large organizations (e.g., businesses, hospitals, police departments), wants to integrate a broad range of practical knowledge to use to inform many current and future decisions. By contrast, the *narrow practitioner* wants targeted findings that will address a specific, pressing problem.

Researcher Autonomy and Commissioned Social Research. In the idealized and romantic image of research, there is complete freedom to pursue knowledge without restriction. The ideal researcher is independent, has sufficient funds, and has complete control over how to conduct a study. The opposite of this image is research with many restrictions. This describes hired researcher-employee

---

Instrumental knowledge Knowledge narrowly focused to answer a basic or applied research question, issue, or concern with an outcome or task-oriented orientation.

Reflexive knowledge Knowledge used to broadly examine the assumptions, context, and moral-value positions of basic or applied social research, including the research process itself and the implications of what is learned.

TABLE 2.2 Expanded Set of Basic and Applied Research Types

AUDIENCE	FORM OF KNOWLEDGE		
	REFLEXIVE	INSTRUMENTAL	INSTRUMENTAL
	Autonomous	*Commissioned*	*Autonomous*
Basic Research Type			
Scientific community	Basic critical	Basic contract	Basic professional
Applied Research Types			
General public	Public intellectual	Dedicated policy	Democratic policy
Participants	Public educator	Consultant	Participatory researcher
Generalist practitioner	Democratic deliberation	Democratic contract	Democratic applied research
Narrow practitioner	Dedicated deliberation	Dedicated contract	Dedicated applied research

or **commissioned research**. Most commissioned studies put limitations on researcher autonomy. Someone else provides the funds, and specifies the scope of the research question and the dissemination of findings. Other "strings" may include restriction to examine certain issues but not others. Researchers may face strict limits on the time to complete a study. Alternatively, they may be told which research techniques to use or which people to contact in the study.

Expanded Set of Basic and Applied Research Types. We can now combine the form of knowledge, audience, and commissioned versus autonomous research to create an expanded set of basic and applied research and researcher roles (see Table 2.2). Basic research for the scientific community can produce reflexive or instrumental knowledge—critical and professional research, respectively.[13] A large private foundation or government agency might commission a researcher to conduct basic research. This is basic contract research. At times, researchers assume a public intellectual role and produce reflexive knowledge to advance general discussion and public debate. At other times, they produce instrumental knowledge, sometimes from a commissioned or autonomous study. The knowledge might be dedicated to a specific policy and contribute to a policy debate.

A researcher who designs reflexive research for participants is in a public educator role. When the knowledge is instrumental, the researcher may act as a consultant to the participants or be a participatory researcher who is equal to the participants. On some occasions, generalist and targeted practitioners create and apply reflexive knowledge in debates and deliberations over issues or decision options. More often practitioners focus on instrumental knowledge. Sometimes a generalist practitioner creates and uses knowledge as a contributor to open, democratic decisions. At other times, a practitioner narrowly focuses on a particular targeted issue that has little application or distribution of findings.[14] An outside group or employer could commission a study, or a researcher could create it autonomously.

PURPOSE OF RESEARCH

We conduct studies for many reasons: my boss told me to; it was a class assignment; I was curious; my roommate thought it would be a good idea. There

---

Commissioned research Research funded and conducted at the behest of someone other than the researcher; the person conducting the study often has limited control over the research question, methods of a study, and presentation of results.

are nearly as many reasons to conduct a study as there are researchers. We can organize the purposes of research into three groups: explore a new topic, describe a social phenomenon, or explain why something occurs.[15] Studies may have multiple purposes (e.g., both to explore and to describe), but one purpose is usually dominant (see Summary Review Box 2.2, Purposes of Research Types).

Exploration

We use **exploratory research** when the subject is very new, we know little or nothing about it, and no one has yet explored it (see Example Box 2.4, Exploratory Research). Our goal with it is to formulate more precise questions that we can address in future research. As a first stage of inquiry, we want to know enough after the exploratory study so we can design and execute a second, more systematic and extensive study. Exploratory research rarely yields definitive answers. It addresses the "what" question: What is this social activity really about? It is difficult to conduct because it has few guidelines, everything is potentially important, steps are not well defined, and the direction of inquiry changes frequently.

Researchers who conduct exploratory research must be creative, open minded, and flexible; adopt an investigative stance; and explore all sources of information. They ask creative questions and take advantage of serendipity (i.e., unexpected or chance factors that have large implications). For example, an expectation might be that the impact of immigration to a new nation would be more negative on younger children than on older ones. Instead, the unexpected finding was that children of a specific

Exploratory research Research whose primary purpose is to examine a little understood issue or phenomenon and to develop preliminary ideas about it and move toward refined research questions.

Descriptive research Research in which the primary purpose is to "paint a picture" using words or numbers and to present a profile, a classification of types, or an outline of steps to answer questions such as who, when, where, and how.

SUMMARY REVIEW BOX 2.2

Purposes of Research Types

EXPLORATORY

- Become familiar with the basic facts, setting, and concerns
- Create a general mental picture of conditions
- Formulate and focus questions for future research
- Generate new ideas, conjectures, or hypotheses
- Determine the feasibility of conducting research
- Develop techniques for measuring and locating future data

DESCRIPTIVE

- Provide a detailed, highly accurate picture
- Locate new data that contradict past data
- Create a set of categories or classify types
- Clarify a sequence of steps or stages
- Document a causal process or mechanism
- Report on the background or context of a situation

EXPLANATORY

- Test a theory's predictions or principle
- Elaborate and enrich a theory's explanation
- Extend a theory to new issues or topics
- Support or refute an explanation or prediction
- Link issues or topics to a general principle
- Determine which of several explanations is best

age group (between ages six and eleven) who immigrate are most vulnerable to its disruption—more so than either older or younger children.[16]

Description

You may have a well-developed idea about a social phenomenon and want to describe it. **Descriptive research** presents a picture of the specific details of a situation, social setting, or relationship. Much of the social research found in scholarly journals or used for making policy decisions is descriptive (see Example Box 2.5, Descriptive Research on page 40).

Descriptive and exploratory research blur together in practice. A descriptive research study starts with a well-defined issue or question and tries

EXAMPLE BOX 2.4

Exploratory Research

Most exploratory research uses qualitative data. In general, qualitative research tends to be more open to using a wide range of evidence and discovering new issues. Troshynski and Blank (2008) conducted an exploratory study of men who engage in illegal sex trafficking. The study was unusual because the research participants had actively engaged in an illegal activity. The authors had a chance meeting with someone who knew people "in the business." Over a 3-month period, the authors were able to meet and conduct open-ended interviews with five traffickers. Their goal was to explore how the traffickers saw their business and learn about their backgrounds.

Other exploratory qualitative studies are more complex. Gavlee (2005) conducted an exploratory ethnographic study of racial classification in Puerto Rico. The study was motivated by previous studies that had found that the way people dealt with race in Brazil and much of Latin American differed from ideas about race on the mainland United States. Brazilians emphasized phenotype (outward appearance) over descent, which produced numerous categories that are fluid and uncertain. The study's research questions were these: What categories do people in Puerto Rico use? What are the organizing principles of the categories? Gavlee focused on one small city in Puerto Rico. He spent time in the city and conducted open-ended interviews with twenty-four people to learn terms and categories they used to talk about others. Next, he asked forty-two people to organize a set of pictures of faces that he analyzed using computer software. He discovered that local people organize primarily in terms of appearance rather than race, using five shades of color as categories. Other physical appearance features (hair texture, nose shape) also had minor roles.

Some exploratory studies use quantitative techniques. Krysan (2008) analyzed survey data in an exploratory study of how people of different races in the United States search for housing. The study asked several hundred people in the Detroit area about their recent housing search including how long it took, how many possibilities they inspected during the search, and how many offers or applications they completed. Krysan compared renters and buyers as well as Whites and Blacks with regard to search strategies (e.g., talk to friends, family, or neighbors, look at yard signs, search newspapers or the Internet, use a real estate professional or search service). She looked at percentages and found many similarities but a few differences with regard to race pertaining to type of real estate agent used, Internet use, and length or difficulty of search. People tended to use an agent of their own race. Whites were more likely to use the Internet and more likely to restrict their searchers to White majority neighborhoods. Blacks searched a wider range of locations, had longer searchers, and filed more applications before they had success.

---

to describe it accurately. The study's outcome is a detailed picture of the issue or answer to the research question. For example, the focused issue might be the relationship between parents who are heavy alcohol drinkers and child abuse. Results could show that 25 percent of heavy-drinking parents had physically or sexually abused their children compared to 5 percent of parents who never drink or drink very little.

A descriptive study presents a picture of types of people or of social activities and focuses on "how" and "who" questions (How often does it happen? Who is involved?). Exploring new issues or explaining why something happens (e.g., why do heavy-drinking parents abuse their children) is less of a concern than describing how things are. A great deal of social research is descriptive. Descriptive researchers use most data-gathering techniques: surveys, field research, content analysis, and historical-comparative research.

Explanation

When encountering an issue that is known and with a description of it, we might wonder *why* things are the way they are. Addressing the "why" is the

Descriptive Research

The experimental study by Lowery and colleagues (2007) on priming and academic performance, the survey research study by Edgell and Tranby (2007) on religion and beliefs about racial inequality, and the ethnographic study of gangs by Venkatesh (2008) discussed in Chapter 1 were all descriptive research. The primary focus of each study was to describe patterns rather than address the why question or to test an existing theory.

Another example of a descriptive study is the Unnever and Cullen (2007) study on support for the death penalty. The authors observed that many public opinion polls revealed a sharp racial divide in Americans' support for the death penalty. White racism is often cited as a reason for this difference, yet "there is no systematic theory of why white racism fosters support for capital punishment" (page 1283). The authors conducted a secondary data analysis (see later in this chapter) of survey data with a national sample of 1,500 people. In statistical analysis, they found that while many factors (authoritarian personality, conservative ideology, religious belief, and anti-egalitarian views) contribute to a person's support for death penalty, the strongest predictor of support among Whites was a high score on White racism. Among nonracist Whites, support for the death penalty is similar to levels found among African Americans. The authors briefly discussed theory, but they used theories for only general ideas and primarily described the characteristics of death penalty supporters. They did not directly test any theories or use them to create an explanation (see the next section).

---

purpose of **explanatory research**. It builds on exploratory and descriptive research and goes on to identify the reason something occurs (see Example Box 2.6, Explanatory Research). Going beyond providing a picture of the issue, an explanatory

Explanatory research Research whose primary purpose is to explain why events occur and to build, elaborate, extend, or test theory.

study looks for causes and reasons. For example, a descriptive study would document the numbers of heavy-drinking parents who abuse their children whereas an explanatory study would be interested in learning *why* these parents abuse their children. We focus on exactly what is it about heavy drinking that contributes to child abuse.

We use multiple strategies in explanatory research. In some explanatory studies, we develop a novel explanation and then provide empirical evidence to support it or refute it. In other studies, we outline two or more competing explanations and then present evidence for each in a type of a "head-to-head" comparison to see which is stronger. In still others, we start with an existing explanation derived from social theory or past research and then extend it to explain a new issue, setting, or group of people to see how well the explanation holds up or whether it needs modification or is limited to only certain conditions.

WITHIN OR ACROSS CASES

Studies vary according to the number of cases we examine and the depth-intensity of investigation into features of the cases. Sometimes we carefully select or sample a smaller number cases out of a much larger pool of cases or population. These studies may still involve hundreds or thousands of cases. In other studies (especially experiments), we analyze a few dozen people and manipulate conditions for those people. In still another type of study, we intensively examine one or a small handful of cases, perhaps fewer than ten. While the number of cases in a study is important, the more critical issue is whether a study primarily focuses on features within cases or across cases. As Ragin (1994:93) observed, "often there is a trade-off between the number of cases and the number of features of cases researchers typically can study."

The concept of "case" is central but can be complex. Gerring (2007:17) calls a case a "definitional morass." The complication arises because many possible things can be cases. They can be determined by a study's perspective and research

EXAMPLE BOX **2.6**

Explanatory Research

The historical-comparative study on the movement for jury rights by McCammon and colleagues (2008) described in Chapter 1 was explanatory. The study focused on explaining why movements were more successful in some states than others. The existing-statistics study by McVeigh and Sobolewski (2007) in Chapter 1 was also explanatory because the authors tested ethnic competition theory and split labor market theory to explain county voting patterns.

Explanatory studies usually outline an existing theory and test it or extend the theory to a new area or group. A well-known social psychological theory for the past 50 years has been the contact hypothesis. It has primarily been used to study interracial relations. It explains the degree of prejudice and negative attitudes by saying that people tend to hold negative views toward an "out-group" because of ignorance and negative stereotypes. Once people have contact with and get to know out-group members, they replace their ignorance and negative stereotypes with more positive views. It answers the question why people hold negative feelings toward out-groups with the contact hypothesis: their lack of contact with the out-group. Many studies examined this hypothesis, by investigating specific conditions of contact and the degree to which an out-group is perceived as threatening.

Lee, Farrel, and Link (2004) extended the contact hypothesis to explain a new topic, people in U.S. cities who are homeless. They looked at fourteen measures of exposure to these people. The measures ranged from having information (e.g., articles, television) about them, personal observation, and personal interaction, to having been homeless oneself or having a family member who was or is. They also developed comprehensive measures of a person's view on people who are homeless. These included beliefs about why people become homeless, seeing them as dangerous, feeling empathy and having positive emotions, and supporting their rights. Using telephone survey data from a random sample of 1,388 adults in 200 U.S. metropolitan areas in 1990, they found clear evidence supporting the contact hypothesis. People who had more contact and more intimate types of contact with people who are homeless held the most favorable views of them and were more likely to support programs that helped people who are homeless compared to people who had little or no contact with them. They also found some variation in views about people who are homeless based on a person's race, age, education level, and political ideology.

question. Formally, a case is bounded or delimited in time and space; it is often called a "unit" or "observation." An individual person can be a case as can a family, company, or entire nation. What serves as a case in one study may not be a case in a different study. For example, the nation might be a case that can examine aspects of it or aspects of individuals as cases within one nation's population.

A case is not simply any individual person, family, company, or nation; we select it as part of a "class of events" or because it belongs to a category of cases (see George and Bennett, 2005:17). We study a case because it is part of some grouping—type or kind—that we study to develop knowledge about causes of similarities and differences among

a type or kind of case. For example, I would not study my neighbor Alex as a case just because he lives next to me; however, I might include Alex as a case within a class of similar cases: middle-aged men with a physical disability that prevents them from working and who became full-time "househusbands" to a professional spouse. Likewise, I might study the 1962 Cuban missle crisis as a case, but it would be as one case within a category of cases: international crisis management and deterrance situations.

In any study, researchers should ask both how many cases are involved and whether the emphasis is more on a detailed examination within a few cases or across many cases.

Case-Study Research

Case-study research examines many features of a few cases. The cases can be individuals, groups, organizations, movements, events, or geographic units. The data on the case are detailed, varied, and extensive. It can focus on a single point in time or a duration of time. Most case-study research is qualitative, but it does not have to be. By contrast, almost all cross-case (or noncase research) is quantitative. Qualitative and case-study research are not identical, but "almost all qualitative research seeks to construct representations based on in-depth, detailed knowledge of cases" (Ragin, 1994a:92).[17] The ethnography on urban gangs by Venkatesh (2008) described in Chapter 1 was a case study. It described how specific events and relationships unfolded over the course of 8 years in and around one gang in a limited geographic area of South Chicago.

Case-study research intensively investigates one or a small set of cases, focusing on many details within each case and the context. In short, it examines both details of each case's internal features as well as the surrounding situation. Case studies enable us to link micro level, or the actions of individuals, to the macro level, or large-scale structures and processes (Vaughan, 1992). As Walton (1992b:122) remarked, "The logic of the case study is to demonstrate a causal argument about how general social forces shape and produce results in particular settings."

Case-study research has many strengths. It clarifies our thinking and allows us to link abstract ideas in specific ways with the concrete specifics of cases we observe in detail. It also enable us to calibrate or adjust the measures of our abstract concepts to actual lived experiences and widely accepted standards of evidence. Other case-study strengths involve theory. As Walton (1992b:129) noted, "Case studies are likely to produce the best theory." This occurs for three reasons. First, as we become very familiar with the in-depth detail of

specific cases, we can create/build new theories as well as reshape current theories to complex cases or new situations. Second, when we examine specific cases, the intricate details of social processes and cause-effect relations become more visible. The increased visibility allows us to develop richer, more comprehensive explanations that can capture the complexity of social life. In addition, case studies provide evidence that more effectively depicts complex, multiple-factor events/situations and processes that occur over time and space. Case-study research also can incorporate an entire situation and multiple perspectives within it.

Case study research has the following six strengths:[18]

1. *Conceptual validity.* Case studies help to "flush out" and identify concepts/variables that are of greatest interest and move toward their core or essential meaning in abstract theory.
2. *Heuristic impact.* Case studies are highly heuristic (i.e., providing further learning, discovery, or problem solving). They help with constructing new theories, developing or extending concepts, and exploring the boundaries among related concepts.
3. *Causal mechanisms identification.* Case studies have the ability to make visible the details of social processes and mechanisms by which one factor affects others.
4. *Ability to capture complexity and trace processes.* Case studies can effectively depict highly complex, multiple-factor events/situations and trace processes over time and space.
5. *Calibration.* Case studies enable researchers to adjust measures of abstract concepts to dependable, lived experiences and concrete standards.
6. *Holistic elaboration.* Case studies can elaborate on an entire situation or process holistically and permit the incorporation of multiple perspectives or viewpoints.

Case studies have a detailed focus but tell a larger story (see Example Box 2.7, Case-Study Research). Walton remarked (1992a) in his case study of one community, Owens Valley, California,

Case-study research Research that is an in-depth examination of an extensive amount of information about very few units or cases for one period or across multiple periods of time.

EXAMPLE BOX **2.7**

EXAMPLE BOX **2.7**

Case-Study Research

Perhaps you have seen the prize-winning 2002 movie *The Pianist,* about Wladyslaw Szpilman and the 1943 Jewish uprising in Warsaw, Poland. Einwohner (2003) conducted a historical case study of a single event—the 1943 Jewish uprising—to examine widely accepted social movement theory. The theory builds on three ideas: political opportunity structure (POS), threat, and motivational frame. *POS* is the overall set of options and constraints in institutions and resource control. When new opportunities arise (e.g., the opposition is divided, stalled, distracted, or runs short of supplies), the POS "opens," increasing the odds that a movement can grow or be successful. POS theory also recognizes threat. *Threat* is defined as increased costs to a movement for taking certain actions (e.g., new law restricting protest activity and many people being arrested) or not taking certain actions. A third concept is "motivational frame." A *frame* refers to how people think about and perceive something. A *motivational frame* is what participants perceive to be acceptable reasons or moral justifications for taking an action. The theory says a social movement advances when all three conditions occur: an opening occurs in the POS, the level of threat is low, and people have a frame that motivates them to take action.

Einwohner (2003) studied diaries and historical reports in the specific case of the Warsaw Jewish ghetto in 1943. She found a tightly closed POS and a situation of great threat. The Jews of the ghetto faced highly effective and overwhelming military power, and the Nazis began a policy of systematic extermination. Thus, two of the three conditions required for a successful movement were missing, yet the Jews of the ghetto formed a new and radical motivational frame. They redefined death in struggle as their only acceptable, honorable option. Instead of seeing death as an event to fear and avoid, their view shifted to seeing death in an uprising as a highly courageous, dignified, and honorable action. They redefined being killed in an impossible fight as being honorable and necessary both for each individual and for the entire Jewish people. Thus, the case study found that although two essential factors predicted by the theory (an open opportunity and low threat) were absent, a mass movement emerged. In fact, there was a complete lack of opportunity and extreme threat. In this case, the mass movement depended on the massive and widespread redefinition of what action all of the people had to pursue in a completely hopeless situation. Thus, Einwohner's detailed case study modified a widely accepted and well-documented existing theory.

"I have tried . . . to tell a big story through the lens of a small case" (p. xviii). The community engaged in social protest as it attempted to control its key resource (water) and destiny. The protest took different forms for more than 100 years. In the study, Walton examined diverse forms of data including direct observation, formal and informal interviews, census statistics, maps, old photos and newspapers, various historical documents, and official records.

Across-Case Research

Most quantitative research studies gather information from a large number of cases (30 to 3,000) and focus on a few of features of the cases. Rather than

carry out a detailed investigation of each case, across-case research compares select features across numerous cases. It treats each case as the carrier of the feature of interest.

While certain issues lend themselves to one or another approach, it is sometimes possible to study the same issue using a case study and an across-case research design. Let us say we are interested in how a family decides whether to move to a different town. One strategy is to use a case study of five families. We conduct highly detailed observations and in-depth interviews of each family's decision-making process. Another strategy would be to use an across-case study of the relationship between the husband's job and family income and a decision to relocate to a different town. We look across 1,000 families, identifying the husband's job and income of 250 families that had moved and 750 that had not moved during the past five years. In the across-case study, the family unit acts as a carrier of the features of interest: husband's job, income level, and decision to move or not. Across-case research focuses on the relation among features (job, income, and decision), not on what happens within specific families.

SINGLE OR MULTIPLE POINTS IN TIME

Time is a dimension of every study. We incorporate time in two ways, cross-sectionally and longitudinally. **Cross-sectional research** gathers data at one time point and creates a kind of "snapshot" of social life. **Longitudinal research** gathers data at multiple time points and provides more of a "moving picture" of events, people, or social relations across time. In general, longitudinal studies are more difficult to conduct and require more resources. Researchers may collect data on many units at many time points and then look for patterns across the units or cases.[19]

Cross-Sectional Research

Cross-sectional research can be exploratory, descriptive, or explanatory, but it is most consistent with a descriptive approach. It is usually the simplest and least costly alternative but rarely captures social processes or change. Of the studies described in Chapter 1, both the survey by Edgell and Tranby (2007) on religion and beliefs about racial inequality and the existing statistics study of red and blue states by McVeigh and Sobolewski (2007) are cross-sectional. Of studies described in this chapter, the

Cross-sectional research   Any research that examines information on many cases at one point in time.

Longitudinal research   Any research that examines information from many units or cases across more than one point in time

Time-series research   Longitudinal research in which information can be about different cases or people in each of several time periods.

exploratory study on race in Puerto Rico (Gavlee 2005) and on housing in Detroit (Krysan, 2008) were also cross-sectional. The descriptive study on death penalty views by Unnever and Cullen (2007) is also cross-sectional.

Deciding whether a study is cross-sectional or longitudinal is not always simple. It is more than simply a matter of length of time. The experiment on priming by Lowery and associates (2007) described in Chapter 1 has "long-term effects" (4 days) in its title and is longtitudinal. Data in the survey study by Edgell and Tranby (2007) and the existing statistics study by McVeigh and Sobolewski (2007) were collected over several days or months but are cross-sectional studies. The priming experiment is longitudinal not because of the specific length of time involved but because the study's design incorporated time. Researchers gathered data at two distinct time points and compared these data in the data analysis. In the survey and existing statistics studies, researchers could not collect data all at once. They treated the minor time differences in when they gathered data as irrelevant and ignored the time differences in their study design.

Longitudinal Research

We can use longitudinal studies for exploratory, descriptive, and explanatory purposes. Usually more complicated and costly to conduct than cross-sectional research, longitudinal studies are more powerful. The study on the jury rights movement by McCammon and colleagues (2008) was longitudinal. It focused on explaining the pace and pattern of change across several decades. The authors gathered data from multiple time points, and their design compared data from them.

We now consider three types of longitudinal research: time series, panel, and cohort.

1. Time-series research is a longitudinal study in which data are collected on a category of people or other units across multiple time points. It enables researchers to observe stability or change in the features of the units or can track conditions over time (see Example Box 2.8, Time-Series Studies).

Even simple descriptive information on one item of time-series data can be very revealing. For

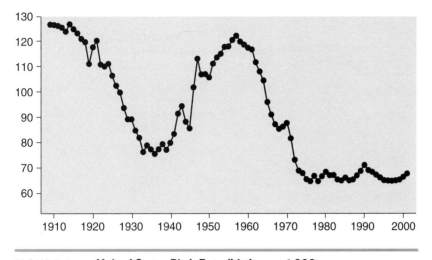

FIGURE 2.1 **United States Birth Rate (births per 1,000 women ages 15–44) 1910 to 2000**

Source: Calculated by author from U.S. census data.

example, time-series data on the U.S. birth rate since 1910 (Figure 2.1) shows that the number of births per woman declined steadily in the 1920s, continued to drop in the 1930s and early 1940s, but sharply reversed direction after World War II ended (1945). This increase began the dramatic upsurge called the "baby boom" of the 1950s to 1960s before declining and becoming stable in the 1970s. Time series can reveal changes not easily seen otherwise. For example, since 1967 the Higher Education Research Institute (2004) has gathered annual survey data on large samples of students entering American colleges for use in applied research by colleges. Time-series results on the percentage of students answering which value was very important for them (Figure 2.2) show a clear reversal of priorities between the 1960s and 1970s. The students ceased to value developing a meaningful philosophy of life and instead sought material-financial success.

2. The panel study, a powerful type of longitudinal research (see Example Box 2.9, Panel Studies on page 47), is more difficult to conduct than time-series research. Researchers conducting a panel study observe or gather data on exactly the same people, group, or organization across time points. Panel research is formidable to conduct and very costly. Tracking people over time is difficult

EXAMPLE BOX **2.8**
Time-Series Studies

A time-series study by Pettit and Western (2004) on imprisonment rates among Black and White men in the United States from 1964 to 1997 found that during a major rise in incarceration rates in the 1980s (up by 300%), Black men were six to eight times more likely than White men to go to jail. Young Black men who did not attend college were more likely to be incarcerated, and nearly one in three spent some time behind bars; these rates doubled for Black men who failed to complete high school. By looking across time, the study authors showed that the expansion of the number of jailed people was uneven, and that increasing numbers of jailed people came from certain parts of the U.S. population.

because some people die or cannot be located. Nevertheless, the results of a well-designed panel study are very valuable. Even short-term panel studies can clearly show the impact of a particular life event.

Panel study Longitudinal research in which information is about the identical cases or people in each of several time periods.

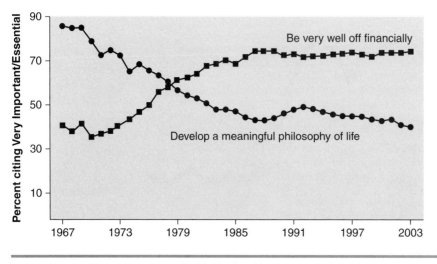

FIGURE 2.2   Value Priorities of U.S. College Freshmen, 1967–2003

Source: From Higher Education Research Institute. (2004). *Recent findings,* Figure 4. Retrieved September 25, 2004, from www.gseis.ucla.edu/heri/findings.html.

However, we learn distinct things from panel studies because we are studying the same people. For example, Brewer et al. (2005) looked at the impact of the September 11, 2001, terrorist attack on attitudes. The researchers asked about trust in other nations and resurveyed the same Americans in a three-wave panel study (October 2001, March 2002, and September 2002). They found that people's feelings toward other nations after the September 11 attack was not temporary but that people's distrust increased over time and was higher one year later. This showed that the attack had ended an entire era of positive feelings and had triggered a much deeper xenophobia among many in the U.S. population.

3. A **cohort study** is similar to the panel study, but rather than observing the exact same people, it studies a category of people who share a similar life experience in a specified period (see Example Box 2.10, Cohort Studies on page 48). Cohort analysis is "explicitly macroanalytic" (i.e., researchers examine

the category as a whole for important features [Ryder, 1992:230]). We focus on the "cohort," or a defined category. Commonly used cohorts include all people born in the same year (called *birth cohorts*), all people hired at the same time, all people who retire in a 1- or 2-year period, and all people who graduate in a given year. Unlike panel studies, we do not have to locate the exact same people for each year in a cohort study but identify only those who experienced a common life event. A cohort study could, for example, compare three marriage cohorts—all people married in each of three years (1970, 1990, and 2010) to see whether they differ as to the features of the marriage ceremony, whether the bride was pregnant at the time of marriage, and other features.

DATA COLLECTION TECHNIQUES

This section is a brief overview of the main data collection techniques. In later chapters, you will read about these techniques in detail and learn how to use them. We can group them into two categories based on the type of data you gather: *quantitative,* collecting data in the form of numbers, and *qualitative,* collecting data in the form of words or pictures. Certain techniques are more effective at addressing specific

Cohort study Longitudinal research that traces information about a category of cases or people who shared a common experience at one time period across subsequent time periods.

EXAMPLE BOX **2.9**

Panel Studies

In many large U.S. cities, as many as 50 percent of students who begin high school do not graduate. Neild, Stoner-Eby, and Furstenberg (2008) studied the issue of dropping out by focusing on ninth grade students. They used panel data from the Philadelphia Education Longitudinal Study (PELS) that followed 10 percent of youth in one high school district over time. Students and their parents within those schools were randomly selected to participate in half-hour telephone interviews during the summer after the students had completed the eighth grade. Both parents and students were again interviewed (in English or Spanish) during the fall/winter of the ninth grade year (Wave 2 of the survey), during the summer after ninth grade (Wave 3) and after each subsequent school year until the fall/winter of 2000–2001 (about 6 months after what would have been their fourth year in high school). By the end of the fourth year, 48.9 percent of students who had started in the ninth grade had graduated. The study tried to determine whether ninth grade course failure and attendance added substantially to predicting dropout. They statistically analyzed the data and found that the ninth grade year contributed substantially to the probability of dropping out. It was a key "turning point" in the process. Many students who eventually dropped out had difficulty with the social and academic transition. They had social adjustment difficulties indicated by a rise in behavior and attendance problems, and a high proportion failed key ninth grade classes (math and English) because their preparation for high school–level standards had been inadequate. This is a panel study because the same parents and students were repeatedly interviewed year after year.

Jennings and Zeitner (2003) studied civic engagement, but they focused on the influence of Internet usage among Americans. They noted that cross-sectional data showed that Internet users had high levels of civic engagement, yet more educated people tended to use the Internet more and to be more engaged in civic organizations. Past studies could not identify whether over time increasing usage of the Internet influenced a person's level of civic engagement. By using panel data collected from a survey of high school seniors in 1965 who were again studied in 1973, 1982, and 1997 (by which time they were in their fifties), the researchers could measure levels of civic engagement before and after Internet use. The Internet was not available until after 1982 but was in wide use by 1997. Both people previously interviewed and their offspring were surveyed. The measure of civic engagement included a wide range of behaviors and attitudes. In general, the authors found that those who were more engaged in civic organizations prior to the availability of the Internet were more likely to use it, and people who used the Internet also increased their civic engagement once they started using the Internet. Whereas Internet users among people in the panels since 1965, who are now in their fifties, increased all forms of civic engagement as they adopted the Internet, their offspring who use the Internet are less likely to be volunteers or become engaged in their local community. Internet use increases levels of civic engagement for the older more than the younger generation, especially younger generation Internet users who use it for purposes other than following public affairs.

kinds of research questions or topics. It takes skill, practice, and creativity to match a research question to an appropriate data collection technique.

Quantitative Data

Experiments. **Experimental research** uses the logic and principles found in natural science research (see Chapter 9 on experimental research). Experiments can be conducted in laboratories or in

real life. They usually involve a small number of people (thirty to one hundred) and address a well-focused question. Experiments are highly effective for explanatory research.

> **Experimental research** Research in which the researcher manipulates conditions for some research participants but not others and then compares group responses to see whether doing so made a difference.

Cohort Studies

Anderson and Fetner (2008) used data from a cross-national survey of people in various countries conducted in the 1981–1982, 1990, and 2000 periods and examined a question regarding tolerance of homosexuality in the United States and Canada. The authors found that tolerance for homosexuality increased both by birth cohort and over time. Thus, people born later in the twentieth century were more tolerant than people born earlier and everyone was more tolerant in the later time periods. For example, people born in the 1920–1929 era were less tolerant when asked in 1981–1982 than when they were asked 20 years later in 2000. People born in 1960–1963 tended to be more tolerant than the 1920–1929 cohort when they were asked in 1980 and in 2000, and their tolerance increased over time as well. An interesting aspect of this study is the comparison between Canada and the United States. In 1980–1982, Canadians were less tolerant than Americans for every birth cohort. Thus, Canadians born in the 1920s or 1940s or 1960s, who were then in their 60s, 40s, or 20s were all less tolerant than Americans when asked in the 1981–1982 survey. When asked in the 1990 and 2000 surveys, Canadians at every birth cohort were much more tolerant than Americans. In fact, increased tolerance between 1990 to 2000 for Americans was small compared to that of the Canadians. Moreover, the youngest Canadian cohort (people born in the 1960s) increased tolerance far more dramatically than other cohorts and Americans of that cohort. A more detailed analysis showed that Canadians from rural areas, small towns, and large cities all became more tolerant; however, Americans in rural areas and very small towns did not become

tolerant; only those in larger towns or urban areas did so. A researcher who studied only cross-sectional data in 1981–1982 would see small cohort difference with the Americans being slightly more tolerant. Consideration of only cross-sectional data in 2000 would identify very large cohort differences and that the Canadians were much more tolerant than the Americans. By looking longitudinally, it is possible to see how opinions changed by cohort and over time very differently in the two countries.

In another cohort study, Bratter and King (2008) examined data from a 2002 U.S. nationally representative sample of people ages 15–44 who were ever married and who had valid information on the race of their first spouse (1,606 males and 4,070 females). The authors studied marriage cohorts (i.e., all people married in a certain year or set of adjoining years), comparing interracial and same-racial group marriage partners. They investigated whether the marriage was intact or had ended at a later time point. In this study, six cohorts were examined (earlier than 1980, 1980–1984, 1985–1989, 1990–1994, 1995–1999, and after 2000). Comparisons across the cohorts showed that interracial couples tended to have higher divorce rates. However, this was not the case for people married across all years but it was especially strong for those marrying during the late 1980s. The researchers found that White female/Black male and White female/Asian male marriages had higher divorce rates than White/White couples but marriages involving non-White females and White males and Hispanics and non-Hispanic persons had similar or lower risks of divorce.

In most experiments, such as the ones you read about on priming and academic performance in Chapter 1 (Lowery et al., 2007), a researcher divides the people being studied (about seventy people in the study) into two or more groups. The researcher then treats both groups identically except that he or she gives one group but not the other a specific condition: the "treatment." The Lowery et al. experiment was "priming" students with words

related to being smart. The researchers measure the reactions of both groups precisely. By controlling the setting and giving only one group the treatment, she or he can conclude that differences in group reactions are due to the treatment alone.

Surveys. As researchers, we utilize questionnaires or interviews to learn people's beliefs or opinions in many research situations (e.g., experiments, field research). **Survey research** uses a written questionnaire or formal interview to gather information on the backgrounds, behaviors, beliefs, or attitudes of a large number of people (see Chapter 10 on survey research). Usually, we ask a large number of people (100 to 5,000) dozens of questions in a short time frame. The survey by Engell and Tanby (2007) discussed in Chapter 1 on religious belief and racial inequality had gathered data in 30-minute-long telephone interviews with 2,081 people in the fall of 2003. Unlike an experiment, we do not manipulate a situation or condition to see how people react; we only carefully record answers from many people who have been asked the same questions. Often we select the people for a survey using a random sampling technique (random sampling is discussed in Chapter 8). This allows us to generalize information legitimately from a few people (e.g., 1,000) to many more (e.g., several million). We usually present survey data in charts, graphs, or tables and analyze them with statistics. Most frequently, we use surveys in descriptive research, sometimes in explanatory research, and only rarely in exploratory research.

Nonreactive Research. In experimental and survey research, we actively engage the people we study by creating experimental conditions or directly asking questions. These are called *reactive* methods because a research participant could react in some way because he or she is aware of being in a study. Other quantitative research is called **nonreactive research** because the study participants are not aware that information about them is part of a study. Four types of nonreactive studies are unobtrusive research, existing statistical information, content analysis, and secondary data analysis. (You will learn about unobtrusive research in Chapter 11.) *Secondary data analysis* is the statistical analysis of quantitative data that were previously collected and stored (often originally from a survey). Here we briefly consider two types of nonreactive research: content analysis and existing statistical information.

Content Analysis. **Content analysis** is a technique for examining the content or information and symbols contained in written documents or other communication media (e.g., photographs, movies, song lyrics, advertisements). To conduct a content analysis, we identify a body of material to analyze (e.g., school textbooks, television programs, newspaper articles) and then create a system for recording specific aspects of its content. The system might include counting how often certain words or themes appear. After we systematically record what we find, we analyze it, often using graphs or charts. Content analysis is a nonreactive method because the creators of the content didn't know whether anyone would analyze it. Content analysis lets us discover and document specific features in the content of a large amount of material that might otherwise go unnoticed. We most frequently use content analysis for descriptive purposes, but exploratory or explanatory studies are also possible (see Example Study Box 2.11, Content Analysis on page 51).

Existing Statistics. Using **existing statistics research**, we locate a source of previously collected information, often in the form of official government reports (existing statistics research is discussed in Chapter 11). We then reorganize the information in new ways to address a research question. Locating the sources and verifying their quality can be time consuming. Frequently, we do not know whether the needed information is available when we begin a study. We can use existing statistics research for exploratory, descriptive, or explanatory purposes but most frequently for descriptive research.

Survey research   Quantitative research in which the researcher systematically asks a large number of people the same questions and then records their answers.

Nonreactive research   Research methods in which people are not aware of being studied.

Content analysis   Research in which the content of a communication medium is systematically recorded and analyzed.

Existing statistics research   Research in which one reexamines and statistically analyzes quantitative data that have been gathered by government agencies or other organizations.

CROSS-SECTIONAL: Observe a collection of people at one time.

February 2011

TIME SERIES: Observe different people at multiple times.

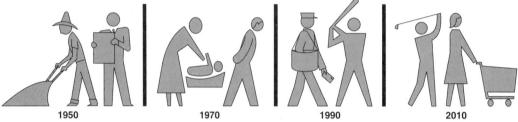

1950   1970   1990   2010

PANEL: Observe the exact same people at two or more times.

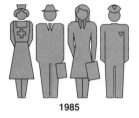      

1985   1995   2005

COHORT: Observe people who shared an experience at two or more times.

Married in 1962   1982   2002

CASE STUDY: Observe a small set intensely across time.

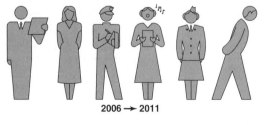

2006 → 2011

FIGURE 2.3   The Time Dimension in Social Research

Content Analysis

Lawrence and Birkland (2004) conducted a content analysis of school shootings after the ones in 1999 at Columbine High School. The researchers were interested in how media coverage shaped eventual legislation on the issue. They examined and coded the content of four data sources: newspaper articles in two leading newspapers between April and August 1999 that mentioned the incident, television news stories in 1999, Congressional debates on the issue in 1999–2000, and legislation introduced in the U.S. Congress in 1999–2000. The authors discovered that some reasons for the shooting that the media and the debates emphasized (influence of pop culture and peer pressure) did not appear in legislation but other issues did (school security and access to guns). An issue (law enforcement measures) not evident in media stories became prominent in debates and legislation.

Qualitative Data

Qualitative data come in a vast array of forms: photos, maps, open-ended interviews, observations, documents, and so forth. We can simplify such data into two major categories: field research (including ethnography, participant observation, depth interviewing) and historical-comparative research.

Field Research. **Field research** involves conducting ethnographic case studies on a small group of people for a length of time (field research is discussed in Chapter 13). Field research begins with a loosely formulated question, then selects a group or site for study, gains access to, and then adopts a social role in the setting and begin observing. Field researchers carefully observe and interact in the field setting for a few months to several years. They get to know personally the people being studied and conduct informal interviews. Data are in the form of detailed notes taken on a daily basis. While observing, researchers constantly consider what they observed and refine ideas about its significance. Finally, the researchers leave the field site, review notes, and prepare written reports. Field research is usually used for exploratory and descriptive

Field Research

Mitchell Duneier (1999) conducted a field research of street vendors in Greenwich Village, New York City. He gained entree by browsing through books at one vendor whom he had befriended. The vendor introduced him to other vendors, panhandlers, people who were homeless, and others. Duneier observed them on and off over 4 years, periodically working as a magazine vendor and scavenger. As a White college professor, it took adjustment to learn the daily life and win acceptance among low-income African American men who made a living selling used books and magazines on the sidewalk. In addition to observing and tape-recording life on the sidewalk, Duneier conducted many informal interviews, read related documents, and had a photojournalist take numerous photos of the field site and its people.

Duneier concluded with a critique of the popular "broken window" theory of social control and crime reduction. Where others saw only a disorderly street environment causing deviant behavior and crime, Duneier found a rich informal social life with honor, dignity, and entrepreneurial vigor among poor people who were struggling to survive. He noted that upper-middle-class government officials and corporate leaders often advocate for laws and regulations that threaten to destroy the fluid, healthy informal social structure he discovered because they do not know the people or understand life on the sidewalk. They see only social disorganization because the vibrant daily lives of those who make a living among the flow of people on the sidewalk do not mesh with the upper-middle-class world that is centered in large complex organizations with formal regulations, official procedures, fixed hierarchies, and standardized occupations.

studies; it is sometimes used for explanatory research. (In Chapter 1, you read about gang research Venkatesh [2008]; also see Example Box 2.12, Field Research).

Field research   Qualitative research in which the researcher directly observes and records notes on people in a natural setting for an extended period of time.

Historical-Comparative Research

Mahoney (2003) presented a puzzle about the countries of Spanish America, specifically 15 countries that had been mainland territories of the Spanish colonial empire. He observed that their relative ranking, from most to least developed in 1900, remained unchanged in 2000; that is, the least developed country in 1900 (Bolivia) remained the least developed in 2000. This picture of great stability contrasts with dramatic changes and improvements in the region during the twentieth century. Going back to the height of the Spanish empire in the seventeenth century, Mahoney noted that the richest, most central colonies in that period later became the poorest countries while marginal, backwater, poor colonies became the developed, richest countries by the late nineteenth century.

To solve this puzzle, Mahoney used two qualitative data analysis tools, path dependency and qualitative comparative analysis (QCA) (both are discussed later in Chapter 15). His data included maps, national economic and population statistics, and several hundred historical studies on the specific countries. He concluded that the most central, prosperous Spanish colonies were located where natural resources were abundant (for extraction and shipment to Europe) and large indigenous populations existed (to work as coerced labor). In these colonies, local elites arose and created rigid racial-ethnic stratification systems. The elites concentrated economic-political power with themselves and excluded broad parts of society. The systems continued into the nineteenth century when new political events, trade patterns, and economic conditions appeared. In the 1700–1850 era, liberal-minded elites who were open to new ideas did not succeed in the central, prosperous colonies. In contrast, colonies that had been on the fringe of the Spanish empire in South America were less encumbered by rigid systems. New elites who were able to innovate and adapt arose in a "great reversal" of positions. After this historical "turning point," some countries had a substantial head start toward social-economic development in the late 1800s. These countries built political-economic systems and institutions that propelled them forward; that is, they "locked into" a particular direction or path that brought increasing returns.

Mahoney (2003:53) argued, "Explanations of differences in units that draw on the current attributes of those units will often be inadequate." In other words, a cross-sectional approach that tries to explain differences among the countries by using data at only one point in time cannot capture significant long-term dynamic processes. An explanation that includes the impact of distant historical events and takes a long-term view is superior.

Historical-Comparative Research. **Historical-comparative research** is a collection of related types of research. Some studies investigate aspects of social life in a past historical era in one society or in a few. Other studies examine a different culture or compare two or more cultures (we examine historical-comparative research in Chapter 14). We might focus on one historical period or several, compare one or more cultures, or mix historical periods and cultures. As with field research, we start with a loosely formulated question and then refine and elaborate on it during the research process. We often use a mix of evidence, including existing statistics, documents (e.g., books, newspapers, diaries, photographs, and maps), observations, and interviews. Historical-comparative research can be exploratory, descriptive, or explanatory, but it is usually descriptive. Not all historical-comparative research follows a qualitative approach; some examine quantitative data (e.g., survey data) in a different time point or a different culture.

You read in Chapter 1 about a historical-comparative study on the jury-rights movement in the United States, and earlier in this chapter on the Warsaw uprising (Example Study Box 2.2). In

> **Historical-comparative research** Qualitative research in which the researcher examines data on events and conditions in the historical past and/or in different societies.

both, the researched examined past events in one country/culture. It is also possible to look across multiple countries and time (see Example Box 2.13, Historical-Comparative Research).

CONCLUSION

This chapter provided an overview of the dimensions of social research. You saw that one research study can be classified in a number of different ways (e.g., by its purpose, research technique) and that the dimensions loosely overlap with each other (see Chart 2.1). The dimensions of research are a "road map" through the terrain of social research.

In the next chapter, we turn to social theory. You read about theory in Chapter 1 and heard about it again in this chapter. In Chapter 3, you will learn how theory and research methods work together and about several types of theory.

KEY TERMS

action research
applied research
basic research
case-study research
cohort study
commissioned research
content analysis
cost-benefit analysis
cross-sectional research

descriptive research
evaluation research
existing statistics research
experimental research
explanatory research
exploratory research
field research
historical-comparative research
instrumental knowledge

longitudinal research
needs assessment
nonreactive research
panel study
participatory action research
reflexive knowledge
social impact assessment
survey research
time-series research

REVIEW QUESTIONS

1. When is exploratory research used, and what can it accomplish?
2. What types of results does a descriptive research study produce?
3. What is explanatory research? What is its primary purpose?
4. What are the major differences between basic and applied research?
5. Who is likely to conduct basic research, and where are results likely to appear?
6. Explain the differences among the three types of applied research.
7. How do time-series, panel, and cohort studies differ?
8. What are some potential problems with cost-benefit analysis?
9. What is a needs assessment? What complications can occur when conducting one?
10. Explain the differences between qualitative and quantitative research.

NOTES

1. Abbott (2004:40–79) offers a more comprehensive and complex organization of methods.
2. See Finsterbusch and Motz (1980), Freeman (1983), Lazarsfeld and Reitz (1975), Olsen and Micklin (1981),

and Rubin (1983) on applied research. Whyte (1986) critiques social research that is not applied. McGrath and colleagues (1982) discuss judgment calls relevant in applied research.

3. See Crespi (1987) and Dutka (1982) on the use of survey research in legal proceedings.

4. See Turner and Turner (1991:181).

5. For a brief introduction to evaluation research, see Adams and Schvaneveldt (1985:315–328), Finsterbusch and Motz (1980:119–158), and Smith and Glass (1987). A more complete discussion can be found in Burnstein and associates (1985), Freeman (1992), Rossi (1982), Rossi and Freeman (1985), Saxe and Fine (1981), and Weiss (1972).

6. See Oliker (1994).

7. Smith and Glass (1987:41–49) discuss PPBS and related evaluation research.

8. See Reinharz (1992:252).

9. See Cancian and Armstead (1992), Reason (1994), and Whyte (1989).

10. On participatory action research, see Cassell and Johnson (2006), Kemmis and McTaggart (2003), and Stoecker (1999).

11. Social impact research is discussed in Chadwick and associates (1984:313–342), Finsterbusch and Motz (1980:75–118), and Finsterbusch and Wolf (1981). Also see Rossi and colleagues (1982) and Wright and Rossi (1981) on "natural hazards" and social science.

12. See Becker and Vanclay (2003) and *Guidelines and Principles For Social Impact Assessment* by The Interorganizational Committee on Guidelines and Principles for Social Impact Assessment (1994). http://www.nmfs.noaa.gov/sfa/social_impact_guide.htm

13. See Burawoy and colleagues (2004).

14. Hammersley (2000) makes this generalist versus narrow practitioner distinction.

15. Babbie (1998), Bailey (1987:38–39), and Churchill (1983:56–77) also discuss explanatory, exploratory, and descriptive research.

16. See Guy and colleagues (1987:54–55) for discussion.

17. For discussions of case-study research, see George and Bennett (2005), Gerring (2007), Miller (1992), Mitchell (1984), Ragin (1992a, 1992b), Stake (1994), Vaughan (1992), Walton (1992b), and Yin (1988).

18. (see George and Bennett 2005:19–22; Gerring 2007; McKeown 2004; Ragin 2008:71–84; Snow and Trom 2002).

19. See Mitchell (1984) and Stake (1994).

CHAPTER 3

Theory and Research

> *One of the major functions of theory is to order experience with the help of concepts.*
> *It also selects relevant aspects and data among the enormous multitude of "facts"*
> *that confront the investigator of social phenomena.*
> —Lewis Coser, *"The Uses of Classical Sociological Theory,"* p. 170

The percent of people who regularly smoke cigarettes has declined in the United States. We suspect that the decline is due to public campaigns that warned about the dangers of smoking to health. We find that more educated, higher income people tend to smoke less than less educated and low-income people. A theory of social resources suggests that this is because people who are educated and have higher incomes read more, have a long-term time horizon, and have more resources to make lifestyle adjustments compared to less educated and low-income people. However, smoking is more than a health issue. It can also be a symbolic fashion statement and lifestyle issue of cultural taste. Likewise, education and income level indicate more than knowledge and resources but also suggest membership in different class cultures (i.e., the ways people of different social classes culturally distinguish themselves). A theory of cultural taste suggests that people adopting an upper-middle-class lifestyle would not smoke because it is culturally less fashionable for their class. In contrast, people who adopt a working-class lifestyle would be more likely to smoke in part because it is a feature of their class culture. Other aspects of class culture include music taste. Highly educated, high-income people tend to prefer classical music while less educated, low-income prefer bluegrass and heavy metal music. Logically, a theory of cultural taste implies that taste in music is related to smoking because of the different class lifestyles. This is exactly what Pampel (2006) found is happening. But the results are even more interesting. Both well-educated, high-income people and less educated, low-income people tend to enjoy jazz. The jazz subculture has long included smoking. Consistent with cultural taste theory, Pampel found that jazz lovers are more likely to smoke than nonjazz lovers of the same social class.

The connection between a person's musical taste and his or her smoking behavior outlined in the preceding box may be unexpected, but it illustrates the power of theory and its influence on research. Theory helps us to understand the complexities of social life. It not only explains why people do what they do but also offers us insights and suggests directions for inquiry. As the theory of cultural taste that led Pampel to ask new questions and reexamine smoking behavior illustrated, a theory can provide concepts with which we can explore and think about the social world in novel ways. It also shows how different theories provide competing ways to explain events.

Many beginning students fear theory. They feel it is a maze of obscure jargon and many abstractions that are irrelevant to daily life. I hope you come to see that theory is not only useful but also vital for comprehending the social world around you. Theory does many things: It clarifies thinking, extends understanding, deepens discussion, and enriches analysis. It has a critical role in advancing knowledge and in organizing the way that we conduct research. This chapter is an elementary introduction to social theory, and later chapters will include more about theory as well.

My students share their anxieties and confusion over social theory with me. One source of confusion is that few understand what social theory really involves. It does not help that *theory* has multiple meanings and takes several forms. Even professionals debate the meaning of theory and have given it several meanings.

1. A *theory* is a logically connected set of general propositions that establishes a connection between two or more variables.
2. A *theory* is an explanation of a specific social phenomenon that identifies a set of causally relevant factors or conditions.
3. A *theory* provides insights into the real meaning of a social phenomenon by offering an illuminating interpretation and by telling us "what it is all about."
4. A *theory* is what a famous social thinker really meant.

5. A *theory* is an entire worldview, or a way of seeing, interpreting, and understanding events in the world.
6. A *theory* is a criticism based on a political-moral viewpoint; it presents and stands for a set of beliefs-values from which it critiques the position and arguments of opponents.
7. A *theory* is a philosophical commentary on key questions or issues about core issues of how we develop knowledge about the social world (e.g., how we really construct a sense of social reality).

Source: Gabriel Abend, The Meaning of 'Theory,' *Sociological Theory*, Volume 26 Issue 2, May 28, 2008, pages 173–199.

A source of confusion regarding theory is that most of us encounter and use similar-looking but nontheory explanations in daily life. Theories are explanations but not the only source of explanations. Explanations offer ideas for making sense of things and tell us what is important, why people do what they do, and how events in the world fit together. We can hear explanations in conversations with friends, on television shows, from politicians and business leaders, in newspaper reports, and even via films. They are explanations but fall short of ones offered by social theory.

Many people become anxious when encountering unfamiliar abstract ideas. We all recognize that the world has both concrete events and physical objects that we can touch and see (e.g., holding this book) as well as abstract ideas that reside in our minds (e.g., the meaning of freedom and justice). When we encounter many unfamiliar abstract ideas and the ideas are poorly defined, whether intentionally or not, we quickly experience anxiety and frustration. Social theory consists of interconnected abstract ideas. Some of the ideas are linked only loosely to the observable world or familiar ideas. Until we learn a theory's ideas and see their connections, it is no surprise that discussing abstract ideas can make us feel uncomfortable.

A last source of confusion relates directly to doing research. A few of us as researchers fail to make theory explicit and easy to see. Although it takes a little more time and effort, when a study's theory is clear and visible, we can all more easily evaluate the study's strengths and weaknesses.

WHAT IS THEORY?

Chapter 1 discussed the fact that *social theory* is a system of interconnected ideas. It condenses and organizes knowledge about the social world. We can also think of it as a type of systematic "story telling" that explains how some aspect of the social world works and why.

Many courses in social theory emphasize the history of social thought or teach us what great thinkers said. Classical social theorists (e.g., Durkheim, Marx, Mills, Tonnies, and Weber) generated many innovative ideas. They radically changed how we see and understand the social world around us by developing highly original, broad theories that laid the foundation for subsequent generations. We continue to study their writings because they offered many creative and interrelated ideas. Such true geniuses who can generate many insightful ideas and fundamentally shift how we see the social world are very rare. Despite the value of their contributions, theory is more than what the classical social theorists wrote. It is also more than we learn from recent leading theorists (e.g., Jeffrey Alexander, Pierre Bourdieu, James Coleman, Michel Foucault, Anthony Giddens, and Erving Goffman). Although theorists generate many new ideas and theories, we all can use theory.

Theories are not static. We are constantly modifying older theories and developing new ones. Theories come in many shapes and sizes. Some are broad systems of thought while others are narrow and specific explanations of one particular issue. At their core, we use social theories to organize and systematize our thinking and to deepen and extend understanding. Because they organize knowledge, theories also become a way to communicate effectively with one another.

Most likely, we all encounter social theories in daily life, although few are explicit or labeled as such. For example, newspaper articles or television reports on social issues usually rely on implicit social theories or partial theories. Such theories may be shallow and incomplete, but they contain assumptions, interconnected concepts, and explanations. For example, a news report might discuss public support or opposition over an issue such as legalizing same-sex marriage. The report might provide a type of social theory to explain why legalizing it is controversial; it might say that opposition originates with religious organizations and people who are afraid of disrupting traditional social values. This theory has several assumptions: Religious organizations can influence new laws, some people fight to preserve past or current social norms, and some religious organizations and some people have strong views about laws regarding marriage. This theory includes concepts such as traditional values, forms of marriage, laws, or religious organizations. It offers an explanation: Vocal political opposition by some organizations or by people with strong beliefs can prevent elected government officials from passing a law. The media are not the only sources of theories in daily life. Political leaders frequently express social theories as they discuss public issues. A politician who says that inadequate schooling causes poverty is expressing a type of theory. Compared to the theories we use in social science research, these implicit, partial theories are less systematic, not as sharply formulated, and more difficult to evaluate with empirical evidence.

Social science theory is often more complex and abstract than a typical layperson's theory; however, a principle of good theory, **parsimony**, is helpful. It means that simpler is better, that better theories have minimal complexity. Good theories lack redundant or excess elements. If we have to two equally convincing theories, the simpler one is better.

Most research studies have theory somewhere. The question is less *whether* we use theory in a study than *how* we use it, or which *type* of theory we use. The place of theory is less prominent in applied or descriptive research than in basic or explanatory research. The studies we conduct will be better designed and stronger once we are aware of how

Parsimony   The idea that simple is better; everything else being equal, a social theory that explains more with less complexity is better.

theory and research fit together. Theory also helps to sharpen our thinking about what we are doing in a study. If we are clear and explicit about our study's theory, others will find it easier to read and understand our research. One indicator of a weak research study is that its theory remains unclear, incomplete, or poorly formulated.

SOCIAL THEORY VERSUS IDEOLOGY

Many people confuse social scientific theory with either a sociopolitical ideology or a moral-religious doctrine. This is understandable. In daily life, we encounter many doctrines and ideologies that share features with social theory. The debate over evolution and "creationism" in the United States illustrates the misunderstanding of scientific theory by many laypeople. Opinion polls show that more than half of the U.S. public want schools to teach both evolution and creationism because people say both are "theories" (Pew Forum, 2005). However, evolution qualifies as a scientific theory because of its logical coherence, openness, integration with other scientific knowledge, and empirical tests. Creationism (or its reinvention into something called "intelligent design") does not qualify; instead, it is part of an ideology grounded in a moral-religious doctrine.

Moral-religious doctrines are faith-based belief systems. They rely on sacred teachings or writings that believers accept as being absolute truth and largely do not question. These doctrines are a type of ideology, or a nonscientific belief system. Debates over many public issues involve ideology, either a moral-religious one, a social-political one, or both. The doctrines frequently appear in the mass media from advocates of various political-moral viewpoints, in corporate or interest group media campaigns, or in justifications by politicians for public policies or new laws.

> **Ideology** A nonscientific quasi-theory, often based on political values or faith with assumptions, concepts, relationships among concepts, and explanations. It is a closed system that resists change, cannot be directly falsified with empirical data, and makes normative claims.

Their many shared features make mistaking an ideology for a social scientific theory easy. Both tell us why things are the way they are: why crime occurs, why some people are poor but not others, why divorce rates are high in some places, and so on. Both contain assumptions about the fundamental nature of human beings and of the social world. Both tell us what is or is not important. Both offer systems of ideas or concepts, and both interconnect the ideas.

The scientific community recognizes theory as essential to the scientific enterprise. Good theory is essential to clarify thinking, to extend and deepen our understanding, and to build knowledge over time. The scientific community views ideology differently, as a nonscientific worldview. Ideology may be appropriate to address nonscientific questions but is an illegitimate way to evaluate truth claims or build knowledge on many issues or questions of social science. To many in the scientific community, ideology is a source of obfuscation that is antithetical to the fundamental principles of science. Defenders of ideologies at times become antagonistic toward social science when the social science refutes aspects of their ideological belief system.

As an "almost" theory, **ideology** lacks critical features required of a true scientific theory. We can distinguish ideologies from theories in seven ways (also see Summary Review Box 3.1 on page 61):

1. *Certainty of answers.* Many people find comfort in ideologies because they offer absolute truth and certain answers. They provide people with feelings of assurance and sense of security. In contrast, social scientific theories offer only tentative answers and admit to uncertainty. Many people are uneasy with the persistent uncertainty, hesitation, and tentativeness of scientific theories. Social science theories require us to have a high tolerance for ambiguity, to ask questions continuously, and to live with persistent doubt.

2. *Type of knowledge system differs.* Ideologies offer a closed system of knowledge that changes little. Ideologies claim to have all of the answers and do not require improvement. In contrast, science is an open-ended knowledge system that is always growing and changing. Its answers are incomplete and subject to revision as we acquire new evidence and knowledge. We are constantly modifying and reconsidering theories. Theories continuously evolve, grow, or develop toward higher levels—sometimes slowly, sometimes quickly; sometimes directly, sometimes only after a temporary reversal or diversion.

3. *Type of assumptions differ.* Both ideologies and social scientific theories contain assumptions. The assumptions in ideologies tend to be fixed, inflexible, and unquestioned. Most ideological assumptions originate in one of three sources: religious belief or faith (e.g., a specific form of Christianity or Islam), a value-based position (e.g., libertarian, socialist, or fascist), or the point of view of particular social position (e.g., a wealthy powerful elite, persons who are homeless and destitute). When they originate in a particular social location, ideologies protect and advance that one sector of society (e.g., wealthy investors, people who are destitute). In contrast, the assumptions of social scientific theory originate in open debates and discussions within the scientific community, and they evolve over time. We will examine issues of value neutrality and objectivity later (in Chapters 4 and 16). For now, we can recognize that social science theory differs from ideology by an attempt to be neutral with regard to assumptions or, if not entirely neutral, very explicit and open about its assumptions.

As noted here, ideologies often reflect the worldview of one sector of society. Might the social position of researcher-scientists affect social theory? Some say that researchers must remain detached and separate from all specific societal interests in their theory; others allow social-political views in some areas of the research process so long as they are explicit; still others say researchers occupy a unique "relational" position in society (Mannheim, 1936). A *relational position* means that social researchers come from diverse areas of society, are highly conscious of the full range of all social areas, and self-consciously reflect on their unique social position.

4. *Use of normative statements differ.* Ideologies contain many normative assumptions, statements, and ideas. They advance a normative stance or position. A *normative statement* is one that contains "what ought to be." It tells us what is desirable, proper, moral, and right versus undesirable,

improper, immoral, or wrong. An ideology, like a social theory, tells us what is and why but goes beyond that to have a "what should be." (See Expansion Box 3.1, Explaining Divorce on page 60.) Ideologies blur the distinction between a descriptive, fact-based assertion—*this is what happened or how people live*—an explanation—*this is why it happened or why people live this way*—and a normative position—*this should have occurred or is how people should live.*

In contrast, few social science theories advance a specific normative claim. They offer descriptive statements ("this is how the world operates") and explanations. In social theory, there are separate normative positions. We can connect a theory's descriptions (e.g., some people are starving) or explanations (e.g., some people withhold food supplies to get higher prices and this causes others to starve) to one or more normative positions (e.g., no one should go hungry, starvation of the weak makes humankind stronger). Although description, explanation, and normative positions do not have to occur in a theory, if one occurs, it is not rigid or fixed.

In sum, in social theory, normative-moral positions are detached or separated from the descriptive statements and explanations, while in ideologies, the normative positions are integral to and embedded within the descriptive statements and explanations. This makes it impossible to remove the normative positions from ideologies.

5. *Use of empirical evidence differs.* A critical distinction between scientific theory and ideology involves empirical evidence. Supporters of an ideology will selectively present and interpret the evidence in ways to protect an ideological belief. Often they emphasize personal experience, conformity to a core value conviction, or religious faith as an ultimate type of evidence that overrides careful empirical observation. As a closed belief system that already has "the answers," ideologies resist or deny contradictory evidence. When an ideology confronts overwhelmingly negative or contradictory evidence, the ideologies do not bend or change. From an ideological worldview, believers will selectively reinterpret, treat as an exception, or declare negative evidence as irrelevant to the ideology's claims. Believers in an ideology can always find

EXPANSION BOX **3.1**

Explaining Divorce

How an Ideology Might Explain Divorce

American society has experienced a moral-social break-down over the past 30 years. Families were strong, mothers did not work away from home but spent much more time taking care of their children and husband. Because of religious and moral teachings, families were strong, and divorce was rare. In the recent decades, however, moral decay has spread. There is less respect for religious and moral authority. Negative behaviors, government policy, and mass media have weakened the family and caused divorce to increase.

An Evaluation   This explanation uses the concepts of *moral-social breakdown, strength of family, divorce, time that mothers spend with their children and husband, moral decay, loss of respect,* and *media messages*. These concepts lack precise meanings and measurement, and their exact timing is not certain. The concepts are vague and highly evaluative (e.g., *decay, breakdown, bad*). Testing the explanation would not be easy, and a long time frame suggests that alternative factors occurred in the same period that also might have an impact.

Example of Social Theory

Whether or not a family remains intact (i.e., married adults do not divorce) and is strong (i.e., expresses affection toward one another and spends time together, devotes more time nurturing children, exhibits positive social interaction patterns) depends on the level of resources and social-emotional stress. Resources include factors that are material (income, education, housing), social (friends and extended family, involvement in community organizations), cognitive (e.g., schooling, knowledge, following current events), and psychological (positive self-images, maturity, and respect for others). Stress includes uncertainty about the future and instability of life conditions (e.g., irregularly employed family members, poor or declining health, victims of crime, or emotional instability). Families with both sufficient resources and low levels of stress tend to be stronger than those with a combintion of low resources and high stress, and strong families are more likely to remain intact than weak families.

An Evaluation   This explanation uses four concepts: *resources* (three types), *stress, family strength,* and *remaining intact*. It suggests definitions or how we measure each concept. The relationship among concepts is straightforward and can be empirically tested.

---

ways to reject contrary evidence. It is a "Don't confuse me with facts; I know I'm right" position. In fact, when presented with negatives, believers in an ideology react with fear and hostility toward people who disagree.

Social theories are open systems of belief and explanation; they welcome all evidence. Because social science theories are open to continuous debate, modification, or change, they are constantly evolving. Evidence from studies may support, extend, reject, or modify a theory. We regularly confront theory with empirical evidence—*all* of the relevant evidence—both supporting and contrary. We use evidence to evaluate a theory, not to defend it. We

never know in advance whether the evidence will support the theory. Any study could uncover evidence suggesting that a theory has weaknesses and needs modification.

In social science, we assume that over time, social research produces cumulative knowledge and evidence; it builds over time. Because research and theory are cumulative, we do not automatically toss out a theory if we encounter any negative evidence. We evaluate all evidence together. If after years of research and dozens of studies, we have accumulated widespread empirical support for a theory, we may only slowly adjust it to new negative evidence. Nonetheless, any negative evidence raises some questions about a theory. If the new evidence repeatedly fails to support a theory, we are compelled to modify or replace it.

6. *Demand for logical consistency differs.* Ideologies often contain logical contradictions, and many ideologies rely on circular reasoning. There are many forms of circular reasoning; some are logical fallacies or errors in true logical reasoning. They simply repeat a statement in slightly different or stronger terms as "evidence" or reasoning for it. The typical response to finding a logical contradiction or fallacy in an ideology is to deny it or cover it up. In contrast, we as social scientists insist that theories be logically consistent. We are constantly trying to root out and remove all logical fallacies. If we discover a fallacy or contradiction, we revise the theory or replace it with a different one that does not contain a fallacy or contradiction.

7. *Transparency differs.* The distinction between ideology and theory has implications for the way we conduct research studies. In social scientific research, we are aware of a theory's assumptions, concepts, and relationships and make them explicit. Theory and its place in research are very public; we as scientists hide nothing. Combined with visibility

is a welcome to challenges and open debate. In contrast, ideologies often contain features that are obscure or difficult to pinpoint. Ideologies frequently contain areas clouded in mystery or secrecy; they seek obedience and deference, not serious challenge or debate.

THE PARTS OF SOCIAL THEORY

Assumptions

All theories contain built-in **assumptions**, which are statements about the nature of things that we cannot observe or do not empirically evaluate. They are necessary starting points. In social science we make assumptions about the nature of human beings (e.g., people are essentially competitive or kind and cooperative), social reality (e.g., it is easy to see or contains hidden elements), or a particular phenomenon or issue.

> **Assumption**   An untested starting point or belief in a theory that is necessary in order to build a theoretical explanation.

Social Theory versus Ideology

BASIS OF DIFFERENCE	IDEOLOGY	THEORY
Certainty of answers	Absolute, certain answers with few questions	Tentative, conditional answers that are incomplete and open ended
Type of knowledge	Closed, fixed belief system	Open, expanding belief system
Type of assumptions	Implicit assumptions based on faith, moral belief, or social position	Explicit, changing assumptions based on open, informed debate and rational discussion
Use of normative statements	Merger of descriptive claims, explanations, and normative statements	Separation of descriptive claims, explanations, and normative statements
Empirical evidence	Selective use of evidence, avoidance of direct tests of claims, resistance, denial, or ignorance of contrary evidence	Consideration of all evidence, seeking repeated tests of claims, changing, based on new evidence
Logical consistency	Contradictions and logical fallacies	Highest levels of consistency and congruity, avoiding logical fallacies
Transparency	Avoidance of transparency	Encouragement of transparency

One type of assumption is the *background assumption*: It must exist for us to continue inquiry. Theories about complex social issues, such as racial prejudice, rely on several implicit background assumptions. Some of them related to racial prejudice are as follows: The people of a society recognize racial categories or racial distinctions; they see distinctions among individuals based on the person's membership in a racial group; they attach traits, motivations, and characteristics to being a member of a racial group; and they evaluate the goodness of members' traits, motivations, and characteristics. These are background assumptions because if people did not distinguish among "races" (i.e., certain physical appearance features related to ancestry), never attached characteristics to members of a racial group, and so forth, then the concept of *racial prejudice* would cease to be useful. Thus, the concept and a theory to explain it build on background assumptions.

In addition to background assumptions, we may have *"tractable"* assumptions (i.e., they have traction and allow us to take an argument further [see Abbott 2004:152]). A tractable assumption may or may not hold. If we wanted to study racial prejudice, we might assume that people have it in varying degrees, and some people may not have it at all. We might assume that a person's racial prejudice applies to people in other racial groups but not to their own racial group. We might assume that racial prejudice persists over time in a person and does not instantly appear or disappear.

Concepts

Concepts are the building blocks of theory.[1] A **theoretical concept** is an idea we can express as a symbol or in words. We often express theoretical concepts in natural science and mathematics in symbolic forms, such as Greek letters (e.g., π or Σ) or as formulas (e.g., $s = d/t$; s = speed, d = distance, t = time). In contrast, most social scientists express their concepts in words. While the exotic symbols of mathematics and natural science make

---

Theoretical concept   An idea that is thought through, carefully defined, and made explicit in a theory.

---

many people nervous, using everyday words in specialized ways for social science concepts can create confusion. The distinction between concepts expressed as words and concepts expressed as symbols should not be exaggerated. Words, after all, are symbols, too; they are symbols we learn with language.

Let us look at a simple example concept with which you are already familiar, *height*. You can say the word *height* or write it as a symbol, *h*. The combination of letters in the word or its sound symbolizes, or stands for, an idea in your head. The Chinese characters 高度, the French word *hauteur*, the German word *höhe*, the Spanish word *altura* all symbolize the same idea. In a sense, a language is an agreement to represent ideas by sounds or written characters that people learned at some point in their lives. Learning concepts and theory is like learning a language.[2]

Concepts exist outside of social science theory. They are everywhere, and we use them all the time. *Height* is a simple concept from everyday life, but what does it mean? We may find it easy to use the concept *height* but difficult to define or describe the concept itself. This is often the case: We may use concepts but find it difficult to think through their full meaning and give them good definitions. The concept *height* is an abstract idea about a physical relationship. As a characteristic of a physical object, it indicates the distance from top to bottom. We typically define concepts both by using other concepts and with examples. We can define *height* by using the concepts of top, bottom, and distance and can illustrate it with numerous examples in the physical world.

Height is a very familiar concept. All people, buildings, trees, mountains, books, and so forth have a height. We can measure the height of any object or living thing or compare their heights. A height of zero is rare but possible, and height can increase or decrease over time. As with many words, we use *height* and its concept in several ways. We use the word *height* in many expressions: the *height* of the battle, the *height* of the summer, and the *height* of fashion.

The word *height* refers to an abstract idea. We associate a sound and written form of the word with that idea. Nothing inherent in the sounds of the word connects it to the idea. The connection is arbitrary, but it is still very useful. Symbols allow us to express an abstract idea to one another by using the symbol alone. This is an important point: We communicate the abstract, invisible concepts in our heads to each other by using visible symbols.

Concepts have two parts: a *symbol* (a word, term, or written character) and a *definition*. We learn definitions in many ways. We probably learned the word *height* and the idea it represents, or its definition, from our parents. We learn many concepts as we learn to speak and learn to be socialized to a culture. Our parents probably did not give us a dictionary definition. Instead they taught us through a diffuse, nonverbal, informal process. They showed us many examples; we observed and listened to others use the word. We used the word incorrectly and got confused looks or someone corrected us. We used it correctly, and others understood us. Eventually, we mastered the concept. This is how we learn most concepts in everyday language. Had our parents isolated us from television and other people and then taught us that the word for the idea of distance from top to bottom was *zodige*, we would have had difficulty communicating with others. To be of value, people must share the symbols/terms for concepts and their definitions with others.

Most of the concepts we use in everyday life have vague, unclear definitions. Likewise, the values and experiences of people in a specific culture can influence or limit everyday concepts. Preindustrial people in a remote area without electricity who never used a telephone have trouble understanding the concept of a computer or the Internet. Also, some everyday concepts (e.g., evil spirits, demons) have roots in misconceptions, ancient myth, or folklore.

Everyday concepts and those used in social science differ, but the difference is not rigid or sharp. Some social science concepts first developed in research studies with precise technical definitions have diffused into the larger culture and language. Over time, they have become less precise or developed an altered meaning. Concepts such as sexism, lifestyle, peer group, urban sprawl, and social class started as technical concepts in a social theory.

Where do social science concepts originate? Many started as ideas from everyday life, personal experiences, creative thought, or daily observations. Someone elaborated on the idea, offered a definition, and others discussed the idea, trying to make it clearer and more precise. Some social science concepts originated in classical theory. People developed some new concepts out of deep contemplation and reflective thought, sometime after examining the findings in research studies or by synthesizing findings and ideas from many diverse situations. Taken together, the numerous social science concepts form a specialized language. We use it for discussing, analyzing, and examining the social world around us. Many people call this language *jargon,* which has a bad reputation.

Specialists in many fields use jargon. It is a shorthand way to communicate with one another. Physicians, lawyers, artists, accountants, plumbers, anime fans, orchid growers, and auto mechanics all have specialized languages, or jargon. They use it to refer to the ideas and objects with which they deal on a regular basis, some of which are not widely known or shared. For example, publishers and printers have a jargon: terms such as *idiot tape, fonts, cropping, halftone, galley proof, kiss impression, hickeys, widows,* and *kerning.* For people on the inside, jargon is a fast, effective, and efficient way to communicate. However, when people misuse a specialized language to confuse, exclude, or denigrate others, the specialized language acquires a negative reputation, and we call it *jargon.* Use of jargon with people who do not know the specialized language fails to communicate and often generates resentment.

Once we learn social science concepts and begin to use them among others who know their meaning, we will find them to be an efficient, concise, and precise way to discuss ideas and issues. To the novice or an outsider who has not yet learned the concepts, a discussion filled with the terms for social science concepts will sound like incomprehensible jargon.

Level of Abstraction. Concepts vary according to their **level of abstraction**. Some concepts are very concrete and refer to objects we can see and touch: pizza, trees, cats, cell phones, or a college test. Others are abstract mental creations removed from direct,

Level of abstraction   A characteristic of a concept that ranges from empirical and concrete, often easily observable in daily experience, to very abstract, unseen mental creations.

daily empirical life. Abstract concepts refer to aspects of the world we do not easily experience or cannot easily express. Nonetheless, they have great value because they organize our thoughts and expand our understanding. We cannot directly see concepts such as patriotism, social capital, self-esteem, emotional pain, panic, fear, cognitive dissonance, political power, or organizational authority, but we might "feel" them or recognize them operating in daily life.

To define simple, concrete concepts, we use many examples and point to visible physical features. In contrast, complex, abstract concepts often require formal, dictionary-like definitions. Their definitions combine several other, less abstract or low-level concepts. The concept of *height* is not very abstract, but we still use the slightly less abstract concepts of *top, bottom,* and *distance* to define it. Similarly, the concept of *aggression* is more abstract than ones we might use to define it, such as *hit, slap, scream, push, yell, punch, physically injure,* or *threaten serious bodily harm.* We might define *racial prejudice* using other abstract concepts such as *attitude* or *stereotype.*

As social scientists, we tend to define concepts more precisely than the ones in daily life. We link concepts in a theory with research studies and empirical data. This happens because knowledge advances only if we have clear, logically consistent definitions of our ideas.

Having clear, explicit, and precisely defined concepts is essential for advancing knowledge and conducting research. A few studies or theoretical essays develop entirely new concepts, but usually we rely on existing concepts. However, many concepts have multiple definitions, so we must decide which one to use. Even after we choose one, we may wish to modify or clarify the existing definition. Wimmer (2008:973) explored and refined the concept of *ethnic boundary* (i.e., the boundaries that divide ethnic groups). He defined the concept of ethnicity "as a subjectively felt sense of belonging based on the belief in shared culture and common ancestry."

This is one among many definitions, and other people have used it. Social researchers have debated how to define the concepts of *ethnicity* and *race.* Wimmer says that ethnicity is a very broad idea. He defines *race* and *nationhood* as subtypes of ethnicity. Race is ethnicity based on phenotype features; nation is ethnicity based on a community's nationalist aspirations. Other subtypes include ethnicity based on a belief in a shared religious, regional, or linguistic heritage.

Wimmer (2008) explicitly rejects the idea of using common everyday understandings of ethnicity or race. Americans' understanding of these concepts is overlapping, vague, and contradictory (for recent evidence, see Hitlin, Brown, and Elder, 2007; Morning, 2009). Wimmer wanted to avoid defining the concepts as they are used in a single culture because doing so would limit cross-cultural comparisons and theory building. He noted that there are

> *societies with phenotypical variation among the population but without racialized groups, societies without phenotypical variation but racially defined groups in stark opposition to one another, and nonracialized systems of ethnic differentiation that are as exclusionary as race is in the United States. (p. 975)*

This example illustrates how we define concepts. It also highlights a tension between the public's use of concepts in daily life and concepts in social theory and research. The public defines many concepts in overlapping, vague, or contradictory ways. To deepen understanding of the social world and create clear theories, we want precise, nonoverlapping, and noncontradictory theoretical definitions, yet we study how the public sees and thinks about the world. If we borrow the public's definitions, our definitions may be close to how the public uses the concepts in daily life but may be vague, overlapping, and contradictory. If we use academic definitions, they may not closely match the public's understanding of the concept, but our definitions can be precise, nonoverlapping, and noncontradictory, permitting clearer thinking and real advances in knowledge. An additional source of confusion is that words that the public uses (e.g., race) are the same as the ones we use in social theories. In the end, such issues mean we want to be very clear in our own minds about concepts and carefully define them.

In sum, an important research task is to think through ideas or concepts carefully and precisely and to assign them explicit, clear definitions (we will look at this more in Chapter 7). Such theorizing provides a crucial foundation for carrying out research studies and advances our understanding of the world around us.

Single versus Concept Clusters. We rarely use concepts in isolation from one another. Concepts form interconnected groups, or **concept clusters**. This is true for concepts in daily life as well as for those in social theory. Theories have collections of associated concepts that are consistent and mutually reinforcing. Together, the collections can form a broader web of meaning. For example, in a discussion of the *urban decay,* we may read about associated concepts such as urban expansion, economic growth, urbanization, suburbs, center city, revitalization, ghetto, mass transit, crime rate, unemployment, White flight, and racial minorities. Used together, these concepts form a mutually reinforcing collection of ideas that we use in theorizing and research studies.

We can simplify the concepts in daily life and social theory into two types. One type has a range of values, quantities, or amounts. Examples include *amount of income, temperature, density of population, years of schooling,* and *degree of violence.* These are *variables,* or *variable concepts,* that you will read about in Chapter 6. The other type expresses categories or nonvariable phenomena (e.g., *bureaucracy, family, college degree, homelessness,* and *cold*).

Simple versus Complex Concepts. In addition to ranging from concrete to abstract and being a variable or nonvariable type, concepts can be categorized as simple or complex. *Simple concepts* have only one dimension and vary along a single continuum. *Complex concepts* have multiple dimensions or many subparts. We can break complex concepts down into several simple, or single-dimension, concepts. In general, the more complex concepts tend to be more abstract and simple ones more concrete, although this is not always true.

Here is an example of a complex concept. Rueschemeyer and associates (1992:43–44) stated that democracy has three dimensions: (1) regular, free elections with universal suffrage; (2) an elected legislative body that controls government; and (3) freedom of expression and association. They recognized that each dimension varies by degree (very regular and wide-open or free elections in which everyone votes versus irregular restricted elections with only a minority allowed to vote). By combining the three simpler concepts or dimensions, Rueschemeyer et al. created the idea of different types of political regimes. Regimes considered to be very low on all three dimensions are totalitarian, those high on all three are democracies, and ones with other mixes are either authoritarian or liberal oligarchies. The regime types refer to more complex concepts than the three concepts for the dimensions.

Another type of complex concept is the **ideal type**. It is a broader, more abstract concept that organizes a set of more concrete concepts. Ideal types are pure, abstract models that try to define the core of the phenomenon in question. They are mental pictures that outline the central aspects of what is of interest. They are smaller than a theory but help to build a full one. Ideal types are not explanations because they do not tell why or how something occurs. Qualitative researchers often use ideal types to see how well observable phenomena match the ideal model. A very famous ideal type is that of Max Weber, who developed an ideal type of the concept *bureaucracy* (see Example Box 3.1, Max Weber's Ideal Type of Bureaucracy). It distinguishes a bureaucracy from other organizations. No real-life organization perfectly matches the ideal type, but this model helps us to think about and study bureaucracy.

A **concept classification** is partway between a simple concept and a full-blown theory.[3] It helps to

---

Concept cluster A collection of interrelated concepts that share common assumptions, refer to one another, and operate together in a social theory.

Ideal type A type of concept classification that presents a pure, abstract model of an event, process, or idea. It is used in building social theory and in the analysis of data.

Concept classification A complex, multidimensional concept that has subtypes that are between a single concept and a complete theoretical explanation.

EXAMPLE BOX **3.1**

Max Weber's Ideal Type of Bureaucracy

- Bureaucracy is a continuous organization governed by a system of rules.
- Conduct is governed by detached, impersonal rules.
- There is division of labor in which different offices are assigned different spheres of competence.
- Hierarchical authority relations prevail; that is, lower offices are under control of higher ones.
- Administrative actions, rules, and so on are in writing and maintained in files.
- Individuals do not own and cannot buy or sell their offices.
- Officials receive salaries rather than receiving direct payment from clients in order to ensure loyalty to the organization.
- Property of the organization is separate from personal property of officeholders.

Source: Adapted from Chafetz. *A primer on the construction and testing of theories in sociology* (1978: 72). F. E. Peacock Publishers.

TABLE 3.1 Robert Merton's Modes of Individual Adaptation

MODE OF ADAPTION	SOCIETAL GOALS	INSTITUTIONAL MEANS
I Conformity	Accept	Accept
II Innovation	Accept	Reject
III Ritualism	Reject	Accept
IV Retreatism	Reject	Reject
V Revolution	Substitute new	Substitute new

organize abstract, complex concepts. By logically combining the simpler concepts, we can create a type of complex concept that is a classification. You can best grasp this idea by considering some examples. A major type of classification is the **typology**, or taxonomy,[4] in which a researcher logically combines two or more unidimensional, simple concepts so that a new concept is formed where the two simple concepts intersect. The new concept expresses the interrelation or overlap of the simple concepts.

Merton's (1938) anomie theory of deviance is a widely used typology that is simple and elegant. It allows us to understand both nondeviance and deviance by using two simpler concepts: (a) the goals that a society defines as worth pursuing and (b) the means that people use to achieve goals. The typology rests on two relationships: (1) whether people

Typology A theoretical classification or quasi-theory that is created by cross-classifying or combining two or more simple concepts to form a set of interrelated subtypes.

accept or reject society's goals and (2) whether people use socially approved means (i.e., legitimate) to reach the goals. Merton's typology identifies conformity and several types of deviance based on these concepts (see Table 3.1). Conformity, or nondeviance, occurs when people accept societal goals (e.g., obtaining a high income) and use a socially legitimate means to reach them (e.g., getting a good job and working hard). Various forms of deviance occur when this is not the case. Merton's classification of how individuals adapt to goals and means to reach them summarizes his complex concept and labels each subpart. For example, *retreatism* describes a person who rejects both societal goals and the socially legitimate means to achieve them—such as a chronic alcohol user or a religious hermit. This type of deviant rejects the societal goal of appearing respectable and acquiring material possessions (e.g., house, car) and the legitimate means of reaching the goal (e.g., being honest, working at a job).

A different concept classification builds on classical social theory. Wright (1978) updated Marx's theory of social classes in capitalism and later tested his theoretical updating with empirical data from contemporary U.S. society. Wright noted that, for Marx, inequality and exploitation are based on control over three types of resources: (1) investments (i.e., profit-making property or capital), (2) the organization of production, and (3) labor power (i.e., the work of other people). Wright said that the organization of a class society creates positions or places that confer power (i.e. directing the work of other people). He also said that the organization of a class society creates positions

TABLE 3.2   Erik Wright's System of Social Classes

SOCIAL CLASS	CONTROL OVER SOCIETAL RESOURCE		
	Investments	Production	Labor
Capitalists	+	+	+
Managers	−	+	+
Supervisors	−	−	+
Workers	−	−	−
Petite bourgeoisie	+	+	−

+ means has control, − means has little or no control

that confer control over the three types of resources (see Table 3.2). People in positions that control all three resources constitute the most powerful people or become the society's dominant social class. In market economies, this is the capitalist class. Its members include the major investors, owners, and presidents of banks or corporations. Capitalists make investment decisions (e.g., whether and where to build a new factory), determine how to organize production (e.g., use robots or low-wage workers), and give orders to others. The class near the bottom consists of workers. They occupy positions in which they have no say over investments or how to organize production. They lack authority over others and must follow orders from other people to keep their jobs. Managers and supervisors, who assist the capitalists, are between the two major classes. They are a quasi-class that had not yet fully appeared in the mid-1800s when Marx developed his theory. This class controls some but not all of society's major resources. The classification also points out another class about which Marx wrote, the petite (small) bourgeoisie. It consists of small-scale self-employed proprietors or farmers. Members of this class own and operate their own businesses but employ no one except family members. Marx thought this class would decrease and disappear, but it is still with us today. Like Merton, Wright combined simple concepts (i.e., types of resources owned or not owned) to generate a theoretically powerful, complex classification (i.e., the structure of social classes in capitalist society).

A final example of a concept classification comes from Walder (2003), who wanted to understand transition from a communist regime with a command economy to postcommunist regime with a market economy. He used two factors—(1) limits on seizing private assets and (2) the amount of political change that took place—to create a classification of four types of postcommunist regimes. He cross-classified the two factors to create a conceptual typology. He used this typology with other ideas to explain the smoothness of the transition from communism and to identify which social-political groups gained power in the various postcommunist societies (see Table 3.3). Note that concept classifications are not, in themselves, full theoretical explanations. We need to add other theoretical ideas to them for them to tell us why outcomes occurred.

Scope. Concepts vary as to scope. Some are very narrow and apply only to specific social settings or activities or are restricted in time or place. We cannot easily use them beyond a particular setting. Other concepts are very broad. They apply to many diverse settings or activities across large expanses of time and space. Broad concepts tend to be more abstract than narrow ones.

An example concept with a narrow scope is "football hooliganism." It refers to acts of violence by British and, to a degree, other European soccer fans that have accelerated since the late 1960s. The concept is restricted in time and location. Fans of other mass spectator events have engaged in rioting or acts of violence and property destruction, but this

TABLE 3.3   Four Transition Paths from a Communist to a Postcommunist Economy

		HOW EXTENSIVE WAS POLITICAL CHANGE?	
		High	Low
Limits on taking assets	High	1	2
	Low	3	4

concept is rather specific to rioting British soccer fans. Another example is the Japanese phenomena of *karoshi,* or death by overwork. People have died from excessive labor throughout history and across cultures, but this concept narrowly refers to males working in white-collar jobs who are under intense social pressure to work many hours (e.g. 16–18 hours per day) for their company without rest for a period of one or more years. The concept is associated with Japanese company work culture in the 1970s–1990s. In contrast, similar concepts of broader scope, such as physical labor or clerial work, widely apply across historical time and in diverse cultural settings.

Concepts with a narrow scope are closest to concrete everyday life. This makes them easily recognized. We can incorporate specific contextual features and the texture of a social setting into them. At the same time, doing so makes it difficult to generalize them and use them easily to build a general theoretical understanding of social life. Concepts with a broad scope (e.g., social participation, emotional warmth) have the opposite advantages and disadvantages. These concepts bridge diverse settings and times, and they facilitate our general understanding. However, they disregard significant contextual details in particular social settings and historical conditions.

Relationships

Social theories are more than collections of assumptions and concepts; they also specify relationships among the concepts. They tell us whether the concepts are connected to one another, and, if so, how. By outlining an entire complex of assumptions, concepts, and relationships, a theory provides a complete picture of why specific relationships do or do not exist.

> **Proposition** A theoretical statement about the relationship between two or more concepts.
>
> **Hypothesis** An empirically testable version of a theoretical proposition that has not yet been tested or verified with empirical evidence. It is most used in deductive theorizing and can be restated as a prediction.

Kinds of Relationships. Beyond telling us whether concepts are or are not related, theories specify the relationships. For example, a theory may tell us whether a relationship is strong or weak, direct or indirect, positive or negative. It might tell us that one concept accelerates or decelerates/diminishes the other or that its impact is immediate or delayed. Good theories indicate whether one concept is a necessary (i.e., essential and required) precondition for another concept or only sufficient (i.e., it is involved but does not have to be present). Sometimes a theory states that one concept relates to another but only under certain conditions (these are called *contingent relationships* and are discussed later in this book). A theory also specifies the form of explanation (e.g., causal, structural, and so forth) in which a relationship operates (see later in this chapter).

Propositions and Hypotheses. Social theories contain propositions about the relationships among concepts. A **proposition** is a theoretical statement that two or more factors or concepts are related and the type of relationship it is. It is a belief that may or may not have been tested. A major purpose of doing research is to find out whether a theory's proposition conforms to empirical evidence or data. Some theoretical propositions are in the form of assumptions; others can be tested with empirical data. A **hypothesis** is an empirically testable version of a proposition. It is a tentative statement about a relationship because when we start a study, we are uncertain as to whether the hypothesis actually holds in the empirical world. After repeated empirical evaluations of a hypothesis in many situations, our certainty in its truthfulness grows. By empirically evaluating a hypothesis, we learn whether a theoretical proposition is supported, or we may decide to revise it or remove it from the theory entirely. While many research studies are designed to test hypotheses, some types of research proceed without a hypothesis.

Units of Analysis

The social world comprises many units, such as individual people, groups, organizations, movements, institutions, countries, and so forth. Researchers tailor theoretical concepts to apply to one or more of these **units of analysis**. For example, the concept *aggression* can be applied to several units: an individual, group, organization, or country. This is illustrated by these statements: Jamie is an *aggressive* child; the basketball team was very *aggressive* last night; the XYZ Corporation has *aggressively* moved into a new market; and the United Nations condemned country X for acts of *aggression* toward its neighbor. Aggression by a child (slapping another four-year-old and kicking the teacher) seems different than aggression by a sports team (physical contact and blocking), a company (lowering prices and launching a massive advertising campaign that targets a competing product), or a nation (moving troops and tanks across an international border).

When we conduct a study, we must fit a concept to the specific type of unit we wish to analyze, like a glove fitting over a hand. This means fitting concepts with units as we design a study and measure concepts (discussed in Chapters 6 and 7). If we consider an abstract concept, such as aggression, that is applicable across various units of analysis, we must decide the unit to focus on and tailor the way we define the concept to that unit before proceeding.

Aspects of Theory

Now that you know the parts of social theory, you can consider its other forms. Social theory can be baffling because it has many aspects. To simplify matters, we can divide them into five major ones:

1. *Direction of theorizing.* Either deductive or inductive
2. *Level of analysis.* Either micro, macro, or meso
3. *Theoretical focus.* Either substantive or formal theory
4. *Form of explanation.* Either causal, structural, or interpretative
5. *Range of a theory.* Either an empirical generalization, a middle-range theory, or a framework

The aspects may seem intimidating at first. Fortunately, only a few major combinations of them are frequently used. As you become familiar with the aspects, you will find that they help to clarify and simplify how you apply theory when conducting a research study.

Direction of Theorizing

In an ideal sense, you can approach the building and testing of theory from two directions: (1) begin with abstract thinking and then logically connect the ideas in theory to concrete evidence or (2) begin with specific observations of empirical evidence and then generalize from the evidence to build toward increasingly abstract ideas. In practice, most researchers are flexible and tend use both directions, perhaps at different points in a study (see Figure 3.1).

Deductive. To theorize in a **deductive direction**, we start with abstract concepts or a theoretical proposition that outlines the logical connection among concepts. We move next to evaluate the concepts and propositions against concrete evidence. We go from ideas, theory, or a mental picture toward observable empirical evidence. The studies of the contact hypothesis discussed in Chapter 2 used deductive theorizing. The researchers began with a theoretical proposition: The absence of interpersonal contact between people and others in a social "out-group" causes negative views of an out-group to arise because of ignorance and negative stereotypes. The researchers turned the proposition into a testable empirical hypothesis: that increased social contact with, knowledge of, and familiarity among individuals in an out-group will lessen the negative beliefs, attitudes, and statements of people in the "in-group." The theorizing proceeded from the abstract level to a concrete, empirical level that

---

Units of analysis   The units, cases, or parts of social life that are under consideration. They are key to developing concepts, empirically measuring or observing concepts, and using data analysis.

Deductive direction   An approach to developing or confirming a theory that begins with abstract concepts and theoretical relationships and works toward more concrete empirical evidence.

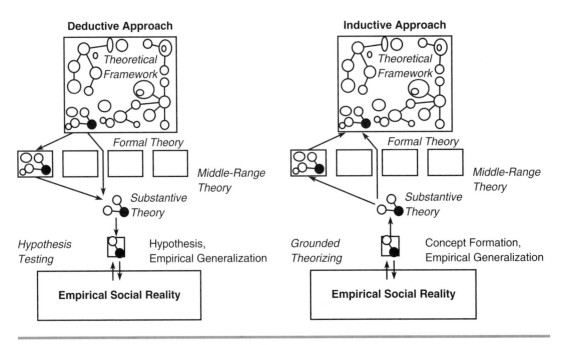

FIGURE 3.1   Deductive and Inductive Theorizing

included specific out-groups, forms of social contact, and beliefs or attitudes.

Inductive. To theorize in an **inductive direction**, we begin with observing the empirical world and then reflecting on what is taking place and thinking in increasingly more abstract ways. We move toward theoretical concepts and propositions. We can begin with a general topic and a few vague ideas that we later refine and elaborate into more precise concepts when operating inductively. We build from empirical observations toward more abstract

thinking. In his study of street vendors in New York City presented in Chapter 2, Duneier (1999) used inductive theorizing. He developed a theoretical understanding only during and after he had collected empirical data. He stated, "I began to get ideas from the things I was seeing and hearing on the street" (p. 341). Duneier (p. 342) described the process as being like the method used by a medical professional who sees patients with many diverse symptoms. Only after analyzing the symptoms does the professional make a diagnosis or coherent story that explains the underlying reason for the many symptoms visible on the surface.

Many researchers use a specific type of inductive theorizing called grounded theory. It involves formulating new theoretical ideas from the ground up instead of testing existing theoretical ideas. You will learn more about this theory in Chapters 6 and 14.

Inductive direction   An approach to developing or confirming a theory that begins with concrete empirical evidence and works toward more abstract concepts and theoretical relationships.

Grounded theory   A type of inductive social theory often used in qualitative research that builds toward abstract theory, often by making comparisons of empirical observations.

Grounded theory is a widely used approach in qualitative research. It is not the only approach and it is not used by all qualitative researchers.

Grounded theory is "a qualitative research method that uses a systematic set of procedures to develop an inductively derived theory about a phenomenon" (Strauss and Corbin, 1990:24). The purpose of grounded theory is to build a theory that is faithful to the evidence. It is a method for discovering new theory. With it, the researcher compares unlike phenomena in order to learn their similarities. He or she sees micro-level events as the foundation for a more macro-level explanation. Grounded theory shares several goals with more positivist-oriented theory. (Postivist theory is discussed in Chapter 4.) It seeks a theory that is comparable with the evidence that is precise and rigorous, capable of replication, and generalizable. A grounded theory approach pursues generalizations by making comparisons across social situations.

Qualitative researchers use alternatives to grounded theory. Some qualitative researchers offer an in-depth depiction that is true to an informant's worldview. They excavate a single social situation to elucidate the micro processes that sustain stable social interaction. The goal of other researchers is to provide a very exacting depiction of events or a setting. They analyze specific events or settings to gain insight into the larger dynamics of a society. Still other researchers apply an existing theory to analyze specific settings that they have placed in a macro-level historical context. They show connections among micro-level events and between micro-level situations and larger social forces for the purpose of reconstructing the theory and informing social action (for a summary of several alternatives, see Burawoy, 1991:271–287; Charmaz, 2003; and Hammersley, 1992.)

Level of Analysis

Social reality exists on many levels, ranging from the micro to macro levels. The micro level of social life includes short-term face-to-face interactions of a few individuals, usually in a small-scale setting (e.g., a female customer at a fast-food restaurant chats briefly with an employee and a male customer behind her in line). At the micro-level of social reality, people engage in direct personal contact, usually in a close physical setting. Social

scientists develop **micro-level theory** and concepts tailored to analyze this level of social reality. For example, McFarland (2004) developed a micro-level theory of disruptive behaviors in high school classrooms. Based on detailed observations of interactions inside classrooms among students and teachers, he noted the way protagonists and antagonists acted in patterned ways and had different outcomes. (Also see Example Box 3.2, Inductive, Micro-Level Theory on page 72.)

The macro level, which is at the opposite extreme of the micro level, includes large-scale societal events (e.g., the patterns of encounters between western European imperialist powers and Chinese civilization during the eighteenth century) and entire social institutions (e.g., the entire criminal justice system of a nation). **Macro-level** theorizing explains events, processes, patterns, and structures that operate among large-scale social units, usually over decades or longer and often covering large expanses of geographic space. The study of Spanish America for over a century of time by Mahoney (2003) in Chapter 2, Example Box 2.13, illustrates macro-level theorizing.

Between the micro level and macro levels is the meso level, an intermediate level. **Meso-level theory** focuses on the level of organizations, social movements, or communities. As we examine different levels of the social world, we develop theories and concepts that operate at a corresponding level of analysis.

Micro-level theory Social theory focusing on the micro level of social life that occurs over short durations (e.g., face-to-face interactions and encounters among individuals or small groups).

Macro-level theory Social theory focusing on the macro level of social life (e.g., social institutions, major sectors of society, entire societies, or world regions) and processes that occur over long durations (many years, multiple decades, or a century or longer).

Meso-level theory Social theory focusing on the relations, processes, and structures at a midlevel of social life (e.g., organizations, movements, and communities) and events operating over moderate durations (many months, several years, or a decade).

EXAMPLE BOX 3.2

Inductive, Micro-Level Theory

In her study of two very different toy stores, Williams (2006) developed a micro-level theory inductively from her observations made while working for six weeks at each store. Her goal was "to describe and analyze the rules that govern giant toy stores" (pp. 19–20) from observing day-to-day interactions. Williams observed and documented hundreds of ways males, Whites, and high-income people were treated better in daily workplace routines, informal store rules, and customer–staff interactions. These actions reinforced the prevailing societal hierarchy: Males dominated and had privileges when compared with females, Whites compared with non-Whites, and high-income individuals compared with low-income people. In both stores, all directors were White males; everyone employed in a "masculine" job (e.g., security guards, loading dock laborers, backroom assem-

blers) were male (half being non-White), and everyone in a "feminine" job (e.g., cash register clerk, customer service worker) was female. An exception was the electronics section of one store. It was a separate area, and every employee in that section was an Asian man. One store was "high end" and had expensive toys. The other was like a warehouse with working-class customers. In both, the clerks and managers engaged in identical "customer profiling": They treated White female customers as potential "big spenders" and Black male customers as potential thieves. Williams' micro-level theory showed how informal daily rules in very different settings perpetuated inequalities of class, race, and gender. Mundane shopping/selling interactions continuously reproduced, and almost never reversed, any relations of the social hierarchies.

Theoretical Focus

We construct, elaborate, and test or verify two types of theory, substantive and formal. **Substantive theory** focuses on a particular content or topic area in social reality, such as family relations, delinquent behavior, or racial-ethnic relations. We might have a theory that focuses on economic development as with Mahoney's (2003) study of Spanish America (Chapter 2) or a theory that focuses on how social inequalities are reproduced in everyday face-to-face interactions as with Williams' (2006) study of toy stores (see Example Box 3.2).

Formal theory focuses on general processes or structures that operate across multiple topic areas, such as forming a social identity, engaging in conflict, or exercising power. It is more general and abstract. A formal theory about access to resources and holding onto power and authority might apply

to several areas. It might explain how wealthy business owners use their access to valued resources in advanced capitalist societies to maintain economic and social power (see Table 3.2), how government elites used resource control to try to hold onto power during the transition from communism to a post-community world (see Table 3.3), and how colonial elites in a rigid system of resource control held onto local power in the nineteenth century in a way that stalled later national development (see Example Box 2.13). In all three situations, a similar social-economic dynamic operated: Powerful elite groups used their ownership and control over valued resources to maintain a position of power and resist challenges to their authority.

The two types of theory intersect. Substantive theory on a topic often draws on and combines formal theories, and a formal theory may have applications in several substantive areas. As Layder (1993:44) remarked, "The cumulative process of theory is enhanced by the encouragement of multiple substantive and formal theories."

Each theoretical focus has strengths and limitations. Substantive theory offers powerful explanations for a specific topic area. It incorporates

Substantive theory A type of theory that is specifically tailored to a particular topic area.

Formal theory A type of theory that is general and applies across many specific topic areas.

details from specific settings, processes, or events. Nonetheless, it may be difficult to generalize across topic areas. Compared to formal theory, concepts in a substantive theory tend to be at lower levels of abstraction and narrower in scope. Compared to formal theory, we can see the relevance of a substantive theory for ongoing events more easily. Formal theory's strength is its ability to bridge across multiple topic areas and advance general knowledge. Its weakness is that by being less rooted in specific issues and social settings, we have to adjust the theory to see how it relates to a particular issue or topic. Formal theories help us to recognize and explain similar features across multiple topics. They are more abstract, making them more complex and easier to express in a purely logical, analytic form.

Forms of Explanation

Prediction and Explanation. The primary purpose of theory is to explain. However, explanation has two meanings: theoretical and ordinary. Researchers focus on **theoretical explanation**, a logical argument that tells why something takes a specific form or why it occurs. Usually when we do this, we refer to a general rule or principle, and we connect it to a theoretical argument with many connections among concepts. An *ordinary explanation* makes something clear or describes something in a way that illustrates it and makes it intelligible for other people. For example, a good teacher "explains" in the ordinary sense. The two kinds of explanation can blend together, as when we explain (i.e., make intelligible) an explanation (i.e., a logical argument involving theory). Before we examine forms of theoretical explanation, we will take a short detour because many people confuse prediction with explanation.

Prediction is a statement that something will occur. An *explanation* logically connects what occurs in a specific situation to a more abstract or basic principle about "how things work" to answer the why question. The particular situation is shown to be an instance or specific case of the more general principle. It is easier to predict than to explain, and an explanation has more logical power than prediction because good explanations also predict. A specific explanation rarely predicts more than one

> **Theoretical explanation** A logical argument or "story" that tells why something takes a specific form or occurs and does so by referring to more general ideas and abstract principles.

outcome, but competing explanations can predict the same outcome. Although it is less powerful than an explanation, many people are entranced by the dramatic visibility of a prediction.

A gambling example illustrates the difference between explanation and prediction. If I enter a casino and consistently and accurately predict the next card to appear or the next number on a roulette wheel, this will be sensational. I may win a lot of money, at least until the casino officials realize that I am always winning and expel me. Yet my method of making the predictions is more interesting than the fact that I can do so. Telling you what I do to predict the next card is more fascinating than being able to predict. Here is another example. You know that the sun "rises" each morning. You can predict that at some time, every morning, whether or not clouds obscure it, the sun will rise. But why is this so? One explanation is that the Great Turtle carries the sun across the sky on its back. Another explanation is that a god sets his arrow ablaze, which appears to us as the sun, and shoots it across the sky. Few people today believe these ancient explanations. The explanation you probably accept involves a theory about the rotation of the earth and the position of the sun, a star in our solar system. In this explanation, the sun only appears to rise, but it does not move. Its apparent movement depends on the earth's rotation. We are on a planet that both spins on its axis and orbits around a star millions of miles away in space. All three explanations make the same prediction: The sun rises each morning. As you can see, a weak explanation can produce an accurate prediction. A good explanation depends on a well-developed theory and is confirmed by empirical observations.

Nobel Prize–winning physicist Steven Weinberg (2001:47) has given a "hard science" view of explanation:

> *Scientists who do pure rather than applied research commonly tell the public and funding agencies that*

*their mission is the explanation of something or other. . . .Within the limited context of physics, I think one can . . . [distinguish] explanation from mere description, which captures what physicists mean when they say that they have explained some regularity. . . .We **explain** a physical principle when we show that it can be deduced from a more fundamental physical principle.* [emphasis added]

Theoretical explanations take three forms: causal, structural, and interpretative. Each explains, or answers, the question of why events occur. Each connects a specific case to some type of general principle.

Causal Explanation A **causal explanation** indicates a cause-effect relationship among concepts/ variables. We use this type of explanation in everyday language, although everyday language tends to be rather sloppy and ambiguous. Here is a causal explanation: You say that poverty *causes* crime or that weakening societal morals *causes* divorce to increase. These are elementary causal explanations. Social scientists try to be more precise and exact when they discuss causal relations. They also try to determine how or why the causal process works (e.g., how and why poverty causes crime).

At least since the time of eighteenth century Scottish philosopher David Hume (1711–1776), philosophers have debated the idea of cause. Some people argue that causality occurs in the empirical world. Although we cannot see it easily, it is "out there" in objective reality, and we can find indirect evidence of it. Others argue that causality does not exist in objective reality. It is a mental construction "in our heads." We have subjectively created the idea of causality to help us think about events in objective reality. Without entering into the philosophical debate, many social scientists theorize and conduct studies on causal relationships.

Requirements for Causality. We need three things to establish causality: temporal order, empirical

Causal explanation A type of theoretical explanation about why events occur and how things work expressed in terms of causes and effects or as one factor producing certain results.

association, and the elimination of plausible alternatives (see Example Box 3.3, Three Elements of Causality). An implicit fourth condition is that the causal relationship makes sense or fits with broader assumptions or a theoretical framework. Let us examine the three basic conditions. In addition to these three, a full explanation also requires specifying the causal mechanism and outlining a causal chain.

1. *Temporal order* means that the cause must come earlier in time than an effect. This common-sense assumption establishes the direction of causality: from the cause toward the effect. You may ask how the cause can come after what it is to affect. It cannot, but temporal order is only one of the conditions needed for causality. Temporal order is necessary but not sufficient to infer causality. Sometimes people make the mistake of talking about "cause" on the basis of temporal order alone. For example, race riots occurred in a dozen U.S. cities in 1968 one day after an intense wave of sunspots happened. The temporal ordering does not establish a causal link between sunspots and race riots. Eventually, all of prior human history occurred before some specific event. The temporal order condition simply eliminates from consideration potential causes that occurred later in time.

Establishing temporal order can be tricky in cross-sectional research. For example, a researcher finds that people who have considerable formal schooling express less prejudiced attitudes than others. Does more schooling cause a reduction in prejudice, or do people who are highly prejudiced avoid school? Here is another example. The students who get high grades in my class say I am an excellent teacher. Am I doing a great job, students learn a lot, and this causes high grades, or does getting high grades make them happy, so they return the favor by saying that I am an excellent teacher (i.e., high grades cause a positive evaluation)? It is a chicken-and-egg problem. To resolve it, a researcher needs to bring in other information or design research to test for the temporal order. Simple causal relations are unidirectional, operating in a single direction from the cause to the effect. More complex theories specify reciprocal-effect

EXAMPLE BOX **3.3**
Three Elements of Causality

I read that several politicians visited a Catholic school in Chicago that had a record of being much more successful than public schools in educating children. The next day, the politicians called a news conference and advocated new laws and the redirection of tax money to Catholic schools. As a person who wants children to get a good education, I was interested in the story, but as a social scientist, I critically evaluated it. The politicians' theory said Catholic schools cause more learning than public schools. They had two elements of causality: temporal order (first the children attended a Catholic school, then learning improved) and association (those attending Catholic schools performed better than those attending public school). Social researchers know this is not enough information. They first try to eliminate alternative explanations and then try to understand the causal mechanism (i.e., what happens in Catholic schools that helps students learn more). For example, the politicians failed to

eliminate the alternative explanation that children in the two types of schools had different family circumstances that affect learning and that this caused learning differences. If the family circumstances (e.g., parents' education and income, family religious belief and intensity of belief, two-parent versus single-parent households, degree of parental interest in child's education) are the same for children who attend both types of schools, then the politicians are on the right track. The focus, then, is on what Catholic schools are doing that improves learning. If the family circumstances are very different, then the politicians are making a big mistake. Unfortunately, politicians are rarely trained in social research and most make quick, high-publicity decisions without the careful reasoning or the patience for precise empirical investigation. Fortunately, sociologist James S. Coleman and others have studied this issue (see Coleman and Hoffer, 1987).

---

causal relations—that is, a mutual causal relationship or simultaneous causality. For example, studying a lot can cause a student to get good grades, but getting good grades also motivates the student to continue to study. Theories often have reciprocal or feedback relationships, but these are difficult to test. Some researchers call unidirectional relations *nonrecursive* and reciprocal-effect relations *recursive.*[5]

   2. An *association* means that two phenomena occur together in a patterned way or appear to act together. People often confuse the word *correlation* with association. Correlation has a specific technical meaning and there are certain statistical requirements for it. Association is the more general idea. The correlation coefficient is a statistical measure that indicates the strength of association, but there are other ways to measure an association. Sometimes researchers call association *concomitant variation* because two variables vary together. Figure 3.2 (on page 76) depicts 38 people from a lower-income neighborhood and 35 people from an upper-income neighborhood. Can you see an association between

race (represented by lighter and darker shaded figures) and income level? Some people mistake association for true causality. For example, when I was in college, I got high grades on the exams I took on Fridays but low grades on those I took on Mondays. Thus, an association existed between the day of the week and the exam grade. This association did not mean that the day of the week caused the exam grade. Instead, the reason for the association was that I worked 20 hours each weekend and was very tired on Mondays. If you cannot find an association, a causal relationship is very unlikely. This is why you want to find correlations and other measures of association. Yet just because you find an association does not mean you have causality. It is a necessary but not a sufficient condition. In other words, you need it for causality, but it is not enough alone.

> **Association**   The co-occurrence of two events, characteristics, or factors so that when one happens or is present, the other one is likely to happen or be present as well.

Lower Income   **Upper Income**

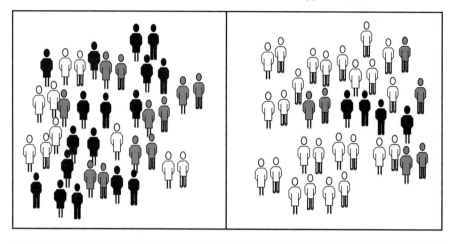

FIGURE 3.2   Association of Income and Race

To show causality, an association does not have to be perfect (i.e., every time one variable is present, the other is also). In the example involving exam grades and days of the week, there is an association if on ten Fridays I got seven As, two Bs, and one C, whereas my exam grades on ten Mondays were six Ds, two Cs, and two Bs. An association exists, but the days of the week and the exam grades are not perfectly associated. The race and income-level association shown in Figure 3.2 is also an imperfect association.

3. *Eliminating alternatives* means that we must show that the effect is due to the causal variable, not to something else. It is also called *no spuriousness* because an apparent causal relationship that is actually due to an alternative but unrecognized cause is called a spurious relationship, which is discussed in Chapter 6. While we can observe temporal order and associations, we cannot empirically eliminate all logical alternatives. Eliminating possible alternatives is an ideal. This means we can demonstrate this only indirectly or rule out the more obvious alternative

> **Causal mechanism**   The part of a causal explanation that specifies the process by which the primary independent variable(s) influence the primary dependent variable(s).

explanations. In an experiment, we build controls into the study design itself to eliminate alternative causes and isolate the experimental situation from the influence of all variables except the main causal variable. Nonexperimental research eliminates alternatives by identifying possible alternative causes and measuring them. This is common in survey research. Once we measure potential alternatives, we use statistical techniques to learn whether the causal variable or something else operates on the effect variable.

4. *Specifying the mechanism in a causal relationship* means that when we create a causal explanation, we must have more than two variables that are correlated, which is "a satisfactory explanation requires that we also specify the social 'cogs and wheels'" (Hedstrom and Swedberg, 1998:7). We go beyond saying that an independent and dependent variable are linked, as if the connection were through a "black box" of unknown processes. A full causal explanation identifies a causal relationship and specifies a **causal mechanism**.

Let us say we find a strong association between a person's social class and her health. We may state our "theory" as high-class people live longer and get sick less often than low-class people. However, it is not enough to say that a person's social class causes health outcomes. We must also explain why and how social class does this. In short, we should describe exactly what it is about social class that makes the health outcomes happen. We may *believe* that higher class provides people with more social resources (knowledge, social connections, leisure time, flexible schedule) that enables them to eat healthy food, experience less stress, engage in physical exercise, and so forth, which produce better health. Social resources are the mechanism that connects class and outcomes (resources include "being in the know," "knowing the right people," and having access to opportunities).

Seeing the mechanism of a full causal explanation may be difficult, especially in the natural sciences. We may posit unseen mechanisms among subatomic particles or off in distant galaxies to explain what we can observe. As research advances, we observe the outline of a mechanism whose existence we first only predicted in theory. Even if we cannot directly observe the mechanism now, we can still describe how we think it operates.

We can use models of a process that we believe connects inputs with outcomes to clarify mechanisms. In economics, the market is a common mechanism; it is a process of making exchanges between independent buyers and sellers, each with desires and resources. The market explains how the supply–demand relationship operates. In sociology, a commonly used mechanism is Merton's self-fulfilling prophecy. A self-fulfilling prophecy occurs when a definition of a situation stimulates behavior that makes a false definition come true. A "negative feedback" mechanism in a prophecy connects people's beliefs and behaviors at one point in time to later outcomes. A classic example of a self-fulfilling prophecy is a run on a bank. A bank may be very financially stable, but a false rumor starts that it will fail. This new definition of the situation, although inaccurate, causes many people to withdraw their money quickly. As people withdraw large amounts of money, the bank weakens. The weakened bank stimulates even more rumors of bank failure. The new rumors in turn stimulate more withdrawals. Eventually, accelerating fear (false definition of the situation) and withdrawals (behavior based on the definition) cause the bank to fail (the false definition becomes true).

Sometimes we state theories as a lawlike generalization: When *X* occurs, *Y* will occur. However, such "theories" are not a full explanation (Elster 1998). They need the causal mechanism. The mechanism is often more specific than a general law, but it is more general than a specific instance. In a full explanation, the mechanism may be an arrangement of opportunities or individual desires, which are more general than a particular opportunity or one desire but less general than a lawlike statement. Mechanisms add complexity. Instead of a simple law (if *B* then *R*), we find in specific situations that if *B* sometimes *R* but at other times *P* or *D*. The mechanism explains why *B* does not always cause *R* but can create other outcomes. Perhaps we believe that when economic conditions are bad (*B*), people rebel (*R*). However, as we study many specific situations, we find this is not always true. Sometimes people rebel, but at other times they become passive and accept their fate (*P*) and at still other times they fight one another and become self-destructive (*D*). For a complete explanation, we must include the mechanism that tells us when bad conditions produce each of the outcomes.

5. *Outlining the causal chain* is a process in evaluating each part of the chain. Here is an association in a causal theory: A rise in unemployment causes child abuse to increase. We want to explain these increases. We explain them as being caused by a rise in unemployment. To "explain" increased child abuse, we must identify its primary cause, but a full explanation also requires specifying how this happens (i.e., identify a causal mechanism and put it in a casual chain). The mechanism in this theory is the situation of people losing their jobs. Once they lose their jobs, they feel a loss of self-worth and increased stress. As they lose self-worth and experience high stress, they are more easily frustrated and become angry more quickly. Inner social control weakens, and the pattern of living is disrupted. Highly frustrated people with lower inner social control may express their anger by directing violent acts toward those with whom they have close personal contact (e.g., friends, spouse, children). This is especially true if they cannot direct their anger in actions against its source (e.g., an employer, government policy, or "economic forces"). The mechanism is part of a larger process or causal chain, and it occurs after the initial cause (unemployment) and before the effect (child abuse).

We can test each part of a causal chain. In addition to determining whether unemployment rates and child abuse occur together, we can consider whether unemployment increases frustration, and frustrated people become violent toward family members. A typical research strategy is to divide the causal chain into its parts and then to evaluate each part of the chain against the data.

Diagrams of Causal Relations. We can express causal relationships and theories using words, pictures, or both. We often present diagrams of the causal relations to provide a simple picture of a relationship. This makes it easier for others to see the causal relation quickly at a glance. Such symbolic representations supplement verbal descriptions and are shorthand for conveying complex information.

The simplest diagram is a two-variable model as the one in Figure 3.3(a). We represent variables using letters, circles, or boxes. The convention is to represent a cause by an X and the effect by a Y. The arrow shows the direction of causality (e.g., from cause to effect). Sometimes we use subscripts when there is more than one cause (e.g., X_1, X_2). We symbolize relationships by lines with directional arrows. Causal relations are represented by straight lines. The convention is to use curved lines with arrows on both ends to show an association that does not imply that a causal relationship goes in one direction.

> **Positive relationship**   An association between two concepts or measures so that as one increases, the other also increases, or when one is present, the other is also present.
>
> **Negative relationship**   An association between two concepts or measures so that as one increases, the other decreases, or when one is present, the other is absent.
>
> **Structural explanation**   A type of theoretical explanation about why events occur and how things work expressed by outlining an overall structure and emphasizing locations, interdependences, distances, or relations among positions in that structure.

Positive and Negative Causal Relationships. Causal relationships can be positive or negative. Many people imply a positive relationship between the cause and effect variables if they say nothing. A **positive relationship** means that a higher value on the cause goes with a higher value on the effect or outcome. For example, as the number of years of a person's schooling increases, the longer the person's life expectancy is. A **negative relationship** means that a higher value on the cause goes with a lower value on the effect or outcome. For example, as the number of years of a person's schooling increases, his or her bigotry and prejudice decreases. In diagrams, a plus sign ($+$) signifies a positive relationship and a negative sign ($-$) signifies a negative relationship. Figure 3.3 presents some samples of relationships that can be diagrammed. Researchers would not use a diagram for a very simple relationship like the one in Figure 3.3(a) but find it helpful as they increase the number and complexity of causal relationships.

At times, the impact of a cause on an outcome is mediated or conditioned. This means that the cause operates under some conditions but not others. For example, early marriage causes divorce in modern societies that permit individual freedoms and allow for legal divorce but not in highly traditional societies. A third factor that mediates the basic cause-effect relationship is diagrammed as a third line with an arrow that intersects the line with an arrow between the cause and effect. In Chapter 2 the study on the contact hypothesis that you read used a causal explanation. The researchers found that more contact caused negative attitudes to decline (also see Example Box 3.4, Explaining Racial Conflict on page 80).

Structural Explanation. In a causal explanation, one or more factors may cause a response in other factors. This is like one ball that rolls and hits others, causing them to begin rolling. In contrast, the logic of a **structural explanation** locates a social process, event, or factor within a larger structure. The structure is like a spiderweb, a wheel with spokes, or a machine with interconnected parts. A structural explanation explains social life by noting how one part fits within the larger structure. A causal expla-

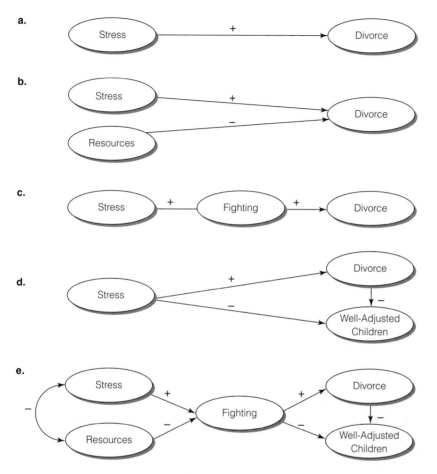

Explanation of relationship in each diagram

a. Level of stress (financial, social, emotional, etc.) is positively associated with the likelihood that a couple will divorce.

b. Level of stress is positively associated with the likelihood that a couple will divorce, but the amount of resources (financial, social, emotional, etc.) they possess is negatively associated with it.

c. Level of stress is positively associated with the frequency of fighting by a couple, which is associated with the likelihood that the couple will divorce.

d. Level of stress is positively associated with the likelihood that a couple will divorce and negatively associated with the likelihood that the couple will have emotionally well-adjusted children. In addition, the divorce process itself has a negative effect on the emotional adjustment of children.

e. Level of stress and amount of resources are negatively associated with each other (i.e., people who tend to have many resources are less likely to experience or better able to deal with stress). Level of stress is positively associated with the frequency of fighting by a couple, but the amount of resources is negatively associated with it. Amount of fighting is positively associated with the likelihood that a couple will divorce. Both fighting and the divorce itself are negatively associated with the likelihood that the couple will have emotionally well-adjusted children.

FIGURE 3.3   Causal Diagrams

Sequential theory   A type of theory that uses a structural explanation, outlines a sequential pattern, and specifies the ordered sequence, stages, steps, or phases by which events occur.

Three major types of theories that use a structural explanation are sequential theories, network theories, and functional theories (see Figure 3.4).

nation says, B happens because A causes B. A structural explanation may say that B happens because B is positioned inside a larger structure that either blocks off or provides B openings to other areas in the structure.

1. Sequential theory emphasizes the order or sequence by which events occur; it identifies the necessary earlier steps and possible subsequent steps in an unfolding pattern of development across time. A sequential theory maps out an ordered set of stages. Almost all people, organizations, or events follow the sequence. There may be a single path or

EXAMPLE BOX 3.4
Explaining Racial Conflict

Behrens, Uggen, and Manza (2003) provided a causal explanation of felon disenfranchisement in the United States. They noted that the United States has the most restrictive voting laws for people convicted of committing a crime among advanced democracies. State-level voting laws vary widely: Some states have no restrictions, others bar incarcerated felons from voting, and others bar felons who have served their sentences from voting for life. The authors extended an existing theory, the "racial threat hypothesis," to explain why some states have highly restrictive voting laws while others do not. Others have developed the theory to explain interracial economic competition. These authors measured a high racial threat as a potentially angry, powerful Black presence (e.g., large Black populations and many Blacks in prisons) in a state where a White majority prevented Blacks from voting in the pre–Civil Rights era but can no longer do so after the passage of civil rights laws. The authors looked at the year in which a restrictive voting law was passed, the types of restrictions it included, and the percentage of Blacks in the state population and in its prisons. The role of imprisonment is pertinent because Blacks are far more likely than Whites to be felons. The theory suggests the states with the highest "racial threat" would have the most restrictive voting laws because restrictive voting laws replaced more direct forms of denying voting rights to Blacks. The authors documented temporal order and found an association between racial composition and restrictive laws that fit the hypothesis. In this macro-level study, the main cause was a large Black

population in prisons, the main effect was restrictive voting laws, and the unit of analysis was the state (see Example Box 3.4 Figure).

McVeigh (2004) also used a causal explanation to study why White racist organizations succeed in some areas of the United States more than in other areas. Racist organizations appealed to Whites who experience downward social mobility and offered messages that blamed non-Whites for the difficulties. McVeigh hypothesized that racist organizations would be most successful where local conditions matched the racist claims. He predicted that the White racist messages would succeed in areas of more racial diversity, unstable economic conditions, and rising income inequality. In addition, he expected racist messages that lacked an alternative, nonracist diagnosis of the conditions to be most successful. He argued that alternatives would be in the highest numbers where White education levels were mixed, the more educated Whites would spread to other Whites information of alternative reasons for their economic decline (e.g., global competition, changing technology, lack of relevant skills). He hypothesized that a combination of two causes— Whites economically falling behind visible, nearby non-Whites and the absence of an nonracist diagnosis—explained the success of racial organizations in some areas. In the study, McVeigh measured economic conditions, racial organizational success, and mixed White education level by county, which was the study's unit of analysis (see Example Box Figure 3.4 Figure).

(continued)

EXAMPLE BOX 3.4

continued

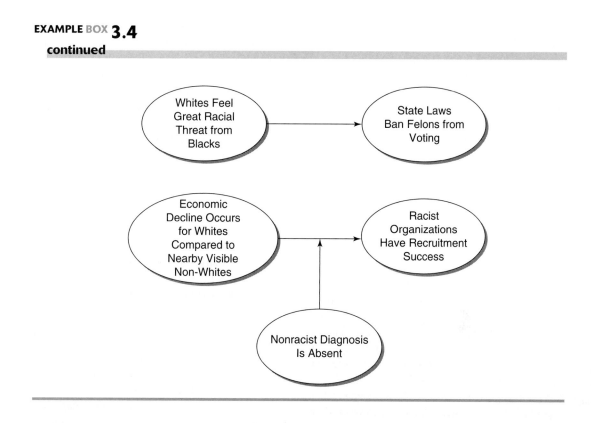

a narrow range of paths for a specific process, such as the moral development of a child, the maturing of an intimate relationship, family formation, urban expansion, organizational growth or death, conflict intensification or resolution, or societal development. In addition to identifying the steps or stages of a process, sequential theories explain the speed of movement along the steps, stagnations at a stage,

and key turning points of a process that trigger a different direction or steps. A sequential theory may identify essential versus optional steps, or how a specific prior step restricts possible next steps. It is not a causal theory; being in an earlier step does not *cause* movement along the sequence; instead, the structure of a staged sequence constrains what can occur. Thus, a sequential theory may state that

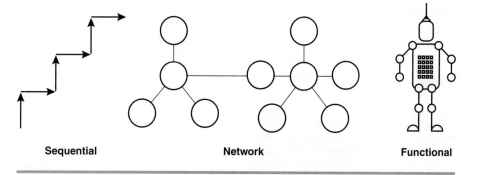

FIGURE 3.4 Forms of Structural Explanation

unless step A was completed, movement to step B is impossible, and the only way to get from step A to step C is to pass through step B.

The study of Spanish American countries by Mahoney (2003) that you read about in Chapter 2 used a sequential theory. He found that events at an early stage in a Spanish American country's development, during colonialism, shaped the direction of its path in later stages. Oesterle, Johnson, and Mortimer (2004) offer a sequential theory in their panel study on voluntarism among young people. The authors adopted a "life course" perspective in which "the meaning of roles and activities differs across life stage" (p. 1124). Thus, the impact of an event at a specific phase of a person's life differs from the same event happening in other phases, and the same impact will shape events in later phases. The authors noted that the transition to adulthood is a critical stage when a person learns new social roles and adult expectations. They examined panel data of ninth-grade students (15–16 years old) begun in 1988 that continued across 9 years when the research subjects were 18–19 and 26–27. The authors found that prior stage activities strongly influenced what happened at the last stage. People who worked or who were parenting full-time at an earlier stage (18–19 years old) were less likely to volunteer at a later stage (26–27 years old) than people whose major activity was to attend school full-time. Also, having volunteered at an earlier stage predicted whether a person volunteered at a later stage.

2. Network theory explains social relations in terms of placement in a network. It explains by referring to relational positions within a network or its size and shape, type and existence of connections among positions, overlap or density of connections, centrality in a network, or flows among positions or nodes in a network.[6] The positions might be points or nodes in a network of relationships among people, organizations, cities, or nations. The positions and structure of a network help to explain ease of communication, power relationships, hierarchical relations, and speed of flows in the network.

A network theorist explains by referring to a pattern, a set of syntax rules, or structures. The explanation shows events fitting into a larger pattern or within a much larger system of linkages. Network theory is a form of reasoning similar to that used to explain why people use language in specific way. For example, a language has syntax rules that state that X goes with Y or that sentences need a noun and a verb. To explain is to identify the syntax rule that covers a situation.

Many studies examine social networks and map network structures as a way to explain social life. Entwisle, Faust, Rindfuss, and Kaneda (2007) studied networks in villages in a region of Thailand. The authors found that the networks connecting people, through kinship or other social ties, varied by village: "Networks are sparse in some, dense in others; porous in some, less so in others. Moreover, this variability matters" (p. 1524). The networks had many consequences for relations with nearby villages, for the economic activities in a village, for whether people migrated out of a village, and so forth. Network structure shaped the flow of activities and degree of intravillage cooperation. To illustrate these findings, the authors provide a diagram with six households (on page 83). Solid lines indicate people related as brother or sister, and dotted lines indicate those helping with the rice harvest. They show that households a, b, d and e work together. There is no direct family connection between a and d, or between b and e, but they cooperate due to their indirect connections in the network through d. A key network impact was on social cohesion. As the authors noted, "Networks in which actors have more ties, on average, are more cohesive than those in which actors have fewer ties. . . . The more cohesive a network, the more likely that information can travel through social ties to all members and that activities can be coordinated among network members" (p. 1508). In other words, networks influenced how activities in a village occur. More important, dense overall networks with many interconnections were more socially cohesive than loose

Network theory   A type of theory that uses a structural explanation in which the emphasis is on locations and connections within an interconnected web or network and on the shape or overall pattern of the network.

networks. *Cohesion* meant that people shared information, cooperated, and accomplished tasks faster and with fewer difficulties compared to people in villages that have sparse networks (*American Journal of Sociology,* 2007:1515).

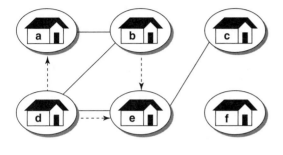

—— Siblings

--➤ People Helping with Rice Harvest

From The Construction of a Global Profession: The Transnationalization of Economics, by Marion Fourcade. *American Journal of Sociology,* Volume 112 Number 1 (July 2006): 145–94 (page 151).

---

3. Functional theory uses the idea of a system with a set of mutually interdependent relations.[7] Various parts of a system depend on other parts, and in combination, all parts function together as a whole. Success or failure of one part has ramifications for other parts and for the entire system. The system might refer to a family, a social group, a formal organization, or an entire society. Functional theories suggest that long-term system survival requires a balance or equilibrium to continue smooth operation. If a critical part fails, the system is unable to fulfill a vital function unless a replacement for the vital function is found. Parts of a system tend to be specialized or more efficient/effective in fulfilling different system needs or functions and therefore fit a patterned division of labor. The theory explains parts by the way they fit into the structure of all functions. Like the part of a human body or part of a robot, each part (e.g., head, hand, foot) performs specialized functions.

A functional theory of social change says that society moves through developmental stages, from traditional to modern. Over time, society becomes increasingly differentiated and complex and evolves

> **Functional theory** A type of theory that uses a structural explanation in which the emphasis is on how interdependent parts fit into and operate to sustain an overall system with specific parts serving complementary and specialized supporting roles for the whole.

a more specialized division of labor with individualism. These developments create more efficiency for the system as a whole. Specialization and individualism may create disruptions and require system adjustments. They might weaken traditional ways of performing system functions. However, new types of social relations will emerge to replace traditional ways, and they will perform the same function to satisfy the needs of the system for continuity.

Kalmijn (1991) explained a shift in the way that Americans select marriage partners using a functional explanation. He relied on modernization theory, which holds that the historical processes of modernization (industrialization, urbanization, and secularization) shape societal development. As part of modernization, people rely less on traditional ways of doing things. Traditional religious beliefs and local community ties weaken as does the family's control over young adults. People cease to live their entire lives in small, homogeneous communities. Young adults gain independence from their parents and from local religious organizations. In order to function, every society has a way to organize how people select marriage partners and locate partners with whom they share fundamental values. In the past, parents and religion had a major role in selecting marriage partners. In modern society, people spend time away from small local settings and more time in school settings. In school settings, especially in college, they meet other unmarried people who are potential marriage partners. Education is a major socialization agent in modern society. It affects a person's future earnings, moral beliefs and values, and leisure time interests. Over time, the trend in the United States has been that people are less likely to marry within the same religion and increasingly likely to marry persons with a similar level of education. The functions of socializing people to moral values and linking people to marriage partners that the family and religious organization had performed in traditional society has been replaced by higher education in modern society.

Interpretive Explanation. The purpose of **interpretive explanation** is to foster understanding. It does so by placing what we wish to explain (e.g., a social relationship, event, cultural practice) within a specific social context and setting that have a meaning system. The explanatory goal is for others to mentally grasp how some area of the social world operates and to place what we want to explain within that would. This goal is reached by helping others comprehend what we want to explain within an entire worldview and system of meaning. Each person's subjective worldview shapes how he or she acts, so the goal is to discern others' reasoning and view of things. The process is similar to decoding a text or work of literature in which meaning comes from the context of a cultural symbol system.

Futrell and Simi (2004) used an interpretative explanation to study the U.S. White power movement. The authors focused on movement, collective identity, or a shared sense of "we." They examined members of racist movements that are fragmented into many organizations (e.g., Ku Klux Klan, Christian identity groups, Aryan Nation, neo-Nazi groups) and whose members are marginalized from larger society. The authors investigated how members communicate their beliefs and engage in activism when their radical beliefs can result in losing their jobs and destroying most personal relations. After interviewing and collecting data on fifty-six activists from 1996 and 2003, the authors discovered that the members participated in small domestic gatherings (e.g., study groups, ritual parties) at which they reaffirmed their commitments to the group and discouraged conformity to the mainstream of outsiders. The gatherings were small, inclusive, and rooted in ongoing personal relations. In them members felt that they could safely and openly express racial ideologies. Family members and close friends supported these "cultural havens." Thus, members created and sought out "free spaces" in which they could affirm their radical beliefs among like-minded people. By embedding opportunities for political expressions in what looked on the surface to be "normal" activities (homeschooling, study groups, camping trips, parties), they reduced the distance between themselves and the outside world. They built a protective social environment so they could maintain and celebrate a radical ideology and identity that was camouflaged to appear mainstream.

Range of Theorizing

Theoretical statements also vary by range. At one extreme is the empirical generalization, a narrow statement that relies on concrete concepts and fits into a substantive theory; it is a low-level descriptive statement about a relationship believed to operate empirically. It generalizes beyond a specific case or set of observations but not by very much. For example, people who marry when they are very young (under age 21) are more likely to divorce than those who marry when they are older (over age 31). We might wish to qualify the generalization by specifying historical, cultural, or other conditions that make a divorce more or less likely. If empirical generalization includes an explanation, it is simple and concrete, not a full social theory. For example, people who marry when they are younger are more likely to divorce because they are less mature.

Middle-range theorizing has a broader theoretical range and uses more abstract concepts in a substantive or formal theory. A **middle-range theory** about divorce would include a number of empirical generalizations interlocked with more abstract concepts. Divorce might become part of the

Interpretative explanation A type of theoretical explanation about why events occur and how things work expressed in terms of the socially constructed meanings and subjective worldviews.

Empirical generalization A narrow, quasi-theoretical statement that expresses empirical patterns or describes empirical regularities using concepts that are not very abstract.

Middle-range theory Social theory that falls between general frameworks and empirical generalization, that has limited abstraction/range, and that is in the form of empirically verifiable statements capable of being connected to observable phenomena.

large idea of marital instability, and age of marriage might be linked to the person's stage in the life cycle and the social roles she or he learns. Maintaining a marital relationship may be placed in a context of other social forces (e.g., gender ideologies, societal disapproval or acceptance, laws affecting divorce, friendship or kinship groups, religious pressures). A study may elaborate and test specific parts of the middle-range theory, and accumulating empirical support for many parts of the theory over time helps the theory to advance as an explanation.

Theoretical frameworks (also called *theoretical systems* or *paradigms*) are at the widest range and the opposite extreme from empirical generalizations. A theoretical framework is more than a formal or substantive theory and includes many specific formal and substantive theories that may share basic assumptions and general concepts in common. Sociology has several major frameworks.[8] They are orientations or sweeping ways to see and think about the social world. They provide assumptions, concepts, and forms of explanation.

> **Theoretical framework**   A very general theoretical system with assumptions, concepts, and specific social theories.

For example, each framework may have its own theory of the family, of crime, or of social change. Some frameworks (e.g., symbolic interactionism) are more oriented toward the micro level of analysis whereas others (e.g., conflict) are stronger at the macro level. Specific studies rarely test or contrast entire frameworks. More often, studies seek evidence for one part of a theory within one framework (e.g., one proposition from a conflict theory of crime). Example Box 3.5, Kalmijn's Levels of Theory, illustrates the ranges of theory with Kalmijn's study of changing marriage partner selection. As you will see in Chapter 4, each framework is associated with an overall approach to doing research. Expansion Box 3.2, Major Theoretical Frameworks, briefly describes the key concepts of assumption of the four major theoretical frameworks of sociology.

EXAMPLE BOX **3.5**
Kalmijn's Levels of Theory in "Shifting Boundaries"

Theoretical framework. Structural functionalism holds that the processes of industrialization and urbanization change human society from a traditional to a modern form. In this process of modernization, social institutions and practices evolve. This evolution includes those that fill the social system's basic needs, socialize people to cultural values, and regulate social behavior. Institutions that filled needs and maintained the social system in a traditional society are superseded by modern ones.

Formal theory. Secularization theory says that during modernization, people shift away from a reliance on traditional religious beliefs and local community ties. In traditional society, institutions that conferred ascribed social status (family, church, and community) also controlled socialization and regulated social life. In modern society, they are superseded by secular institutions (e.g., education, government, and media) that confer achievement-oriented status.

Middle-range substantive theory. A theory of intermarriage patterns notes that young adults in modern society spend less time in small, local settings where family, religion, and community all have a strong influence. Instead, young adults spend increasing amounts of time in school settings. In these settings, especially in college, young adults have opportunities to meet other unmarried people. In modern society, education has become a major socialization agent. It affects future earnings, moral beliefs and values, and leisure interests. Thus, young adults select marriage partners less on the basis of shared religious or local ties and more on the basis of common educational levels.

Empirical generalization. Americans once married others with similar religious beliefs and affiliation. This practice is being replaced by marriage to others with similar levels of education.

EXPANSION BOX **3.2**

Major Theoretical Frameworks

Structural Functionalism

Major concepts.   System, equilibrium, dysfunction, division of labor.

Key assumptions.   Society is a system of interdependent parts that is in equilibrium or balance. Over time, society has evolved from a simple to a complex type, which has highly specialized parts. The parts of society fulfill different needs or functions of the social system. A basic consensus on values or a value system holds society together.

Exchange Theory (Also Rational Choice)

Major concepts.   Opportunities, rewards, approval, balance, credit

Key assumptions.   Human interactions are similar to economic transactions. People give and receive resources (symbolic, social approval, or material) and try to maximize their rewards while avoiding pain, expense, and embarrassment. Exchange relations tend to be balanced. If they are unbalanced, persons with credit can dominate others.

Symbolic Interactionism

Major concepts.   Self, reference group, role-playing, perception

Key assumptions.   People transmit and receive symbolic communication when they socially interact. People create perceptions of each other and social settings. People largely act on their perceptions. How people think about themselves and others is based on their interactions.

Conflict Theory

Major concepts.   Power, exploitation, struggle, inequality, alienation

Key assumptions.   Society is made up of groups that have opposing interests. Coercion and attempts to gain power are ever-present aspects of human relations. Those in power attempt to hold onto their power by spreading myths or by using violence if necessary.

The Dynamic Duo

You have seen the many aspects of theory (see Summary Review Box 3.2). Only those of us who are naive, new researchers mistakenly believe that theory is irrelevant to conducting research or that we just collect the data. If we try to proceed without using theory, we may find that we are adrift as we attempt to design a study. We may waste time collecting useless data, lack precise ideas, and fall into the trap of hazy and vague thinking. We may find organizing arguments, converging on research issues, or generating a lucid account of our study for other people to be difficult.

The reason for all of these difficulties is simple. Theory frames how we investigate and think about a topic. It gives us concepts, provides basic assumptions, directs us to the important questions, and

suggests ways for us to make sense of data. Theory helps us make connections and see the broader significance of findings. To use an analogy, theory is what helps us see the forest instead of just a single tree.

Theory has a place in virtually all research, but its prominence varies. It is generally less central in applied-descriptive research than in basic-explanatory research. The role of theory in applied and descriptive research may be indirect. The concepts are often more concrete, and the goal is not to create general knowledge. Nevertheless, we use theory in descriptive research to refine concepts, evaluate assumptions of a theory, and indirectly test hypotheses.

Theory does not remain fixed; it is provisional and open to revision. Theories grow into more accurate and comprehensive explanations about the

SUMMARY REVIEW BOX **3.2**

SUMMARY REVIEW BOX **3.2**
The Parts and Aspects of Social Theory

Four Parts of Social Theory

1. *Assumptions*
2. *Concepts.* Vary by level of abstraction (concrete versus abstract), single versus concept clusters, simple versus complex (e.g., classifications, typologies), and scope (narrow versus broad)
3. *Relationships.* Forms of relationships, propositions, and hypotheses
4. *Units of analysis*

Five Aspects of Social Theory

1. *Direction of theorizing.* Deductive (abstract to concrete) or inductive (concrete to abstract)
2. *Level of analysis.* Micro level, meso level, macro level
3. *Focus of theory.* Substantive theory or formal theory
4. *Forms of explanation.* Causal, structural (sequential, network, functional), or interpretative
5. *Range of theorizing.* Empirical generalization, middle-range theory, or theoretical framework

---

makeup and operation of the social world in two ways. Theories advance as we toil to think clearly and logically, but this effort has limits. The way a theory makes significant progress is by interacting with research findings.

The scientific community expands and alters theories based on empirical results. If we adopt a deductive approach, theory guides study design and the interpretation of results. We refute, extend, or modify the theory based on results. Only by continuing to conduct empirical research that tests a theory can we develop confidence that some parts of it are true. A theory's core propositions and central tenets are more difficult to test and are refuted less often. In a slow process, we may decide to abandon or change a theory as the evidence against it mounts over time and cannot be logically reconciled.

If we adopt an inductive approach, we follow a slightly different process. Inductive theorizing begins with a few assumptions and broad orienting concepts. Theory develops from the ground up as we gather and analyze the data. Theory in a specific area emerges slowly, concept by concept, proposition by proposition. The process is similar to a long pregnancy. Over time, the concepts and empirical generalizations emerge and mature. Soon, relationships become visible, and we weave together knowledge from different studies into more abstract theory.

Theories are relevant because they provide explanations. Different theories provide different explanations, and the types of explanations tell us that the world works in different ways. Some studies evaluate one theory. Other studies expand on a theory or find a theory incomplete and add to it. You saw this in this chapter's opening box: Education and income alone do not explain smoking behaviors. Still other studies set forth two or more competing theoretical explanations and attempt to create a head-to-head competition to see which one better explains events.

Sometimes a study contrasts the competing predictions offered by two or more theoretical explanations. For example, Kraeger (2008) contrasted two explanations about the relationship between a high school boy engaging in antisocial behavior (fighting and delinquency) and in participating in high school sports teams: social control theory and social learning theory. Social control theory suggests that participation in school sports will reduce antisocial behavior. This is so because school sports are an institutionally approved behavior governed by adults. Sports create social bonds among adolescent males and tie them to conventional behavior. Engaging in deviance can cause a loss of athletic status and lower peer social standing. The time required by sports participation also reduces idle time available for performing antisocial behavior. In addition, organized school sports promote prosocial values, such as teamwork and fair play. Social control theory suggests that reports of violent behavior by male high school athletes can be attributed to a few mavericks who lack sufficient control and social integration.

By contrast, social learning theory says we learn either prosocial or antisocial behavior from our peers and family. High school athletics promote both prosocial and antisocial values: play through the pain, do not accept limits, and glorify nonacademic achievements. Certain games or sports, such as the game of chicken, more than others can encourage aggressive physical behavior, use of intimidation, loyalty to insiders, and "character contests." A sub-part of learning theory, masculinity theory, notes that certain sports are "hypermasculine" (such as football, rugby, and ice hockey versus swimming, track, baseball, and tennis). Hypermasculine sports emphasize engaging in individual violence, such as the use of the body as a weapon, brutal body contact, and raw physical domination. These sports link success and prestige among peers to a particular form of "maleness." This form of maleness is insulated from alternative forms of masculinity, which it labels as "weak" or "effeminate." Together social learning and masculinity theory predict that boys who participate or have friends in hypermasculine sports will engage in antisocial behavior, such as fighting, more than those who participate in other sports or who are not engaged in high school sports.

The two theories offer competing predications: (1) participating in school sports or having peers in them reduces antisocial behavior, (2) participating in certain sports or having peers in those sports increases antisocial behavior. Kraeger (2008) examined data from a national sample of 6,397 male high school students. He investigated males who participated in twelve high school sports or had friends in those sports to identify any connections with the students' engaging in antisocial behavior

(i.e., fighting or other acts of delinquency). The findings suggest that high school males with many friends in hypermasculine sports (such as football), especially those also active in such sports themselves, had a high likelihood of fighting. By contrast, the high school males in other school-based sports, such as tennis, had a low tendency to fight. His findings showed more support for social learning than for social control theory.

CONCLUSION

In this chapter, you learned about social theory—its parts, purposes, and types. The dichotomy between theory and research is an artificial one. The value of theory and its necessity for conducting good research should be clear. Researchers who proceed without theory rarely conduct top-quality research and frequently find themselves in a quandary. Likewise, theorists who proceed without linking theory to research or anchoring it to empirical reality are in jeopardy of floating off into incomprehensible speculation and conjecture. You now should be familiar with the scientific community, the dimensions of research, and social theory. In the next chapter, you will examine the competing approaches that researchers adopt when they do social science.

KEY TERMS

association	ideal type	positive relationship
assumption	ideology	proposition
causal explanation	inductive direction	sequential theory
causal mechanism	interpretative explanation	structural explanation
concept classification	level of abstraction	substantive theory
concept cluster	macro-level theory	theoretical concept
deductive direction	meso-level theory	theoretical explanation
empirical generalization	micro-level theory	theoretical framework
formal theory	middle-range theory	typology
functional theory	negative relationship	unit of analysis
grounded theory	network theory	
hypothesis	parsimony	

REVIEW QUESTIONS

1. How do concrete and abstract concepts differ? Give examples.

2. How do researchers use ideal types and classifications to elaborate concepts?

3. How do concepts contain built-in assumptions? Give examples.

4. What is the difference between inductive and deductive approaches to theorizing?

5. Describe how the micro, meso, and macro levels of social reality differ.

6. Discuss the differences between prediction and theoretical explanation.

7. What are the three conditions for causality? Which one is never completely demonstrated? Why?

8. Why do researchers use diagrams to show causal relationships?

9. How do structural and interpretive explanations differ?

10. What is the role of the major theoretical frameworks in research?

NOTES

1. For more detailed discussions of concepts, see Chafetz (1978:45–61), Hage (1972:9–85), Kaplan (1964:34–80), Mullins (1971:7–18), Reynolds (1971), and Stinchcombe (1973).

2. Turner (1980) has provided an interesting discussion of how sociological explanation and theorizing can be conceptualized as translation.

3. Classifications are discussed in Chafetz (1978: 63–73) and Hage (1972).

4. For more on typologies and taxonomies, see Blalock (1969:30–35), Chafetz (1978:63–73), Reynolds (1971: 4–5), and Stinchcombe (1968:41–47).

5. *Recursive* refers to a procedure that can repeat itself indefinitely or an iterative process that reoccurs with a feedback loop. Applied to a causal relationship, recursive suggests that a cause (X) operates on an effect (Y) to produce an effect (Y), but this process repeats with the effect (Y), at a later time, itself acting as a cause influencing the original cause (X).

6. Network theory is discussed in Collins (1988: 412–428), Fuhse (2009), Galaskiewicz and Wasserman (1993), and Schweizer (1997).

7. A basic introduction to functional explanation can be found in Chafetz (1978:22–25).

8. See Craib (1984), Phillips (1985:44–59), and Skidmore (1979). Chapter 1 of Bart and Frankel (1986) also offers an elementary introduction. Jasso (2004) offers a tripartite model of social science knowledge that consists of empirical analysis, theoretical analysis, and framework analysis, arguing that the advance of knowledge takes place on all three levels and their interrelationship.

The Meanings of Methodology

*The confusion in the social sciences—it should now be obvious—is wrapped up with
the long-continuing controversy about the nature of Science.*
—C. Wright Mills, *The Sociological Imagination,* p. 119

Many people ask whether the social sciences are *real* science. They think only of the natural sciences (e.g., physics, chemistry, and biology). The meaning of *science* significantly shapes how we do social scientific research. We can define science in two ways: (1) what practicing scientists actually do and how the institutions of science operate and (2) what philosophers have dissected as the core meaning of twenty-first-century science. One thing is clear. The many studies in the sociology and philosophy of science tell us that the practice and meaning of social science are more nuanced and complex than what most people think. As Collins (1989:134) remarked, "Modern philosophy of science does not destroy sociological science; it does not say that science is impossible, but gives us a more flexible picture of what science is."

The question regarding *what makes social science scientific* has a long history of debate and is relevant for learning about social research. It bridges across the various social sciences and considers whether a disjuncture or unity exists between natural and human sciences. Philosophers and great social theorists such as Auguste Comte, Émile Durkheim, David Hume, Karl Marx, John Stuart Mill, and Max Weber have pondered this question. Despite more than two centuries of discussion and debate, the question is still with us today. Obviously, it does not have one simple answer.

The question does not have one answer because there is no one way to do science; rather, there are multiple sciences, or several *alternative approaches.* "Approaches is a general term, wider than theory or methodology. It includes epistemology or questions about the theory of knowledge, the purposes of research, whether understanding, explanation, or normative evaluation . . ." (Della Porta and Keating, 2008:1). Each approach to social science rests on philosophical assumptions and has a stance on what constitutes the best research. The approaches are found in social science fields across nations, although as Abend (2006) has argued, very different approaches to social research may predominate in different nations. More specifically, the prevailing approach found in the United States may not be widely accepted or used among social scientists elsewhere.

You may find the pluralism of approaches confusing at first, but once you learn them, you will find that other aspects of research and theory become clearer. Specific research techniques (e.g., experiments and participant observation) make more sense if you are aware of the logic and assumptions on which they rest. In addition, the approaches will help you understand the diverse perspectives you may encounter as you read social research studies. Equally important, the approaches give you an opportunity to make an informed choice among alternatives for the type of research you may want to pursue. You might feel more comfortable with one approach or another.

Learning about the approaches is not simple. When you read reports on research studies, the author rarely tells you which approach was used. Many professional researchers are only vaguely aware of the alternatives. They learn an approach's principles and assumptions indirectly as they receive training in research methods (Steinmetz 2005a:45). The approaches operate across the social sciences and applied areas and make a very big difference in the way to do research.[1]

The major approaches I present here are ideal types, and I have highlighted their differences so that you can see what each is about more clearly. Although the approaches operate relying on different core assumptions, competing principles, and contrasting priorities, a person could conduct research studies using more than one approach and learn a great deal. Each approach makes significance advances to knowledge on its own terms. As Roth and Mehta (2002) argued, we can study the same social events using alternative approaches and learn a great deal from each approach used. Each offers a different perspective or viewpoint not only on the social event we wish to study but also on the most important questions, the types of relevant data, and the general way to go about creating knowledge.

PHILOSOPHICAL FOUNDATIONS

In this chapter, we link abstract issues in philosophy to concrete research techniques. The abstract issues proscribe what good social research involves, justify why we do research, relate moral-political values to research, and guide ethical research behavior. The alternative approaches are broad frameworks within which all researchers conduct studies. Couch (1987:106) summarized the different approaches as follows:

> The ontological and epistemological positions of these . . . research traditions provide the foundation

> of one of the more bitter quarrels in contemporary sociology. . . . Each side claims that the frame of thought they promote provides a means for acquiring knowledge about social phenomena, and each regards the efforts of the other as at best misguided. . . . They [the positions] differ on what phenomena should be attended to, how one is to approach phenomena, and how the phenomena are to be analyzed.

The quote mentions two areas of philosophy, ontology and epistemology. All scientific research rests on assumptions and principles from these two areas whether or not a researcher acknowledges them. We do not need a deep discussion over philosophical assumptions to conduct research; however, we make choices implicitly among them when we do a study. Most of us accept assumptions without question. However, by becoming aware of the assumptions, you can better understand what underlies your choices about research. Different philosophical assumptions highlight how and why the approaches to social research differ.

This is not a book about the philosophy of science, but research methodology rests on a foundation of ontological and epistemological assumptions. Once you learn them, you can start to recognize the bases of many disputes and differences among social scientists. You will become a better researcher by considering assumptions and being explicit about them. This is so because being reflexive and aware of assumptions—rather than accepting them without awareness—will help you to think more clearly. As Collier remarked (2005:327),

> existing sciences, particularly social sciences, are not innocent of philosophy. Many of them from their onset assumed some philosophical position about what a science should look like, and tried to imitate it. Further, their practitioners have often forgotten their philosophical premises . . . thereby turning these premises into unchallengeable dogmas.

A division of labor between the practical activity of doing research and being aware of the root philosophical issues in science has had unfortunate consequences. Most practicing researchers focus on mastering specific research techniques. This has left "the question of what empirical research might be or entail to philosophers of social science," and this gap "obscured what might otherwise be a more accurate picture of the range of extant research practices: the actuality of divergent approaches . . ." (Mihic, Engelmann, and Wingrove 2005:483).

We now turn to the two areas of philosophy and some basic divisions within them that relate directly to the major approaches to social science research.

Ontology concerns the issue of what exists, or the fundamental nature of reality. When we do a study, we are making assumptions about what we will study and its place in the world. Two basic positions within ontology are the realist and nominalist. Realists see the world as being "out there." The world is organized into preexisting categories just waiting for us to discover. A realist assumes is that the "real world" exists independently of humans and their interpretations of it. This makes accessing what is in the real world less difficult. To use a cliché, "What you see is what you get." A subgroup of realists, critical realists, modify this assumption. They say that it is not easy to capture reality directly and that our inquiry into reality "out there" can easily become distorted or muddied. Our preexisting ideas, subjectivity, or cultural interpretations contaminate our contact with reality. The critical realist adds a few safeguards or adjustments to control the effect of such interpretations.

The nominalist assumes that humans never directly experience a reality "out there." Our experience with what we call "the real world" is always occurring through a lens or scheme of interpretations and inner subjectivity. Subjective-cultural beliefs influence what we see and how we experience reality. Our personal biography and cultural worldview are always organizing our experiences into categories and patterns. They do this without our realizing it. Nominalists recognize that some interpretative schemes are more opaque than others, yet they hold that we can never entirely remove the interpretative lens. We are always limited in how far we can reach

beyond our inner thoughts, cultural background, and subjectivity.

Let us make this abstract distinction between realists and nominalists more concrete. A realist sees a rug. She says reality presents her a rug—something to cover a floor and walk upon. She looks at a person's facial features, hair, and skin tone and recognizes that the person belongs to one of the world's racial groupings. She examines a person's body in depth—such as skeleton, genitals, breasts, results of chemical tests for hormones, and hair coverage—and sees that the person is a biological male or female. By contrast, a nominalist looks at a rug and asks what might this be. He asks what is it made of, how was it created, in what ways is it used, why is it here, and how does a specific historical-cultural setting and people's practices with it shape what we see. Is it only something to wipe his feet on and walk upon? Do some people sit, sleep, and eat on the rug all day? Do people hang it on walls to keep a room warm? Can it be a work of art to be admired and provide aesthetic pleasure? Do people see the rug as a religious object and worship it? When the nominalist sees a person's skin tone and facial features, he is perplexed. Why are there categories of racial distinction? What might such categories contain when the entire idea of race varies greatly by culture and historical era? Likewise, a nominalist looks at a human body and worries about ambiguities in the physical differences. Is everyone clearly one or another of the biological sexes? How well do biological-physical differences match the gender-social differences of a society? As with racial categories, the number of gender categories and what distinguishes one from another varies greatly by culture and era. What a nomialist sees largely comes from imposing a subjective viewpoint onto the visible physical appearances, and what other people might see could be very different.

We can put realist-nominalist ontological assumptions on a continuum (see Figure 4.1). A hardcore realist says we see what exists, and we can easily capture it to produce objective knowledge. A critical realist is more cautious and recognizes that subjective-culture interpretations may color some of our experiences with reality. A moderate

Ontology   An area of philosophy that deals with the nature of being, or what exists; the area of philosophy that asks what really is and what the fundamental categories of reality are.

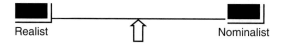

Realist ⇧ Nominalist

FIGURE 4.1   Ontological Assumptions

nominalist says subjective-cultural factors greatly shape all of our experiences with the physical and social world, and we can never totally remove such factors. An extreme nominalist says our basic understanding of every physical-social experience is depends so heavily on interpretative-cultural factors that the experiences make no sense without these factors and any form of objective knowledge is impossible.

Epistemology is the issue of how we know the world around us or what makes a claim about it true. How we can learn about or know the world is rooted in our ontological assumptions. Epistemology includes what we need to do to produce knowledge and what scientific knowledge looks like once we have produced it.

If we adopt a realist position, we can produce knowledge and learn about reality by making careful observations of it. A realist says there is an empirical world "out there" that exists apart from our inner thoughts and perceptions of it. As we gather empirical evidence we find that some of our ideas about reality can be verified or found consistent with the evidence, while other ideas are false because they lack supporting empirical evidence. As we investigate empirical reality, we can distinguish truth from myth or illusion and produce objective knowledge. After we pull together and organize the ideas that have been verified, we will discover broad principles or laws to explain what reality contains and how it works. We produce new knowledge deductively by testing preexisting ideas and conjectures about reality against empirical data. We can also work inductively to gather together and organize empirical evidence into higher order generalizations. Working inductively and deductively, over time we can distinguish true from false ideas about broad areas of reality.

If we adopt a nominalist position, making observations will not lead to knowledge about reality because interpretations and subjective views greatly influence all observations. The same holds true for people we might observe—their interpretations and subjective views shape all they say and do. What we and other people experience as reality is constructed from the outcome of a constant process of actions and interpretations that take place in particular locations and times. It is impossible to separate an objective "out there" reality from interpretations or effects of the time/place in which it occurs. The best we can do is to recognize our own viewpoints and interpretations. We might try to discover other people's inner, subjective views and interpretations as they carry out their daily lives. General laws of social life, laws that hold across all people and places, are not possible to create. The best knowledge about the world that we can produce is to offer carefully considered interpretations of specific people in specific settings. We can offer interpretations of what we think other people are doing and what we believe to be their reasons in specific settings. To produce social science knowledge, we must inductively observe, interpret, and reflect on what other people are saying and doing in specific social contexts while we simultaneously reflect on our own experiences and interpretations.

THE THREE APPROACHES

Science is a human creation. It is not something handed down like a sacred text written in stone. Until the early 1800s, only philosophers and religious scholars engaging in armchair speculation wrote about human behavior. Early social thinkers argued that we could study the social world using principles from science. These thinkers held that rigorous, systematic observation of the social world combined with careful, logical thinking could provide a new, valuable form of knowledge.

Slowly the idea that we could examine the social world by using scientific principles gained

Epistemology An area of philosophy concerned with the creation of knowledge; focuses on how we know what we know or what are the most valid ways to reach truth.

broad acceptance. The next issue was how to conduct scientific research to study social reality. A simple answer was to borrow from the natural sciences (e.g., physics, biology, and chemistry) and copy/adapt their assumptions and research methods as much as possible.

Many social researchers embraced this answer, but it posed several difficulties. First, even natural scientists debate the meaning of science. The so-called *scientific method* is little more than a loose set of abstract, vague principles that offer limited guidance, and working scientists use several methods. Second, some people said that human beings have qualitative differences from the types of objects studied in natural science (stars, rocks, plants, chemical compounds, fish, etc.). Humans have the ability to think and learn. They are aware of themselves as well as their past and possess motives and reasons. Some asked whether such human characteristics require only some adjustments to the natural science approach or require an entirely separate, special kind of science.

The three approaches in this chapter are core ideas distilled from many specific arguments.[2] They are ideal types. In practice, we as social researchers may mix elements from each approach, yet these approaches represent differences in outlook and alternative assumptions about doing social science research.[3] The approaches are evolving positions that offer different ways to observe, measure, and understand social reality.

To simplify the discussion, the assumptions and ideas of the three approaches have been organized into answers to ten questions (see Chart 4.1).

The three approaches are *positivist social science, interpretive social science,* and *critical social science.* Most ongoing social research is based on the first two. Positivism is the oldest and the most widely used approach. The other two nonpositivist alternatives represent a different outlook and

---

Paradigm A general organizing framework for theory and research that includes basic assumptions, key issues, models of quality research, and methods for seeking answers.

CHART 4.1   Ten Questions

1. What is the ultimate purpose of conducting social scientific research?
2. What is the fundamental nature of social reality?
3. What is the basic nature of human beings?
4. What is the view on human agency (free will, volition, and rationality)?
5. What is the relationship between science and common sense?
6. What constitutes an explanation or theory of social reality?
7. How does one determine whether an explanation is true or false?
8. What does good evidence or factual information look like?
9. What is the relevance or use of social scientific knowledge?
10. Where do sociopolitical values enter into science?

---

assumptions about social science research that go back more than a century.

Each approach is associated with different social theories and diverse research techniques. Connections among the approaches to science, social theories, and research techniques are not strict. The approaches are similar to a research program, research tradition, or scientific paradigm. A **paradigm**, an idea made famous by Thomas Kuhn (1970), means a basic orientation to theory and research. There are many definitions of *paradigm.* In general, a scientific paradigm is a whole system of thinking. It includes basic assumptions, the important questions to be answered or puzzles to be solved, the research techniques to be used, and examples of what good scientific research is like. Positivism has been a dominant paradigm in social science, especially as practiced in the United States since 1945. Anthropology and history are the least positivist fields and economics and experimental psychology the most positivist with political science and sociology somewhat mixed. Several paradigms compete in sociology,[4] but it "has been predominantly positivist since 1945, aside from a brief period of epistemological turmoil . . ." (Steinmetz, 2005a:25).

POSITIVIST SOCIAL SCIENCE

Positivist social science (PSS) is used widely, and *positivism,* broadly defined, is the approach of the natural sciences. In fact, most people assume that a positivist approach *is* science. Many versions of positivism exist and it has a long history within the philosophy of science and among researchers.[5] Yet for many researchers, positivism has come to be a pejorative label to be avoided. Turner (1992:1511) observed, "*Positivism* no longer has a clear referent, but it is evident that, for many, being a positivist is not a good thing." Varieties of PSS go by names such as logical empiricism, the accepted or conventional view, postpositivism, naturalism, the covering law model, and behaviorism. Steinmetz (2005b:227) calls "the special cluster of ontological, epistemological and methodological assumptions that has prevailed in U.S. sociology for the past half century" *methodological positivism.*

Western European philosophers developed positivism in the late eighteenth and early nineteenth centuries. Two British philosophers, David Hume (1711–1776) in *A Treatise of Human Nature* (1739–1740) and John Stuart Mill (1806–1873) in *A System of Logic* (1843), outlined the fundamentals of positivist science. The French founder of sociology—Auguste Comte (1798–1857)—wrote *Cours de Philosophie Positivistic* (*The Course of Positive Philosophy*) (1830–1842), which elaborated principles of social science positivism. French sociologist Émile Durkheim (1858–1917) used positivist assumptions in his *Rules of the Sociological Method* (1895), a core text for early social researchers.

Positivism sets up a certain model of science as value-free, atomistic; discovering causal laws. . . . These are supposed to be characteristic of the natural sciences that have made them so successful, and the assumption is that if the social sciences could only imitate them, they would achieve similar success. (Collier 2005:328)

Positivism is associated with several social theories and structural-functional, rational choice, and exchange-theory frameworks. PSS researchers prefer precise quantitative data and often use experiments, surveys, and statistics. They seek rigorous, exact measures and "objective" research. They test causal hypotheses by carefully analyzing numbers from the measures. Researchers in many fields (public health administration, criminal justice, market research, policy analysis, program evaluation) rely on positivist social science.

PSS dominated the articles of major sociology journals in Britain, Canada, Scandinavia, and the United States during the 1960s and 1970s. By the 1980s and 1990s, it had declined sharply in European journals but remained dominant in North American journals.[6]

In positivism, "there is only *one* logic of science, to which any intellectual activity aspiring to the title of 'science' must conform" (Keat and Urry, 1975:25, emphasis in original). Thus, the social sciences and the natural sciences use the same method. In this view, any differences between the social and natural sciences are due to the immaturity of the social sciences and their subject matter. There is an assumption that eventually all science, including the social sciences, will become like the most advanced science, physics. Some differences remain among the sciences because of the subject matter (e.g., studies of geology require techniques different from astrophysics or microbiology because of the objects being examined), but all sciences share a common set of principles and logic.

Positivist social science is an *organized method for combining deductive logic with precise empirical observations of individual behavior in order to discover and confirm a set of probabilistic causal laws that can be used to predict general patterns of human activity.*

Positivist social science (PSS)   One of three major approaches to social research that emphasizes discovering causal laws, careful empirical observations, and value-free research.

The Questions

1. *What is the ultimate purpose of conducting social scientific research?*

The ultimate purpose of research is to obtain scientific explanation—to discover and document universal **causal laws** of human behavior. As Turner (1985:39) stated, the "social universe is amenable to the development of abstract laws that can be tested through the careful collection of data" and researchers need to "develop abstract principles and models about invariant and timeless properties of the social universe." Scientists engage in a never-ending quest for knowledge. As we learn more and discover new complexities, we still have more to learn. Some versions of PSS maintain that humans can never know everything: Only God possesses such knowledge; however, God gave humans the capacity for knowledge, and we have a duty to discover as much as we can.

2. *What is the fundamental nature of social reality?*

Modern positivists adopt a realist ontology. They hold that reality exists "out there" and is waiting to be discovered. Human perception and intellect may be flawed, and reality may be difficult to pin down, but it exists, is patterned, and has a natural order. Without this assumption (i.e., if the world were chaotic and without regularity), logic and prediction would be impossible. Science lets humans discover this order and the laws of nature. "The basic, observational laws of science are considered to be true, primary and certain, because they are built into the fabric of the natural world. Discovering a law is like discovering America, in the sense that

both are already waiting to be revealed" (Mulkay, 1979:21).

The assumptions of realist ontology (also called *essentialist, objectivist,* or *empirical realist*) about reality prevail in commonsense thinking, especially in Anglo-European societies. The assumption is that what we can see and touch (i.e., empirical reality) is not overly complex. What we observe reflects the deeper essence of things, people, and relations in the world. It is a "what-you-see-is-what-you-get" or "show-me" type of stance. Things are as they appear, created out of a natural order of the world. Thus, race, gender, and measurements of space and time just "are." This view has many implications. For example, males commit more crime than females do because of something involving their "maleness." A related assumption about time is that it is linear or flows in a straight line. What happened in the past always differs somewhat from the present because time flows in only one direction—forward to the future.

Other PSS assumptions are that social reality is stable and our knowledge about reality is additive. While time flows, the core regularity in social reality does not change, and laws we discover today will hold in the future. The additive feature of knowledge means we can study many separate parts of reality one at a time, then add the fragments together to get a picture of the whole. Over time, we add more and more knowledge, ever expanding our understanding of the world.

3. *What is the basic nature of human beings?*

PPS assumes that humans are self-interested, pleasure-seeking/pain-avoiding, rational mammals. A cause will have the same effect on everyone. We can learn about people by observing their behavior that we see in external reality. This is more important than what happens in internal, subjective reality. Sometimes, this is called a **mechanical model of man** or a behaviorist approach. It means that people respond to external forces that are as real as physical forces on objects. Durkheim (1938:27) stated, "Social phenomena are things and ought to be studied as things." This emphasis on observable, external reality suggests that researchers do not have to examine unseen, internal motivations.

Causal laws General cause–effect rules used in causal explanations of social theory and whose discovery is a primary objective of positivist social science.

Mechanical model of man A model of human nature used in positivist social science stating that observing people's external behaviors and documenting outside forces acting on them are sufficient to provide adequate explanations of human thought and action.

4. *What is the view on human agency (free will, volition, and rationality)?*

PSS emphasizes the **determinism** of relationships and looks for determining causes or mechanisms that produce effects. PSS investigates how external forces, pressures, and structures that operate on individuals, groups, organizations, or societies produce outcomes (e.g., behaviors, attitudes). PSS downplays an individual's subjective or internal reasons and any sense of free choice or volition. Mental processes are less central than the structural forces or conditions beyond individual control that exert influence over choices and behavior. While individual people may believe that they can act freely and can make any decisions, positivists emphasize the powerful social pressures and situations that operate on people to shape most if not all of their actions. Even positivists who use rational choice explanations focus less on how individuals reason and make choices than on identifying sets of conditions that allow them to predict what people will choose. Positivists assume that once they know external factors, individual reasoning largely follows a machinelike rational logic of decision making.

Few positivists believe in a strict or absolute determinism in which people are mere robots or puppets who must always respond similarly. Rather, the causal laws are probabilistic. Laws hold for large groups of people or occur in many situations. Researchers can estimate the odds of a predicted behavior. In other words, the laws enable us to make accurate predictions of how often a social behavior will occur within a large group. The causal laws cannot predict the specific behavior of a specific person in each specific situation. However, they can say that under conditions X, Y, and Z, there is a 95 percent probability that one-half of the people will engage in a specified behavior. For example, researchers cannot predict how John Smith will vote in the next election. However, after learning dozens of facts about John Smith and using laws of political behavior, researchers can accurately state that there is an 85 percent chance that he (and people like him) will vote for candidate C. This does not mean that Mr. Smith cannot vote for whomever he wants. Rather, his voting behavior is patterned and shaped by outside social forces.

5. *What is the relationship between science and common sense?*

PSS sees a clear separation between science and nonscience. Of the many ways to seek truth, science is special—the "best" way. Scientific knowledge is better than and will eventually replace the inferior ways of gaining knowledge (e.g., magic, religion, astrology, personal experience, and tradition). Science borrows some ideas from common sense, but it replaces the parts of common sense that are sloppy, logically inconsistent, unsystematic, or full of bias. The scientific community—with its special norms, scientific attitudes, and techniques—can regularly produce "Truth," whereas common sense does so only rarely and inconsistently.

Many positivist researchers create an entirely new vocabulary that is more logically consistent, carefully considered, and refined than terms of everyday common sense. The positivist researcher "should formulate new concepts at the outset and not rely on lay notions. . . . There is a preference for the precision which is believed possible in a discipline-based language rather than the vague and imprecise language of everyday life" (Blaikie, 1993:206). In his *Rules of the Sociological Method*, Durkheim warned the researcher to "resolutely deny himself the use of those concepts formed outside of science" and to "free himself from those fallacious notions which hold sway over the mind of the ordinary person" (quoted in Gilbert, 1992:4).

6. *What constitutes an explanation or theory of social reality?*

A PSS explanation is **nomothetic** (*nomos* means *law* in Greek); it is based on a system of general laws. Science explains why social life is the way it is by discovering causal laws. Explanation takes this form: Y is caused by X because Y and X are specific instances of a causal law. In other

---

Determinism   An approach to human agency and causality that assumes that human actions are largely caused by forces external to individuals that can be identified.

Nomothetic   A type of explanation used in positivist social science that relies heavily on causal laws and lawlike statements and interrelations.

words, a PSS explanation states the general causal law that applies to or covers specific observations about social life. This is why PSS is said to use a **covering law model** of explanation.

PSS assumes that the laws operate according to strict, logical reasoning. Researchers connect causal laws and can deductively connect the many facts that they observe. Many positivists believe that it may be possible eventually to express the laws and theories of social science in formal symbolic systems with axioms, corollaries, postulates, and theorems. Someday social science theories could look similar to those in mathematics and the natural sciences.

The laws of human behavior should be universally valid, holding in all historical eras and in all cultures. As noted before, the laws are in a probabilistic form for aggregates of people. For example, a PSS explanation of a rise in the crime rate in Toronto in 2010 refers to factors (e.g., rising divorce rate, declining commitment to traditional moral values) that could be found anywhere at any time: in Buenos Aires in the 1890s, Chicago in the 1940s, or Singapore in the 2020s. The factors logically obey a general law (e.g., the breakdown of a traditional moral order causes an increase in the rate of criminal behavior).

7. *How does one determine whether an explanation is true or false?*

Positivism developed during the Enlightenment (post–Middle Ages) period of Western thinking.[7] It includes an important Enlightenment idea: People can recognize truth and distinguish it from falsehood by applying reason, and, in the long run, the human condition can improve through the use of reason and the pursuit of truth. As knowledge increases and ignorance declines, conditions will improve. This optimistic belief that knowledge accumulates over time plays a role in how positivists sort out true from false explanations.

PSS explanations must meet two conditions: They must (1) have no logical contradictions and (2) be consistent with observed facts, yet this is not

sufficient. Replication is also needed.[8] Any researcher can replicate or reproduce the results of others. This puts a check on the whole system for creating knowledge. It ensures honesty because it repeatedly tests explanations against hard, objective facts. An open competition exists among opposing explanations. In the competition, we use impartial rules, accurately observe neutral facts, and rigorously apply logic. Over time, scientific knowledge accumulates as different researchers conduct independent tests and add up the findings. For example, a researcher finds that rising unemployment is associated with increased child abuse in San Diego, California. We cannot conclusively demonstrate a causal relationship between unemployment and child abuse with just one study, however. Confirming a causal law requires finding the same relationship elsewhere with other researchers conducting independent tests and careful measures of unemployment and child abuse.

8. *What does good evidence or factual information look like?*

PSS adopts a dualist view; it assumes that the cold, observable facts are fundamentally distinct from ideas, values, or theories. Empirical facts exist apart from personal ideas or thoughts. We can experience them by using our sense organs (sight, smell, hearing, and touch) or special instruments that extend the senses (e.g., telescopes, microscopes, and Geiger counters). Some researchers express this idea as two languages: a language of empirical fact and a language of abstract theory. If people disagree over facts, the dissent must be due to the improper use of measurement instruments or to sloppy or inadequate observation. "Scientific explanation involves the accurate and precise measurement of phenomena" (Derksen and Gartell, 1992:1714). Knowledge of observable reality obtained using our senses is superior to other knowledge (e.g., intuition, emotional feelings); it allows us to separate true from false ideas about social life.

Positivists assign a privileged status to empirical observation. They assume that we all share the same fundamental experience of the empirical world. This means that factual knowledge is not based on just one person's observations and subjective reasoning. It must be communicated to and

---

Covering law model   A positivist social science principle that a few high-level, very abstract theories cover and allow deducing to many low-level, more concrete situations.

shared with others. Rational people who independently observe facts will agree on them subjectively. This is called **intersubjectivity**, or the shared subjective acknowledgment of the observable facts.

Many positivists also endorse the falsification doctrine outlined by the Anglo-Austrian philosopher Sir Karl Popper (1902–1991) in *The Logic of Scientific Discovery* (1934). Popper argued that claims to knowledge "can never be proven or fully justified, they can only be refuted" (Phillips, 1987:3). Evidence for a causal law requires more than piling up supporting facts; it involves looking for evidence that contradicts the causal law. In a classic example, if I want to test the claim that all swans are white, and I find 1,000 white swans, I have not totally confirmed a causal law or pattern. Locating one black swan is all it takes to refute my claim—one piece of negative evidence. This means that researchers search for disconfirming evidence, and even then, the best they can say is, "Thus far, I have not been able to locate any, so the claim is probably right."

9. *What is the relevance or use of social scientific knowledge?*

Positivists try to learn about how the social world works to enable people to exercise control over it and make accurate predictions about it. In short, as we discover the laws of human behavior, we can use that knowledge to alter and improve social conditions. This instrumental form of knowledge (discussed in Chapter 2) sees research results as tools or instruments that people use to satisfy their desires and control the social environment. Thus, PSS uses an **instrumental orientation** in which the relevance of knowledge is its ability to enable people to master or control events in the world around them.

PSS has a **technocratic perspective** to the application of knowledge. The word *technocratic* combines *technology* and *bureaucracy*. PSS says that after many years of professional training, researchers develop in-depth technical expertise. As an expert, the researcher tries to satisfy the information needs of large-scale bureaucratic organizations (e.g., hospitals, business corporations, government agencies). The questions such organizations ask tend to be oriented to improving the efficiency of operations and effectiveness of

reaching organizational goals or objectives. In a technical expert role the researcher provides answers to questions asked by others but *not* to ask different questions, redirect an inquiry into new areas, challenge the basic premises of questions, or defy the objectives set by leaders in control of the bureaucratic organizations.

10. *Where do sociopolitical values enter into science?*

PSS argues for objectives of **value-free science**. The term *objective* has two meanings: (1) that observers agree on what they see and (2) that scientific knowledge is not based on values, opinions, attitudes, or beliefs.[9] Positivists see science as a special, distinctive part of society that is free of personal, political, or religious values. Science is able to operate independently of the social and cultural forces affecting other human activity because science involves applying strict rational thinking and systematic observation in a manner that transcends personal prejudices, biases, and values. Thus, the norms and operation of the scientific community keep science objective. Researchers accept and internalize the norms as part of their membership in the scientific community. The scientific community has an elaborate system of checks and balances to guard against value bias. A researcher's

---

Intersubjectivity   A principle for evaluating empirical evidence in positivist social science stating that different people can agree on what is in the empirical world by using the senses.

Instrumental orientation   A means–end orientation toward social knowledge in which knowledge is like an instrument or tool that people can use to control their environment or achieve some goal. The value of knowledge is in its use to achieve goals.

Technocratic perspective   An applied orientation in which the researcher unquestioningly accepts any research problem and limits on the scope of study requested by government, corporate, or bureaucratic officials, uncritically conducts applied research for them, and obediently supplies the officials with information needed for their decision making.

Value-free science   A positivist social science principle that social research should be conducted in an objective manner based on empirical evidence alone and without inference from moral-political values.

proper role is to be a "disinterested scientist."[10] PSS has had an immense impact on how people see ethical issues and knowledge:

> To the degree that a positivist theory of scientific knowledge has become the criterion for all knowledge, moral insights and political commitments have been delegitimized as irrational or reduced to mere subjective inclination. Ethical judgments are now thought of as personal opinion. (Brown, 1989:37)

Summary

Positivist social science is widely taught as being the same as science. Few people are aware of the origins of PSS assumptions. Scholars in western Europe during the eighteenth and nineteenth centuries who developed these assumptions had religious training and lived in a cultural-historical setting that assumed specific religious beliefs. Many PSS assumptions will reappear when you read about quantitative research techniques and measurement in later chapters. A positivist approach implies that a researcher begins with a cause–effect relationship that he or she logically derives from a possible causal law in general theory. He or she logically links the abstract ideas to precise measurements of the social world. The researcher remains detached, neutral, and objective as he or she measures aspects of social life, examines evidence, and replicates the research of others. These processes lead to an empirical test and confirmation of the laws of social life as outlined in a theory. Chart 4.2 provides a summary of PSS.

When and why did PSS become dominant? The story is long and complicated. Many present it as a natural advance or the inevitable progress of pure knowledge. PSS expanded largely due to changes in the larger political-social context. Positivism gained dominance in the United States and became the model for social research in many nations after World War II once the United States became the leading world power. A thrust toward objectivism—a strong version of positivism—developed in U.S. sociology during the 1920s. Objectivism grew as researchers shifted away from social reform–oriented studies with less formal or precise techniques toward rigorous techniques in a "value-free" manner modeled on the natural sciences. Researchers

---

CHART 4.2   Summary of Positivist Social Science

1. The purpose of social science is to discover laws.

2. An *essentialist* view is that reality is empirically evident.

3. Humans are rational thinking, individualistic mammals.

4. A *deterministic* stance is taken regarding human agency.

5. Scientific knowledge is different from and superior to all other knowledge.

6. Explanations are *nomothetic* and advance via deductive reasoning.

7. Explanations are verified using *replication* by other researchers.

8. Social science evidence requires *intersubjectivity*.

9. An *instrumental orientation* is taken toward knowledge that is used from a *technocratic perspective*.

10. Social science should be *value free* and objective.

---

created careful measures of the external behavior of individuals to produce quantitative data that could be subjected to statistical analysis. Objectivism displaced locally based studies that were action oriented and largely qualitative. It grew because competition among researchers for prestige and status combined with other pressures, including the need for funds from private foundations (e.g., Ford Foundation, Rockefeller Foundation), university administrators who wanted to avoid unconventional politics, a desire by researchers for a public image of serious professionalism, and the information needs of expanding government and corporate bureaucracies. These pressures combined to redefine social research. The less technical, applied local studies conducted by social reformers (often women) were often overshadowed by apolitical, precise quantitative research by male professors in university departments.[11] Decisions made during a large-scale expansion of federal government funding for research after World War II also pushed the social sciences in a positivist direction.

INTERPRETIVE SOCIAL SCIENCE

We can trace **interpretive social science (ISS)** to the German sociologist Max Weber (1864–1920) and German philosopher Wilhelm Dilthey (1833–1911). In his major work, *Einleitung in die Geisteswissenshaften (Introduction to the Human Sciences)* (1883), Dilthey argued that there were two fundamentally different types of science: *Naturwissenschaft* and *Geisteswissenschaft.* The former rests on *Erklärung,* or abstract explanation. The latter is rooted in an empathetic understanding, or **verstehen**, of the everyday lived experience of people in specific historical settings. Weber argued that social science should study social action with a purpose. He embraced *verstehen* and felt that we must learn the personal reasons or motives that shape a person's internal feelings and guide decisions to act in particular ways.

> We shall speak of "social action" wherever human action is subjectively related in meaning to the behavior of others. An unintended collision of two cyclists, for example, shall not be called social action. But we will define as such their possible prior attempts to dodge one another. . . . Social action is not the only kind of action significant for sociological causal explanation, but it is the primary object of an "interpretive sociology." (Weber, 1981:159)

Interpretive social science is related to **hermeneutics**, a theory of meaning that originated in the nineteenth century. The term comes from a god in Greek mythology, Hermes, who had the job of communicating the desires of the gods to mortals. It "literally means making the obscure plain" (Blaikie, 1993:28). The humanities (philosophy, art history, religious studies, linguistics, and literary criticism) use hermeneutics. It emphasizes conducting a very close, detailed reading of *text* to acquire a profound, deep understanding. *Text* can mean a conversation, written words, or pictures. We conduct "a reading" to discover deeper, richer meanings that are embedded within the text. Each reader brings her or his subjective experience to the text. When studying the text, the researcher/reader tries to absorb or get inside the viewpoint the text presents as a whole and then to develop an understanding of how each of the parts relates to the whole. In other words, true meaning is rarely obvious on the surface. We can reach it only through a detailed examination and study of the text, by contemplating its many messages, and seeking the connections among its parts.[12]

Interpretive social science (ISS) has several varieties: hermeneutics, constructionism, ethnomethodology, cognitive, idealist, phenomenological, subjectivist, and qualitative sociology.[13] An interpretive approach is associated with the symbolic interactionist Chicago school in sociology of the 1920s–1930s. Often people just call ISS qualitative research because most interpretive researchers use participant observation and field research. These techniques require researchers to devote many hours in direct personal contact with the people they study. Other ISS researchers analyze transcripts of conversations or study videotapes of behavior in extraordinary detail, looking for subtle nonverbal communication to understand the details of interactions in their context. The positivist researcher may precisely measure selected quantitative details about thousands of people and use statistics whereas an interpretive researcher may live for a year with a dozen people to gather mountains of highly detailed qualitative data so that he or she can acquire an in-depth understanding of how the people create meaning in their everyday lives.

Interpretive social science concerns how people interact and get along with each other. In general, the interpretive approach is *the systematic*

Interpretative social science (ISS) One of three major approaches to social research that emphasizes meaningful social action, socially constructed meaning, and value relativism.

Verstehen A word from German that means empathetic understanding (i.e., a deep understanding with shared meaning) and that is a primary goal for social research according to interpretative social science.

Hermeneutics A method associated with interpretative social science that originates in religious and literary studies of textual material in which in-depth inquiry into text and relating its parts to the whole can reveal deeper meanings.

analysis of socially meaningful action through the direct detailed observation of people in natural settings in order to arrive at understandings and interpretations of how people create and maintain their social worlds.

The Questions

1. *What is the ultimate purpose of conducting social scientific research?*

For interpretive researchers, the goal of social research is to develop an understanding of social life and discover how people construct meaning in natural settings. The ISS researcher wants to learn what is meaningful or relevant to the people he or she is studying and how they experience everyday life. To do this, he or she gets to know people in a particular social setting in great depth and works to see the setting from the viewpoint of the people in it. He or she tries to know in the most intimate way the feelings and interpretations of people being studied, and to see events through their eyes. Summarizing the goal of his ten-year study of Willie, a repair shop owner in a rural area, interpretive researcher Harper (1987:12) said, "The goal of the research was to share Willie's perspective."

ISS researchers study **meaningful social action**, not just people's visible, external behavior. Social action is the action to which people attach subjective meaning and is activity with a purpose or intent. Nonhuman species lack culture and the reasoning to plan things and attach purpose to their behavior; therefore, social scientists should study what is unique to human social behavior. The researcher must take into account the social actor's reasons and the social context of action. For example, a physical reflex such as eye blinking is

Meaningful social action   Social action in social settings to which people subjectively attach significance and that interpretive social science treats as being the most important aspect of social reality.

Constructionist orientation   An orientation toward social reality that assumes the beliefs and meaning that people create and use fundamentally shape what reality is for them.

human behavior that is rarely an intentional social action (i.e., done for a reason or with human motivation), but in some situations, it can be such a social action (i.e., a wink). More than simply having a purpose, the actions must also be social and "for action to be regarded as social and to be of interest to the social scientist, the actor must attach subjective meaning to it and it must be directed towards the activities of other people" (Blaikie, 1993:37).

Most human actions have little inherent meaning; they acquire meaning in a social context among people who share a meaning system. The common system of meaning allows people to interpret the action as being a socially relevant sign or action. For example, raising one finger in a situation with other people can express social meaning; the specific meaning it expresses (e.g., a direction, an expression of friendship, a vulgar sign) depends on the cultural meaning system that the social actors share.

2. *What is the fundamental nature of social reality?*

ISS sees human social life as an accomplishment. People intentionally create social reality with their purposeful actions of interacting as social beings. In contrast to the positivist view that social life is "out there" waiting to be discovered, ISS adopts a more nominalist ontology. Social reality is largely what people perceive it to be; it exists as people experience it and assign meaning to it. Social reality is fluid and fragile, and people construct it as they interact with others in ongoing processes of communication and negotiation. People rely on many untested assumptions and use taken-for-granted knowledge about the people and events around them. Social life arises in people's subjective experiences as they interact with others and construct meaning. Capturing people's subjective sense of reality to really understand social life is crucial. In ISS, "access to other human beings is possible, however, only by indirect means: what we experience initially are gestures, sounds, and actions and only in the process of understanding do we take the step from external signs to the underlying inner life" (Bleicher, 1980:9).

A **constructionist orientation** in ISS assumes that people construct reality out of their interactions and beliefs. No inner essence causes the reality people see. For example, when you see a chair, there is no "chairness" in it; rather, what you see to be a chair arises from what the people of particular society and time define, accept, and understand to be a chair. Yes there is a physical object of wood or metal or cloth configured in a particular shape, but what you see as the empirical reality of a chair arises out of cultural-social processes that tell you to define the object as a chair.

In general, what people see and experience in the social world is socially constructed. Just because people's experiences are socially constructed does not make them illusionary, immaterial, or unimportant. Once people accept social creations as being facts, or as real, the creations have very real consequences. For example, if socially constructed reality tells me that the person moving into an apartment next to mine has committed violent crimes and carries a gun, I will behave accordingly whether or not my constructed belief fits actual physical reality. For the constructionists, people live in, believe, and accept the constructed reality that has links to but is somewhat distinct from physical reality.

A constructionist notes that people take the social world around them "for granted" and behave as if the social world were a natural, objective, part of fixed reality. For example, people accept that a week has 7 days. Very few people realize that a week could be very different. Cultures have had 3-day, 5-day, and even 10-day weeks. The 7-day week is not a physical reality, but people take it for granted and treat it as a natural, fixed part of reality. The week that we now accept is a social construction. People created it in particular places and under specific historical circumstances.

PSS language connects directly to reality, and there is an attempt to make language as pure, logical, and precise as possible so that it accurately reflects reality. By contrast, the constructionist sees language as comprising social constructions. As we learn language, we learn to think and see the world in certain ways. Language has little direct connection to essential reality; it contains a worldview that colors how we see and experience the world. The difference continues to affect others' social concepts, such as gender and race. For example, Anglo-European society divides gender into two categories and race into

six categories, primarily based on shades of skin color. The PSS realist ontology suggests that genders and races are real (i.e., males and females or races are essential distinctions in reality). In contrast, the constructionist says that language and habitual ways of thinking dictate what people see. They might see a world with two genders and six races, but other cultures see more than two genders or a different number of races and base racial differences on something other than skin color. In contrast to the PSS demand for "cold hard facts," constructionists emphasize the processes by which people create social construction and use them as if they were real "things."[14]

PSS assumes that everyone experiences the world in the same way. The interpretive approach questions whether people experience social or physical reality in the same way. These are key questions for an ISS researcher: How do people experience the world? Do they create and share meaning? Interpretive social science points to numerous examples in which several people have seen, heard, or even touched the same physical object yet come away with different meanings or interpretations of it. The interpretive researcher argues that positivists impose one way of experiencing the world on others. In contrast, ISS assumes that multiple interpretations of human experience, or realities, are possible. In sum, the ISS approach defines social reality as consisting of people who construct meaning and create interpretations through their daily social interaction.

3. *What is the basic nature of human beings?*

Ordinary people are engaged in an ongoing process of creating systems of meaning through social interaction. They then use such meanings to interpret their social world and make sense of their lives. Human behavior may be patterned and regular but this is not because of preexisting laws that are waiting for us to discover them. The patterns result from evolving meaning systems or social conventions that people generate as they interact socially. Important questions for the interpretive researcher are these: What do people believe to be true? What do they hold to be relevant? How do they define what they are doing?

Interpretive researchers want to discover what actions mean to the people who engage in them. It makes little sense to try to deduce social life from abstract, logical theories that may not relate to the daily feelings and experiences of ordinary people. People have their own reasons for their actions, and we need to learn the reasons that people use. Individual motives are crucial to consider even if they are irrational, carry deep emotions, and contain mistaken beliefs and prejudices. Some ISS researchers say that the laws sought by positivists may be found only after the scientific community understands how people create and use meaning systems, how common sense develops, and how people apply their common sense to situations. Other ISS researchers do not believe that such laws of human social life exist, so searching for them is futile. For example, an ISS researcher sees the desire to discover laws of human behavior in which unemployment causes child abuse as premature at best and dangerous at worst. Instead, he or she wants to understand how people subjectively experience unemployment and what the loss of a job means in their everyday lives. Likewise, the interpretive researcher wants to learn how child abusers account for their actions, what reasons they give for abuse, and how they feel about abusing a child. He or she explores the meaning of being unemployed and the reasons for abusing a child in order to understand what is happening to the people who are directly involved.

4. *What is the view on human agency (free will, volition, and rationality)?*

Whereas PSS emphasizes deterministic relations and external forces, ISS emphasizes voluntary individual free choice, sometimes called *human agency*. ISS adopts **voluntarism** and sees people as having volition (being able to make conscious choices). Social settings and subjective points of view help to shape the choices a person makes, but

Voluntarism   An approach to human agency and causality assuming that human actions are based on the subjective choices and reasons of individuals.

Natural attitude   An idea used in ISS that we assume that the world of commonsense understanding is stable and real and continues from the past into the future without dramatic change; we do this from the practical need to accomplish everyday tasks.

people create and change those settings and have the ability to develop or form a point of view. ISS researchers emphasize the importance of considering individual decision-making processes, subjective feelings, and ways to understand events. In ISS, this inner world and a person's way of seeing and thinking are equally if not more significant for a person's actions than the external, objective conditions and structural forces that positivists emphasize.

5. *What is the relationship between science and common sense?*

Positivists see common sense as being inferior to science. By contrast, ISS holds that ordinary people use common sense to guide them in daily life. Common sense is a stockpile of everyday theories that people use to organize and explain events in the world. It is critical for us to understand common sense because it contains the meanings that people use when they engage in everyday routine social interactions.

ISS says that common sense and the positivist's laws are alternative ways to interpret the world; that is, they are distinct meaning systems. Neither common sense nor scientific law has all of the answers. Instead, interpretive researchers see both scientific laws and common sense as being important in their own domains; we create scientific laws and common sense in different ways for different purposes. Ordinary people could not function in daily life if they tried to base their actions on science alone. For example, to boil an egg, people use unsystematic experiences, habits, and guesswork. A strict application of natural science would require people to know the laws of physics that determine heating water and the chemical laws that govern the changes in an egg's internal composition. Even natural scientists use common sense when they are not "doing science" in their area of expertise.

Common sense is a vital source of information for understanding people. A person's common sense emerges from a pragmatic orientation and set of assumptions about the world. People assume that common sense is true because they need to use it to accomplish anything. The interpretive philosopher Alfred Schutz (1899–1959) called this the **natural attitude**. It is the assumption that the world existed before you arrived and it will continue to exist after you depart. People develop ways to maintain or re-produce a sense of reality based on systems of meaning that they create in the course of social interactions with others.

6. *What constitutes an explanation or theory of social reality?*

PSS theory tries to mimic theory in natural science. It may have deductive axioms, theorems, and interconnected causal laws. Instead of interconnected laws and propositions, theory for ISS tells a story. ISS describes and interprets how people conduct their daily lives. While it may contain social science concepts and limited generalizations, it does not dramatically depart from the lived experiences and inner reality of the people being studied.

ISS is idiographic and inductive. **Idiographic** means that the approach provides a symbolic representation or "thick" description of something else. An interpretive research report may read like a novel or a biography. It is rich in detailed description and limited in abstraction. Like the interpretation of a literary work, it has internal coherence and is rooted in the text, which here refers to the meaningful everyday experiences of the people being studied.

The purpose of ISS theory is to provide an interpretative explanation (see Chapter 2). ISS attempts to provide readers a deep feeling for another person's social reality by revealing the meanings, values, interpretive schemes, and rules of daily living. For example, ISS theory may describe major typifications that people use in a setting to recognize and interpret their experiences. A **typification** is an informal model, scheme, or set of beliefs that people use to categorize and organize the flow of the daily events they experience.

ISS theory resembles a map that outlines a social world and describes local customs and norms. For example, an interpretive report on professional gamblers tells the reader about the careers and daily concerns of such people. The report describes the specific individuals studied, the locations and activities observed, and the strategies used to gamble. The reader learns how professional gamblers speak, how they view others, and what their fears or ambitions are. The researcher provides some generalizations and organizing concepts, but the bulk of the report is a detailed description of the gambling world. The theory and evidence are interwoven to create a unified whole; the concepts and generalizations are wedded to their context.

7. *How does one determine whether an explanation is true or false?*

PSS logically deduces from theory, collects data, and analyzes facts in ways that allow replication. For ISS, a theory is true if it makes sense to those being studied and if it allows others to enter the reality of those being studied. The theory or description is accurate if the researcher conveys a deep understanding of the way others reason, feel, and see things. Prediction may be possible but it is a type of prediction that occurs when two people are very close as when they have been married for a long time. An interpretive explanation documents the actor's point of view and translates it into a form that is intelligible to readers. Smart (1976:100) calls this the **postulate of adequacy**:

> *The postulate of adequacy asserts that if a scientific account of human action were to be presented to an individual actor as a script it must be understandable to that actor, translatable into action by the actor and furthermore comprehensible to his fellow actors in terms of a common sense interpretation of everyday life.*

Like a traveler telling about a foreign land, the researcher is not a native. Such an outside view never equals the insider account that people who are

---

Idiographic   A type of explanation used in interpretive social science in which the explanation is an in-depth description or picture with specific details but limited abstraction about a social situation or setting.

Typification   An informal model or scheme people use in everyday life to categorize and organize the flow of the events and situations that they experience; often part of common knowledge or common sense, it simplifies and helps to organize the complexity and flow of life.

Postulate of adequacy   An interpretive social science principle that explanations should be understandable in commonsense terms by the people being studied.

being studied might give; however, the closer it is to the native's account, the better. For example, one way to test the truthfulness of an ISS study of professional gambling is to have professional gamblers read it and verify its accuracy. A good report tells a reader enough about the world of professional gambling so that if the reader absorbed it and then met a professional gambler, the understanding of gambling jargon, outlook, and lifestyle might lead the gambler to ask whether the reader was also a professional gambler.

8. *What does good evidence or factual infor-mation look like?*

Good evidence in positivism is observable, pre-cise, and independent of theory and values. In con-trast, ISS sees the features of specific contexts and meanings as essential to understand social mean-ing. Evidence about social action cannot be isolated from the context in which it occurs or the meanings assigned to it by the social actors involved. As Weber (1978:5) said, "Empathic or appreciative ac-curacy is attained when, through sympathetic par-ticipation, we can adequately grasp the emotional context in which the action took place."

For ISS, facts are fluid and embedded within a meaning system; they are not impartial, objective, or neutral. Facts are contingent and context specific; they depend on combinations of specific events with particular people in a specific setting. What PSS assumes—that neutral outsiders observe behavior and see unambiguous, objective facts—ISS takes as a question to be addressed: How do people observe ambiguities in social life and assign meaning? In-terpretive researchers say that social situations are filled with ambiguity. Most behaviors or statements can have several meanings and can be interpreted in multiple ways. In the flow of social life, people are constantly "making sense" by reassessing clues in the situation and assigning meanings until they

"know what's going on." For example, I see a woman holding her hand out, palm forward. Even this simple act carries multiple potential meanings; I do not know its meaning without knowing the so-cial situation. It could mean that she is warding off a potential mugger, drying her nail polish, hailing a taxi, admiring a new ring, telling oncoming traffic to stop for her, or requesting five bagels at a deli counter.[15] People are able to assign appropriate meaning to an act or statement only if they consider the social context in which it occurs.

ISS researchers rarely ask survey questions, aggregate the answers of many people, or claim to obtain something meaningful to the questions. To ISS researchers, each person's interpretation of the survey question must be placed in a context (e.g., the individual's previous experiences or the survey interview situation), and the true meaning of a per-son's answer will vary according to the interview or questioning context. Moreover, because each per-son assigns a somewhat different meaning to the question and answer, combining answers produces only nonsense.

When studying a setting or data, interpretive re-searchers of the ethnomethodological school often use **bracketing**. It is a mental exercise in which the researcher identifies and then sets aside taken-for-granted assumptions used in a social scene. ISS re-searchers question and reexamine ordinary events that have an "obvious" meaning to those involved. For example, at an office work setting, one male co-worker in his late twenties says to the male re-searcher, "We're getting together for softball after work tonight. Do you want to join us?" What is *not said* is that the researcher should know the rules of softball, own a softball glove, and change from a business suit into other clothing before the game. Bracketing reveals what "everyone knows": what people assume but rarely say. It makes visible sig-nificant features of the social scene that make other events possible and is the underlying scaffolding of understandings on which actions are based.

9. *What is the relevance or use of social sci-entific knowledge?*

Interpretative social scientists want to learn how the world works so they can acquire an in-depth

Bracketing A strategy of interpretive social science researchers to identify the taken-for-granted assump-tions of a social scene and then set them aside or hold them in temporary abeyance. By recognizing and sep-arating the ordinary, "obvious" meanings people use in daily life, researchers can better understand their role.

understanding of other people, appreciate the wide diversity of lived human experience, and better acknowledge shared humanity. Instead of viewing knowledge as a type of tool or instrument, ISS researchers try to capture the inner lives and subjective experiences of ordinary people. This humanistic approach focuses on how people manage their practical affairs in everyday life and treats social knowledge as a pragmatic accomplishment.

According to the ISS **practical orientation**, the relevance of social science knowledge comes from its ability to reflect in an authentic and comprehensive way how ordinary people do things in commonplace situations. ISS also emphasizes incorporating the social context of knowledge creation and creates a reflexive form of knowledge (discussed in Chapter 2).

ISS researchers tend to apply a **transcendent perspective** toward the use and application of new knowledge. To *transcend* means to go beyond ordinary material experiences and perceptions. In social research, it means not stopping at the surface or observable level but going on to an inner and subjective level of human experience. Rather than treating people as external objects that a researcher studies, the transcendant perspective urges researchers to examine people's complex inner lives. Also, rather than study social conditions as they now appear, researchers should examine processes by which people actively construct and can transform existing conditions. ISS researchers try to engage and participate with the people being studied as a way to gain an intimate familiarity of them. A transcendent perspective emphasizes that researchers and people being studied should work together to create mutual understandings and affect conditions.

10. *Where do sociopolitical values enter into science?*

The PSS researcher calls for eliminating values and operating within an apolitical environment. The ISS researcher, by contrast, argues that researchers should reflect on, reexamine, and analyze personal points of view and feelings as a part of the process of studying others. The ISS researcher needs, at least temporarily, to empathize with and share in the social and political commitments or values of people

whom he or she studies. This is why ISS adopts the position of **relativism** with regard to values.

ISS questions the possibility of being value free because interpretive research sees values and meaning infused everywhere in everything. What PSS calls value freedom is just another meaning system and value—the value of positivist science. The interpretive researcher adopts relativism and does not assume that any one set of values is better or worse. Values should be recognized and made explicit.

Summary

ISS existed for many years as the loyal opposition to positivism. Although some positivist social researchers accept the interpretive approach as being useful in exploratory research (see Chapter 2), few positivists consider it as being scientific. You will read again about the interpretive outlook when you examine field research and, to a lesser degree, historical-comparative research in later chapters. The interpretive approach is the foundation of social research techniques that are sensitive to context, that get inside the ways others see the world, and that are more concerned with achieving an empathic understanding than with testing laws such as theories of human behavior. Chart 4.3 (page 108) provides a summary of the interpretive approach.

Practical orientation A pragmatic orientation toward social knowledge in which people apply knowledge in their daily lives; the value of knowledge is the ability to be integrated with a person's practical everyday understandings and choices.

Transcendent perspective The researcher develops research together with the people being studied, examines people's inner lives to gain an intimate familiarity with them, and works closely with people being studied to create mutual understandings.

Relativism A principle used in interpretive social science that no single point of view or value position is better than others, and all are equally valid for those who hold them.

CHART 4.3 Summary of Interpretative Social Science

1. The purpose of social science is to understand social meaning in context.
2. A *constructionist* view is that reality is socially created.
3. Humans are interacting social beings who create and reinforce shared meaning.
4. A *voluntaristic* stance is taken regarding human agency.
5. Scientific knowledge is different from but no better than other forms.
6. Explanations are *idiographic* and advance via *inductive reasoning*.
7. Explanations are verified using the *postulate of adequacy* with people being studied.
8. Social scientific evidence is contingent, context specific, and often requires *bracketing*.
9. A *practical orientation* is taken toward knowledge that is used from a *transcendent perspective*.
10. Social science should be *relativistic* regarding value positions.

CRITICAL SOCIAL SCIENCE

Versions of **critical social science (CSS)** are called *dialectical materialism, class analysis,* and *critical structuralism.*[16] CSS mixes nomothetic and ideographic approaches. It agrees with many of the criticisms the interpretive approach directs at PSS, but it adds some of its own and disagrees with ISS on some points. We can trace this approach to the writings of Karl Marx (1818–1883) and Sigmund Freud (1856–1939). Later, Theodor Adorno (1903–1969), Erich Fromm (1900–1980), and Herbert Marcuse (1898–1979) elaborated on it. Often CSS is associated with conflict theory, feminist analysis, and radical psychotherapy and is tied to critical theory first developed by the Frankfurt School in Germany in the 1930s.[17] Critical social science criticized positivist science as being narrow, antidemocratic, and

> **Critical social science (CSS)** One of three major approaches to social research that emphasizes combating surface-level distortions, multiple levels of reality, and value-based activism for human empowerment.

nonhumanist in its use of reason. This was outlined in Adorno's essays "Sociology and Empirical Research" (1976a) and "The Logic of the Social Sciences" (1976b). A well-known living representative of the school, Jürgen Habermas (1929–), advanced CSS in his *Knowledge and Human Interests* (1971). In the field of education, Paulo Freire (1921–1997) and his *Pedagogy of the Oppressed* (1970) also falls within the CSS approach.

Another example is the French sociologist Pierre Bourdieu (1930–2002) with his writings such as *Outline of A Theory of Practice* (1977).[18] Bourdieu rejected both the objective, lawlike quantitative empirical approach of positivists and the subjective, voluntarist approach of ISS. He argued that social research must be reflexive (i.e., study and criticize itself as well as its subject matter) and is necessarily political. He also held that a goal of research is to uncover and demystify ordinary events.

ISS criticizes PSS for failing to deal with the meanings of real people and their capacity to feel and think, for ignoring social context, and for being antihumanist. CSS agrees with most such criticisms of PSS and believes that PSS defends the status quo. CSS criticizes ISS for being too subjective and relativist, treating people's ideas as more important than actual conditions (e.g., real poverty, oppression, violence). CSS also says that ISS focuses too much on localized, microlevel, short-term settings while ignoring the broader and long-term structural conditions. To CSS, ISS is amoral and passive. ISS fails to take a strong value position or actively help people to see false illusions around them. CSS does become involved so that ordinary people can improve their lives. In general, CSS defines social science as a *critical process of inquiry that goes beyond surface illusions to uncover the real structures in the material world in order to help people change conditions and build a better world for themselves.*

The Questions

1. *What is the ultimate purpose of conducting social scientific research?*

In the CSS view, the primary purpose of research is not simply to study the social world but to change it. CSS researchers conduct studies to critique and transform social relations by revealing the underlying sources of social control, power relations, and inequality. By uncovering conditions, CSS empowers people, especially those in society who are less powerful and marginalized. More specifically, CSS wants to expose myths, reveal hidden truths, and assist people in improving their lives. For CSS, the purpose of doing research is "to explain a social order in such a way that it becomes itself the catalyst which leads to the transformation of this social order" (Fay, 1987:27).

A CSS researcher asks embarrassing questions, exposes hypocrisy, and investigates conditions to stimulate grassroots action. "The point of all science, indeed all learning, is to change and develop out of our understandings and reduce illusion. . . . Learning is the reducing of illusion and ignorance; it can help free us from domination by hitherto unacknowledged constraints, dogmas and falsehoods" (Sayer, 1992:252).

For example, a CSS researcher conducts a study concerning racial discrimination in rental housing: Do White landlords refuse to rent to minority tenants? A critical researcher does not just publish a report and then wait for the fair housing office of the city government to act. The researcher gives the report to newspapers and meets with grassroots organizations to discuss the results of the study. He or she works with activists to mobilize political action in the name of social justice. When grassroots people picket the landlords' offices, flood the landlords with racial minority applicants for apartments, or organize a march on city hall demanding action, the critical researcher predicts that the landlords will be forced to rent to minorities. The goal of research is to empower. Kincheloe and McLaren (1994:140) stated:

> *Critical research can be best understood in the context of the empowerment of individuals. Inquiry that aspires to the name critical must be connected to an attempt to confront the injustice of a particular society or sphere within the society. Research thus becomes a transformative endeavor unembarrassed by the label "political" and unafraid to consummate a relationship with an emancipatory consciousness.*

2. *What is the fundamental nature of social reality?*

CSS shares aspects of PSS's premise that there is an empirical reality independent of our perceptions and of ISS's focus that we construct what we take to be reality from our subjective experiences, cultural beliefs, and social interactions. CSS adopts a critical realist ontology that views reality as being composed of multiple layers: the empirical, the real, and the actual.[19] We can observe the empirical reality using our senses. However, the surface empirical layer we experience is being generated by deeper structures and causal mechanisms operating at unobservable layers. Theories and research over time can help us to understand structures operating at the real level and causal mechanisms at the actual level that generate and modify structures.

We can directly observe structures at the real level. Such structures are not permanent but can evolve, and we can modify them. For example, gender structures at the real level shape the specific actions of people at the surface level that we can observe. With theoretical insight and careful investigation, researchers can slowly uncover these deep structures, but the task is complicated because the structures can change. Structures at deeper levels do not produce a direct and immediate surface appearance at the empirical level. They can lie inactive or dormant and then become activated and emerge on the surface. Also, various structures are not insulated from one another. Counteracting structures may suppress or complicate the surface appearances of another structure.

Causal mechanisms operating at the actual level can have internal contradictions and operate in a paradoxical manner creating structural conflicts. These mechanisms may contain forces or processes that appear to be opposites or to be in conflict but are actually parts of a single larger process. A biological analogy helps illustrate this idea. We see birth and life as the opposites of death, yet death begins the day we are born and each day of living moves us toward death as our body ages and decays. There is a contradiction between life and death; to live, we move toward life's opposite, death. Living and dying appear to be opposites, but actually they are two parts of a single process. Discovering and understanding such paradoxical processes, called the **dialectic**, is a central task in CSS.

CSS says that our observations and experiences with empirical reality are not pure, neutral, and unmediated; rather, ideas, beliefs, and interpretations color or influence what and how we observe. Our knowledge of empirical reality can capture the way things really are, yet in an incomplete manner because our experiences of it depend on ideas and beliefs. CSS states that our experiences of empirical reality are always theory or concept dependent. Our theories and concepts, both commonsense and scientific, sensitize us to particular aspects of empirical reality, inform what we recognize as being relevant in it, and influence how we categorize and divide its features. Over time, new theoretical insights and concepts enable us to recognize more aspects in the surface, empirical reality and to improve our understandings of the deeper levels of reality.

In sum, PSS emphasizes how external reality operates on people whereas ISS emphasizes the inner subjective construction of reality. CSS states that there is a deeper reality that is prestructured, not invented by us. It existed before we experience or think about it and has real effects on people. At the same time, we construct ways of seeing and thinking that shape our experience of empirical reality. Our thinking can lead to us to take actions that will change the structures in deeper levels of reality. CSS views our ability to understand reality as an interactive process in which thoughts, experiences, and actions interact with one another over time.

CSS notes that social change and conflict are not always apparent or easily observable. The social world is full of illusion, myth, and distortion. Initial observations of the world are only partial and often misleading because the human senses are limited. The appearances in surface reality do not have to be based on conscious deception. The immediately perceived characteristics of objects, events, or social relations rarely reveal everything. These illusions allow some groups in society to hold power and exploit others. Karl Marx, German sociologist and political thinker, stated this forcefully (Marx and Engels, 1947:39):

> *The ideas of the ruling class are in every epoch the ruling ideas; . . . The class which has the means of material production at its disposal, has control at the same time over the means of mental production, so that . . . the ideas of those who lack the means of mental production are subject to it.*

CSS states that although subjective meaning is important, real, objective relations shape social relations. The critical researcher probes social situations and places them in a larger historical context.

For example, an ISS researcher studies the interactions of a male boss and his female secretary and provides a rich account of their rules of behavior, interpretive mechanisms, and systems of meaning. By contrast, the CSS researcher begins with a point of view (e.g., feminist) and notes issues that an interpretive description ignores: Why are bosses male and secretaries female? Why do the roles of boss and secretary have unequal power? Why do large organizations create such roles throughout society? How did the unequal power come about historically, and were secretaries always female? Why can the boss make off-color jokes that humiliate the secretary? How are the roles of boss and secretary in conflict based on the everyday conditions faced by the boss (large salary, country club membership, new car, large home, retirement plan, stock investments, etc.) and those of the secretary (low hourly pay, children to care for, concerns about how to pay bills, television as her only recreation, etc.)? Can the secretary join with others to challenge the power of her boss and similar bosses?

3. *What is the basic nature of human beings?*

PSS sees humans as mammals and focuses on their behavior as rationally acting individuals. ISS sees humans as fundamentally social beings defined by their capacity to create and sustain social meanings. CSS recognizes that people are rational decision makers who are shaped by social structures and creative beings who construct meaning and social structures. Society exists prior to and apart from people, yet it can exist only with their active

Dialectic   A change process emphasized in critical social science in which social relationships contain irresolvable inner contradictions; over time they will trigger a dramatic upset and a total restructuring of the relationship.

involvement. People create society and society creates people, who in turn create society in a continuous process.[20] Thus, human beings exist within an ongoing relational process.

CSS notes that humans can be misled and have unrealized potential. One important way this happens is through **reification**, which occurs when we become detached from and lose sight of our connection or relationship to something that we created ourselves. By severing connections to our own creations, we no longer recognize ourselves in them but treat them as being alien, external forces that have control over us. By "forgetting" and not seeing connections, we lose control over our creations. Humans have tremendous potential that often goes unrealized because we find breaking free from beliefs, conditions, and situations largely of our own making difficult. To realize their full potential, people must look beyond immediate surface appearance and break through what they reified to see how they possess the capacity to change situations.

4. *What is the view on human agency (free will, volition, and rationality)?*

CSS blends determinism and voluntarism to emphasize **bounded autonomy**, or how agency and structure cooperate. Bounded autonomy suggests that free will, choices, and decision making are not unlimited or open ended; rather, they either must stay within restricted boundaries of options or are confined within limits, which can be cultural or material boundaries. A CSS researcher identifies a range of options, or at least what people see as being realistic alternatives, and allows for some volition among those options. People make choices, but the choices are confined to what they believe is possible. Material factors (e.g., natural resources, physical abilities) and cultural-subjective schemes (e.g., beliefs, core values, deeply felt norms) set what people believe to be possible or impossible, and people act based on what they believe is possible.

Sewell (1992) observed that social structures are simultaneously cultural and material. What a person sees, thinks, or feels (i.e., culture) shapes a person's action in the material world. Material objects, conditions, and resources depend on the cultural schemas. Researchers recognized that "so-called hard data were themselves cultural products that required

interpretation" (Sewell, 2005:190). If a person's worldview defines an action as being impossible, a material resource as being unavailable, or a choice as being blocked, his or her "free will" choices are limited. If for reasons of culture a person does not see an insect as a source of food or having three wives simultaneously as morally possible, cultural beliefs restrict the use of material resources and make some actions impossible. Material and subjective-cultural factors interact. Cultural-subjective beliefs that define material resources as available restrict volition, and material conditions can shape people's cultural-subjective experiences and beliefs. Under certain conditions, collective human actions can alter deep structures of the material conditions and cultural beliefs, and this can expand the range of volition.

5. *What is the relationship between science and common sense?*

CSS sees common sense as containing **false consciousness**: the idea that people are often mistaken and act against their own true best interests as defined in objective reality. Objective reality lies behind myth and illusion. False consciousness is meaningless for ISS because it implies that a social actor uses a meaning system that is false or out of touch with objective reality. ISS states that people create and use such systems and that researchers can only describe such systems, not judge their value. CSS states that social researchers should study subjective ideas and common sense because these shape human behavior, yet they contain myth and illusion that can mask an objective world in which there is unequal control over resources and power.

The structures that critical researchers talk about are not easy to see. Researchers must first

---

Reification An idea used in critical social science referring to when people become detached from and lose sight of their connection to their own creations and treat them as being alien, external forces.

Bounded autonomy An approach to human agency and causality used in critical social science that assumes human action is based on subjective choices and reasons but only within identifiable limits.

False consciousness An idea used by critical social science that people often have false or misleading ideas about empirical conditions and their true interests.

demystify them and pull back the veil of surface appearances. Careful observation is not enough. It does not tell what to observe, and observing an illusion does not dispel it. A researcher must use theory to dig beneath surface relations, to observe periods of crisis and intense conflict, to probe interconnections, to look at the past, and to consider future possibilities. Uncovering the deeper level of reality is difficult but is essential because surface reality is full of ideology, myth, distortion, and false appearances. "Common sense tends to naturalize social phenomena and to assume that what is, must be. A social science which builds uncritically on common sense . . . reproduces these errors" (Sayer, 1992:43).

6. *What constitutes an explanation or theory of social reality?*

Beyond deduction and induction, CSS uses abduction to create explanatory critiques. American philosopher Charles S. Peirce (1839–1914) developed **abduction** by extending the other forms of reasoning. Instead of beginning with many observations or with a theoretical premise, abduction "tries on" a potential rule and asks what might follow from this rule. Both ideas and observations are placed into alternative frames and then examined, and the "what-if" question is asked. A researcher using abduction applies and evaluates the efficacy of multiple frameworks sequentially and creatively recontexualizes or redescribes both data and ideas in the process.

Abduction rarely produces a single, definitive truth; instead, it eliminates some alternatives as it advances a deeper understanding. In certain ways, it is an aspect of all human perception. Abduction is similar to how an insightful, creative detective might solve a crime—by taking the data (clues) and putting them into alternative possible scenarios (what might have caused the crime). Considering alternative scenarios gives the same observations new meanings. Thus, abduction means making repeated reevaluations of ideas and data based on applying alternative rules or schemes and learning from each.

Explanatory critique begins with the premise that when we study social life, we study both the thing "itself" and how people think about or understand the "thing" we are studying. Actual conditions and people's beliefs about conditions are both relevant, and the two may not match. An explanatory critique has practical, moral, and political implications because it can differ from the prevailing beliefs. The explanation simultaneously explains conditions (or tells why events occur) and critiques conditions (or points out discrepancies, reveals myths, or identifies contradictions).

When we render social conditions in an explanatory critique, we often enlighten and help to emancipate people. As the explanation reveals aspects of reality beyond the surface level, people may awaken to the underlying structures of society. The explanatory critique reveals deep causal mechanisms and once exposed, people can learn how to influence the mechanisms to change larger social structures. In this way, explanatory critiques show a pathway for taking action and achieving social change.

7. *How does one determine whether an explanation is true or false?*

PSS deduces hypotheses, tests hypotheses with replicated observations, and then combines results to confirm or refute causal laws. ISS asks whether the meaning system and rules of behavior make sense to those being studied. CSS tests theory by accurately describing conditions generated by underlying structures and then by applying that knowledge to change social relations. A CSS theory teaches people about their own experiences, helps them understand their historical role, and can be used to improve conditions.

CSS theory informs practical action; at the same time CSS theory is modified on the basis of using it. A CSS theory grows and interacts with the world it seeks to explain. Because CSS tries to explain and change the world by penetrating hidden structures,

Abduction An approach to theorizing in which several alternative frameworks are applied to data and theory, which are redescribed in each and evaluated.

Explanatory critique A type of explanation used in critical social science in which the explanation simultaneously explains conditions (or tells why) events occur and critiques conditions (or points out discrepancies, reveals myths, or identifies contradictions).

the test of an explanation is not static. Testing theory is a dynamic, ongoing process of applying and modifying theory. Knowledge grows with the use of an ongoing process of eroding ignorance and enlarging insights through action.

CSS separates good from bad theory by putting the theory into practice and then uses the outcome of these applications to reformulate theory. **Praxis** means that explanations are valued when they help people understand the world and to take action that changes it. As Sayer (1992:13) argued, "Knowledge is primarily gained through activity both in attempting to change our environment (through labor or work) and through interaction with other people."

Critical praxis tries to eliminate the division between the researcher and the people being studied, the distinction between science and daily life. For example, a CSS researcher develops an explanation for housing discrimination. He or she tests the explanation by using it to try to change conditions. If the explanation says that underlying economic relations cause discrimination and that landlords refuse to rent to minorities because it is profitable to rent only to nonminorities, then political actions that make it profitable to rent to minorities should change the landlords' behavior. By contrast, if the explanation says that an underlying racial hatred causes landlords to discriminate, then actions based on profit will be unsuccessful. The critical researcher would then examine race hatred as the basis of landlord behavior through new studies combined with new political action.

8. What does good evidence or factual information look like?

PSS assumes that there are incontestable neutral facts on which all rational people agree. Its dualist doctrine says that social facts are like objects. They exist separately from values or theories. ISS sees the social world as made up of created meaning with people creating and negotiating meanings. It rejects positivism's dualism, but it substitutes an emphasis on the subjective. Evidence is whatever resides in the subjective understandings of those involved. The critical approach bridges the object–subject gap. It says that the facts of material conditions exist

independently of subjective perceptions, but that facts are not theory neutral. Instead, facts require an interpretation from within a framework of values, theory, and meaning.

For example, it is a "fact" that the United States spends a much higher percentage of its gross national product (GNP) on health care than any other advanced industrial nation, yet it ranks as the twenty-ninth lowest for infant death rate (7 deaths per 1,000 live births). A CSS interprets the fact by noting that the United States has many people without health care and no system to cover everyone. The fact includes the way the health care is delivered to some through a complex system of for-profit insurance companies, pharmaceutical firms, hospitals, and others who benefit greatly from the current arrangement. Some powerful groups in the system are getting rich while weaker or poor sectors of society are getting low-quality or no health care. CSS researchers look at the facts and ask who benefits and who loses.

Theory helps a critical researcher find new facts and separate the important from the trivial ones. The theory is a type of map telling researchers where to look for facts and how to interpret them once they are uncovered. The critical approach says that theory does this in the natural sciences, as well. For example, a biologist looks into a microscope and sees red blood cells—a "fact" based on a theory about blood and cells and a biologist's education about microscopic phenomena. Without this theory and education, a biologist sees only meaningless spots. Clearly, then, facts and theories are interrelated.

CSS notes that only some theories are useful for finding and understanding key facts. Theories rest on beliefs and assumptions about what the world is like and on a set of moral-political values. CSS states that some values are better than others.[21] Thus, to interpret facts, we must understand history, adopt a set of moral-political values, and know where to look for underlying structures. Different

---

Praxis A way to evaluate explanations in critical social science by putting theoretical explanations into real-life practice and the subsequent outcome is used to refine explanation.

versions of critical science offer different value positions (e.g., Marxism versus feminism).

9. *What is the relevance or use of social scientific knowledge?*

As CSS researchers learn how the world works, they link subjective understandings with ways to analyze objective conditions to reveal unseen forces and unrecognized injustices. This spurs people to take action. For CSS, knowledge is not an instrument for people to manipulate, nor is it a capturing and rendering of people's inner, subjective experiences; instead, knowledge means active involvement in the world. Knowledge can free people from the shackles of past thinking and help them take control of events around them. It is not a thing to be possessed but a process that combines increased awareness with taking action.

CSS researchers blend aspects of the instrumental and practical orientations and bridge duality of the positivist's external, empirical reality and the inner, subjective reality emphasized in ISS. CSS uses reflexive knowledge (see Chapter 2) to offer a "third way," **reflexive-dialectic orientation**. This third way is "not a conflation of, or compromise between these perspectives; it represents a standpoint in its own right" (Danermark et al., 2002:202). Instead of treating external and internal reality as being opposites, a reflexive-dialectic orientation sees them as two sides of a single dynamic whole that is in a process of becoming. An external or internal orientation alone is incomplete. The two sides work together as one and are interwoven to affect each other.

Reflexive-dialectic orientation An orientation toward social knowledge used in critical social science in which subjective and objective sides are blended together to provide insights in combination unavailable from either side alone; the value of knowledge as a process that integrates making observations, reflecting on them, and taking action.

Transformative perspective The view that the researcher probes beyond the surface level of reality in ways that can shift subjective understandings and provide insights into how engaging in social-political action may dramatically improve the conditions of people's lives.

CSS adopts a **transformative perspective** toward applying knowledge. To *transform* means to *change fundamentally, to reorganize basic structures,* and *to breach current limits.* The perspective goes beyond a surface level of reality to realign subjective understandings with the external reality and then uses renewed consciousness as a basis for engaging in actions that have the potential to modify external conditions and future consciousness. The relevance of knowledge is its ability to connect consciousness to people engaging in concrete actions, reflecting on the consequences of those actions, and then advancing consciousness to a new level in an ongoing cycle.

10. *When do sociopolitical values enter into science?*

CSS has an activist orientation. Social research is a moral-political activity that requires the researcher to commit to a value position. CSS rejects the PSS value freedom as a myth. It also attacks ISS for its relativism. In ISS, the reality of the genius and the reality of the idiot are equally valid and important. There is little, if any, basis for judging between alternative realities or conflicting viewpoints. For example, the interpretive researcher does not call a racist viewpoint wrong because any viewpoint is true for those who believe in it. CSS states that there is only one, or a very few, correct points of view. Other viewpoints are plain wrong or misleading. All social research *necessarily* begins with a value or a moral point of view. For CSS, being objective is not being value free. Objectivity requires a nondistorted, true picture of reality; "it challenges the belief that science must be protected from politics. It argues that some politics—the politics for emancipatory social change—can increase the objectivity of science" (Harding, 1986:162).

CSS holds that to deny that a researcher has a point of view is itself a point of view. It is a technician's point of view: Conduct research and ignore the moral questions, satisfy a sponsor, and follow orders. Such a view says that science is a tool or instrument that anyone can use. This view was strongly criticized when Nazi scientists committed inhumane experiments and then claimed that they were blameless because they "just followed orders"

EXPANSION BOX 4.1

The Extended Case Method and CSS

Michael Burawoy's (1998) extended case method is an example of critical social science. He says it applies *reflexive science* to ethnography or field research. Reflexive science is a type of CSS that states social research should be a dialogue between the researcher and the people being studied. Thus, intersubjectivity is not only among scientists, as in positivism; rather, it occurs between the researcher and people under study. Burawoy identifies four features of reflexive science:

1. The researcher interacts with subject-participants. Disruptions or disturbances that develop out of their mutual interaction help to expose and better illuminate social life.
2. The researcher adopts the subject-participant's view of the world in specific situations, but does not stop there. The researcher adds together many views from individual subjects and specific situations, aggregating them into broader social processes.
3. The researcher sees the social world simultaneously from inside outward (i.e., from the subjective viewpoint of the people being studied) and from the outside inward (i.e., from the viewpoint of external forces that act on people).
4. The researcher constantly builds and rebuilds theory. This takes place in a dialogue with the people studied and in a dialogue with other researchers in the scientific community.

Burawoy used the extended case method to study mine workers in Zambia. He argued that positivist social science best fits situations in which people are "powerless to resist wider systems of economy and polity" (p. 30)—in other words, situations in which people are dominated and have little control over their lives. The CSS approach strives in contexts in which people try to resist or reduce power distinctions and domination. It highlights conditions of emancipation in which people come to question or challenge the external forces of power and control under which they live.

and were "just scientists." PSS adopts such an approach and produces technocratic knowledge—a form of knowledge best suited for use by the people in power to dominate or control other people.[22]

CSS rejects PSS and ISS for being detached and concerned with studying the world instead of acting on it. CSS holds that knowledge is power. Social science knowledge can be used to control people, it can be hidden in ivory towers for intellectuals to play games with, or it can be given to people to help them take charge of and improve their lives. What a researcher studies, how he or she studies it, and what happens to the results involve values and morality because knowledge has tangible effects on people's lives. The researcher who studies trivial behavior, who fails to probe beneath the surface, or who buries the results in a university library is making a moral choice. The choice is to take information from the people being studied without involving them or liberating them (see Expansion Box 4.1, The Extended Case Method and CSS). CSS questions the morality of such a choice, even if it is not a conscious one.

Summary

Although few full-time academic researchers adopt CSS, community action groups, political organizations, and social movements often follow a CSS approach. It only rarely appears in scholarly journals. CSS researchers may use any research technique, but they tend to favor the historical-comparative method. This is so because of its emphasis on change and because it helps researchers uncover underlying structures. CSS researchers differ from the others less in the research techniques they use than in how they approach a research problem, the types of questions they ask, and their purposes for doing research. Chart 4.4 provides a summary of CSS.

FEMINIST AND POSTMODERN RESEARCH

Two additional, less well-known approaches are feminist and postmodern social research. Both criticize PSS and offer alternatives that build on

CHART 4.4   Summary of Critical Social Science

1. The purpose of social science is to reveal what is hidden to liberate and empower people.

2. Social reality has multiple layers.

3. People have unrealized potential and are misled by reification; social life is relational.

4. A *bounded autonomy* stance is taken toward human agency.

5. Scientific knowledge is imperfect but can fight *false consciousness*.

6. *Abduction* is used to create *explanatory critiques*.

7. Explanations are verified through *praxis*.

8. All evidence is theory dependent, and some theories reveal deeper types of evidence.

9. A *reflexive-dialectic orientation* is adopted toward knowledge that is used from a *transformative perspective*.

10. Social reality and the study of it necessarily contain a moral-political dimension, and moral-political positions are unequal in advancing human freedom and empowerment.

emphases on individual competition, on dominating and controlling the environment, and on the "hard facts." It reflects a patriarchal orientation that emphasizes finding forces that act on the world rather looking for ways to interact with and cooperate within the world.

In contrast, women emphasize accommodation and gradually developing human bonds. They see the social world as a web of interconnected human relations, full of people linked together by feelings of trust and mutual obligation. Women emphasize the subjective, empathetic, process-oriented, and inclusive sides of social life. Feminist research is also action oriented and seeks to advance feminist values (see Expansion Box 4.2, Characteristics of Feminist Social Research).

Feminist researchers argue that much of non-feminist research is sexist. This largely happened as a result of broader cultural beliefs and a preponderance of male researchers. The research generalizes from the experience of men to all people, ignores gender as a fundamental social division, focuses on men's problems, uses males as points of reference, and assumes traditional gender roles. For example, a traditional researcher would say that a family has a problem of unemployment when the adult male in

ISS and CSS. They have gained visibility only since the 1980s.

Feminist Research

Feminist research is conducted by people, most of them women, who hold a feminist self-identity and consciously use a feminist perspective. They use multiple research techniques, attempt to give a voice to women, and work to correct the predominant male-oriented perspective. Works such as *Women's Ways of Knowing* (Belenky et al., 1986) argue that women learn and express themselves differently than men do.

Feminist research assumes that the subjective experience of women differs from that of men.[23] Many feminist researchers see PSS as presenting a male point of view; it is objective, logical, task oriented, and instrumental. It reflects masculine

EXPANSION BOX 4.2

Characteristics of Feminist Social Research

■ Advocacy of a feminist value position and perspective
■ Rejection of sexism in assumptions, concepts, and research questions
■ Creation of empathic connections between the researcher and those he or she studies
■ Sensitivity to how relations of gender and power permeate all spheres of social life
■ Incorporation of the researcher's personal feelings and experiences into the research process
■ Flexibility in choosing research techniques and crossing boundaries between academic fields
■ Recognition of the emotional and mutual-dependence dimensions in human experience
■ Action-oriented research that seeks to facilitate personal and societal change

it cannot find stable work. When a woman in the same family cannot find stable work outside the home, it is not considered an equal family problem. Likewise, traditional researchers often use the concept *unwed mother,* but it is not a parallel of *unwed father.*

The feminist approach sees researchers as fundamentally gendered beings. Researchers necessarily have a gender that shapes how they experience reality, and therefore it affects their research. In addition to gender's impact on individual researchers, basic theoretical assumptions and the scientific community appear as gendered cultural contexts. Gender has a pervasive influence in culture and shapes basic beliefs and values that cannot be isolated and insulated in the social processes of scientific inquiry.[24]

Feminist researchers are not objective or detached; they interact and collaborate with the people they study. They fuse their personal and professional lives. For example, feminist researchers will attempt to comprehend an interviewee's experiences while sharing their own feelings and experiences. This process may give birth to a personal relationship between researcher and interviewee that might mature over time. Reinharz (1992:263) argued, "This blurring of the disconnection between formal and personal relations, just as the removal of the distinction . . . between the research project and the researcher's life, is a characteristic of much, if not all, feminist research."

The impact of a woman's perspective and her desire to gain an intimate relationship with what she studies occurs even in the biological sciences. Feminist researchers tend to avoid quantitative analysis and experiments. They use multiple methods, often qualitative research and case studies. Gorelick (1991) criticized the affinity of many feminist researchers for interpretive social science. ISS is limited to the consciousness of those being studied and fails to reveal hidden structures. Gorelick wants feminist researchers to adopt a critical approach and to advocate social change more assertively.

Feminist researchers reject the value-neutral claim of positivists. For example, Risman (2001) criticized a study that tried to explain gender differences almost entirely with biological factors. She argued (p. 606) that "the positivist model of science not only failed in this particular instance to recognize and exclude the expression of particular political values, but that value-free science as such is not only an impossible goal but it is an inappropriate one that distorts the research and publication." She noted (p. 609) that "value-neutrality can be a cloak that hides (perhaps even from scientists themselves) values that are so embedded in the folk wisdom of our culture so as to be invisible. Researchers who believe they are working within an apolitical, value-neutral version of science are, often without any conscious decision at all, simply ignoring the ways in which dominant presumptions frame their questions."

Postmodern Research

Postmodern research is part of the larger postmodern movement that includes art, music, literature, and cultural criticism. It began in the humanities and has roots in the philosophies of existentialism, nihilism, and anarchism and in the ideas of Martin Heidegger (1889–1976), Michel Foucault (1926–1984), Friedrich Nietzsche (1844–1900), Jean-Paul Sartre (1905–1980), and Ludwig Wittgenstein (1889–1951). Postmodernism is a rejection of modernism. *Modernism* refers to basic assumptions, beliefs, and values that arose in the Enlightenment era. Modernism relies on logical reasoning; it is optimistic about the future and believes in progress; it has confidence in technology and science; and it embraces humanist values (i.e., judging ideas based on their effect on human welfare). Modernism holds that most people can agree about standards of beauty, truth, and morality.[25]

Postmodern researchers see no separation between the arts or humanities and social sciences. They share the critical social science goal of demystifying the social world, and want to deconstruct or tear apart surface appearances and reveal the hidden structure. Like extreme forms of ISS, postmodernism distrusts abstract explanation and holds that research can never do more than describe and that all descriptions are equally valid. A researcher's description is neither superior nor inferior to anyone else's and describes only the researcher's personal experiences. Going beyond interpretive and critical social science, modernism attempts to dismantle social science. Extreme postmodernists reject the possibility of a science of the social world, distrust all systematic empirical observation, and doubt that knowledge is generalizable or accumulates over time. They see knowledge as taking numerous forms and as unique to particular people or specific locales. Rosenau (1992:77) argued,

> Almost all postmodernists reject truth as even a goal or ideal because it is the very epitome of modernity.... Truth makes reference to order, rules, and values; depends on logic, rationality and reason, all of which the postmodernists question.

Postmodernists object to presenting research results in a detached and neutral way. The researcher or author of a report should never be hidden when someone reads it, but his or her presence needs to be unambiguously evident in the report. Thus, a postmodern research report is similar to a work of art. Its purpose is to stimulate others, to give pleasure, to evoke a response, or to arouse curiosity. Postmodern

reports often have a theatrical, expressive, or dramatic style of presentation. They may be in the form of a work of fiction, a movie, or a play. The postmodernist argues that the knowledge about social life created by a researcher may be better communicated through a short story, a skit, or a musical piece than by a scholarly journal article. The value of the skit, story or music lies in telling a story that may stimulate experiences within the people who read or encounter it. Postmodernism is antielitist and rejects the use of science to predict and to make policy decisions. Postmodernists oppose those who use positivist science to reinforce power relations and bureaucratic forms of control over people (see Expansion Box 4.3, Characteristics of Postmodern Social Research).

CONCLUSION

This chapter has presented two important concepts. First, there are competing approaches to social research based on philosophical assumptions about the purpose of science and the nature of social reality. Second, the ideal-type approaches answer basic questions about research differently (see Table 4.1). Most researchers operate primarily within one approach, but many also combine elements from the others.

Remember that you can study the same topic from any of these approaches, but each approach implies going about it differently. This can be illustrated with the topic of discrimination and job competition between minority and majority groups in four countries: aborigines in the Australian outback, Chinese in western Canada, African Americans in the midwestern United States, and Pakistanis in London.

PSS researchers first deduce hypotheses from a general theory about majority–minority relations. The theory is probably in the form of causal statements or predictions. The researchers next gather data from existing government statistics or conduct a survey to precisely measure the factors that the theory identifies, such as the form of initial contact, the ratio of numbers in majority versus minority groups, or the visibility of racial differences. Finally, PSS researchers use statistics to formally test the theory's predictions about the degree of discrimination and the intensity of job competition.

EXPANSION BOX 4.3

Characteristics of Postmodern Social Research

- Rejection of all ideologies and organized belief systems, including all formal social theory
- Strong reliance on intuition, imagination, personal experience, and emotion
- Sense of meaninglessness and pessimism; belief that the world will never improve
- Extreme subjectivity in which there is no distinction between the mental and the external worlds
- Ardent relativism in which there are infinite interpretations, none superior to another
- Espousal of diversity, chaos, and complexity that is constantly changing
- Rejection of studying the past or different places because only the here and now is relevant
- Belief that causality cannot be studied because life is too complex and rapidly changing
- Assertion that research can never truly represent what occurs in the social world

TABLE 4.1   A Summary of Differences among the Three Approaches to Social Research

	POSITIVISM	INTERPRETIVE SOCIAL SCIENCE	CRITICAL SOCIAL SCIENCE	FEMINIST	POSTMODERN
1. Reason for research	To discover natural laws so people can predict and control events	To understand and describe meaningful social action	To smash myths and empower people to change society	To empower people to advance values of nurturing others and equality	To express the subjective self, to be playful, and to entertain and stimulate
2. Nature of social reality	Stable preexisting patterns or order that can be discovered	Fluid definitions of a situation created by human interaction	Multiple layers and governed by hidden, underlying structures	Gender-structured power relations that keep people oppressed	Chaotic and fluid without real patterns or master plan
3. Human nature	Self-interested and rational individuals who are shaped by external forces	Social beings who create meaning and who constantly make sense of their worlds	Creative, adaptive people with unrealized potential, trapped by illusion.	Gendered beings with unrealized potential often trapped by unseen forces	Creative, dynamic beings with unrealized potential
4. Human agency	Powerful external social pressures shape people's actions; free will is largely illusion	People have significant volition; they develop meanings and have freedom to make choices	Bounded autonomy and free choice structurally limited, but the limits can be moved	Structural limits based on gender confines choices, but new thinking and action can breach the limits	People have great volition, and all structures are illusionary
5. Role of common sense	Clearly distinct from and less valid than science	Powerful everyday theories used by ordinary people	False beliefs that hide power and objective conditions	False beliefs that hide power and objective conditions	The essence of social reality that is superior to scientific or bureaucratic forms of reasoning
6. Theory looks like	A logical, deductive system of interconnected definitions, axioms, and laws	A description of how a group's meaning system is generated and sustained	A critique that reveals true conditions and helps people take action	A critique that reveals true conditions and helps people see the way to a better world	A performance or work of artistic expression that can amuse, shock, or stimulate others
7. An explanation that is true	Is logically connected to laws and based on facts	Resonates or feels right to those who are being studied	Supplies people with tools needed to change the world	Supplies ideas/tools to help liberate people from oppressive relations	No one explanation is more true; all are true for those who accept them
8. Good evidence	Is based on precise observations that others can repeat	Is embedded in the context of fluid social interactions	Is informed by a theory that penetrates the surface level	Is informed by theory that reveals gender structures	Has aesthetic properties and resonates with people's inner feelings
9. Relevance of knowledge	An instrumental orientation is used; knowledge enables people to master and control events	A practical orientation is used; knowledge helps us embrace/share empathetically others' life worlds and experiences	A dialectiical orientation is used; knowledge lets people see and alter deeper structures	Knowledge raises awareness and empowers people to make change	Formal knowledge has no special value; it can amuse or bring personal enjoyment
10. Place for values	Science is value free, and values have no place except when choosing a topic	Values are an integral part of social life: no group's values are wrong, only different	All science must begin with a value position; some positions are right, some are wrong	Values are essential to research, and feminist ones are clearly preferred	Values are integral to research, but all value positions are equal

An ISS researcher personally talks with and observes specific people from both the minority groups and the majority groups in each of the four countries. His or her conversations and observations are used to learn what each group believes to be its major problem and whether group members feel that discrimination or job competition is an everyday concern. The researcher puts what people say into the context of their daily affairs (e.g., paying rent, getting involved in family disputes, having run-ins with the law, getting sick). After he or she sees what the minority or majority people think about discrimination, how they get jobs, how people in the other group get jobs, and what they actually do to get or keep jobs, he or she describes findings in terms that others can understand.

A CSS researcher begins by looking at the larger social and historical context. This includes factors such as the invasion of Australia by British colonists and the nation's history as a prison colony, the economic conditions in China that caused people to migrate to Canada, the legacy of slavery and civil rights struggles in the United States, and the rise and fall of Britain's colonial empire and the migration of people from its former colonies. He or she inquires from a moral-critical standpoint: Does the majority group discriminate against and economically exploit the minority? The researcher looks at many sources to document the underlying pattern of exploitation and to measure the amount of discrimination in each nation. He or she may examine statistical information on income differences between groups, personally examine living situations and go with people to job interviews, or conduct surveys to find out what people now think. Once the researcher finds out how discrimination keeps a minority group from getting jobs, he or she gives results to minority group organizations, gives public lectures on the findings, and publishes results in newspapers read by minority group members in order to expose the true conditions and to encourage political-social action.

What does all of this about three approaches mean to you in a course on social research? First, it means that there is no single, correct approach to social science research. This does not mean that anything goes, nor that there is no ground for

agreement (see Expansion Box 4.4, Common Features of the Three Major Approaches to Social Science). Rather, it means that the basis for doing social research is not settled. In other words, more than one approach is currently "in the running." Perhaps this will always be the case. An awareness of the approaches will help you to read research reports. Often researchers rely on one approach, but rarely do they tell you which one they are using.

EXPANSION BOX **4.4**

Common Features of the Three Major Approaches to Social Science

1. *All are empirical.* Each is rooted in the observable reality of the sights, sounds, behaviors, situations, discussions, and actions of people. Research is never based on fabrication and imagination alone.
2. *All are systematic.* Each emphasizes meticulous and careful work. All reject haphazard, shoddy, or sloppy thinking and observation.
3. *All are theoretical.* The nature of theory varies, but all emphasize using ideas and seeing patterns. None holds that social life is chaos and disorder; all hold that explanation or understanding is possible.
4. *All are public.* All say a researcher's work must be candidly expressed to other researchers; it should be made explicit and shared. All oppose keeping the research processes hidden, private, or secret.
5. *All are self-reflective.* Each approach says researchers need to think about what they do and be self-conscious. Research is never done in a blind or unthinking manner. It involves serious contemplation and requires self-awareness.
6. *All are open-end processes.* All see research as constantly moving, evolving, changing, asking new questions, and pursuing leads. None sees it as static, fixed, or closed. Current knowledge or research procedures are not "set in stone" and settled. They involve continuous change and an openness to new ways of thinking and doing things.

Thus, despite their differences, all of the approaches say that the social sciences strive to create systematically gathered, empirically based theoretical knowledge through public processes that are self-reflective and open ended.

Second, the three approaches mean that what you try to accomplish when you do research (i.e., discover laws, identify underlying structures, describe meaning systems) will vary with the approach you choose. The fit between the three approaches and types of research discussed in Chapter 2 is loose. For example, PSS is likely to conduct cost-benefit analysis, ISS researchers tend to do exploratory research, and CSS researchers favor action-oriented research. By being aware of the approaches when you do social research, you can make an informed decision about the type of study to conduct.

Third, the various techniques used in social research (sampling, interviewing, participant observation, etc.) are ultimately based on assumptions and ideas from the approaches. Often you will see a research technique presented without the background reasoning on which it was originally based. By knowing about the approaches, you can better understand the principles on which the specific research techniques are based. For example, the precise measures and logic of experimental research flow directly from positivism whereas field research is based on an interpretive approach.

So far, we have looked at the overall operation of the research process, different types of studies and theory, and the three fundamental approaches to social research. By now, you should have a grasp of the basic contours of social research. In the next chapter, you will see how to locate reports of specific research projects.

KEY TERMS

abduction
bounded autonomy
bracketing
causal laws
constructionist orientation
covering law model
critical social science (CSS)
determinism
dialectic
epistemology
explanatory critique
false consciousness
hermeneutics

idiographic
instrumental orientation
interpretative social science
  (ISS)
intersubjectivity
meaningful social action
mechanical model of man
natural attitude
nomothetic
ontology
paradigm
positivist social science (PSS)
postulate of adequacy

practical orientation
praxis
reflexive-dialectic orientation
reification
relativism
technocratic perspective
transcendent perspective
transformative perspective
typification
value-free science
verstehen
voluntarism

REVIEW QUESTIONS

1. What is the purpose of social research according to each of the three approaches?
2. How does each approach define social reality?
3. What is the nature of human beings according to each approach?
4. How are science and common sense different in each approach?
5. What is social theory according to each approach?
6. How does each approach test a social theory?
7. What does each approach say about facts and how to collect them?

8. How is value-free science possible in each approach? Explain.

9. In what way(s) are the criticisms of positivism by the interpretive and critical science approaches similar?

10. How does the model of science and the scientific community presented in Chapter 1 relate to each of the three approaches?

NOTES

1. This book is primarily concerned with sociology (Steinmetz, 2005a). For anthropology, see Kean (2005); for educational research, see Bredo and Feinberg (1982) and Guba and Lincoln (1994); for psychology, see Harré and Secord (1979) and Rosnow (1981); for political science, see Hauptmann (2005) and Sabia and Wallulis (1983); and for economics, see Hollis (1977), Mitchell (2005), and Ward (1972). A general discussion of alternatives can be found in Nowotny and Rose (1979).

2. See especially Friedrichs (1970), Giddens (1976), Gouldner (1970), and Phillips (1971). General introductions are provided by Harré (1972), Suppe (1977), and Toulmin (1953).

3. Divisions of the philosophies of social science similar to the approaches discussed in this chapter can be found in Benton (1977), Blaikie (1993), Bredo and Feinberg (1982), Fay (1975), Fletcher (1974), Guba and Lincoln (1994), Keat and Urry (1975), Lloyd (1986), Miller (1987), Mulkay (1979), Sabia and Wallulis (1983), Smart (1976), and Wilson (1970).

4. For discussions of paradigms, see Eckberg and Hill (1979), Kuhn (1970, 1979), Masterman (1970), Ritzer (1975), and Rosnow (1981).

5. In addition to the works listed in note 3, Halfpenny (1982), Steinmetz (2005), and Turner (1984) have provided overviews of positivism in sociology. Also see Giddens (1978). Lenzer (1975) is an excellent introduction to Auguste Comte.

6. See Gartell and Gartell (1996, 2002).

7. From Bernard (1988:12–21).

8. See Hegtvedt (1992).

9. For a discussion, see Derksen and Gartell (1992:1715).

10. See Couch (1987). Also see Longino (1990:62–82) for an excellent analysis of objectivity in positivism.

11. For a discussion, see Bannister (1987), Blumer (1991a, 1991b, 1992), Deegan (1988), Geiger (1986), Gillespie (1991), Lagemann (1989), Ross (1991), Schwendinger and Schwendinger (1974), Silva and Slaughter (1980), and Smith (1996).

12. For a further discussion of hermeneutics see Bleicher (1980) and Schwandt (1994; 1997). Sewell (1996; 2005) also discusses the significance of "reading" text.

13. In addition to the works in note 3, interpretive science approaches are discussed in Berger and Luckman (1967), Bleicher (1980), Cicourel (1973), Garfinkel (1967, 1974b), Geertz (1979), Glaser and Strauss (1967), Holstein and Gubrium (1994), Leiter (1980), Mehan and Wood (1975), Silverman (1972), and Weber (1974, 1981).

14. See Roy (2001:7–13) on the essentialist versus constructionist orientation.

15. See Brown (1989:34) for more examples and explanation.

16. In addition to the works in note 3, critical science approaches are discussed in Burawoy (1990), Dickson (1984), Fay (1987), Glucksmann (1974), Harding (1986), Harvey (1990), Keat (1981), Lane (1970), Lemert (1981), Mayhew (1980, 1981), Sohn-Rethel (1978), Veltmeyer (1978), Wardell (1979), Warner (1971), and Wilson (1982).

17. For a discussion of the Frankfurt School, see Bottomore (1984), Held (1980), Martin (1973), and Slater (1977). For more on the works of Habermas, see Holub (1991), McCarthy (1978), Pusey (1987), and Roderick (1986).

18. See Swartz (1997) on Bourdieu.

19. For discussions of realism, see Bhaskar (1975), Miller (1987), and Sayer (1992).

20. For discussions of critical realism, see Archer et al. (1998), Bhaskar (2003), Danermark et al. (2002), and Groff (2004).

21. See Sprague and Zimmerman (1989) on feminists' privileged perspectives of women and see Rule (1978a, 1978b) on constituencies that researchers favor.

22. See Habermas (1971, 1973, 1979) for a critical science critique of positivism as being technocratic and used for domination. He has suggested an emancipatory alternative.

23. See Olsen (1994).

24. See Evelyn Fox Keller's (1983) biography of Barbara McClintock and her other essays on gender and science (1985, 1990). Also see Longino (1990), Chapters 6 and 7.

25. From Brannigan (1992).

CHAPTER 5

How to Review the Literature and Conduct Ethical Studies

The Literature Review
Ethics in Social Research

Conclusion

But since we do not as yet live in a period free from mundane troubles and beyond history, our problem is not how to deal with a kind of knowledge which shall be "truth in itself," but rather how man deals with his problems of knowing, bound as he is in his knowledge by his position in time and society.

—Karl Mannheim, *Ideology and Utopia*, p. 188

In his field research study of a drug-dealing gang in Chicago housing projects, Venkatesh (2008:185–186) realized "Four years deep into my research, it came to my attention that I might get into a lot of trouble if I kept doing what I've been doing. . . . I did see a lawyer, and I learned a few important things. First, if I became aware of a plan to physically harm anyone, I was obligated to tell the police . . . there was no such thing as 'research-client confidentiality,' akin to the privilege conferred upon lawyers, doctors, or priests. This meant that if I were ever subpoenaed to testify against the gang, I would be legally obligated to participate. . . . This legal advice was ultimately helpful in that it led me to seriously take stock of my research. . . ."

You are ready to design a study on the topic of gangs. As you narrow the broad topic into a specific research question (e.g., Do drug-dealing gangs in a housing project provide services or protection to other residents or do they only exploit them?), you encounter two issues. First, are any past studies relevant to this question (i.e., review the scholarly literature on gangs)? In practice, the process of focusing a topic into a research question overlaps nicely with reviewing the literature. Second, as you gather data on gangs, what must you do to be ethical? Specific ethical concerns depend on the research question and the data collection technique. Human subject issues are most salient in survey research, experiments, and field research and least salient in existing documents, secondary data analysis, content analysis, or historical-comparative research. Ethical issues are more significant for controversial topics or areas that might violate a person's privacy or involve illegal behavior than for "safe topics." To study illegal gangs, you need not only to protect yourself from physical attack but also to be aware of the legal implications. Ideally, unlike Venkatesh's study mentioned in the opening box, you do not want to be doing research for four years before you learn about the legal-ethical issues of your research study and need to change direction.

Previous chapters discussed the foundations of research: how the scientific community operates, various types of studies, theory-research connections, and broad approaches to doing social science. In this chapter and the three that follow, we move to practical matters that you will encounter as you begin to do your own research study: reviewing the literature, considering ethical issues, designing a study, measuring aspects of the social world, and deciding on what data to collect.

THE LITERATURE REVIEW

An early and essential step in doing a study is to review the accumulated knowledge on your research question. This applies to all research questions and all types of studies. As in other areas of life, it is wise to find out what others have already learned about an issue before you address it on your own. Clichés reinforce this advice: Do not waste time "reinventing the wheel" and remember to "do your homework" before beginning an endeavor. This holds true whether you are a consumer of research or will be beginning a study yourself.

We begin by looking at the various purposes the review might serve. We will also discuss what *the literature* is, where to find it, and what it contains. Next we will explore techniques for systematically conducting a review. Finally, we will look at how to write a review and what its place is in a research report.

Doing a literature review builds on the idea that knowledge accumulates and that we can learn from and build on what others have done. The review rests on the principle that scientific research is a collective effort, one in which many researchers contribute and share results with one another. Although some studies may be especially important and a few individual researchers may become famous, one study is just a tiny part of the overall process of creating knowledge. Today's studies build on those of yesterday. We read studies to learn from, compare, replicate, or criticize them.

Literature reviews vary in scope and depth. Different kinds of reviews are stronger at fulfilling one or another of four goals (see Expansion Box 5.1, Goals of a Literature Review). Doing an extensive professional summary review that covers all of the research literature on a broad question could take years by a skilled researcher. On the other hand,

---

EXPANSION BOX 5.1
Goals of a Literature Review

1. *To demonstrate a familiarity with a body of knowledge and establish credibility.* A review tells a reader that the researcher knows the research in an area and knows the major issues. A good review increases a reader's confidence in the researcher's professional competence, ability, and background.
2. *To show the path of prior research and how a current project is linked to it.* A review outlines the direction of research on a question and shows the development of knowledge. A good review places a research project in a context and demonstrates its relevance by making connections to a body of knowledge.
3. *To integrate and summarize what is known in an area.* A review pulls together and synthesizes different results. A good review points out areas in which prior studies agree, disagree, and major questions remain. It collects what is known up to a point in time and indicates the direction for future research.
4. *To learn from others and stimulate new ideas.* A review tells what others have found so that a researcher can benefit from the efforts of others. A good review identifies blind alleys and suggests hypotheses for replication. It divulges procedures, techniques, and research designs worth copying so that a researcher can better focus hypotheses and gain new insights.

---

the same person could finish a narrowly focused review in a specialized area in a week. To begin a review, you must pick a topic area or research question, determine how much time and effort you can devote to the study, settle on the appropriate level of depth, and decide on the best type of review for your situation (see Expansion Box 5.2, Six Types of Literature Reviews). You can combine features of each type in a specific review.

Literature Meta-Analysis

A literature **meta-analysis** is a special technique used to create an integrative review or a methodological review.[1] Meta-analysis involves gathering the details about a large number of previous studies

EXPANSION BOX **5.2**

Six Types of Literature Reviews

1. *Context review.* A common type of review in which the author links a specific study to a larger body of knowledge. It often appears at the beginning of a research report and introduces the study by situating it within a broader framework and showing how it continues or builds on a developing line of thought or study.
2. *Historical review.* A specialized review in which the author traces an issue over time. It can be merged with a theoretical or methodological review to show how a concept, theory, or research method developed over time.
3. *Integrative review.* A common type of review in which the author presents and summarizes the current state of knowledge on a topic, highlighting agreements and disagreements within it. This review is often combined with a context review or may be published as an independent article as a service to other researchers.
4. *Methodological review.* A specialized type of integrative review in which the author compares and evaluates the relative methodological strength of various studies and shows how different methodologies (e.g., research designs, measures, samples) account for different results.
5. *Self-study review.* A review in which an author demonstrates his or her familiarity with a subject area. It is often part of an educational program or course requirement.
6. *Theoretical review.* A specialized review in which the author presents several theories or concepts focused on the same topic and compares them on the basis of assumptions, logical consistency, and scope of explanation.

and synthesizing the results. A meta-analysis proceeds in five steps:

1. Locate all potential studies on a specific topic or research question
2. Develop consistent criteria and screen studies for relevance and/or quality
3. Identify and record relevant information for each study

4. Synthesize and analyze the information into broad findings
5. Draw summary conclusions based on the findings

For a meta-analysis of quantitative studies, relevant information in step 3 often includes sample size, measures of variables, methodological quality, and size of the effects of variables, and in step 4, this information is analyzed statistically (see Example Box 5.1, Meta-Analysis of Quantitative Studies on page 126). A meta-analysis of qualitative studies is a little different. The relevant information in step 3 includes qualitative descriptions that are coded into a set of categories, and in step 4 the results are synthesized qualitatively to reveal recurrent themes (see Example Box 5.2, Meta-Analysis of Qualitative Studies on page 126).

In addition to using meta-analysis to identify major findings across many studies, we can also use it to identify how contributors in a research case define and use major concepts. For example, Fulkerson and Thompson (2008) examined the concept of "social capital" over 18 years (1988–2006). They identified 1,218 articles in 450 academic journals with the term *social capital* in the title or abstract. They coded the articles in seven ways to define the concept and identified the "founding scholar" on the concept that the article cited. They also used statistical techniques to analyze the patterns that show use of definition across time and by specialty area.

Where to Find Research Literature

Researchers can find reports of research studies in several formats: books, scholarly journal articles, dissertations, government documents, and policy reports. Researchers also present findings as papers at the meetings of professional societies. This section discusses each format and provide a simple road map on how to access them.

Meta-analysis A special type of literature review in which a writer organizes the results from many studies and uses statistical techniques to identify common findings in them.

Meta-Analysis of Quantitative Studies

Cheng and Chan (2008) conducted a meta-analysis of 133 studies on the issue of job insecurity. Their interest was in the impact of job insecurity on health outcomes. They considered three factors: job tenure (i.e., how long a person worked at a job), age, and gender. Their purpose was to learn how job tenure, age, and gender might weaken or intensify how job insecurity influenced outcomes. First, they identified possible relevant studies by searching the keywords *job security* and *job insecurity* in several databases of studies published from 1980 to 2006. They also manually searched fifteen academic journals, searched for unpublished dissertations, and contacted leading scholars about any unpublished studies they had conducted. Next the researchers screened the potential studies using

selection criteria. To be included the study, a report had to be in English, use the term *job insecurity* in a way that matched the authors' definition, report certain types of statistical results, and include all variables of interest. After they had identified 133 acceptable studies, two graduate student raters coded results from each. Information coded included sample size, measures of key variables, correlations among variables, and size of statistical effects. Next Cheng and Chan statistically analyzed the coded information. From their statistical analysis of results, the authors concluded that compared to younger and less experienced employees, older employees and those with longer job tenure experience suffered more negative physical and psychological health outcomes due to job insecurity.

Meta-Analysis of Qualitative Studies

Marston and King (2006) conducted a meta-analysis of 268 qualitative studies published between 1990 and 2004 of young people's sexual behavior. Their interest was in how sexual behaviors among young people might influence the spread of HIV infections because almost half of all such infections occur within this age group. The authors wanted to examine qualitative studies because they were interested in what happened during a sexual encounter, reasons for the behavior, and the context of the behavior. In contrast, most quantitative studies examined only simple, isolated questions such as the percentage of young people who use condoms. They identified all studies in English published between 1990 and 2004 that provided qualitative empirical evidence about sexual relations among persons 10–25 years old. The authors included studies that concentrated on other issues (e.g., drug use) but also included sexual behavior. They searched numerous databases of articles and books and investigated the catalogs of 150 academic libraries in the United Kingdom. They found 5,452

potential reports based on a search of titles but narrowed these to 2,202 based on relevance of the title. They narrowed them further to 268 studies (246 journal articles and 22 books) based on inclusion criteria: excluding studies on child sexual abuse and commercial sex work, or those that were not available in full. They also classified documents as primary and high quality (e.g., very specific descriptions of sexual encounters with contexts) and secondary (e.g., reports of attitudes, lacking evidence for statements made). Of the 268 documents, 121 were classified as primary. Martson and King used a method of comparative thematic analysis in which they reviewed and coded the documents/studies that represented themes found in the studies (e.g., violence against women, fear of embarrassment), and then collapsed these codes into broad overall themes. They identified seven broad themes, such as gender stereotypes that were critical in determining social expectations (e.g., women, not men, should be chaste; men are expected to seek physical pleasure and women romantic love).

Periodicals. Study results appear in newspapers, in popular magazines, on television or radio broadcasts, and in Internet news summaries, but these are not the full, complete reports of research you need to prepare a literature review. They are selected, condensed summaries prepared by journalists for a general audience. They lack many essential details that we require to seriously evaluate the study. Textbooks and encyclopedias also present condensed summaries as introductions to readers who are new to a topic. These too are inadequate for preparing a literature review because many essential details about the study are absent.

Navigating the world of published scholarly articles can be intimidating at first. When asked to do a "literature review," many beginning students Google the topic on the Internet or go to familiar nonprofessional, nonscholarly magazines or newspaper articles. Social science students need to learn to distinguish between scholarly publications that report on research studies and popular or layperson entertainment or news articles for the lay public (see Table 5.1 on page 128). They need to move from lay public sources and rely on serious scholarly publications written for a professional audience.

Professional researchers present the results of studies in one of several forms: academic research books (often called *monographs*), articles in scholarly journals, chapters in edited academic books, and papers presented at professional meetings. Simplified, abbreviated, and "predigested" versions of articles appear in textbooks written for students who are first learning about a topic or in journalistic summaries in publications for the public. Unfortunately, the simplified summaries can give an incomplete or distorted picture of a complete study. Researchers must locate the original scholarly journal article to see what the author said and the data show.

Upper-level undergraduates and graduate students writing a serious research paper should rely on the academic literature, that is, original articles published in academic scholarly journals. Unfortunately, students may find some of the scholarly articles too difficult or technical to follow. The upside is that the articles are the "real McCoy," or original reports, not another person's (mis)reading of the original.

Researchers also may find a type of nonresearch publication with commentaries on topics or research questions. These are discussion-opinion magazines (e.g., *American Prospect, Cato Journal, Commentary, Nation, National Review, New Republic, New York Review of Books, Policy Review,* and *Public Interest*). In them, professionals write essays expressing opinions, beliefs, value-based ideas, and speculation for the educated public or professionals. They do not contain original empirical research or actual scientific studies. They may be classified as "academic journals" (versus general magazines) and may be "peer reviewed," but they do not contain original reports of empirical research. For example, *Policy Review* covers many topics: law enforcement, criminal justice, defense and military, politics, government and international relations, and political science. The leading conservative "think tank," the Heritage Foundation, publishes material as a forum for conservative debate on major political issues. At times, professors or professional researchers who also conduct serious research studies contribute their opinions and speculation in such publications. These publications must be used with caution. They present debates, opinions, and judgments, not the official reports of serious empirical research. If you want to write a research paper based on empirical research (e.g., an experiment, survey data, field research), you need to rely on specialized sources. If you use an opinion essay article, you need to treat it as such and never confuse it with an empirical social science study.

Researchers use specialized computer-based search tools to locate articles in the scholarly literature. They also must learn the specialized formats or citation styles for referring to sources. Professional social scientists regularly use search tools to tap into and build on a growing body of research studies and scientific knowledge. Knowing how to locate studies; recognize, read, and evaluate studies; and properly cite scholarly sources is a very important skill for serious consumers of research and researchers to master.

Scholarly Journals. The primary source to use for a literature review is the scholarly journal. It is filled

TABLE 5.1   Types of Publications

TYPE	EXAMPLE	AUTHOR	PURPOSE	STRENGTH	WEAKNESS
Peer-reviewed scholarly journal	*Social Science Quarterly, Social Forces, Journal of Contemporary Ethnography*	Professional researchers	Report on empirical research studies to professionals and build knowledge	Highest quality, most accurate, and most objective with complete details	Technical, difficult to read, requires background knowledge, not always current issues
Semischolarly professional publication	*American Prospect, Society, American Demographics*	Professors, professional policymakers, politicians	Share and discuss new findings and implications with the educated public	Generally accurate, somewhat easy to read	Lacks full detail and explanation, often includes opinion mixed in with discussion
Newsmagazines and newspapers	*Wall Street Journal, Christian Science Monitor, Newsweek, Time*	Respected journalists	Report on current events in an easy-to-read, accessible way for the lay public	Easy to read, accessible, very current	Semiaccurate, incomplete, distorted, or one-sided views
Serious opinion magazines	*Nation, Human Events, Public Interest, Commentary*	Professors, professional policymakers, politicians	Offer value-based ideas and opinions to the educated public	Carefully written and reasoned	One-sided view and highly value based
Popular magazines for the public	*Esquire, Ebony, Redbook, Forbes, Fortune*	Journalists, other writers	Entertain, present and discuss current events for lay public	Easy to read, easy to locate	Often shallow, inaccurate, and incomplete

with peer-reviewed reports of research. (See the back inside cover of this book for a list.) One can rarely find these journals outside of college and university libraries. Recall from Chapter 1 that most researchers disseminate new findings in scholarly journals. They are the heart of the scientific community's communication system.

Some scholarly journals are specialized and have only book reviews that provide commentary and evaluations on academic books (e.g., *Contemporary Sociology, Law and Politics Book Review*), or only literature review essays (e.g., *Annual Review of Sociology, Annual Review of Psychology, Annual Review of Anthropology*) in which researchers give a "state of the field" essay for others. Publications that specialize in literature reviews can offer useful introductions or overviews on a topic. Many scholarly journals include a mix of literature reviews, book reviews, reports on research studies, and theoretical essays.

No simple solution or "seal of approval" separates scholarly journals from other periodicals or instantly distinguishes a research study report from other types of articles. To identify a research study you need to develop judgment skills or ask experienced researchers or professional librarians. Nonetheless, learning to distinguish among types of publications is an essential skill to master. One of the best ways to distinguish among types of publications is to read many articles in scholarly journals.

The number of scholarly journals varies widely according to academic field. Psychology has more than 400 scholarly journals, sociology has about 250, political science and communication have fewer than sociology, anthropology-archaeology and social work each has about 100, urban studies and women's studies have about 50, and criminology has only about a dozen. The "pure" academic fields usually have more than the "applied" or practical fields such as marketing or social work. Each journal publishes from a few dozen to more than 100 articles each year.

You may wonder whether anyone ever reads all of these articles. One study found that in a sample of 379 sociology articles, 43 percent were cited in another study in the first year after publication and 83 percent within 6 years.[2] As mentioned in Chapter 1, scholarly journals vary by prestige and acceptance rates. Prestigious journals accept only 10 percent of the research reports submitted to them. Overall rejection rates are higher in the social sciences than in other academic fields and have been rising.[3] This does not mean that researchers are doing low-quality studies. Rather, the review process is becoming more rigorous, standards are rising, and more studies are being conducted. This means that the competition to publish an article in a highly respected journal has increased.

You can find the full text of many scholarly journal articles on the Internet. Usually, to access them you need to go through libraries that pay special subscription fees for online article searching services, or a source tool. Some journals or publishers offer limited articles or sell them. For example, I was able to view current articles in *Social Science Quarterly* (a respected scholarly journal) free on the Internet, but when I tried to read an article in *Politics and Society* online, I was asked to pay $25 per article; however, if I had access to it through my university library, the article was free.

Article search services may have full, exact copies of scholarly journal articles. For example, JSTOR and Project MUSE provide exact copies but only for a limited number of scholarly journals and only for past years. Other source tools, such as Anthrosource, Proquest, EBSCO HOST, or Wilson Web offer a full-text version of recent articles. Most articles are in the same format as their print versions. In addition to searching the database of articles using a source tool, you can also select a particular journal and browse its table of contents for particular issues. This can be very useful for generating new ideas for research topics, seeing an established topic in creative ways, or expanding an idea into new areas. Each online source tool has its own search procedure and list of scholarly journals. None has all articles from all journals for all years.

Some recent Internet-only scholarly journals, called *e-journals* (e.g., *Sociological Research Online, Current Research in Social Psychology,* and *Journal of World Systems Research*), present peer-reviewed research studies. Eventually, the Internet format may replace print versions. But for now, about 95 percent of scholarly journals are available in print form and most are available in a full-text version over the Internet. Internet access nearly always requires that you use an online service through a library that pays an annual fee to use it. Certain journals and certain years are not yet available online.

Once you locate a scholarly journal that contains empirical research studies, you next locate specific articles. You need to make sure that a particular article presents the results of a study because journals often publish several other types of article. It is easier to identify quantitative studies because they usually have a methods or data section as well as charts, statistical formulas, and tables of numbers. Qualitative research articles are more difficult to identify, and many students confuse them with theoretical essays, literature review articles, idea-discussion essays, policy recommendations, book reviews, and legal case analyses. To distinguish among these types requires a grasp of the varieties of research and experience in reading many articles.

Most college libraries have a section for scholarly journals and magazines, or, in some cases, they mix the journals with books. Look at a map of library facilities or ask a librarian to identify this section. The most recent issues, which look like magazines, are often physically separate in a "current periodicals" section where they are temporarily available until the library receives all issues of a volume.

Libraries place scholarly journals from many fields together with popular, nonscholarly magazines. All are periodicals, or "serials" in the jargon of librarians. Thus, you will find popular magazines (e.g., *Time, Road and Track, Cosmopolitan,* and *The Atlantic*) next to journals for astronomy, chemistry, mathematics, literature, sociology, psychology, social work, and education. Libraries list journals in their catalog system by title and can provide a list of the periodicals to which they subscribe.

Scholarly journals are published as rarely as once a year or as frequently as weekly. Most appear four to six times a year. For example, *Social Science Quarterly,* like other journals with the word *quarterly* in their title, is published four times a year. To assist in locating articles, each journal issue has a date, volume number, and issue number. This information makes it easier to locate an article. Such information—along with details such as author, title, and page number—is called an article's *citation* and is used in bibliographies or lists of works cited. The very first issue of a journal begins with volume 1, number 1. It continues increasing the numbers thereafter. Most journals follow a similar system, but enough exceptions exist that you need to pay close attention to citation information. For most journals, each volume includes one year of articles. If you see a journal issue with volume 52, it probably means that the journal has been in existence for 52 years. Most, but not all, journals begin their publishing cycle in January.

Most journals number pages by volume, not by issue. The first issue of a volume usually begins with page 1, and page numbering continues throughout the entire volume. For example, the first page of volume 52, issue 4, may be page 547. Most journals have an index for each volume and a table of contents for each issue that lists the title, the author's or authors' names, and the page on which the article begins. Issues contain as few as one or two articles or as many as fifty. Most have eight to eighteen articles, which each may be five to fifty pages long. The articles often have **abstracts**, short summaries on the first page of the article or grouped together at the front of the issue.

Many libraries do not retain physical paper copies of older journals, but to save space and costs they keep only electronic or microfilm versions. Because each field may have hundreds of scholarly journals, with each costing the library $100 to $3,500 per year in subscription fees, only the large research libraries subscribe to most of them. You can also obtain a copy of an article from a distant library through an *interlibrary loan service,* a system by which libraries lend books or materials to other libraries. Few libraries allow people to check out recent issues of scholarly journals.

If you go to the library and locate the periodicals section, it is fun to wander down the aisles and skim what is on the shelves. You will see volumes containing many research reports. Each title of a scholarly journal has a call number like that of a regular library book. Libraries often arrange the journals alphabetically by title. However, journals sometimes change titles, creating confusion if they have been shelved under their original titles.

Scholarly journals contain articles on research in an academic field. Thus, most mathematics journals contain reports on new mathematical studies or proofs, literature journals contain commentary and literary criticism on works of literature, and sociology journals contain reports of sociological research. Some journals cover a very broad field (e.g., social science, education, public affairs) and contain reports from the entire field. Others specialize in a subfield (e.g., the family, criminology, early childhood education, or comparative politics).

Citation   Details of a scholarly publication's location that helps people to find it quickly.

Abstract   A short summary of a scholarly journal article that usually appears at its beginning; also a reference tool for locating journal articles.

Citation Formats.   An article's citation is the key to locating it. Suppose you want to read the study by Pampel on cultural taste, music, and smoking behavior that opened Chapter 4. Its citation says the following: Pampel, Fred C. 2006. "Socioeconomic Distinction, Cultural Tastes, and Cigarette Smoking." *Social Science Quarterly,* 87(1):19–35. It tells you to go to an issue of the scholarly journal *Social Science Quarterly* published in 2006. The citation does not provide the month, but it gives the volume number (87), the issue as 1, and the page numbers (319–335).

Formats for citing literature vary in many ways. The most popular format in the text is the internal citation format of using an author's last name and date of publication in parentheses. A full citation appears in a separate bibliography or reference section. There are many styles for full citations of journal articles with books and other types of works each having a separate style. When citing articles, it is best to check with an instructor, journal, or other outlet for the required form. Almost all include the names of authors, article title, journal name, and volume and page numbers. Beyond these basic elements, there is great variety. Some include the authors' first names while others use initials only. Some include all authors; others give only the first one. Some include information on the issue or month of publication; others do not (see Figure 5.1 on page 132).

Citation formats can be complex. Two major reference tools on the topic in social science are *Chicago Manual of Style,* which has nearly 80 pages on bibliographies and reference formats, and *American Psychological Association Publication Manual,* which devotes about 60 pages to the topic. In sociology, the *American Sociological Review* style, with two pages of style instructions, is widely followed.

Books.   Books communicate many types of information, provoke thought, and entertain. The many types of books include picture books, textbooks, short story books, novels, popular fiction or nonfiction, religious books, and children's books. Our concern here is with those books containing reports of original research or collections of research articles. Libraries shelve these books and assign call numbers to them, as they do with other types of books. You can find citation information on them (e.g., title, author, publisher) in the library's catalog system.

Distinguishing a book reporting on research from other books can be difficult. You are more likely to find such books in a college or university library. Some publishers, such as university presses, specialize in publishing research reports. Nevertheless, there is no guaranteed method for identifying one on research without reading it. Some types of research are more likely to appear in book form than others. For example, studies by anthropologists and historians are more likely to appear in book-length reports than are those of economists or psychologists. However, some anthropological and historical studies are reported in articles, and some economic and psychological studies appear as books. In education, social work, sociology, and political science, the results of long, complex studies may appear both in two or three articles and in book form. Studies that involve detailed clinical or ethnographic descriptions and complex theoretical or philosophical discussions usually appear as books. Finally, an author who wants to communicate to scholarly peers and to the educated public may write a book that bridges the scholarly, academic style and a popular nonfiction style. Locating original research articles in books can be difficult because no single source lists them.

Three types of books contain collections of articles or research reports. The first type, for teaching, called a *reader,* may include original research reports. Usually, articles on a topic from scholarly journals are gathered and edited to be easier for students to read and understand. The second type of collection gathers journal articles or may contain original research or theoretical essays on a specific topic. Some collections contain original research reports organized around a specialized topic in journals that are difficult to locate. The table of contents lists the titles and authors. Libraries shelve these collections with other books, and some library catalog systems include article or chapter titles. Finally, annual research books that are hybrids between scholarly journals and collections of articles contain reports on studies not found elsewhere. They

---

FIGURE 5.1   Different Reference Citations for a Journal Article

---

The oldest journal of sociology in the United States, *American Journal of Sociology,* reports on a study of virginity pledges by Peter Bearman and Hannah Bückner. It appeared on pages 859 to 912 of the January 2001 issue (number 4) of the journal, which begins counting issues in March. It was in volume 106, or the journal's 106th year. Here are ways to cite the article. Two very popular styles are those of American Sociological Review (ASR) and American Psychological Association (APA).

ASR STYLE

Bearman, Peter and Hannah Bückner. 2001. "Promising the Future: Virginity Pledges and First Intercourse." *American Journal of Sociology* 106:859–912.

APA STYLE

Bearman, P., and Bückner, H. (2001). Promising the future: Virginity pledges and first intercourse. *American Journal of Sociology 106,* 859–912.

OTHER STYLES

Bearman, P., and H. Bückner. "Promising the Future: Virginity Pledges and First Intercourse," *American Journal of Sociology* 106 (2001), 859–912.

Bearman, Peter and Hannah Bückner, 2001.
    "Promising the future: Virginity pledges and first intercourse." *Am.J. of Sociol.* 106:859–912.

Bearman, P. and Bückner, H. (2001). "Promising the Future: Virginity Pledges and First Intercourse." *American Journal of Sociology* 106 (January): 859–912.

Bearman, Peter and Hannah Bückner. 2001.
    "Promising the future: Virginity pledges and first intercourse." *American Journal of Sociology* 106 (4):859–912.

Bearman, P. and H. Bückner. (2001). "Promising the future: Virginity pledges and first intercourse." *American Journal of Sociology* 106, 859–912.

Peter Bearman and Hannah Bückner, "Promising the Future: Virginity Pledges and First Intercourse," *American Journal of Sociology* 106, no. 4 (2001): 859–912.

---

appear year after year with a volume number for each year. These volumes, such as the *Review of Research in Political Sociology* and *Comparative Social Research,* are shelved with books. Some annual books specialize in literature reviews (e.g., *Annual Review of Sociology* and *Annual Review of Anthropology*). No comprehensive list of these books is available as there is for scholarly journals. The only way to find out is by spending a lot of time in the library or asking a researcher who is already familiar with a topic area.

Citations or references to books are shorter than article citations. They include the author's name, book title, year and place of publication, and publisher's name.

Dissertations. All graduate students who receive the doctor of philosophy (Ph.D.) degree are required to complete a work of original research, called a *dissertation thesis.* The dissertation is bound and shelved in the library of the university that granted the degree. About half of all dissertations are eventually published as books or articles. Because dissertations report on original research, they can be valuable sources of information. Some students who receive the master's degree also conduct original research and write a master's thesis, but fewer master's theses involve serious research, and they are much more difficult to locate than unpublished dissertations.

Specialized indexes list dissertations completed by students at accredited universities. For example, *Dissertation Abstracts International* lists dissertations with their authors, titles, and universities. The organization of the index is by topic with an abstract of each dissertation. You can borrow most dissertations via interlibrary loan from the degree-granting university if it permits this. An alternative is to purchase a copy from a national dissertation microfilm/photocopy center such as the one at the University of Michigan, Ann Arbor, for U.S. universities. Some large research libraries contain copies of dissertations from other libraries if someone previously requested them.

Government Documents. The federal government of the United States, the governments of other nations, state- or provincial-level governments, the United Nations, and other international agencies such as the World Bank, sponsor studies and publish reports of the research. Many college and university libraries have these documents in their holdings, usually in a special "government documents" section. These reports are rarely found in the catalog system. You must use specialized lists of publications and indexes, usually with the help of a librarian, to locate these reports. Most college and university libraries hold only the most frequently requested documents and reports.

Policy Reports and Presented Papers. If you are conducting a thorough literature review, you may look at these two sources. Some are on the Internet, but most are difficult for all but the trained specialist to obtain. Research institutes and policy centers (e.g., Brookings Institute, Institute for Research on Poverty, Rand Corporation) publish papers and reports. Some major research libraries purchase these and shelve them with books. The only way to

be sure of what has been published is to write directly to the institute or center and request a list of reports.

Each year the professional associations in academic fields (e.g., anthropology, criminal justice, geography, political science, psychology, sociology) hold annual meetings. Thousands of researchers assemble to give, listen to, or discuss oral reports of recent research. Most oral reports are also available as written papers. People who do not attend the meetings but who are members of the association receive a program of the meeting, listing each paper to be presented with its title, author, and author's place of employment. These people can write directly to the author and request a copy of the paper. Many, but not all, of the papers later appear as published articles. Sometime the papers are in online services (to be discussed).

How to Conduct a Systematic Literature Review

Define and Refine a Topic. Just as you must plan and clearly define a topic and research question as you begin a research project, you need to begin a literature review with a clearly defined, well-focused research question and a plan. A good review topic should be in the form of a research question. For example, "divorce" or "crime" is much too broad. A more appropriate review topic might be "What contributes to the stability of families with stepchildren?" or "Does economic inequality produce crime rates across nations?" If you conduct a context review for a research project, it should be slightly broader than the specific research question being examined. Often, a researcher will not finalize a specific research question for a study until he or she has reviewed the literature. The review usually helps to focus on the research question.

Design a Search. After choosing a focused research question for the review, the next step is to plan a search strategy. You must decide on the type of review, its extensiveness, and the types of materials to include. The key is to be careful, systematic, and organized. Set parameters on your search: how much time you will devote to it, how far back in time you will look, the minimum number of research reports you will examine, how many libraries you will visit, and so forth.

Also decide how to record the bibliographic citation for each reference and how to take notes (e.g., in a notebook, on 3" × 5" cards, in a computer file). You should begin a file folder or computer file in which you can place possible sources and ideas for new sources. As your review proceeds, you should more narrowly focus on a specific research question or issue.

Locate Research Reports. Locating research reports depends on the type of report or research "outlet" for which you are searching. As a general rule, use multiple search strategies to counteract the limitations of a single search method.

Articles in Scholarly Journals. As discussed earlier, most social research is published in scholarly journals. With hundreds of journals, each containing hundreds of articles, an article search can be formidable. Luckily, online services and specialized publications make the task easier.

Perhaps you have used an index for general publications, such as *Reader's Guide to Periodical Literature.* Many academic fields have "abstracts" or "indexes" for the scholarly literature (e.g., *Psychological Abstracts, Social Sciences Index, Sociological Abstracts,* and *Gerontological Abstracts*). For education-related topics, the Educational Resources Information Center (ERIC) system is especially valuable. More than one hundred such source tools are available now. With a source tool or online service, you can look up articles by title, author name, or subject.

It may sound as though all you have to do is to go find the source tool and look up a topic. Sometimes that is how it works, but at other times, things are more complicated. The subjects or topics in source tools are broad. The specific research question that interests you may fit into several subject areas. You should check each one. For example, for the topic of illegal drugs in high schools, you might look up these subjects: drug addiction, drug abuse, substance abuse, drug laws, illegal drugs, high schools, and secondary schools. Many of the articles

under a subject area will not be relevant for your literature review. Also, many times there is a 3- to 12-month time lag between the publication of an article and its appearance in a source tool.

Major research-oriented libraries subscribe to the *Social Science Citation Index (SSCI)* of the Institute for Scientific Information. This valuable resource has information on more than 1,400 journals. It is similar to other indexes and abstracts, but it takes time to learn how to use it. The *SSCI* comes in four books. One is a source index, which provides complete citation information on journal articles. The other three books refer to articles in the source book. The organization is by subject, by university or research center for which the researcher works, or by authors who are cited in the reference sections of other articles.

You can conduct an online search by author, by article title, by subject, or by keyword. A keyword is an important term for a topic and is often part of a title. You will want to use six to eight keywords in searches and consider several synonyms. The computer's searching method can vary and most look for a keyword only in a title or abstract. If you choose too few words or very narrow terms, you will miss relevant articles. If you choose too many words or very broad terms, you will get a huge number of irrelevant articles. The best way to learn the appropriate breadth and number of keywords is by trial and error.

Years ago, I conducted a study on the way that college students define *sexual harassment* (Neuman, 1992). I used the following keywords: *sexual harassment, sexual assault, harassment, gender equity, gender fairness,* and *sex discrimination.* I later discovered a few important studies that lacked any of these keywords in their titles. I also tried the keywords *college student* and *rape* but got huge numbers of unrelated articles that I could not even skim.

Numerous computer-assisted search databases or systems are available. A person with a computer and an Internet hookup can search article index collections, the catalogs of libraries, and other information sources around the globe that are accessible on the Internet.

All computerized searching methods share a similar logic, but each has its own method of operation to learn. In my study, I looked for sources in the previous 7 years and used five computerized databases of scholarly literature: *Social Science Index, CARL (Colorado Area Research Library), Sociofile, Social Science Citation Index,* and *PsychLit.*

Often you will locate the same article in several source tool databases; however, if you use several for your search, you will see that one has articles not found in the others. A critical lesson is: "Do not rely exclusively on computerized literature searches, on abstracting services, [or] on the literature in a single discipline, or on an arbitrarily defined time period" (Bausell, 1994:24). For example, I discovered several new excellent sources not in any databases by studying the bibliographies of the most relevant articles. My literature search process was fairly typical. Based on my keyword search, I quickly skimmed or scanned the titles or abstracts of more than 200 sources. From these, I selected about 80 articles, reports, and books to read. I found about 49 of the 80 sources valuable, and they are included in the bibliography of the published article.

Scholarly Books.   Finding scholarly books on a subject can be difficult. The subject topics of library catalog systems are usually incomplete and too broad to be useful. Moreover, they list only books that are in a particular library system, although you may be able to search other libraries for interlibrary loan books. Libraries organize books by call numbers based on subject matter. Again, the subject matter classifications may not reflect the subjects of interest to you or all of the subjects discussed in a book. Librarians can help you locate books from other libraries. For example, the *Library of Congress National Union Catalog* lists all books in the U.S. Library of Congress. Librarians have access to sources that list books at other libraries, or you can use the Internet. There is no surefire way to locate relevant books. Use multiple search methods, such as checking journals that have book reviews and the bibliographies of articles.

Dissertations.   The publication *Dissertation Abstracts International* lists most dissertations. Like the indexes and abstracts for journal articles, it organizes dissertations by broad subject category, author, and date. Researchers look up all titles in the subject areas that include their topic of interest. Unfortunately, after you have located the dissertation title and abstract, you may find that obtaining a copy of it takes time and involves added costs.

Government Documents.   The "government documents" sections of libraries contain specialized lists of these documents. A useful index for publications issued by the U.S. federal government is the *Monthly Catalog of Government Documents,* which is often available online. It has been issued since 1885, but other supplemental sources should be used for research into documents more than a decade old. The catalog has an annual index, and monthly issues have subject, title, and author indexes. *Indexes to Congressional Hearings,* another useful source, lists committees and subjects going back to the late 1930s. The *Congressional Record* contains debates of the U.S. Congress with synopses of bills, voting records, and changes in bills. *United States Statutes* lists each individual U.S. federal law by year and subject. The *Federal Register,* a daily publication of the U.S. government, contains all rules, regulations, and announcements of federal agencies. It has both monthly and annual indexes. Other indexes include treaties, technical announcements, and so forth. Other governments have similar lists. For example, the British government's *Government Publications Index* lists government publications issued during a year. *Parliamentary Papers* lists official social and economic studies going back 200 years. It is usually best to rely on the expertise of librarians for assistance in using these specialized indexes. The topics used by index makers may not be the best ones for your specific research question.

Policy Reports and Presented Papers.   Policy reports and presented conference papers are difficult to locate. You may see them listed in the bibliographies of published studies and in some source tools. Often you must write to research centers and ask for lists of their publications, obtain lists of papers presented at professional meetings, and so forth. Once you locate a research report, try writing to the relevant author or institute.

How to Evaluate Research Articles

After you locate a published study, you need to read and evaluate it. At first, this is difficult but becomes easier over time. Guidelines to help you read and evaluate reports you find and locate models for writing your own research reports follow.

1. *Examine the title.* A good title is specific, indicates the nature of the research without describing the results, and avoids asking a yes or no question. It describes the topic, may mention one or two major variables, and tells about the setting or participants. An example of a good title is "Parental Involvement in Schooling and Reduced Discipline Problems among Junior High School Students in Singapore." A good title informs readers about a study whereas a bad title either is vague or overemphasizes technical details or jargon. The same study could have been titled "A Three-Step Correlation Analysis of Factors That Affect Segmented Behavioral Anxiety Reduction."

2. *Read the abstract.* A good abstract summarizes critical information about a study. It gives the study's purpose, identifies methods used, and highlights major findings. It avoids vague references to future implications. After an initial screening by title, you should be able to determine a report's relevance from a well-prepared abstract. In addition to screening for relevance, a title and abstract prepare you for examining a report in detail. I recommend a two-stage screening process. Use the title and abstract to determine the article's initial relevance. If it appears relevant, quickly scan the introduction and conclusion sections to decide whether it is a real "keeper" (i.e., worth investing in a slow, careful reading of the entire article). Most likely, you will discover a few articles that are central to your purpose and many that are tangential. They are only worth skimming to locate one or two specific relevant details. Exercise caution not to pull specific details out of context.

3. *Read the article.* Before reading the entire article, you may want to skim the first several paragraphs at the beginning and quickly read the conclusion. This will give you a picture of what the article is about. Certain factors affect the amount of time and effort and overall payoff from reading a scholarly article. The time and effort are lower and results higher under three conditions: (1) the article is a high-quality article with a well-defined purpose, clear writing, and smooth, logical organization, (2) you are sharply focused on a particular issue or question, and (3) you have a solid theoretical background, know a lot about the substantive topic, and are familiar with research methodology. As you see, a great deal depends on reader preparation. You can develop good reader preparation to quickly "size up" an article by recognizing the dimensions of a study (see Chapter 2), its use of theory (Chapter 3), and the approach used (Chapter 4). Also, be aware that authors write with different audiences in mind. They may target a narrow, highly specialized sector of the scientific community; write for a broad cross-section of students and scholars in several fields; or address policymakers, issue advocates, and applied professionals.

When you read a highly relevant article, begin with the introduction section. It has three purposes: (1) to introduce a broad topic and make a transition to a specific research question that will be the study's primary focus, (2) to establish the research question's significance (in terms of expanding knowledge, linking to past studies, or addressing an applied concern), and (3) to outline a theoretical framework and define major concepts. Sometimes an article blends the introduction with a context literature review; at other times the literature review is a separate section.

To perform a good literature review, you must be selective, comprehensive, critical, and current. By being selective, you do not list everything ever written on a topic, only the most relevant studies. By being comprehensive, you include past studies that are highly relevant and do not omit any important ones. More than merely recounting past studies, you should be critically evaluative, that is, you comment on the details of some specific studies and evaluate them as they relate to the current study. You will not know everything about your study until it is finished, so plan to fine-tune and rewrite it after it is completed.

You should include recent studies in your literature review. Depending on its size and complexity, you may distinguish among theory, methods, findings, and evaluation. For example, you might review theoretical issues and disputes, investigate the methods previous researchers used, and summarize the findings, highlighting any gaps or inconsistencies. An evaluation of past studies can help you to justify the importance of conducting the current study.

Depending on the type of research approach used in an article, a hypothesis or methods section may follow the literature review. These sections outline specific data sources or methods of data collection, describe how variables were measured, whether sampling was used, and, if so, the details about it. You may find these sections tightly written and packed with technical details. They are longer in quantitative than qualitative studies.

After a methods section comes the results section. If the study is quantitative research, it should do more than present a collection of statistical tables or coefficients and percentages. It should discuss what the tables and data show. If it is qualitative research, it should be more than a list of quotations or straight description. The organization of data presentation usually begins simply by painting a broad scope and then goes into complexities and specific findings. Data presentation includes a straightforward discussion of the central findings and notes their significance. In quantitative research, it is not necessary to discuss every detail in a table or chart. Just note major findings and any unexpected or unusual findings. In a good article, the author will guide the reader through the data, pointing out what is in the study, and show all data details. In qualitative research, the organization of data often tells a story or presents a line of reasoning. Readers follow the author's story but are free to inquire about it.

In some articles, the author combines the discussion and results sections. In others, they are separate. A discussion section moves beyond simple description. It elaborates on the implications of results for past findings, theory, or applied issues. The section may include implications for building past findings from the literature review, and implications for the specific research question. The discussion section may also include commentary on any unexpected findings.

Most researchers include methodological limitations of the study in the discussion. This often includes how the specific measures, sampling, cases, location, or other factors restrict the generalizability of findings or are open to alternative explanations. Full candor and openness are expected. In a good article, the author is self-critical and shows an awareness of the study's weaknesses.

After you have read the discussion and results sections, read the article's conclusion or summary for a second time. A good conclusion/summary reviews the study's research question, major findings, and significant unexpected results. It also outlines future implications and directions to take. You may want to look for an appendix that may include additional study details and review the reference or bibliography section. An article's bibliography can give you leads to related studies or theoretical statements.

Reading and critically evaluating scholarly articles takes concentration and time, and it improves with practice. Despite the peer-review process and manuscript rejection rates, articles vary in quality. Some may contain errors, sloppy logic, or gaps. Be aware that a title and introduction may not mesh with specific details in the results section. Authors do not always describe all findings. The reader with a clearly focused purpose may notice new details in the findings by carefully poring over an article. For example, an author may not mention important results evident in a statistical table or chart or may place too much attention on minor or marginal results. As you evaluate an article, notice exactly how the study it reports was conducted, how logically its parts fit together, and whether the conclusions really flow from all of the findings.

How to Take Notes

As you gather the relevant research literature, you may feel overwhelmed by the quantity of information, so you need a system for taking notes. The old-fashioned note-taking approach was to write the notes onto index cards and then shift and sort the note cards, place them in piles, and so forth while looking for connections among them or developing an outline for a report or paper. This method still works. Today, however, most people use word processing software and gather photocopies or printed versions of many articles.

As you discover new sources, you may want to create two file types for note cards or computer documents, a *source file* and a *content file*. Record *all* bibliographic information for each source in the source file even though you may not use some of it. Do not forget anything in a complete bibliographic citation, such as a page number or the name of the second author; if you do, you will regret it later. It is far easier to erase a source you do not use than to try to locate bibliographic information later for a source you discover that you need or from which you forgot one detail. I suggest creating two kinds of source files, or dividing a master file into two parts: *have file* and *potential file*. The have file is for sources that you have found and for which you have already taken content notes. The potential file is for leads and possible new sources that you have yet to track down or read. You can add to the potential file anytime you come across a new source or a new article's bibliography. Toward the end of writing a report, the potential file will disappear and the have file will become your bibliography.

The content file contains substantive information of interest from a source, usually its major findings, details of methodology, definitions of concepts, or interesting quotes. If you quote directly from a source or want to take some specific information from it, you must record the specific page number(s) on which it appears. Link the files by putting key source information, such as author and date, on each content file.

What to Record. You must decide what to record about an article, book, or other source. It is better to err in the direction of recording too much rather than too little. In general, record the hypotheses tested, the measurement of major concepts, the main findings, the basic design of the research, the group or sample used, and ideas for future study (see Figure 5.2). It is wise to examine the report's

bibliography and note sources that you can add to your search.

Photocopying all relevant articles or reports will save you time recording notes and will ensure that you will have an entire report. Also, you can make notes on the photocopy, but consider several facts about this practice. First, photocopying can be expensive for a large literature search. Second, be aware of and obey copyright laws. U.S. copyright laws permit photocopying for personal research use. Third, remember to record or photocopy the entire article, including all citation information. Fourth, organizing a large pile of articles can be cumbersome, especially if you want to use several different parts of a single article. Finally, unless you highlight carefully or take good notes, you may have to reread the entire article later.

Organize Notes. After you have gathered many references and notes, you need an organizing method. One approach is to group various studies or specific findings by skimming notes and creating a mental map of how they fit together. Try several organizational plans before you settle on a final one. Organizing is a skill that improves with practice. For example, place notes into piles representing common themes or draw charts comparing what different reports state about the same question, noting any agreements and disagreements.

In the process of organizing notes, you will find that some references and notes do not fit anywhere. You should discard them as being irrelevant. You may discover gaps or areas and topics that are relevant but you have not examined yet. This necessitates return visits to the library.

The best organizational method depends on the purpose of the review. A *context review* implies organizing recent reports around a specific research question. A *historical review* implies organizing studies by major theme and by the date of publication. An *integrative review* implies organizing studies around core common findings of a field and the main hypotheses tested. A *methodological review* implies organizing studies by topic and, within each topic, by the design or method used. A *theoretical review* implies organizing studies by theories and major thinkers.

FIGURE 5.2   Example of Notes on an Article

FULL CITATION ON BIBLIOGRAPHY (SOURCE FILE)

> Bearman, Peter, and Hannah Bückner. 2001. "Promising the Future: Virginity Pledges and First Intercourse." *American Journal of Sociology* 106:859–912. (January, issue no. 4).

NOTE CARD (CONTENT FILE)

> Bearman and Bückner 2001   **Topics:**   Teen pregnancy & sexuality, pledges/promises, virginity, first sexual intercourse, S. Baptists, identity movement
>
> Since 1993, the Southern Baptist Church sponsored a movement among teens whereby the teens make a public pledge to remain virgins until marriage. Over 2.5 million teens have made the pledge. This study examines whether the pledge affected the timing of sexual intercourse and whether pledging teens differ from nonpledging teens. Critics of the movement are uncomfortable with it because pledge supporters often reject sex education, hold an overly romanticized view of marriage, and adhere to traditional gender roles.
>
> **Hypothesis**
> Adolescents will engage in behavior that adults enjoy but that is forbidden to them based on the amount of social controls that constrain opportunities to engage in forbidden behavior. Teens in nontraditional families with greater freedom and less supervision are more likely to engage in forbidden behavior (sex). Teens in traditional families and who are closer to their parents will delay sexual activity. Teens closely tied to "identity movements" outside the family will modify behavior based on norms the movements teach.
>
> **Method**
> Data are from a national health survey of U.S. teens in grades 7–12 who were in public or private schools in 1994–1995. A total of 90,000 students in 141 schools completed questionnaires. A second questionnaire was completed by 20,000 of the 90,000 students. The questionnaire asked about a pledge, importance of religion, and sexual activity.
>
> **Findings**
> The study found a substantial delay in the timing of first intercourse among pledgers, yet the effect of pledging varies according to the age of the teen. In addition, pledging works only in some social contexts (i.e., where it is at least partially a social norm). Pledgers tend to be more religious, less developed physically, and from more traditional social and family backgrounds.

Planning and Writing the Review

A literature review requires planning and clear writing, and it requires rewriting. All rules of good writing (e.g., clear organizational structure, an introduction and conclusion, transitions between sections) apply to writing a literature review. Keep your purposes in mind when you write, and communicate clearly and effectively.

You want to communicate a review's purpose to readers by the review's organization. The *wrong* way to write a review is to list a series of research reports with a summary of the findings of each. This fails to communicate a sense of purpose. It reads as a set of notes strung together. When I see these, I think that the review writer was sloppy and skipped over an important organizational step in writing the review. The *correct* way to write a review is to synthesize and organize common findings together. A well-accepted approach is to address the most important ideas first, logically link common statements or findings, and note discrepancies or weaknesses (see Example Box 5.3, Examples of Bad and Good Reviews).

How to Use the Internet for Social Research

The Internet has revolutionized how social researchers work. A little more than a decade ago, it was rarely used; today, all social researchers use the Internet regularly to help them review the literature, communicate with other researchers, and search for other information. The Internet continues to expand and change. However, it has been a mixed blessing, not the panacea that some people first thought it might be. It provides new, fast, and important ways to find information, but it remains one tool among others. Using the Internet for social research has its advantages and disadvantages.

The Advantages.

1. *The Internet is easy, fast, and cheap.* It is widely accessible, and can be used from many locations. This nearly free resource allows people to find source material from almost anywhere: local public libraries, homes, labs or classrooms, coffee shops, or anywhere a computer can connect to the Internet. It operates 24 hours a day, 7 days a week. With minimal training, most people can quickly perform searches and get information that a few years ago would have required them to take a trip to large research libraries. Searching a vast quantity of information electronically is easier and faster than a manual search. The Internet greatly expands the amount and variety of source material. In addition, once the information is located, a researcher can often store it electronically or print it at a local site.

2. *The Internet has "links" that provide additional ways to find and connect to other sources of information.* Web sites, home pages, and other Internet resource pages have links that can call up information from related sites or sources simply by clicking on the link indicator (usually a button or a highlighted word or phrase). This connects the user to more information and provides access to cross-referenced material. Links embed one source within a network of related sources.

3. *The Internet greatly speeds the flow of information around the globe and has a "democratizing" effect.* It provides rapid transmission of information (e.g., text, news, data, and photos) across long distances and national borders. Accessing some reports 10 years ago required waiting a week or month and spending some money; today you obtain them within seconds at no cost. Almost no restrictions limit who puts material on the Internet or what appears on it. This means that people who had difficulty publishing or disseminating materials can now do so with ease. Because of its openness, the Internet reinforces the norm of universalism.

4. *The Internet provides access to a vast range of information sources, some in formats that are quite dynamic and interesting.* You can access a report in black-and-white text, as in traditional academic journals and sources, or with bright colors, graphics, moving images, photos, and even audio and video clips. Authors and other creators of information can be creative in their presentations.

The Disadvantages.

1. *There is no quality control over what can be put on the Internet.* Unlike standard academic

EXAMPLE BOX **5.3**
Examples of Bad and Good Reviews

EXAMPLE OF BAD REVIEW

Sexual harassment has many consequences. Adams, Kottke, and Padgitt (1983) found that some women students said they avoided taking a class or working with certain professors because of the risk of harassment. They also found that men and women students reacted differently. The research was a survey of 1,000 men and women graduate and undergraduate students. Benson and Thomson's study in *Social Problems* (1982) lists many problems created by sexual harassment. In their excellent book, *The Lecherous Professor,* Dziech and Weiner (1990) give a long list of difficulties that victims have suffered.

Researchers study the topic in different ways. Hunter and McClelland (1991) conducted a study of undergraduates at a small liberal arts college. They had a sample of 300 students to whom they gave multiple vignettes that varied by the reaction of the victim and the situation. Jaschik and Fretz (1991) showed 90 women students at a mideastern university a videotape with a classic example of sexual harassment by a teaching assistant. Before it was labeled as *sexual harassment,* few women called it that. When asked whether it was sexual harassment, 98 percent agreed. Weber-Burdin and Rossi (1982) replicated a previous study on sexual harassment using students at the University of Massachusetts. They had 59 students rate 40 hypothetical situations. Reilley, Carpenter, Dull, and Bartlett (1982) conducted a study of 250 female and 150 male undergraduates as well as 52 faculty members at the University of California at Santa Barbara. All three sample groups (two of students and one of faculty) completed a questionnaire in which respondents were presented vignettes of sexual-harassing situations that they were to rate. Popovich et al. (1986) created a nine-item scale of sexual harassment. They studied 209 undergraduates at a medium-size university in groups of 15 to 25. They found disagreement and confusion among students.

EXAMPLE OF GOOD REVIEW

The victims of sexual harassment suffer a range of consequences from lowered self-esteem and loss of self-confidence to withdrawal from social interaction, changed career goals, and depression (Adams et al., 1983; Benson and Thomson, 1982; Dziech and Weiner, 1990). For example, Adams et al. noted that 13 percent of women students said they avoided taking a class or working with certain professors because of the risk of harassment.

Research into campus sexual harassment has taken several approaches. In addition to survey research, many have experimented with vignettes or presented hypothetical scenarios (Hunter and McClelland, 1991; Jaschik and Fretz, 1991; Popovich et al., 1986; Reilley et al., 1982; Rossi and Anderson, 1982; Valentine-French and Radtke, 1989; Weber-Burdin and Rossi, 1982). Victim verbal responses and situational factors appear to affect whether observers label a behavior as harassment. There is confusion over the application of a sexual harassment label for inappropriate behavior. For example, Jaschik and Fretz (1991) found that only 3 percent of the women students shown a videotape with a classic example of sexual harassment by a teaching assistant initially labeled it as *sexual harassment.* Instead, they called it "sexist," "rude," "unprofessional," or "demeaning." When asked whether it was sexual harassment, 98 percent agreed. Roscoe et al. (1987) reported similar labeling difficulties.

publications, information is subject to no peer-review or any other review process. Anyone can put almost anything on a Web site. It may be poor quality, undocumented, highly biased, invented fiction, or plain fraudulent. Once you locate material on the Internet, it takes skill to distinguish the "trash" from valid information. You need to treat a Web page with the same caution that one applies to a paper flyer someone hands out on the street; it could contain the drivel of a "nut" or be really valuable information. A less serious problem is that the "glitz" of bright colors, music, or moving images found on sites can distract unsophisticated users from serious content, and they may confuse glitz with high-caliber information. Also, the Internet is better for a quick look and short attention

EXPANSION BOX **5.3**

Web Sites: Surfer Beware

The rapid diffusion of Internet access and increased reliance on the Internet for information have provided many benefits. The Internet is unregulated, so almost anyone can create a Web site saying almost anything. In 2000, over 60 million U.S. residents went online in search of health information. Among those who use the Internet, more than 70 percent report the health information they find will influence a decision about treatment. A study (Berland et al., 2001) on health information available on the Internet found that health information is often incomplete or inaccurate. The researchers used ten English and four Spanish search engines looking for four search terms: breast cancer, childhood asthma, depression, and obesity. They found that less than one-fourth of the linked background information on health Web pages provided valid, relevant information.

Thirty-four physicians evaluated the quality of 25 health Web sites. They concluded that less than one-half more than minimally covered a topic and were completely accurate. The researchers found that, more than half the time, information in one part of a site contradicted information elsewhere on the same site and same topic. They also found wide variation in whether the site provided full source documentation. On average, only 65 percent of the site provided accurate documentation of the author and date of its sources.

---

spans rather than the slow, deliberative, careful reading and study of content (see Expansion Box 5.3, Websites: Surfer Beware).

2. *Many excellent sources and some critical resource materials are* not *available on the Internet.* Contrary to popular belief, the Internet has *not* made all information free and accessible to everyone. Often what is free is limited, and fuller information is available only to those who pay.

3. *Finding sources on the Internet can be time consuming.* It is not easy to locate specific source materials. The several search engines (e.g., Google, Bing, Yahoo, Altavista, Lycos, AskJeeves.com) work somewhat differently and can produce very different results. I searched for the same term, *voter disenfranchisement,* using four different search engines, all within 5 minutes. I looked at the first three results for each engine. Each search engine produced one or more sites that the others missed. Only two Web sites appeared in more than one search engine; all of the others were unique. Of the two Web sites that were among the top three "hits" more than once, one of them was a broken link. Obviously, you want to use multiple search engines and go beyond the first page of results. Most search engines simply look for specific words in a short description of the Web page. Search engines can come up with tens of thousands of sources, far too many for anyone to examine. The ones at the "top" may be there because their short description had several versions of the search word. Your "best" Web source might be buried as the 150th item found in a search.

4. *Internet sources can be "unstable" and difficult to document.* You can conduct a Web search and find Web pages with useful information. You can return a week later and find that several of them have disappeared. Be sure to note the specific uniform resource locator (url) or "address" (usually starts http://) where the Web page resides. The address refers to an electronic file sitting in a computer somewhere. Unlike a journal article that will be stored on a shelf or on microfiche in hundreds of libraries for many decades to come and are available for anyone to read, Web pages can quickly vanish. This can make it impossible to easily check someone's Web references, verify a quote in a document, or go back to original materials. Also, it is easy to copy, modify, or distort a source and then reproduce copies of it. For example, a person could alter a text passage or a photo image and then create a new Web page to disseminate the false information. This raises issues about copyright protection and the authenticity of source material.

Understanding the Internet, its jargon, and ways to identify a worthwhile site takes time and practice.

There are few rules for locating the best sites on the Internet that have useful and truthful information. Sources that originate at universities, research institutes, or government agencies usually are more trustworthy for research purposes than ones that are individual home pages of unspecified origin or location or that a commercial organization or a political/social issue advocacy group sponsors. In addition to moving or disappearing, many Web pages or sources fail to provide complete information to make citation easy. Quality sources provide fuller or more complete information about the author, date, location, and so on.

ETHICS IN SOCIAL RESEARCH

We now turn to a second major concern that you need to address before designing a study. Social research has an ethical-moral dimension, although as you saw in Chapter 4, different approaches to science address the values issue differently. All approaches recognize the ethical dimension to research. It is difficult to appreciate fully the ethical dilemmas until you are doing research, but waiting until the middle of doing a study is too late. You need to prepare and consider ethical concerns as you design a study so you can build sound ethical practice into the design.

Codes of ethics and other researchers provide guidance, but ethical conduct ultimately depends on an individual researcher. You have a moral and professional obligation to be ethical even when research participants are unaware of or unconcerned about ethics. Indeed, many participants are little concerned about protecting their privacy and other rights.[4]

The ethical issues are the concerns, dilemmas, and conflicts that arise over the proper way to conduct research. Ethics defines what is or is not legitimate to do or what "moral" research procedure involves. There are few ethical absolutes but there are many agreed-on principles. These principles may conflict in practice. Many ethical issues require you to balance two values: the pursuit of scientific knowledge and the rights of those being studied or of others in society. You must weigh potential benefits—such as advancing the understanding of social life, improving decision making,

or helping research participants— against potential costs—such as a loss of dignity, self-esteem, privacy, or democratic freedoms.

Ethical standards for doing research can be stricter than standards in many organizations (e.g., collection agencies, police departments, advertisers). Professional social research requires that you both know proper research techniques (e.g., sampling) and be sensitive to ethical concerns in research.

The Individual Researcher

Ethics begins and ends with you, the researcher. Your personal moral code is the best defense against unethical behavior. Before, during, and after conducting a study, you will have opportunities to and *should* reflect on research actions and consult your conscience. Ethical research depends on the integrity and values of individual researchers. "If values are to be taken seriously, they cannot be expressed and laid aside but must instead be guides to actions for the sociologist. They determine who will be investigated, for what purpose and in whose service" (Sagarin, 1973:63).

Reasons for Being Ethical

Because most people who conduct social research are genuinely concerned about others, why would a researcher act in an ethically irresponsible manner? Except for the rare disturbed individual, the causes of most unethical behavior result from a lack of awareness and pressures to take ethical shortcuts. Many researchers face intense pressures to build a career, publish, advance knowledge, gain prestige, impress family and friends, hold on to a job, and so forth. Ethical research takes longer to complete, costs more money, is more complicated, and is more likely to end before completion. Moreover, written ethical standards are in the form of vague principles. In many situations, it is possible to act unethically, and the odds of getting caught are small.

Also, no one rewards you for being ethical and doing the right thing. The unethical researcher, if caught, faces public humiliation, a ruined career, and possible legal action, but the ethical researcher wins no praise. Most researchers internalize ethical behavior during professional training, while having a professional role, and from having personal contact with other researchers. Moreover, the scientific community's norms of honesty and openness reinforce ethical behavior. Someone who is genuinely oriented toward a professional researcher role, who believes in the scientific ethos, and who interacts regularly with serious researchers is most likely to act ethically.

Scientific Misconduct. The research community opposes scientific misconduct, which includes research fraud and plagiarism. **Scientific misconduct** occurs when a researcher falsifies or distorts the data or the methods of data collection or plagiarizes the work of others. It also includes significant departures from the generally accepted practices of the scientific community for doing or reporting on research. Research institutes and universities have policies and procedures to detect misconduct, report it to the scientific community and funding agencies, and penalize researchers who engage in it (e.g., through a pay cut or loss of job).[5]

Research fraud occurs when a researcher fakes or invents data that were not really collected or falsely reports how research was conducted. Although rare, it is treated very seriously. The most famous case of fraud was that of Sir Cyril Burt, the father of British educational psychology. Burt died in 1971 as an esteemed researcher who was famous for his studies with twins that showed a genetic basis of intelligence. In 1976, it was discovered that he had falsified data and the names of coauthors. Unfortunately, the scientific community had been misled for nearly 30 years.

LEGAL	ETHICAL	
	Yes	*No*
Yes	Ethical and legal	Legal but unethical
No	Illegal but ethical	Unethical and illegal

FIGURE 5.3   Typology of Legal and Moral Actions in Social Research

Plagiarism is fraud that involves someone stealing the ideas or writings of another or using them without citing the source. A special type of plagiarism is stealing the work of another researcher, an assistant, or a student, and misrepresenting it as one's own. These are serious breaches of ethical standards.[6] Plagiarism is discussed further in Chapter 16.

Unethical but Legal. Behavior may be unethical but not break the law. The distinction between legal and ethical behavior is illustrated in a plagiarism case. The American Sociological Association documented that a 1988 book without footnotes by a dean from Eastern New Mexico University contained large sections of a 1978 dissertation written by a sociology professor at Tufts University. The copying was not *illegal;* it did not violate copyright law because the sociologist's dissertation did not have a copyright filed with the U.S. government. Nevertheless, it was clearly *unethical* according to standards of professional behavior.[7] (See Figure 5.3.)

Power

The relationship between a researcher and research participants involves power and trust. The experimenter, survey director, or research investigator has power relative to participants and assistants. Credentials, expertise, training, and the role of science in modern society legitimate the power relation and trust. Some ethical issues involve an abuse of power and trust.

A researcher's authority to conduct research comes with a responsibility to guide, protect, and oversee the interests of the people he or she is studying. For example, a physician was discovered to

---

Scientific misconduct   Action of someone who engages in research fraud, plagiarism, or other unethical conduct that significantly deviates from the accepted practices for conducting and reporting research established by the scientific community.

Research fraud   A type of unethical behavior in which a researcher fakes or creates false data, or falsely reports on the research procedure.

have conducted experimental gynecological surgery on thirty-three women without their permission. This was both unethical and a breach of trust. The women had trusted the doctor, but he had abused the trust that his patient, the medical community, and society had placed in him.[8]

If you seek ethical guidance, you can turn to a number of resources: professional colleagues, ethical advisory committees, institutional review boards or human subjects committees at a college or institution, codes of ethics from professional associations, and writings on ethics in research.

Ethical Issues Involving Research Participants

Have you ever been a participant in a research study? If so, how were you treated? More than any other issue, the discussion of research ethics has focused on possible negative effects on research participants. Being ethical requires that we balance the value of advancing knowledge against the value of noninterference in the lives of other people. If research participants had an absolute right of noninterference, most empirical research would be impossible. If researchers had an absolute right of inquiry, it could nullify participants' basic human rights. The moral question is when, if ever, researchers are justified in taking risks with the people being studied, possibility causing embarrassment, loss of privacy, or some kind of harm.

The law and codes of ethics recognize a few clear prohibitions: Never cause unnecessary or irreversible harm to participants, secure prior voluntary consent when possible, and never unnecessarily humiliate, degrade, or release harmful information about specific individuals that was collected for research purposes. These are minimal standards and are subject to interpretation (e.g., what does *unnecessary* mean in a specific situation?).

Origins of Research Participant Protection. Concern over the treatment of research participants arose after revelations of gross violations of basic human rights in the name of science. The most notorious violations were "medical experiments" that Nazi researchers conducted on Jews and others. In these experiments, research scientists committed acts of terrible torture in the name of scientific research. People were placed in freezing water to see how long it took them to die, others were purposely starved to death, and children had limbs severed and transplanted onto others.[9]

Such human rights violations did not occur only in Germany, nor did they happen only long ago. The Tuskegee Syphilis Study, also known as Bad Blood, took place in the United States nearly 30 years after Nazi concentration camps had been closed. Until the 1970s, when a newspaper report caused a scandal to erupt, the U.S. Public Health Service sponsored a study in which poor, uneducated African American men in Alabama suffered and died of untreated syphilis while researchers studied the severe physical disabilities that appear in advanced stages of the disease. The study began in 1929 before penicillin was available to treat the disease, but it continued long after treatment was available. Despite their unethical treatment of the subjects, the researchers were able to publish their results for 40 years. The study ended in 1972, but the President of the United States did not admit wrongdoing or apologize to the participant-victims until 1997.[10]

Unfortunately, the Bad Blood scandal is not unique. During the Cold War era, the U.S. government periodically compromised ethical research principles for military and political goals. In 1995, reports revealed that the government authorized injecting unknowing people with radioactive material in the late 1940s. In the 1950s, the government warned Eastman Kodak and other film manufacturers about nuclear fallout from atomic tests to prevent fogged film, but it did not provide health warnings to citizens who lived near the test areas. In the 1960s, the U.S. army gave unsuspecting soldiers LSD (a hallucinogenic drug), causing serious trauma. Today these are widely recognized to be violations of two fundamental ethical principles: avoid physical harm and get informed consent.[11]

Physical Harm, Psychological Abuse, and Legal Jeopardy. Social research can harm a research participant physically, psychologically, legally, and economically, affecting a person's career or income.

Physical harm is rare, even in biomedical research, in which the intervention is much greater. Specific types of harm are more likely in different types of research (e.g., in experimental versus field research). Researchers must be aware of all types of harm and work to minimize them at all times.[12]

Physical Harm. A core ethical principle is that researchers should never cause physical harm to participants. This means we must anticipate risks before beginning research, including basic safety concerns (safe buildings, furniture, and equipment). We screen out high-risk subjects (those with heart conditions, mental illness, or seizure disorders) if the study involves stress, and anticipate the danger of injury and even physical attacks on research participants or assistants. We accept moral and legal responsibility for any injury that occurs as a result of research participation. This means that we must immediately terminate a study if we cannot guarantee the physical safety of participants (see the Zimbardo study in Example Box 5.4, Three Cases of Ethical Controversy).

Psychological Abuse, Stress, or Loss of Self-Esteem. Although the risk of physical harm is rare, social researchers may place people in stressful, embarrassing, anxiety-producing, or unpleasant situations. To learn about how people respond in real-life, high anxiety-producing situations, social researchers have placed research participants in realistic situations of psychological discomfort or stress. The ethics of the famous Milgram obedience study is still debated (see Example Box 5.4). Some say that the precautions taken by Milgram and the knowledge gained outweighed the stress and potential psychological harm that research participants experienced. Others believe that the extreme stress and the risk of permanent harm were too great.

Some researchers have created high levels of anxiety or discomfort by exposing participants to gruesome photos, falsely telling male students that they have strongly feminine personality traits, falsely telling students that they have failed, creating a situation of high fear (e.g., smoke entering a room in which the door is locked), asking participants to harm others, placing people in a situation in which they face social pressure to deny their convictions, and having participants lie, cheat, or steal.[13] Researchers who study helping behavior may place participants in emergency situations to see whether they will lend assistance to "victims." For example, Piliavin and associates (1969) studied helping behavior in subways by faking someone's collapse onto the floor. In the field experiment, the riders in the subway car were unaware of the experiment and did not volunteer to participate in it.

A sensitive researcher is also aware of harm to a person's self-esteem. For example, Walster (1965) wanted to see whether feelings of female self-worth affected romantic liking. She gave undergraduate women personality tests followed by phony feedback. She told some that they lacked imagination and creativity. Next, a handsome male graduate student who pretended to be another research participant struck up a conversation with the women. He acted very interested in one woman and asked her out for a dinner date. Walster wanted to measure the woman's romantic attraction to the male. After the experiment, the woman learned that there was no date and the man was just working in an experiment and was not really interested in her. Although the participants were debriefed, they suffered a loss of self-esteem and possible psychological harm.[14]

Only experienced researchers who take precautions before inducing anxiety or discomfort should consider conducting studies that induce stress or anxiety. They should consult with others who have conducted similar studies and mental health professionals when planning the study, screen out high-risk populations (e.g., people with emotional problems or a weak heart), and arrange for emergency interventions or termination of the research if dangerous situations arise. Researchers should always obtain informed consent (to be discussed) before the research and debrief the subjects immediately afterward.

A core ethical principle is that researchers should never create *unnecessary* stress in participants. *Unnecessary* means beyond the minimal amount required to create the desired effect, or stress without a direct, legitimate research purpose. Knowing the minimal amount comes with experience. It is better to begin with too little stress, risking finding no effect than to create too much. If the level of

EXAMPLE BOX 5.4

Three Cases of Ethical Controversy

Stanley Milgram's *obedience study* (Milgram, 1963, 1965, 1974) attempted to discover how the horrors of the Holocaust under the Nazis could have occurred by examining the strength of social pressure to obey authority. After signing "informed consent forms," subjects were assigned, in rigged random selection, to be a "teacher" while a confederate was the "pupil." The teacher was to test the pupil's memory of word lists and increase the electric shock level if the pupil made mistakes. The pupil was located in a nearby room, so the teacher could hear but not see the pupil. The shock apparatus was clearly labeled with increasing voltage. As the pupil made mistakes and the teacher turned switches, the pupil also made noises as if in severe pain. The researcher was present and made comments such as "You must go on" to the teacher. Milgram reported, "Subjects were observed to sweat, tremble, stutter, bite their lips, groan and dig their fingernails into their flesh. These were characteristic rather than exceptional responses to the experiment" (Milgram, 1963:375). The percentage of subjects who would shock to dangerous levels was dramatically higher than expected. Ethical concerns arose over the use of deception and the extreme emotional stress experienced by subjects.

In Laud Humphreys' (1975) *tearoom trade study* (a study of male homosexual encounters in public restrooms), about 100 men were observed engaging in sexual acts as Humphreys pretended to be a "watchqueen" (a voyeur and lookout). Subjects were followed to their cars, and their license numbers were secretly recorded. Names and addresses were obtained from police registers when Humphreys posed as a market researcher. One year later, in disguise,

Humphreys used a deceptive story about a health survey to interview the subjects in their homes. Humphreys was careful to keep names in safety deposit boxes, and identifiers with subject names were burned. He significantly advanced knowledge of homosexuals who frequent "tearooms" and overturned previous false beliefs about them. There has been controversy over the study: The subjects never consented; deception was used; and the names could have been used to blackmail subjects, to end marriages, or to initiate criminal prosecution.

In the *Zimbardo prison experiment* (Zimbardo, 1972, 1973; Zimbardo et al., 1973, 1974), male students were divided into two role-playing groups: guards and prisoners. Before the experiment, volunteer students were given personality tests, and only those in the "normal" range were chosen. Volunteers signed up for two weeks, and prisoners were told that they would be under surveillance and would have some civil rights suspended but that no physical abuse would be allowed. In a simulated prison in the basement of a Stanford University building, prisoners were deindividualized (dressed in standard uniforms and called only by their numbers) and guards were militarized (with uniforms, nightsticks, and reflective sunglasses). Guards were told to maintain a reasonable degree of order and served 8-hour shifts; prisoners were locked up 24 hours per day. Unexpectedly, the volunteers became too caught up in their roles. Prisoners became passive and disorganized, while guards became aggressive, arbitrary, and dehumanizing. By the sixth day, Zimbardo called off the experiment for ethical reasons. The risk of permanent psychological harm, and even physical harm, was too great.

---

stress might have long-term effects, a researcher should follow up and offer free counseling. Another danger is that researchers might develop a callous or manipulative attitude toward the research participants. Researchers report guilt and regret after conducting experiments that caused psychological harm to participants. Experiments that place research participants in anxiety-producing situations often produce discomfort for an ethical researcher.

Legal Harm. As researchers, we are responsible for protecting research participants from increased risk of arrest. The fact that participating in a research study increases the risk that a participant will face arrest will destroy trust in social scientific research, causing future participants not to be willing to participate in studies. Researchers may be able to secure clearance from law enforcement authorities before conducting certain types of research. For example, the U.S. Department of Justice sometimes provides written waivers for researchers studying criminal behavior. However, as this chapter's opening box on the study of gangs suggests, the protection to researchers is limited, and researchers need to be cautious.

Potential legal harm is one criticism of the 1975 "tearoom trade" study by Humphreys (Example Box 5.4). In the New Jersey Negative Income Tax Experiment, some participants received income supplements. However, the researchers did not monitor whether they were also receiving public assistance checks. A local prosecuting attorney requested data on participants to identify "welfare cheats." In other words, participants were at legal risk because they were participating in the study. Eventually, the conflict was resolved, but it illustrates the need for researchers to be aware of potential legal issues while designing a study.

A related ethical issue arises when a researcher learns of illegal activity when collecting data. We must weigh the value of protecting the researcher–subject relationship and the benefits to future researchers against potential harm to innocent people. For example, in his field research on police, Van Maanen (1982:114–115) reported seeing police beat people and witnessing illegal acts and irregular procedures, but said, "On and following these troublesome incidents . . . I followed police custom: I kept my mouth shut."

Field researchers often face difficult ethical decisions. For example, when studying a mental institution, Taylor (1987) discovered the mistreatment and abuse of patients by the staff. He had two choices: Abandon the study and call for an investigation, or keep quiet and continue with the study for several months, publicize the findings afterward, and then advocate an end to the abuse. After weighing the situation, he followed the latter course and is now an activist for the rights of mental institution patients.

The issue of protecting confidentiality (discussed later) complicated a similar ethical dilemma in a study of restaurants in New York. A sociology graduate student was conducting a participant observation study of waiters. During the study, the field site, a restaurant, burned down and arson was suspected. Local legal authorities requested the researcher's field notes and wanted to interrogate him about activities in the restaurant. He had two choices: cooperate with the investigation and violate the trust of participants, confidentiality, and basic research ethics or uphold confidentiality and act ethically but face contempt of court and obstruction of justice penalties, including fines and jail. He wanted to behave ethically but also wanted to stay out of jail. After years of legal battles, the situation was resolved with limited cooperation by the researcher and a judicial ruling upholding the confidentiality of field notes. Nevertheless, the issue took years to resolve, and the researcher bore substantial financial and personal costs.[15]

Observing illegal behavior may be central to a research project. A researcher who covertly observes and records illegal behavior and then supplies information to law enforcement authorities violates ethical standards regarding research participants and undermines future research. A researcher who fails to report illegal behavior indirectly permits criminal behavior and could be charged as an accessory to a crime. Is the researcher a professional seeking knowledge or a freelance undercover informant?

Other Harm to Participants. Research participants may face other types of harm. For example, participating in a survey interview may create anxiety and discomfort among people who are asked to recall unpleasant events. We need to be sensitive to any harm to participants, consider possible precautions, and weigh potential harm against potential benefits. Participants could face negative effects on their careers or incomes due to involvement with a study. For example, assume that a researcher surveys employees and concludes that the supervisor's performance is poor. As a consequence of the researcher's communication of this fact, the supervisor is discharged. Or a researcher studies people on public assistance. Based on the findings, some of them lose the benefits and their quality of life declines. What is the researcher's responsibility? We need to consider the consequences of research for those being studied, but there is no fixed answer to such questions. We must evaluate each case, weigh potential harm against potential benefits, and bear the responsibility for the decision.

Deception.   Has anyone ever told you a half-truth or lie to get you to do something? How did you feel about it? A major ethical tenet is the **principle of voluntary consent**: never force anyone to participate in research. A related ethical rule is do not lie to research participants unless it is required for legitimate research reasons. A very serious ethical standard is that participants should explicitly agree to participate in a study. The right not to participate becomes a critical issue when we use deception, disguise the research, or use covert research methods.[16]

Social researchers sometimes deceive or lie to participants in field and experimental research. We might misrepresent our actions or true intentions for legitimate methodological reasons: If participants knew the true purpose, they would modify their behavior, making it impossible to learn of their real behavior or access to a research site might be impossible if the researcher told the truth. Deception is never preferable if we can accomplish the same thing without deception.

Deception is acceptable only if it has a specific methodological purpose, and even then, we can use it only to the minimal degree necessary. If we use deception, we should obtain informed consent, never misrepresent risks, and always debrief the participants after the study. We can describe the basic procedures involved and conceal only some information about the study.

Informed Consent.   A fundamental ethical principle is: Never coerce anyone into participating; all research participation *must* be voluntary. It is not enough to obtain permission; people need to know what they are being asked to participate in. Only then can they make an informed decision. Participants can become aware of their rights and what they are getting involved in when they read and sign a statement giving **informed consent**, a written agreement to participate given by people after they have learned some basic details about the research procedure.

The U.S. federal government does not require informed consent in all research involving human subjects. Nevertheless, researchers should obtain

EXPANSION BOX **5.4**

Informed Consent

Informed consent statements contain the following:

1. A brief description of the purpose and procedure of the research, including the expected duration of the study
2. A statement of any risks or discomfort associated with participation
3. A guarantee of anonymity and the confidentiality of records
4. The identification of the researcher and of the location of information about participants' rights or questions about the study
5. A statement that participation is completely voluntary and can be terminated at any time without penalty
6. A statement of alternative procedures that may be used
7. A statement of any benefits or compensation provided to participants and the number of subjects involved
8. An offer to provide a summary of findings

written consent unless there are good reasons for not doing so (e.g., covert field research, use of secondary data) as judged by an **institutional review board (IRB)** (see the later discussion of IRBs).

Informed consent statements provide specific information (see Expansion Box 5.4, Informed Consent).[17] A general statement about the procedures or questions involved and the uses of the data are

Principle of voluntary consent   An ethical principle that people should never participate in research unless they explicitly and freely agree to participate.

Informed consent   A statement, usually written, that explains aspects of a study to participants and asks for their voluntary agreement to participate before the study begins.

Institutional review board (IRB)   A committee at U.S. colleges, hospitals, and research institutes required by federal law to ensure that research involving humans is conducted in a responsible, ethical manner; examines study details before the research begins.

sufficient for informed consent. In a study by Singer (1978), one random group of survey respondents received a detailed informed consent statement and another did not. She found no significant differences between the groups in response rates. If anything, people who refused to sign such a statement were more likely to guess or answer "no response" to questions. In their analysis of the literature, Singer and colleagues (1995) found that ensuring confidentiality modestly improved responses when asking about highly sensitive topics. In other situations, extensive assurances of confidentiality failed to affect how or whether the subjects responded.

Signed informed consent statements are optional for most survey, field, and secondary data research but often are required in experimental research. They are impossible to obtain in documentary research and in telephone interviews. The general rule is that the greater the risk of potential harm, the greater the need for a written consent statement. In sum, there are many reasons to get informed consent but few reasons not to.

Covert Observation. Obtaining informed consent may be easy in survey and experimental research, but some field researchers believe that it is inappropriate when observing real-life field settings and say they could not gain entry or conduct a study unless it were covert. In the past, field researchers used covert observation, such as feigning alcoholism so they could join a group seeking treatment to be able to study it. Field researchers have three choices blurring the line between informed consent and not fully informed acquiescence. Borrowing from the language of espionage, Fine (1980) distinguished deep cover (the researcher tells nothing of the research role but acts as a full participant), shallow cover (the researcher reveals that research is taking place but is vague about details), and explicit cover (the researcher fully reveals his or her purpose and asks permission).

Some favor covert observation and exempting field research from informed consent (Herrera, 1999). One reason is that informed consent is impractical and disruptive in field research. It may even create some harm by disturbing the participants or the location by disrupting the ongoing

activities. The difficulty with this reasoning is the moral principle that ensuring participant dignity outweighs practical expediency for researchers. The reasoning is self-serving; it places a higher value on doing research than on upholding honesty or privacy. It assumes that a researcher is better at judging study risks than the participants. The moral-ethical standard says we must respect the freedom/autonomy of all people we study and let them make their own decisions. Participants may not remain naïve and may be offended once they learn of an unauthorized invasion of their "privacy" for research purposes.

Another reason given for covert observations is that human communication and daily affairs are filled with covert activity. Daily activities involve some amount of covert activity with many "people watchers" or harmless eavesdroppers. Covert and deceptive behaviors are pervasive in daily life by many retail sales outlets, law enforcement, or security personnel, and people almost expect it. It is expected and harmless, so why must social researchers act differently? Using "everyone else is doing it" and "it would happen anyway" are not valid justifications for exemption. The issue here involves moral-ethical standards for doing research. Perhaps voyeurism, surveillance, and the use of undercover informants are increasing in some societies. Does that make them morally right and ensure personal privacy? Should we take them as a model for the ensuring integrity and trust in social research? Growing covert surveillance may increase public cynicism, distrust, and noncooperation. An absence of informed consent is an ethical gray area, and many believe that the moral-ethical risk of not getting informed consent is likely to cause greater harm than getting informed consent.

Covert research remains controversial, and many researchers believe that all covert research is unethical.[18] The code of ethics of the American Anthropological Association condemns such research as "impractical and undesirable." Even those who accept covert research as being ethical in some situations argue that it should be used only when overt observation is impossible. In addition, we should inform participants afterward and give them an opportunity to express concerns.

Deception and covert research may increase mistrust and cynicism and diminish public respect for social research. Misrepresentation in field research is analogous to being an undercover agent or informer in nondemocratic societies. Deception can increase distrust by people who are frequently studied. In one case, the frequent use of deception reduced helping behavior. When a student was shot at the University of Washington in Seattle in 1973, students crossing the campus made no attempt to assist the victim. Later it was discovered that many of the bystanders did not help because they thought that the shooting was staged as part of an experiment.[19]

Special Populations and New Inequalities

Special Populations and Coercion. Some populations or research participants are not capable of giving true voluntary informed consent. **Special populations** may lack the necessary competency or may be indirectly coerced. Students, prison inmates, employees, military personnel, the homeless, welfare recipients, children, or the mentally disabled may agree to participate in research, yet they may not be fully capable of making a decision or may agree to participate only because some desired good—such as higher grades, early parole, promotions, or additional services—requires an agreement to participate.

It is unethical to involve "incompetent" people (e.g., children, mentally disabled) in our study unless we have met two conditions: A legal guardian grants written permission, and we follow all ethical principles against harm to participants. For example, we want to conduct a survey of smoking and drug/alcohol use among high school students. If the study is conducted on school property, school officials must give permission. Written parental permission for all participants who are legal minors is also required. It is best to ask permission from each student as well.

Coercing people to participate, including offering them special benefits that they cannot otherwise attain, is unethical. For example, it is unethical for a commanding officer to order a soldier to participate in a study, for a professor to require a student to be a research subject in order to pass a course, and for an employer to expect an employee to complete a survey as a condition of continued employment. It is unethical even if someone other than the researcher (e.g., an employer) coerced people (e.g., employees) to participate in research.

Determining whether coercion to participate is involved can be a complex issue, and we must evaluate each case. For example, a researcher offers a convicted criminal the alternative of continued imprisonment or participation in an experimental rehabilitation program. The convicted criminal may not believe in the benefits of the program, but the researcher believes that it will help the criminal. This is a case of coercion, but the researcher must judge whether the benefits to the subject and to society outweigh the ethical prohibition on coercion.

Teachers sometimes require students in social science courses to participate in research projects. This is a special case of coercion. Three arguments have been made in favor of requiring participation: (1) It would be difficult and prohibitively expensive to get participants otherwise, (2) the knowledge created from research with students serving as participants will benefit future students and society, and (3) students will learn more about research by experiencing it directly in a realistic research setting. Of the three arguments, only the third justifies limited coercion. It is acceptable only as long as it has a clear educational objective, the students are given a choice of research experience, and all other ethical principles are upheld.[20]

Creating New Inequalities. Another type of possible harm is when one group of people is denied a service or benefit as a result of participation in a study. For example, say that you have a new treatment for subjects with a terrible disease, such as acquired immune deficiency syndrome (AIDS). To learn the effects of the new treatment, you provide

Special population Research participants who, because of age, incarceration, potential coercion, or less than full physical, mental, emotional, or other capabilities, may lack complete freedom or awareness to grant voluntary consent to participate in a study.

it to some individuals but give others a placebo, or empty pill. The study is designed to demonstrate whether the drug is effective, but participants who get the placebo may die. Of course, those receiving the drug may also die until more is known about whether the drug is effective. Is it ethical for you to deny a potential lifesaving treatment to people who have been randomly assigned in a study to learn more?

We can reduce new inequality among research participants in three ways. First, participants who do not receive the "new, improved" treatment continue to receive the best previously acceptable treatment. In other words, no one is denied all assistance, but everyone receives the best treatment available prior to the new one being tested. This ensures that no one suffers in absolute terms even if they temporarily fall behind others in relative terms. Second, we can use **crossover designs**, whereby a control group (i.e., those who do not get the new treatment) for a first phase of the study receive it in the second phase, and vice versa. Finally, we carefully and continuously monitor results. If it appears early in the study that the new treatment is highly effective, we give the new treatment to everyone. Also, in high-risk studies with medical treatments or possible physical harm, researchers may use animal or other surrogates for humans.

Privacy, Anonymity, and Confidentiality. How would you feel if private details about your personal life were shared with the public without your knowledge? Because social researchers transgress the privacy of subjects in order to study social behavior, they must take precautions to protect participants' privacy.

Privacy. Survey researchers invade a person's privacy when they probe into beliefs, backgrounds, and behaviors in a way that reveals intimate private details. Experimental researchers sometimes use two-way mirrors or hidden microphones to "spy" on participants. Even if people are told they are being studied, they are unaware of what the experimenter is looking for. Field researchers may observe very private aspects of another's behavior or eavesdrop on conversations. In field experimentation and ethnographic field research, privacy can be violated without advance warning. When Humphreys (1975) served as a "watchqueen" in a public restroom where homosexual contacts took place, he observed very private behavior without informing the participants. When Piliavin and colleagues (1969) had people collapse on subways to study helping behavior, those in the subway car had the privacy of their ride violated. People have been studied in public places (e.g., in waiting rooms, walking down the street, in classrooms), but some "public" places are more private than others (consider, for example, the use of periscopes to observe people who thought they were alone in a public toilet stall).[21]

The ethical researcher violates privacy only to the minimum degree necessary and only for legitimate research purposes. In addition, he or she protects the information on research participants from public disclosure.

In some situations, the law protects privacy. One case of the invasion of privacy led to the passage of a federal law. In the *Wichita Jury Study* of 1954, University of Chicago Law School researchers recorded jury discussions to examine group processes in jury deliberations. Although the findings were significant and researchers took precautions, a Congressional investigation followed and passed a law in 1956 to prohibit the "bugging" of any grand or petit jury for any purpose, even with the jurors' consent.[22]

Anonymity. Researchers protect privacy by not disclosing a participant's identity after information is gathered. This takes two forms: anonymity and confidentiality. **Anonymity** means that people remain anonymous, or nameless. For example, a field researcher provides a social picture of a particular

Crossover design A type of experimental design in which all groups receive the treatment but at different times so that discomfort or benefits are shared and inequality is not created.

Anonymity The ethical protection that participants remain nameless; their identity is protected from disclosure and remains unknown.

individual but uses a fictitious name and location of the individual and alters some characteristics. The person's identity is protected, and the individual is unknown or anonymous. Survey and experimental researchers discard the names or addresses of participants as soon as possible and refer to participants by a code number only to protect anonymity. If a researcher using a mail survey includes a code on the questionnaire to determine who failed to respond, the respondent's anonymity is not being protected fully. In panel studies, in which the same individuals are tracked over time, anonymity is not possible. Likewise, historical researchers use specific names in historical or documentary research. They may do so if the original information was from public sources; if the sources were not publicly available, they must obtain written permission from the owner of the documents to use specific names.

It is difficult to protect research participant anonymity. In one study about a fictitious town, "Springdale," in *Small Town in Mass Society* (Vidich and Bensman, 1968), it was easy to identify the town and specific individuals in it. Town residents became upset about how the researchers portrayed them and staged a parade mocking the researchers. In the famous Middletown study of Muncie, Indiana, people recognized their town. A researcher who protects the identities of individuals with fictitious information, however, creates a gap between what was studied and what is reported to others. This raises questions about what a researcher found and what he or she made up.

Confidentiality. Even if anonymity is not possible, we should protect confidentiality. Anonymity protects the identity of specific individuals from being known. **Confidentiality** means that we may attach names to information, but we hold it in confidence or keep it secret from the public. We never release the information in a way that permits linking specific individuals to it. We present results publicly only in an aggregate form (e.g., percentages, means).

We can provide anonymity without confidentiality, or vice versa, although the two usually go together. Anonymity without confidentiality happens if we make details about a specific individual public but withhold the individual's name and certain details that would make it possible to identify the individual. Confidentiality without anonymity happens if we do not release individual data public but privately link individual names to data on specific individuals.

Researchers have undertaken elaborate procedures to protect the identity of participants from public disclosure: eliciting anonymous responses, using a third-party list custodian who holds the key to coded lists, or using the random-response technique (discussed in Chapter 10). Past abuses suggest that such measures may be necessary. Diener and Crandall (1978:70) reported that during the 1950s, the U.S. State Department and the FBI requested research records on individuals who had been involved in the famous Kinsey sex study. The Kinsey Sex Institute refused to comply with the government and threatened to destroy all records rather than release any of them. Eventually, the government agencies backed down. The moral and ethical duty of researchers obligated them to destroy the records to protect confidentiality.

Confidentiality may protect participants from physical harm. For example, I met a researcher who had studied the inner workings of the secret police in a nondemocratic society. Had he released the names of informants, they would have faced certain death or imprisonment. To protect the research participants, he wrote all notes in code and kept all records secretly locked away. Although he resided in the United States, he received physical threats by the foreign government and discovered attempts to burglarize his office. In other situations, some principles may take precedence over protecting confidentiality.

> **Confidentiality** The ethical protection for those who are studied by holding research data in confidence or keeping them secret from the public; not releasing information in a way that permits linking specific individuals to specific responses; researchers do this by presenting data only in an aggregate form (e.g., percentages, means).

Some researchers pay high personal costs for being ethical. Although he was never accused or convicted of breaking any law and he closely followed the ethical principles outlined by the American Sociological Association, Rik Scarce, a doctoral sociology student at Washington State University, spent 16 weeks in a Spokane jail for contempt of court. He was jailed because he refused to testify before a grand jury and break the confidentiality of social research data. Scarce had been studying radical animal liberation groups and had already published one book on the subject. He had interviewed a research participant who was suspected of leading a group that had broken into animal facilities and caused $150,000 damage. Two judges refused to acknowledge the confidentiality of social research data.[23]

Participants' Information as Private Property. If you freely give information about yourself for research purposes, do you lose all rights to it? Can it be used against you? Research participants have knowledge about them taken and analyzed by others. The information can then be used for a number of purposes, including actions against the subjects' interests. Large businesses collect, buy, sell, analyze, and exchange information on people everyday. Private businesses and government agencies use information about buying habits, personal taste, spending patterns, credit ratings, voting patterns, Internet surfing, and the like. Information is a form of private property. Like other "intellectual" property (copyrights, software, patents, etc.) and unlike most physical property, information continues to have value after it is exchanged.

Most people give their time and information to a researcher for little or no compensation, yet concerns about privacy and the collection of information make it reasonable to consider personal information as private property. If it is private property, a person clearly has the right to keep, sell, or give it away. The ethical issue is strongest in situations in which someone could use the information in ways that participants would disapprove of if they were fully informed. For example, a group of committed nonsmokers participate in a study about their habits and psychological profiles. A market research

firm obtains the information, and a tobacco company asks the market research firm to design a campaign that promotes smoking to the nonsmokers. Had the nonsmokers been informed about the uses of their responses, they might have chosen not to participate. Ethical researchers can increase protections by offering participants a copy of the findings and describing all uses to which the information will be put in an informed consent statement.

The issue of who controls data on research participants is relevant to the approaches to social science outlined in Chapter 4. Positivism implies the collection and use of information by experts separate from research participants and the ordinary citizen. Each of the two alternatives to positivism in its own way argues for the involvement and participation of those who are studied in the research process and in the use of research data and findings.[24]

Mandated Protections of Research Participants. The U.S. federal government and governments of other nations have regulations and laws to protect research participants and their rights. In the United States, the legal restraint is found in rules and regulations issued by the U.S. Department of Health and Human Services Office for the Protection from Research Risks. Although this is only one federal agency, most researchers and other government agencies look to it for guidance. Current U.S. government regulations evolved from Public Health Service policies adopted in 1966 and expanded in 1971. The National Research Act (1974) established the National Commission for the Protection of Human Subjects in Biomedical and Behavioral Research, which significantly expanded regulations, and required informed consent in most social research. The responsibility for safeguarding ethical standards was assigned to research institutes and universities. The Department of Health and Human Services issued regulations in 1981 that are still in force. Regulations on scientific misconduct and protection of data confidentiality were expanded in 1989.

Federal regulations follow a biomedical model and protect subjects from physical harm. Other rules require institutional review boards (IRBs) at all research institutes, colleges, and universities to review all uses of human subjects. Researchers and community members staff the IRB. Similar committees oversee the use of animals in research. The board also oversees, monitors, and reviews the impact of all research procedures on human participants and applies ethical guidelines. The board also reviews research procedures when a study is first proposed. Educational tests, "normal educational practice," most surveys, most observation of public behavior, and studies of existing data in which individuals cannot be identified are exempt from the IRB.[25]

Ethics and the Scientific Community

Physicians, attorneys, counselors, and other professionals have a **code of ethics** and peer review boards or licensing regulations. The codes formalize professional standards and provide guidance when questions arise in practice.[26] Social researchers do not provide a service for a fee, receive limited ethical training, and are rarely licensed. However, they incorporate ethical concerns into research because it is morally and socially responsible. Doing so also helps to protect social research from charges of insensitivity or abusing people. Professional social science associations around the world have codes of ethics. The codes state proper and improper behavior and represent a consensus of professionals on ethics. All researchers may not agree on all ethical issues, and ethical rules are subject to interpretation, but researchers are expected to uphold ethical standards as part of their membership in a professional community.

Codes of research ethics can be traced to the **Nuremberg code**, which was adopted during the Nuremberg Military Tribunal on Nazi war crimes held by the Allied Powers immediately after World War II. The code, developed as a response to the cruelty of concentration camp experiments, outlines ethical principles and rights of human research participants. The principles in the Nuremberg code focused on medical experimentation. They have become the foundation for the ethical codes in social research. Similar codes of human rights, such as the 1948 Universal Declaration of Human Rights by the United Nations and the 1964

EXPANSION BOX **5.5**

Basic Principles of Ethical Social Research

■ Recognize that ethical responsibility rests with the individual researcher.

■ Do not exploit research participants or students for personal gain.

■ Some form of informed consent is highly recommended or required.

■ Honor all guarantees of privacy, confidentiality, and anonymity.

■ Do not coerce or humiliate research participants.

■ Use deception only if needed, and always accompany it with debriefing.

■ Use a research method that is appropriate to the topic.

■ Detect and remove undesirable consequences to research subjects.

■ Anticipate repercussions of the research or publication of results.

■ Identify the sponsor who funded the research.

■ Cooperate with host nations when doing comparative research.

■ Release the details of the study design with the results.

■ Make interpretations of results consistent with the data.

■ Use high methodological standards and strive for accuracy.

■ Do not conduct secret research.

Declaration of Helsinki, also have implications for social researchers.[27] (See Expansion Box 5.5, Basic Principles of Ethical Social Research.)

Professional social science associations (e.g., the American Psychological Association, American Anthropological Association, American Political Science Association, and American Sociological

---

Code of ethics   Principles and guidelines developed by professional organizations to guide research practice and clarify the line between ethical and unethical behavior.

Nuremberg code   An international code of moral, ethical behavior adopted after the war crime trials of World War II in response to inhumane Nazi medical experiments; was the beginning of codes of ethics for human research.

Association) adopted codes of ethics beginning in the 1960s or 1970s. Professional social science associations have committees that review codes of ethics and hear about possible violations but does not strictly enforcement the codes. The penalty for a minor violation rarely goes beyond a letter. If no laws are violated, the main penalty is the negative publicity surrounding a well-documented and serious ethical violation. The publicity may result in the loss of employment, a refusal to publish research findings in scholarly journals, and a prohibition from receiving funding for research—in other words, banishment from the community of professional researchers.

Codes of ethics do more than systemize thinking and provide guidance; they also help universities and other institutions defend ethical research. For example, after interviewing twenty-four staff members and conducting observations, a researcher in 1994 documented that the staff at the Milwaukee Public Defenders Office were seriously overworked and could not effectively provide legal defense for poor people. Learning of the findings, top officials at the office contacted the university and demanded to know who on its staff had talked to the researcher with implications that there could be reprisals to those employees. The university administration defended the researcher and refused to release the information, citing widely accepted codes that protect human research participants.[28]

Ethics and the Sponsors of Research

Whistle-Blowing. You might find a job in which you do research for a sponsor—an employer, a government agency, or a private firm that contracts with you to conduct research. Special ethical prob-

lems can arise when someone else is paying for a study, especially if it is applied research. You may be asked to compromise ethical or professional research standards as a condition for receiving a contract or for continued employment. This means that you must set ethical boundaries beyond which you will refuse sponsor demands. When confronted with an illegitimate demand, you have three basic choices: be loyal to an organization or larger group, exit from the situation, or voice opposition.[29] These three choices present themselves as caving in to the sponsor, quitting, or becoming a **whistle-blower**. You must choose your own course of action, but it is best to consider ethical issues early in a relationship with a sponsor and to express concerns up front.

Whistle-blowing can be strenuous and risky. Three parties are involved: the researcher who sees ethical wrongdoing, an external agency or the media, and supervisors in an employing organization. The researcher must be convinced that the breach of ethics is serious and approved by the organization. After exhausting internal avenues to resolve the issue, he or she turns to outsiders. The outsiders may or may not be interested in the problem or able to help. Outsiders often have their own priorities (not making an organization look bad or sensationalizing the problem) that differ from the researcher's main concern (ending unethical behavior). Supervisors or managers may try to discredit or punish anyone who exposes problems and acts disloyal (see Example Box 5.5, The Story of a Whistle-Blower). As Frechette-Schrader (1994:78) noted, "An act of whistle blowing is a special kind of organizational disobedience or, rather, obedience to a higher principle than loyalty to an employer." Under the best of conditions, an issue may take a long time to be resolved and create great emotional strain. By acting morally, a whistle-blower needs to be prepared to make sacrifices: losing a job or promotions, receiving lower pay or an undesirable transfer, being abandoned by friends at work, or incurring legal costs. There is no guarantee that doing the right thing will change the unethical behavior or protect the researcher from retaliation.

Whistle-blower A person who recognizes unethical or illegal practices in an organization, voices opposition to them, and attempts to stop the practices through organizational channels but is not successful and may be punished for the attempt, but continues to voice opposition to the unethical or illegal practices beyond the organization.

EXAMPLE BOX 5.5

The Story of a Whistle-Blower

A Ph.D. microbiologist, David Franklin, was hired by Warner-Lambert to be a medical liaison. His job was to gain the trust of physicians and provide them with scientific information to sell pharmaceuticals. During his training, he was asked to make false claims about a drug and told how to circumvent legal-ethical rules to increase sales. He was also told to exaggerate the results of studies that did show a few benefits of the drug and hide reports of side effects. When he raised concerns and showed published reports of dangerous side effects to his superiors, his complaints were dismissed. He observed that the company paid tens of thousands of dollars to physicians to give testimonials as to the drug's benefits or to be the authors of articles that were actually written by the firm's marketing department. He felt that the company was acting illegally and endangering people. He resigned after just 4 months on the job but was threatened should he reveal anything about the company. It took 7 years to settle his whistle-blower legal case against the firm.

Source: Excerpt from Melody Petersen, "Doctor Explains Why He Blew the Whistle," *New York Times* (March 12, 2003).

Applied social researchers in sponsored research settings must think seriously about their professional roles and maintain a degree of independence from their employer. Many find a defense against sponsor pressures by participating in professional organizations (e.g., the Evaluation Research Society), maintaining regular contacts with researchers outside the sponsoring organization, and staying current with the best research practices. The researcher least likely to uphold ethical standards in a sponsored setting is someone who is isolated and professionally insecure. Whatever the situation, unethical behavior is never justified by the argument, If I didn't do it, someone else would have.

Arriving at Particular Findings. What should you do if a sponsor tells you, directly or indirectly, what your results should be? An ethical researcher refuses to participate if he or she must arrive at specific results as a precondition for doing research. All research should be conducted without restrictions on the findings that the research yields. For example, a survey organization obtained a contract to conduct research for a shopping mall association. The association was engaged in a court battle with a political group that wanted to demonstrate at a mall. An interviewer in the survey organization objected to many survey questions that he believed were invalid and slanted to favor the shopping mall association. After contacting a newspaper and exposing the biased questions, the interviewer was fired. Several years later, however, in a whistle-blower lawsuit, the interviewer was awarded more than $60,000 for back pay, mental anguish, and punitive damages against the survey organization.[30]

Another example of pressure to arrive at particular findings is in the area of educational testing. Standardized tests to measure achievement by U.S. school children have come under criticism. For example, children in about 90 percent of school districts in the United States score "above average" on such tests. This was called the *Lake Wobegon effect* after the mythical town of Lake Wobegon, where, according to radio show host Garrison Keillor, "all the children are above average." The main reason for this finding was that the researchers compared current students to standards based on tests taken by students many years ago. The researchers faced pressure from teachers, school principals, superintendents, and school boards for results that would allow them to report to parents and voters that their school district was "above average."[31]

Limits on How to Conduct Studies. Can a sponsor limit research by defining what can be studied or by limiting the techniques used, either directly or indirectly (by limiting funding)? Sponsors can legitimately set some conditions on research techniques used (e.g., survey versus experiment) and limit costs for research. However, we must follow generally accepted research methods. We should give a realistic appraisal of what can be accomplished for a given level of funding.

The issue of limits is common in **contract research**, as when a firm or government agency asks for work on a particular research project. A trade-off may develop between quality and cost in contract research. Abt (1979), the president of a major private social research firm, Abt Associates, argued that it is difficult to receive a contract by bidding what the research actually costs. Once the research begins, we may need to redesign the project, to lower costs. The contract procedure makes midstream changes difficult. We may find that we are forced by the contract to use research procedures that are less than ideal. We then confront a dilemma: Complete the contract and do low-quality research or fail to fulfill the contract and lose money and future jobs.

You should refuse to continue work on a study if you cannot uphold generally accepted standards of research. If a sponsor wants biased samples or leading questions, to be ethical, you must refuse to cooperate. If legitimate research shows the sponsor's pet idea or project to be a bad course of action, you may even anticipate the end of employment or pressure to violate professional research standards. In the long run, you, the sponsor, the scientific community, and the larger society would be harmed by the violation of sound research practice. You must decide whether you are a "hired hand" who will give the sponsors whatever they want, even if it is ethically wrong, or a professional who is obligated to teach, guide, or even oppose sponsors in the service of higher moral principles.

We should ask why sponsors would want the social research conducted if they are not interested in using the findings or in the truth. The answer is that such sponsors do not view social research as a means to knowledge or truth. They see it only as a cover they can use to legitimate a decision or practice that they could not otherwise do easily. These sponsors are abusing the researcher's status as being a serious trustworthy professional by being deceit-

ful and trying to "cash in" on the reputation of the scientific researchers' honesty and integrity. When this occurs, the ethical course of action is to expose and end the abuse.

Suppressing Findings. What happens if you conduct research and the findings make the sponsor look bad or the sponsor refuses to release the results? This is not an uncommon situation. For example, a sociologist conducted a study for the Wisconsin Lottery Commission on the effects of state government-sponsored gambling. After she completed the report but before it was released to the public, the commission asked her to remove sections that outlined many negative social effects of gambling and to eliminate her recommendations to create social services to help compulsive gamblers. The researcher was in a difficult position. Which ethical value took precedence: covering up for the sponsor that had paid for the research or revealing the truth for all to see but then suffering the consequences?[32] A Roman Catholic priest who surveyed American bishops on their dissatisfaction with official church policy was ordered by his superiors to suppress findings and destroy the questionnaires. Instead, he resigned after 24 years in the priesthood and made his results public.[33] Researchers pay high personal and economic costs for being ethical.

Government agencies may suppress scientific information that contradicts official policy or embarrasses high officials. Retaliation against social researchers employed by government agencies who make the information public also occurs. For example, a social researcher employed by the U.S. Census Bureau who studied deaths caused by the 1991 Gulf War against Iraq reported that government officials suppressed findings for political reasons. The researcher, whom the agency attempted to fire, reported that findings of high death rates had been delayed and underestimated by the U.S. government agency that provided statistics. Before information could be released, it had to go through an office headed by a political appointee. The researcher charged that the political appointee was most interested in protecting the administration's foreign policy. In another example, the U.S. Defense Department ordered the destruction of studies that

---

Contract research   A type of applied research that is sponsored (paid for) by a government agency, foundation, company, and so on; the researcher agrees to conduct a study on the sponsor's research question and finish the study by a set deadline for a fixed price.

showed 10 percent of the U.S. military to be a person who is gay or lesbian and the military provided no support for the banning of gays from the military. In 2005, the White House threatened the head of the little-known Bureau of Justice Statistics with dismissal and eventually demoted him for releasing law enforcement data on racial profiling. The government agency produces dozens of reports each year on crime patterns, drug use, police tactics, and prison populations. The data documented clear disparities in how racial groups were treated once they were stopped by the police. Political supervisors demanded deleting references to the disparities from reports. The data were based on interviews with 80,000 people in 2002. It showed that White, Black, and Hispanic drivers nationwide were stopped by the police that year at about the same rate, roughly 9 percent. However, once the police had made a stop, what happened next differed depending on driver's race and ethnicity.[34]

In sponsored research, we can negotiate conditions for releasing findings *prior to beginning* the study and sign a contract to that effect. It may be unwise to conduct the study without such a guarantee, although competing researchers who have fewer ethical scruples may do so. Alternatively, we can accept the sponsor's criticism and hostility and release the findings over the sponsor's objections. Most researchers prefer the first choice because the second one may scare away future sponsors.

Social researchers sometimes restrict or delay the release of findings to protect the identity of informants, to maintain access to a research site, to hold on to their jobs, or to protect the personal safety of themselves or of family members.[35] This is a less disturbing type of censorship because it is not imposed by an outside power. It is done by someone who is close to the research and who is knowledgeable about possible consequences. Researchers shoulder the ultimate responsibility for their research. Often, they can draw on many different resources, but they face many competing pressures as well. (See Expansion Box 5.6, Common Types of Misuse in Evaluation Research.)

Concealing the True Sponsor. Is it ethical to keep the identity of a sponsor secret? For example, an

---

EXPANSION BOX **5.6**
Common Types of Misuse in Evaluation Research

■ Asking "wrong" research questions (e.g., asking summative yes/no questions when formulative questions are most appropriate or asking questions that exclude major stakeholders)

■ Requesting an evaluation study after a decision on a program has been made, using the study only as a way to delay or justify the decision already made

■ Demanding the use of a research design/data collection technique that is inappropriate for the program evaluation task

■ Interfering with the research design or data collection process to ensure that it produces desired results

■ Continuing a program when the evaluation results unambiguously show it to be ineffective or ending a program when the results unambiguously show it to be highly effective

■ Suppressing/deleting positive results to eliminate/reduce a program, or suppressing/deleting negative results to continue/expand a program

Source: Adapted from Stevens and Dial (1994), who also provide examples of misuse.

---

abortion clinic funds a study on the attitudes of religious groups opposed to abortion. We must balance the ethical value of making the sponsor's identity public to subjects and releasing results against the sponsor's desire for confidentiality and the likelihood of reduced cooperation from subjects. If the results are published, there is a clear overriding ethical mandate to reveal the true sponsor. There is less agreement on the ethical issue of revealing the true sponsor to subjects. Presser and colleagues (1992) found that the answers given by survey respondents may depend on its sponsor. If a respondent believes a survey is conducted by a newspaper that has taken a strong position on an issue, the respondent is less likely to contradict the newspaper's public stand on the issue. This is less a problem if the respondent believes the survey sponsor is a neutral academic organization. It is ethical to inform the subjects of the sponsor unless one has a good methodological reason for not doing so.

Feminist Communitarian Research Ethics

Some researchers who adopt the interpretative or critical social science approaches (see Chapter 4) view most ethical debates, codes of ethics, and review boards as inadequate and rooted in positivist assumptions. They propose a feminist communitarian model of research ethics as an alternative to research ethics based on formal procedures and a rational utilitarian balancing of costs versus benefits and abstract principles of moral good. They hold that "the moral task cannot be reduced to professional ethics" (Christians 2003:232). Aligned with participatory action research (see Chapter 2), they argue that research participants should have a say in how research is conducted and be actively involved in conducting it. Ethics should reflect the ultimate purpose of research—to empower research participants in terms of their own everyday experiences and advance the goal of human freedom.

The feminist communitarian model rests on three moral principles. First, ethical research is multivocal, that is, it recognizes a diversity of human experiences and incorporates that diversity. It begins with the premise that all human life is situated in the socially constructed contexts of gender, race, class, and religion. People live in multiple communities, and each has something important to say. Second, ethical research requires engaging in a dialogue over moral concerns that is phrased in terms of the participants' everyday life experiences. Researchers must engage and participate in the ongoing moral debates and discussions occurring within the communities of the people they wish to study, and they should not superimpose their own abstract legalistic rights or principles. Third, research processes that involve researchers and participants on open, equal terms will unmask power relations and generate social criticism that can facilitate greater reflection and mutual awareness. In the end, a collaborative relationship between researcher and participant will emerge in which "invasion of privacy, informed consent, and deception are non-issues" (Christians 2003:234).

The feminist communitarian model of research ethics is still in an early stage of development and has yet to be implemented. Nonetheless, it critiques the dominant approach to research ethics for being overly formal-legalistic, procedure based, and abstract. It also highlights how an approach to social sciences, as outlined in Chapter 4, is connected with moral issues in research ethics.

CONCLUSION

This chapter is a transition between the general foundation of social research and the specifics of study design. We discussed two issues that are part of the preparation for designing a study: the literature review and ethical concerns. Both involve placing your study in the context of the larger community of researchers and attaching a specific study to larger concerns.

In Chapter 1, we discussed the distinctive contribution of science to society and the ways in which social research is a source of knowledge about the social world. The perspectives and techniques of social research can be powerful tools for understanding the world. Nevertheless, with that power comes responsibility—to yourself, your sponsors, the community of researchers, and the larger society. These responsibilities can and do come into conflict with each other at times.

Ultimately, you personally must decide to conduct research in an ethical manner, to uphold and defend the principles of the social science approach you adopt, and to demand ethical conduct by others. The truthfulness of knowledge produced by social research and its use or misuse depends on individual researchers like you, reflecting on their actions and on how social research fits into society.

In the next chapter, we examine basic design approaches and issues that appear in both qualitative and quantitative research.

KEY TERMS

abstract	crossover design	principle of voluntary
anonymity	informed consent	consent
citation	institutional review board	research fraud
code of ethics	(IRB)	scientific misconduct
confidentiality	meta-analysis	special population
contract research	nuremberg code	whistle-blower

REVIEW QUESTIONS

1. What are the four major goals of a literature review?
2. Which outlets of research are easiest to locate and which are the most difficult?
3. How would you locate a Ph.D. dissertation?
4. What distinguishes a strong from a weak literature review?
5. What are the major advantages and disadvantages of using the Internet for social research?
6. What is the primary defense against unethical conduct in research?
7. How do deceiving and coercing individuals to participate in research conflict with the principle of voluntary consent?
8. Explain the ethical issues in the Milgram, Humphreys, and Zimbardo examples.
9. What is *informed consent,* and how does it protect research subjects?
10. What is the difference between *anonymity* and *confidentiality*?

NOTES

1. See Hunt (1997) and Hunter and associates (1982).
2. From Hargens (1988).
3. Based on Hargens (1991).
4. See Reynolds (1979:56–57) and Sieber (1993).
5. See research fraud discussion in Broad and Wade (1982), Diener and Crandall (1978:154–158), and Weinstein (1979). Also see Hearnshaw (1979) and Wade (1976) on Cyril Burt. Kusserow (1989) and the September 1, 1989, issue of the National Institutes of Health weekly *Guide* summarize some recent scientific misconduct issues.
6. See "Noted Harvard Psychiatrist Resigns Post after Faculty Group Finds He Plagiarized," *Chronicle of Higher Education* (December 7, 1988).
7. See Blum (1989) and D'Antonio (1989) on this case of plagiarism.
8. See "Doctor Is Accused of 'Immoral' Tests,'" *New York Times* (December 9, 1988). For a more general discussion of power and trust, see Reynolds (1979:32).

9. Lifton (1986) provided an account of Nazi medical experimentation.
10. See Jones (1981) and Mitchell (1997) on the Bad Blood case.
11. Diener and Crandall (1978:128) discuss these examples.
12. See Warwick (1982) on types of harm to research participants. See Reynolds (1979:62–68) on rates of harm in biomedical research. Kelman (1982) discusses different types of harm from different types of research.
13. College counselors report that anxiety and low self-esteem over dating are major problems among college women (Diener and Crandall, 1978:21–22). Also see Kidder and Judd (1986:481–484).
14. See Dooley (1984:330) and Kidder and Judd (1986: 477–484).
15. See Hallowell (1985) and "Threat to Confidentiality of Fieldnotes," *ASA Footnotes,* 12:6.

16. For more on the general issue of the right not to be researched, see Barnes (1979), Boruch (1982), Moore (1973), and Sagarin (1973).

17. Informed consent requirements and regulations are discussed in detail in Maloney (1984). Also see Capron (1982) and Diener and Crandall (1978:64–66).

18. The debate over covert research is discussed in Denzin and Erikson (1982), Homan (1980), and Sieber (1982). Also see Miller and Tewksbury (2000), especially Sections 1 and 4.3.

19. See Diener and Crandall (1978:87) and Warwick (1982:112).

20. See Diener and Crandall (1978:173–177) and Kidder and Judd (1986:469).

21. See Boruch (1982), Caplan (1982), Katz (1972), and Vaughan (1967) on privacy.

22. For more on the Wichita Jury Study, see Dooley (1984:338–339), Gray (1982), Robertson (1982), Tropp (1982:391), and Vaughan (1967).

23. See Monaghan (1993a, 1993b, 1993c).

24. See Gustavsen (1986).

25. IRBs are discussed in Maloney (1984) and Chadwick and associates (1984:20). See Taylor (1994) for an international survey of ethical standards.

26. See Abbott (1988), Brint (1994), and Freidson (1986, 1994) on professionals.

27. See Beecher (1970:227–228) and Reynolds (1979:28–31, 428–441).

28. See "UW Protects Dissertation Sources," *Capital Times* (December 19, 1994):4. Greenwald (1992: 585–586) remarked, "Sociology stands out among the learned professions as critical of the authority of established institutions such as government or large business firms" and in its provision to "explicitly state the shortcoming of methodologies and the openness of findings to varying interpretations."

29. See Hirschman (1970) on loyalty, exit, and voice. Also see Rubin (1983:24–40) on ethical issues in applied research.

30. Additional discussion can be found in Schmeling and Miller (1988).

31. See Fiske (1989), Koretz (1988), and Weiss and Gruber (1987) on educational statistics.

32. See "State Sought, Got Author's Changes in Lottery Report," *Capital Times* (July 28, 1989), p. 21.

33. See Chambers (1986).

34. See Dale W. Nelson, "Analyst: War Death Counts Falsified," *Wisconsin State Journal* (April 14, 1992:3A); "Ex-Official Says Pentagon Dumped Findings on Gays," *Capital Times* (April 1, 1993); and Eric Lichtblau, "Profiling Report Leads to a Clash and a Demotion, " *New York Times* (August 24, 2005).

35. See Adler and Adler (1993).

CHAPTER 6

Strategies of Research Design

Triangulation

**Qualitative and Quantitative
Orientations Toward Research**

Qualitative Design Issues

Quantitative Design Issues

Conclusion

*Substantive problems must thus be translated into the vocabulary of social
inquiry. . . . Working out a way of thinking through the choices and some
appropriate sequence of tasks will allow you to answer a research question.*
—Robert Alford, *The Craft of Inquiry,* p. 25

In 1995 more than 700 people died in a few days in a Chicago heat wave. News reports
and officials lacked answers about why it happened. Public and media discussions of
the disaster disappeared shortly after it happened. Klinenberg (2002) conducted a
"social autopsy" of this "extreme event" in a study using the tools of sociological
inquiry—ethnographic field work, interviews, examination of archival documents
(newspapers, statistical reports, various records, maps), and analysis of statistical data.
The study was designed to answer a question: why and how so many died so quickly.
He used social research to dissect the event and reveal its underlying social, political,
and economic causes. The study informs us about why and how the disaster occurred.
It shows how to design a social research study that answers a significant question
(reasons for the unnecessary deaths of hundreds of people in a few days) but that had
remained unanswered or ignored.

This chapter focuses on issues involved in designing a study and developing a strategy to guide
you during the research process. Your strategy for
designing and conducting a study will vary depending on whether it is primarily quantitative or qualitative. You need to plan a quantitative study in
detail before you collect or analyze the data.
You may ask how you can best create a logically
rigorous design that defines and measures all variables precisely, select a representative sample, collect data, and conduct statistical analysis? For a
qualitative study, you try to immerse yourself fully
in a range of data while being very alert to new
insights throughout the process of gathering data.
You may ask how you can best capture the richness,
texture, and feeling of dynamic social life. Of course,
you can mix the features of quantitative and qualitative studies to build on their complementary
strengths. Mixing approaches has advantages but
adds complexity and is more time consuming. We
can see the advantages in triangulation, which is
described in the next section.

TRIANGULATION

Surveyors and sailors measure distances between objects by taking observations from multiple positions. By observing the object from several different angles or viewpoints, the surveyors and sailors can obtain a good fix on an object's true location (see Figure 6.1). Social researchers employ a similar process of **triangulation**. In social research, we build on the principle that we learn more by observing from multiple perspectives than by looking from only a single perspective.

Social researchers use several types of triangulation (see Expansion Box 6.1, Example of Four Types of Triangulation). The most common type is *triangulation of measure,* meaning that we take multiple measures of the same phenomena. For example, you want to learn about a person's health. First, you ask the person to complete a questionnaire with multiple-choice answers. Next you conduct an open-ended informal interview. You also ask a live-in partner/caregiver about the person's health. You interview the individual's physician and together examine his or her medical records and lab

Triangulation The idea that looking at something from multiple points of view improves accuracy.

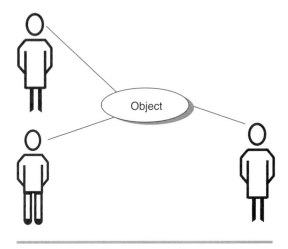

FIGURE 6.1 Triangulation: Observing from Different Viewpoints

test results. Your confidence that you have an accurate picture grows from the multiple measures you used compared to relying on just one, especially if each measure offers a similar picture. Differences you see among the measures stimulates questions as well.

Triangulation of observers is a variation on the first type. In many studies, we conduct interviews or are the lone observer of events and behavior.

EXPANSION BOX 6.1

Example of Four Types of Triangulation

TOPIC

The amount of violence in popular American films

Measures: Create three quantitative measures of violence: the frequency (e.g., number of killings, punches), intensity (e.g., volume and length of time screaming, amount of pain shown in face or body movement), and level of explicit, graphic display (e.g., showing a corpse with blood flowing, amputated body parts, close-ups of injury) in films.

Observers: Have five different people independently watch, evaluate, and record the forms and degrees of violence in a set of ten highly popular American films.

Theory: Compare how a feminist, a functional, and a symbolic interaction theory explains the forms, causes, and societal results of violence that is in popular films.

Method: Conduct a content analysis of a set of ten popular films, as an experiment to measure the responses of experimental subjects to violence in each film, to survey attitudes toward film violence among the movie-going public, and to make field observations on audience behavior during and immediately after showing the films.

Any limitations of a single observer (e.g., lack of skill in an area, a biased view on an issue, inattention to certain details) become restrictions of the study. Multiple observers bring alternative perspectives, backgrounds, and social characteristics. They thereby reduce the limitations. For example, two people interact with and observe the behavior of ten 5-year-old children at a child care center. One of the observers is a 60-year-old White male pediatrician with 25 years of experience working in a large city hospital. The other is a 31-year-old Hispanic female mother of two children who has 6 years of experience as an elementary school teacher in a small town. Each observer may notice and record different data. Combining what both see and experience will produce a fuller picture than relying on either one alone.

Triangulation of theory requires using multiple theoretical perspectives to plan a study or interpret the data. Each theoretical perspective has assumptions and concepts. They operate as a lens through which to view the social world. For example, a study of work relations in a bank could use conflict theory with its emphasis on power differences and inequality. The study could highlight the pay and working condition inequalities based on positions of authority (e.g., manager versus teller). The study reveals relevant differences in social backgrounds: a middle-aged White male manager with an MBA and a young African American female teller with an associate's degree. Next, rational choice theory is applied to focus on decision-making and rational strategies individuals use to maximize personal benefits. This perspective highlights how the bank manager varies the time/effort he devotes to various customers depending on their loan or savings account size. It also presents a better picture of how the teller invests her time and energy differently with various supervisors, depending on whether she believes they might help her get a promotion. Each perspective guides the study: It identifies relevant data, provides a set of concepts, and helps to interpret the meaning and significance of the data.

Triangulation of method mixes the qualitative and quantitative research approaches and data. Most researchers develop an expertise in one approach, but the approaches have complementary strengths. A study that combines both tends to be richer and more comprehensive. Mixing them occurs in several ways:[1] by using the approaches sequentially, first one and then the other, or by using them in parallel or simultaneously. In the study that opened this chapter, Klinenberg mixed a statistical analysis of quantitative data on deaths with interviews and document analysis. (see Example Box 6.1, A Multimethod Study on page 166).

QUALITATIVE AND QUANTITATIVE ORIENTATIONS TOWARD RESEARCH

In all research, we strive to collect empirical data systematically and to examine data patterns so we can better understand and explain social life, yet differences between research approaches can create miscommunication and misunderstandings. They are mutually intelligible; grasping both approaches and seeing how each complements the other simply takes more time and effort. Next we will look at some sources of differences.

A first difference originates in the nature of the data itself. *Soft data* (i.e., words, sentences, photos, symbols) dictate qualitative research strategies and data collection techniques that differ from *hard data* (in the form of numbers) for which quantitative approaches are used. Such differences may make the tools for a quantitative study inappropriate or irrelevant for a qualitative study and vice versa.

Another difference between qualitative and quantitative research originates in principles about the research process and assumptions about social life. Qualitative and quantitative research principles give rise to different "languages of research" with different emphases. In a quantitative study, we rely more on positivist principles and use a language of variables and hypotheses. Our emphasis is on precisely measuring variables and test hypotheses. In a qualitative study, we rely more on the principles from interpretive or critical social science. We speak a language of "cases and contexts" and of cultural meaning. Our emphasis is on conducting detailed examinations of specific cases that arise in the natural flow of social life. Interestingly, more female

EXAMPLE BOX **6.1**

A Multimethod Study

Lee and Bean (2007) mixed quantitative and qualitative research approaches in a study of multiracial identity in the United States. They observed that social diversity has increased because of growing immigration since 1970, and for the first time in 2000, the United States census offered the option of classifying oneself as multiracial. The new diversity contrasts to the long history of single-race categories and a dominant White-Black dichotomous racial division. Lee and Bean asked whether multiracial people feel free or highly constrained when they pick a single racial-ethnic or multiracial identity. They also asked whether selecting a multiracial category on the census form is a symbolic action or a reflection of a person's multiracial daily existence. In the quantitative part of the study, the authors statistically analyzed 2000 census data on the numbers and mixes of people who classified themselves as multiracial. In the qualitative part of the study, they conducted forty-six in-depth semi-structured interviews with multiracial adults from northern and southern California. In the interviews, Lee and Bean asked how and why a person chose to identify herself or himself as she or he did, whether that identity changed over time or by context, and about language use and other practices associated

with race and ethnicity. They interviewed adults of various mixtures of Asian, White, Latino, and Black races. Based on the interviews, Lee and Bean found that multiracial Blacks were less likely to call themselves multiracial than people of other mixed race categories. This restriction is consistent with the U.S. historical pattern of the public identifying a person with only some Black heritage as being Black. Persons of mixed White and Asian or Latino or Latino-Asian heritage had more flexibility. Some mixed Asian-White or Latino-White people self-identified as White because of public perceptions and a narrow stereotypical definition of proper Asian or Latino appearance. Other White-Asian and White-Latino people said that they are proud of their mixed heritage even if it made little difference in their daily encounters. People did not stick with one label but claimed different racial-ethnic backgrounds in different situations. Pulling together the quantitative and qualitative findings, Lee and Bean suggested that racial-ethnic group boundaries are fading faster for Latinos and Asians than for Blacks. They concluded that a new Black versus non-Black divide is emerging to replace the old White-Black division but that Blacks are still in a disadvantaged position relative to all racial categories.

than male social researchers adopt the qualitative approach.[2]

A third difference between qualitative and quantitative research lies in what we try to accomplish in a study. "The heart of good work"—whether it is quantitative or qualitative—"is a puzzle and an idea" (Abbott, 2003:xi). In all studies, we try to solve a puzzle or answer a question, but depending on the approach, we do this in different ways. In the heat wave study that opened this chapter, Klinenberg (2002) asked why so many people died. But he also asked how they died, and why some categories of people were greatly affected but others were not. In a quantitative study, we usually try to verify or falsify a relationship or hypothesis we already have in mind. We focus on an outcome or effect found across numerous cases.

The test of a hypothesis may be more than a simple true or false answer; frequently it includes learning that a hypothesis is true for some cases or under certain conditions but not others. In the heat wave study, Klinenberg asked whether a person's social class influenced an outcome: being likely to die during the heat wave. Using quantitative data, he tested the relationship between class and death rate by comparing the social class of the roughly 700 who died with thousands who did not.

In many qualitative studies, we often generate new hypotheses and describe details of the causal mechanism or process for a narrow set of cases. Returning to the heat wave study, Klinenberg (2002) tested existing hypotheses about class and death rates. He also developed several new hypotheses as he looked closely into the mechanism that caused some to die but not others. He learned that high death rates occurred in poverty- and crime-ridden neighborhoods. More males than females died, and more African Americans died than Latinos or Whites. By walking around in different low-income neighborhoods and interviewing many people first-hand, he identified the mechanisms of urban isolation that accounted for very different heat wave survival rates among people of the same social class. He examined the social situations of older African American men and discovered the local social environment to be the critical causal mechanism. He also looked at larger forces that created the social situations and local environments in Chicago in the mid-1990s.

A fourth difference between quantitative and qualitative studies is that each has a distinct "logic" and path of conducting research. In a quantitative study, we employ a logic that is systematic and follows a linear research path. In a qualitative study, the logic arises from ongoing practice and we follow a nonlinear research path. In the next section, we examine the logics and paths of research.

Reconstructed Logic and Logic in Practice

How we learn and discuss research tends to follow one of two logics.[3] The logics summarize the degree to which our research strategy is explicit, codified, and standardized. In specific studies, we often mix the two logics, but the proportion of each varies widely by study.

A **reconstructed logic** emphasizes using an explicit research process. Reconstructed logic has been "reconstructed" or restated from the many messy details of doing a real-life study into an idealized, formal set of steps with standard practices and consistent principles, terms, and rules. You can think of it as a "cleansed model" of how best to do a high-quality study. Following this logic is like cooking by exactly following a printed recipe. Thus, the way to conduct a simple random sample (discussed in Chapter 7) is straightforward and follows a clear step-by-step procedure.

The **logic in practice** is messy and closer to the concrete practice of doing research. Logic in

practice includes advice that comes from the practical activities of doing specific real-life studies more than a set of restated, ideal rules. This logic relies heavily on "judgment calls" and "tricks of the trade" that active, experienced researchers share. We learn it best by reading many studies and being an apprentice researcher and from the folk wisdom that passes informally among experienced researchers. It is like cooking without a written recipe—adding a pinch of an ingredient here, stirring until something "looks right," and adjusting while cooking until we reach a certain smell or taste.

You can see the reconstructed logic in the distinct research methods section of a quantitative research report. In contrast, in qualitative research reports, you may not see the research method (common for historical-comparative research) discussed or find it mixed with a personal autobiographical account of a particular study (common for field research). The absence of a standard method does not make qualitative study less valid; however, it often requires more time and a different style of thinking for the newcomer to master.

Linear and Nonlinear Paths

The path is a metaphor for a sequence of things to do: what you finish first or where you have been and what comes next. You can follow a straight, well-worn, and marked path that has clear signposts and is where many others have trod before. Alternatively, you may follow a path that meanders into unknown territory where few others have gone. The path has few signs, so you move forward, veer off to the side, and sometimes backtrack a little before going forward again.

Reconstructed logic   A logic of research based on reorganizing, standardizing, and codifying research knowledge and practices into explicit rules, formal procedures, and techniques; it is characteristic of quantitative research.

Logic in practice   A logic of research based on an apprenticeship model and the sharing of implicit knowledge about practical concerns and specific experiences; it is characteristic of qualitative research.

When using the **linear research path**, we follow a fixed sequence of steps that are like a staircase that leads upward in one direction. By following a linear path, we move in a direct, narrow, and straight way toward a conclusion. This pathway toward task completion is the dominant approach in western European and North American cultures. It is most widely used in quantitative research. By contrast, a **nonlinear research path** requires us to make successive passes through the steps. We may move forward, backward, and sideways before advancing again. It is more of a spiral than a straight staircase. We move upward but slowly and indirectly. With each cycle or repetition, we may collect new data and gain new insights.

People who are accustomed to a direct, linear approach often become impatient with a less direct cyclical path. Although a nonlinear path is not disorganized, undefined chaos, the cyclical path appears inefficient and without rigor. People who are used to a nonlinear path often feel stifled and "boxed in" by a linear approach. To them, a linear path feels artificial or rigid. They believe that this approach prevents them from being naturally creative and spontaneous.

Each path has its strengths. The linear path is logical, easy to follow, and efficient. The nonlinear path can be highly effective in creating an authentic feeling for understanding an entire setting, for grasping subtle shades of meaning, for integrating divergent bits of information, and for switching perspectives. Each path has its own discipline and rigor. The linear path borrows from the natural sciences with their emphasis on logic and precision. A nonlinear path borrows devices from the humanities (e.g., metaphor, analogy, theme, motif, and irony) and is suited for tasks such as translating languages, a process in which delicate shades

of meaning, subtle connotations, or contextual distinctions can be important (see Figure 6.2 for a graphic representation of each path).

Objectivity and Integrity

We try to be fair, honest, truthful, and unbiased in our research activity, yet, we also have opportunities to be biased, dishonest, or unethical in all knowledge production including social research. The two major research approaches address the issue of reducing difficulties and ensuring honest, truthful studies in different ways.

In qualitative research, we often try to acquire intimate, firsthand knowledge of the research setting. Thus, we do not want to distance ourselves from the people or events we are studying. Acquiring an intimate understanding of a setting does not mean that we can arbitrarily interject personal opinion, be sloppy about data collection, or use evidence selectively to support our prejudices. Rather, we take maximum advantage of personal insight, inner feelings, and life perspective to understand social life. We "walk a fine line" between intimacy and detachment and place personal integrity and honesty at the forefront. Some techniques may help us walk a fine line. One technique is to become highly sensitive to our own views, preconceptions, and prior assumptions and then "bracket" them, or put them aside, so we can see beyond them better. Instead of trying to bury or deny our assumptions, viewpoints, and values, we find that acknowledging them and being open about them is best. We can then recognize how they might influence us. We try to be forthright and candid in our involvement in the research setting, in dealing with the people in the study, and with any relevant issues that arise. We do this in the way that we conduct the study and report on the findings.

Personal openness and integrity by the individual researcher are central to a qualitative study. By contrast, in a quantitative study, we stress neutrality and objectivity. In a quantitative study, we rely on the principle of replication, adhere to standardized procedures, measure with numbers, and analyze the data with statistics.[4] In a sense, we try to minimize or eliminate the subjective human

---

Linear research path Research that proceeds in a clear, logical, step-by-step straight line; often used in quantitative research.

Nonlinear research path Research that proceeds in a cyclical, iterative, or back-and-forth pattern and is often used in qualitative research.

Reconstructed Logic, Linear Path

Logic in Practice, Nonlinear Path

FIGURE 6.2   Graphic Representation of Linear and Nonlinear Paths

factor in a quantitative study. As Porter (1995:7, 74) has argued,

> *Ideally, expertise should be mechanized and objectified . . . grounded in specific techniques. . . . This ideal of objectivity is a political as well as scientific one. Objectivity means rule of law, not of men. It implies the subordination of personal interests and prejudices to public standards.*

The issue of integrity in quantitative research mirrors the natural science approach. It relies on using an explicit and objective technology, such as making statements in precise neutral terms, using well-documented standard techniques, and making replicable, objective numerical measures.

Quantitative social research shares the hallmarks of natural science validation: explicit, standard procedures; precise numerical measurement; and replication. By contrast, validation in qualitative research relies more on a dependable, credible researcher and her or his personal integrity, self-discipline, and trustworthiness.[5] Four other forms of validation in qualitative research somewhat parallel the objective procedures found in quantitative studies.[6]

The first form indicates that the researcher has carefully evaluated various forms of evidence and checked them for consistency. For example, a field researcher listens to and records a student who says, "Professor Smith threw an eraser at Professor Jones." The researcher must consider the evidence carefully. This includes considering what other people say about the event. The field researcher also looks for confirming evidence and checks for internal consistency. The researcher asks whether the student has firsthand knowledge of the event, that is, directly witnessed it, and asks whether the student's feelings or self-interest might lead him or her to lie (e.g., the student dislikes Professor Smith).

A second form of validation arises from the great volume of detailed written notes in most qualitative studies. In addition to verbatim description of the evidence, other documentation includes references to sources, commentaries by the researcher, and quotes, photographs, videos, maps, diagrams, paraphrasing, and counts. The huge volume of information, its great diversity, and its interlocking and mutually reinforcing presentation help to validate its authenticity.

A third kind of validation comes from other observers. Most qualitative researchers work alone, but many others know about the evidence. For example, we study people in a specific setting who are alive today. Other researchers can visit the same setting and talk to the same people. The people we studied can read study details and verify or raise questions about it. Likewise, historical-comparative researchers cite historical documents, archival sources, or visual material. By leaving a careful "audit trail" with precise citations, others can check the references and verify sources.

A fourth type of truthfulness is created by the way we publicly disclose results. In a quantitative study, we adhere to a standard format for writing a research report. We explain in detail how we followed accepted procedures. We describe each step of the study, display the quantitative data in charts, graphs, or tables, and make data files available to others to reanalyze. We offer to answer any questions about the study. In a qualitative study, we cannot publicly display or share the many mountains of detailed notes, recorded interviews, photos, or original source materials in a research report. They might fill an entire room! Instead, we "spin a web" of interlocking details and use tightly cross-referenced material. Through our writing and presentation, we provide sufficient texture and detail to build an "I-was-there" sense within readers. By providing rich specific descriptions supplemented with maps, photos, and verbatim quotations, we convey an intimate knowledge of a setting. We build a sense of shared familiarity in readers. A skilled qualitative researcher can recreate the visual images, voices, smells, sounds, tensions, and entire atmosphere that existed by referring to the mountains of empirical evidence.

Preplanned and Emergent Research Questions

Studies start in many ways, but the usual first step is to select a topic.[7] We have no formula for how to do this task. Whether we have experience or are just a beginning researcher, the best guide is to pick something that interests us. There are many ways to select topics (see Expansion Box 6.2, Sources of Topics). We may begin with one topic, but it is too large and is only a starting point. We must narrow it into a focused research question. How we do this varies by whether our study is primarily qualitative or quantitative. Both kinds of studies work well with some topics; we can study poverty by examining official statistics, conducting a survey, doing ethnographic field research, or completing a historical-comparative analysis. Some topics are best suited for a qualitative study (e.g., how do people reshape their self-identity through participating in goth youth subculture) and others for a quantitative study (e.g., how has public opinion on the death penalty shifted over the past 50 years and whether one's opinion on this issue is influenced by views on related issues or by the amount of exposure the news media gives to certain topics).

Most qualitative studies start with a vague or loosely defined topic. The specific topic emerges slowly during the study, and it may change direction based on new evidence. This was the case for Venkatesh's study (2008) that opened Chapter 5. He began with an interest in studying poverty in an inner-city housing project but shifted to studying a drug-selling gang. Focusing on a specific research question continues while we gather data. Venkatesh increasingly focused his topic of gang activity into sharper questions: How and why did gangs in a low-income housing project sustain an underground economy and provide housing project residents with protection and aid services?

Flexibility in qualitative research encourages us to continuously focus throughout a study. An emergent research question may become clear only during the research process. We can focus and refine the research question after we gather some data and begin a preliminary analysis. In many qualitative studies, the most important issues and

EXPANSION BOX **6.2**

Sources of Topics

1. *Personal experience.* You can choose a topic based on something that happens to you or those you know. For example, while you work a summer job at a factory, the local union calls a strike. You do not have strong feelings either way, but you are forced to choose sides. You notice that tensions rise. Both management and labor become hostile toward each other. This experience suggests unions or organized labor as a topic.

2. *Curiosity based on something in the media.* Sometimes you read a newspaper or magazine article or see a television program that leaves you with questions. What you read raises questions or suggests replicating what others' research found. For example, you read a *Newsweek* article on people who are homeless, but you do not really know much about who they are, why they are homeless, whether this has always been a problem, and so forth. This suggests homeless people as a topic.

3. *The state of knowledge in a field.* Basic research is driven by new research findings and theories that push at the frontiers of knowledge. As theoretical explanations are elaborated and expanded, certain issues or questions need to be answered for the field to move forward. As such issues are identified and studied, knowledge advances. For example, you read about attitudes toward capital punishment and realize that most research points to an underlying belief in the innate wickedness of criminals among capital punishment supporters. You notice that no one has yet examined whether people who belong to certain religious groups that teach such a belief in wickedness

support capital punishment, nor has anyone mapped the geographic location of these religious groups. Your knowledge of the field suggests a topic for a research project: beliefs about capital punishment and religion in different regions.

4. *Solving a problem.* Applied research topics often begin with a problem that needs a solution. For example, as part of your job as a dorm counselor, you want to help college freshmen establish friendships with each other. Your problem suggests friendship formation among new college students as a topic.

5. *Social premiums.* This is a term suggested by Singleton and colleagues (1988:68). It means that some topics are "hot" or offer an opportunity. For example, you read that a lot of money is available to conduct research on nursing homes, but few people are interested in doing so. Your need of a job suggests nursing homes as a topic.

6. *Personal values.* Some people are highly committed to a set of religious, political, or social values. For example, you are strongly committed to racial equality and become morally outraged whenever you hear about racial discrimination. Your strong personal belief suggests racial discrimination as a topic.

7. *Everyday life.* Potential topics can be found throughout everyday life in old sayings, novels, songs, statistics, and what others say (especially those who disagree with you). For example, you hear that the home court advantage is very important in basketball. This statement suggests home court advantage as a topic for research.

---

most interesting questions become clear only after we become immersed in the data. We need to remain open to unanticipated ideas, data, and issues. We should periodically reevaluate our focus early in a study and be ready to change direction and follow new lines of evidence. At the same time, we must exercise self-restraint and discipline. If we constantly change the focus of our research without end, we will never complete a study. As with most things, a balance is required.

Typical qualitative research questions include these: How did a certain condition or social situation originate? How do people, events, and conditions sustain a situation over time? By what processes does the situation change, develop, or end? Another type of question seeks to confirm existing beliefs or assumptions (e.g., do Southern and Northern Whites act differently around people of other races as those in McDermott's [2006] study of working class neighborhoods in Atlanta and Boston). A last type of research question tries to discover new ideas.[8]

In a quantitative study, we narrow a topic into a focused question as a discrete planning step before we finalize the study design. Focusing the question is a step in the process of developing a testable hypothesis (to be discussed later). It guides the study design before you collect any data.[9]

In a qualitative study, we can use the data to help narrow the focus. In a quantitative study, we must focus without the benefit of data and use other techniques. After picking a topic, we ask ourselves: What is it about the topic that is of greatest interest? For a topic about which we know little, we must first acquire background knowledge by reading studies about the topic. Reading the research literature can stimulate many ideas for how to focus a research question.

In most quantitative studies, research questions refer to relationships among a small number of variables. This means that we should list variables as we try to focus the topic into a research question (see Expansion Box 6.3, Techniques for Narrowing a Topic into a Research Question). For example, the question what causes divorce? is not a good research question. A better one is, is age at marriage associated with divorce? The second question has two variables: age of marriage and whether or not a divorce occurred (also see Example Box 6.2, Examples of Bad and Good Research Questions).

Personal experience can suggest topics. Perhaps personal experience suggests people released from prison as a topic as it did for Pager (2007). We can read about former inmates and their reentry and about probation in dozens of books and hundreds of articles. A focused research question might be whether it is more difficult for someone who has a nonviolent criminal record to get a job offer than someone without a criminal record. This question is more specific in terms of type of criminal record and the specific outcome for a former prisoner. It focuses on two variables, whether a person has a criminal record and whether the person gets a job offer. A common type of research question asks which factor among several had the most significant impact on an outcome. We might ask, as Pager did,

---

EXPANSION BOX **6.3**

Techniques for Narrowing a Topic into a Research Question

1. *Examine the literature.* Published articles are excellent sources of ideas for research questions. They are usually at an appropriate level of specificity and suggest research questions that focus on the following:
   a. Replicating a previous research project exactly or with slight variations.
   b. Exploring unexpected findings discovered in previous research.
   c. Following suggestions an author gives for future research at the end of an article.
   d. Extending an existing explanation or theory to a new topic or setting.
   e. Challenging the findings or attempting to refute a relationship.
   f. Specifying the intervening process and considering any linking relations.

2. *Talk over ideas with others.*
   a. Ask people who are knowledgeable about the topic for questions about it that they have thought of.
   b. Seek out those who hold opinions that differ from yours on the topic and discuss possible research questions with them.

3. *Apply to a specific context.*
   a. Focus the topic onto a specific historical period or time period.
   b. Narrow the topic to a specific society or geographic unit.
   c. Consider which subgroups or categories of people/units are involved and whether there are differences among them.

4. *Define the aim or desired outcome of the study.*
   a. Will the research question be for an exploratory, explanatory, or descriptive study?
   b. Will the study involve applied or basic research?

---

how does racial category (Black versus White) and whether a person had a criminal record affect the chances of getting a job? Did race make a difference, did being a former prisoner make a difference, did the two factors operate separately, cancel out one another, or intensify one another in their impact on getting a job offer?

Examples of Bad and Good Research Questions

BAD RESEARCH QUESTIONS

Not Empirically Testable, Nonscientific Questions
- Should abortion be legal?
- Is it right to have capital punishment?

General Topics, Not Research Questions
- Treatment of alcohol and drug abuse
- Sexuality and aging

Set of Variables, Not Questions
- Capital punishment and racial discrimination
- Urban decay and gangs

Too Vague, Ambiguous
- Do police affect delinquency?
- What can be done to prevent child abuse?

Need to Be Still More Specific
- Has the incidence of child abuse risen?
- How does poverty affect children?
- What problems do children who grow up in poverty experience that others do not?

GOOD RESEARCH QUESTIONS

Exploratory Questions
- Has the incidence of new forms of child abuse appeared in Wisconsin in the past 10 years?

Descriptive Questions
- Is child abuse, violent or sexual, more common in families that have experienced a divorce than in intact, never-divorced families?
- Are the children raised in impoverished households more likely to have medical, learning, and social-emotional adjustment difficulties than children who are not living in poverty?

Explanatory Questions
- Does the emotional instability created by experiencing a divorce increase the chances that divorced parents will physically abuse their children?
- Is a lack of sufficent funds for preventive treatment a major cause of more serious medical problems among children raised in families in poverty?

We also want to specify the **universe** to which we generalize answers to a research question. All research questions and studies apply to some category of people, organizations, or other units. The universe is the set of all units that the research question covers or to which we can generalize. For example, in Pager's (2007) study, his units were individuals, specifically young White and Black men. The universe to which we might generalize his findings includes all U.S. males in their twenties of these two racial categories.

As we refine a topic into a research question and design a study, we also need to consider practical limitations. Designing the perfect research project is an interesting academic exercise, but if we expect to carry out a study, practical limitations must shape its design. Major limitations include time, costs, access to resources, approval from authorities, ethical concerns, and expertise. If we have 10 hours a week for 5 weeks to conduct a research project but answering the research question will require 2 years,

we must narrow the question to fit the practical limitations.

Time is always a consideration. However, it is very difficult to estimate the time required for a study. A specific research question, the research techniques used, the complexity of the study, and the amount and types of data we plan to collect all affect the amount of time required. Experienced researchers are the best source for getting good estimates of time requirements.

Cost is another limitation, and we cannot answer some research questions because of the great expense involved. For example, our research question asks whether sports fans develop strong positive feelings toward team mascots if the team has a winning season but negative feelings if it has

Universe The entire category or class of units that is covered or explained by a relationship or hypothesis.

TABLE 6.1   Quantitative Research versus Qualitative Research

QUANTITATIVE RESEARCH	QUALITATIVE RESEARCH
Researchers test hypotheses that are stated at the beginning.	Researchers capture and discover meaning once they become immersed in the data.
Concepts are in the form of distinct variables.	Concepts are in the form of themes, motifs, generalizations, and taxonomies.
Measures are systematically created before data collection and are standardized.	Measures are created in an ad hoc manner and are often specific to the individual setting or researcher.
Data are in the form of numbers from precise measurement.	Data are in the form of words and images from documents, observations, and transcripts.
Theory is largely causal and is deductive.	Theory can be causal or noncausal and is often inductive.
Procedures are standard, and replication is frequent.	Research procedures are particular, and replication is very rare.
Analysis proceeds by using statistics, tables, or charts and discussing how what they show relates to hypotheses.	Analysis proceeds by extracting themes or generalizations from evidence and organizing data to present a coherent, consistent picture.

a losing season. To examine the question for all sports teams across a nation across a decade would require a great investment of time and money. The focus could be narrowed to one sport (football), to sports played in college, and to student fans at just four colleges across three seasons. As with time, experienced researchers can help provide estimates of the cost to conduct a study.

Access to resources is a common limitation. Resources include expertise, special equipment, and information. For example, a research question about burglary rates and family income in many different nations is nearly impossible to answer. Data on burglary and income are not collected or available for many countries. Other questions require the approval of authorities (e.g., to see medical records) or involve violating basic ethical principles (e.g., lying to a person and endangering her or him). Our expertise or background as researchers is also a limitation. Answering some research questions involves the use of data collection techniques, statistical methods, knowledge of a foreign language, or skills we may not have. Unless we acquire the necessary training or can

pay for another person's services, the research question may not be practical.

In sum, qualitative and quantitative studies share a great deal, but they differ on several design issues: logic, research path, mode of verification, and way to arrive at a research question (see Table 6.1). In addition, the research approaches speak different "languages" and emphasize distinct study design features, issues that we consider in the next section.

QUALITATIVE DESIGN ISSUES

The Language of Cases and Contexts

Most qualitative studies involve a language of cases and contexts, employ *bricolage* (discussed later in this chapter), examine social processes and cases in their social context, and study interpretations or meanings in specific socio-cultural settings. We examine social life from multiple points of view and explain how people construct identities. Only rarely do we use variables, test hypotheses, or create precise measures in the form of numbers.

Most qualitative studies build on the assumption that certain areas of social life are intrinsically qualitative. For this reason, qualitative data are not imprecise or deficient but are very meaningful. Instead of trying to convert fluid, active social life into variables or numbers, we borrow ideas and viewpoints from the people we study and situate them in a fluid natural setting. Instead of variables, we examine motifs, themes, distinctions, and perspectives. Most often, our approach is inductive and relies on a form of *grounded theory* (discussed in Chapter 3).

Qualitative data may appear to be soft, intangible, and elusive. This does not mean that we cannot capture them. We gather qualitative data by documenting real events, recording what actual people say (with words, gestures, and tone), observing specific behaviors, examining written documents, and studying visual images. These are specific, concrete aspects of the social world. As we closely scrutinize photos or videotapes of people or social events, we are looking at "hard" physical evidence.[10] The evidence is just as "hard" and physical as the numeric measures of attitudes, social pressure, intelligence, and the like found in a quantitative study.

Grounded Theory

In qualitative research, we may develop theory during the data collection process. This largely inductive method means that we are building theory from data or ground the theory in the data. Grounded theory adds flexibility and allows the data and theory to interact. This process also helps us remain open to the unexpected. We can change direction of study and even abandon the original research question in the middle of a project if we discover something new and exciting.[11]

We build theory by making comparisons. For example, we observe an event (e.g., a police officer confronting a speeding motorist who has stopped). We may ponder questions and look for similarities and differences. When watching a police officer, we ask: Does the police officer always radio in the car's license number before proceeding? After radioing the car's location, does the officer ask the motorist to get out of the car or some times casually walk up to the car and talk to the seated driver? When we intersperse data collection and theorizing, new

theoretical questions may arise that suggest future observations. In this way, we tailor new data to answer theoretical questions that arose only from thinking about previous data.

In grounded theory, we build from specific observations to broader concepts that organize observational data and then continue to build principles or themes that connect the concepts. Compared to other ways of theorizing, grounded theory tends to be less abstract and closer to concrete observations or specific events. Building inductively from the data to theory creates strong data-theory linkages. However, this can be a weakness as well. It may make connecting concepts and principles across many diverse settings difficult, and it may slow the development of concepts that build toward creating general, abstract knowledge. To counteract this weakness, we become familiar with the concepts and theories developed in other studies to apply shared concepts when appropriate and to note any similarities and differences. In this way, we can establish cross-study interconnections and move toward generalized knowledge.

The Context Is Critical

In qualitative research, we usually emphasize the social context because the meaning of a social action, event, or statement greatly depends on the context in which it appears. If we strip social context from an event, social action, or conversation, it is easy to distort its meaning and alter its social significance.

Social context includes time context (when something occurs), spatial context (where something occurs), emotional context (the feelings regarding how something occurs), and socio-cultural context (the social situation and cultural milieu in which something occurs). For example, a social activity (a card game, sexual act, or disagreement) occurs late at night on the street in a low-income area of a large city, a setting for drug use, fear and anger, violent crime, and prostitution within a cultural milieu of extreme racial-economic inequality. The same activity occurs midday in the backyard of a large house in an affluent suburban neighborhood in a social setting of relaxation and leisure, surrounded by trust and emotional closeness, and within a cultural milieu of established affluence and privilege. The context will significantly color the activity's meaning. With different contextual meanings, the same activity or behavior may have different consequences.

In a quantitative study, we rarely treat context as important. We often strip it away as being "messy" or just "noise" and instead concentrate on precise counts or numerical measures. Thus, what a qualitative study might treat as essential may be seen as irrelevant noise in a quantitative study. For example, if a quantitative study counts the number of votes across time or cultures, a qualitative researcher might consider what voting means

in the context. He or she may treat the same behavior (e.g., voting for a presidential candidate) differently depending on the social context in which it occurs (see Example Box 6.3, Example of Importance of Context for Meaning).

Context goes beyond social events, behaviors, and statements to include physical objects. One handgun could be an art object, part of a recreational hobby, a key element in committing a violent crime, evidence of an irresponsible parent, a suicide facilitator, or a means of social peace and community protection, each depending on the context. Without including the surrounding context, we cannot assign meaning to an object.

EXAMPLE BOX **6.3**

Example of the Importance of Context for Meaning

"Voting in a national election" has different meanings in different contexts:

1. *A one-party dictatorship with unopposed candidates, where people are required by law to vote.* The names of nonvoters are recorded by the police. Nonvoters are suspected of being antigovernment subversives. They face fines and possible job loss for not voting.
2. *A country in the midst of violent conflict between rebels and those in power.* Voting is dangerous because the armed soldiers on either side may shoot voters they suspect of opposing their side. The outcome of the vote will give power to one or the other group and dramatically restructure the society. Anyone over the age of 16 can vote.
3. *A context in which people choose between a dozen political parties of roughly equal power that represent very different values and policies.* Each party has a sizable organization with its own newspapers, social clubs, and neighborhood organizers. Election days are national holidays when no one has to work. A person votes by showing up with an identification card at any of many local voting locations. Voting itself is by secret ballot, and everyone over age 18 can vote.
4. *A context in which voting is conducted in public by White males over age 21 who have regular jobs.* Family, friends, and neighbors see how one another vote. Political parties do not offer distinct policies; instead, they are tied to ethnic or religious groups and are part of a person's ethnic-religious identity. Ethnic and religious group identities are very strong. They affect where one lives, where one works, whom one marries, and the like. Voting follows massive parades and week-long community events organized by ethnic and religious groups.
5. *A context in which one political party is very powerful and is challenged by one or two very small, weak alternatives.* The one party has held power for the past 60 years through corruption, bribery, and intimidation. It has the support of leaders throughout society (in religious organizations, educational institutions, businesses, unions, and the mass media). The jobs of anyone working in any government job (e.g., every police officer, post office clerk, schoolteacher, and garbage collector) depend on the political party staying in power.
6. *A context in which the choice is between two parties with little difference between them.* People select candidates primarily on the basis of television advertising. Candidates pay for advertising with donations by wealthy people or powerful organizations. Voting is a vague civic obligation that few people take seriously. Elections are held on a workday. In order to vote, a person must meet many requirements and register to vote several weeks in advance. Recent immigrants and anyone arrested for a crime are prohibited from voting.

Bricolage

A *bricoleur* is someone who has learned to be adept in diverse areas, can draw on a variety of sources, and makes do with whatever is at hand.[12] The **bricolage** technique involves working with one's hands and combining odds and ends in a practical, skilled, and inventive way to accomplish a task. A successful *bricoleur* possesses a deep knowledge of materials, a set of esoteric skills, and a capacity to combine or create flexibly. The typical *bricoleur* is often a highly inventive and skilled craftsperson, repairperson, or jack-of-all-trades.

A qualitative study draws on a variety of skills, materials, and approaches as needed. This usually happens when we are unable to anticipate the need for them. The process of mixing diverse source materials, applying disparate approaches, and assembling bits and pieces into a whole is analogous to the bricolage of a skilled craftsperson who is able to create or repair many things by using whatever is available at the time.

The Case and Process

We can divide all empirical social research into two groups: *case study* (with one or a few cases) or *cross-case* (comprising many cases).[13] Most qualitative studies use a "case-oriented approach [that] places cases, not variables, center stage" (Ragin, 1992a:5). Thus, we examine many aspects of a few cases. The intensive, in-depth study a handful of cases replaces the extensive, surface-level study of numerous cases as is typical in quantitative research. Often a case-oriented analysis emphasizes contingencies in "messy" natural settings (i.e., the co-occurrence of many specific factors and events in one place and at one time). Rather than precise measures of a huge number of cases, as is typical of quantitative research, we acquire in-depth of knowledge and an astute insight into a small number of cases.

The study of cases tends to produce complex explanations or interpretations in the form of an unfolding plot or a narrative story about particular people or specific events. This makes the passage of time integral to the explanation. Often the empha-

sis becomes the sequence of events: what occurred first, second, third, and so on. This focus on process helps to reveal how an issue evolves, a conflict emerges, or a social relationship develops.

Interpretation

To interpret means to assign significance or coherent meaning. In quantitative research, meaning comes from using numbers (e.g., percentages or statistical coefficients), and we explain how the numerical data relate to the hypotheses. Qualitative studies rarely include tables with numbers. The only visual presentations of data may be maps, photographs, or diagrams showing how ideas are related. We instead weave the data into discussions of the ideas' significance. The data are in the form of words, including quotes or descriptions of particular events. Any numerical information is supplementary to the textual evidence.

Qualitative studies give data meaning, translate them, or make them understandable. We begin with the point of view of the people we study and then find out how they see the world and define situations. We learn what events, behaviors, and activities mean for them. To begin qualitative interpretation, we first must learn the meanings of things for the people we are studying.[14]

People who create social activities and behavior have personal reasons or motives for what they do. This is **first-order interpretation**. As we discover and reconstruct this first-order interpretation, it becomes a **second-order interpretation** because we come from the outside to discover what has occurred. In a second-order interpretation, we elicit an underlying coherence or sense of meaning in the

Bricolage   Improvisation by drawing on diverse materials that are lying about and using them in creative ways to accomplish a pragmatic task.

First-order interpretation   Interpretations from the point of view of the people being studied.

Second-order interpretation   Qualitative interpretations from the point of view of the researcher who conducted a study.

data. Meaning develops only in relation to a large set of other meanings, not in a vacuum. In a second-order interpretation, we place the human action being studied into a "stream of behavior" or events to which it is related: its context.

If we were to adopt a very strict interpretive approach, we might stop at a second-order inter-pretation, that is, once we understand the signifi-cance of the action for the people we study. Most qualitative researchers go further. They want to generalize or link the second-order interpretation to a theory or general knowledge. They move to a broad level of interpretation, or **third-order interpretation** by which they assign general theo-retical significance to the data.

Because interpreting social meaning in context is often a major purpose and outcome of qualitative studies, keep in mind that the three steps or orders of interpretation help provide a way to organize the research process.

QUANTITATIVE DESIGN ISSUES

The Language of Variables and Hypotheses

Variation and Variables. Simply defined, a **variable** is a concept that varies. In quantitative research, we use a language of variables and relationships among variables.

In Chapter 3, we discussed two types of con-cepts: those that refer to a fixed phenomenon (e.g., the ideal type of bureaucracy) and those that vary in quantity, intensity, or amount (e.g., amount of edu-cation). Variables are this second type of concept and measures of the concepts.

A variable must have two or more values. Once we become aware of them, we see variables every-where. For example, gender is a variable; it can take one of two values: male or female. Marital status is

a variable; it can take the value of never married single, married, divorced, or widowed. Type of crime committed is a variable; it can take values of robbery, burglary, theft, murder, and so forth. Fam-ily income is a variable; it can take values from zero to billions of dollars. A person's attitude toward abortion is a variable; as a woman's basic right can range from strongly favoring legal abortion to strongly believing in the sanctity of fetal life.

A variable's values or categories are its **attri-butes**. It is easy to confuse variables with attributes. The confusion arises because one variable's attri-bute can itself be a separate variable in its own right with only a slight change in definition. This rests on a distinction between concepts that vary and the conditions within concepts that vary. For example, "male" is not a variable; it describes a category of gender. Male is an attribute of the variable gender, yet a related idea, degree of masculinity, is a variable. It describes the intensity or strength of attachment to a set of beliefs, orientations, and behaviors that are associated with the concept of masculine within a culture. Likewise, "married" is not a variable; it is an attribute of the variable marital status. Related ideas such as number of years married or depth of commitment to a mar-riage are variables. In a third example, "robbery" is not a variable; but an attribute of the variable type of crime. Number of robberies, robbery rate, amount taken during a robbery, and type of robbery are all variables because they vary or take on a range of values.

In quantitative research, we redefine all con-cepts into the language of variables. As the examples of variables and attributes illustrate, the redefini-tion often requires only a slight change in defi-nition. As noted in Chapter 3, concepts are the building blocks of theory; they organize thinking about the social world. Clear concepts with careful definitions are essential in theory.

Types of Variables. As we focus on causal rela-tions among variables, we usually begin with an effect and then search for its cause(s). We can clas-sify variables depending on their location in a causal relationship or chain of causality. The cause variable, or the force or condition that acts on something else,

---

Third-order interpretation   Qualitative interpreta-tions made by the readers of a research report.

Variable   A concept or its empirical measure that can take on multiple values.

Attributes   The categories or levels of a variable.

is the **independent variable**. The variable that is the effect, result, or outcome of another variable is the **dependent variable**. The independent variable is "independent of" prior causes that have acted on it whereas the dependent variable depends on the cause.

It is not always easy to determine whether a variable is independent or dependent. Two questions can help to identify the independent variable. First, does it come before other variables in time? Independent variables must come before any other type. Second, if two variables occur at the same time, does one variable have an impact on another variable? Independent variables affect or have an impact on other variables. We often phrase research topics and questions in terms of the dependent variable because dependent variables are the phenomena we want to explain. For example, an examination of the reasons for an increase in the crime rate in Dallas, Texas would have the dependent variable as the crime rate in Dallas.

A simple causal relationship requires only an independent and a dependent variable. A third variable type, the **intervening variable**, appears in more complex causal relations. Coming between the independent and dependent variables, this variable helps to show the link or mechanism between them. As noted in Chapter 3, advances in knowledge depend not only on documenting cause-and-effect relationships but also on specifying the mechanisms that account for the causal relation. In a sense, the intervening variable acts as a dependent variable with respect to the independent variable and acts as an independent variable toward the dependent variable.

For example, French sociologist Émile Durkheim developed a theory of suicide that specified a causal relationship between marital status and suicide rate. Durkheim found evidence that married people are less likely to commit suicide than single people. He believed that married people have more social integration (i.e., feelings of belonging to a group or family). He thought that a major cause of one type of suicide was that people lacked a sense of belonging to a group. Thus, his theory can be restated as a three-variable relationship: marital status (independent variable) causes the degree of

social integration (intervening variable), which affects suicide (dependent variable). Specifying the chain of causality makes the linkages in a theory clearer and helps a researcher test complex explanations.[15]

Simple theories have one dependent and one independent variable whereas complex ones can contain dozens of variables with multiple independent, intervening, and dependent variables. For example, a theory of criminal behavior (dependent variable) identifies four independent variables: an individual's economic hardship, opportunities to commit crime easily, membership in a deviant subgroup that does not disapprove of crime, and lack of punishment for criminal acts. A multicause explanation usually specifies which independent variable has the most significant causal effect.

A complex theoretical explanation has a string of multiple intervening variables. For example, family disruption causes lower self-esteem among children, which causes depression, which causes poor grades in school, which causes reduced prospects for a good job, which causes a lower adult income. The chain of variables is family disruption (independent), childhood self-esteem (intervening), depression (intervening), grades in school (intervening), job prospects (intervening), adult income (dependent).

Two theories on the same topic can differ as to the number of independent variables. In addition, theories might agree about the independent and dependent variables but differ on the intervening variable or causal mechanism. For example, two theories say that family disruption causes lower adult income, each for different reasons. One theory

Independent variable   A type of variable that produces an effect or results on a dependent variable in a causal hypothesis.

Dependent variable   The effect or result variable that is caused by an independent variable in a causal hypothesis.

Intervening variable   A variable that comes logically or temporally after the independent variable and before the dependent variable and through which their causal relation operates.

holds that disruption encourages children to join deviant peer groups, which are not socialized to the norms of work and thrift. Another theory emphasizes the impact of the disruption on childhood depression and poor academic performance. In the second theory, depression and limited school learning directly cause poor job performance.

In one study, we usually test only one or a few parts of a causal chain. For example, a research project examining six variables may take the six from a large, complex theory with two dozen variables. Explicit links to a larger theory strengthen and clarify a research project.

Causal Theory and Hypotheses

The Hypothesis and Causality. A **causal hypothesis** is a proposition to be tested or a tentative statement of a relationship between two variables. Hypotheses are guesses about how the social world works; they are stated in a value-neutral form. Kerlinger (1979:35) noted that,

> *Hypotheses are much more important in scientific research than they would appear to be just by knowing what they are and how they are constructed. They have a deep and highly significant purpose of taking man out of himself. . . . Hypotheses are powerful tools for the advancement of knowledge, because, although formulated by man, they can be tested and shown to be correct or incorrect apart from man's values and beliefs.*

A causal hypothesis has five characteristics (see Expansion Box 6.4, Five Characteristics of Causal Hypotheses). For example, we can restate the hypothesis that attending religious services reduces the probability of divorce as a prediction: Couples who attend religious services frequently have a lower divorce rate than do couples who rarely attend religious services. We can test the prediction against the empirical evidence. We should logically

> **Causal hypothesis** A statement of a causal explanation or proposition that has at least one independent and one dependent variable and has yet to be empirically tested.

EXPANSION BOX 6.4

Five Characteristics of Casual Hypotheses

1. They have at least two variables.
2. They express a causal or cause–effect relationship between the variables.
3. They can be expressed as a prediction or an expected future outcome.
4. They are logically linked to a research question and a theory.
5. They are falsifiable; that is, they are capable of being tested against empirical evidence and shown to be true or false.

---

connect the hypothesis to a research question and to a broader theory; after all, we test hypotheses to answer the research question or to find empirical support for a theory. Statements that are logically or necessarily true, or questions that are impossible to answer through empirical observation (e.g., What is the "good life"? Is there a God?) are not scientific hypotheses.

We can state causal hypotheses in several ways. Sometimes we use the word *cause,* but it is not necessary. For example, we can state a causal hypothesis between religious attendance and a reduced likelihood of divorce in ten different ways (see Example Box 6.4, Ways to State Causal Relations).

In scientific research, we avoid using the term *proved* when talking about testing hypotheses. Journalism, courts of law, and advertisements use the word *proof,* but a research scientist almost never uses it. A jury says that the evidence "proves" someone guilty, or a television commercial will state, "Studies prove that our aspirin cures headaches the fastest." This is not the language of scientific research. In science, we recognize that knowledge is tentative and that creating knowledge is an ongoing process that avoids premature closure. The word *proof* implies finality, absolute certainty, or something that does not need further investigation. It is too strong a term for the cautious world of science. We might say that the evidence supports or confirms, but does not prove, the hypothesis. Even after hundreds of studies show the same results, such as

EXAMPLE BOX **6.4**

Ways to State Casual Relations

- Religious attendance *causes* reduced divorce.
- Religious attendance *leads to* reduced divorce.
- Religious attendance *is related to* reduced divorce.
- Religious attendance *influences* the reduction of divorce.
- Religious attendance *is associated with* reduced divorce.
- Religious attendance *produces* reduced divorce.
- Religious attendance *results in* reduced divorce.
- *If* people attend religious services, *then* the likelihood of divorce will be reduced.
- *The higher* religious attendance, *the lower* the likelihood of divorce.
- Religious attendance *reduces* the likelihood of divorce.

the link between cigarette smoking and lung cancer, scientists do not say that we have absolute proof. Instead we can say that overwhelming evidence, or all studies to date, support or are consistent with the hypothesis. Scientists never want to close off the possibility of discovering new evidence that might contradict past findings. They do not want to cut off future inquiry or stop exploring intervening mechanisms. History contains many examples of relationships that people once thought to be proved but were later found to be in error. We can use *proof* when referring to logical or mathematical relations, as in a mathematical proof, but not for empirical research.

Testing and Refining a Hypothesis. Knowledge rarely advances on the basis of one test of a single hypothesis. In fact, researchers can get a distorted picture of the research process by focusing on a single study that tests one hypothesis. Knowledge develops over time as many researchers across the scientific community test many hypotheses. It slowly grows from shifting and winnowing through many hypotheses. Each hypothesis represents an explanation of a dependent variable. If the evidence fails to support some hypotheses, they are gradually eliminated from consideration. Those that receive support remain in

contention. Theorists and researchers constantly create new hypotheses to challenge those that have received support (see Figure 6.3 on page 182). From Figure 6.3 we see that in 2010, three hypotheses are in contention, but from 1970 to 2010, eleven hypotheses were considered, and over time, eight of them were rejected in one or more tests.

Scientists are a skeptical group. Supporting a hypothesis in one study is not sufficient for them to accept it. The principle of replication says that a hypothesis needs several tests with consistent and repeated support before it can gain broad acceptance. Another way to strengthen confidence in a hypothesis is to test related causal linkages in the theory from which it comes.

As scientists, we accept the strongest contender with the greatest empirical support as the best explanation at the time. The more alternatives we test a hypothesis against, the more confidence we have in it. Some tests are called **crucial experiments** or crucial studies. This is a type of study whereby

> *two or more alternative explanations for some phenomenon are available, each being compatible with the empirically given data; the crucial experiment is designed to yield results that can be accounted for by only one of the alternatives, which is thereby shown to be "the correct explanation." (Kaplan, 1964:151–152)*

Thus, the infrequent crucial experiment is an important test of theory. Hypotheses from two different theories confront each other in crucial experiments, and one is knocked out of the competition. It is rare, but significant, when it occurs.

Types of Hypotheses. Hypotheses are links in a theoretical causal chain and are used to test the direction and strength of a relationship between variables. When a hypothesis defeats its competitors, it supports the researcher's explanation. A curious aspect of hypothesis testing is that researchers treat

Crucial experiment A direct comparison and evaluation of competing explanations of the same phenomenon designed to show that one is superior to the other.

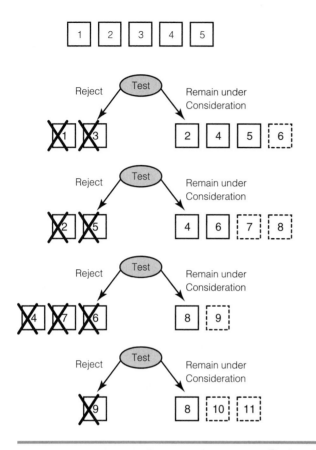

1970

There are five possible hypotheses.

1980

Two of the original five hypotheses are rejected.
A new one is developed.

1990

Two hypotheses are rejected.
Two new ones are developed.

2000

Three hypotheses are rejected.
A new one is developed.

2010

One hypothesis is rejected.
Two new ones are developed.

FIGURE 6.3 **How the Process of Hypotheses Testing Operates over Time**

evidence that supports a hypothesis differently from evidence that opposes it: They give negative evidence more importance. The idea that negative evidence is critical when evaluating a hypothesis comes from the **logic of disconfirming hypotheses**.[16] It is associated with Karl Popper's idea of falsification

> **Logic of disconfirming hypothesis** The logic for the null hypothesis based on the idea that confirming empirical evidence makes a weak case for the existence of a relationship; instead of gathering supporting evidence, testing that no relationship exists provides more cautious, indirect support for its possible existence.

(see Chapter 4 under positivism) and with the use of null hypotheses (see later in this section).

Recall the preceding discussion of proof. We never prove a hypothesis; however, we can disprove it. With supporting evidence, we can say only that the hypothesis remains a possibility or that it is still being considered. Negative evidence is more significant. With it, the hypothesis becomes "tarnished" or "soiled" because a hypothesis makes predictions. Negative and disconfirming evidence shows that the predictions are wrong. Positive or confirming evidence for a hypothesis is less critical because various alternative hypotheses may make the same prediction. When we find confirming evidence for a prediction, we may elevate one explanation over its alternatives that could also have confirming evidence.

For example, a man stands on a street corner with an umbrella and claims that his umbrella protects him from falling elephants. He has supporting evidence for his hypothesis that the umbrella provides protection. He has not had a single elephant fall on him in all of the time he has had his umbrella open, yet such supportive evidence is weak; it also is consistent with an alternative hypothesis: elephants do not fall from the sky. Both hypotheses predict that the man will be safe from falling elephants. Negative evidence for the hypothesis—the one elephant that falls on him and his umbrella, crushing both—would destroy the hypothesis for good!

We can test hypotheses in two ways: in a straightforward way and in a null hypothesis way. Many quantitative researchers, especially experimenters, frame hypotheses in terms of a **null hypothesis** based on the logic of the disconfirming hypotheses. These researchers look for evidence that will allow them to accept or reject the null hypothesis. Most people talk about a hypothesis as a way to predict a relationship. The null hypothesis does the opposite. It predicts no relationship. For example, Sarah believes that students who live on campus in dormitories get higher grades than students who live off campus and commute to college. Her null hypothesis is that there is no relationship between residence and grades. Researchers use the null hypothesis with a corresponding **alternative hypothesis** or experimental hypothesis. The alternative hypothesis says that a relationship exists. Sarah's alternative hypothesis is that students' on-campus residence has a positive effect on grades.

For most people, the null hypothesis approach seems like a backward way to think about hypothesis testing. Using a null hypothesis rests on the assumption that we want to discover a relationship. Because of our inner desire to find relationships, we need to design hypothesis testing to make finding relationships very demanding. When we use the null hypothesis approach, we directly test only the null hypothesis. If evidence supports or leads us to accept the null hypothesis, we conclude that

the tested relationship does not exist. This implies that the alternative hypothesis is false. On the other hand, if we find evidence to reject the null hypothesis, the alternative hypotheses remain a possibility. We cannot prove the alternative; rather, by testing the null hypotheses, we keep the alternative hypotheses in contention. When we add null hypothesis testing to confirming evidence, the argument for alterative hypotheses can become stronger over time.

If all this discussion of null hypothesis is confusing to you, remember that the scientific community is extremely cautious. After all, it is in the business of creating genuine, verified truth. It would prefer to consider a causal relationship as false until mountains of evidence show it to be true. This is similar to the Anglo-American legal idea of innocent until proved guilty. We assume, or act as though, the null hypothesis is correct until *reasonable doubt* suggests otherwise. When we use null hypotheses, we can also use specific statistical tests (e.g., *t*-test or *F*-test) designed for this way of thinking. Thus, we say there is reasonable doubt in a null hypothesis if a statistical test suggests that the odds of it being false are 99 in 100. This is what we mean when we say that statistical tests allow us to "reject the null hypothesis at the .01 level of significance" (we will discuss statistical significance further in Chapter 12).

Another type of hypothesis is the **double-barreled hypothesis**.[17] It shows unclear thinking and creates unnecessary confusion and should be

---

Null hypothesis A hypothesis stating that there is no significant effect of an independent variable on a dependent variable.

Alternative hypothesis A hypothesis paired with the null hypothesis that says an independent variable has a significant effect on a dependent variable.

Double-barreled hypothesis A confusing and poorly designed hypothesis with two independent variables in which it is unclear whether one or the other variable or both in combination produce an effect.

avoided. A double-barreled hypothesis puts two separate relationships into one hypothesis. For example, we say that poverty and a high concentration of teenagers in an area cause property crime to increase. This is double barreled. We might mean either of two things: that poverty *or* a high concentration of teenagers causes property crime or that *only* the combination of poverty with a high concentration of teenagers causes property crime. If "either one" is intended and only one independent variable has an effect, the results of hypothesis testing are unclear. For example, if the evidence shows that poverty causes crime but a concentration of teenagers does not, is the hypothesis supported? If we intend the combination hypothesis, then we really mean that the joint occurrence of poverty with a high concentration of teenagers only, but neither alone, causes property crime. If we intend the combination meaning, it is not double barreled. We need to be very clear and state the combination hypothesis explicitly. The term for a combination hypothesis is the *interaction effect* (interaction effects are discussed later; also see Figure 6.4).

Potential Errors in Causal Explanation

Developing a good explanation for any theory (i.e., causal, interpretive, or network) requires avoiding some common logical errors. These errors can enter while starting a study, while interpreting and analyzing quantitative data, or while collecting and analyzing qualitative data. Such errors can be referred to as *fallacies* or *false explanations* that may deceptively appear to be legitimate on the surface but have serious problems once they are more deeply investigated.

Tautology An error in explanation in which the causal factor (independent variable) and the result (dependent variable) are actually the same or restatements of one another, making an apparent causal relationship true by definition.

Teleology An error in explanation in which the causal relationship is empirically untestable because the causal factor does not come earlier in time than the result or because the causal factor is a vague, general force that cannot be empirically measured.

Tautology. A **tautology** is a form of circular reasoning. We appear to say something new but are really talking in circles and making a statement that is *true by definition*. We cannot test tautologies with empirical data. For example, I heard a news report about a representative in the U.S. Congress who argued for a new crime law that would send many more 14- and 15-year-olds to adult courts. When asked why he was interested only in harsh punishment, not prevention, the representative said that offenders would learn that crime does not pay and that would prevent crime. He believed that the only prevention that worked was harsh punishment. This sounded a bit odd when I heard it. So, I reexamined the argument and realized it was tautological (i.e., it contained a logic error). The representative essentially said punishment resulted in prevention because he had redefined *prevention* as being the same as *punishment*. Logically, he said punishment caused prevention because harsh punishment was prevention. Politicians may confuse the public with circular reasoning, but social researchers need to learn how to see through and avoid such garble.

Example. A conservative is a person with certain attitudes, beliefs, and values (desires less government regulation, no taxes on upper income people, a strong military, religion taught in public schools, an end to antidiscrimination laws, etc.). It is a tautology to say that wanting less regulation, a strong military, and so on *causes* conservatism. In sloppy everyday usage, we can say, "Sally is conservative *because* she believes that there should be less regulation." This appears to be a causal statement, but it is not. The set of attitudes is a *reason* to label Sally as a conservative, but those attitudes cannot be the *cause* of Sally's conservatism. Her attitudes *are* conservatism, so the statement is true by definition. It would be impossible ever to obtain evidence showing that those attitudes were not associated with conservatism.

Teleology. A **teleology** is something directed by an ultimate purpose or goal. It can take two forms. First, it is associated with an event that occurs because it is in "God's plan" or in some overarching, mysterious unseen and unknowable force. In other

HYPOTHESIS: Poverty and a high concentration of teenagers in an area cause property crime to increase.

DOUBLE-BARRELED HYPOTHESIS: This can mean one of three things:

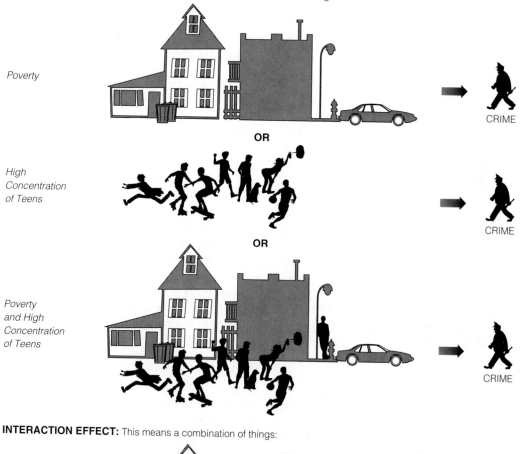

Poverty

OR

High
Concentration
of Teens

OR

Poverty
and High
Concentration
of Teens

INTERACTION EFFECT: This means a combination of things:

Poverty
and High
Concentration
of Teens
Together

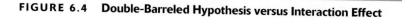

FIGURE 6.4   Double-Barreled Hypothesis versus Interaction Effect

words, an event occurs because God, or an unseen, unknowable master force has predetermined that it must occur. It is a teleology to say that something occurs because it is part of the "natural unfolding" of some all-powerful inner spirit or *Geist* (German for *spirit*). Thus, it is a teleology to say that a society develops in a certain direction because of the "spirit of the nation" or a "manifest destiny." Similar teleogical arguments rely on human nature as a cause, such as "Crime occurs because it is just human nature." Teleology has appeared in theories of history when someone says we are moving toward an "ideal society" or a utopia, and this movement explains events that are occurring today. Teleology has also been found in functional arguments. It is a teleology to say the family takes a certain form (e.g., nuclear) because the nuclear family fulfills social system "needs" for societal continuation. Logically, this says that the functional needs of the social system's survival into the distant future are the cause of the family form we see today. It is impossible to measure the cause and empirically test teleologies.

Teleology violates the temporal order requirement of causality. There is no true independent variable because the "causal factor" is extremely vague, distant, and unseen. Many people confuse goal motivation (i.e., a desire for something yet to occur) with teleology. I might say a goal causes an action. For example, my goal to get an A in a class caused me to get a good grade. My conscious goal or desire could be a legitimate cause and not be teleological. To show this, I need to outline the causal chain. First, we can empirically measure my mental condition (e.g., goals, desires, or aspirations) at some time point. This clarifies both the empirical evidence and temporal order issue. Second, we can compare my mental condition to future events that may or may not occur, such as getting a specific grade in a course. The mental condition can be a motivation that causes me to engage in certain behaviors, such as studying (an intervening variable). The studying behaviors could increase the chances that a future event (a course grade) will occur. Conscious human goals differ from the will of God, a society's *Geist,* or system needs, which we cannot empirically measure, have no fixed existence in time, and always match what occurs.

Example. The statement *The nuclear family is the dominant family form in Western industrial societies* because *it is functional for the survival of the society* is an untestable teleological statement from structural functional theory. It is saying "society's survival" *causes* "development of family form," yet the only way we can observe whether a society survives is after the fact, or as a consequence of its having had a form of the family. Here is another example of a teleological statement: *Because it was the destiny of the United States to become a major world power, we find thousands of immigrants entering the Western frontier during the early nineteenth century.* This says that "becoming a major world power," which occurred from 1920 to 1945, caused "westward migration," which took place between 1850 and 1890. It uses the obscure term *destiny,* which, like other similar terms (e.g., "in God's plan"), cannot be observed in causal relationships.

Ecological Fallacy. The **ecological fallacy** arises from a mismatch of units of analysis. It refers to a poor fit between the units for which we have empirical evidence and the units for which we want to make general statements. Ultimately, it comes down to imprecise reasoning and generalizing well beyond what the evidence warrants. Ecological fallacy occurs when we gather data at a *higher* or an *aggregated* unit of analysis but want to say something about a *lower* or *disaggregated* unit. It is a fallacy because what happens in one unit of analysis does not always hold for a different unit of analysis.[18] Thus, when we gather data for large aggregates (e.g., organizations, entire countries) and draw conclusions about the behavior of individuals from those data, we are creating an ecological fallacy. To

Ecological fallacy   An error in explanation in which empirical data about associations found among large-scale units of analysis are greatly overgeneralized and treated as evidence for statements about relationships among much smaller units.

avoid this error, we must ensure that the unit of analysis we use in an explanation is the same as or very close to the unit on which we collect data (see Example Box 6.5, The Ecological Fallacy).

Example.   About 45,000 people live in Tomsville and in Joansville. Tomsville has a high percentage of upper income people. More than half of the households in the town have family incomes of over $160,000. The town also has more motorcycles registered in it than any other town of its size. The town of Joansville has many poor people. Half of its households live below the poverty line. The town also has fewer motorcycles registered in it than any other town of its size. But it is a *fallacy* to say, on the basis of this information alone, that rich people are more likely to own motorcycles or that the evidence shows a relationship between family income and motorcycle ownership. The reason is that we do not know which families in Tomsville or Joansville own motorcycles. We know about only the two variables—average income and number of motorcycles—for the towns as a whole. The unit of analysis for observing variables is each town as a whole. Perhaps all of the low- and middle-income families in Tomsville belong to a motorcycle club, but not a single upper income family belongs to

one. Or perhaps one rich family and five poor ones in Joansville own motorcycles. To make a statement about the relationship between family ownership of motorcycles and family income, we have to collect information on families, not on towns as a whole.

Reductionism.   Another problem that involves a mismatch of units of analysis and imprecise reasoning about evidence is **reductionism**, also called the *fallacy of nonequivalence* (see Example Box 6.6, Error of Reductionism on page 188). This error occurs in an explanation of macro-level events using evidence about specific individuals. It occurs when a person observes a *lower* or *disaggregated* unit of analysis but makes statements about the operations of *higher* or *aggregated* units. In a way, it is a mirror image of the mismatch error in the ecological fallacy. A person makes this error when he

> **Reductionism**   An error in explanation in which empirical data about associations found among small-scale units of analysis are greatly overgeneralized and treated as evidence for statements about relationships among much larger units.

Researchers have criticized the famous study *Suicide* ([1897] 1957) by Émile Durkheim for the ecological fallacy of treating group data as though they were individual-level data. In the study, Durkheim compared the suicide rates of Protestant and Catholic districts in nineteenth-century western Europe and explained observed differences as due to dissimilarity between people's beliefs and practices in the two religions. He said that Protestants had a higher suicide rate than Catholics because the Protestants were more individualistic and had lower social integration. Durkheim and early researchers had data only by district. Because people tended to reside with others of the same religion, Durkheim used group-level data (i.e., region) for individuals.

Later researchers (van Poppel and Day, 1996) reexamined nineteenth century suicide rates with only individual-level data that they discovered for some areas. They compared the death records and looked at the official reason of death and religion, but their results differed from Durkheim's. Apparently, local officials at that time recorded deaths differently for people of different religions. They recorded "unspecified" as a reason for death far more often for Catholics because of the religion's strong moral prohibition against suicide. Durkheim's larger theory may be correct, yet the evidence he had to test it was weak because he used data aggregated at the group level while trying to explain the actions of individuals.

EXAMPLE BOX 6.6
Error of Reductionism

Suppose you pick up a book and read the following:

American race relations changed dramatically during the Civil Rights Era of the 1960s. Attitudes among the majority, White population shifted to greater tolerance as laws and court rulings changed across the nation. Opportunities that had been legally and officially closed to all but the White population—in the areas of housing, jobs, schooling, voting rights, and so on—were opened to people of all races. From the Brown vs. Board of Education *decision in 1955, to the Civil Rights Act of 1964, to the War on Poverty from 1966 to 1968, a new, dramatic outlook swept the country. This was the result of the vision, dedication, and actions of America's foremost civil rights leader, Dr. Martin Luther King, Jr.*

This says: *dependent variable* = major change in U.S. race relations over a 10- to 13-year period; *independent variable* = King's vision and actions.

If you know much about the civil rights era, you see a problem. The entire civil rights movement and its successes are attributed to a single individual. Yes, one individual does make a difference and helps build and guide a movement, but the *movement* is missing. The idea of a social-political movement as a causal force is reduced to its major leader. The distinct social phenomenon—a movement—is obscured. Lost are the actions of hundreds of thousands of people (marches, court cases, speeches, prayer meetings, sit-ins, rioting, petitions, beatings, etc.) involved in advancing a shared goal and the responses to them. The move-

ment's ideology, popular mobilization, politics, organization, and strategy are absent. Related macro-level historical events and trends that may have influenced the movement (e.g., Vietnam War protest, mood shift with the killing of John F. Kennedy, African American separatist politics, African American migration to urban North) are also ignored.

This error is not unique to historical explanations. Many people think in terms of only individual actions and have an individualist bias, sometimes called *methodological individualism*. This is especially true in the extremely individualistic U.S. culture. The error is that it disregards units of analysis or forces beyond the individual. The *error of reductionism* shifts explanation to a much lower unit of analysis. One could continue to reduce from an individual's behavior to biological processes in a person, to micro-level neurochemical activities, to the subatomic level.

Most people live in "social worlds" focused on local, immediate settings and their interactions with a small set of others, so their everyday sense of reality encourages seeing social trends or events as individual actions or psychological processes. Often, they become blind to more abstract, macro-level entities—social forces, processes, organizations, institutions, movements, or structures. The idea that all social actions cannot be reduced to individuals alone is the core of sociology. In his classic work *Suicide,* Émile Durkheim fought methodological individualism and demonstrated that larger, unrecognized social forces explain even highly individual, private actions.

---

or she has data on how individuals behave but wants to talk about the dynamics of macro-level units. It occurs because it is often easier to obtain data on individuals. Also, the operation of macro-level units is more abstract and nebulous. Lieberson argued that this error produces inconsistencies, contradictions, and confusion. He (1985:108, 113–114) forcefully stated:

Associations on the lower level are irrelevant for determining the validity of a proposition about processes operating on the higher level. As a mat-

ter of fact, no useful understanding of the higher-level structure can be obtained from lower-level analysis. . . . If we are interested in the higher-level processes and events, it is because we operate with the understanding that they have distinct qualities that are not simply derived by summing up the subunits.

As with the ecological fallacy, to avoid the error of reductionism, we must make certain that the unit of analyses in our explanation and for which we have empirical evidence are very close. When we fail to think precisely about the units of analysis and fail to couple the data closely with the theory, we might commit the ecological fallacy or error of reductionism. These are mistakes about having data that are appropriate for a research question and seriously overgeneralizing from the data.

It is possible to make assumptions about units of analysis other than the ones we study empirically. Thus, research on individuals rests on assumptions that individuals act within a set of social institutions. We base research on social institutions on assumptions about individual behavior. We know that many micro-level units join to form macro-level units. The danger is that it is easy to slide into using the behavior of micro units, such as individuals, to explain the actions of macro units, such as social institutions. What happens among units at one level does not necessarily hold for different units of analysis. Sociology as a field rests on the belief that a distinct level of social reality exists beyond the individual. Explanations of this level require data and theory that go beyond the individual alone. We cannot reduce the causes, forces, structures, or processes that exist among macro units to individual behavior.

Example.   Why did World War I occur? You may have heard that it was because a Serbian shot an archduke in the Austro-Hungarian Empire in 1914. This is reductionism. Yes, the assassination was a factor, but the macro-political event between nations—war—cannot be reduced to a specific act of one individual. If it could, we could also say that the war occurred because the assassin's alarm clock worked and woke him up that morning. If it had not worked, there would have been no assassination, so the alarm clock caused the war! The cause of the event, World War I, was much more complex and was due to many social, political, and economic forces that came together at a point in history. The actions of specific individuals had a role, but only a minor one compared to these macro forces. Individuals affect events, which eventually, in combination with large-scale social forces and organizations, affect others and move nations, but individual actions alone are not the cause. Thus, it

is likely that a war would have broken out at about that time even if the assassination had not occurred.

Spuriousness.   To call a relationship between variables *spurious* means that it is false, a mirage. We often get excited if we think we have found a spurious relationship because we can show the world to be more complex than it appears on the surface. Because any association between two variables might be spurious, we must be cautious when we discover that two variables are associated; upon further investigation, it may not be the basis for a causal relationship. It may be an illusion, just like the mirage that resembles a pool of water on a road during a hot day.

Spuriousness occurs when two variables are associated but are not causally related because an unseen third factor is the real cause (see Example Box 6.7, Spuriousness and Example Box 6.8, Night-Lights and Spuriousness on page 190). The third variable is the cause of both the apparent independent and the dependent variable. It accounts for the observed association. In terms of conditions for causality, the unseen third factor represents a more powerful alternative explanation.

How can you tell whether a relationship is spurious? How do you find out what the mysterious third factor might be? You will need to use statistical techniques (discussed later in this book) to test whether an association is spurious. To use them, you need a theory or at least a guess about possible third factors. Actually, spuriousness is based on some commonsense logic that you already use. For example, you know that an association exists between the use of air conditioners and ice cream cone consumption. If you measured the number of air conditioners in use and the number of ice cream cones sold each day, you would find a strong

Spuriousness   An apparent causal relationship that is illusionary due to the effect of an unseen or initially hidden causal factor; the unseen factor has a causal impact on both an independent and dependent variable, and produces the false impression that a relationship between them exists.

EXAMPLE BOX **6.7**

Spuriousness

In their study of the news media, Neuman and colleagues (1992) found a correlation between type of news source and knowledge. People who prefer to get their news from television are less knowledgeable than those who get it from print sources. This correlation is often interpreted as the "dumbing down" of information. In other words, television news causes people to know little.

The authors found that the relationship was spurious, however. "We were able to show that the entire relationship between television news preference and lower knowledge scores is spurious" (p. 113). They found that a third variable, initially unseen, explained both a preference for television news and a level of knowledge about current events. They said, "We find that what is really causing the television-is-the-problem effect is the preference for people with lower cognitive skill to get their news from television" (p. 98). The missing or hidden variable was "cognitive skill." The authors defined *cognitive skill* as a person's ability to use reason and manipulate abstract ideas. In other words, people who find it difficult to process abstract, complex information turn to television news. Others may also use the high-impact, entertaining television news sources, but they use them less and heavily supplement them with other more demanding, information-rich print sources. People who have weak information skills also tend to be less knowledgeable about current events and about other topics that require abstract thought or deal with complex information.

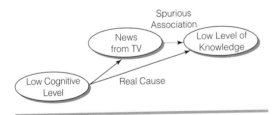

EXAMPLE BOX **6.8**

Night-Lights and Spuriousness

For many years, researchers observed a strong positive association between the use of a night-light and children who were nearsighted. Many thought that the night-light was somehow causing the children to develop vision problems (illustrated below). Other researchers could think of no reason for a causal link between night-light use and developing nearsightedness. A 1999 study provided the answer. It found that nearsighted parents are more likely to use night-lights; they also genetically pass on their vision deficiency to their children. The study found no link between night-light use and nearsightedness once parental vision was added to the explanation (see **b** below). Thus the initial causal link was misleading or spurious (from *New York Times,* May 22, 2001).

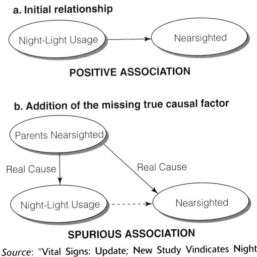

Source: "Vital Signs: Update; New Study Vindicates Night Lights" from *The New York Times,* Health Section, 5/22/2001 Issue, Page(s) 6.

correlation with more cones being sold on the days when more air conditioners are in use. But you know that eating ice cream cones does not cause people to turn on air conditioners. Instead, a third variable, hot days, causes both variables. You could verify this by measuring the daily temperature, ice cream consumption, and air conditioner use. In social research, opposing theories help us figure out which third factors are relevant for many topics (e.g., the causes of crime or the reasons for war or child abuse).

Example. Some people argue that taking illegal drugs causes suicide, school dropouts, and violent acts. Advocates of "drugs-are-the-problem" position point to the positive correlations between taking drugs and being suicidal, dropping out of school, and engaging in violence. The supporters argue that ending drug use will greatly reduce suicide, dropouts, and violence. Others argue that many people turn to drugs because of their emotional problems or high levels of disorder of their communities (e.g., high unemployment, unstable families, high crime, few community services, lack of civility). The people with emotional problems or who live in disordered communities are also more likely to commit suicide, drop out, and engage in violence. This means that reducing emotional problems and community disorder will cause illegal drug use, dropping out, suicide, and violence to decline greatly. Reducing drug taking alone will have only a limited effect because it ignores the root cause, which is not drugs. The "drugs-are-the-problem" argument is spurious because the initial relationship between taking illegal drugs and the problems that advocates identify is misleading. The emotional problems and community disorder are the true and often unseen causal variables.

We can now turn from the errors in causal explanation to avoid and move to other issues involving hypotheses. Table 6.2 provides a review of the major errors, and Figure 6.5 illustrates them.

From the Research Question to Hypotheses

It is difficult to move from a broad topic to hypotheses, but the leap from a well-formulated research question to hypotheses is a short one. A good research question has hypotheses embedded within it. In addition, hypotheses are tentative answers to research questions.

Consider this example of a research question: "Is age at marriage associated with divorce?" The question has two variables: "age at marriage" and "divorce." To develop a hypothesis, we must determine which is the independent variable. The independent variable is age at marriage because marriage must logically precede divorce. We may also ask what the direction of the relationship is. The hypothesis could be the following: "The lower the age at time of marriage, the higher the chances that the marriage will end in divorce." This hypothesis answers the research question and makes a

---

TABLE 6.2 Summary of Errors in Explanation

TYPE OF ERROR	SHORT DEFINITION	EXAMPLE
Tautology	The relationship is true by definition and involves circular reasoning.	Poverty is caused by having very little money.
Teleology	The cause is an intention that is inappropriate, or it has misplaced temporal order.	People get married in religious ceremonies because society wants them to.
Ecological fallacy	The empirical observations are at too high a level for the causal relationship that is stated.	New York has a high crime rate. Joan lives in New York. Therefore, she probably stole my watch.
Reductionism	The empirical observations are at too low a level for the causal relationship that is stated.	Because Steven lost his job and did not buy a new car, the country entered a long economic recession.
Spuriousness	An unseen third variable is the actual cause of both the independent and dependent variable.	Hair length is associated with TV programs. People with short hair prefer watching football; people with long hair prefer romance stories. (*Unseen:* Gender)

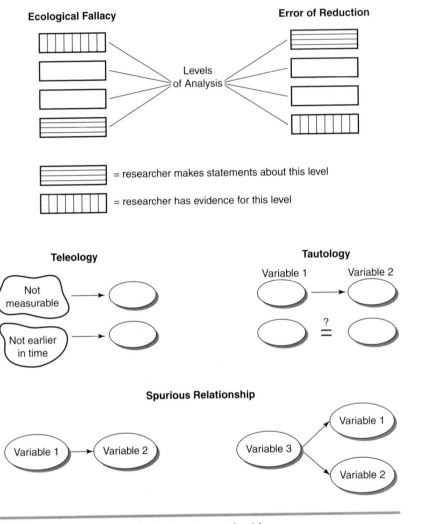

FIGURE 6.5 **Five Errors in Explanation to Avoid**

prediction. Notice that we can reformulate and better focus it now into: "Are couples who marry younger more likely to divorce?"

We can create several hypotheses for one research question. Another hypothesis from the same research question is as follows: "The smaller the difference between the ages of the marriage partners at the time of marriage, the less likely that the marriage will end in divorce." In this case, we specify the variable age at marriage differently.

We can have a hypothesis that specifies that a relationship holds under some conditions but not others. As Lieberson (1985:198) remarked, "In order to evaluate the utility of a given causal proposition, it is important that there be a clear-cut statement of the conditions under which it will operate." For example, a hypothesis states: The lower the age of the partners at time of marriage, the higher are the chances that the marriage will end in divorce, unless it is a marriage between members of a tight-knit traditional religious community in which early marriage is the norm.

Formulating a research question and a hypothesis does not have to proceed in fixed stages. We can formulate a tentative research question and then develop possible hypotheses; the hypotheses will help us to state the research question more precisely. The process is interactive and requires our creativity.

You may be wondering where theory fits into the process of moving from a topic to a testable hypothesis. Recall from Chapter 3 that theory takes many forms. We use general theoretical issues as a source of topics. Theories provide concepts that we turn into variables as well as the reasoning or mechanism that helps us connect variables together to produce a research question. A hypothesis can both answer a research question and be an untested proposition from a theory. We can express a hypothesis at an abstract, conceptual level or restate it in a more concrete, measurable form. Examples of specific studies may help to illustrate the parts of the research process. For examples of three quantitative studies, see Chart 6.1 on page 194; for two qualitative studies, see Chart 6.2 on page 195.

CONCLUSION

In this chapter, you encountered the groundwork needed to begin a study. You saw how differences in the qualitative and quantitative styles direct us to prepare for a study differently. In all types of research, you must narrow a topic into a more specific, focused research question. Each of the major approaches to doing research implies a different form and sequence of decisions as well as different answers as to when and how to focus on a research question. The most effective approach will depend on the topic you select, your purpose and intended use of study results, the orientation toward social science you adopt, and the your own assumptions and beliefs.

A quantitative study generally takes a linear path and emphasizes objectivity. In it you will use explicit, standardized procedures and a causal explanation. It uses the language of variables and hypotheses that is found across many areas of science that are based on a positivist tradition. The process is often deductive with a sequence of discrete steps that precede data collection: Narrow the topic to a more focused question, transform nebulous theoretical concepts into more exact variables, and develop one or more hypotheses to test. In actual practice, you will move back and forth, but the general process flows in a single, linear direction. In addition, you should take special care to avoid logical errors in hypothesis development and causal explanation.

In a qualitative study, you will likely follow a nonlinear path and emphasize becoming intimate with the details of a natural setting or a particular cultural-historical context. There are fewer standardized procedures or explicit steps, and you must often devise on-the-spot techniques for one situation or study. The language of cases and contexts directs you to conduct detailed investigations of particular cases or processes in a search for authenticity. Planning and design decisions are rarely separated into a distinct predata collection stage but continue to develop throughout early data collection. In fact, you use a more inductive qualitative style that encourages a slow, flexible evolution toward a specific focus based on what you learn from the data. Grounded theory emerges from your continuous reflections on the data and the context.

The qualitative and quantitative distinction is often overdrawn. Too often, it appears as a rigid dichotomy. Adherents of one approach judge the studies of the other approach on the basis of its own assumptions and standards. The quantitative researcher demands to know the variables used and the hypothesis tested. The qualitative researcher balks at turning humanity into cold numbers. A well-versed, prudent social researcher will understand and appreciate each approach to research on its own terms and recognize the strengths and limitations of each. The ultimate goal of developing a better understanding and explanation of the social world comes from an appreciation of what each has to offer.

CHART 6.1   Examples of Quantitative Studies

Study citation and title	Ridgeway and Erickson (2000), "Creating and Spreading Status Beliefs"	Musick, Wilson, and Bynum (2000), "Race and Formal Volunteering: The Differential Effects of Class and Religion"	Barlow, Barlow, and Chiricos (1995), "Economic Conditions and Ideologies of Crime in the Media"
Methodological technique used	Experiment	Survey	Content analysis
Topic	Processes by which people develop beliefs about the social status of others	Rates of volunteering by White and Black adults	U.S. mass media portrayals of law-breakers
Research question	As individuals interact, do external, structural factors that affect the interaction mold the beliefs they come to hold about entire categories of people in the future?	What different kinds of resources are available to Blacks and Whites that explain why Blacks are less likely to volunteer?	Do economic conditions affect how the media portray offenders?
Main hypothesis tested	People can be "taught" to make status distinctions among categories of people, who are actually equal, based on limited interaction in which one category exerts more skill.	Social class and religion affect whether Blacks volunteer differently than Whites.	The media distortion of crime shows offenders in a more negative way (blames them) when economic conditions are bad.
Main independent variable(s)	Whether a person's interaction with someone in a category that shows members of the category to have superior or inferior skill at tasks	Social class, religious attendance, race	Unemployment rate in several years, 1953–1982
Main dependent variable	Whether individuals develop and apply a belief of inequality to an entire category of people	Whether a person said he or she volunteered for any of five organizations (religious, education, political or labor, senior citizen, or local)	Whether distortion occurred, measured as a mismatch between media attention (articles in *Time* magazine) and crime statistics for several years
Unit of analysis	Individual undergraduate student	Individual adults	The media report
Universe	All individuals	All adult Whites and Blacks in the United States	All U.S. mass media reports

CHART 6.2   Examples of Qualitative Studies

Study citation and title	Lu and Fine (1995), "The Presentation of Ethnic Authenticity: Chinese Food as a Social Accomplishment"	Molotch, Freudenburg, and Paulsen (2000), "History Repeats Itself, but How? City Character, Urban Tradition, and the Accomplishment of Place"
Methodological technique used	Field research	Historical-comparative research
Topic	The ways ethnic cultures are displayed within the boundaries of being acceptable in the United States and how they deploy cultural resources	The ways cities develop a distinct urban "character"
Research question	How do Chinese restaurants present food to balance authenticity and to satisfy non-Chinese U.S. customers?	Why did the California cities of Santa Barbara and Ventura, which appear very similar on the surface, develop very different characters?
Grounded theory	Ethnic restaurants Americanize their food to fit local tastes but also construct an impression of authenticity. This is a negotiated process of meeting the customer's expectations/taste conventions and the desire for an exotic and authentic eating experience.	The authors use two concepts, "lash up" (interaction of many factors) and structure (past events create constraints on subsequent ones), to elaborate on character and tradition. Economic, political, cultural, and social factors combine to create distinct cultural-economic places. Similar forces can have opposite results depending on context.
Bricolage	The authors observed and interviewed at four Chinese restaurants but relied on evidence from past studies.	The authors used historical records, maps, photos, official statistical information, and interviews. In addition to economic and social conditions, they examined voluntary associations and physical materials.
Process	Restaurants make modifications to fit available ingredients, their market niche, and the cultural and food tastes of local customers.	Conditions in the two cities contributed to two different economic development responses to oil and highways. Ventura formed an industrial-employment base around oil and allowed new highways. Santa Barbara limited both and instead focused on creating a tourism industry.
Context	Chinese restaurants, especially four in Athens, Georgia	The middle part of California's coast over the past 100 years

KEY TERMS

alternative hypothesis	dependent variable	intervening variable
attributes	double-barreled hypothesis	linear research path
bricolage	ecological fallacy	logic in practice
causal hypothesis	first-order interpretation	logic of disconfirming
crucial experiment	independent variable	hypothesis

nonlinear research path
null hypothesis
reconstructed logic
reductionism

second-order interpretation
spuriousness
tautology
teleology

third-order interpretation
triangulation
universe
variable

REVIEW QUESTIONS

1. What are the implications of saying that qualitative research uses more logic in practice than a reconstructed logic?

2. What does it mean to say that qualitative research follows a nonlinear path? In what ways is a nonlinear path valuable?

3. Describe the differences between independent, dependent, and intervening variables.

4. Why don't we *prove* results in social research?

5. Take a topic of interest and develop two research questions for it. For each research question, specify the units of analysis and universe.

6. What two hypotheses are used if a researcher uses the logic of disconfirming hypotheses? Why is negative evidence stronger?

7. Restate the following in terms of a hypothesis with independent and dependent variables: The number of miles a person drives in a year affects the number of visits a person makes to filling stations, and there is a positive unidirectional relationship between the variables.

8. Compare the ways in which quantitative and qualitative researchers deal with personal bias and the issue of trusting the researcher.

9. How do qualitative and quantitative researchers use theory?

10. Explain how qualitative researchers approach the issue of interpreting data. Refer to first-, second-, and third-order interpretations.

NOTES

1. See Tashakkori and Teddlie (1998).

2. Ward and Grant (1985) and Grant and colleagues (1987) analyzed research in sociology journals and suggested that journals with a higher proportion of qualitative research articles address gender topics but that studies of gender are not themselves more likely to be qualitative.

3. See Kaplan (1964:3–11) for a discussion.

4. On the issue of using quantitative, statistical techniques as a substitute for trust, see Collins (1984), Porter (1995), and Smith and Heshusius (2004).

5. For discussion, see Schwandt (1997), Swanborn (1996), and Tashakkori and Teddlie (1998:90–93).

6. For examples of checking, see Agar (1980) and Becker (1970c).

7. Problem choice and topic selection are discussed in Campbell and associates (1982) and Zuckerman (1978).

8. See Flick (1998:51).

9. *Exceptions* are secondary data analysis and existing statistics research. In working with them, a quantitative researcher often focuses the research question and develops a specific hypothesis to test after she or he examines the available data

10. See Ball and Smith (1992) and Harper (1994).

11. For place of theory in qualitative research, see Hammersley (1995).

12. See Harper (1987:9, 74–75) and Schwandt (1997: 10–11).

13. See Gerring (2007:20) and George and Bennett (2005).

14. See Blee and Billings (1986), Ricoeur (1970), and Schneider (1987) on the interpretation of text in qualitative research.

15. See Lieberson (1985:185–187) for a discussion of basic and superficial variables in a set of causal linkages. Davis (1985) and Stinchcombe (1968) provide good general introductions to making linkages among variables in social theory.

16. The logic of disconfirming hypothesis is discussed in Singleton and associates (1988:56–60).

17. See Bailey (1987:43) for a discussion of this term.

18. The general problem of aggregating observation and making causal inferences is discussed in somewhat technical terms in Blalock (1982:237–264) and in Hannan (1985). O'Brien (1992) argues that the ecological fallacy is one of a whole group of logical fallacies in which levels and units of analysis are confused and overgeneralized.

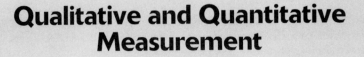

CHAPTER 7

Qualitative and Quantitative Measurement

The Need for Measurement	**Reliability and Validity**
Quantitative and Qualitative Measurement	**A Guide to Quantitative Measurement**
	Scales and Indexes
The Measurement Process	**Conclusion**

Measurement, in short, is not an end in itself. Its scientific worth can be appreciated only in an instrumentalist perspective, in which we ask what ends measurement is intended to serve, what role it is called upon to play in the scientific situation, what functions it performs in inquiry.
—Abraham Kaplan, *The Conduct of Inquiry*, p. 171

Who is poor and how much poverty exists? U.S. government officials in the 1960s answered these questions using the poverty line to measure poverty. New programs were to provide aid to poor people (for schooling, health care, housing assistance, and so forth). They began with the idea of being so impoverished that a family was unable to buy enough food to prevent malnourishment. Studies at the time showed that low-income people were spending one-third of their income on food. Officials visited grocery stores and calculated how much low-cost nutritional food for a family would cost and multiplied the amount by 3 to create a poverty line. Since then, the number has been adjusted for inflation. When Brady (2003:730) reviewed publications from 1990–2001, he found that 69.8 percent of poverty studies in the United States used the official government rate. However, numerous studies found that the official U.S. measure of poverty has major deficiencies. When the National Research Council examined the measure in 1995, members declared it outdated and said it should not be retained. The poverty measure sets an arbitrary income level and "it obscures differences in the extent of poverty among population groups and across geographic contexts and provides an inaccurate picture of trends over time" (Brady, 2003:718). It fails to capture the complex nature of poverty and does not take into account new family situations, new aid programs, changes in taxes, and new living expenses. Adding to the confusion, we cannot compare U. S. poverty reduction over time to those in other countries because each country uses different poverty measures. All of the methodological improvements as to how we measure poverty would result in counting far more people as being poor, so few government officials want to change the measure.

THE NEED FOR MEASUREMENT

As researchers, we encounter measures everyday such as the Stanford Binet IQ test to measure intelligence, the index of dissimilarity to measure racial segregation, or uniform crime reports to measure the amount of crime. We need measures to test a hypothesis, evaluate an explanation, provide empirical support for a theory, or study an applied issue. The way we measure a range of social life—aspects such as self-esteem, political power, alienation, or racial prejudice—is the focus of this chapter. We measure in both quantitative and qualitative studies, but quantitative researchers are most concerned with measurement. In *quantitative studies,* measurement is a distinct step in the research process that occurs prior to data collection. Quantitative measurement has a special terminology and set of techniques because the goal is to precisely capture details of the empirical social world and express what we find in numbers.

In *qualitative studies,* we measure with alternatives to numbers, and measurement is less a separate research step. Because the process is more inductive, we are measuring and creating new concepts simultaneously with the process of gathering data.

Measuring is not some arcane, technical issue (like pulling out a tape measure to determine an object's length or putting an object on a scale to check its weight) that we can skip over quickly. Measurement intimately connects how we perceive and think about the social world with what we find in it. Poor-quality measures can quickly destroy an otherwise good study. Measurement also has consequences in everyday life. For example, psychologists and others debate the meaning and measures of intelligence. We use IQ "tests" to measure a person's intelligence in schools, on job applications, and in statements about racial or other inherited superiority. But what is intelligence? Most such IQ "tests" measure only analytic reasoning (i.e., one's capacity to think abstractly and to infer logically). However, we recognize other types of intelligence: artistic, practical, mechanical, and creative. Some people suggest even more types, such as social-interpersonal, emotional, body-kinesthetic, musical,

or spatial. If there are many forms of intelligence but we narrowly measure only one type, we limit the way schools identify and nurture learning; the way we select, evaluate, and promote employees; and the way society as a whole values diverse human capabilities.

As the chapter opening indicated, the way we measure poverty determines whether people receive assistance from numerous social programs (e.g., subsidized housing, food aid, health care, childcare). Some say that people are poor if they cannot afford to buy food required to prevent malnutrition. Others say that *poor* means having an annual income that is less than one-half of the average (median) income. Still others say that *poor* means someone who earns less than a "living wage" based on a judgment about an income needed to meet minimal community standards of health, safety and decency in hygiene, housing, clothing, diet, transportation, and so forth. Decisions about measuring poverty can greatly influence the daily living conditions of millions of people.

We use many measures in daily life. For example, this morning I woke up and hopped onto a bathroom scale to see how well my diet is working. I glanced at a thermometer to find out whether to wear a coat. Next, I got into my car and checked the gas gauge to be sure I could make it to campus. As I drove, I watched the speedometer so I would not get a speeding ticket. By 8:00 A.M., I had measured weight, temperature, gasoline volume, and speed—all measures about the physical world. Such precise, well-developed measures of daily life are fundamental in the natural sciences.

Our everyday measures of the nonphysical world are usually less exact. We are measuring when we say that a restaurant has excellent food, that Pablo is really smart, that Karen has a negative attitude toward life, that Johnson is really prejudiced, or that last night's movie contained lots of violence. Such everyday judgments as "really prejudiced" or "lots of violence" are sloppy and imprecise.

Measurement instruments also extend our senses. The astronomer or biologist uses the telescope or the microscope to extend natural vision.

Measuring helps us see what is otherwise invisible, and it lets us observe things that were once unseen and unknown but predicted by theory. For example, we may not see or feel magnetism with our natural senses. Magnetism comes from a theory about the physical world. We see its effects indirectly; for instance, metal flecks move near a magnet. The magnet allows us to "see" or measure the magnetic fields. In contrast to our natural senses, scientific measurement is more sensitive and varies less with the specific observer and yields more exact information. We recognize that a thermometer gives more specific, precise information about temperature than touch can. Likewise, a good bathroom scale gives us more specific, constant, and precise information about the weight of a 5-year-old girl than we can get by lifting her and then calling her "heavy" or "light."

Before we can measure, we need to have a very clear idea about what we are interested in. This is a key principle; measurement connects ideas we carry in our heads with specific things we do in the empirical world to make those ideas visible. Natural scientists use many theories, and they created measures to "see" very tiny things (molecules or insect organs) or very large things (huge geological land masses or planets) that are not observable through ordinary senses. All researchers are constantly creating new measures.[1]

We might easily see age, sex, and race that are measured in social research (e.g., physical wrinkles of age, body parts of each sex, skin tones, and eye shape), but many aspects of the social world (e.g., attitudes, ideology, divorce rates, deviance, social roles) are difficult to observe directly. Just as natural scientists created indirect measures of the "invisible" molecules and the force of gravity, social scientists created measures for difficult-to-observe parts of the social world.

QUANTITATIVE AND QUALITATIVE MEASUREMENT

In all social research—both qualitative and quantitative studies—we connect data to ideas or concepts. We can think of the data in a study as the empirical representation of a concept. Measurement links the data to the concepts, yet the measurement process differs depending on whether our data and research approach are primarily quantitative or qualitative. Three features separate quantitative from qualitative approaches to measurement.

The first difference is timing. In quantitative research, we think about variables and convert them into specific actions during a planning stage that is before and separate from gathering or analyzing data. In qualitative research, we measure while in the data collection phase.

A second difference involves the data itself. In a quantitative study, we use techniques that will produce data in the form of numbers. Usually this happens by moving deductively from abstract ideas to specific data collection techniques, and to precise numerical information that the techniques yield. Numerical data represent a uniform, standardized, and compact way to empirically represent abstract ideas. In a qualitative study, data sometimes come in the form of numbers; more often, the data are written or spoken words, actions, sounds, symbols, physical objects, or visual images (e.g., maps, photographs, videos). Unlike a quantitative study, a qualitative study does not convert all observations into a single, common medium such as numbers but leaves the data in a variety of nonstandard shapes, sizes, and forms. While numerical data convert information into a standard and condensed format, qualitative data are voluminous, diverse, and nonstandard.

A third difference involves how we connect concepts with data. In quantitative research, we contemplate and reflect on concepts before we gather data. We select measurement techniques to bridge the abstract concepts with the empirical data. Of course, after we collect and examine the data, we do not shut off our minds and continue to develop new ideas, but we begin with clearly thought-out concepts and consider how we might measure them.

In qualitative research, we also reflect on concepts before gathering data. However, many of the concepts we use are developed and refined during or after the process of data collection. We reexamine and reflect on the data and concepts simultaneously and interactively. As we gather data, we are simultaneously reflecting on it and generating new ideas. The new ideas provide direction and suggest new ways to measure. In turn, the new ways to measure shape how we will collect additional data. In short, we bridge ideas with data in an ongoing, interactive process.

To summarize, we think about and make decisions regarding measurement in quantitative studies before we gather data. The data are in a standardized, uniform format: numbers. In contrast, in a qualitative study, most of our thinking and measurement decisions occur in the midst of gathering data, and the data are in a diffuse forms.

THE MEASUREMENT PROCESS

When we measure, we connect an invisible concept, idea, or construct in our minds with a technique, process, or procedure with which we observe the idea in the empirical world.[2] In quantitative studies, we tend to start with abstract ideas and end with empirical data. In qualitative studies, we mix data and ideas while gathering data. However, in a specific study, things are messy and tend to be more interactive than this general statement suggests.

We use two major processes in measurement: conceptualization and operationalization. **Conceptualization** refers to taking an abstract construct and refining it by giving it a conceptual or theoretical definition. A **conceptual definition** is a statement of the idea in your head in specific words or theoretical terms that are linked to other ideas or constructs. There is no magical way to turn a construct into a precise conceptual definition; doing so involves thinking carefully, observing directly, consulting with others, reading what others have said, and trying possible definitions.

A good definition has one clear, explicit, and specific meaning. There is no ambiguity or vagueness. Sometimes conceptualization is highly creative and produces new insights. Some scholarly articles have been devoted to conceptualizing key concepts. Melbin (1978) conceptualized *night* as a frontier, Gibbs (1989) analyzed the meaning of the concept of *terrorism,* and Ball and Curry (1995) discussed what *street gang* means. The key point is this: We need clear, unambiguous definitions of concepts to develop sound explanations.

A single construct can have several definitions, and people may disagree over definitions. Conceptual definitions are linked to theoretical frameworks. For example, a conflict theorist may define *social class* as the power and property that a group of people in society has or lacks. A structural functionalist defines *social class* in terms of individuals who share a social status, lifestyle, or subjective identification. Although people disagree over definitions, we as researchers should always state explicitly which definition we are using.

Some constructs (e.g., alienation) are highly abstract and complex. They contain lower level concepts within them (e.g., powerlessness), which can be made even more specific (e.g., a feeling of little power concerning where one can live). Other constructs are concrete and simple (e.g., age). We need to be aware of how complex and abstract a construct is. For example, it is easier to define a concrete construct such as *age* (e.g., number of years that have passed since birth) than a complex, abstract concept such as *morale.*

Before we can measure, we must distinguish exactly what we are interested in from other nearby things. This is common sense. How can we measure something unless we know what we are looking for? For example, a biologist cannot observe a cancer cell unless he or she first knows what a cancer cell is, has a microscope, and can distinguish the cell from noncell "stuff" under the microscope. The process of measurement involves more than simply having a measurement instrument (e.g., a microscope). We need three things in the measurement process: a construct, a measure, and the ability to recognize what we are looking for.[3]

For example, let us say that I want to measure teacher morale. I must first define *teacher morale.* What does the construct of *morale* mean? As a variable construct, morale takes on different values: high versus low or good versus bad. Next I must

---

Conceptualization The process of developing clear, rigorous, systematic conceptual definitions for abstract ideas/concepts.

Conceptual definition A careful, systematic definition of a construct that is explicitly written down.

create a measure of my construct. This could take the form of survey questions, an examination of school records, or observations of teachers. Finally, I must distinguish morale from other things in the answers to survey questions, school records, or observations.

The social researcher's job is more difficult than that of the natural scientist because social measurement involves talking with people or observing their behavior. Unlike the planets, cells, or chemicals, the answers people give and their actions can be ambiguous. People can react to the very fact that they are being asked questions or observed. Thus, the social researcher has a double burden: first, to have a clear construct, a good measure, and an ability to recognize what is being looked for, and second, to try to measure fluid and confusing social life that may change just because of an awareness that a researcher is trying to measure.

How can I develop a conceptual definition of *teacher morale,* or at least a tentative working definition to get started? I begin with my everyday understanding of morale: something vague such as "how people feel about things." I ask some of my friends how they define it. I also look at an unabridged dictionary and a thesaurus. They give definitions or synonyms such as "confidence, spirit, zeal, cheerfulness, esprit de corps, mental condition toward something." I go to the library and search the research literature on morale or teacher morale to see how others have defined it. If someone else has already given an excellent definition, I might borrow it (citing the source, of course). If I do not find a definition that fits my purposes, I turn to theories of group behavior, individual mental states, and the like for ideas. As I collect various definitions, parts of definitions, and related ideas, I begin to see the boundaries of the core idea.

By now, I have many definitions and need to sort them out. Most of them say that morale is a spirit, feeling, or mental condition toward something, or a group feeling. I separate the two extremes of my construct. This helps me turn the concept into a variable. High morale involves confidence, optimism, cheerfulness, feelings of togetherness, and willingness to endure hardship for the common good. Low morale is the opposite; it is a lack of

confidence, pessimism, depression, isolation, selfishness, and an unwillingness to put forth effort for others.

Because I am interested in *teacher* morale, I learn about teachers to specify the construct to them. One strategy is to make a list of examples of high or low teacher morale. High teacher morale includes saying positive things about the school, not complaining about extra work, or enjoying being with students. Low morale includes complaining a lot, not attending school events unless required to, or looking for other jobs.

Morale involves a feeling toward something else; a person has morale with regard to something. I list the various "somethings" toward which teachers have feelings (e.g., students, parents, pay, the school administration, other teachers, the profession of teaching). This raises an issue that frequently occurs when developing a definition. Are there several types of teacher morale, or are all of these "somethings" aspects of one construct? There is no perfect answer. I have to decide whether morale means a single, general feeling with different parts or dimensions or several distinct feelings.

What unit of analysis does my construct apply to: a group or an individual? Is morale a characteristic of an individual, of a group (e.g., a school), or of both? I decide that for my purposes, morale applies to groups of people. This tells me that my unit of analysis will be a group: all teachers in a school.

I must distinguish the construct of interest from related ideas. How is my construct of teacher morale similar to or different from related concepts? For example, does *morale* differ from *mood?* I decide that mood is more individual and temporary than morale. Likewise, morale differs from optimism and pessimism. Those are outlooks about the future that individuals hold. Morale is a group feeling. It may include positive or negative feelings about the future as well as related beliefs and feelings.

Conceptualization is the process of thinking through the various possible meanings of a construct. By now, I know that teacher morale is a mental state or feeling that ranges from high (optimistic, cheerful) to low (pessimistic, depressed); morale has several dimensions (regarding students, regarding other teachers); it is a characteristic of a group;

and it persists for a period of months. I have a much more specific mental picture of what I want to measure than when I began. If I had not conceptualized, I would have tried to measure what I started with: "how people feel about things."

Even with all of the conceptualization, some ambiguity remains. To complete the conceptualization process, boundaries are necessary. I must decide exactly what I intend to include and exclude. For example, what is a teacher? Does a teacher include guidance counselors, principals, athletic coaches, and librarians? What about student teachers or part-time or substitute teachers? Does the word *teachers* include everyone who teaches for a living, even if someone is not employed by a school (e.g., a corporate trainer, an on-the-job supervisor who instructs an apprentice, a hospital physician who trains residents)? Even if I restrict my definition to people in schools, what is a school? It could include a nursery school, a training hospital, a university's Ph.D. program, a for-profit business that prepares people to take standardized tests, a dog obedience school, a summer camp that teaches students to play basketball, and a vocational school that teaches how to drive semitrailer trucks.

Some people assume *teacher* means a full-time, professionally trained employee of a school teaching grades 1 through 12 who spends most of the day in a classroom with students. Others use a legal or official government definition that could include people certified to teach, even if they are not in classrooms. It excludes people who are uncertified, even if they are working in classrooms with students. The central point is that conceptualization requires me to be very clear in my own thinking. I must know exactly what I mean by *teachers* and *morale* before I can begin to measure. I must state what I think in very clear and explicit terms that other people can understand.

Operationalization links a conceptual definition to a set of measurement techniques or procedures, the construct's **operational definition** (i.e., a definition in terms of the specific operations or actions). An operational definition could be a survey questionnaire, a method of observing events in a field setting, a way to measure symbolic content in the mass media, or any process that reflects,

---

EXPANSION BOX 7.1

Five Suggestions for Coming Up with a Measure

1. *Remember the conceptual definition.* The underlying principle for any measure is to match it to the specific conceptual definition of the construct that will be used in the study.
2. *Keep an open mind.* Do not get locked into a single measure or type of measure. Be creative and constantly look for better measures. Avoid what Kaplan (1964:28) called the "law of the instrument," which means being locked into using one measurement instrument for all problems.
3. *Borrow from others.* Do not be afraid to borrow from other researchers, as long as credit is given. Good ideas for measures can be found in other studies or modified from other measures.
4. *Anticipate difficulties.* Logical and practical problems often arise when trying to measure variables of interest. Sometimes a problem can be anticipated and avoided with careful forethought and planning.
5. *Do not forget your units of analysis.* Your measure should fit with the units of analysis of the study and permit you to generalize to the universe of interest.

---

documents, or represents the abstract construct as it is expressed in the conceptual definition.

We often can measure a construct in several ways; some are better and more practical than other ways. The key point is that we must fit the measure to the specific conceptual definition by working with all practical constraints within which we must operate (e.g., time, money, available participants). We can develop a new measure from scratch or use one that other researchers are using (see Expansion Box 7.1, Five Suggestions for Coming Up with a Measure).

Operationalization   The process of moving from a construct's conceptual definition to specific activities or measures that allow a researcher to observe it empirically.

Operational definition   A variable in terms of the specific actions to measure or indicate it in the empirical world.

Operationalization connects the language of theory with the language of empirical measures. Theory has many abstract concepts, assumptions, definitions, and cause-and-effect relations. By contrast, empirical measures are very concrete actions in specific, real situations with actual people and events. Measures are specific to the operations or actions we engage in to indicate the presence or absence of a construct as it exists in concrete, observable reality.

Quantitative Conceptualization and Operationalization

Quantitative measurement proceeds in a straightforward sequence: first conceptualization, next operationalization, and then application of the operational definition or the collection of data. We must rigorously link abstract ideas to measurement procedures that can produce precise information in the form of numbers. One way to do this is with rules of correspondence or an auxiliary theory. The purpose of the rules is to link the conceptual definitions of constructs to concrete operations for measuring the constructs.[4]

Rules of correspondence are logical statements of the way an indicator corresponds to an abstract construct. For example, a rule of correspondence says that we will accept a person's verbal agreement with a set of ten specific statements as evidence that the person strongly holds an anti-feminist attitude. This auxiliary theory may explain how and why indicators and constructs connect. Carmines and Zeller (1979:11) noted,

"The auxiliary theory specifying the relationship between concepts and indicators is equally important to social research as the substantive theory linking concepts to one another." Perhaps we want to measure alienation. Our definition of the alienation has four parts, each in a different sphere of life: family relations, work relations, relations with community, and relations with friends. An auxiliary theory may specify that certain behaviors or feelings in each sphere of life are solid evidence of alienation. In the sphere of work, the theory says that if a person feels a total lack of control over when, where, and with whom he or she works, what he or she does when working, or how fast he or she must work, that person is alienated.

Figure 7.1 illustrates the measurement process linking two variables in a theory and a hypothesis. We must consider three levels: conceptual, operational, and empirical.[5] At the most abstract level, we may be interested in the causal relationship between two constructs, or a **conceptual hypothesis**. At the level of operational definitions, we are interested in testing an **empirical hypothesis** to determine the degree of association between indicators. This is the level at which we consider correlations, statistics, questionnaires, and the like. The third level is the empirical reality of the lived social world. As we link the operational indicators (e.g., questionnaire items) to a construct (e.g., alienation), we capture what is taking place in the lived social world and relate it back to the conceptual level.

As we measure, we link the three levels together and move deductively from the abstract to the concrete. First, we conceptualize a variable, giving it a clear conceptual definition; next we operationalize it by developing an operational definition or set of indicators for it; and lastly, we apply indicators to collect data and test empirical hypotheses.

Let us return to the example mentioned earlier. How do I give my teacher morale construct an operational definition? First, I read the research reports of others and see whether a good indicator already exists. If there are no existing indicators, I must invent one from scratch. Morale is a mental state or feeling, so I measure it indirectly through people's words and actions. I might develop a questionnaire

---

Rules of correspondence Strandards that researchers use to connect abstract constructs with measurement operations in empirical social reality.

Conceptual hypothesis A type of hypothesis that expresses variables and the relationships among them in abstract, conceptual terms.

Empirical hypothesis A type of hypothesis in which the researcher expresses variables in specific empirical terms and expresses the association among the measured indicators in observable, empirical terms.

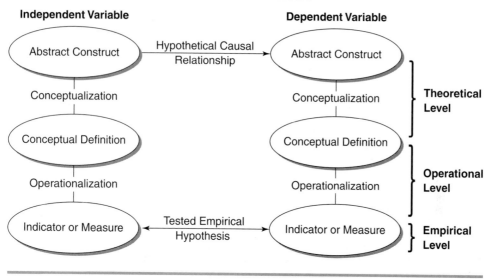

FIGURE 7.1   Conceptualization and Operationalization

for teachers and ask them about their feelings toward the dimensions of morale in my definition. I might go to the school and observe the teachers in the teachers lounge, interacting with students, and attending school activities. I might use school personnel records on teacher behaviors for statements that indicate morale (e.g., absences, requests for letters of recommendation for other jobs, performance reports). I might survey students, school administrators, and others to find out what they think about teacher morale. Whichever indicator I choose, I further refine my conceptual definition as I develop it (e.g., write specific questionnaire questions).

Conceptualization and operationalization are necessary for each variable. In the preceding example, morale is one variable, not a hypothesis. It could be a dependent variable caused by something else, or it could be an independent variable causing something else. It depends on my theoretical explanation.

Qualitative Conceptualization and Operationalization

Conceptualization. In qualitative research, instead of refining abstract ideas into theoretical definitions

early in the research process, we refine rudimentary "working ideas" during the data collection and analysis process. *Conceptualization* is a process of forming coherent theoretical definitions as we struggle to "make sense" or organize the data and our preliminary ideas about it.

As we gather and analyze qualitative data, we develop new concepts, formulate definitions for major constructs, and consider relationships among them. Eventually, we link concepts and constructs to create theoretical relationships. We form and refine constructs while examining data (e.g., field notes, photos and maps, historical documents), and we ask theoretical questions about the data (e.g., Is this a case of class conflict? What is the sequence of events and could it be different? Why did this happen here but not somewhere else?).

We need clear, explicit definitions expressed in words and descriptions of specific actions that link to other ideas and are tied to the data. In qualitative research, conceptualization flows largely from the data.

Operationalization. In qualitative studies, operationalization often precedes conceptualization

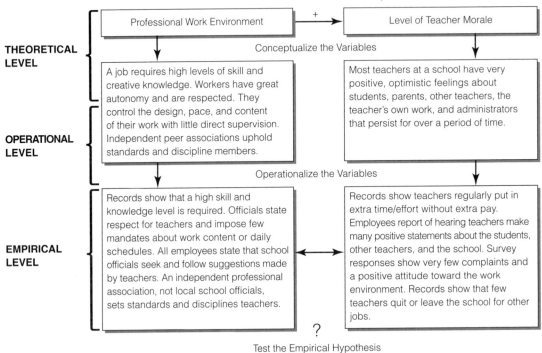

FIGURE 7.2   Example of the Deductive Measurement Process for the Hypothesis: A Professional Work Environment Increases the Level of Teacher Morale

(see Figure 7.2) and gives deductive measurement (see Figure 7.3 for inductive measurement). We may create conceptual definitions out of rudimentary "working ideas" while we are making observations or gathering data. Instead of turning refined conceptual definitions into measurement operations, we operationalize by describing how specific observations and thoughts about the data contribute to working ideas that are the basis of conceptual definitions.

Thus, qualitative research operationalization largely involves developing a description of how we use working ideas while making observations. Oerationalization describes how we gathered specific observations or data and we struggled to understand the data as the data evolved into abstract constructs. In this way, qualitative operationalization is more an after-the-fact description than a preplanned technique.

Just as quantitative operationalization deviates from a rigid deductive process, qualitative researchers may draw on ideas from beyond the data of a specific research setting. Qualitative operationalization includes using preexisting techniques and concepts that we blend with those that emerged during the data collection process.

Fantasia's (1988) field research on contested labor actions illustrates qualitative operationalization. Fantasia used *cultures of solidarity* as a central construct. He related this construct to ideas of conflict-filled workplace relations and growing class consciousness among nonmanagerial workers. He defined a culture of solidarity as a type of cultural expression created by workers that evolves in particular places over time. The workers over time develop shared feelings and a sense of unity that is in opposition to management and business owners. It is an interactive process. Slowly over

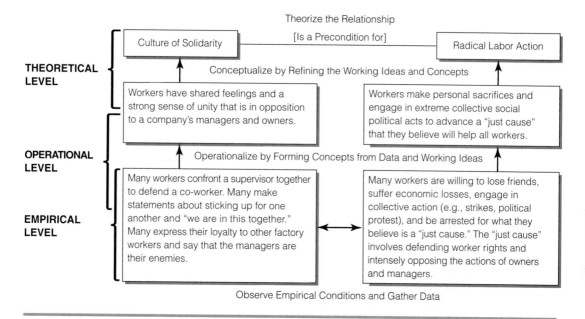

FIGURE 7.3   Example of the Inductive Measurement Process for the Proposition: Radical Labor Action Is Likely to Occur Where a Culture of Solidarity Has Been Created

time, the workers arrive at common ideas, understandings, and actions. It is "less a matter of disembodied mental attitude than a broader set of practices and repertoires available for empirical investigation" (Fantasia:14).

To operationalize the construct, Fantasia describes how he gathered data. He presents them to illustrate the construct, and explains his thinking about the data. He describes his specific actions to collect the data (e.g., he worked in a particular factory, attended a press conference, and interviewed people). He also shows us the data in detail (e.g., he describes specific events that document the construct by showing several maps indicating where people stood during a confrontation with a foreperson, retelling the sequence of events at a factory, recounting actions by management officials, and repeating statements that individual workers made). He gives us a look into his thinking process as he reflected and tried to understand his experiences and developed new ideas drawing on older ideas.

Casing. In qualitative research, ideas and evidence are mutually interdependent. This applies particularly to case study analysis. Cases are not given preestablished empirical units or theoretical categories apart from data; they are defined by data and theory. By analyzing a situation, the researcher organizes data and applies ideas simultaneously to create or specify a case. Making or creating a case, called **casing**, brings the data and theory together. Determining what to treat as a case resolves a tension or strain between what the researcher observes and his or her ideas about it. "Casing, viewed as a methodological step, can occur at any phase of the research process, but occurs especially at the beginning of the project and at the end" (Ragin, 1992b:218).

RELIABILITY AND VALIDITY

All of us as researchers want reliability and validity, which are central concerns in all measurement. Both connect measures to constructs. It is not

Casing	Developing cases in qualitative research.

possible to have perfect reliability and validity, but they are ideals toward which we strive. Reliability and validity are salient because our constructs are usually ambiguous, diffuse, and not observable. Reliability and validity are ideas that help to establish the truthfulness, credibility, or believability of findings. Both terms also have multiple meanings. As used here, they refer to related, desirable aspects of measurement.

Reliability means dependability or consistency. It suggests that the same thing is repeated or recurs under the identical or very similar conditions. The opposite of reliability is an erratic, unstable, or inconsistent result that happens because of the measurement itself. *Validity* suggests truthfulness. It refers to how well an idea "fits" with actual reality. The absence of validity means that the fit between the ideas we use to analyze the social world and what actually occurs in the lived social world is poor. In simple terms, validity addresses the question of how well we measure social reality using our constructs about it.

All researchers want reliable and valid measurement, but beyond an agreement on the basic ideas at a general level, qualitative and quantitative researchers see reliability and validity differently.

Reliability and Validity in Quantitative Research

Reliability. **Measurement reliability** means that the numerical results an indicator produces do not vary because of characteristics of the measurement process or measurement instrument itself. For example, I get on my bathroom scale and read my weight. I get off and get on again and again. I have

---

Measurement reliability   The dependability or consistency of the measure of a variable.

Stability reliability   Measurement reliability across time; a measure that yields consistent results at different time points assuming what is being measured does not itself change.

Representative reliability   Measurement reliability across groups; a measure that yields consistent results for various social groups.

---

a reliable scale if it gives me the same weight each time, assuming, of course, that I am not eating, drinking, changing clothing, and so forth. An unreliable scale registers different weights each time, even though my "true" weight does not change. Another example is my car speedometer. If I am driving at a constant slow speed on a level surface but the speedometer needle jumps from one end to the other, the speedometer is not a reliable indicator of how fast I am traveling. Actually, there are three types of reliability.[6]

Three Types of Reliability

1. Stability reliability is reliability across time. It addresses the question: Does the measure deliver the same answer when applied in different time periods? The weight-scale example just given is of this type of reliability. Using the test-retest method can verify an indicator's degree of stability reliability. Verification requires retesting or readministering the indicator to the same group of people. If what is being measured is stable and the indicator has stability reliability, then I will have the same results each time. A variation of the test-retest method is to give an alternative form of the test, which must be very similar to the original. For example, I have a hypothesis about gender and seating patterns in a college cafeteria. I measure my dependent variable (seating patterns) by observing and recording the number of male and female students at tables, and noting who sits down first, second, third, and so on for a 3-hour period. If, as I am observing, I become tired or distracted or I forget to record and miss more people toward the end of the 3 hours, my indicator does not have a high degree of stability reliability.

2. Representative reliability is reliability across subpopulations or different types of cases. It addresses the question: Does the indicator deliver the same answer when applied to different groups? An indicator has high representative reliability if it yields the same result for a construct when applied to different subpopulations (e.g., different classes, races, sexes, age groups). For example, I ask a question about a person's age. If people in their twenties answered my question by overstating their true age whereas people in their fifties understated their true age, the indicator has a low degree of representative reliability. To have representative reliability, the measure needs to give accurate information for every age group.

A *subpopulation analysis* verifies whether an indicator has this type of reliability. The analysis compares the indicator across different subpopulations or subgroups and uses independent knowledge about them. For example, I want to test the representative reliability of a questionnaire item that asks about a person's education. I conduct a subpopulation analysis to see whether the question works equally well for men and women. I ask men and women the question and then obtain independent information (e.g., check school records) and check to see whether the errors in answering the question are equal for men and women. The item has representative reliability if men and women have the same error rate.

3. Equivalence reliability applies when researchers use **multiple indicators**—that is, when a construct is measured with multiple specific measures (e.g., several items in a questionnaire all measure the same construct). Equivalence reliability addresses the question: Does the measure yield consistent results across different indicators? If several different indicators measure the same construct, then a reliable measure gives the same result with all indicators.

We verify equivalence reliability with the *split-half method*. This involves dividing the indicators of the same construct into two groups, usually by a random process, and determining whether both halves give the same results. For example, I have fourteen items on a questionnaire. All measure political conservatism among college students. If my indicators (i.e., questionnaire items) have equivalence reliability, then I can randomly divide them into two groups of seven and get the same results. For example, I use the first seven questions and find that a class of fifty business majors is twice as conservative as a class of fifty education majors. I get the same results using the second seven questions. Special statistical measures (e.g., Cronbach's alpha) also can determine this type of reliability. A special type of equivalence reliability, intercoder reliability,

can be used when there are several observers, raters, or coders of information (explained in Chapter 11). In a sense, each observer is an indicator. A measure is reliable if the observers, raters, or coders agree with each other. This measure is a common type of reliability reported in content analysis studies. For example, I hire six students to observe student seating patterns in a cafeteria. If all six are equally skilled at observing and recording, I can combine the information from all six into a single reliable measure. But if one or two students are lazy, inattentive, or sloppy, my measure will have lower reliability. Intercoder reliability is tested by having several coders measure the exact same thing and then comparing the measures. For instance, I have three coders independently code the seating patterns during the same hour on three different days. I compare the recorded observations. If they agree, I can be confident of my measure's intercoder reliability. Special statistical techniques measure the degree of intercoder reliability.

How to Improve Reliability. It is rare to have perfect reliability. We can do four things to improve reliability: (1) clearly conceptualize constructs, (2) use a precise level of measurement, (3) use multiple indicators, and (4) use pilot tests.

1. *Clearly conceptualize all constructs.* Reliability increases when each measure indicates one and only one concept. This means we must develop unambiguous, clear theoretical definitions. Constructs should be specified to eliminate "noise" (i.e., distracting or interfering information) from other constructs. For example, the indicator of a pure chemical compound is more reliable than the indicator in which the chemical is mixed with other

Equivalence reliability Measurement reliability across indicators; a measure that yields consistent results using different specific indicators, assuming that all measure the same construct.

Multiple indicators The use of multiple procedures or several specific measures to provide empirical evidence of the levels of a variable.

material or dirt. In the latter case, separating the "noise" of other material from the pure chemical is difficult.

Let us return to the example of teacher morale. I should separate morale from related ideas (e.g., mood, personality, spirit, job attitude). If I did not do this, I could not be sure what I was really measuring. I might develop an indicator for morale that also indicates personality; that is, the construct of personality contaminates that of morale and produces a less reliable indicator. Bad measurement occurs by using one indicator to operationalize different constructs (e.g., using the same questionnaire item to indicate morale and personality).

2. *Increase the level of measurement.* Levels of measurement are discussed later in this chapter. Indicators at higher or more precise levels of measurement are more likely to be reliable than less precise measures because the latter pick up less detailed information. If more specific information is measured, it is less likely that anything other than the construct will be captured. The general principle is: Try to measure at the most precise level possible. However, quantifying at higher levels of measurement is more difficult. For example, if I have a choice of measuring morale as either high or low, or in ten categories from extremely low to extremely high, it would be better to measure it in ten refined categories.

3. *Use multiple indicators of a variable.* A third way to increase reliability is to use multiple indicators because two (or more) indicators of the same construct are better than one.[7] Figure 7.4 illustrates the use of multiple indicators in hypothesis testing. Three indicators of the one independent variable construct are combined into an overall measure, A, and two indicators of a dependent variable are combined into a single measure, B. For example, I have three specific measures of A, which is teacher morale: (a1) the answers to a survey question on attitudes about school, (a2) the number of absences for reasons other than illness and (a3) the number of complaints others heard made by a teacher. I also have two measures of my dependent variable B, giving students extra attention: (b1) number of hours a teacher spends staying after school hours to meet individually with students and (b2) whether the teacher inquires frequently about a student's progress in other classes.

With multiple indicators, we can build on triangulation and take measurements from a wider range of the content of a conceptual definition (i.e., sample from the conceptual domain). We can measure different aspects of the construct with its own indicator. Also, one indicator may be imperfect, but several measures are less likely to have the same error. James (1991) provides a good example of this principle applied to counting persons who are homeless. If we consider only where people sleep (e.g., using sweeps of streets and parks and counting people in official shelters), we miss some because many people who are homeless have temporary shared housing (e.g., sleep on the floor of a friend or family member). We also miss some by

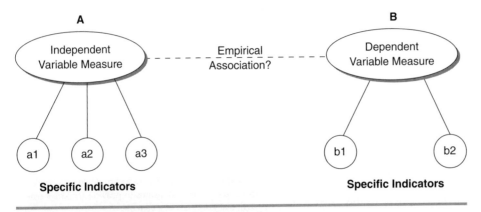

FIGURE 7.4   Measurement Using Multiple Indicators

using records of official service agencies because many people who are homeless avoid involvement with government and official agencies. However, if we combine the official records with counts of people sleeping in various places and conduct surveys of people who use a range of services (e.g., street clinics, food lines, temporary shelters), we can get a more accurate picture of the number of people who are homeless. In addition to capturing the entire picture, multiple indicator measures tend to be more stable than single item measures.

4. *Use pilot studies and replication.* You can improve reliability by first using a pilot version of a measure. Develop one or more draft or preliminary versions of a measure and try them before applying the final version in a hypothesis-testing situation. This takes more time and effort. Returning to the example discussed earlier, in my survey of teacher morale, I go through many drafts of a question before the final version. I test early versions by asking people the question and checking to see whether it is clear.

The principle of using pilot tests extends to replicating the measures from researchers. For example, I search the literature and find measures of morale from past research. I may want to build on and use a previous measure if it is a good one, citing the source, of course. In addition, I may want to add new indicators and compare them to the previous measure (see Example Box 7.1, Improving the Measure of U.S. Religious Affiliation). In this way, the quality of the measure can improve over time as long as the same definition is used (see Table 7.1 on page 212 for a summary of reliability and validity types).

Validity. Validity is an overused term. Sometimes, it is used to mean "true" or "correct." There are several general types of validity. Here we are concerned with **measurement validity**, which also has several types. Nonmeasurement types of validity are discussed later.

When we say that an indicator is valid, it is valid for a particular purpose and definition. The same indicator may be less valid or invalid for other purposes. For example, the measure of morale discussed above (e.g., questions about feelings toward school) might be valid for measuring morale among

EXAMPLE BOX **7.1**

Improving the Measure of U.S. Religious Affiliation

Quantitative researchers measure individual religious beliefs (e.g., Do you believe in God? in a devil? in life after death? What is God like to you?), religious practices (e.g., How often do you pray? How frequently do you attend services?), and religious affiliation (e.g., If you belong to a church or religious group, which one?). They have categorized the hundreds of U.S. religious denominations into either a three-part grouping (Protestant, Catholic, Jewish) or a three-part classification of fundamentalist, moderate, or liberal that was introduced in 1990.

Steensland and colleagues (2000) reconceptualized affiliation, and, after examining trends in religious theology and social practices, argued for classifying all American denominations into six major categories: Mainline Protestant, Evangelical Protestant, Black Protestant, Roman Catholic, Jewish, and Other (including Mormon, Jehovah's Witnesses, Muslim, Hindu, and Unitarian). The authors evaluated their new six-category classification by examining people's religious views and practices as well as their views about contemporary social issues. Among national samples of Americans, they found that the new classification better distinguished among religious denominations than did previous measures.

teachers but invalid for measuring morale among police officers.[8]

At its core, measurement validity tells us how well the conceptual and operational definitions mesh with one other: The better the fit, the higher is the measurement validity. Validity is more difficult to achieve than reliability. We cannot have absolute confidence about validity, but some measures are *more valid* than others. The reason is that constructs are abstract ideas, whereas indicators refer to concrete observation. This is the gap between our mental pictures about the world and the specific

Measurement validity How well an empirical indicator and the conceptual definition of the construct that the indicator is supposed to measure "fit" together.

TABLE 7.1   Summary of Measurement Reliability and Validity Types

RELIABILITY (DEPENDABLE MEASURE)	VALIDITY (TRUE MEASURE)
Stability—over time (verify using test-retest method)	Face—makes sense in the judgment of others
Representative—across subgroups (verify using split-half method)	Content—captures the entire meaning
Equivalence—across indicators (verify using subpopulation analysis)	Criterion—agrees with an external source ▪ Concurrent—agrees with a preexisting measure ▪ Predictive—agrees with future behavior
	Construct—has consistent multiple indicators ▪ Convergent—alike ones are similar ▪ Discriminant—different ones differ

things we do at particular times and places. Validity is part of a dynamic process that grows by accumulating evidence over time, and without it, all measurement becomes meaningless.

Some researchers use rules of correspondence (discussed earlier) to reduce the gap between abstract ideas and specific indicators. For example, a rule of correspondence is: A teacher who agrees with statements that "things have gotten worse at this school in the past 5 years" and that "there is little hope for improvement" is indicating low morale. Some researchers talk about the *epistemic correlation,* a hypothetical correlation between an indicator and the construct that the indicator measures. We cannot empirically measure such correlations, but they can be estimated.[9]

Four Types of Measurement Validity.

1. Face validity is the most basic and easiest type of validity to achieve. It is a judgment by the

> **Face validity**   A type of measurement validity in which an indicator "makes sense" as a measure of a construct in the judgment of others, especially in the scientific community.
>
> **Content validity**   A type of measurement validity that requires that a measure represent all aspects of the conceptual definition of a construct.

scientific community that the indicator really measures the construct. It addresses the question: On the face of it, do people believe that the definition and method of measurement fit? For example, few people would accept a measure of college student math ability by asking students what 2 + 2 equals. This is not a valid measure of college-level math ability on the face of it. Recall that the principle of organized skepticism in the scientific community means that others scrutinize aspects of research.[10]

2. Content validity addresses this question: Is the full content of a definition represented in a measure? A conceptual definition holds ideas; it is a "space" containing ideas and concepts. Measures should sample or represent all ideas or areas in the conceptual space. Content validity involves three steps. First, specify the content in a construct's definition. Next, sample from all areas of the definition. Finally, develop one or more indicators that tap all of the parts of the definition.

Let us consider an example of content validity. I define *feminism* as a person's commitment to a set of beliefs creating full equality between men and women in areas of the arts, intellectual pursuits, family, work, politics, and authority relations. I create a measure of feminism in which I ask two survey questions: (1) Should men and women get equal pay for equal work? and (2) Should men and women share household tasks? My measure has low content validity because the two questions ask only about pay and household tasks. They ignore the other areas (intellectual pursuits, politics, authority relations, and other aspects of work and family). For a content-valid measure, I must either expand the measure or narrow the definition.[11]

3. Criterion validity uses some standard or criterion to indicate a construct accurately. The validity of an indicator is verified by comparing it with another measure of the same construct in which a researcher has confidence. The two subtypes of this type of validity are concurrent and predictive.[12]

To have **concurrent validity**, we need to associate an indicator with a preexisting indicator that we already judge to be valid (i.e., it has face validity). For example, we create a new test to measure intelligence. For it to be concurrently valid, it should be highly associated with existing IQ tests (assuming the same definition of intelligence is used). This means that most people who score high on the old measure should also score high on the new one, and vice versa. The two measures may not be perfectly associated, but if they measure the same or a similar construct, it is logical for them to yield similar results.

Criterion validity by which an indicator predicts future events that are logically related to a construct is called **predictive validity**. It cannot be used for all measures. The measure and the action predicted must be distinct from but indicate the same construct. Predictive measurement validity should not be confused with prediction in hypothesis testing in which one variable predicts a different variable in the future. For example, the Scholastic Assessment Test (SAT) that many U.S. high school students take measures scholastic aptitude: the ability of a student to perform in college. If the SAT has high predictive validity, students who achieve high SAT scores will subsequently do well in college. If students with high scores perform at the same level as students with average or low scores, the SAT has low predictive validity.

Another way to test predictive validity is to select a group of people who have specific characteristics and predict how they will score (very high or very low) vis-à-vis the construct. For example, I create a measure of political conservatism. I predict that members of conservative groups (e.g., John

Birch Society, Conservative Caucus, Daughters of the American Revolution, Moral Majority) will score high on it whereas members of liberal groups (e.g., Democratic Socialists, People for the American Way, Americans for Democratic Action) will score low. I "validate" it by pilot-testing it on members of the groups. It can then be used as a measure of political conservatism for the public.

4. Construct validity is for measures with multiple indicators. It addresses this question: If the measure is valid, do the various indicators operate in a consistent manner? It requires a definition with clearly specified conceptual boundaries. The two types of construct validity are convergent and discriminant.

Convergent validity applies when multiple indicators converge or are associated with one another. It means that multiple measures of the same construct hang together or operate in similar ways. For example, I measure the construct "education" by asking people how much education they have completed, looking up school records, and asking the people to complete a test of school knowledge. If the measures do not converge (i.e., people who claim to have a college degree but have no records of attending college or those with college degrees perform no better than high school dropouts on my tests), my measure has weak convergent validity, and I should not combine all three indicators into one measure.

Criterion validity   Measurement validity that relies on some independent, outside verification.

Concurrent validity   Measurement validity that relies on a preexisting and already accepted measure to verify the indicator of a construct.

Predictive validity   Measurement validity that relies on the occurrence of a future event or behavior that is logically consistent to verify the indicator of a construct.

Construct validity   A type of measurement validity that uses multiple indicators and has two subtypes: how well the indicators of one construct converge or how well the indicators of different constructs diverge.

Convergent validity   A type of measurement validity for multiple indicators based on the idea that indicators of one construct will act alike or converge.

Discriminant validity is the opposite of convergent validity and means that the indicators of one construct "hang together," or converge, but also are negatively associated with opposing constructs. Discriminant validity says that if two constructs *A* and *B* are very different, measures of *A* and *B* should not be associated. For example, I have ten items that measure political conservatism. People answer all ten in similar ways. But I also put five questions that measure political liberalism on the same questionnaire. My measure of conservatism has discriminant validity if the ten conservatism items converge and are negatively associated with the five liberalism ones. (See Figure 7.5 for a review of measurement validity.)

Reliability and Validity in Qualitative Research

Qualitative research embraces the core principles of reliability and validity, but we rarely see the terms in this approach because they are so closely associated with quantitative measurement. In addition, in qualitative studies, we apply the principles differently.

Reliability.   Recall that *reliability* means dependability or consistency. We use a wide variety of techniques (e.g., interviews, participation, photographs, document studies) to record observations consistently in qualitative studies. We want to be consistent (i.e., not vacillating or being erratic) in how we make observations, similar to the idea of stability reliability. One difficulty with reliability is that we often study processes that are unstable over time. Moreover, we emphasize the value of a changing or developing interaction between us as researchers and the people we study. We believe that the subject matter and our relationship to it is an evolving process. A metaphor for the relationship is one of an evolving relationship or living organism (e.g., a plant) that naturally matures over time. Many qualitative researchers see the quantitative approach to

reliability as a cold, fixed mechanical instrument that one applies repeatedly to static, lifeless material.

In qualitative studies, we consider a range of data sources and employ multiple measurement methods. We do not become locked into the quantitative-positivist ideas of replication, equivalence, and subpopulation reliability. We accept that different researchers or researchers who use alternative measures may find distinctive results. This happens because data collection is an interactive process in which particular researchers operate in an evolving setting whose context dictates using a unique mix of measures that cannot be repeated. The diverse measures and interactions with different researchers are beneficial because they can illuminate different facets or dimensions of a subject matter. Many qualitative researchers question the quantitative researcher's quest for standard, fixed measures and fear that such measures ignore the benefits of having a variety of researchers with many approaches and may neglect key aspects of diversity that exist in the social world.

Validity.   *Validity* means truthfulness. In qualitative studies, we are more interested in achieving authenticity than realizing a single version of "Truth." *Authenticity* means offering a fair, honest, and balanced account of social life from the viewpoint of the people who live it every day. We are less concerned with matching an abstract construct to empirical data than with giving a candid portrayal of social life that is true to the lived experiences of the people we study. In most qualitative studies, we emphasize capturing an inside view and providing a detailed account of how the people we study understand events (see Expansion Box 7.2, Meanings of Validity in Qualitative Research).

There are qualitative research substitutes for the quantitative approach to validity: ecological validity or natural history methods (see Chapter 13). Both emphasize conveying an insider's view to others. Historical researchers use internal and external criticisms (see Chapter 14) to determine whether the evidence is real. Qualitative researchers adhere to the core principle of validity, to be truthful (i.e., avoid false or distorted accounts) and try to create a tight fit between understandings, ideas, and statements about the social world and what is actually occurring in it.

Discriminant validity   A type of measurement validity for multiple indicators based on the idea that indicators of different constructs diverge.

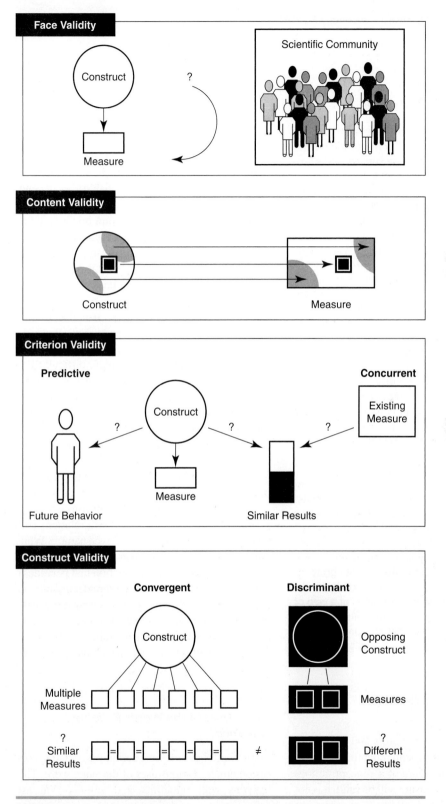

FIGURE 7.5   Types of Validity

EXPANSION BOX **7.2**

Meanings of Validity
in Qualitative Research

Measurement validity in qualitative research does not require demonstrating a fixed correspondence between a carefully defined abstract concept and a precisely calibrated measure of its empirical appearance. Other features of the research measurement process are important for establishing validity.

First, to be considered valid, a researcher's truth claims need to be plausible and, as Fine (1999) argued, intersubjectively "good enough" (i.e., understandable by many people). *Plausible* means that the data and statements about it are not exclusive; they are not the only possible claims, nor are they exact accounts of the one truth in the world. This does not make them mere inventions or arbitrary. Instead, they are powerful, persuasive descriptions that reveal a researcher's genuine experiences with the empirical data.

Second, a researcher's empirical claims gain validity when supported by numerous pieces of diverse empirical data. Any one specific empirical detail alone may be mundane, ordinary, or "trivial." Validity arises out of the cumulative impact of hundreds of small, diverse details that only together create a heavy weight of evidence.

Third, validity increases as researchers search continuously in diverse data and consider the connections among them. Raw data in the natural social world are not in neatly prepackaged systematic scientific concepts; rather, they are numerous disparate elements that "form a dynamic and coherent ensemble" (Molotch et al., 2000:816). Validity grows as a researcher recognizes a dense connectivity in disparate details. It grows with the creation of a web of dynamic connections across diverse realms, not only with the number of specifics that are connected.

Relationship between Reliability and Validity

Reliability is necessary for validity and is easier to achieve than validity. Although reliability is necessary to have a valid measure of a concept, it does not guarantee that the measure will be valid. It is not a sufficient condition for validity. A measure can

yield a result over and over (i.e., has reliability), but what it truly measures may not match a construct's definition (i.e., validity).

For example, I get on a scale to check my weight. The scale registers the same weight each time I get on and off during a 2-hour period. I next go to another scale—an "official" one at a medical clinic—and it reports my weight to be twice as much. The first scale yielded reliable (i.e., dependable and consistent) results, but it was not a valid measure of my weight. A diagram might help you see the relationship between reliability and validity. Figure 7.6 illustrates the relationship between the concepts by using the analogy of a target. The bull's-eye represents a fit between a measure and the definition of the construct.

Validity and reliability are usually complementary concepts, but in some situations, they conflict with each other. Sometimes, as validity increases, reliability becomes more difficult to attain and vice versa. This situation occurs when the construct is highly abstract and not easily observable but captures the "true essence" of an idea. Reliability is easiest to achieve when a measure is precise, concrete, and observable. For example, *alienation* is a very abstract, subjective construct. We may define it as a deep inner sense of loss of one's core humanity; it is a feeling of detachment and being without purpose that diffuses across all aspects of life (e.g., the sense of self, relations with other people, work, society, and even nature). While it is not easy, most of us can grasp the idea of alienation, a directionless disconnection that pervades a person's existence. As we get more deeply into the true meaning of the concept, measuring it precisely becomes more difficult. Specific questions on a questionnaire may produce reliable measures more than other methods, yet the questions cannot capture the idea's essence.

Other Uses of the Words *Reliable* and *Valid*

Many words have multiple definitions, creating confusion among various uses of the same word. This happens with reliability and validity. We use *reliability* in everyday language. A *reliable* person

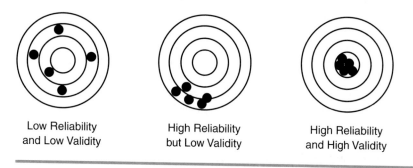

A Bull's-Eye = A Perfect Measure

Low Reliability
and Low Validity

High Reliability
but Low Validity

High Reliability
and High Validity

FIGURE 7.6   Illustration of Relationship between Reliability and Validity

Source: Adapted version of Figure 5-2 An Analogy to Validity and Reliability, page 155 from Babbie, E. R. 1986. *The Practice of Social Research*, Fourth Edition. Belmont, CA: Wadsworth Publishing Company.

is a dependable, stable, and responsible person who responds in similar, predictable ways in different times and conditions. A *reliable* car is dependable and trustworthy; it starts and peforms in a predicable way. Sometimes, we say that a study or its results are *reliable*. This means that other researchers can reproduce the study and will get similar results.

Internal validity means we have not made errors internal to the design of a research project that might produce false conclusions.[13] In experimental research, we primarily talk about possible alternative causes of results that arise despite our attempts to institute controls (see Chapter 9 for discussion).

External validity is also used primarily in experimental research. It refers to whether we can generalize a result that we found in a specific setting with a particular small group beyond that situation or externally to a wider range of settings and many different people. External validity addresses this question: If something happens in a laboratory or among a particular set of research participants (e.g., college students), does it also happen in the "real" (nonlaboratory) world or among the general population (nonstudents) (discussed in Chapter 9)? External validity has serioius implications for evaluating theory. If a general theory is true, it implies that we can generalize findings from a single test of the theory to many other situations and populations (see Lucas, 2003).

Statistical validity means that we used the proper statistical procedure for a particular purpose

and have met the procedure's mathematical requirements. This validity arises because different statistical tests or procedures are appropriate for different situations as is discussed in textbooks on statistical procedures. All statistical procedures rest on assumptions about the mathematical properties of the numbers being used. A statistic will yield nonsense results if we use it for inappropriate situations or seriously violate its assumptions even if the computation of the numbers is correct. This is why we must know the purposes for which a statistical procedure is designed and its assumptions to use it. This is also why computers can do correct computations but produce output that is nonsense.

A GUIDE TO QUANTITATIVE MEASUREMENT

Thus far, we have discussed principles of measurement. Quantitative researchers have specialized measures that assist in the process of creating operational definitions for reliable and valid measures. This section of the chapter is a brief guide to these ideas and a few of the specific measures.

Levels of Measurement

We can array possible measures on a continuum. At one end are at "higher" ones. These measures contain a great amount of highly specific information with many exact and refined distinctions. At the opposite end are "lower" ones. These are rough, less precise measures with minimal information and a few basic distinctions. The level of measurement affects how much we can learn when we measure features of the social world and limits the types of indicator we can use as we try to capture empirical details about a construct.

The **level of measurement** is determined by how refined, exact, and precise a construct is in our assumptions about it. This means that how we conceptualize a construct carries serious implications. It influences how we can measure the construct and restricts the range of statistical procedures that we can use after we have gathered data. Often we see a trade-off between the level of measurement and the ease of measuring. Measuring at a low level is simpler and easier than it is at a high level; however, a low level of measurement offers us the least refined information and allows the fewest statistical procedures during data analysis. We can look at the issue in two ways: (1) continuous versus discrete variable, and (2) the four levels of measurement.

Continuous and Discrete Variables. Variables can be continuous or discrete. **Continuous variables** contain a large number of values or attributes that flow along a continuum. We can divide a continuous variable into many smaller increments; in mathematical theory, the number of increments is infinite. Examples of continuous variables include temperature, age, income, crime rate, and amount of schooling. For example, we can measure the amount of your schooling as the years of schooling you completed. We can subdivide this into the total number of hours you have spent in classroom instruction and out-of-class assignments or

Levels of measurement A system for organizing information in the measurement of variables into four levels, from nominal level to ratio level.

Continuous variables Variables that are measured on a continuum in which an infinite number of finer gradations between variable attributes are possible.

Discrete variables Variables in which the attributes can be measured with only a limited number of distinct, separate categories.

preparation. We could further refine this into the number of minutes you devoted to acquiring and processing information and knowledge in school or due to school assignments. We could further refine this into all of the seconds that your brain was engaged in specific cognitive activities as you were acquiring and processing information.

Discrete variables have a relatively fixed set of separate values or variable attributes. Instead of a smooth continuum of numerous values, discrete variables contain a limited number of distinct categories. Examples of discrete variables include gender (male or female), religion (Protestant, Catholic, Jew, Muslim, atheist), marital status (never married single, married, divorced or separated, widowed), or academic degrees (high school diploma, or community college associate, four-year college, master's or doctoral degrees). Whether a variable is continuous or discrete affects its level of measurement.

Four Levels of Measurement. Levels of measurement build on the difference between continuous and discrete variables. Higher level measures are continuous and lower level ones are discrete. The four levels of measurement categorize its precision.[14]

Deciding on the appropriate level of measurement for a construct is not always easy. It depends on two things: how we understand a construct (its definition and assumptions), and the type of indicator or measurement procedure.

The way we conceptualize a construct can limit how precisely we can measure it. For example, we might reconceptualize some of the variables listed earlier as continuous to be discrete. We can think of temperature as a continuous variable with thousands of refined distinctions (e.g., degrees and fractions of degrees). Alternatively, we can think of it more crudely as five discrete categories (e.g., very hot, hot, cool, cold, very cold). We can think of age as continuous (in years, months, days, hours, minutes, or seconds) or discrete categories (infancy, childhood, adolescence, young adulthood, middle age, old age).

While we can convert continuous variables into discrete ones, we cannot go the other way around, that is, convert discrete variables into continuous

TABLE 7.2   Characteristics of the Four Levels of Measurements

LEVEL	DIFFERENT CATEGORIES	RANKED	DISTANCE BETWEEN CATEGORIES MEASURED	TRUE ZERO
Nominal	Yes			
Ordinal	Yes	Yes		
Interval	Yes	Yes	Yes	
Ratio	Yes	Yes	Yes	Yes

ones. For example, we cannot turn sex, religion, and marital status into continuous variables. We can, however, treat related constructs with slightly different definitions and assumptions as being continuous (e.g., amount of masculinity or femininity, degree of religiousness, commitment to a marital relationship). There is a practical reason to conceptualize and measure at higher levels of measurement: We can collapse higher levels of measurement to lower levels, but the reverse is not true.

Distinguishing among the Four Levels.   The four levels from lowest to highest precision are nominal, ordinal, interval, and ratio. Each level provides a different type of information (see Table 7.2). **Nominal-level measurement** indicates that a difference exists among categories (e.g., religion: Protestant, Catholic, Jew, Muslim; racial heritage: African, Asian, Caucasian, Hispanic, other). **Ordinal-level measurement** indicates a difference *and* allows us to rank order the categories (e.g., letter grades: A, B, C, D, F; opinion measures: strongly agree, agree, disagree, strongly disagree). **Interval-level measurement** does everything the first two do *and* allows us to specify the amount of distance between categories (e.g., Fahrenheit or celsius temperature: 5°, 45°, 90°; IQ scores: 95, 110, 125). **Ratio-level measurement** does everything the other levels do, *and* it has a true zero. This feature makes it possible to state relationships in terms of proportion or ratios (e.g., money income: $10, $100, $500; years of formal schooling: 1, 10, 13). In most practical situations, the distinction between interval and ratio levels makes little difference.

One source of confusion is that we sometimes use arbitrary zeros in interval measures but the zeros are only to help keep score. For example, a rise in temperature from 30 to 60 degrees is not really a doubling of the temperature, although the numbers appear to double. Zero degrees in Fahrenheit or centigrade is not the absence of any heat but is just a placeholder to make counting easier. For example, water freezes at 32° on a Fahrenheit temperature scale, 0° on a celsius or centigrade scale, and 273° on a Kelvin scale. Water boils at 212°, 100°, or 373.15°, respectively. If there were a true zero, the actual relation among temperature numbers would be a ratio. For example, 25° to 50° Fahrenheit would be "twice as warm," but this is not true because a ratio relationship does not exist without a true zero. We can see this in the ratio of boiling to freezing water temperatures. The ratio is 6.625 times higher in Fahrenheit, 100 times in Celsius, and 1.366 times

Nominal-level measurement   The lowest, least precise level of measurement for which there is a difference in type only among the categories of a variable.

Ordinal-level measurement   A level of measurement that identifies a difference among categories of a variable and allows the categories to be rank ordered as well.

Interval-level measurement   A level of measurement that identifies differences among variable attributes, ranks categories, and measures distance between categories but has no true zero.

Ratio-level measurement   The highest, most precise level of measurement; variable attributes can be rank ordered, the distance between them precisely measured, and there is an absolute zero.

in Kelvin. The Kelvin scale has an absolute zero (the absence of all heat), and its ratio corresponds to physical conditions. While this physical world example may be familiar, another example of arbitrary—not true—zeros occurs when measuring attitudes with numbers. We may assign a value to statements in a survey questionnaire (e.g., −1 = disagree, 0 = no opinion, +1 = agree). Just because our data are in the form of numbers does not allow us to use statistical procedures that require the mathematical assumption of a true zero.

Discrete variables are nominal and ordinal, whereas we can measure continuous variables at the interval or ratio level. There is an interesting unidirectional relationship among the four levels. We can convert a ratio-level measure into the interval, ordinal, or nominal level; an interval level into an ordinal or nominal level; and an ordinal into a nominal level; but the process does not work in the opposite way! This happens because higher levels of measurement contain more refined information than lower levels. We can always toss out or ignore the refined information of a high-level measure, but we cannot squeeze additional refined information out of a low-level measure.

For ordinal measures, we generally want to have at least five ordinal categories and try to obtain many observations for each. This is so because a distortion occurs as we collapse a continuous construct into few ordered categories. We minimize the distortion as the number of ordinal categories and the number of observations increase.[15] (See Example Box 7.2, Example of Four Levels of Measurement).

Before continuing, keep two things in mind. First, we can measure nearly any social phenomenon. We can measure some constructs directly and create precise numerical values (e.g., family income) while other constructs are less precise and require the use of surrogates or proxies to indirectly measure a variable (e.g., predisposition to commit a crime). Second, we can learn a great deal from the measures created by other researchers. We are fortunate to have the work of other researchers to draw on. It is not always necessary to start from scratch. We can use a past scale or index or modify it for our own purposes. Measuring aspects of social life is an ongoing process. We are constantly creating ideas, refining theoretical definitions, and improving measures of old or new constructs.

EXAMPLE BOX **7.2**
Example of Four Levels of Measurement

VARIABLE (LEVEL OF MEASUREMENT)	HOW VARIABLE IS MEASURED
Religion (nominal)	Different religious denominations (Jewish, Catholic, Lutheran, Baptist) are not ranked but are only different (unless one belief is conceptualized as closer to heaven).
Attendance (ordinal)	"How often do you attend religious services? (0) Never, (1) less than once a year, (3) several times a year, (4) about once a month, (5) two or three times a week, or (8) several times a week." This might have been measured at a ratio level if the exact number of times a person attended were asked instead.
IQ score (interval)	Most intelligence tests are organized with 100 as average, middle, or normal. Scores higher or lower indicate distance from the average. Someone with a score of 115 has somewhat above average measured intelligence for people who took the test, whereas 90 is slightly below. Scores of below 65 or above 140 are rare.
Age (ratio)	Age is measured by years. There is a true zero (birth). Note that a 40-year-old has lived twice as long as a 20-year-old.

Principles of Good Measurement.   Three features of good measurement whether we are considering using a single-indicator or a scale or index (discussed next) to measure a variable are that (1) the attributes or categories of a variable should be mutually exclusive, (2) they should also be exhaustive, and (3) the measurement should be unidimensional.

1. Mutually exclusive attributes means that an individual or a case will go into one and only one variable category. For example, we wish to measure the variable type of religion using the four attributes Christian, non-Christian, Jewish, and Muslim. Our measure is not mutually exclusive. Both Islam and Judaism are non-Christian religious faiths. A Jewish person and a Muslim fit into two categories: (1) the non-Christian and (2) Jewish or Muslim. Another example without mutually exclusive attributes is to measure the type of city using the three categories of river port city, state capital, and access to an international airport. A city could be all three (a river port state capital with an international airport), any combination of the three, or none of the three. To have mutually exclusive attitudes, we must create categories so that cases cannot be placed into more than one category.

2. Exhaustive attribute means that every case has a place to go or fits into at least one of a variable's categories. Returning to the example of the variable religion, with the four categorical attributes of Christian, non-Christian, Jewish, and Muslim, say we drop the non-Christian category to make the attributes mutually exclusive: Christian, Jewish, or Muslim. These are not exclusive attributes. The Buddhist, Hindu, atheist, and agnostic do not fit anywhere. We must create attributes to cover every possible situation. For example, Christian, Jewish, Muslim, or Other attributes for religion would be exclusive and mutually exclusive.

3. Unidimensionality means that a measure fits together or measures one single, coherent construct. Unidimensionality was hinted at in the previous discussions of construct and content validity. Unidimensionality states that if we combine several specific pieces of information into a single score or measure, all of the pieces should measure the same thing. We sometimes use a more advanced technique—factor analysis —to test for the unidimensionality of data.

We may see an apparent contradiction between the idea of using multiple indicators or a scale or index (see next section) to capture diverse parts of a complex construct and the criteria of unidimensionality. The contraction is apparent only because constructs vary theoretically by level of abstraction. We may define a complex, abstract construct using multiple subdimensions, each being a part of the complex construct's overall content. In contrast, simple, low-level constructs that are concrete typically have just one dimension. For example, "feminist ideology" is a highly abstract and complex construct. It includes specific beliefs and attitudes toward social, economic, political, family, and sexual relations. The ideology's belief areas are parts of the single, more abstract and general construct. The parts fit together as a whole. They are mutually reinforcing and collectively form one set of beliefs about the dignity, strength, and power of women. To create a unidimensional measure of feminist ideology requires us to conceptualize it as a unified belief system that might vary from very antifeminist to very profeminist. We can test the convergence validity of our measure with multiple indicators that tap the construct's subparts. If one belief area (e.g., sexual relations) is consistently distinct from all other areas in empirical tests, then we question its unidimensionality.

It is easy to become confused about unidimensionality because an indicator we use for a simple

Mutually exclusive attribute   The principle that variable attributes or categories in a measure are organized so that responses fit into only one category and there is no overlap.

Exhaustive attributes   The principle that attributes or categories in a measure should provide a category for all possible responses.

Unidimensionality   The principle that when using multiple indicators to measure a construct, all indicators should consistently fit together and indicate a single construct.

construct in one situation might indicate one part of a different, complex construct in another situation. We can combine multiple simple, concrete constructs into a complex, more abstract construct. The principle of unidimensionality in measurement means that for us to measure a construct, we must conceptualize it as one coherent, integrated core idea *for its level of abstraction*. This shows the way that the processes of conceptualization and measurement are tightly interwoven.

Here is a specific example. A person's attitude about gender equality with regard to getting equal pay for work is a simpler, more specific and less abstract idea than gender ideology (i.e., a general set of beliefs about gender relations in all areas of life). We might measure attitude regarding equal pay as a unidimensional construct in its own or as a less abstract subpart of the complex, broader construct of gender ideology. This does not mean that gender ideology ceases to be unidimensional. It is a complex idea with several parts but can be unidimensional at a more abstract level.

SCALES AND INDEXES

In this section, we look at scales and indexes, specialized measures from among the hundreds created by researchers.[16] We have scales and indexes to measure many things: the degree of formalization in bureaucratic organizations, the prestige of occupations, the adjustment of people to a marriage, the intensity of group interaction, the level of social activity in a community, the degree to which a state's sexual assault laws reflect feminist values, and the level of socioeconomic development of a nation. We will examine principles of measurement, consider principles of index and scale construction, and then explore a few major types of index and scale.

You might find the terms *index* and *scale* confusing because people use them interchangeably. One researcher's scale is another's index. Both produce ordinal- or interval-level measures. To add to the confusion, we can combine scale and index techniques into a single measure. Nonetheless, scales and indexes are very valuable. They give us more information about a variable and expand the quality of measurement (i.e., increase reliability and

validity) over using a simple, single indictor measure. Scales and indexes also aid in data reduction by condensing and simplifying information (see Expansion Box 7.3, Scales and Indexes: Are They Different?).

Index Construction

You hear about indexes all the time. For example, U.S. newspapers report the Federal Bureau of Investigation (FBI) crime index and the consumer price index (CPI). The FBI index is the sum of police reports on seven so-called index crimes (criminal homicide, aggravated assault, forcible rape, robbery, burglary, larceny of $50 or more, and auto theft). The index began as part of the Uniform Crime Report in 1930 (see Rosen, 1995). The CPI, which is a measure of inflation, is created by totaling the cost of buying a list of goods and services (e.g., food, rent, and utilities) and comparing the

---

EXPANSION BOX **7.3**

Scales and Indexes: Are They Different?

For most purposes, researchers can treat scales and indexes as being interchangeable. Social researchers do not use a consistent nomenclature to distinguish between them.

A *scale* is a measure in which a researcher captures the intensity, direction, level, or potency of a variable construct and arranges responses or observations on a continuum. A scale can use a single indicator or multiple indicators. Most are at the ordinal level of measurement.

An *index* is a measure in which a researcher adds or combines several distinct indicators of a construct into a single score. This composite score is often a simple sum of the multiple indicators. It is used for content and convergent validity. Indexes are often measured at the interval or ratio level.

Researchers sometimes combine the features of scales and indexes in a single measure. This is common when a researcher has several indicators that are scales (i.e., that measure intensity or direction). He or she then adds these indicators together to yield a single score, thereby creating an index.

total to the cost of buying the same list in the previous period. The CPI has been used by the U.S. Bureau of Labor Statistics since 1919; wage increases, union contracts, and social security payments are based on it. An **index** is a combination of items into a single numerical score. Various components or subparts of a construct are each measured and then combined into one measure.

There are many types of indexes. For example, the total number of questions correct on an exam with 25 questions is a type of index. It is a composite measure in which each question measures a small piece of knowledge and all questions scored correct or incorrect are totaled to produce a single measure. Indexes measure the most desirable place to live (based on unemployment, commuting time, crime rate, recreation opportunities, weather, and so on), the degree of crime (based on combining the occurrence of different specific crimes), the mental health of a person (based on the person's adjustment in various areas of life), and the like.

Creating indexes is so easy that we must be careful to check that every item in an index has face validity and excludes any without face validity. We want to measure each part of the construct with at least one indicator. Of course, it is better to measure the parts of a construct with multiple indicators.

An example of an index is a college quality index (see Example Box 7.3, Example of Index). A theoretical definition says that a high-quality college has six distinguishing characteristics: (1) few students per faculty member, (2) a highly educated faculty, (3) high number of books in the library, (4) few students dropping out of college, (5) many students who go on to seek advanced degrees, and (6) faculty members who publish books or scholarly articles. We score 100 colleges on each item and then add the scores for each to create an index score of college quality that can be used to compare colleges.

We can combine indexes. For example, to strengthen my college quality index, I add a subindex on teaching quality. The index contains eight items: (1) average size of classes, (2) percentage of class time devoted to discussion, (3) number of different classes each faculty member teaches, (4) availability of faculty to students outside the classroom, (5) currency and amount of reading assigned, (6) degree to which assignments promote learning, (7) degree to which faculty get to know each student, and (8) student ratings of instruction. Similar subindex measures can be created for other parts of the college quality index. They can be combined into a more global measure of college quality. This further elaborates the definition of the construct "quality of college."

Next we look at three issues involved when we construct an index: weight of items, missing data, and the use of rates and standardization.

1. *Weighting* is an important issue in index construction. Unless otherwise stated, we assume that the items in an index are unweighted. Likewise, unless we have a good theoretical reason for assigning different weights to items, we use equal weights. An *unweighted index* gives each item equal weight. We simply sum the items without modification, as if each were multiplied by 1 (or –1 for items that are negative). A *weighted index* values or weights some items more than others. The size of weights can come from theoretical assumptions, the theoretical definition, or a statistical technique such as factor analysis.

For example, we can elaborate the theoretical definition of the college quality index. We decide that the student/faculty ratio and number of faculty with Ph.D.s are twice as important as the number of books in the library per student or the percentage of students pursuing advanced degrees. Also, the percentage of freshmen who drop out and the number of publications per faculty member are three times more important than books in the library or percentage of students pursuing an advanced degree. This is easier to see when it is expressed as a formula (refer to Example Box 7.3).

The number of students per faculty member and the percentage who drop out have negative signs because, as they increase, the quality of the college declines. The weighted and unweighted indexes can

---

Index The summing or combining of many separate measures of a construct or variable to create a single score.

EXAMPLE BOX **7.3**

Example of Index

In symbolic form, where:

Q = overall college quality

A quality-of-college index is based on the following six items:

R = number of students per faculty member
F = percentage of faculty with Ph.D.s
B = number of books in library per student
D = percentage of freshmen who drop out or do not finish
A = percentage of graduates who seek an advanced degree
P = number of publications per faculty member

Unweighted formula: $(-1) R + (1) F + (1) B + (-1) D + (1) A + (1) P = Q$
Weighted formula: $(-2) R + (2) F + (1) B + (-3) D + (1) A + (3) P = Q$

Old Ivy College

Unweighted: $(-1) 13 + (1) 80 + (1) 334 + (-1) 14 + (1) 28 + (1) 4 = 419$
Weighted: $(-2) 13 + (2) 80 + (1) 334 + (-3) 14 + (1) 28 + (3) 4 = 466$

Local College

Unweighted: $(-1) 20 + (1) 82 + (1) 365 + (-1) 25 + (1) 15 + (1) 2 = 419$
Weighted: $(-2) 20 + (2) 82 + (1) 365 + (-3) 25 + (1) 15 + (3) 2 = 435$

Big University

Unweighted: $(-1) 38 + (1) 95 + (1) 380 + (-1) 48 + (1) 24 + (1) 6 = 419$
Weighted: $(-2) 38 + (2) 95 + (1) 380 + (-3) 48 + (1) 24 + (3) 6 = 392$

produce different results. Consider Old Ivy College, Local College, and Big University. All have identical unweighted index scores, but the colleges have different quality scores after weighting.

Weighting produces different index scores in this example, but in most cases, weighted and unweighted indexes yield similar results. Researchers are concerned with the relationship between variables, and weighted and unweighted indexes usually give similar results for the relationships between variables.[17]

2. *Missing data* can be a serious problem when constructing an index. Validity and reliability are threatened whenever data for some cases are missing. There are four ways to attempt to resolve the problem (see Expansion Box 7.4, Ways to Deal with Missing Data), but none fully solves it.

For example, I construct an index of the degree of societal development in 1985 for 50 nations. The index contains four items: life expectancy, percentage of homes with indoor plumbing, percentage of population that is literate, and number of telephones per 100 people. I locate a source of United Nations statistics for my information. The values for Belgium are $68 + 87 + 97 + 28$ and for Turkey are $55 + 36 + 49 + 3$; for Finland, however, I discover that literacy data are unavailable. I check other sources of information, but none has the data because they were not collected.

3. *Rates and standardization* are related ideas. You have heard of crime rates, rates of population growth, or the unemployment rate. Some indexes and single-indicator measures are expressed as rates. Rates involve standardizing the value of an item to make comparisons possible. The items in an

EXPANSION BOX **7.4**

Ways to Deal with Missing Data

1. *Eliminate all cases for which any information is missing.* If one nation in the discussion is removed from the study, the index will be reliable for the nations on which information is available. This is a problem if other nations have missing information. A study of 50 nations may become a study of 20 nations. Also, the cases with missing information may be similar in some respect (e.g., all are in eastern Europe or in the Third World), which limits the generalizability of findings.
2. *Substitute the average score for cases in which data are present.* The average literacy score from the other nations is substituted. This "solution" keeps Finland in the study but gives it an incorrect value. For an index with few items or for a case that is not "average," this creates serious validity problems.
3. *Insert data based on nonquantitative information about the case.* Other information about Finland (e.g., percentage of 13- to 18-year-olds in high school) is used to make an informed guess about the literacy rate. This "solution" is marginally acceptable in this situation. It is not as good as measuring Finland's literacy, and it relies on an untested assumption—that one can predict the literacy rate from other countries' high school attendance rate.
4. *Insert a random value.* This is unwise for the development index example. It might be acceptable if the index had a very large number of items and the number of cases was very large. If that were the situation, however, then eliminating the case is probably a better "solution" that produces a more reliable measure.

Source: Allison (2001).

index frequently need to be standardized before they can be combined.

Standardization involves selecting a base and dividing a raw measure by the base. For example, City A had ten murders and City B had thirty murders in the same year. In order to compare murders in the two cities, we will need to standardize the raw number of murders by the city population. If the cities are the same size, City B is more dangerous. But City B may be safer if it is much larger. For example, if City A has 100,000 people and City B has 600,000, then the murder rate per 100,000 is ten for City A and five for City B.

Standardization makes it possible for us to compare different units on a common base. The process of standardization, also called *norming*, removes the effect of relevant but different characteristics in order to make the important differences visible. For example, there are two classes of students. An art class has twelve smokers and a biology class has twenty-two smokers. We can compare the rate or incidence of smokers by standardizing the number of smokers by the size of the classes. The art class has 32 students and the biology class has 143 students. One method of standardization that you already know is the use of percentages, whereby measures are standardized to a common base of 100. In terms of percentages, it is easy to see that the art class has more than twice the rate of smokers (37.5 percent) than the biology class (15.4 percent).

A critical question in standardization is deciding what base to use. In the examples given, how did I know to use city size or class size as the base? The choice is not always obvious; it depends on the theoretical definition of a construct. Different bases can produce different rates. For example, the unemployment rate can be defined as the number of people in the workforce who are out of work. The overall unemployment rate is

$$\text{unemployment rate} = \frac{\text{number of unemployed people}}{\text{total number of people working}}$$

We can divide the total population into subgroups to get rates for subgroups in the population such as

Standardization Procedures to adjust measures statistically to permit making an honest comparison by giving a common basis to measures of different units.

White males, African American females, African American males between the ages of 18 and 28, or people with college degrees. Rates for these subgroups may be more relevant to the theoretical definition or research problem. For example, we believe that unemployment is an experience that affects an entire household or family and that the base should be households, not individuals. The rate will look like this:

$$\text{unemployment rate} = \frac{\begin{array}{c}\text{number of households}\\ \text{with one}\\ \text{unemployed person}\end{array}}{\begin{array}{c}\text{total number}\\ \text{of households}\end{array}}$$

Different conceptualizations suggest different bases and different ways to standardize. When combining several items into an index, it is best to standardize items on a common base (see Example Box 7.4, Standardization and the Real Winners at the 2000 Olympics).

Scales

We often use scales when we want to measure how an individual feels or thinks about something. Some call this the *hardness or potency of feelings*. Scales also help in the conceptualization and operationalization processes. For example, you believe a single ideological dimension underlies people's judgments about specific policies (e.g., housing, education, foreign affairs). Scaling can help you determine whether a single construct—for instance, "conservative/liberal ideology"—underlies the positions that people take on specific policies.

> **Scale** A class of quantitative data measures often used in survey research that captures the intensity, direction, level, or potency of a variable construct along a continuum; most are at the ordinal level of measurement.
>
> **Likert scale** A scale often used in survey research in which people express attitudes or other responses in terms of ordinal-level categories (e.g., agree, disagree) that are ranked along a continuum.

Scaling measures the intensity, direction, level, or potency of a variable. Graphic rating **scales** are an elementary form of scaling. People indicate a rating by checking a point on a line that runs from one extreme to another. This type of scale is easy to construct and use. It conveys the idea of a continuum, and assigning numbers helps people think about quantities. Scales assume that people with the same subjective feeling mark the graphic scale at the same place. Figure 7.7 is an example of a "feeling thermometer" scale that is used to find out how people feel about various groups in society (e.g., the National Organization of Women, the Ku Klux Klan, labor unions, physicians). Political scientists have used this type of measure in the national election study since 1964 to measure attitudes toward candidates, social groups, and issues.[18]

We next look at five commonly used social science scales: Likert, Thurstone, Borgadus social distance, semantic differential, and Guttman scale. Each illustrates a somewhat different logic of scaling.

1. *Likert scaling.* You have probably used **Likert scales**; they are widely used in survey research. They were developed in the 1930s by Rensis Likert to provide an ordinal-level measure of a person's attitude.[19] Likert scales are called *summated-rating* or *additive scales* because a person's score on the scale is computed by summing the number of responses he or she gives. Likert scales usually ask people to indicate whether they agree or

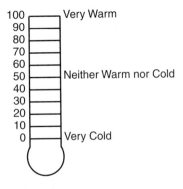

FIGURE 7.7   **"Feeling Thermometer" Graphic Rating Scale**

EXAMPLE BOX **7.4**

Standardization and the Real Winners at the 2000 Olympics

Sports fans in the United States were jubilant about "winning" at the 2000 Olympics by carrying off the most gold medals. However, because they failed to *standardize,* the "win" is an illusion. Of course, the world's richest nation with the third largest population does well in one-on-one competition among all nations. To see what really happened, one must standardize on a base of the population or wealth. Standardization yields a more accurate picture by adjusting the results as if the nations had equal populations and wealth. The results show that the Bahamas, with fewer than 300,000 citizens (smaller than a medium-sized U.S. city), proportionately won the most gold. Adjusted for its population size or wealth, the United States is not even near the top; it appears to be the leader only because of its great size and wealth. Sports fans in the United States can perpetuate the illusion of being at the top only if they ignore the comparative advantage of the United States.

TOP TEN GOLD MEDAL WINNING COUNTRIES AT THE 2000 OLYMPICS IN SYDNEY

Unstandardized Rank			Standardized Rank*			
RANK	COUNTRY	TOTAL	COUNTRY	TOTAL	POPULATION	GDP
1	USA	39	Bahamas	1.4	33.3	20.0
2	Russia	32	Slovenia	2	10	10.0
3	China	28	Cuba	11	9.9	50.0
4	Australia	16	Norway	4	9.1	2.6
5	Germany	14	Australia	16	8.6	4.1
6	France	13	Hungry	8	7.9	16.7
7	Italy	13	Netherlands	12	7.6	3.0
8	Netherlands	12	Estonia	1	7.1	20.0
9	Cuba	11	Bulgaria	5	6.0	41.7
10	Britain	11	Lithuania	2	5.4	18.2
	EU15**	80	EU15	80	2.1	0.9
			USA	39	1.4	0.4

*Population is gold medals per 10 million people and GDP is gold medals per $10 billion.

**EU15 is the 15 nations of the European Union treated as a single unit.

Source: Adapted from *The Economist,* October 7, 2000, p. 52. Copyright 2000 by Economist Newspaper Group. Reproduced with permission of Economist Newspaper Group in the format Textbook via Copyright Clearance Center.

disagree with a statement. Other modifications are possible; people might be asked whether they approve or disapprove or whether they believe something is "almost always true" (see Example Box 7.5, Examples of Types of Likert Scales on page 228).

To create a Likert scale, you need a minimum of two categories, such as "agree" and "disagree." Using only two choices creates a crude measure and forces distinctions into only two categories. It is usually better to use four to eight categories. You can combine or collapse categories after the data have been collected, but once you collect them using crude categories, you cannot make them more precise later. You can increase the number of categories at the end of a scale by adding "strongly agree," "somewhat agree," "very strongly agree," and so forth. You want to keep the number of choices to eight or nine at most. More distinctions than that are not meaningful, and people will become confused. The choices should be evenly

EXAMPLE BOX **7.5**

Examples of Types of Likert Scales

THE ROSENBERG SELF-ESTEEM SCALE

All in all, I am inclined to feel that I am a failure:

(1) Almost always true   (4) Seldom true
(2) Often true   (5) Never true
(3) Sometimes true

A STUDENT EVALUATION OF INSTRUCTION SCALE

Overall, I rate the quality of instruction in this course as:

Excellent   Good   Average   Fair   Poor

A MARKET RESEARCH MOUTHWASH RATING SCALE

Brand	Dislike Completely	Dislike Somewhat	Dislike a Little	Like a Little	Like Somewhat	Like Completely
X	_____	_____	_____	_____	_____	_____
Y	_____	_____	_____	_____	_____	_____

WORK GROUP SUPERVISOR SCALE

My supervisor:

	Never	Seldom	Sometimes	Often	Always
Lets members know what is expected of them	1	2	3	4	5
Is friendly and approachable	1	2	3	4	5
Treats all unit members as equals	1	2	3	4	5

balanced (e.g., "strongly agree," "agree," "strongly disagree," "disagree"). Nunnally (1978:521) stated:

> As the number of scale steps is increased from 2 up through 20, the increase in reliability is very rapid at first. It tends to level off at about 7, and after about 11 steps, there is little gain in reliability from increasing the number of steps.

Researchers have debated about whether to offer a neutral category (e.g., "don't know," "undecided," "no opinion") in addition to the directional

categories (e.g., "disagree," "agree"). A neutral category implies an odd number of categories.

We can combine several Likert scale items into a composite index if they all measure the same construct. Consider the Index of Equal Opportunity for Women and the Self-Esteem Index created by Sniderman and Hagen (1985) (see Example Box 7.6, Examples of Using the Likert Scale to Create Indexes). In the middle of large surveys, they asked respondents three questions about the position of women. The researchers later scored answers and combined items into an index that ranged from 3 to 15. Respondents also answered questions about self-esteem. Notice that when scoring these items, they scored one item (question 2) in reverse. The reason for switching directions in this way is to avoid the problem of the **response set**. The response

Response set   A tendency to agree with every question in a series rather than carefully thinking through one's answer to each.

EXAMPLE BOX **7.6**

Examples of Using the Likert Scale to Create Indexes

Sniderman and Hagen (1985) created indexes to measure beliefs about equal opportunity for women and self-esteem. For both indexes, scores were added to create an unweighted index.

INDEX OF EQUAL OPPORTUNITY FOR WOMEN

Questions

1. Women have less opportunity than men to get the education they need to be hired in top jobs.

Strongly Agree	Somewhat Agree	Somewhat Disagree	Disagree a Great Deal	Don't Know

2. Many qualified women cannot get good jobs; men with the same skills have less trouble.

Strongly Agree	Somewhat Agree	Somewhat Disagree	Disagree a Great Deal	Don't Know

3. Our society discriminates against women.

Strongly Agree	Somewhat Agree	Somewhat Disagree	Disagree a Great Deal	Don't Know

Scoring: For all items, Strongly Agree = 1, Somewhat Agree = 2, Somewhat Disagree = 4, Disagree a Great Deal = 5, Don't Know = 3.

Highest Possible Index Score = 15, respondent feels opportunities for women are equal
Lowest Possible Index Score = 3, respondent feels opportunities are not equal

SELF-ESTEEM INDEX

Questions

1. On the whole, I am satisfied with myself.   Agree   Disagree   Don't Know

2. At times, I think I am no good at all.   Agree   Disagree   Don't Know

3. I sometimes feel that (other) men do not take my opinion seriously.   Agree   Disagree   Don't Know

Scoring: Items 1 and 3: 1 = Disagree, 2 = Don't Know, 3 = Agree, Item 2: 1 = Disagree, 2 = Don't Know, 1 = Agree.

Highest Possible Index Score = 9, high self-esteem
Lowest Possible Index Score = 3, low self-esteem

---

set, also called *response style* and *response bias,* is the tendency of some people to answer a large number of items in the same way (usually agreeing) out of laziness or a psychological predisposition. For example, if items are worded so that saying "strongly agree" always indicates self-esteem, we would not know whether a person who always strongly agreed had high self-esteem or simply had a tendency to agree with questions. The person might be answering "strongly agree" out of habit or a tendency to agree. We word statements in alternative directions so that anyone who agrees all the time appears to answer inconsistently or to have a contradictory opinion.

We often combine many Likert-scaled attitude indicators into an index. Scale and indexes can improve reliability and validity. An index uses multiple indicators, which improves reliability. The use of multiple indicators that measure several aspects of a construct or opinion improves content validity. Finally, the index scores give a more precise quantitative measure of a person's opinion. For example, we can measure a person's opinion with a number from 10 to 40 instead of in four categories: "strongly agree," "agree," "disagree," and "strongly disagree."

Instead of scoring Likert items, as in the previous example, we could use the scores $-2, -1, +1, +2$. This scoring has an advantage in that a zero implies neutrality or complete ambiguity whereas a high negative number means an attitude that opposes the opinion represented by a high positive number.

The numbers we assign to the response categories are arbitrary. Remember that the use of a zero does not give the scale or index a ratio level of measurement. Likert scale measures are at the ordinal level of measurement because responses indicate only a ranking. Instead of 1 to 4 or -2 to $+2$, the numbers 100, 70, 50, and 5 would have worked. Also, we should not be fooled into thinking that the distances between the ordinal categories are intervals just because numbers are assigned. The numbers are used for convenience only. The fundamental measurement is only ordinal.[20]

The real strength of the Likert Scale is its simplicity and ease of use. When we combine several ranked items, we get a more comprehensive multiple indicator measurement. The scale has two limitations: Different combinations of several scale items produce the same overall score, and the response set is a potential danger.

Thurstone scaling Measuring in which the researcher gives a group of judges many items and asks them to sort the items into categories along a continuum and then considers the sorting results to select items on which the judges agree.

---

2. *Thurstone scaling.* This scale is for situations when we are interested in something with many ordinal aspects but would like a measure that combines all information into a single interval-level continuum. For example, a dry cleaning business, Quick and Clean, contacts us; the company wants to identify its image in Greentown compared to that of its major competitor, Friendly Cleaners. We conceptualize a person's attitude toward the business as having four aspects: attitude toward location, hours, service, and cost. We learn that people see Quick and Clean as having more convenient hours and locations but higher costs and discourteous service. People see Friendly Cleaners as having low cost and friendly service but inconvenient hours and locations. Unless we know how the four aspects relate to the core attitude—image of the dry cleaner—we cannot say which business is generally viewed more favorably. During the late 1920s, Louis Thurstone developed scaling methods for assigning numerical values in such situations. These are now called **Thurstone scaling** or the *method of equal-appearing intervals*.[21]

Thurstone scaling uses the law of comparative judgment to address the issue of comparing ordinal attitudes when each person makes a unique judgment. The law anchors or fixes the position of one person's attitude relative to that of others as each makes an individual judgment. The law of comparative judgment states that we can identify the "most common response" for each object or concept being judged. Although different people arrive at different judgments, the individual judgments cluster around a single most common response. The dispersion of individual judgments around the common response follows a statistical pattern called the *normal distribution*. According to the law, if many people agree that two objects differ, then the most common responses for the two objects will be distant from each other. By contrast, if many people are confused or disagree, the common responses of the two objects will be closer to each other.

With Thurstone scaling, we develop many statements (e.g., more than 100) regarding the object of interest and then use judges to reduce the number to a smaller set (e.g., 20) by eliminating ambiguous statements. Each judge rates the statements on an underlying continuum (e.g., favorable to unfavorable). We examine the ratings and keep some statements based on two factors: (1) agreement among the judges and (2) the statement's location on a range of possible values. The final set of statements is a measurement scale that spans a range of values.

Thurstone scaling begins with a large number of statements that cover all shades of opinion. Each statement should be clear and precise. "Good" statements refer to the present and are not capable of being interpreted as facts. They are unlikely to be endorsed by everyone, are stated as simple sentences, and avoid words such as *always* and *never*. We can get ideas for writing the statements from reviewing the literature, from the mass media, from personal experience, and from asking others. For example, statements about the dry cleaning business might include the four aspects listed before plus the following:

- I think X Cleaners dry cleans clothing in a prompt and timely manner.
- In my opinion, X Cleaners keeps its stores looking neat and attractive.
- I do not think that X Cleaners does a good job of removing stains.
- I believe that X Cleaners charges reasonable prices for cleaning coats.
- I believe that X Cleaners returns clothing clean and neatly pressed.
- I think that X Cleaners has poor delivery service.

We would next locate 50 to 300 judges who should be familiar with the object or concept in the statements. Each judge receives a set of statement cards and instructions. Each card has one statement on it, and the judges place each card in one of several piles. The number of piles is usually 7, 9, 11, or 13. The piles represent a range of values (e.g., favorable to neutral to unfavorable) with regard to the object or concept being evaluated. Each judge places cards in rating piles independently of the other judges.

After the judges place all cards in piles, we create a chart cross-classifying the piles and the

statements. For example, 100 statements and 11 piles results in an 11×100 chart, or a chart with $11 \times 100 = 1,100$ boxes. The number of judges who assigned a rating to a given statement is written into each box. Statistical measures (beyond the present discussion) are used to compute the average rating of each statement and the degree to which the judges agree or disagree. We keep the statements with the highest between-judge agreement, or interrater reliability, as well as statements that represent the entire range of values. (See Example Box 7.7, Example of Thurstone Scaling on page 232.)

With Thurstone scaling, we can construct an attitude scale or select statements from a larger collection of attitude statements. The method has four limitations:

- It measures agreement or disagreement with statements but not the intensity of agreement or disagreement.
- It assumes that judges and others agree on where statements appear in a rating system.
- It is time consuming and costly.
- It is possible to get the same overall score in several ways because agreement or disagreement with different combinations of statements can produce the same average.

3. *Bogardus social distance scale.* A measure of the "social distance" that separates social groups from each other is the **Bogardus social distance scale**. We use it with one group to learn how much distance its members feel toward a target or "outgroup." Emory Bogardus developed this technique in the 1920s to measure the willingness of members of different ethnic groups to associate with each other. Since then it has been used to see how close or distant people in one group feel toward some other group (e.g., a religious minority or a deviant group).[22]

Bogardus social distance scale A scale measuring the social distance between two or more social groups by having members of one group indicate the limit of their comfort with various types of social interaction or closeness with members of the other group(s).

Example of Thurstone Scaling

Variable Measured: Opinion with regard to the death penalty.

Step 1: Develop 120 statements about the death penalty using personal experience, the popular and professional literature, and statements by others.

Example Statements
1. I think that the death penalty is cruel and unnecessary punishment.
2. Without the death penalty, there would be many more violent crimes.
3. I believe that the death penalty should be used only for a few extremely violent crimes.
4. I do not think that anyone was ever prevented from committing a murder because of fear of the death penalty.
5. I do not think that people should be exempt from the death penalty if they committed a murder even if they are insane.
6. I believe that the Bible justifies the use of the death penalty.
7. The death penalty itself is not the problem for me, but I believe that electrocuting people is a cruel way to put them to death.

Step 2: Place each statement on a separate card or sheet of paper and make 100 sets of the 120 statements.

Step 3: Locate 100 persons who agree to serve as judges. Give each judge a set of the statements and instructions to place them in one of 11 piles, from 1 = highly unfavorable statement through 11 = highly favorable statement.

Step 4: The judges place each statement into one of the 11 piles (e.g., Judge 1 puts statement 1 into pile 2; Judge 2 puts the same statement into pile 1; Judge 3 also puts it into pile 2, Judge 4 puts it in pile 3, and so on).

Step 5: Collect piles from judges and create a chart summarizing their responses. See the example chart that follows.

NUMBER OF JUDGES RATING EACH STATEMENT RATING PILE

Statement	Unfavorable				Neutral				Favorable			Total
	1	2	3	4	5	6	7	8	9	10	11	
1	23	60	12	5	0	0	0	0	0	0	0	100
2	0	0	0	0	2	12	18	41	19	8	0	100
3	2	8	7	13	31	19	12	6	2	0	0	100
4	9	11	62	10	4	4	0	0	0	0	0	100

Step 6: Compute the average rating and degree of agreement by judges. For example, the average for question 1 is about 2, so there is high agreement; the average for question 3 is closer to 5, and there is much less agreement.

Step 7: Choose the final 20 statements to include in the death penalty opinion scale. Choose statements if the judges showed agreement (most placed an item in the same or a nearby pile) and ones that reflect the entire range of opinion, from favorable to neutral to unfavorable.

Step 8: Prepare a 20-statement questionnaire, and ask people in a study whether they agree or disagree with the statements.

The scale has a simple logic. We ask people to respond to a series of ordered statements. We place more socially intimate or close situations at one end and the least socially threatening situations at the opposite end. The scale's logic assumes that a person who is uncomfortable with another social group and might accept a few nonthreatening (socially distant) situations will express discomfort or refusal regarding the more threatening (socially intimate) situations.

We can use the scale in several ways. For example, we give people a series of statements: People from Group X are entering your country, are in your town, work at your place of employment, live in your neighborhood, become your personal friends, and marry your brother or sister. We ask people whether they feel comfortable with the situation in the statement or the contact is acceptable. We ask people to respond to all statements until they are at a situation with which they do not feel comfortable. No set number of statements is required; the number usually ranges from five to nine.

We can use the Bogardus scale to see how distant people feel from one outgroup versus another (see Example Box 7.8, Example of Bogardus Social Distance Scale). We can use the measure of social distance as either an independent or a dependent variable. For example, we might believe that social distance from a group is highest for people who have some other characteristic, such as education. Our hypothesis might be that White people's feelings of social distance toward Vietnamese people is negatively associated with education; that is, the least educated Whites feel the most social distance. In this situation, social distance is the dependent variable, and amount of education is the independent variable.

The social distance scale has two potential limitations. First, we must tailor the categories to a specific outgroup and social setting. Second, it is not easy for us to compare how a respondent feels toward several different groups unless the respondent completes a similar social distance scale for all outgroups at the same time. Of course, how a respondent completes the scale and the respondent's actual behavior in specific social situations may differ.

4. *Semantic differential.* Developed in the 1950s as an indirect measure of a person's feelings about a concept, object, or other person, **semantic differential** measures subjective feelings by using many adjectives because people usually communicate evaluations through adjectives. Most adjectives have polar opposites (e.g., *light/dark, hard/soft, slow/fast*). The semantic differential attempts to capture evaluations by relying on the connotations of adjectives. In this way, it measures a person's feelings and evaluations in an indirect manner.

To use the semantic differential, we offer research participants a list of paired opposite adjectives with a continuum of 7 to 11 points between them. We ask participants to mark the spot on the continuum between the adjectives that best expresses their evaluation or feelings. The adjectives can be very diverse and should be mixed (e.g., positive items should not be located mostly on either the right or the left side). Adjectives in English tend to fall into three major classes of meaning: evaluation *(good–bad),* potency *(strong–weak),* and activity *(active–passive).* Of the three classes, evaluation is usually the most significant.

The most difficult part of the semantic differential is analyzing the results. We need to use advanced statistical procedures to do so. Results from the procedures inform us as to how a person perceives different concepts or how people view a concept, object, or person. For example, political analysts might discover that young voters perceive their candidate to be traditional, weak, and slow, and midway between good and bad. Elderly voters perceive the candidate as leaning toward strong, fast, and good, and midway between traditional and modern. In Example Box 7.9, Example of Semantic Differential on page 235, a person rated two concepts. The pattern of responses for each concept

---

Semantic differential   A scale that indirectly measures feelings or thoughts by presenting people a topic or object and a list of polar opposite adjectives or adverbs and then having them indicate feelings by marking one of several spaces between the two adjectives or adverbs.

EXAMPLE BOX **7.8**

Example of Bogardus Social Distance Scale

A researcher wants to find out how socially distant freshmen college students feel from exchange students from two different countries: Nigeria and Germany. She wants to see whether students feel more distant from students coming from Africa or from Europe. She uses the following series of questions in an interview:

> Please give me your first reaction, yes or no, whether you personally would feel comfortable having an exchange student from (name of country):
>
> ———— As a visitor to your college for a week
>
> ———— As a full-time student enrolled at your college
>
> ———— Taking several of the same classes you are taking
>
> ———— Sitting next to you in class and studying with you for exams
>
> ———— Living a few doors down the hall on the same floor in your dormitory
>
> ———— As a same-sex roommate sharing your dorm room
>
> ———— As someone of the opposite sex who has asked you to go out on a date

Hypothetical Results

| | Percentage of Freshmen Who Report Feeling Comfortable | |
	Nigeria	Germany
Visitor	100%	100%
Enrolled	98	100
Same class	95	98
Study together	82	88
Same dorm	71	83
Roommate	50	76
Go on date	42	64

The results suggest that freshmen feel more distant from Nigerian students than from German students. Almost all feel comfortable having the international students as visitors, enrolled in the college, and taking classes. Feelings of distance increase as interpersonal contact increases, especially if the contact involves personal living settings or activities not directly related to the classroom.

illustrates how this individual feels. This person views the two concepts differently and appears to feel negatively about divorce.

Guttman scaling index   A scale that researchers use after data are collected to reveal whether a hierarchical pattern exists among responses so that people who give responses at a "higher level" also tend to give "lower level" ones.

Statistical techniques can create three-dimensional diagrams of results.[23] The three aspects are diagrammed in a three-dimensional "semantic space." In the diagram, "good" is up and "bad" is down, "active" is left and "passive" is right, "strong" is away from the viewer and "weak" is close.

5. *Guttman scaling.* Also called *cumulative scaling,* the **Guttman scaling index** differs from the previous scales or indexes in that we use it to

EXAMPLE BOX **7.9**

Example of Semantic Differential

Please read each pair of adjectives below and then place a mark on the blank space that comes closest to your first impression feeling. There are no right or wrong answers.

How do you feel about the idea of divorce?

	1	2	3	4	5	6	7	8	9	
Bad		X								Good
Deep								X		Shallow
Weak			X							Strong
Fair								X		Unfair
Quiet									X	Loud
Modern	X									Traditional
Simple						X				Complex
Fast		X								Slow
Dirty		X								Clean

How do you feel about the idea of marriage?

	1	2	3	4	5	6	7	8	9	
Bad									X	Good
Deep		X								Shallow
Weak								X		Strong
Fair		X								Unfair
Quiet			X							Loud
Modern									X	Traditional
Simple						X				Complex
Fast								X		Slow
Dirty							X			Clean

evaluate data after collecting them. This means that we must design a study with the Guttman scaling technique in mind. Louis Guttman developed the scale in the 1940s to determine whether there was a structured relationship among a set of indicators. He wanted to learn whether multiple indicators about an issue had an underlying single dimension or cumulative intensity.[24]

To use Guttman scaling, we begin by measuring a set of indicators or items. These can be questionnaire items, votes, or observed characteristics. We usually measure three to twenty indicators in a simple yes/no or present/absent fashion. We select items for which we believe there could be a logical relationship among all of them. We place the results into a Guttman scale chart and next determine whether there is a hierarchical pattern among items.

After we have the data, we can consider all possible combinations of responses. For example, we have three items: whether a child knows (1) her age, (2) her telephone number, and (3) three local elected political officials. The little girl could know her age but no other answer, or all three, or only her age and telephone number. Three items have eight possible combinations of answers or patterns of responses from not knowing any through knowing all three. There is a mathematical way to compute the number of combinations (e.g., twenty-three); you can write down all combinations of yes or no for three questions and see the eight possibilities.

An application of Guttman scaling known as *scalogram analysis* allows us to test whether a patterned hierarchical relationship exists in the data. We can divide response patterns into scaled items and errors (or nonscalable). A scaled pattern for the child's knowledge example would be as follows: not knowing any item, knowing age only, knowing only age plus phone number, and knowing all three. All other combinations of answers (e.g., knowing the political leaders but not her age) are logically possible but nonscalable. If we find a hierarchical relationship, then most answers fit into the scalable patterns. The items are scalable, or capable of forming a Guttman scale, if a hierarchical pattern exists. For higher order items, a smaller number would agree but all would also agree to the lower order ones but not vice versa. In other words, higher order items build on the middle-level ones, and middle-level build on lower ones.

Statistical procedures indicate the degree to which items fit the expected hierarchical pattern. Such procedures produce a coefficient that ranges from zero to 100 percent. A score of zero indicates a random pattern without hierarchical structure; one of 100 percent indicates that all responses fit the hierarchical pattern. Alternative statistics to measure scalability have also been suggested.[25] (See Example Box 7.10, Guttman Scale Example.)

EXAMPLE BOX **7.10**

Guttman Scale Example

Crozat (1998) examined public responses to various forms of political protest. He looked at survey data on the public's acceptance of forms of protest in Great Britain, Germany, Italy, the Netherlands, and the United States in 1974 and 1990. He found that the pattern of the public's acceptance formed a Guttman scale. Those who accepted more intense forms of protest (e.g., strikes and sit-ins) almost always accepted more modest forms (e.g., petitions or demonstrations), but not all who accepted modest forms accepted the more intense forms. In addition to showing the usefulness of the Guttman scale, Crozat also found that people in different nations saw protest similarly and the degree of Guttman scalability increased over time. Thus, the pattern of acceptance of protest activities was Guttman "scalable" in both time periods, but it more closely followed the Guttman pattern in 1990 than in 1974.

	FORM OF PROTEST				
	Petitions	*Demonstrations*	*Boycotts*	*Strikes*	*Sit-Ins*
Guttman Patterns					
	N	N	N	N	N
	Y	N	N	N	N
	Y	Y	N	N	N
	Y	Y	Y	N	N
	Y	Y	Y	Y	N
	Y	Y	Y	Y	Y
Other Patterns (examples only)					
	N	Y	N	Y	N
	Y	N	Y	Y	N
	Y	N	Y	N	N
	N	Y	Y	N	N
	Y	N	N	Y	Y

Clogg and Sawyer (1981) studied U.S. attitudes toward abortion using Guttman scaling. They examined the different conditions under which people thought abortion was acceptable (e.g., mother's health in danger, pregnancy resulting from rape). They discovered that 84.2 percent of responses fit into a scaled response pattern.

CONCLUSION

This chapter dicussed the principles and processes of measurement. Central to measurement is how we conceptualize—or refine and clarify ideas into conceptual definitions and operationalize conceptual variables into specific measures—or develop procedures that link conceptual definitions to empirical reality. How we approach these processes varies depending on whether a study is primarily qualitative or quantitative. In a quantitative study, we usually adopt a more deductive path, whereas with a qualitative study, the path is more inductive. Nonetheless, they share the same goal to establish an unambiguous connection between abstract ideas and empirical data.

The chapter also discussed the principles of reliability and validity. *Reliability* refers to a measure's dependability; *validity* refers to its truthfulness or the fit between a construct and data. In both quantitative and qualitative studies, we try to measure in a consistent way and seek a tight fit between the abstract ideas and the empirical social world. In addition, the principles of measurement are applied in quantitative studies to build indexes and scales. The chapter also discussed some major scales in use.

Beyond the core ideas of reliability and validity, we now know principles of sound measurement: Create clear definitions for concepts, use multiple indicators, and, as appropriate, weigh and standardize the data. These principles hold across all fields of study (e.g., family, criminology, inequality, race relations) and across the many research techniques (e.g., experiments, surveys).

As you are probably beginning to realize, a sound research project involves doing a good job in each phase of research. Serious mistakes or sloppiness in any one phase can do irreparable damage to the results, even if the other phases of the research project were conducted in a flawless manner.

KEY TERMS

bogardus social distance scale
casing
conceptual definition
conceptual hypothesis
conceptualization
concurrent validity
construct validity
content validity
continuous variables
convergent validity
criterion validity
discrete variables
discriminant validity
empirical hypothesis

equivalence reliability
exhaustive attributes
face validity
guttman scaling index
index
interval-level measurement
level of measurement
likert scale
measurement reliability
measurement validity
multiple indicators
mutually exclusive attributes
nominal-level measurement
operational definition

operationalization
ordinal-level measurement
predictive validity
ratio-level measurement
representative reliability
response set
rules of correspondence
scale
semantic differential
stability reliability
standardization
thurstone scaling
unidimensionality

REVIEW QUESTIONS

1. What are the three basic parts of measurement, and how do they fit together?
2. What is the difference between reliability and validity, and how do they complement each other?
3. What are ways to improve the reliability of a measure?
4. How do the levels of measurement differ from each other?
5. What are the differences between convergent, content, and concurrent validity? Can you have all three at once? Explain your answer.
6. Why are multiple indicators usually better than one indicator?
7. What is the difference between the logic of a scale and that of an index?
8. Why is unidimensionality an important characteristic of a scale?
9. What are advantages and disadvantages of weighting indexes?
10. How does standardization make comparison easier?

NOTES

1. Duncan (1984:220–239) presented cautions from a positivist approach on the issue of measuring anything.
2. The terms *concept, construct,* and *idea* are used more or less interchangeably, but their meanings have some differences. An *idea* is any mental image, belief, or impression. It refers to any vague impression, opinion, or thought. A *concept* is a thought, a general notion, or a generalized idea about a class of objects. A *construct* is a thought that is systematically put together, an orderly arrangement of ideas, facts, and impressions. The term *construct* is used here because its emphasis is on taking vague concepts and turning them into systematically organized ideas.
3. See Grinnell (1987:5–18) for further discussion.
4. See Blalock (1982:25–27) and Costner (1985) on the rules of correspondence or the auxiliary theories that connect an abstract concept with empirical indicators. Also see Zeller and Carmines (1980:5) for a diagram that illustrates the place of the rules in the measurement process. In his presidential address to the American Sociological Association in 1979, Hubert Blalock (1979a:882) said, "I believe that the most serious and important problems that require our immediate and concerted attention are those of conceptualization and measurement."
5. See Bailey (1984, 1986) for a discussion of the three levels.
6. See Bohrnstedt (1992a,b) and Carmines and Zeller (1979) for discussions of reliability and its various types.

7. See Sullivan and Feldman (1979) on multiple indicators. A more technical discussion can be found in Herting (1985), Herting and Costner (1985), and Scott (1968).
8. See Carmines and Zeller (1979:17). For a discussion of the many types of validity, see Brinberg and McGrath (1982).
9. The epistemic correlation is discussed in Costner (1985) and in Zeller and Carmines (1980:50–51, 137–139).
10. Kidder (1982) discussed the issue of disagreements over face validity, such as acceptance of a measure's meaning by the scientific community but not the subjects being studied.
11. This was adapted from Carmines and Zeller (1979:20–21).
12. For a discussion of types of criterion validity, see Carmines and Zeller (1979:17–19) and Fiske (1982) for construct validity.
13. See Cook and Campbell (1979) for elaboration.
14. See Borgatta and Bohrnstedt (1980) and Duncan (1984:119–155) for a discussion and critique of the topic of levels of measurement.
15. Johnson and Creech (1983) examined the measurement errors that occur when variables that are conceptualized as continuous are operationalized in a series of ordinal categories. They argued that errors are not serious if more than four categories and large samples are used.

16. For compilations of indexes and scales used in social research, see Brodsky and Smitherman (1983), Miller (1991), Robinson and colleagues (1972), Robinson and Shaver (1969), and Schuessler (1982).

17. For a discussion of weighted and unweighted index scores, see Nunnally (1978:534).

18. Feeling thermometers are discussed in Wilcox and associates (1989).

19. For more information on Likert scales, see Anderson and associates (1983:252–255), Converse (1987:72–75), McIver and Carmines (1981:22–38), and Spector (1992).

20. Some researchers treat Likert scales as interval-level measures, but there is disagreement on this issue. Statistically, whether the Likert scale has at least five response categories and an approximately even proportion of people answer in each category makes little difference.

21. McIver and Carmines (1981:16–21) have an excellent discussion of Thurstone scaling. Also see discussions in Anderson and colleagues (1983:248–252), Converse (1987:66–77), and Edwards (1957). The example used here is partially borrowed from Churchill (1983:249–254), who described the formula for scoring Thurstone scaling.

22. The social distance scale is described in Converse (1987:62–69). The most complete discussion can be found in Bogardus (1959).

23. The semantic differential is discussed in Nunnally (1978:535–543). Also see Heise (1965, 1970) on the analysis of scaled data.

24. See Guttman (1950).

25. See Bailey (1987:349–351) for a discussion of an improved method for determining scalability called *minimal marginal reproducibility*. Guttman scaling can involve more than yes/no choices and a large number of items, but the complexity increases quickly. A more elaborate discussion of Guttman scaling can be found in Anderson and associates (1983:256–260), Converse (1987:189–195), McIver and Carmines (1981:40–71), and Nunnally (1978:63–66). Clogg and Sawyer (1981) presented alternatives to Guttman scaling.

CHAPTER 8

Qualitative and Quantitative Sampling

Reasons for Sampling
Sampling Strategies
Conclusion

Sampling is a major problem for any type of research. We can't study every case of whatever we're interested in, nor should we want to. Every scientific enterprise tries to find out something that will apply to everything *of a certain kind by studying a few examples,* the results of the study being, as we say, "generalizable."

—Howard Becker, *Tricks of the Trade,* p. 67

In *Promises I Can Keep,* an in-depth study of low-income mothers, Edin and Kefalas (2005) first identified eight low-income neighborhoods in the Philadelphia, Pennsylvania, area through extensive qualitative fieldwork and quantitative analysis of census data. Each neighborhood met three selection criteria: at least 20 percent of householders were below the poverty line, at least 20 percent of all households had a single parent, and each had a large number of Black, White, and Hispanic residents. In each neighborhood, Edin and Kefalas recruited half of the mothers to interview through referrals from local experts (teachers, social workers, public nurses, clergy, business owners, and public housing officials) and half by posting fliers on public phone booths or personally contacting mothers on street corners. All mothers had incomes putting them below the poverty line in the previous year. Edin and Kefalas tried to get a mixture: 50 Whites, 50 African Americans, and 50 Puerto Ricans, and tried to get one-half over 25 and one-half under 25 years old. They eventually had 162 mothers, 52 whites, 63 African American, and 47 Puerto Rican. Only 40 were over 25 years old, but ages ranged from 15 to 56. They say, "The resulting sample is not random or representative but is quite heterogeneous" (238).

REASONS FOR SAMPLING

When we sample, we select some cases to examine in detail, and then we use what we learn from them to understand a much larger set of cases. Most, but

Sample A small set of cases a researcher selects from a large pool and generalizes to the population.

not all, empirical studies use sampling. Depending on the study, the method we use for sampling can differ. Most books on sampling emphasize its use in quantitative research and contain applied mathematics and quantitative examples. The primary use of sampling in quantitative studies is to create a representative sample (i.e., a **sample**, a selected small collection of cases or units) that closely reproduces or represents features of interest in a larger collection of cases, called the **population**.

We examine data in a sample in detail, and if we sampled correctly, we can generalize its results to the entire population. We need to use very precise sampling procedures to create representative samples in quantitative research. These procedures rely on the mathematics of probabilities and hence, are called *probability sampling*.

In most quantitative studies, we want to see how many cases of a population fall into various categories of interest. For example, we might ask how many in the population of all of Chicago's high school students fit into various categories (e.g., high-income family, single-parent family, illegal drug user, delinquent behavior arrestee, musically talented person). We use probability samples in quantitative research because they are very efficient. They save a lot of time and cost for the accuracy they deliver. A properly conducted probability sample may cost 1/1000 the cost and time of gathering information on an entire population, yet it will yield virtually identical results. Let us say we are interested in gathering data on the 18 million people in the United States diagnosed with diabetes. From a well-designed probability sample of 1,800, we can take what we learned and generalize it to all 18 million. It is more efficient to study 1,800 people to learn about 18 million than to study all 18 million people.

Probability samples can be highly accurate. For large populations, data from a well-designed, carefully executed probability sample are often equally if not more accurate than trying to reach every case in the population, but this fact confuses many people. Actually, when the U.S. government planned its 2000 census, all of the social researchers and statistically trained scientists agreed that probability sampling would produce more accurate data than the traditional census method of trying to count every person. A careful probability sample of 30,000 has a very tiny and known error rate. If we try to locate every single person of 300,000,000, systematic errors will slip in unless we take extraordinary efforts and expend huge amounts of time and money. By the way, the government actually conducted the census in the traditional way, but it was for political, not scientific, reasons.

Sampling proceeds differently in qualitative studies and often has a different purpose from quantitative studies. In fact, using the word *sampling* creates confusion in qualitative research because the term is closely associated with quantitative studies (see Luker, 2008:101). In qualitative studies, to allow us to make statements about categories in the population, we rarely sample to gather a small set of cases that is a mathematically accurate reproduction of the entire population. Instead, we sample to identify relevant categories at work in a few cases. In quantitative sampling, we select cases/units. We then treat them as carriers of aspects/features of the social world. A sample of cases/units "stands in" for the much larger population of cases/units. We pick a few to "stand in" for the many. In contrast, the logic of the qualitative sample is to sample aspects/features of the social world. The aspects/features of our sample highlight or "shine light into" key dimensions or processes in a complex social life. We pick a few to provide clarity, insight, and understanding about issues or relationships in the social world. In qualitative sampling, our goal is to deepen understanding about a larger process, relationship, or social scene. A sample gives us valuable information or new aspects. The aspects accentuate, enhance, or enrich key features or situations. We sample to open up new theoretical insights, reveal distinctive aspects of people or social settings, or deepen understanding of complex situations, events, or relationships. In qualitative research, "it is their relevance to the research topic rather than their representativeness which determines the way in which the people to be studied are selected" (Flick, 1998: 41).

We should not overdo the quantitative-qualitative distinction. In a few situations, a study that is primarily quantitative will use the qualitative-sampling

---

Population   The abstract idea of a large group of many cases from which a researcher draws a sample and to which results from a sample are generalized.

strategy and vice versa. Nonetheless, most quantitative studies use probability or probability-like samples while most qualitative studies use a nonprobability method and nonrepresentative strategy.

SAMPLING STRATEGIES

We want to avoid two types of possible sampling mistakes. The first is to conduct sampling in a sloppy or improper manner; the second is to choose a type of sample inappropriate for a study's purpose. The first mistake reminds us to be very meticulous and systematic when we sample. To avoid the second mistake, we need a sampling strategy that matches our specific study's purpose and data. Sampling strategies fall into two broad types: a sample that will accurately represent the population of cases, and all others. We primarily use the first strategy in quantitative studies and the latter in qualitative studies.

Strategies When the Goal Is to Create a Representative Sample

In a representative sample, our goal is to create sample data that mirror or represent many other cases that we cannot directly examine. We can do this in two ways. The first is the preferred method and considered the "gold standard" for representative samples, the *probability sample*. It builds on more than a century of careful reasoning and applied mathematics plus thousands of studies in natural science and quantitative social science. With a probability sampling strategy, we try to create an accurate representative sample that has mathematically predictable errors (i.e., precisely known chances of being "off target"). This sampling approach is complex with several subtypes. Before we examine it, let us look at the second, simpler way to produce a representative sample: to use a nonprobability

technique. It is a less accurate substitute when we want a representative sample; however, it is acceptable when probability sampling is impossible, too costly, time consuming, or impractical.

Nonprobability Sampling Techniques. Ideally, we would prefer probability samples when we want to create a representative sample, as a less demanding alternative there are two nonprobability alternatives: convenience and quota samples. In **convenience sampling** (also called *accidental, availability,* or *haphazard sampling*), our primary criteria for selecting cases are that they are easy to reach, convenient, or readily available. This sample type may be legitimate for a few exploratory preliminary studies and some qualitative research studies when our purpose is something other than creating a representative sample. Unfortunately, it often produces very nonrepresentative samples, so it is *not recommended* for creating an accurate sample to represent the population.

When we select cases based on convenience, our sample can seriously misrepresent features in the entire population.[1] You may ask why, if this method is so bad and samples can be seriously nonrepresentative, anyone would use it. The reason is simple: convenience samples are easy, cheap, and quick to obtain. Another reason might be that people are ignorant about how to create a good representative sample. An example of such sampling is the person-on-the-street interview conducted by television programs. Television interviewers go out on the street with camera and microphone to talk to a few people who are convenient to interview. The people walking past a television studio in the middle of the day do not represent everyone. Likewise, television interviewers tend to pick people who look "normal" to them and avoid people who are unattractive, disabled, impoverished, elderly, or inarticulate. Another example is a newspaper that asks readers to clip a questionnaire and mail it in, a Web site that asks users to click on a choice, or a television program that asks viewers to call in their choices. Such samples may have entertainment value, but they easily yield highly misleading data

---

Convenience sampling   A nonrandom sample in which the researcher selects anyone he or she happens to come across.

that do not represent the population even when a large number of people respond.

Maybe you wonder what makes such a sample nonrepresentative. If you want to know about everyone in city XYZ that has a population of 1 million, only some read the newspaper, visit a Web site, or tuned into a program. Also, not everyone who is reading the newspaper, visiting the Web site, or has tuned in is equally interested in an issue. Some people will respond, and there may be many of them (e.g., 50,000), but they are self-selected. We cannot generalize accurately from self-selected people to the entire population. Many in the population do not read the newspaper, visit specific Web sites, or tune into certain television programs, and even if they did, they may lack the interest and motivation to participate. Two key ideas to remember about representative samples are that: (1) self-selection yields a nonrepresentative sample and (2) a big sample size alone is not enough to make a sample representative.

For many purposes, well-designed **quota sampling** is an acceptable nonprobability substitute method for producing a quasi-representative sample.[2] In quota sampling, we first identify relevant categories among the population we are sampling to capture diversity among units (e.g., male and female; or under age 30, ages 30 to 60, over age 60). Next we determine how many cases to get for each category—this is our "quota." Thus, we fix a number of cases in various categories of the sample at the start.

Let us return to the example of sampling residents from city XYZ. You select twenty-five males and twenty-five females under age 30 years of age, fifty males and fifty females aged 30 to 60, and fifteen males and fifteen females over age 60 for a 180-person sample. While this is a start as a population's diversity, it is difficult to represent all possible population characteristics accurately (see Figure 8.1 on page 244). Nonetheless, quota sampling ensures that a sample has some diversity. In contrast, in convenience sampling, everyone in a sample might be of the same age, gender, or background. The description of sampling in the

Promises I Can Keep study at the opening of this chapter used quota sampling (also see Example Box 8.1, Quota Samples on page 245).

Quota sampling is relatively easy. My students conducted an opinion survey of the undergraduate student body using quota sampling. We used three quota categories—gender, class, and minority/majority group status—and a convenience selection method (i.e., a student interviewer approached anyone in the library, a classroom, the cafeteria). We set the numbers to be interviewed in each quota category in advance: 50 percent males and 50 percent females; 35 percent freshman, 25 percent sophomores, 20 percent juniors, and 20 percent seniors; and 10 percent minority and 90 percent majority racially. We picked the proportions based on approximate representation in the student body according to university official records. In the study, a student interviewer approached a person, confirmed that he or she was a student, and verified his or her gender, class, and minority/majority status. If the person fit an unfilled quota (e.g., locate five freshman males who are racial-ethnic minorities), the person was included in the sample and the interviewer proceeded to ask survey questions. If the person did not fit the quota, the interviewer quickly thanked the person without asking survey questions and moved on to someone else.

Quota samples have three weaknesses. First, they capture only a few aspects (e.g., gender and age) of all population diversity and ignore others (e.g., race-ethnicity, area of residence in the city, income level). Second, the fixed number of cases in each category may not accurately reflect the proportion of cases in the total population for the category. Perhaps 20 percent of city residents are over 60 years old but are 10 percent of a quota. Lastly, we use convenience sampling selection for each

---

Quota sampling A nonrandom sample in which the researcher first identifies general categories into which cases or people will be placed and then selects cases to reach a predetermined number in each category.

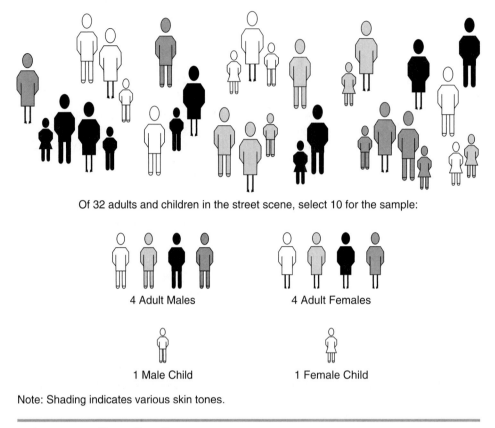

Of 32 adults and children in the street scene, select 10 for the sample:

4 Adult Males

4 Adult Females

1 Male Child

1 Female Child

Note: Shading indicates various skin tones.

FIGURE 8.1   Quota Sampling

quota category. For example, we include the first twenty-five males under age 30 we encounter—even if all twenty-five are high-income White lawyers who just returned from a seminar on financial investments. Nothing prevents us from sampling only "friendly"-acting people who want us to pick them.

Probability Sampling Techniques. Probability sampling is the "gold standard" for creating a representative sample. It has a specialized vocabulary

that may make it difficult to understand until you learn it, so next we will review some of its vocabulary.

The Language of Probability Sampling. You draw a sample from a large collection of cases/units. Each case/unit is your **sampling element**. It is the unit of analysis or a case in a population. It could be a person, a family, a neighborhood, a nation, an organization, a written document, a symbolic message (television commercial, display of a flag), or a social action (e.g., an arrest, a divorce, or a kiss).

The large collection is the population, but sometimes the word *universe* (defined in Chapter 6) is used. To define the population, you specify the elements and identify its geographical

Sampling element The name for a case or single unit to be sampled.

EXAMPLE BOX **8.1**
Quota Samples

Two studies illustrate different uses of quota sampling in quantitative research. In a study, McMahon, McAlaney, and Edgar (2007) wanted to examine public views of binge drinking in the United Kingdom. They noted that most past research was on young adults and campaigns to curb binge drinking had been ineffective. The authors wanted to learn about public perceptions of binge drinking among the entire adult population. They developed a survey that asked how people defined binge drinking, the extent to which they saw it as a concern, and reasons for and solutions to it. They combined quota sampling with another sampling method to interview 586 people in one city (Inverclyde, Scotland). For quota sampling, interviewers approached potential participants in the streets surrounding a shopping center and invited them to take part in the survey. The quota was based on getting a balance of gender and six age categories. The other method was to go door-to-door in several low-income neighborhoods. The authors learned useful information about views on binge drinking across age groups in both genders in one city. They found wide variation in definitions of binge drinking and support for a "false consensus effect" in which a small number of the heaviest drinkers see their behavior as normal and socially accepted. Nonetheless, the sample is not representative, so findings on the extent of binge drinking in the public and views about it may not reflect the behaviors or views within the city's overall population.

A second study in China by Bian, Breiger, Davis, and Galaskiewicz (2005) employed a targeted use of quota sampling. Their interest was in the difference between the social networks and social ties (e.g.,

friends, family) among people in different social classes in major Chinese cities. They selected households in four of China's largest metropolitan areas (Shanghai, Shenzhen, Tianjin, and Wuhan), identified a set of neighborhoods in each, and then sampled 100 people per city. They had a list of thirteen occupational titles that represented the full range of the class system in China and 88 percent of all working people in the four cities. Their quota was to get an equal number in each city and a sufficient number of households in each of the thirteen occupational categories for careful analysis. Thus, only 4 percent of the people held the position as manager, but nearly 10 percent of the sample were managers, and 40 percent of people held an industrial worker occupation, but close to 10 percent of people in the sample were industrial workers. The study goal was to test hypotheses about whether a household's social ties are with others of similar or different social classes. They asked households to maintain a written log of social visits (in person or via phone) with other people and recorded the occupation of visitors. This process lasted a year, and researchers interviewed people every three months. The primary interest in the study was to compare patterns of social networks across the various social classes. For example, did managers socialize only with other managers or with people from a wide range of classes? Did industrial workers socialize with industrial workers as well as people in various lower occupations but not in higher occupations? Because the study goal was to compare social network patterns across the various classes, not to have a representative sample that described the Chinese population, it was a highly effective use of quota sampling.

---

and temporal boundaries as well as any other relevant boundaries.

Most probability studies with large samples of the entire U.S. population have several boundaries. They include adults over 18 who are residents of the forty-eight continental states and exclude the institutionalized population (i.e., people in hospitals, assisted living and nursing homes, military

housing, prisons and jails, homeless and battered women's shelters, college dormitories). Ignoring people in Alaska, Hawaii, and Puerto Rico and excluding the institutionalized population can throw off statistics—for example, the unemployment rate would be higher if the millions of people in prison were included in calculations (see Western and Pettit, 2005). Many studies include only English speakers, yet as of 2007, roughly 5 percent of U.S. households were "linguistically isolated" (no one over 14 spoke English very well (U.S. Census Bureau, 2007).

To draw a probability sample we start with a population, but *population* is an abstract concept. We must conceptualize and define it more precisely in a process similar to conceptualization in the measurement process (see Chapter 7), for example, all people in Tampa, Florida, or all college students in the state of Nevada. A **target population** is the specific collection of elements we will study (e.g., noninstitutionalized persons 18 years of age and older with legal residences with the city limits of Tampa on May 15, 2011; students enrolled full-time in an accredited two- or four-year postsecondary educational facility in the state of Nevada in October 2010). In some ways, the target population is analogous to our use of a conceptual definition of the measurement process.

Populations are in constant motion, so we need a temporal boundary. For example, in a city at any given moment, people are dying, boarding or getting off airplanes, and driving across city boundaries in cars. Whom should we count? Do we exclude a long-time city resident who happens to be on vacation when the time is fixed? A population (e.g., persons over the age of 18 who are in the city limits of Milwaukee, Wisconsin, at 12:01 A.M. on March 1, 2011), is an abstract idea. It exists in the mind but is difficult to pinpoint concretely (see Example Box 8.2, Examples of Populations).

After we conceptualize our population, we need to create an operational definition for the abstract population idea in a way that is analogous to operationalization in the measurement process (see Chapter 7). We turn the abstract idea into an empirically concrete specific list that closely approximates all population elements. This is our **sampling frame**.

There are many types of sampling frames: telephone directories, tax records, driver's license records, and so on. Listing the elements in a population sounds simple, but it is often difficult because often there is no accurate, up-to-date list of all elements in a population.

A good sampling frame is crucial for accurate sampling. Any mismatch between a sampling frame and the conceptually defined population can create errors. Just as a mismatch between our theoretical and operational definitions of a variable weakens measurement validity, a mismatch between the abstract population and the sampling frame weakens our sampling validity. The most famous case in the history of sampling involved an issue of sampling frames.[3] (See Expansion Box 8.1, Sampling Frames and the History of Sampling.)

Let us say that our population is all adult residents in the Pacific coast region of the United States in 2010. We contact state departments of transportation to obtain lists of everyone with a driver's

---

Target population The concretely specified large group of many cases from which a researcher draws a sample and to which results from the sample are generalized.

Sampling frame A list of cases in a population, or the best approximation of them.

EXAMPLE BOX 8.2

Examples of Populations

1. All persons ages 16 or older living in Australia on December 2, 2009, who were not incarcerated in prison, asylums, and similar institutions
2. All business establishments employing more than 100 persons in Ontario Province, Canada, that operated in the month of July 2005
3. All admissions to public or private hospitals in the state of New Jersey between August 1, 1988, and July 31, 1993
4. All television commercials aired between 7:00 A.M. and 11:00 P.M. Eastern Standard Time on three major U.S. networks between November 1 and November 25, 2004
5. All currently practicing physicians in the United States who received medical degrees between January 1, 1960, and the present
6. All African American male heroin addicts in the Vancouver, British Columbia, or Seattle, Washington, metropolitan areas during 2004

EXPANSION BOX 8.1
Sampling Frames and the History of Sampling

A famous case in the history of sampling illustrates the limitations of quota sampling and of sampling frames. The *Literary Digest,* a major U.S. magazine, sent postcards to people before the 1920, 1924, 1928, and 1932 U.S. presidential elections. The magazine took the names for its sample from automobile registrations and telephone directories. People returned the postcards indicating for whom they would vote. The magazine correctly predicted all four election outcomes. The magazine's success with predictions was well known, and in 1936, it increased the sample from about 1 million to 10 million. 2.4 million people returned postcards they were sent. The magazine predicted a huge victory for Alf Landon over Franklin D. Roosevelt. But the *Literary Digest* was wrong; Roosevelt won by a landslide. Another random sample of 50,000 by George Gallup was accurate within 1 percent of the result.

The prediction was wrong for several reasons, but the sampling mistakes were central. Although the magazine sampled a very large number of people, its sampling frame did not accurately represent the target population (i.e., all voters). It excluded people without telephones or automobiles, a sizable percentage of the population in 1936. The frame excluded as much as 65 percent of the population, particularly a section of the voting population (lower income) that tended to favor Roosevelt. The magazine had been accurate in earlier elections because people with higher and lower incomes did not differ in the way they voted. Also, during earlier elections before the Great Depression, more low-income people could afford to have telephones and automobiles.

The *Literary Digest* mistake teaches us two lessons. First, an accurate sampling frame is crucial. Second, the size of a sample is less important than how accurately it represents the population. A representative sample of 50,000 can give more accurate predictions about the U.S. population than a nonrepresentative sample of 10 million or 50 million.

---

license in California, Oregon, and Washington. We know some people do not have driver's licenses, although some people drive illegally without them or do not drive. The lists of people with licenses, even if updated regularly, quickly goes out of date as people move into or out of a state. This example shows that before we use official records, such as driver's licenses, as a sampling frame, we must know how officials produce such records. When the state of Oregon instituted a requirement that people show a social security number to obtain a driver's license, the number applying for licenses dropped by 10 percent (from 105,000 issued over three months of 2007 to 93,000 in the same three months of 2008). Thus, thousands disappeared from official records. We could try income tax records, but not everyone pays taxes. Some people cheat and do not pay, others have no income and do not have to file, others have died or have not begun to pay taxes, and still others have entered or left the area since taxes were due. Voter registration records exclude as much as half of the population. In the United States

between 53 and 77 percent of eligible voters are registered (Table 401, Statistical Abstract of the United States, 2009). Telephone directories are worse. Many people are not listed in a telephone directory, some people have unlisted numbers, and others have recently moved. With a few exceptions (e.g., a list of all students enrolled at a university), it is difficult to get a perfectly accurate sampling frame. A sampling frame can include those outside the target population (e.g., a telephone directory that lists people who have moved away) or it may omit those within it (e.g., those without telephones). (See Example Box 8.3, Sampling Frame on page 248.)

The ratio of a sample size to the size of the target population is the **sampling ratio**. If the target

---

Sampling ratio The number of cases in the sample divided by the number of cases in the population or the sampling frame, or the proportion of the population in a sample.

Sampling Frame

A study by Smith, Mitchell, Attebo, and Leeder (1997) in Australia shows how different sampling frames can influence a sample. The authors examined 2,557 people aged 49 and over living in a defined post code area recruited from a door-to-door census. Of all addresses, people in 80.9 percent were contacted and 87.9 percent of the people responded. The authors searched the telephone directory and the electoral roll for each person. The telephone directory listed 82.2 percent and the electoral roll contained 84.3 percent. Younger people, those who did not own their own homes, and those born outside of Australia were significantly less likely to be included in either sampling frame. The telephone directory was also likely to exclude people with higher occupational prestige while the electoral roll was likely to exclude unmarried persons and males.

population has 50,000 people and the sample has 150, then the sampling ratio is 150/50,000 = 0.003, or 0.3 percent. For a target population of 500 and sample of 100, the sampling ratio is 100/500 = 0.20,

Parameter A characteristic of the entire population that is estimated from a sample.

Statistic A word with several meanings including a numerical estimate of a population parameter computed from a sample.

or 20 percent. Usually, we use the number of elements in a sampling frame as our best estimate of the size of the target population.

Except for small specialized populations (e.g., all students in a classroom), when we do not need to sample, we use data from a sample to estimate features in the larger population. Any characteristic of a population (e.g., the percentage of city residents who smoke cigarettes, the average height of all women over the age of 21, the percent of people who believe in UFOs) is a population **parameter**. It is the true characteristic of the population. We do not know the parameter with absolute certainty for large populations (e.g., an entire nation), so we can estimate it by using sample data. Information in the sample used to estimate a population parameter is called a **statistic**. (See Figure 8.2.)

Random Sampling

In applied mathematics, probability theory relies on random processes. The word *random* has several meanings. In daily life, it can mean unpredictable, unusual, unexpected, or haphazard. In mathematics, random has a specific meaning: a selection process without any pattern. In mathematics, random processes mean that each element will have an equal probability of being selected. We can mathematically calculate the probability of outcomes over many cases with great precision for true random processes.

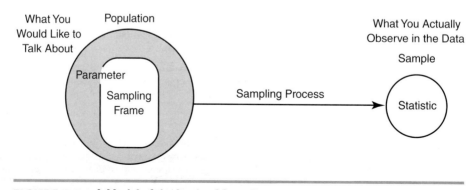

FIGURE 8.2   A Model of the Logic of Sampling

Random samples yield samples most likely to truly represent the entire population. They also allow us to calculate statistically the relationship between the sample and the population—that is, the size of the **sampling error**. The sampling error is the deviation between what is in the sample data and an ideal population parameter due to random processes.

Probability samples rely on random selection processes. Random selection for sampling requires more precision, time, and effort than samples with nonrandom selection. The formal mathematical procedure specifies exactly which person to pick for the sample, and it may be very difficult to locate that specific person! In sampling, random is not anyone, nor does it mean thoughtless or haphazard. For example, if we are using true random sampling in a telephone survey, we might have to call back six or seven times at different times of the days and on different days, trying to get a specific person whom the mathematically random process identified.[4]

This chapter does not cover all technical and statistical details of random sampling. Instead, we discuss the fundamentals of how probability sampling works, the difference between good and bad samples, how to draw a sample, and basic principles of sampling in social research. If you plan to pursue a career in quantitative research, you will need more mathematical and statistical background on probability and sampling than space permits here.

Five Ways to Sample Randomly

Simple Random. All probability samples are modeled on the **simple random sample** that first specifies the population and target population and identifies its specific sampling elements (e.g., all households in Prescott, Arizona, in March 2011). Next we create an accurate sampling frame and we then use a true random process (discussed later) to pick elements from the sampling frame. Beyond creating an accurate sampling frame, the next difficulty is that we must locate the specific sampled element selected by a random process. If the sampled element is a household, we may have to revisit or call back five times to contact that specific selected household.

To select elements from a sampling frame, we will need to create a list of random numbers that will tell us which elements on it to select. We will need as many random numbers as there are elements to be sampled. The random numbers should range from 1 (the first element on the sampling frame) to the highest number in our sampling frame. If the sampling frame lists 15,000 households, and we want to sample 150 from it, we need a list of 150 random numbers (i.e., numbers generated by a true random process, from 1 to 15,000).

There are two main ways to obtain a list of random numbers. The "old-fashioned" way is to use a **random-number table**. Such tables are available in most statistics and research methods books including this one (see Appendix). The numbers are generated by a pure random process so that any number has an equal probability of appearing in any position. Today most people use computer programs to produce lists of random numbers. Such programs are readily available and often free.

You may ask, once we select an element from the sampling frame, do we then return it to the sampling frame, or do we keep it separate? Unrestricted random sampling is called "random sampling with replacement"—that is, replacing an element after sampling it so it has a chance to be selected again. In simple random sampling without replacement, we "toss out" or ignore elements

---

Random sample   A sample using a mathermatically random method, such as a random-number table or computer program, so that each sampling element of a population has an equal probablity of being selected into the sample.

Sampling error   How much a sample deviates from being representative of the population.

Simple random sample   A random sample in which a researcher creates a sampling frame and uses a pure random process to select cases so that each sampling element in the population will have an equal probability of being selected.

Random-number table   A list of numbers that has no pattern and that researchers use to create a random process for selecting cases and other randomization purposes.

already selected for the sample. For almost all practical purposes in social science, random sampling is without replacement.

We can see the logic of simple random sampling with an elementary example: sampling marbles from a jar. Let us say I have a large jar full of 5,000 marbles, some red and some white. The marble is my sampling element, the 5,000 marbles are my population (both target and ideal), and my sample size is 100. I do not need a sampling frame because I am dealing with small physical objects. The population parameter I want to estimate is the percentage of red marbles in the jar.

I need a random process to select 100 marbles. For small objects, this is easy; I close my eyes, shake the jar, pick one marble, and repeat the procedure 100 times. I now have a random sample of marbles. I count the number of red marbles in my sample to estimate the percentage of red versus white marbles in the population. This is a lot easier than counting all 5,000 marbles. My sample has 52 white and 48 red marbles.

Does this mean that the population parameter is exactly 48 percent red marbles? Maybe or maybe not; because of random chance, my specific sample might be off. I can check my results by dumping the 100 marbles back in the jar, mixing the marbles, and drawing a second random sample of 100 marbles. On the second try, my sample has 49 white marbles and 51 red ones. Now I have a problem. Which is correct? You might ask how good this random sampling business is if different samples from the same population can yield different results. I repeat the procedure over and over until I have drawn 130 different samples of 100 marbles each (see Chart 8.1 for results). Most people might find it easier to empty the jar and count all 5,000 marbles, but

I want to understand the process of sampling. The results of my 130 different samples reveal a clear pattern. The most common mix of red and white marbles is 50/50. Samples that are close to that split are more frequent than those with more uneven splits. The population parameter appears to be 50 percent white and 50 percent red marbles.

Mathematical proofs and empirical tests demonstrate that the pattern found in Chart 8.1 always appears. The set of many different samples is my **sampling distribution**. It is a distribution of different samples. It reveals the frequency of different sample outcomes from many separate random samples. This pattern appears if the sample size is 1,000 instead of 100, if there are 10 colors of marbles instead of 2, if the population has 100 marbles or 10 million marbles instead of 5,000, and if the sample elements are people, automobiles, or colleges instead of marbles. In fact, the "bell-shaped" sampling distribution pattern becomes clearer as I draw more and more independent random samples from a population.

The sampling distribution pattern tells us that over many separate samples, the true population parameter (i.e., the 50/50 split in the preceding example) is more common than any other outcome. Some samples may deviate from the population parameter, but they are less common. When we plot many random samples as in the graph in Chart 8.1, the sampling distribution always looks like a normal or bell-shaped curve. Such a curve is theoretically important and is used throughout statistics. The area under a bell-shaped curve is well known or, in this example, we can quickly figure out the odds that we will get a specific number of marbles. If the true population parameter is 50/50, standard statistical charts tell what the odds of getting 50/50 or a 40/50 or any other split in a random sample are.

The **central limit theorem** from mathematics tells us that as the number of different random samples in a sampling distribution increases toward infinity, the pattern of samples and of the population parameter becomes increasingly predictable. For a huge number of random samples, the sampling distribution always forms a normal curve, and the midpoint of the curve will be the population parameter.

Sampling distribution   A distribution created by drawing many random samples from the same population.

Central limit theorem   A mathematical relationship that states when many random samples are drawn from a population, a normal distribution is formed, and the center of the distribution for a variable equals the population parameter.

CHART 8.1 Example of Sampling Distribution

RED	WHITE	NUMBER OF SAMPLES
42	58	1
43	57	1
45	55	2
46	54	4
47	53	8
48	52	12
49	51	21
50	50	31
51	49	20
52	48	13
53	47	9
54	46	5
55	45	2
57	43	1
	Total	130

Number of red and white marbles that were randomly drawn from a jar of 5,000 marbles with 100 drawn each time, repeated 130 times for 130 independent random samples.

NUMBER OF SAMPLES

```
31                                                *
30                                                *
29                                                *
28                                                *
27                                                *
26                                                *
25                                                *
24                                                *
23                                                *
22                                                *
21                                        *       *
20                                        *       *       *
19                                        *       *       *
18                                        *       *       *
17                                        *       *       *
16                                        *       *       *
15                                        *       *       *
14                                        *       *       *
13                                        *       *       *       *
12                                *       *       *       *       *
11                                *       *       *       *       *
10                                *       *       *       *       *
 9                                *       *       *       *       *       *
 8                        *       *       *       *       *       *       *
 7                        *       *       *       *       *       *       *
 6                        *       *       *       *       *       *       *
 5                        *       *       *       *       *       *       *       *
 4                *       *       *       *       *       *       *       *       *
 3                *       *       *       *       *       *       *       *       *
 2        *       *       *       *       *       *       *       *       *       *
 1    *       *       *       *       *       *       *       *       *       *       *       *
     42  43  44  45  46  47  48  49  50  51  52  53  54  55  56  57
```

NUMBER OF RED MARBLES IN A SAMPLE

You probably do not have the time or energy to draw many different samples and just want to draw one sample. You are not alone. We rarely draw many random samples except to verify the central limit theorem. We draw only one random sample, but the central limit theorem lets us generalize from one sample to the population. The theorem is about many samples, but it allows us to calculate the probability that a particular sample is off from the population parameter. We will not go into the calculations here.

The important point is that random sampling does not guarantee that every random sample perfectly represents the population. Instead, it means that most random samples will be close to the population parameter most of the time. In addition, we can calculate the precise probability that a particular sample is inaccurate. The central limit theorem lets us estimate the chance that a particular sample is unrepresentative or how much it deviates from the population parameter. It lets us estimate the size of the sampling error. We do this by using information from one sample to estimate the sampling distribution and then combine this information with knowledge of the central limit theorem and area under a normal curve. This lets us create something very important, **confidence intervals**.

The confidence interval is a simple but very powerful idea. When television or newspaper polls are reported, you may hear about what journalists call the "margin of error" being plus or minus 2 percentage points. This is a version of confidence interval, which is a range around a specific point that we use to estimate a population parameter.

We use a range because the statistics of random processes are based on probability. They do not let us predict an exact point. They do allow us to say with a high level of confidence (e.g., 95 percent) that the true population parameter lies within a certain range (i.e., the confidence interval). The calculations for sampling errors or confidence intervals are beyond the level of the discussion here. Nonetheless, the sampling distribution is the key idea that tells us the sampling error and confidence interval. Thus, we cannot say, "This sample gives a perfect measure of the population parameter," but we can say, "We are 95 percent certain that the true population parameter is no more than 2 percent different from what was have found in the sample." (See Expansion Box 8.2, Confidence Intervals.)

Going back to the marble example, I cannot say, "There are precisely 2,500 red marbles in the jar based on a random sample." However, I can say, "I am 95 percent certain that the population parameter lies between 2,450 and 2,550." I combine the characteristics of my sample (e.g., its size, the variation in it) with the central limit theorem to predict specific ranges around the population parameter with a specific degree of confidence.

Systematic Sampling. **Systematic sampling** is a simple random sampling with a shortcut selection procedure. Everything is the same except that instead of using a list of random numbers, we first calculate a **sampling interval** to create a quasi-random selection method. The sampling interval (i.e., 1 in k, where k is some number) tells us how to select elements from a sampling frame by skipping elements in the frame before selecting one for the sample.

For instance, we want to sample 300 names from 900. After a random starting point, we select every third name of the 900 to get a sample of 300. The sampling interval is 3. Sampling intervals are easy to compute. We need the sample size and the population size (or sampling frame size as a best estimate). We can think of the sampling interval as the inverse of the sampling ratio. The sampling ratio for 300 names out of 900 is $300/900 = .333 = 33.3$ percent. The sampling interval is $900/300 = 3$.

Confidence intervals   A range of values, usually a little higher and lower than a specific value found in a sample, within which a researcher has a specified and high degree of confidence that the population parameter lies.

Systematic sampling   A random sample in which a researcher selects every kth (e.g., third or twelfth) case in the sampling frame using a sampling interval.

Sampling interval   The inverse of the sampling ratio that is used when selecting cases in systematic sampling.

EXPANSION BOX **8.2**

Confidence Intervals

The confidence interval is a simple and very powerful idea; it has excellent mathematics behind it and some nice formulas. If you have a good mathematics background, this concept could be helpful. If you are nervous about complex mathematical formulas with many Greek symbols, here is a simple example with a simple formula (a minimum of Greek). The interval is a range that goes above and below an estimate of some characteristic of the population (i.e., population parameters), such as its average or statistical mean. The interval has an upper and lower limit. The example illustrates a simplified way to calculate a confidence interval and shows how sample size and sample homogeneity affect it.

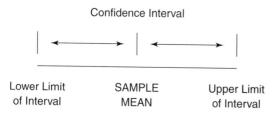

Confidence Interval

Lower Limit   SAMPLE   Upper Limit
of Interval   MEAN   of Interval

Let us say you draw a sample of nine 12-year-old children. You weigh them and find that their average weight, the mean, is 90 pounds with a standard deviation of 36 pounds (mean and standard deviation are statistical measures discussed in Chapter 12). You want to create a confidence interval around your best estimate of the population parameter (the mean weight for the population of all 12-year-olds). You symbolize the population parameter with the Greek letter μ.

Here is how to figure out a confidence interval for the population mean based on a simple random sample. You estimate a confidence level around μ by adding and subtracting a range above and below the sample mean, your best estimate of μ.

To calculate the confidence interval around the sample mean, you first calculate something called the *standard error of the mean*. Call it standard error for short. It is your estimate of variability in the sampling distribution. You use another Greek letter,

σ, to symbolize the standard deviation and add the letter m as a subscript to it, indicating that it is your estimate of the standard deviation in the sampling distribution. Thus, the standard error comes from the standard deviation in the sampling distribution of all possible random samples from the population.

You estimate the standard deviation of the sampling distribution by getting the standard deviation of your sample and adjusting it slightly. To simplify this example, you skip the adjustment and assume that it equals the sample standard deviation. To get the standard error, you adjust it for your sample size symbolized by the letter N. The formula for it is:

$$\sigma_m = \frac{\sigma}{\sqrt{N}}$$

Let us make the example more concrete. For the example, let us look at weight among nine 12-year-olds. For the sampling distribution of the mean you use a mean of 90 pounds and a standard deviation of $36/3 = 12$ (note the square root of $9 = 3$). The confidence interval has a low and upper limit. Here are formulas for them.

Lower limit $M - Z_{.95}\sigma_m$
Upper limit $M + Z_{.95}\sigma_m$

In addition to the σ_m there are two other symbols now:

M in the formula stands for mean in your sample.
$Z_{.95}$ stands for the z-score (discussed in Chapter 12) under a bell-shaped or normal curve at a 95 percent level of confidence (the most typical level). The z-score for a normal curve is a standard number (i.e., it is always the same for 95 percent level of confidence, and it happens to be 1.96). We could pick some confidence level other than 95 percent, but it is the most typical one used.

You now have everything you need to calculate upper and lower limits of the confidence interval. You compute them by adding and subtracting 1.96 standard deviations to/from the mean of 90 as follows:

Lower limit $90 - (1.96)(12) = 66.48$
Upper limit $90 + (1.96)(12) = 113.52$

(continued)

EXPANSION BOX 8.2

(continued)

This says you can be 95 percent confident that the population parameter lies somewhere between 66.48 and 113.52 pounds. You determined the upper and lower limits by adding and subtracting an amount to the sample mean (90 pounds in your example). You use 1.96 because it is the z-score when you want to be 95 percent confident. You calculated 12 as the standard error of the mean based on your sample size and the standard deviation of your sample.

You might see the wide range of 66 to 113 pounds and think it is large, and you might ask why is the sample small, with just nine children?

Here is how increasing the sample size affects the confidence interval. Let us say that instead of a sample of nine children you had 900 12-year-olds (luckily the square root of 900 is easy to figure out: 30). If everything remained the same, your σ_m with a sample of 900 is 36/30 = 1.2. Now your confidence interval is as follows

Lower limit   90 − (1.96)(1.2) = 87.765
Upper limit   90 + (1.96)(1.2) = 92.352

With the much larger sample size, you can be 95 percent confident that the population parameter of average weight is somewhere between 87.765 and 92.352 pounds.

Here is how having a very homogeneous sample affects the confidence interval. Let us say that you had a standard deviation of 3.6 pounds, not 36 pounds. If everything else remained the same, your σ_m with a standard deviation of 3.6 is 3.6/9 = 0.4

Now your confidence interval is as follows

Lower limit   90 − (1.96)(0.4) = 89.215
Upper limit   90 + (1.96)(0.4) = 90.784

With the very homogeneous sample, you can be 95 percent confident that the population parameter of average weight is somewhere between 89.215 and 90.784 pounds.

Let us review the confidence intervals as sample size and standard deviation change:

Sample size = 9, standard deviation = 36. Confidence interval is 66 to 113 pounds.
Sample size = 900, standard deviation = 36. Confidence interval is 87.765 to 92.352 pounds.
Sample size = 9, standard deviation = 3.6 pounds. Confidence interval is 89.215 to 90.784 pounds.

In most cases, a simple random sample and a systematic sample yield equivalent results. One important situation in which systematic sampling cannot be substituted for simple random sampling occurs when the elements in a sample are organized in some kind of cycle or pattern. For example, our sampling frame is organized as a list of married couples with the male first and the female second (see Table 8.1). Such a pattern gives us an unrepresentative sample if systematic sampling is used. Our systematic sample can be nonrepresentative and include only wives because of the organization of the cases. When our sample frame is organized as couples, even-numbered sampling intervals result in samples with all husbands or all wives.

Figure 8.3 illustrates simple random sampling and systematic sampling. Notice that different names were drawn in each sample. For example, H. Adams appears in both samples, but C. Droullard

TABLE 8.1   Problems with Systematic Sampling of Cyclical Data

CASE	
1	Husband
2[a]	Wife
3	Husband
4	Wife
5	Husband
6[a]	Wife
7	Husband
8	Wife
9	Husband
10[a]	Wife
11	Husband
12	Wife

Random start = 2; Sampling interval = 4.
[a]Selected into sample.

FIGURE 8.3 How to Draw Simple Random and Systematic Samples

1. Number each case in the sampling frame in sequence. The list of 40 names is in alphabetical order, numbered from 1 to 40.

2. Decide on a sample size. We will draw two 25 percent (10-name) samples.

3. For a *simple random sample*, locate a random-number table (see excerpt to this figure; a fuller table appears in Appendix B). Before using the random-number table, count the largest number of digits needed for the sample (e.g., with 40 names, two digits are needed; for 100 to 999, three digits; for 1,000 to 9,999, four digits). Begin anywhere on the random-number table (we will begin in the upper left) and take a set of digits (we will take the last two). Mark the number on the sampling frame that corresponds to the chosen random number to indicate that the case is in the sample. If the number is too large (over 40), ignore it. If the

number appears more than once (10 and 21 occurred twice in the example), ignore the second occurrence. Continue until the number of cases in the sample (10 in our example) is reached.

4. For a *systematic sample*, begin with a random start. The easiest way to do this is to point blindly at the random-number table, then take the closest number that appears on the sampling frame. In the example, 18 was chosen. Start with the random number and then count the sampling interval, or 4 in our example, to come to the first number. Mark it, and then count the sampling interval for the next number. Continue to the end of the list. Continue counting the sampling interval as if the beginning of the list were attached to the end of the list (like a circle). Keep counting until ending close to the start, or on the start if the sampling interval divides evenly into the total of the sampling frame.

No.	Name (Gender)	Simple Random	Systematic	No.	Name (Gender)	Simple Random	Systematic
01	Abrams, J. (M)			21	Hjelmhaug, N. (M)	Yes*	
02	Adams, H. (F)	Yes	Yes (6)	22	Huang, J. (F)	Yes	Yes (1)
03	Anderson, H. (M)			23	Ivono, V. (F)		
04	Arminond, L. (M)			24	Jaquees, J. (M)		
05	Boorstein, A. (M)			25	Johnson, A. (F)		
06	Breitsprecher, P. (M)	Yes	Yes (7)	26	Kennedy, M. (F)		Yes (2)
07	Brown, D. (F)			27	Koschoreck, L. (F)		
08	Cattelino, J. (F)			28	Koykkar, J. (M)		
09	Cidoni, S. (M)			29	Kozlowski, C. (F)	Yes	
10	Davis, L. (F)	Yes*	Yes (8)	30	Laurent, J. (M)		Yes (3)
11	Droullard, C. (M)	Yes		31	Lee, R. (F)		
12	Durette, R. (F)			32	Ling, C. (M)		
13	Elsnau, K. (F)	Yes		33	McKinnon, K. (F)		
14	Falconer, T. (M)		Yes (9)	34	Min, H. (F)	Yes	Yes (4)
15	Fuerstenberg, J. (M)			35	Moini, A. (F)		
16	Fulton, P. (F)			36	Navarre, H. (M)		
17	Gnewuch, S. (F)			37	O'Sullivan, C. (M)		
18	Green, C. (M)		START, Yes (10)	38	Oh, J. (M)		Yes (5)
19	Goodwanda, T. (F)	Yes		39	Olson, J. (M)		
20	Harris, B. (M)			40	Ortiz y Garcia, L. (F)		

Excerpt from a Random-Number Table (for Simple Random Sample)

150<u>10</u>	18590	001<u>02</u>	42<u>10</u>	94174	22099
901<u>22</u>	38221	215<u>29</u>	000<u>13</u>	047<u>34</u>	60457
67256	13887	941 <u>19</u>	11077	01061	27779
13761	23390	12947	21280	445<u>06</u>	36457
81994	666<u>11</u>	16597	44457	076<u>21</u>	51949
79180	25992	46178	23992	62108	43232
07984	47169	88094	82752	15318	11921

*Numbers that appeared twice in random numbers selected.

is in only the simple random sample. This is because it is rare for any two random samples to be identical.

The sampling frame contains twenty males and twenty females (gender is in parentheses after each name). The simple random sample yielded three males and seven females, and the systematic sample yielded five males and five females. Does this mean that systematic sampling is more accurate? No. To check this, we draw a new sample using different random numbers, taking the first two digits and beginning at the end (e.g., 11 from 11921 and then 43 from 43232). Also, we draw a new systematic sample with a different random start. The last time the random start was 18, but we now try a random start of 11. What did we find? How many of each gender?[5]

Stratified Sampling. When we use **stratified sampling**, we first divide the population into sub-populations (strata) on the basis of supplementary information.[6] After dividing the population into strata, we draw a random sample from each sub-population. In stratified sampling, we control the relative size of each stratum rather than letting random processes control it. This guarantees representativeness or fixes the proportion of different strata within a sample. Of course, the necessary information about strata is not always available.

In general, if the stratum information is accurate, stratified sampling produces samples that are more representative of the population than those of simple random sampling. A simple example illustrates why this is so. Imagine a population that is 51 percent female and 49 percent male; the population parameter is a gender ratio of 51 to 49. With stratified sampling, we draw random samples among females and among males so that the sample contains a 51 to 49 percent gender ratio. If we had used simple random sampling, it would be possible for a random sample to be off from the true gender ratio

in the population. Thus, we have fewer errors representing the population and a smaller sampling error with stratified sampling.

We use stratified sampling when a stratum of interest is a small percentage of a population and random processes could miss the stratum by chance. For example, we draw a sample of 200 from 20,000 college students using information from the college registrar's office. It indicates that 2 percent of the 20,000 students, or 400, are divorced women with children under the age of 5. For our study, this group is important to include in the sample. There would be four such students (2 percent of 200) in a representative sample, but we could miss them by chance in one simple random sample. With stratified sampling, we obtain a list of the 400 such students from the registrar and randomly select four from it. This guarantees that the sample represents the population with regard to the important strata (see Example Box 8.4, Illustration of Stratified Sampling).

In special situations, we may want the proportion of a stratum in a sample to differ from its true proportion in the population. For example, the population contains 0.5 percent Aleuts, but we want to examine Aleuts in particular. We oversample so that Aleuts make up 10 percent of the sample. With this type of disproportionate stratified sample, we cannot generalize directly from the sample to the population without special adjustments.

In some situations, we want the proportion of a stratum or subgroup to differ from its true proportion in the population. For example, Davis and Smith (1992) reported that the 1987 General Social Survey (explained in Chapter 11) oversampled African Americans. A random sample of the U.S. population yielded 191 Blacks. Davis and Smith conducted a separate sample of African Americans to increase it to 544. The 191 Black respondents are about 13 percent of the random sample, roughly equal to the percentage of Blacks in the U.S. population. The 544 Blacks are 30 percent of the disproportionate sample. The researcher who wants to use the entire sample must adjust it to reduce the number of sampled African Americans before generalizing to the U.S. population. Disproportionate sampling helps the researcher who wants

> **Stratified sampling**   A random sample in which the researcher first identifies a set of mutually exclusive and exhaustive categories, divides the sampling frame by the categories, and then uses random selection to select cases from each category.

EXAMPLE BOX **8.4**

Illustration of Stratified Sampling

Sample of 100 Staff of General Hospital, Stratified by Position

	POPULATION		SIMPLE RANDOM SAMPLE	STRATIFIED SAMPLE	ERRORS COMPARED
POSITION	N	Percent	n	n	TO THE POPULATION
Administrators	15	2.88	1	3	−2
Staff physicians	25	4.81	2	5	−3
Intern physicians	25	4.81	6	5	+1
Registered nurses	100	19.23	22	19	+3
Nurse assistants	100	19.23	21	19	+2
Medical technicians	75	14.42	9	14	+5
Orderlies	50	9.62	8	10	−2
Clerks	75	14.42	5	14	+1
Maintenance staff	30	5.77	3	6	−3
Cleaning staff	25	4.81	3	5	−2
Total	520	100.00	100	100	

Randomly select 3 of 15 administrators, 5 of 25 staff physicians, and so on.

Note: Traditionally, N symbolizes the number in the population and n represents the number in the sample. The simple random sample overrepresents nurses, nursing assistants, and medical technicians but underrepresents administrators, staff physicians, maintenance staff, and cleaning staff. The stratified sample gives an accurate representation of each position.

to focus on issues most relevant to a subpopulation. In this case, he or she can more accurately generalize to African Americans using the 544 respondents instead of a sample of only 191. The larger sample is more likely to reflect the full diversity of the African American subpopulation.

Cluster Sampling. We use **cluster sampling** to address two problems: the lack of a good sampling frame for a dispersed population and the high cost to reach a sampled element.[7] For example, there is no single list of all automobile mechanics in North America. Even if we had an accurate sampling frame, it would cost too much to reach the sampled mechanics who are geographically spread out. Instead of using a single sampling frame, we use a sampling design that involves multiple stages and clusters.

A *cluster* is a unit that contains final sampling elements but can be treated temporarily as a sampling element itself. First we sample clusters, and then we draw a second sample from within the clusters selected in the first stage of sampling. We randomly sample clusters and then randomly sample elements from within the selected clusters. This has a significant practical advantage when we can create a good sampling frame of clusters even if it is impossible to create one for sampling elements. Once we have a sample of clusters, creating a sampling frame for elements within each cluster becomes manageable. A second advantage for geographically dispersed populations is that elements within each cluster are physically closer to one another, which can produce a savings in locating or reaching each element.

> **Cluster sampling** A type of random sample that uses multiple stages and is often used to cover wide geographic areas in which aggregated units are randomly selected and then samples are drawn from the sampled aggregated units or clusters.

We draw several samples in stages in cluster sampling. In a three-stage sample, stage 1 is a random sampling of large clusters; stage 2 is a random sampling of small clusters within each selected large cluster; and the last stage is a sampling of elements from within the sampled small clusters. For example, we want a sample of individuals from Mapleville. First, we randomly sample city blocks, then households within blocks, and then individuals within households (see Chart 8.2). Although there is no accurate list of all residents of Mapleville, there is an accurate list of blocks in the city. After selecting a random sample of blocks, we count all households on the selected blocks to create a sample frame for each block. Then we use the list of households to draw a random sample at the stage of sampling households. Finally, we choose a specific individual within each sampled household.

Cluster sampling is usually less expensive than simple random sampling, but it is less accurate. Each stage in cluster sampling introduces sampling errors, so a multistage cluster sample has more sampling errors than a one-stage random sample.[8]

When we use cluster sampling, we must decide the number of clusters and the number of elements within clusters. For example, in a two-stage cluster sample of 240 people from Mapleville, we could randomly select 120 clusters and select 2 elements from each or randomly select two clusters and select 120 elements in each. Which is better? A design with more clusters is better because elements within clusters (e.g., people living on the same block) tend to be similar to each other (e.g., people on the same block tend to be more alike than those on different blocks). If few clusters are chosen, many similar elements could be selected, which would be less representative of the total population. For example, we could select two blocks with relatively wealthy people and draw 120 people from each block. This would be less representative than a sample with 120 different city blocks and 2 individuals chosen from each.

When we sample from a large geographical area and must travel to each element, cluster sampling significantly reduces travel costs. As usual, there is a trade-off between accuracy and cost. For example, Alan, Ricardo, and Barbara each

personally interview a sample of 1,500 students who represent the population of all college students in North America. Alan obtains an accurate sampling frame of all students and uses simple random sampling. He travels to 1,000 different locations to interview one or two students at each. Ricardo draws a random sample of three colleges from a list of all 3,000 colleges and then visits the three and selects 500 students from each. Barbara draws a random sample of 300 colleges. She visits the 300 and selects 5 students at each. If travel costs average $250 per location, Alan's travel bill is $250,000, Ricardo's is $750, and Barbara's is $75,000. Alan's sample is highly accurate, but Barbara's is only slightly less accurate for one-third the cost. Ricardo's sample is the cheapest, but it is not representative.

Within-Household Sampling. Once we sample a household or similar unit (e.g., family or dwelling unit) in cluster sampling, the question arises as to whom we should choose. A potential source of bias is introduced if the first person who answers the telephone, the door, or the mail is used in the sample. The first person who answers should be selected only if his or her answering is the result of a truly random process. This is rarely the case. Certain people are unlikely to be at home, and in some households one person (e.g., a husband) is more likely than another to answer the telephone or door. Researchers use within-household sampling to ensure that after a random household is chosen, the individual within the household is also selected randomly.

We can randomly select a person within a household in several ways.[9] The most common method is to use a selection table specifying whom you should pick (e.g., oldest male, youngest female) after determining the size and composition of the household (see Table 8.2 on page 260). This removes any bias that might arise from choosing the first person to answer the door or telephone or from the interviewer's selection of the person who appears to be friendliest.

Probability Proportionate to Size (PPS). There are two ways we can draw cluster samples. The method just described is proportionate or unweighted

---

CHART 8.2   Illustration of Cluster Sampling

Goal: Draw a random sample of 240 people in Mapleville.

Step 1: Mapleville has 55 districts. Randomly select 6 districts.

1 2 3* 4 5 6 7 8 9 10 11 12 13 14 15* 16 17 18 19 20 21 22 23 24 25 26
27* 28 29 30 31* 32 33 34 35 36 37 38 39 40* 41 42 43 44 45 46 47 48
49 50 51 52 53 54* 55
* = Randomly selected.

Step 2: Divide the selected districts into blocks. Each district contains 20 blocks. Randomly select 4 blocks from the district.

Example of District 3 (selected in step 1):

1 2 3 4* 5 6 7 8 9 10* 11 12 13* 14 15 16 17* 18 19 20
* = Randomly selected.

Step 3: Divide blocks into households. Randomly select households.

Example of Block 4 of District 3 (selected in step 2):

Block 4 contains a mix of single-family homes, duplexes, and four-unit apartment buildings. It is bounded by Oak Street, River Road, South Avenue, and Greenview Drive. There are 45 households on the block. Randomly select 10 households from the 45.

1	#1 Oak Street	16	"	31*	"
2	#3 Oak Street	17*	#154 River Road	32*	"
3*	#5 Oak Street	18	#156 River Road	33	"
4	"	19*	#158 River Road	34	#156 Greenview Drive
5	"	20*	"	35*	"
6	"	21	#13 South Avenue	36	"
7	#7 Oak Street	22	"	37	"
8	"	23	#11 South Avenue	38	"
9*	#150 River Road	24	#9 South Avenue	39	#158 Greenview Drive
10*	"	25	#7 South Avenue	40	"
11	"	26	#5 South Avenue	41	"
12	"	27	#3 South Avenue	42	"
13	#152 River Road	28	#1 South Avenue	43	#160 Greenview Drive
14	"	29*	"	44	"
15	"	30	#152 Greenview Drive	45	"

* = Randomly selected.

Step 4: Select a respondent within each household.

Summary of cluster sampling:
1 person randomly selected per household
10 households randomly selected per block
4 blocks randomly selected per district
6 districts randomly selected in the city
1 x 10 x 4 x 6 = 240 people in sample

TABLE 8.2   Within-Household Sampling

Selecting individuals within sampled households. Number selected is the household chosen in Chart 8.2.

NUMBER	LAST NAME	ADULTS (OVER AGE 18)	SELECTED RESPONDENT
3	Able	1 male, 1 female	Female
9	Bharadwaj	2 females	Youngest female
10	DiPiazza	1 male, 2 females	Oldest female
17	Wucivic	2 males, 1 female	Youngest male
19	Cseri	2 females	Youngest female
20	Taylor	1 male, 3 females	Second oldest female
29	Velu	2 males, 2 females	Oldest male
31	Wong	1 male, 1 female	Female
32	Gray	1 male	Male
35	Mall-Krinke	1 male, 2 females	Oldest female

EXAMPLE SELECTION TABLE (ONLY ADULTS COUNTED)

MALES	FEMALES	WHOM TO SELECT	MALES	FEMALES	WHOM TO SELECT
1	0	Male	2	2	Oldest male
2	0	Oldest male	2	3	Youngest female
3	0	Youngest male	3	2	Second oldest male
4+	0	Second oldest male	3	3	Second oldest female
0	1	Female	3	4	Third oldest female
0	2	Youngest female	4	3	Second oldest male
0	3	Second oldest female	4	4	Third oldest male
0	4+	Oldest female	4	5+	Youngest female
1	1	Female	5+	4	Second oldest male
1	2	Oldest female	5+	5+	Fourth oldest female
1	3	Second oldest female			
2	1	Youngest male			
3	1	Second oldest male			

+ = or more

cluster sampling. It is proportionate because the size of each cluster (or number of elements at each stage) is the same. The more common situation is for the cluster groups to be of different sizes. When this is the case, we must adjust the probability for each stage in sampling.

The foregoing example with Alan, Barbara, and Ricardo illustrates the problem with unweighted cluster sampling. Barbara drew a simple random sample of 300 colleges from a list of all 3,000 colleges, but she made a mistake—unless every college has an identical number of students. Her method gave each college an equal chance of being selected—a 300/3,000, or 10 percent chance. But colleges have different numbers of students, so each student does not have an equal chance to end up in her sample.

Barbara listed every college and sampled from the list. A large university with 40,000 students and a small college with 400 students had an equal chance of being selected. But if she chose the large university, the chance of a given student at that college being selected was 5 in 40,000 (5/40,000 = 0.0125 percent), whereas a student at the small college had a 5 in 400 (5/400 = 1.25 percent) chance of being selected. The small-college student was 100 times more likely to be in her sample. The total probability of a student from the large university being selected was 0.125 percent (10 × 0.0125) while it was 12.5 percent (10 × 1.25) for the small-college student. Barbara violated a principle of random sampling: that each element has an equal chance to be selected into the sample.

If Barbara uses **probability proportionate to size (PPS)** and samples correctly, then each final sampling element or student will have an equal probability of being selected. She does this by adjusting the chances of selecting a college in the first stage of sampling. She must give large colleges with more students a greater chance of being selected and small colleges a smaller chance. She adjusts the probability of selecting a college on the basis of the proportion of all students in the population who attend it. Thus, a college with 40,000 students will be 100 times more likely to be selected than one with 400 students. (See Example Box 8.5, Probability Proportionate to Size (PPS) Sampling.)

Random-Digit Dialing. **Random-digit dialing (RDD)** is a sampling technique used in research projects in which the general public is interviewed by telephone.[10] It does not use the published telephone directory as the sampling frame. Using a telephone directory as the sampling frame misses three kinds of people: those without telephones, those who have recently moved, and those with unlisted numbers. Those without phones (e.g., the poor, the uneducated, and transients) are missed in any telephone interview study, but 95 percent of people in advanced industrialized nations have a telephone. Several types of people have unlisted numbers: those who want to avoid collection agencies; those who are very wealthy; and those who want to have privacy and to avoid obscene calls, salespeople, and prank calls. In some urban areas in the United States, the percentage of unlisted numbers is 50 percent. In addition, people change

their residences, so annual directories have numbers for people who have moved away and do not list those who have recently moved into an area.

If we use RDD, we randomly select telephone numbers, thereby avoiding the problems of telephone directories. The population is telephone numbers, not people with telephones. RDD is not difficult, but it takes time and can frustrate the person doing the calling.

Here is how RDD works in the United States. Telephone numbers have three parts: a three-digit area code, a three-digit exchange number or central office code, and a four-digit number. For example, the area code for Madison, Wisconsin, is 608, and there are many exchanges within the area code (e.g., 221, 993, 767, 455), but not all of the 999 possible three-digit exchanges (from 001 to 999) are active. Likewise, not all of the 9,999 possible four-digit numbers in an exchange (from 0000 to 9999) are being used. Some numbers are reserved for future expansion, are disconnected, or are temporarily withdrawn after someone moves. Thus, a possible U.S. telephone number consists of an active area code, an active exchange number, and a four-digit number in an exchange.

In RDD, a researcher identifies active area codes and exchanges and then randomly selects four-digit numbers. A problem is that the researcher can select any number in an exchange. This means that some selected numbers are out of service, disconnected, pay phones, or numbers for businesses; only some numbers are what the researcher wants: working residential phone numbers. Until the researcher calls, it is not possible to know whether the number is a working residential number. This means spending much time reaching numbers that are disconnected, are for businesses, and so forth. Research organizations often use

---

Probability proportionate to size (PPS) An adjustment made in cluster sampling when each cluster does not have the same number of sampling elements.

Random-digit dialing (RDD) A method of randomly selecting cases for telephone interviews that uses all possible telephone numbers as a sampling frame.

Probability Proportionate to Size (PPS) Sampling

Henry wants to conduct one-hour, in-person interviews with people living in the city of Riverdale, which is spread out over a large area. Henry wants to reduce his travel time and expenses, so he uses a *cluster sampling design*. The last census reported that the city had about 490,000 people. Henry can interview only about 220 people, or about 0.05 percent of the city population. He first gathers maps from the city tax office and fire department, and retrieves census information on city blocks. He learns that there are 2,182 city blocks. At first, he thinks he can randomly select 10 percent of the blocks (i.e., 218), go to a block and count housing units, and then locate one person to interview in each housing unit (house, apartment, etc.), but the blocks are of unequal geographic and population size. He studies the population density of the blocks and estimates the number of people in each, and then develops a five-part classification based on the average size of a block as in the following chart.

Block Type	Number of Clusters	Average Number People per Block
Very high density	20	2,000
High density	200	800
Medium density	800	300
Low density	1,000	50
Semirural	162	10

Henry realizes that randomly selecting city blocks without adjustment will not give each person an equal chance of being selected. For example, 1 very high-density block has the same number of people as 40 low-density blocks. Henry adjusts proportionately to the block size. The easiest way to do this is to convert all city blocks to equal-size units based on the smallest cluster, or the semirural city blocks. For example, there are 2,000/10 or 200 times more people in a high-density block than a semirural block, so Henry increases the odds of selecting such a block to make its probability 200 times higher than a semirural block. Essentially, Henry creates adjusted cluster units of 10 persons each (because that is how many there are in the semirural blocks) and substitutes them for city blocks in the first stage of sampling. The 162 semirural blocks are unchanged, but after adjustment, he has 20 X 200 = 4,000 units for the very high density blocks, 200 X 80 = 16,000 units for the high-density blocks, and so forth, for a total of 49,162 such units. Henry now numbers each block, using the adjusted cluster units, with many blocks getting multiple numbers. For example, he assigns numbers 1 to 200 to the first very high density block, and so forth, as follows:

1	Very high density block #1
2	Very high density block #1
3	Very high density block #1

. . . and so forth

3,999	Very high density block #20
4,000	Very high density block #20
4,001	High-density block #1
4,002	High-density block #2

. . . and so forth

49,160	Semirural block #160
49,161	Semirural block #161
49,162	Semirural block #162

Henry still wants to interview about 220 people and wants to select one person from each adjusted cluster unit. He uses simple random sample methods to select 220 of the 49,162 adjusted cluster units. He can then convert the cluster units back to city blocks. For example, if Henry randomly selected numbers 25 and 184, both are in very high density block #1, telling him to select two people from that block. If he randomly picked the number 49,161, he selects one person in semirural block #161. Henry now goes to each selected block, identifies all housing units in that block, and randomly selects among housing units. Of course, Henry may use within-household sampling after he selects a housing unit.

computers to select random digits and dial the phone automatically. This speeds the process, but a human must still listen and find out whether the number is a working residential one (see Expansion Box 8.3, Random Digit Dialing.)

The sampling element in RDD is the phone number, not the person or the household. Several families or individuals can share the same phone number, and in other situations, each person may have a separate phone number. This means that after a working residential phone is reached, a second stage of sampling, within household sampling, is necessary to select the person to be interviewed.

Example Box 8.6, (Example Sample, the 2006 General Social Survey on page 264) illustrates how the many sampling terms and ideas can be used together in a specific real-life situation.

EXPANSION BOX **8.3**

Random-Digit Dialing (RDD)

During the past decade, participation in RDD surveys has declined. This is due to factors such as new call-screening technologies, heightened privacy concerns due to increased telemarketing calls, a proliferation of nonhousehold telephone numbers, and increased cell telephone users (most RDD samples include only landline numbers). When they compared a new technique, address-based sampling (ABS), to RDD for the U.S. adult population, Link et al. (2008) estimated that RDD sampling frames may be missing 15–19 percent of the population. Although the alternative was superior to RDD in some respects, ABS had other limitations including overrepresentation of English-speaking non-Hispanics and more educated persons than RDD. One issue in RDD sampling involves reaching someone by phone. A researcher might call a phone number dozens of times that is never answered. Does the nonanswer mean an eligible person is not answering or that the number is not really connected with a person? A study (Kennedy, Keeter, and Dimock, 2008) of this issue estimates that about half (47 percent) of unanswered calls in which there are six call-back attempts have an eligible person who is not being reached.

Decision Regarding Sample Size

New social researchers often ask, "How large does my sample have to be?" The best answer is, "It depends." It depends on population characteristics, the type of data analysis to be employed, and the degree of confidence in sample accuracy needed for research purposes. As noted, a large sample size alone does not guarantee a representative sample. A large sample without random sampling or with a poor sampling frame creates a less representative sample than a smaller one that has careful random sampling and an excellent sampling frame.

We can address the question of sample size in two ways. One method is to make assumptions about the population and use statistical equations about random sampling processes. The calculation of sample size by this method requires a statistical discussion that goes beyond the level of this text.[11] We must make assumptions about the degree of confidence (or number of errors) that is acceptable and the degree of variation in the population. In general, the more diverse a population, the more precise is the statistical analysis, the more variables will be examined simultaneously, and the greater confidence is required in sample accuracy (e.g., it makes a difference in critical health outcomes, huge financial loss, or the freedom or incarceration of innocent people), the larger the required sample size. The flip side is that samples from homogeneous populations with simple data analysis of one or a few variables that are used for low-risk decisions can be equally effective when they are smaller.

A second method to decide a sample size is a rule of thumb, a conventional or commonly accepted amount. We use rules of thumb because we rarely have the information required by the statistical estimation method. Also, these rules give sample sizes close to those of the statistical method. Rules of thumb are based on past experience with samples that have met the requirements of the statistical method.

A major principle of sample size is that the smaller the population, the larger the sampling ratio has to be for a sample that has a high probability of yielding the same results as the entire population. Larger populations permit smaller sampling ratios for equally good samples because as the population

EXAMPLE BOX **8.6**

Example Sample, the 2006 General Social Survey

Sampling has many terms for the different types of samples. A complex sample illustrates how researchers use them. We can look at the 2006 sample for the best-known national U.S. survey in sociology, the General Social Survey (GSS) (discussed in Chapter 11). It has been conducted since 1972. Its sampling has been updated several times over the years based on the most sophisticated social science sampling techniques to produce a representative population within practical cost limits. The *population* consists of all resident adults (18 years of age or older) in the United States for the *universe* of all Americans. The *target population* consists of all English- or Spanish-speaking mentally competent adults who live in households but excludes people living in institutional settings. The researchers used a complex multistage area probability sample to the block or segment level. At the block level, they used *quota sampling* with quotas based on gender, age, and employment status. They selected equal numbers of men and women as well as persons over and under 35 years of age.

The sample design combined a *cluster sample* and a *stratified sample*. U.S. territory was divided into standard metropolitan statistical areas (SMSAs, a U.S. Census Bureau classification) and nonmetropolitan counties. The SMSAs and counties were stratified by region, age, and race before selection. Researchers adjusted clusters using *probability proportionate to size (PPS)* based on the number of housing units in each county or SMSA.

The sampling design had three basic stages. *Stage 1*: Randomly select a "primary sampling unit" (a U.S. census tract, a part of a SMSA, or a county) from among the stratified "primary sampling units." Researchers also classified units by whether there were stable mailing addresses in a geographic area or others. *Stage 2*: Randomly select smaller geographic units (e.g., a census tract, parts of a county), and *Stage 3*: Randomly select housing units on blocks or similar geographic units. As a final stage, researchers used the household as the sampling element and randomly selected households from the addresses in the block. After selecting an address, an interviewer contacted the household and chose an eligible respondent from it. The interviewer looked at a quota selection table for possible respondents and interviewed a type of respondent (e.g., second oldest) based on the table. Interviewers used computer-assisted personal interviewing (CAPI) (see Chapter 10).

In the 2006 sample, researchers first identified 9,535 possible household addresses or locations. However, this number dropped to 7,987 after they eliminated vacant addresses and ones where no one who spoke either English or Spanish lived. After taking into account people who refused to participate, were too ill, were ineligible, or did not finish an interview (23.3%), the final sample included 4,510 persons (for details, see http://publicdata.norc.org: 41000/gss/Documents/Codebook/A.pdf)

---

size grows, the returns in accuracy for sample size decrease.

In practical terms, this means for small populations (under 500), we need a large sampling ratio (about 30 percent) or 150 people, while for large populations (over 150,000), we can obtain equally good accuracy with a smaller sampling ratio (1 percent), and samples of about 1,500 can be equally accurate, all things being the same. Notice that the population of 150,000 is 30 times larger but the sample is just 10 times larger. Turning to very large populations (more than 10 million), we can achieve accuracy with tiny sampling ratios (0.025 percent),

or samples of about 2,500. The size of the population ceases to be relevant once the sampling ratio is very small, and samples of about 2,500 are as accurate for populations of 200 million as for 10 million. These are approximate sizes, and practical limitations (e.g., cost) also play a role.

A related principle is that for small samples, a small increase in sample size produces a big gain in accuracy. Equal increases in sample size produce an increase in accuracy more for small than for large samples. For example, an increase in sample size from 50 to 100 reduces errors from 7.1 percent to 2.1 percent, but an increase from 1,000 to 2,000

TABLE 8.3 Sample Size of a Random Sample for Different Populations with a 99 Percent Confidence Level

POPULATION SIZE	SAMPLE SIZE	% POPULATION IN SAMPLE
200	171	85.5%
500	352	70.4%
1,000	543	54.3%
2,000	745	37.2%
5,000	960	19.2%
10,000	1,061	10.6%
20,000	1,121	5.6%
50,000	1,160	2.3%
100,000	1,173	1.2%

decreases errors from only 1.6 percent to 1.1 percent.[12] (See Table 8.3.)

Notice that our plans for data analysis influence the required sample size. If we want to analyze many small subgroups within the population, we need a larger sample. Let us say we want to see how elderly Black females living in cities compare with other subgroups (elderly males, females of other ages and races, and so forth). We will need a large sample because the subgroup is a small proportion (e.g., 10 percent) of the entire sample. A rule of thumb is to have about 50 cases for each subgroup we wish to analyze. If we want to analyze a group that is only 10 percent of our sample, then we will need a sample 10 times 50 (500 cases) in the sample for the subgroup analysis. You may ask how you would know that the subgroup of interest is only 10 percent of the sample until you gather sample data? This is a legitimate question. We often must use various other sources of information (e.g., past studies, official statistics about people in an area), then make an estimate, and then plan our sample size requirements from the estimate.

Making Inferences. The reason we draw probability samples is to make inferences from the sample to the population. In fact, a subfield of statistical data analysis is called *inferential statistics* (see

Chapter 12). We directly observe data in the sample but are not interested in a sample alone. If we had a sample of 300 from 10,000 students on a college campus, we are less interested in the 300 students than in using information from them to infer to the population of 10,000 students. Thus, a gap exists between what we concretely have (variables measured in sample data) and what is of real interest (population parameters) (see Figure 8.4 on page 266).

In Chapter 7, you saw how we can express the logic of measurement in terms of a gap between abstract constructs and concrete indicators. Measures of concrete, observable data are approximations for abstract constructs. We use the approximations to estimate what is of real interest (i.e., constructs and causal laws). Conceptualization and operationalization bridge the gap in measurement just as the use of sampling frames, the sampling process, and inference bridge the gap in sampling.

We can integrate the logic of sampling with the logic of measurement by directly observing measures of constructs and empirical relationships in samples (see Figure 8.4). We infer or generalize from what we observe empirically in samples to the abstract causal laws and parameters in the population. Likewise, there is an analogy between the logic of sampling and the logic of measurement for validity. In measurement, we want valid indicators of constructs: that is, concrete observable indicators that accurately represent unseen abstract constructs. In sampling, we want samples that have little sampling error: that is, concrete collections of cases that accurately represent unseen and abstract populations. A valid measure deviates little from the construct it represents. A good sample has little sampling error, and it permits estimates that deviate little from population parameters.

We want to reduce sampling errors. For equally good sampling frames and precise random selection processes, the sampling error is based on two factors: the sample size and the population diversity. Everything else being equal, the larger the sample size, the smaller the sampling error. Likewise, populations with a great deal of homogeneity will have smaller sampling errors. We can think of it this way: if we had a choice between

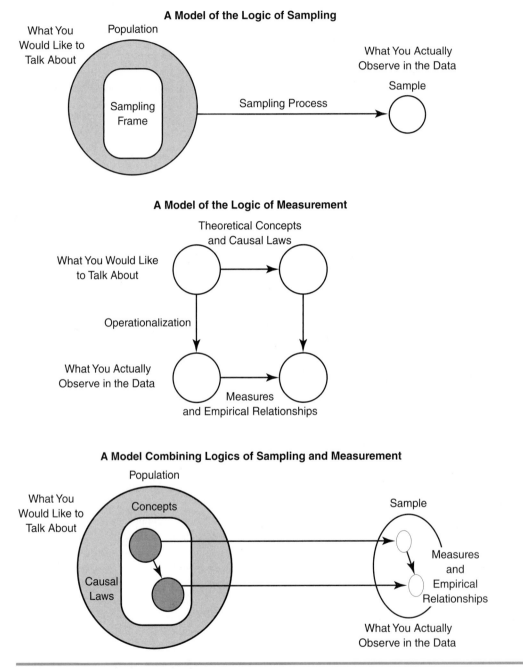

A Model of the Logic of Sampling

What You Would Like to Talk About

Population

Sampling Frame

Sampling Process

What You Actually Observe in the Data

Sample

A Model of the Logic of Measurement

Theoretical Concepts and Causal Laws

What You Would Like to Talk About

Operationalization

What You Actually Observe in the Data

Measures and Empirical Relationships

A Model Combining Logics of Sampling and Measurement

Population

What You Would Like to Talk About

Concepts

Causal Laws

Sample

Measures and Empirical Relationships

What You Actually Observe in the Data

FIGURE 8.4   Model of the Logic of Sampling and of Measurement

sampling/picking 10 or 50 marbles out of a jar of 1000 red and white marbles to determine the number of red marbles, it would be better to pick 50. Likewise, if there are ten colors of marbles in a jar, we are less able to predict accurately the number of red marbles than if there were only two colors of marbles.

Sampling error is related to confidence intervals. If two samples are identical except one is much larger, the larger one will have a smaller sampling error and narrower confidence intervals. Likewise, if two samples are identical except that the cases in one are more similar to each other, the one with greater homogeneity will have a smaller sampling error and narrower confidence intervals. A narrow confidence interval means that we are able to estimate more precisely the population parameter for a given level of confidence.

Here is an example: You want to estimate the annual income of bricklayers. You have two samples. Sample 1 gives a confidence interval of $30,000 to $36,000 around the estimated population parameter of $33,000 for an 80 percent level of confidence. However, you want a 95 percent level of confidence. Now the range is $25,000 to $45,000. A sample that has a smaller sampling error (because it is much larger) might give the $30,000 to $36,000 range for a 95 percent confidence level.

Strategies When the Goal Differs from Creating a Representative Sample

In qualitative research, the purpose of research may not require having a representative sample from a huge number of cases. Instead, a nonprobability sample often better fits the purposes of a study. In nonprobability samples, you do not have to determine the sample size in advance and have limited knowledge about the larger group or population from which the sample is taken. Unlike a probability sample that required a preplanned approach based on mathematical theory, nonprobability sampling often gradually selects cases with the specific content of a case determining whether it is chosen. Table 8.4 shows a variety of nonprobability sampling techniques.

TABLE 8.4   Types of Nonprobability Samples

TYPE OF SAMPLE	PRINCIPLE
Convenience	Get any cases in any manner that is convenient.
Quota	Get a preset number of cases in each of several predetermined categories that will reflect the diversity of the population, using haphazard methods.
Purposive	Get all possible cases that fit particular criteria, using various methods.
Snowball	Get cases using referrals from one or a few cases, then referrals from those cases, and so forth.
Deviant case	Get cases that substantially differ from the dominant pattern (a special type of purposive sample).
Sequential	Get cases until there is no additional information or new characteristics (often used with other sampling methods).
Theoretical	Get cases that will help reveal features that are theoretically important about a particular setting/topic.
Adaptive	Get cases based on multiple stages, such as snowball followed by purposive. This sample is used for hidden populations.

Purposive or Judgmental Sampling

Purposive sampling (also known as *judgmental sampling*) is a valuable sampling type for special situations. It is used in exploratory research or in field research.[12] It uses the judgment of an expert in

> **Purposive sampling**   A nonrandom sample in which the researcher uses a wide range of methods to locate all possible cases of a highly specific and difficult-to-reach population.

selecting cases, or it selects cases with a specific purpose in mind. It is inappropriate if the goal is to have a representative sample or to pick the "average" or the "typical" case. In purposive sampling, cases selected rarely represent the entire population.

Purposive sampling is appropriate to select unique cases that are especially informative. For example, we want to use content analysis to study magazines to find cultural themes. We can use three specific popular women's magazines to study because they are trend setting. In the study *Promises I Can Keep* that opened this chapter, the researchers selected eight neighborhoods using purposive sampling. We often use purposive sampling to select members of a difficult-to-reach, specialized population, such as prostitutes. It is impossible to list all prostitutes and sample randomly from the list. Instead, to locate persons who are prostitutes, a researcher will use local knowledge (e.g., locations where prostitutes solicit, social groups with whom

prostitutes associate) and local experts (e.g., police who work on vice units, other prostitutes) to locate possible prostitutes for inclusion in the research project. A researcher will use many different methods to identify the cases because the goal is to locate as many cases as possible.

We also use purposive sampling to identify particular types of cases for in-depth investigation to gain a deeper understanding of types (see Example Box 8.7, Purposive Sampling).

Snowball Sampling

We are often interested in an interconnected network of people or organizations.[13] The network could be scientists around the world investigating the same problem, the elites of a medium-size city, members of an organized crime family, persons who sit on the boards of directors of major banks and corporations, or people on a college campus who

---

EXAMPLE BOX **8.7**

Purposive Sampling

In her study *Inside Organized Racism,* Kathleen Blee (2002) used purposive sampling to study women who belong to racist hate organizations. The purpose of her study was to learn why and how women became actively involved in racist hate organizations (e.g., neo-Nazi, Ku Klux Klan). She wanted "to create a broadly based, national sample of women racist group members" (p. 198). A probability sample was not possible because no list of all organizations exists, and the organizations keep membership lists secret.

Blee avoided using snowball sampling because she wanted to interview women who were not connected to one another. To sample women for the study, she began by studying the communication (videotapes, books, newsletters, magazines, flyers, Web sites) "distributed by every self-proclaimed racist, anti-Semitic, white supremacist, Christian Identity, neo-Nazi, white power skinhead, and white separatist organization in the United States for a one-year period" (p. 198). She also obtained lists from antiracist organizations that monitor racist groups

and examined the archives at the libraries of Tulane University and the University of Kansas for right-wing extremism. She identified more than one hundred active organizations. From these, she found those that had women members or activists and narrowed the list to thirty racist organizations. She then tried to locate women who belonged to organizations that differed in ideological emphasis and organizational form in fifteen different states in four major regions of the United States.

In a type of cluster sampling, she first located organizations and then women active in them. To find women to interview, she used personal contacts and referrals from informed persons: "parole officers, correctional officials, newspaper reporters and journalists, other racist activists and former activists, federal and state task forces on gangs, attorneys, and other researchers" (p. 200). She eventually located thirty-four women aged 16 to 90 years of age and conducted two 6-hour life history interviews with each (see Chapter 13).

Source: Excerpt from page 198 of *Inside Organized Racism: Women in the Hate Movement,* by Kathleen M. Blee. © 2002 by the Regents of the University of California. Published by the University of California Press.

have had sexual relations with each other. The crucial feature is that each person or unit is connected with another through a direct or indirect linkage. This does not mean that each person directly knows, interacts with, or is influenced by every other person in the network. Rather, taken as a whole, with direct and indirect links, most people are within an interconnected web of linkages.

For example, Sally and Tim do not know each other directly, but each has a good friend, Susan, so they have an indirect connection. All three are part of the same friendship network. Researchers represent such a network by drawing a *sociogram,* a diagram of circles connected with lines. The circles represent each person or case, and the lines represent friendship or other linkages (see Figure 8.5).

Snowball sampling (also called *network, chain referral, reputational,* and *respondent-driven sampling*) is a method for sampling (or selecting) the cases in a network. The method uses an analogy to a snowball, which begins small but becomes larger as we roll it on wet snow and it picks up additional snow. Snowball sampling is a multistage technique. It begins with one or a few people or cases and spreads out based on links to the initial cases.

For example, we want to study friendship networks among the teenagers in our community. We might start with three teenagers who do not know each other. We ask each teen to name four close friends. Next we go to each set of four friends and ask each person to name four close friends. This continues to the next round of four people and repeats again. Before long, a large number of people have been identified. Each person in the sample is directly or indirectly tied to the original teenagers, and several people may have named the same person. The process stops, either because no new names are given, indicating a closed network, or because the network is so large that it is at the limit of what can be studied. The sample includes those named by at least one other person in the network as being a close friend.

Deviant Case Sampling

We use **deviant case sampling** (also called *extreme case sampling*) when we are interested in cases that

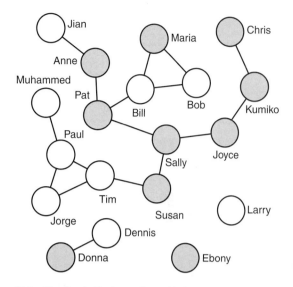

Note: Shading indicates various skin tones.

FIGURE 8.5   Sociogram of Friendship Relations

differ from the dominant pattern, mainstream, or predominant characteristics of other cases. Similar to purposive sampling, we use a variety of techniques to locate cases with specific characteristics. The goal is to locate a collection of unusual, different, or peculiar cases that are not representative of the whole. We select cases because they are unusual. We can sometimes learn more about social life by considering cases that fall outside the general pattern or including what is beyond the main flow of events.

For example, we want to study high school dropouts. Let us say that previous research suggested that a majority of dropouts come from low-income,

---

Snowball sampling A nonrandom sample in which the researcher begins with one case and then, based on information about interrelationships from that case, identifies other cases and repeats the process again and again.

Deviant case sampling A nonrandom sample, especially used by qualitative researchers, in which a researcher selects unusual or nonconforming cases purposely as a way to provide increased insight into social processes or a setting.

single-parent families and tend to be racial minorities. The family environment is one in which parents and/or siblings have low education or are themselves dropouts. In addition, many dropouts engage in illegal behavior. We might seek dropouts who are members of the majority racial group, who have no record of illegal activities, and who are from stable two-parent, upper-middle-income families. By looking at atypical dropouts we might learn more about the reasons for dropping out.

Sequential Sampling

Sequential sampling is also similar to purposive sampling. We use purposive sampling to try to locate as many relevant cases as possible. Sequential sampling differs because we continue to gather cases until the amount of new information ends or a certain diversity of cases is reached. The principle is to gather cases until we reach a saturation point. In economic terms, information is gathered until the marginal utility, or incremental benefit for additional cases, levels off or drops significantly. It requires that we continuously evaluate all collected cases. For example, we locate and plan in-depth interviews of sixty widows over 70 years of age who have been living without a spouse for 10 or more years. Depending on our purposes, getting an additional twenty widows whose life experiences, social

backgrounds, and worldviews differ little from the first sixty may be unnecessary.

Theoretical Sampling

In **theoretical sampling**, what we sample (e.g., people, situations, events, time periods) comes from grounded theory. A growing theoretical interest guides the selection of sample cases. The researcher selects cases based on new insights that the sample could provide. For example, a field researcher could be observing a site and a group of people during weekdays. Theoretically, the researcher may question whether the people act the same at other times or aspects of the site change. He or she could then sample other time periods (e.g., nights and weekends) to have a fuller picture and learn whether important conditions are the same.

Adaptive Sampling and Hidden Populations

In contrast to sampling the general population or visible and accessible people, sampling **hidden populations** (i.e., people who engage in clandestine or concealed activities) is a recurrent issue in the studies of deviant or stigmatized behavior (such as victims of sexual violence, illegal drug users). This method illustrates the creative application of sampling principles, mixing qualitative and quantitative styles of research and combining probability with nonprobability techniques.

Adaptive sampling is a design that adjusts based on early observations.[15] For example, we ask illegal drug users to refer other drug users as in snowball sampling. However, we adjust the way that we trace through the network based on our research topic. We might identify a geographic area, divide it into sections randomly, and then select participants in that area through strategies such as random-digit dialing or by posting recruitment fliers. Once we identify members of the targeted hidden population, we use them in a snowball technique to find others. AIDS researchers or studies of illegal drug users that have sampled "hidden populations" are instructive, often relying on modified snowball techniques. (See Example Box 8.8, Hidden Populations).

Sequential sampling   A nonrandom sample in which a researcher tries to find as many relevant cases as possible until time, financial resources, or his or her energy is exhausted or until there is no new information or diversity from the cases.

Theoretical sampling   A nonrandom sample in which the researcher selects specific times, locations, or events to observe in order to develop a social theory or evaluate theoretical ideas.

Hidden population   A population of people who engage in clandestine, socially disapproved of, or concealed activities and who are difficult to locate and study.

Adaptive sampling   A nonprobability sampling technique used for hidden populations in which several approaches to identify and recruit, including a snowball or referral method, may be used.

EXAMPLE BOX **8.8**

Hidden Populations

Three studies of hidden populations illustrate the difficulties of sampling. Martin and Dean (1993) sampled gay men from New York City. The men had to live in the city, be over age 18, not be diagnosed as having AIDS, and engage in sex with other men. The authors began with a purposive sample using five diverse sources to recruit 291 respondents. They first contacted 150 New York City organizations with predominately homosexual or bisexual members. They next screened these to 90 organizations that had men appropriate for the study. From the 90, the researchers drew a stratified random sample of 52 organizations by membership size. They randomly selected five members from each of the organizations. Reports of Martin and Dean's study appeared in local news sources. This brought calls from forty-one unsolicited volunteers. They also found thirty-two men as referrals from respondents who had participated in a small pilot study, seventy-two men from an annual New York City Gay Pride Parade, and fifteen eligible men whom they contacted at a New York City clinic and asked to participate. They next used snowball sampling by asking each of the 291 men to give a recruitment packet to three gay male friends. Each friend who agreed to participate was also asked to give packets to three friends. This continued until it had gone five levels out from the initial 291 men. Eventually, Dean recruited 746 men into the study. The researchers checked their sample against two random samples of gay men in San Francisco, a random-digit dialing sample of 500, and a cluster sample of 823 using San Francisco census tracts. Their sample paralleled those from San Francisco on race, age, and the percent being "out of the closet."

Heckathorn (1997, 2002) studied active drug injectors in two small Connecticut cities and the surrounding area. As of July 1996, medical personnel had diagnosed 390 AIDS cases in the towns; about half of the cases involved drug injection. The sampling was purposive in that each sampled element had to meet certain criteria. Heckathorn also used a modified snowball sampling with a "dual reward system." He gave each person who completed an interview a monetary reward and a second monetary reward for recruiting a new respondent. The first person was asked not to identify the new person to the researcher, a practice sometimes referred to as *masking* (i.e., protecting friends). This avoids the "snitching" issue and "war on drugs" stigma, especially strong in the U.S. context. This modified snowball sampling is like sequential sampling in that after a period of time, fewer and fewer new recruits are found until the researcher comes to saturation or an equilibrium.

Wang et al. (2006) used a respondent-driven sampling method to recruit 249 illicit drug users in three rural Ohio counties to examine substance abuse and health care needs. To be eligible for the sample, participants had to be over 18 years of age, not be in drug abuse treatment, and not have used cocaine or methamphetamines in the past month. After locating an eligible participant, the researchers paid him or her $50 dollars to participate. The participant could earn an additional $10 by recruiting eligible peers. In a snowball process, each subsequent participant was also asked to make referrals. The authors identified nineteen people to start. Only a little more than half (eleven of the nineteen) referred peers for the study who were eligible and participated. Over roughly 18 months, the researchers were able to identify 249 participants for their study. They compared the study sample with characteristics of estimates of the illegal drug–using population and found that the racial composition of the originally identified participants (White) led to overrepresentation of that racial category. Otherwise, it appeared that the method was able to draw a reasonable sample of the hidden population.

CONCLUSION

This chapter discussed probability and nonprobability sampling (see Summary Review Box 8.1, Types of Samples on page 272). A key point is that a sampling strategy should match in a specific study's purpose. In general, probability sampling is preferred for a representative sample; it allows for using statistical tests in data analysis. In addition to simple random sampling, the chapter referred to other probability samples: systematic, stratified, RDD, and

Types of Samples

EIGHT TYPES OF NONPROBABILITY SAMPLES

Type of Sample	Principle
Adaptive	Get a few cases using knowledge of likely locations of a hidden population, use random techniques or recruit, and then use a snowball sample to expand from a few cases.
Convenience	Get any cases in any manner that is convenient.
Deviant case	Get cases that substantially differ from the dominant pattern (a special type of purposive sample).
Purposive	Get all possible cases that fit particular criteria using various methods.
Quota	Using haphazard methods, get a preset number of cases in each of several predetermined categories that will reflect the diversity of the population.
Sequential	Get cases until there is no additional information or new characteristics (often used with other sampling methods).
Snowball	Get cases using referrals from one or a few cases, then referrals from those cases, and so forth.
Theoretical	Get cases that will help reveal features that are theoretically important about a particular setting/topic.

FOUR TYPES OF PROBABILITY SAMPLES

Type of Sample	Technique
Cluster	Create a sampling frame for large cluster units, draw a random sample of the cluster units, create a sampling frame for cases within each selected cluster unit, then draw a random sample of cases, and so forth.
Simple random	Create a sampling frame for all cases and then select cases using a purely random process (e.g., random-number table or computer program).
Stratified	Create a sampling frame for each of several categories of cases, draw a random sample from each category, and then combine the several samples.
Systematic	Create a sampling frame, calculate the sampling interval 1/k, choose a random starting place, and then take every 1/k case.

cluster sampling. Although this book does not cover the mathematics or statistical theory at the foundation of random sampling, the discussions of sampling error, the central limit theorem, and sample size indicated that probability sampling produces most accurate sampling when the goal is creating a representative sample.

The chapter also discussed several types of nonprobability samples: convenience, deviant case quota, sequential, snowball, and theoretical. Except for convenience, these types are best suited for studies in which the purpose is other than creating a sample that is highly representative of a population.

Before moving to the next chapter, it may be useful to restate a fundamental principle of all social research: Do not compartmentalize the steps of the research process; rather, learn to see the interconnections among the steps. Research design, measurement, sampling, and specific research techniques are interdependent. Unfortunately, the constraints of presenting information in a textbook necessitate presenting the parts separately, in sequence. In practice, we need to think about data collection as we design research and develop measures. Likewise, sampling issues influence research design, measurement, and data collection strategies. As you will see in future chapters, good social research depends on simultaneously controlling quality at several different steps: research design, conceptualization, measurement, sampling, and data collection and handling. Making serious errors at any one stage could make an entire research project worthless.

KEY TERMS

adaptive sampling
central limit theorem
cluster sampling
confidence intervals
convenience sampling
deviant case sampling
hidden populations
parameter
population
probability proportionate to
    size (PPS)

purposive sampling
quota sampling
random-digit dialing (RDD)
random-number table
random sample
sample
sampling distribution
sampling element
sampling error
sampling frame
sampling interval

sampling ratio
sequential sampling
simple random sample
snowball sampling
statistic
stratified sampling
systematic sampling
target population
theoretical sampling

REVIEW QUESTIONS

1. When is purposive sampling used?
2. When is the snowball sampling technique appropriate?
3. What is a sampling frame and why is it important?
4. Which sampling method is best when the population has several groups and a researcher wants to ensure that each group is in the sample?
5. How can researchers determine a sampling interval from a sampling ratio?
6. When should a researcher consider using probability proportionate to size?
7. What is the population in random-digit dialing? Does this type avoid sampling frame problems? Explain.
8. How do researchers decide how large a sample to use?
9. How are the logic of sampling and the logic of measurement related?
10. When is random-digit dialing used, and what are its advantages and disadvantages?

NOTES

1. See Stern (1979:77–81) and Beck (1983) on biased samples.

2. Babbie (1998:196), Kalton (1983:91–93), and Sudman (1976a:191–200) discuss quota sampling.

3. For a discussion of the *Literary Digest* sampling error, see Babbie (1998:192–194), Dillman (1978:9–10), Frey (1983:18–19), and Singleton and colleagues (1988: 132–133).

4. See Traugott (1987) on the importance of persistence in reaching sampled respondents for a representative sample. Also see Kalton (1983:63–69) on the importance of nonresponse.

5. Only one name appears in both. The stratified sample has six males and four females; the simple random sample has five males and five females. (Complete the lower block of numbers and then begin at the far right of the top block.)

6. Stratified sampling techniques are discussed in more detail in Frankel (1983:37–46), Kalton (1983:19–28), Mendenhall and associates (1971:53–88), Sudman (1976a:107–130), and Williams (1978:162–175).

7. Cluster sampling is discussed in Frankel (1983: 47–57), Kalton (1983:28–38), Kish (1965), Mendenhall and associates (1971:121–141, 171–183), Sudman (1976a: 69–84), and Williams (1978:144–161).

8. For a discussion, see Frankel (1983:57–62), Kalton (1983:38–47), Sudman (1976a:131–170), and Williams (1978:239–241).

9. Czaja and associates (1982) and Groves and Kahn (1979:32–36) discuss within-household sampling.

10. For more on random-digit dialing issues, see Dillman (1978:238–242), Frey (1983:69–77), Glasser and Metzger (1972), Groves and Kahn (1979:20–21, 45–63), Kalton (1983:86–90), and Waksberg (1978). Kviz (1984) reported that telephone directories can produce relatively accurate sampling frames in rural areas, at least for mail questionnaire surveys. Also see Keeter (1995).

11. See Grosof and Sardy (1985:181–185), Kalton (1983: 82–90), Kraemer and Thiemann (1987), Sudman (1976a:85–105), and Williams (1978: 211–227) for a technical discussion of selecting a sample size.

12. For further discussion on purposive sampling, see Babbie (1998:195), Grosof and Sardy (1985:172–173), and Singleton and associates (1988:153–154, 306). Bailey (1987:94–95) describes "dimensional" sampling, which is a variation of purposive sampling.

13. Snowball sampling is discussed in Babbie (1998:194–196), Bailey (1987:97), and Sudman (1976a:210–211). For discussions of sociometry and sociograms, also see Bailey (1987:366–367), Dooley (1984:86–87), Kidder and Judd (1986:240–241), Lindzey and Byrne (1968:452–525), and Singleton and associates (1988:372–373). Network sampling issues are discussed in Galaskiewicz (1985), Granovetter (1976), and Hoffmann-Lange (1987).

14. On adaptive sampling, see Martsolf et al. (2006), Thompson and Geber (1996), Thompson (2002), and Thompson and Collins (2002).

Experimental Research

*The experiment is distinguished by the activity of the researcher who determines
the conditions under which investigation will take place. Wholly or in part,
the researcher . . . creates, builds or controls the research setting.*
— Willer and Walker, *Building Experiments, Testing Social Theory*, p. 2

Pager (2007) wanted to examine the impact of imprisonment on the chances of getting
a job after release. In addition, he was curious about whether race had an effect. He
created a field experiment in which he hired college-age male "testers." Half the testers
were White and half were Black. In 2001, the testers applied for entry-level jobs that
had been advertised in the newspaper in the Milwaukee metropolitan area. The jobs
required no experience and only a high school diploma. Pager matched testers of each
race on age, physical appearance, and presentation style. He trained the testers, checked
their interview skills, and created a fake résumé for each. For one-half of the testers of
each race, he created résumés that showed a felony conviction for drug possession and
18 months of prison time. The other half had a virtually identical résumé but no
criminal record. Pager randomly assigned testers to the advertised jobs. In this study,
the independent variables were tester race and criminal record. The dependent variable
was whether an employer called back to offer a job to a tester. Pager found that testers
with a criminal record on their résumé and the Black testers received far fewer job offers.
When he looked at the two independent variables together, he learned that a White tester
with a criminal record was more likely to be offered a job than an equally qualified Black
tester who had no criminal record. In Wisconsin as in many other states, laws bar hiring
discrimination by race and by criminal conviction when the conviction has no relevance
to a job. Pager also looked at data suggesting the large racial effect he found in
Milwaukee may be larger in other major urban areas.

In previous chapters, you learned about the foundations of research design. This chapter and the three that follow it focus on research techniques that yield quantitative data. We begin with experiments.

Experimental research builds on the principles of a positivist approach.[1] Natural scientists (e.g., chemists or biologists) and researchers in related applied fields (e.g., agriculture, engineering, and medicine) conduct experiments. We use experiments in education, criminal justice, journalism, marketing, nursing, political science, psychology, social work, and sociology to examine many social issues and theories. As Pager's (2007) experiment on race and criminal record on job seeking in the opening box illustrates, the experiment provides us powerful evidence about how one or two variables affect a dependent variable.

In commonsense language, to *experiment* means to modify one thing in a situation and then compare an outcome to what existed without the modification. For example, I try to start my car. To my surprise, it does not start. I "experiment" by cleaning off the battery connections because I have a simple hypothesis that it is causing the problem. I try to start it again. I had modified one thing (cleaned the connections) and compared the outcome (whether the car started) to the previous situation (it did not start). An experiment begins with a "hypothesis about causes." My hypothesis was that a buildup of crud on the battery connections was blocking the flow of electricity and the cause of the car not starting, so once I had cleared off the crud, the car could start. This commonsense experiment is simple, but it illustrates three critical steps in an experiment: (1) start with causal hypothesis, (2) modify one specific aspect of a situation that is closely connected to the cause, and (3) compare outcomes.

In the chapter's opening box, Pager's (2007) hypothesis was that racial heritage and criminal record influence whether a qualified person will receive job offers. He selected testers by race and created false résumés to modify the job-seeking situation in ways connected to racial heritage and criminal record. He then compared the job offers by racial background and criminal record.

Compared to other social research techniques, experimental research offers the strongest tests of causal relationships. This is so because we consciously design an experiment to satisfy the three conditions for causality (i.e., temporal order in which the independent precedes the dependent variable, evidence of an association, and ruling out alternative causes).

APPROPRIATE TECHNIQUE

People new to social research may anguish over which research technique best fits a specific research question. It can be a difficult decision because there is no ready-made, fixed match between technique and question. Deciding requires making an "informed judgment." You can develop judgment skills by learning the strengths and weaknesses of the various research techniques, reading the methodology section of many published studies, assisting an experienced social researcher, and acquiring practical experience by conducting studies yourself.

An experiment can powerfully test and focus evidence about causal relationships. Compared to other research techniques, it has both advantages and limitations, and these help to see where it is most appropriate.

The experiment is often artificial. It is a purposeful simplification of the complex social world. We tend to think that "artificial" means something negative, but Webster and Sell (2007:11) argue,

> *The greatest benefits of experiments reside in the fact that they are artificial. That is, experiments allow observation in a situation that has been designed and created by investigators rather than one that occurs in nature.*

Artificial means that the experimenter consciously controls the study situation and purposely incorporates theoretically relevant variables while removing variables without a causal importance for a hypothesis. *Artificial* also means a sharpened focus and narrowly targeted effects that we may not easily encounter in the natural world. We include the independent and dependent variables, but exclude irrelevant or **confounding variables** (i.e., variables not a part of our hypothesis test). An analogy is the chemist who finds pure sodium in the natural world. In a controlled laboratory setting, the chemist mixes it precisely with another pure chemical to study its effects. The controlled, sterile laboratory is artificial, pure sodium is artificial, and what the chemist mixes it with is artificial, yet the outcome can produce new knowledge and compounds that have great utility in the real world.

Social science experiments have a very powerful logic; however, we face many practical and ethical limitations. In an experiment, we manipulate some aspects of the world and then examine the outcomes; however, we cannot manipulate many areas of human life for the sake of gaining scientific knowledge. With experiments, we are limited to questions that have specific conditions that we can manipulate and that clearly fall within ethical standards for research with humans. Thus, an experiment cannot directly answer questions such as these: Do people who complete a college education increase their annual income more than people who do not attend college? Do children raised with younger siblings develop better leadership skills than only children? Do people who belong to more organizations vote more often in elections? We cannot allow some people to attend college and prevent others from attending to discover who earns more income later in life. We cannot induce couples to have either many children or a single child in order to examine how leadership skills develop in the children. We cannot compel people to join or quit organizations or never join them and then see whether they vote. Although we cannot manipulate many of the situations or variables we find of interest, we are able to be creative in simulating such interventions or conditions.

The experimental technique is usually best for issues that have a narrow scope or scale. We can often assemble and conduct numerous experiments with limited resources in a short period yet still test theoretically significant hypotheses. For example, we could replicate a study like that of Niven (see Example Box 9.1, News Reports on Death Penalty Opinions on page 278) in less than a month and at very low cost.

In general, an experiment is suited for micro-level (e.g., individual psychological or small-group phenomena) more than for macro-level theoretical concerns. This is why social psychologists and political psychologists conduct experiments. Experiments cannot easily address questions that require consideration of conditions operating across an entire society or over many years.

Experiments encourage us to isolate and target one or a few causal variables. Despite the strength to demonstrate the causal effect of one or two variables, experiments are not effective if we want to consider dozens of variables simultaneously. It is rarely appropriate for questions requiring us to examine the impact of many of variables together or to assess conditions across a range of complex settings or numerous social groups.

Experiments provide focused tests of hypotheses with each experiment considering one or two variables in a specific setting. Knowledge advances slowly by compiling, comparing, and synthesizing the findings from numerous separate experiments. This strategy for building knowledge differs from that of other research techniques in which one study might examine fifteen to twenty variables simultaneously in a diverse range of social settings.

Convention also influences the research questions that best align with the experimental method. Researchers have created vast research literature on many topics by using the experimental method. This has facilitated rapid, smooth communication about those topics. It has also facilitated replicating past experiments with minor adjustments and precisely isolating the effects of specific variables. Expertise in experiments can be a limitation because researchers who specialize in such topics tend to expect everyone to use the experimental method. These researchers evaluate new studies by the standards of a good experiment and may more slowly accept and assimilate new knowledge coming from a nonexperimental study.

Confounding variables In experimental research, factors that are not part of the intended hypothesis being tested, but that have effects on variables of interest and threaten internal validity.

News Reports on Death Penalty Opinions

Niven (2002) noted the overwhelming support (75–80 percent) in opinion polls for the death penalty among Americans in recent decades. However, if people have a choice between supporting the death penalty for a murder or a sentence of life imprisonment without parole (LIWP), their support for the death penalty drops by nearly one-half. Niven found that more than 90 percent of media stories on death penalty opinions report overwhelming public support for it, but very few stories report that many people would prefer LIWP as an alternative punishment for the same crimes. Niven hypothesized that support for the death penalty might change if people had exposure to media stories that told them about high levels of public support for the LIWP alternative. To test his hypothesis, he went to waiting areas in the Miami International Airport for more than a two-week period and recruited 564 participants for his study. He randomly assigned people to read one of three newspaper articles, which were his independent variable. One newspaper article told about overwhelming support for the death penalty, another reported public support for LIWP, and the third was unrelated to the death penalty issue and about airport expansion plans. He told respondents a cover story: that the study was about newspaper article writing style. Participants completed a questionnaire about the clarity and organization of the article to disguise the purpose of the experiment. He also had a section on political beliefs under the premise that he wanted to know whether people with different political beliefs reacted the same way to the article. This section included his dependent variable, three questions about determining support or opposition for the death penalty for the crime of murder, preference for the death penalty or LIWP, and an estimate as to whether more or fewer states would adopt the death penalty in the future. His results showed no differences on the death penalty questions between participants who read about overwhelming death penalty support and the control group that read about airport expansion. More than 80 percent of both groups supported the death penalty, a little over one-half preferred it to LIWP, and most thought more states would adopt the death penalty in the future. People who read about LIWP showed much less support for the death penalty (62 percent), preferred LIWP over the death penalty (by a 57 to 43 percent margin), and predicted that fewer states would have the death penalty in the future. Thus, Nevin found support for his hypothesis that media stories that report on public support for the death penalty only perpetuate public opinion for it over the LIWP alternative.

We also can conduct mixed experimental and nonexperimental methods in a study to expand understanding. For example, we want to study attitudes toward people in wheelchairs. We could survey a thousand people about their views on people in wheelchairs. We could conduct a field research study and observe how people react to us while we are in a wheelchair in real-life settings. We can also design an experiment in which we interact with others—sometimes while in a wheelchair and at other times standing or walking without a wheelchair and then noting how people respond to each situation. To best test theories and develop a fuller understanding, we combine knowledge from all types of studies (see Example Box 9.2, Experimental and Survey Methods to Test and Apply Identity Theory).

A SHORT HISTORY OF THE EXPERIMENT

The social sciences, starting with psychology, borrowed the experimental method from the natural sciences. Psychology did not fully embrace the experiment until after 1900.[2] Wilhelm M. Wundt (1832–1920), a German psychologist and physiologist, introduced the experimental method into psychology. During the late 1800s, Germany was the center of graduate education, and social scientists came from around the world to study there. Wundt established a laboratory for experimentation in psychology that became a model for social research. By 1900, universities in the United States and elsewhere established psychology laboratories to conduct experimental research. However, William

EXAMPLE BOX **9.2**

Experimental and Survey Methods to Test and Apply Identity Theory

Transue (2007) combined experimental logic with survey research methods in one study and tested an abstract social science theory by applying it to a real public policy issue. His work contributed to a growing literature showing how a subtle emphasis on racial differences among Americans tends to accentuate divisions along racial lines regarding public issues.

According to social identity theory, we automatically categorize other people into in-groups (groups to which we belong) and out-groups (groups to which we do not belong). These groups form the basis of social boundaries and feelings of social distance from or closeness to other people. We also have multiple identities. A subset of the broader theory, self-categorization, says we recategorize others as members of in-groups or out-groups based on which of our identities is more active. Social boundaries and feelings of social distance depend on the most salient in-group. We feel closer to members of an in-group and farther from people in salient out-groups. *Priming* is a process by which something happens to activate a particular identity. Once activated, this identity tends to have greater influence over subsequent behavior or thinking. Once reminded of an identity (i.e., it has been primed) it moves to the forefront of how we think about ourselves and therefore influences our behavior.

In most past studies on social identity theory, researchers used laboratory experiments with small convenience samples of students and tested the effect of a temporary, artificially created identity on a contrived issue. Transue (2007) sought more external validity. To obtain it, he used a large random sample of adults, an actual social identity, and a real public policy issue. His study used a telephone survey of a random sample of 405 White U.S. citizens in the Minneapolis metropolitan area in summer 1998 relying on random-digit dialing (see Chapter 8; Chapter 10 discusses telephone surveys). Transue considered two actual identities, race and nation. He built on past studies that showed racially prejudiced Whites who had been primed or reminded of their race to be more likely to think in racist ways when they voted. The real policy issue he examined was support for paying taxes for public schools.

For the independent variable, social identity, Transue asked randomly assigned subsets of survey respondents one of two questions: "How close do you feel to your ethnic or racial group?" or "How close do you feel to other Americans?" This question primed or raised awareness of an identity. Later in the survey, he asked randomly assigned subsets of two questions about paying school taxes, "to improve education in public schools" or "to improve opportunities for minorities." This was the main dependent variable. Transue hypothesized that Whites who were primed about their racial identity would reject paying taxes to help minorities more than Whites who were primed about their American national identity. He also thought that Whites primed about an American national identity would more strongly support taxes for public schools generally than those primed about their racial identity.

Transue found that Whites primed with a racial identity and asked about helping minorities had the least amount of support for paying school taxes. The most support came from Whites primed with an American national identity and asked about helping public schools generally. Tensue also looked at the Whites who had identified more strongly with their racial-ethnic group and compared them with Whites having a weak or no racial identification. Consistent with social identity theory, he found that Whites with the strongest racial identity showed the most resistance to paying taxes to improve minority opportunities. In this study, a primed racial self-identity increased the salience of a person's racial in-group and heightened social boundaries associated with racial categories. A strong identity with one's racial in-group increased social distance for people in racial out-groups and lowered a desire to provide them with assistance.

James (1842–1910), a prominent philosopher and psychologist, did not use or embrace the experimental method. The experiment displaced a more philosophical, introspective, integrative approach in psychology that was closer to the interpretive social science approach discussed in Chapter 4.

From 1900 to 1950, social researchers elaborated on the experimental method until it became entrenched in some areas. The experiment's appeal was its objective, unbiased, scientific approach to studying mental and social life in an era when the scientific study of social life was just gaining broad public acceptance. Four trends sped the expansion of experimental social research: the rise of behaviorism, the spread of quantification, the changes in research participants, and the method's practical applications. Let us briefly consider each trend.

1. *Behaviorism* is an approach in psychology founded by the American James B. Watson (1878–1958) and expanded by B. F. Skinner (1904–1990). It emphasizes creating precise measures of observable behavior or outward manifestations of inner mental life and advocates the experiment to conduct rigorous empirical tests of hypotheses.

2. *Quantification,* or measuring social phenomena with numbers, expanded between 1900 and 1950. Researchers conceptualized social constructs as quantified measures and jettisoned other nonquantifiable constructs (e.g., spirit, consciousness, will) from empirical research. An example is measuring mental ability by using the IQ test. Originally developed by Alfred Binet (1857–1911), a Frenchman, researchers translated the test into English and revised it by 1916. It soon had widespread use and appeal as a way to represent something as subjective as a person's mental ability with a single score and became an objective, scientific way to rank people. Between the years of 1921 and 1936, more than 5,000 articles were published on intelligence tests.[3] Many scaling and index techniques were developed in this period, and social researchers began to use applied statistics.

3. Over time, the people used as participants changed. Early social research reports contained the names of the specific individuals who participated in a study, and most were professional researchers. Later reports treated participants anonymously and reported only the results of their actions. Over time, there was a shift to use college students or schoolchildren as research participants. The relationship between a researcher and the people studied became more distant. Such distancing reflected a trend for the experimenters to be more detached, remote, and

objective from the people under study. Researchers saw reducing emotional engagement with research participants in their studies as becoming more neutral or value-free and truly "scientific" in a positivist sense.

4. As researchers became aware of an experiment's practical applications, businesses, governments, health care facilities, and schools increasingly used experimental methods for applied purposes. For example, the U.S. Army adopted intelligence tests during World War I to sort thousands of soldiers into different military positions. The leader of the "scientific management" movement in factories, Frederick W. Taylor (1856–1915), advocated using experiments in factories. He worked with management to modify factory conditions as a way to increase worker productivity. In the 1920s, educational researchers conducted many experiments on teaching methods and the effect of class size on learning.

By the 1950s and 1960s, researchers became more concerned with possible sources of alternative explanations, or confounding variables, that might slip into experimental design. Researchers designed experiments to reduce such potential errors and increasingly used statistical procedures in data analysis. A turning point in the increasingly rigorous design of social science experiments was a book by Campbell and Stanley (1963), who defined basic designs and issues in experimental methods.

By the 1970s, researchers increasingly evaluated the methodological rigor of studies. A related trend was the increased use of deception and a corresponding rise in concern about ethical issues. For example, the now common practice of debriefing did not come into use until the 1960s.[4] Over the last three decades, the trend has been to use more sophisticated experimental designs and statistical techniques for data analysis.

Experiments and Theory

We conduct two types of social science experiments: empirically based and theory-directed (see Willer and Walker, 2007a, 2007b). The practical process of doing an experiment differs little, but each type has different purposes. Most studies are empirically based.

In the empirically based experiment, our goal is to determine whether an independent variable has a significant effect on a specific dependent variable. We want to document and describe an effect (i.e., its size, direction, or form). Often we empirically demonstrate the effect in a controlled setting from which we can generalize to "real-life" conditions (see the discussion of external validity later in this chapter). We generalize our findings to natural or "real-world" settings. For example, Solomon Asch's (1955) famous experiment demonstrated the effect of conformity to group pressure by having eight students look at three lines. Once Asch demonstrated the power of group conformity, we generalized its effects beyond his specific study of eight students looking at three lines to many sizes of groups of all types of people engaged in most real-life tasks. The study by Pager (2007) that opened this chapter was an empirically based study. It demonstrated the effects of race and a criminal record on job seeking, as did the study by Niven (2002) on news reports and death penalty opinions (see Example Box 9.1). Niven's study demonstrated the effect of reading news reports on death penalty opinions.

In a theory-directed experiment, we proceed deductively by converting an abstract model of how we believe the world operates (i.e., theory) into a specific study design with specific measures. The experiment is a replica of the theoretical model. When we generalize from a theory-directed experiment, we generalize the theory as a model of how the world operates. Our primary task is to test the theory and learn whether there is empirical evidence for it. We are not concerned with finding a large effect of the independent variable; rather, we are concerned with finding that a theory's specific expectations or predictions closely match empirical findings. We worry less whether the experimental test of theory is highly artificial and nonrealistic to the natural world. Our primary concern is whether the empirical results match our theory. We seek many replication experiments to show repeatedly that the evidence matches the theory or that the theory can survive numerous tests. Indeed, as Webster and Sell (2007:21) argue, "experimental results themselves are really not interesting except as they bear on a theory."

We often use statistical techniques in experiments to see how likely the result predicted by the theory occurs. If the theory-predicted outcome has a low probability but occurs regularly, our confidence in the theory's correctness grows. Here is a simple example. My friend believes he can tell the difference between five brands of diet colas. I have him drink twenty cups of them over 4 days. One-fifth of the cups is one brand and their order is totally mixed. If he is correct twenty of the twenty times, I am confident that he really can tell the difference. By chance alone, he would be correct only 20 percent of the time. If a theory such as the one regarding my friend is correct 100 percent of the time, our confidence in it grows, but 100 percent is rare. However, if my friend was correct 90 percent of the time, I would think his evaluation was very good but not perfect. If he was correct just 30 percent of the time, this is little better than chance alone, so my confidence in his evaluation is low. In theory testing, our confidence in an explanation varies by whether the theory's predictions far exceed what we expect by chance alone and whether it survives repeated tests.

The study by Transue reported in Example Box 9.2 has features of a theory-directed experiment. He sought to replicate tests of a theory that had survived many previous experimental tests, self-categorization theory. He applied the priming effect to activate self-categorization to select an in-group identity and then provided evidence that supported the theory. His study was unusual in that it combined survey methods and a realistic policy issue. Another study on the contact hypothesis described later in this chapter (see Example Box 9.7, A Field Experiment on College Roommates) is also a theory-directed experiment, although applied in a real-life situation. Although we usually begin theory-directed experiments in highly controlled artificial settings, we may extend and replicate them in naturalistic settings.

RANDOM ASSIGNMENT

As researchers, we are always making comparisons. The cliché "Compare apples to apples; don't compare apples to oranges" is not about fruit; it is about comparisons. It means that a valid comparison depends on comparing what is fundamentally alike.

There are many ways to compare.[5] We can compare the same person over time (e.g., before and after completing a training course)—a within-subject experiment. However, we are often less interested whether a treatment or independent variable results in one person changing than whether it generally has an effect. We can compare a group of people at two times (e.g., the group average of thirty people before and after a training course). We can also compare the same group of thirty people over a series treatments (e.g., three training programs in sequence) to see whether each time we get an effect. These are within-group experiments. Alternatively, we can also compare two groups of fifteen participants: fifteen who have had and another fifteen who have not had the treatment (e.g., the training course). This is a between-group experiment.

Random assignment facilitates between-group comparisons by creating similar groups. For comparative purposes, we do not want the group to differ with regard to variables that may present alternative explanations for a causal relationship. For example, we want to compare two groups to determine the causal effect of completing a firefighting training course on each person's ability to respond to a fire. We want the two groups to be similar in all respects except for taking the course. If the groups were identical except for the course, we can compare outcomes with confidence and know that the course caused any of the differences we found. If the groups differed (e.g., one had experienced firefighters or one had much younger and more physically fit participants) we could not be certain when we compared them that the training course was the only cause of any differences we observe.

Why Assign Randomly

Random assignment is a method for assigning cases (e.g., individuals, organizations) to groups to make comparisons. It is a way to divide a collection of participants into two or more groups to increase your confidence that the groups do not differ in a systematic way. It is a purely mechanical method; the assignment is automatic. You cannot assign based on your or a participant's personal preference or his or her features (e.g., you thought the person acted friendly, someone wants to be in a group with a friend, put all people who arrived late in one group).

Random assignment is random in a statistical or mathematical sense, not in an everyday sense. We may say *random* to mean unplanned, haphazard, or accidental. In probability theory, *random* is a process in which each case has an equal chance of being selected. With random selection, you can mathematically calculate the odds that a specific case appears in one group over another. For example, you have fifty people and use a random process (such as the toss of a balanced coin) to place some in one (the coin that was always heads) or another group (the coin indicates tails). This way all participants have an equal chance of ending up in one or the other group.

The great thing about a random process is that over many separate random occurrences, very predictable things happen. Although the process is entirely due to chance and it is impossible to predict a specific outcome at a specific time, we can make highly accurate predictions when looking over many situations.

Random assignment is *unbiased* because our desires to confirm a hypothesis or a research participant's personal interests do not enter into the selection process. *Unbiased* does not mean the groups will be identical in each specific random assignment selection but is something close to this: We can determine the probability of selecting a case mathematically and, in the long run, across many separate selections, the average across all the groups will be identical.

Random sampling and random assignment are both processes for selecting cases for inclusion in a study. When we randomly assign, we sort a collection of cases into two or more groups using a random process. When we randomly sample, we select a smaller subset of cases from a far larger collection of cases (see Figure 9.1). We can both sample and

> **Random assignment** Participants divided into groups at the beginning of experimental research using a random process so the experimenter can treat the groups as equivalent.

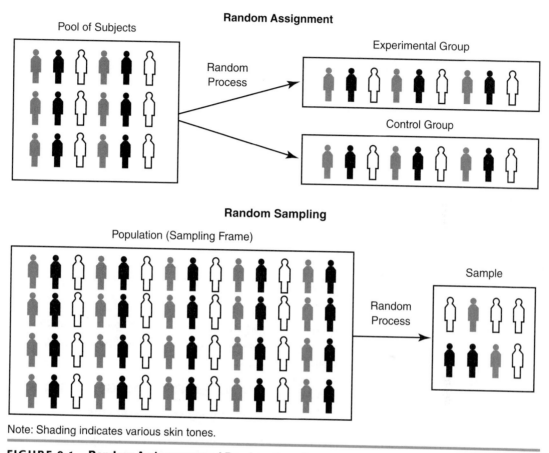

FIGURE 9.1   Random Assignment and Random Sampling

randomly assign. We can first sample to obtain a smaller set of cases (e.g., 150 people out of 20,000) and then use random assignment to divide the smaller set into groups (e.g., divide the 150 people into three groups of 50).

How to Randomly Assign

Random assignment is simple in practice. We begin with a collection of cases (i.e., individuals, teams, companies, or whatever the unit of analysis is) and then divide the collection into two or more groups using a random process, such as asking people to count off, tossing a coin, or throwing dice. For example, we want to divide thirty-two people into two groups of sixteen. We could have each write his or her name on a standard size slip of paper, put all slips in a hat, mix the slips with our eyes closed, and then with eyes still closed, draw the first sixteen names for group 1 and the second sixteen for group 2. A specific situation can be unusual and the groups may differ. For example, it is possible although extremely unlikely that all cases with one characteristic will end up in one group. For example, we have thirty-two people with sixteen males and sixteen females, but all of the males end up in one group and all of the females in another. This is possible by random chance but extremely rare (see in Figure 9.2 [page 284] on random assignment).

Matching versus Random Assignment

If the purpose of random assignment is to get two (or more) equivalent groups, you may ask whether

Step 1: Begin with a collection of subjects.

Step 2: Devise a method to randomize that is purely mechanical (e.g., flip a coin).

Step 3: Assign subjects with "Heads" to one group   and "Tails" to the other group.

Control Group   **Experimental Group**

Note: Shading indicates various skin tones.

FIGURE 9.2   How to Randomly Assign

it would not be simpler to match the characteristics of cases in each group. Some researchers match cases in groups on certain characteristics, such as age and gender. Matching is an alternative to random assignment, but it is an infrequently used one.

Matching presents a problem: What are the relevant characteristics on which to match, and can one locate exact matches? Individual cases differ in thousands of ways, and we cannot know which might be relevant. For example, we compare two groups of fifteen students. Group 1 has eight males, so we need eight males in group 2. Two males in group 1 are only children; one is from a divorced family, one from an intact family. One is tall, slender, and Jewish; the other is short, heavy, and Catholic. To match groups, do we have to find a tall Jewish male only child from a divorced home and a short Catholic male only child from an intact home? The tall, slender, Jewish male child is only 22 years old, and he is a premed major. The short, heavy Catholic male is 20 years old and is an accounting major. Do we also need to match the age

and career aspirations of the two males? True matching soon becomes an impossible task.

EXPERIMENTAL DESIGN LOGIC

The Language of Experiments

In experimental research, many studies call the participants **subjects**, although in recent years, *research participant* has been more commonly used**.**

Parts of the Experiment. Experiments have seven parts. Not all experiments have all of these parts, and some have all seven parts plus others.

1. Treatment or independent variable
2. Dependent variable
3. Pretest
4. Posttest
5. Experimental group
6. Control group
7. Random assignment

In most experiments, we create a situation or enter into an ongoing situation and modify it. The **treatment** (or the stimulus or manipulation) is what we do. The term comes from medicine: a physician administers a treatment to patients; the physician

Subjects   A traditional name for participants in experimental research.

Treatment   The independent variable in experimental research.

intervenes with a physical or psychological treatment to change it. The treatment is the independent variable or a combination of independent variables. In the study described in this chapter's opening box, Pager (2007) had two independent variables: one was a fixed characteristic (the tester's race) and the other was manipulated (a criminal conviction on a false résumé). In Niven's study (2002) (Example Box 9.1), the treatment was which of three news stories participants received to read while in an airport waiting area. In Transue's study (2007) (Example Box 9.2), the treatment was which of two questions about identity participants heard in a telephone survey.

At times, we go to great lengths to create treatments. While some may use reading different false records, reading different news stories, hearing different survey questions, or seeing different videos (see Example Box 9.4). Other treatments can be as complex, such as putting participants into situations with elaborate equipment, staged physical settings, or contrived social situations. You saw this in the famous Milgram and Zimbardo experiments that you read about in Chapter 4 (also see Example Box 9.6 later in this chapter). We want the treatment to have an impact and produce specific reactions, feelings, or behaviors (see the section on experimental realism later in this chapter).

Dependent variables, or outcomes in experimental research, are the physical conditions, social behaviors, attitudes, feelings, or beliefs of participants that change in response to a treatment. We can measure dependent variables by using paper-and-pencil indicators, observations, interviews, or physiological responses (e.g., heartbeat or sweating palms).

Frequently, we measure the dependent variable more than once during an experiment. The **pretest** is the measurement of the dependent variable prior to the introduction of the treatment. The **posttest** is the measurement of the dependent variable after the treatment has been introduced into the experimental situation.

We often divide participants into two or more groups for purposes of comparison. A simple experiment has two groups, only one of which receives the treatment. The **experimental group** is the group that receives the treatment or in which the treatment is present. The group that does not receive the treatment is the **control group**. When the independent variable takes on many different values, more than one experimental group is used.

Steps in Conducting an Experiment. Following the basic steps of the research process, we decide on a topic, narrow it into a testable research problem or question, and then develop a hypothesis with variables. A crucial early step is to plan a specific experimental design (to be discussed). As we plan, we decide the number of groups to use, how and when to create treatment conditions, the number of times to measure the dependent variable, and what the groups of participants will experience from beginning to end of the study. We often *pilot test* the experiment (i.e., conduct it as a "dry run").

The experiment begins after we locate volunteer participants and randomly assign them to groups. We give them precise, preplanned instructions. Next we may measure the dependent variable in a pretest before the treatment. We then expose one group only to the treatment (or a high level of it). Finally, we measure the dependent variable in a posttest. We also interview participants about the experiment before they leave. We record measures of the dependent variable and examine the results for each group to see whether the hypothesis is supported.

Control in Experiments. Control is crucial in experimental research.[6] We want to control all aspects of the experimental situation to isolate the effects of the treatment. By controlling confounding

---

Pretest   An examination that measures the dependent variable of an experiment prior to the treatment.

Posttest   An examination that measures the dependent variable of an experiment after the treatment.

Experimental group   The participants who receive the treatment in experimental research.

Control group   The participants who do not receive the treatment in experimental research.

variables, we eliminate alternative explanations that could undermine our attempts to establish causality.

We sometimes use deception to control the experimental setting (see the section A Word on Ethics later in this chapter). **Deception** occurs when we intentionally mislead research participants through written or verbal instructions, the actions of others, or aspects of the setting. Using deception may involve the use of a **confederate**—someone who pretends to be another research participant or bystander but who actually works for the researcher and deliberately misleads participants. Milgram's experiment used confederates as did the study described in Example Box 9.6 later in this chapter about disabled co-workers.

The purpose of deception is to control what the participants see and hear and what they believe is occurring. This usually means creating a **cover story**, a false explanation of the study's purpose that we tell participants to mislead them about its true purpose. The cover story helps satisfy curiosity but reduces demand characteristics (see later in this chapter). Many studies use a cover story (see studies in Example Boxes 9.1, 9.4, 9.6, and 9.7).

Types of Design

We combine parts of an experiment (e.g., pretests, control groups) into an **experimental design**. Some designs lack pretests, some do not have control

> **Deception**   A lie by an experimenter to participants about the true nature of an experiment or the creation of a false impression through his or her actions or the setting.
>
> **Confederate**   A person working for the experimenter who acts as another participant or in a role in front of participants to deceive them with an experiment's cover story.
>
> **Cover story**   A type of deception in which the experimenter tells a false story to participants so they will act as wanted and do not know the true hypothesis.
>
> **Experimental design**   The planning and arranging of the parts of an experiment.
>
> **Classical experimental design**   An experimental design that has random assignment, a control group, an experimental group, and a pretest and posttest for each group.

groups, and others have many experimental groups. We have given widely used standard designs names. It is important to learn the standard design for two reasons. First, when reading research reports, researchers may name a standard design instead of describing it. Second, the standard designs illustrate common ways to combine design parts. We can use them for experiments we conduct or create variations.

We illustrate the various designs with a simple example. Let us say that you want to learn whether waitstaff (waiters and waitresses) receive more in tips if they first introduce themselves by first name and return 8 to 10 minutes after delivering the food to ask, "Is everything fine?" The dependent variable is the size of the tip received. Your study occurs in two identical restaurants on different sides of a town that have had the same types of customers and average the same amount in tips.

Classical Experimental Design.   All designs are variations of the **classical experimental design**, the type of design discussed so far, which has random assignment, a pretest and a posttest, an experimental group, and a control group.

Example.   You give forty newly hired waitstaff an identical 2-hour training session and instruct the members to follow a script in which they are not to introduce themselves by first name and not to return during the meal to check on the customers. You next randomly divide the servers into two equal groups of twenty and send each group to one of the two restaurants to begin employment. You record the amount in tips for all participants for one month (pretest score). Next, you "retrain" the twenty participants at restaurant 1 (experimental group). You instruct them henceforth to introduce themselves to customers by first name and to check on the customers, asking, "Is everything fine?" 8 to 10 minutes after delivering the food (treatment). You remind the group at restaurant 2 (control group) to continue without an introduction or checking during the meal. Over the second month, you record the amount of tips for both groups (posttest score).

Preexperimental Designs.   Some designs lack random assignment and are compromises or shortcuts.

We use these **preexperimental designs** in situations in which it is difficult to use the classical design. The designs have weaknesses that make inferring a causal relationship difficult.

One-Shot Case-Study Design. Also called the *one-group posttest-only design,* the **one-shot case-study design** has only one group, a treatment, and a posttest. Because there is only one group, there is no random assignment.

Example. You take a group of forty newly hired waitstaff and give all a 2-hour training session in which you instruct them to introduce themselves to customers by first name and to check on the customers, asking, "Is everything fine?" 8 to 10 minutes after delivering the food (treatment). The participants begin employment, and you record the amount in tips for all for one month (posttest score).

One-Group Pretest-Posttest Design. This design has one group, a pretest, a treatment, and a posttest. It lacks a control group and random assignment.

Example. You take a group of forty newly hired wait staff and give all a 2-hour training session. You instruct the staff members to follow a script in which they are not to introduce themselves by first name and not to return during the meal to check on the customers. All begin employment, and you record the amount in tips for all for one month (pretest score). Next, you "retrain" all 40 participants and instruct them henceforth to introduce themselves to customers by first name and to check on the customers, asking, "Is everything fine?" 8 to 10 minutes after delivering the food (treatment). Over the second month, you record the amount of tips for both groups (posttest score).

This is an improvement over the one-shot case study because you measure the dependent variable before and after the treatment. But it lacks a control group. We cannot know whether something other than the treatment occurred between the pretest and the posttest to cause the outcome.

Static Group Comparison. Also called the *posttest-only nonequivalent group design,* a **static group comparison** has two groups, a posttest, and treatment. It lacks random assignment and a pretest. A weakness is that any posttest outcome difference between the groups could be due to group differences prior to the experiment instead of to the treatment.

Example. You give forty newly hired waitstaff an identical 2-hour training session and instruct all to follow a script in which servers are not to introduce themselves by first name and but to return during the meal to check on the customers. They can choose one of the two restaurants at which to work, as long as each restaurant has twenty people. All begin employment. After one month, you "retrain" the twenty participants at restaurant 1 (experimental group) and instruct them henceforth to introduce themselves to customers by first name and to check on the customers, asking, "Is everything fine?" 8 to 10 minutes after delivering the food (treatment). The group at restaurant 2 (control group) is "retrained" to continue without an introduction or checking during the meal. Over the second month, you record the amount of tips for both groups (posttest score).

Quasi-Experimental and Special Designs. These designs, like the classical design, make identifying a causal relationship more certain than do preexperimental designs. **Quasi-experimental designs** help us test for causal relationships in situations in which the classical design is difficult or inappropriate. We call them *quasi* because they

---

Preexperimental designs Experimental plans that lack random assignment or use shortcuts and are much weaker than the classical experimental design; are substituted in situations in which an experimenter cannot use all of the features of a classical experimental design but the design has weaker internal validity.

One-shot case-study design An experimental plan with only an experimental group and a posttest but no pretest.

Static group comparison design An experimental plan with two groups, no random assignment, and only a posttest.

Quasi-experimental designs Plans that are stronger than preexperimental ones; variations on the classical experimental design used in special situations or when an experimenter has limited control over the independent variable.

TABLE 9.1   A Comparison of the Classical Experimental Design

DESIGN	RANDOM ASSIGNMENT	PRETEST	POSTTEST	CONTROL GROUP	EXPERIMENTAL GROUP
Classical	Yes	Yes	Yes	Yes	Yes
One-shot case study	No	No	Yes	No	Yes
One-group pretest/postest	No	Yes	Yes	No	Yes
Static group comparison	No	No	Yes	Yes	Yes
Two-group posttest only	Yes	No	Yes	Yes	Yes
Time-series designs	No	Yes	Yes	No	Yes

are variations of the classical experimental design. Some have randomization but lack a pretest, some use more than two groups, and others substitute many observations of one group over time for a control group. In general, the researcher has less control over the independent variable than in the classical design (see Table 9.1).

Two-Group Posttest-Only Design.   This design is identical to the static group comparison with one exception: You randomly assign. It has all parts of the classical design except a pretest. Random assignment reduces the chance that the groups differed before the treatment, but without a pretest, you cannot be as certain that the groups began the study at the same level on the dependent variable.

In a study using a two-group posttest-only design with random assignment, Rind and Strohmetz (1999) examined restaurant tips. The treatment involved messages about an upcoming special written on the back of customers' checks. The participants were eighty-one dining parties eating at an upscale restaurant in New Jersey. The treatment was whether

a female server wrote a message about an upcoming restaurant special on the back of a check and the dependent variable was the size of the tip. The researchers gave a server with two years' experience a randomly shuffled stack of cards. One-half said No Message and one-half said Message. Just before she gave a customer his or her check, she randomly pulled a card from her pocket. If it said Message, she wrote about an upcoming special on the back of the customer's check. If it said No Message, she wrote nothing. The experimenters recorded the amount of the tip and the number of people at the table. They instructed the server to act the same toward all customers. The results showed that higher tips came from customers who received the message about upcoming specials.

Interrupted Time Series.   In an **interrupted time-series design**, you measure the dependent variable on one group over time using many multiple dependent variable measures before (prettests) and after a treatment (posttests).

Equivalent Time Series.   An **equivalent time-series design** is a one-group design similar to the interrupted time series design. It extends over a time period, but instead of a single treatment, the equivalent time series design has the same treatment multiple times. Like the interrupted time series design, we measure the dependent variable several times before and after the treatments. The study on alcohol sales and suicide rates (Example Box 9.3,

---

Interrupted time-series design   An experimental plan in which the dependent variable is measured periodically across many time points and the treatment occurs in the midst of such measures, often only once.

Equivalent time-series design   An experimental plan with several repeated pretests, posttests, and treatments for one group often over a period of time.

EXAMPLE BOX **9.3**

Interrupted Time Series, Alcohol Sales, and Suicide Rates

Governments face strong pressures by economic interests to modify laws to allow them to collect increased profits from alcohol sales. In most of western Canada, a public monopoly controlled alcohol sales and distribution through most of the twentieth century. Proponents of privatization point to its economic benefits, including selling previously government-owned retail outlets and the sale of licenses to merchandise alcohol. Others point to the impact of privatization on consumption and health. Studies of privatization of sales of alcoholic beverages indicate that privatization greatly expands alcohol availability and consumption.

Alberta moved to privatize alcohol sales in three stages: the opening of privately owned wine stores in 1985, the opening of privately owned cold beer stores and sale of spirits and wine in hotels in the rural area in 1989–1990, and finally the privatization of all liquor stores in 1994. The number of alcohol outlets increased substantially, and consumption of spirits increased dramatically at a time when consumption was decreasing elsewhere in the country. Privatization in Alberta has been associated with an increase in criminal offenses, such as liquor store break-ins and less strict enforcement of underage purchase laws. Alberta also has some of the highest rates of

drunk-driving fatalities in the country. Many past studies also showed a strong relationship between suicide rates and alcohol consumption.

Zalcman and Mann (2007) used a three-stage interrupted time-series design to examine the influence of Alberta's privatization of alcohol sales on suicide rates between 1976 and 1999. They considered whether suicide rates changed after each privatization phase. They also compared Alberta's suicide levels to those for the same years in Ontario where alcohol sales remained a government monopoly.

The researchers found that the 1985 privatization of wine retailers increased male and female suicide rates in Alberta by 51 percent for males and 35 percent for females. After the 1989–1990 privatization of spirits and wine a significant increase occurred in male and female suicide rates, estimated to be 17 percent and 52 percent, respectively. The 1994 privatization event significantly increased male suicide mortality rates, estimated at 19 percent, but not female suicide rates. Part of the increase was a short-term spurt but long-term suicide raises also rose. By tracing the rates both over time by comparing those in a "control group" or to those in Ontario, the authors provided evidence of the effect of alcohol privatization.

Interrupted Time Series, Alcohol Sales, and Suicide Rates) illustrated equivalent time series.

Latin Square Design. At times, we are interested in how several independent variables in different sequences or time orders affect a dependent variable. The **Latin square design** enables us to examine this type of situation. For example, a geography instructor has three units to teach students: map reading, using a compass, and the longitude/latitude (LL) system. The units can be taught in any order, but the teacher wants to know which order most helps students learn. In one class, students first learn to read maps, then how to use a compass, and then the LL system. In another class, using a compass comes first, then map reading, and then using the LL system. In a third class, the instructor first teaches the LL system, then compass

usage, and ends with map reading. The teacher gives tests to each class after each unit, and students take a comprehensive exam at the end of the term. The students were randomly assigned to classes, so the instructor could see whether presenting units in one sequence or another resulted in improved learning.

Solomon Four-Group Design. We believe that the pretest measure may have an influence on the treatment or dependent variable. A pretest can sometimes sensitize participants to the treatment or improve their performance on the posttest (see the

> **Latin square design** An experimental plan to examine whether the order or sequence in which participants receive versions of the treatment has an effect.

discussion of testing effect to come). Richard L. Solomon developed the **Solomon four-group design** to address the issue of pretest effects. It combines the classical experimental design with the two-group posttest-only design and randomly assigns participants to one of four groups. For example, a mental health worker wants to find out whether a new training method improves clients' coping skills. The worker measures coping skills with a 20-minute test of reactions to stressful events. Because the clients might learn coping skills from taking the test itself, a Solomon four-group design is used. The mental health worker randomly divides clients into four groups. Two groups receive the pretest; one of these groups gets the new training method and the other gets the old method. Another two groups receive no pretest; one of them gets the new method and the other the old method. All four groups are given the same posttest, and the posttest results are compared. If the two treatment (new method) groups have similar results, and the two control (old method) groups have similar results, then the mental health worker knows pretest learning is not a problem. If the two groups with a pretest (one treatment, one control) differ from the two groups without a pretest, then the worker concludes that the pretest itself may have had an effect on the dependent variable.

Factorial Designs. Sometimes we are curious about the simultaneous effects of two or more independent variables. A **factorial design** uses two or more independent variables in combination.

Solomon four-group design An experimental plan in which participants are randomly assigned to two control groups and two experimental groups; only one experimental group and one control group receive a pretest; all four groups receive a posttest.

Factorial design An experimental plan that considers the impact of several independent variables simultaneously.

Interaction effect A result of two independent variables operating simultaneously and in combination on a dependent variable; is larger than a result that occurs from the sum of each independent variable working separately.

We look at each combination of the categories in variables (sometimes called *factors*). When each variable contains several categories, the number of combinations grows quickly. In this type of design, the treatment is not each independent variable; rather, it is each combination of the variable categories. Researchers discuss factorial design in a shorthand way. A "two by three factorial design" is written 2×3. It means that there are two treatments with two categories in one and three categories in the other. A $2 \times 3 \times 3$ design means that there are three independent variables, one with two categories and two with three categories each.

For example, Krysan and associates (2009) wanted to study neighborhood preferences, but it was difficult to examine both racial and social class features of a neighborhood at the same time, so they used a factorial design (see Example Box 9.4, Factorial Experiment on Neighborhood Preference). The three independent variables of their study were participant race (two categories, Black or White), neighborhood composition (three types, all White, all Black, racially mixed), and social class (5 levels). The dependent variable was the desirability of a neighborhood based on a rating of 1 to 7. They had a $2 \times 3 \times 5$ factorial design. (The authors also asked participants about the strength of their identity with their own racial group.)

In a factorial design, treatments can have two types of effects on the dependent variable: main effects and interaction effects. Only *main effects* are present in one-factor or single-treatment designs. In other words, we simply examine the impact of the treatment on the dependent variable. In a factorial design, specific combinations of independent variable categories can have an effect beyond a single factor effect. We call them **interaction effects** because the categories in a combination interact to produce an effect beyond that of each variable alone. Interaction effects are of special interest because they suggest that not only an independent variable has an impact but also specific combinations have unique effects, or variables only have an impact under certain conditions.

Mueller-Johnson and Dhami (2010) (see Example Box 9.5, Mock Jury and Interaction Effects by Age and Crime on page 292) created a mock jury

EXAMPLE BOX **9.4**

Factorial Experiment on Neighborhood Preference

Krysan and associates (2009) created an experiment to study neighborhood preferences among Blacks and White adults in the United States. Past studies had looked at this issue; however, examining both racial and social class factors at the same time was very difficult, and telling whether people preferred a neighborhood for its social class or its racial features was not possible. The authors said, "At the core of our analysis are two research questions: (1) Are neighborhood preferences color blind or race conscious? (2) If preferences are race conscious, do they reflect a desire to be in a neighborhood with one's 'own kind' or to avoid being in a neighborhood with another racial group?" (p. 529). In 2004–2005, the authors selected more than 700 participants in the Detroit region and nearly 800 in the Chicago metropolitan area. To disentangle the class and race effects in neighborhoods, the authors showed participants videotaped neighborhoods that varied by social class and racial mix. They created thirteen videos in total. The neighborhoods varied by five social class levels and three racial mix levels.

We selected different neighborhoods to convey the different social class levels, relying on this assumption that respondents infer social class based on features such as home and property size, upkeep of the houses, and other cues gleaned from observation. Each of the different neighborhoods had, in turn, three variants in terms of the race of the individuals shown: (1) all residents are white; (2) all residents are black; (3) three residents are white and two residents are black. (p. 537)

One video was a control without people. In each other video, five people (actors) appeared as residents engaged in ordinary activities. They noted (p. 537),

In each neighborhood, there was one scene in which three individuals were shown together talking in the driveway, in the front yard, at the mailbox, or surrounding a car that was being repaired. Residents wore short-sleeved shirts and no hats to increase the likelihood that the respondents could detect their racial/ethnic identity. Residents within each neighborhood social class level were matched on approximate age, gender, and style of dress.

As a manipulation check, the authors showed videos to a small group of other participants prior to the actual study to verify that people saw the class and race composition of neighborhoods as intended. After viewing videos, the authors asked participants to rate each neighborhood on a seven-point Likert scale from very desirable to very undesirable. They said (p. 539), "Our dependent variables are the desirability ratings of the four neighborhoods, and thus our unit of analysis is the video. Given that each respondent saw and rated the same baseline video— an upper-working-class neighborhood with no residents—we include the ratings of this neighborhood as a respondent-level control." The authors used a factorial design with three independent variables: research participant race, neighborhood social class, and neighborhood racial mix. The authors randomly assigned participants to view different racial compositions in the same neighborhoods. Among their many findings, the authors note (p. 538), "Our fundamental conclusion is that race, per se, shapes how whites and, to a lesser extent, blacks view residential space. Residential preferences are not simply a reaction to class-based features of a neighborhood; they are shaped by the race of the people who live there."

---

with a trial-like situation and participants as a jury. The researchers presented various combinations of characteristics of offenders to see their impact on sentencing decisions (see Figure 9.3). The authors varied the age, health, offense severity, and prior convictions of an offender to create a $2 \times 2 \times 2 \times 2$ factorial design. They found main effects for severity of

crime, age, and prior conviction. People committing more severe crimes, younger offenders, and those with prior convictions received longer sentences than people committing less serious crime, older offenders, and those with no prior convictions. They also found a few interaction effects; one was age and severity of crime for those with a past conviction.

Mock Jury and Interaction Effects by Age and Crime

Mueller-Johnson and Dhami (2010) created a mock jury. They formed a trial-like situation and had participants form a jury. The authors presented various combinations of characteristics of offenders to see how they impacted jury sentencing decisions. Sentencing was length of prison term. Their jurors were forty-seven students (thirty-six women and eleven men) from an English university. The authors varied the age, health, offense severity, and prior convictions of an offender to create a $2 \times 2 \times 2 \times 2$ factorial design. In past experiments, they had found main effects for health, prior convictions, and severity of offense. People in poor health received shorter sentences, and older (66- to 72-year-old) received shorter sentences than younger (21- to 26-year-old) offenders regardless of the number of prior convictions. Younger offenders with prior convictions and more severe offences received longer sentences. In the current study, they investigated child sex offenders. Prior offense was either no prior conviction or one for sexual contact with a child 4 years earlier, and offense severity was either once touching a 7-year-old girl's genitals over her clothing or touching naked genitalia ten times over the course of a year. The participants usually decided on a sentence in 15 minutes. The authors found interesting interaction effects among age, offense severity, and previous convictions. For those with a prior conviction, older offenders received a longer sentence than younger offenders with less serious offenses, but shorter sentences if the offense was more serious. In other words, the combination of a prior conviction and less serious offense for older offenders resulted in a longer sentence. This is consistent with the "dirty-old-man" stereotype.

Design notation   A symbol system used to show parts of an experiment and to make diagrams of them.

Internal validity   The ability of experimenters to strengthen the logical rigor of a causal explanation by eliminating potential alternative explanations for an association between the treatment and dependent variable through an experimental design.

FIGURE 9.3   Sentence in Mock Jury Trial for Sex Offenders with One Prior Conviction

Design Notation

We can design experiments in many ways. **Design notation** is a shorthand system for symbolizing the parts of experimental design.[7] It expresses a complex, paragraph-long description of the parts of an experiment in five or six symbols arranged in two lines. Once you learn design notation, you will find it easier to think about and compare designs. Design notation uses the following symbols: O = observation of dependent variable; X = treatment, independent variable; R = random assignment. The Os are numbered with subscripts from left to right based on time order. Pretests are O_1, posttests O_2. When the independent variable has more than two levels, the Xs are numbered with subscripts to distinguish among them. Symbols are in time order from left to right. The R is first, followed by the pretest, the treatment, and then the posttest. We arrange symbols in rows with each row representing a group of participants. For example, an experiment with three groups has an R (if random assignment is used) followed by three rows of Os and Xs. The rows are on top of each other because the pretests, treatment, and posttest occur in each group at about the same time. Table 9.2 gives the notation for many standard experimental designs.

INTERNAL AND EXTERNAL VALIDITY

The Logic of Internal Validity

Internal validity occurs when the independent variable, and nothing else, influences the dependent

TABLE 9.2   Summary of Experiment Designs with Notation

NAME OF DESIGN	DESIGN NOTATION
Classical experimental design	R → O X O → O O
Preexperimental designs	
One-shot case study	X O
One-group pretest/posttest	O X O
Static group comparison	X O O
Quasi-experimental designs	
Two-group posttest only	R ⟶ X O O
Interrupted time series	O O O O X O O O
Equivalent time series	O X O X O X O X O

Latin square designs	R → O X_a O X_b O X_c O
	   → O X_b O X_a O X_c O
	   → O X_c O X_b O X_a O
	   → O X_a O X_c O X_b O
	   → O X_b O X_c O X_a O
	     O X_c O X_a O X_b O

Solomon four-group design	R → O X O
	   → O O
	   → X O
	   → O

Factorial designs	R → X_1 Z_1 O
	   → X_1 Z_2 O
	   → X_2 Z_1 O
	   → X_2 Z_2 O

Note: Subscripts with letters indicate different treatment variables. Subscripts with numbers indicate different categories of the same treatment variable, such as male or female for gender.

variable. Anything other than the independent variable influencing the dependent variable threatens internal validity. These are confounding variables; they confound the logic of an experiment to exclude everything except the relationship between the variables in your hypothesis. They threaten your ability to say that the treatment was the true causal factor that produced a change in the dependent variable. You may also hear them called **artifacts**. This is

Artifact   An object in experimental research studies; refers to the type of confounding variable that is not part of the hypothesis but affects the experiment's operation or outcome. In field research studies, it refers to physical objects that humans created that have cultural significance; specifically, objects that members use or to which they attach meaning that we study to learn more about a cultural setting or its members.

because the unwanted or confounding variables do not come from the natural relationship you are examining but are due to the particular experimental arrangement. An artifact appears by accident because during preparation of the study, you unintentionally introduce something that alters things. For example, you clean a room before participants arrive for an experiment on the emotional effects of going without sleep, but the cleaning solution you used to wipe down tables and chairs causes irritability in many people. Your results show increased irritability among people who had little sleep. However, it is not because of sleep loss but an unintended side effect of your cleaning solution. You want to rule out artifacts and confounding variables—everything that could possibly affect the dependent variable other than the treatment. You rule out artifacts and confounding variables by controlling experimental conditions and by using experimental designs. Next we examine major threats to internal validity.

Threats to Internal Validity

The following are 12 threats to internal validity.[8]

1. *Selection bias.* **Selection bias** can arise when an experiment has more than one group of participants. You want to compare the groups, but they differ or do not form equivalent groups. This is a problem in designs without random assignment. For example, you design a two-group experiment on aggressiveness. If you do not use randomization

or randomization is not effective, the treatment group could by chance differ. You may have sixty research participants who are active in various campus activities. By chance, many of your volunteers for the experimental group have participated in football, rugby, hockey, and wrestling whereas volunteers in your control group are musicians, chess club members, ballet dancers, and painters. Another example of selection bias is an experiment on the ability of people to dodge heavy traffic. Selection bias would occur if participants assigned to one group are from rural areas with little traffic experience and those in the other grew up in large cities and have traffic experience. You can often detect selection bias by comparing pretest scores. If you see no group differences in the pretest scores, selection bias is probably not a problem.

2. *History.* **History effect** is the result of an event unrelated to the treatment will occur during the experiment and influence the dependent variable. History effects are more likely in experiments that continue over a long time. For example, halfway through a two-week experiment to evaluate feelings about pet dogs, a fire at a nearby dog kennel kills and injures many puppies with news reports showing injured animals and many local people crying over the incident.

3. *Maturation.* A **maturation effect** is a result of a threat that a biological, psychological, or emotional process within participants other than the treatment occurs during the experiment and influences the dependent variable. The time period for maturation effects to occur can be hours, months, or years depending on the dependent variable and study design. For example, during a daylong eight-hour experiment on reasoning ability, participants become bored and sleepy and, as a result, their scores are lower. Another example is an experiment on the styles of children's play between grades 1 and 6. Play styles are affected by physical, emotional, and maturational changes that occur as the children grow older instead of or in addition to the effects of a treatment. Designs with a pretest and control group help to determine whether maturation or history effects are present because both experimental and control groups will show similar changes over time.

Selection bias A preconception that threatens internal validity when groups in an experiment are not equivalent at the beginning of the experiment with regard to the dependent variable.

History effect Result that presents a threat to internal validity because of something that occurs and affects the dependent variable during an experiment; is unplanned and outside the control of the experimenter.

Maturation effect A result that is a threat to internal validity in experiments because of natural processes of growth, boredom, and so on that occur during the experiment and affect the dependent variable.

4. *Testing.* Sometimes the pretest measure itself affects an experiment. This **testing effect** threatens internal validity because more than the treatment alone affects the dependent variable. The Solomon four-group design helps to detect testing effects. For example, you pretest to determine how much participants know about geology and geography. Your treatment is a series of videos about geology and geography viewed over 2 days. If participants remember the pretest questions and this affects what they learned (i.e., paid attention to) or how they answered questions on the posttest, a testing effect is present. If testing effects occur, you cannot say that the treatment alone has affected the dependent variable. The dependent variable was influenced by both memory of the pretest and the treatment.

5. *Instrumentation.* This threat is related to stability reliability. It occurs when the *instrument* or dependent variable measure changes during the experiment. For example, in a weight-loss experiment, the springs on the scale weaken during the experiment, giving lower readings in the posttest. Another example is a treatment to show a video, but the video equipment failed to work for some participants.

6. *Experimental mortality.* When some research participants do not continue throughout the entire experiment, **experimental mortality**, or attrition, arises. Although the word *mortality* means death, it does not necessarily mean that they have died. If many participants leave partway through an experiment, we cannot know whether the results would have been different had they stayed. For example, you begin a weight-loss experiment with sixty people. At the end of the program, forty remain, each of whom lost 5 pounds with no side effects. The twenty who left could have differed from the thirty who stayed, changing the results. Perhaps the program was effective for those who left, and they withdrew after losing 25 pounds. Or perhaps the program made them sick and forced them to quit, or they saw no improvement and dropped out. We need to notice and report the number of participants at all stages of an experiment to detect this threat to internal validity.

7. *Statistical regression effect.* This is not easy to grasp intuitively. It is a problem of extreme values or a tendency for random errors to move group results toward the average. It can occur in two ways.

One situation in which **statistical regression effect** occurs is when participants are unusual with regard to the dependent variable. Because they are unusual, they do not respond further in one direction. For example, you want to see whether playing violent video games makes people more aggressive. Your participants are a group of convicts from a high-security prison. You give them a pretest, have them play 60 hours of extremely violent video games, and then administer a posttest. To your surprise, there is no change. It could be that the convicts started as extremely aggressive so your treatment could not make them any more aggressive. By random chance alone, some may even appear to be less aggressive when measured in the posttest.[9]

A second statistical regression effect situation involves a problem with the measurement instrument. If your measure is such that most people score very high (at the ceiling) or very low (at the floor) on a variable, random chance alone will produce a change between the pretest and the posttest. For example, you give eighty participants a simple math test, and seventy-seven get perfect scores. You give a treatment to improve math scores. Because so many already had perfect scores, random errors could reduce the group average because the seventy-seven who got perfect scores can move in only one direction—to get an answer wrong, and only three could improve. As a result, the group average may appear lower in the posttest due to chance alone. You need to monitor the range of scores to detect statistical regression.

Testing effect   A result that threatens internal validity because the very process of measuring in the pretest can have an impact on the dependent variable.

Experimental mortality   Threat to internal validity because participants fail to participate through the entire experiment.

Statistical regression effect   A threat to internal validity from measurement instruments providing extreme values and a tendency for random errors to move extreme results toward the average.

8. *Diffusion of treatment or contamination.* **Diffusion of treatment** is the threat that research participants in different groups will communicate with each other and learn about the other's treatment. You can avoid this by isolating groups or having them promise not to reveal anything to other participants. For example, you have eighty participants in a daylong experiment on ways to memorize words. The treatment group is taught a simple method, but the control group is told to use any technique the members want to use. During a break, participants in the treatment group tell those in the control group about the new method. After the break, control group particpants start using it too. You might ask about possible diffusion in a post-experiment interview with participants to reduce this threat.

9. *Compensatory behavior.* In experiments that provide something of value to one group of participants but not to another and the difference becomes known, **compensatory behavior** is said to occur. The inequality between groups may create a desire to reduce differences, competitive rivalry between groups, or resentful demoralization. Such behavior can affect the dependent variable in addition to the treatment. For example, students in one school receive a treatment of longer lunch breaks to produce gains in learning, but students in another school have a regular lunchtime. Once the inequality is known, stundents in the control group (school without long lunch breaks) work extra hard to learn and to overcome the inequality. Alternatively, the control group students could become demoralized by the unequal treatment and put less effort into learning. It is difficult to detect this threat unless you obtain outside information (see the discussion of diffusion of treatment).

10. *Experimenter expectancy.* An experimenter's behavior might threaten internal validity if the experimentor indirectly communicates a desired outcome.[10] This is called **experimenter expectancy**. Because of a strong belief in the hypothesis, even the honest experimenter might unintentionally communicate desired findings. For example, you study participants' reactions to people with disabilities. You deeply believe that females are more sensitive to those with disabilities than males are. Through eye contact, tone of voice, pauses, and other nonverbal communication, you might unconsciously encourage female research participants to report positive feelings toward those with disabilities; your nonverbal behavior is the opposite for male participants.

The **double-blind experiment** is a design intended to control experimenter expectancy. In this experiment, the only people who have direct contact with participants do not know the details of the hypothesis or the treatment. It is *double* blind because both the participants and those in contact with them are blind to details of the experiment (see Figure 9.4). For example, you want to see whether a new drug is effective. Using pills of three colors—green, yellow, and pink—you put the new drug in the yellow pill, an old drug in the pink one, and make the green pill a *placebo* (i.e., an empty or nonactive treatment). Assistants who give the pills and record the effects do not know which color pill contains the new drug. They just administer the pills and record results by color of pill. Only you know which color pill contains the drug and examine the results, but you have no contact with the research participants. The double-blind design is nearly mandatory in medical research because experimenter expectancy effects are well recognized.

11. *Demand characteristics.* A threat to internal validity related to reactivity (discussed in next

---

Diffusion of treatment   The spread of a threat to internal validity that occurs when the treatment "spills over" from the experimental group and control group participants modify their behavior because they learn of the treatment.

Compensatory behavior   Conduct that is a threat to internal validity when participants in the control group modify their behavior to make up for not getting the treatment.

Experimenter expectancy   A type of reactivity that occurs because the experimenter indirectly makes participants aware of the hypothesis or desired results.

Double-blind experiment   A type of experimental research in which neither the participants nor the person who directly deals with them for the experimenter knows the specifics of the experiment.

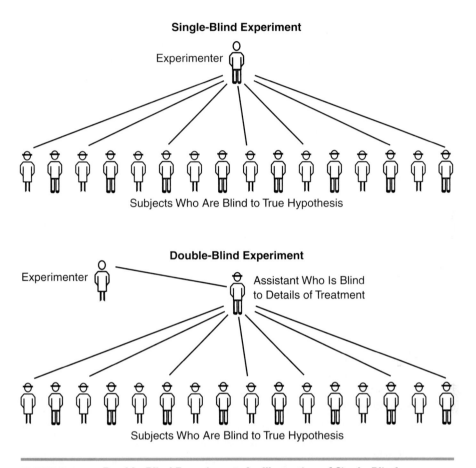

FIGURE 9.4   Double-Blind Experiment: An Illustration of Single-Blind, or Ordinary, and Double-Blind Experiments

section of this chapter) is called a **demand characteristic**. It occurs when research participants pick up clues about the hypothesis or an experiment's purpose and then modify their behavior to what they think the research demands of them (i.e., support the hypothesis). Participants often do this to please the researcher, which is why we often use mild deception in the form of cover stories.

12. *Placebo effect.* The last type of threat to internal validity is the **placebo effect**. A *placebo* is an empty or nonactive treatment, such as a sugar pill in medical research. It occurs when you give some participants a placebo but they respond as if they have received the real treatment. For example, you create an experiment on stopping smoking for heavy smokers. You give some participants a pill with an antini-

cotine drug to reduce their nicotine dependence and others a placebo (empty pill). If participants who received the placebo also stop smoking, then merely participating in the experiment and taking something that they believed would help them quit smoking had an effect. The belief in the placebo alone may have affected the dependent variable (see Table 9.3 on page 298 for a summary of internal validity threats).

Demand characteristic   A type of reactivity in which participants in experimental research pick up clues about the hypothesis and alter their behavior accordingly.

Placebo effect   A result that occurs when participants do not receive the real treatment but receive a nonactive or imitation treatment but respond as though they have received the real treatment.

TABLE 9.3   Internal Validity and External Validity Issues

INTERNAL VALIDITY	EXTERNAL VALIDITY
Selection bias	Population generalization
History effect	Naturalistic generalization
Testing effect	Theoretical generalization
Maturation effect	Mundane realism
Instrumentation	Experimental realism
Experimental mortality	Hawthorne effect
Statistical regression effect	
Diffusion of treatment	
Compensatory behavior	
Experimenter expectancy	
Demand characteristics	
Placebo effect	

Experimenters often undertake manipulation checks to increase internal validity. A **manipulation check** is a process to verify theoretically salient variables (e.g., independent, dependent, and intervening variables in hypotheses). Its purpose is to verify measurement validity (e.g., variables truly measure the theoretical concepts) of whether the conditions of the experiment had the intended effects, or the degree of its experimental realism (experimental realism is discussed later in this chapter). We have manipulation checks to make certain that the variables and conditions in our experiment operate as we intended and help us rule out possible threats to internal validity.

We check "manipulations" (our measures and interventions in an experimental situation) with pretests, pilot tests, and experimental debriefing. We might create a pretest of certain experimental conditions. For example, you have a confederate act as if he or she is disabled and have preliminary research participants observe the confederate. As a

Manipulation check A separate measure of independent or dependent variables to verify their measurement validity and/or experimental realism.

check, you ask whether the participants believed the confederate was truly disabled or just acting. In the study on neighborhood preference (see Example Box 9.3), the researchers showed videos of neighborhoods to a small number of people before using the videos in the study. This was done to verify that people recognized the racial mix and neighborhood's social class as the researchers intended. If you plan to provide participants with written or oral instructions in an experiment, you might pretest them with a few preliminary participants. You can inquire about the clarity of the instructions and whether the participants understood them as you intended.

A "dry-run" or pilot test of the entire experimental procedure can be a manipulation check. During and after the pilot test, you look for potential flaws, mishaps, or misunderstandings. You ask whether all parts of the experimental situation went smoothly and had their intended effects on participants. You may check to see whether participants paid attention and accepted the "cover story" if you used deception.

Experimental debriefing after a pilot test or the actual experiment can be a manipulation check. To conduct an experimental debriefing (unlike ethical debriefing that emphasizes removing a lie or deception), you interview participants about details of the experiment. You want to learn what they thought was happening, whether they felt fully engaged and took the situation seriously, and whether they felt any confusion, anxiety, or discomfort. You may discuss compensatory behavior and demand characteristics or diffusion of treatment in such interviews. At times, experimenters drop a participant from study data if they learn that the participant misunderstood a critical aspect of the experiment, saw through the cover story of deception, or modified responses because of demand characteristics (also see discussions on reactivity later in this chapter). For example, an experimenter may drop data of a participant who revealed that she or he did not accept the deception cover study but believed the study was about reactions toward disabled people (which it was) and responded based on that belief (i.e., showed demand characteristics) (see Example Box 9.6, Who Helps a Co-Worker Who Is Disabled?).

EXAMPLE BOX 9.6
Who Helps a Co-Worker Who Is Disabled?

Miller and Werner (2007) conducted a laboratory experiment on helping behavior with two treatment conditions and a control group. The authors wanted to learn what types of people would be likely to assist a co-worker who is disabled. Past studies have found a positive relationship between personality traits and attitudes toward persons with disabilities. The researchers measured three personality traits: equity preference, feminine traits, and impression management. *Equity preference* comes from the idea that each person must do an amount of work for a reward. Some people are more benevolent (i.e., people who try harder should get equal rewards even if they produce less) and some feel more entitled (i.e., no one should receive a bigger reward if they do less). Traditional *feminine traits* are to be kind, helpful, and understanding. *Impression management* is a conscious representation of oneself to others. Those who score high on impression management act consciously to display an intended image in a public setting. The authors had more than 500 students in three sections of an undergraduate business management course complete a survey that measured personality traits. From these, the authors selected 133 volunteers for the experiment. They manipulated three levels of disability, their key independent variable: no disability, a mental disability, and a physical disability. They also did a *manipulation check* by asking a separate group of eighty-four participants to read descriptions of various people and rate the descriptions of the persons as being physically disabled, mentally disabled, or not disabled. The authors reported (p. 2668) that

> to reduce the confounding of variables, the same confederate was used in each session of the experiment. This confederate was a male graduate student in a nonbusiness doctoral program at the university. The same confederate was used so that there was no variability on race, physical attractiveness, personality, and other characteristics that might have elicited differences in responses from participants. The confederate was a White student with a slight build who was 25 years old.

At the beginning, each participant and the confederate prepared and read an autobiography. In the physical disability condition, the confederate was in a wheelchair and had an autobiography that included a past automobile accident that had left him wheelchair bound. In the mental disability condition, the confederate displayed difficulty with the autobiography and reported that he was in an automobile accident that had left him with a brain injury and short-term memory difficulties. Next, the participants and the confederate were to complete a complex paper-folding and envelope-stuffing task that required some physical movement and mental counting. Each person was told she or he would be paid for completing the task and had to finish it in exactly 5 minutes. The task required rapid work but was fairly easy to complete in the allotted time. In the physical disability condition, the wheelchair-bound confederate had difficulty moving to complete the task. In the mental disability condition, the confederate showed great difficulty in performing the mental calculations needed to complete the task in time. In the no-disability condition, the confederate just moved slowly. For all three conditions, it was clear to participants that the confederate could not complete the task on time. The dependent variable was whether any participants assisted the confederate. The researchers videotaped sessions and a trained, independent observer scored the amount of assistance participants gave to the confederate. Results showed that equity preference and impression management but not feminine traits had an effect. People high on benevolent equity preference and impression management helped more. The physically disabled condition received more help than the mentally disabled condition, and both disabled conditions received more than the nondisabled condition. In a debriefing interview after the experiment, researchers told participants the study's true purpose and asked what they thought the study was about. Researchers discarded data for five participants, "because they offered a comment that revealed that their ratings might have been biased. Examples of such comments include 'I thought that the disabled student was a decoy,' 'I think you wanted to see how we react to working with a disabled person. . . .'" (p. 2671).

External Validity and Field Experiments

Even if we eliminated all internal validity concerns, external validity would remain an issue. **External validity** is the effectiveness of generalizing experimental findings. If a study lacks external validity, the findings may hold true for only a specific experiment. Because we seek general theoretical knowledge in basic research and findings that relate to real-life problems in applied research, findings lacking external validity are nearly useless. However, in the widely cited article "In Defense of External Invalidity," Mook (1983) argued that generalizing from an experiment to natural, real-life settings is not a goal for many experiments. Instead, we may have other theoretical purposes (see later section on theoretical generalization).

The issue of external validity can be complex. Indeed, Thye (2007:81) says, "Perhaps the most misunderstood issue surrounding experiments is that of external validity." The reason is that external validity can involve several forms of generalization.[11] External validity addresses three questions about generalizing: Can we generalize from the specific collection of participants in an experiment to an entire population? Can we generalize from what occurs in a highly controlled and artificial experimental setting to most natural, "real-world" situations? Can we generalize from the empirical evidence of a specific experiment to an abstract theoretical model about relationships among variables? To address these questions, we can think of external validity as involving three forms of generalization that do not always overlap: populational, naturalistic, and theoretical (see Figure 9.5).

Populational Generalization. The key question for this form of external validity is whether we can accurately generalize from what we learn with a specific collection of people in one study to a universe or population of people/cases. To generalize the findings, we should specify the universe to which we wish to generalize and consider providing evidence to support such a generalization. For example, we conduct an experiment with one hundred undergraduate volunteers from one course in one university. To whom can we generalize these findings? To all undergraduate students in all courses at the same university during the same year, to all college students in the same country in the same decade, or to all humanity for all time? To improve the populational generalization form of external validity in an experiment, we would draw a random sample from a population and conduct the experiment on sampled participants.

Naturalistic generalization is what most people first think of when hearing the term *external validity*. The key question of naturalistic generalization is whether we can generalize accurately from what we learn in an artificially created, controlled laboratory-like setting to "real-life" natural settings. For naturalistic generalization, we need to consider two issues: mundane realism and reactivity.

Mundane realism asks whether an experiment or a situation is like the real world. For example, your study of learning has participants memorize four-letter nonsense syllables. Mundane realism would be stronger if you had them learn real-life factual information rather than nonsense syllables invented for an experiment alone.[12]

Reactivity is the effect of people responding because they are aware that they are in a study. Research participants might react differently in an experiment than in real life because they know someone is studying them. The **Hawthorne effect** is a specific kind of reactivity.[13] The name comes from a series of experiments by Elton Mayo at the Hawthorne, Illinois,

---

External validity   The ability to generalize findings beyond a specific study.

Naturalistic generalization   The ability to generalize accurately from what was learned in an artificially created controlled laboratory-like experimental settings to "real life" natural settings.

Mundane realism   A type of external validity in which the experimental conditions appear to be real and very similar to settings or situations outside a lab setting.

Reactivity   A result that occurs because of a general threat to external validity that arises because participants are aware that they are in an experiment and being studied.

Hawthorne effect   A reactivity result named after a famous case in which participants responded to the fact that they were in an experiment more than to the treatment.

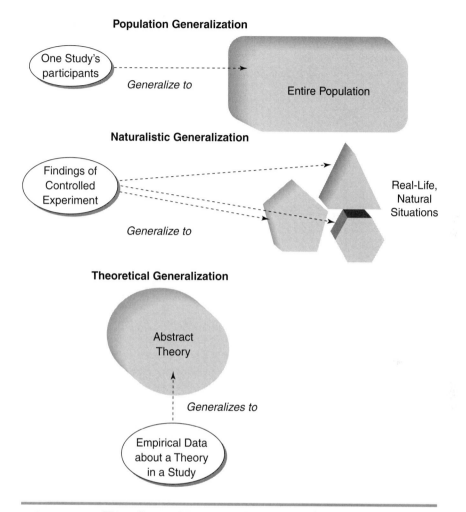

FIGURE 9.5   Three Types of External Validity Generalization

plant of Westinghouse Electric during the 1920s and 1930s. Researchers modified many aspects of working conditions (e.g., lighting, time for breaks) and measured productivity. They discovered that productivity rose after each modification, no matter what it was. This curious result occurred because the workers did not respond to the treatment but to the additional attention they received from being part of the experiment and knowing that they were being watched. Later research questioned whether the reported worker response had in fact occurred, but the name is still used for an effect that results from the attention of researchers.

For external validity concerns, the issue of reactivity is whether we can accurately generalize from activities that occur in a setting in which people are aware they are being studied to natural settings. Reactivity is most likely to occur in a highly controlled experiment in which the research participants know that an experimenter has created the conditions and is observing their behaviors or responses.

Let us say that you conduct an experiment in a college classroom or laboratory in which the participants know they are participating in a study. You ask the participants to engage in some artificially created tasks (e.g., assemble a puzzle) or create artificial status using deception (e.g., tell participants that a confederate working for you has a genius IQ score). After working on the task, you ask participants to complete a questionnaire in which you have questions about their feelings regarding people with high IQ scores. To what settings in daily life might you generalize your study's findings? To all real-life workplace settings with people of varying intelligence levels, to all types of work tasks and all social statuses, or to all attitudes about other people naturally formed in daily life and retained in everyday thoughts, behavior, or conversations? To improve the naturalistic generalization form of external validity in an experiment, you would need to conduct a field experiment.

Theoretical generalization asks whether we can accurately generalize from the concepts and relations in an abstract theory that we wish to test to a set of measures and arrangement of activities in a specific experiment. This is probably the most difficult type of generalization because it includes several other ideas: experimental realism, measurement validity, and control-confounding variables (high internal validity). **Experimental realism** is the impact of an experimental treatment or setting on people; it occurs when participants are caught up in the experiment and are truly influenced by it. It is weak if they remain unaffected and the experiment has little impact on them.

Field Experiments. We conduct experiments under the controlled conditions of a laboratory and in real-life or field settings in which we have less control over the experimental conditions. The amount of control varies on a continuum. At one end is the highly controlled **laboratory experiment**, which takes place in a specialized setting or laboratory; at the opposite end is the **field experiment**, which takes place in the "field"—natural settings such as a subway car, a liquor store, or a public sidewalk. Participants in field experiments are usually unaware that they are involved in an experiment and react in a natural way. For example, researchers have had a confederate fake a heart attack on a subway car to see how the bystanders react.[14]

Some field experiments, such as those by Transue on racial identity and school taxes or Krysan and colleagues on neighborhood preference (see Example Boxes 9.2 and 9.3), involved gathering participants and presenting them with realistic choices. Others are "natural experiments" in which experimental-like situations arise without total researcher control as with the Alberta privitization of alcohol sales (see Example Box 9.4). A related type of natural experiment in the field occurs when a researcher can take advantage of random assignment conditions of a key variable, as in the case of racial mixing of college roomates (see Example Box 9.7, A Field Experiment on College Roommates)

The amount of experimenter control is related to internal and external validity. Laboratory experiments tend to have higher internal validity but lower external validity. They are logically tighter and better controlled but less generalizable. Field experiments tend to have high external validity but low internal validity. They are more generalizable but less controlled. Quasi-experimental designs are more common. For example, in the experiment involving college roommates, the roommate situation was very real and lasted several months. The experiment had more external validity than putting people in a laboratory setting and asking them what they would do hypothetically.

PRACTICAL CONSIDERATIONS

Every research technique has "tricks of the trade" that are pragmatic strategies learned from experience. They account for the difference between the successful studies of an experienced researcher and the difficulties a novice researcher faces. Three are discussed here.

Planning and Pilot Tests

All social research requires planning. During the planning phase, we anticipate alternative explanations or threats to internal validity, develop a

---

Experimental realism   External validity in which the experiment is made to feel realistic so that experimental events have a real impact on participants.

Laboratory experiment   An experimental study in an artificial setting over which the experimenter has great control.

Field experiment   A study that takes place in a natural setting.

EXAMPLE BOX **9.7**

A Field Experiment on College Roommates

Contact hypothesis states that intimate, long-term contact with an out-group reduces prejudice. Shook and Fazio (2008) wanted "to assess the nature of interracial relationship and test the effect of intergroup contact" (p. 719). However, when we measure prejudice with self-report attitude measures, people often control prejudice reactions so they do not appear prejudicial even though they may harbor prejudicial attitudes. An indirect technique for measuring hidden or "automatic" racial prejudice measures the response time in seconds as a person sees visual images of people of different races matched with various adjectives (see Fazio et al., 1995). Speed of response indirectly measures racial prejudice because we respond more slowly as we try to hide true attitudes. To create a long-term field experiment, the authors took advantage of random assignment to college dormitory rooms and room shortage that prevented roommates from switching. The study had 136 White and 126 African American college freshmen. By random assignment, some had a same-race roommate, and others had a different race roommate. Roommate race was the independent variable. The authors had the students attend one session during the first two weeks and another during the last two weeks of the academic term. They asked students about several issues, including roommate

satisfaction, activities with roommates, and social networks. The students also completed a questionnaire on racial attitudes and intergroup anxiety. In addition, the authors created a series of tasks asking students to respond to various images on a computer screen. After several such computer tasks to create a "cover story," a final task was to respond to images of faces matched with adjectives; one-half of the faces were African American and one-half White. This was the indirect measure of racial prejudice. Thus, the authors had multiple pretest and posttest measures of racial attitudes and interracial social interactions. As in past roommate studies, their results showed less social interaction and lower roommate satisfaction among the different race roommate pairs than same-race pairs. Over the academic term, satisfaction with same-race roommates declined slightly but for the different race roommates increased slightly. For roommates of a different race, intergroup anxiety declined and roommate social interactions increased over the three-month term. Both the direct and indirect measures of racial prejudice remained unchanged for same-race roommates. However, levels of prejudice declined significantly between the pretest and posttest for the students who had different race roommates, just as predicted by the contact hypothesis.

---

well-organized system for recording data, and pilot test any apparatus (e.g., computers, video cameras, tape recorders) that we will use. After the pilot test, we interview participants to uncover aspects of the experiment that need refinement.

Instructions to Participants

Most experiments involve giving instructions to participants to "set the stage." We must word instructions carefully and follow a prepared script so that all participants hear the exact same thing. This ensures reliability. The instructions are also important in creating a realistic cover story when deception is used. Aronson and Carlsmith (1968:46) noted, "One of the most common mistakes the novice experimenter makes is to present his instructions too briefly."

Postexperiment Interview

At the end of an experiment, we should interview participants for three reasons. First, if we used deception, we must ethically **debrief** the research participants (i.e., explain the true purpose of the experiment and answer any participants' questions). Second, we can learn what participants thought and how their definitions of the situation affected their behavior. Finally, we can explain the importance of not revealing the true nature of the experiment to other potential participants.

> **Debrief** To gather information by talking with participants after an experiment to give a true explanation of the experiment if deception has been used or to learn their perceptions.

RESULTS OF EXPERIMENTAL RESEARCH: MAKING COMPARISONS

Comparison is critical to all research. By carefully examining the results of experimental research, we can learn about possible threats to internal validity and treatment effects on the dependent variable. In each study discussed in this chapter, the researchers carefully analyzed quantitative data to examine the effects of independent variables and considered potential internal validity concerns.

Here is an illustration of such comparisons (see Figure 9.6) based on the results of a series of five weight-loss experiments using the classical experimental design. In the example, the thirty research participants in the experimental group at Enrique's Slim Clinic lost an average of 50 pounds, whereas the thirty in the control group did not lose a single pound. Only one person dropped out during the experiment. Susan's Scientific Diet Plan had equally dramatic results, but eleven people in her experimental group dropped out. This suggests a problem with experimental mortality. People in the experimental group at Carl's Calorie Counters lost eleven pounds, compared to 2 pounds for the control group, but the control group and the experimental group began with an average of 31 pounds' difference in weight. This suggests a problem with selection bias. Natalie's Nutrition Center had no experimental mortality or selection bias problems, but those in the experimental group lost no more weight than those in the control group. It appears that the treatment was not effective. Pauline's Pounds' Off also avoided selection bias and experimental mortality problems. People in her experimental group lost 32 pounds but so did those in the control group. This suggests that the maturation, history, or diffusion of treatment effects may have occurred. Thus, the treatment at Enrique's Slim Clinic appears to be the most effective one.

A WORD ON ETHICS

Ethical consideration is a significant issue in most experiments because they are often intrusive (i.e., interfere with ordinary activity). Experimental treatments may involve putting people in contrived social settings, asking them to engage in specific activities, or manipulating their feelings or behaviors. While doing this, we listen to what they say, observe their actions, and record responses. Ethical requirements limit the amount and type of allowable intrusion. We must never place research participants in physical danger, and we must take precautions when we put them in embarrassing or anxiety-inducing situations. It is essential to continuously monitor and control experimental events to ensure safe and ethical study.[15]

Sometimes we might use deception in social experiments by temporarily misleading participants. Such dishonesty might be acceptable but only if there is no other way to achieve a specific research goal. Even for a highly worthy goal, we only use deception with restrictions. The amount and type of deception cannot exceed the minimum needed for the specific purpose. In addition, we must always debrief research participants as soon as possible, telling them that they had been temporarily deceived and explaining the real situation to them.

CONCLUSION

This chapter discussed experimental research. In most experimental designs, we use random assignment to create two (or more) groups that we can treat as equivalent and hence compare. Experimental research provides precise and relatively unambiguous evidence for a causal relationship. It closely follows principles of a positivist approach to social science and produces quantitative results that we can analyze with statistics.

This chapter also examined how the parts of an experiment can be combined to produce different experimental designs. In addition to the classical experimental design, preexperimental and quasi-experimental designs and design notation were discussed.

Various threats to internal validity that are possible alternative explanations to the treatment were identified as were external validity and the ways that field experiments maximize naturalistic generalization in external validity.

The real strength of experimental research is its control and logical rigor in establishing evidence

FIGURE 9.6   Comparisons of Results, Classical Experimental Design, Weight-Loss Experiments

	ENRIQUE'S SLIM CLINIC			NATALIE'S NUTRITION CENTER	
	Pretest	*Posttest*		*Pretest*	*Posttest*
Experimental	190 (30)	140 (29)	Experimental	190 (30)	188 (29)
Control group	189 (30)	189 (30)	Control group	192 (29)	189 (28)

	SUSAN'S SCIENTIFIC DIET PLAN			PAULINE'S POUNDS OFF	
	Pretest	*Posttest*		*Pretest*	*Posttest*
Experimental	190 (30)	141 (19)	Experimental	190 (30)	158 (30)
Control group	189 (30)	189 (28)	Control group	191 (29)	159 (28)

	CARL'S CALORIE COUNTERS			SYMBOLS FOR COMPARISON PURPOSES	
	Pretest	*Posttest*		*Pretest*	*Posttest*
Experimental	160 (30)	152 (29)	Experimental	A (A)	C (C)
Control group	191 (29)	189 (29)	Control group	B (B)	D (D)

COMPARISONS

	A–B	C–D	A–C	B–D	(A)–(C)	(B)–(D)
Enrique's	1	49	−50	0	−1	0
Susan's	1	48	−49	0	−11	0
Carl's	31	37	−8	−2	−1	0
Natalie's	2	1	−2	−3	−1	−1
Pauline's	1	1	−32	−32	0	−1

A–B   Do the two groups begin with the same weight? If not, selection bias may be possibly occurring.

C–D   Do the two groups end the same way? If not, the treatment may be ineffective, or there may be strong history, maturation, diffusion, or treatment effects.

A–C   Did the experimental group change? If not, treatment may be ineffective.

(A)–(C) and (B)–(D)   Did the number of participants in the experimental group or control group change? If a large drop occurs, experimental mortality may be a threat to internal validity.

INTERPRETATION

Enrique's: No internal validity threats evident, shows effects of treatment
Susan's: Experimental mortality threat likely problem
Carl's: Selection bias likely problem
Natalie's: No internal validity threat evident, shows no treatment effects
Pauline's: History, maturation, diffusion of treatment threats are a likely problem

Note: Numbers are average number of pounds. Numbers in parentheses ( ) are number of participants per group. Random assignment is made to the experimental or control group.

for causality. In general, experiments tend to be easier to replicate, less expensive, and less time consuming than other research techniques. Experimental research also has limitations. First, some questions cannot be addressed using experimental methods because control and experimental manipulation are impossible. Another limitation is that experiments usually test one or a few hypotheses at a time. This fragments knowledge and makes it necessary to synthesize results across many research reports. External validity is a potential problem because many experiments rely on small nonrandom samples of college students.[16]

The chapter explained that careful examination and comparison of results can alert us to potential problems in research design. Finally, the chapter presented some practical and ethical considerations in experiments.

In the next chapters, you will examine other research techniques. The logic of the nonexperimental methods differs from that of the experiment. Experimenters focus narrowly on a few hypotheses, target one or two independent variables operating on a single dependent variable, and usually examine small numbers of participants. In contrast, by using other techniques, we often test many hypotheses at once, measure many independent and dependent variables, and use a larger number of randomly sampled research participants.

KEY TERMS

artifacts
classical experimental design
compensatory behavior
confederate
confounding variables
control group
cover story
debrief
deception
demand characteristic
design notation
diffusion of treatment
double-blind experiment
equivalent time-series design
experimental design
experimental group

experimental mortality
experimental realism
experimenter expectancy
external validity
factorial design
field experiment
hawthorne effect
history effects
interaction effect
internal validity
interrupted time-series design
laboratory experiment
latin square design
manipulation check
maturation effect
mundane realism

naturalistic generalization
one-shot case-study design
placebo effect
posttest
preexperimental designs
pretest
quasi-experimental designs
random assignment
reactivity
selection bias
solomon four-group design
static group comparison design
statistical regression effect
subjects
testing effect
treatment

REVIEW QUESTIONS

1. What are the seven elements or parts of an experiment?
2. What distinguishes preexperimental designs from the classical design?
3. Which design permits the testing of different sequences for several treatments?
4. A researcher says, "It was a three by two design with the independent variables being the level of fear (low, medium, high) and ease of escape (easy/difficult) and the dependent variable being anxiety." What does this mean? What is the design notation, assuming that random assignment with a posttest only was used?

5. How do the interrupted and the equivalent time series designs differ?

6. What is the logic of internal validity, and how does the use of a control group fit into that logic?

7. How does the Solomon four-group design show the testing effect?

8. What is a double-blind experiment, and why is it used?

9. Do field or laboratory experiments have higher internal validity? External validity? Explain.

10. What is the difference between experimental and mundane realism?

NOTES

1. Cook and Campbell (1979:9–36, 91–94) argued for a modification of a more rigid positivist approach to causality for experimental research. They suggested a "critical-realist" approach, which shares some features of the critical approach outlined in Chapter 4.

2. For discussions of the history of the experiment, see Danziger (1988), Gillespie (1988), Hornstein (1988), O'Donnell (1985), Scheibe (1988), and Webster and Sell (2007:6–9).

3. See Hornstein (1988:11).

4. For events after World War II, see Harris (1988) and Suls and Rosnow (1988). For a discussion of the increased use of deception, see Reynolds (1979:60).

5. See Field and Hole (2003) for a review of different comparisons.

6. Cook and Campbell (1979:7–9) and Spector (1981:15–16) discuss control in experiments.

7. The notation for research design is discussed in Cook and Campbell (1979:95–96), Dooley (1984:132–137), and Spector (1981:27–28).

8. For additional discussions of threats to internal validity, see Cook and Campbell (1979:51–68), Kercher (1992), Spector (1981:24–27), Smith and Glass (1987), and Suls and Rosnow (1988).

9. This example is borrowed from Mitchell and Jolley (1988:97).

10. Experimenter expectancy is discussed in Aronson and Carlsmith (1968:66–70), Dooley (1984:151–153), and Mitchell and Jolley (1988:327–329).

11. For discussions of external validity, see Aronson and Carlsmith (1968:22–25), Cook and Campbell (1979:70–80), Lucas (2003), and Zelditch (2007).

12. For a discussion of external validity, see Lucas (2003), Mook (1983), Willer and Walker (2007b), and Vissersi et al. (2001).

13. The Hawthorne effect is described in Roethlisberger and Dickenson (1939), Franke and Kaul (1978), and Lang (1992). Also see the discussion in Cook and Campbell (1979:123–125) and Dooley (1984:155–156). Gillespie (1988, 1991) discussed the political context of the experiments and how it shaped them.

14. See Piliavin and associates (1969).

15. See Hegtvedt (2007) for a recent review of ethical issues in experiments.

16. See Graham (1992).

Survey Research

> *Every method of data collection, including the survey, is only an approximation to knowledge. Each provides a different glimpse of reality, and all have limitations when used alone. Before undertaking a survey the researcher would do well to ask if this is the most appropriate and fruitful method for the problem at hand. The survey is highly valuable for studying some problems, such as public opinion, and worthless for others.*
>
> —Donald P. Warwick and Charles A. Lininger, *The Sample Survey,* pp. 5–6

In public opinion polls, most Americans say they would vote for a qualified female presidential candidate. Support for a qualified female candidate has steadily risen from 33 percent in 1937 to more than 92 percent in 2005. However, when survey researchers ask about controversial issues, they know that social desirability effects are a possibility (i.e., people give a false opinion so they will conform to general social norms). Streb et al. (2008) hypothesized that many Americans were being untruthful about this issue on surveys. Testing such a hypothesis required creativity. They created a list of four issues (e.g., gasoline prices rising, being required to wear seat belts) and asked how many "make you angry or upset." They created a second identical list with the same questions, but including a fifth issue, "A woman serving as president." They randomly selected more than 1,000 people for each list and conducted telephone interviews. The authors learned that when the woman as president item was on the list, the number of items that make people angry or upset was 26 percent higher. This suggests that about one in four people are giving a false, socially desirable answer on opinion polls and actually oppose a female presidential candidate.

The survey is the most widely used social science data-gathering technique. Surveys have many uses and take many forms—phone interviews, Internet opinion polls, and various types of questionnaires. All rely on the principles of the professional social research survey. Many people say that they will do a survey to get information when they should say that they need the most appropriate way to get good data.

Surveys can provide us accurate, reliable, and valid data, but to do this they require serious effort and thought. General public familiarity with the survey technique and the ease of conducting a survey can be a drawback. Despite their widespread use and popularity, without care, surveys can easily yield misleading results. As the issue of social desirability bias (discussed later in the chapter) described in the chapter's opening box shows, the survey methodology requires diligence. In this chapter, you will learn about survey research as well as its limitations.

Survey research grew within a positivist approach to social science.[1] As Groves remarked, "Surveys produce information that is inherently statistical in nature. Surveys are quantitative beasts" (1996:389). Most surveys ask a large number of people (usually called *respondents*) about their beliefs, opinions, characteristics, and past or present behaviors (see Expansion Box 10.1, What Is Asked in a Survey). For this reason, surveys are appropriate when we want to learn about self-reported beliefs or behaviors. Most surveys ask many questions at once, thereby measuring many variables. This allows us to gather descriptive information and test multiple hypotheses in a single survey

We can use surveys for exploratory, descriptive, or explanatory research. However, we should be cautious when asking "why" questions of respondents (e.g., Why do you think crime occurs?).[2] Such questions may tell us about people's beliefs and subjective understandings, but people often have incomplete, mistaken, or distorted views. We do not want confuse what people say or believe about why things occur with actual cause-effect relations in the social world.

A HISTORY OF SURVEY RESEARCH

The modern survey goes back to ancient forms of the census.[3] A *census* is government-collected information on characteristics of the entire population in a territory. For example, the *Domesday Book* was a census of England conducted from 1085 to 1086 by William the Conqueror. The early census assessed property for taxation or young men for

Although the categories overlap, the following can be asked in a survey:

1. *Behavior.* How frequently do you brush your teeth? Did you vote in the last city election? When did you last visit a close relative?
2. *Attitudes/beliefs/opinions.* What type of job do you think the mayor is doing? Do you think other people say many negative things about you when you are not there? What is the biggest problem facing the nation these days?
3. *Characteristics.* Are you married, never married, single, divorced, separated, or widowed? Do you belong to a union? What is your age?
4. *Expectations.* Do you plan to buy a new car in the next 12 months? How much schooling do you think your child will get? Do you think the population in this town will grow, decrease, or stay the same?
5. *Self-classification.* Do you consider yourself to be liberal, moderate, or conservative? Into which social class would you put your family? Would you say you are highly religious or not religious?
6. *Knowledge.* Who was elected mayor in the last election? About what percentage of the people in this city are non-White? Is it legal to own a personal copy of Karl Marx's *Communist Manifesto* in this country?

military service. After representative democracy developed, officials used the census to assign elected representatives based on the population in a district and to allocate funds for public improvements.

Surveys for social research started with nineteenth century social reform movements in the United States and Great Britain. Surveys helped people document urban conditions and poverty produced by early industrialization. The early surveys were descriptive and did not use scientific sampling or statistical analyses. For example, between 1851 and 1864, Henry Mayhew published the four-volume *London Labour and the London Poor* based on conversations with street people and observations of daily life. Later studies by Charles Booth's seventeen-volume (1889–1902) *Labour and Life of the People of London* and B. Seebohm Rowntree's *Poverty* (1906) documented urban poverty in England; the *Hull House Maps and Papers of 1895* and W. E. B. DuBois's *Philadelphia Negro* (1899) documented urban conditions in the United States.

In the early twentieth century, the Social Survey Movement in Canada, Great Britain, and the United States used the survey method as part of qualitative community field studies. The Social Survey Movement was an action-oriented community research program that interviewed people and documented conditions to gain support for sociopolitical reforms. By the 1940s, the positivist, quantitative survey had largely displaced this early form of survey research.

Early social surveys offered a detailed empirical picture of specific areas and combined sources of quantitative and qualitative data. Their goal was to inform the public of the problems of rapid industrialization. Early leaders of the social survey—Florence Kelly and Jane Addams of the Hull House and settlement movement and African American W. E. B. DuBois—were outside the mainstream of academic life. Kelly, Addams, and Dubois had difficulties securing regular academic employment because of race and gender discrimination of that era. The early social surveys provide impressive pictures of daily community life in the early twentieth century. For example, the six-volume *Pittsburgh Survey* published in 1914 includes data from face-to-face interviews, statistics on health, crime, and industrial injury, and direct observations.

By the 1920s and 1930s, researchers began to use statistical sampling techniques, especially after the *Literary Digest* debacle (discussed in Chapter 8). They created attitude scales and indexes (discussed in Chapter 7) to measure opinions and subjective beliefs in more precise, quantitative ways. Professionals in applied areas (e.g., agriculture, education, health care, journalism, marketing, public service, and philanthropy) adapted the survey technique for measuring consumer behavior, public opinion, and local needs.

By the 1930s, professional researchers who embraced a positivist orientation were fast displacing

the social reformers who had used the survey to document local social problems. The professional researchers incorporated principles from the natural sciences and sought to make the survey method more objective, quantitative, and nonpolitical. Many academic researchers sought to distance themselves from social reform politics after the Progressive Era (1895–1915) ended. Competition among researchers and universities for status, prestige, and funds accelerated a reorientation or positivist "modernization" of the survey method. This period saw the creation of several survey research centers: the Office of Public Opinion Research at Princeton University, the Division of Program Surveys in the U.S. Department of Agriculture under Rensis Likert (whom you read about in Chapter 7), and the Office of Radio Research at Columbia University. A publication devoted to advancing the survey research method, *Public Opinion Quarterly,* began in 1937. Several large private foundations (Carnegie, Rockefeller, and Sage) funded the expansion of quantitative, positivist-oriented social research.[4]

Survey research dramatically expanded during World War II, especially in the United States. Academic social researchers and practitioners from industry converged in Washington, D.C., to work for the war effort. Survey researchers received generous funding and government support to study civilian and soldier morale, consumer demand, production capacity, enemy propaganda, and the effectiveness of bombing. Wartime cooperation helped academic researchers and applied practitioners learn from one another and gain valuable experience in conducting many large-scale surveys. Academic researchers helped practitioners appreciate precise measurement, sampling, and statistical analysis. Practitioners helped academics learn the practical side of organizing and conducting surveys. Officials in government and business executives saw the practical benefits of using information from large-scale surveys. Academic social scientists realized they could advance understanding of social events and test theories with survey data.

After World War II, officials quickly dismantled the large government survey establishment. This was done to cut costs and because political conservatives feared that reformers might use survey methods to document social problems. They feared such information about ill treatment and poor conditions could be used to advance policies that conservatives opposed, such as helping unemployed workers or promoting racial equality for African Americans in the segregated southern states.

After the war, many researchers returned to universities and founded new social research organizations such as the National Opinion Research Center at the University of Chicago in 1947. Likert moved from the Department of Agriculture to create what became the Institute for Survey Research at the University of Michigan in 1949.

At first, universities were hesitant to embrace the new survey research centers. They were expensive and employed many people. Traditional social researchers were wary of quantitative research and skeptical of bringing a technique popular within private industry into the university. The culture of applied research and business-oriented poll takers clashed with an academic culture of basic researchers, yet survey use quickly increased in the United States and other advanced nations. By 1948, France, Norway, Germany, Italy, the Netherlands, Czechoslovakia, and Britain had each established national survey research institutes.[5]

Publications including survey research accelerated in the 1950s to 1960s. For example, about 18 percent of articles in sociology journals used the survey method in the period 1939–1950; this rose to 55 percent by 1964–1965. In the 1960s, higher education and social science rapidly expanded, also spurring survey research. During the 1970s, computers first became available; they provided the statistical analysis of large-scale quantitative datasets, and hundreds of graduate students learned survey research techniques.[6]

Since the 1970s, quantitative survey research has become huge in private industry, government, and in many academic fields (e.g., communication, education, economics, political science, public health, social psychology, and sociology). The professional survey industry employs more than 60,000 people in the United States alone. Most are part-time workers, assistants, or semiprofessionals. About 6,000 full-time professional survey researchers design and analyze surveys.[7] Weissberg (2005:11)

sees survey research becoming a separate discipline from the many fields (e.g., sociology, political science, marketing) that use it.

Professionals in education, health care, management, marketing, policy research, and journalism use survey research. Governments from the local to national levels around the world sponsor surveys to inform policy decisions. The private-sector survey industry includes opinion polling (e.g., Gallup, Harris, Roper, Yankelovich and Associates), marketing (e.g., Nielsen, Market Facts, Market Research Corporation), and nonprofit research (e.g., Mathematica Policy Research, Rand Corporation, etc.).[8] In addition, survey research has several professional organizations.[9]

Over the past two decades, researchers have increasingly studied the survey process itself and developed theories of the communication-interaction process of a survey interview. They can pinpoint the effectiveness of visual and other clues in questionnaire design, recognize the impact of question wording or ordering, adjust for social desirability, incorporate computer-related technologies, and theorize about survey respondent cooperation or refusals.[10]

THE LOGIC OF SURVEY RESEARCH

As discussed in Chapter 9, in experimental research we divide small numbers of people into equivalent groups, test one or two hypotheses, manipulate conditions so that certain participants receive the treatment, and control the setting to reduce threats to internal validity (i.e., confounding variables). At the end of an experiment, we have quantitative data and compare participant responses on the dependent variable. Survey research follows a different logic. We usually sample many respondents and ask all of them the same questions. We measure many variables with the questions and test multiple hypotheses simultaneously. We infer temporal order from questions about past behavior, experiences, or characteristics. For example, years of schooling completed or race are prior in time to a person's current attitudes. We statistically analyze associations among the variables to identify causal relationships. We also anticipate possible alternative explanation and measure them with other survey questions (i.e. control variables). Later, we statistically examine their effects to rule out alternative explanations. Surveys are sometimes called correlational because the researchers do not control and manipulate conditions as in an experiment. In survey research, we use control variables to statistically approximate an experimenter's physical controls on confounding variables.

Steps in Conducting a Survey

To conduct a survey, researchers start with a theoretical or applied research problem. We can divide the steps in a survey study as outlined in Figure 10.1. The first phase is to create an instrument—a survey questionnaire or interview schedule. Respondents read the questions in a questionnaire themselves and mark the answers themselves. An *interview schedule* is a set of questions read to the respondent by an interviewer, who also records responses. To simplify the discussion, I will use only the term *questionnaire.*

Survey research proceeds deductively. First, we conceptualize variables and then operationalize each variable as one or more survey questions. This means we write, rewrite, and again rewrite survey questions for clarity and completeness. Once we have a collection of survey questions, we must organize them on the questionnaire and group and sequence the questions. Our research question, the types of respondents, and the type of survey (see types of surveys later in this chapter) should guide how we do this.

Let us say you are going to conduct a survey. As you prepare a questionnaire, think ahead to how you will record and organize the data. You also should pilot test the questionnaire with a small set of respondents who are similar to those in the final survey. If you use interviewers, you must train them with the questionnaire. In the pilot test and interviewer training, you ask respondents and interviewers whether the questions were clear, and you need to explore their interpretations to see whether your intended meaning was clear (see pilot testing and cognitive interviewing later in this chapter).[11]

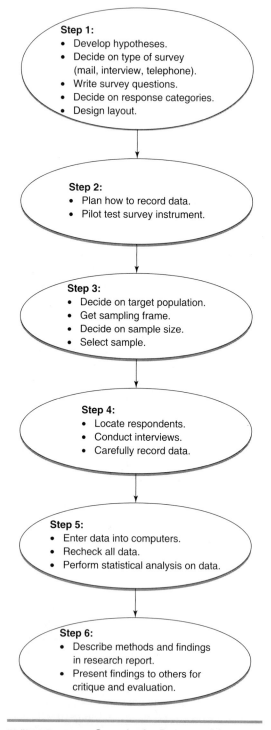

FIGURE 10.1   Steps in the Process of Survey Research

This is the stage at which you would draw the sample of respondents. After the planning phase, you are ready to collect data. You must locate sampled respondents in person, by telephone, by mail, or over the Internet. You provide respondents the instructions on completing the questionnaire or interview. The questions usually follow a simple stimulus/response or question/answer pattern. You must accurately record the answers or responses immediately after they are given. After all respondents have completed the questionnaire and you thank them for participating, you organize the quantitative data and prepare them for statistical analysis.

Conducting survey research requires good organization. A large survey can be complex and expensive. It involves coordinating other people, moving through multiple steps, and accurate record keeping.[12] You must keep track of each respondent's answer to every question on each questionnaire. To help with this task, you should assign each sampled respondent an identification number and attach the number to the questionnaire.

After collecting all of the data, you will want to review responses on individual questionnaires, store original questionnaires, and transfer information from questionnaires to a computer-readable format for statistical analysis. Meticulous bookkeeping and labeling are essential. If you are sloppy, you can lose the data or end up with worthless, inaccurate data.

There are many ways to make mistakes or errors in survey research (see Expansion Box 10.2, Sources of Errors in Survey Research). Errors can occur in sampling and respondent selection (discussed in Chapter 8), in creating questionnaires or interviewing, and in handling or processing the data. Next we look at possible errors to avoid when you write questions for a survey research questionnaire.

CONSTRUCTION OF THE QUESTIONNAIRE

Principles of Good Question Writing

Dozens of books have been published on writing survey questionnaires, so only the basics are reviewed here. Writing good survey questions involves a

EXPANSION BOX 10.2

Sources of Errors in Survey Research

Error is the difference between obtained values and "true values." It occurs when survey data (obtained values) do not accurately reflect the actual behaviors, beliefs, and understandings of respondents in a population that a survey researcher seeks to understand (true values).

1. Errors in selecting the respondent
   a. Sampling errors (e.g., using a nonprobability sampling method)
   b. Coverage errors (e.g., a poor sampling frame omits certain groups of people)
   c. Nonresponse errors at the level of a sampled unit (e.g., a respondent refuses to answer)
2. Errors in responding to survey questions
   a. Nonresponse errors specific to a survey item (e.g., certain questions are skipped or ignored)
   b. Measurement errors caused by respondent (e.g., respondent does not listen carefully)
   c. Measurement errors caused by interviewers (e.g., interviewer is sloppy in reading questions or recording answers)
3. Survey administration errors
   a. Postsurvey errors (e.g., mistakes in cleaning data or transferring data into an electronic form)
   b. Mode effects (e.g., differences due to survey method: by mail, in person, over the Internet)
   c. Comparability errors (e.g., different survey organizations, nations, or time periods yield different data for the same respondents on the same issues).

See: Weisberg (2005:10–28) and Willis (2005:13–17).

mixture of art and science. It is best to see the entire questionnaire as an integrated whole with the questions flowing smoothly from one to another after a few introductory remarks and instructions for ease of entry and clarity.

Two key principles guide writing good survey questions: Avoid possible confusion and keep the respondent's perspective in mind. Avoiding confusion is easier said than done. You want the survey questions to provide a valid and reliable measure.

Being valid and reliable means that the respondents should quickly grasp each question's meaning as you intended, answer completely and honestly, and believe that their answers are meaningful.

You do not want questions that confuse or frustrate respondents. This means that you must exercise extra care if the respondents are heterogeneous, come from life situations unfamiliar to you, or have different priorities than yours. You must be vigilant if the respondents use a different vocabulary or think in different ways than you do.

You want the questions to be equally clear, relevant, and meaningful to all respondents, but you face a dilemma. If the respondents have diverse backgrounds and frames of reference, the same question wording may not have the same meaning for everyone, yet you want everyone to hear the same question because you will combine all answers into numerical data for analysis. If each question is tailored to each respondent, you would not know whether variations in the data are due to question wording or real differences among the respondents.

Survey question writing takes skill, practice, patience, and creativity. You can understand principles of question writing by knowing ten things to avoid when you write survey questions. The list includes only frequently encountered potential problems.[13]

1. *Avoid jargon, slang, and abbreviations.* Jargon and technical terms come in many forms. Plumbers talk about *snakes,* lawyers about a contract of *uberrima fides,* and psychologists about the *Oedipus complex.* Slang is a kind of jargon within a subculture. For example, people who are homeless talk about a *snowbird,* and snowboarders talk about *goofy foot.* People inside a profession or members of a distinct subculture may be familiar and comfortable with the jargon or slang terms but only confuse outsiders. Also, avoid using abbreviations and acronyms. The same ones often have many meanings. For example, I received a letter from the Midwest Sociological Society (MSS). Look up the acronym, and you will see that MSS refers to Manufacturers Standardization Society, Marine Systems Simulator, Medical Student Society, and Minnesota Speleological Society, among a

dozen others that use the MSS abbreviation. I belong to a professional association, the Association for Asian Studies, or AAS. Six other academic organizations use the same acronym: American Astronomical Society, American Association of Suicidology, American Audiology Society, American Astronautical Society, American Antiquarian Society, and the Assyrian Academic Society.

When you survey the public, you should use the language of popular culture (i.e., what is on television or in a local newspaper with about an eighth-grade reading vocabulary). Survey researchers have found that respondents often misunderstand basic terms and are confused by many words. For example, a survey asked respondents whether they thought television news was impartial. Researchers later learned that large numbers of respondents had ignored the word *impartial*—a term the researchers assumed everyone would know. Less than half of the respondents had interpreted the word as intended with its proper meaning. More than one-fourth had no idea of its meaning; others gave it unusual meanings, and one-tenth thought it was directly opposite to its true meaning. In another case, one in four respondents who had less than a high school degree (about 20 percent of the U.S. adult population) did not know what *vaginal intercourse* meant.[14]

2. *Avoid ambiguity, confusion, and vagueness.* Ambiguity and vagueness plague most question writers. It is very easy to make implicit assumptions that can confuse respondents. For example, the question "What is your income?" could mean weekly, monthly, or annually; family or personal; before taxes or after taxes; for this year or last year; from salary or from all sources. Such confusion can cause inconsistencies in respondents' answers to the question. If you want before-tax annual family income for last year, you should explicitly ask for it. Many respondents may not know this, but they tell you their weekly take-home pay (see item 6 following as to questions beyond respondent capabilities).[15] Indefinite words or response categories are also sources of ambiguity. For example, an answer to the question "Do you jog regularly? Yes _____ No _____ " hinges on the meaning of the word *regularly.* Some respondents

may define *regularly* as every day, others as once a week. To reduce confusion and get more information, be more specific: Rather than ask if a person *regularly* jogs, ask whether a person jogs "about once a day," "a few times a week," "once a week," and so on. (See Expansion Box 10.3, Improving Unclear Questions.)

3. *Avoid emotional language and prestige bias.* Words have implicit connotative as well as explicit denotative meanings. Likewise, titles or positions in society (e.g., president, expert) carry prestige and status. Words with strong emotional connotations and issues connected to high-status people can color how respondents answer survey questions. It is best to use neutral language and avoid words with emotional "baggage" because respondents may be reacting to the emotional words rather than the substantive issue. For example, the question "What do you think about paying murderous terrorists who threaten to steal the freedoms of peace-loving people?" is full of emotional words: *murderous, freedoms, steal,* and *peace.*

Prestige bias occurs when questions include terms about a highly prestigious person, group, or institution and a respondent's feelings toward the

Prestige bias A problem in survey research question writing that occurs when a highly respected group or individual is associated with an answer choice.

EXPANSION BOX 10.3

Improving Unclear Questions

Here are three survey questions written by experienced professional researchers. They revised the original wording after a pilot test revealed that 15 percent of respondents asked for clarification or gave inadequate answers (e.g., don't know). As you can see, question wording is an art that may improve with practice, patience, and pilot testing.

ORIGINAL QUESTION	PROBLEM	REVISED QUESTION
Do you exercise or play sports regularly?	What counts as exercise?	Do you do any sports or hobbies, physical activities, or exercise, including walking, on a regular basis?
What is the average number of days each week you have butter?	Does margarine count as butter?	This next question is just about butter—not including margarine. How many days a week do you have butter?
[Following question on eggs] What is the number of servings in a typical day?	How many eggs is a serving? What is a typical day?	On days when you eat eggs, how many eggs do you usually have?

	PERCENTAGE OF RESPONSES TO QUESTION		PERCENTAGE ASKING FOR CLARIFICATION	
	Original	*Revision*	*Original*	*Revision*
Exercise question (saying "yes")	48%	60%	5%	0%
Butter question (saying "none")	33	55	18	13
Egg question (saying "one")	80	33	33	0

Source: Survey questions adapted from Fowler, *Survey Research Methods,* Sage Publications. 1992.

prestigious person or group overshadows how he or she answers a question. You would not know whether you are measuring their feelings about a prestigious person or their real thoughts on the issue. For example, you ask, "Most doctors say that cigarette smoke causes lung disease for those who are near a smoker. Do you agree?" People who think it best to agree with doctors might agree even if they personally disagree.

4. *Avoid double-barreled questions.* This is a version of avoiding ambiguity. You want each question to be about one and only one topic. A **double-barreled question** consists of two or more questions mixed together. For example, you ask, "Does your employer offer pension and health insurance benefits?" A respondent working for a company that offers health insurance benefits but not a pension could answer either yes or no. A respondent who hears the word *and* and thinks it means *and/or* will say yes. A respondent who hears *and* and thinks it means *both* or *and also* will say "no." With double-barreled questions, you cannot be certain of the respondent's intention. If you want to ask about the joint occurrence of two things, ask two separate questions, each about a single issue. During data analysis, you can see whether people who answered yes to one question also answered yes to another.

5. *Avoid leading questions.* You always want respondents to believe that all response choices are equally legitimate and never want them to become aware of an answer that you expect or want. A *leading* (or *loaded*) *question* is one that leads the respondent to one response over another by its wording. There are many kinds of leading questions. For example, the question "You don't smoke, do you?" leads respondents to state that they do not smoke.

Loaded questions can lead respondents to either positive or negative answers. For example, "Should the mayor spend even more tax money to keep the city's excellent streets in super shape?"

Double-barreled question A survey enquiry that contains more than one issue and can create respondent confusion or ambiguous answers.

leads respondents to answering no. A question phrased, "Should the mayor allocate funds to fix streets with large potholes that have become dangerous and are forcing drivers to make costly repairs?" leads respondents to say yes.

6. *Avoid questions beyond respondents' capabilities.* Asking something that respondents do not know creates confusion, frustration, and inaccurate responses. Respondents cannot always recall past details and may not know specific information. For example, asking a 40-year-old, "How did you feel about your brother when you were 6 years old?" is probably worthless, as is asking about an issue respondents know nothing about (e.g., a technical issue in foreign affairs or an internal policy of an organization). Respondents may give you an answer but an unreliable and meaningless one. When many respondents are unlikely to know about an issue, use special question formats (we discuss this later in the chapter).

Try to rephrase questions into the terms in which respondents think. For example, few respondents can answer, "How many gallons of gasoline did you buy last year for your car?" Yet they might be able to answer a question about gasoline purchases in a typical week. You can do the calculations to estimate annual purchases.[16]

Clear, relevant questions increase accuracy and reduce errors. Clear questions contain built-in clues and make contrasts explicit. Instead of asking "Do you pay money to the children of your past marriage?" it would be better to ask "Do you pay child support?" For those answering yes, follow-up questions could be "Did you pay alimony in addition to child support?" and "Did you have any other financial obligations, such as paying health insurance, tuition, or contributing to the mortgage or rent payments?"[17]

7. *Avoid false premises.* If you begin a question with a premise with which respondents disagree and offer choices regarding it, respondents may become frustrated and not know how to answer. About two years ago, I experienced a false premise question, but it was not in a survey. I was an airline passenger shortly after the airlines ceased providing free in-flight snacks. A flight attendant handed me an optional snack, and asked, "Will you

be paying by cash or credit card?" I hesitated a second and then realized that it was a ploy to get me to purchase the now optional snack that I did not want. I replied "neither" and returned it quickly. The false premise in this situation was that I wanted to buy the snack. I became a little irritated with this premise. Apparently, the false premise had irritated others because six months later, flight attendants no longer tried to trick passengers into buying the snacks.

8. *Avoid asking about distant future intentions.* Avoid asking people about what they might do under hypothetical circumstances. Questions such as "Suppose a new grocery store opened down the road. Would you shop at it?" are usually a waste of time. It is best to ask about current or recent attitudes and behavior. Respondents give more reliable answers to specific, concrete, and relevant questions than to questions about things remote from immediate experiences.

9. *Avoid double negatives.* Double negatives in ordinary language are grammatically incorrect and confusing. For example, "I ain't got no job" grammatically and logically means that I have a job. Some people use the second negative for emphasis. Such blatant errors are rare, but subtle forms of the double negative are also confusing. They can arise when we ask respondents to agree or disagree with a statement. For example, you ask "Do you agree or disagree that students should not be required to take a comprehensive exam to graduate?" This is confusing. To disagree is a double negative; it is to *disagree* with *not* doing something. You always want to keep questions simple and straightforward.

10. *Avoid overlapping or unbalanced response categories.* Make response categories or choices mutually exclusive, exhaustive, and balanced (you read about mutually exclusive and exhaustive attributes in Chapter 7). *Mutually exclusive* means that the response categories do not overlap. It is easy to fix overlapping categories that are numerical ranges (e.g., 5–10, 10–20, 20–30 become 5–9, 10–19, 20–29). Ambiguous verbal choices can be overlapping response categories: for example, "Are you satisfied with your job, or are there things you do not like about it?" Assume that I am satisfied overall with my job, but it has some specific things I really

dislike. *Exhaustive* means that every respondent has a choice—a place to go. For example, asking respondents, "Are you working or unemployed?" omits respondents who are not working and who are not unemployed, such as full-time homemakers, people on vacation, full-time students, people who are permanently disabled and cannot work, and people who are retired. To avoid such problems, first think seriously about what you really want to measure and consider the circumstances of all possible respondents. For example, if you ask about employment, do you want information on a primary job or on all jobs, on full-time work only or both full- and part-time work, on jobs for pay only or on unpaid or volunteer jobs as well?

Keep response categories *balanced.* Unbalanced response categories create a type of leading question. An unbalanced choice is "What kind of job is the mayor doing: outstanding, excellent, very good, or satisfactory?" Another type of unbalanced question omits information—for example, "Which of the five candidates running for mayor do you favor: Eugene Oswego or one of the others?"

You can balance categories by offering polar opposites. It is easy to see that the terms *honesty* and *dishonesty* have different meanings and connotations. If you ask whether a mayor is highly, somewhat, or not very honest is not the same as asking whether a mayor is very honest, somewhat honest, neither honest nor dishonest, somewhat dishonest, or very dishonest. The way that you ask a question could give you very different pictures of what people think. Unless you have a specific reason for doing otherwise, offer polar opposites at each end of a continuum[18] (see Table 10.1 on page 318).

Respondent Recall

We often want to ask respondents about past behaviors or events. Respondents vary in their ability to recall accurately when answering survey questions.[19] Recalling past events often takes more time and effort than the few seconds we give respondents to answer a survey question. Also, the ability of people to recall accurately declines quickly over time. They might accurately recall a significant event that occurred 2 weeks ago, but

TABLE 10.1   Summary of Survey Question Writing Pitfalls

THINGS TO AVOID	NOT GOOD	A POSSIBLE IMPROVEMENT
Jargon, slang, abbreviations	Did you drown in brew until you were totally blasted last night?	Last night, about how much beer did you drink?
Vagueness	Do you eat out often?	In a typical week, about how many meals do you eat away from home, at a restaurant, cafeteria, or other eating establishment?

Emotional language and prestige bias	"The respected Grace Commission documents that a staggering $350 BILLION of our tax dollars are being completely wasted through poor procurement practices, bad management, sloppy bookkeeping, 'defective' contract management, personnel abuses and other wasteful practices. Is cutting pork barrel spending and eliminating government waste a top priority for you?"*	How important is it to you that Congress adopt measures to reduce government waste?
		  Very Important
		  Somewhat Important
		  Neither Important or Unimportant
		  Somewhat Unimportant
		  Not Important at All

Double-barreled questions	Do you support or oppose raising Social Security benefits and increased spending for the military?	Do you support or oppose raising Social Security benefits? Do you support or oppose increasing spending on the military?
Leading questions	Did you do your patriotic duty and vote in the last election for mayor?	Did you vote in last month's mayoral election?
Issues beyond respondent capabilities	Two years ago, how many hours did you watch TV every month?	In the past two weeks, about how many hours do you think you watched TV on a typical day?
False premises	When did you stop beating your girl- or boyfriend?	Have you ever slapped, punched, or hit your girl- or boyfriend?
Distant future intentions	After you graduate from college, get a job, and are settled, will you invest a lot of money in the stock market?	Do you have definite plans to put some money into the stock market within the coming two months?
Double negatives	Do you disagree with those who do not want to build a new city swimming pool?	There is a proposal to build a new city swimming pool. Do you agree or disagree with the proposal?
Unbalanced responses	Did you find the service at our hotel to be Outstanding, Excellent, Superior, or Good?	Please rate the service at our hotel: Outstanding, Very Good, Adequate, or Poor.

*Actual question taken from a mail questionnaire that was sent to the author in May 1998 by the National Republican Congressional Committee. It is also a double-barreled question.

few can be accurate about minor events that happened 2 years ago.

Survey researchers recognize that memory is less trustworthy than was once assumed. Many factors influence recall: the topic (threatening or socially desirable), events occurring simultaneously and subsequently, the significance of an event for a person, the situational condition (question wording and interview style), and a respondent's need for internal consistency. Also, recall (e.g., what is the name of your town's mayor) is more difficult than recognition (e.g., look at this list of names and please identify which one is your town's mayor).

The issue of respondent recall does not mean that we cannot ask about past events; rather, we must write survey questions specifically for that purpose and interpret results with caution. To improve recall, we can offer special instructions and extra thinking time. We can provide aids to respondent recall, such as a fixed timeframe or location references. Rather than ask "How often did you attend a sporting event last winter?" you should say, "I want to know how many sporting events you attended last winter. Let's go month by month. Think back to December. Did you attend any sporting events for which you paid admission in December? Now, think back to January. Did you attend any sporting events that charged admission in January?" (See Example Box 10.1, How to Measure TV Watching in a Survey.)

EXAMPLE BOX **10.1**
How to Measure TV Watching in a Survey

Two studies by Prior (2009a, 2009b) illustrate the difficulty of using recall survey questions to measure television watching. The primary way we measure media usage is by self-reports on surveys. In the past 10 years, nearly fifty studies in leading scholarly journals used survey self-reports of media usage as data. Unfortunately, people do not recall accurately and can dramatically overstate media usage in surveys. Survey self-reports of watching television news during the past week are three times higher than the media company Nielsen has found based on its in-set usage-monitoring technology. While most demographic groups overreport, Prior found overreporting was highest in the 18–34-year-old age group. About thirty-five percent in this age group said they watch TV news on each day, but the Nielsen technology shows that only 5 percent really do. Even older age groups who are much more accurate overstate by a factor of 2. Prior looked at three explanations for inaccurate recall of behavior on surveys from the literature on how respondents answer in survey: satisficing, flawed estimates, and social desirability. *Satisficing* is a word that describes people having inaccurate recall because they lack motivation or do not try hard enough to search their memories. *Flawed estimates* result when people do not use good memory searching strategies to remember. *Social desirability* indicates that people report what they believe to be a socially appropriate or normative answer. In a series of experiments with survey question formats, Prior found little support for satisficing or social desirability, at least for TV news recall. Even when given extra time to think, told that their answer was important, and asked a second time, people highly overstated. When people were told how much others watched TV news, they changed answers dramatically to conform. However, when given some assistance in recall, extreme overstating decreased. When people were given an "anchor" or some additional factual information to assist their recall, their estimates improved. Respondents were asked, "The next question is about the nightly national network news on CBS, ABC, and NBC. This is different from local news shows about the area where you live and from cable news channels such as CNN or Fox News channel. How many days in the past week did you watch national network news on television?" One group of respondents heard the following introductory statement. "Television news audiences have declined a lot lately. Less than one out of every ten Americans watches the national network news on a typical weekday evening." Respondents who heard this introductory statement took longer to answer and gave lower reports of news watching. Prior's research suggests that respondents may give more accurate recalls in survey questions if they are both given more time to respond and are helped along in the recall process.

Respondents often **telescope**, or compress time, when asked about past events. They recall an event but earlier (backward telescope) or later (forward telescope) than it actually occurred. Several techniques reduce telescoping (see Expansion Box 10.4, Four Techniques to Reduce Telescoping).

Honest Answers

Questions about Sensitive Topics. We sometimes ask about sensitive issues or ones that people believe threaten their presentation of themselves. These include questions about sexual behavior, drug or alcohol use, mental health problems, law violations, or socially unpopular behavior. Respondents may be reluctant to answer completely and truthfully. To ask about such issues, we adjust how we ask and are especially cautious about the results[20] (see Table 10.2).

Questions on sensitive issues are part of the larger issue of ego protection. Most of us try to

Telescoping Survey research respondents' compressing time when answering about past events, overreporting recent events, and underreporting distant past ones.

EXPANSION BOX 10.4
Four Techniques to Reduce Telescoping

1. *Situational framing.* Ask the respondent to recall a specific situation and ask details about it ("Tell me what happened on the day you were married, starting with the morning").
2. *Decomposition.* Ask the respondent several specific events and then add them up ("Last week did you buy anything from a vending machine? Now, for the week before that, did you buy any items?").
3. *Landmark anchoring.* Ask the respondent whether something occurred before or after a major event ("Did that occur before or after the major earthquake here in June 2010?").
4. *Bounded recall.* (for panel surveys). Ask the respondent about events that occurred since the last interview ("We last talked 2 years ago; since that time, what jobs have you held?").

TABLE 10.2 Threatening Questions and Sensitive Issues

TOPIC	PERCENTAGE VERY UNEASY
Masturbation	56
Sexual intercourse	42
Use of marijuana or hashish	42
Use of stimulants and depressants	31
Getting drunk	29
Petting and kissing	20
Income	12
Gambling with friends	10
Drinking beer, wine, or liquor	10
Happiness and well-being	4
Education	3
Occupation	3
Social activities	2
General leisure	2
Sports activity	1

Source: Adapted from *Improving Interview Method and Questionnaire Design.* Bradburn and Sudman. 1980. JosseyBass. ISBN 10: 087589402X

present a positive image of ourselves to others. We may be ashamed, embarrassed, or afraid to give truthful answers, or may find confronting our actions honestly to be emotionally painful, let alone admitting them to others. When this occurs, we underreport the behaviors or attitudes we wish to hide or believe to violate social norms. People often underreport having an illness or disability (e.g., cancer, mental illness, venereal disease), engaging in illegal or deviant behavior (e.g., evading taxes, taking drugs, consuming alcohol, engaging in uncommon sexual practices), or revealing their financial status (e.g., income, savings, debts)

We can increase honest answering about sensitive topics in four ways: create comfort and trust, use enhanced phrasing, establish a desensitizing context, and use anonymous questioning methods. Each is discussed next.

1. *Create comfort and trust.* Establish trust and a comfortable setting before asking questions. Before starting an interview we can explicitly restate guarantees of anonymity and confidentiality and emphasize the need for obtaining honest

answers from respondents. We also can ask sensitive questions only after a "warm-up period" of asking nonthreatening questions and creating feelings of trust or comfort.

2. *Use enhanced phrasing.* Modify question wording to reduce threat. For example, you could ask "Have you ever shoplifted?" which carries an accusatory tone and uses the emotional word *shoplift* that names an illegal act. You could get at the same behavior by asking "Have you ever taken anything from a store without paying for it?" This only describes the behavior, avoids using emotional words, and leaves open the possibility that it happened under acceptable conditions (e.g., accidentally forgetting to pay).

3. *Establish a desensitizing context.* We can also reduce threat and make it easier for respondents to answer honestly about sensitive topics by providing desensitized contextual information. One way is to first asking about behaviors more serious than ones of real interest to us. For example, a respondent may hesitate to answer a question about shoplifting, but if it follows questions regarding a long list of serious crimes (e.g., armed robbery, burglary), it will appear less serious and might be answered honestly.

4. *Use anonymous questioning methods.* The questioning format significantly affects how respondents answer sensitive questions. Formats that permit increased anonymity, such as a self-administered questionnaire or a Web-based survey, increase the likelihood of honest responses to sensitive questions over formats that require interacting with another person as in a face-to-face interview.[21]

Technological innovations such as **computer-assisted self-administered interviewing (CASAI)** and **computer-assisted personal interviewing (CAPI)** enable respondents to have a degree of anonymity. CASAI "interviews" a respondent by having the person read questions on a computer screen or listen to them with earphones. The respondent answers by moving a computer mouse or typing on a keyboard. Even when an interviewer or others are present in the same room, the respondent is semi-insulated from human contact and interacts only with an automated system. In CAPI, the respondent uses a laptop computer, and an interviewer is available to help or answer questions. Respondents hear questions over earphones and/or read them on a screen and then enter answers without the interviewer directly observing. While completing computer-based interviews, respondents appear to believe they have privacy even if others are present.[22]

A complicated method for asking sensitive questions in face-to-face interview situations is the **randomized response technique (RRT)**. The technique uses statistics beyond the level of this book but is similar to the method described in the chapter's opening box on female presidential candidates. The basic idea is to use known probabilities to estimate unknown proportions. Here is how RRT works. An interviewer gives the respondent two questions: One is threatening (e.g., "Do you use heroin?"), the other not threatening (e.g., "Were you born in September?"). A random method (e.g., toss of a coin, using heads to indicate the heroin question and tails for the birthdate question) is used to select the question to answer. The interviewer does not see the question and records the respondent's answer (yes or no). By using the probability of the random outcomes (e.g., the percent of people born in September), we can estimate the frequency of the sensitive behavior.

We want honest answers to questions on sensitive topics and want to reduce the chances that respondents will give a less-than-honest socially

Computer-assisted self-administered interviewing (CASAI) Technique in which a respondent reads questions on a computer screen or listens over earphones and then answers by moving a computer mouse or typing on a keyboard.

Computer-assisted personal interviewing (CAPI) Technique in which an interviewer sets up a laptop computer and is available to help respondents who hear questions over earphones and/or read them on a screen and then enter answers.

Randomized response technique (RRT) A specialized method in survey research used for very sensitive topics; the random receipt of a question by the respondent without the interviewer being aware of the question to which the respondent is answering.

acceptable answer as described in this chapter's opening box. However, **social desirability bias** is widespread. It occurs when respondents distort answers to conform to popular social norms. People tend to overstate being highly cultured (e.g., reading, attending cultural events), giving money to charity, having a good marriage, loving their children, and so forth. One study found that 34 percent of people who reported in a survey that they gave money to a local charity really did not.[23] Because a norm says that one should vote in elections, many report voting when they did not. In the United States, those under the greatest pressure to vote (i.e., highly educated, politically partisan, highly religious people who had been contacted by an organization that urged them to vote) are the people most likely to overreport voting. This patterned misrepresentation of voting "substantially distorts" studies of voting that rely on self-reported survey data (Bernstein et al., 2001:41).

One way to reduce social desirability bias is to phrase questions in ways that make norm violation appear less objectionable or give respondents "face-saving" alternatives. For example, Belli et al. (1999) reduced overreporting of voting and permitted respondents to "save face" by including in their voting question statements such as "A lot of people were not able to vote because they were not registered, were sick, or just didn't have time." They offered four response choices: "I did not vote in the November 5 election; I thought about voting but did not vote; I usually vote but did not vote this time; I am sure I voted on November 5." Only the last response choice is a clear, unambiguous indication that the person voted. Phrased in this manner, more people admitted that they did not vote.

Knowledge Questions. Studies suggest that a large majority of the public cannot correctly answer elementary geography questions, name their elected leaders, or identify major documents (e.g., the

Declaration of Independence). If we use knowledge questions to learn what respondents know, we need to be careful because respondents may lie because they do not want to appear ignorant.[24] Knowledge questions are important because they address the basis on which people make judgments and form opinions. They tell us whether people are forming opinions based on inaccurate information.

Nadeau and colleagues (1993) found that most Americans seriously overestimate the percent of racial minorities in the population. Only 15 percent (plus or minus 6 percent) of U.S. adults accurately report that 12.1 percent of the U.S. population is African American. More than half believe it is above 30 percent. Similarly, Jews make up about 3 percent of the U.S. population, but a majority (60 percent) of Americans believe the proportion to be 10 percent. A follow-up study by Sigelman and Niemi (2001:93) found that "African Americans themselves overestimate the black population by at least as much" as other respondents. Nearly twice as many African Americans (about 30 percent) versus 15 percent of Whites thought that African Americans were one-half of the U.S. population. Apparently, many Americans have a distorted view of the true racial composition of their country.

Race is not the only issue of which the public has a distorted picture. For example, when we ask Americans about government spending for foreign aid, a large percentage will say that it is too high. However, if we ask them how much the government should be spending on foreign aid, people report an amount that is actually more than the government is currently spending. This situation creates a dilemma. If we ask about the issue in one way, we find that the public says the spending is too high, but if we ask in a different way, we find the public says (indirectly) that it is lower than it should be. Such a dilemma is not unique to the foreign aid issue. In many issue areas—university expenses, health care programs, aid to poor people—respondents offer an opinion to support or oppose an issue or policy position, but if we ask them about the issue in a different way, their position reverses.

This dilemma does not mean that we cannot obtain valid measures of public opinions with surveys. It reminds us that social life is complex and

Social desirabilty bias   A problem in survey research in which respondents give a "normative" response or a socially acceptable answer rather than an honest answer.

writing good surveys to learn about what people think requires effort and diligence. If we carelessly ask for an opinion, we may receive a superficial one offered without serious thought or based on inaccurate knowledge. Or we might get an opinion parroted from what a neighbor said or what was heard in a television advocacy "sound bite."

You may think having an inaccurate view of the country's racial composition or foreign aid spending occurs because the information is beyond people's everyday experiences, but people can also give inaccurate answers to questions about the number of people living in their household. This is not due to ignorance but comes from the complexity of their daily lives. Some people will not report as part of their households marginal persons (e.g., a boyfriend who left for a week, the adult daughter who ran out after an argument about her pregnancy, or the uncle who walked out after a dispute over money). However, such marginal people may not have another permanent residence. If we asked them where they live, they would say they are still living in the household that did not include them, and they plan to return to it.[25]

Our goal in survey research is to obtain accurate information (i.e., a valid and reliable measure of what a person really thinks, does, or feels). Pilot testing questions (discussed later in this chapter) helps to achieve this. Pilot tests reveal whether questions are at an appropriate level of difficulty. We gain little if 99 percent of respondents cannot answer the question. We must word questions so that respondents feel comfortable saying they do not know the answer—for example, "How much, if anything, have you heard about . . .?"

We can check whether respondents are overstating their knowledge with a **sleeper question** to which a respondent could not possibly know the answer. For example, in a study to determine which U.S. civil rights leaders respondents recognized, researchers added the name of a fictitious person. This person was "recognized" by 15 percent of the respondents. This implies that 15 percent of the actual leaders that respondents "recognized" were probably unknown. Another method is to ask respondents an open-ended question after they recognize a name, such as "What can you tell me about

the person" (see the next section, open- versus closed-ended questions).

Contingency Questions. Some questions apply only to specific respondents, and researchers should avoid asking questions that are irrelevant for a respondent. A **contingency question** (sometimes called a *screen* or *skip* question) is a two- (or more) part question.[26] The answer to the first part of the question determines which of two different questions to ask a respondent next. Contingency questions identify respondents for whom a second question is relevant. On the basis of the answer to a first question, the researchers instruct the respondent or the interviewer to go to another or to skip certain questions (see Expansion Box 10.5, Example of a Contingency Question on page 324).

Open-Ended versus Closed-Ended Questions

Researchers actively debate the merits of open versus closed survey questions.[27] An **open-ended question** (requiring an unstructured, free response) asks a question (e.g., "What is your favorite television program?") to which respondents can give any answer. A **closed-ended question** (asking for a structured, fixed response) asks a question and offers a fixed set of responses from which a respondent can choose (e.g., "Is the president doing a very good, good, fair, or poor job, in your opinion?").

Sleeper question   Survey research inquiry about nonexistent people or events to check whether respondents are being truthful.

Contingency question   A two-part survey item in which a respondent's answer to a first question directs him or her either to the next questionnaire item or to a more specific and related second question.

Open-ended question   A type of survey research inquiry that allows respondents freedom to offer any answer they wish to the question.

Closed-ended question   A type of survey research inquiry in which respondents must choose from a fixed set of answers.

10.5

Example of a Contingency Question

QUESTION VERSION 1 (NOT CONTINGENCY QUESTION)

In the past year, how often have you used a seat belt when you have ridden in the backseat of a car?

QUESTION VERSION 2 (CONTINGENCY QUESTION)

In the past, have you ridden in the backseat of a car?

> No [Skip to next question]
>
> Yes → When you rode in the backseat, how often did you use a seat belt?

Results	Always Use	Never Use
Version 1	30%	24%
Version 2	42	4

During pilot testing, researchers learned that many respondents who answered "never" to Version 1 did not ride in the backseat of a car. Version 1 created ambiguity because respondents who never rode in the backseat plus those who rode there but did not use a seat belt both answered "Never." Version 2 using a contingency question format clarified the question.

Source: Adapted from Presser, *Evaluating Survey Questionnaires,* Hoboken, NJ: Wiley. (2004). Reprinted by permission of John Wiley & Sons, Inc.

Each question form has advantages and disadvantages (see Table 10.3). The crucial issue is not which form is better, but which form is most appropriate for a specific situation. Your choice of an open- or closed-ended question depends on the purpose and the practical limits of a study. The demands of using open-ended questions requiring interviewers to write verbatim answers followed by

> **Partially open question**   A type of survey research enquiry in which respondents are given a fixed set of answers to choose from, but the addition an "other" category is offered so that they can specify a different answer.

time-consuming coding may make them impractical for many studies.

We use closed-ended questions in large-scale surveys because they are faster and easier for both respondents and researchers, yet we can lose something important whenever we force an individual's beliefs and feelings into a few fixed, predetermined categories. To learn how a respondent thinks and discover what is important to him or her or for questions with numerous answer categories (e.g., age), open questions are best.

You can reduce the disadvantages of a question format by mixing open-ended and closed-ended questions in a questionnaire. Mixing them also offers a change of pace and helps interviewers establish rapport. Periodic probes (i.e., follow-up questions by interviewers, discussed later) with closed-ended questions can reveal a respondent's reasoning. Having interviewers periodically use probes to ask about a respondent's thinking can check on whether the respondent understands the questions as you intended. However, probes are not substitutes for writing clear questions or creating a framework of understanding for the respondent. Unless carefully stated, probes might influence a respondent's answers or obtain answers for respondents who have no opinion, yet flexible or conversational interviewing (discussed later in this chapter) encourages many probes. For example, to the question "Did you do any work for money last week?" a respondent might hesitate and then reply, "Yes." An interviewer probes, "Could you tell me exactly what work you did?" The respondent may reply "On Tuesday and Wednesday, I spent a couple of hours helping my buddy John move into his new apartment. For that he gave me $40, but I didn't have any other job or get paid for doing anything else." If your intention is to get reports of only regular employment, the probe revealed a misunderstanding. We also use **partially open questions** (i.e., a set of fixed choices with a final open choice of "other"), which allows respondents to offer an answer other than one of the fixed choices.

A total reliance on closed questions can distort results. For example, a study compared open and closed versions of the question "What is the major problem facing the nation?" Respondents

TABLE 10.3   Closed versus Open Questions

ADVANTAGES OF CLOSED
- They are easier and quicker for respondents to answer.
- The answers of different respondents are easier to compare.
- Answers are easier to code and statistically analyze.
- The response choices can clarify a question's meaning for respondents.
- Respondents are more likely to answer about sensitive topics.
- There are fewer irrelevant or confused answers to questions.
- Less articulate or less literate respondents are not at a disadvantage.
- Replication is easier.

DISADVANTAGES OF CLOSED
- They can suggest ideas that the respondent would not otherwise have.
- Respondents with no opinion or no knowledge can answer anyway.
- Respondents can be frustrated because their desired answer is not a choice.
- It is confusing if many (e.g., 20) response choices are offered.
- Misinterpretation of a question can go unnoticed.
- Distinctions between respondent answers may be blurred.
- Clerical mistakes or marking the wrong response is possible.
- They force respondents to give simplistic responses to complex issues.
- They force respondents to make choices they would not make in the real world.

ADVANTAGES OF OPEN
- They permit an unlimited number of possible answers.
- Respondents can answer in detail and can qualify and clarify responses.
- They can help us discover unanticipated findings.
- They permit adequate answers to complex issues.
- They permit creativity, self-expression, and richness of detail.
- They reveal a respondent's logic, thinking process, and frame of reference.

DISADVANTAGES OF OPEN
- Different respondents give different degrees of detail in answers.
- Responses may be irrelevant or buried in useless detail.
- Comparisons and statistical analysis become very difficult.
- Coding responses is difficult.
- Articulate and highly literate respondents have an advantage.
- Questions may be too general for respondents who lose direction.
- Responses are written verbatim, which is difficult for interviewers.
- An increased amount of respondent time, thought, and effort is necessary.
- Respondents can be intimidated by questions.
- Answers take up a lot of space in the questionnaire.

ranked different problems as most important depending on the form of the question. As Schuman and Presser (1979:86) reported, "Almost all respondents work within the substantive framework of the priorities provided by the investigators, *whether or not it fits their own priorities*" [emphasis added]. In a study that asked respondents open and closed questions about what was important in a job, half of the respondents who answered the open-ended version gave answers outside closed-ended question responses.

Open-ended questions are especially valuable in early or exploratory stages of research. For large-scale surveys, we can use open questions in pilot tests and later develop closed-ended questions from the open question answers.

Closed-ended questions require us to make many decisions. How many response choices do we provide? Should we offer a middle or neutral choice? What should be the order of responses? What types of response choices should be included? Answers to these questions are not easy. For example, two response choices are too few, but more than seven are rarely a benefit. We want to measure meaningful distinctions, not collapse them. More specific answer choices yield more information, but too many specifics create respondent confusion. For example, rephrasing the question "Are you satisfied with your dentist?" (which has a yes/no answer) to "How satisfied are you with your dentist: very satisfied, somewhat satisfied, somewhat dissatisfied, or not satisfied at all?" gives us more information and a respondent more choices.

Neutral Positions, Floaters, and Selective Refusals

Failing to get valid responses from each respondent weakens a survey. Respondents may answer three ways that yield invalid responses.

1. *Swayed opinion.* This involves falsely overstating a position as with the social desirability bias, or falsely understating or withholding a position as with sensitive topics.
2. *False positive.* This results from selecting an attitude position but lacking any knowledge on

an issue and really having no true opinion or view on it.
3. *False negative.* Caused when a respondent refuses to answer some questions or withholds an answer when he or she actually has information or really holds an opinion.

The three types of responses overlap. The first involves an inaccurate direction of a response toward a normative position, the second substitutes wild guesses for a serious response, and the last type is the partial and selective nonresponse to the survey.[28]

Neutral Positions. Survey researchers debate whether they should offer respondents who lack knowledge or have no position a neutral position and a "no opinion" choice.[29]

Some argue against offering a neutral or middle position and the no opinion option and favor pressuring respondents to give a response.[30] This perspective holds that respondents engage in **satisficing**; that is, they pick no opinion or a neutral response to avoid the cognitive effort of answering. Those with this position maintain that the least educated respondents may pick a no opinion option when they actually have one they believe that pressuring respondents for an answer does not lower data quality.

Others argue that it is best to offer a neutral ("no opinion") choice because people often answer questions to please others or not to appear ignorant. Respondents may give opinions on fictitious issues, objects, and events. By offering a nonattitude (middle or no opinion) choice, we can identify respondents without an opinion and separate them from respondents who really have one.

Floaters. Survey questions address the issue of nonattitudes with three types of attitude questions: standard-format, quasi-filter, and full-filter questions (see Expansion Box 10.6, Standard-Format, Quasi-Filter, and Full-Filter Questions). The **standard-format question** does not offer a "don't know" choice; a respondent must volunteer it. A **quasi-filter question** offers a "don't know" alternative. A **full-filter question** is a special type of contingency question. It first asks whether respondents have an opinion, and then asks for the opinion of those who state that they do have one.

Satisficing Avoiding exerting cognitive effort when answering survey questions and giving the least demanding answer that will satisfy the minimal requirements of a survey question or interview situation.

Standard-format question A survey research inquiry for which the answer categories do not include a "no opinion" or "don't know" option.

Quasi-filter question A survey research inquiry that includes the answer choice "no opinion," "unsure," or "don't know."

Full-filter question A survey research inquiry that first asks respondents whether they have an opinion or know about a topic; then only those with an opinion or knowledge are asked specifically about the topic.

EXPANSION BOX **10.6**

Standard-Format, Quasi-Filter, and Full-Filter Questions

STANDARD FORMAT

Here is a question about another country. Do you agree or disagree with this statement? "The Russian leaders are basically trying to get along with America."

QUASI-FILTER

Here is a statement about another country: "The Russian leaders are basically trying to get along with America." Do you agree, disagree, or have no opinion on that?

FULL FILTER

Here is a statement about another country. Not everyone has an opinion on this. If you do not have an opinion, just say so. Here's the statement: "The Russian leaders are basically trying to get along with America." Do you have an opinion on that? No (go to next question), Yes (continue). Do you agree or disagree?

Example of Results from Different Question Forms

	Standard Format (%)	Quasi-Filter (%)	Full Filter (%)
Agree	48.2	27.7	22.9
Disagree	38.2	29.5	20.9
No opinion	13.6*	42.8	56.3

*Volunteered

Source: Adapted from Schuman and Presser (1981). *Questions and Answers in Attitude Surveys: Experiments in Question Form, Wording, and Context* (116–125). Academic Press. With permission from Elsevier. Standard format is from Fall 1978; quasi- and full-filter forms are from February 1977.

The logic behind these three formats is that many respondents will answer a question if a "no-opinion" choice is missing, but they pick "don't know" when we offer it, or say they do not have an opinion if asked directly. These respondents are **floaters** because they "float" from responding to questions they understand and have knowledge about responding to questions which they have no knowledge and do not understand. Minor wording changes are likely to change their answers. Quasi-filter or full-filter questions help screen out floaters. Filtered questions may not eliminate all respondents answering to nonexistent issues, but they reduce the problem.

Middle alternative floaters will choose a middle position when we offer it but another alternative if we do not. They feel ambivalent or less intense about an issue. There may be a slight **recency effect**; that is, respondents tend to choose the last alternative offered. The recency effect suggests that we should present responses on a continuum and place the neutral position in the middle.

Attitudes have two aspects: direction (for or against) and intensity (strongly held or weakly held). For example, two respondents both oppose abortion. One is fiercely attached to the opinion and strongly committed to it; the other holds the opinion weakly and is wavering. If we ask only an

Floaters   Survey research respondents without the knowledge or an opinion to answer a survey question but who answer it anyway, often giving inconsistent answers.

Recency effect   A result in survey research that occurs when respondents choose the last answer response offered rather than seriously considering all answer choices.

agree/disagree question, respondents may respond in the same way; however, we can capture both aspects of the opinion by offering more choices (strongly agree, agree) or with a contingency question (agree/disagree and then how strongly do you hold that opinion).

Selective Refusals. In addition to the issue of satisficing, by which respondents pick no or a neutral response to avoid the effort of answering, some respondents refuse to answer certain questions. This often is the case involving a sensitive issue. Respondents refuse rather than indicate a socially inappropriate answer.

For example, in 1992 more than one-third of Americans refused to answer a sensitive question about racial integration. When many respondents do not answer a question, the findings may be misleading if the nonresponding people actually hold an opinion. For example, if the respondents who opposed racial integration answered "don't know," the results appeared more favorable to integration than if all respondents had answered the question. After adjusting for nonresponses, Berinsky (1999) found that the percentage of Americans who favored racial integration dropped from 49.4 to 34.9 percent. He warned (p. 1225) that "the opinions respondents express in the survey interview are not necessarily identical to the opinions they construct when coming to grips with a survey question."

Agree/Disagree, Rankings or Ratings? Survey researchers who measure values and attitudes have debated two issues about responses offered.[31] Should a questionnaire item make a statement and ask respondents whether they agree or disagree with it, or should it offer respondents specific alternatives? Should the questionnaire include a set of items and ask respondents to rate them (e.g., approve, disapprove), or should it give them a list of items and force them to rank order them (e.g., from most favored to least favored)?

Offering respondents explicit alternatives is best. For example, instead of asking, "Do you agree or disagree with the statement, 'Men are better suited to run the nation?'" ask instead, "Do you think men are better suited to run the nation, women

are better suited, or both are equally suited?" Less well-educated respondents tend to agree with a statement. Explicit forced-choice alternatives encourage thought and avoid the *response set* bias—the tendency of some respondents to agree (you read about the response set in Chapter 7).

Survey respondents asked about values often show little differentiation and their responses pile up at the extremes. One solution is to use a "rank-then-rate" procedure. We first ask respondents to rank values, most to least important. Next, we ask them to assign each a rating. For example, respondents rank values (e.g., world peace, personal wealth, family security) in importance. Next they assign a value, 1 to 10, from extremely important to not important at all. A respondent may rank the value of world peace ahead of personal wealth, but when asked to rate the importance of world peace or its personal significance, a respondent may give world peace a 4 but personal wealth an 8.[32]

Remember that we must present the alternatives fairly and not offer a reason for respondents to choose one alternative. For example, if you ask "Do you support the law for energy conservation or do you oppose it because the law would be difficult to enforce?" instead of simply "Do you support or oppose the law for energy conservation?" you created a leading question against the energy conservation law. This is why we ask respondents to choose among alternatives by ranking (e.g., please give me you first choice, second choice, and third choice) instead of rating items along an imaginary continuum (e.g., which of these is best). Respondents can rate several items equally high but place them in a hierarchy if we ask them to rank the items compared to one another.[33]

Attaching numbers to a response scale can assist respondents and give them a clue for understanding. Positive and negative numbers at the extremes (e.g., $+5$ to -5) are best when we conceptualize the variables as polar. It is best to use a series of positive numbers (e.g., 0 to 10) if we conceptualize the variable as a single continuum. Again, how we do this tells us how we should organize the question and its answer choices.

Visual presentations, including the use of colors, symbols, and pictures, can influence respondents' reactions to questionnaires. Visuals sometimes may have a larger impact than question wording changes. Respondents tend to interpret the middle of a set of responses as a typical or middle option, treat closeness in space on a questionnaire as indicating similar meaning, view the top items in a vertical list as being most desirable, and see differences in space between answers or the use of different colors as indicating more significant differences in meaning. Also, respondents find that organizing response categories vertically is less confusing than if they are organized horizontally.[34]

Question format and questionnaire design may influence the results we obtain. Rockwood, Sangster, and Dillman (1997) asked college students how many hours they studied per day. Some students got a "low set" of five answer choices, ranging from 0.5 hour to more than 2.5 hours per day. Other students received a "high set" of five answer choices, ranging from less than 2.0 hours to more than 4.5 hours per day. Of students who received the "low" set of choices, 28 percent said they studied over 2.5 hours. Of students who got the "high" set of choices, 69 percent studied over 2.5 hours. Apparently, answer choices had influenced answers. The researchers also compared survey format for the same question and answer choices. They sent some students mail questionnaires and interviewed others by telephone. Answers changed with the survey format. Of students asked about studying with the "low" set of five answer choices by mail questionnaire, 23 percent said they studied over 2.5 hours per day. Of students interviewed by phone with the "low" set of choices, 42 percent gave the answer of 2.5 hours per day. For students who received the "high" set of five answer choices, answers by mail questionnaire and phone interview were similar. In the same study, the researchers asked students about the number of hours they watched television with similar "high" and "low" response category sets, comparing mail questionnaires and telephone interviews. For the topic of television watching, ranges of response categories or format did not affect answers.

This study shows us three things. Respondents rely on the range of response categories in a question for guidance; they answer more honestly with more anonymous survey formats, such as a mail questionnaire, compared to less anonymous formats, such as interviews; and both response categories and survey format shape answers about some topics more than other topics.[35]

Wording Issues

We face two wording issues in creating questionnaires. The first, discussed earlier, is to use simple vocabulary and grammar to minimize confusion. The second issue involves the effects of specific words or phrases. This is trickier because we do not know in advance whether a word or phrase affects responses.[36]

A well-documented difference between *forbid* and *not allow* illustrates the problem. Both terms have the same meaning, but many more people are willing to "not allow" something than to "forbid" it. In general, less well-educated respondents are influenced more by minor wording differences than educated ones.

Certain words trigger an emotional reaction, and we are just beginning to learn of them. For example, Smith (1987) found large differences (e.g., twice as much support) in U.S. survey responses depending on whether a question asked about spending "to help the poor" or "for welfare." He suggested that for Americans, the word *welfare* has such strong negative connotations (lazy people, wasteful and expensive programs, etc.) that it is best to avoid it.

Possible **wording effects** are illustrated by what appears to be a noncontroversial question. Peterson (1984) examined four ways to ask about age: "How old are you?" "What is your age?" "In what year were you born?" and "Are you . . . 18–24, 25–34, . . . ?" He checked responses against birth certificate records and found that from 98.7 to 95.1 percent of respondents gave correct responses depending on the form of question used. He also found that the form of the question that had the

Wording effects Results in survey research when the use of a specific term or word strongly influences how some respondents answer a survey question.

fewest errors had the highest percentage of refusals to answer, and the form with the most errors had the lowest refusal rate. This example suggests that errors in a noncontroversial factual question may vary with minor wording changes.

Questionnaire Design Issues

Length of Survey or Questionnaire. How long should a questionnaire be or an interview last?[37] We prefer long questionnaires or interviews because they are more cost effective. The cost for a few extra questions once a respondent has been sampled, has been contacted, and has completed other questions is small. There is no absolute proper length. It depends on the survey format (to be discussed) and on the respondent's characteristics. A 5-minute telephone interview is rarely a problem. Mail questionnaires are more variable. A short (three-page) questionnaire is appropriate for the general population. Some researchers have had success with questionnaires as long as ten pages (about one hundred items), but responses drop significantly for longer questionnaires. For highly educated respondents and a very salient topic, a fifteen-page questionnaire may be possible. Face-to-face interviews can be long, with ones lasting an hour not uncommon. In special situations, researchers have conducted face-to-face interviews as long as 3 or 5 hours.

Question Order or Sequence. We face three question sequence issues: organization of the overall questionnaire, question order effects, and context effects.

1. *Organization of questionnaire.* In general, you should sequence questions to minimize respondent discomfort and confusion. A questionnaire has opening, middle, and ending questions. After an introduction explaining the survey, it is best to make opening questions pleasant, interesting, and easy to answer. This helps a respondent to feel comfortable

---

Order effect   A result in survey research in which a topic or some questions asked before others influence respondents' answers to later questions.

---

about the questionnaire. Avoid asking many boring background questions or sensitive questions at the beginning. Organize questions in the middle into common topics. Mixing questions on different topics causes confusion. Orient respondents by placing questions on the same topic together after introducing the section with a short statement (e.g., "Now I would like to ask you questions about housing"). Make question topics flow smoothly and logically, and organize them to assist respondents' memory or comfort levels. Do not end with sensitive issue questions, and always say "thank you."

2. *Order effects.* The order in which questions appear in a questionnaire can influence respondent answers.[38] Such **order effects** appear to be strongest for people who lack strong views, for less educated respondents, and for older respondents or those with memory loss.[39] For example, opinions that support a single woman having an abortion regularly rises if the question follows a question about abortion being acceptable when a fetus has serious defects but not when the question is alone or before a question about fetus defects. A classic example of order effects is presented in Expansion Box 10.7, Question Order Effects.

Answers to earlier questions can influence later ones in two ways: through their content (i.e., the issue) and through the respondent's response. For example, you ask a student, "Do you support or favor educational contributions for students?" Answers vary depending on the preceding question topic. If it comes after "How much tuition does the average U.S. student pay?" respondents will interpret "contributions" to mean what students will pay. If the question comes after "How much does the Swedish government pay to students?" respondents interpret "contributions" to mean those the government will make. Previous answers can also influence responses because having already answered one part respondents will assume no overlap. For example, you ask a respondent, "How is your wife?" The next question is, "How is your family?" Most respondents assume that the second question means family members other than the wife because they already answered about her.[40]

3. *Context effects.* Survey researchers have observed powerful **context effects** in surveys.[41]

Question Order Effects

QUESTION 1

"Do you think that the United States should let Communist newspaper reporters from other countries come in here and send back to their papers the news as they see it?"

QUESTION 2

"Do you think a Communist country like Russia should let U.S. newspaper reporters come in and send back to America the news as they see it?"

PERCENTAGE SAYING YES

Heard First	Yes to Question 1 (Communist Reporter)	Yes to Question 2 (American Reporter)
Question 1	54%	75%
Question 2	64	82

The context created by answering the first question affects the answer to the second question.

Source: Adapted from Schuman and Presser (1981). *Questions and Answers in Attitude Surveys: Experiments in Question Form, Wording, and Context,* p. 29. New York: Academic Press. With permission from Elsevier.

"Context includes more than just the influence of one question on another. It includes the effects of the interviewer, the interview setting, and indeed the historical setting. . . . At present, we do not have a good grasp of how questionnaire context effects relate to response effects on surveys" (Schuman, 1992:18). The context has a more significant impact in mail versus phone surveys because a respondent can see all of the questions in the former.[42]

You can do two things regarding context effects. Use a **funnel sequence** of questions; that is, ask general questions before specific ones (e.g., about health in general before specific diseases). Alternatively, you can divide respondents in half and give one half questions in one order and the other half questions in an alternative order and then examine the results to see whether question order mattered. If you discover question order effects, which order tells you what the respondents really think? The answer is that you cannot know for sure.

For example, a few years ago, my students conducted a telephone survey on two topics: concern about crime and attitudes toward a new antidrunk-driving law. A random half of the respondents heard questions about the drunk-driving law first; the other half heard about crime first. I examined the results to see whether there was any context effect—a difference resulting from topic order. I found that respondents asked about the antidrunk-driving law first expressed less fear about crime than did those who were asked about crime first. Likewise, respondents were more supportive of the antidrunk-driving law than were those who first heard about crime. The first topic created a context within which respondents answered questions on the second topic. After we asked respondents about crime in general and they

Context effect A result in survey research when an overall tone, setting, or set of topics heard by respondents affect how they interpret the meaning of subsequent questions.

Funnel sequence Organization of survey research questions in a questionnaire from general to specific questions.

thought about violent crimes, drunk driving may have appeared to be a less important issue to them. By contrast, after we asked about drunk driving as a crime, respondents may have expressed less concern about crime in general.

We need to remember that context effects are strong if the question is ambiguous because respondents will draw on the context to interpret and understand the question. Previous questions on the same topic and ones immediately preceding a question can have a large context effect. For example, Sudman et al. (1996:90–91) contrasted three ways of asking how much a respondent followed politics. When they asked the question alone, about 21 percent of respondents said they followed politics "now and then" or "hardly at all." When they asked the question after asking about something that the respondent's elected representative recently did, the percentage who said they did not follow nearly doubled (39 percent). The knowledge question made many respondents feel that they did not really know much. When a question about the amount of "public relations work" the elected representative provided to the area came between the two questions, 29 percent of respondents said they did not follow politics. This question gave respondents an excuse for not knowing the first question; they could blame their representative for their ignorance. The context of a question can make a difference, and researchers need to be aware of it at all times: "Question comprehension is not merely a function of the wording of a question. Respondents use information provided by the context of the question to determine its intended meaning" (Sudman et al., 1996:69).

Layout and Format. There are two format or layout issues: the overall physical layout of the questionnaire and the format of questions and responses.

Questionnaire Layout. Layout of a questionnaire is important both to an interviewer and for the respondent.[43] Questionnaires should be clear, neat, and easy to follow. Put identifying information (e.g., name of organization) on questionnaires and give each question a number. Never cramp questions together or create a confusing appearance. A few cents saved in postage or printing will ultimately

cost more in terms of lower validity resulting from a lower response rate or of confusion of interviewers and respondents. A professional appearance with high-quality graphics, space between questions, and good layout encourages accuracy and completeness and helps the questionnaire flow. If using an interview format, create a *face sheet* (the face sheet is discussed in Chapter 13) as part of the questionnaire for administrative use. The face sheet should include the time and date of the interview, the interviewer's name, the respondent's identification number, and the interviewer's comments and observations on the interview.

Give interviewers and respondents instructions. It is best to print instructions in a different style from the questions (e.g., in a different color or font) to distinguish them. This helps an interviewer to distinguish between questions for respondents and instructions intended for the interviewer alone.

Layout is crucial for mail and Web questionnaires because there is no friendly interviewer to interact with the respondent. Instead, the questionnaire's appearance persuades the respondent.

Include a polite, professional cover letter on letterhead stationery with mail surveys, identifying the researcher and offering a telephone number for questions. Details matter. Respondents will be turned off if they receive a bulky brown envelope with bulk postage addressed to Occupant or if the questionnaire does not fit into the return envelope.

Web surveys are still new, and researchers are just learning which design features are most effective, but visual design details matter (see Web survey discussion later in this chapter).

Question Format. You must decide on a format for questions and responses. Should respondents circle responses, check boxes, fill in dots, or write in a blank? The principle is to make responding clear and unambiguous. Boxes or brackets to be checked and numbers to be circled are usually clearest. Also, listing responses down a page rather than across makes them easier to see (see Expansion Box 10.8, Question Format Examples). Use arrows and instructions for contingency questions. Visual aids are helpful. For example, hand out thermometer-like drawings to respondents when asking whether their feeling

EXPANSION BOX **10.8**
Question Format Examples

EXAMPLE OF HORIZONTAL VERSUS VERTICAL RESPONSE CHOICES

Do you think it is too easy or too difficult to get a divorce, or is it about right?
○ Too Easy   ○ Too Difficult   ○ About Right

Do you think it is too easy or too difficult to get a divorce, or is it about right?
○ Too Easy
○ Too Difficult
○ About Right

EXAMPLE OF A MATRIX QUESTION FORMAT

	Strongly Agree	Agree	Disagree	Strongly Disagree	Don't Know
The teacher talks too fast.	○	○	○	○	○
I learned a lot in this class.	○	○	○	○	○
The tests are very easy.	○	○	○	○	○
The teacher tells many jokes.	○	○	○	○	○
The teacher is organized.	○	○	○	○	○

EXAMPLES OF SOME RESPONSE CATEGORY CHOICES

Excellent, Good, Fair, Poor

Approve/Disapprove

Favor/Oppose

Strongly Agree, Agree, Somewhat Agree, Somewhat Disagree, Disagree, Strongly Disagree

Too Much, Too Little, About Right

Better, Worse, About the Same

Regularly, Often, Seldom, Never

Always, Most of the Time, Some of the Time, Rarely, Never

More Likely, Less Likely, No Difference

Very Interested, Interested, Not Interested

---

toward someone is warm or cool. A **matrix question** (or *grid question*) is a compact way to present a series of questions using the same response categories. It saves space and makes it easier for the respondent or interviewer to note answers for the same response categories.

Nonresponse. The failure to get a valid response from every sampled respondent weakens a survey. In addition to research surveys, people are asked to respond to many surveys from charities, marketing firms, candidate polls, and so forth. Charities and marketing firms generally have low response rates, whereas government organizations have much higher rates. Nonresponse can be a major problem because if a high proportion of the sampled respondents do not respond, results may not be generalizable, especially if those who do not respond differ from those who do.

Matrix question A survey research inquiry that groups together a set of questions that share the same answer categories in a compact form.

Almost all people complete surveys at some time, and the reporting of survey or poll results in major newspapers grew rapidly after the 1960s. By the 1970s, it seemed that every day a newspaper story cited survey or poll results. As surveys became increasingly used, response rates have declined. Nonresponse rates in surveys vary greatly; for academic organizations, they range from 25 to 33 percent. In the United States, nonresponse rates for major academic surveys rose from less than 10 percent in the 1950s to 25 percent in the 1980s. Public cooperation in survey research has declined across most countries with the Netherlands having the highest refusal rate; it is as high as 30 percent in the United States.[44] The nonresponse rates to commercial polls (Roper, Gallup, CBS, etc.) and campaign polls tend to be higher, however, reaching as high as 50 percent.

Researchers discovered a growing group of "hard core" refusing people who decline all surveys. In addition, general survey participation has declined because people believe there are too many surveys. Other reasons for declining survey participation include a fear of strangers, a more hectic lifestyle, a loss of privacy, and a rising distrust of authority. The misuse of a survey to sell products or persuade people, poorly designed questionnaires, and inadequate explanations of surveys also increase refusals for legitimate, serious ones.

The most interested, informed, and active members of society tend to participate in surveys. This means that nonresponse both harms survey validity and omits a particular segment of the population. In the United States, nonrespondents tend to be young non-White males and the less educated.

Nonresponse rates have five components (see Expansion Box 10.9, Confusion about Response Rates).[45]

1. *Location*—Could a sampled respondent be located?
2. *Contact*—Was a located respondent at home or reached after many attempts?
3. *Eligibility*—Was the contacted respondent the proper age, race, gender, citizenship, and so on for the survey purpose?
4. *Cooperation*—Was an eligible respondent willing to be interviewed or fill in a questionnaire?

EXPANSION BOX **10.9**

Confusion about Response Rates

There is some confusion about response rates because the total response rate depends on the success rate of five component responses, each of which has its own rate:

Location rate: Percentage of respondents in the sampling frame who are located.

Contact rate: Percentage of located respondents who are contacted.

Eligibility rate: Percentage of contacted respondents who are eligible.

Cooperation rate: Percentage of contacted, eligible respondents who agree to participate.

Completion rate: Percentage of cooperating respondents who complete the survey.

Total response rate: Percentage of all respondents in the initial sampling frame who were located, contacted, eligible, agreed to participate, and completed the entire questionnaire.

For example, researchers begin with 1,000 respondents in a sampling frame, locate 950 by telephone or an address, are able to contact 800 (by an interviewer or successful mailing), and determine that 780 are eligible (i.e., meet basic criteria, speak the language, are mentally competent). They find that 700 people cooperate with the questionnaire or interview, and 690 complete the entire questionnaire or interview. This yields the following rates: *location rate:* 95 percent; *contact rate:* 84.2 percent; *eligibility rate:* 97.5 percent; *cooperation rate:* 89.8 percent; *completion rate:* 98.6 percent; *total response rate:* 69 percent. The *total response rate* is the product of all of the individual rates: $.95 \times .842 \times .975 \times .898 \times .986 = .690$.

---

5. *Completion*—Did a cooperating respondent stop answering before the end or start answering most questions with "do not know" or "no opinion"?

Improving the overall survey response rate requires us to reduce each type of nonresponse.

Location Rate. Improving location means using better sampling frames and maps or phone directories. Improving contact necessitates making many repeat calls, varying the time of day for calls, and lengthening the period to make contact. Several factors are associated with noncontact in the United States: high population density, urban central city, nonowner-occupied housing (i.e., rental), high crime rate, high percentage of minority race population, presence of physical barriers (i.e., fences, bars on windows, beware of dog or no trespassing signs), and a single adult living alone or households without young children. Although they may be easier to locate and contact, people who have higher income and more education may be less likely to cooperate once contacted. As Groves and Couper (1998:130) observed, "We find support in our data for the notion that those in high SES [socioeconomic status] households cooperate less with surveys than those in low SES groups." Although caller ID has increased, few respondents use caller ID and telephone machine screening technologies to block survey research in a significant way.[46]

Contact Rate. A critical area of nonresponse or refusal to participate occurs with the initial contact between an interviewer and a respondent. Cooperation increases when a respondent believes that the survey topic or results will be salient to him or her (i.e., are of great interest or will produce direct benefits), or when interviewers use "tailoring" (discussed later in this chapter) in their introductions to respondents, or offer a small incentive (e.g., a few dollars).

Eligibility Rate. We can improve eligibility rates by creating careful respondent screening, using better sample-frame definitions, and having multilingual interviewers. We can decrease refusals by sending letters in advance of an interview, offering to reschedule interviews, using small incentives (i.e., small gifts or amounts of money, as noted), adjusting interviewer behavior and statements (i.e., making eye contact, expressing sincerity, explaining the sampling or survey, emphasizing importance of the interview, clarifying promises of confidentiality). We can also use alternative interviewers (i.e., different demographic characteristics, age, race,

gender, or ethnicity), use alternative interview methods (i.e., phone versus face to face), or accept alternative respondents in a household.

Cooperation Rate. Cooperation among inner-city residents, low-income persons, and racial-ethnic minorities have increased as a result of using a journalistic-style letter and a personal phone call compared to using a standard academic letter. Respondents who were pessimistic about government and social service agencies and who felt misunderstood were more likely to participate after someone explained the nature of the survey to them in terms to which they could easily relate.[47]

As mentioned, small prepaid incentives increase respondent cooperation in all types of surveys and appear to have no negative effects on survey composition or future participation. For example, Brehm (1994) found that without advance contact, 71 percent of respondents cooperated, but the rate rose to 78 percent with advance contact (a letter) and an incentive ($1) and the respondents were more talkative. Moreover, respondents do not feel that differential payments for participation are unfair.[48]

Instead of seeing respondents as already having well-developed attitudes, beliefs, and opinions that they are ready to retrieve and deliver when asked in a survey, we see a survey as involving several processes. The first is to win cooperation-motivation so that people will participate fully in the survey process. A second is assisting respondents in correctly interpreting the survey question and assembling an appropriate and accurate response from memory or past experiences. A third is helping respondents properly answer or deliver the appropriate response (also see Example Box 10.1 earlier in this chapter).

Two related theories help explain the cooperation-motivation process. Social exchange theory, or the total design method (see Dillman, 1978, 2000), sees the formal survey as a special type of social interaction. A respondent behaves based on what he or she expects to receive in return for cooperation. To increase response rates and accuracy, we need to minimize the burdens of cooperating by making participation very easy and to maximize rewards by providing benefits (i.e., feelings of esteem, material incentives, and emotional rewards) for cooperation.

Leverage saliency theory holds that the salience or interest/motivation varies by respondent. Different people value, either positively or negatively, specific aspects of the survey process differently (e.g., length of time, topic of survey, sponsor). To maximize survey cooperation, we need to identify and present positively valued aspects early in the survey process. Two practical implications are sponsorship and tailoring. *Sponsorship* refers to the organization that conducts or pays for the survey. **Tailoring** occurs when interviewers adjust what they say in an introduction to specific respondents, highlighting what they believe will encourage a respondent to cooperate. Tailoring is achieved by training survey interviewers to be sensitive to a range of household types and concerns so they can "read" the setting and the various verbal and nonverbal cues. Interviewers should be able to shift quickly to alternative scripts for persuading a respondent and tailor the persuasion to a specific respondent.[49]

Completion Rate. Dillman (2000:252) reports higher self-administered questionnaire completion rates if someone is personally handed the questionnaire as opposed to receiving it on the doorstep or via the mail. He was able to achieve response rates of 77 percent with a combination of personally handing a questionnaire to a respondent, sending two follow-up reminders, and including a monetary incentive for completion (compared to 53 to 71 percent rates when one or more technique was not included).

Leverage saliency theory A hypothesis of survey research cooperation that states that different respondents find different aspects of a survey interview to be salient and decide whether to cooperate based on different specific aspects of the interview.

Tailoring Encouraging a respondent's cooperation in survey research interviews by having interviewers highlight specific aspects of the interview that a respondent finds salient and values positively.

Total Response Rate. A large body of literature examines how to increase response rates for mail questionnaires (see Expansion Box 10.10, Ten Ways to Increase Mail Questionnaire Response).[50]

A meta-analysis (explained in Chapter 5) of 115 articles on mail survey responses taken from 25 journals published between 1940 and 1988 revealed that cover letters, questionnaires of four pages or less, a return envelope with postage, and a small monetary reward all increase returns (Yammarino et al., 1991). Another meta-analysis comparing mail with Web surveys found that mail surveys have higher response rates. College respon-

---

EXPANSION BOX 10.10
Ten Ways to Increase Mail Questionnaire Response

1. Address the questionnaire to a specific person, not "Occupant," and send it first class.
2. Include a carefully written, dated cover letter on letterhead stationery. In it, request respondent cooperation, guarantee confidentiality, explain the purpose of the survey, and give the researcher's name and phone number.
3. *Always* include a postage-paid, addressed return envelope.
4. The questionnaire should have a neat, attractive layout and reasonable page length.
5. The questionnaire should be professionally printed, be easy to read, and have clear instructions.
6. Send two follow-up reminder letters to those not responding. The first should arrive about one week after sending the questionnaire, the second a week later. Gently ask for cooperation again and offer to send another questionnaire.
7. Do not send questionnaires during major holiday periods.
8. Do not put questions on the back page. Instead, leave a blank space and ask the respondent for general comments.
9. Sponsors that are local and are seen as legitimate (e.g., government agencies, universities, large firms) get a better response.
10. Include a small monetary inducement ($1) if possible.

dents are more responsive to Web surveys, but other respondents (e.g., medical doctors, teachers, consumers) prefer mail surveys. Follow-up reminders appear to be less effective for Web than for mail surveys (Shih and Fan, 2008). Many of the techniques suggested follow the total design method and help to make the task easy and interesting for respondents.

TYPES OF SURVEYS: ADVANTAGES AND DISADVANTAGES

Mail and Self-Administered Questionnaires

Advantages. We can give or mail questionnaires directly to respondents, who read the instructions and questions and then record their answers. A single researcher can conduct this type of survey at very low cost and cover a wide geographical area. The respondent can complete the questionnaire when it is convenient and can check personal records for information if necessary. Mail questionnaires offer anonymity and avoid interviewer bias. They are very effective and can achieve acceptable response rates from an educated sample that has a strong interest in the topic or the survey organization.

Disadvantages. Because many people do not complete and return mail questionnaires, their biggest problem is a low response rate. Most questionnaires are returned within 2 weeks, but others trickle in for up to 2 months. We can improve response rates by sending nonrespondents reminder letters, but this adds to the time and cost of data collection.

We lack control over the conditions under which a mail questionnaire is completed. A questionnaire completed during a drinking party by a dozen laughing people may be returned along with one filled out by an earnest respondent. Also, no one is present to clarify questions or to probe for more information when respondents give incomplete answers. Someone other than the sampled respondent (e.g., spouse, new resident) may open the mail and complete the questionnaire without

the researcher's knowledge. We cannot visually observe the respondent's reactions to questions, physical characteristics, or the setting. For example, an impoverished 70-year-old White woman living alone on a farm could falsely state that she is a prosperous 40-year-old Asian male doctor with three children living in a town. Such extreme lies are rare, but serious errors can go undetected. In addition, different respondents can complete the questionnaire weeks apart or answer questions in a different order than intended. Incomplete questionnaires can also be a serious problem.

The mail questionnaire format limits the questions that we can use. Those that require visual aids (e.g., look at this picture and tell me what you see), open-ended questions, many contingency questions, and complex questions cannot be used in most mail questionnaires. Likewise, mail questionnaires are ill suited for people who are illiterate or nearly illiterate (see Table 10.4 on page 338).

Telephone Interviews

Advantages. The telephone interview is a popular survey method because about 95 percent of the population can be reached by telephone. An interviewer calls a respondent (usually at home), asks questions, and records answers. Researchers sample respondents from lists and telephone directories or use RDD and can quickly reach many people across all geographic areas. A staff of interviewers can interview 1,500 respondents across a nation within a few days and, with a dozen callbacks, achieve response rates as high as 80 percent. The telephone survey is more expensive than a mail questionnaire because it requires interviewer time. In general, the telephone interview is a flexible method with most of the strengths of face-to-face interviews but at a much lower cost. Interviewers control the sequence of questions and can use some probes. A specific respondent is chosen and is likely to answer all questions alone. We know when the questions were answered and can use contingency questions effectively.

Most researchers use computer-assisted technologies in telephone interviews, two of which

TABLE 10.4   Types of Surveys and Their Features

FEATURES	TYPE OF SURVEY			
	Mail Questionnaire	*Telephone Interview*	*Face-to-Face Interview*	*Web Survey*
Administrative Issues				
Cost	Cheap	Moderate	Expensive	Cheapest
Speed	Slowest	Fast	Slow to moderate	Fastest
Length (number of questions)	Moderate	Short	Longest	Moderate
Response rate	Lowest	Moderate	Highest	Moderate
Research Control				
Probes possible	No	Yes	Yes	No
Specific respondent	No	Yes	Yes	No
Question sequence	No	Yes	Yes	Yes
Only one respondent	No	Yes	Yes	No
Visual observation	No	No	Yes	Yes
Success with Different Questions				
Visual aids	Limited	None	Yes	Yes
Open-ended questions	Limited	Limited	Yes	Yes
Contingency questions	Limited	Yes	Yes	Yes
Complex questions	Limited	Limited	Yes	Yes
Sensitive questions	Some	Limited	Limited	Yes
Sources of Bias				
Social desirability	No	Some	Worse	No
Interviewer bias	No	Some	Worse	No
Respondent's reading skill level	Yes	No	No	Some

we discuss here. **Computer-assisted telephone interviewing (CATI)** systems are widely used.[51] When using CATI, the interviewer sits in front of a computer, which makes the calls. Wearing a headset and microphone, the interviewer reads the questions from a computer screen for the specific respondent called and then enters the answer via the computer keyboard. The computer program will control which question next appears and will allow for complex contingency questions. CATI speeds the process and reduces interviewer errors. It also eliminates the separate step of having the interviewer write responses on paper and then having someone else enter information into a computer, and speeds data collection.

Interactive voice response (IVR) includes several computer-automated systems available through phone technology and is widely used in marketing. IVR has a respondent listen to questions and response options over the telephone and indicate responses by touch-tone entry or by voice (the computer uses voice recognition software). IVR may

> **Computer-assisted telephone interviewing (CATI)** Technique in which the interviewer sits before a computer screen and keyboard, reads questions from the screen, and enters answers directly into the computer.
>
> **Interactive voice response (IVR)** A technique in telephone interviewing in which respondents hear computer-automated questions and indicate their responses by touch-tone phone entry or voice-activated software.

have some advantages over live interviewers, such as rapid and automated data collection, no interviewer reading or recording errors, and high anonymity. Some IVR interviewers have a live interviewer to recruit and set up the respondent and then records the questions following the setup. IVR can be successful for very short and very simple surveys.

Disadvantages. IVR has a sharp drop-off rate (as many as 40 percent not completing the long questionnaires).[52] Moderately high cost and limited interview length are also disadvantages of both CATI and traditional telephone interviews. In addition, the call may come at an inconvenient time and respondents without a telephone are impossible to reach. The use of an interviewer reduces anonymity but introduces potential interviewer bias. Open-ended questions are difficult to use, and questions requiring visual aids are impossible. Interviewers can note only serious disruptions (e.g., background noise) and respondent tone of voice (e.g., anger or flippancy) or hesitancy.

Survey researchers developed telephone interviewing when people had only landline phones. Increased cell phone use since 2000 has become an issue. As of 2006, about one in four adults aged 18 to 24 years in the United States lived in cell-phone-only households and are not covered by current RDD landline sampling procedures. The cell-phone-only population is likely to increase, suggesting a growing need to combine samples that include both cell phone and landline phone respondents. In comparison to landline surveys, cell phone surveys tend to have lower response rates, higher refusal rates, and lower rates of turning an initial refusal into participation. Early studies provide some suggestions for cell phone interviews such as calling during evening weekday hours, letting a cell phone ring longer than a landline, being extra alert to cues that suggest it is a bad time to do the interview (e.g., the respondent is operating a motor vehicle), needing to schedule a callback, and deciding how long to wait before recontacting the cell phone number.[53]

Face-to-Face Interviews

Advantages. Face-to-face interviews have the highest response rates and permit the longest and most complex questionnaires. They have all the advantages of the telephone interview and allow interviewers to observe the surroundings and to use nonverbal communication and visual aids. Well-trained interviewers can ask all types of questions and can use extensive probes.

Disadvantages. High cost is the biggest disadvantage of face-to-face interviews. The training, travel, supervision, and personnel costs for interviews can be high. Interviewer bias is also greatest in face-to-face interviews. The interviewer's appearance, tone of voice, question wording, and so forth may affect the respondent. In addition, interviewer supervision is lower than for telephone interviews that supervisors monitor by listening in.[54]

A variation on the face-to-face survey with questions on sensitive issues is CAPI (described earlier in the chapter). A CAPI interviewer with a laptop computer is present, and the respondent completes questions on the laptop. The interviewer serves to motivate completion and to clarify questions.

Web Surveys

The public did not have widespread access to the Internet and e-mail until the end of the 1990s. For example, in 1994, only 3 percent of the U.S. population had e-mail at home or work; by 2007, 62 percent of households had both e-mail and Internet connections. By 2012, some projections suggest that 77 percent of households will be connected. Internet connection rates are higher in other nations, for example, 97 percent in South Korea, 82 percent in the Netherlands, 81 percent in Hong King, 79 percent in Canada, and 77 percent in Japan.[55]

Advantages. Web-based or e-mail surveys are very fast and inexpensive; they allow flexible design and can use visual images and even audio or video. The two types of Web surveys are static and interactive. A static Web or e-mail survey is like the presentation of a page of paper but on the computer screen. An interactive Web or e-mail survey has contingency questions and may present different questions to different respondents based on prior answers.

Disadvantages. An unusual disadvantage of Web surveys is that they are cheap and easy. As Weisberg (2005:38) remarked: "Putting a poll up on the Internet can be inexpensive, so many groups put up polls without paying attention to quality." Web surveys have three disadvantages or areas of concern: coverage, privacy and verification, and design issues. The first concern involves sampling and unequal access to and use of the Internet. Older, less educated, low-income, and rural people are less likely to have access, and a majority without access now say that they do not plan to acquire it in the future. In addition, many people have multiple e-mail addresses.

A second concern involves protecting respondent privacy. Secure Web sites with passwords or PINs and high confidentiality protection can help. Respondent verification is needed to ensure that the sampled respondent alone participates and only once.

A third concern involves design complexity and flexibility. The compatibility of various Web software and hardware combinations must be verified. We are just beginning to learn the most effective way to design Web surveys. For example, it appears best to provide one or a few questions per screen, making the entire question visible on the screen at one time in a consistent format with drop-down boxes for answer choices. It is best to include a progress indicator (as motivation) such as a clock or symbol indicating progress (how far respondents have gone and how much questionnaire remains). Keeping visual appearance simple (limited colors and fonts) and maintaining consistency is best. Very clear instructions are needed for any computer action (e.g., use of drop-down screens) and they should include "click here" instructions. Also, making it easy for respondents to move back and forth across questions is best. Providing detailed questions and a large space for answers in open-ended questions on Internet surveys helps elicit longer and more complete answers. Avoiding technical glitches and "bugs" at the implementation stage with dedicated servers and sufficient broadband to handle demand is important.[56]

Special Situations

There are many kinds of special surveys. One is a survey of organizations (e.g., businesses, schools). We write questions to ask about the organization but also to learn who in the organization has necessary information. Making the significance of the survey clear is also essential because officials in an organization receive many requests for information and do not answer all of them.

Surveying white-collar elites requires special techniques.[57] Powerful leaders in business, the media, and government are difficult to reach. Assistants frequently intercept mail questionnaires or restrict access to face-to-face or telephone interviewing. One way to facilitate access is to have a respected source call or send a letter of introduction. After making an appointment, the researcher him- or herself, not a hired interviewer, needs to conduct the interview. Personal interviews with a high percentage of open-ended questions are usually more successful than those with all closed-ended questions. Confidentiality is a crucial issue because elites often have information that few others do and are very sensitive about being identified as having provided specific information.

The **time budget survey** is a special type used to study how people allocate their time. Studies of urban planning, the gender division of labor, quality of life, mass media usage, and leisure use time budget surveys. A respondent to a time budget survey agrees to record her or his activities in detail over several days, usually in a diary, noting activities for each 10- or 15-minute period. For example, about 10 years ago, several professors who work at my university were asked to be part of a time budget survey. Government officials who wanted to learn how much time professors devoted to academic work activities initiated the survey. The professors filled in a detailed diary, recording what they did for each 15-minute period at home and work for a two-week period. The officials thought that professors

---

Time budget survey A specialized type in which respondents record details about the timing and duration of their activities over a period of time.

worked too little. As with dozens of other such time budget surveys when all meetings, community service activities, research work, course preparation and planning, exam writing and grading, paper evaluation, student advising, and direct teaching time are totaled, most professors work 55 to 60 hours a week. By the way, undergraduate students tend to believe that professors put in about 40 hours a week.[58]

Costs

Professional-quality survey research can be expensive if we consider all of the costs, which vary according to the type of survey used. A simple formula is that for every $1 in cost for a mail survey, a telephone interview survey costs about $5 and a face-to-face interview about $25. Internet surveys can cost almost nothing except setup time.

Costs vary greatly.[59] Beyond modest supply costs, the highest expenses are labor costs to hire professional staff (who develop and pilot test a questionnaire) to hire clerical staff and interviewers, and to train interviewers. Beginning researchers tend to underestimate all of the expenses and time required. In 2008, a two-page mail questionnaire sent to 300 respondents cost me $2,500, or about $8.30 each. This did not include payment for writing and checking the questionnaire or for statistically analyzing the data. With a 60 percent response rate (180 returns), the real cost was closer to $13.90 per completed questionnaire.

Professional survey organizations often charge $75 or more for a completed 15-minute telephone interview. The costs for a face-to-face interview study are higher. A professionally completed face-to-face interview can cost more than $200, depending on the interview length and travel expenses. At one extreme, a face-to-face survey of 1,000 geographically dispersed respondents from the public can cost more than $300,000 and require a year to complete. At the other extreme, a simple one-page, self-administered questionnaire that a teacher photocopies and distributes to 100 students in one school can cost very little except for the teacher's time and effort. The teacher might be able to prepare and distribute the questionnaire, collect responses, and tabulate results in as little as one week.

SURVEY INTERVIEWING

Over the decades, our knowledge of interviewing errors evolved in three stages. During the 1960s and 1970s, we focused on how to stop mistakes because a respondent was not being fully committed to the seriousness of the survey interview situation. To improve survey interviews, we told interviewers to emphasize the importance of complete and accurate answers or to model proper respondent behavior. By the 1980s–1990s, improving interviews shifted to standardizing interviewer behavior. We carefully trained interviewers to read each survey question exactly as written, to use neutral probes, to record respondent answers verbatim, and to be very nonjudgmental. We emphasized making each interview situation an identical experience.

The standard interview is based on the **naïve assumption model** (see Foddy, 1993:13). We sought to reduce any gap between actual experience in conducting surveys and the ideal survey as expressed in the model's assumptions (see Expansion Box 10.11, Naïve Assumption Model of Survey Interviews on page 342).

By 2000, some researchers advocated abandoning the standardized approach and using an alternative interview format, a flexible or **conversational interview**, which is based on the collaborative encounter model (discussed later in this chapter). The interview is treated as a social situation in which respondents must interpret the meaning of a survey question. Interviewers collaborate with respondents or assist so that respondents accurately grasp the researcher's intent in a question. The interviewers actively work to improve accuracy on questions about complex issues or

Naïve assumption model   A particular standardized survey research type in which there are no communication problems and respondents' responses perfectly match their thoughts.

Conversational interview   A flexible technique based on the collaborative encounter model in which interviewers adjust interviewing questions to the understanding of specific respondents but maintain the resesearcher's intent in each question.

Naïve Assumption Model of Survey Interviews

1. Researchers have clearly conceptualized all variables being measured.
2. Questionnaires have no wording, question order, or related effects.
3. Respondents are motivated and willing to answer all questions asked.
4. Respondents possess complete information and can accurately recall events.
5. Respondents understand each question exactly as the reseacher intends it.
6. Respondents give more truthful answers if they do not know the hypotheses.
7. Respondents give more truthful answers if they receive no hints or suggestions.
8. The interview situation and specific interviewers have no effects on answers.
9. The process of the interview has no impact on the respondents' beliefs or attitudes.
10. Respondents' behaviors match perfectly their verbal responses in an interview.

about which respondents have difficulty expressing their thoughts.

Most professional survey researchers still rely on standardized interviewing and question the validity of conversational interviewing. They believe interviewer effects will distort or bias respondent answers. However, both approaches to interviewing have their defenders. Advocates of a standardized interview approach believe more refined survey question wording can resolve any respondent misinterpretations. Advocates of conversational interviewing emphasize the fluid nature of social interactions and the different social realities or understandings held by socially diverse respondents. These advocates say that the goal is to create a common interpretation of the survey researcher's intent behind a question, not to repeat the same words in a question. To achieve a common interpretation among diverse respondents, an interviewer may have to ask some respondents the question in different ways. Only a highly trained, socially adept interviewer who has a deep understanding of the researcher's intent in each survey question may be able to reach a shared understanding of that intent with many diverse respondents. We can trace the cause of the standard versus the conversational interview disagreement to the assumptions of the positivist versus interpretative approaches to social science that you read about in Chapter 4.[60]

The Role of the Interviewer

Interviews to gather information occur in many settings. Employers interview prospective employees, medical personnel interview patients, mental health professionals interview clients, social service workers interview people who are needy, reporters interview politicians and others, police officers interview witnesses and crime victims, and talk show hosts interview celebrities (see Expansion Box 10.12, Types of Nonresearch Interviews). Survey research interviewing is a specialized type of interviewing. As with most interviewing, its goal is to obtain accurate information from another person.[61]

The interview is a short-term, secondary social interaction between two strangers with the explicit purpose of one person obtaining specific information from the other. The social roles are those of the interviewer and the interviewee or respondent. Interaction takes the form of a structured conversation in which the interviewer asks prearranged questions and the respondent gives answers, which the interviewer records. It differs in several ways from ordinary conversation (see Table 10.5 on page 344).

Interviewers often find that respondents are unfamiliar with a survey respondent's role and "respondents often do not have a clear conception of what is expected of them" (Turner and Martin, 1984:282). As a result, respondents may substitute a role with which they are familiar (e.g., an intimate conversation or therapy session, a bureaucratic exercise in completing forms, a citizen referendum on policy choices, a testing situation, or a form of deceit in which interviewers are try to entrap respondents). Even for a well-designed, professional survey, follow-up studies found that only half of respondents understand questions exactly as intended by researchers. Respondents often

EXPANSION BOX 10.12

Types of Nonresearch Interviews

1. *Job interview.* An employer asks open-ended questions to gather information about a candidate for a job and to observe how the candidate presents himself or herself. The candidate (respondent) initiates the contact and attempts to present a positive self-image. The employer (interviewer) tries to discover the candidate's true talents and flaws. A serious, judgmental tone exists with the employer having the power to accept or reject the candidate. This often creates tension and limited trust. The parties may have conflicting goals, and each may use some deception. The results are not confidential.

2. *Assistance interview.* A helping professional (counselor, lawyer, social worker, medical doctor, etc.) seeks information on a client's problem, including background and current conditions. The helping professional (interviewer) uses the information to understand and translate the client's (respondent's) problem into professional terms for problem resolution. The tone is serious and concerned. There is usually low tension and high mutual trust. The parties share the goal of resolving the client's problem, and deception is rare. The interview results are usually confidential.

3. *Journalistic interview.* A journalist gathers information from a celebrity, newsmaker, witness, or background person for later use in constructing a newsworthy story. The journalist (interviewer) uses various skills in attempting to get novel information, some that may not be easily revealed, and "quotable quotes" from the news source (respondent). The journalist uses the interview information selectively in combination with other information, usually beyond the respondent's control. The tone and degree of trust and tension vary greatly. The goals of the parties may diverge, and each may use deception. The interview results are not confidential and they may get a lot of publicity.

4. *Interrogation or investigative interview.* A criminal justice official, auditor, or other person in authority seriously asks questions to obtain information from an accused person or others with information about wrongdoing. The official (interviewer) will use the information as evidence to construct a case against someone (possibly the respondent). The tension is often extreme with mutual distrust. The goals of the parties diverge sharply, and each often uses deception. Interview results are rarely confidential and may become part of an official, public record.

5. *Entertainment interview.* An emcee or show host offers comments and asks open-ended questions to a celebrity or other person who may digress in answers or begin a monologue. The primary goal is to stimulate interest, enjoyment, or gaiety among an audience. Often, the style displayed by each is more central than any information revealed. The host (interviewer) seeks an immediate response or reaction in the audience, while the celebrity (respondent) tries to increase his or her fame or reputation. The tone is light, tension is low, and trust is moderately high. The limited goals of each often converge. They may deceive each other or join in deceiving the audience. The situation is the opposite to one in which confidentiality can occur.

People can mix the types of interviews, and people often use several types. For example, the social worker in a social control role instead of a helping role may conduct an investigative interview. Or a police officer helping a crime victim may use an assistance interview instead of an interrogation.

---

reinterpreted questions to make them applicable to their own idiosynactic, personal situations or to make them easy to answer.[62]

Interviewers have a difficult role. They encroach on the respondents' time and privacy, seeking cooperation and building rapport to obtain information that may not directly benefit the respondents. They may have to explain the nature of survey research or give hints about social roles in an interview. At the same time, interviewers must remain neutral and objective. They try to reduce embarrassment, fear, and suspicion so that respondents feel comfortable revealing information. Good interviewers monitor the pace and direction of the social interaction as well as the content of answers and the behavior of respondents.

TABLE 10.5   Differences between Ordinary Conversation and a Structured Survey Interview

ORDINARY CONVERSATION	THE SURVEY INTERVIEW
1. Questions and answers from each participant are relatively equally balanced.	1. Interviewer asks and respondent answers most of the time.
2. There is an open exchange of feelings and opinions.	2. Only the respondent reveals feelings and opinions.
3. Judgments are stated and attempts made to persuade the other of particular points of view.	3. Interviewer is nonjudgmental and does not try to change respondent's opinions or beliefs.
4. A person can reveal deep inner feelings to gain sympathy or as a therapeutic release.	4. Interviewer tries to obtain direct answers to specific questions.
5. Ritual responses are common (e.g., "Uh huh," shaking head, "How are you?" "Fine").	5. Interviewer avoids making ritual responses that influence a respondent and seeks genuine answers, not ritual responses.
6. The participants exchange information and correct the factual errors that they are aware of.	6. Respondent provides almost all information. Interviewer does not correct a respondent's factual errors.
7. Topics rise and fall, and either person can introduce new topics. The focus can shift directions or digress to less relevant issues.	7. Interviewer controls the topic, direction, and pace. He or she keeps the respondent "on task," and irrelevant diversions are contained.
8. The emotional tone can shift from humor, to joy, to affection, to sadness, to anger, and so on.	8. Interviewer attempts to maintain a consistently warm but serious and objective tone throughout.
9. People can evade or ignore questions and give flippant or noncommittal answers.	9. Respondent should not evade questions and should give truthful, thoughtful answers.

Source: Adapted from Gorden (1980:19–25) and Sudman and Bradburn (1983:5–10).

Survey interviewers are nonjudgmental and do not reveal their opinions, verbally or nonverbally. For example, if the respondent gives a shocking answer (e.g., "I was arrested three times for beating my infant daughter and burning her with cigarettes"), the interviewer does not show shock, surprise, or disdain but treats the answer in a matter-of-fact manner. Interviewers help respondents feel that they can give any truthful answer. If a respondent asks for an interviewer's opinion, he or she politely redirects the respondent and indicates that such questions are inappropriate. For example, if a respondent asks "What do you think?" the interviewer may answer "Here we are interested in what *you* think; what I think doesn't matter."

An interviewer helps define the situation and ensures that respondents have the information sought, understand what is expected, give relevant and serious answers, and are motivated to cooperate. Interviewers do more than interview respondents. Face-to-face interviewers spend only about 35 percent of their time interviewing. About 40 percent is spent locating the correct respondent, 15 percent traveling, and 10 percent studying survey materials and dealing with administrative and recording details.[63]

Stages of an Interview

The interview proceeds through stages, beginning with an introduction and entry. For a face-to-face interview, the interviewer gets in the door, shows authorization, and reassures the respondent and secures his or her cooperation. The interviewer is prepared for reactions such as "How did you pick me?" "What good will this do?" "I don't know about this." "What's this about, anyway?" The interviewer explains why a specific respondent, not a substitute, must be interviewed.

The interview's main part consists of asking questions and recording answers. In a standard interview (not conversational), the interviewer uses the exact wording on the questionnaire, adds or omits no words, does not rephrase, and asks questions in order without returning to or skipping questions. He or she goes at a comfortable pace and gives nondirective feedback to maintain interest.

In addition to asking questions, the interviewer accurately records answers. This is easy for closed-ended questions, for which interviewers just mark the correct box. For open-ended questions, the interviewer's job is more difficult. He or she listens carefully, must write legibly, and must record what is said verbatim without correcting grammar or slang. More important, the interviewer never summarizes or paraphrases. Doing so causes a loss of information or distorts answers. For example, the respondent says, "I'm really concerned about my daughter's heart problem. She's only 10 years old and already she has trouble climbing stairs. I don't know what she'll do when she gets older. Heart surgery is too risky for her and it costs so much. She'll have to learn to live with it." If the interviewer writes, "concerned about daughter's health," much is lost.

The interviewer knows how and when to use a **probe**, a neutral request to clarify an ambiguous answer, to complete an incomplete answer, or to obtain a relevant response. Interviewers recognize an irrelevant or inaccurate answer and use probes as needed.[64] There are many types of probes. A 3- to 5-second pause is often effective. Nonverbal communication (e.g., tilt of head, raised eyebrows, or eye contact) also works well. The interviewer can repeat the question or repeat the reply and then pause. She or he can ask a neutral question, such as "Any other reasons?" "Can you tell me more about that?" "How do you mean that?" "Could you explain more for me?" (see Expansion Box 10.13, Example of Probes and Recording Full Responses to Closed Questions).

Respondents often interpret straightforward questions differently than the survey designer intended. For example, "Inaccurate reporting is not a response tendency or a predisposition to be untruthful. Individuals who are truthful on one occasion or in response to particular questions may not be truthful at other times or to other questions" (Wentworth, 1993:130).

Techniques to reduce misunderstanding, such as conversational interviewing, deviate from the standardized interview model. Beyond concerns about introducing bias, conversational interviewing requires more time and more intense interviewer training. Yet as Conrad and Schober (2000:20) have observed, respondent "comprehension can be made more consistent—and responses more comparable—when certain interviewer behaviors (discussions about the meaning of questions) are *less* consistent." Paradoxically, nonstandardized interviewing can increase reliability by improving the consistency in how respondents interpret the meaning of survey questions and responses.

Given this complexity and possible distortion, what should the diligent survey researcher do? We should at least supplement closed-ended questionnaires with open-ended questions and probes. Open-ended questions take more time, require better-trained interviewers, and produce responses that may be less standardized and more difficult to quantify. Fixed-answer questionnaires based on the naïve assumption model imply a more simple and mechanical way of responding than occurs in many situations. The inquiry into interviewer bias, cultural meanings, and the interview as a social situation provides a lesson in how qualitative and quantitative styles of social research complement one another. In all research we strive to eliminate sources of interviewer bias and respondent confusion. In the past decade quantitative survey researchers discovered that qualitative researchers offer valuable insights into how people construct meaning in diverse social settings.

Probe   A follow-up question asked by an interviewer to elicit an appropriate response when a respondent's answer is unclear or incomplete.

EXPANSION BOX 10.13
Example of Probes and Recording Full Responses to Closed Questions

Interviewer question: What is your occupation?

Respondent answer: I work at General Motors.
  Probe: What is your job at General Motors? What type of work do you do there?

Interviewer question: How long have you been unemployed?

Respondent answer: A long time.
  Probe: Could you tell me more specifically when your current period of unemployment began?

Interviewer question: Considering the country as a whole, do you think we will have good times during the next year, or bad times, or what?

Respondent answer: Maybe good, maybe bad, it depends, who knows?
  Probe: What do you expect to happen?

Record Response to a Closed Question
Interviewer question: On a scale of 1 to 7, how do you feel about capital punishment or the death penalty, where 1 is strongly in favor of the death penalty, and 7 is strongly opposed to it? (Favor) 1 _ 2 _ 3 _ 4 _ 5 _ 6 _ 7 _ (Oppose)

Respondent answer: About a 4. I think that all murderers, rapists, and violent criminals should get death, but I don't favor it for minor crimes like stealing a car.

The last interview stage is the exit when the interviewer thanks the respondent and leaves. The interviewer usually goes to a quiet, private place to edit the questionnaire and record other details such as the date, time, and place of the interview. Often interviewers write a thumbnail sketch of the respondent and interview situation, including the respondent's attitude (e.g., serious, angry, or laughing) and any unusual circumstances (e.g., "Telephone rang at question 27 and respondent talked for 4 minutes before the interview started again"). He or she notes anything disruptive that happened during the interview (e.g., "Teenage son entered room, sat at opposite end, turned on television with the volume loud, and watched a baseball game"). The interviewer also records his or her personal feelings and anything that was suspected (e.g., "Respondent became nervous and fidgeted when questioned about his marriage").

Training of Interviewers

A large-scale survey requires hiring multiple interviewers.[65] A professional-quality interview requires carefully selecting interviewers and providing them with rigorous training. As with any employment situation, adequate pay and good supervision are important for consistent high-quality performance. Unfortunately, professional interviewing has not always paid well or provided regular employment. In the past, most interviewers were middle-aged women willing to accept irregular part-time work. Good interviewers are pleasant, honest, accurate, mature, responsible, moderately intelligent, stable, and motivated. They have a nonthreatening appearance, have experience with many types of people, and possess poise and tact. If the survey involves interviewing in high-crime areas, interviewers need to be protected.

We may consider interviewers' physical appearance, age, race, gender, languages spoken, and even the voice (see interviewer bias discussion later in this chapter). For example, in a study using trained female telephone interviewers from homogeneous social backgrounds, Oksenberg and colleagues (1986) found fewer refusals for interviewers whose voices had higher pitch and more pitch variation and who spoke louder and faster with clear pronunciation and sounded more pleasant and cheerful. Most training programs for professional interviewers are 2 weeks long. They usually include a mix of lectures and reading, observation of expert interviewers, mock interviews in the office and in the field that are recorded and critiqued, many practice interviews, and role-playing. The interviewers learn about survey research and the role of the interviewer. They become familiar with the questionnaire and the purpose of questions, although not with the answers expected.

Although interviewers largely work alone, researchers use an interviewer supervisor in large-scale surveys with multiple interviewers. Supervisors are familiar with the location, assist with problems, oversee the interviewers, and ensure that work is completed on time. For telephone interviewing, supervisors help with calls, check when interviewers arrive and leave, and monitor interview calls. In face-to-face interviews, supervisors check to find out whether the interview actually took place. This means calling back or sending a confirmation postcard to a sample of respondents. Supervisors can also check the response rate and incomplete questionnaires to see whether interviewers are obtaining cooperation, and they may reinterview a small subsample, analyze answers, or observe interviews to see whether interviewers are accurately asking questions and recording answers.

Interviewer Bias

Survey researchers proscribe interviewer behavior to reduce bias. Ideally, the actions of a particular interviewer will not affect how a respondent answers, and responses will not vary from what they would have been if asked by any other interviewer.

Proscribed behavior for interviewers goes beyond instructions to read each question exactly as worded, and interview bias takes many forms (see Expansion Box 10.14, Six Categories of Interview Bias).

We are still learning about the factors that influence survey interviews. We know that interviewer expectations can create significant bias. Interviewers who expect difficult interviews have them, and those who expect certain answers are more likely to get them (see Chart 10.1 on page 348). Proper interviewer behavior and exact question reading may be difficult, but there are many other forms of interview bias.

Interviewer bias can arise from expectations based on a respondent's age and race. In a major national U.S. survey, researchers learned that interviewers regularly coded Black respondents as being less intelligent and coded younger respondents as both less intelligent and less informed. Better interviewer training is needed to reduce such bias in survey results.[66]

EXPANSION BOX 10.14
Six Categories of Interview Bias

1. *Errors by the respondent.* Forgetting, embarrassment, misunderstanding, or lying because of the presence of others
2. *Unintentional errors or interviewer sloppiness.* Contacting the wrong respondent, misreading a question, omitting questions, reading questions in the wrong order, recording the wrong answer to a question, or misunderstanding the respondent
3. *Intentional subversion by the interviewer.* Purposeful alteration of answers, omission or rewording of questions, or choice of an alternative respondent
4. *Influence due to the interviewer's expectations* about a respondent's answers based on the respondent's appearance, living situation, or other answers
5. *Failure of an interviewer to probe* or to probe properly
6. *Influence on the answers due to the interviewer's appearance,* tone, attitude, reactions to answers, or comments made outside the interview schedule

CHART 10.1 Interviewer Characteristics Can Affect Responses

EXAMPLE OF INTERVIEWER EXPECTATION EFFECTS

Asked by Female Interviewer Whose Own	*Female Respondent Reports That Husband Buys Most Furniture*
Husband buys most furniture	89%
Husband does not buy most furniture	15

EXAMPLE OF RACE OR ETHNIC APPEARANCE EFFECTS

	PERCENTAGE ANSWERING YES TO	
Interviewer	*"Do you think there are too many Jews in government jobs?"*	*"Do you think that Jews have too much power?"*
Looked Jewish with Jewish-sounding name	11.7%	5.8%
Looked Jewish only	15.4	15.6
Non-Jewish appearance	21.2	24.3
Non-Jewish appearance and non-Jewish-sounding name	19.5	21.4

Note: Racial stereotypes held by respondents can affect how they respond in interviews.

Source: Adapted from *Interviewing in social research* by Herbert H. Hyman with William J. Cobb et al.; foreword by Samuel A. Stouffer. © 1954, 1975 University of Chicago Press, p. 153.

The interview setting can affect answers. For example, high school students answer differently depending on whether we interview them at home or at school. The presence of other people often affects responses, so usually we do not want others present.[67] For example, Zipp and Toth (2002) found greater agreement on numerous attitude items when a spouse was present at an interview; wives modified their answers to conform to their husbands' responses and husbands' changed little.

An interviewer's visible physical characteristics, including race and gender, can affect respondent answers, especially for questions about issues related to race or gender. For example, African American and Hispanic American respondents express different policy positions on race- or ethnic-related issues depending on the apparent race or ethnicity of the interviewer. This occurs even with telephone interviews when a respondent has clues about the interviewer's race or ethnicity. In general, interviewers of the same racial-ethnic group get

more accurate answers than does an interviewer of a different background. Gender also affects interviews both in terms of obvious issues, such as sexual behavior, as well as support for gender-related collective action or gender equality. Yet, as Weisberg (2006:61) noted, "Interviewer matching is rarely used in the United States, except when it is necessary to use interviewers who can speak another language. . . . Interview matching is more necessary in some other countries, as in Arab countries where it would be considered inappropriate for an interviewer of one gender to speak with a respondent of another gender."[68]

Interviewer characteristics can influence answers in many ways. For example, when the interviewer was a person with disabilities, respondents lowered their self-reported level of "happiness" compared to answering a self-administered questionnaire. Apparently, they did not want to sound too well off compared to the interviewer. However, when respondents completed a self-administered questionnaire while a person with disabilities was in the same room, they reported higher levels of happiness. Apparently, respondents felt comparatively better off due to the physical presence of the person with the disability compared to situations in which there was no immediate reminder of the life situations of others.[69] A respondent who answers identical questions differently depending on features of an interviewer threatens representative reliability (you read about representative reliability in Chapter 7).

Cultural Meanings and Survey Interviews

Research into survey errors and interview bias has advanced information about how people create meaning and achieve cultural understanding.[70] We are troubled when a word has different meanings and implications depending on the social situation, who speaks it, how it is spoken, and the social distance between the speaker and listener. Survey research is complicated when respondents misinterpret the nature of survey research and seek clues for how to answer in the wording of questions or subtle actions of the interviewer. Moreover, "it is important not to lose sight of the fact that the interview setting is itself distinct from other settings in which attitudes are expressed, and hence we should not expect to find complete congruence between attitudes expressed in interviews and in other social contexts."[71]

We face a dilemma: An interviewer who strives to act in a neutral and uniform way reduces the type of bias that causes unreliability because of individual interviewer behavior, yet such attempts cause other problems according to interpretive or critical social science researchers, including feminist researchers (see Expansion Box 10.15, Interviewing: Positivist and Feminist Approaches on page 350).[70]

Nonpositivist researchers argue that meaning is created in social context; therefore, standard survey question wording will not produce the same meaning for all respondents. For example, some respondents express feelings by telling stories instead of answering straightforward questions with fixed answers. Nonpositivist researchers advocate the **collaborative encounter model** of the survey

situation. This model views all human encounters as highly dynamic, complex mutual interactions in which even minor, unintended forms of feedback (e.g., saying hmmm, laughing, smiling, nodding) have an influence, and suggests conversational interviewing. The collaborative encounter model also allows interviewers to incorporate information offered by respondents in response to fixed-choice questions that the standardized interview prohibits or treats as an error because it does not correspond to a preset, standardized format.

According to the collaborative encounter model, in complex human interactions, people add interpretative meaning to simple questions. For example, my neighbor asks me the simple question, "How often do you mow your lawn?" I could interpret his question in the following ways:

How often do I personally mow the lawn (versus having someone else mow it for me)?

How often do I mow it to cut grass (versus run my lawnmower over it to chop up leaves)?

How often do I mow the entire lawn (versus cutting the quick-growing parts only)?

How often do I mow it during an entire season, a month, a week?

How often do I mow it most seasons (versus last year when my lawnmower was broken several times and it was very dry and the grass grew less, so I did not mow it as frequently)?

Within seconds, I make an interpretation and give an answer, but the open-ended, ongoing interaction between myself and the neighbor permits me to ask for clarification and for several follow-up questions that help us arrive at mutual understanding.

A survey interview interaction differs from ordinary conversation. The standard survey research interview is an artificial interaction that treats diverse

---

Collaborative encounter model   A particular survey interview in which the respondent and interviewer work together to reach the meaning of the survey question as intended by the researcher and produce an accurate response to it.

Interviewing: Positivist and Feminist Approaches

In this chapter, we have mostly considered the positivist approach to survey research interviewing. In the ideal survey interview, the interviewer withholds her or his own feelings and beliefs. The interviewer should be so objective and neutral that it should be possible to substitute another interviewer and obtain the same responses.

Feminist researchers approach interviewing very differently. Feminist interviewing is similar to qualitative interviewing (to be discussed in Chapter 14). Oakley (1981) criticized positivist survey interviewing as being part of a masculine paradigm. It is a social situation in which the interviewer exercises control and dominance while suppressing the expression of personal feelings. The interview is manipulative and instrumental. The interviewer and the respondent become merely the vehicles for obtaining the objective data.

The goals of feminist research vary, but two common goals are to give greater visibility to the subjective experience of women and to increase the involvement of the respondent in the research process. Features of feminist interviewing include the following:

- A preference for an unstructured and open-ended format
- A preference for interviewing a person more than once
- Creation of social connections and building a trusting social relationship
- Disclosure of personal experiences by the interviewer
- Encouragement of female skills of being open, receptive, and understanding
- Avoidance of control and encouragement of equality by downplaying professional status
- Careful listening; interviewers become emotionally engaged with respondents
- Respondent-oriented direction, not researcher oriented or questionnaire oriented
- Encouragement of respondents to express themselves in ways they are most comfortable—for example, by telling stories or following digressions
- Creation of a sense of empowerment and an esprit de corps among women

respondents alike to control the communication situation and yield a uniform measure. Ordinary interaction contains built-in features to detect and correct misinterpretation; it relies on nuance and give and take. People achieve social meaning in ordinary conversation by relying on clues in the context, adjusting the interaction flow to specific people involved, and building on a cultural frame (often based on race, class, gender, region, or religion). The fluid interaction of ordinary conversation is self-adjusting because different people do not always assign the same meaning to the same words, phases, and questions. For example, men and women report health differently. A man saying he is in excellent health

means something different from a woman answering the same question with the same response. By standardizing human interaction, the survey interview strips away features in ordinary conversation that provide self-correction, promote the construction of a shared meaning among different people, and increase human mutual understanding.[73]

Pilot Testing and Cognitive Interviews

It is important to pilot test survey interviews and questionnaires prior to implementation. Systematic study of pilot tests in the survey process and models of cognitive processing has helped us better understand the survey process. We see that the process of answering survey questions has several steps: interpret and comprehend the question, retrieve relevant information, integrate and evaluate the information, and select a response category. A recent area of study is cognitive testing or **cognitive interviewing** in which we study how respondents answer questions in pilot test situations.[74]

Cognitive interviewing   A technique used in pilot testing surveys in which researchers try to learn about a questionnaire and improve it by interviewing respondents about their thought processes or having respondents "think out loud" as they answer survey questions.

Cognitive interviewing helps us to identify problems in questionnaires under development by asking a small number of pretest participants to verbally report their thinking while answering the draft questions. It provides a window into respondents' thinking and problems they face when answering survey questions. Cognitive interviewers probe for additional information about the process of answering questions. We use this information to refine the questionnaire or interviewing process (see Expansion Box 10.16, Methods of Improving Questionnaire with Pilot Tests).

Another related development draws on ethnomethodology (see Chapter 13 for a discussion of this) and conversation analysis to study the interview process as a special type of social interaction

and speech event. These approaches support the collaborative encounter model and suggest treating nonstandardized interview behaviors, such as respondent queries or minor forms of interviewer feedback (saying hmmm, laughing, smiling) as opportunities to learn more about the interview.[75]

THE ETHICAL SURVEY

Like all social research, we can conduct surveys in ethical or unethical ways. A major ethical issue in survey research is the invasion of privacy.[76] People have a right to privacy. Respondents have a right to decide when and to whom to reveal personal information. We intrude into a respondent's privacy by asking about intimate actions and personal beliefs. Respondents are likely to provide such information accurately and honestly when asked for it in a comfortable context with mutual respect and trust. They are most likely to answer when they believe we want serious answers for legitimate research purposes and when they believe answers will remain confidential. We need to treat all respondents with dignity, reduce discomfort, and protect the confidentiality of survey data.

A second issue involves voluntary participation by respondents. Respondents can agree to answer questions or refuse to participate at any time. They give "informed consent" to participate in research. We depend on respondents' voluntary cooperation and need to ask well-developed questions in a sensitive way, treat respondents with respect, and be very sensitive to confidentiality.

A third ethical issue is the exploitation of surveys and pseudosurveys. Because of its popularity, some organizations and people have used surveys to mislead others. A **pseudosurvey** is a survey format that is used in an attempt to persuade someone to do something and has little or no real interest in learning information from a respondent. Charlatans

---

EXPANSION BOX 10.16

Methods of Improving Questionnaire with Pilot Tests

1. *Think aloud interviews.* A respondent explains his or her thinking out loud during the process of answering each question.
2. *Retrospective interviews and targeted probes.* After completing a questionnaire, the respondent explains to researchers the process used to select each response or answer.
3. *Expert evaluation.* An independent panel of experienced survey researchers reviews and critiques the questionnaire.
4. *Behavior coding.* Researchers closely monitor interviews, often using audio or videotapes, for misstatements, hesitations, missed instructions, nonresponse, refusals, puzzled looks, answers that do not fit any of the response categories, and so forth.
5. *Field experiments.* Researchers administer alternative forms of the questionnaire items in field settings and compare results.
6. *Vignettes and debriefing.* Interviewers and respondents are presented with short, invented "lifelike" situations and asked which questionnaire response category they would use.

Sources: Dillman and Redine (2004), Fowler (2004), Martin (2004, Tourangeau (2004a, 2004b), van der Zouwen and Smit (2004), and Willis (2004).

Pseudosurvey A false and deceptive survey-like instrument using the format of a survey interview but whose true purpose is to persuade a respondent.

use the guise of conducting a survey to invade privacy, gain entry into homes, or "suggle" (sell in the guise of a survey). An example of a pseudosurvey occurred during the 1994 U.S. election campaign with "suppression polls" in which an unknown survey organization telephoned a potential voter and asked whether the voter supported a given candidate. If the voter supported the candidate, the interviewer asked whether the respondent would still support the candidate if he or she knew that the candidate had an unfavorable characteristic (e.g., had been arrested for drunk driving, used illegal drugs, raised the wages of convicted criminals in prison). The goal of the interview was not to measure candidate support; rather, it was to identify a candidate's supporters and then attempt to suppress voting. I received such calls, as did an unsuccessful candidate for governor who was the object of the suppression poll. No one has been prosecuted for using this campaign tactic.

Another ethical issue is the misuse of survey results or use of poorly designed or purposely rigged surveys. People may demand answers from surveys that surveys cannot provide or they do not appreciate the limitations of survey data. Also, people who design and prepare surveys may lack sufficient training about conducting a legitimate survey. Policy decisions made based on careless or poorly designed surveys may result in waste and human hardship. Such misuse makes it important for you to learn about the complexity of survey research and to conduct only methodologically sound survey research studies.

Another issue is that the mass media's reporting of survey results can permit abuse.[77] Few people reading survey results may appreciate them, but we should always include details about the survey (see Expansion Box 10.17, Ten Items to Include When Reporting Survey Research) to reduce the misuse of survey research and increase questions about surveys that lack such information. More than 88 percent of reports on surveys in the mass media fail to reveal the researcher who conducted the survey, and only 18 percent provide details on how the survey was conducted.[78] We urge the media to include such information, especially because the

---

EXPANSION BOX **10.17**

Ten Items to Include When Reporting Survey Research

1. The sampling frame used (e.g., telephone directories)
2. The dates on which the survey was conducted
3. The population that the sample represents (e.g., U.S. adults, Australian college students)
4. The size of the sample for which information was collected
5. The sampling method (e.g., random)
6. The exact wording of the questions asked
7. The method of the survey (e.g., face to face, telephone)
8. The organization(s) that sponsored the survey (who paid for it and conducted it)
9. The response rate or percentage of those contacted who actually completed the questionnaire
10. Any missing information or "don't know" responses when results on specific questions are reported

---

media report more surveys than other types of social research.

Currently, there are no quality-control standards to regulate the U.S. media's reporting of opinion polls or surveys. For nearly 50 years the professional survey research community has sought, without success, to have media only report studies with adequate scientific samples, rigorous interviewer training and supervision, satisfactory questionnaire design, public availability of data, and controls on the integrity of survey organizations.[79] Unfortunately, the mass media report both biased, misleading survey results and results from rigorous, professional surveys without distinction. It is not surprising that public confusion regarding and a distrust of all surveys occur.

CONCLUSION

In this chapter, you read about survey research. The survey is the most widely used social research technique. You also read about some principles of writing good survey questions. There are many things to avoid and to include when writing questions. The chapter presented the advantages and disadvantages of various types of survey research and noted that interviewing, especially face-to-face interviewing, can be difficult.

Although this chapter focused on survey research, we use questionnaires to measure variables in other types of quantitative research (e.g., experiments). The survey, often called the *sample survey* because random sampling is usually used with it, is a distinct technique. It is a process of asking many people the same questions and examining their answers.

Survey researchers try to minimize errors, but survey data often contain them. Errors in surveys can compound each other. For example, errors can arise in sampling frames, from nonresponse, from question wording or order, and from interviewer bias. Do not let the potential for errors discourage you from using the survey, however. Instead, learn to be very careful when designing survey research and cautious about generalizing from its results.

KEY TERMS

closed-ended question
cognitive interviewing
collaborative encounter model
computer-assisted personal
  interviewing (CAPI)
computer-assisted self-
  administered interviewing
  (CASAI)
computer-assisted telephone
  interviewing (CATI)
context effect
contingency question
conversational interview

double-barreled question
floaters
full-filter question
funnel sequence
interactive voice response (IVR)
leverage salience theory
matrix question
naïve assumption model
open-ended question
order effects
partially open question
prestige bias
probe

pseudosurvey
quasi-filter question
randomized response technique
  (RRT)
recency effect
satisficing
sleeper question
social desirability bias
standard-format question
tailoring
telescope
time budget survey
wording effects

REVIEW QUESTIONS

1. What are the six types of information that surveys often ask about? Give an example of each that is different from the examples in the book.

2. Why are surveys called *correlational,* and how do these differ from experiments?

3. Identify five of the ten things to avoid in question writing.

4. What topics are commonly threatening to respondents, and how can a researcher ask about them?

5. What are advantages and disadvantages of open-ended versus closed-ended questions?

6. What are filtered, quasi-filtered, and standard-format questions? How do they relate to floaters?

7. What are differences between and relative merits of a standard versus a conversational interview?

8. What is cognitive interviewing, and how does it improve survey research?

9. Under what conditions are mail questionnaires, telephone interviews, Web surveys, and face-to-face interviews best?

10. What are CATI and IVR, and when might they be useful? How do they differ from CASAI or CAPI?

NOTES

1. See Carr-Hill (1984b), Denzin (1989), Mishler (1986), and Phillips (1971) for criticisms of a strict positivist approach in surveys.
2. "Why" questions require special techniques. See Barton (1995) and Wilson and colleagues (1996).
3. The history of survey research is discussed in Converse (1987), Hyman (1991), Marsh (1982:9–47), Miller (1983:19–125), Moser and Kalton (1972:6–15), Rossi and colleagues (1983), Sudman (1976b), and Sudman and Bradburn (1987).
4. See Bannister (1987), Blumer (1991a, 1991b), Blumer et al. (1991), Camic and Xie (1994), Cohen (1991), Deegan (1988), Ross (1991), Sklar (1991), Turner (1991), and Yeo (1991). Also see R. Smith (1996) on how political ideological conflicts and private foundations affected the development of survey research.
5. See Scheuch (1990) on national surveys conducted in various countries.
6. See Converse (1987:383–385), *Statistical Abstract of the United States,* and Rossi et al. (1983:8).
7. See Rossi et al. (1983:10).
8. See Bayless (1981) on the Research Triangle Institute.
9. Some organizations include the American Association for Public Opinion Research, founded in 1947. The Council of American Survey Research Organization is an organization for U.S. commercial polling firms and the World Association of Public Opinion Research is an international organization for commercial polling. See Bradburn and Sudman (1988).
10. Bishop et al. (1983, 1984, 1985), Bradburn (1983), Bradburn and Sudman (1980), Cannell et al. (1981), Converse and Presser (1986), Groves and Kahn (1979), Groves et al. (2000), Groves and Couper (1998), Hyman (1991), Lacy (2001), Lyberg et al. (1997), Schacter (2001), Schuman and Presser (1981), Schwarz and Sudman (1992, 1994), Sniderman and Grob (1996), Sudman and Bradburn (1983), Sudman et al. (1996), and Tanur (1992).
11. For a discussion of pilot testing techniques, see Bishop (1992), Bolton and Bronkhorst (1996), Fowler and Cannell (1996), and Sudman et al. (1996).
12. On the administration of survey research, see Backstrom and Hursh-Cesar (1981:38–45), Dillman (1978:200–281; 1983), Frey (1983:129–169), Groves and Kahn (1979:40–78, 186–212), Prewitt (1983), Tanur (1983), and Warwick and Lininger (1975:20–45, 220–264).
13. Similar lists of prohibitions can be found in Babbie (1990:127–132), Backstrom and Hursh-Cesar (1981: 140–153), Bailey (1987:110–115), Bradburn and Sudman (1988:145–153), Converse and Presser (1986: 13–31), deVaus (1986:71–74), Dillman (1978:95–117), Fowler (1984:75–86), Frey (1983:116–127), Moser and Kalton (1972:318–341), Sheatsley (1983:216–217), Sudman and Bradburn (1983:132–136), and Warwick and Lininger (1975:140–148).
14. Binson and Catania (1998), Foddy (1993), and Presser (1990).
15. Sudman and Bradburn (1983:39) suggest that even simple questions (e.g., "What brand of soft drink do you usually buy?") can cause problems. Respondents who are highly loyal to one brand answer the question easily.
16. See Schaeffer (2000) and Sudman et al. (1996: 197–226).
17. See Dykema and Schaeffer (2000).
18. On using a continuum, see Ostrom and Gannon (1996).
19. See Abelson and associates (1992), Auriat (1993), Bernard et al. (1984), Croyle and Loftus (1992), Gaskell et al. (2000), Krosnick and Abelson (1992), Loftus et al. (1990), Loftus et al. (1992), Pearson and Dawes (1992), Sudman et al. (1996), and Weisberg (2005:76–81, 127).
20. See Bradburn (1983), Bradburn and Sudman (1980), and Sudman and Bradburn (1983) on threatening or sensitive questions. Backstrom and Hursh-Cesar (1981:219) and Warwick and Lininger (1975:150–151) provide useful suggestions as well. Fox and Tracy (1986) discuss the randomized response technique. Also see DeLamater and MacCorquodale (1975) on measuring sexual behavior and Herzberger (1993) on sensitive topics.
21. For studies on survey format and answer honesty, see Holbrook et al. (2004), Johnson et al. (1989), Schaeffer and Presser (2003:75), and Tourangeau et al. (2002).
22. See Couper et al. (2003), DeMaio (1984), and Sudman and Bradburn (1983:59).

23. For more on surveys with threatening or sensitive topics and computer-assisted techniques, see Aquilino and Losciuto (1990), Couper and Rowe (1996), Johnson et al. (1989), Tourangeau and Smith (1996), and Wright et al. (1998).

24. For a discussion of knowledge questions, see Backstrom and Hursh-Cesar (1981:124–126), Converse and Presser (1986:24–31), Sudman and Bradburn (1983: 88–118), and Warwick and Lininger (1975:158–160).

25. On how "Who knows who lives here?" can be complicated, see Martin (1999) and Tourangeau et al. (1997).

26. Contingency questions are discussed in Babbie (1990:136–138), Bailey (1987:135–137), de Vaus (1986:78–80), Dillman (1978:144–146), and Sudman and Bradburn (1983:250–251).

27. For further discussion of open and closed questions, see Bailey (1987:117–122), Converse (1984), Converse and Presser (1986:33–34), de Vaus (1986:74–75), Geer (1988), Moser and Kalton (1972:341–345), Schuman and Presser (1979; 1981:79–111), Sudman and Bradburn (1983:149–155), and Warwick and Lininger (1975: 132–140).

28. See Gilljam and Grandberg (1993). Moors (2008) notes that generally five versus six choices are equally effective in statistical tests but six is sometimes better, and the "optimal" solution depends on the content of the survey items.

29. For a discussion of the "don't know," "no opinion," and middle positions in response categories, see Backstrom and Hursh-Cesar (1981:148–149), Bishop (1987), Bradburn and Sudman (1988:154), Brody (1986), Converse and Presser (1986:35–37), Duncan and Stenbeck (1988), Poe et al. (1988), Sudman and Bradburn (1983: 140–141), and Schuman and Presser (1981:113–178). For more on filtered questions, see Bishop et al. (1983, 1984), Bishop et al. (1986), and Weisberg (2005:134-136).

30. See Krosnick et al. (2002), Schaefer and Presser (2003:79–80), and Tourganeau (2004:786).

31. The disagree/agree versus specific alternatives debate is discussed in Bradburn and Sudman (1988: 149–151), Converse and Presser (1986:38–39), Schuman and Presser (1981:179–223), and Sudman and Bradburn (1983: 119–140). Backstrom and Hursh-Cesar (1981:136–140) discuss asking Likert, agree/disagree questions.

32. See McCarty and Shrum (2000) and Narayan and Krosnick (1996).

33. The ranking versus ratings issue is discussed in Alwin and Krosnick (1985), Krosnick and Alwin (1988), and Presser (1984). Also see Backstrom and Hursh-Cesar (1981:132–134) and Sudman and Bradburn (1983:156–165) for formats of asking rating and ranking questions.

34. For more on specific design issues, see Christian and Dillman (2004), Dillman and Redline (2004), Kaplowitz et al. (2004), Ostrom and Gannon (1996), Schwarz et al. (1991), and Tourangeau et al. (2004).

35. See Dillman (2000:32–39) and Dillman and Christian (2005) for discussion.

36. For a discussion of wording effects in questionnaires, see Bradburn and Miles (1979), Peterson (1984), Schuman and Presser (1981:275–296), Sheatsley (1983), and Smith (1987). Hippler and Schwarz (1986) found the same difference between *forbid* and *not allow* in the Federal Republic of Germany.

37. The length of questionnaires is discussed in Dillman (1978:51–57; 1983), Frey (1983:48–49), Herzog and Bachman (1981), and Sudman and Bradburn (1983: 226–227).

38. For a discussion of the sequence of questions or question order effects, see Backstrom and Hursh-Cesar (1981:154–176), Bishop et al. (1985), Bradburn (1983: 302–304), Bradburn and Sudman (1988:153–154), Converse and Presser (1986:39–40), Dillman (1978: 218–220), McFarland (1981), McKee and O'Brien (1988), Moser and Kalton (1972:346–347), Schuman and Ludwig (1983), Schuman and Presser (1981:23–74), Schwartz and Hippler (1995), and Sudman and Bradburn (1983:207–226). Also see Knäuper (1999), Krosnick (1992), Lacy (2001), and Smith (1992) on the issue of question-order effects.

39. A study by Krosnick (1992) and a meta-analysis by Narayan and Krosnick (1996) show that education reduces response-order (primacy or recency) effects, but Knäuper (1999) found that age is strongly associated with response-order effects.

40. This example comes from Strack (1992).

41. For additional discussion of context effects, see Schuman (1992), Smith (1992), Todorov (2000a, 2000b), and Tourangeau (1992).

42. Tarnai and Dillman (1992) discuss how the method of survey affects context effects.

43. For a discussion of format and layout, see Babbie (1990), Backstrom and Hursh-Cesar (1981:187–236), Dillman (1978, 1983), Mayer and Piper (1982), Sudman and Bradburn (1983:229–260), Survey Research Center (1976), and Warwick and Lininger (1975:151–157).

44. For a discussion, see Couper et al. (1998), de Heer (1999), Keeter et al. (2000), Sudman and Bradburn (1983:11), and "Surveys Proliferate, but Answers Dwindle," *New York Times* (October 5, 1990), p. 1. Smith (1995) and Sudman (1976b:114–116) also discuss refusal rates.

45. For additional discussion of nonresponse and refusal rates, see Backstrom and Hursh-Cesar (1981:140–141, 274–275), DeMaio (1980), Frey (1983:38–41), Groves and Couper (1998), Groves and Kahn (1979:218–223), Martin (1985:701–706), Nederhof (1986), Oksenberg et al. (1986), Schuman and Presser (1981:331–336), Sigelman (1982), Stech (1981), Sudman and Bradburn (1983), and Yu and Cooper (1983). For a discussion of methods for calculating response rates, see Bailey (1987:169), Dillman (1978:49–51), Fowler (1984:46–52), and Frey (1983:38).

46. Link and Oldendick (1999) examined telephone screening.

47. See Pottick and Lerman (1991) for a discussion of the study.

48. Introductions and incentives are discussed in Brehm (1994), Couper (1997), De Leeuw et al. (2007), Goldstein and Jennings (2002), Singer (1999), Singer et al. (1998), Singer et al. (1999), Singer et al. (2000), and Trussell and Lavrakas (2004). Dillman et al. (1996) discuss mandatory appeals.

49. Tailoring is discussed in Brehm (1994), Groves and Couper (1996, 1998, 2004), and Groves, Presser, and Dipko (2004).

50. On increasing mail questionnaire return rates, see Bailey (1987:153–168), Church (1993), Dillman (1978, 1983), Fox et al. (1988), Goyder (1982), Heberlein and Baumgartner (1978, 1981), Hubbard and Little (1988), Jones (1979), and Willimack et al. (1995).

51. CATI is discussed in Bailey (1987:201–202), Bradburn and Sudman (1988:100–101), Freeman and Shanks (1983), Frey (1983:24–25, 143–149), Groves and Kahn (1979:226), Groves and Mathiowetz (1984), and Karweit and Meyers (1983).

52. See Tourangeau et al. (2002), Tourangeau (2004a:791–792), and Weisberg (2005:30–37).

53. On cell phone survey interviewing issues, see Brick et al. (2007), Lavrakas et al. (2007), and Link et al. (2007).

54. For comparison of surveys, see Backstrom and Hursh-Cesar (1981:16–23), Bradburn and Sudman (1988:94–110), Dillman (1978:39–78), Fowler (1984: 61–73), and Frey (1983:27–55).

55. For discussions of Web and e-mail surveys, see Birnhaum (2004), Couper (2000), Couper (2008), Couper et al. (2001), Fox and associates (2003), Koch and Emrey (2001), and Tourangeau (2004a:792–794). On Internet usage see "Internet Use Triples in Decade, U.S. Census Bureau Reports," June 3, 2009 [http://www.census.gov/Press-Release/www/releases/archives/communication_industries/013849.html] and "Broadband Internet to Reach 77 Percent of Households by 2012," TMC net, July 29, 2008 [http://www.tmcnet.com/voip/ip-communications/articles/35393-gartner-broadband-internet-reach-77-percent-households-2012.htm].

56. See Couper, Conrad, and Tourangeau (2007), Couper (2008), Dillman (2000:376–400), and Smyth et al. (2009).

57. Elite interviewing is discussed in Dexter (1970). Also see Galaskiewicz (1987), Useem (1984), Verba and Orren (1985), and Zuckerman (1972).

58. On time budget surveys, see Andorka (1987), Bittman and Wajcman (2000), ERIC (1976), Hornsby-Smith (1974), Jordan and Layzell (1992), Mattingly and Bianchi (2003), Meyer (1998), Milem et al. (2000), and Wiedmer (1993) for faculty hours.

59. Dillman (1983) and Groves and Kahn (1979: 188–212) discuss costs.

60. See Maynard et al. (2002), Schwartz (1996), and Weisberg (2005:72–91).

61. For more on interviewing, see Brenner et al. (1985), Cannell and Kahn (1968), Converse and Schuman (1974), Dijkstra and van der Zouwen (1982), Foddy (1993), Gorden (1980), Hyman (1975), Moser and Kalton (1972:270–302), and Survey Research Center (1976). For a discussion of telephone interviewing, see Frey (1983), Groves and Mathiowetz (1984), Jordan et al. (1980), and Tucker (1983).

62. See Turner and Martin (1984:262–269, 282).

63. From Moser and Kalton (1972:273).

64. The use of probes is discussed in Backstrom and Hursh-Cesar (1981:266–273), Foddy (1995), Gorden (1980:368–390), Hyman (1975:236–241), Schober and Conrad (1997), and Smith (1989).

65. On interviewer training, see Backstrom and Hursh-Cesar (1981:237–307), Billiet and Loosveldt (1988), Bradburn and Sudman (1980), Oksenberg et al. (1986), Singer and Kohnke-Aguirre (1979), and Tucker (1983). Olson and Peytchev (2007) found negative effects from more interviewer experience, suggesting interviewers become sloppy or rush as they gain more experience.

66. See Leal and Hess (1999).

67. See Bradburn and Sudman (1980), Pollner and Adams (1997), and Zane and Matsoukas (1979).

68. See Anderson et al. (1988), Bradburn (1983), Catania et al. (1996), Cotter et al. (1982), Finkel et al. (1991), Gorden (1980:168–172), Kane and MacAulay (1993), Reese et al. (1986), Schaeffer (1980), Schuman and Converse (1971), and Weeks and Moore (1981). Davis (1997) found that when African Americans are interviewed by Whites, they put "self-imposed limits on free expression" and are less likely to say that Whites keep

Blacks down or that Blacks do not have the power to effect change.

69. Sudman et al. (1996:74–76).

70. See Bateson (1984), Clark and Schober (1992), Foddy (1993), Lessler (1984), and Turner (1984).

71. From Turner and Martin (1984:276).

72. See Briggs (1986), Cicourel (1982), and Mishler (1986) for critiques of survey research interviewing.

73. For additional discussion of ordinary conversation and survey interviews, see Beatty (1995), Conrad and Schober (2000), Groves el al. (1992), Moore (2004), Schaeffer (2004), Schober and Conrad (2004), Smith (1984), and Suchman and Jordan (1992).

74. On cognitive interviews, see Conrad and Blair (2009), Willis, (2004, 2005), and van der Zouwen and Smit (2004).

75. See Maynard et al. (2002), Maynard and Schaeffer (2004), Moore (2004), Schaeffer (2004), Schober and Conrad (2004), and Willis (2005) on pilot testing methods such as the cognitive interview and related techniques.

76. For a discussion of ethical concerns specific to survey research, see Backstrom and Hursh-Cesar (1981: 46–50), Fowler (1984:135–144), Frey (1983:177–185), Kelman (1982:79–81), Marsh (1982:125–146), Miller (1983:47–96), Reynolds (1982:48–57), and Weisberg (2005:311-324). The use of informed consent is discussed in Singer and Frankel (1982) and in Sobal (1984).

77. On reporting survey results in the media, see Channels (1993) and MacKeun (1984).

78. See Singer (1988).

79. From Turner and Martin (1984:62).

CHAPTER 11

Nonreactive Research and Secondary Analysis

There are a number of research conditions in which the sole use of the interview or questionnaire leaves unanswerable rival explanations. The purpose of those less popular measurement classes emphasized here is to bolster these weak spots and provide intelligence to evaluate threats to validity. The payout for using these measures is high, but the approach is more demanding of the investigator.

—Eugene Webb et al., *Nonreactive Measures in the Social Sciences,* pp. 315–316

Behm-Morawitz and Mastro (2008) explored media exposure on young adults, particularly a "mean girls" trend. "Mean girls," based on a 2004 movie, are teen females who obtain rewards and feel pleasure by being socially aggressive. The authors searched the Internet to identify ninety U.S. teen films released between 1995 and 2005. A teen film stars teen characters and is marketed to a teen audience. From the ninety, they picked the twenty with the highest box office sales. The authors trained three coders for 48 hours on teen films outside the sample. Coders learned to identify primary and secondary characters, socially cooperative behavior (help a friend, resolve conflict), socially aggressive behavior (humiliating others, excluding others), and positive or negative consequences of the behaviors. In data collection, the coders found 139 primary or secondary characters, most (87%) ages 15 to 18, in the twenty films. Slightly more than one-half (55%) were female. Coders identified 337 incidents of socially aggressive behavior and 534 incidents of socially cooperative behavior. In a statistical analysis of the data, the authors found in the films that "both males and females were more often rewarded than punished for engaging in social aggression with females significantly more likely to be rewarded" (p. 136). The authors next conducted a survey of 136 college undergraduates (19–20 years old). They found that the undergraduates who watched the most teen movies and who most identified with teen movie characters were more likely to believe that social aggression is rewarded by increased popularity with peers.

Experiments and survey research are both reactive; that is, the people we study are aware of that fact. In this chapter, we look at **nonreactive research**, or research in which the people we study are not aware that they are being studied. We will consider four nonreactive techniques that usually rely on positivist principles but interpretative and critical researchers also use the techniques. We first look at a collection of inventive nonreactive measures and then *content analysis*. *Existing statistics* and *secondary analysis,* the last two techniques, refer to collecting information from government documents or previous surveys. Although the data may have been reactive when first collected, we can address new questions without reactive effects.

NONREACTIVE RESEARCH

Nonreactive research begins when we notice something that indicates a variable of interest. When we take nonreactive or **unobtrusive measures** (i.e., measures that are not obtrusive or intrusive), the people we study are not aware of it but leave evidence of their social behavior or actions "naturally." We infer from the evidence to behavior or attitudes without disrupting the people we study. Unnoticed observation is also a type of nonreactive measure, which indicates a construct indirectly.

For example, Rosenbloom et al. (2009) unobtrusively observed and recorded information on 1,062 drivers in two cities (population 300,000), two towns (population 3,000), and two villages (population 800) in Israel. They noted five types of traffic violations: (1) not wearing a seat belt, (2) not using a safety child seat, (3) driving while using a cell phone, (4) failing to comply with a "give way" or yield sign, and (5) stopping in an undesignated area. Based on anonymity in cities they hypothesized that more traffic violations would occur in more urban areas. They found, however, that more traffic violations occurred in towns and villages, and that males committed many more violations than females. The study was nonreactive because the drivers that researchers observed never knew they were part of a study.

EXAMPLE BOX 11.1
Finding Data on Tombstones

Foster and colleagues (1998) examined the tombstones in ten cemeteries in an area of Illinois for the period 1830 to 1989. They retrieved data on birth and death dates and gender from more than 2,000 of the 2,028 burials. The researchers learned that some trends in the area differed from national ones. They found that conceptions had two peaks (spring and winter), females ages 10 to 64 had a higher death rate than males, and younger people died in late summer but older people in late winter.

Varieties of Nonreactive or Unobtrusive Observation

Nonreactive measures are varied, and researchers have invented creative ways to measure indirectly social behavior (see Example Box 11.1, Finding Data on Tombstones). Because the measures have little in common except being nonreactive, we can best learn about them by studying many examples. One type is the **erosion measure**, which considers the wear or deterioration of surfaces. Another is the **accretion measure**, which studies things that have been left behind.[1]

Researchers have examined family portraits in different historical eras to see how gender relations within the family are reflected in seating patterns. Urban anthropologists have examined the contents of garbage dumps to learn about lifestyles from

Nonreactive research   A type of social research in which people being studied are unaware of the fact.

Unobtrusive measures   Another name for nonreactive measures that emphasize the fact that the people being studied are not aware of it because the measures do not intrude.

Erosion measure   Nonreactive measures of the wear or deterioration on surfaces due to the activity of people.

Accretion measure   Nonreactive measure of the residue of the activity of people or what they leave behind.

EXPANSION BOX **11.1**
Examples of Nonreactive Measures

PHYSICAL TRACES

Erosion: Wear suggests use.
Example: A researcher examines children's toys at a day care that were purchased at the same time. Worn-out toys suggest higher interest in them by the children.

Accretion: Accumulation of physical evidence suggests behavior.
Example: A researcher examines the brands of aluminum beverage cans in trash or recycling bins in male and female dormitories. This indicates the brands and types of beverages favored by each gender.

ARCHIVES

Running records: Regularly produced public records may reveal much.
Example: A researcher examines marriage records for the bride and groom's ages. Regional differences suggest that the preference for males marrying younger females is higher in certain areas of the country.

Other records: Irregular or private records can reveal a lot.

Example: A researcher finds the number of reams of paper purchased by a college dean's office for 10 years when student enrollment was stable. A sizable increase suggests that bureaucratic paperwork has increased.

OBSERVATION

External appearance: How people appear may indicate social factors.
Example: A researcher watches students to see whether they are more likely to wear their school's colors and symbols after the school team has won or lost.

Count behaviors: Counting how many people do something can be informative.
Example: A researcher counts the number of men and women who come to a full stop and those who come to a rolling stop at a stop sign. This suggests gender difference in driving behavior.

Time duration: How long people take to do things may indicate their attention.
Example: A researcher measures how long men and women pause in front of the painting of a nude man and in front of a painting of a nude woman. Time may indicate embarrassment or interest in same or cross-gender nudity by each gender.

---

what is thrown away (e.g., liquor bottles indicate level of alcohol consumption). Based on information obtained by their garbage, people underreport their liquor consumption by 40 to 60 percent (Rathje and Murphy, 1992:71). Researchers studied the listening habits of drivers by checking what stations their radios are tuned to when cars are repaired. They measured interest in different museum exhibits by noting worn tiles on the floor in different parts of a museum. They studied differences in graffiti in male versus female high school restrooms to show gender differences in themes. Some researchers examined high school yearbooks to compare the high school activities of those who had psychological problems later in life versus those who did not. Researchers have noted bumper stickers in support of different political candidates

to see whether one candidate's supporters are more likely to obey traffic laws than those of the opposing candidate. Researchers have even measured television-watching habits by noting changes in water pressure due to the use of toilets during television commercials.[2] (Also see Expansion Box 11.1, Examples of Nonreactive Measures.)

Recording and Documentation

Creating a nonreactive measure follows the logic of quantitative measurement, although qualitative researchers also use nonreactive observation. You first conceptualize a construct. Next, you link the construct to a nonreactive measure. The variable's operational definition is how you systematically record observations.

As with other studies, you must rule out reasons for the observation other than the construct of interest. For example, your construct is level of customer interest in ten products displayed in a store. Your operational definition is the amount of customer traffic in front of each of ten store product displays. You measure customer traffic with a hidden video camera. You will need to clarify what the customer traffic means (e.g., the location is near an outside entrance causing more to pass by; people are looking at something beyond the display; people are pausing at the display to put on coats, not looking at the products on it; the floor is a path to another department; or traffic simply indicates a good location for a visual display). Next, you systematically consider what is on the video: Compare it to that in other store locations, look at the number of people at the display, note their speed of walking past or time stopping at the display, and count how many customers turned their heads toward it. You want to record results on a regular basis (e.g., hourly, daily, weekly).

CONTENT ANALYSIS

Content Analysis Definition

In a content analysis study, you gather and analyze the content of text. The content can be words, meanings, pictures, symbols, ideas, themes, or any communicated message. The **text** is anything written, visual, or spoken that serves as a medium for communication. It includes books, newspaper or magazine articles, advertisements, speeches, official documents, films or videotapes, musical lyrics, photographs, articles of clothing, Web sites, or works of art. In Chapter 2, you read about a content analysis study of school shootings after the 1999 Columbine High School shootings. The study about "mean girls" in the box that opened this chapter was an example of a content analysis study. (Also see Example Box 11.2, What Is the Message of Antiaging Product Web Sites?)

Content analysis has been around for about a century and is used in many fields—literature, history, journalism, political science, education, psychology, and so on. At the first meeting of the

EXAMPLE BOX 11.2

What Is the Message of Antiaging Product Web Sites?

Ageism, like sexism and racism, requires a set positive or negative stereotypes and messages to reinforce power relations, inequalities, and social privileges. Calasanti (2007) examined Web sites to see what their marketing discourse communicated to older consumers. She identified a sample of 96 antiaging Web sites, coding the pictures and text from each into a set of categories. Coded categories included problems of old age/aging; solutions for problems/old age; gendered aspects of old age; aspects of aging bodies on the site; and depictions of class, race, and sexual orientation. A key message of ageism is that if you can fix your body to forestall aging, you should do so; otherwise, you are a marginal person or loser. Calasanti discovered the antiaging advertisements not only promoted various ways to hide the physical signs of aging but also consistently showed the ideal person as a particular race (White), class (middle class or higher), and sexual orientation (heterosexual). The ads showed men as being dominant in athletic competition or work and sexually assertive. Ads displayed aging women as being alluring sexual partners, competitors with younger women, and sexually receptive to men. The ads suggest that people cannot be old and possess a specific gender at the same time, at least in terms of a White, middle-class, heterosexual ideal. They tell viewers that to look old means losing both gender and sexuality (i.e., becoming a neutral genderless person who is neither male nor female) and that only by appearing younger can they restore these socially valued assets.

German Sociological Society, in 1910, Max Weber suggested using it to study newspapers.[3] In quantitative content analysis, you use objective and systematic counting and recording procedures to produce a numerical description of the content in a text. There are also qualitative or interpretive versions of

Text A general name for a communication medium from which symbolic meaning is measured in content analysis.

EXPANSION BOX **11.2**
How Qualitative Researchers Study Documents or Statistical Reports

Qualitative researchers who use interpretative or critical approaches also study documents and reports with statistical information, but they tend to do so differently from positivists. They consider documents and statistical reports to be cultural objects, or media that communicate social meaning. They see the documents as belonging to a range of other cultural objects (e.g., monuments, diaries, musical scores, shopping lists, films, photographs, paintings, engineering drawings, Web pages) that carry meaning. For example, an architectural floor plan is a document that expresses spatial arrangements that convey social meanings. Some offices are located in desirable locations with large windows designed for holders of certain highly ranked job positions.

Instead of treating a document or statistical report as a neutral container of content, qualitative researchers examine the larger context of its creation, distribution, and reception. Consistent with a constructionist perspective (discussed in Chapter 4), qualitative researchers emphasize the entire process from a document's creation (including the intentions of creators) through its consumption or reception by various receivers/consumers and then situate the document in a social context. In short, they treat the document or report as a cultural object that carries social meaning in its own right. Although they may examine the content of a document or report, they do not limit themselves to it.

Qualitative researchers emphasize that people think and interact on the basis of meaning as well as with words or numbers. For example, the content in one document may convey medical information to health care workers, grant a person access to a social service, sell products to a consumer, inform officials of geographic areas where problems exist, or allow/prevent a person's entry into a country. Different people may put the same document or report to different uses at different times, and processes of "reading" or interpreting documents often depend on training and following rules. For example, people learn what to look for in a medical record, statistical report, or passport. People looking at the same document may see different things, follow different rules, and use it for different purposes (e.g., grant insurance reimbursement or prescribe a medical treatment, test a hypothesis or allocate funds for a new public building, allow someone into a country, or cash a check). Qualitative researchers look at multiple facets of a document and its content. For example, a magazine article can carry content that entertains readers, is a vehicle that allows an author to build a reputation, triggers a public controversy, and is a way to boost magazine sales; (see Griswold (1987, 1994) and Prior (2003) on the study of cultural objects and documents).

content analysis (see Expansion Box 11.2, How Qualitative Researchers Study Documents or Statistical Reports). Here the focus is on quantitative data about a text's content.

Content analysis is nonreactive because the process of placing words, messages, or symbols in a text to communicate to a reader or receiver is without any awareness of the researcher. For example, I, as author of this book, wrote words or drew diagrams to communicate research method content to you, the student. The way I wrote this book and the way you read it are without any knowledge or intention of its ever being content analyzed.

Content analysis lets you see and reveal the content (i.e., messages, meanings, symbols) within a communication source (i.e., a book, article,

movie). You probe into and discover content in a manner different from the ordinary way of reading a book or watching a television program. Content analysis can document—in objective, quantitative terms—whether feelings based on unsystematic observation are true. It yields repeatable, precise results about the text. After you gather the data, you analyze them with statistics in the same way that an experimenter or survey researcher would.

Topics Appropriate for Content Analysis

Content analysis is used for many purposes: to study themes in popular songs and religious symbols in hymns, trends in the topics that newspapers cover and the ideological tone of newspaper editorials, gender role stereotypes in textbooks or feature films, frequency with which people of different races appear in television commercials and programs, answers to open-ended survey questions, enemy propaganda during wartime, the covers of popular magazines, personality characteristics from suicide notes, themes in advertising messages, gender differences in conversations, and so on.

Generalizations you make on the basis of content analysis are limited to the cultural communication itself. Content analysis cannot determine the truthfulness of an assertion or evaluate the aesthetic qualities of literature. It reveals the content in text but cannot interpret the content's significance. You should examine the text directly. Holsti (1968a:602) warned, "Content analysis may be considered as a supplement to, not as a substitute for, subjective examination of documents."

Content analysis is useful for three types of research questions: those regarding a large volume of text, content that may be at a distance or scattered, and content that is difficult to see or document with casual observation. You can measure large amounts of text (e.g., 20 years of newspaper articles) with sampling and multiple coders. You can study topics "at a distance" such as broadcasts in a hostile foreign country or scattered such as common themes in fifteen films produced by the same director over a 20-year period. Most important, content analysis can reveal messages in a text that are difficult to see with casual observation. Even the creator of the text or those who read it may be unaware of all its themes, biases, or characteristics. For example, authors of preschool picture books may not consciously intend to portray children in traditional stereotyped gender roles, but a high degree of such stereotyping has been revealed through content analysis.[4] Another example is that of conversations in all-male versus all-female groups. Although people may be unaware of it, in same-gender groups, women talk more about interpersonal matters and social relationships whereas men talk more about achievement and aggressive themes.[5]

Measurement and Coding

As in most quantitative research, careful measurement is crucial in content analysis. You take diffuse and murky symbolic communication and convert it into precise, objective, quantitative data. To do this, you must very carefully design and document procedures for coding to make replication possible. For example, you want to determine how frequently television dramas portray elderly characters in terms of negative stereotypes. You must develop a measure of the construct "negative stereotypes of the elderly." The conceptualization may be a list of stereotypes or negative generalizations about older people (e.g., senile, forgetful, cranky, frail, hard of hearing, slow, ill, in nursing homes, inactive, conservative) that may or may not accurately reflect elderly people. For example, if 5 percent of people over age 65 are in nursing homes yet 50 percent of those over age 65 on television shows are portrayed as being in nursing homes, evidence supports negative stereotyping.[6]

In a content analysis study, you operationalize constructs with a **coding system**. It is a set of instructions or rules describing how to observe and record content from text. You tailor it to the type of text or communication medium you are studying (e.g., television drama, novels, photos in magazine advertisements). It also depends on your unit of analysis.

The unit of analysis can vary a great deal in content analysis. It can be a word, a phrase, a theme, a plot, a newspaper article, a character, and so forth. In the study on "mean girls" in this chapter's opening box, the unit of analysis was film characters. In addition to units of analysis, you use other units in content analysis that may or may not be the same as units of analysis: recording units, context units, and enumeration units. There are few differences among them, and they are easily confused, but each has a distinct role. In simple projects, all three are the same. For example, you may note features of television commercials for cars or trucks (commercial is recording unit) and what television show or other commercial appeared before or after it (context unit) and count the number and features of people

> **Coding system** A set of instructions or rules used in content analysis to explain how a researcher systematically converted the symbolic content from text into quantitative data.

appearing in each commercial (person is an enumeration unit).

Measurement in content analysis uses **structured observation**: systematic, careful observation based on written rules. The rules explain how to categorize and classify observations. As with other measurement, categories should be mutually exclusive and exhaustive. Written rules make replication possible and improve reliability. Although researchers begin with preliminary coding rules, they often conduct a pilot study and refine coding based on it. Coding systems identify four characteristics of text content: frequency, direction, intensity, and space. A researcher measures from one to all four characteristics in a content analysis research project (see Expansion Box 11.3, What We Measure).

Coding, Validity, and Reliability

Coding requires carefully looking at text and converting it in a very systematic manner into measures of significant words, symbols, or messages. There are two major types of content analysis coding: manifest and latent.

Manifest coding involves the visible, surface content in a text. For example, you count the number of times a phrase or word (e.g., red) appears in written text or whether a specific action (e.g., a kiss) appears in a video scene. The manifest coding system has a list of terms or actions that you want to locate. For written words, you can scan the information into an electronic form and use a computer program to search for words or phrases and let a computer count the number of times they appear. To do this, you first create a comprehensive list of relevant words or phrases.[7]

Structured observation A method of watching what is happening in a social setting that is highly organized and follows systematic rules for observation and documentation.

Manifest coding A type of content analysis coding in which a researcher first develops a list of words, phrases, or symbols and then locates them in a communication medium.

EXPANSION BOX 11.3
What We Measure

1. *Frequency* refers to whether or not something occurs and, if it occurs, how often. For example, how many elderly people appear on a television program within a given week? What percentage of all characters are they, or in what percentage of programs do they appear?
2. *Direction* refers to the direction of messages in the content along some continuum (e.g., positive or negative, supporting or opposing). For example, we devise a list of ways an elderly television character can act. We classify the actions into three categories: positive (e.g., friendly, wise, kind, considerate), neutral, or negative (e.g., nasty, dull, selfish, slow, forgetful).
3. *Intensity* is the strength or power of a message in a direction. A television character may be active, (e.g., running about, speaking quickly and loudly) or passive (e.g., standing nearly still and saying a few words quietly). A characteristic, such as forgetfulness, can be minor (e.g., not remembering to take car keys when leaving home, taking longer time to recall the name of someone who has not been seen in 10 years) or major (e.g., not remembering one's own name, not recognizing one's children).
4. *Space* is the size of a text message, amount of time, or the amount of space allocated to a message. It is easy to measure size or space of a print advertisement or a photo. We can measure space in written text by counting words, sentences, paragraphs, or the space it covers on a page (e.g., square inches). For video or audio text, we measure the amount of time allocated. For example, a TV character may be present for a few seconds or in every scene of an hour-long program.

Manifest coding is highly reliable because the phrase or word either is or is not present. Unfortunately, manifest coding does not consider the connotations of words or phrases. The same word can take on different meanings depending on the context. The possibility that there are multiple meanings of a word limits the measurement validity of manifest coding.

For example, I read a book with a ***red*** cover that is a real ***red*** herring. Unfortunately, its publisher drowned in *red* ink because the editor could not deal with the *red* tape that occurs when a book is *red* hot. The book has a story about a *red* fire truck that stops at *red* lights only after the leaves turn *red*. There is also a group of *Red*s who carry *red* flags to the little *red* schoolhouse. They are opposed by *red*-blooded *red*necks who eat *red* meat and honor the *red*, white, and blue. The main character is a *red*-nosed matador who fights *red* foxes, not bulls, with his *red* cape. *Red*-lipped Little *Red* Riding Hood is also in the book. She develops *red* eyes and becomes *red*-faced after eating a lot of *red* peppers in the *red* light district. She is given a *red* backside by her angry mother, a *red*head.

Latent coding (also called *semantic analysis*) looks for the underlying, implicit meaning in the content of a text. For example, you read an entire paragraph and decide whether it contains erotic themes or a romantic mood. Your coding system contains general rules to guide your interpretation of the text and to determine whether particular themes or moods are present. The study on "mean girls" in the chapter's opening box used latent coding, which tends to be less reliable than manifest coding. It depends on a coder's knowledge of language and social meaning.[8] Training, practice, and written rules improve reliability, but still it is difficult to consistently identify themes, moods, and the like. However, the validity of latent coding can exceed that of manifest coding because we communicate meaning in many implicit ways that depend on context, not just specific words.

You may want to use both manifest and latent coding to study the content of text. Agreement from the two approaches strengthens your final result; if they disagree, you should reexamine the operational and theoretical definitions.

In many studies, you will need to code information from a very large number of units. You might look at the content in thirty books, hundreds of hours of television programming, or about one hundred Web sites (as in the opening box). In addition to coding the information personally, you may hire assistants to help with the coding. You teach coders the coding system and train them to fill out a recording sheet. Coders should understand the variables, follow the coding system, and ask about ambiguities. You must record all decisions about how to treat a new specific coding situation after coding begins so that you can be consistent.

If you use several coders, you must always check for consistency across coders. To do this, you ask coders to code the same text independently and then check for consistency across coders. You measure **intercoder reliability**, a type of equivalence reliability, with a statistical coefficient that identifies the degree of consistency among coders (see Expansion Box 11.4, Krippendorff's Alpha on page 366).[9] You always report the coefficient with the results of content analysis research. The study described in the chapter's opening box reported an intercoder reliability measure (*Krippendorff's alpha*) for each variable measured. To create the coefficient, the three coders each coded 10 percent of all the films used in the study. The alpha coefficient ranged from 0.72 to 1.0, with most over 0.80.

If the coding process stretches over considerable time (e.g., more than 3 months), you should also check stability reliability by having each coder independently code samples of text that were previously coded to see whether the coding is stable or changing. For example, you have 6 hours of television episodes coded in April. You ask the coders to code the 6 hours again in September without allowing the coders to look at their original coding decisions. If the results are the same, you have stability reliability. If you see large deviations in coding, you may need to retrain coders and recode a second time.

Researchers have studied many forms of visual "text," such as photographs, paintings, statues, buildings, clothing, videos, and film. Visual "text" is more difficult to analyze than written text because it communicates messages or emotional content indirectly through images, symbols, and metaphors.

Latent coding A type of content analysis coding in which a researcher identifies subjective meaning such as themes or motifs and then systematically locates them in a communication medium.

Intercoder reliability Equivalence reliability in content analysis with multiple content coders that requires a high degree of consistency across coders.

EXPANSION BOX **11.4**

Krippendorff's Alpha

Krippendorff's alpha (α) is the most widely used and best known measure of intercoder agreement or interrater reliability. Klaus Krippendorff developed this intercoder reliability coefficient to measure the agreement between observers, coders, judges, raters, and measuring instruments. When observers agree perfectly, observed disagreement of $\alpha = 1$ and indicates perfect reliability. Agreement by observers as if chance had produced the results indicates the absence of reliability, $\alpha = 0$. It is as if the coders failed to observe the text or information and made up their data by throwing dice.

α's general from is : $\alpha = 1 - \dfrac{D_o}{D_e}$

where D_o is the observed disagreement and D_e is the disagreement one would expect when the coding of units is attributable to chance rather than to the properties of these units.

The mathematics behind the formula and its more advanced details are beyond the level of this book (see Hayes and Krippendorf, 2007, and Krippendorf, 2004). The data for this formula come from two or more jointly trained coders working independently to assign values to a variable for a common set of units of analysis. Details of the coefficient will change based on the number of coders, range of values in variables, and so forth. The coefficient α applies to many situations: any number of coders, any number of variable categories or measures, any level of measurement (nominal, ordinal, interval, ratio), any incomplete or missing data, and any sample size. Several statistical computer programs can compute the statistic.

Moreover, visual images often contain mixed messages and operate at multiple levels of meaning.

Most people share a common meaning for key symbols of the dominant culture, but people may read a symbol differently. For example, should you "read" a nation's flag to mean patriotism, duty to nation, and honor of tradition, or domination, abuse of power, and police or military aggression? Japan rarely displayed its national flag in public schools from 1945 to 1999. Then government officials enacted a law that required its display and the playing of the national anthem, causing great controversy. Conservative politicians wanted the flag displayed to instill more patriotism among the nation's youth. However, many teachers and others objected because of the flag was strongly associated with Japan's past military aggression and suppression of democracy, and extremist right-wing groups in Japan often promoted the display of the flag.

The confederate flag in the United States contains sharply divergent meanings for different social groups.[10] To many African Americans, it symbolizes racial segregation, slavery, and violent oppression by Whites during the Jim Crow era. For many older Whites, it symbolizes regional heritage and a genteel "Old-South" lifestyle. For others, it symbolizes rebelliousness, individual freedom, and rejection of externally imposed authority. For some people outside the United States, it is simply a colorful fashion statement with connections to the United States. There are several possible readings of the flag as a symbol.

To study visual images, you must learn to "read" multiple meanings of visual text and to interpret various symbolic images. Such a "reading" is not mechanical (i.e., image X always means G) but depends on the cultural context because the meaning of an image is culture bound. It also depends on the interrelationships within a field of many symbols. The meaning of the confederate flag may vary by age, racial group, geographic location, and so forth. It also varies by how it is displayed. Displaying the flag at a Klu Klux Klan rally, at a University of Mississippi football game, as part of the Georgia state flag, and on the back of a motorcycle "biker" jacket may not carry the same meaning. In my hometown, I read a newspaper article stating that the police are tracking a high school gang advocating racial hate that fights and intimidates non-Whites. The gang symbol (on hats and jackets) is the confederate flag. National symbols, such as the Statue of Liberty, are also used to convey social or political messages (see Example Box 11.3, Magazine Covers and Immigration).

Sociopolitical groups construct new symbols or wrestle for control of the meaning of major existing symbols. For example, some people want

EXAMPLE BOX **11.3**
Magazine Covers and Immigration

Chavez (2001) conducted a content analysis of the covers of major U.S. magazines that dealt with the issue of immigration into the country. Looking at the covers of ten magazines from the mid-1970s to the mid-1990s, he classified the covers as having one of three major messages: affirmative, alarmist, or neutral or balanced. Beyond his classification and identifying trends in messages, he noted how the mix of people (i.e., race, gender, age, and dress) in the photographs and the recurrent use of major symbols, such as the Statue of Liberty or the U.S. flag, communicated messages. Chavez argued that magazine covers are a site, or location, where cultural meaning is created. Visual images on magazine covers have multiple levels of meaning, and viewers construct specific meanings as they read the image and use their cultural knowledge. Collectively, the covers convey a worldview and express messages about a nation and its people. For example, a magazine cover that displayed the icon of the Statue of Liberty as strong and full of compassion (message: welcome immigrants) was altered to have strong Asian facial features (message: Asian immigrants distorted the national culture and altered the nation's racial makeup), or holding a large stop sign (message: go away immigrants). Chavez (p. 44) observed that "images on magazines both refer to and, in the process, help to structure and construct contemporary 'American' identity."

to assign a religious meaning to the Christmas tree; others want it to represent a celebration of tradition and family values without religious content; still others want it to mean a festive holiday season for commercial reasons. Because of the complex, multilayered meanings of symbols, you need to combine qualitative judgments about the images with quantitative data in content analysis.

How to Conduct a Content Analysis Study

1. *Formulate the research question.* You begin with a topic and a research question. When the question involves variables that are messages or symbols, content analysis may be appropriate. For example, you want to study how local television covers a campaign for mayor of the city. Your question may be whether each candidate has equal coverage. The construct "coverage" includes the amount of coverage (time on television), the prominence of the coverage, and whether the coverage favors one candidate over another. You could survey people and ask what they think of the coverage, but a better strategy is to examine the news reports directly using content analysis.

2. *Decide on units of analysis.* You must decide on the units of analysis. For example, for a political campaign, each day of a news show on each of several local stations could be your unit of analysis, or each news report or segment during each of two evening news programs each day on all local stations. You could also count television advertisements by candidates or issue groups. You could study debate or interview programs on television that featured the candidates.

3. *Develop a sampling plan.* Random sampling is very useful in content analysis. First, you must define the population and the sampling element. For example, the population might be all words, all sentences, all paragraphs, or all articles in certain types of documents over a specified period. Likewise, it could include each conversation, situation, scene, or episode of certain types of television programs over a particular period. For example, you may want to see how the candidates are covered on television news programs, commercials, and in debate or interview programs during the one year leading up to the election and the month following it. You must decide whether to include news programs during the daytime and special reports on just two Monday through Friday evening news programs. Should you include commercials aired any time of the day any day of the week or limit your population to times when more people view television? Your unit of analysis could be the news program segment that focuses on the campaign and names a candidate, a commercial in which a candidate's image or name appears, or the interview program featuring one or more candidates. Your population may include all news program segments, commercials, and interview programs aired on four local television stations during a 13-month period.

After you have specified the target population and your sampling elements, you will need to plan in detail. This includes constructing sampling frames and determining sample size and the sampling ratios. As you may recall from Chapter 8, the sampling frame is a critical step in creating an accurate random sample. To sample coverage of mayoral candidates over a 13-month period, you should list all news segments, commercials, and debate-interview programs. Practically, you might have three separate samples, one for commercials, one for news segments, and one for debates. Because the same commercial could appear many times, you might create a list (sampling frame) of all possible time slots when commercials could appear and randomly sample the time slots. Because a news program could have none, one, or several segments focusing the election and candidates, you may have to search each station's program log to obtain a list of all possible segments and then use that as a sampling frame. If there are only a few debate-interview programs, you might include the entire population.

As you plan a project, you should calculate the work required. For example, during a pilot test, you might find that it takes an average of 15 minutes to view and code a 30- or 60-second commercial, 20 minutes for a 3- to 5-minute news program segment, and 2 hours for a 30-minute debate or interview program. This does not include time for sampling or locating the commercial, segment, or debate. Let us say the sampling frame had 300 commercials, 80 news segments, and five debates, and you sampled 100 of the commercials, 40 segments, and all five debates. Your coding time would be (15 minutes × 100 commercials) + (20 minutes × 40 segments) + (180 minutes × 5 debates) = 2,200 minutes, or about 37 hours after you have gathered and organized all of the video feeds. You might consider hiring assistants as coders.

4. *Construct coding categories and a recording sheet.* You need to identify all variables of interest. Often they will come from ideas in a literature review, from your own thinking or theory, or from a preliminary analysis of pilot data. You should create a very explicit coding system for yourself and for coders if you use them. The manifest or latent coding system will describe exactly how to convert what a coder sees

or hears into a few code categories. To organize codes, you should create a recording sheet. This is a grid or page with a place to record the identification number of the unit and spaces for coding information about each variable (see Figure 11.1). You should always test your coding system and recording sheets with some pilot data (about a dozen units).

5. *Coding and intercoder reliability check.* Finally, if you use multiple coders, check intercoder reliability. Usually this means selecting 10 percent of your total sample and having each coder use the coding system with the same units but independently of one another. If necessary, discard and recode information for inaccurate coders.

6. *Data collection and analysis.* After you have prepared the coding system and recording sheets and trained all coders, you are ready to gather and check the data. You enter the data into a computer for statistical analysis, interpret the results, and prepare a report.

Inferences

The inferences that you can make based on the results is a critical issue in content analysis, which describes what is in the text. It cannot reveal the intentions of those who created the text or the effects that messages in the text have on those who receive them. For example, content analysis shows that children's books contain gender stereotypes. That does not necessarily mean that the stereotypes in the books shape the beliefs or behaviors of children; you need to conduct a separate study on children's perceptions to verify that inference. In the study described in this chapter's opening box, the authors conducted a second study with the survey method to see how their content analysis results affected the viewers of teen movies.

EXISTING STATISTICS/DOCUMENTS

Appropriate Topics

Many types of information about the social world are already available in the form of statistical documents (books, reports, etc.) or as published compilations available in libraries or on computerized records. In either case, you can search through

FIGURE 11.1   Example TV Commercial Recording Sheet for Content Analysis on Mayoral Election

Commercial ID _____   Date of commercial _____   Time of commercial _____   Coder # ___

Station on which commercial aired _____ Duration ____ Sponsor of commercial _____

Visual of Candidate A shown? _____   Voice of Candidate A heard? _____
Visual of Candidate B shown? _____   Voice of Candidate B heard? _____
Visual of Candidate C shown? _____   Voice of Candidate C heard? _____

Number of people shown other than the candidates _____
Number who appear elderly ___   Number of nonelderly adults ___   Number of children ___
Gender mix _____ Racial-ethnic mix W__ B__ H__ A___ O___
Occupational mix _____

Check all issues referenced in commercial that apply.

 1. Taxes _____
 2. Schools _____
 3. Crime _____
 4. Housing _____
 5. Public transport _____
 6. Roads _____
 7. Social services _____
 8. Parks _____
 9. Business _____
10. Urban sprawl _____
11. Water/air quality _____
12. Vision for future _____
13. Neighborhoods _____
14. Fire/police _____
15. Zoning _____
16. Library _____
17. Quality of life _____
18. Elderly services _____
19. Youth services _____
20. Multicultural issues_____
21. Public health _____
22. Job creation _____
23. Efficient government _____
24. Public voice _____
25. Cooperation with other government agencies _____

Endorsements of candidate A made by _____
Endorsements of candidate A made by _____
Endorsements of candidate A made by _____

Criticism of candidate A made by _____ on issue number above _____
Criticism of candidate B made by _____ on issue number above _____
Criticism of candidate C made by _____ on issue number above _____

such collections of information with a research question and variables in mind and then reassemble and statistically analyze the information in new ways to address a research question.

It is difficult to specify topics that are appropriate for existing statistics research because they are so varied. You can study any topic on which an organization collected information and made it publicly available. In fact, existing statistics projects do not fit neatly into a deductive model of research design. Rather, you creatively reorganize the existing information into the variables for a research question after first finding what data are available.

Recall that experiments are best for topics that can be controlled and manipulated as independent variables. Survey research is best for topics about which we ask questions to learn about reported attitudes or behaviors. Content analysis is best for topics that involve the content of messages in cultural communication. Existing statistics research is best for topics that involve information collected by large bureaucratic organizations. Public or private organizations systematically gather many types of information for policy decisions or as a public service. Rarely do they collect data for purposes directly related to a specific research question. Thus, existing statistics research is appropriate for testing hypotheses that involve variables in official reports of social, economic, and political conditions. These include descriptions of organizations or the people in them. Often organizations collect the information over long time periods. For example, you can use existing statistics to see whether unemployment and crime rates are associated in 150 cities across a 20-year period.

Existing statistics are valuable for looking over time and across nations. You read about an existing statistics study about red and blue states by McVeigh and Sobolewski (2007) in Chapter 1. The census (see Expansion Box 11.5, The Census) is a valuable type of existing statistical data (see Example Box 11.4, Existing Census Statistics and Naturalization in the Early Twentieth Century).

Social Indicators

During the 1960s, many social scientists, dissatisfied with the information available to decision

EXPANSION BOX 11.5

The Census

Almost every country conducts a census, or a regular count of its population. For example, Australia has done so since 1881, Canada since 1871, and the United States since 1790. Most nations conduct a census every 5 or 10 years. In additon to the number of people, census officials collect information on topics such as housing conditions, ethnicity, religious affiliation, education, and so forth.

The census is a major source of high-quality existing statistical data, but it can be controversial. In Canada, an attempt to count the number of same-sex couples living together evoked public debate about whether the government should document the changes in society. In Great Britain, the Muslim minority welcomed questions about religion in the 2001 census because they felt that they had been officially ignored. In the United States, the measurement of race and ethnicity was hotly debated, so in the 2000 census, people could place themselves in multiple racial-ethnic categories.

The U.S. 2000 census also generated a serious public controversy because it missed thousands of people, most from low-income areas with concentrations of recent immigrants and racial minorities. Some double counting of people in high-income areas where many owned second homes also occurred. A contentious debate arose among politicians to end miscounts by using scientific sampling and adjusting the census. The politicians proved to be less concerned about improving the scientific accuracy of the census than retaining traditional census methods that would benefit their own political fortunes or help their constituencies because the government uses census data to draw voting districts and allocate public funds to areas.

makers, spawned the "social indicators' movement" to measure social well-being. They wanted to expand understanding by combining information about social well-being with generally used indicators of economic performance (e.g., gross national product) to better inform policy-making officials. Members of this movement hoped that measuring the quality of social life would influence public policy decisions.[11] Today, many books, articles,

EXAMPLE BOX **11.4**

Existing Census Statistics and Naturalization in the Early Twentieth Century

Bloemraad (2006) studied existing statistical records to examine citizenship acquisition, or naturalization, in early twentieth century America. She noted that many commentators contrast low levels of citizenship acquisition among today's immigrants with the assumed rapid and uniform naturalization of European migrants 80 to 100 years ago. However, there is little solid evidence about the earlier process, and myths have filled the void. Bloemraad examined data on adult male immigrants from the 1900, 1910, and 1920 U.S. censuses. The U.S. government gathers census data and makes them available to the public for statistical analysis. Naturalization is a legal process that enables noncitizens to become citizens. It requires a specific length of residence, a clean legal record, passage of a language test, and several other features. Between 1900 and 1920, the proportion of immigrants who held U.S. citizenship fell from 67 percent to 49 percent due to large-scale immigration from Europe. Bloemraad used sophisticated statistical analysis to

investigate four explanations for naturalization: individuals' resources and skills, regulatory and bureaucratic barriers to citizenship, relative costs and benefits of citizenship, and the degree of political mobilization directed to immigrants. The census had measures of years of residence, age, literacy, and English ability. Bloemraad found that naturalization rates varied widely by geographic area. The key factor that made a difference was the warmth of the welcome extended to newcomers. Although some local histories suggested this process, we did not have the nationwide, generalizable findings until her large-scale national study that statistically analyzed millions of cases. Her most notable result was that where an immigrant lived had a more significant effect on naturalization than the immigrant's birthplace, ability to speak English, or literacy. In short, the local reception of immigrants determined how fast they became citizens, not features of the individual immigrants as was emphasized in past studies or by political commentators.

and reports discuss social indicators. A scholarly journal, *Social Indicators Research,* is devoted to the creation and evaluation of social indicators. Since 1976 every three years, the U.S. Census Bureau has published a report, *Social Indicators,* and the United Nations collects many measures of social well-being across nations.

A **social indicator** is any measure of social well-being that can inform policy decisions. Many specific indicators can measure well-being related to the following areas: population, family, housing, social security and welfare, health and nutrition, public safety, education and training, work, income, culture and leisure, social mobility, voting, and participation in social and religious organizations. The FBI's uniform crime index indicates the amount of crime in U.S. society. Social indicators can measure negative aspects of social life, such as the infant mortality rate (the death rate of infants during the first year of life) and alcoholism, or they can indicate positive aspects, such as job satisfaction or the percentage of housing units with indoor

plumbing. Social indicators often involve implicit value judgments (e.g., which crimes are serious or what constitutes a good quality of life).

The Institute for Innovation in Social Policy now at Vassar College created an Index of Social Well-Being for the United States. It combines measures of sixteen social problem areas (see Chart 11.1 on page 372) from various existing U.S. government statistical documents. With it you can compare each year to the best level recorded for an item, on a scale of 0 to 100 with 100 being the highest score, since 1970 when the index began. The United States reached its highest level of social well-being in 1973 (index score = 77.5) and has since declined. Overall, between 1970 and 2007, the Index declined from 66 to 56. The current social well-being is lower than in the recent past and varies greatly by state.[12]

Social indicator A quantitative indicator of social well-being.

CHART 11.1   Social Health Index of United States

SIXTEEN SOCIAL INDICATORS USED TO CREATE SOCIAL HEALTH INDEX

Infant mortality	Health insurance coverage
Child poverty	Aging: poverty among the elderly
Child abuse	Suicide among the elderly
Teenage suicide	Homicide
Teenage drug abuse	Alcohol-related traffic fatalities
High school completion	Food stamp coverage
Unemployment	Affordable housing
Average wages	Income inequality

Social Health of States in 2008

RANK	SOCIAL HEALTH SCORE	RANK	SOCIAL HEALTH SCORE
1. Minnesota	75.0	26. Missouri	51.4
2. Iowa	71.1	27. Michigan	48.9
3. New Hampshire	67.2	28. Oregon	47.8
4. Nebraska	67.0	29. Rhode Island	46.8
5. Hawaii	63.1	30. Colorado	44.6
6. Vermont	62.7	31. New York	43.9
7. Connecticut	61.2	32. Georgia	43.7
8. North Dakota	61.1	33. Alaska	43.6
9. Utah	60.6	34. Nevada	42.6
10. New Jersey	59.9	35. California	41.7
11. Idaho	59.7	36. West Virginia	40.8
12. Virginia	59.7	37. Oklahoma	40.1
13. Pennsylvania	58.6	38. Montana	39.4
14. Maine	57.4	39. Alabama	38.8
15. Indiana	55.9	40. South Carolina	38.0
16. Kansas	55.9	41. Texas	37.8
17. Delaware	55.7	42. Louisiana	37.5
18. Illinois	55.2	43. Arkansas	36.4
19. Wisconsin	55.2	44. Kentucky	36.2
20. Maryland	54.9	45. Tennessee	35.5
21. South Dakota	54.4	46. Florida	34.3
22. Ohio	53.8	47. North Carolina	33.4
23. Wyoming	53.4	48. Arizona	32.8
24. Massachusetts	53.1	49. Mississippi	31.0
25. Washington	52.2	50. New Mexico	26.8

Source: From http://iisp.vassar.edu/socialhealth08.html. Institute for Innovation in Social Policy. Vassar College. Reprinted by permission.

Locating Data

Government or international agencies and private sources are the main providers of existing statistics. If you plan to conduct an existing statistics study, it is wise to discuss your interests with an information professional—in this case, a reference librarian, who can direct you to possible sources. Most existing documents are "free"—that is, available at public libraries—but the time and effort required to search for specific information can be substantial. Researchers who conduct existing statistics research spend many hours in libraries or on the Internet. After they locate the information, they record it on computer files or recording sheets for later analysis. Often it is already available in an electronic format. For example, instead of recording voting data from reference books, researchers might use a social science data archive at the University of Michigan (to be discussed). Also see Expansion Box 11.6, Newspaper Reports as a Data Source.

Researchers can be very creative using existing statistics. (See Example Box 11.5, Existing Statistics, Androgynous First Names, and Collective Behavior.) With many sources available, I will discuss only a small sample of them here. The

EXPANSION BOX 11.6
Newspaper Reports as a Data Source

Many social researchers use reports in newspapers as a data source, not only to analyze the content of articles but also as a way to identify and count key events, such as social protests. Newspapers can be an invaluable source of public information even if they do not cover all events (i.e., selection bias) or do not report all information on the events covered (i.e., description bias). In addition, these types of bias may vary by geographic area or historical period. Although major newspapers have subject indexes, these are not always organized to be useful for social research purposes. Especially in countries with a free press, newspapers can be a way to measure social events across time. In particular, "for many historical and comparative research designs, newspapers remain the only source of data on protest events" (Earl et al., 2004:76).

EXAMPLE BOX 11.5
Existing Statistics, Androgynous First Names, and Collective Behavior

An androgynous first name is one that can be for either a girl or boy without clearly marking the child's gender. Some argue that the feminist movement decreased gender marking in a child's name as part of its broader societal influence to reduce gender distinctions and inequality. Others observe that gender remains the single most predominant feature of naming in most societies. Even when racial groups or social classes invent distinctive new first names, the gender distinctions are retained.

Lieberson et al. (2000) examined existing statistical data in the form of computerized records from the birth certificates of 11 million births of White children in the state of Illinois from 1916 to 1989. They found that androgynous first names are rare (about 3 percent) and that there has been a very slight historical trend toward androgyny, but only in very recent years. In addition, parents give androgynous names to girls more than to boys, and gender segregation in naming is unstable (i.e., a name tends to lose its androgynous meaning over time). The authors noted that the way parents name children mimics a pattern of collective behavior found to operate in another research area: the racial segregation of neighborhoods. Change in residence is unequal among races with less movement by the dominant group; the less powerful group moves to occupy areas that the dominant group has abandoned; and integration is unstable with new segregation reappearing after some time.

single most valuable source of statistical information about the United States is *The Statistical Abstract of the United States*. It has been published annually (with a few exceptions) since 1878 and is available in all libraries and on the Internet. It is a selected compilation of the many reports and statistical tables of data that U.S. government agencies collect. It has summary information from hundreds of more detailed government reports, which could be examined further. With 1,400 charts, tables, and statistical lists from hundreds of government and private agencies, it is difficult to grasp all it contains until you spend time skimming through its many tables.

Most governments publish similar statistical information such as *Yearbook Australia, Canada Yearbook, New Zealand Official Yearbook,* and in the United Kingdom, the *Annual Abstract of Statistics.*[13] Many other nations also publish books with historical statistics.

Locating government statistical documents is an art in itself and some publications exist solely to assist the researcher: the *American Statistics Index: A Comprehensive Guide and Index to the Statistical Publications of the U.S. Government* and *Statistics Sources: A Subject Guide to Data on Industrial, Business, Social Education, Financial and Other Topics for the United States and Internationally.*[14] The United Nations and international agencies such as the World Bank have their own publications with statistical information (e.g., literacy rates, percentage of the labor force working in agriculture, birth rates) for various countries, for example, the *Demographic Yearbook, UNESCO Statistical Yearbook,* and *United Nations Statistical Yearbook.*

Other publications offer sources of data on specialized topics. For example, there are publications that contain social background, career, and other biographical information on famous individuals identified as important by some criteria. These publications depend on voluntary information provided by those deemed important. Another source of information covers businesses or their executives.[15] Finally, there are publications that specialize in information about politics, voting, and politicians (see Expansion Box 11.7, Specialized Publications That Provide Social Data, for source publications covering the United States).

SECONDARY ANALYSIS OF SURVEY DATA

Secondary analysis is a special case of existing statistics. It statistically analyzes survey data originally gathered by someone else as opposed to primary research (e.g., experiments, surveys, and content analysis) that collects quantitative data. During the past two decades, many more social scientists have conducted secondary analysis as more data have become available. It is relatively inexpensive; it permits comparisons across groups, nations, or time; it facilitates replication; and it permits asking about issues not considered by the original researchers, such as using a health survey of teens to study religion (see Example Box 11.6, Secondary Data Analysis, Answering New Questions from Old Data on page 376).

Large-scale survey data collection can be very expensive and difficult to conduct. For most researchers, the cost and time required for a major national survey that uses rigorous techniques are prohibitive. Fortunately, the organization, preservation, and dissemination of major survey data sets have improved. Today, archives of past surveys are open to researchers.

The Inter-University Consortium for Political and Social Research (ICPSR) at the University of Michigan is the world's major archive of social science data. More than 17,000 survey research and related sets of information are stored and made available to researchers at modest costs. Various centers in the United States and other nations also hold survey data.[16]

A widely used source of survey data for the United States is the General Social Survey (GSS). The National Opinion Research Center at the University of Chicago conducted the survey about every other year since 1973. In recent years, it has covered other nations as well. The data are made publicly available for secondary analysis at a low cost[17] (see Expansion Box 11.8, The General Social Survey on page 376).

Limitations

Despite the growth and popularity of secondary data analysis and existing statistics research, they have limitations. The use of such techniques is not trouble free simply because a government agency or research organization gathered the data.

One danger is that the secondary data or existing statistics may be inappropriate for your research question. Before proceeding, you need to consider the units in the data (e.g., types of people, organizations), the time and place of data collection, the sampling methods used, and the specific issues or topics covered in the data such as the census. For example, you want to examine racial-ethnic

EXPANSION BOX **11.7**

Specialized Publications That Provide Social Data

PUBLISHED INFORMATION SOURCES ON FAMOUS INDIVIDUALS

Who's Who in America is a popular biographic source that has been published since 1908. It lists the name, birth date, occupation, honors, publications, memberships, education, positions held, spouse, and children's names for those included. Specialized editions are devoted to regions of the United States (e.g., *Who's Who in the East*), to specific occupations (e.g., *Who's Who in Finance and Industry*), and to specific subgroups (e.g., women, Jews, African Americans).

Dictionary of American Biography is a more detailed listing on fewer people than *Who's Who*. It began in 1928 and has supplements to update information. For example, Supplement 7 lists 572 people and devotes about a page to each. It has details about careers, travels, the titles of publications, and relations with other famous people.

Biographical Dictionaries Master Index is an index listing names in the various *Who's Who* publications and many other biographic sources (e.g., *Who's Who in Hockey*). If a researcher knows a name, the index tells where biographic information can be found for the person.

SOURCES ON BUSINESSES AND COMPANIES

Dun and Bradstreet Principal Industrial Businesses is a guide to approximately 51,000 businesses in 135 countries with information on sales, number of employees, officers, and products.

Who Owns Whom comes in volumes for nations or regions (e.g., North America, the United Kingdom, Ireland, and Australia). It lists parent companies, subsidiaries, and associated companies.

Standard and Poor's Register of Corporations, Directors and Executives lists about 37,000 U.S. and Canadian companies. It has information on corporations, products, officers, industries, and sales figures.

SOURCES ON POLITICAL ISSUES (UNITED STATES)

Almanac of American Politics is a biannual publication that includes photographs and a short biography of U.S. government officials. Committee appointments, voting records, and similar information are provided for members of Congress and leaders in the executive branch.

America Votes: A Handbook of Contemporary American Election Statistics contains detailed voting information by county for most statewide and national offices. Primary election results are included down to the county level.

Vital Statistics on American Politics provides dozens of tables on political behavior, such as the campaign spending of every candidate for Congress, their primary and final votes, ideological ratings by various political organizations, and a summary of voter registration regulations by state.

---

tensions between Latinos and Anglos across the United States but have only secondary data that includes the Pacific Northwest and New England states. In this situation, you should reconsider the question or the use of data.

A second danger is that you must understand the substantive topic to use the data. Because they are easily accessible, you might have data but know very little about a topic. As a result, you make erroneous assumptions or false interpretations about the results. Before using any data, you should study details of the substantive topic. For example, if you use data on high school graduation rates in Germany but you do not know much about the German secondary education system with its distinct academic and vocational tracks and assume the German and U.S. system are the same, you can easily make serious errors in interpreting results.

A third danger is to quote statistics in excessive detail to give others an impression of scientific rigor. This can lead to the **fallacy of misplaced concreteness,** which occurs when someone gives a false impression of precision by quoting statistics in more

> **Fallacy of misplaced concreteness** Use of too many digits in a quantitative measure in an attempt to create the (mis)impression that data are accurate.

Secondary Data Analysis, Answering New Questions from Old Data

To perform secondary data analysis, researchers can use already collected survey data to address new research questions unrelated to the survey's original purpose. Uecker et al. (2007) used data from a health survey to study religion. Data were from National Longitudinal Study of Adolescent Health, a school-based three-part panel survey on health and related social behaviors (you read about panel studies in Chapter 2). The authors used data from the first panel of the survey, a random sample in 1994–1995 of 132 schools with 20,745 U.S. adolescents in grades 7–12 and from the third part of the panel, interviews in 2001–2002 with 15,197 of the original respondents (who were then aged 18–25). The authors' interest was to explain declines in religious involvement that occur as young adults move from adolescence to adulthood, not in health. However, the health survey had questions about religious involvement, importance of religion in one's life, and feelings about organized religion. The authors used these three questions as their dependent variable measure. Past research had explained the decline in religion during the young adult years as being due to the secularizing effects of going to college. After statistically analyzing the data, the authors found that people who went to college remained as religious as those who did not go. The authors found that cohabitation, nonmarital sex, and drug and alcohol use among the young people reduced the importance of religion in the young person's life, not whether they attended college, and that contrary to what people had thought, higher education itself had little effect on religious belief.

---

detail than warranted and "overloading" the details. For example, existing statistics report that the population of Australia is 19,169,083, but it is better to say that it is a little more than 19 million. You might calculate the percentage of divorced people as 15.65495 in a secondary data analysis of the 2000 General Social Survey, but it is better to report that about 15.7 percent of people are divorced.[18]

Units of Analysis and Variable Attributes. A common problem in existing statistics is finding the

The General Social Survey

The General Social Survey (GSS) is the best-known set of survey data used by social researchers for secondary analysis. The mission of the GSS is "to make timely, high quality, scientifically relevant data available to the social science research community" (Davis and Smith, 1992:1). It is available in many computer-readable formats and is widely accessible for a low cost. Neither datasets nor codebooks are copyrighted. Users may copy or disseminate them without obtaining permission. You can find results using the GSS in more than 2,000 research articles and books.

The National Opinion Research Center (NORC) has conducted the GSS almost every year since 1972. A typical year's survey contains a random sample of about 1,500 adult U.S. residents. A team of researchers selects some questions for inclusion, and individual researchers can recommend questions. The Center repeats some questions and topics each year, includes some on a four- to six-year cycle, and adds other topics in specific years. For example, in 1988, the special topic was religion, and in 1990, it was intergroup relations.

Interviewers collect the data through face-to-face interviews. The NORC staff carefully selects interviewers and trains them in social science methodology and survey interviewing. About 120 to 140 interviewers work on the GSS each year. About 95 percent are women, and most are middle-aged. The NORC recruits bilingual and minority interviewers. Interviewers are race-matched with respondents. Interviews are typically 90 minutes long and contain approximately 500 questions. The response rate has been 71 to 79 percent. The major reason for nonresponse is a refusal to participate.

The International Social Survey Program conducts similar surveys in other nations. Beginning with the German ALLBUS and British Social Attitudes Survey, participation has grown to include Australia, Austria, Italy, Hungary, Ireland, Israel, the Netherlands, Switzerland, Poland and others. The goal is to conduct on a regular basis large-scale national general surveys in which some common questions are asked across cooperating nations.

---

appropriate units of analysis. Many statistics are published for aggregates, not the individual. For example, a table in a government document has information (e.g., unemployment rate, crime rate) for a state, but the unit of analysis for the research question is the individual (e.g., "Are unemployed people more likely to commit property crimes?"). The potential for committing the ecological fallacy is very real in this situation. It is less of a problem for secondary survey analysis because we can obtain raw information on each respondent from archives.

A related problem involves the categories of variable attributes used in existing documents or survey questions. This is not a problem if organizations that gathered the initial data used many highly refined categories. The problem arises when the organizations collected the original data in broad categories or ones that do not match the needs of current research. For example, you are interested in people of Asian heritage. If the racial and ethnic heritage categories in a document are White, Black, and Other, you have a problem. The Other category includes people of Asian and other heritages. Sometimes organizations gather information in refined categories but publish it only in broad categories. You need to dig more deeply to discover whether the organization collected refined information.

Validity. Validity problems can occur when your theoretical definition does not match that of the government agency or organization that collected the information. Official policies and procedures specify definitions for official statistics. For example, you define a work injury as including minor cuts, bruises, and sprains that occur on the job, but the official definition in government reports includes only injuries that require a visit to a physician or hospital. Many work injuries that you define as relevant will not be included in official statistics. Another example occurs when you define as unemployed people who would work if a good job were available, who have to work part-time when they want full-time work, and who have given up looking for work, but the official definition of unemployed includes only those who are actively seeking work (full- or part-time). The official statistics exclude those whom you define as unemployed. In both cases, your definition differs from that in official statistics.

Another validity problem arises when you rely on official statistics as a proxy for a construct. This is necessary because you cannot collect original data. For example, you want to know how many people are victims of hate crimes, so you use police statistics on hate crime as a proxy, but the measure is not entirely valid. Many victims do not report hate crimes to the police, and official reports do not always reveal all that occurred (see Expansion Box 11.9, Official Statistics on Hate Crime, Slow Improvements in Accuracy on page 378).

Perhaps you want to measure marriages "forced" by a premarital pregnancy. You can use the date of marriage and the date of the birth of a child in official records to estimate whether such a marriage occurred. This does not tell you that pregnancy was the motivation for the marriage, however. A couple may have planned to marry and the pregnancy was irrelevant, or the pregnancy may have been unknown at the date of marriage. Likewise, some marriages that show no record of a birth could have been forced by a false belief in pregnancy, or a pregnancy that ended in a miscarriage or abortion instead of a birth. In addition, a child might be conceived after the date of marriage, but be born very prematurely. If you measure forced marriages as those in which a child was born less than nine months after a marriage date, some will be mislabeled, thereby lowering your study's validity.

A third validity problem arises because you lack control over how information is collected. Ordinary people who work in bureaucracies collect information that appears in official government reports. You depend on these people to collect, organize, report, and publish data accurately. Systematic errors in collecting the initial information (e.g., census workers who avoid poor neighborhoods and make up information or people who put a false age on a driver's license), in organizing and reporting information (e.g., a police department that is sloppy about filing crime reports and loses some), and in publishing information (e.g., a typographical error in a table) all reduce measurement validity.

Such a problem happened in U.S. statistics regarding the number of people permanently laid off from their jobs. A university researcher reexamined the methods used to gather data by the U.S. Bureau of Labor Statistics and found an error. Data on permanent job losses came from a survey of 50,000 people, but the government agency failed to adjust for a high survey nonresponse rate. The

Official Statistics on Hate Crime, Slow Improvements in Accuracy

Government statistics on crime is one of the many types of existing statistics frequently used in social research. The Uniform Crime Reporting (UCR) program, operating since 1920, is the most-used source of national crime statistics in the United States. Each state and local law enforcement agency sends its crime statistics (i.e., crimes reported to police and arrests made) for most major crimes to the Federal Bureau of Investigation. In 1973, the Department of Justice added a second source of crime data, the National Crime Victimization Survey (NCVS). It is an annual survey conducted with a representative sample of 49,000 households. The survey asks household members whether anyone over the age of 12 had been a crime victim. In the 1980s, a new program supplemented the simple crime counts from the UCR. The National Incident-Based Reporting System (NIBRS) includes many more details about crime circumstances (e.g., location, participants, time). It now covers about 15 percent of the U.S. population, but is slowly expanding.

In 1990, the United States enacted a new hate crime law in which crimes committed that include bias or prejudice regarding a victim's race, religion, ethnicity, or sexual orientation result in added penalties. The FBI publishes a summary of such crimes in its annual report *Hate Crime Statistics,* the primary source of national information on such crime. The accuracy of reporting this new crime illustrates some complexities with official statistics.

After enactment of the national hate crime law, the FBI trained local law officials on enforcing the new

law. In 1991, only 29 percent of the U.S. population had a law enforcement agency that had participated in this training program. By 1999, this had risen to 85 percent of the population. However, a majority of participating agencies report zero hate crimes each year. Since 1994, about 85 percent of trained law enforcement agencies reported zero hate crimes. These zero reports may not be entirely accurate. One study of locations with zero reports discovered that 37 percent of them had hate crimes, but a breakdown occurred in the reporting system. Large regional reporting differences exist. Southern states, with the highest general crime rates, have the lowest reports of hate crimes. Some studies suggest that local attitudes about hate crimes influence the willingness of victims to report them to the police. In addition, not all local police agencies take the hate crime violations equally seriously. Starting in 2000, the National Victimization Survey began to add hate crime questions.

In summary, a dozen years after hate crime legislation was enacted, such crime data are limited. Reporting accuracy is uneven by geographic area and police agency. The data collection, which provides a basic understanding about the numbers and types of hate crimes, is improving slowly. Researchers who want to study hate crime seriously need to combine official national reports with other sources of information that contain more detail and focus on local geographic areas (see Nolan, Akiyama, and Berhanu, 2002).

---

corrected figures showed that instead of a 7 percent decline in the number of people laid off between 1993 and 1996, as had been first reported, there had been no change.[19]

Reliability. Reliability problems can plague existing statistics research; they occur when official definitions or the method of collecting information changes over time. Official definitions of work injury, disability, unemployment, and the like change periodically. Even if we learn of such changes, consistent measurement over time is impossible. For example, during the early 1980s, the method for

calculating the U.S. unemployment rate changed. Previously, the government had calculated the unemployment rate as the number of unemployed persons divided by the number in the civilian workforce. The new method divided the number of unemployed by the civilian workforce plus the number of people in the military. Likewise, when police departments computerize their records, the number of crimes reported appears to increase, simply because of improved record-keeping.

Equivalence reliability can also be a problem. For example, a measure of crime across a nation depends on each police department's providing accurate information. If departments in one region of a country have sloppy bookkeeping, the measure reported loses equivalence reliability. Likewise, studies of police departments suggest that political pressures to increase arrests are closely related to the number of arrests. For example, political pressure in one city may increase arrests (e.g., a crackdown on crime) whereas pressures in another city may decrease arrests (e.g., to show a drop in crime shortly before an election in order to make officials look better).

Representative reliability can be a problem in official government statistics. For example, the U.S. Bureau of Labor Statistics found a 0.6 percent increase in the female unemployment rate after it used gender-neutral measurement procedures. Until the mid-1990s, interviewers asked women only whether they had been keeping house or doing something else. Researchers categorized women who answered "keeping house" as being housewives, not as being unemployed, even if the women had been seeking work. Once they asked women the same question as men, "Were you working or doing something else?" many women reported not working but doing "something else" such as looking for work. This shows the importance of methodological details in how officials create government statistics.

Official statistics allow for international comparisons but national governments collect data differently and the quality of data collection varies. For example, in 1994, the official unemployment rate reported for the United States was 7 percent, 2.9 percent in Japan, and 12 percent in France. If the nations defined and gathered data the same way, including rates of discouraged workers and involuntary part-time workers, the rates would have been 9.3 percent for the United States, 9.6 percent for Japan, and 13.7 percent for France. To evaluate the quality of official government statistics, *The Economist* magazine asked a team of 20 leading statisticians to evaluate the statistics of thirteen nations based on freedom from political interference, reliability, statistical methodology, and coverage of topics. The top five nations in order were Canada, Australia, Holland, France, and Sweden. The United States tied for sixth with Britain and Germany. The quality of U.S. statistics suffered from being highly decentralized, having fewer

statisticians than any other nation, and experiencing politically motivated cutbacks on the range of data collected.

Data collected internationally can be controversial. The International Labor Organization of the United Nations reported that the official statistics of total economic activity for several nations are inaccurate because they exclude the sex industry. In some countries (especially Thailand and the Philippines), millions of workers (primarily young women) are employed and billions of dollars in revenue are generated from prostitution and the sex industry. This has a large impact on the economy, but it does not appear in any official reports or statistics.[20]

Missing Data. One problem that plagues researchers who use existing statistics and documents is that of missing data (discussed in Chapter 7). Sometimes the data were collected but lost. More frequently, the data were never collected. The data may be missing because researchers and officials in government agencies decided not to collect information. Those who decide what to collect may not collect what later researchers will need in order to address new questions. Government agencies start or stop collecting information for political, budgetary, or other reasons. For example, during the early 1980s, cost-cutting measures by the U.S. federal government stopped the collection of information that social researchers found valuable. Missing information is a problem especially when researchers cover long periods. For instance, someone interested in studying the number of work stoppages and strikes in the United States can obtain data from the 1890s to the present except for a 5-year period after 1911 when the federal government did not collect the data.

ISSUES OF INFERENCE AND THEORY TESTING

You need to take extra care when inferring causality or testing a theory based on nonreactive data. It is difficult to establish temporal order and eliminate alternative explanations with nonreactive and unobtrusive measures. In content analysis, you cannot generalize from the content to its effects on those who read the text, but can use the correlation logic of survey research only to show an association among variables.

ETHICAL CONCERNS

Ethical concerns are not at the forefront of most nonreactive research because the people you study are not directly involved. The primary ethical concern is the privacy and confidentiality of using information that someone else gathers. Another larger ethical issue is that official statistics are social and political products. Some researchers or official agencies gather data based on implicit theories and value assumptions. Official measures or statistics can be the objects of political conflict and a way to push policy in certain political directions. Once government agencies define a measure as official, it can influence public policy and lead to outcomes that would be different had an alternative but equally valid measure been used. For example, political activism during the Great Depression of the 1930 simulated the collection of information on many social conditions (e.g., the number of patients who died while in public mental hospitals). Before the political activism of the time, governments and others did not see the conditions as sufficiently important to warrant public attention. Likewise, information on the percentage of non-White students enrolled in U.S. schools at various ages is available only since 1953 and for various non-White races only since the 1970s. Earlier, such information was not salient for public policy.

The collection of official statistics can stimulate public attention toward an issue, and public concern about a social issue can stimulate the collection of new official statistics. For example, drunk driving became a public issue only after government agencies started to maintain statistics on the number of automobile accidents in which alcohol was a factor.

Political and social values influence decisions about which statistics government agencies collect. The design and collection of most official statistics is for top-down administrative planning purposes. The data may not conform to your purposes or the purposes of people who disagree with the thinking

of bureaucratic decision makers. For example, a government agency measures the number of tons of steel produced, miles of highway paved, and the average number of people in a household. Information on other conditions such as drinking-water quality, time needed to commute to work, stress related to a job, and number of children needing child care may not be collected because political officials consider it to be unimportant. In many countries, officials see gross national product (GNP) as a critical measure of societal progress, but GNP ignores noneconomic aspects of social life (e.g., time spent playing with one's children) and types of work (e.g., housework) that are free. The information available reflects the outcome of political debate and the values of officials who decide which statistics to collect.[21]

CONCLUSION

In this chapter, you read about several types of nonreactive research techniques. They are ways to measure or observe aspects of social life without affecting those who are being studied. They result in objective, numerical information that you can analyze to address research questions. You can use the techniques in conjunction with other types of quantitative or qualitative social research to address a large number of questions.

As with any form of quantitative data, we need to be concerned with measurement issues. It is easy to take available information from a survey or government document, but this does not mean that it measures the construct of interest to us.

You should be aware of two potential problems in nonreactive research. First, the availability of existing information restricts the questions that we can address. Second, the nonreactive variables often have weak validity because they do not measure the construct of interest. Although existing statistics and secondary data analysis are low-cost research techniques, the researcher lacks control over, and substantial knowledge of, the data collection process. This potential source of errors means that researchers need to be especially vigilant and cautious.

In the next chapter, we move from designing research projects and collecting data to analyzing data. The analysis techniques apply to the quantitative data presented in the previous chapters. So far, you have seen how to move from a topic, to a research design and measures, to collecting data. Next you look at data and see what they can tell you about a hypothesis or research question.

KEY TERMS

accretion measure
coding system
erosion measure
fallacy of misplaced
   concreteness

intercoder reliability
latent coding
manifest coding
nonreactive research
social indicator

structured observation
text
unobtrusive measures

REVIEW QUESTIONS

1. For what types of research questions is content analysis appropriate?
2. What are the four characteristics of content that are observed and recorded in coding systems?
3. Of what reliability problems should the researcher using existing statistical data be aware?
4. What are the advantages and disadvantages of secondary data analysis?
5. Why do content analysis researchers use multiple coders, and what is a possible problem with doing this?
6. How are inferences limited in content analysis?
7. What units of analysis are used in content analysis?
8. What is the aggregation problem in existing statistics?
9. What are the three validity problems in content analysis?
10. Of what limitations of using existing statistics should researchers be aware?

NOTES

1. See Webb and colleagues (1981:7–11).
2. For an inventory of nonreactive measures, see Bouchard (1976) and Webb et al. (1981).
3. See Krippendorff (1980:13). For definitions of content analysis, see Holsti (1968a:597), Krippendorff (1980:21–24), Markoff et al. (1974:5–6), Stone and Weber (1992), and Weber (1985:81, note 1).
4. Weitzman et al. (1972) is a classic in this type of research.
5. See Ariés (1977) for an example.
6. Examples of content analysis studies can be found in Berelson (1952), Carney (1972), McDiarmid (1971),

Myers and Margavio (1983), Namenwirth (1970), Sepstrup (1981), Stewart (1984), and Stone et al. (1966). Harwood (2000) described elderly people on television. Also see Weber (1983) for a discussion of measurement issues in content analysis.
7. Stone and Weber (1992) and Weber (1984, 1985) review computerized content analysis techniques.
8. See Andren (1981:58–66) and Holsti (1969:94–126) on reliability and latent or semantic analysis.
9. See Krippendorff (1980) for various measures of intercoder reliability. Also see Fiske (1982) for the related issue of convergent validity.

10. For information on the confederate flag issue, see Cooper and Knotts (2006), Holyfield, Moltz, and Bradley (2009), and Newman (2007).

11. On social indicators, see Bauer (1966), Carley (1981), Duncan (1984:233–235), Juster and Land (1981), Land (1992), Rossi and Gilmartin (1980), and Taylor (1980). Also see Ferriss (1988) on using social indicators for planning and social forecasting.

12. See Herbert (2003), Miringoff and Opdycke (2007), and Ravo (1996).

13. Many non-English language yearbooks are also produced; for example, *Statistisches Jahrbuch* for the Federal Republic of Germany, *Annuaire Statistique de la France* for France, Year Book Australia for Australia, and Denmark's *Statiskisk Ti Arsoversigt*. Japan produces an English version of its yearbook called the *Statistical Handbook of Japan*.

14. Guides to government include the *Guide to British Government Publications*, Australian official publications, and Irish official publications. Similar publications exist for most nations. For example, *DOD's Parliamentary Companion for the United Kingdom* and the *Parliamentary Handbook of the Commonwealth of Australia* are both similar to the *Almanac of American Politics*.

15. See Churchill (1983:140–167) and Stewart (1984) for lists of business information sources.

16. Other major U.S. archives of survey data include the National Opinion Research Center, University of Chicago; the Survey Research Center, University of California–Berkeley; the Behavioral Sciences Laboratory, University of Cincinnati; Data and Program Library Service, University of Wisconsin–Madison; the Roper Center, University of Connecticut–Storrs; and the Institute for Research in Social Science, University of North Carolina–Chapel Hill. Also see Kiecolt and Nathan (1985) and Parcel (1992).

17. See Alwin (1988) and Davis and Smith (1992).

18. For a discussion of these issues, see Dale et al. (1988:27–31), Horn (1993:138), Maier (1991), and Parcel (1992).

19. See Stevenson (1996).

20. See *The Economist,* "The Good Statistics Guide" (September 11, 1993); "The Overlooked Housekeeper" (February 5, 1994); and "Fewer Damned Lies?" (March 30, 1996). Also see "U.N. Urges Fiscal Accounting to Include Sex Trade," *New York Times* (August 20, 1998).

21. See Block and Burns (1986), Carr-Hill (1984a), Hindess (1973), Horn (1993), Maier (1991), and Van den Berg and Van der Veer (1985). Discussions by Norris (1981) and Starr (1987) are also helpful.

CHAPTER 12

Analysis of Quantitative Data

Dealing with Data
Results with One Variable
Results with Two Variables

More than Two Variables
Inferential Statistics
Conclusion

> *Statistics may also be regarded as a method of dealing with data.*
> *This definition stresses the view that statistics is a tool concerned*
> *with the collection, organization, and analysis of numerical facts*
> *or observations. . . . The major concern of descriptive statistics is to*
> *present information in a convenient, usable, and understandable form.*
> —Richard Runyon and Audry Haber, *Fundamentals of Behavioral Statistics*, p. 6.

If you read a research report or article based on quantitative data, you will probably see many charts, graphs, and tables full of numbers. Do not be intimidated by them. The author provides the charts, graphs, and tables to give you, the reader, a condensed picture of the data. The charts and tables allow you to see the evidence collected by the researcher and examine it for yourself. When you collect your own quantitative data, you will use similar techniques to reveal what is inside the data. You will need to organize and manipulate the quantitative data to get them to disclose things of interest about the social world. In this chapter, you will be introduced to the fundamentals of organizing and analyzing quantitative data. Its analysis is a complex field of knowledge. This chapter cannot substitute for a course in social statistics. It covers only the basic statistical concepts and data-handling techniques necessary to understand social research.

Data collected using the techniques in the past chapters are in the form of numbers. The numbers represent values of variables, which measure characteristics of participants, respondents, or other cases. The numbers are in a raw form on questionnaires,

note pads, recording sheets, or computer files. We do several things to the raw data in order to see what they can say about the hypotheses: reorganize them into a form suitable for computer entry, present them in charts or graphs to summarize their features, and interpret or give theoretical meaning to the results.

DEALING WITH DATA

Coding Data

Before we examine quantitative data to test hypotheses, we must put them in a specific form. You encountered the idea of coding data in the last chapter. Here data coding means systematically reorganizing raw data into a format that is easy to analyze using statistics software on computers. As with coding in content analysis, researchers create and consistently apply rules for transferring information from one form to another.[1]

Coding can be a simple clerical task when you have recorded the data as numbers on well-organized recording sheets, but it is very difficult if you want to code answers to open-ended survey questions into numbers in a process similar to latent content analysis. To code open-ended survey data or other data that are not already in the form of numbers requires a coding procedure and a codebook. The **coding procedure** is a set of rules stating that you will assign certain numbers to variable attributes. For example, you code males as 1 and females as 2, or for a Likert scale, you code strongly agree as 4, agree as 3, and so forth. You need a code for each category of all variables and missing information. The coding procedure explains in detail how you converted non-numerical information into numbers.

A **codebook** is a document (i.e., one or more pages) describing the coding procedure and the computer file location of data for variables in a specific format. When you code data, it is essential to create a well-organized, detailed codebook and make multiple copies of it. If you do not write down the details of the coding procedure or if you misplace the codebook, you have lost the key to the data and may have to recode them again.

You should begin to think about a coding procedure and codebook before you collect any data. For example, many survey researchers precode a questionnaire before interviewing or collecting data. Precoding involves placing the code categories (e.g., 1 for male, 2 for female) on the questionnaire and building the features of a codebook into it.[2] If you do not precode, your first step after collecting data is to create a codebook. You also must assign an identification number to each case to keep track of the cases. Next you transfer the information from each questionnaire into a computer-readable format.

Entering Data

Most computer programs designed for numerical data analysis require that the data be in a grid format. In the grid, each row represents a respondent, participant, or case. In computer terminology, these are called **data records**. Each data record is for a single case. A column or a set of columns represents specific variables. It is possible to go from a column and row location (e.g., row 7, column 5) back to the original source of data (e.g., a questionnaire item on marital status for respondent 8). A column or a set of columns assigned to a variable is called a **data field**, or simply *field*.

For example, you code survey data for three respondents in a format for computers like the start of a data file presented in Figure 12.1. People cannot easily read data in this format and without the codebook, it is worthless. The data file condenses answers to 50 survey questions for three respondents into three lines or rows. The raw data for many research projects look like this, except that there may be more than 1,000 rows, and the lines may be more than 100 columns long. For example, a 15-minute telephone survey of 250 students produces a grid of data that is 250 rows by 240 columns.

The codebook in Figure 12.1 states that the first two numbers are identification numbers. Thus, the example data are for the first (01), second (02), and third (03) respondents. Notice that we use zeros as placeholders to reduce confusion between 1 and 01. The 1s are always in column 2; the 10s are in column 1. The codebook states that column 5 contains the variable "gender": Cases 1 and 2 are male and Case 3 is female. Column 4 tells us that Carlos interviewed Cases 1 and 2 and Sophia Case 3.

There are four ways to enter raw quantitative data into a computer:

1. *Code sheet.* Gather the information, then transfer it from the original source onto a grid

---

Coding procedure   A set of rules created by a quantitative researcher for assigning numbers to specific variable attributes, usually in preparation for statistical analysis and carefully recorded in a codebook.

Codebook   A document that describes the procedure for coding variables and their location in a format that computers can use.

Data records   The units or reports in computer-based data that contain information on the variables for a case.

Data field   One or more columns in data organized for a computer representing the location of information on a specific variable.

FIGURE 12.1   Coded Data for Three Cases and Codebook

EXCERPT FROM SURVEY QUESTIONNAIRE

Respondent ID _____   Interviewer Name _____

Note the Respondent's Gender: _____ Male _____ Female

1. The first question is about the President of the United States. Do you Strongly Agree, Agree, Disagree, Strongly Disagree, or Have No Opinion About the following statement:

   The President of the United States is doing a great job.

   _____ Strongly Agree _____ Agree _____ Disagree _____ Strongly Disagree _____ No Opinion

2. How old are you? _____

EXCERPT OF CODED DATA

Column

```
00000000011111111112222222222333333333444 ... etc. (tens)
123456789012345678901234567890123456789012 ... etc. (ones)
01 212736302 182738274 10239 18.82 3947461 ... etc.
02 213334821 124988154 21242 18.21 3984123 ... etc.
03 420123982 113727263 12345 17.36 1487645 ... etc.
etc.
```
Raw data for first three cases, columns 1 through 42.

EXCERPT FROM CODEBOOK

Column	Variable Name	Description
1–2	ID	Respondent identification number
3	BLANK	
4	Interviewer	Interviewer who collected the data:
		1 = Susan
		2 = Carlos
		3 = Juan
		4 = Sophia
		5 = Clarence
5	Gender	Interviewer report of respondent's sex
		1 = Male, 2 = Female
6	PresJob	The President of the United States is
		doing a great job.
		1 = Strongly Agree
		2 = Agree
		3 = No Opinion
		4 = Disagree
		5 = Strongly Disagree
		Blank = Missing Information

---

format (code sheet). Next, enter what is on the code sheet into a computer line by line.

2. *Direct-entry method (including CATI).* As information is being collected, sit at a computer keyboard (or similar recording device) while listening to or observing the information and enter or have a respondent/participant enter the information him- or herself. To use the

direct-entry method, the computer must be preprogrammed to accept the information.

3. *Optical scan.* Gather the information and then enter it onto optical scan sheets (or have a respondent/participant enter the information) by filling in the correct "dots." Next use an optical scanner or reader to transfer the information into a computer.

4. *Bar code.* Gather the information and convert it into different widths of bars that are associated with specific numerical values; then use a bar-code reader to transfer the information into a computer.

Cleaning Data

Accuracy is extremely important when coding data (see Example Box 12.1, Example of Dealing with Data). Errors you make when coding or entering data into a computer threaten the validity of the measures and cause misleading results. If you have a perfect sample, perfect measures, and no errors in gathering data but make errors in the coding process or in entering data into a computer, you can ruin an entire research project.

After very careful coding, you must check the accuracy of coding, or "clean" the data. Often you want to code random sample of 10 to 15 percent of the data a second time. If you discover no coding

errors in the recoded sample, you can proceed. If you find errors, you need to recheck all of the coding.

You can verify coding after the data are in a computer in two ways. **Possible code cleaning** (or *wild code checking*) involves checking the categories of all variables for impossible codes. For example, respondent gender is coded 1 = Male, 2 = Female. A 4 for a case found in the field for the gender variable indicates a coding error. A second method, **contingency cleaning** (or *consistency checking*), involves cross-classifying two variables and looking for logically impossible combinations. For example, you cross-classify school level by occupation. If you find a respondent coded never having passed the eighth grade and recorded as being a medical doctor, you must check for a coding error.

You can modify data in some ways after they are in a computer, but you cannot use more refined categories than those used collecting the original data. For example, you may group ratio-level income data into five ordinal categories, and you can collapse variable categories and combine information from several indicators to create a new index variable.

RESULTS WITH ONE VARIABLE

Frequency Distributions

The word *statistics* can refer to a set of collected numbers (e.g., numbers telling how many people live in a city) as well as a branch of applied mathematics we use to manipulate and summarize the features of numbers. Social researchers use both types of statistics. Here we focus on the second type: ways to manipulate and summarize numbers that represent data from a research project.

Descriptive statistics describe numerical data. We can categorize them by the number of variables involved: univariate, bivariate, or multivariate (for one, two, and three or more variables). Univariate statistics describe one variable (*uni-* refers to one; *-variate* refers to variable). The easiest way to describe the numerical data of one variable is with a **frequency distribution**. You can use the frequency

---

Direct-entry method Process of entering data directly into a computer by typing them without bar codes or optical scan sheets.

Possible code cleaning Clarifying data using a computer by searching for responses or answer categories that cannot have cases.

Contingency cleaning Flushing data using a computer in which the researcher reviews the combination of categories for two variables for logically impossible cases.

Descriptive statistics A general type of simple statistics used by researchers to describe basic patterns in the data.

Frequency distribution A table that shows the dispersion of cases into the categories of one variable, that is, the number or percent of cases in each category.

EXAMPLE BOX **12.1**
Example of Dealing with Data

There is no good substitute for getting your hands dirty with the data. Here is an example of data preparation from a study I conducted with my students. My university surveyed about one-third of the students to learn their thinking about and experience with sexual harassment on campus. A research team drew a random sample and then developed and distributed a self-administered questionnaire. Respondents put answers on optical scan sheets that were similar to the answer sheets used for multiple-choice exams. The story begins with the delivery of more than 3,000 optical scan sheets.

After the sheets arrived, we visually scanned each one for obvious errors. Despite instructions to use pencil and fill in each circle neatly and darkly, we found that about 200 respondents used a pen, and another 200 were very sloppy or used very light pencil marks. We cleaned up the sheets and redid them in pencil. We also found about 25 unusable sheets that were defaced, damaged, or too incomplete (e.g., only the first 2 of 70 questions answered).

Next we read the usable optical scan sheets into a computer. We had the computer produce the number of occurrences, or frequency, of the attributes for each variable. Looking at them, we discovered several kinds of errors. Some respondents had filled in two responses for a question to which only one answer was requested or possible. Some had filled in impossible response codes (e.g., the numeral 4 for gender, when the only legitimate codes were 1 for male and 2 for female), and some had filled in every answer in the same way, suggesting that they did not take the survey seriously. For each case with an error, we returned to the optical scan sheet to see whether we could recover any information. If we could not recover

information, we reclassified the case as a nonresponse or recoded a response as missing information.

The questionnaire had two contingency questions. For each, a respondent who answered "no" to one question was to skip the next five questions. We created a table for each question. We looked to see whether all respondents who answered "no" to the first question skipped or left blank the next five. We found about 35 cases in which the respondent answered "no" but then went on to answer the next five questions. We returned to each sheet and tried to figure out which the respondent really intended. In most cases, it appeared that the respondent meant the "no" but failed to read the instructions to skip questions.

Finally, we examined the frequency of attributes for each variable to see whether they made sense. We were very surprised to learn that about 600 respondents had marked "Native American" for the racial heritage question. In addition, more than half of those who had done so were freshmen. A check of official records revealed that the university enrolled a total of about 20 Native Americans or American Indians, and that over 90 percent of the students were White, non-Hispanic Caucasians. The percentage of respondents marking Black, African-American, or Hispanic-Chicano matched the official records. We concluded that some White Caucasian respondents had been unfamiliar with the term "Native American" for "American Indian." Apparently, they had mistakenly marked it instead of "White, Caucasian." Because we expected about 7 Native Americans in the sample, we recoded the "Native American" responses as "White, Caucasian." This meant that we reclassified Native Americans in the sample as Caucasian. At this point, we were ready to analyze the data.

---

distribution with nominal-, ordinal-, interval-, or ratio-level data. For example, I have data for 400 respondents and want to summarize the information on the gender at a glance. The easiest way is with a raw count or a percentage frequency distribution (see Figure 12.2 on page 388). I can present the same information in graphic form.

Some common types of graphic representations are the histogram, bar chart, and pie chart. Bar

charts or graphs are used for discrete variables. They can have a vertical or horizontal orientation with a small space between the bars. The terminology is not exact, but the **histogram** is

> **Histogram** A graphic display of univariate frequencies or percentages, usually with vertical lines indicating the amount or proportion.

FIGURE 12.2   Examples of Univariate Statistics

RAW COUNT FREQUENCY DISTRIBUTION

Gender	Frequency
Male	100
Female	300
Total	400

PERCENTAGE FREQUENCY DISTRIBUTION

Gender	Percentage
Male	25%
Female	75%
Total	100%

BAR CHART OF SAME INFORMATION

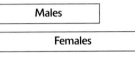

EXAMPLE OF GROUPED DATA FREQUENCY DISTRIBUTION

First Job Annual Income	N
Under $5,000	25
$5,000 to $9,999	50
$10,000 to $15,999	100
$16,000 to $19,999	150
$20,000 to $29,999	50
$30,000 and over	25
Total	400

EXAMPLE OF FREQUENCY POLYGON

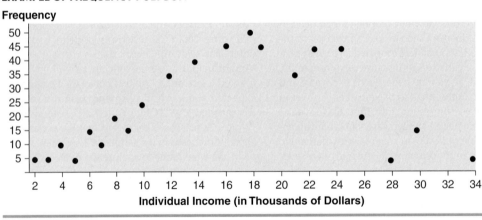

---

usually a set of upright bar graphs for interval or ratio data.[3]

For interval- or ratio-level data, we often group the information into several categories. The grouped categories must be mutually exclusive. We also can plot interval- or ratio-level data in a **frequency polygon** with the number of cases or frequency along the vertical axis and the values of the variable or scores along the horizontal axis. A polygon appears when we connect the dots.

Measures of Central Tendency

Often, we want to summarize the information about one variable into a single number. To do this, we use three **measures of central tendency** (i.e. measures of the center of the frequency distribution: mean, median, and mode). Many people call them *averages,* a less precise or clear way of saying the same thing.

The **mode** is the easiest to use and we can use it with nominal, ordinal, interval, and ratio data. It is simply the most common or frequently occurring number. For example, the mode of the following list is 5: 6, 5, 7, 10, 9, 5, 3, 5. A distribution can have more than one mode. For example, the mode of this list is both 5 and 7: 5, 6, 1, 2, 5, 7, 4, 7. If the list gets long, it is easy to spot the mode in a frequency distribution; just look for the most frequent score. There is always at least one case with a score equal to the mode.

The **median** is the middle point. It is also the 50th percentile, or the point at which half the cases are above it and half below it. We can use it with ordinal-, interval-, or ratio-level data (but not nominal level). We can "eyeball" the mode, but computing a median requires a little more work. The easiest way is first to organize the scores from highest to lowest and then count to the middle. If there is an odd number of scores, it is simple. Seven people are waiting for a bus; their ages are 12, 17, 20, 27, 30, 55, 80. The median age is 27. Note that the median does not change easily. If the 55-year-old and the 80-year-old both got on one bus and the remaining people were joined by two 31-year-olds, the median remains unchanged. If there is an even number of scores, things are a bit more complicated. For example, six people at a bus stop have the following ages: 17, 20, 26, 30, 50, 70. The median is halfway between 26 and 30. Compute the median by adding the two middle scores together and dividing by 2 (26 + 30 = 56/2 = 28). The median age is 28, even though no person is 28 years old. Note that there is no mode in the list of six ages because each person has a different age.

The **mean** (also called the *arithmetic average*) is the most widely used measure of central tendency. We can use it only with interval- or ratio-level data.[4] To compute the mean, we add up all scores and then divide by the number of scores. For example, the mean age in the previous example is 17 + 20 + 26 + 30 + 50 + 70 = 213; 213/6 = 35.5. No one in the list is 35.5 years old, and the mean does not equal the median.

Changes in extreme values (very large or very small) can greatly influence the mean. For example, the 50-year-old and 70-year-old left and were replaced with two 31-year-olds. The distribution now looks like this: 17, 20, 26, 30, 31, 31. The median is unchanged: 28. The mean is 17 + 20 + 26 + 30 + 31 + 31 = 155; 155/6 = 25.8. Thus, the mean dropped a great deal when a few extreme values were removed.

If the frequency distribution forms a **normal distribution** or bell-shaped curve, the three measures of central tendency equal each other. If the distribution is a **skewed distribution** (i.e., more cases are in the upper or lower scores), then the three will not be equal. If most cases have lower scores with a few extreme high scores, the mean will be the highest, the median in the middle, and the mode the

Frequency polygon   A graph of connected points showing how many cases fall into each category of a variable.

Measures of central tendency   A class of statistical measures that summarizes information about the distribution of data for one variable into a single number.

Mode   A measure of central tendency for one variable that indicates the most frequent or common score.

Median   A measure of central tendency for one variable that indicates the point or score at which half of the cases are higher and half are lower.

Mean   A measure of central tendency for one variable that indicates the arithmetic average, that is, the sum of all scores divided by the total number of them.

Normal distribution   A bell-shaped frequency polygon for a dispersion of cases with a peak in the center and identical curving slopes on either side of the center; distribution of many naturally occurring phenomena and a basis of much statistical theory.

Skewed distribution   A dispersion of cases among the categories of a variable that is not normal, that is, not a bell shape; instead of an equal number of cases on both ends, more are at one of the extremes.

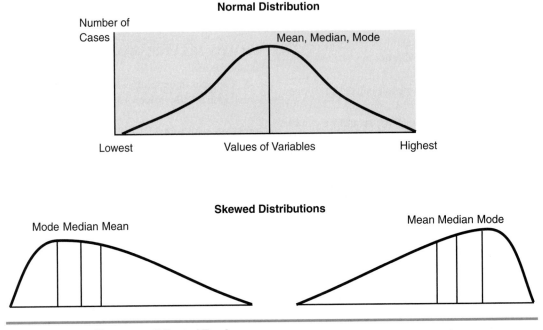

FIGURE 12.3   Measures of Central Tendency

lowest. If most cases have higher scores with a few extreme low scores, the mean will be the lowest, the median in the middle, and the mode the highest. In general, the median is best to use for a skewed distribution, although the mean is used in most other statistics (see Figure 12.3).

Measures of Variation

The measure of central tendency is a single-number summary of a distribution; however, the measures give only its center. Another characteristic of a distribution is its *spread, dispersion,* or *variability* around the center. Two distributions can have identical measures of central tendency but differ in their spread about the center. For example, seven people are at a bus stop in front of a bar. Their ages are 25, 26, 27, 30, 33, 34, 35. Both the median and the mean are 30. At a bus stop in front of an ice cream store, seven people have the identical median and mean, but their ages are 5, 10, 20, 30, 40, 50, 55. The ages of the group in front of the ice cream store are spread more from the center, or the distribution has more variability.

Variability has important social implications. For example, in city X, the median and mean family income is $37,600 per year, and it has zero variation. *Zero variation* means that every family has an income of exactly $37,600. City Y has the same median and mean family income, but 96 percent of its families have incomes of $14,000 per year and 4 percent have incomes of $350,000 per year. City X has perfect income equality whereas there is great inequality in city Y. If we do not know the variability of income in the two cities, we miss very important information.

We measure variation in three ways: range, percentile, and standard deviation. **Range** is the simplest. It consists of the largest and smallest scores. For example, the range for the bus stop in front of the bar is from 25 to 35, or $35 - 25 = 10$ years. If

Range   A measure of dispersion for one variable indicating the highest and lowest scores.

the 35-year-old got onto a bus and was replaced by a 60-year-old, the range would change to $60 - 25 = 45$ years. Range has limitations because it only tells us the extreme high and low. For example, here are two groups of six with a range of 35 years: 30, 30, 30, 30, 30, 65 and 20, 45, 46, 48, 50, 55.

Percentiles tell us the score at a specific place within the distribution. One percentile you already studied is the median, the 50th percentile. Sometimes the 25th and 75th percentiles or the 10th and 90th percentiles are used to describe a distribution. For example, the 25th percentile is the score at which 25 percent of cases in the distribution have either that score or a lower one. The computation of a percentile follows the same logic as the median. If you have 100 people and want to find the 25th percentile, you rank the scores (i.e. measures in numbers of variables) and count up from the bottom until you reach number 25. If the total is not 100, you simply adjust the distribution to a percentage basis.

Standard deviation is the most difficult to compute measure of dispersion; it is also the most comprehensive and widely used. The range and percentile are for ordinal-, interval-, and ratio-level data, but the standard deviation requires an interval or ratio level of measurement. It is based on the mean and gives an "average distance" between all scores and the mean. People rarely compute the standard deviation by hand for more than a handful of cases because computers do it in seconds.

Look at the calculation of the standard deviation in Figure 12.4 (page 392). If you add the absolute difference between each score and the mean (i.e., subtract each score from the mean), you get zero because the mean is equally distant from all scores. Also notice that the scores that differ the most from the mean have the largest effect on the sum of squares and on the standard deviation.

The standard deviation is of limited usefulness by itself. It is used for comparison purposes. For example, the standard deviation for the schooling of parents of children in class A is 3.317 years; for class B, it is 0.812; and for class C, it is 6.239. The standard deviation tells a researcher that the parents of children in class B are very similar, whereas those for class C are very different. In fact, in class

B, the schooling of an "average" parent is less than a year above or below the mean for all parents, so the parents are very homogeneous. In class C, however, the "average" parent is more than six years above or below the mean, so the parents are very heterogeneous.

We use the standard deviation and the mean to create **z-scores**, which let you compare two or more distributions or groups. The z-score, also called a *standardized score*, expresses points or scores on a frequency distribution in terms of a number of standard deviations from the mean. Scores are in terms of their relative position within a distribution, not as absolute values (see Expansion Box 12.1, Calculating Z-Scores on page 393). Z-scores can tell us a lot. For example, Katy, a sales manager in firm A, earns $70,000 per year, whereas Mike in firm B earns $60,000 per year. Despite the $10,000 absolute income differences between them, the managers are paid equally relative to others in the same firm. Both Katy and Mike are paid more than two-thirds of other employees in each of their respective firms.

Here is another example of how to use z-scores. Hans and Heidi are twin brother and sister, but Hans is shorter than Heidi. Compared to other girls her age, Heidi is at the mean height; she has a z-score of zero. Likewise, Hans is at the mean height among boys his age. Thus, within each comparison group, the twins are at the same z-score, so they have the same relative height.

Z-scores are easy to calculate from the mean and standard deviation. For example, an employer interviews students from Kings College and Queens College. She learns that the colleges are similar and that both grade on a 4.0 scale, yet the mean grade-point average at Kings College is 2.62 with

---

Percentile   A measure of dispersion for one variable that indicates the percentage of cases at or below a score or point.

Standard deviation   A measure of dispersion for one variable that indicates an average distance between the scores and the mean.

Z-score   A standardized location of a score in a distribution of scores based on the number of standard deviations it is above or below the mean.

FIGURE 12.4   The Standard Deviation

STEPS IN COMPUTING THE STANDARD DEVIATION

1. Compute the mean.
2. Subtract the mean from each score.
3. Square the resulting difference for each score.
4. Total up the squared differences to get the sum of squares.
5. Divide the sum of squares by the number of cases to get the variance.
6. Take the square root of the variance, which is the standard deviation.

EXAMPLE OF COMPUTING THE STANDARD DEVIATION

[8 respondents, variable = years of schooling]

Score	Score – Mean	Squared (Score – Mean)
15	15 – 12.5 = 2.5	6.25
12	12 – 12.5 = −0.5	.25
12	12 – 12.5 = −0.5	.25
10	10 – 12.5 = −2.5	6.25
16	16 – 12.5 = 3.5	12.25
18	18 – 12.5 = 5.5	30.25
8	8 – 12.5 = 4.5	20.25
9	9 – 12.5 = −3.5	12.25

Mean = 15 + 12 + 12 + 10 + 16 + 18 + 8 + 9 = 100, 100/8 = 12.5
Sum of squares = 6.25 + .25 + .25 + 6.25 + 12.25 + 30.25 + 20.25 + 12.25 = 88
Variance = Sum of squares/Number of cases = 88/8 = 11
Standard deviation = Square root of variance = $\sqrt{11}$ = 3.317 years.
Here is the standard deviation in the form of a formula with symbols.

Symbols:
X = SCORE of case Σ = Sigma (Greek letter) for sum, add together
$\bar{X}$ = MEAN N = Number of cases

Formula:[a]

$$\text{Standard deviation} = \sqrt{\frac{\Sigma(X-\bar{X})^2}{N-1}}$$

---

[a] There is a slight difference in the formula depending on whether one is using data for the population or a sample to estimate the population parameter.

---

a standard deviation of .50, whereas the mean grade-point average at Queens College is 3.24 with a standard deviation of .40. The employer suspects that grades at Queens College are inflated. Suzette from Kings College has a grade-point average of 3.62; Jorge from Queens College has a grade-point average of 3.64. Both students took the same courses. The employer wants to adjust the grades for the grading practices of the two colleges (i.e., create standardized scores). She calculates z-scores by subtracting each student's score from the mean and then divides by the standard deviation. For example, Suzette's z-score is 3.62 − 2.62 = 1.00/.50 = 2, whereas Jorge's z-score is 3.64 − 3.24. = .40/.40 = 1. Thus, the employer learns that Suzette is two standard deviations above the mean in her

EXPANSION BOX **12.1**

Calculating Z- Scores

Personally, I do not like the formula for z-scores, which is:

Z-score = (Score − Mean)/Standard Deviation, or in symbols:

$$z = \frac{X - \bar{X}}{\delta}$$

where: X = score, $\bar{X}$ = mean, δ = standard deviation

I usually rely on a simple conceptual diagram that does the same thing and that shows what z-scores really do. Consider data on the ages of schoolchildren with a mean of 7 years and a standard deviation of 2 years. How do I compute the z-score of 5-year-old Miguel, or what if I know that Yashohda's z-score is a +2 and I need to know her age in years? First, I draw a little chart from −3 to +3 with zero in the middle. I will put the mean value at zero, because a z-score of zero is the mean and z-scores measure distance above or below it. I stop at 3 because virtually all cases fall within 3 standard deviations of the mean in most situations. The chart looks like this:

```
|___|___|___|___|___|___|
-3  -2  -1   0  +1  +2  +3
```

Now, I label the values of the mean and add or subtract standard deviations from it. One standard deviation above the mean (+1) when the mean is 7 and standard deviation is 2 years is just 7 + 2, or 9 years. For a −2 z-score, I put 3 years. This is because it is 2 standard deviations, of 2 years each (or 4 years), lower than the mean of 7. My diagram now looks like this:

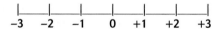
```
1    3   5   7    9    11   13   age in years
|____|___|___|____|____|____|
-3  -2  -1   0   +1   +2   +3
```

It is easy to see that Miguel, who is 5 years old, has a z-score of −1, whereas Yashohda's z-score of +2 corresponds to 11 years old. I can read from z-score to age, or age to z-score. For fractions, such as a z-score of −1.5, I just apply the same fraction to age to get 4 years. Likewise, an age of 12 is a z-score of +2.5.

college, whereas Jorge is only one standard deviation above the mean for his college. Although Suzette's absolute grade-point average is lower than Jorge's, relative to the students in each of their colleges, Suzette's grades are much higher than Jorge's.

RESULTS WITH TWO VARIABLES

A Bivariate Relationship

Univariate statistics describe a single variable in isolation. **Bivariate statistics** are much more valuable. They let us consider two variables together and describe the relationship between variables. Even simple hypotheses require two variables. Bivariate statistical analysis shows a **statistical relationship** between variables—that is, things that tend to appear together. For example, a relationship exists between water pollution in a stream and the fact that people who drink the water get sick. It is a statistical relationship between two variables: pollution in the water and the health of the people who drink it.

Statistical relationships are based on two ideas: covariation and statistical independence. **Covariation** means that things go together or are associated. To *covary* means to vary together; cases with certain values on one variable are likely to have certain values on the other one. For example, people with higher values on the income variable are likely to have higher values on the life expectancy variable. Likewise, those with lower incomes have lower life expectancy. This is usually

---

Univariate statistics Statistical measures that deal with one variable only.

Bivariate statistics Statistical measures that involve two variables only.

Statistical relationship Expression of whether two or more variables affect one another based on the use of elementary applied mathematics, that is, whether there is an association between them or independence.

Covariation The concept that two variables vary together, such that knowing the values on one variable provides information about values found on another.

stated in a shorthand way by saying that income and life expectancy are related to each other, or covary. We could also say that knowing one's income tells us one's probable life expectancy, or that life expectancy depends on income.

Statistical independence is the opposite of covariation. It means there is no association or no relationship between variables. If two variables are independent, cases with certain values on one variable do not have a special value on the other variable. For example, Rita wants to know whether number of siblings is related to life expectancy. If the variables are independent, then people with many brothers and sisters have the same life expectancy as those who are only children. In other words, knowing how many brothers or sisters someone has tells Rita nothing about the person's life expectancy.

We usually state hypotheses in terms of a causal relationship or expected covariation; if we use the null hypothesis, it is that there is independence. It is used in formal hypothesis testing and is frequently found in inferential statistics (to be discussed).

We use several techniques to decide whether a relationship exists between two variables. Three elementary ones are a scattergram, or a graph or plot of the relationship; a percentaged table; and measures of association, or statistical measures that express the amount of covariation by a single number (e.g., correlation coefficient). Also see Chart 12.1 on graphing data.

Statistical independence The absence of a statistical relationship between two variables, that is, when knowing the values on one variable provides no information about the values found on another variable; no association between the variable.

Scattergram A diagram to display the statistical relationship between two variables based on plotting each case's values for both of the variables.

Linear relationship An association between two variables that is positive or negative across the levels of variables; when plotted in a scattergram, the pattern of the association forms a straight line, without a curve.

The Scattergram

Definition of Scattergram. A **scattergram** (or *scatterplot*) is a graph on which you plot each case or observation. Each axis represents the value of one variable. It is used for variables measured at the interval or ratio level, rarely for ordinal variables, and never if either variable is nominal. There is no fixed rule for determining which variable (independent or dependent) to place on the horizontal or vertical axis, but usually the independent variable (symbolized by the letter X) goes on the horizontal axis and the dependent variable (symbolized by Y) on the vertical axis. The lowest value for each should be the lower left corner and the highest value should be at the top or to the right.

Constructing a Scattergram. Begin with the range of the two variables. Draw an axis with the values of each variable marked and write numbers on each axis (graph paper is helpful). Next label each axis with the variable name and put a title at the top. You are now ready to enter the data. For each case, find the value of each variable and mark the graph at a place corresponding to the two values. For example, you want to make a scattergram of years of schooling by number of children. You look at the first case to see years of schooling (e.g., 12) and number of children (e.g., 3). Then you go to the place on the graph where 12 for the "schooling" variable and 3 for the "number of children" variable intersect and put a dot for the case. You repeat this for each case until all are plotted on the scattergram.

The scattergram in Figure 12.5 (page 396) is a plot of data for 33 women. It shows a negative relationship between the years of education the woman completed and the number of children she gave birth to.

A scattergram shows us three aspects of a bivariate relationship: form, direction, and precision.

1. *Form.* Relationships can take three forms: independence, linear, and curvilinear. Independence or no relationship is the easiest to see. It looks like a random scatter with no pattern, or a straight line that is exactly parallel to the horizontal or vertical axis. A **linear relationship** means that a straight line can be visualized in the middle of a maze of

CHART 12.1 Graphing Accurately

The pattern in graph A shows drastic change. A steep drop in 1990 is followed by rapid recovery and instability. The pattern in graph B is much more constant. The decline from 1989 to 1990 is smooth, and the other years are almost level. Both graphs are for identical data, the U.S. business failure rate from 1985 to 2002. The X axis (bottom) for years is the same.

The scale of the Y axis is 60 to 160 in graph A and 0 to 400 in graph B. The pattern in graph A only looks more dramatic because of the Y axis scale. When reading graphs, be careful to check the scale. Some people purposely choose a scale to minimize or dramatize a pattern in the data.

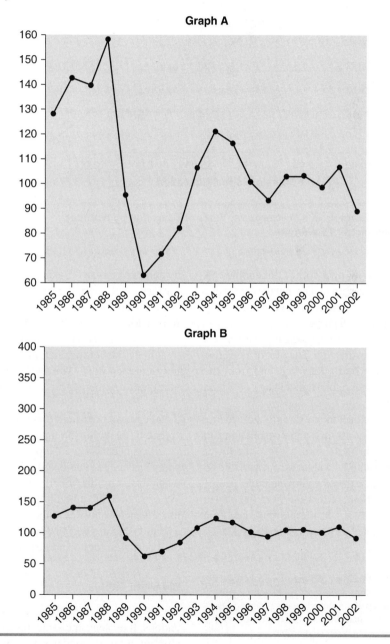

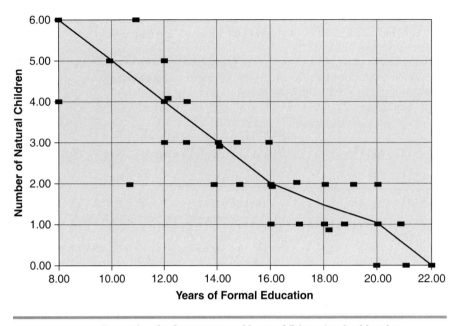

FIGURE 12.5 Example of a Scattergram: Years of Education by Number of Natural Children for 33 Women

cases running from one corner to another. A **curvilinear relationship** means that the center of a maze of cases would form a U curve, right side up or upside down, or an S curve.

2. *Direction.* Linear relationships can have a positive or negative direction. The plot of a positive relationship looks like a diagonal line from the lower left to the upper right. Higher values on X tend to go with higher values on Y, and vice versa. The income and life expectancy example described a positive linear relationship. A negative relationship looks like a line from the upper left to the lower right. It means that higher values on one variable go with lower values on the other. For example, people with more education are less likely to have been arrested. If we look at a scattergram of data on a group of males that plots years of schooling (X axis)

by number of arrests (Y axis), we see that most cases (or men) with many arrests are in the lower right because most of them completed fewer years of school. Most cases with few arrests are in the upper left because most have had more schooling. The imaginary line for the relationship can have a shallow or a steep slope. More advanced statistics provide precise numerical measures of the line's slope.

3. *Precision.* Bivariate relationships differ in their degree of precision. *Precision* is the amount of spread in the points on the graph. A high level of precision occurs when the points hug the line that summarizes the relationship. A low level occurs when the points are widely spread around the line. We can "eyeball" a highly precise relationship or use advanced statistics to measure the precision of a relationship in a way that is analogous to the standard deviation for univariate statistics.

Curvilinear relationship An association between two variables so that as the values of one variable increase, the values of the second show a changing pattern, for example, first decrease, then increase, and finally decrease; not a linear relationship.

Bivariate Tables

We use the bivariate **contingency table** in many situations. It presents the same information as a scattergram in a more condensed form. One advantage of it over the scattergram is that the data can be measured at any level of measurement, although interval and ratio data must be grouped.

The bivarate contingency table is based on **cross-tabulation** (i.e., tabulating two or more variables simultaneously). It is "contingent" because the cases in each category of a variable are distributed into each category of a second (or additional) variable. The table distributes cases into the categories of multiple variables at the same time and shows us how the cases, by category of one variable, are "contingent upon" the categories of other variables.

Constructing Percentaged Tables. Contingency tables made up of the counts of a case are of limited use because seeing patterns or variable relationships with the counts of cases is difficult. By "standardizing" data, or turning them into percentages, we can see patterns and relationships among variables more easily even if the counts of cases vary greatly. It is not difficult to construct a percentaged table, and there are ways to make it look professional. We first review the steps for constructing a table by hand. The same principles apply if a computer makes the table for you. We begin with the raw data (see data from an imaginary survey in Example Box 12.2 on page 398, Raw Data and Frequency Distributions).

If you create a table by hand, you may find an intermediate step between raw data and the table useful (i.e., create a compound frequency distribution [CFD]). It is similar to the frequency distribution except that it is for each combination of the values of two variables. For example, you want to see the relationship between age and attitude about the legal age to drink alcohol. Age is a ratio measure, so you group it to treat the ratio-level variable as if it were ordinal. In percentage tables, we group ratio- or interval-level data to convert them into the ordinal level. Otherwise, we might have 50 categories for a variable and a table that is impossible to read.

The CFD has every combination of category. Age has four categories and Attitude three, so there are 3 × 4 = 12 rows. The steps to create a CFD are as follows:

1. Determine all possible combinations of variable categories.

2. Make a mark next to the combination category into which each case falls.
3. Add the marks for the number of cases in a combination category.

If there is no missing information problem, add the numbers of categories (e.g., all the "Agree"s, or all the "61 and Older"s). In the example, missing data are an issue. The four "Agree" categories in the CFD add to 37 (20 + 10 + 4 + 3), not 38, as in the univariate frequency distribution, because one of the 38 cases has missing information for age.

The next step is to set up the parts of a table (see Figure 12.6 on page 399) by labeling the rows and columns. The independent variable usually is placed in the columns, but this convention is not always followed. Next, each number from the CFD is placed in a cell in the table that corresponds to the combination of variable categories. For example, the CFD shows that 20 of the under-30-year-olds agree (top number) as does Figure 12.6 (upper left cell).

Figure 12.6 is a raw count or frequency table. Its cells contain a count of the cases. It is easy to make but very difficult to interpret because the rows or columns can have different totals. What is of real interest is the relative size of cells compared to others.

Raw count tables can be converted into percentaged tables in three ways: percent by row, by column, and by total. The first two are often used to show relationships. The percent by total is almost never used and does not reveal relationships easily.

Is it best to percentage by row or column? Either can be appropriate. Here are the mechanics of making a percentage table. When calculating column percentages, compute each cell's percentage

Contingency table A summary format of the cross-tabulation of two or more variables showing bivariate quantitative data for variables in the form of percentages across rows or down columns for the categories of one variable.

Cross-tabulation The process of placing data for two variables in a contingency table to show the percentage or number of cases at the intersection of variable categories.

Raw Data and Frequency Distributions

EXAMPLE OF RAW DATA

Case	Age	Gender	Schooling	Attitude	Political Party, etc. . . .
01	21	F	14	1	Democrat
02	36	M	8	1	Republican
03	77	F	12	2	Republican
04	41	F	20	2	Independent
05	29	M	22	3	Democratic Socialist
06	45	F	12	3	Democrat
07	19	M	13	2	Missing Information
08	64	M	12	3	Democrat
09	53	F	10	3	Democrat
10	44	M	21	1	Conservative

(Attitude scoring, 1 = Agree, 2 = No Opinion, 3 = Disagree)

TWO FREQUENCY DISTRIBUTIONS:
AGE AND ATTITUDE TOWARD CHANGING THE DRINKING AGE

Age Group	Number of Cases	Attitude	Number of Cases
Under 30	26		
30–45	30	Agree	38
46–60	35	No Opinion	26
61 and older	15	Disagree	40
Missing	3	Missing	5
Total	109	Total	109

COMPOUND FREQUENCY DISTRIBUTION:
AGE GROUP AND ATTITUDE TOWARD CHANGING THE DRINKING AGE

Age	Attitude	Number of Cases
Under 30	Agree	20
Under 30	No Opinion	3
Under 30	Disagree	3
30–45	Agree	10
30–45	No Opinion	10
30–45	Disagree	5
46–60	Agree	4
46–60	No Opinion	10
46–60	Disagree	21
61 and older	Agree	3
61 and older	No Opinion	2
61 and older	Disagree	10
	Subtotal	101
Missing on either variable		8
Total		109

FIGURE 12.6   Age Group by Attitude about Changing the Drinking Age, Raw Count Table

RAW COUNT TABLE (a)

ATTITUDE (b)	AGE GROUP (b)				
	Under 30	30–45	46–60	61 and Older	TOTAL (c)
Agree	20	10	4	3	37
No opinion	3 (d)	10	10	2	25
Disagree	3	5	21	10	39
Total (c)	26	25	35	15	101

Missing cases (f) = 8.   (e)

THE PARTS OF A TABLE
(a) Give each table a *title,* which names variables and provides background information.
(b) Label the row and column variable and give a name to each of the variable categories.
(c) Include the totals of the columns and rows. These are called the **marginals.** They equal the univariate frequency distribution for the variable.
(d) Each number or place that corresponds to the intersection of a category for each variable is a **cell of a table.**
(e) The numbers with the labeled variable categories and the totals are called the **body of a table.**
(f) If there is missing information (cases in which a respondent refused to answer, ended interview, said, "don't know," etc.), report the number of missing cases near the table to account for all original cases.

of the column total. This includes the total column or **marginal,** which is the name for totals of a row or of a column variable. For example, look at the column marginals in Table 12.1 (page 300). The first column total is 26 (there are 26 people under age 30), and the first cell of that column is 20 (there are 20 people under age 30 who agree). The percentage is 20/26 = 0.769, or 76.9 percent. Or, for the first number in the row marginal, which is 37, 37/101 = 0.366 = 36.6 percent. This tells you that 36.6 percent of cases agree. Except for rounding, the total should equal 100 percent.

Computing row percentages is similar. Compute the percentage of each cell as a percentage of the row total. For example, using the same cell with 20 in it, you now want to know what percentage 20 is of the row total of 37, or 20/37 = 0.541 = 54.1

percent. Percentaging by row or column gives different percentages for a cell unless the marginals are the same.

Row and column percentages let you address different questions. The row-percentaged table answers the question: Among those who want to lower the drinking age, what percentage comes from each age group? It says of respondents who agree, 54.1 percent are in the under-30 age group. The column-percentaged table addresses the question: Among those in each age group, what percentage holds different attitudes? It says that among

Marginal   In a contingency table, the row of totals or the column of totals.

TABLE 12.1   Age Group by Attitude about Changing the Drinking Age, Percentaged Tables

COLUMN-PERCENTAGED TABLE

	AGE GROUP				
ATTITUDE	*Under 30*	*30–45*	*46–60*	*61 and Older*	TOTAL
Agree	76.9%	40.0%	11.4%	20.0%	36.6%
No opinion	11.5	40.0	28.6	13.3	24.8
Disagree	11.5	20.0	60.0	66.7	38.6
Total	99.9%	100%	100%	100%	100%
(N)	(26)*	(25)*	(35)*	(15)*	(101)*

Missing cases = 8

ROW-PERCENTAGED TABLE

	AGE GROUP					
ATTITUDE	*Under 30*	*30–45*	*46–60*	*61 and Older*	TOTAL	*(N)*
Agree	54.1%	27%	10.8%	8.1%	100.0%	(37)*
No opinion	12.0	40.0	40.0	8.0	100.0	(25)*
Disagree	7.7	12.8	53.8	25.6	99.9	(39)*
Total	25.7%	24.8%	34.7%	14.9%	100.1%	(101)*

Missing cases = 8

*For percentaged tables, provide the number of cases or *N* on which percentages are computed in parentheses near the total of 100%. This makes it possible to go back and forth from a percentaged table to a raw count table and vice versa.

those who are under 30, 76.9 percent agree. From the row percentages, you learn that a little over half of those who agree are under 30 years old. From column percentages, you learn that among the under-30 people, more than 75 percent agree. The first way of percentaging tells you about people with specific attitudes; the second tells you about people in specific age groups and lets you compare them.

Your hypothesis often tells you to look at either the row or column percentages. When beginning, you may want to calculate percentages each way and practice interpreting what each says. For example, your hypothesis is that a person's age affects his or her legal alcohol age attitude, and you are interested in the age of people most/least supportive. This suggests that you look at column percentages because you want to compare attitudes

across the different age groups. However, if your interest is in describing the age makeup of groups of people with different attitudes, then row percentages are appropriate. Perhaps you want to buy TV advertising about the issue and you want to know what age group will be viewing the commercials. As Zeisel (1985:34) noted, whenever one factor in a cross-tabulation can be considered the cause of the other, the most illuminating percentage will be obtained by computing percentages in the direction of the causal factor. So, if age is your causal variable, create the percentage table by rows.

Unfortunately, there is no "industry standard" for putting the independent and dependent variable in a percentage table as row or column, or for percentage by row and column. A majority of researchers place the independent variable on the column and percentage by column, but a large minority put the independent variable as row and percentage by row.

Reading a Percentaged Table. Once you understand how to make a table, you will find it easier to read and figure out what the table says. To read a percentage table, first look at the title, the variable labels, and any background information. Next, look at the direction in which percentages have been computed: in rows or columns. Notice that the headings in Table 12.1 are the same. This is so because the same variables are used. It would be easier if headings included how the data are percentaged, but this is not done. Sometimes you will see abbreviated tables that omit the 100 percent total or the marginals, which adds to the confusion. When you create a table, it is best to include all the parts of a table and use clear labels.

When you read percentaged tables, you will make comparisons in the opposite direction from that in which percentages are computed. This sounds confusing but is simple in practice. A rule of thumb is to compare across rows if the table is percentaged down (i.e., by column) and to compare up and down in columns if the table is percentaged across (i.e., by row).

For example, in row-percentaged Table 12.1, compare columns or age groups. Most of those who agree are in the youngest group. The proportion saying they agree declines as age increases. Most no-opinion people are in the middle-age groups whereas those who disagree are older, especially in the 46-to-60 group. When reading column-percentaged Table 12.1, compare across rows. You can see that a majority of the youngest group agree, and they are the only group in which most people agree. Only 11.5 percent disagree, compared to a majority in the two oldest groups.

Seeing a relationship in a percentaged table takes practice. If there is no relationship in a table, the cell percentages look approximately equal across rows or columns. A linear relationship appears like larger percentages in the diagonal cells. If there is a curvilinear relationship, the largest percentages form a pattern across cells. For example, the largest

cells might be the upper right, the bottom middle, and the upper left. It is easiest to see a relationship in a moderate-size table (9 to 16 cells) in which most cells have some cases (at least five are recommended) and the relationship is strong and precise.

Principles of reading a scattergram can help you see a relationship in a percentage table. Imagine a scattergram divided into 12 equal-size sections. The cases in each section correspond to the number of cases in the cells of a table that is superimposed onto the scattergram. You can think of the table as a condensed form of the scattergram. The bivariate relationship line in a scattergram corresponds to the diagonal cells in a percentaged table. Thus, a simple way to see strong relationships is to circle the largest percentage in each row (for row-percentaged tables) or column (for column-percentaged tables) and see whether a line appears.

The circle-the-largest-cell rule works—with one important caveat. The categories in the percentages table must be ordinal or interval and in the same order as in a scattergram. In scattergrams the lowest variable categories begin at the bottom left. If the categories in a table are not ordered the same way, the rule does not work.

For example, Table 12.2a (page 402) looks like a positive relationship and Table 12.2b like a negative relationship. Both use the same data and are percentaged by row. The actual relationship is negative. Look closely: Table 12.2b has age categories ordered as in a scattergram. When in doubt, return to the basic difference between positive and negative relationships. A positive relationship means that as one variable increases, so does the other. A negative relationship means that as one variable increases, the other decreases.

Bivariate Tables without Percentages. Another kind of bivariate table condenses information—a measure of central tendency (usually the mean). You can use it when one variable is nominal or ordinal and another is measured at the interval or ratio level. The mean (or a similar measure) of the interval or ratio variable is presented for each category of the nominal or ordinal variable. Do not construct the measure of central tendency from the CFD. Instead, divide the cases into the ordinal or

TABLE 12.2A   Age by Schooling

YEARS OF SCHOOLING

AGE	0–11	12	13–14	16+	TOTAL
Under 30	5%	25	30	40	100
30–45	15	25	40	20	100
46–60	35	45	12	8	100
61+	45	35	15	5	100

TABLE 12.2B   Age by Schooling

YEARS OF SCHOOLING

AGE	0–11	12	13–14	16+	TOTAL
61+	45%	35	15	5	100
46–60	35	45	12	8	100
30–45	15	25	40	20	100
Under 30	5	25	30	40	100

TABLE 12.3   Attitude about Changing the Drinking Age by Mean Age of Respondent

DRINKING AGE ATTITUDE	MEAN AGE	(N)
Agree	26.2	(37)
No opinion	44.5	(25)
Disagree	61.9	(39)

Missing cases = 8

nominal variable categories; then calculate the mean for the cases in each variable category from the raw data. Table 12.3 shows the mean age of people in each of the attitude categories. The results suggest that the mean age of those who disagree is much higher than for those who agree or have no opinion.

Measures of Association

A *measure of association* is a single number that expresses the strength, and often the direction, of a relationship. It condenses information about a bivariate relationship into a single number. There are many measures of association. The correct one to use depends on the level of measurement of the data and specific research purposes. Many measures are

> **Proportionate reduction in error**   A logic in many statistics that measures the strength of association between two variables. A strong association reduces most errors in predicting the dependent variable using information from the independent variable.

identified by letters of the Greek alphabet. Lambda, gamma, tau, chi (squared), and rho are commonly used measures. The emphasis here is on interpreting the measures, not on their calculation. To understand each measure, you will need to complete at least one statistics course. Some measures of association, such as gamma, are for data measured at the ordinal level (see Expansion Box 12.2, Gamma). Other measures, such as the correlation coefficient, assume data measured at the ratio-level (see Expansion Box 12.3, Correlation, on page 404).

Most of the elementary measures discussed here follow a **proportionate reduction in error** logic. The logic asks how much does knowledge of one variable reduce the errors that are made when guessing the values of the other variable. *Independence* means that knowledge of one variable does not reduce the chance of errors on the other variable. Measures of association equal zero if the variables are independent.

If there is a strong association or relationship between the independent and dependent variable, we make few errors in predicting a dependent variable based on knowledge of the independent variable, or the proportion of errors reduced is large. A large number of correct guesses suggests that the measure of association is a nonzero number if an association exists between the variables. Table 12.4 describes five commonly used bivariate measures of association. Notice that most range from −1 to +1, with negative numbers indicating a negative relationship and positive numbers a positive relationship. A measure of 1.0 means a 100 percent reduction in errors, or perfect prediction.

EXPANSION BOX 12.2

Gamma

Gamma is a comparatively simple statistic that measures the strength of an association between two ordinal-level variables. This bivariate measure requires you to specify which variable is independent and which is dependent in a hypothesis. It illustrates the basic logic of other measures of association.

Gamma allows you to predict the rank of one variable based on knowledge of the rank of another variable. Essentially, it answers this question: If you know how I rank on variable 1, how good is your prediction of my rank on variable 2? For example, if you know my letter grade in mathematics, how accurately can you predict my grade in literature? Perfect prediction or the highest possible gamma is +1 or −1, depending on whether the ranks are the same (positive) or the opposite on another (negative). Perfect statistical independence of the two variables is a gamma of zero. The formula for calculating gamma uses data in the cells in the body of a cross-tabulation.

Let us look at a simple example using real data from a national sample of adults in United States in 2008 (the GSS). A total of 672 people were asked questions about their happiness and health. Many health care professionals and social scientists noted that emotional happiness is associated with being healthier, so we can test the hypothesis that happy people are healthier.

By looking at the raw count or frequency table, we see from the marginals that most people are pretty happy and more say they are in good health.

Would You Say Your Own Health in General Is:	Taking All Things Together, How Would You Say Things Are these Days?			
	Very Happy	Pretty Happy	Not Too Happy	Total
Excellent	63 A	100 D	19 G	182
Good	93 B	190 E	53 H	336
Fair or poor	27 C	77 F	50 I	154
Total	183	327	122	672

Gamma is based on the idea of "paired observations" (i.e., observations compared in terms of their relative rankings on the independent and dependent variables). Concordant (same-order) paired observations show a positive association, that is, when the member of the pair ranked higher on the independent variable is also ranked higher on the dependent variable. Discordant (inverse-order) paired observations show a negative association. The member of the pair ranked higher on the independent variable is ranked lower on the dependent variable

The formula for gamma is

$$\text{Gamma} = [(P\text{-}Q)/(P + Q)]$$

Where P = concordant and Q = discordant pairs.

Gamma ranges from −1.0 to zero to +1.0 and is a proportionate reduction in error statistic. If Gamma = 0 means the extra information provided by the independent variable does not help prediction. The higher the gamma, the more strength there is in predicting the dependent variable. Gamma can be positive or negative, giving a direction of the association between the variables. When there are more concordant pairs, gamma will be positive; when there are more discordant pairs, gamma will be negative.

Gamma compares cells that are concordant (i.e., same ranked) on the independent and dependent variables to those that are discordant (i.e., opposite ranked) and ignores tied cells (i.e., cells where the independent and dependent variable are ranked the same). The table shown on the left has nine cells. First, let us identify all "concordant" pairs of cells (each cell has a letter).

Cell A in the upper left and Cell F are concordant. Because they are along a diagonal from upper left to lower right, this is predicted in the hypothesis (i.e., very happy people have excellent health, pretty happy have good health, etc.). Other concordant pairs are E:I, B:F, and D:H for the same reason. In the opposite direction are discordant pairs center, G:E, E:C, D:B, and H:F. We multiply the number of cases in each pair. In the formula these are (A x (E + F + H + I)) + (D x (H + I)) + (B x (F + I)) + (E x I) for concordant pairs and (G x (B + E + C + F)) + (D x (B + C)) + (H x (C + F)) + (E x C) for discordant pairs. Substituting the number of cases for each cell, this becomes (63 x (190 + 77 + 53 + 50)) + (100 x (53 + 50)) + (93 x

(continued)

(continued)

$(77 + 50)) + (190 \times 50) = 23310 + 10300 + 11811 + 9500 = 54921$ concordant pairs. Also $(19 \times (93 + 190 + 27 + 77) + (100 \times (93 + 27)) + (53 \times (77 + 27)) + (190 \times 27) = 7353 + 5512 + 12000 + 5130 = 29995$ discordant pairs. Putting this into the formula, $(54921 - 29995)/(54921 + 29995) = 0.2935$. Computers usually do the calculations for us. A gamma of .2935 suggests a weak positive relationship or that health and happiness tend to go together somewhat.

Interpreting gamma (+ means positive relation, − means negative relation):

GAMMA	MEANING
0.00 to 0.24	No relationship
0.25 to 0.49	Weak relationship (positive or negative)
0.50 to 0.74	Moderate relationship (positive or negative)
0.75 to 1.00	Strong relationship (positive or negative)

Correlation

The formula for a correlation coefficient (rho) looks awesome to most people. Calculating it by hand, especially if the data have multiple digits, can be a very long and arduous task. Nowadays, computers do the calculation. However, the problem with relying on computers to do the work is that a researcher may not understand what the coefficient means. Here is a short, simplified example to show how it is done.

The purpose of a correlation coefficient is to show how much two variables "go together" or covary. Ideally, the variables have a ratio level of measurement (some use variables at the interval level). To calculate the coefficient, we first convert each score on a variable into its z-score. This "standardizes" the variable based on its mean and standard deviation. Next we multiply the z-scores for each case together. This tells us how much the variables for a case vary together—cases with high z-scores on both variables are much larger, while those low on both are much smaller. Finally, we divide the sum of the multiplied z-scores

by the number of cases. It yields a type of "average" covariation that has been standardized. In short, a correlation coefficient is the product of z-scores added together and then divided by the number of cases. It is always between +1.0 and −1.0 and summarizes scattergram information about a relationship into a single number.

Let us look at the correlation between the age and price for five small bottles of red wine. First, anyone who is brave or lacks math-symbol phobia can look at one of the frequently used formulas for a correlation coefficient:

$$(\Sigma\ [z\text{-score}_1][z\text{-score}_2])/N$$

where: Σ = sum, $z\text{-score}_1$ = z-score for 1st variable (see Expansion Box 12.1), $z\text{-score}_2$ = z-score for 2nd variable, N = number of cases

Here is how to calculate a correlation coefficient without directly using the formula:

WINE	AGE	PRICE	(DIFFERENCE) Age	(DIFFERENCE) Price	SQUARED DIFF. Age	SQUARED DIFF. Price	Z-SCORES Age	Z-SCORES Price	Z-SCORE Product
A	2	$10	−2	−5	4	25	−1.43	−0.70	1.00
B	3	5	−1	−10	1	100	−0.71	−1.41	1.00
C	5	20	+1	+5	1	25	0.71	+0.70	0.50
D	6	25	+2	+10	4	100	+1.43	+1.41	2.00
E	4	15	0	0	0	0	0.00	0.00	0.00
Total	20	$75			10	250			4.50

(continued)

EXPANSION BOX **12.3**

(continued)

Mean: Age = 4; Price = $15
Variance: Age = 10/5 = 2; Price = 250/5 = 50.
Stnd. Dev.:   Age = square root of 2 = 1.4; Price = square root of 50 = 7.1
Correlation: 4.50/5 = .90

Step 1: Calculate the mean and standard deviation for each variable. (For the standard deviation, first subtract each score from its mean, next square the difference, sum squared differences, and then divide the sum by the number of cases for the variance. Then take the square root of the variance.)

Step 2: Convert each score for the variables into their z-scores. (Just subtract each score from its mean and divide by its standard deviation.)

Step 3: Multiply the z-scores together for each case.

Step 4: Sum the products of z-scores and then divide by the number of cases.

TABLE 12.4   Five Measures of Association

Lambda is used for nominal-level data. It is based on a reduction in errors based on the mode and ranges between zero (independence) and 1.0 (perfect prediction or the strongest possible relationship).

Gamma is used for ordinal-level data. It is based on comparing pairs of variable categories and seeing whether a case has the same rank on each. Gamma ranges from −1.0 to +1.0 with zero meaning no association.

Tau is also used for ordinal-level data. It is based on a different approach than gamma and takes care of a few problems that can occur with gamma. Actually, there are several statistics named tau (it is a popular Greek letter), and the one here is Kendall's tau. Kendall's tau ranges from −1.0 to +1.0, with zero meaning no association.

Rho is also called Pearson's product moment correlation coefficient (named after the famous statistician Karl Pearson and based on a product moment statistical procedure). It is the most commonly used measure of correlation, the correlation statistic people mean if they use the term *correlation* without identifying it further. It can be used only for data measured at the interval or ratio level. Rho is used for the mean and standard deviation of the variables and tells how far cases are from a relationship (or regression) line in a scatterplot. Rho ranges from −1.0 to +1.0 with zero meaning no association. If the value of rho is squared, sometimes called R-squared (R^2), it has a unique proportion reduction in error meaning. R-squared tells how the percentage in one variable (e.g., the dependent) is accounted for, or explained by, the other variable (e.g., the independent). Rho measures linear relationships only. It cannot measure nonlinear or curvilinear relationships. For example, a rho of zero can indicate either no relationship or a curvilinear relationship (see Expansion Box 12.3).

Chi-square has two different uses. It can be used as a measure of association in descriptive statistics like the others listed here or in inferential statistics. As a measure of association, chi-square can be used for nominal and ordinal data. It has an upper limit of infinity and a lower limit of zero, meaning no association (see Expansion Box 12.3).

(continued)

TABLE 12.4   continued

SUMMARY OF MEASURES OF ASSOCIATION

Measure	Greek Symbol	Type of Data	High Association	Independence
Lambda	λ	Nominal	1.0	0
Gamma	γ	Ordinal	+1.0, −1.0	0
Tau (Kendall's)	τ	Ordinal	+1.0, −1.0	0
Rho	ρ	Interval, ratio	+1.0, −1.0	0
Chi-square	χ^2	Nominal, ordinal	Infinity	0

MORE THAN TWO VARIABLES

Statistical Control

Demonstrating an association between two variables is an important first step for understanding the data. However, it is not sufficient for you to say that an independent variable causes a dependent variable. In addition to temporal order and association, we must eliminate alternative explanations that can make the hypothesized relationship spurious. Experimental researchers do this by choosing a research design that physically controls potential alternative explanations for results (i.e., that threaten internal validity).

In nonexperimental research, we can statistically control for alternative explanations with control variables (discussed shortly). We examine the control variables with multivariate tables and statistics that help us decide whether a bivariate relationship might be spurious. We can also show the relative size of the effect of multiple independent variables on a dependent variable.

A **control variable** is a third (or fourth or fifth) variable that represents an alternative explanation for a two-variable relationship. It is a "control" in that is adjusts for, or takes into account, the effects of variables other than the primary independent and dependent variable of a hypothesis. For example,

your bivariate table shows that taller teenagers like baseball more than shorter ones do. But the bivariate relationship between height and attitude toward baseball might be spurious. Why is this; because you suspect that teenage males are taller than females and you suspect that males like baseball more than females do? To test whether the relationship is actually due to height, you must control for gender. By controlling for gender, you are statistically removing their effect. Once you do this, you can see whether the bivariate relationship between height and attitude toward baseball remains or whether the association between height and baseball attitude was really due to gender.

You can "control for" a third variable by seeing whether the bivariate relationship persists within categories of the control variable. For example, you control for gender, and the relationship between height and baseball attitude persists. This means that tall males and tall females both like baseball more than short males and short females do. In other words, the control variable has no effect. When this is so, the bivariate relationship is not spurious, and the control variable (suspected alternative explanation) has no effect.

What if the bivariate relationship weakens or disappears after you control for gender? It means that tall males are no more likely than short males to like baseball, and tall females are no more likely to like baseball than short females. It indicates that the initial bivariate relationship is spurious and suggests that the third variable (in this case gender), not height, is the true cause of differences in attitudes toward baseball.

Control variable   A "third" factor that shows whether a bivariate relationship holds up to alternative explanations; can occur before or between other variables.

Statistical control is a central idea used in many advanced statistical techniques. A measure of association such as the correlation coefficient only suggests a relationship. Until you consider control variables, the bivariate relationship might be spurious. This is why researchers are cautious in interpreting bivariate relationships until they have considered control variables.

After you introduce control variables, you see the **net effect** of an independent variable, that is, the effect of the independent variable "net of," or in spite of, the control variable. We briefly look at two ways to introduce control variables: trivariate percentaged tables and multiple regression analysis.

The Elaboration Model of Percentaged Tables

Constructing Trivariate Tables. To meet the conditions needed for causality, we want to "control for" or see whether an alternative explanation eliminates a causal relationship. If an alternative explanation accounts for a relationship, then the bivariate relationship may be spurious. We operationalize alternative explanations as third or control variables.

You can consider such third variables by statistically introducing control variables in trivariate or three-variable tables. Trivariate tables differ only slightly from bivariate tables. In a sense, they consist of multiple bivariate tables. A trivariate table consists of a separate bivariate table of the independent and dependent variables created for each category of the control variable. The multiple tables of your independent and dependent variable, one for each control variable category, are its **partials**. The tables partial out the effects based on the control variable. The number of partials depends on the number of categories in the control variable. Partial tables look just like bivariate tables, but they use a subset of the cases. Only cases with a specific value on the control variable are in the partial. Thus, you can combine the partials to restore the initial bivariate table without a control variable.

Trivariate tables have three limitations. First, they are difficult to interpret if a control variable has more than four categories. Second, control variables can be at any level of measurement, but you must

group interval-level or ratio-level control variables (i.e., convert them to the ordinal level). Finally, the total number of cases is a limiting factor because the cases are divided among cells in partials. The number of cells in the partials equals the number of cells in the bivariate relationship multiplied by the number of categories in the control variable. For example, a control variable has three categories, and a bivariate table has 12 cells, so the partials have $3 \times 12 = 36$ cells. An average of five cases per cell is recommended, so $5 \times 36 = 180$ cases at minimum are required.

Like bivariate table construction, a trivariate table begins with a CFD but a three-way instead of a two-way CFD. An example of a trivariate table with "gender" as a control variable for the bivariate relation in Table 12.1 is shown in Table 12.5 (page 406).

As with the bivariate tables, each combination in the CFD represents a cell in the final (here the partial) table. Each partial table has the variables in an initial bivariate table. For three variables, three bivariate tables are logically possible. In the example of Table 12.5, the combinations are (1) gender by attitude, (2) age group by attitude, and (3) gender by age group. The partials are set up on the basis of the initial bivariate relationship. The independent variable in each is age group, the dependent variable is attitude, and gender is the control variable. Thus, the trivariate table consists of a pair of partials, each showing the age/attitude relationship for a given gender.

Your theory and understanding of the social world suggest both the hypothesis in the initial bivariate relationship and which variables might be alternative explanations (i.e., the control variables).

As with bivariate tables, the CFD provides the raw count for cells (partials here). You convert them

---

Net effect The result of one variable (usually independent) on another (usually dependent) after the impact of control variables that affects both has been statistically removed.

Partials In contingency tables for three variables, tables between the independent and dependent variables for each category of a control variable.

TABLE 12.5 CFD and Tables for a Trivariate Analysis

COMPOUND FREQUENCY DISTRIBUTION FOR TRIVARIATE TABLE

MALES			FEMALES		
Age	*Attitude*	*Number of Cases*	*Age*	*Attitude*	*Number of Cases*
Under 30	Agree	10	Under 30	Agree	10
Under 30	No opinion	1	Under 30	No opinion	2
Under 30	Disagree	2	Under 30	Disagree	1
30–45	Agree	5	30–45	Agree	5
30–45	No opinion	5	30–45	No opinion	5
30–45	Disagree	2	30–45	Disagree	3
46–60	Agree	2	46–60	Agree	2
46–60	No opinion	5	46–60	No opinion	5
46–60	Disagree	11	46–60	Disagree	10
61 and older	Agree	3	61 and older	Agree	0
61 and older	No opinion	0	61 and older	No opinion	2
61 and older	Disagree	5	61 and older	Disagree	5
	Subtotal	51		Subtotal	50
Missing on either variable		4	Missing on either variable		4
Number of males		55	Number of females		54

PARTIAL TABLE FOR MALES

	AGE GROUP				
ATTITUDE	*Under 30*	*30–45*	*46–60*	*61 and Older*	**TOTAL**
Agree	10	5	2	3	20
No Opinion	1	5	5	0	11
Disagree	2	2	11	5	20
Total	13	12	18	8	51

Missing cases = 4

PARTIAL TABLE FOR FEMALES

	AGE GROUP				
ATTITUDE	*Under 30*	*30–45*	*46–60*	*61 and Older*	**TOTAL**
Agree	10	5	2	0	17
No Opinion	2	5	5	2	14
Disagree	1	3	10	5	19
Total	13	13	17	7	50

Missing cases = 4

into percentages in the same way as for a bivariate table (i.e., divide cells by the row or column total). For example, in the partial table for females, the upper left cell has a 10. The row percentage for that cell is 10/17 = 58 percent.

The **elaboration paradigm** is a system for reading percentaged trivariate tables.[5] It describes five possible patterns that might emerge after you add a control variable. The patterns describe how the partial tables compare to the initial bivariate table, or how the original bivariate relationship changes after you add the control variable (see Example Box 12.3, Summary of Elaboration Paradigm). The examples of patterns presented here show strong cases. You will need to use advanced statistics when the differences are not as obvious.

Of the five patterns, the **replication pattern** is the easiest to understand. It occurs when the partials replicate or reproduce the same relationship that existed in the bivariate table before considering the control variable, and means that the control variable has no effect. The **specification pattern** is the next easiest pattern. It occurs when one partial replicates the initial bivariate relationship but other partials do not. For example, you find a strong (negative) bivariate relationship between automobile accidents and college grades. You control for gender and discover that the relationship holds only for males (i.e., the strong negative relationship was in the partial for males, not for females). This is the *specification* because you specify the category of the control variable in which the initial relationship persists.

The control variable has a large effect in both the interpretation and explanation patterns. In both, the bivariate table shows a relationship that disappears or greatly weakens in the partials. In other words, you saw a relationship between the independent and dependent variables in a bivariate table, but the relationship disappears and the variables appear to be independent in the partial tables. You cannot distinguish between the two patterns by looking at the tables alone. The difference between the patterns depends on the location of the control variable in the causal order of variables. Theoretically, a control variable can be in one of two places, either between the original independent and dependent variables (i.e., the control variable

is intervening), or before the original independent variable.

The **interpretation pattern** describes the situation in which the control variable intervenes between the original independent and dependent variables. For example, you examine a relationship between religious upbringing and abortion attitude. Political ideology is a control variable. You reason that religious upbringing affects current political ideology and abortion attitude. You theorize that political ideology is logically prior to an attitude about a specific issue, such as abortion. Thus, religious upbringing causes political ideology, which in turn has an impact on abortion attitude. The control variable is an intervening variable, which helps you interpret the meaning of the complete relationship.

The **explanation pattern** looks the same as the interpretation pattern. The difference is the temporal order of the control variable. In the explanation pattern, a control variable comes before the independent variable in the initial bivariate relationship. For example, the original relationship is between religious upbringing and abortion attitude, but now gender is the control variable. Gender comes before

---

Elaboration paradigm   A system for describing patterns evident among tables when the bivariate contingency table is compared with partials after the control variable has been added.

Replication pattern   An arrangement in the elaboration paradigm in which the partials show the same relationship as in a bivariate contingency table of the independent and dependent variable alone.

Specification pattern   An arrangement in the elaboration paradigm in which the bivariate contingency table shows a relationship; one of the partial tables but others do not.

Interpretation pattern   An arrangement in the elaboration paradigm in which the bivariate contingency table shows a relationship, but the partials show no relationship and the control variable is intervening in the causal explanation.

Explanation pattern   A pattern in the elaboration paradigm in which the bivariate contingency table shows a relationship, but the partials show no relationship, and the control variable occurs prior to the independent variable.

Summary of the Elaboration Paradigm

Pattern Name	Pattern Seen When Comparing Partials to the Original Bivariate Table
Replication	Relationship in both partials is same as in bivariate table.
Specification	Bivariate relationship is seen only in one of the partial tables.
Interpretation	Bivariate relationship weakens greatly or disappears in the partial tables (control variable is intervening).
Explanation	Bivariate relationship weakens greatly or disappears in the partial tables (control variable is before independent variable).
Suppressor variable	No bivariate relationship exists; relationship appears in partial tables only.

EXAMPLES OF ELABORATION PATTERNS

Replication (percentages)

	BIVARIATE TABLE			**PARTIALS**			
				Control = Low		*Control = High*	
	Low	*High*		*Low*	*High*	*Low*	*High*
Low	85%	15%	Low	84%	16%	86%	14%
High	15%	85%	High	16%	84%	14%	86%

Interpretation or Explanation (percentages)

	BIVARIATE TABLE			**PARTIALS**			
				Control = Low		*Control = High*	
	Low	*High*		*Low*	*High*	*Low*	*High*
Low	85%	15%	Low	45%	55%	55%	45%
High	15%	85%	High	55%	45%	45%	55%

Specification (percentages)

	BIVARIATE TABLE			**PARTIALS**			
				Control = Low		*Control = High*	
	Low	*High*		*Low*	*High*	*Low*	*High*
Low	85%	85%	Low	95%	5%	50%	50%
High	15%	15%	High	5%	95%	50%	50%

Suppressor Variable (percentages)

	BIVARIATE TABLE			**PARTIALS**			
				Control = Low		*Control = High*	
	Low	*High*		*Low*	*High*	*Low*	*High*
Low	54%	46%	Low	84%	16%	14%	86%
High	46%	54%	High	16%	84%	86%	14%

religious upbringing because one's gender is fixed at birth. The explanation pattern changes how a researcher explains the results. It implies that the initial bivariate relationship is spurious (see the discussion of spuriousness in Chapter 6).

The **suppressor variable pattern** occurs when the bivariate tables suggest independence but a relationship appears in one or both of the partials. For example, religious upbringing and abortion attitude are independent in a bivariate table. Once you introduce the control variable region of the country, you see that religious upbringing is associated with abortion attitude in the partial tables. The control variable suppressed the true relationship, and the true relationship appears in the partials.

Multiple Regression Analysis

Multiple regression is a popular statistical technique whose calculation is beyond the level of this book. Although by using appropriate statistics software you can compute multiple regression quickly, a background in statistics is needed to prevent you from making errors in its calculation and interpretation. Multiple regression requires interval- or ratio-level data.

Multiple regression's great advantage is its ability to adjust for several control variables (i.e., alternative explanations) simultaneously. With percentaged tables, you can rarely use more than one control variable at a time. In addition, multiple regression is widely used, and you are likely to encounter it when reading research reports or articles. Multiple regression results tell the reader two things. First, it tells the overall predictive power of the set of independent and control variable on the dependent variable. A statistic, R-squared (R^2), tells us how well a set of variables "explains" a dependent variable. *Explain* here means making fewer errors when predicting the dependent variable scores on the basis of information about the independent variables. A good model with several variables might account for, or explain, a large percentage of variation in a dependent variable. For example, an R^2 of 0.50 means that knowing the independent and control variables improves the accuracy of predicting the dependent variable by 50 percent and that you would make one-half as

many errors in predicting the dependent variable with the variable as you would not knowing about the independent and control variables.

Second, multiple regression results give the direction and size of the effect of each variable on a dependent variable. The effect is measured precisely with a numerical value. The higher the value, the larger the effect of a variable on predicting the dependent variable. The sign (positive or negative) of the effect tells you the direction of the impact on the dependent variable. For example, you can see how five independent or control variables simultaneously affect a dependent variable with all variables controlling for the effects of one another. This is especially valuable for testing theories that state that multiple independent variables cause one dependent variable. (See Chapter 3 for examples of causal diagrams.)

We measure effect of an independent or control variable on the dependent variable by using a standardized regression coefficient or the Greek letter beta (ß). It is similar to a correlation coefficient, and ranges from zero to +0.99 or –0.99 with zero meaning no effect. We can perform statistical tests to determine the statistical significance (discussed later in this chapter) of a coefficient. The beta coefficient for two variables equals the correlation coefficient.

We use the beta regression coefficient to determine whether control variables have an effect. For example, the bivariate correlation between X and Y is 0.75. Next, we statistically add four control variables. If the beta remains at 0.75, the four control variables have no effect. However, if the beta for X and Y becomes smaller (e.g., drops to 0.20), the control variables have an effect on the dependent variable.

Consider an example of regression analysis with age, income, education, and region as independent variables. The dependent variable is a score on a political ideology index. The multiple regression results show that income and religious attendance have large effects, education and region minor effects, and age no effect. All independent variables together have a 38 percent accuracy in predicting a person's political

Supressor variable pattern   Occurs when the bivariate tables suggest independence but a relationship appears in one or both partials.

Example of Multiple Regression Results

DEPENDENT VARIABLE IS POLITICAL IDEOLOGY INDEX (HIGH SCORE MEANS VERY LIBERAL)

Independent Variable	Standardized Regression Coefficients
Region = South	−.19
Age	.01
Income	−.44
Years of education	.23
Religious attendance	−.39
$R^2 = .38$	

ideology (see Example Box 12.4, Example of Multiple Regression Results).[6] The example suggests that high income, frequent religious attendance, and a southern residence are positively associated with conservative opinions, whereas having more education is associated with liberal opinions. The impact of income is more than twice the size of the impact of living in a southern region.

Chart 12.2 summarizes the types and techniques of descriptive statistics. Next we turn our attention to inferential statistics.

INFERENTIAL STATISTICS

The Purpose of Inferential Statistics

The statistics discussed so far in this chapter are descriptive statistics. But we often want to do more than just describe; we want to test hypotheses, to find out whether sample results hold true in a population, and decide whether results (e.g., between the mean scores of two groups) are big enough to indicate that a relationship truly exists and is not due to chance alone. **Inferential statistics** build on probability theory to test hypotheses formally, permit inferences from a sample to a population, and test whether descriptive results are likely to be due to random factors or to a real relationship. This section explains the basic ideas of inferential statistics but does not deal with inferential statistics in any detail. This area is more complex than descriptive statistics and requires a background in statistics.

Inferential statistics rely on principles from probability sampling by which we use a random process (e.g., a random-number table, random computer process) to select cases from the entire population. Inferential statistics are a precise way to talk about how confident we can be when inferring from the results in a sample to the population.

You have already encountered inferential statistics if you have read or heard about "statistical significance" or results "significant at the 0.05 level." We use them to conduct various statistical tests (e.g., a *t*-test or an *F*-test). We use statistical significance in formal hypothesis testing, which is a precise way to decide whether to accept or to reject a null hypothesis.[7]

Statistical Significance

The term *statistically significant results* means that the results are not likely to be due to chance factors. **Statistical significance** indicates the probability of finding a relationship in the sample when there is none in the population. Because probability samples involve a random process, it is always possible that sample results will differ from a population parameter. We want to estimate the odds that sample results are due to a true population parameter or to chance factors of random sampling. With some probability theory from mathematics and specific statistical tests, we can tell whether the results (e.g., an association, a difference between two means, a regression coefficient) are likely to be produced by random error in random sampling

Inferential statistics A branch of applied mathematics based on random sampling that allows researchers to make precise statements about the level of confidence they can have that measures in a sample are the same as a population parameter.

Statistical significance The likelihood that a finding or statistical relationship in a sample's results is due to random factors rather than to the existence of an actual relationship in the entire population.

CHART 12.2   Summary of Major Types of Descriptive Statistics

TYPE OF TECHNIQUE	STATISTICAL TECHNIQUE	PURPOSE
Univariate	Frequency distribution, measures of central tendency, standard deviation, z-score	Describe one variable.
Bivariate	Correlation, percentage table, chi-square	Describe a relationship or the association between two variables
Multivariate	Elaboration paradigm, multiple regression	Describe relationships among several variables, or see how several independent variables have an effect on a dependent variable.

or are likely to show effects actually occurring in the social world.

Statistical significance tells us only what is likely. It cannot prove anything with absolute certainty. It states that particular outcomes are more or less probable. Statistical significance is not the same as practical, substantive, or theoretical significance. Results can be statistically significant but theoretically meaningless or trivial. For example, two variables can have a statistically significant association due to coincidence with no logical connection between them (e.g., length of fingernails and ability to speak French).

Levels of Significance

We usually express statistical significance in terms of levels (e.g., a test is statistically significant at a specific level) rather than giving the specific probability. The **level of statistical significance** (usually .05, .01, or .001) is an easy way of talking about the likelihood that results are due to chance factors, that is, that a relationship appears in the sample when there is none in the population. When we say that results are significant at the .05 level, we mean the following:

- Results like these are due to chance factors only 5 in 100 times.
- There is a 95 percent chance that the sample results are not due to chance factors alone but reflect the population accurately.

- The odds of such results based on chance alone are .05, or 5 percent.
- One can be 95 percent confident that the results are due to a real relationship in the population, not chance factors.

These all say the same thing in different ways. This may sound a bit like the discussion of sampling distributions and the central limit theorem in the chapter on sampling. It is no accident! Both are based on probability theory, which we use to link sample data to a population. Probability theory lets us predict what happens in the long run over many events when a random process is used. In other words, it allows us to make precise predictions over many situations in the long run but not for a specific situation. Because we have just one sample and we want to infer to the population, probability theory helps us estimate the odds that our particular sample represents the population. We cannot know for certain unless we have the whole population, but probability theory lets us state our confidence: how likely it is that the sample shows one thing while something else is true in the population.

Level of statistical significance   A set of numbers that researchers use as a simple way to measure the degree to which a statistical relationship results from random factors rather than the existence of a true relationship among variables.

For example, a sample shows that college men and women differ in how many hours they study. Is the result due to having an unusual sample, and in reality there is no difference in the population, or does it reflect a true difference between the men and women? (See Example Box 12.5, Chi-Square.)

Type I and Type II Errors

The logic of statistical significance rests on whether chance factors might have produced the results. You may ask, why use the .05 level? We use it to mean a 5 percent chance that randomness could cause the results. Why not use a more certain standard—for example, a 1 in 1,000 probability of random chance? This gives a smaller chance that randomness versus a true relationship caused the results.

> **Type I Error** The mistake made in saying that a relationship exists when in fact none exists; a false rejection of a null hypothesis.
>
> **Type II Error** The mistake made in saying that a relationship does not exist when in fact it does; false acceptance of a null hypothesis.

There are two answers to this way of thinking. The simple answer is that the scientific community has informally agreed to use .05 as a rule of thumb for most purposes. Being 95 percent confident of results is the accepted standard for explaining the social world. A second, more complex answer involves a trade-off between making Type I and Type II errors. We can make two kinds of logical mistakes. A **Type I error** occurs when we say that a relationship exists when in fact none exists. It means falsely rejecting a null hypothesis. A **Type II error** occurs when we say that a relationship does not exist, when in fact it does. It means falsely accepting a null hypothesis (see Table 12.6). Of course, we want to avoid both errors and say a relationship is in the data only when it does indeed exist and there is no relationship only when there really is none. However, we face a dilemma: As the odds of making one type of error decline, the odds of making the opposite error increase.

You may find the ideas of Type I and Type II errors difficult at first, but the same logical dilemma appears outside research settings. For example, a jury can err by deciding that an accused person is guilty when in fact he or she is innocent, or the jury

EXAMPLE BOX 12.5

Chi-Square

The chi-square (χ^2) is used in two ways. This creates confusion. As a *descriptive statistic*, it tells us the strength of the association between two variables; as an *inferential statistic*, it tells us the probability that any association we find is likely to be due to chance factors. The chi-square is a widely used and powerful way to look at variables measured at the nominal or ordinal level. It is a more precise way to tell whether there is an association in a bivariate percentaged table than by just "eyeballing" it.

Logically, we first determine "expected values" in a table. We do this based on information from the marginals alone. Recall that marginals are frequency distributions of each variable alone. An expected value can be thought of as our "best guess" without examining the body of the table. Next we consider the data to see how much differs from the "expected value." If they differ a lot, then there may be an association between the variables. If the data in a table are identical or very close to the expected values, then the variables are not associated; they are independent. In other words, *independence* means "what is going on" in a table is what we would expect based on the marginals alone. Chisquare is zero if there is independence increases as the association gets stronger. If the data in the table greatly differ from the expected values, then we know something is "going on" beyond what we would expect from the marginals alone (i.e., an association between the variables). See the example of an association between height and grade.

EXAMPLE BOX 12.5

(continued)

Raw or Observed Data Table

STUDENT HEIGHT	GRADE IN RESEARCH METHODS			
	C	B	A	TOTAL
Tall	30	10	10	50
Medium	10	30	10	50
Short	30	20	50	100
Total	70	60	70	200

Expected Values Table

Expected value = (Column total × Row total)/Grand total). EXAMPLE (70 × 50)/200 = 17.5

STUDENT HEIGHT	GRADE IN RESEARCH METHODS			
	C	B	A	TOTAL
Tall	17.5	15.0	17.5	50.0
Medium	17.5	15.0	17.5	50.0
Short	35.0	30.0	35.0	100.0
Total	70.0	60.0	70.0	200.0

Difference Table

Difference = (Observed − Expected). EXAMPLE (30 − 17.5) = 12.5

STUDENT HEIGHT	GRADE IN RESEARCH METHODS			
	C	B	A	TOTAL
Tall	12.5	−5.0	−7.5	0.0
Medium	−7.5	15.0	−7.5	0.0
Short	−5.0	−10.0	15.0	0.0
Total	0.0	0.0	0.0	0.0

Chi-square = Sum of each difference squared, then divided by the expected value of the cell. Example: 12.5 squared = 156.25, divided by 17.5 = 8.93.

Chi-square = 1st row (8.93 + 1.67 + 3.21) +
2nd row (3.21 + 15 + 3.21) +
3rd row (.71 + 3.33 + 6.43) = 45.7

Because chi-square is not zero, the data are not independent; there is an association. The chi-square coefficient cannot tell us the direction (e.g., negative) of the association. For inferential statistics, we need to use a chi-square table or computer program to evaluate the association (i.e., to see how likely such a large chi-square is to occur by chance alone). Without going into all the details about the chi-square table, this association is rare; it occurs by chance less than 1 in 1,000 times. For a table with nine cells, a chi-square of 45.7 is significant at the .001 level.

TABLE 12.6   Type I and Type II Errors

WHAT THE RESEARCHER SAYS	TRUE SITUATION IN THE WORLD	
	No Relationship	*Causal Relationship*
No relationship	No error	Type II error
Causal relationship	Type I error	No error

can err by deciding that a person is innocent when in fact she or he is guilty. The jury does not want to make either error. It does not want to jail the innocent or to free the guilty, but it must make a judgment using limited information. Likewise, a pharmaceutical company has to decide whether to sell a new drug. The company can err by stating that the drug has no side effects when, in fact, it has the side effect of causing blindness, or it can err by holding back a drug because of fear of serious side effects when in fact there are none. The company does not want to make either error. If it makes the first error, the company will face lawsuits and injure people. The second error will prevent the company from selling a drug that may cure illness and produce profits.

Combining the ideas of statistical significance and the two types of error together: If you are overly cautious and set a very high level of significance, you are likely to make one type of error. For example, you use the .0001 level. You attribute the results to chance only if they are so rare that they would occur by chance only 1 in 10,000 times. Such a high standard means that you are most likely to err by saying results are due to chance when in fact they are not. You may falsely accept the null hypothesis when there is a causal relationship (a Type II error). By contrast, if you are a risk-taking researcher and set a low level of significance, such as .10, your results indicate that a relationship would occur by chance 1 in 10 times. You are likely to err by saying that a causal relationship exists, when in fact random factors (e.g., random sampling error) actually cause the results. You are likely to falsely reject the null hypothesis (Type I error). In sum, the .05 level is a compromise between Type I and Type II errors.

This section has outlined the basics of inferential statistics. The statistical techniques are precise and rely on the relationship between sampling error, sample size, and central limit theorem. The power of inferential statistics is their ability to let us state, with specific degrees of certainty, that specific sample results are likely to be true in a population. For example, you conduct statistical tests and learn that a relationship is statistically significant at the .05 level. You can state that the sample results are probably not due to chance factors. Indeed, there is a 95 percent chance that a true relationship exists in the social world. Tests for inferential statistics are useful but limited. The data must come from a random sample, and tests consider only sampling errors. Nonsampling errors (e.g., a poor sampling frame or a poorly designed measure) are not considered. Do not be fooled into thinking that such tests offer easy, final answers. See the discussion presented in Expansion Box 12.4, Statistical Programs on Computers.

CONCLUSION

This chapter discussed organizing quantitative data to prepare them for analysis and then analyzing them (organizing data into charts or tables, or summarizing them with statistical measures). We use statistical analysis to test hypotheses and answer research questions. You saw how data must first be coded and then analyzed using univariate or bivariate statistics. Bivariate relationships might be spurious, so control variables and multivariate analyses are often necessary. You also saw some basics about inferential statistics.

Beginning researchers sometimes believe they have done something wrong if their results do not

EXPANSION BOX **12.4**

Statistical Programs on Computers

Almost every social researcher who needs to calculate many statistics does so with a computer program. One can calculate some statistics using a basic spreadsheet program, such as Excel. Unfortunately, spreadsheets are designed for accounting and bookkeeping functions; they include statistical functions but are clumsy and limited for that purpose. There are many computer programs designed for calculating general statistics. The marketplace can be confusing to a beginner for products rapidly evolve with changing computer technology. One or two decades ago, one had to know a computer language or do simple programming to have a computer calculate statistics.

In recent years, the software has become less demanding for a user. The most popular programs in the social sciences are Minitab, Microcase, and Statistical Package for the Social Sciences (SPSS). Others include Statistical Analysis System (SAS), BMPD (bought by SPSS, Inc.), STATISTICA by StratSoft, and Strata. Many began as simple, low-cost programs for research purposes. Today private corporations own many of these and are interested in selling a sophisticated set of software products to many diverse corporate and government users.

The most widely used program for statistics in the social sciences is SPSS. Its advantages are that social researchers have used it extensively for more than three decades, it includes many ways to manipulate quantitative data, and it contains most statistical measures. Its disadvantage is that it can take a long time to learn because of its many options and complex statistics. Also, it is expensive to purchase except for an inexpensive, "stripped down" student version included with a textbook or workbook.

As computer technology makes using statistics programs easier, the danger increases that some people will use the programs but not understand statistics or what the programs are doing. These people can easily violate basic assumptions required by a statistical procedure, use the statistics improperly, and produce results that are pure nonsense yet look very technically sophisticated.

---

support a hypothesis. There is nothing wrong with rejecting a hypothesis. The goal of scientific research is to produce knowledge that truly reflects the social world, not to defend pet ideas or hypotheses. Hypotheses are theoretical guesses based on limited knowledge; they need to be tested. Excellent-quality research can find that a hypothesis is wrong, and poor-quality research can support a hypothesis. Good research depends on high-quality methodology, not on supporting a specific hypothesis.

Good research means guarding against possible errors or obstacles to true inferences from data to the social world. Errors can enter into the research process and affect results at many places: research design, measurement, data collection, coding, calculating statistics and constructing tables, or interpreting results. Even if you can design, measure, collect, code, and calculate without error, you must also complete another step in the research process: interpret the tables, charts, and statistics, and answer the question: What does it all mean? The only way to assign meaning to facts, charts, tables, or statistics is to use theory, insight, and understanding.

Data, tables, or computer output alone cannot answer research questions. The facts do not speak for themselves. As a researcher, you must return to your theory (i.e., concepts, relationships among concepts, assumptions, theoretical definitions) and give the results meaning. Do not lock yourself into the ideas with which you began. There is room for creativity, and new ideas are generated by trying to figure out what results really say. It is important to be careful in designing and conducting research so that you can look at the results as a reflection of something in the social world and not worry about whether they are due to an error or an artifact of the research process itself.

Before we leave quantitative research, we must present one last issue. Journalists, politicians, and others increasingly use statistical results to make a point or bolster an argument. This has not produced increased accuracy or clarity in public debate. More often, it has increased confusion; this makes knowing what statistics can and cannot do essential. The cliché that you can prove anything with statistics is false; however, some people can and do misuse statistics to pretend to prove anything. Through ignorance or conscious deceit, some people use statistics to fool others. The best way to protect yourself from being misled by statistics is not to ignore them or hide from the numbers but to understand the research process and statistics, think about what you hear, and ask questions.

We turn next to qualitative research. The logic and purpose of qualitative research differ from those of the quantitative, positivist approach of the past chapters. It is less concerned with numbers, hypotheses, and causality and more concerned with words, norms and values, and meaning.

KEY TERMS

bivariate statistics
codebook
coding procedure
contingency cleaning
contingency table
control variable
covariation
cross-tabulation
curvilinear relationship
data field
data records
descriptive statistics
direct-entry method
elaboration paradigm
explanation pattern
frequency distribution

frequency polygon
histogram
inferential statistics
interpretation pattern
level of statistical
    significance
linear relationship
marginal
mean
measures of central tendency
median
mode
net effect
normal distribution
partials
percentile

possible code cleaning
proportionate reduction in error
range
replication pattern
scattergram
skewed distribution
specification pattern
standard deviation
statistical independence
statistical relationship
statistical significance
suppressor variable pattern
Type I error
Type II error
univariate statistics
z-score

REVIEW QUESTIONS

1. What is a codebook, and how is it used in research?
2. How do researchers clean data and check their coding?
3. Describe how researchers use optical scan sheets.
4. In what ways can a researcher display frequency distribution information?
5. Describe the differences between mean, median, and mode.
6. What three features of a relationship can be seen from a scattergram?
7. What is a covariation, and how is it used?
8. When can a researcher generalize from a scattergram to a percentaged table to find a relationship among variables?
9. Discuss the concept of control as it is used in trivariate analysis.
10. What does it mean to say "statistically significant at the .001 level," and what type of error is more likely, Type I or Type II?

NOTES

1. Practical advice on coding and handling quantitative data comes from survey research. See discussions in Babbie (1998:366–372), Backstrom and Hursh-Cesar (1981:309–400), Fowler (1984:127–133), Sonquist and Dunkelberg (1977:210–215), and Warwick and Lininger (1975:234–291).

2. Note that coding gender as $1 = $ Male, $2 = $ Female, or as $0 = $ Male, $1 = $ Female, or reversing the gender for numbers is arbitrary. The only reason one uses numbers instead of letters (e.g., M and F) is that many computer programs work best with all numbers. Sometimes coding data as a zero can create confusion, so the number 1 is usually the lowest value.

3. For discussions of many different ways to display quantitative data, see Fox (1992), Henry (1995), Tufte (1983, 1991), and Zeisel (1985:14–33).

4. Other statistics measure special types of means for ordinal data and for other special situations, which are beyond the level of discussion in this book.

5. On the elaboration paradigm and its history, see Babbie (1998:400–409) and Rosenberg (1968).

6. Beginning students and people outside the social sciences are sometimes surprised at the low (10 to 50 percent) predictive accuracy in multiple regression results. There are three responses to this. First, a 10 to 50 percent reduction in errors is really not bad compared to purely random guessing. Second, positivist social science is still developing. Although the levels of accuracy may not be as high as those of the physical sciences, they are much higher than for any explanation of the social world possible 10 or 20 years ago. Finally, the theoretically important issue in most multiple regression models is less the accuracy of overall prediction than the effects of specific variables. Most hypotheses involve the effects of specific independent variables on dependent variables.

7. In formal hypothesis testing, we test the null hypothesis and usually want to reject the null because rejection of the null indirectly supports the alternative hypothesis to the null, the one we deduce from theory as a tentative explanation. The null hypothesis was discussed in Chapter 6.

Field Research and Focus Group Research

Field research is the study of people acting in the natural courses of their daily lives. The fieldworker ventures into the worlds of others in order to learn firsthand about how they live, how they talk and behave, and what captivates and distresses them. . . . It is also seen as a method of study whose practitioners try to understand the meanings that activities observed have for those engaging in them.

—Robert Emerson, *Contemporary Field Research*, p. 1

Gender is an identy and performance that we reproduce and recreate through daily interactions. *Marriage* is a gendered relationship, and weddings are ritualized events with clear norms to reinforce traditional masculinity and femininity. Likewise, the bridal shower is gendered. The word *bridal* rather than *wedding* shower indicates that it is a woman's ritual. A man's complementary prewedding ritual has been the bachelor party. In the past decade, a new social form, the mixed or coed bridal shower, has spread. Montemurro (2005) studied mixed and traditional bridal showers. She conducted in-depth interviews with 51 women using snowball sampling. The women had been guests of honor, planned, hosted, or attended more than 280 bridal showers in 5 years before the interview, but she focused on 148 in the previous year. She also attended five bridal showers as a participant observer; three were traditional (all female) and two were mixed. She noted who attended the shower (age, gender, and relationships), what happened in sequence, what gifts were given, and how attendees acted and felt. In a traditional bridal shower, men were peripheral or absent, together in another area of the home from where the shower was held or in another place. This signified the shower as exclusively feminine space. Many women reported being bored in the traditional shower. Montemurro identified three types of mixed showers: fiancé-only, couples, and groom-centered (a "groomal shower"). Mixed gender showers tended to be a different time (weekend evening) and more informal than traditional showers. They were likely to serve alcohol and not make gift opening the central or exclusive activity. Also, gifts were more varied and less exclusively feminine at mixed than at bridal showers. Gender roles were distinct at mixed showers but tended to be egalitarian. While women-only showers retained formality and expectations that women "do" femininity, mixed showers tended to be lavish and oriented toward status display more than gender transformation.

With this chapter, we shift from the quantitative to the qualitative research and discuss field research and focus group research. *Field research* encompasses many specific techniques but usually the researcher directly observes and participates in small-scale social settings, most often in his or her home culture. You read about field research on Chicago gangs (Venkatesh, 2008) in Chapter 1 and on street vendors in New York City (Duneier 1999) in Chapter 2. As the study of bridal showers in this chapter's opening box illustrates, field research is not just about the urban poor.

Many people enjoy field research because it involves "hanging out" with people. It has no cold mathematics or complicated statistics and no abstract deductive hypotheses. Instead, in involves direct, face-to-face social interaction with "real people" in a natural social setting. Field research appeals to those who like people watching. Field research reports can be fascinating, revealing accounts of unfamiliar social worlds: nude beaches, people who are homeless or professional gamblers, street gangs, police squads, emergency rooms, artists' colonies, and so on. Some field studies are as engaging to read as a work of fiction with the excitement of a thriller or mystery novel.

Field research requires directly talking with and observing the people being studied. Through personal interactions over months or years, you learn about these people and their life histories, hobbies, habits, hopes, fears, and dreams. Meeting new people and discovering new social worlds can be fun. Field research is also difficult, intense, time consuming, emotionally draining, and sometimes physically dangerous.

UNDERSTANDING FIELD RESEARCH

Field research is appropriate when we want to learn about, understand, or describe a group of interacting people. It helps us answer research questions such as: How do people do Y in the social world? or What is the social world of X like? We can use field research to identify aspects of the world that are inaccessible using other methods (e.g., survey, experiments) as in studying street gangs or bridal showers.

Most field research studies focus on a particular location or setting. These range from a small group (twenty or thirty people) to entire communities. Beginning field researchers should start with a relatively small group who interact with each other on a regular basis in a fixed setting (e.g., a street corner, church, barroom, beauty salon, baseball field). Some researchers used amorphous social experiences that are not fixed in place but where intensive interviewing and observation are the only way we can gain access to the experience, for example, the feelings of a person who has been mugged or who is the widow of someone who committed suicide.[1]

To use consistent terminology, I will call the people studied in a field setting *members*. They are insiders or natives in the field and belong to a group, subculture, or social setting that the outside field researcher wants to learn about.

Field researchers have explored a wide variety of social settings, subcultures, and aspects of social life[2] (see Figure 13.1 on page 422). Places where my students have conducted successful short-term, small-scale field research studies include a beauty salon, day care center, bakery, bingo parlor, bowling alley, church, coffee shop, laundromat, police dispatch office, nursing home, strip club, tattoo parlor, and weight room.

A Short History of Field Research

We can trace field research to the reports of travelers to distant lands.[3] Since the thirteenth century, European explorers and missionaries have written descriptions of the strange cultures and peoples they have encountered. Others read these descriptions to learn about foreign cultures. By the eighteenth and nineteenth centuries with European expansion, the travelers had become more literate. The number and quality of such reports of strange lands and peoples grew.

Academic field research began in the late nineteenth century with anthropology. The first anthropologists only read the reports of explorers, government officials, or missionaries. They lacked direct contact with the people they studied. Many travel reports focused on the exotic and were racist and ethnocentric. Travelers rarely spoke the local language and relied on interpreters. Not until the 1890s did European anthropologists begin to travel to faraway lands to learn about other cultures.

FIGURE 13.1   Examples of Field Research Sites/Topics

SMALL-SCALE SETTINGS

Passengers in an airplane
Bars or taverns
Battered women's shelters
Camera clubs
Laundromats
Social movement organizations
Social welfare offices
Television stations
Waiting rooms

COMMUNITY SETTINGS

Retirement communities
Small towns
Urban ethnic communities
Working-class neighborhoods

CHILDREN'S ACTIVITIES

Playgrounds
Little League baseball
Youth in schools
Junior high girl groups
Summer camps

OCCUPATIONS

Airline attendants
Artists
Cocktail waitresses
Dog catchers

Door-to-door salespersons
Factory workers
Gamblers
Medical students
Female strippers
Police officers
Restaurant chefs
Social workers
Taxi drivers

DEVIANCE AND CRIMINAL ACTIVITY

Body/genital piercing and branding
Cults
Drug dealers and addicts
Hippies
Nude beaches
Occult groups
Prostitutes
Street gangs, motorcycle gangs
Street people, homeless shelters

MEDICAL SETTINGS AND MEDICAL-RELATED EVENTS

Death
Emergency rooms
Intensive care units
Pregnancy and abortion
Support groups for Alzheimer's caregivers

British social anthropologist Bronislaw Malinoski (1844–1942) was the first researcher to live with a group of people for a long period of time and write about collecting data. In the 1920s, he presented intensive fieldwork as a new method and argued for separating direct observation and native statements from the observer's inferences. He held that the best way to develop an in-depth understanding of a community or culture was for a researcher to directly interact with and live among the native peoples, learning their customs, beliefs, and social processes.

Soon researchers were applying field research techniques to study their own societies. In the 1890s, Charles Booth and Beatrice Webb used both survey research and field research to study poor people in London. They directly observed people in natural settings and used an inductive data-gathering approach. The field research technique of participant observation may have originated in Germany in 1890. Paul Gohre worked and lived as a factory apprentice for three months and took detailed notes each night at home to study factory life. His published work influenced university scholars including the sociologist Max Weber.

We can trace field research in the United States to the University of Chicago Department of Sociology in what is known as the *Chicago School of sociology*. Its influence on field research had two phases. In the first, from the 1910s to 1930s, researchers used a variety of methods based on the case study or life history approach including direct observation, informal interviews, and reading documents or official records. In 1916, Robert E. Park (1864–1944) drew up a research program for the social investigation of the city of Chicago. Influenced by his background as a newspaper reporter, he urged researchers to leave the libraries and "get their hands dirty" by making direct observations and listening to conversations on street corners, in barrooms, and in luxury hotel lobbies. Early studies such as *The Hobo* (Anderson, 1923), *The Jack Roller* (Shaw, 1930), and *The Gang* (Thrasher, 1927) established early Chicago School sociology as the descriptive study of street life with little analysis.

Early field research blended journalistic and anthropological techniques. Journalistic techniques require getting behind surface appearances and behavior, using informants, noticing conflicts, and exposing what is "really happening." Anthropological techniques tell us to remain with a small group for an extended time, conduct detailed observations, and then produce a report on how group members interact and see the world.

In the Chicago School's second phase, from the 1940s to the 1960s, scholars developed participant observation as a distinct technique by expanding anthropological technique to study a researcher's own society. Three principles emerged: (1) Study people in their natural settings, or *in situ;* (2) study people by directly interacting with them repeatedly over time; and (3) develop broad theoretical insights based on an in-depth understanding of members' perspectives of the social world.

After World War II, field research faced increased competition from survey and quantitative research. Field research declined as a proportion of all social research until the 1970–1980s. Field researchers began to borrow and adapt ideas and techniques from cognitive psychology, cultural anthropology, folklore, and linguistics. Field researchers also reexamined the epistemological roots and philosophical assumptions of social science (see Chapter 4) to elaborate on the qualitative methods. In addition, these researchers became more self-conscious about research techniques and were more systematic about elaborating on field research as a distinct scientific approach for the study of social life.

Today field researchers directly observe and interact with members in natural settings to acquire an "inside" perspective. Many of these researchers embrace an activist or social constructionist perspective on social life. Instead of viewing people as a neutral medium through which social forces operate or social life as something "out there" to measure, they hold that people continuously create and define social life through their daily interactions. Field researchers assume that people filter human experiences through an ongoing, fluid, subjective sense of reality that shapes how we see and act on events. Such assumptions about social life suggest that we must focus on the everyday, face-to-face social processes of negotiation, discussion, and bargaining by which people construct and modify social meanings. To do field research is simultaneously to describe the social world and to be an actor within it. When the researcher is a part of a social setting, conducting field research is more than a passive or neutral data-gathering activity. It becomes a self-aware lived social experience in itself.

Ethnography and Ethnomethodology

Two extensions of field research, ethnography and ethnomethodology, build on the social constructionist perspective. **Ethnography** comes from cultural anthropology.[4] *Ethno* means people or folk, and *graphy* refers to writing about or describing something. Ethnography is a description of a people and/or their culture. We constantly make inferences—that is, go beyond what is explicitly said or obvious to see—and move toward what is really meant or implied indirectly. People display their culture (i.e., what they think, ponder, or believe) through external behaviors (e.g., speech and actions) in specific social contexts, yet we cannot capture full social meaning from explicit, externally displayed behavior alone. Thus, by using

Ethnography   Field research that emphasizes providing a very detailed description of a different culture from the viewpoint of an insider in the culture to facilitate understanding of it.

ethnography, we describe people's lives and behavior but also try to infer the meaning of behavior (i.e., the thoughts or beliefs that reside behind it). The major goal of ethnography is to move from what we can easily observe externally to what the people we observe truly feel and mean internally. For example, someone invites you to a "bridal shower." Based on your cultural knowledge, you may infer that it will be an informal party and you should bring a gift for a person who will soon marry. Cultural knowledge includes symbols, songs, sayings, facts, ways of behaving, and objects (e.g., cell phones, hamburgers). We learn the culture by watching television, listening to parents and friends, observing others, and so on.

Cultural knowledge includes both *explicit knowledge* (i.e., what we know and talk about) and *tacit knowledge* (i.e., what we implicitly know but rarely acknowledge directly). For example, explicit knowledge includes the social event (e.g., a shower). Most people can describe what happens at one. Tacit knowledge includes the unspoken cultural norm for appropriate gifts and method of presenting them. People may not even think about the norm or if uncertain may feel anxious about how to use the norm properly. They feel discomfort when someone violates the norm, but it is difficult to pinpoint the source of discomfort. Ethnographers describe the explicit and tacit cultural knowledge that members use. They use detailed descriptions and careful analysis to disassemble and reassemble the events.

The anthropologist Clifford Geertz (1926–2006) stated that a critical part of ethnography is **thick description**.[5] It is a rich, highly detailed

---

Thick description Qualitative data in which a researcher attempts to capture all details of a social setting in an extremely detailed description and convey an intimate feeling for the setting and the inner lives of people in it.

Ethnomethodology A social science approach that combines philosophy, social theory, and method to study commonsense knowledge; investigates ordinary social interaction in small-scale settings to reveal the rules that people use to construct and maintain their everyday social reality.

---

description of specifics (as opposed to a summary, or generalization, or use of standard variables). A thick description of a 3-minute event may take several pages. It captures exactly what has occurred and places the drama of events in a larger context. It permits multiple interpretations or perspectives and gives the broader social-cultural context, allowing the reader to infer deeper cultural meanings.

Ethnomethodology, a distinct approach developed in the 1960s, is the study of commonsense knowledge.[6] To study common sense, ethnomethodologists observe its creation and use in ongoing social interactions in natural settings. Ethnomethodology is an extreme form of field research based on phenomenological philosophy and a social constructionist approach that blends theory, philosophy, and method. In Mehan and Wood (1975:3, 5) we see a description of ethnomethodology.

> *[E]thnomethodology is not a body of findings, nor a method, nor a theory, nor a world view. I view ethnomethodology as a form of life. . . . Ethnomethodology is an attempt to display the reality of a level which exists beyond the sociological level. . . . It differs from sociology much as sociology differs from psychology.*

Ethnomethodology involves the specialized, highly detailed analysis of microsituations (e.g., transcripts of short conversations or videotapes of social interactions). Compared to Chicago School field research, it is more self-conscious about method and sees research findings arising as much from the specific method we use to study as from the social life we study.

A core assumption of ethnomethodology is that social meaning is fragile and fluid, not fixed, stable, or solid. We constantly create and recreate meaning as an ongoing process. For this reason, ethnomethodologists closely analyze what we say, including our pauses and the context of our speech. They assume that people "accomplish" commonsense understanding by applying tacit social-cultural rules. Ethnomethodologists wish to reveal the unspoken rules that we follow but about which we are not explicitly conscious. They see us as constantly interpreting (i.e., figuring out or assigning meaning to) everyday events by applying our cultural knowledge and drawing on clues in specific social contexts.

By examining ordinary social interaction in great detail, ethnomethodologists seek to identify the rules for constructing social reality and common sense. They want to document how we apply micro-level social rules and create new rules "on the fly." For example, a positivist, quantitative researcher sees standardizing tests or formal survey interviews as producing objective facts about a person while the ethnomethodologist sees them as demonstrating the person's ability to pick up implicit clues and apply commonsense cultural knowledge.

One technique used by ethnomethodologists is the **breaching experiment**, a method to make visible and to demonstrate the power of simple tacit rules that we rely on to create a sense of reality in everyday life. In the "experiment," the ethnomethodologist purposefully violates a tacit social norm. The breach usually elicits a powerful social response (e.g., people become anxious and confused, laugh nervously, or express irritation and anger). The response both verifies the rule's existence and demonstrates that such tacit rules are an essential feature of the flow of ordinary social life. The breach also shows the fragility of social reality. In a famous breaching experiment, Harold Garfinkel (1917–) sent his students to nearby stores. He told them to "mistake" other customers for salesclerks. At first, the customers became confused and stammered explanations, but as the students persisted in the misinterpretation, many bewildered customers reluctantly accepted the new definition of the situation and awkwardly tried to fill the salesclerk role. Others "blew up" and "lost their cool," violating the larger social norm of maintaining polite disinterested interactions with other customers. Such a social breach illustrates how we greatly depend on tacit knowledge for the ongoing operation of social life (e.g., distinguishing salesclerks from other customers). Filmmakers have used similar social situations for comic effect. They have people from a different culture who do not share the same tacit, unspoken rules of proper behavior violate social norms.[7] This is humorous because a capable adult violating a common everyday tacit norm disrupts the flow of everyday social reality and generates

social tension that we release through laughter. If a very young child or person who is cognitively impaired were to violate the tacit norm, few see it as humorous but perhaps as "cute" or "sad." Mental health practitioners use a person's ability to recognize and apply everyday tacit cultural knowledge as an indicator of the person's mental competence.

The Logic of Field Research

Field research is an orientation toward doing social research more than a specific research technique. Field researchers draw on an wide array of specific techniques.[8] As Schatzman and Strauss (1973:14) said, "Field method is more like an umbrella of activity beneath which any technique may be used for gaining the desired knowledge, and for processes of thinking about this information." A field researcher is a resourceful, talented individual with ingenuity and an ability to think on her or his feet while in the field. The field research involves bricolage (discussed in Chapter 6), which is more than combining diverse pieces of information. It connects what the researcher studies to the contexts in which it appears, links the researcher with people studied, and integrates meaning with experience (Kincheloe, 2005).

Field research rests on the principle of **naturalism**. It applies to the study phenomena such as oceans, animals, plants. Naturalism tells us to observe ordinary events in natural settings, not in contrived, invented, or researcher-created settings. The best way for us to learn is to capture events as they occur in authentic reality, so we must conduct our research in "the field," leaving the predictable, safe settings such as an office, laboratory, or classroom.

Another principle of field research is that ongoing social life contains numerous perspectives that people use in natural social settings. To understand

---

Breaching experiment   Research technique by which a field researcher intentionally breaks social rules and patterns of behavior to reveal aspects about social meanings and relationships.

Naturalism   The principle that researchers should examine events as they occur in natural, everyday, ongoing social settings.

social life, we must include all perspectives. Field researchers try to get inside the "heads" or meaning systems of diverse members and then switch back to an outsider or research viewpoint. As Van Maanen (1982:139) noted, "Fieldwork means involvement and detachment, both loyalty and betrayal, both openness and secrecy, and most likely, love and hate." You want to be able to smoothly and quickly switch perspectives and see events from multiple points of view simultaneously. Usually a single individual conducts a field research study alone, although small teams have been effective. The person must do many things at once and be highly attentive (see Expansion Box 13.1, What Do Field Researchers Do?)

Because you are directly engaged in "real" social life as you study it, personal characteristics

are very relevant in field research, unlike most quantitative research. Wax (1979:509) noted:

> *Informal and quantitative methods, the peculiarities of the individual tend to go unnoticed. Electronic data processing pays no heed to the age, gender, or ethnicity of the research director or programmer. But, in fieldwork, these basic aspects of personal identity become salient; they drastically affect the process of field research.*

Such direct involvement in the field can have an emotional impact. Field research can be fun and exciting, but it can also disrupt your personal life, physical security, or mental well-being. More than other types of social research, it reshapes friendships, family life, self-identity, or personal values:

> *The price of doing fieldwork is very high, not in dollars (fieldwork is less expensive than most other kinds of research) but in physical and mental effort. It is very hard work. It is exhausting to live two lives simultaneously. (Bogdan and Taylor, 1975:vi)*

Field research requires much time. A study may require hundreds, if not thousands, of hours in direct observation and interaction over several months or years with nearly daily visits to a field setting. As Fine (1996: 244) remarked in his study of four restaurant kitchens: "I attempted to be present six days each week . . . and I attempted to stagger my observation times. . . . I spent a month observing in the kitchen in each restaurant then interviewed all the full-time cooks for a total of thirty in-depth interviews. Each interview lasted from one to three hours."

EXPANSION BOX **13.1**
What Do Field Researchers Do?

A field researcher does the following:
1. Observes ordinary events and everyday activities as they happen in natural settings, in addition to any unusual occurrences
2. Becomes directly involved with the people being studied and personally experiences the process of daily social life in the field setting
3. Acquires an insider's point of view while maintaining the analytic perspective or distance of an outsider
4. Uses a variety of techniques and social skills in a flexible manner as the situation demands
5. Produces data in the form of extensive written notes as well as diagrams, maps, or pictures to provide very detailed descriptions
6. Sees events holistically (i.e., as a whole unit, not in pieces) and individually in their social context
7. Understands and develops empathy for members in a field setting and does not record only "cold" objective facts
8. Notices both explicit (recognized, conscious, spoken) and tacit (less recognized, implicit, unspoken) aspects of culture
9. Observes ongoing social processes without imposing an outside point of view
10. Copes with high levels of personal stress, uncertainty, ethical dilemmas, and ambiguity

Steps in Performing Field Research

The process of doing a field research study is more flexible and less structured than quantitative research. This makes it essential for you to be well organized and prepared for the field. The steps of a project serve as only an approximate guide or road map (see Expansion Box 13.2, Steps in Field Research). We can divide the overall process into six parts: preparation, field site selection and access, field strategies, relations in the field, data gathering, and exit.

EXPANSION BOX **13.2**
Steps in Field Research

1. Prepare oneself, read the literature, and defocus.
2. Select a field site and gain access to it.
3. Enter the field and establish social relations with members.
4. Adopt a social role, learn the ropes, and get along with members.
5. Watch, listen, and collect quality data.
   - Begin to analyze data and to generate and evaluate working hypotheses.
   - Focus on specific aspects of the setting and use theoretical sampling.
   - Conduct field interviews with member informants.
6. Disengage and physically leave the setting.
   - Complete the analyses and write the research report.

Note: There is no fixed percentage of time needed for each step. For a rough approximation, Junker (1960:12) suggested that, once in the field, the researcher should expect to spend approximately one-sixth of his or her time observing, one-third recording data, one-third of the time analyzing data, and one-sixth reporting results. Also see Denzin (1989:176) for eight steps of field research.

Step 1: Prepare to Enter the Field. There are four aspects of preparing for the field: learning to be flexible, preparing, defocusing, and being self-aware and having knowledge of yourself.

Be Flexible. Agility is a virtue when doing field research. In field research, you will not follow clearly laid-out, preset, fixed steps. Rather than having a set of methods to apply or explicit hypotheses to test, you select techniques based on their value in providing valuable information in specific situations. At the beginning, you should expect little control over data and little focus. You want to be able to shift directions and follow leads as needed, learn to recognize and seize opportunities, and adjust quickly to fluid social situations. You do not want to lock yourself into initial misconceptions; instead, learn to be open to discovering new ideas. Finding the most fruitful questions to ask about a part of social life in the field often requires patience, time, sensitivity, and reflection.

Organize Yourself. Human and personal factors can play a role in any research project, but they are crucial ingredients in a field research study. Field projects often begin with chance occurrences or a personal interest, such as working at a job, having a hobby, or being a patient or an activist.[9] To conduct field research, you must refine the skills of careful looking and listening, short-term memory, and regular writing. Before you enter the field site, you will want to practice observing the ordinary details of situations and later writing them down. Extreme attention to details and short-term memory can improve with practice. Likewise, keeping a daily diary or personal journal is good practice for writing field notes. As with all social research, reading the scholarly literature will help you to learn concepts, potential pitfalls, data collection methods, and techniques for resolving conflicts. A beginning field researcher should read dozens of field research reports before starting a study. In addition, you may find diaries, novels, movies, journalistic accounts, and autobiographies valuable tools to gain greater familiarity with and prepare yourself emotionally for entering the field.

Defocus. To begin, you need to empty your mind of preconceptions and take a broad view rather than focusing narrowly. Once socialized to the setting, however, you can begin to focus the inquiry. **Defocusing** means consciously beginning fresh, highly aware and curious, unburdened by assumptions and prejudgments. It comes in two types.[10] The first is casting a wide net in order to witness a broad range of situations, people, and settings—getting a feel for the overall setting before deciding what to include or exclude. The second is going beyond the narrow researcher role and not restricting yourself exclusively to being the researcher. As Douglas (1976:122) noted, it is important to extend your experience beyond a strict professional role.

Defocusing   A technique early in field research by which the researcher removes his or her past assumptions and preconceptions to become more open to events in a field site.

You want to go beyond your "comfort zone" to experience the field as much as possible without betraying a primary commitment to being a researcher.

Be Self-Aware. A good field researcher is a highly self-aware person. As a field researcher, you need to know yourself and reflect on your personal experiences. You can expect to feel anxiety, self-doubt, frustration, and uncertainty in the field. Especially in the beginning, you may feel that you are collecting the wrong data and may suffer emotional turmoil, isolation, and confusion. You may feel doubly marginal: an outsider in the field setting and someone distant from friends, family, and other researchers.[11] Your emotional makeup, personal biography, and cultural experiences are very relevant in field research. This makes it essential to know your limitations, personal commitments, and inner conflicts (see the later section on stress).

As Eliasoph discovered when studying a country and western bar, self awareness is essential (see Example Box 13.1, Field Research at a Country and Western Bar).

Fieldwork can have a powerful impact on your identity and outlook. Many researchers report having been transformed by their field research experiences. Some adopted new values, interests, and moral commitments or changed their religion or political ideology.[12] McDermott (2006:161) studied Black–White racial relations by working in convenience stores in Atlanta and Boston. She remarks that, "I felt like a very different person by the time I completed my work at Quickie Mart." Hayano (1982:148) says something similar after conducting intensive field research on professional gambling:

> By this time I felt more comfortable sitting at a poker table than I did at faculty meetings and in my classes. Most of my social life focused on poker

EXAMPLE BOX **13.1**

Field Research at a Country and Western Bar

Eliasoph (1998) conducted field research on several groups in a California community to understand how Americans avoid political expression. One was a social club. Eliasoph describes herself as an "urban, bicoastal, bespectacled, Jewish, Ph.D. candidate from a long line of communists, atheists, liberals, bookreaders, ideologues, and arguers" (p. 270). The social club's world was very foreign to her. The social club, the Buffalos, centered on country and western music at a bar, the Silverado Club. She describes it:

> The Silverado huddled on a vast, rutted parking lot on what was once wetlands and now was a truck stop, a mile and a half from Amargo's [town name] nuclear battleship station. Occasional gulleys of salt water cattails poked through the wide flat miles of paved malls and gas stations. Giant four-wheeled-drive vehicles filled the parking lot, making my miniature Honda look like a toy. . . . Inside the windowless Silverado, initial blinding darkness gave way to a huge Confederate flag pinned up behind the bandstand, the standard collection of neon beer signs and beer mirrors, men in

> cowboy hats, cowboy shirts and jeans, women in curly perms and tiered flounces of lace or denim skirts, or jeans, and belts with their names embroidered in glitter on the back. (1998:92)

Eliasoph introduced herself as a student. During her two years of research, she endured smoke-filled rooms as well as expensive beer and bottled-water prices; attended a wedding and many dance lessons; and participated in countless conversations and heard many abusive sexist/racist jokes. She listened, asked questions, observed, and took notes in the bathroom. When she returned home after spending hours with club members, it was to a university crowd who had little understanding of the world she was studying. For them, witty conversation was central and being bored was to be avoided. By contrast, club members used more nonverbal than verbal communication and being bored, or sitting and doing nothing, was just fine. The research forced Eliasoph to reexamine her own views and tastes, which she had taken for granted.

playing, and often, especially after a big win, I felt the desire to give up my job as a university professor in order to spend more time in the cardroom.

Step 2: Choose a Field Site and Gain Access. Most field research occurs in a particular setting. In the early stages of a study, you need to select a site, deal with gatekeepers, enter and gain access, assume a social role, adopt a level of involvement, and build rapport with members.

Select a Site. We often talk about doing field research on a setting, or **field site**, but this term is misleading. A site is the context in which events or activities occur, a socially defined territory with flexible and shifting boundaries. The case, activity, or group of interest may span several physical sites. For example, a college football team may interact on the playing field, in the locker room, in a dormitory, at a training camp, and at a local hangout. The team's field site includes all five locations. Selecting a field site is an important decision, and you should take notes on the site selection processes.

Your research question should guide you. Three factors are relevant when you choose a field research site: richness of data, unfamiliarity, and suitability.[13] Some sites are more likely than others to provide rich data. Sites that present a web of social relations, a variety of activities, and diverse events over time provide richer, more interesting data. It is usually easier for a beginning field researcher to choose an unfamiliar setting because it is easier to see cultural events and social relations in a new site. Bogdan and Taylor (1975:28) noted, "We would recommend that researchers choose settings in which the subjects are strangers and in which they have no particular professional knowledge or expertise." At the same time, the novice field researcher can be overwhelmed or intimidated by an entirely new social setting. As you "case out" possible field sites, consider practical issues such as your time and skills, serious conflicts among people in the site, your personal characteristics and feelings, and access to parts of a site.

Your ascriptive characteristics can limit access to some sites. For example, an African American researcher cannot hope to study the Ku Klux Klan

or neo-Nazis, although some researchers have successfully crossed ascriptive lines.[14] Sometimes "insider" and "outsider" teams can work together. For example, the outsider Douglas teamed with a member insider, Flanagan, for a study of nude beaches, and a White collaborated with a Black to study a Black housing project.[15]

Physical access to a site can be an issue. Sites are on a continuum, with open and public areas (e.g., public restaurants, airport waiting areas) at one end and closed and private settings (e.g., private firms, clubs, activities in a person's home) at the other. You may find that you are not welcome or not allowed on the site, or there are legal and political barriers to access. Laws and regulations in institutions (e.g., public schools, hospitals, prisons) restrict access. In addition, institutional review boards may limit field research on ethical grounds (discussed in Chapter 5).

Field research is often a case study, but choosing a field site is not identical to focusing on a case for study. A field site is a social space or location in which activities occur. A case is a type of social relationship or activity. A case can extend beyond the boundaries of one site and link to other social settings. You can select a site and then identify cases to examine within it.

Deal with Gatekeepers. Most field sites have **gatekeepers**. They are people with the formal or informal authority to control access to a site.[16] It can be the thug on the corner, an administrator of a hospital, or the owner of a business. Informal public areas (e.g., sidewalks, public waiting rooms) rarely have gatekeepers; formal organizations have authorities from whom you must obtain permission. A gatekeeper is a leader, with or without a formal title, that members in the field obey, and it may take time to discover who the gatekeeper is

---

Field site A natural location where a researcher conducts field research.

Gatekeeper A person in an official or unofficial role who controls access to a setting.

Gatekeepers and Access

In his study of a crack-dealing gang, the Black Kings, in Chicago's low-income housing projects, Venkatesh (2008) had difficulty in gaining access. He describes in detail how he gained access and luckily came upon the sympathetic gang leader, J.T., who was the critical gatekeeper for both the gang's activities and the housing project. A graduate student of South Asian ancestry from middle-class California suburbs, Venkatesh naïvely entered the projects with a pile of survey questionnaires. He was not prepared for the extreme poverty, perils, and everyday reality of life in the dilapidated high-rise housing projects. Soon after he entered a building, a gang of menacing young men accosted him in a dark, dirty, urine-smelling stairwell. They mistook him for a Mexican-American (and member of rival gang, Latin Kings) and appeared ready to harm him, until J.T. arrived. As Venkatesh (2008:17-19) reports,

J.T. shot the young man a look, then turned to me. "You're not from Chicago," he said. "You should really not be walking through the projects. People

get hurt." J.T. started tossing questions at me. . . . I spent most of the night sitting on the cold steps, trying to avoid protruding shards of metal. I would have liked to sleep also, but I was too nervous.

The next afternoon Venkatesh returned with a six-pack of beer.

"Beer?" I said, tossing him a bottle. "You said I should hang out with folks if I want to know what their life was like." J.T. didn't answer. A few of the guys burst out laughing in disbelief. "He's crazy, I told you!" said one. "Nigger thinks he's going to hang out with us! I still think he's a Latin King." Finally J.T. spoke up. "All right, the brother wants to hang out," he said, unfazed. "Let him hang out." (p. 23)

In gaining access to the site, Venkatesh made many missteps and mistakes, confronted serious physical danger, overcame uncertainty and fear, and had some fantastic good luck, particularly with the gatekeeper.

(see Example Box 13.2, Gatekeepers and Access). You should expect to negotiate with gatekeepers and bargain for access. Gatekeepers may not appreciate the need for conceptual distance or ethical balance. You need to set nonnegotiable limits to protect research integrity. If there are many restrictions initially, you can often reopen negotiations later, and gatekeepers may forget their initial demands as trust develops. It is ethically and politically astute to call on gatekeepers. Many of them do not care about the findings except so far as these findings might provide evidence for someone to criticize them.

Dealing with gatekeepers is a recurrent issue as you enter new levels or areas of a field site. In addition, a gatekeeper can shape the direction of research. "Even the most friendly and co-operative gatekeepers or sponsors will shape the conduct and development of research. To one degree or another, the ethnographer will be channeled in line

with existing networks of friendship and enmity, territory, and equivalent boundaries" (Hammersley and Atkinson, 1983:73). In some sites, gatekeeper approval creates a stigma that inhibits the cooperation of members. For example, prisoners may not be cooperative if they know that the prison warden gave approval to the researcher.

Enter and Gain Access. Entering and gaining access to a field site requires commonsense judgment and social skills. Field sites usually have different levels or areas, and entry to each is an issue. Entry is more analogous to peeling the layers of an onion than to opening a door. Moreover, bargains and promises of entry may not remain stable over time. You need fallback plans or may have to return later for renegotiation. Because the specific focus of research may not emerge until later in the research process or may change, it is best to avoid being locked into specifics by gatekeepers.

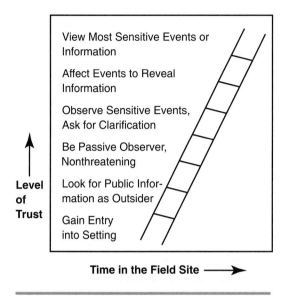

View Most Sensitive Events or Information

Affect Events to Reveal Information

Observe Sensitive Events, Ask for Clarification

Be Passive Observer, Nonthreatening

Look for Public Information as Outsider

Gain Entry into Setting

Level of Trust

Time in the Field Site ⟶

FIGURE 13.2   The Access Ladder

We can visualize entry and access as an **access ladder** (see Figure 13.2). You begin at the bottom rung. Here access is easy, and you are the naïve outsider looking for visible, public information. The next rung requires increased access. It occurs after serious on-site observation begins. You are a passive observer, not questioning what members say, but you slowly penetrate into local social life. With time in the field, you move up a rung. You observe or hear things that are potentially sensitive, and you begin to seek clarification of what you see or hear. Reaching this access rung is difficult. Finally, you may try to shape interaction so that it reveals specific information to you. You may request to see highly sensitive material. Few attain this highest rung of the access ladder, which requires deep trust.[17]

Assume a Social Role. You play many social roles in daily life—daughter/son, student, customer, sports fan—and maintain social relations with others. You choose some roles, and others are structured for you. Few people have a choice but to play the role of son or daughter. Some roles are formal (e.g., bank teller, police chief); others are informal (flirt, elder statesperson, buddy, etc.). You can switch roles, play multiple roles, and play a role in a particular way.

You occupy two types of roles in the field: a social role in the site (e.g., customer, patient, employee) and your field researcher role (to be discussed in the next section). Harrington (2003) noted that a field researcher's success depends on how skillfully he or she negotiates symbolic interaction processes, such as presentation of self and performing social roles. She observed (p. 609):

Researchers entering a field site encounter not only participants but participants' preexisting categories for understanding the world—categories which will be applied to researchers as a way of getting a definitional "handle" on their presence, and figuring out how to interact with them . . . researchers must be defined in terms that either enhance or do not threaten participants' group identity.

You must negotiate for preexisting social roles that field site members assign you in early field site interactions. The assigned role and your performance in it influences the ease and degree of access, as well as your success in developing social trust and securing cooperation. Some existing roles provide more access than other roles. The roles give you an ability to observe and interact with all members, the freedom to move around, and a way to balance the requirements of researcher and member. At times, you might be able to introduce a new role or modify an existing one. For example, Fine (1987) created a role of the "adult friend" and performed it with little adult authority when studying preadolescent boys. He was able to observe parts of their culture and behavior that were otherwise inaccessible to adults. You may adopt several different field roles over time in the field.

Your ascriptive features and physical appearance can limit social roles. You can change some aspects of appearance, such as dress or hairstyle, but not ascriptive features such as age, race, gender, and attractiveness. Nevertheless, such factors can

Access ladder Field researchers may be able to see and learn about only public, noncontroversial events in the beginning, but with time and effort, they can gain entry to more hidden, intimate, and controversial information.

be important in gaining access and can restrict the available roles. For example, Gurney (1985) reported that being a female in a male-dominated setting required extra negotiations and "hassles." Nevertheless, her gender provided insight and created situations that a male researcher would not have had.

Because many roles are gender-typed, gender is an important consideration. Female researchers often have more difficulty when the setting is perceived as dangerous or seamy and where males are in control (e.g., police work, fire fighting). Female researchers may be shunned or pushed into limiting gender stereotypes (e.g., "sweet kid," "mascot," "loud mouth"). Male researchers have more problems in routine and administrative sites where males are in control (e.g., courts, large offices), nor may they be accepted in female-dominated territory. In sites where both males and females are involved, both genders may be able to enter and gain acceptance.[18]

Almost any role limits access to some parts of a field site. For example, the role of a bartender in a bar limits knowledge of intimate customer behavior or presence at customer gatherings in other locations. You want to take care when choosing a role (or having it assigned) but should recognize that all roles involve trade-offs.

Most social settings contain cliques, informal groups, hierarchies, and rivalries. A role can help you gain acceptance into or be excluded from a clique, be treated as a person in authority or as an underling, or be a friend or an enemy of some members. You need to be aware that by adopting a role, you may be forming allies and enemies who can assist or limit research.

Danger and high risk are aspects of some settings (e.g., police work, violent criminal gangs) and influence social roles. You should be aware of risks to safety, assess them, and then decide what you are willing to do. Some observers argue that the field researcher should share in the risks and danger of a setting to understand it and its members. For example, Westmarland (2000) argued that a field researcher could acquire police officers' viewpoints only by putting on a safety vest while rushing to the scene of violent crime and then dodging bullets along with them. Taking risks has meant that some researchers have had "near misses" or have been injured.

In addition to physical injury, you can face legal or financial risks and damage to your professional or personal reputation based on actions in the field. Research into some settings (e.g., mental hospitals, trauma centers, war zones) may create emotional-psychological discomfort and damage a researcher's sense of inner well-being. Field researchers who have studied high-risk settings, such as inner-city drug dealers, offer suggestions for staying safe (see Expansion Box 13.3, Staying Safe in Unsafe Settings).

EXPANSION BOX **13.3**

Staying Safe in Unsafe Settings

1. First impressions matter; adopt a personal style and demeanor appropriate to the setting.
2. Learn "street life" and fit in; do not dress or act too much like an outsider.
3. Explain yourself, who you are, and why you are there.
4. Scan the physical environment for obvious signs of danger (e.g., floors likely to collapse, a ceiling likely to fall).
5. Stay alert and be prepared to respond quickly to potentially dangerous circumstances (paranoia, sexual approaches, robbery, theft, shootings, police raids, and arrests).
6. Find a "protector" (i.e., a powerful person in the setting with whom you create strong trust and who will provide verbal/physical protection).
7. Develop an assertive, confident mind-set and do not act like a victim; overly fearful behavior can invite aggression.
8. Acquire a "sixth sense" and use prudence or common sense for changing conditions. Keep some money hidden for an emergency.
9. Develop a "safety zone" of people whom you trust and feel comfortable with and who accept you.
10. If feeling discomfort, leave the setting and return another time. The threat of sexual assault or rape is often a real concern for female researchers and should be taken seriously.

Sources: Adapted from Bourgeois (1996), Lee-Treweek and Linkogle (2000), and Williams and Dunlap (1992).

Adopt a Level of Involvement. We can arrange researcher roles along a continuum by their degree of involvement with members. At one extreme is a detached outsider observer; the opposite extreme is an intimately involved insider participant. Several authors have developed systems for discussing the researcher roles (see Chart 13.1).

Your level of involvement will vary based on negotiations with members, specifics of the field setting, your personal comfort level, and the social role you occupy within the field site. You may move from outsider to insider levels with more time in the field. Each level has its advantages and disadvantages. Different field researchers advocate different levels of involvement. For example, some criticize the Adlers' (1978) complete member role for overinvolvement and loss of a researcher's perspective. Others argue that it is the only way to understand a member's social world.

Roles at the outsider end of the continuum reduce the time needed for acceptance, make over-rapport less an issue, and can sometimes help members open up. These roles facilitate detachment and protect the researcher's self-identity. Rueben May assumed this role over the 18 months as he studied Trena's bar, visiting it three to four times a week. He reports (2001:174), "My goal as an ethnographer was to document the daily lifestyle of Trena's regulars, while being as unobtrusive as possible. . . . I spent most of my time listening to the patrons' exchanges and documenting those topics patrons thought important." Although there is less risk of going native (see later discussion on the subject) the outsider is less likely to capture the full depth of an insider's experience and is more likely to make misinterpretations.

Many reject the outsider observer role and argue that the only way to acquire an understanding

---

CHART 13.1   Involvement in the Field

Junker (1960, also see Denzin, 1989, Gold, 1969, and Roy, 1970) describes four researcher roles:

1. *Complete observer.* The researcher is behind a one-way mirror or taking on an "invisible role" such as an eavesdropping janitor.
2. *Observer as participant.* The researcher is known from the beginning but has limited contact.
3. *Participant as observer.* The researcher is overt and an intimate friend of participants.
4. *Complete participant.* The researcher acts as a member and shares secret information of insiders.

Gans (1982) offers a similar scheme but collapses the two middle categories into researcher participant. He emphasizes the degree of attachment/emotional involvement or detachment at each level.

Adler and Adler (1987) suggest three roles:

1. *Peripheral membership.* The researcher maintains distance between her- or himself and the members studied or sets limits based on her or his beliefs or discomfort with the members' activities.
2. *Active membership.* The researcher assumes a membership role and goes through a typical member induction and participates as a member, maintaining high levels of trust and withdrawing from the field periodically.
3. *Complete member.* The researcher converts to become a fully committed member, experiencing the same emotions as others. He or she "goes native" and finds it very difficult or impossible to leave the field and return to being a researcher.

of members is to engage them and participate in the field setting. Holy (1984:29–30) observed:

> *The researcher does not participate in the lives of subjects in order to observe them, but rather observes while participating fully in their lives . . . through living with the people being studied. . . . She comes to share the same meanings with them in the process of active participation in their social life. . . . Research means, in this sense, socialization to the culture being studied.*

A role at the insider end of the continuum facilitates empathy and sharing of a member's lived experience. It helps you to experience fully the intimate social world of a member. Nevertheless, a lack of distance from, too much sympathy for, or over-involvement with members have risks. Readers may question your reports, gathering data is more difficult, the impact on the self can be dramatic, and you may lack the social distance required for serious data analysis.[19]

Build Rapport. You want to begin to build rapport as soon as you enter the field. At one level, doing so simply means getting along with members in the field and takes time, tenacity, and openness. To build rapport, you want to forge a friendly relationship, share the same language, and learn to laugh and cry with members. Doing these things is a step toward obtaining an understanding of members and moving beyond understanding toward empathy—that is, seeing and feeling events from another's perspective.

It is not always easy to build rapport. The social world is not all in harmony and does not necessarily have warm, friendly people. A setting may provoke fear, tension, and conflict. Members may be unpleasant, untrustworthy, or untruthful; they may do things that disturb or disgust you. You want to prepare for a range of events and relationships. You may find, however, that it is impossible to penetrate a setting or get really close to members. Settings in which cooperation, sympathy, and collaboration are impossible require different techniques.[20] Also, you accept what you hear or see at face value but without being gullible. As Schatzman and Strauss (1973: 69) remarked, "The researcher believes 'everything' and 'nothing' simultaneously."

Step 3: Apply Strategies. Once in a field site, you will soon need to apply a range of strategies: negotiate, normalize research decide how much to disclose, sample and focus, use the attitude of strangeness, notice social breakdowns, and cope with stress.

Negotiate. You will negotiate and form new social relations throughout the fieldwork process.[21] You will negotiate with members until you establish a stable relationship as you gain more access, build trust, obtain information, and contain resistance or hostility. Expect to negotiate and explain what you are doing over and again in the field. People who are marginalized, those engaged in illegal or illicit activities, and those who are elites often require more intense negotiations to increase access. For example, to gain access to deviant subcultures, field researchers have used contacts from their private lives, gone to social welfare or law enforcement agencies, advertised for volunteers, offered a service (e.g., counseling) in exchange for access, or gone to a location where deviants hang out and joined a group. Harper (1982) gained access by living in a skid-row mission without any money and befriending homeless men who knew street life. Bart (1987) argued that her background as a feminist activist and nonprofessional demeanor were essential for gaining access to an illegal feminist abortion clinic. McDermott (2006:160) says,

> *"I was able to fit in at the Atlanta site, as I grew up in South Carolina and had previously worked as a convenience store clerk there. I was thus able to speak and easily understand the local accent, and the fact that we were required to wear uniforms . . . meant that I fit in with everyone else in terms of dress, as well."*[22]

After developing social relations, you may maintain them for months or years. Access to elite people and professional people often depends on luck or personal ties.[23] Hoffmann (1980) gained access to wealthy individuals on the boards of directors by using her family ties and including personal references in letters requesting interviews. Danziger (1979) gained access to physicians' activities because her father was a doctor. Johnson's

(1975) access to a social work agency was aided by mentioning that someone in the agency was a friend of his wife.

Normalize Research. A field researcher not only observes and investigates members in the field but is observed and investigated by members as well. "While the fieldworker is undertaking a study of others, others are undertaking a study of the fieldworker" (Van Maanen, 1982:110). The isolated researcher does not perform fieldwork alone, but everyone in the field setting helps to create it (Wax 1979:363). In overt field research, members are usually initially uncomfortable with the presence of a researcher. Most are unfamiliar with field research and fail to distinguish between sociologists, psychologists, counselors, and social workers. They may see you as an outside critic or dangerous spy or as a savior or all-knowing expert.

When you adopt an overt role, you must **normalize social research**—that is, help members redefine social research from something unknown and threatening to something normal and predictable. You can help members do this by presenting your own biography, explaining field research a little at a time, appearing nonthreatening, or accepting minor deviance in the setting (e.g., minor violations of official rules).[24] For example, in a study of social workers, Johnson (1975:99–104) was accepted after the social workers realized that he accepted their minor deviance (e.g., leaving work early to go swimming) and after he said that he thought others did it also. Co-workers accepted McDermott (2006) after she caught shoplifters and agreed to work the night shift at the convenience store alone, proving her toughness and that she was not afraid of "mundane, thankless work."

Another way to normalize research is to explain it in terms members understand. Sometimes members' excitement about being written up in a book is useful, as Fine and Glassner (1979), LeMasters (1975), and Venkatesh (2008) found. In his study of a neighborhood tavern in Wisconsin, LeMasters became a regular over a 5-year period, going to the bar several nights a week. He (1975:7) stated how he explained what he was doing to members:

Initially assumed the role of patron—just another person who liked to drink beer and shoot some pool.

This finally became difficult because the amount of time I spent in the tavern began to raise questions. Some of the regular customers, I learned later, had decided I must be an undercover agent from the state liquor commission. . . . I adopted the following stance when queried about being in the tavern: that sociologists have to have some knowledge of various aspects of American society to be effective teachers, that I found The Oasis men and women to be helpful in understanding how blue-collar people feel about American society, and, further, that I became bored by constant association with white-collar people and that the tavern contacts were refreshing. All of the above statements were true.

Decide on Disclosure. You must decide how much to reveal about yourself and the research project. Disclosing your personal life, hobbies, interests, and background can build trust and close relationships, but you also lose privacy and need to ensure that the focus remains on events in the field.

Disclosure ranges on a continuum from fully covert research, in which no one in the field is aware that research is taking place, to the opposite end, where everyone knows the specifics of the research project (see Chapter 5 on covert research). The degree and timing of disclosure depends on your judgment and particulars in the setting. Disclosure may unfold over time as you feel more secure.

It is best to disclose the project to gatekeepers and others unless there is a very good reason for not doing so. Even then, you may disclose your identity as a researcher but may pose as one who seems submissive, harmless, and interested in nonthreatening issues (see later discussion on being an acceptable incompetent). McDermott (2006) developed a cover story, telling people she wanted to study the effects of economic restructuring on working people and did not reveal that her real interest was in racial attitudes. She states (p. 36), "If I had stated my true research intentions at the onset,

> **Normalize social research** Technique in field research that attempts to make the people being studied feel more comfortable with the research process and to help them accept the researcher's presence.

it would have very likely have affected the validity of the data. . . ." She debriefed people she worked with and revealed the true purpose of her study when she left the field site.

After you select a field site and obtain access, you must learn the ropes, develop rapport with members, adopt a role in the setting, and maintain social relations. Before confronting such issues, you should ask: How will I present myself? What does it mean for me to be a "measurement instrument"? How can I assume an "attitude of strangeness"?

People explicitly and implicitly present themselves to others. We display who we are—the type of person we are or would like to be—through our physical appearance, what we say, and how we act. The presentation of self sends a symbolic message. It may be, "I'm a serious, hard-working student," "I'm a warm and caring person," "I'm a cool jock," or "I'm a rebel and party animal." Many selves are possible, and presentations of them can differ depending on the occasion.

You should be very conscious of the presentation of self in the field. For example, how should you dress in the field? The best guide is to respect both yourself and the members in the field. Do not overdress in a manner that offends or stands out. Copying the dress of the people you study is not always necessary. A professor who studies street people does not have to dress or act like one; dressing and acting informally is sufficient. Likewise, more formal dress and professional demeanor are usually required when studying corporate executives or top officials.[25]

Self-presentation can influence field relations to some degree. However, honesty is usually the best policy. It is difficult to present a highly deceptive front or to present yourself in a way that deviates sharply from who you are normally.

For example, being herself and revealing her personal background as a Jewish woman helped Myerhoff (1989) to gain access and develop rapport in a field site of elderly residents in a Jewish senior citizen home. At the same time, her understanding and awareness of her identity changed as a result of her field interactions. Stack (1989) began as an outsider, a White woman studying a low-income Black industrial community. Eventually,

members accepted her into a kinlike relationship. Being assigned the nickname "White Caroline" was a signal of acceptance and endearment. She performed many small favors, such as driving people to the hospital or welfare office, shopping, and visiting sick children. She achieved this by how she interacted with others—her openness and willingness to share personal feelings. Anderson (1989) found social class to be a barrier, although he was a Black man in a Black bar. The setting was a corner bar and liquor store on the south side of Chicago in a poor African American neighborhood. Anderson developed a social relationship of trust with members, and an insider whom he befriended, Herman, "sponsored" him. Herman was a witty, easygoing person who was street smart and socially well connected in the setting. Anderson succeeded by "the low-key, nonassertive role I assumed . . . not to disrupt the consensual definition of the social order in this type of setting" (Anderson, 1989:19).

Focus and Sample. Once in the field, you first acquire a general picture. Only then can you gradually focus on a few specific problems or issues (see Figure 13.3).[26] You can decide on specific research questions and develop tentative "hypotheses" only after experiencing the field firsthand. At first, everything may appear relevant; later, however, you can selectively focus attention on specific questions and themes.

Field research sampling differs from that in survey research, although sometimes both use snowball sampling (see Chapter 8).[27] The study on bridal showers that opened this chapter used snowball

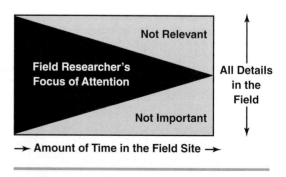

FIGURE 13.3   Focusing in Field Research

sampling. In field research, we often use theoretical sampling, which is guided by developing theory and sampling times, situations, types of events, locations, types of people, or contexts of interest.

McDermott (2006) sampled a working class, mixed race neighborhood in Boston and one in Atlanta because she theoretically wanted to compare conditions in a northern and a southern city. To get a full sense of how the field site stays the same or changes, you can observe what happens at a setting at various times: the times of the day, each day of the week, and all seasons. It is often best to overlap when sampling (e.g., to have sampling times from 7 A.M. to 9 A.M., from 8 A.M. to 10 A.M., from 9 A.M. to 11 A.M.).

You sample different locations because one may give depth but a narrow perspective. Sitting or standing in different locations helps you get a sense of the whole site. For example, the peer-to-peer behavior of schoolteachers usually occurs in a faculty lounge as well as at a local bar or cafe when teachers gather or in a classroom temporarily used for a teachers meeting. In addition, researchers trace the paths of members to various field locations.

We sample people by focusing attention or interaction on different types of people (old-timers and newcomers, old and young, males and females, leaders and followers). As you identify types of people, or people with opposing outlooks, you may try to interact with and learn about all types.

For example, you might sample three kinds of field events: routine, special, and unanticipated. Routine events (e.g., opening a store for business) happen every day and should not be considered unimportant simply because they are routine. Special events (e.g., annual office party) are announced and planned in advance. They focus attention on members and reveal aspects of social life not otherwise visible. Unanticipated events are those that just happen to occur while a researcher is present (e.g., workers being unsupervised when the manager gets sick and cannot oversee workers at a store for a day). In this case, you see something unusual, unplanned, or rare by chance.

Assume the Attitude of Strangeness. It is difficult to recognize what we are very close to. The everyday

world we inhabit is filled with thousands of details. If we paid attention to everything all of the time, we would suffer from severe information overload. We manage by ignoring much of what is around us and by engaging in habitual thinking. Unfortunately, we fail to see the familiar as distinctive and assume that others experience reality just as we do. We tend to treat our own way of living as natural or normal. This "blindness" to the familiar makes field research in familiar surroundings difficult. In fact, "intimate acquaintance with one's own culture can create as much blindness as insight" (McCracken, 1988:12). By studying other cultures or subcultures, you can encounter very different assumptions about what is important and how to accomplish tasks. This confrontation of cultures, or culture shock, makes seeing cultural elements easier and facilitates self-discovery.

Field researchers adopt the **attitude of strangeness** to gain these benefits. This means that you question and notice ordinary details or look at the ordinary through the eyes of a stranger. It helps you to overcome the boredom of observing ordinary details. In addition, it helps reveal aspects of the setting of which members are not consciously aware.

People rarely recognize customs they take for granted. For example, when someone gives us a gift, we say thank you and praise the gift. In contrast, gift-giving customs in many cultures include complaining that the gift is inadequate. The attitude of strangeness helps make the tacit culture visible—for example, that gift givers expect to hear "thank you" and "the gift is nice," and become upset otherwise. You adopt both a stranger's and an insider's point of view. The stranger sees events as specific social processes whereas they seem natural to an insider. Davis (1973) called this the Martian and the convert: The Martian sees everything as strange and questions assumptions, whereas the convert accepts everything and wants to become

> **Attitude of strangeness**   A field research technique in which researchers mentally adjust to "see" events in the field as if for the first time or as an outsider.

a believer. You need both views as well as an ability to swiftly switch between them.[28]

The attitude of strangeness also encourages you to reconsider your own social world. Immersion in a different setting breaks old habits of thought and action. You will find reflection and introspection easier and more intense when encountering the unfamiliar, whether it is a different culture or a familiar one seen through a stranger's eyes.

Notice Social Breakdowns. A **social breakdown** occurs when two cultural traditions or social assumptions fail to mesh. It highlights social meanings because hidden routine expectations and assumptions become explicit in the breakdown. Such expectations appear as misunderstandings or confusion over which of several implicit social rules to apply. For example, I go to a restaurant and sit down. I wait for a server to appear. Ten minutes later, having gotten no service, I become angry. I look around and notice that I have not seen any servers. I see customers enter from a doorway carrying their own food and realize my misunderstanding. My implicit expectation was that the restaurant had table service; in fact, it is one where patrons must go to a counter, order, and pick up their own food. Once I recognize which rules to apply in the context, I can resolve the breakdown.

Social breakdowns produce embarrassment because the mismatch of cultural meanings often causes a person to look foolish, ignorant, or uninformed. For example, you are invited to a party that begins at 8:00 P.M. You show up in your usual attire, old jeans and a wrinkled sweater, and arrive at your usual time for an 8:00 party—8:30. The door opens and you enter. Shocked, you see that everyone else is formally dressed and sitting at a formal dinner, which the host served about 30 minutes ago. People stare at you, and you feel out of place. Your cultural

expectation (this is an informal student party with loud music, dancing, beer, and informal dress) does not match the setting (this is a formal dinner party, at which people expect to eat, engage in polite conversation, and act professionally). The breakdown makes explicit the unspoken social rules that "everyone knows" or assumes.

Social breakdowns can be unexpected or you can purposefully create them to test working hypotheses. As with an ethnomethodologist's breaching experiments, you may violate social rules to expose the existence of tacit rules and their importance. You can observe unplanned breakdowns or create mini-social breakdowns and then watch reactions to pinpoint implicit social expectations.

Cope with Stress. Fieldwork can be highly rewarding, exciting, and fulfilling, but it also can be difficult:

> It must certainly rank with the more disagreeable activities that humanity has fashioned for itself. It is usually inconvenient, to say the least, sometimes physically uncomfortable, frequently embarrassing, and, to a degree, always tense (Shaffir et al., 1980:3).

New researchers face embarrassment, experience discomfort, and are overwhelmed by the details in the field. For example, in her study of U.S. relocation camps for Japanese Americans during World War II, respected field researcher Wax (1971) reported that she endured the discomfort of 120-degree Fahrenheit temperatures, filthy and dilapidated living conditions, dysentery, and mosquitoes. She felt isolated, she cried a lot, and she gained 30 pounds from compulsive eating. After months in the field, she thought she was a total failure; she was distrusted by members and got into fights with the camp administration.

Maintaining a "marginal" status is stressful; it is difficult to be an outsider who is not fully involved, especially when studying settings full of intense feelings (e.g., political campaigns, religious conversions). The loneliness and isolation of fieldwork may combine with the desire to develop rapport and empathy to cause over-involvement. You may **go native** and abandon the professional researcher's role to become a full member of the group being studied. Or you may feel guilt about learning intimate details as

Social breakdown The failure of social rules and patterns of behavior in a field site to operate as expected, revealing a great deal about social meanings and relationships.

Go native Action in which a field researcher becomes overly involved with the people being studied and loses all distance or objectivity and becomes joined with them.

members drop their guard and overidentify with members.[29] As Venkatesh (2008:176-177) remarked about his Chicago gang study:

> I was starting to feel schizophrenic, as if I were one person in the projects—sometimes I caught myself even talking in a different way—and another back in Hyde Park. Increasingly I found that I was angry at the entire field of social science. . . . I felt as though the other scholars were living in a bubble . . . Rather than sharing my frustration with my girlfriend, my roommates, and my friends—most of whom were actually quite supportive—I just kept my experiences to myself. . . . When I did try talking about my fieldwork, I felt awkward. In fact, I sometimes came off as defending gangs and their violent practices or as romanticizing the conditions of the projects. . . . I was growing quieter and more solitary. My fellow graduate students and even some faculty members thought of me as unapproachable. Rumors circulated that I was too ambitious, too aloof, but I figured I'd just have to live with them.

Some degree of emotional stress is inevitable in field research. Instead of suppressing emotional responses, remain sensitive to emotional reactions. Some ways to help you cope in the field include keeping a personal diary, emotional journal, or written record of inner feelings or having a few sympathetic people outside the field site in whom you can confide.[30]

Step 4: Maintaining Relations in the Field. You need to use many social strategies and skills as you work to maintain relations in the field.

Adjust and Adapt. With time, you develop and modify social relationships. Members who are cool at first may warm up later, or they may put on a front of initial friendliness, and their fears and suspicions surface only later. You are in a delicate position. Early in a project when not yet fully aware of everything about a field site, you should not rush to form close relationships because circumstances may change; yet if you develop close friends, they can become allies who will defend your presence and help you gain access.

You need to monitor how your actions or appearance affects members. For example, a physically attractive researcher who interacts with members of the opposite sex may encounter crushes, flirting, and jealousy. He or she develops an awareness of these field relations and learns to manage them.[31]

In addition to developing social relationships, you must be able to break or withdraw from relationships as well. You may have to break ties with one member to forge new ties with others or to explore other aspects of the setting. As with the end of any friendly relationship, the emotional pain of social withdrawal can affect both the researcher and the member. You must balance social sensitivity and the research goals.

Use Charm and Nurture Trust. You need social skills and personal charm to build rapport. Trust, friendly feelings, and being well liked facilitate communication and can help you understand the inner feelings of others. There is no magical way to do this. Showing a genuine concern for and an interest in others, being honest, and sharing feelings are good strategies, but they are not foolproof and depend on the specific setting and members. Your demeanor should always be non-threatening, and if possible and appropriate, warm and friendly.

Many factors affect trust and rapport: how you present yourself; your role in the field; and the events that encourage, limit, or make achieving trust impossible. Trust is not gained once and for all. It is a process built up over time through many social nuances (e.g., sharing of personal experiences, storytelling, gestures, hints, facial expressions). Trust is constantly recreated and seems easier to lose once it has been built than to gain in the first place. Establishing trust is important, but it does not ensure that all information will be revealed. Trust may be limited to specific areas. For example, it can be built regarding financial matters but not disclosure of intimate dating behavior. Trust may have to be created anew in each area of inquiry; it requires constant reaffirmation.

Some members may not be open and cooperative. **Freeze-outs** are members who express an uncooperative attitude or an overt unwillingness to

> **Freeze-outs**   People studied in field research who refuse to cooperate with the researcher or to become involved in the study.

participate. You may never gain the cooperation of everyone, or a lukewarm relationship may develop only after prolonged persistence.

Rapport helps you understand members, but understanding is a precondition for greater depth, not an end in itself. It slowly develops in the field as you overcome an initial bewilderment with a new or unusual system of social meaning. Once you attain an understanding of a member's point of view, the next step is to learn how to think and act from within the member's perspective. This is empathy, or adopting, at least temporarily, another's perspective. Empathy does not necessarily mean being sympathetic, agreeing, or approving; it means feeling things as another does.[32] Rapport helps create understanding and ultimately empathy, and the development of empathy facilitates greater rapport. The novel *To Kill a Mockingbird* notes the connection between rapport and empathic understanding:

> *"First of all," [Atticus] said, "if you can learn a simple trick, Scout, you'll get along a lot better with all kinds of folks. You never really understand a person until you consider things from his point of view."*
> *"Sir?"*
> *"—until you climb into his skin and walk around in it." (Lee, 1960:34)*

Perform Small Favors. Exchange relationships develop in the field in which small tokens or favors, including deference and respect, are exchanged.[33] You may gain acceptance by helping in small ways. Exchange helps when access to sensitive issues is limited. You may offer small favors but not burden members by asking for any in return. As you and members share experiences and see each other again, members recall the favors and reciprocate by allowing access. For example, Fine (1987:242) learned a lot when he was providing small favors (e.g., driving the boys to the movies) as part of his "adult friend" role. He (1996:x) also reported that

---

Appearance of interest A technique that field researchers use to maintain relations in a field site in which they pretend to be interested in and excited by the activities of those studied even though they are actually not interested.

---

he washed potatoes, cleaned beans, and performed many small chores during his study of restaurant kitchens.

Avoid Conflicts. Fights, conflict, and disagreements can erupt in the field, or you may study groups with opposing positions. In such situations, you will feel pressure to take sides and may be tested to see whether you can be trusted. On such occasions, you usually want to stay on the neutral side and walk a tightrope between opposing sides because once you become aligned with one side, you will be cut off from access to the other side.[34] In addition, you will see the situation from only one point of view. Nevertheless, some (e.g., Van Maanen, 1982:115) argue that true neutrality is illusory. Avoiding conflict entirely is not possible as you become involved with members and embroiled in webs of relationships and commitments.

Appear Interested. We try to maintain an **appearance of interest** in the field. An experienced researcher appears to be interested in and involved with field events by statements and behaviors (e.g., using facial expression, going for coffee, organizing a party) even if he or she is not truly interested. This is so because you can weaken field relationships if members see you as bored or distracted. When you appear uninterested in field site activities, you are sending a message that the members are dull, boring people and you do not want to be there—hardly a way to build trust, intimacy, and strong social bonds. Putting up a temporary front of involvement is a common small deception we use in daily life and is part of the more general social norm of being polite.[35]

Of course, selective inattention (i.e., not staring or appearing not to notice) is also part of acting polite. If a person makes a social mistake (e.g., accidentally uses an incorrect word, passes gas), the polite thing to do is to ignore it. Selective inattention works in the field; if you are alert, it gives you an opportunity to casually eavesdrop on conversations or observe events not meant to be public.

Be the Acceptable Incompetent. As a researcher, you are in the field to learn, not to be an expert.

Depending on the setting, you should be a friendly but naïve outsider, an **acceptable incompetent**—someone interested in learning about the social life of the field but only partially competent (skilled or knowledgeable) in the setting and whom members accept as a nonthreatening person who needs to be guided or taught.[36]

You may know little about the setting or local culture at first. You may be seen as a fool who is hoodwinked or shortchanged and may be the butt of jokes for your lack of adeptness in the setting. Even when you are knowledgeable, you can display less than full information to draw out a member's knowledge. Of course, you might overdo this and appear so ignorant that you are not taken seriously.

Step 5: Gather and Record Data. This section considers how to obtain good qualitative field data. Field data are what you experience, remember, and record in field notes.

Absorb and Experience. The researcher is the instrument for measuring field data. As Lofland et al. (2006:3) observed, "In subjecting him- or herself to the lives of others and living and feeling those lives along with them, the researcher becomes the primary instrument or medium through which research is conducted." This has two implications. First, it puts pressure on you to be alert and sensitive to what happens in the field and to be disciplined about recording data. Second, it has personal consequences. Fieldwork involves social relationships and personal feelings. You include your own subjective insights and feelings, or "experiential data."[37] Personal, subjective experiences are part of field data. They are valuable both in themselves and for interpreting events in the field. Instead of trying to be objective and eliminate personal reactions, your feelings toward field events are data. For example, Karp's (1973, 1980) personal feelings of tension in his study of pornographic bookstores were a critical part of the data. His personal discomfort in the field revealed some dynamics of the setting. In addition, according to Kleinman and Copp (1993:19), "If we avoid writing about our reactions, we cannot examine them. We cannot

achieve immersion without bringing our subjectivity into play."

Field research can heighten awareness of personal feelings. For example, you may not be fully aware of personal feelings about nudity until you are in a nudist colony or about personal possessions until you are in a setting in which others regularly "borrow" many items. Your surprise, indignation, or questioning then may become an opportunity for reflection and insight.[38]

Watch and Listen. A great deal of what you do in the field is to pay close attention, watch, and listen carefully. You must use all of the senses, noticing what is seen, heard, smelled, tasted, or touched. You should become an instrument that absorbs all sources of information. You want to scrutinize the physical setting to capture its atmosphere. What is the color of the floor, walls, ceiling? How large is a room? Where are the windows and doors? How is the furniture arranged, and what is its condition (e.g., new, old and worn, dirty, or clean)? What type of lighting is there? Are there signs, paintings, plants? What are the sounds or smells?

Why bother with such details? You may have noticed that stores and restaurants often plan lighting, colors, and piped-in music to create a certain atmosphere. Maybe you know that used-car salespeople spray a new-car scent into cars or that shopping malls stores intentionally send out the odor of freshly made cookies. These subtle signals influence human behavior.

Observing in field research is often detailed, tedious work. You need patience and an ability to concentrate on the slow particulars of everyday life. Silverman (1993:30) noted, "If you go to the cinema to see action [car chases, hold-ups, etc.], then it is unlikely that you will find it easy to be a good observer." Instead of the quick flash, motivation in field research arises out of a deep curiosity about the details. Good field researchers are intrigued about details that reveal "what's going on here" by

Acceptable incompetent A field researcher who pretends to be less skilled or knowledgeable in order to learn more about a field site.

carefully listening and watching. Remember that we communicate the core of social life through the mundane, trivial, everyday minutia. Most people overlook the constant flow of details, but you need to learn to notice it.

In addition to physical surroundings, you want to observe people and their actions, noting each person's observable physical characteristics: age, gender, race, and stature. People socially interact differently depending on whether another person is 18, 40, or 70 years old; male or female; White or non-White; short and frail or tall, heavyset, and muscular. When noting such characteristics, include yourself. For example, an attitude of strangeness heightens sensitivity to a group's racial composition. A researcher who ignores the racial composition of a group of Whites in a multiracial society because he or she too is White is being racially insensitive. Likewise, "Gender insensitivity occurs when the sex of participants in the research process is neglected" (Eichler, 1988:51).

You want to record such details because they might reveal something of significance. It is better to err by including everything than to ignore potentially significant details. For example, "the tall, White muscular 19-year-old male in a torn tee shirt and dirty jeans sprinted into the brightly lit room just as the short, overweight light-skinned Black woman in her sixties who was professionally dressed eased into a battered chair" says much more than "one person entered, another sat down."

You should note aspects of physical appearance such as neatness, dress, and hairstyle because they express messages that can affect social interactions. People spend a great deal of time and money selecting clothes, styling and combing hair, grooming with makeup, shaving, ironing clothes, and using deodorant or perfumes. These are part of their presentation of self. Even people who do not groom, shave, or wear deodorant present themselves and send a symbolic message by their appearance. No one dresses or looks "normal." Such a statement suggests that you are insensitive to social signals.

What people do is also significant. You want to notice where people sit or stand, the pace at which they walk, and their nonverbal communication.

People express social information, feelings, and attitudes through nonverbal communication including gestures, facial expressions, and standing or sitting (standing stiffly, sitting in a slouched position, etc.). People express relationships by how they position themselves in a group and through eye contact. You may read social communication by noting that people are standing close together, looking relaxed, and making eye contact.

You can also notice the context in which events occur: Who was present? Who just arrived or left the scene? Was the room hot and stuffy? Such details may help you assign meaning and understand why an event occurred. If you do not notice details, they are lost as is a full understanding of the event.

Serendipity and chance encounters are important in field research. Many times, you do not know the relevance of what you are observing until later. This has two implications. First is the importance of keen observation and excellent notes at all times even when nothing seems to be happening. Second is the importance of looking back over time and learning to appreciate wait time. Most field researchers say that they spend a lot of time waiting. Novice field researchers get frustrated with the amount of time they seem to waste, waiting either for other people or for events to occur. What novices need to learn is that wait time is a necessary part of fieldwork, and it can be valuable.

You need to learn the rhythms of the setting, to operate on other people's schedules, and to observe how events occur within their own flow of time. Also, wait time is not always wasted time. Wait time is time for reflection, observing details, developing social relations, building rapport, and becoming a familiar sight to people in the field setting. Wait time also displays that you are committed and serious; perseverance is a significant trait to cultivate. You may be impatient to get in, get the research over, and get on with your "real life," but this is "real life" for the people in the field site. You should subordinate your personal wants to the demands of the field site.

A good field researcher listens carefully both to what is said and how it is said or what was implied, and to phrases, accents, and incorrect grammar. For example, people often use phrases such as "you know" or "of course" or "et cetera." You want to learn the meaning behind such phrases. You can try to hear everything, but listening is difficult when many conversations occur at once or when you are eavesdropping. Luckily, significant events and themes usually recur.

People who interact with each other over a time period develop shared symbols and terminology. They create new words or assign new meanings to ordinary words. New words develop out of specific events, assumptions, or relations. Knowing and using the language can signal membership in a distinct subculture. You want to learn the specialized language, or **argot**.[39]

You should start with the premise that words and symbols used in your world may have different meanings in the world of the people you study. You must also be attuned to new words and their use in contexts other than the ones with which you are familiar (Bogdan and Taylor, 1975:53).

You want to recognize how the argot fits into social relations or meanings. The argot gives you clues to what is important to members and how they see the world. For example, Douglas (1976:125) discovered the term "vultching" in a study of nude beaches. It was a member's label for the practice of some males who sat around an attractive nude woman on the beach.

In their study of sales practices of a vacation condominium ownership firm, Katovich and Diamond (1986) conducted observations and informal interviews over 6 months when one researcher was employed and the other was a trainee. They analyzed the salesroom as a stage in which a series of events are presented to prospective buyers and discussed the argot used. For example, "drops" occur when the finance manager enters and "drops" information during a discussion between the salesperson and potential buyers. The purpose of such staged events is to stimulate sales. Common revelations were that a major corporation that had bought twenty units just decided it needed only fifteen, so five are suddenly available at a special price; a previous client was denied financing, so a property can be offered at a reduced price; or only a few charter members can qualify for a special deal.

A field researcher translates back and forth between the field argot and the outside world. Spradley (1970:80) offered an example when quoting an "urban nomad." He said, "If a man hasn't made the bucket, he isn't a tramp." This translates: A man is not considered a true member of the subculture (i.e., a tramp) until he has been arrested for public drunkenness and spent the night in the city or county jail (i.e., "made the bucket"). After you have been in the field for some time, you may feel comfortable using the argot, but it is unwise to use it too soon and risk looking foolish.

Record the Data. Information overload is common in field research and stretches an individual's ability, not matter how skilled the person is in recording data. Most field research data are in the form of notes. Full field notes can contain maps, diagrams, photographs, interviews, tape recordings, videotapes, memos, objects from the field, notes jotted in the field, and detailed notes written away from the field. You can expect to fill many notebooks or the equivalent in computer memory. You may spend more time writing notes than being in the field. Some researchers produce forty single-spaced pages of notes for 3 hours of observation. With practice, you should produce several pages of notes for each hour in the field.

Writing notes is often boring, tedious work that requires self-discipline. The notes contain extensive descriptive detail drawn from memory. Emerson and colleagues (1995) argued that good field notes are as much a mind-set as an activity and remarked (p. 40), "Perhaps more crucial than how long the ethnographer spends in the field is the timing of writing up field notes. . . . Writing field notes *immediately* after leaving the setting provides fresher, more detailed recollections . . ." (emphasis in original). If possible, always write notes before the day's thoughts and excitement begin to fade, without retelling events to others. Pouring fresh

---

Argot The special language or terminology used by the members of a subculture or group who interact regularly.

memories into the notes with an intense immediacy often triggers an emotional release and stimulates insightful reflection. Begin by allocating about a half hour to writing your field notes for each hour you spend in the field site.

You must keep notes and must organize them because you will return to them over and again. Once written, the notes are private and valuable. You must treat them with care and protect confidentiality. Members have the right to remain anonymous, and most researchers use pseudonyms (false names) in notes. Field notes may be of interest to hostile parties, blackmailers, or legal officials, so some researchers write field notes in code.

Your state of mind, level of attention, and conditions in the field affect note taking. Begin with relatively short 1- to 3-hour periods in the field before writing notes. Johnson (1975:187) remarked:

The quantity and quality of the observational records vary with the field worker's feelings of restedness or exhaustion, reactions to particular events, relations with others, consumption of alcoholic beverages, the number of discrete observations, and so forth.

Types of Field Notes. Field researchers take notes in many ways.[40] The recommendations here (also see Expansion Box 13.4, Recommendations for Taking Field Notes) are only suggestions. Full field notes have several types. Five major types (see Figure 13.4) and supplemental types are discussed here. It is usually best to keep all notes for an observation period together and to distinguish various types of notes by putting them on separate pages. Some researchers include inference notes with direct observation notes, but distinguish them by a visible device such as brackets or colored ink.

EXPANSION BOX 13.4
Recommendations for Taking Field Notes

1. Record notes as soon as possible after each period in the field, and do not talk with others until observations are recorded.
2. Begin the record of each field visit with a new page, and note the date and time.
3. Use jotted notes only as a temporary memory aid, with keywords or terms, or the first and last things said.
4. Use wide margins to make it easy to add to notes at any time. Go back and add to the notes if you remember something later.
5. Plan to type notes and keep each level of notes separate so it will be easy to go back to them later.
6. Record events in the order in which they occurred, and note how long they lasted (e.g., a 15-minute wait, a 1-hour ride).
7. Make notes as concrete, complete, and comprehensible as possible.
8. Use frequent paragraphs and quotation marks. Exact recall of phrases is best, with double quotes; use single quotes for paraphrasing.
9. Record small talk or routines that do not appear to be significant at the time; they may become important later.

10. "Let your feelings flow" and write quickly without worrying about spelling or "wild ideas." Assume that no one else will see the notes, but use pseudonyms.
11. Never substitute tape recordings completely for field notes.
12. Include diagrams or maps of the setting, and outline your own movements and those of others during the period of observation.
13. Include your own words and behavior in the notes. Also record emotional feelings and private thoughts in a separate section.
14. Avoid evaluative summarizing words. Instead of "The sink looked disgusting," say, "The sink was rust-stained and looked as though it had not been cleaned in a long time. Pieces of food and dirty dishes looked as though they had been piled in it for several days."
15. Reread notes periodically and record ideas generated by the rereading.
16. Always make one or more backup copies, keep them in a locked location, and store the copies in different places in case of fire, flood, or theft.

Direct Observation	Inference	Analytic	Personal Journal
Sunday, October 4. Kay's Kafe 3:00 pm. Large White male in mid-40s, overweight, enters. He wears worn brown suit. He is alone; sits at booth #2. Kay comes by, asks, "What'll it be?" Man says, "Coffee, black for now." She leaves and he lights cigarette and reads menu. 3:15 pm. Kay turns on radio.	Kay seems friendly today, humming. She becomes solemn and watchful. I think she puts on the radio when nervous.	Women are afraid of men who come in alone since the robbery.	It is raining. I am feeling comfortable with Kay but am bored today.

FIGURE 13.4   Types of Field Notes

The quantity of notes varies across types. For example, 6 hours in the field might result in one page of jotted notes, forty pages of direct observation, five pages of researcher inference, and two pages total for methodological, theoretical, and personal notes.

1. *Jotted notes.* It is nearly impossible to take good notes in the field. Even a known observer in a public setting looks strange when furiously writing. More important, when looking down and writing, you cannot see and hear what is happening. The attention given to note writing is taken from field observation where it belongs. The specific setting determines whether you can take notes in the field. You may be able to write, and members may expect it, or you may have to be secretive (e.g., go to the restroom). As McDermott (2006:88) noted after an important interaction in her field site, "I hastily improvised a trip to the restroom to scribble furiously. . . ."

You write **jotted notes** while in the field. They are very short memory triggers such as words, phrases, or drawings you make inconspicuously, perhaps scribbling on a convenient item (e.g., napkin, matchbook). Later you will incorporate them into your direct observation notes, but never substitute them for the direct observation notes.

2. *Direct observation notes.* The basic source of field data are **direct observation notes**. You write them immediately after leaving the field, which you can add to later. You want to order the notes chronologically with the date, time, and place written on each entry. They serve as a detailed description of what you heard and saw in very concrete, specific terms. To the extent possible, they are an exact recording of the particular words, phrases, or actions.

Your memory improves with practice, and you will soon remember exact phrases from the field. Verbatim statements should be written with double quote marks to distinguish them from paraphrases. Dialogue accessories (nonverbal communication, props, tone, speed, volume, gestures) should be recorded as well. Record what was actually said and do not clean it up; include ungrammatical speech, slang, and misstatements (e.g., write, "Uh, I'm goin' home, Sal," not "I am going home, Sally").

Put concrete details, not summaries, in notes. For example, instead of "We talked about sports,"

Jotted notes   Field notes inconspicuously written while in the field site on whatever is convenient in order to "jog the memory" later.

Direct observation notes   Field research notes that attempt to include all details and specifics of what the researcher heard or saw in a field site and that are written to permit multiple interpretations later.

write "Anthony argued with Sam and Jason. He said that the Cubs would win next week because they traded for a new shortstop, Chiappetta. He also said that the team was better than the Mets, who he thought had inferior infielders. He cited last week's game where the Cubs won against Boston by 8 to 3." You should note who was present, what happened, where it occurred, when, and under what circumstances. New researchers may not take notes because "nothing important happened." An experienced researcher knows that events when "nothing happened" can reveal a lot. For example, members may express feelings and organize experience into folk categories even in trivial conversations.

A useful way to think of time in the field comes from Zerubavel (1981), who looked at the rhythms of social life and argued that the coordination of social activities is based on the organization of time.

Four temporal patterns that you may try to notice and record in your direct observations notes are the following: (1) sequential structure—what comes first, second, third and so on—the order in which events happen (out of order, before versus after); (2) duration—the length of time of social events (too long, too short); (3) temporal locations—social meaning of certain times of the day, week, month, year (too early, too late); and (4) reoccurance—the repetition of certain events or a cycle of time that has been attached to social norms (too often, not enough).

3. *Inference notes.* You should listen to members in order to "climb into their skin" or "walk in their shoes."[41] This involves a three-step process: listen without applying analytical categories; compare what you hear to what you heard at other times and to what others say; and then apply your own interpretation to infer or figure out what the information means. In ordinary interaction, we do all three steps simultaneously and jump quickly to our own inferences. In field research, you learn to look and listen without inferring or imposing an interpretation. Your observations without inferences go into direct observation notes.

You can record inferences in a separate section that is keyed to direct observations. We never see social relationships, emotions, or meaning. We see specific physical actions and hear words, then use background cultural knowledge, clues from the context, and what is done or said to assign social meaning. For example, we do not see love or anger; we see and hear specific actions (red face, loud voice, wild gestures, obscenities) and draw inferences from them (the person is angry).

We constantly infer social meaning on the basis of what we see and hear—but not always correctly. For example, my niece visited me and accompanied me to a store to buy a kite. The clerk at the cash register smiled and asked her whether she and her "daddy" (looking at me) were going to fly the kite that day. The clerk observed our interaction and then inferred a father/daughter, not an uncle/niece, relationship. She saw and heard a male adult and a female child, but she inferred the social meaning incorrectly. You want to keep inferred meaning separate from direct observation because the meaning of actions is not always self-evident. Sometimes people try to deceive others. For example, an unrelated couple register at a motel as Mr. and Mrs. Smith. More frequently, social behavior is ambiguous or multiple meanings are possible. For example, I see a White male and female, both in their late twenties, get out of a car and enter a restaurant together. They sit at a table, order a meal, and talk with serious expressions in hushed tones, sometimes leaning forward to hear each other. As they get up to leave, the woman, who has a sad facial expression and appears ready to cry, is briefly hugged by the male. They then leave together. Did I witness a couple breaking up, two friends discussing a third, two people trying to decide what to do because they have discovered that their spouses are having an affair with each other, or a brother and sister whose father just died? The **separation of inference** allows multiple meanings to arise on rereading direct observation notes. If you record inferred meaning without separation, you lose other possible meanings. Tjora (2006:433) observed that

Separation of inference A process by which a field researcher writes direct observation notes in a way that keeps what was observed separate from what was inferred or believed to have occurred.

you want to "both record 'what you "know" has happened and what you "think" has happened' . . . not mix them with actual observations."

4. *Analytic memos.* We make many decisions about how to proceed while in the field. We plan some acts (e.g., to conduct an interview, to observe a particular activity) while others seem to occur almost out of thin air. Most field researchers keep analytic notes to have a record of plans, tactics, ethical and procedural decisions, and self-critiques of tactics.

Theory emerges in field research during data collection and when reviewing field notes. Theoretical notes are a running account of your attempts to give meaning to field events. You "think out loud" in the notes. In them, you might suggest new linkages between ideas, create hypotheses, propose conjectures, and develop new concepts.

Analytic memos include methodological strategies and theoretical notes. They are collections of your thoughts, systematic digressions into theory, and a record of your decisions. You use them to elaborate and expand on ideas while still in the field, and to modify or develop more complex theory by rereading and thinking about the memos.

5. *Personal notes.* As discussed earlier, personal feelings and emotional reactions become part of the data and color what you see or hear in the field. You should keep a section of notes that is like a personal diary. You record personal life events and feelings in it ("I'm tense today, I wonder if it's because of the fight I had yesterday with . . ."; "I've got a headache on this gloomy, overcast day").

Personal notes provide a way to cope with stress; they are a source of data about personal reactions; they help to evaluate direct observation or inference notes when you later reread the notes. For example, being in a good mood during observations might color what you observed.

6. *Interview notes.* If you conduct field interviews (to be discussed), you keep the interview notes separate.[42] In addition to recording questions and answers, you create a **face sheet**. This is a page at the beginning of the notes with information such as the date, place of interview, characteristics of interviewee, content of the interview, and so on. It helps you to make sense of the notes when rereading them.

7. *Maps, diagrams, and artifacts.* You may wish to make maps and draw diagrams or pictures of the features of a field site.[43] This serves two purposes: It helps organize events in the field and it helps convey a field site to others. For example, a researcher observing a bar with 15 stools may draw and number 15 circles to simplify recording (e.g., "Yosuke came in and sat on stool 12; Phoebe was already on stool 10").

Three types of maps are helpful: spatial, social, and temporal. The first helps orient the data; the latter two are preliminary forms of data analysis. A *spatial map* locates people, equipment, and the like in terms of physical space to show where activities occur (Figure 13.5a on page 448). A *social map* shows the number or variety of people and the arrangements among them according to power, influence, friendship, division of labor, and so on (Figure 13.5b). A *temporal map* shows the ebb and flow of people, goods, services, and communications or schedules (Figure 13.5c).

In addition to the maps that we create to analyze the field site, many researchers gather artifacts, or items from the field site. These items of physical evidence (e.g., a brochure, menu, coffee cup, T-shirt, program or roster of participants, party hat) are visible reminders from the site. You can use them to trigger a memory, illustrate a theme, or symbolize some activity or event.

8. *Machine-recorded data.* Photos, tape recorders, and videotapes can be helpful supplements in field research. They never substitute for field notes or your presence in the field. You cannot introduce them into all field sites, and you can use them only after you develop some rapport. Recorders and videotapes provide a close approximation to what occurred and a permanent record that others can review. They help you recall events and observe

---

Analytic memos Notes a qualitative researcher takes while developing more abstract ideas, themes, or hypotheses from an examination of details in the data.

Face sheet A page at the beginning of interview or field notes with information on the date, place of observations, interviews, the context, and so on.

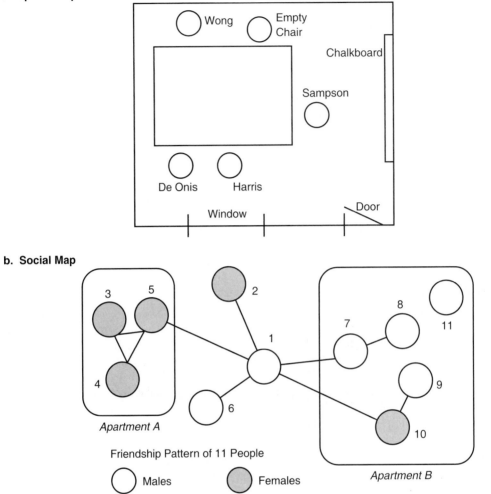

a. Spatial Map

Wong

Empty Chair

Chalkboard

Sampson

De Onis   Harris

Window

Door

b. Social Map

3   5

2

8

7   11

1

4

6

9

10

Apartment A

Friendship Pattern of 11 People

Males   Females

Apartment B

c. Temporal Map

Day of Week, Buzz's Bar

	Mon	Tue	Wed	Thr	Fri	Sat
Open 10:00	Old Drunks	Old Drunks	Old Drunks	Old Drunks	Skip Work or Leave Early	Going to Fish
5:00	Football Watchers	Neighbors and Bridge Players	Softball Team (All-Male Night)	Young Crowd	Loud Music, Mixed Crowd	Loners and No Dates
Close 1:00						

FIGURE 13.5 **Types of Maps Used in Field Research**

what does not happen, or nonresponses, which are easy to miss. Nevertheless, these items create disruption and an increased awareness of surveillance. Researchers who rely on them must address associated problems (e.g., ensure that batteries are fresh, the supply of blank tapes is adequate). Also, relistening to or viewing tapes can be time consuming. For example, it may take more than 100 hours to listen to 50 hours recorded in the field. Transcriptions of tape are expensive and not always accurate; they do not always convey subtle contextual meanings or mumbled words.[44]

Step 6: Exit the Field Site. Work in the field can last from a few weeks to a dozen years.[45] In either case, at some point, it ends. Some researchers suggest that the end comes naturally when theory building ceases or reaches a closure; others believe that fieldwork could go on without end and that a firm decision to cut it off is needed.

Experienced field researchers anticipate a process of disengaging and exiting the field. Depending on the intensity of involvement and the length of time in the field, the process can be disruptive or emotionally painful for both them and the members. You may experience the emotional pain of breaking intimate friendships when leaving the field. You may feel guilty and depressed immediately before and after leaving. You may find letting go difficult because of personal and emotional entanglements. If the involvement in the field was intense and long and the field site differed from your native culture, you may need months of adjustment before feeling at home with your original cultural surroundings.

Once you decide to leave—because the project reaches a natural end and little new is being learned or because external factors force it to end (e.g., end of a job, gatekeepers order you out)—choose a method of exiting. You can leave by a quick exit (simply not return one day) or slowly withdraw, reducing involvement over weeks. You also need to decide how to tell members and how much advance warning to give.

The exit process depends on the specific field setting and the relationships developed. In general, let members know a short period ahead of time. You

should fulfill any bargains or commitments that were made and leave with a clean slate. Sometimes a ritual or ceremony, such as a going-away party or shaking hands with everyone, helps signal the break for members. Feminist researchers advocate maintaining friendships with members after exiting.

Leaving affects members. Some may feel hurt or rejected because a close social relationship is ending. They may react by trying to pull you back into the field and make you more a member, or they may become angry and resentful. They may grow cool and distant because of an awareness that you really are an outsider. In any case, fieldwork is not finished until the process of disengagement and exiting is complete. (See Summary Review Box 13.1, Overview of the Field Research Process on page 450.)

THE FIELD RESEARCH INTERVIEW

So far, you have read about how field researchers observe and take notes. They also interview members, but field interviews differ from survey research interviews. This section introduces the field interview.

Unstructured, nondirective, in-depth interviews in field research differ from formal survey research interviews in many ways (see Table 13.1 on page 451).[46] The field interview involves asking questions, listening, expressing interest, and recording what was said.

The field interview is a joint production of a researcher and one or more members. Members are active participants whose insights, feelings, and cooperation are essential parts of a discussion process that reveals subjective meanings. "The interviewer's presence and form of involvement—how she or he listens, attends, encourages, interrupts, digresses, initiates topics, and terminates responses—is integral to the respondent's account" (Mishler, 1986:82).

Field research interviews go by many names: *unstructured, depth, ethnographic, open ended, informal,* and *long.* Generally, they involve one or more people being present, occur in the field, and are informal and nondirective (i.e., a member may take the interview in various directions).[47]

Overview of the Field Research Process

Step 1: Prepare To Enter the Field
- Be flexible
- Organize
- Defocus
- Be self-aware

Step 2. Choose a Field Site and Gain Access
- Select a site
- Deal with gatekeepers
- Enter and gain access
- Assume a social role
- Adopt a level of involvement
- Build rapport

Step 3. Apply Strategies
- Negotiate
- Normalize research
- Decide on disclosure
- Focus and sample
- Assume the attitude of strangeness
- Notice social breakdowns
- Cope with stress

Step 4. Maintain Relations in the Field
- Adjust and adapt

- Use charm and nurture trust
- Perform small favors
- Avoid conflicts
- Appear interested
- Be the acceptable incompetent

Step 5. Gather and Record Data
- Absorb and experience
- Watch and listen
- Record the data
- Types of field notes
1. Jotted notes
2. Direct observation notes
3. Inference notes
4. Analytic memos
5. Personal notes
6. Interview notes
7. Maps, diagrams, and artifacts
8. Machine-recorded data

Step 6. Exit the Field Site

A field interview involves a mutual sharing of experiences. You might share your background to build trust and encourage the informant to open up, but do not force answers or use leading questions. You want to encourage and guide a process of mutual discovery. In her study of youth subculture, Wilkins (2008:21) says that her own unexpected pregnancy and single motherhood during her field research study "changed my social location in significant and often unexpected ways," including facilitating her research opportunities with wannabes (i.e., white teens who acted Puerto Rican).

In field interviews, members express themselves in the forms in which they normally speak, think, and organize reality. You want to retain members' jokes and narrative stories in their natural form and not repackage them into a standardized format. Focus on the member's perspective and

experiences. To stay close to the member's experience, ask questions in terms of concrete examples or situations—for example, "Could you tell me things that led up to your quitting in June?" instead of "Why did you quit your job?"

Field interviews occur in a series over time. Begin by building rapport and steering conversation away from evaluative or highly sensitive topics. Avoid probing inner feelings until you establish intimacy, and even then, expect apprehension. After several meetings, you may be able to probe more deeply into sensitive issues and seek clarification of less sensitive issues. In later interviews, you may return to topics and check past answers by restating them in a nonjudgmental tone and asking for verification—for example, "The last time we talked, you said that you started taking things from the store after they reduced your pay. Is that right?"

TABLE 13.1   Survey Interviews versus Field Research Interviews

TYPICAL SURVEY INTERVIEW	TYPICAL FIELD INTERVIEW
1. It has a clear beginning and end.	1. The beginning and end are not clear. The interview can be picked up at a later time.
2. The same standard questions are asked of all respondents in the same sequence.	2. The questions and the order in which they are asked are tailored to specific people and situations.
3. The interviewer appears neutral at all times.	3. The interviewer shows interest in responses and encourages elaboration.
4. The interviewer asks questions, and the respondent answers.	4. It is like a friendly conversational exchange but with more interviewer questions.
5. It is almost always with one respondent alone.	5. It can occur in a group setting or with others in the area but varies.
6. It has a professional tone and businesslike focus; diversions are ignored.	6. It is interspersed with jokes, asides, stories, diversions, and anecdotes, which are recorded.
7. Closed-ended questions are common with infrequent probes.	7 Open-ended questions are common, and probes are frequent.
8. The interviewer alone controls the pace and direction of the interview.	8. The interviewer and member jointly control the pace and direction of the interview.
9. The social context in which the interview occurs is ignored and assumed to make little difference.	9. The social context of the interview is noted and seen as important for interpreting the meaning of responses.
10. The interviewer attempts to mold the communication pattern into a standard framework.	10. The interviewer adjusts to the member's norms and language usage.

Sources: Adapted from Briggs (1986), Denzin (1989), Douglas (1985), Mishler (1986), Spradley (1979a).

The field interview is a "speech event," closer to a friendly conversation than the stimulus/response model found in a survey research interview (see Chapter 10). You are familiar with a friendly conversation, which has its own informal rules and the following elements: (1) a greeting ("Hi, it's good to see you again"); (2) the absence of an explicit goal or purpose (we don't say, "Let's now discuss what we did last weekend"); (3) avoidance of explicit repetition (we don't say, "Could you clarify what you said about . . ."); (4) question asking ("Did you see the race yesterday?"); (5) expressions of interest ("Really? I wish I could have been there!"); (6) expressions of ignorance ("No, I missed it. What happened?"); (7) turn taking so the encounter is balanced (one person does not always ask questions and the other only answers); (8) abbreviations ("I missed the Derby, but I'm going to the Indy," not "I missed the Kentucky Derby horse race but I will go to the Indianapolis 500 automotive race"); (9) a pause or brief silence when neither person talks is acceptable; (10) a closing (we don't say, "Let's end this conversation"; instead, we give a verbal indicator before physically leaving—"I've got to get back to work now. See ya tomorrow.").

The field interview differs from a friendly conversation. It has an explicit purpose: to learn about the member and setting. You include explanations or requests that diverge from friendly conversations. For example, you may say, "I'd like to ask you about . . ." or "Could you look at this and see if I've written it down right?" The field interview is less balanced. A higher proportion of questions come from you, and you express more ignorance and interest. Also, it includes repetition, and you may often ask the member to elaborate about unclear abbreviations.[48]

Field research interviewers watch for **markers**, "a passing reference made [in a field interview] by a respondent to an important event or feeling state" (Weiss, 1994:77). For example, during an interview with a 45-year-old physician, the physician mentions casually while describing having difficulty in a high school class, "It was about that time that my sister was seriously injured in a car accident." The physician had never mentioned the sister or the accident before. By dropping it in, the physician is indicating it was an important event at the time. You should pick up on the marker. You later may ask, "Earlier, you mentioned that your sister was seriously injured in a car accident. Could you tell me more about that?" Most important, you must listen. Do not interrupt frequently, repeatedly finish a member's sentences, offer associations (e.g., "Oh, that is just like X"), insist on finishing asking your question after the member has started an answer, fight for control over the interview process, or stay fixed with a line of thought and ignore new leads.[49] Perhaps you will learn something unexpected, such as the sister's accident started an interest in medicine by the physician and was critical to choosing a medical career.

Life History

Life history, life story, or a biographical interview is a special type of field interviewing. It overlaps with oral history (see Chapter 14).[50] Stories of the past have multiple purposes and may shape the forms of interview. In a **life history interview**, we

interview and gather documentary material about a particular individual's life. The person, referred to as an informant, usually is elderly. "The concept of life story is used to designate the retrospective information itself without the corroborative evidence often implied by the term life history" (Tagg, 1985:163). We ask open-ended questions to capture how the person understands his or her own past. Exact accuracy in the story is less critical than the story itself. We recognize that the informant may reconstruct or add present interpretations to the past; the person may "rewrite" his or her story. The main purpose of this interview is to get at how the informant sees/remembers the past, not some kind of objective truth (see Expansion Box 13.5, The Life History Interview).

We sometimes use a *life story grid* when we ask the person what happened at various dates and in several areas of life. A grid may consist of categories such as migration, occupation, education, or family events for each of ten different ages in the person's life. We can supplement the interview information with artifacts (e.g., old photos) and present them during the interview to stimulate discussion or recollection. "Life writing as an empirical exercise feeds on data: letters, documents, interviews" (Smith, 1994:290).

McCracken (1988:20) gave an example of how objects aided an interview by helping him understand how the person being interviewed saw things. When interviewing a 75-year-old woman in her living room, McCracken initially thought the room just contained a lot of cluttered physical objects. After having the woman explain the meaning of each item, it was clear that she saw each as a memorial or a memento. The room was a museum to key events in her life. Only after the author looked at the objects in this new way did he begin to see the furniture and objects not as inanimate things but as objects that radiated meaning.

Sometimes we find an existing archive with a person; other times, we search out the documents and create an archive. Locating such documentary data can be a tremendous task followed by reviewing, cataloging, and organizing the information. The interview and documentary data together form the basis of the life story.

Marker   A passing reference by a person in a field interview that actually indicates a very important event or feeling.

Life history interview   Open-ended interview with one person who describes his or her entire life, a subtype of oral history.

EXPANSION BOX **13.5**
The Life History Interview

Life history or life story interviews typically involve two to ten open-ended interviews, usually recorded, of 60 to 90 minutes each. These interviews serve several purposes. First, they can assist the informant being interviewed in reconstructing his or her life memories. Retelling and remembering one's life events as a narrative story can have therapeutic benefits and pass on personal wisdom to a new generation. Second, these interviews can create new qualitative data on the life cycle, the development of self, and how people experience events that can be archived and added to similar data (e.g., The Center for Life Stories at University of Southern Maine is such an archive). Third, life story interviews can provide the interviewer with an in-depth look at another's life. This is often an enriching experience that creates a close personal relationship and encourages self-reflection in ways that enhance personal integrity. Steps in the process are as follows:

1. The researcher prepares with background reading, refines his or her interview skills, contacts the informant, gets permission for the interview, and promises anonymity.
2. The researcher conducts a series of interviews, audio- or video-recording them. The interviewer suspends any prior history with an informant and gives his or her total respect, always showing sincere interest in what another says. He or she asks open-ended questions, but is flexible and never forces a question. The interviewer acts as a guide, knowing when to ask a question that will open up stories; gives intense attentiveness; and is completely nonjudgmental and supportive. Often the interviewer offers photographs or objects to help spark memories and past feelings.
3. The researcher transcribes the recorded interviews in four stages: (a) prepares a summary of each session; (b) makes a verbatim transcription, with minor editing (e.g., adds punctuation for sentences, paragraphs) and stage directions (e.g., laughter, coughing); (c) reviews the whole transcript for clarity of meaning and does further editing and minor rearranging; and (d) has the informant review the transcript for any corrections and modifications.
4. The researcher sends a note of appreciation to the informant and prepares a commentary on major themes and/or sends it to an archive.

Source: Adapted from A. B. Atkinson & John Hills, 1998. "Exclusion, Employment and Opportunity," *CASE Papers* 04, Centre for Analysis of Social Exclusion, LSE. http://sticerd.lse.ac.uk/case/

Types of Questions Asked in Field Interviews

We ask three types of questions in a field interview: descriptive, structural, and contrast questions. We ask all concurrently, but each type is more frequent at a different stage in the research process (see Figure 13.6 on page 454). During the early stage, ask descriptive questions and gradually add structural questions until, in the middle stage after analysis has begun, they make up a majority of the questions. Ask contrast questions in the middle of a study and increase them until, by the end, you ask them more than any other type.[51]

You ask a descriptive question to explore the setting and learn about members. Descriptive questions can be about time and space—for example,

"Where is the bathroom?" "When does the delivery truck arrive?" "What happened Monday night?" They can also be about people and activities: "Who is sitting by the window?" "What is your uncle like?" "What happens during the initiation ceremony?" They can be about objects: "When do you use a saber saw?" "Which tools do you carry with you on an emergency water leak job?" Questions asking for examples or experiences are descriptive questions: for example, "Could you give me an example of a great date?" "What were your experiences as a postal clerk?" Descriptive questions may ask about hypothetical situations: "If a student opened her book during the exam, how would you deal with it?" Another type of descriptive question asks members about the argot of the setting: "What

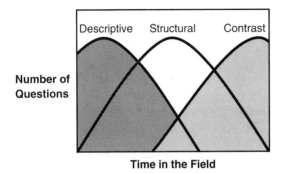

Number of Questions

Descriptive   Structural   Contrast

Time in the Field

FIGURE 13.6   Types of Questions in Field Research Interviews

do you call a deputy sheriff?" (The answer is a "county Mountie.")

You use a structural question after spending time in the field and starting to analyze data, especially with a domain analysis (to be discussed in Chapter 15). It begins after you organize specific field events, situations, and conversations into categories. For example, your observations of a highway truck-stop restaurant revealed that the employees informally classify customers who patronize the truck stop. In a preliminary analysis, you create a conceptual category, "kinds of customers" and then you talk to members using structural questions to verify types.

One way to pose a structural question is to ask the members whether a category includes elements in addition to those you already have identified. You might ask, "Are there any types of customers other than regulars, greasers, pit stoppers, and long haulers?" In addition, you ask for confirmation: "Is a greaser a type of customer that you serve?" "Would you call a customer who . . . a greaser?" "Would a pit stopper ever eat a three-course dinner?"

The contrast question builds on the analysis that you verified by structural questions. Contrast questions focus on similarities or differences between elements in categories or between categories that you ask members to verify: "You seem to have a number of different kinds of customers come in here. I've heard you call some customers 'regulars' and others 'pit stoppers.' How are a regular and a pit stopper alike?" or "Is the difference

between a long hauler and a greaser that the greaser doesn't tip?" or "Two types of customers just stop to use the restroom—entire families and a lone male. Do you call both pit stoppers?"

Informants. An informant in field research is a member with whom a field researcher develops a relationship and who tells about, or informs on, the field.[52] The ideal informant has four characteristics (see Expansion Box 13.6, The Ideal Field Research Informant).

You may interview several types of informants. Contrasting types who provide useful perspectives include rookies and old-timers; people in the center of events and those on the fringes of activity; people who recently changed status (e.g., through promotion) and those who are static; frustrated or needy people and happy or secure people; and the leader in charge and the subordinate who

EXPANSION BOX 13.6

The Ideal Field Research Informant

1. The person who is totally familiar with the culture and is in position to witness significant events makes a good informant. He or she lives and breathes the culture and engages in routines in the setting without thinking about them. The individual is not a novice but has years of intimate experience in the culture.

2. The individual is currently involved in the field. Former members who have reflected on the field may provide useful insights, but the longer they have been away from direct involvement, the more likely it is that they have reconstructed their recollections.

3. The person can spend time with the researcher. Interviewing may take many hours, and some members are simply not available for extensive interviewing.

4. Nonanalytic individuals make better informants. A nonanalytic informant is familiar with and uses native folk theory or pragmatic common sense. This is in contrast to the analytic member who preanalyzes the setting using categories from the media or education. Even members educated in the social sciences can learn to respond in a nonanalytic manner but only if they set aside their education and use the member perspective.

follows. Expect mixed and inconsistent messages when you interview a range of informants.

Interview Context. We recognize that a conversation in a private office may not occur in a crowded lunchroom.[53] Often, interviews take place in the informant's home environment so that he or she is comfortable. This is not always best. If an informant is preoccupied or there is no privacy, you move to another setting (e.g., quiet restaurant or university office).

Meaning in an interview is shaped by its Gestalt; that is, the whole interaction of a researcher and an informant in a specific context. Also, nonverbal forms of communication (e.g., shrugs, gestures, etc.) that add meaning should be noted.

DATA QUALITY

The Meaning of Quality

What does the term high-quality data mean in field research, and what does a qualitative researcher do to get such data?[54] For the researcher following a positivist, quantitative approach, high-quality data are reliable and valid; they give precise, consistent measures of the same "objective" truth for all researchers. By contrast, a field researcher following an interpretive approach believes that instead of assuming one single, objective truth, members subjectively interpret experiences within a social context. What a member takes to be true flows from social interaction and interpretation. Thus, high-quality field data capture such processes and provide an understanding of the member's viewpoint. You want "rich" data. This means the data are diverse and you gathered data systematically over a prolonged period. We do not eliminate subjective views to get quality data; rather, quality data include subjective responses and experiences. Quality field data are detailed descriptions from your immersion into the authentic experiences in the social world of members.[55]

Reliability in Field Research

The reliability of field data addresses whether your observations about a member or field event are internally and externally consistent. **Internal consistency** refers to data that are plausible given all that is known about a person or event and eliminating common forms of human deception. In other words, the data fit together into a coherent picture. For example, a member's actions are consistent over time and in different social contexts.

External consistency refers to data that have been verified or cross-checked with other, divergent sources of data. In other words, the data all fit into the overall context. For example, others can verify what you observed about a person. It asks: Does other evidence confirm your observations?

Reliability in field research also includes what is not said or done but is expected or anticipated. Such omissions or null data can be significant but are difficult to detect. For example, when observing a cashier end her shift, you notice that she did not count the money in the drawer. You may notice the omission only if other cashiers always count money at the end of the shift (see the discussion of negative case method in Chapter 15).

Reliability in field research depends on your insight, awareness, suspicions, and questions. You look at members and events from different angles (legal, economic, political, personal) and mentally ask questions: Where does the money come from for that? What do those people do all day?

You depend on what members tell you. This makes the credibility of members and their statements part of reliability. To check member credibility, you must ask: Does the person have a reason to lie? Is she or he in a position to know that? What are the person's values, and how might that shape what she or he says? Is the person just saying

---

Internal consistency Reliability in field research determined by having a researcher examine the plausibility of data to see whether they form a coherent whole, fit all else that is known about a person or event, and avoid common forms of deception.

External consistency Reliability of data in field research demonstrated by having the researcher cross-check and verify qualitative data using multiple sources of information.

that to please me? Is there anything that might limit her or his spontaneity?

Take subjectivity and context into account as you evaluate credibility. A person's subjective perceptions influence his or her statements or actions, which are colored by an individual's point of view and past experiences. Instead of evaluating each statement to see whether it is true, you may find statements useful in themselves. Even inaccurate statements and actions can be revealing.

As mentioned before, the context shapes actions and statements. What is said in one setting may differ in other contexts. For example, when asked, "Do you dance?" a member may say no in a public setting full of excellent dancers but yes in a semiprivate setting with few dancers and different music. It is not that the member is lying but that the answer is shaped by the context. Four other obstacles to reliability include behaviors that can mislead you: misinformation, evasions, lies, and fronts (see Expansion Box 13.7, Obstacles to Reliable Field Data).[56]

Validity in Field Research

Validity in field research comes from your analysis of data as accurate representations of the social world in the field. Replicability is not a criterion because field research is virtually impossible to replicate. Essential aspects of the field change: The social events and context change, the members are different, the individual researcher differs, and so on. There are four types of validity or tests of research accuracy: ecological validity, natural history, member validation, and competent insider performance.

Fronts People in a field site who engage in actions and say things that give an impression or appearance that differs from what is actually occurring.

Ecological validity Authenticity and trustworthiness of a study; demonstrated by showing that the researcher's descriptions of the field site match those of the members and that the field researcher's presence was not a disturbance.

Natural history A detailed description of how a project was conducted.

EXPANSION BOX **13.7**
Obstacles to Reliable Field Data

1. *Misinformation* is an unintended falsehood caused by the uncertainty and complexity of life. For example, nurses in a hospital state something as "official hospital policy" when, in fact, there is no such written policy.
2. *Evasions* are intentional acts of not revealing information. Common evasions include not answering questions, answering a different question than was asked, switching topics, or answering in a purposefully vague and ambiguous manner. For example, a salesperson appears uncomfortable when the topic of using call girls to get customers comes up at a dinner party. He says, "Yes, a lot of people use them." But later, alone, after careful questioning, the salesman is drawn out and reveals that he himself uses the practice.
3. *Lies* are untruths intended to mislead or to give a false view. For example, a gang member gives you a false name and address, or a church minister gives an inflated membership figure in order to look more successful. Douglas (1976:73) noted, "In all other research settings I've known about in any detail, lying was common, both among members and to researchers, especially about the things that were really important to the members."
4. **Fronts** are shared and learned lies and deceptions. They can include the use of physical props and collaborators. An example is a bar that is really a place to make illegal bets. The bar appears to be legitimate and sells drinks, but its true business is revealed only by careful investigation. Fronts are not always malicious. A common example is that of Santa Claus—a "front" put on for small children.

---

1. **Ecological validity** is the degree to which the social world you describe matches the members' world. It asks whether the natural setting described is relatively undisturbed by your presence or procedures. A study has ecological validity if events would have occurred without your presence.
2. **Natural history** is a detailed description of how you conducted the project. It is a full and candid disclosure of your actions, assumptions,

and procedures for others to evaluate. A study is valid in terms of natural history if outsiders see and accept the field site and your actions.

3. **Member validation** occurs when you take field results back to members and they judge the adequacy of the results. A study is "member valid" if many members recognize and understand your description as reflecting their intimate social world. Member validation has limitations because conflicting perspectives in a setting produce disagreement with your observations, and members may object when results do not portray their group in a favorable light. In addition, members may not recognize the description because it is not from their perspective or does not fit with their purposes.[57]

4. **Competent insider performance** is the ability of a nonmember to interact effectively as a member or pass as one. This includes the ability to tell and understand insider jokes. A valid study gives enough of a flavor of the social life in the field and sufficient detail so that an outsider can act as a member. Its limitation is that it is not possible to know the social rules for every situation. Also, an outsider might be able to pass simply because members are being polite and do not want to point out social mistakes.[58]

ETHICAL DILEMMAS OF FIELD RESEARCH

Your direct, personal involvement in the social lives of other people during field research introduces ethical dilemmas. Some of them arise when you are alone in the field and have little time to deliberate over ethics. You may be aware of general ethical issues before entering the field, but they often arise unexpectedly in the course of observing and interacting in the field. We consider five ethical issues in field research: covert research, confidentiality, involvement with illegal behavior, the powerful, and publishing reports.[59]

1. *Covert research.* The most debated of the ethical issues is that of covert versus overt field research.[60] It involves the broader issue of deception both in fully secret or covert research and when the researcher assumes a false role, name, or identity, or lies to members in some way. Some in the research community support covert research or deception and see it as necessary to enter into and gain a full knowledge of some areas of social life. Others oppose it absolutely. They argue that it undermines a trust between researchers and society.[61] Although its moral status is questionable, some field sites or activities can be studied only covertly (see Chapter 15).

Covert research is never preferable and rarely easier than overt research because of the difficulties of maintaining a front and the constant fear of being caught. Lofland et al. (2006:39) note, "the ethical sensitive, thoughtful, and knowledgeable investigator is the best judge of whether covert research is justified. However . . . we suggest you undertake no covert research . . . before you have acquainted yourself with the problems, debates, and dilemmas associated with such research and local IRB protocols and mandates."

2. *Confidentiality.* You may learn intimate knowledge revealed in confidence and have a strong moral obligation to uphold the confidentiality of data. This obligation includes keeping information confidential from others in the field and disguising members' names in field notes. Sometimes you cannot directly quote a person in a research report. One strategy is to find documentary evidence that says the same thing and use the document (e.g., an old memo, a newspaper article) as the source of the information instead of the member.

A more serious ethical difficulty arises when a field researcher and a member develop a close,

> **Member validation** A method that field researchers use to demonstrate the authenticity and trustworthiness of a study by having the people who were studied read and confirm as being true what the researchers have reported.
>
> **Competent insider performance** Action that field researchers use to demonstrate the authenticity and trustworthiness of a study by having the researcher "pass" as a member of the group under study.

personal relationship in addition to their researcher-researched person relationship. Based on deep trust, a member may share intimate secrets with the field researcher alone. As Howell (2004:346) found in her study of women from Oaxaca, Mexico:

> *Ethnographers typically present detailed descriptions of their subjects' lives and circumstances to portray fully the cultural and personal events. Yet informants may try to hide from the general public the more sensitive of the myriad topics . . . including infidelity, wealth accumulation, criminal activities, and violence . . . culturally and personally sensitive subjects—such as sexual assault—may be difficult, if not impossible, to probe with strangers and acquaintances. . . . When informants volunteer information about these experiences, standard channels for maintaining ethical guidelines are invoked. . . . The situation becomes more delicate when information is volunteered as a confidence between "friends," one of whom is also an ethnographer in a position to publish potentially damaging secrets from another's life. . . . The importance of presenting as accurately as possible the realities—including violence and fear of violence—that affect informants' opportunities and choices compels ethnographers to discuss these carefully guarded secrets that are not necessarily revealed within the researcher-researched paradigm. Yet doing so reinforces the importance of considering anew the issues of confidentiality, betrayal, and power. . . .*

3. *Involvement with illegal behavior.* Researchers who conduct field research on people who engage in illegal, immoral, or unethical behavior know of and are sometimes involved in illegal activity. Fetterman (1989) called this **guilty knowledge**. Such knowledge is of interest not only to law enforcement officials but also to other field site

---

Guilty knowledge Information of illegal, unethical, or immoral actions by the people in the field site that are not widely known but the researcher learns.

Hierarchy of credibility Concept of ranking of believeability that refers to situations in which a researcher who learns much about weaker members of society whose views are rarely heard is accused of "bias" while the views of powerful people are accepted as "unbiased" based on their high social status.

---

members. The researcher faces a dilemma of building trust and rapport with the members, yet not becoming so involved as to violate his or her basic personal moral standards. Usually, the researcher makes an explicit arrangement with the deviant members.

4. *The powerful.* Many field researchers study society's people who are marginal and powerless (e.g., people who live on the street, the impoverished, children, low-level workers in bureaucracies). Some criticize researchers for ignoring the powerful, yet the wealthy and powerful people in society have effective gatekeepers and can easily block access. At the same time, elites and officials criticize researchers for being biased in favor of the less powerful.

Becker (1970c) explained this by the **hierarchy of credibility**. It says that those who study people who are powerless, criminals, or low-level subordinates are often viewed as being biased, whereas people with official authority are assumed to be credible. Many people assume that people at the top of organizations have the right to define the way things are going to be, have a broader view than people at lower levels, and are in a position to do something. Thus, "the sociologist who favors officialdom will be spared the accusation of bias" (Becker, 1970c:20). Researchers who immerse themselves in the world of people who are disadvantaged by developing an in-depth understanding of that side of social life and then publicize a rarely heard perspective may be accused of bias simply because they are giving a voice to a rarely heard sector of society.

5. *Publishing field reports.* The intimate knowledge researchers obtain and report on can create a dilemma between the right of privacy and the right to know. Researchers cannot always reveal all secrets they learn without violating privacy or harming reputations, yet failure to make public what the researchers have learned keeps that information and details hidden. When the researchers are not giving a complete and accurate account of events, others may question a report that omits critical details.

Some researchers suggest asking members to look at a report to verify its accuracy and to approve of their portrayal in print. Such reviews of studies that involve marginal groups (e.g., those who are addicts, prostitutes, crack users) may not be possible because we must always respect member privacy. On the other hand, censorship or self-censorship can be a danger. A compromise position is to reveal truthful but unflattering material only if it is essential to a larger argument or to present an accurate total picture.[62]

FOCUS GROUP RESEARCH

The **focus group** is a special qualitative research technique in which people are informally "interviewed" in a group discussion setting.[63] Focus group research has rapidly grown in the past 20 years. The procedure is that a researcher gathers together six to twelve people in a room with a moderator to discuss issues, generally for about 90 minutes. The moderator is trained to be nondirective and to facilitate free, open discussion by all group members (i.e., not let one person dominate the discussion). Group members should be homogeneous but not include close friends or relatives. A typical study uses four to six separate groups. Focus group topics might include public attitudes (e.g., race relations, workplace

equality), personal behaviors (e.g., dealing with AIDS), a new product (e.g., breakfast cereal), or a political candidate (see Example Box 13.3, Focus Group on Father Loss and Manhood). We often combine focus groups with quantitative research, and the combination has its own specific strengths and weaknesses (see Expansion Box 13.8, Advantages and Limitations of Focus Groups on page 460).

Providing very clear instructions and carefully selecting participants for focus groups can greatly shape their outcome. As Wibeck, Dahlgren, and Öberg (2007:262) observed, "Since the interpretative frames and the previous experience of the participants may differ, it is crucial to ensure that the preconditions for focus group participation are clear to all participants before the discussion starts." Although participants should be moderately homogeneous, this does not always ensure an openness and a willingness to share beliefs and opinions candidly. For example, to discuss gender-sensitive

> **Focus group**   A group of people informally "interviewed" in a discussion setting that is participating in a qualitative research technique.

EXAMPLE BOX **13.3**
Focus Group on Father Loss and Manhood

Hunter et al. (2006) conducted focus group research with young African American men about what it is like to grow up without a father. Because fewer than 40 percent of African Americans grow up in two-parent households, the researchers were interested in how adolescent boys and young men acquire their sense of manhood. The authors held two focus groups at a local community recreation center where the youth and their families received social services and where many of the youth played basketball. Each session was 75 to 90 minutes long and was audiotaped and later transcribed. The groups had twenty African American men aged 15 to 22. The authors recruited participants through counselors and other connections to the center. Most participants (92%) had less than a high school education and were currently in school. Most (91%) grew up in households without a father. All had a low

income or were from a low working class situation. The primary question to the focus groups was what participants thought "being a man" meant, and what type of man they wanted to become. In their analysis of the transcripts, the authors learned that father loss was central to the young men's perspectives about becoming a man. This information came out in two ways: general perspectives about fatherhood and manhood and specific autobiographical reflections about fathers who had influenced the participants as young men. Father loss was a recurrent issue linking general perspectives and autobiography. The authors found several themes expressed in the narratives of the young men, including the following four: (1) some things only a daddy can teach you; (2) if daddy could have taught you anything, he would still be here; (3) momma's both my momma and my daddy; and (4) I will be the man, my father was not.

EXPANSION BOX **13.8**

Advantages and Limitations of Focus Groups

ADVANTAGES

- The natural setting allows people to express opinions/ideas freely.
- Open expression among members of social groups who are marginalized is encouraged.
- People tend to feel empowered, especially in action-oriented research projects.
- Survey researchers have a window into how people talk about survey topics.
- The interpretation of quantitative survey results is facilitated.
- Participants may query one another and explain their answers to one another.

LIMITATIONS

- A "polarization effect" exists (attitudes become more extreme after group discussion).
- Only one or a few topics can be discussed in one focus group session.
- A moderator may unknowingly limit open, free expression of group members.
- Focus groups can produce fewer ideas than individual interviews.
- Focus group studies rarely report all details of study design/procedure.
- Researchers cannot reconcile the differences that arise between individual-only and focus group–context responses.

issues the presence of one gender is not enough. Hollander (2004) found that many participants still fear disclosing stigmatized, traumatic experiences (rape, domestic abuse). She (p. 626) argued, "What individual participants say during focus groups cannot necessarily be taken as a reliable indicator of experience. Participants may exaggerate, minimize, or withhold experiences depending on the social contexts." Context includes not only other participants but also the facilitator, as well as the larger social context (e.g., major social events and trends), the institutional context (e.g., location and

sponsor of the focus group), and the status context (e.g. people of different social status or position). Focus groups should be segmented by status. For example, rather than mixing supervisors and their employees, each should be in different group. Likewise, mixing teachers and their students together in the same focus group is unwise because people often respond very differently when people of higher or lower status are present.

CONCLUSION

In this chapter, you read about field research and the field research process (choosing a site and gaining access, creating relations in the field, observing and collecting data, and conducting the field interview). Field researchers begin with data analysis and theorizing during the data collection phase.

You can now appreciate implications of saying that a field researcher is directly involved with those being studied and is immersed in a natural setting. Doing field research has a greater impact on the researcher's emotions, personal life, and sense of self more than doing other types of research. Field research is difficult to conduct, but it is the best way to study many parts of the social world that we otherwise could not study.

Performing good field research requires a combination of skills. In addition to a strong sense of self, the researcher needs an incredible ability to listen and absorb details, tremendous patience, sensitivity and empathy for others, superb social skills, a talent to think very quickly "on your feet," the ability to see subtle interconnections among people/events, and a superior ability to express oneself in writing.

Field research is strongest when used to study a small group of people interacting in the present. It is valuable for micro-level or small-group face-to-face interaction. It is less effective when the concern is macro-level processes and social structures. It is nearly useless for events that occurred in the distant past or processes that stretch across decades. Historical-comparative research, discussed in the next chapter, is better suited to investigating these types of concerns.

KEY TERMS

acceptable incompetent	ethnography	internal consistency
access ladder	ethnomethodology	jotted notes
analytic memos	external consistency	life history interview
appearance of interest	face sheet	marker
argot	field site	member validation
attitude of strangeness	focus group	natural history
breaching experiment	freeze-outs	naturalism
competent insider	fronts	normalize social research
performance	gatekeeper	separation of inference
defocusing	go native	social breakdown
direct observation notes	guilty knowledge	thick description
ecological validity	hierarchy of credibility	

REVIEW QUESTIONS

1. What were the two major phases in the development of the Chicago School, and what are its journalistic and anthropological models?

2. List five of the ten things that the "methodological pragmatist" field researcher does.

3. Why is it important for a field researcher to read the literature before beginning fieldwork? How does this relate to defocusing?

4. Identify the characteristics of a field site that make it a good one for a beginning field researcher.

5. How does the "presentation of self" affect a field researcher's work?

6. What is the attitude of strangeness, and why is it important?

7. What are relevant considerations when choosing roles in the field, and how can the degree of researcher involvement vary?

8. Identify three ways to ensure quality field research data.

9. Compare differences between a field research and a survey research interview and between a field interview and a friendly conversation.

10. What are the different types or levels of field notes, and what purpose does each serve?

NOTES

1. See Lofland et al. (2006:2–20).
2. For studies of these sites or topics, see Neuman (2000: 345–346). On studies of children or schools, see Corsaro (1994), Corsaro and Molinari (2000), Eder (1995), Eder and Kinney (1995), Kelle (2000), and Merten (1999). On studies of people who are homeless, see Lankenau (1999) and on studies of female strippers, see Wood (2000).

3. For a background in the history of field research, see Adler and Adler (1987:8–35), Burgess (1982a), Douglas (1976:39–54), Holy (1984), and Wax (1971:21–41). On the Chicago School, see Blumer (1984) and Faris (1967).
4. Ethnography is described in Agar (1986), Franke (1983), Hammersley and Atkinson (1983), Sanday (1983), and Spradley (1979a:3–12; 1979b:3–16).

5. See Geertz (1973, 1979) on "thick description." Also see Denzin (1989:159–160) for additional discussion.

6. For more on ethnomethodology, see Cicourel (1964), Denzin (1970), Leiter (1980), Mehan and Wood (1975), and Turner (1974). Also see Emerson (1981:357–359) and Lester and Hadden (1980) on the relationship between field research and ethnomethodology. Garfinkel (1974a) discussed the origins of the term *ethnomethodology*.

7. The misunderstandings of people resulting from the disjuncture of different cultures is a common theme.

8. For a general discussion of field research and naturalism, see Adler and Adler (1994), Georges and Jones (1980), Holy (1984), and Pearsall (1970). For discussions of contrasting types of field research, see Clammer (1984), Gonor (1977), Holstein and Gubrium (1994), Morse (1994), Schwandt (1994), and Strauss and Corbin (1994).

9. See Georges and Jones (1980:21–42) and Lofland et al. (2006:11–15).

10. Johnson (1975:65–66) has discussed defocusing.

11. See Lofland (1976:13–23) and Shaffir et al. (1980: 18–20) on feeling marginal.

12. See Adler and Adler (1987:67–78).

13. See Hammersley and Atkinson (1983:42–45) and Lofland et al. (2006:17–32).

14. Jewish researchers have studied Christians (Kleinman, 1980), Whites have studied African Americans (Liebow, 1967), and adult researchers have become intimate with youngsters (Fine, 1987; Fine and Glassner, 1979; Thorne and Luria, 1986). Also see Eichler (1988), Hunt (1989), and Wax (1979) on the role of race, gender, and age in field research.

15. See Douglas and Rasmussen (1977) and Yancey and Rainwater (1970).

16. For more on gatekeepers and access, see Beck (1970:11–29), Bogdan and Taylor (1975:30–32), Corra and Willer (2002), and Wax (1971:367).

17. Adapted from Gray (1980:311). See also Hicks (1984) and Schatzman and Strauss (1973:58–63).

18. For discussions of ascribed status (and, in particular, gender) in field research, see Adler and Adler (1987), Ardener (1984), Ayella (1993), Denzin (1989:116–118), Douglas (1976), Easterday et al. (1982), Edwards (1993), Lofland et al. (2006:22-24), and Van Maanen (1982).

19. Roy (1970) argued for the "Ernie Pyle" role based on his study of union organizing in the southern United States. In this role, named after a World War II war correspondent, the researcher "goes with the troops" as a type of participant as observer. Trice (1970) discussed the advantages of an outsider role. Schwartz and Schwartz (1969) discussed various roles.

20. See Douglas (1976), Emerson (1981:367–368), and Johnson (1975:124–129) on being patient, polite, and considerate.

21. Negotiation in the field is discussed in Gans (1982), Johnson (1975:58–59, 76–77), and Schatzman and Strauss (1973:22–23).

22. On entering and gaining access to field sites with deviant groups, see Becker (1970a:31–38), Hammersley and Atkinson (1983:54–76), Lofland et al. (2006:30–47), and West (1980). Elite access is discussed by Hoffman (1980).

23. See Lofland et al. (2006:22-25).

24. For discussion of "normalizing," see Gans (1982: 57–59), Georges and Jones (1980:43–164), Hammersley and Atkinson (1983:70–76), Harkens and Warren (1993), Johnson (1975), and Wax (1971). Mann (1970) discussed how to teach members about a researcher's role.

25. For more on roles in field settings, see Barnes (1970:241–244), Emerson (1981:364), Hammersley and Atkinson (1983:88–104), Warren and Rasmussen (1977), and Wax (1979). On dress, see Bogdan and Taylor (1975: 45) and Douglas (1976).

26. See Lofland (1976) and Lofland et al. (2006) on focusing. Spradley (1979b:100–111) also provides a helpful discussion.

27. See Denzin (1989:71–73, 86–92), Glaser and Strauss (1967), Hammersley and Atkinson (1983: 45–53), Honigmann (1982), and Weiss (1994:25–29) on sampling in field research.

28. See Gurevitch (1988), Hammersley and Atkinson (1983), and Schatzman and Strauss (1973:53) on "strangeness" in field research.

29. See Gans (1982), Goward (1984b), and Van Maanen (1983b:282–286).

30. See Douglas (1976:216) and Corsino (1987).

31. See Warren and Rasmussen (1977) for a discussion of cross-gender tension.

32. See Wax (1971:13).

33. Also see Adler and Adler (1987:40–42), Bogdan and Taylor (1975:35–37), Douglas (1976), and Gray (1980: 321).

34. See Bogdan and Taylor (1975:50–51), Lofland et al. (2006:57–60), Shupe and Bromley (1980), and Wax (1971).

35. See Johnson (1975:105–108).

36. The acceptable incompetent or learner role is discussed in Bogdan and Taylor (1975:46), Douglas (1976), Hammersley and Atkinson (1983:92–94), Lofland et al. (2006:55-57), and Schatman and Strauss (1973:25).

37. See Strauss (1987:10–11).

38. See Georges and Jones (1980:105–133) and Johnson (1975:159). Clarke (1975) noted that it is not necessarily "subjectivism" to recognize this in field research.

39. See Becker and Geer (1970), Spradley (1979a, 1979b), and Schatzman and Strauss (1973) on argot.

40. For more on recording and organizing data, see Bogdan and Taylor (1975:60–73), Hammersley and Atkinson (1983:144–173), and Kirk and Miller (1986:49–59).

41. See Schatzman and Strauss (1973:69) on inference.

42. See Burgess (1982b), Lofland et al. (2006:99-108), and Spradley (1979a, 1979b) on notes for field interviews.

43. See Denzin (1989:87), Lofland et al. (2006: 88), Schatzman and Strauss (1973:34–36), and Stimson (1986) on maps in field research.

44. See Albrecht (1985), Bogdan and Taylor (1975:109), Denzin (1989:210–233), and Jackson (1987) for more on taping in field research.

45. Altheide (1980), Bogdan and Taylor (1975:75–76), Lofland et al. (2006), Maines et al. (1980), and Roadburg (1980) discuss leaving the field.

46. Discussion of field interviewing can be found in Banaka (1971), Bogdan and Taylor (1975:95–124), Briggs (1986), Burgess (1982c), Denzin (1989:103–120), Douglas (1985), Lofland et al. (2006), Spradley (1979a), and Whyte (1982).

47. See Fontana and Frey (1994).

48. On comparisons with conversations, see Briggs (1986:11), Spradley (1979a:56–68), and Weiss (1994:8).

49. See Weiss (1994:78).

50. See Atkinson (1998), Denzin (1989:182–209), Nash and McCurdy (1989), Smith (1994), and Tagg (1985) on life history interviews.

51. The types of questions are adapted from Spradley (1979a, 1979b).

52. Field research informants are discussed by Dean et al. (1969), Kemp and Ellen (1984), Lofland et al. (2006: 93-94), Schatzman and Strauss (1973), Spradley (1979a:46–54), and Whyte (1982).

53. Interview contexts are discussed in Hammersley and Atkinson (1983:112–126) and in Schatzman and Strauss (1973:83–87). Briggs (1986) argued that nontraditional populations and females communicate better in unstructured interviews.

54. For additional discussion of data quality, see Becker (1970b), Dean and Whyte (1969), Douglas (1976:7), Kirk and Miller (1986), and McCall (1969).

55. Douglas (1976:115) argued that it is easier to "lie" with "hard numbers" than with detailed observations of natural settings.

56. Adapted from Douglas (1976:56–104).

57. See Bloor (1983) and Douglas (1976:126).

58. For more on validity in field research, see Briggs (1986:24), Bogdan and Taylor (1975), Douglas (1976), Emerson (1981:361–363), and Sanjek (1990).

59. See Lofland et al. (2006), Miles and Huberman (1994:288–297), and Punch (1986).

60. Covert, sensitive study is discussed in Ayella (1993), Edwards (1993), and Mitchell (1993).

61. See Douglas (1976), Erikson (1970), and Johnson (1975).

62. See Barnes (1970), Becker (1969), Fichter and Kolb (1970), Goward (1984a), Lofland et al. (2006), Miles and Huberman (1994:298–307), and Wolcott (1994) on publishing field research results.

63. For a discussion of focus groups, see Bischoping and Dykema (1999), Churchill (1983:179–184), Krueger (1988), Labaw (1980:54–58), and Morgan (1996).

CHAPTER 14

Historical-Comparative Research

> *Sociological explanation is necessarily historical. Historical sociology is thus not some special kind of sociology; rather, it is the essence of the discipline.*
> —Philip Abrams, Historical Sociology, p. 2

> *Thinking without comparisons is unthinkable. And, in the absence of comparisons, so is all scientific thought and all scientific research. No one should be surprised that comparisons, implicit and explicit, pervade the work of social scientists and have done so from the beginning.*
> —Guy Swanson, "Frameworks for Comparative Research," p. 145

People looking at East Asia see only two countries with a high percentage of Christians despite 300 years of activity by Christian missionaries: the Philippines and South Korea. Two hundred years of Spanish Catholic rule helps to explain the many Catholics in the Philippines, but Christianity in South Korea is Protestant. Korea had little Western influence until after the Korean War (1953). Today, one in three Koreans are Christian. This compares to about 2 percent in Japan and China. Kane and Park (2009) asked why Korea has so many Protestant Christians. They thought that micro-level theories of religious conversion could not explain the Korean situation, so they developed a geopolitical cultural theory to explain it. Their data came from about 150 historical, cultural, and political books on Korea and East Asia written in English and Korean. They noted that the imposition of unequal treaties and domination by Western imperialist powers across East Asia in the nineteenth century generated nationalist, antiforeign movements. Japan, not the West, colonized Korea in 1910, and Japan instituted harsh repression. Korean nationalists directed antiforeign feelings toward Japan. Japan distrusted the small number of Protestant missionaries in Korea. The missionaries later joined with nationalists who had a passion for freedom from Japan. By comparing how

Christianity operated in Japan, China, and Korea during the late nineteenth and first half of the twentieth centuries, Kane and Park showed how Protestant Christianity in Korea became fused with a nationalist movement for independence. Unlike China and Japan where antiforeign feelings precluded Christian conversion, Korean protestant missionaries resisted foreign (Japanese) domination and became a vehicle for expressing nationalist sentiments. Thus, the strength of Korean Christianity today is explained by Korea's position in geopolitical networks meshed with the diffusion of certain religious beliefs at a particular time in history.

Sometimes we wish to examine macro-level issues or those of long-term social change. We cannot experiment with entire societies, surveys are largely limited to the present, and existing statistical measures are available for some countries only on some topics. Field research is best to examine on small-scale settings in the present. To compare entire cultures or societies to learn about macro patterns or long-term trends across decades or a century, we turn to historical-comparative (H-C) research (also called *comparative-historical*). This method allows us to address many exciting "big" questions about patterns in entire societies or over time. An additional benefit is that it brings clarity to many methodological concerns found in other research techniques.

Founders of the social sciences, such as Émile Durkheim, Karl Marx, and Max Weber, who wanted to explain the transformation of society from a preindustrial to a modern industrial form, used a historical and comparative method. It helps us understand why an entire society operates in particular ways by revealing processes that operate over long periods and across societies. H-C research greatly advanced concept development and theory, often causing major revisions in past thinking. As Mahoney (2004:93) remarked, "In terms of conceptual innovation, comparative-historical researchers have offered leading definitions for many of the most important social science concepts." H-C research often causes us to modify theories and understandings. For example, Ingram and Lifschitz (2006) studied the shipbuilding industry in Scotland across two hundred years. They found that the family-run firms and personal connections among firms created profitable, thriving firms. The rise of the modern corporation and shift to a corporate organizational form was believed to "modernize" old businesses and raise profits. The authors found that rather than improving profitability and advancing the industry, the corporate form had the opposite effect in this instance, slowing growth and profitability.

H-C research is a powerful tool for addressing many of the central issues in social theory. Basic researchers more than applied researchers examine many issues in social science using historical-comparative research because H-C research is vital to the expansion of fundamental knowledge.

A SHORT HISTORY OF HISTORICAL-COMPARATIVE RESEARCH

The nineteenth century founders of sociology conducted H-C research. At that time, the areas of cultural anthropology, human geography, sociology, history, political science, and economics had little separation. This produced a great sharing of concepts, theories, and research methods. As the social sciences specialized and separated in the early twentieth century, historical-comparative research declined. Anthropologists increasingly focused on culture and comparison, historians studied the past, and so forth. H-C research was relegated to small subfields of other disciplines. With a few exceptions (Marc Bloch, George Homans, Robert Merton, and Karl Polanyi), sociology saw few H-C studies prior to World War II.[1]

After World War II, improved international communication, the breakup of colonial empires, and the new geopolitics of the Cold War stimulated interest in comparative research. By the 1950s, we began to see a few H-C studies of major theoretical significance.[2]

By the 1960–1970s, several factors stimulated a return to H-C research. First, several historians imported quantitative research techniques from the social sciences. This increased the interchange between fields. Statistical studies of mobility, railroad expansion, and voting showed historians the power of quantitative data and gave quantitative researchers new questions to address with their techniques. Second, studies using the survey technique spread across nations, and researchers used advanced quantitative techniques to seek crossnational generalizations. Third, several historical-comparative works of Max Weber and Karl Marx were translated into English for the first time. "The translation of Weber probably did more to influence the writing of history in the 1960s than any other single influence from the social sciences" (Stone, 1987:13). Fourth, H-C studies in the 1960s made theoretical breakthroughs, stimulating interest in it as a research technique.[3] By the 1970s, new models of how to conduct H-C research appeared.[4]

H-C expanded greatly in the 1980s. In 1983, the American Sociological Association created a special H-C section and in his presidential address to the association, Melvin Kohn (1987) observed that cross-national research was experiencing a major revival. Articles using some form of historical-comparative research grew in leading scholarly journals. For example, in the late 1970s, H-C articles were 18 percent of articles of leading sociology journals. This increased to 28 percent in the 1980s and 40 percent in the 1990s and early 2000s.[5]

RESEARCH QUESTIONS APPROPRIATE FOR HISTORICAL-COMPARATIVE RESEARCH

Historical-comparative research is a powerful method for addressing big questions such as these: How did major societal change take place? Why did current social arrangements take a certain form in some societies but not in others? We can address macro-level questions, as did the study in this

chapter's opening box regarding why Christianity has a big presence in Korea, but not in nearby East Asian countries. In Chapter 2, you read about the study on the Warsaw ghetto in the 1940s that considered why some people facing extermination fight while others do not. You also read about why some former colonies in Latin America remained poor while others did not.[6]

H-C research is well suited for examining the combinations of social factors that produce a specific outcome (e.g., a civil war, a system of taxation, a religion). It is also appropriate for comparing entire social systems to find what is common across societies and what is unique as well as to study long-term societal change. An H-C researcher often builds or applies a theory to specific cases. For example, France has a highly centralized national government and government involvement in the economy, and leftist parties often win elections. However, the United States has a decentralized system, strong free markets, and weak leftist politics. A theory might suggest France would tax its citizens with high incomes more than the United States does, but researchers found the opposite (see Example Box 14.1, Why Two Countries Tax People Differently). We can use H-C research to build a theory that explains the differences and unexpected outcomes in the two cases. With H-C research, we can compare cultural units or countries, and build theoretical generalizations and analysis across time.[7]

Historical-comparative research strengthens conceptualization and theory building. By looking at historical events or diverse cultural contexts, we generate new concepts and broaden understanding. We are less likely to have concepts restricted to a single historical era or to a single culture yet simultaneously base our ideas in the experiences of people in specific cultural and historical contexts.[8]

One difficulty in reading H-C studies is that a reader often needs some knowledge of the past or other cultures to understand the study fully. A person who knows about only her or his own culture or who lacks historical knowledge may find H-C studies, and even the classical theorists, difficult. For example, understanding Karl Marx's "The Communist Manifesto" is difficult without knowing about the conditions of feudal Europe and the world

EXAMPLE BOX **14.1**
Why Two Countries Tax People Differently

Morgan and Prasad (2009) looked at why France and the United States adopted different systems of taxation. Two major types of taxation are consumption taxes and income taxes. *Consumption taxes* tend to be regressive (i.e., lower income people pay more) but advance economic growth and avoid the political protests that *income taxes* are progressive (i.e, higher income people paymore) but generate. Governments that use consumption taxes develop a larger welfare state. In contrast, *income taxes* are progressive (i.e., higher income people pay more) but hinder economic growth, generate political protest, and limit the size of the state. To explain why a nation relies on one or the other, the authors compared how the national governments of France and the United States developed their taxing systems. Among advanced nations, the United States is near the highest in relying on a national income tax while France is the lowest. Paradoxically, among advanced nations, the United States has the strongest "free market" economy with the least government interference and almost an absence of leftist political parties. By contrast, France has a very strong central government, extensive involvement in the economy, and powerful leftist political parties that often win elections. One

might expect to see a progressive tax such as an income tax in France, not the United States Instead, France relies for most of its revenue on a type of national sales tax. Before 1920, the United States shifted away from indirect consumption taxes to rely primarily on income taxes. The authors explain the divergent paths of the two nations by examining the politics, economy, and government patterns in the two nations during the late nineteenth and early twentieth centuries. They show that protest movements to resist industrialization and specific form of government centralization explain the taxation system and other features of the two nations today. The authors develop a theory that applies beyond the two cases, and they conclude that we cannot explain major aspects of today's societies unless we examine what happened in the decades before World War I. The main form of evidence in the study consists of rich historical details about the events and patterns in the two nations. The authors build a rigorous theoretical argument with the evidence while presenting and rejecting various alternative explanations. Their bibliography lists about 100 books and articles in English and French; about two-thirds of its cited works are on historical topics in the two countries.

in which Marx was writing. In that time and place, serfs lived under severe oppression. Feudal society included caste-based dress codes in cities and a system of peonage that forced serfs to give a large percent of their product to landlords. The one and only Church had extensive landholdings, and tight familial ties existed among the aristocracy, landlords, and Church. Modern readers might ask why the serfs did not flee if conditions were so bad. The answer requires an understanding that serfs had little chance to survive in European forests living on roots, berries, and hunting. Also, no one would have aided a fleeing serf because the traditional societies did not embrace strangers but feared them. To understand H-C studies by classical theorists, "one must appreciate what they took for granted as characteristic of their time and their interpretations of the past" (Tuchman, 1994:310).

THE LOGIC OF HISTORICAL-COMPARATIVE RESEARCH

Confusion over terms reigns in H-C research and terminology is inconsistent. Researchers call their method *historical, comparative, cross-national, cross-cultural,* or *historical-comparative.* Researchers use a great diversity in specific techniques to carry out studies on H-C issues. Another source of confusion is whether there is a distinct historical-comparative method or we use the same research method but it happens to examine social life in the past or in several societies. Mahoney (2004: 81, footnote1) called H-C research "a field of research characterized by the use of systematic comparison and the analysis of processes over time to explain large-scale outcomes such as revolutions, political regimes, and welfare states."

He distinguishes it from other approaches within historical sociology, such as rational choice analysis and interpretive analysis, game theory, and ethnography.

Some social researchers use a positivist, quantitative approach to study historical or comparative issues while others rely on the qualitative, interpretative, or critical approaches. According to Ragin and Zaret (1983), the Durkheimian (or positivist) approach and the Weberian (or interpretative) approach to H-C research use different logics.[9] Øyen (1990:7) summarized the confusion:

> The vocabulary for distinguishing between different kinds of comparative research is redundant and not very precise. Concepts such as cross-country, cross-national, cross-societal, cross-systemic, cross-institutional, as well as trans-national, trans-societal, trans-cultural, and comparisons on the macro-level, are used both as synonymous with comparative research in general and as denoting specific kinds of comparisons.

We can organize H-C research along three dimensions that you read about in Chapter 2: cases, time, and type of data. The research can focus within a case, or what occurs in one country; compare a small set of countries (two to six); or examine many countries (twelve to one hundred). The research focuses on the present, a single time period in the past, or across many years. Finally, the data can be primarily quantitative or qualitative. If we cross-classify the three dimensions, we get a typology of eighteen logically possible types of H-C research (see Table 14.1). No wonder there is so much confusion over what constitutes H-C research. While most social science research is on the researcher's home country in the present, H-C research is very diverse.

Most H-C research is in ten of the eighteen cells (1, 4, 5, 7, 8, 10, 11, 13, 14, 15, and 16). This includes the entire single-nation column. Many H-C studies try to identify universal or near-universal processes. They want to find processes or relationships operating across all human societies or at least within a major type of society (i.e., highly industrial, agricultural) for a long time period (see Ember and Ember, 2001). However, most studies consider data for only one society and one time period and there-

TABLE 14.1 Logically Possible Kinds of Historical-Comparative Research

TIME DIMENSION AND KIND OF DATA	COMPARATIVE DIMENSION		
	Single Nation*	Few Nations	Many Nations
One Time in Past			
Quantatitive	1	2	3
Qualitative	4	5	6
Across Time			
Quantitative	7	8	9
Qualitative	10	11	12
Present			
Quantitative	13	14	15
Qualitative	16	17	18

*Nation different than researcher's and audience of results for present time.

fore have the least generalizability. We cannot say with confidence whether an explanation based on such data applies only to that one society, is found across most human societies, or is specific to one time point or holds across a stretch of history.

Some researchers try to obtain data for many of the world's approximately 170 nations, such as the (2004) data Schofer identified for more than 120 nations for a study of the world expansion of science, or Sung's (2003) data gained from a study of women's political participation that included 99 countries. However, data on many societies are unavailable or not comparable, so most comparative studies are limited to between 10 and 20 nations. Mahoney (2003) (discussed in Chapter 2) studied fifteen South American nations, Sutton (see Example Box 14.2, Imprisonment Rate Across Fifteen Countries) considered imprisonment across fifteen nations, and Mandel and Shalev (2009) investigated the size of the male-female gap in earnings across sixteen nations (see Example Box 14.3, The Gender Earning Gap Across Seventeen Countries).

Other researchers focus on comparing two to four cases. For example, Fretzer (2000) studied public attitudes toward immigration in France, Germany, and the United States; Gangl (2004)

EXAMPLE BOX 14.2
Imprisonment Rates Across Fifteen Countries

Many cross-national studies that use the nation as the unit of analysis rely on existing statistical data. For example, Sutton (2004) conducted a quantitative, statistical study on fifteen nations between 1960 and 1990. Many researchers have long observed that imprisonment rates do not closely follow changes in crime rates. Sutton tested the Rusche and Kirchheimer thesis, which says that unemployment rates cause a rise in imprisonment rates because imprisonment is a government attempt to control a surplus of unemployed working class males in the population who could be potentially unruly. Basically, prisons are filled when many workers are out of work but are empty when the economy is booming. Sutton gathered data from government statistical yearbooks of the fifteen countries, from publications by international organizations such as the World Health Organization and the International Labor

Organization, and from prior social science studies that identified features of several nations, such as their unionization pattern, political party structure, and so forth. Sutton found only limited support for the original thesis, but he documented a strong effect from several other factors. He argued that the effect of unemployment on imprisonment was probably spurious (see the discussion of a spurious relationship in Chapters 2, 4, and 10 of this book). He found that specific features of a nation's politics and labor market structure appeared to be a cause of both specific unemployment patterns and different imprisonment policies. In short, when low-income people and workers were politically weak compared to wealthy people and corporate owners, both unemployment and imprisonment rates rose compared to times when low-income people and workers had more political power.

EXAMPLE BOX 14.3
The Gender Earning Gap Across Seventeen Countries

Mandel and Shalev (2009) studied the size of the male-female gap in earnings across nations. They noted,

> In recent decades feminist scholars have drawn attention to the importance of welfare state policies for women's economic autonomy. . . . The welfare state powerfully affects the life chances of women relative to men, as well as ameliorating class inequalities. This insight has substantially extended the study of gender inequality and the welfare state, particularly research informed by a comparative perspective. (p. 1873)

Mandel and Shalev divided the earnings gender gap into its class-based and gender-based components. In other words, the gender gap in earning depends on how many women reached the top of the class structure in a country and the degree of class inequality in the country. The authors considered how welfare state

policies in seventeen advanced countries affected each component. Welfare states take three forms: liberal, social democratic, and conservative. Some policies encourage family responsibility for social welfare, others rely on government employment, and others encourage private-market solutions. By examining gender inequality in countries with very diverse social programs and class structures, the authors were able to separate the several causes of gender inequality. They found that a country's class structure and its mix of social programs combine in specific ways to create levels of gender earnings inequality. The role of the welfare state affects women in different class positions differently. The authors argue that we cannot treat "family policy" (gender) as separate from "social policy" (class).

compared welfare state policies and unemployment in Germany and the United States. Viterna and Fallon (2008) investigated political movements for gender equality in South Africa, Argentina, Ghana, and El Salvador. They chose the four cases because

they clearly demonstrate successes and failures in improving gender equity and differ on features in their theoretical framework.

Many investigations focus on the present, but others are limited to one society at one point in the

EXAMPLE BOX **14.4**
Decline in Coresidence over 150 Years in the United States

In the middle 1800s, nearly 70 percent of elderly people lived with their adult children. By 2000, less than 15 percent did so. The reason for this has been subject to debate. The main reason given is that elderly people were no longer poor and in later years can afford independent living. Ruggles (2007) examined this question and found that the situation has more to do with younger generations than with their elderly parents. Coresidence is linked to changes in the economy with less household-based production and more wage labor, more education, and greater geographic mobility by younger generations. New family patterns with more divorce or separation and increased opportunities for working women also are factors. Ruggles examined detailed census files over the years for data on family composition, occupation, and geographic location. Obtaining data from 1850 to 1950 required him to enter data from microfilm copies of handwritten census enumerators' manuscripts.

past, such as Einwohner's (2003) study of Warsaw, Poland, in 1943 (discussed in Chapter 2) and Emigh's (2003) study on fifteenth century Tuscany (discussed in Chapter 15). A few studies consider long time periods, such as Lachman's (2003) research of elites in four European states from the 1500s to the 1700s, Mahoney's (2003) investigation of South America across two centuries (described in Chapter 2), Pettit and Western's (2004) research on imprisonment rates among Black and White men in the United States in 1964–1997 (described in Chapter 2), and Ruggles' (2007) investigation of a decline of coresidence in the United States from 1850 to 2000 (see Example Box 14.4, Decline in Coresidence over 150 Years in the United States).

A distinct, qualitative historical-comparative type of social research differs from the positivist approach and from an extreme interpretive approach. H-C studies that use case studies and qualitative data depart from strict positivist principles. Case studies can be very important. Without them scholars "would continue to advance theoretical arguments that are inappropriate, outdated, or totally irrelevant for a specific region" (Bradshaw and Wallace, 1995:155). Case studies can elaborate historical processes and specify concrete historical details, yet researchers who adhere strictly to a positivist approach to social science criticize the H-C for using a small number of cases because it cannot produce the types of probabilistic causal generalizations of a positivist science.[10]

Both field research based on interpretative social science and H-C research focus on culture. Each asks us to see through the eyes of those we study, reconstruct their lives, and examine particular individuals or groups in depth. An extreme interpretive approach assumes that each social setting is unique and that comparisons are impossible. This approach recreates specific subjective experiences and describes particulars. As Stone (1987:31) noted, traditional history "deals with a particular problem and a particular set of actors at a particular time and a particular place." A distinct H-C approach borrows from ethnography and cultural anthropology, and some varieties of H-C attempt to recreate the reality of another time or place, yet borrowing from the strengths of ethnography does not require adopting the extreme interpretive approach.[11]

A distinct H-C research method combines sensitivity to specific historical or cultural contexts with theoretical generalization by using quantitative data to supplement qualitative data and analysis. The logic and goals of H-C research are closer to those of field research than to those of traditional positivist approaches (see Table 14.2).

Similarities to Field Research

In both H-C research and field research, the researcher's point of view is an unavoidable part of research. In both types of research, interpretation is central. The researcher-interpreter's location in time, place, and worldview matter. H-C research does not

TABLE 14.2 Summary of a Comparison of Approaches to Research: The Qualitative versus Quantitative Distinction

TOPIC	BOTH FIELD AND H-C	QUANTITATIVE
Researcher's perspective	Include as an integral part of the research process	Removes from research process
Approach to data	Immerse in many details to acquire understanding	Precisely operation-alizes variables
Theory and data	Use grounded theory with dialogue between data and concepts	Tests deductive theory with empirical data
Present findings	Translate a meaning system	Tests hypotheses
Action/structure	Meaning acted and constructed by people but within structures	Examines how social forces shape behavior
Laws/generalization	Use limited generalizations that depend on context	Discovers universal, context-free laws

FEATURES OF DISTINCT H-C RESEARCH APPROACH

TOPIC	HISTORICAL-COMPARATIVE RESEARCHER'S APPROACH
Evidence	Reconstructs from fragments and incomplete evidence
Distortion	Guards against using researcher's own awareness of factors outside the social or historical context
Human role	Includes the consciousness of people in a context and uses their motives as causal factors
Causes	Sees cause as contingent on conditions, beneath the surface, and resulting from a combination of elements
Micro/macro	Compares whole cases and links the micro to macro levels or layers of social reality
Cross-contexts	Moves between concrete specifics in a context and across contexts for more abstract comparisons

try to produce a single, unequivocal set of objective facts but confronts old with new ideas and evidence or considers multiple worldviews. Our reading of historical or comparative evidence is influenced by an awareness of the past and by living in the present.

Second, both field and H-C research examine a great diversity of data. In both, as researchers, we immerse ourselves in data to gain an empathic understanding of events and people. We try to capture subjective feelings and see how ordinary activities signify important social meanings.

We inquire, select, and focus on specific aspects of social life from a vast array of events, actions, symbols, and words. This means that we must organize data and focus attention on the basis of evolving concepts. We examine rituals and symbols that dramatize culture (e.g., parades, clothing, placement of objects) and investigate the motives, reasons, and justifications for behaviors. For example, Burrage and Corry (1981) measured changes in occupation status in London between the fourteenth and seventeenth centuries using records of the official order of appearance of guilds at major public events (parades, pageants, feasts, royal visits, etc.).[12]

Third, in both field and H-C, we use *grounded theory*. Theory usually emerges during the process of data collection. We begin to examine data without fixed hypotheses. Instead, we develop and modify concepts and theory through a dialogue with the data and then apply theory to reorganize the evidence. Thus, data collection and theory building interact. Thompson (1978:39) called this "a dialogue between concept and evidence, a dialogue conducted by successive hypotheses, on the one hand, and empirical research on the other."[13]

In addition, both field and H-C research involve translation. Our meaning system usually differs from that of the people we study, yet we try to penetrate and understand their point of view. After we master the life, language, and perspective of the people we study, our job is then to "translate" it for others who read a research report.

Fifth, both field and H-C researchers focus on action, process, and sequence. They see the passage of time as essential in a study. Both researchers are sensitive to an ever-present tension between agency (i.e., people and organizations actively engaged in change) and structure (i.e., the fixed regularities that constrain actions and perceptions). Both see social reality simultaneously as people creating and transforming life and something that imposes restrictions on human choice.[14]

Sixth, generalization and abstract theory in both types of research are limited. In micro-level field research and macro-level H-C studies, our knowledge is incomplete and provisional. Replication is unrealistic, and we rarely can deduce propositions or test hypotheses to uncover fixed laws. Rather, each researcher assembles a unique body of evidence to build plausible accounts and offer limited generalizations that slowly advance knowledge.

Unique Features of Historical-Comparative Research

Despite its many similarities to field research, H-C research is distinguished by a number of important differences. H-C research "is inherently a field in which researchers marshal a great deal of over time data to infer causation. In fact, a common view is that the analysis of processes over time is the central basis for causal inference . . ." (Mahoney 2004:88). We can identify six unique features of H-C research: types of evidence, distortion control, recognition of human agency, specification of causation, linking of micro-macro levels, and alternative use of contexts and comparisons.

1. *Types of evidence.* H-C research evidence is limited and indirect. We can rarely directly observe or become closely involved with people we study but reconstruct what occurred from the evidence. Historical evidence depends on the survival of data from the past, usually in the form of documents (e.g., letters and newspapers). We are limited to what has not been destroyed and what leaves a trace, record, or other evidence behind.

We must interpret the evidence by becoming immersed in and absorbing details about a context. For example, we want to study the working of families either 100 years ago or in a very different culture. To do this, you need to understand the families' full social context (e.g., the nature of work, forms of communication, transportation technology). You should examine maps, learn the laws and policies in effect, and study people's cooking and eating practices. You want to find out about child's play, schooling, medical care, life expectancy, and common social practices. For example, you need to know what "a visit by a family member" means. It is affected by conditions such as roads of dirt and mud as well as an inability to call ahead of time. The lives of people who work on a farm with animals that need constant watching may follow a different rhythm and priorities than what you are used to. You need to acquire a feel for the pace of daily life and ordinary experiences of people.

2. *Control distortion.* Our reconstruction of the past or another culture can be distorted easily. Compared to the people we study, we are usually more aware of events that occurred in the past and in places far from the location studied as well as after the period studied. This awareness can create a greater sense of coherence than people living in the past or in an isolated social setting might have

had. "In short, historical explanation surpasses any understanding while events are still occurring. The past we reconstruct is more coherent than the past when it happened" (Lowenthal, 1985:234). Our broader awareness can create an illusion that events happened because they had to, or that they fit together neatly, and this may or may not be how ordinary people experienced them.

We cannot easily see through the eyes of those we study. Knowledge of the present and changes over time can distort how we perceive events, people, laws, and even physical objects. For example, the old buildings that survive into the present are more permanent and solid than those that did not survive. Moreover, a surviving building looks different in 2010 than it did in 1810 because of the context in which it appears. When the 1810 building was newly built and standing among similar or older buildings, the people living at the time saw it differently than we do in the twenty-first century. We may view it as quaint or historic, but they experienced it differently.

3. *Recognition of human agency.* In all studies, we recognize the capacity of people to learn, make decisions, and act on what they learn in order to modify the course of events. When we study processes over time, we need to consider the ability of people to be conscious and to act on events. This limits our ability to assert lawlike generalizations that will hold across all societies,[15] for example, whether a group of people is aware of or gain consciousness of their own past history. As a result of having such knowledge, they avoid the mistakes of the past and act consciously to alter the course of events. Of course, people will not necessarily learn or act on what they have learned, and if they do act, they will not necessarily be successful. Nevertheless, we need to incorporate people's capacity to learn, which introduces a degree of indeterminacy into historical-comparative explanations.

We want to find out whether the people involved saw various courses of action as plausible. The people's worldview and knowledge are conditioning factors. They shape what the people saw as possible or impossible. We must ask whether people were conscious of certain things. For example, if an army knew an enemy attack was coming and so decided to cross a river in the middle of the night, the action of crossing the river would have a different meaning than if the army did not know the enemy was approaching.

4. *Specifications of causation.* In H-C studies, to establish causal connections we often adopt combinational explanations, use process analysis, and examine contingency. A **combinational explanation** is analogous to a chemical reaction in which we must add together several ingredients (chemicals, oxygen) under specified conditions (temperature, pressure) to produce an outcome (explosion). This differs from a simple linear causal explanation. The logic is more "A, B, and C appeared together in time and place Z that had conditions G, then D resulted" rather than "A caused B, and B caused C, and C caused D." As Ragin (1987:13) summarized:

> *Most comparativists, especially those who are qualitatively oriented, are interested in specific historical sequences or outcomes and their causes across a set of similar cases. Historical outcomes often require complex, combinational explanations, and such explanations are very difficult to prove in a manner consistent with the norms of mainstream quantitative social science.*

For example, Max Weber's explanations gave cultural factors equal weight to economic, demographic, and social structural factors. He employed a combination of causal factors through the ideal type. It was neither a deductive formal theory to test nor an inductive, problem-specific theory.[16]

Our thinking about cause-effect often relies on process analysis.[17] **Process analysis** (also called *process tracing*) identifies specific intervening causal mechanisms, their place/role in the process and effect on later events, as well as the duration of

---

Combinational explanation An explanation commonly used in H-C research that emphasizes the coming together of several factors under certain conditions to produce an outcome as opposed to a linear sequence of cause-effect.

Process analysis Examining a causal process in which researchers trace the entire sequence with its intervening mechanisms, including the duration of events and impact of early events on later events.

their effects. In short, we examine exactly how a process unfolds over time. Recall the importance of specifying the causal mechanism when developing a casual explanation (discussed in Chapter 2) and creating a detailed analysis of cases (discussed in the Chapter 6). Process analysis involves outlining a process over time by identifying specific mechanisms through which one or more causes (independent variable) influences an outcome.

Finding an association is not sufficient; we must detail the ways by which one factor influences another. After documenting an association between two events (e.g., rising divorce and improving women's economic opportunities), we look for a mechanism that links cause and effect in particular cases to find whether the association is causal. For example, we observe women both increasingly working outside the home and acquiring property independently and thus gaining control over financial resources (e.g., bank accounts), as well as rising divorce rates. To say that one caused the other, we must analyze the process over time. We must find what specifically is it about financial resource control that ties it to divorce.

H-C research also examines contingency; that is, one factor does not always cause another but is contingent or depends on the presence of other conditions. For example, rising resource control by women and divorce rates may occur only under certain conditions (e.g., legal environments, religious traditions, levels of economic-technological development).

5. *Linking of micro-macro levels.* Historical-comparative research focuses on whole cases versus separate variables across cases. We approach the whole as if it has multiple layers. This means we must grasp surface appearances as well as reveal the general, hidden structures, unseen mechanisms, or causal processes. We integrate micro (small-scale, face-to-face interaction) and macro (large-scale social structures) levels rather than describing micro-

level or macro-level processes alone; we examine and connect both levels or layers of reality.[18] For example, we examine the details of individual biographies by reading diaries or letters to get a feel for the individuals: the food they ate, their recreational pursuits, their clothing, their sicknesses, their relations with friends, and so on. We connect this micro-level view to macro-level processes: increased immigration, mechanization of production, proletarianization, tightened labor markets, and the like.

6. *Alternative use of contexts and comparisons.* H-C research shifts between examining specific contexts and making general comparisons. We examine specific contexts, note similarities and differences, and then generalize by comparing what we found with other situations and contexts. We then look again at the specific contexts using the generalizations we began to develop from the comparisons. Comparative researchers compare across cultural-geographic units (e.g., urban areas, nations, societies).[19] Historical researchers investigate past contexts, usually in one culture (e.g., periods, epochs, ages, eras) for sequence and comparison.[20] Of course, we can combine both to investigate multiple cultural contexts in one or more historical contexts, yet each period or society has its unique causal processes, meaning systems, and social relations. This produces a creative tension between the concrete specifics in a context and the abstract ideas we apply to establish connections across contexts.

The use of transcultural concepts in comparative analysis is analogous to the use of transhistorical ones in historical research.[21] In comparative research, we translate the specifics of a context into a common, theoretical language (see the discussion of etic concepts later in this chapter). "The comparative investigator can thus be regarded as fighting a continuous struggle between the 'culture-boundness' of system-specific categories and the 'contentlessness' of system-inclusive categories" (Smelser, 1976:178).

Annales School A group of French historians that developed a research approach is that holistic, blends attention to the concrete specificity of daily life with abstract theory building, and considers long-term societywide structural change.

The Annales School. H-C research draws from the **Annales School**,[22] a research method associated with a group of French historians (e.g., Marc Bloch, Fernand Braudel, Lucien Febvre, and Emmanuel Le Roy Ladurie) named after the scholarly journal

Annales: Économies, Sociétés, Civilisations, which was founded in 1929. The school's orientation can be summarized by four interrelated characteristics: a holistic-synthetic analysis, incorporation of **mentalities**, concrete-abstract integration, and situating long-term structures called **longue dureé** (see Expansion Box 14.1, Annales School). The Annales School has influenced H-C research in several ways. It encouraged a holistic integration of diverse types of data, emphasized sensitivity to the different subjective consciousness, tied very concrete details to abstract theory, and placed events in a broad context of long-term underling structures.

Mentalities An Annales School idea that a pattern of everyday consciousness and assumptions about ordinary life is pervasive during a particular historical period.

Longue dureé An Annales School idea referring to a long period of time, often a century or longer, across which fundamental patterns or structures in social life remain stable and shape daily life.

few exceptions, does it use complex or specialized techniques.

STEPS IN CONDUCTING A HISTORICAL-COMPARATIVE RESEARCH PROJECT

In this section, we turn to the process of doing H-C research. Conducting historical-comparative research does not involve a rigid set of steps nor, with a

Conceptualizing the Object of Inquiry

To begin an H-C study, you become familiar with the setting and conceptualize what you are studying. You may start with a loose model or set of preliminary concepts and apply them to a specific setting. The provisional concepts contain implicit

EXPANSION BOX 14.1
Annales School

The school's orientation can be summarized by four interrelated characteristics: a holistic-synthetic analysis, incorporation of mentalities, concrete-abstract integration, and long-term structures.

1. *Holistic-synthetic analysis.* The Annales School systematically applies a synthetic, totalizing, holistic, or interdisciplinary approach. Annales researchers combine geography, ecology, economics, and demography with cultural factors to provide a total picture of the past. They blend the diverse conditions of material life and collective beliefs or culture into a comprehensive reconstruction of the past civilization.

2. *Incorporation of mentalities.* The school uses a French term, *mentalities,* which is not directly translatable into English. It means a distinctive worldview, perspective, or set of assumptions about life—the way that thinking was organized or the overall pattern of conscious and unconscious cognition, belief, and values that prevailed in an era. Thus, we try to discover the overall arrangement of thought in a historical period that shaped subjective experience about fundamental aspects of reality: the nature of time, the

relationship of humans to the physical environment, how truth is created, and so on.

3. *Concrete-abstract integration.* The Annales approach mixes concrete historical specificity and abstract theory. Theory takes the form of models or deep underlying structures. Causal or organizing principles account for everyday events. Annales historians look for both the deep-running currents that shape the surface events and individual actions.

4. *Long-term structures.* The school has an interest in recognizing long-term structures or patterns. In contrast to traditional historians who focus on particular individuals or events over several years to a few decades, Annales historians examine long-term changes over periods of a century or more. They assume that the way daily social life occurs usually operates within fundamental organizing principles that change very slowly year-to-year in a location. They use the term *longue dureé* to refer to a long duration or a historical era in geographic space (e.g., feudalism in western Europe, or the fifteenth to eighteenth centuries in the Mediterranean region).

assumptions or organizing categories that you use to see the world, "package" observations, and search through evidence. If you are not already familiar with the historical era or comparative settings, you conduct an orientation reading (of several general works). This will help you grasp the specific setting, assemble organizing concepts, subdivide the main issue, and develop lists of questions to ask.[23] Concepts and evidence interact to stimulate research. For example, Skocpol (1979) began her study of revolution with puzzles in macro-sociological theory and the histories of specific revolutions. The lack of fit between histories of revolutions and existing theories stimulated her research.

Whether we are conscious and explicit about it, we all organize specific details into analytic categories. It is best to recognize this process explicitly and to avoid the **Baconian fallacy**. Named for Francis Bacon (1561–1626), the fallacy assumes that we operate without preconceived questions, hypotheses, ideas, assumptions, theories, paradigms, postulates, prejudices, or presumptions of any kind.

Locating Evidence

The next step is to locate and gather evidence through extensive bibliographic work. You will use many indexes, catalogs, and reference works that list what libraries contain. For comparative research, this means focusing on specific nations or units and on particular kinds of evidence within each. In a major study, you might devote months or even years to searching for sources in libraries, traveling to different specialized research libraries, and reading books and articles. Comparative research often involves learning one or more foreign languages.

As you master the literature and take detailed notes, you complete many specific tasks: create a bibliography list (on cards or computer) with complete citations, take notes that are neither too skimpy nor too extensive (i.e., more than one sentence but less than dozens of pages of quotes), and develop a file on themes or working hypotheses.

You will adjust initial concepts, questions, or focus based on what you discover in the evidence. New issues and questions arise as you read and consider a range of research reports at different levels of analysis (e.g., general context and detailed narratives on specific topics) and multiple studies on a topic, crossing topic boundaries.

Quadagno (1988) conducted a study of old-age and welfare programs. She started with an interest in the history of U.S. programs for the aged. She began with government records on programs for the elderly. Soon she discovered the importance of southern political pressure, so she spent months learning about southern U.S. history. As the issue unfolded, she examined the literature on social programs. Then, as her inquiry expanded, she read theoretical and empirical discussions showing connections to other social welfare programs, which suggested a comparison with extensive western European programs. In Western Europe, social democratic parties represent and work very closely with organized labor. These parties shaped most social programs in those countries. Therefore, Quadagno's research turned to U.S. labor history. The records of labor officials and labor history led her to examine the actions of employers and the power of the private sector. She stated, "I moved back and forth between theory and archival materials, with each new set of empirical observations guiding my generalizations about factors shaping welfare policy" (1988:x).

Evaluating Quality of Evidence

As you gather evidence, you want to ask two questions: How relevant is the evidence to emerging research questions and evolving concepts? How accurate and strong is the evidence? The question of relevance is a difficult one. As the focus of research shifts, evidence that was not relevant can become relevant. Likewise, some evidence may stimulate new avenues of inquiry and a search for additional confirming evidence.

Baconian fallacy   The misconception of assuming that a researcher can operate without any preconceived questions, ideas, assumptions, theories, or presumptions.

As you read the evidence, you are looking for three things: the implicit conceptual framework, particular details, and empirical generalizations (factual statements on which there is agreement). You evaluate alternative interpretations of evidence and look for "silences," or cases in which the evidence fails to address an event, topic, or issue. For example, as you examine a group of leading male merchants, you may find documents that systematically ignore discussing their wives and many servants. This "silence" can be important for developing a full understanding of the subject and suggest new areas for inquiry.

As in all research, you try to avoid fallacies in the evidence. Fischer (1970) provided an extensive list of such fallacies. For example, the fallacy of *pseudoproof* is the failure to place something into its full context. The evidence might state that there was a 50 percent increase in income taxes but its impact is not meaningful outside of a context. The researcher must ask: Did other taxes decline? Did income increase? Did the tax increase apply to all income? Was everyone affected equally?

Another fallacy to avoid with historical evidence is **anachronism,** which indicates that an event, expression, object, person, or situation appears to have occurred before or after the time it actually did, out of its true time context. For example, a movie set in 1939 showed a document with a typeface that had not been created until 1972. Most people did not know when the typeface was created, but its creator who viewed the film immediately recognized the anachronism.[24] You should be precise about the sequence of events and note discrepancies in dating events in evidence.

Organizing Evidence

As you gather evidence and locate new sources, you are already organizing data. Obviously, it is unwise to take notes madly and let them pile up haphazardly. You begin a preliminary analysis by noting low-level generalizations or themes. For example, in a study of revolution, you develop a theme: Rich peasants supported the old regime. You can record this theme in notes and later assign it significance. Next you organize evidence, using theoretical insights to stimulate new ways to organize data and for new questions to ask the evidence. The interaction of data and theory means interrogating the evidence to develop new concepts. This requires you constantly to examine the evidence, questioning what it means. As Clemens and Hughes (2002:207) warned, "The danger lies in reliance on a simple 'reflection' model that takes text or accounts as evidence of what 'really' happened or what people 'really' believed or how society 'really' was."

Synthesizing

The next step is to synthesize the evidence. You continuously refine concepts and move toward a general explanatory model, but this process accelerates after you have most of the evidence. As you do this, revise old themes or concepts and create new ones. Concrete events give meaning to concepts. You want to look for patterns across time or units and draw out similarities and differences with analogies. You can organize divergent events into sequences and group them together to create a larger picture. Then you develop plausible explanations that subsume both concepts and evidence into a coherent whole. You want to read and reread notes and sort and resort them based on organizing schemes. You try to look for connections and see the evidence in different ways.

Synthesis links specific evidence with an abstract model of underlying relations or causal mechanisms. You may use metaphors. For example, mass frustration leading to a revolution is like an emotional roller coaster: Expectations have risen quickly (steep climb), but then there is a sudden letdown (fast, deep drop). The models are sensitizing devices. You develop an explanatory model and then look for new evidence to verify specific links within it, evaluate how well the model approximates the evidence, and make adjustments accordingly. This means you go back and forth from the abstract to the concrete (see Chapter 15).

Anachronism An error by which a historical-comparative researcher locates an event, expression, object, person, or situation before or after it actually occurred.

Many H-C researchers identify critical indicators and supporting evidence for explanations. A **critical indicator** is unambiguous evidence, which is usually sufficient for inferring a specific theoretical relationship. You seek these indicators for key parts of an explanatory model. The indicators critically confirm a theoretical inference and occur when many details suggest a clear interpretation. For example, a critical indicator of hostility between two nations is a formal declaration of war. A critical indicator of the rising political power of a social group is the formation of formal organizations that have a large membership identified with it and advocate its position. Supporting evidence, in contrast, suggests indicators that are less central parts of a model. It builds the overall background or context. Such evidence is usually less abundant or weaker and lacks a clear and unambiguous theoretical interpretation.

Writing a Report

The final step is to combine evidence, concepts, and synthesis into a research report. How you write the report is extremely important in H-C research. Assembling evidence, arguments, and conclusions into a report is always important. More than in quantitative approaches, a careful crafting of evidence and explanation makes or breaks H-C research. You must distill mountains of evidence into exposition and prepare extensive footnotes, weaving together evidence and arguments to communicate a coherent, convincing picture to readers (see Chapter 16).

Critical indicator A clear, unambiguous measure of a concept in a specific cultural or historical setting.

Historiography The theory of using approaches with assumptions, emphases, and a theoretical point of view that historians employ when writing historical studies.

Primary sources Qualitative or quantitative data about past events or social life that were created and used in the past time period.

Archive A specialized library or collection of original records and historical documents that makes them available for research.

DATA AND EVIDENCE IN HISTORICAL CONTEXT

Types of Historical Evidence

History means the events of the past (e.g., it is *history* that the French withdrew troops from Vietnam), a record of the past (e.g., a *history* of French involvement in Vietnam), and a discipline that studies the past (e.g., a department of *history*).[25] **Historiography** is the method of doing historical research or of gathering and analyzing historical evidence. Historical sociology is a part of historical-comparative research. It

> is an approach to historical data, a style of historiography, that seeks to explain and understand the past in terms of sociological models and theories. . . . Alternatively, historical data may be used to illustrate and test the validity of sociological concepts, principles and theories. (Mariampolski and Hughes, 1978:104–105)

We draw on four types of historical evidence: primary sources, secondary sources, running records, and recollections.[26] Traditional historians rely heavily on primary sources. H-C research often uses secondary sources or combines different data types. For example, Quadagno (1984) examined the U.S. Social Security Act to evaluate theories of political power. Of the forty-seven sources she cited for evidence, twenty-three were primary sources (letters, memos, official reports, newspaper or magazine articles of the period), three were recollections (memoirs or oral histories), and twenty-one were secondary sources (books by historians and other researchers).

Primary Sources. The letters, diaries, newspapers, movies, novels, articles of clothing, photographs, and so forth of those who lived in the past and have survived to the present are **primary sources**. We can find them in an **archive** (a specialized location where old records or documents are stored), in private collections, in family closets, and in museums (see Expansion Box 14.2, Using Archival Data). Today's documents and objects (our letters, television programs, commercials, clothing, automobiles) will be primary sources for future historians.

EXPANSION BOX 14.2

Using Archival Data

The archive is the main source for primary historical materials. Archives are accumulations of documentary materials (papers, photos, letters, etc.) in private collections, museums, libraries, or formal archives.

LOCATION AND ACCESS

Finding whether a collection exists on a topic, organization, or individual can be a long, frustrating task of many letters, phone calls, and referrals. If the material on a person or topic does exist, it may be scattered in multiple locations. Gaining access may depend on an appeal to a family member's kindness for private collections or traveling to distant libraries and examining many dusty boxes of old letters. Also, the researcher may discover limited hours (e.g., an archive is open only four days a week from 10 A.M. to 5 P.M., but the researcher needs to inspect the material for 40 hours).

SORTING AND ORGANIZATION

Archive material may be unsorted or organized in a variety of ways. The organization may reflect criteria that are unrelated to the researcher's interests. For example, letters and papers may be in chronological order, but the researcher is interested in letters to only four professional colleagues over three decades, not daily bills, family correspondence, and so on.

TECHNOLOGY AND CONTROL

Archival materials may be in their original form, on microforms, or, more rarely, in an electronic form.

Researchers may be allowed only to take notes, not make copies, or they may be allowed to see only select parts of the whole collection. Researchers become frustrated with the limitations of having to read dusty papers in one specific room and being allowed to take notes by pencil for only the few hours a day the archive is open to the public.

TRACKING AND TRACING

One of the most difficult tasks in archival research is tracing common events or persons through the materials. Even if all materials are in one location, the same event or relationship may appear in several places in many forms. Researchers sort through mounds of paper to find bits of evidence here and there.

DRUDGERY, LUCK, AND SERENDIPITY

Archival research is often painstakingly slow. Spending many hours poring over partially legible documents can be very tedious. Also, researchers will often discover holes in collections, gaps in a series of papers, or documents that have been destroyed. Yet careful reading and inspection of previously untouched material can yield startling new connections or ideas. The researcher may discover unexpected evidence that opens new lines of inquiry (see Elder et al., 1993, and Hill, 1993).

An example of a classic primary source is a bundle of yellowed letters written by a husband at war to his wife, both dead for 10 years, that you find in a dusty attic. In their book on poverty in one Kentucky community, Billings and Blee's (2000) data included manuscripts from a federal census (1850 to 1910) for both individuals and agriculture; tax rolls, deeds, wills, and court records; newspapers; state accounting board records; letters and reports by visiting preachers; and official data at the county and state level. The authors linked individuals, relationships, and households to create longitudinal files on individuals and families for a 60-year period. In his study of how Abraham Lincoln became recognized as a historical figure for racial equality in the African American community, Schwartz (1997:493) said "My analysis is based on a variety of materials, including slave narratives, oratory, prints, photographs, public opinion surveys, biographies, and textbooks. I rely most heavily on the Lincoln's birthday issues of three black newspapers: the liberal *Chicago Defender,* the moderate *New York Age,* and the conservative *Atlanta Daily World*."

Published and unpublished written documents are the most important types of primary source. You may find them in their original paper form or preserved in microfiche or on microfilm. They are often the only surviving records of the words, thoughts, and feelings of people in the past. Written documents are helpful for studying societies and historical periods with writing and literate people. Written sources, especially those that have survived, tend to be written by elites or leaders in official organizations. This means it is easy to overlook the views of people who are illiterate, poor, or outside official social institutions. For example, it was illegal for slaves in the United States to read or write, so written sources on the experience of slavery have been indirect or difficult to find.

The written word on paper was the main medium of communication prior to the widespread use of telecommunications, computers, and video technology to record events and ideas. In fact, the spread of forms of communication that do not leave a permanent physical record (e.g., telephone conversations, computer records, and television or radio broadcasts) and that have largely replaced letters, written ledgers, and newspapers may make the work of future historians more difficult. In April, 2010, the Library of Congress in the United States announced that it would archive public tweets from Twitter social networking that began in March 2006 (http://blogs.loc.gov/loc/2010/04/how-tweet-it-is-library-acquires-entire-twitter-archive/).

Secondary sources Qualitative and quantitative data used in historical research that are reported or written by historians or others who did not directly participate in the events or setting.

Running records Existing files, reports, or documents that are maintained in a relatively consistent manner over a long period of time and are used for statistical research.

Recollections Statements or writings about past experiences collected after time has passed and based on a memory or stimulated by a review of old objects, photos, or notes.

Oral history Chronicle of events obtained during an interview of a person who recollects past events, beliefs, or feelings that he or she experienced.

Secondary Sources. Primary sources have realism and authenticity, but the practical limitation of time can restrict research on many primary sources to a narrow time frame or location. To get a broader picture, we use **secondary sources**, the writings of specialist historians who have spent years studying primary sources.

Running Records. The files or existing statistical documents that organizations maintain on a regular basis are called **running records**. An example is a file in a country church that contains a record of every marriage and every death from 1910 to the present. For example, Roy (1983) used running records when he studied the boards of directors of major U.S. corporations between 1886 and 1905. His evidence came from 150 primary documents, official reports and statistics, and annual business reference books, some of which are still being published.

Recollections. The statements or writings of individuals about their past lives or experiences based on memory are **recollections**. They can be in the form of memoirs, autobiographies, or interviews. Because memory is imperfect, recollections are often distorted in ways that primary sources are not. In gathering an **oral history**, a type of recollection, you conduct unstructured interviews with older people about their lives or events in the past. This approach is especially valuable for nonelite groups or illiterate people. The oral history technique began in the 1930s and now has a professional association and scholarly journal devoted to it.[27] Studies on memory suggest caution when a researcher uses oral history or recollections (see Expansion Box 14.3, Seven Deadly Sins of Memory). As Schacter (2001:9) remarked,

We tend to think of memories as snapshots from family albums that, if stored properly, could be retrieved in precisely the same condition in which they were put away. But we now know that we do not record our experience in the way a camera records them. . . . We extract key elements of our experience and store them. We then recreate or reconstruct our experiences rather than retrieve copies of them. Sometimes, in the process of reconstructing we add on feelings, beliefs, or even knowledge we have obtained after the experience.

EXPANSION BOX **14.3**

Seven Deadly Sins of Memory

Schacter (2001) oberved that memory loss or mistaken memory takes several forms:

1. *Transience.* State of experiencing the slow, continuous decay of memory over time, such that the more distant in the past an event occurred, the less detail is recalled about it
2. *Absentmindedness.* State of focusing on one idea or thing so much that it misdirects one's attention so that other, often simple things, are forgotten (e.g., focusing on a major project but forgetting to pick up the car keys)
3. *Blocking.* Searching unsuccessfully for information that the person possesses but cannot recall despite trying to do so at the moment (often phrased as "it is on the tip of my tongue")
4. *Misattribution.* Mistaking of fantasy for reality, or what one heard from a friend or what one saw in a movie for one's own experience
5. *Suggestibility.* Openness to being asked questions in such a way that a person begins to distort his or her memory and believe things happened that did not.
6. *Bias.* Distortion in recalling things, and often interjecting ideas, feelings, or beliefs that occurred after the remembered event
7. *Persistence.* Inability to forget something despite trying

Two example studies that used oral histories of women in the early twentieth century United States illustrate how researchers combined various documents with oral histories. Blee (1991) studied women in the Klu Klux Klan, and Luken and Vaughan (2006) interviewed women about growing up, forming families, and moving to various homes (see Example Box 14.5, Women of the Klan on page 482 and 14.6, Oral History on Standard American Home and Proper Childrearing on page 483)

Some people "rewrite" the past to make it more consistent with current beliefs or remember it in a self-enhancing way (i.e., inaccurately recall themselves in a more positive way). Older adults (usually beginning sometime in their fifties) tend to lose the memory of specific details about past events more than younger people do. More highly educated, mentally active older adults show less memory loss, but some degree of individual or collective memory distortion is relatively frequent.[28]

Research with Secondary Sources

Uses and Limitations. Social researchers often use secondary sources as well as the books and articles written by history specialists as evidence of past conditions.[29] As Skocpol (1984:382) remarked, the use of such materials is not systematized, and "comparative historical sociologists have not so far worked out clear, consensual rules and procedures for the valid use of secondary sources as evidence." Secondary sources have limitations and need to be used with caution.

The limitations of secondary historical evidence include inaccurate historical accounts and a lack of studies in areas of interest. We cannot use such sources to test hypotheses strictly. *Post facto* (after-the-fact) explanations cannot meet positivist criteria of falsifiability because we cannot use statistical controls or replication.[30] However, historical research by others plays an important role in developing general explanations, among its other uses. For example, such research substantiates the emergence and evolution of tendencies over time.[31]

Potential Problems. The many volumes of secondary sources present a maze of details and interpretations. You must transform the mass of descriptive studies into an intelligible picture that must be consistent with and reflective of the richness of the evidence. It also must bridge the many specific time periods or locales. You face four potential problems with secondary sources: implicit theories, selected evidence, narrative writing, and schools of historiography.

1. *Implicit theories.* Reading the works of historians can be problematic.[32] Historians do not present theory-free, objective "facts." They implicitly frame raw data, categorize information, and use concepts. The historian's concepts often are a mixture from journalism, the language of historical actors, ideologies, philosophy, everyday language in the present, and social science. They may be

EXAMPLE BOX **14.5**

Women of the Klan

In *Women of the Klan,* Kathleen Blee (1991) noted that, prior to her research, no one had studied the estimated 500,000 women in the largest racist, right-wing movement in the United States. She suggested that this may have been due to an assumption that women were apolitical and passive. Her six years of research into the unknown members of a secret society over 60 years earlier shows the ingenuity needed in historical-sociological research.

Blee focused on the state of Indiana, where as many as 32 percent of White Protestant women were members of the Ku Klux Klan at its peak in the 1920s. In addition to reviewing published studies on the Klan, she investigated documents including newspapers, pamphlets, and unpublished reports. She conducted library research on primary and secondary materials at more than half a dozen college, government, and historical libraries. The historical photographs, sketches, and maps in her book give readers a feel for the topic.

Finding information was difficult. Blee did not have access to membership lists. She identified Klan women by piecing together a few surviving rosters, locating newspaper obituaries that identified women as Klan members, scrutinizing public notices or anti-Klan documents for the names of Klan women, and interviewing surviving women of the Klan.

To locate survivors 60 years after the Klan's activity, Blee had to be persistent and ingenious. She mailed a notice about her research to every local newspaper, church bulletin, advertising supplement, historical society, and public library in Indiana. She obtained three written recollections, three unrecorded interviews, and fifteen recorded interviews. Most of her informants were over age 80. They recalled the Klan as an important part of their lives. Blee verified parts of their memories through newspaper and other documentary evidence.

Membership in the Klan remains controversial. In the interviews, Blee did not reveal her opinions about it. Although she was tested, Blee remained neutral and did not denounce the Klan. She stated, "My own background in Indiana (where I lived from primary school through college) and white skin led informants to assume—lacking spoken evidence to the contrary—that I shared their worldview" (p. 5). She did not find Klan women brutal, ignorant, and full of hatred. Blee got an unexpected response to a question on why the women had joined the Klan. Most were puzzled by the question. To them it needed no explanation—it was just "a way of growing up" and "to get together and enjoy."

---

vague, applied inconsistently, and not mutually exclusive or exhaustive.

For example, a historian describes a group of people in a nineteenth century town as being upper class, but never defines the term and fails to link it to a theory of social classes. The methodological problem is that the historian's implicit theories constrain the evidence. You can try to find evidence for explanations that may be contrary to those historians implicitly used in secondary sources by reading through a disorderly set of concepts.

2. *Selected evidence.* The historian's selection procedure is not transparent. Historians select some information from all possible evidence. As Carr (1961:138) noted, "History therefore is a process of selection in terms of historical significance . . . from the infinite oceans of facts the

historian selects those which are significant for his purpose," yet you do not know how this was done. Without knowing the selection process, you must rely on the historian's judgments, which can be biased.[33] For example, a historian who reads 10,000 pages of newspapers, letters, and diaries reduces this information into summaries and selected quotes in a 100-page book. You do not know whether information that the historian left out is relevant to his or her purposes.

The typical historian's research practice also introduces an individualist bias. A heavy reliance on primary sources and surviving artifacts combines with an atheoretical orientation to produce a focus on the actions of specific people. This particularistic, micro-level view directs attention away from integrating themes or patterns. An emphasis on the

EXAMPLE BOX **14.6**

Oral History on Standard American Home and Proper Childrearing

Luken and Vaughan (2006) used oral history and archival research to study how three government agencies (Children's Bureau, Own Your Home, and Better Homes in America) articulated a campaign to create "a proper home environment for raising children" between 1900 and 1930. Together, the agencies had mounted the national Standard American Home movement. It connected proper childrearing with creating a suitable home environment. Often ignoring how people actually lived, the movement sought to coordinate the way parents lived and raised children with the commercial housing and household goods markets. The authors connected the oral histories with their analysis of the Standard American Home movement. They interpreted the movement as discourse that articulated specific class, gender, and racial standards of appropriate housing arrangements for childrearing. The parents owned and did not rent the home; it was a house and not a flat or an apartment. The home was suburban or, if it had to be in a city, it was close to a park. The house was well-ventilated, dry, sunny, temperature controlled, and easily cleaned. Each child had a separate bedroom that had appropriate color schemes, furnishings, and toys appropriate for a specific child's age and gender. The movement had been coordinated with the activities of lumber companies, savings and loans, real estate associations, builders, child development specialists, doctors, home decorators, academics, and newspaper and magazine publishers.

The authors of the study connected how ordinary people talked and thought about their daily activities with extensive archival research including primary documents, records, advertisements, and photos. On four occasions they interviewed for about 2 hours five women in the Phoenix metropolitan area who were at least 60 years of age. Luken and Vaughan asked about "housing work" throughout the women's lives and inquired about living conditions in the homes formed by the women across their life courses. The authors tape-recorded and transcribed approximately 10 to 12 interview hours per woman. They said (p. 302),

"As we examined the transcripts we noticed that the women spoke at length of their girlhood and motherhood experiences. In addition to telling us about the places where they lived as children and where they raised their children, they made us aware of the things that they did, the materials they used, the people with whom they interacted, and their enjoyment or dislike of their activities and circumstances. Their narratives opened up for us connections between housing and childrearing in the everyday world, and they provided an opportunity to explore children's lives vis-à-vis housing and the social relations that shaped these experiences."

activities of specific individuals is a type of theoretical orientation.[34]

3. *Narrative writing.* Historians organize evidence as they write *narrative history* (see Expansion Box 14.4, The Narrative in History on page 484). This compounds problems of undefined concepts and the selection of evidence. In the historical narrative, the writer organizes material chronologically around a single coherent "story." He or she connects each part of the story to each of the other parts by its place in the time order of events. Together, all parts form a unity or whole. Conjuncture and contingency are key elements of the narrative form; that is, if X (or X plus Z) occurred, then Y would occur, and if X (or X plus Z) had not occurred,

something else would have followed. The contingency creates a logical interdependency between earlier and later events. With its temporal logic, the narrative organization differs from quantitative explanation in which the researcher identifies statistical patterns to infer causes.

A difficulty of the narrative is that the organizing tool—time order or position in a story-based sequence of events—does not alone denote theoretical or historical causality. In other words, the narrative meets one of the three criteria for establishing causality, temporal order (see Chapter 3). Narrative method can obscure underlying causal models or processes when a historian includes events in the narrative that have no causal significance. The writer

---

EXPANSION BOX **14.4**

The Narrative in History

Many historians write in the traditional narrative form, which can be a secondary source for the H-C researcher:

CHARACTERISTICS OF THE NARRATIVE FORM

1. It tells a story or tale with a plot and subplots, watersheds, and climaxes.
2. It follows a chronological order and sequence of events.
3. It focuses on specific individuals, not on structures or abstract ideas.
4. It is primarily particular and descriptive, not analytic and general.
5. It presents events as unique, unpredictable, and contingent.

STRENGTHS OF THE NARRATIVE FORM

1. It is colorful, interesting, and entertaining to read.
2. It gives an overall feel for life in a different era so that readers have the sense that they were there.

3. It communicates the way people in the past subjectively experienced reality and helps readers identify emotionally with people in the past.
4. It surrounds individuals and specific events with a mix of many aspects of social reality.

WEAKNESSES OF THE NARRATIVE FORM

1. It hides causal theories and concepts or leaves them as implicit.
2. It uses rhetoric, ordinary language, and common-sense logic to persuade and therefore is subject to logical fallacies of semantic distortion and various rhetorical devices.
3. It tends to ignore the normal or ordinary for the unique, dramatic, extraordinary, or unusual.
4. It rarely builds on previous knowledge and does little to create general knowledge.
5. It tends to be overly individualistic, overstating the role of particular people and their ability to shape events voluntarily.

---

may include events to enrich the background or context or to add color. Such events may have no immediate or delayed causal impact. Also, few narrative historians explicitly state how combination or interaction effects operate. When the historian discusses three conditions for an event, you do not know whether all three conditions must operate together or no two conditions alone, or no single condition alone, to have the same causal impact.[35] The narrative organization can create conflicting findings. You must read through weak concepts, unknown selection criteria, and unclear casual logic. Beneath the narrative may reside the historian's social theory, but it usually remains implicit and hidden.

4. *Schools of historiography.* Historians are influenced by schools of historiography, personal beliefs, social theories, and current events at the time when the historical conducted research. Historians writing today examine primary materials differently from how those writing 30 years ago did. In addition, the field of history has several schools of historiography (e.g., diplomatic, demographic,

ecological, psychological, Marxist, intellectual). Each has it own rules for seeking evidence and asking questions. Carr (1961:54) warned, "Before you study history, study the historian. . . . Before you study the historian, study his historical and social environment."

Research with Primary Sources

The historian becomes a major issue regarding the use of secondary sources. When you use primary sources, a major issue is that only a fraction of all written or used in the past has survived into the present. Moreover, what survived is a nonrandom sample of what once existed. Lowenthal (1985:191–192) observed, "The surviving residues of past thoughts and things represent a tiny fraction of previous generations' contemporary fabric." As you attempt to read primary sources, you want to do so with the eyes and assumptions of a contemporary but who lived in the past. You "bracket" or hold back knowledge of subsequent events and modern values.

Cantor and Schneider (1967:46) wrote, "If you do not read the primary sources with an open mind and an intention to get inside the minds of the writers and look at things the way *they* saw them, you are wasting your time." For example, when you study a source written by a slaveholder, moralizing against slavery or faulting the author for not seeing its evil is not worthwhile. You hold back moral judgments and become a moral relativist. You must "think and believe like . . . subjects, discovering how they performed in their own eyes" (Shafer, 1980:165).

Locating primary documents can be a time-consuming task. You must search through specialized indexes and travel to archives or specialized libraries. Primary sources are often located in a dusty, out-of-the-way room full of stacked cardboard boxes containing masses of fading documents. These may be incomplete, unorganized, and in various stages of decay. Once you locate the documents or other primary sources, you must evaluate them by subjecting them to external and internal criticism (see Figure 14.1).

External criticism means that the authenticity of a document itself has been evaluated to be certain that it is not a fake or a forgery. Criticism involves asking whether the document was created when it is claimed to have been, in the place where it was supposed to be, and by the person who claimed to be its author. Why was the document produced to begin with, and how did it survive?

Once the document passes as being authentic, you use **internal criticism**, an examination of the document's contents to establish credibility. You evaluate whether the document's author directly witnessed events or has passed along secondhand information. This requires you to examine both the literal meaning of what has been recorded and its subtle connotations or intentions. You want to note other events, sources, or people mentioned in the document and ask whether you can verify them. You examine implicit assumptions or value positions and consider relevant conditions under which the document was produced (e.g., during war or under a totalitarian regime). The meaning of words, even in the same language, constantly shifts over time, so you must consider language usage at the time a document was created as well as the context of statements within the document to distill a meaning.

One distortion that can appear in primary documents is **bowdlerization**—a deliberate distortion designed to protect moral standards or furnish a particular image. For example, you find a photograph

External criticism   Evaluation of the authenticity of a primary historical source by accurately locating the place and time of its creation (e.g., determination of whether it is a forgery).

Internal criticism   Evaluation of the authenticity and credibility of primary historical sources to determine their accuracy as accounts of what occurred in the past.

Bowdlerization   A deliberate distortion of the past designed to protect a particular (usually favorable) image.

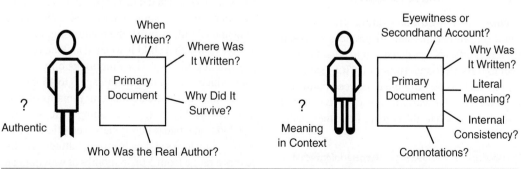

FIGURE 14.1   Internal and External Criticism

taken of the front of a building. In reality, trash and beer cans were scattered all around this building and its paint was peeling. However, the photograph was taken of the one part of the building that has little trash and is framed so that the trash does not show; photo touch-up techniques make the faded, peeling paint look new. Another example is the practice of including famous people on a guest roster published in a newspaper society column study of a wealthy person's party, although they did not actually attend the event.[36]

In addition to primary and secondary sources, you might use what Topolski (1976) called **nonsource-based knowledge**. This is knowledge available to you about the past that does not originate in a specific primary document or secondary source. This can come from logical reasoning. For example, persons A and B are a married couple in a monogamous society that values sexual fidelity. When person B has an extramarital affair, A is likely to become jealous. It also includes knowledge of previous significant events that shape the context of what is studied. For instance, you study France in the late 1920s. You should be aware that a large proportion of French males in the 18- to 40-year-old age group had been killed a few years earlier in World War I. Current knowledge, too, can help you to understand past events. For example, you know that the Black Plague was a disease spread by fleas carried by rats and was the result of poor sanitary conditions. However, people living in the past were unaware of the cause of this disease.

COMPARATIVE RESEARCH

Types of Comparative Research

A Comparative Method. Comparative research focuses on similarities and differences between units. It magnifies issues that occur in other types of research.[37] As Holt and Turner (1970:6) said, "In principle, there is no difference between comparative cross-cultural research and research conducted in a single society. The differences lie, rather, in the

---

Nonsource-based knowledge   General information available to a researcher based on reasoning or an in-depth awareness of historical circumstances.

---

magnitude of certain types of problems." A comparative perspective exposes weaknesses in research design and helps improve the quality of research. Comparative research is more of an orientation than a separate research technique. In this section, we consider its strengths.

Comparative research reveals aspects of social life that operate across units (e.g., cities, nations, cultures) as opposed to features limited to one unit alone. In all research, we want to generalize to some degree. Positivist researchers are interested in discovering general laws or patterns of social behavior that hold across societies. Nonetheless, little positivist research is comparative. Ragin (1994a:107) observed,

> *Comparative researchers examine patterns of similarities and differences across cases and try to come to terms with their diversity. . . . Quantitative researchers also examine differences among cases, but with a different emphasis; the goal is to explain the covariation of one variable with another, usually across many cases. . . . The quantitative researcher typically has only broad familiarity with the cases.*

The comparative orientation improves measurement and conceptualization. Concepts we develop to study many social units or settings are less likely to apply only to a specific culture or setting. It is difficult to detect hidden biases, assumptions, and values until we apply a concept in different cultures or settings. Different social settings provide a wide range of events or behavior. The range in one culture is narrower than for human behavior in general, so research in a single culture focuses on a restricted range of possible social activity. For example, assume that two researchers, Hsi-Ping and Abdul, examine the relationship between the age at which a child is weaned and the onset of emotional problems. Hsi-Ping looks only at U.S. data, which show a range from age 5 to 15 months at weaning and indicate that emotional problems increase steadily as age of weaning increases. She concludes that late weaning causes emotional problems. Abdul looks at data from ten cultures and discovers a range from 5 to 36 months at weaning. He finds that the rate of emotional problems rises with age of weaning until 18 months; it then peaks and falls to a lower level. Abdul arrives at more accurate conclusions: Emotional problems are likely related to weaning between the ages of 8 and 18 months, but weaning either earlier or later reduces the chances of emotional problems. Hsi-Ping reached false conclusions about the relationship because of the narrow range of weaning age in the United States.

A strength of comparative research is its ability to eliminate or offer alternative explanations for causal relationships. For example, Weil (1985) investigated the relationship between years of schooling and intolerance. Past research found such a relationship to exist in the United States, and most researchers thought that education broadened perspectives and decreased intolerance. After looking across countries, Weil (1985:470) concluded that the relationship "is weaker, nonexistent, or sometimes even reverse in nonliberal democracies or countries that did not have liberal-democratic regime forms in earlier decades, compared to countries which have been liberal democratic for some time." In other words, the relationship is not universal but holds only with a certain type of government. Rather than having a universal effect of increasing tolerance, education socializes people to their country's official values. Where the official values include tolerance, education increases it; elsewhere, it does not have that effect. Past studies had considered only a few countries that valued tolerance.

Comparative research is more difficult, more costly, and more time consuming than research that is not comparative. Also, we often encounter problems with equivalence (to be discussed) in comparative research. Comparative researchers can rarely use random sampling. First, if the nation is the unit of analysis, there are only about 170 nations, and sufficient information is not available for all nations in the world. It is unavailable for a nonrandom subset (poor countries, nondemocratic countries, etc.). In addition, can we treat all nations as equal units when some have more than 1 billion people but others only 100,000? With a small number of cases, we tend to particularize and see each case as being unique, but this limits generalization. For example, you examine five cases (e.g., countries), but the units differ from each other in twenty ways. It is difficult to test theory or determine relationships when there are more different characteristics than units.

Comparative researchers often apply, not test, theory. Despite the ability to use combinational theory and to consider cases as whole ones, it is difficult to test theory rigorously, through an experiment. For example, you are interested in the effects of economic recessions, but you cannot cause one group of countries to have a recession while others do not. Instead, you must wait until a recession occurs and then look at other characteristics of the country or unit.

Four Types of Comparative Research. As discussed earlier, there is a great diversity of types of H-C research as well as within comparative research. Kohn (1987) has discussed four types of comparative research. Two fit into a distinct H-C approach: (1) using the nation as object of study or case-study comparative study and (2) using the nation as context of study. The third is positivist in which the nation is the unit of analysis. The final ones are transnational studies.[38] In this section we consider each of the four.

1. *Case-study comparative research.* The **case-study comparative research** approach compares particular societies or cultural units but does not make broad generalizations. Examples of questions addressed by this type follow: How do Canada and the United States differ? How do people experience old age in Japan, Taiwan, and Korea? In what ways are the educational systems of the United States and Russia alike and different? You intensively examine a limited number of cases. The "case" is a culturally defined group, often a nation. By examining in depth a small number of cases, or just one, there is relatively little need to be concerned about the equivalence of units. This method is helpful for identifying factors that are constant or that vary among a few cases.[39] The study of Christianity in Korea that opened this chapter and the comparison of French and U.S. taxation illustrate this type of comparative research.

Case-study comparative research Comparative research in which a researcher compares one or two particular cultures (or cultural units such as regions) in depth.

2. *Cultural-context research.* Study of cases that act as surrogates for types of societies or units is known as **cultural-context research**. Anthony Marx (1998) conducted a study of race relations in the United States, South Africa, and Brazil. He examined some common ideas, race relations, official policies, and laws related to race in the three different cultural settings. He did not arbitrarily or randomly choose the three nations for study. He chose them because they represented three different types of racial regimes or systems for organizing relations among racial groups. Each provided a different cultural context in which he could examine common themes, patterns, and processes.

3. *Cross-national research.* The unit of analysis in this type of study is the nation. You measure variables across many nations without naming them, converting unique features of nations into variables. Two studies discussed earlier fit this type of research: Sutton's study of imprisonment in fourteen nations and Mandel and Shalev's study of the earning gender gap in seventeen nations. Although there are many independent nation-states, data are rarely available for more than fifty, and often we work with far fewer.

4. *Transnational research.* Comparative research that uses a multination unit (e.g., a region of the globe such as the Third World) and focuses on the relations among blocs of nations as units is **transnational research**. It views nations as part of an international system, not as isolated entities. An example of this type of research is Wallerstein's (1974) study on the long-term development of a "world system" since the 1400s. His writings spawned a new school of thought, *world*

system theory, which has stimulated additional H-C research.

The Units Being Compared

Culture versus Nation. For convenience, we often use the nation-state as a unit of analysis. It is the major unit used in thinking about the divisions of people across the globe today. Although it is a dominant unit in current times, the nation-state is neither an inevitable nor a permanent unit; in fact, it has existed for only about 300 years.

The nation-state is a socially and politically defined unit. It refers to one government that has sovereignty (i.e., military control and political authority) over populated territory. Economic relations (e.g., currency, trade), transportation routes, and communication systems are integrated within territorial boundaries. The people of the territory usually share a common language and customs and usually have a common educational system, legal system, and set of political symbols (e.g., flag, national anthem). The government claims to represent the interests of all people in the territory under its control.

We often use the nation-state as a surrogate for culture, which is more difficult to define as a concrete, observable unit. *Culture* refers to a common identity among people based on shared social relations, beliefs, and technology. Cultural differences in language, custom, traditions, and norms often follow national lines. In fact, sharing a common culture is a major factor in the formation of distinct nation-states.

The boundaries of a nation-state may not match those of a culture. In some situations, a single culture crosses into several nations; in other cases, a nation-state contains more than one culture. Over the past centuries, wars and conquests destroyed or diffused distinct vibrant cultures and rearranged boundaries around them. Imperial powers carved land and people into colonies, and wars created new nations from several peoples or cultures. For example, European empires imposed arbitrary boundaries over several cultural groups in nations that were once colonies.[40] Likewise, new immigrants or ethnic minorities may not be assimilated

Cultural-context research Comparative study focused on comparing a small number of societies or cultures that represents theoretical types to permit generalizations to other societies of those same types.

Cross-national research Comparative study that examines data (usually quantitative) for several variables across many nations and analyzes the data.

Transnational research Comparative study approach that examines and compares multinational units.

into the dominant culture in a nation. For example, one region of a nation may have people with a distinct ethnic background, language, set of customs, religion, variety of social institutions, and identity (e.g., the province of Quebec in Canada). Such intranational cultures can create regional conflict because ethnic and cultural identities are the basis for nationalism.[41]

The nation-state is not always the best unit for comparative research. You should ask, What is the relevant comparative unit for my research question: the nation, the culture, a small region, or a subculture? For example, this is a research question: Are income level and divorce related (i.e., are people with higher income less likely to divorce?) A group of people with a distinct culture, language, and religion live in one region of a nation. Among them, income and divorce are not related; elsewhere in the nation, however, where a different culture prevails, income and divorce are related. If you use the nation-state as the unit, the findings could be ambiguous and the explanation weak. Instead of assuming that each nation-state has a common culture, you may find that a unit smaller than the nation-state yields different results.

Cultures may be more relevant than nations for many purposes, but the boundaries between cultures or subcultures are difficult to operationalize. Cultures are difficult to define, are constantly evolving, and blend into each other. Except for cases of border disputes, boundaries between nations are less ambiguous, but they, too, change over time. There is no easy answer to the nation versus culture issue. The issue of the appropriate unit to use remains a serious one.

Galton's Problem. The issue of the units of comparison is related to a problem named after Sir Francis Galton (1822–1911), who raised an issue at the Royal Anthropological Institute in 1889 regarding a paper by E. B. Taylor. Galton's problem states that when we compare units or their characteristics, we want the units to be distinct and separate from one another. If the units are not different but are actually the subparts of a single larger unit, we will find spurious relationships.

For example, let us say you examine 110 units that are the states and provinces in Canada (ten provinces), France (forty provinces), Belgium (ten provinces), and the United States (fifty states). You discover a strong association between speaking English and having the dollar as a currency and between speaking French and using the euro as a currency. Obviously, the association exists because the units of analysis (i.e., states and provinces) are subparts of larger units (i.e., nations). The features of the units are due to their being parts of larger units, not to any relationship among the features. Social geographers also encounter this problem because many social and cultural features diffuse across geographic space.

Galton's problem is an important issue in comparative research because cultures rarely have fixed boundaries.[42] It is difficult to say where one culture ends and another begins, whether one culture is distinct from another, or whether the features of one culture have diffused to another over time. Galton's problem occurs when the relationship between two variables in two different units is actually due to a common origin, and they are not truly distinct units (see Figure 14.2 on page 490).

Galton's problem originated with regard to comparisons across cultures, but it also applies to historical comparisons. It occurs when a researcher asks whether units are really the same or different in different historical periods. For example, is the Cuba of 1885 the same country as the Cuba of 2005? Have 120 years since the end of Spanish colonialism, the rise of U.S. influence, independence, dictatorship, and a communist revolution fundamentally changed the unit?

Data in Cross-Cultural Research

Comparative Field Research. Many comparative researchers use field research in cultures other than their own. Anthropologists are specially trained and prepared for this type of research. Small differences

---

Galton's problem The potential dilemma of finding correlations or associations among characteristics in multiple cases or units that are diffused from a single source and the units (e.g., countries, cultures) are not really independent cases.

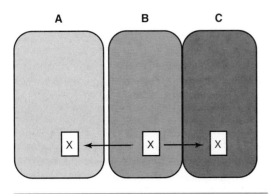

FIGURE 14.2   Galton's Problem *Galton's problem* occurs when a researcher observes the same social relationship (represented by X) in different settings or societies (represented as A, B, and C) and falsely concludes that the social relationship arose independently in these different places. The researcher may believe he or she has discovered a relationship in three separate cases, but the actual reason for the occurrence of the social relation may be a shared or common origin that has diffused from one setting to others. This is a problem because the researcher who finds a relationship (e.g., a marriage pattern) in distinct settings or units of analysis (e.g., societies) may believe that the relationship arose independently in different units. This belief suggests that the relationship is a human universal. The researcher may be unaware that in fact the relationship exists because people have shared it across units.

exist between field research in one's own society and in another culture. Field research in a different culture is usually more difficult and places more requirements on the researcher.

Existing Sources of Qualitative Data.   Comparative researchers can use secondary sources. For example, someone conducting a comparative study of the Brazilian, Canadian, and Japanese education systems can read studies by researchers from many countries, including Brazil, Canada, and Japan, that describe the education systems in the three nations.

> **Human Relations Area Files (HRAF)**   An extensive catalog and comprehensive collection of ethnographies on many cultures (mostly preliterate) that permits a researcher to make comparisons across cultural units.

As many as 5,000 different human cultures may have existed throughout human history; researchers have studied about 1,000 of them. A valuable source of ethnographic data on different cultures is the **Human Relations Area Files (HRAF)** Inc. and the related *Ethnographic Atlas*.[43] The HRAF collection is a unique source of field research reports that anthropologist George Murdock began to gather and organize in 1938. It brings together information from ethnographic studies on various cultures, most of which are primitive or small tribal groupings. The HRAF organizes extensive information on nearly 300 cultures by social characteristics or practices (e.g., infant feeding, suicide, childbirth). A study on a particular culture is divided, and its information on a characteristic is grouped with that from other studies. This makes comparing many cultures on the same characteristic easy. For example, if you are interested in inheritance, you can learn that of 159 different cultures in which it has been studied, 119 have a patrilineal form (father to son), 27 matrilineal (mother to daughter) form, and 13 mixed form.

We can use the HRAF to study relationships among several characteristics of different cultures. For example, to learn whether sexual assault against women, or rape, is associated with patriarchy (i.e., the holding of power and authority by males), you can examine the presence of sexual assault and the strength of patriarchy in many cultures.

Using the HRAF has limitations, however. First, the quality of the original research reports depends on the initial researcher's length of time in the field, familiarity with the language, and prior experience as well as the explicitness of the research report. In addition, the range of behavior the researcher observed and the depth of inquiry can vary. For example, the initial researcher may say that in culture *X*, the children are not punished. In fact, children in the culture are punished but in private; *public* punishment of children is taboo. In addition, the categorization of characteristics in the HRAF can be crude. For example, the importance of sorcery in a culture could be coded on a scale from highly important to not very important.

Another limitation involves the range of cultures included in HRAF. Western researchers have made contact with and conducted field research on a limited number of cultures prior to these cultures' contact with the outside world. The cultures studied are not a representative sample of all human cultures that have existed. In addition, Galton's problem (discussed earlier) can be an issue.

Cross-Cultural Survey Research. Survey research was discussed in Chapter 10. This section examines issues that arise when we use the survey technique in different cultures.[44] The limitations of a cross-cultural survey are not different in principle from those of a survey within one culture. Nevertheless, they are usually so much greater in magnitude and severity that we must carefully consider whether the survey is the best method in a setting.

Survey research in a different culture requires that we possess an in-depth knowledge of its norms, practices, and customs. Without such an in-depth knowledge, it is easy to make serious errors in procedure and interpretation. Knowing another language is not enough. We need to be multicultural and thoroughly know the culture in addition to being familiar with the survey method. We need substantial advance knowledge about the other culture prior to entering it or planning the survey. Close cooperation with the native people of the other culture is also essential. Being intimate with a culture is critical for good survey research in general.

For example, Weinreb (2006) compared "stranger" (i.e., no local outside researcher) versus "insider" (i.e., local researcher) survey interviews in Kenya. He found the single most important characteristic that distinguished insider from stranger interviewers was whether the interviewer knew or was known by a respondent or the respondent's family. He found that in rural areas of Kenya, at least, that having a local, insider interview was necessary to obtain high levels of cooperation and accuracy. While speaking the local language was essential, it was not always enough. Knowing the local customs and culture and having some social connection to the local community proved important.

Your choice of the cultures or nations to include in a cross-cultural survey should be made on both substantive (e.g., theoretical, research question) and practical grounds. You must tailor each step of survey research (question wording, data collection, sampling, interviewing, etc.) to the culture in which you will conduct it. One critical issue is how the people from the other culture experience the survey. In some cultures, the survey and interviewing itself may be a strange, frightening experience analogous to a police interrogation.

Cultural context can affect sampling for a survey. You must consider whether accurate sampling frames are available, the quality of mail or telephone service, and transportation to remote rural areas. You need to be aware of factors such as how often people move, the types of dwellings in which people live, the number of people in a dwelling, or typical rates of refusal. You must tailor the sampling unit to the culture and consider how a culture defines basic units, such as the family. Special samples or methods for locating people for a sample may be required. For example, in his survey in India, Elder (1973) reported that he undersampled people living in servant quarters located behind middle- and upper-income homes.

Although researchers have conducted surveys across cultures and languages for decades, such surveys have been more frequent in recent years, we are still learning about the complex methodological issues involved in cross-cultural survey design and question writing.[45] Problems or concerns encountered when conducting a survey in one's own culture are greatly magnified when two or more cultures are included (see Example Box 14.7, Survey Research in Two Cultures on page 492). Direct language translation is rarely adequate, and many issues of equivalence are involved (equivalence is discussed later in this chapter).

Five issues related to cross-cultural surveys are cultural sensitivity, communication style, situational sensitivity, courtesy bias, and access.

1. Cultural sensitivity. A comparative survey researcher must be very culturally aware. Topics that are noncontroversial in one culture may be highly sensitive or even taboo in another. As Smith (2004) noted, topic sensitivity varies widely by culture. Alcohol use is more sensitive in Islamic than in Judeo-Christian cultures, political questions about the Communist party are forbidden in China, and cohabitation is common in Sweden but still socially

EXAMPLE BOX **14.7**

Survey Research in Two Cultures

Shearman and Dumlao (2008) compared family communication patterns between Japanese and American young adults. They survyed 173 U.S. and 131 Japanese undergraduates. The authors had the questionnaires translated by two bilingual people. They next had the questionnaires back translated to identify discrepancies between the translations. Although past studies and stereotypes suggest that Japanese are "group-oriented," the authors found Japanese youth were no more group-oriented or collectivistic than the U.S. students. They found large differences in family type by country. The U.S. young adults reported that their families were more consensus oriented (coming to an agreement) while the Japanese reported theirs were more laissez-faire (letting each person do what she or he wants). In some ways, these findings are contrary to widely held beliefs. The authors noted limitations of the study (p. 206), "We used country as a proxy measure for culture, assuming that individuals who are natives of a country automatically represent a relatively uniform, general culture." Also, the authors used measurement scales that had been constructed in the United States and then translated. As the authors noted, this could also be an issue in comparative survey research. "A western bias in the scales included in this study might have impacted our results" (p. 206).

sensitive elsewhere. Asking about the king is taboo in Thailand. Cultural settings imply other differences. You can ask about the emperor in Japan or the queen in Great Britain but not in the United States or Germany because there is not one. In some African and Islamic societies, you should ask about a man's wife in the plural. You need to know regional variations; in Scottish law, a person can be found guilty, not proven to have committed the crime, or innocent, but in English law someone is guilty or not guilty. As Braun (2003) emphasized, respondents interpret questions in their own known context and fill in meaning using local knowledge, assumptions, and interpretations, even when the question originated in a different cultural-language setting. For example, the answer to the question "If the mother works, does the child suffer?" can vary widely by culture. For one thing, respondents may envision the child as an infant or a 7-year-old. Maybe their society has many part-time jobs with flexible hours near home widely available to mothers and an extensive system of free, high-quality child care is available in each neighborhood. Or maybe their society is one in which mothers must work full-time some distance away with few or very expensive child-care facilities available and often far from home. What may appear to be the same question, even in the same language, may not have the same meaning in different cultures. Australia, Britain, Canada, Ireland, and the United States all use the English term *social security,* but it has a different meaning in each country and refers to different government programs.

2. *Communication style.* Patterns and styles of communication vary by culture. The pace of talk and use of silence vary both culturally and linguistically. Social desirability (see Chapter 10), the response set (see Chapter 7), and public willingness to answer survey questions varies significantly by culture.[46] In addition to the questions themselves, response scales (e.g., strongly agree, disagree) vary widely across languages and cultural settings.

King et al. (2004) described a method of using short vignettes to anchor responses within a specific cultural setting. For example, asking about someone being elderly or middle aged may vary by societal context. In one society, middle aged may mean 30 years old and elderly may mean 45 because of high death rates, whereas in another society, people think of 50 years old as middle aged and 75 as elderly. Likewise, rather than ask a respondent whether the amount of political influence he or she has is "None at all, A little, or A lot," King et al. suggested providing a set of concrete stories or vignettes and asking a respondent to match his or her response to it. For example, in the standard Likert-form question–response, Mexicans may say they have less political influence than Chinese do. This may occur even though Mexico has a far more open democratic political system, which has voted out the ruling party, than China, which is a one-party, totalitarian state. However, when given five vignettes about their likely response to poor-quality local drinking water—from supporting opposition candidates, to initiating a petition, to feeling it is worthless to vote, to asking local leaders for help, to suffering in silence—the respondents in Mexico and China may answer in ways that reflect their actual political influence. Researchers can statistically calibrate general responses with a few vignettes. Baranik et al. (2008) examined the Rosenberg self-esteem scale used in the United States and seven other countries and found systematic cultural differences. They warn (2008:1891), "When doing this type of cross-cultural research, it is imperative that researchers provide evidence that participants across the countries are responding to the instrument used to measure the construct in a congruent manner."

3. *Situational sensitivity.* Interviewing requires specialization in cross-cultural situations. Selecting and training interviewers depends on the education, norms, and etiquette of the other culture. The interview situation raises issues such as norms of privacy, ways to gain trust, beliefs about confidentiality, and differences in dialect. For example, in some cultures, an interviewer must spend a day in informal discussion before achieving the rapport needed for a short formal interview as Weinreb (2006) experienced in rural Kenya.

4. *Courtesy bias.* Comparative researchers need to be aware of a version of social desirability bias: the **courtesy bias**. It occurs when strong cultural norms cause respondents to hide anything unpleasant or give answers that the respondent thinks that the interviewer wants. Respondents may seriously understate or overstate some characteristics (e.g., income, accomplishments, education) because of cultural norms. In addition, the manner in which answers are given (e.g., tone of voice, situation) may change their meaning (see Expansion Box 14.5, Cross-Cultural Answers to Survey Questions).

5. *Access.* Access can be a serious issue in cultures in which norms limit openness or protect privacy. In addition, your origin from another

---

EXPANSION BOX **14.5**
Cross-Cultural Answers to Survey Questions

The meaning of a statement or answer to a question often depends on the customs of a culture, the social situation, and the manner in which the answer is spoken. The manner of answering can reverse the different meanings of the same answer based on the manner in which the answer was spoken.

MANNER IN WHICH ANSWER IS SPOKEN	ACTUAL RESPONDENT ANSWER TO QUESTION	
	Yes	No
	Spoken Answer	
Polite	"No"	"Yes"
Emphatic	"Yes"	"No"

Source: Adapted from Hymes (1970:329).

---

country or culture may be a significant barrier in itself. Letting local respondents learn your country of origin may open doors or make contact very difficult. Specific problems can involve knowing what agencies and individuals to contact, the appropriate procedures for making contacts (e.g., a formal letter of introduction), how to maintain goodwill (e.g., gift giving), and the effects of such arrangements on the quality and comparability of research. In some cultures, bribery, family connections, or the approval of local political authorities are required for access to sampling frames, certain sections of a town, or specific respondents. In addition, you may have to take special precautions to protect the confidentiality and integrity of data once they have been collected.

Survey Questionnaires and Multiple Languages.
Most survey researchers use an "ask-the-same-question" approach. They use an existing question or develop a question in one language and then

---

Courtesy bias A judgment that occurs when very strong cultural norms exist to "maintain face" or hide unpleasant information from others, including social researchers.

CHART 14.1   Cross-Cultural Survey Question Design

QUESTION SOURCE	ADVANTAGE	DISADVANTAGE
Adapt or adopt existing question	Easy, inexpensive, and fast	Often language and cultural suitability problems
New question methods	High cultural suitability, few language problems	High development cost, more time required

Source: Adapted from *CrossCultural Survey Methods,* Janet A. Harkness, Fons J. R. van de Vijver, Peter Ph. Mohler, 2003, p. 25. Reprinted with permission of John Wiley & Sons, Inc.

translate it into or adapt it to another language. An alternative is to design new questions for multiple languages from the beginning. There is a trade-off between adopting existing questions and creating new ones (see Chart 14.1) that suggests developing new questions is preferred for better quality survey research.

Adapting questions appears straightforward without changes in meaning, such as making minor adjustments as in changing the word *stomach* to *tummy* when a question is adapted to children. However, the adaptation has many possible pitfalls. Ideally, translators are very familiar with survey questionnaire design and the concepts you are attempting to measure. Beyond words, you must be aware of what is left unstated or implied. For example, a simple, everyday question, "Can you open the door?" can have multiple meanings. It can mean do you have the ability to do so, or it can be a request, depending on the language and context. Proper gender is an issue in many languages. German has three genders, whereas French, Italian, and Spanish have two. In some languages, grammatical

Back translation   Translation of written material into a second language by having a different translator translate back into the original language and then comparing the original writing and the translated versions.

rules identify the speaker's gender; in others, it indicates the person or thing about which one is speaking. For example, you might not be able to ask about a "friend" without specifying gender. The English question, "Who is your best friend?" requires asking two questions for English speakers, "Who is your best male friend?" "Who is your best female friend?" Certain occupations, such as secretary, can be so strongly linked to one gender that asking about whether a male or female has the job is very awkward. In some languages, statuses other than gender are embedded in terms. For example, in Japanese, you cannot ask about someone's brother or sister without specifying whether you are referring to an older or younger brother or sister.

Even what appears to be the same word carries different connotations and cultural meanings. For example, *liberty* in English and *liberté* in French translate into the same concept but have different meanings because of historical and political-ideational context. Language and cultural differences may exist within the same country. The English word *education* in the United States primarily refers to academic subjects whereas the similar word *educación* used among Spanish-speaking immigrants to the United States. includes learning social skills not normally included in the content of the English use of the term *education*.

The most common comparative research technique to achieve lexicon equivalence is **back translation**.[47] Back translation involves having a phrase, question, or entire document translated into a foreign language and then having someone else translate from the foreign language version back to the original language. For example, you have a phrase in English translated into Korean and then independently translated from Korean back into English. You then compare the first and second English versions to identify any discrepancies. Even back translation can be limited. In a study to compare knowledge of international issues by U.S. and Japanese college students, the researchers developed a questionnaire in English. They next had a team of Japanese college faculty translate the questionnaire into Japanese. They adjusted the questionnaire. When they used back translation, they discovered "30 translating errors, including some major ones" (Cogan et al., 1988:285).

Back translation does not help when words for a concept do not exist in a different language (e.g., there is no word for *trust* in Hindi, for *loyalty* in Turkish, or for *good quarrel* in Thai). Thus, translation may require complex explanations, or you may not be able to use certain concepts.

Increasingly, comparative research experts advise against simple translation including back translation because it does not identify all problems. Harkness (2003:42) noted that the German phrase *Das Leben in vollen Zügen geißen* was translated accurately into English as "Enjoy life in full trains." The back translation technique did not catch that the actual meaning in English is "Live life to the full" (British English) or "Live life to the fullest" (American English). This happened because the word *Zügen* has two meanings, one of which is "trains." Harkness argues (2003:35), "Whenever possible, translation should be integrated into the study design. In practice, however, translation rarely is seen as part of questionnaire design and usually is treated as an addendum." Modern cross-cultural communication and trans-

lation theory suggest using an integrated approach. Have a team of translators check survey wording with specific techniques, such as in cognitive interviews and with focus groups, to discuss the actual meanings of survey questions. You want to avoid **safari research**, the tendency of a research team from one culture to develop a project and measures in its own cultural-language context and then impose them onto another culture. The alternative is joint research with a multicultural research team.

Back translation is one of several sequential methods that starts with a questionnaire written in one language and created from a single cultural perspective.[48] It is then translated into a new language for use in a different cultural setting (see Expansion Box 14.6, Approaches to Cross-Cultural Survey Translation, and Figure 14.3 on pages 496–497).

Safari research Study by researchers from one culture in which they impose their perspectives, ideas, and issues onto another culture and treat the studied culture as only an exotic object to be studied.

EXPANSION BOX **14.6**

Approaches to Cross-Cultural Survey Translation

1. *Translation-on-the-fly.* Researchers develop and pilot test a questionnaire in one language. Bilingual interviewers are employed and translate each question and response during interviews.

2. *Single translation.* Researchers develop and pilot test a questionnaire in one language. A skilled translator converts it from the original language to the target language.

3. *Back translation.* Researchers develop and pilot test a questionnaire in one language. A translator takes it from the original language to the target language. The translated questionnaire is next translated back to the original language by a second translator. The results are compared with the original questionnaire, and adjustments are made to correct any problems identified.

4. *Parallel translation.* A multicultural group develops a questionnaire with two or more translators independently translating a questionnaire. Each translator incorporates input from multiple target cultural-language sources. Later, the questionnaires

are coordinated and adjusted based on a review and adjudication by a multicultural/lingual team. The questionnaires are then pilot tested in multiple cultural-language contexts.

5. *Simultaneous development.* A team of translators and researchers from different languages/cultures work together, discussing the meanings of concepts and terms in the several languages with alternative translations. The questionnaire items are created for multiple languages/cultural contexts through a decentering process sensitive to *emic/etic* distinctions with culturally specific and multiple-culture ideas/terms. An independent multicultural/lingual team reviews and adjudicates questionnaires in multiple languages. The questionnaires are pilot tested with bilingual-cultural and monolingual-cultural respondents.

Sources: See Smith (2004), Harkness, van de Vijver, and Johnson (2003), Harkness, Pennell, and Schoua-Glusberg (2004).

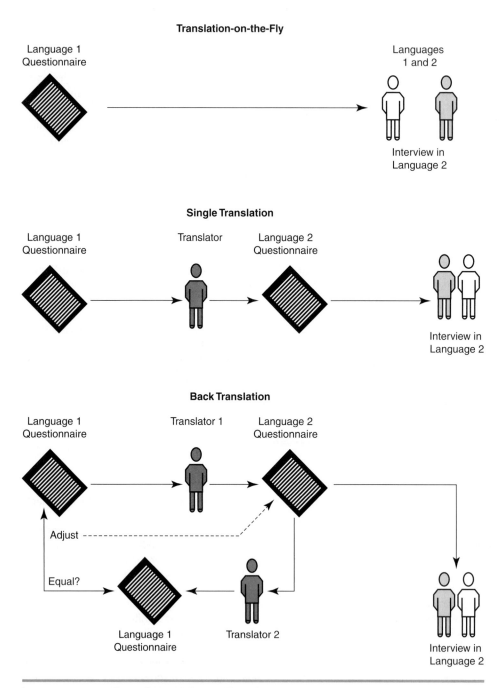

FIGURE 14.3   **Cross-Cultural Survey Translation**

(continued)

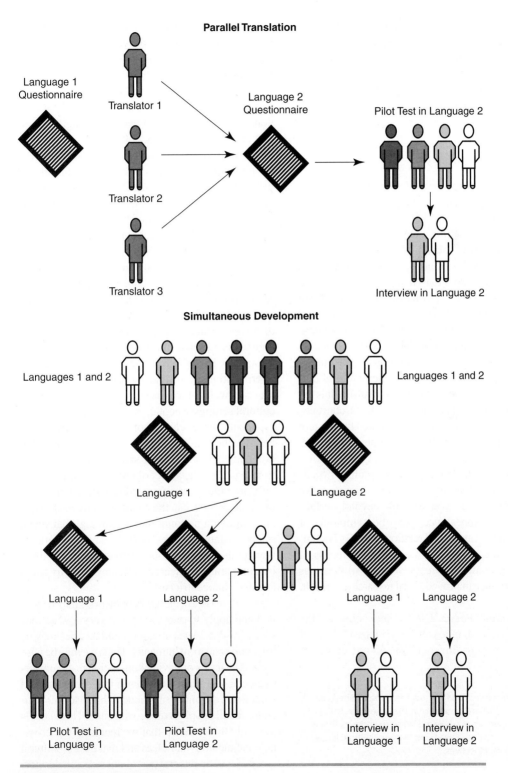

FIGURE 14.3 (Continued)

Newer methods involve parallel or simultaneous survey development. From the beginning, a team of researchers and translators writes questions in multiple languages and designs questionnaires for use in multiple cultural settings. Such new methods are likely to avoid many past questionnaire translation problems.

Western Cultural Bias

Most social research is conducted by people who live, work, or have been educated in any one of a handful of societies in which advanced Western culture is dominant. This creates the danger of a **Western cultural bias** and ethnocentrism. As Myrdal (1973:89) concluded, "A Western approach must be regarded as a biased approach."

Each culture has its own assumptions, modes of thought, orientation toward time, and fundamental values about human life. All of these influence thinking and social relations. If social research were totally free of culture or had a unique professional culture apart from any specific culture, then cultural bias would not be an issue. But this is unrealistic. It is too easy for us to believe that our assumptions, concepts, findings, and values—which are colored by Western culture—apply universally to all people in the world.

A comparative approach encourages you to ask questions that challenge your own cultural tradition.[49] In addition, the need for a comparative perspective causes you to look beyond surface appearances. Appearances may be symptoms of deeper beliefs, values, and relationships. By becoming multicultural, you gain a better awareness of problems in doing social research and of Western bias and can produce improved social research as a result.

An Inverted Focus. Researchers outside the United States and some within it criticize U.S. social science for being "inverted" or too self-centered.

Western cultural bias   A judgment made when conducting comparative research that uses the outlook and perspective of advanced Western societies that is largely insensitive to local, non-Western cultural issues, values, or perspectives.

U.S. theories and ways to conduct social research became dominant during the years following World War II. Many Americans arrogantly assumed that this was natural because their methods and theories were the world's best. The problem is compounded by the U.S. global economic, military, and political dominance and by the international strength of popular and commercial U.S. culture.

Unfortunately, many researchers see concerns from the viewpoint of only their own cultural values and beliefs. They only cite research that was conducted in their home country and ignore concerns relevant to the rest of the world or overlook studies conducted by scholars elsewhere in the world (see Connell, 1990).

The "inverted" focus causes two problems. First, the vast research establishment in the United States produces a large majority of the world's empirical social science research. An inverted focus distorts our understanding about social relations around the planet. It shows conditions or events only through the lens of U.S. culture. This can create misinterpretations or misunderstanding of larger global issues as well as the concerns of people in different cultural settings. Second, many social researchers, especially those who adopt a positivist approach, believe they are discovering universal laws of human behavior. If they formulate research questions based on the views of only one culture, study only one culture, and cite studies conducted in only one culture, how can the results be universal? They are building a national rather than a global social science. Many U.S. researchers cannot generalize beyond the national context except when justified by comparative research, and they need to guard against ethnocentrism.[50]

Certain issues, methods, or theories may be limited and apply to one nation or a very few nations whereas other issues, methods, and theories may be truly universal to all humanity. Thus, we may be wise to think in terms of having both national and universal social sciences.[51] The claim that sociology and other fields are universal sciences that discover principles for all people is often overstated. This claim is true only to the extent that we regularly use cross-national methods and ideas and make cross-cultural comparisons an integral part of our research designs.

Anthropologists distinguish emic from etic concepts and approaches.[52] Although it is an overly simple dichotomy, it clarifies a major comparative research issue. An **emic** approach analyzes cultural elements in terms of a native's explicit or implicit categories and meaning system. It is the "insider's" or "native's" interpretation of customs or beliefs. Emic concepts are developed and used within a specific cultural setting and may not exist elsewhere. They are perceptions and understandings appropriate in the insider's culture. An **etic** approach analyzes cultural elements in terms of cultural-neutral, comparative categories and principles. It applies the interpretation of events, customs, or beliefs and focuses on meaning from a decontextualized perspective. Etic concepts are widely shared across many cultures or are universal in the international scientific community.

Comparative social researchers recognize and apply both the emic and etic approaches. They try to understand and see the world from the insider's view of a specific cultural setting but also try to transcend that setting to establish linkages among and communicate across diverse cultural settings. Racial differences exist around the world, but race is increasingly seen as an emic concept. Based on his detailed study of Puerto Rico's many racial distinctions that differ markedly from those in the rest of the United States, Gravlee (2005:965) argued, "race [is] a cultural-bound concept that presupposes a set of meanings rooted in the American experience. . . . Imposing race as an analytic framework in societies where it is not a salient emic construct poses problems of measurement and interpretation."

There are many other emic examples. Perhaps you want to study labor unions in Japan and the United States. You learn the Japanese word for labor union is *rodo kumiai*; however, as Mouer and Kawanishi (2005:xvii) argued,

> *Many of the concepts used in writing about work in Japan have cultural emic dimensions (i.e., a set of connotations peculiar to the Japanese setting). The word* rodo kumiai, *for example, refers to an organization for and by workers in a generic or etic sense. However, when the term is used in Japan, its connotations for most Japanese suggest a particular approach to union organization, trends in*

> *unionization rates, a history of ideological struggles between left-wing and right-wing groups, an association with a broad range of citizen's movements ad a specific approach to organization both at the national and the grass-roots levels. The term is also used to refer to a range of other self-help or mutual-help organizations, including credit unions and agricultural, consumer or insurance cooperatives.*

EQUIVALENCE IN HISTORICAL-COMPARATIVE RESEARCH

The Importance of Equivalence

Equivalence is a critical issue in all research.[53] It involves whether we can make comparisons across divergent contexts. Although we are living in a specific time period and culture, can we correctly read, understand, or conceptualize data about people from a different historical era or culture. Without equivalence, we cannot use the same concepts or measures in different cultures or historical periods, making comparison difficult if not impossible. It is similar to the problems that arise with measurement validity in quantitative research.

The equivalence issue varies on a continuum. At one extreme, we discover something that is totally foreign to our experience (e.g., head-hunting and cannibalism) or that is unique to a particular time or culture. At the opposite extreme, there are subtle differences that we easily overlook but could affect comparisons. For example, Elder (1973:127) noted this problem when translating the term *friend* across three European languages:

> *Take friend in English,* Freund *in German, and* amigo *in Spanish. Technically, they translate identically. Yet the German* Freund *refers to a few deep, personal associates; the English* friend *refers to a somewhat less intense and wider range of acquaintances; and*

Emic Concept or approach developed and used within a specific cultural setting but that may not exist elsewhere.

Etic Concept or approach that is universal in the international scientific community or widely shared across multiple cultural settings.

the Spanish amigo *refers to a very wide range of persons, some of whom might have been met only that day. Thus, the question, "How many friends do you have?" is asking something different in all three languages.*

Types of Equivalence

The equivalence issue has implications for H-C research because we might misunderstand or misinterpret events in either a different era or a different culture. Assuming that the (emic) interpretation is correct, we may find that making comparisons across times or places (etic) to be difficult. If we fully grasp another time or culture (emic), we may still find communicating with others from our own time and culture (emic) to be difficult. We can divide the equivalence issue into four subtypes: lexicon equivalence, contextual equivalence, conceptual equivalence, and measurement equivalence (see Summary Review Box 14.1, Types of Equivalence).

Lexicon Equivalence. **Lexicon equivalence** refers to the correct translation of words and phrases or the discovery of a word that means the same thing as another word. This is clearest between two languages. For example, many languages and cultures have forms of address and pronouns for intimates (e.g., close friends and family members) and subordinates (e.g., younger persons and lower-status people) that differ from those used in unfamiliar or public settings or for persons of higher social status. There are no directly equal linguistic forms of speech in English, although the idea of close personal versus public relationships exists in English-speaking cultures. In languages such as French, Italian, or Spanish, switching pronouns when saying "How are you today?" might indicate a change in status or in the social relationship. One would

---

Lexicon equivalence Similarity of words or phrases to express their identical meaning in a different language or in the translation from one language to another.

Contextual equivalence Similarity of social roles, norms, or situations across different cultures or historical periods.

SUMMARY REVIEW BOX **14.1**

Types of Equivalence

1. **Lexicon.** Do the same words, ways of communicating, meanings, and expressions exist in two cultures? If not, how do we know whether miscommunication or mistranslations produce differences that we discover, or whether there are real differences?
2. **Contextual.** Does context in each cultural setting influence the substantive meaning of what we study? If so, how can we know whether differences in the cultural contexts account for differences that we discover or whether there are real differences?
3. **Conceptual.** Do the same concepts or ways of understanding social relations, situations, or events exist in two cultures? If not, how can we determine whether a mismatch in concepts produces differences that we discover or whether there are real differences?
4. **Measurement.** Can we measure the same phenomena in the same way in two cultures? If not, how can we know whether different measurement methods produce the differences that we discover or whether there are real differences?

---

have to indicate it in another, perhaps nonverbal, way if speaking in English.

Lexicon equivalence can be significant in historical research because the meaning of words changes over time, even in the same language. The greater the distance in time, the greater the chances are that an expression will have a different meaning or connotation. For example, today the word *weed* refers to unwanted plants or to marijuana, but in Shakespeare's era, the word meant clothing.

Being sensitive to subtle changes in language use can be crucial when you try to understand other perspectives. For example, Sewell (1980) found that differences in how people living about a century and a half ago used certain terms helped him to understand changes in their consciousness and social experiences. However, Jones (1983:24) noted, "Harnessing elementary insights derived from theories of language to problems of substantive historical interpretation is in . . . an extremely primitive state."

Contextual Equivalence. The correct application of terms or concepts in different social or historical contexts is referred to as **contextual equivalence**. It is an attempt to achieve equivalence within specific contexts. For example, in cultures with different dominant religions, a religious leader (e.g., priest, minister, rabbi) can have different roles, training, and authority. In some contexts, priests are full-time male professionals who are wealthy, highly esteemed, well-educated community leaders who also wield political power. In other contexts, a priest is anyone who rises above others in a congregation on a temporary basis but is without power or standing in the community. Priests in such a context may be less well educated, have low incomes, and be viewed as sincere spiritual people. If you ask about "priests" without noticing the context, you could make serious errors in interpretations.

Context also applies across historical eras. For example, *attending college* has a different meaning today than in a historical context in which only the richest 1 percent of the population attended college, most colleges had fewer than 500 students, all were private all-male institutions that did not require a high school diploma for entry, and a college curriculum consisted of classical languages and moral training. Attending college 120 years ago was not the same as it is today, when a majority of high school graduates attend co-educational public colleges offering a wide range of subjects, and college is seen as an extension of high school. The historical context has altered the meaning of *attending college*.

Conceptual Equivalence. The ability to use the same concept across divergent cultures or historical eras is **conceptual equivalence**. We live within specific cultures and historical eras. Our concepts come from our experiences and are shaped by knowledge from our own culture and era. We may try to stretch the concepts by learning about other cultures or eras, but our views of other cultures or eras are colored by our current life situations. This creates a persistent tension and raises the issue of whether we can create concepts that are simultaneously true reflections of life experiences in different cultures or eras and that also make sense to us.

Conceptual equivalence is a special case of larger emic and etic issue because concepts can be incompatible across different periods or cultures. Is it possible to create concepts that are true, accurate, and valid representations of social life in two or more cultural or historical settings that are very different? For example, Thompson (1967) argued that the subjective experience of time and its measurement were radically different in the preindustrial period. The concepts of punctuality and of the workday had a very different meaning or did not exist at all. Someone interested in comparing work in the late twentieth and the early sixteenth centuries is comparing "apples and oranges." For example, the word *class* exists in many societies, but the system of classes (i.e., the role of income, wealth, job, education, status, relation to means of production), the number of classes, the connotations of being in a particular class, and class categories or boundaries differ across societies. This makes the study of social class across several societies difficult.[54]

At times, the same or a similar concept exists across cultures but in different forms or degrees of strength. For example, many Asian societies have a marked difference between the outward, public presentation and definition of self and the private, personal presentation and definition of self. What one reveals and shows externally is often culturally detached from the person's true, internal feelings. Some languages mark this linguistically, as well. The idea of a distinct self for public, nonfamily, or nonprivate situations exists in Western cultures, as well, but it is much weaker and less socially significant than in Japan and other parts of Asia. In addition, many Western cultures assume that the inner self is "real" and should be revealed, an assumption that is not always shared cross-culturally.

At other times, there is no direct cultural equivalence. For example, there is no direct Western conceptual equivalence for the Japanese *ie*. Its English translation is family system. However, as Hendry (2003:26) explained, "The whole notion of 'family system' was a concept created in the face of outside influence to explain Japanese behavior in a comparative context." The *ie* includes a continuing line of familial descent going back generations and continuing into the future with branches created by noninheriting male offspring (or adopted sons). Its

Conceptual equivalence   Similarity of ideas or concepts across divergent cultural or historical settings.

meaning is closer to a European lineage "house" among the feudal nobility than the modern household or even extended family. The word can also include a religious identity and property-holding dimensions (as land or a business passed down for generations). It can include feelings of obligation to one's ancestors, including to uphold any commitments they may have made. The *ie* is also embedded in a web of hierarchical relationships with other *ie* and suggests social position or status in a community. For various reasons, the U.S. occupation government in Japan after World War II legally abolished the *ie*. In doing this, it tried to impose a very different, alien cultural concept, that of the Western nuclear family.

Conceptual equivalence also applies to the study of different historical eras. For example, income is very different in a historical era with a largely noncash society in which most people grew their own food and made their own furniture, clothing, or barter goods. Where money is rarely used, thinking of income as the number of dollars earned makes no sense. Counting hogs, acres of land, pairs of shoes, servants, horse carriages, and the like may be more appropriate. Likewise, poor people today may have finished 8 years of school; may own a black-and-white television; may live in a small, run-down house; and may own a rusted, battered, 15-year-old automobile. Being poor in a past era may have meant sleeping in barns with animals, begging on the streets, being near starvation, never attending school, and owning only the clothing on one's back. Yet despite the material differences, in terms of the specific societies and the concept of poverty, the poor of today and yesterday may be equivalent.

Measurement Equivalence. **Measurement equivalence** refers to using equal measures of the same concept in different settings. If a researcher develops a concept appropriate to different contexts, the question remains: Are different measures necessary in different contexts for the same concept? Armer

(1973:52) defined this idea as follows: "equivalence with respect to measurement refers to whether the instruments used in separate societies in fact measure the same concept, regardless of whether the manifest content and procedures are identical or not." He argued that it may be necessary to use different indicators in different contexts. We might measure the same concept using an attitude survey in one culture but field research in another. The issue then becomes whether we can compare results based on different indicators.

The measurement equivalence issue suggests that we must examine many sources of partial evidence in order to measure or identify a theoretical construct. When evidence exists in fragmentary forms, we must examine extensive amounts of indirect evidence in order to identify constructs. Noting this type of process in his study of early nineteenth-century French works, Sewell (1980:9) remarked:

> *The ideas we were pursuing were stated partially and in fragments, written down in the heat of the action, often by an unknown person or by groups of persons, and are available only in the most heterogeneous forms—in manifest, records of debates at meetings, posts, satirical prints, statutes of associations, pamphlets, and so on. In such situations the coherence of the thought lies not in particular texts . . . but in the entire ideological discourse constituted by a large number of individually fragmentary and incomplete statements, gestures, images and actions.*

ETHICS

Historical-comparative research shares many of the ethical concerns found in nonreactive research techniques. The use of primary historical sources occasionally raises special ethical issues. First, replicating research based on primary material is difficult. Our selection criteria for using evidence and external criticism of documents puts a burden on the integrity of the individual researcher. Novick (1988:220) suggested:

> *The historian has seen, at first hand, a great mass of evidence, often unpublished. The historian develops an interpretation of this evidence based on years of*

Measurement equivalence   Similarity of measures that will accurately represent a construct or variable in divergent cultural or historical settings.

immersion in the material—together, of course, with the perception apparatus and assumptions he or she brings to it. Historians employ devices, the footnote being the most obvious example, to attain for their work something approaching "replicability," but the resemblance is not all that close.

Errors in documentation or the failure to document primary sources sufficiently may lead to an accusation of fraud against historians, especially from opposing schools of historiography.[55]

Second, the right to protect privacy may interfere with the right to gather evidence. A person's descendants may want to destroy or hide private papers or evidence of scandalous behavior. Major political figures (e.g., presidents and top administrators) may want to hide embarrassing official documents.[56]

In comparative research, we must be sensitive to cultural and political issues of cross-cultural interaction. We have to learn what a culture considers offensive. Sensitivity means showing respect for the traditions, customs, and meaning of privacy in a host country; for example, one should respect that it may be taboo for a man to interview a married woman without her husband present.

In general, we want to establish good relations with the host country's government. It is unwise to take data out of the country without giving something (e.g., results) in return. At times, the military or political interests of your home nation or your personal values may conflict with official policy in the host nation. Officials of the host country could suspect you of being a spy or you could be under pressure from your home country to gather covert information.

Sometimes a researcher's presence or findings may cause diplomatic problems. For example, someone who examines abortion practices in a country and then declares that official government policy is to force many women to have abortions can expect serious controversy. Likewise, if the researcher is sympathetic to the cause of groups who oppose the government, that government might imprison or expel her or him from the country. Social researchers who conduct research in another country must be aware of such issues and the consequences of their actions.

Many comparative researchers from "rich," highly industrialized nations who conduct applied economic development research in "poor" industrializing nations emphasize using participatory action research (see Chapter 2). This is as much for practical as ethical reasons. Development researchers learned that unless they work closely with local people, incorporate their popular beliefs, and gain their cooperation, an applied research project is unlikely to be successful or sustained.[57] In addition to usual issues with applied research and learning to respect local customs and culture, this often means that researchers must include teaching local people elements of research design. When working in remote, nonindustrial settings, researchers may need to demonstrate in very basic, visual terms the logic of research and the impact of a project (e.g., use new food-storage methods, eliminate parasites, improve drinking water) on local living conditions.

CONCLUSION

In this chapter, you were introduced to methodological principles for an inquiry into historical and comparative materials and its general approach to research issues. The H-C approach is appropriate when you want to ask "big questions" about macro-level change or to understand social processes that operate across time or across several societies. You can carry out H-C research in several ways, but a distinct qualitative H-C approach is similar to that of field research in important respects.

Historical-comparative research involves having a different orientation toward research more than applying a set of specialized techniques. You may use some specialized techniques, such as the external criticism of primary documents or back translation; nevertheless, the most vital feature is how you approach a question, probe data, and move toward explanations.

Historical-comparative research is more difficult to conduct than research that is neither historical nor comparative, but the difficulties are present to a lesser degree in other types of social research. For example, issues of equivalence exist to some degree in all social research. In H-C research, however, you cannot treat the problems as secondary concerns. They are at the forefront of how you conduct research. They will determine whether you can conduct a study and address a research question.

In the next chapter, we turn to analysis of qualitative data. Many types of H-C research as well as field research produce such data. The form of data and the logic of the research approaches to gathering the data have an influence on the analysis.

KEY TERMS

anachronism
annales School
archive
back translation
baconian fallacy
bowdlerization
case-study comparative
    research
combinational explanation
conceptual equivalence
contextual equivalence
courtesy bias
critical indicator

cross-national research
cultural-context research
emic
etic
external criticism
galton's problem
historiography
human relations area files
    (HRAF)
internal criticism
lexicon equivalence
longue durée
measurement equivalence

mentalities
nonsource-based knowledge
oral history
primary sources
process analysis
recollections
running records
safari research
secondary sources
transnational research
western cultural bias

REVIEW QUESTIONS

1. What are some of the unique features of historical-comparative (H-C) research?
2. What are the similarities between field research and H-C research?
3. What is the Annales School, and what are three characteristics or terms in its orientation toward studying the past?
4. What is the difference between a critical indicator and supporting evidence?
5. What questions does a researcher using external criticism ask?
6. What are the limitations of using secondary sources?
7. What is Galton's problem, and why is it important in comparative research?
8. What strengths or advantages are there to using a comparative method in social research?
9. In what ways is cross-national survey research different from survey research within one's own culture?
10. What is the importance of equivalence in H-C research, and what are its four types?

NOTES

1. The early works include the following: Marc Bloch, *Feudal Society* (1961), transl. L. A. Manyon (University of Chicago Press; original 1939–1940); George Homans (1941), *English Villagers of the Thirteenth Century* (Harvard University Press); Robert K. Merton (1970), *Science, Technology and Society in Seventeenth Century*

England (Harper & Row; originally published in 1938); and Karl Polanyi (1957), *The Great Transformation* (Beacon).

2. They included Bellah's *Tokugawa Religion* (1957), Bendix's *Work and Authority in Industry* (1956), and Smelser's *Social Change in the Industrial Revolution* (1959).

3. Three such works are Tilly's *The Vendee* (1964), Moore's *The Social Origins of Dictatorship and Democracy* (1966), and Thompson's *The Making of the English Working Class* (1963). Tilly's study of France in the 1790s combined quantitative logic and new historical data. Moore's study of England, India, Japan, Germany, the United States, and the former Soviet Union traced how combinations of events and coalitions of social groups caused some nations to develop democractic and others nondemocratic governments. Thompson's study of England prior to 1840 examined the lives, words, and actions of ordinary people. "The inspiration for a good deal of the new social history came from E. P. Thompson's (1963) *The Making of the English Working Class.* Surely, no work in European history ever so profoundly and so rapidly influenced American historians" (Novick, 1988:440).

4. Some influential works of this period include Anderson (1974a, 1974b), Hector (1975), Paige (1975), Skocpol (1979), Tilly et al. (1975), and Wallerstein (1974).

5. This is a large increase over the previous period (1985–1989) when it was about 28 percent. By contrast, the percentage of historical or comparative articles in the journals between 1976 and 1978 was about 18 percent. Additional information on the history of historical-comparative research can be found in Calhoun (1996), Johnson (1982), Kohn (1987, especially footnote 1), Lipset (1968), Novick (1988), Roy (1984), Skocpol (1984), D. Smith (1991), Warwick and Osherson (1973), and Zaret (1978).

6. See Mahoney (1999) for major works of historical-comparative research.

7. For a discussion of differences between generalizations and analysis across temporal units and cultural units, see Firebaugh (1980) and Smelser (1976).

8. See Calhoun (1996), McDaniel (1978), Przeworski and Teune (1970), and Stinchcombe (1978) for additional discussion.

9. Brown (1978), Johnson (1982), Lloyd (1986), McLennan (1981:66–71), and Nowak (1989) provided discussions of the relationship between positivist and nonpositivist approaches to historical-comparative research and the turn toward a realist philosophy of science. See Murphey (1973) with regard to historical research. For comparative research, see Hymes (1970) and Mehan (1973).

10. See Goldthrope (1991, 1997), Lieberson (1991), and Treiman (1977). Counterarguments are made by Burawoy (1977), Goldstone (1997), Mahoney (1999), and Rueschemeyer and Stephens (1997).

11. For more on borrowing from anthropology, see Biersack (1989), Desan (1989), Johnson (1982), Sewell (1980), Stone (1987), and Walters (1980).

12. See also Desan (1989), Griswold (1983), and Ryan (1989) for discussions of ritual and cultural symbolism.

13. Also see Carr (1961:35, 69), McDaniel (1978), Novick (1988:604), and Ragin (1987:164–166) on the dialogue metaphor.

14. For additional discussion, see Sewell (1987).

15. See Roth and Schluchter (1979:205).

16. See Kalberg (1994).

17. See George and Bennett (2005), Gerring (2007), Mahoney (2004) and Munck (2004) on process analysis or process tracing.

18. For an additional discussion of the penetration of surface events, see Bloch (1953:13), Lloyd (1986), McLennan (1981:42–44), and Sewell (1987).

19. See Naroll (1968) on the difficulties in creating distinctions. Also see Whiting (1968).

20. See the discussion on periodization in Chapter 15.

21. Bendix (1963), Przeworski and Teune (1970), and Smelser (1976) discuss transhistorical concepts.

22. For more on the Annales School, see Braudel (1980), Darnton (1978), Hunt (1989), Lloyd (1986), and McLennan (1981).

23. Orientation reading is discussed in Shafer (1980: 46–48).

24. See Wilkinson (2005).

25. Shafer (1980:2) discussed this in depth.

26. See Lowenthal (1985:187).

27. For additional information on oral history, see Dunaway and Baum (1984), Sitton et al. (1983), and P. Thompson (1978). Also see Prucha (1987:78–80) for a guide to major collections of oral histories in the United States.

28. See Schacter (1995) and Schacter (2001:20–21).

29. Bendix (1978:16) distinguished between the *judgments* of historians and the *selections* of sociologists.

30. Merton (1957:93–94) discussed the limitation of *post facto* interpretations.

31. For a discussion of law versus tendency in historical social theory, see Applebaum (1978b) and McLennan

(1981:75). Murphey (1973:86) provided a useful discussion of the issues.

32. As used here, *read* means to bring a theoretical framework and analytic purpose to the text. We read "past" specific details and the historian's interpretations (i.e., passed by, but not without notice) to discover patterns in underlying structures. See Sumner (1979) for discussion. This relates to the objectivity question in historiography in Novick (1988) and Winkler (1989).

33. Bonnell (1980:161), Finley (1977:132), and Goldthorpe (1977:189–190) discussed how historians use concepts. Selection in this context is discussed by Abrams (1982:194) and Ben-Yehuda (1983).

34. See Barzun and Graff (1970), Braudel (1980), Cantor and Schneider (1967), Novick (1988), or Shafer (1980). Most focus on the assembly of historical details that are documented in artifacts, including those of collective biography. This focuses attention on specific historical actors and their actions and motives. It takes on an individualistic-voluntaristic slant, and studies become ideographic accounts. See also Block (1977), Laslett (1980), and MacIver (1968).

35. Abbott (1992), Abell (2004), Gallie (1963), Gotham and Staples (1996), Griffin (1993), McLennan (1981: 76–87), Runciman (1980), and Stone (1987:74–96) discuss the narrative.

36. For more on primary sources, see Barzun and Graff (1970:63–128), Cantor and Schneider (1967:22–91), Dibble (1963), Mariampolski and Hughes (1978), Milligan (1979), Platt (1981), Shafer (1980:127–170), and Topolski (1976). Bloch's (1953:79–137) discussion of historical criticism is still valuable today.

37. On the strengths and limitations of comparative research, see Anderson (1973), Holt and Turner (1970), Kohn (1987), Ragin (1987), Smelser (1976), Vallier (1971a, 1971b), Walton (1973), and Whiting (1968).

38. Bollen et al. (1993), Chase-Dunn (1989:309–333), and Ragin (1994a) provide lists of similar types. Also see Ragin (1989) for a critique of Kohn's typology.

39. See Ragin (1987:49–50).

40. See Wolf (1982) on civilizations around the world between 1400 and 1900. He noted many separate cultures and civilizations that existed prior to European colonization and the rise of nation-states.

41. For examples, see Hector (1975) and See (1986).

42. See Elder (1973) and Whiting (1968) on Galton's problem.

43. For more on the *Human Relations Area Files* and the *Ethnographic Atlas,* see Murdock (1967, 1971) and Whiting (1968).

44. For more on comparative survey research, see Burton and White (1987), Elder (1973), Frey (1970), Verba (1971), Warwick and Lininger (1975), and Williamson et al. (1982:315–319). For an additional discussion of access issues, see Armer (1973:59) and Form (1973).

45. See Harkness, van de Vijver, and Johnson (2003) and Smith (2003, 2004).

46. Couper and de Leeuw (2003) discuss nonresponse, and Johnson and van de Vijver (2003) describe social desirability issues.

47. For more on back translation, see Anderson (1973), Grimshaw (1973), and Hymes (1970).

48. See Harkness, van de Vijver, and Johnson (2003).

49. See Frey (1970), Grimshaw (1973), and McDaniel (1978).

50. See also Bradshaw and Wallace (1996).

51. See Hiller (1979).

52. See Ember (1977), Harris (1976), and Headland et al. (1990).

53. For additional discussions of equivalence, see Anderson (1973), Armer (1973), Frey (1970), Holt and Turner (1970), Przeworski and Teune (1970, 1973), and Warwick and Osherson (1973).

54. See Hazelrigg (1973).

55. See Novick (1988:612–622) for an extensive discussion of the David Abraham case.

56. For a discussion of archived data, see Odette and Mautner (2004) and Richardson and Godfrey (2003).

57. See Mikkelsen (1995).

CHAPTER 15

Analysis of Qualitative Data

> *Much of the best work in sociology has been carried out using qualitative methods*
> *without statistical tests. This has been true of research areas ranging from*
> *organization and community studies to microstudies of face to face interaction*
> *and macrostudies of the world system. Nor should such work be regarded as*
> *weak or initial "exploratory" approaches to those topics.*
> —Randall Collins, "Statistics versus Words," p. 340

In field research, historical-comparative research, and a few other research areas, we collect a great deal of qualitative data to describe details about people, actions, and events in social life. The data are in the form of text from documents, observational notes, open-ended interview transcripts, physical artifacts, audio- or videotapes, and images or photos. It is not enough to collect the data; we also must analyze it. In qualitative approaches to research, analysis begins while gathering data, but such analysis tends to be tentative and incomplete.

To analyze data means systematically to organize, integrate, and examine; as we do this, we search for patterns and relationships among the specific details. To analyze, we connect particular data to concepts, advance generalizations, and identify broad trends or themes. Analysis allows us to improve understanding, expand theory, and advance knowledge.

The data used in quantitative studies are almost exclusively in the form of numbers. Compared to the vast volume, variety, and mutability of nebulous qualitative data, numbers are precise, uniform, standardized, and compact carriers of information. Applied mathematics has a large, highly developed area devoted to the analysis of numbers (you read about statistics in Chapter 12). Moreover, the statistics we use to analyze quantitative social science data are the same as those used across all quantitative science and many applied areas (e.g., business, education, medicine, agriculture, engineering, and so forth). As computer technology has advanced over the past 40 years, statisticians and computer scientists have developed a large array of sophisticated software and widely available programs to assist in quantitative data analysis.

Little of the vast statistical knowledge and related computer software is applicable for the analysis of qualitative data. Qualitative research allows us to be systematic and logically rigorous but often in different ways from statistical analysis.

Until about 20 years ago, qualitative researchers rarely explained how they analyzed data. In fact, a frequent criticism of qualitative research was that data analysis is not explicit or open to inspection, but its analysis has become more explicit and systematic.[1] We now have computer software for qualitative data analysis, some grounded in mathematical and other logical relations. Nonetheless, we use many approaches to qualitative data analysis.

This chapter has four parts. We first compare the similarities and differences between qualitative and quantitative data analysis. Next we discuss how to use coding and concept/theory building to assist in analyzing qualitative data. Third, we review some major analytic strategies that qualitative researchers have used and show how they link data to theory. We also examine the role that absence of direct, observable evidence can have in explanation. Lastly we review a few specific techniques available to examine patterns in the qualitative data.

COMPARISON OF METHODS OF DATA ANALYSIS

Qualitative and quantitative forms of data analysis have similarities and differences. In this section, we look at four similarities and four differences.

Similarities

First, in both types of data analysis, we infer from the empirical details of social life. To *infer* means to pass a judgment, to use reasoning, and to reach a conclusion based on evidence. In both forms of data analysis, we must carefully examine empirical information to reach a conclusion based on reasoning and simplifying the complexity in the data. This process requires some abstraction, or a moving back from the very specific details of concrete data, but how much this occurs varies. In all cases, we remain faithful to what is in the original, raw data.

Both forms of data analysis anchor statements made about the social world in an inquiry that has "adequacy." As Morse (1994:230) observed, "In qualitative research, *adequacy* refers to the amount of data collected, rather than to the number of subjects as in quantitative research. Adequacy is attained when sufficient data has been collected that saturation occurs."

A second similarity is that the analysis involves a public method or process. As we gather large amounts of data, we make our actions accessible to others. We describe the data and document the ways we collected and studied it, and we make how we did these things open to inspection by other members of the scientific community. The degree

to which the method is standardized and visible varies. As King et al. (1994:118) noted, "Research designs in qualitative research are not always made explicit, but they are at least implicit in every piece of research."

Third, comparison is central in all data analysis, qualitative and quantitative. We compare the evidence we gathered internally or with other related evidence. We explore the data and identify multiple process, causes, properties, or mechanisms within it, looking for patterns: similarities and differences, aspects that are alike and unlike:

> [Qualitative] researchers examine patterns of similarities and differences across cases and try to come to terms with their diversity. . . . Quantitative researchers also examine differences among cases, but with a different emphasis, the goal is to explain the covariation of one variable with another, usually across many cases. . . . The quantitative researcher typically has only broad familiarity with the cases. (Ragin, 1994a:107)

Fourth, in both forms of data analysis, we strive to avoid errors, false conclusions, and misleading inferences. We are vigilant and alert for possible fallacies or illusions. As we sort through various explanations, discussions, and descriptions, and evaluate the merits of rival ways to describe and explain, we always seek the most authentic, valid, true, or worthy description and explanation among the alternatives.

Differences

Quantitative researchers can choose from a set of specialized, standardized data analysis techniques. Hypothesis testing and statistical methods are similar across the natural and social sciences. Quantitative analysis is highly developed and builds on a large body of applied mathematics. In contrast, qualitative data analysis is less standardized. The wide variety in qualitative research is matched by the many approaches to data analysis. An added complexity to having many approaches is that qualitative research is often inductive. We do not know the specifics of data analysis when we begin a project. Schatzman and Strauss (1973:108) remarked, "Qualitative analysts do not often enjoy the operational advantages of their quantitative cousins in being able to predict their own analytic processes; consequently, they cannot refine and order their raw data by operations built initially into the design of research."

A second difference is that we do not begin data analysis in quantitative research until we have collected the data. Only then do we manipulate the numbers in seeking patterns or relationships. In qualitative research, we start looking for patterns or relationships while collecting data. We use results from early data analysis to guide subsequent data collection. Thus, analysis is less a distinct final stage of research than a dimension of research that stretches across all stages.

Another difference is the relation to social theory. Quantitative research involves manipulating numbers that represent empirical facts to test abstract hypotheses comprised of variable constructs. In contrast, qualitative research frequently creates new concepts and theory by blending empirical evidence with abstract concepts. Instead of testing a hypothesis, we may illustrate or color evidence to show that a theory, generalization, or interpretation is plausible.

The fourth difference is the degree of abstraction or distance from the details of social life (see Summary Review Box 15.1, Comparing Quantitative and Qualitative Data Analysis). In all data analysis, we place specific raw data into broader categories. We then examine and manipulate categories to identify patterns. In quantitative analysis, this process is clothed in statistics, hypotheses, and variables. We assume that we can capture or measure using numbers and then manipulate the numbers with statistics to reveal key features of social life.

In contrast, data in qualitative analysis are relatively imprecise, diffuse, and context based and can have more than one meaning. This is not always a disadvantage.

> *Words are not only more fundamental intellectually; one may also say that they are necessarily superior to mathematics in the social structure of the discipline. For words are a mode of expression with greater open-endedness, more capacity for connecting various realms of argument and experience, and more capacity for reaching intellectual audiences. (Collins, 1984:353)*

SUMMARY REVIEW BOX **15.1**
Comparing Quantitative and Qualitative Data Analysis

SIMILARITIES	DIFFERENCES
Both infer from empirical data to abstract ideas	*Quantitative* uses a few shared, standardized techniques. *Qualitative* uses many diverse, nonstandard techniques.
Both use a public process and described in detail	*Quantitative* analyzes after all data have been collected. *Qualitative* begins data analysis while still collecting data.
Both make comparisons	*Quantitative* tests preexisting theories and hypotheses. *Qualitative* conceptualizes and builds a new theory.
Both avoid errors and false conclusions	*Quantitative* uses precise and compact abstract data. *Qualitative* uses imprecise, diffuse, relatively concrete data.

Explanations and Qualitative Data

We do not have to choose between a rigid idiographic/nomothetic dichotomy: that is, between describing specifics and verifying universal laws. When analyzing qualitative data, we develop explanations or generalizations that are close to concrete data and contexts, and we usually use less abstract theory. We may build new theory to create a realistic picture of social life and stimulate understanding more than to test causal hypotheses. The explanations tend to be rich in detail, sensitive to context, and capable of showing the complex processes or sequences of social life. They may or may not be causal. Our goal is to organize specific details into a coherent picture, model, or set of tightly interlocked concepts.

Qualitative explanations can be either highly unlikely or highly plausible. We provide supportive evidence to eliminate some theoretical explanations from consideration and to increase the plausibility of others. Qualitative analysis can eliminate an explanation by showing that a wide array of evidence contradicts it. The data might support more than one explanation, but not all explanations will be consistent with it. In addition to eliminating less plausible explanations, we often want to verify a sequence of events or the steps of a process. This temporal ordering is the basis of finding associations among variables, and it supports causal arguments.

A few qualitative researchers are almost entirely descriptive and avoid theoretical analysis. In general, we always want to make theories and concepts explicit. Without an analytic interpretation or theory, the readers of qualitative research may use their own everyday, taken-for-granted ideas. Such ideas rarely advance general knowledge. Moreover, their commonsense framework will contain unexamined assumptions, biases, ethnocentrism, and ill-defined concepts taken from dominant cultural values.[2]

CODING AND CONCEPT FORMATION

Qualitative research often involves the use of general ideas, themes, or concepts as tools for making generalizations. Many are nonvariable concepts or simple nominal-level variables.

Conceptualization

When we perform quantitative research, we conceptualize variables and refine concepts as a step to measure variables. In contrast, when we perform qualitative research, we form new concepts or refine concepts that are grounded in the data. Concept formation is an integral part of data analysis and begins during data collection. Thus, conceptualization is a way to organize and make sense of data.

Those who conduct qualitative studies analyze by organizing data into categories based on themes, concepts, or similar features. While doing this, they may also develop new concepts, formulate conceptual definitions, and examine the relationships among concepts. Eventually, these researchers will link concepts to each other in terms of a sequence, as oppositional sets (X is the opposite of Y), or as sets of similar categories that are interwoven into theoretical statements.

You may begin to form concepts as you read through and ask critical questions of the data (e.g.,

field notes, historical documents, secondary sources). The questions can come from the abstract vocabulary of an academic field discipline such as sociology, for example: Is this a case of class conflict? Was role conflict present in that situation? Is this a social movement? Questions can also be logical, for example: What was the sequence of events? How does the way it happened here compare to the way over there? Are these the same or different, general or specific cases?[3]

Concept and evidence are mutually interdependent, particularly in case-study analysis. Cases are not given preestablished empirical units or theoretical categories apart from data; together, the data and theory define them. As you organize data and apply ideas, you create or specify a case. Making a case, called *casing,* occurs when you bring data and theory together (casing was discussed in Chapter 7). Determining what to treat as a case helps you resolve the tension between what you actually observe and your ideas about what you observe. "Casing viewed as a methodological step, can occur at any phase of the research process, but occurs especially at the beginning of the project and at the end" (Ragin, 1992b:218).

Coding Qualitative Data

When you code quantitative data, you arrange measures of variables into a machine-readable form for statistical analysis. Coding data has a different meaning in qualitative research than in quantitative research. In qualitative research you organize the raw data into conceptual categories and create themes or concepts. Instead of being a clerical task of data management, qualitative coding is an integral part of data analysis. Your research question provides a guide, but the process often leads to new questions. It frees you from entanglement in the details of the raw data and encourages you to think about them at a higher level, moving toward theory and generalizations:

> *Codes are tags or labels for assigning units of meaning to the descriptive or inferential information compiled during a study. Codes usually are attached to "chunks" of varying size—words, phrases, sentences or whole paragraphs, connected*

or unconnected to a specific setting. (Miles and Huberman, 1994:56)

Strauss (1987) defined three types of qualitative data coding and suggests you review the data on three occasions, using a different coding each time. He (p. 55) warned, "Coding is the most difficult operation for inexperienced researchers to understand and to master."[4]

1. *Open coding.* You preform **open coding** during a first pass through recently collected data. You locate themes and assign initial codes in your first attempt to condense the mass of data into categories. As you slowly read field notes, historical sources, or other data, you look for critical terms, central people, key events, or themes. Next you write a preliminary concept or label at the edge of a note card or computer record and highlight it with a different color or in some other distinctive way. You want to remain open to creating new themes and to changing these initial codes in subsequent analysis. A theoretical framework helps if you apply it in a flexible manner. When using open coding you bring themes to the surface from deep inside the data. The themes are at a low level of abstraction and come from your initial research question, concepts in the literature, terms used by members in the social setting, or new thoughts stimulated by an immersion in the data. As Schatzman and Strauss (1973:121) warned, you should see abstract concepts in concrete data and move back and forth between abstract concepts and specific details.

An example of moving between abstract concepts and details is found in LeMasters's (1975) field research study of a working-class tavern when he found that marriage came up in many conversations. If he open coded field notes, he might have coded a block of field notes with the theme "marriage." Following is an example of hypothetical field notes that can be open coded with this theme:

> *I wore a tie to the bar on Thursday because I had been at a late meeting. Sam noticed it immediately and said. "Damn it, Doc. I wore one of them things once—when I got married—and look what happened to me! By God, the undertaker will have to put the next one on." I ordered a beer, then asked*

him, *"Why did you get married?" He replied, "What the hell you goin' to do? You just can't go on shacking up with girls all your life—I did plenty of that when I was single" with a smile and wink. He paused to order another beer and light a cigarette, then continued, "A man, sooner or later, likes to have a home of his own, and some kids, and to have that you have to get married. There's no way out of it—they got you hooked." I said, "Helen [his wife] seems like a nice person." He returned, "Oh, hell, she's not a bad kid, but she's a goddamn woman and they get under my skin. They piss me off. If you go to a party, just when you start having fun, the wife says 'let's go home.'" (Adapted from LeMasters, 1975:36–37)*

Historical-comparative researchers also use open coding. For example, I studied the Knights of Labor, a nineteenth-century U.S. movement for economic and political reform. I read a secondary source about the activities of a local branch of the movement in a specific town. When reading and taking notes, I noticed that the Prohibition Party was important in local elections and that temperance was debated by members of the local branch. My primary interest was in the internal structure, ideology, and growth of the Knights movement. Temperance was a new and unexpected category. I coded the notes with the label "temperance" and included it as a possible theme (also see Expansion Box 15.1, Themes and Coding Qualitative Data on page 512).

In their qualitative content analysis interview data on twenty adults with type 1 diabetes, Graneheim and Lundman (2003) describe the open coding process. The interviews had asked about various aspects of living with type 1 diabetes. The researchers read the interview transcripts several times to obtain a sense of the whole. They then extracted text about the participants' experiences of having hyperglycemia and brought together the relevant passages into one text. This constituted the unit of analysis. They divided the text into meaning units (i.e., the constellation of words or statements that relate to the same central meaning) and then

---

Open coding   The first coding of qualitative data that examines the data to condense them into preliminary analytic categories or codes.

EXPANSION BOX **15.1**

Themes and Coding Qualitative Data

"A good thematic code is one that captures the qualitative richness of the phenomenon. It is usable in the analysis, the interpretation, and the presentation of research" (Boyatzis, 1998:31). To code data into themes, a researcher first needs to learn how "to see" or recognize themes in the data. Seeing themes rests on four abilities: (1) recognizing patterns in the data, (2) thinking in terms of systems and concepts, (3) having tacit knowledge or in-depth background knowledge (e.g., it helps to know Greek myths to understand Shakespeare's plays), and (4) possessing relevant information (e.g., one needs to know a lot about rock musicians and music to code themes about a rock music concert) (see Boyatzis, 1998:7–8).

Three errors to avoid when coding (see Schwandt, 1997:17) are (1) staying at a descriptive level only (not being analytic), (2) treating coding as a purely mechanical process, and (3) keeping codes fixed and inflexible. Codes have five parts: (1) a one- to three-word label or name, (2) a definition with a main characteristic, (3) a "flag" description of how to recognize the code in the data, (4) any exclusions or qualifications, and (5) an example.

ILLUSTRATION OF FIVE PARTS

Label. Gender-role disputes.

Definition. Interpersonal verbal disagreements are an example as are conflicts or disputes over what is proper or acceptable behavior for males and females in their interactions together or separately because he or she is male or female.

Flag. An example is making sarcastic remarks or jokes, or having disagreements (very mild to angry arguments) over what a male or female should do because he or she is male or female.

Qualifications. Only disputes among same gendered persons are considered. Any type of behavior (verbal or nonverbal) can be the target of a dispute. Interactions among overtly homosexual and transgendered persons are not included.

Example. Outside a classroom, Sara and Jessica, 16 years old, discuss their dates last night. Sara says, "We went out for pizza—of course he paid." Jessica remarks, "Of course? You mean you expect the guy to pay?" Sara answers, "Oh, forget it."

---

condensed them. They abstracted the condensed meaning units and labeled each with a code.

Although we can begin coding with a list of concepts, we usually generate most coding themes while reading data notes. Regardless of whether we begin with a list of themes, we list themes *after* finishing the open coding. Such a list serves three purposes:

1. It helps to see the emerging themes at a glance.
2. It stimulates us to find themes in future open coding.
3. We can use the list to build a universe of all themes in the study, which we reorganize, sort, combine, discard, or extend in further analysis.

Axial coding A second stage of coding of qualitative data during which the researcher organizes the codes, links them, and discovers key analytic categories.

We vary in how completely and in how much detail to code. Some researchers code every line or every few words; others code paragraphs or pages. Some of the data are not coded and are dross, or left over. The degree of detail in coding depends on the research question, the "richness" of the data, and the research purposes (see Expansion Box 15.2, The Process of Coding Qualitative Data).

Open-ended coding extends to analytic notes or memos that you write to yourself while collecting data. You should write memos on your codes (see the later discussion of analytic memo writing).

Axial Coding. This is a "second pass" through the data. During open coding, you focus on the actual data and assigning code labels for themes. You are little concerned about making connections among themes or elaborating the concepts that the themes represent. In contrast, you begin **axial coding** with an organized set of initial codes or preliminary

EXPANSION BOX **15.2**
The Process of Coding Qualitative Data

Coding qualitative data, whether it is in the form of observational field notes, video or audio recordings, open-ended interviews, or detailed historical documents, is a challenge despite attempts by Strauss (1987) and others to systematize and simplify the process, making it appear as a fixed three-step sequence with open, axial, and selective coding. Some researchers rely on text-coding software programs (see discussion later in this chapter) that force them to create codes, but the software is just one tool in a larger coding process.

Weston et al. (2001) described their coding process in detail. Weston worked as part of a six-person research team and noted that team collaboration helped to make coding processes more explicit. The ideal associated with grounded theory that a researcher begins with a completely open mind and without prior expectations is just that, an ideal. In reality, a person's academic training, awareness of concepts and theoretical assumptions, and expectations from the audience who will read the research report shape data coding. In Weston's study, the process began with one researcher on the team creating a coding system that had four codes based on a first reading of open-ended interview transcript data. The system had a definition for each coded idea and rules with examples for converting raw data into codes. Others on the research team then used the system to code selections of raw data. Based on experiences with this preliminary system, they revised the coding system and added subtypes of the original codes. The process was repeated several times with the team

members individually coding raw data, meeting together to discuss coding, and revising the coding system. After months of coding and meetings, the initial four codes became three master concepts with two of the three containing two types and each type having four to seven more refined codes. This yielded thirty-four coding distinctions. Over the next 2 years, the research team applied the system to hundreds of pages of raw data. Team members continued the process of reflecting on codes, meeting to discuss coding, and refining the system. Eventually their coding system had four tiers—three master concepts, seven types under the master concepts, two subtypes within three of the seven types, and several refined codes within each of the subtypes. In total, they created fifty-eight codes.

Over the next 2 years, as they continued to examine the data and present findings to the scientific community, the team kept refining and adjusting the coding system. They were following a strategy of *successive approximation* (see later in this chapter). A few new codes emerged and the system's structure shifted a little, but 4 years into the project, after hundreds of hours of meetings and repeated passes through the raw data, the coding system stabilized. As you see, a coding system can be more than a way to code raw data. It offers a system of analysis that provides a structured interpretation. By the way, the research topic Weston et al. studied was improving university teaching, and the team's data were from detailed open-ended interviews with six professors gathered during one semester.

concepts. In this second pass, you focus on the initial coded themes more than on the data. Additional codes or new ideas may emerge during this pass, and you should note them, but your primary task is to review and examine initial codes. You move toward organizing ideas or themes and identify the axis of key concepts in analysis.

Miles and Huberman (1994:62) have warned:

Whether codes are created and revised early or late is basically less important than whether they have some conceptual and structural order. Codes should

relate to one another in coherent, study-important ways; they should be part of a governing structure.

While axial coding, you ask about causes and consequences, conditions and interactions, strategies and processes. You look for categories or concepts that cluster together. You should ask questions such as: Can I divide existing concepts into subdimensions or subcategories? Can I combine several closely related concepts into one more general construct? Can I organize categories into a sequence (i.e., A, then B, then C), or by their physical location (i.e., where they occur), or their relationship to a major topic of interest?

For example, when studying working-class life, LeMasters could have divided the general issue of marriage into subparts (e.g., engagement, weddings). He could mark all notes involving parts of marriage and then relate marriage to themes of sexuality, division of labor in household tasks, views on children, and so on. When the theme reappeared in different places, he could have made comparisons to see new themes (e.g., men and women have different attitudes toward marriage).

In the example of historical research on the Knights of Labor, I looked for themes related to temperance. I looked for discussions of saloons, drinking or drunkenness, and relations between the movement and political parties that supported or opposed temperance. Themes that clustered around temperance included drinking as a form of recreation, drinking as part of ethnic culture, different religious views on drinking, and gender differences regarding drinking.

Graneheim and Lundman (2003) used a process of axial coding in their study of interview data on diabetes. They compared codes based on differences and similarities and sorted them into six subcategories and three categories. The two researchers discussed tentative categories and revised them. A process of reflection and discussion resulted in agreement about how to sort the codes. Finally, the researchers identified underlying meaning—that is, the latent content—of the categories that they formulated into a broader theme.

Axial coding not only stimulates thinking about linkages between concepts or themes, but also raises new questions. It can suggest dropping some themes or examining others in more depth. It also reinforces the connections between evidence and concepts. As you consolidate codes, you may find evidence in many places for core themes and build a dense web of support in the qualitative data for

them. This is analogous to the idea of multiple indicators described with regard to reliability and measuring variables. The connection between a theme and data is strengthened by multiple instances of empirical evidence.[5]

When I studied the Knights of Labor, I made the movement's failure to form alliances with other political groups a major theme. I reviewed notes looking for compromise and conflict between the Knights and other political parties, including temperance groups and the Prohibition Party. The array of concepts and themes related to temperance in axial coding helped me to see how the temperance issue facilitated or inhibited alliances.

Selective Coding.   By the time you are ready for this last pass through the data, you have identified the major themes. **Selective coding** involves scanning all the data and previous codes, looking selectively for cases that illustrate themes, and making comparisons after most or all data collection has been completed. Selective coding should begin after concepts have been well developed and several core generalizations or ideas have been identified.

For example, as LeMasters studied working-class life in a tavern, he decided to make gender relations a major theme. In selective coding, he could have gone through his field notes, looking for differences in how men and women talked about dating, engagements, weddings, divorce, extramarital affairs, or husband/wife relations. He could then compare male and female attitudes on each part of the theme of marriage.

Graneheim and Lundman (2003) may have used selective coding in their study of interview data on diabetes. They provided readers of their study examples of codes, subcategories, categories, and a theme taken from text narratives about hyperglycemia, offering very explicit examples of each.

During selective coding, major themes or concepts ultimately guide the search process. You reorganize specific themes identified in earlier coding and elaborate more than one major theme. For example, in the working-class tavern study, LeMasters could have examined opinions on marriage to understand both the theme of gender relations and the theme of different stages of the life cycle.

Selective coding   The last stage in coding qualitative data that examines previous codes to identify and select data that will support the conceptual coding categories that were developed.

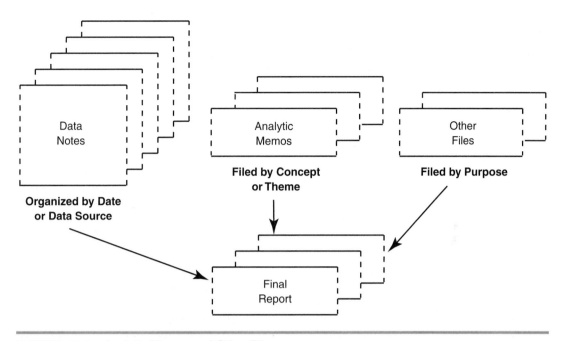

FIGURE 15.1   Analytic Memos and Other Files

Likewise, in the Knights of Labor study, I used temperance to understand the major theme of failed alliances and to understand another theme, sources of division within the movement that were based on ethnic or religious differences among members.

Analytic Memo Writing

In qualitative research, you are always writing notes. You record data in notes, write comments on method or research strategy in notes, and so on. You need to be a compulsive note taker, keep notes organized in files, and create many files with different subjects of the notes: a file on methodological issues (e.g., locations of sources or ethical issues), a file of maps or diagrams, a file on possible overall outlines of a final report or chapter, a file on specific people or events, and so on.

The analytic memo is a special type of note (discussed in Chapter 13).[6] It is a memo or discussion of thoughts and ideas about the coding process that you write to yourself. Each coded theme or concept forms the basis of a separate memo. The memo is a discussion of the concept or theme. Rough theoretical ideas form the beginning of analytic memos.

The analytic memo links concrete data or raw evidence to abstract, theoretical thinking (see Figure 15.1). It contains your reflections on and thinking about the data and coding. Add to the memo and use it as you pass through the data with each type of coding. The memos form the basis for analyzing data in the research report. In fact, rewritten sections from good-quality analytic memos can become sections of the final report.

The tools involved in writing analytic memos are simple: pen and paper, a few notebooks, a stack of file folders, and photocopies of notes. Some researchers use computers, but it is not necessary. There are many ways to write analytic memos; you should develop your own style or method. See Expansion Box 15.3, Suggestions for Analytic Memo Writing (page 516), for concrete suggestions based on the experience of others. Some researchers make multiple copies of notes and then cut them and place various copies into an analytic memo file. This works well if the physical files are large and analytic memos are kept distinct within the file (e.g., on different-colored paper or placed at the beginning of the file). Other researchers list within the analytic memo file locations in the data

EXPANSION BOX **15.3**

Suggestions for Analytic Memo Writing

1. Start to write memos shortly after you begin data collection, and continue memo writing until just before the final research report is completed.
2. Put the date on memo entries so that you can see progress and the development of thinking. This will be helpful when rereading long, complicated memos because you will periodically modify memos as research progresses and add to them.
3. Interrupt coding or data recording to write a memo. Do not wait and let a creative spark or new insight fade away—write it down.
4. Periodically read memos and compare those on similar codes to see whether they can be combined, or whether differences between codes can be made clearer.
5. Keep a separate file for memos on each concept or theme. All memo writing on that theme or concept is kept together in one file, folder, or notebook. Label it with the name of the concept or theme so it can be located easily. It is important to be able to sort or reorganize memos physically as analysis progresses, so you should be able to sort the memos in some way.
6. Keep analytic memos and data notes separate because they have different purposes. The data are

evidence. The analytic memos have a conceptual, theory-building intent. They do not report data but comment on how data are tied together or how a cluster of data is an instance of a general theme or concept.
7. Refer to other concepts within an analytic memo. When writing a memo, think of similarities to, differences between, or causal relationships with other concepts. Note these in the analytic memo to facilitate later integration, synthesis, and analysis.
8. If two ideas arise at once, put each in a separate memo. Try to keep each distinct theme or concept in a separate memo and file.
9. If nothing new can be added to a memo and you have reached a point of saturation in getting any further data on a theme or concept, indicate that in the memo.
10. Develop a list of codes or labels for the memos. This will let you look down the list and see all of the themes of memos. When you periodically sort and regroup memos, reorganize this list of memo labels to correspond to the sorting.

Sources: Adapted from Miles and Huberman (1994:72–76), Lofland and Lofland (1995:193–194), and Strauss (1987:127–129). Also see Lester and Hadden (1980).

notes where a theme appears. Then it is easy to move between the analytic memo and the data. Because data notes contain highlighted or marked themes, it is easy to find specific sections in the data. An intermediate strategy is to keep a running list of locations where a major theme appears in the data and to include copies of a few key sections of the notes for easy reference.[7]

As you review and modify analytic memos, discuss ideas with colleagues and return to the literature with a focus on new issues. Analytic memos may help to generate potential hypotheses, which you can add and drop as needed. These notes also help you develop new themes or modify coding systems.

Outcropping   An aspect of qualitative data analysis that recognizes some event or feature as representing deeper structural relations.

Outcroppings

The specific empirical evidence we gather is related to theoretical ideas and structures that are beneath observable reality. The relationship, modeled in Figure 15.2, shows that data are only samples of everything that happens on the visible, surface level. We use the data to generate and evaluate theories and generalizations and simultaneously assume that beneath the outer surface of reality lie deeper social structures or relationships.

The surface reality that we can easily see only partially reflects what goes on unseen, beneath the surface. To use a term from geology, events on the surface are **outcroppings**.[8] In geology, an outcropping is the part of bedrock that is exposed on the surface for people to see. It is the outward manifestation of central, solid features of the land. Geologists study outcroppings to get clues about what lies beneath the surface.

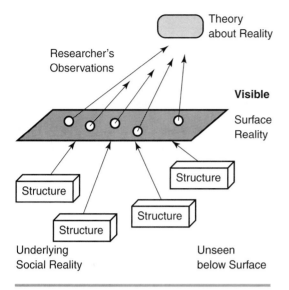

FIGURE 15.2   Theory, Surface Reality, and Underlying Structures

Often we cannot directly observe features of the social world. We cannot observe a deep loving relationship between two people. We can see its outward manifestation only in a kiss, specific deeds of affection, and acts of kindness. Likewise, we cannot directly observe a social structure such as social class. Nonetheless, we see its outward signs in differences in how people act, their career assumptions, their material possessions, and so forth. Sometimes we are misled by outward observation. We analyze data for both the surface level of reality and the deeper structures and forces that may lie unseen beneath the surface.

ANALYTIC STRATEGIES FOR QUALITATIVE DATA

Most qualitative researchers use techniques of coding, memo writing, and looking for outcroppings to some degree. This section introduces you to seven strategies you can use to analyze qualitative data: (1) ideal type, (2) successive approximation, (3) illustrative method, (4) domain analysis, (5) analytic comparison, (6) narrative analysis, and (7) negative case method.

As stated earlier in this chapter, strategies for qualitative data are more diverse, less standardized, and less explicit than in quantitative research. As Mahoney (1999:1192–1193) noted, "The absence of methodological explicitness has made it difficult for many readers to fully understand and appreciate the arguments of [qualitative data] researchers." Some researchers use only one strategy whereas others combine several.

In general, *data analysis* means a search for patterns in data—recurrent behaviors, objects, phases, or ideas. Once you identify a pattern, you need to interpret it in terms of a social theory or the setting in which it occurred. This allows you to move from the particular description of a historical event or social setting to a more general interpretation.

Data take many forms in qualitative research. For example, field research data include raw sense data that a researcher experiences, recorded data in field notes, and selected or processed data that appear in a final report (see Figure 15.3). Data analysis involves examining, sorting, categorizing, evaluating, comparing, synthesizing, and contemplating the coded data as well as reviewing the raw and recorded data.

Ideal Types

One of the most common strategies of qualitative data analysis is Max Weber's *ideal type*. It is a model or mental abstraction of social relations or processes. Ideal types are pure standards against which the data or "reality" can be compared. An ideal type is an artificial device used for comparison because no reality ever fits an ideal type. For example, I develop a mental model of the ideal democracy or an ideal college beer party. These abstractions with lists of characteristics do not describe any specific democracy or beer party; nevertheless, they are useful when applied to many specific cases to see how well each case measures up to the ideal.

Weber's method of ideal types also complements Mills' method of agreement (see analytic comparison). The method of agreement focuses attention on what is common across cases and looks for common causes in cases with a common outcome. By itself, the method of agreement implies a comparison against actual cases. This comparison of cases could also be made against an idealized model. You could develop an ideal type of

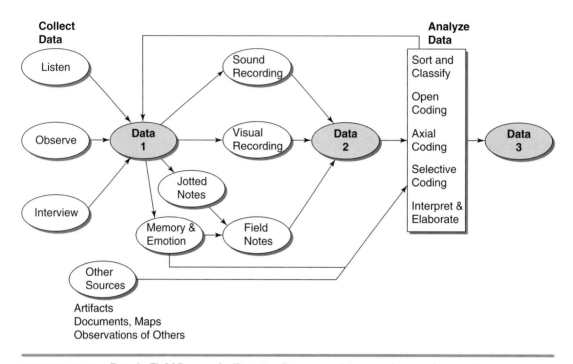

FIGURE 15.3   Data in Field Research (Data 1 = Raw sense data, experiences of researcher;
Data 2 = Recorded data, physical record of experiences; Data 3 = Selected, processed data in a final report)
Source: Adapted from Ellen (1984a:214).

a social process or relationship and then compare specific cases to it.

In qualitative research, we can use ideal types in two ways: contrast contexts and analogy.

1. *Contrast contexts.* Researchers who adopt a strongly interpretive approach may use ideal types to interpret data in a way that is sensitive to the context and cultural meanings of members. Rather than develop hypotheses or create a generalizable theory, they use the ideal type to bring out the specifics of each case and to emphasize the impact of the unique context.[9] As they contrast between contexts, they may choose cases with dramatic contrasts or distinctive features. For example, in *Work and Authority in Industry,* Bendix (1956) compared management relations in very different contexts, Czarist Russia and industrialized England. When comparing contexts, some researchers do not use the ideal type to illustrate a theory in different cases

or to discover regularities. Instead, they accentuate the specific and the unique. In contrast, others use ideal types to show how unique features shape the operation of general processes. As Skocpol and Somers (1980:178) explained:

> "Above all, contrasts are drawn between or among individual cases. Usually such contrasts are developed with the aid of references to broad themes or orienting questions or ideal type concepts. Themes and questions may serve as frameworks for pointing out differences among cases. Ideal types may be used as sensitized devices—benchmarks against which to establish the particular features of each case."

You might use the ideal type to show how specific circumstances, cultural meanings, and the perspectives of specific individuals are central for understanding a social setting or process. The ideal type becomes a foil against which you can highlight unique contextual features.

2. Analogies. We can also use ideal types as analogies to organize qualitative data. An *analogy* is a statement that two objects, processes, or events are similar to each other. We use it to communicate ideas and to facilitate logical comparisons. Analogies transmit information about patterns in data by referring to something that is already known or an experience familiar to the researcher. Analogies can describe relationships buried deep within many details. They are a shorthand method for seeing patterns in a maze of specific events. Making comparison of social processes across different cases or settings are easier.[10] For example, you might say a room went silent after person X spoke and "a chill like a cold gust of air" spread through it. This does not mean that the room temperature dropped or that a breeze was felt, but it succinctly expresses a rapid change in emotional tone. Likewise, you could report that gender relations in society Y were such that women were "viewed like property and treated like slaves." This does not mean that the legal and social relations between genders were identical to those of slave owner and slave. It implies that an ideal type of a slave-and-master relationship would show major similarities to the evidence on relations between men and women if applied to society Y. Ideal type analogies operate as heuristic devices (i.e., a device that helps one learn or see). Analogies are especially valuable when you try to make sense of or explain data by referring to a deep structure or an underlying mechanism.[11] Ideal types do not provide a definitive test of an explanation. Rather, they guide the conceptual reconstruction of the mass of details into a systematic format.

Successive Approximation

Successive approximation is a process that involves making repeated iterations. You cycle through steps, moving toward a final analysis. Over time, or after several iterations, you move from vague ideas and concrete details in the data toward a comprehensive analysis with generalizations. This is similar to coding discussed earlier. You begin with research questions and a framework of assumptions and concepts. You then probe into the data, asking questions of the evidence to see how well the concepts fit the evidence and reveal features of the data. You also create new concepts by abstracting from the evidence and adjusting concepts to fit the evidence better. You then collect additional evidence to address unresolved issues that appeared in the first stage and then repeat the process. At each stage, the evidence and the theory shape each other. The process is called successive approximation because the modified concepts and the model approximate the full evidence and are modified repeatedly to become successively more accurate.

Each pass through the evidence is provisional or incomplete. The concepts are abstract, but they are rooted in the concrete evidence and reflect the context. As the analysis moves toward generalizations that are subject to conditions and contingencies, you can refine generalizations and linkages to reflect the evidence better.[12]

The Illustrative Method

Another method of analysis anchors or illustrates theoretical concepts with empirical evidence. The **illustrative method** applies theory to a concrete historical situation or social setting and organizes data based on theory. Preexisting theory can provide conceptual **empty boxes** that you fill with the empirical evidence.[13] Evidence in the boxes confirms, modifies, or rejects the theory, which can be in the form of a general model, an analogy, or a sequence of steps (see Expansion Box 15.4, Three Variations of the Illustrative Method on page 520).[14]

A single case study with the illustrative method is not a strong test or verification of an explanation because data from one case can illustrate empty boxes from several competing explanations. In addition,

---

Successive approximation   A method of qualitative data analysis that repeatedly moves back and forth between the empirical data and the abstract concepts, theories, or models, adjusting theory and refining data collection each time.

Illustrative method   A method of qualitative data analysis that takes theoretical concepts and treats them as empty boxes to be filled with specific empirical examples and descriptions.

Empty boxes   The conceptual categories in an explanation used as part of the illustrative method.

EXPANSION BOX **15.4**

Three Variations of the
Illustrative Method

1. *Case clarification.* A theoretical model used to illuminate or clarify a specific case or single situation, making the case more understandable by applying theory to it.
2. *Parallel demonstration.* Juxtapositioning of multiple cases (i.e., units or periods) to show that the same theory holds across multiple cases. Paige (1975) used parallel demonstration in a study of rural class conflict. He first developed an elaborate model of conditions that cause class conflict and then provided evidence to illustrate it from Peru, Angola, and Vietnam.
3. *Pattern matching.* This method matches the observations from one case with the pattern or concepts derived from theory or other studies. It allows for partial theory falsification; it narrows the range of possible explanations by eliminating some ideas, variables, or patterns from consideration.

finding evidence to illustrate an empty box using one case does not build a generalized explanation, which requires evidence from numerous cases.

Domain and Scheme Analysis

Cognitive anthropology, which studies relations between human culture and thought, has contributed greatly to qualitative data analysis. It treats cultures as mental creations or the cognitive organization of the physical, material world. Cognitive anthropologists study how people understand and organize material objects, events, and experiences. They note that we make sense of reality based on cognitive categories and that we order events, material life, and ideas based on cultural categories.

Domain analysis   A method of qualitative data analysis that describes and reveals the structure of a cultural domain.

Cultural domain   A cultural setting or site in which people regularly interact and develop a set of shared understandings or "miniculture" that can be analyzed.

Cognitive anthropology seeks to discover and document the rules of behavior or logical systems of thought that we use. To do this, it outlines what people see as culturally expected or appropriate in various situations more than what people actually do. Cognitive anthropology is part of a broader type of data analysis and theorizing that identifies how people or institutions classify and categorize the world, often implicitly. Such classifications then "take on a life of their own" to organize human experience (see Bowker and Leigh-Star, 1999).

Early cognitive anthropologists asked people to arrange colors and plants into categories or to organize relatives into kinship systems. This helped the anthropologists to discover the organizing principles that underlie human social behavior. Cognitive anthropology evolved from studies in the 1950s–1960s (called "ethnoscience") to the study of "folk models" or "domains" in the 1970s, and it later evolved to "scheme analysis." *Schemas* are abstract entities and unconscious models of the world that we use to organize experience. In scheme analysis, we do not view the parts of a culture as either material or symbolic; rather we see culture as being composed of many parts. These parts are not static or integrated into a single whole; instead, we apply schemes to organize the parts. Schemes are cognitive units, such as prototypes, propositions, and cognitive categories. We can analyze the parts of culture to see whether they are shared, examine how they are distributed across people, and look for how the schemas relate to behaviors.

The anthropologist Spradley (1979a, 1979b) developed **domain analysis**. We will examine this system for qualitative data analysis in this section. For Spradley, the basic unit in a cultural setting is a **cultural domain**, an organizing idea or concept. The data analysis system focuses on analyzing domains. Later we can combine domains into taxonomies and broader themes that provide us an interpretation of a cultural scene or social setting.

Cultural domains have three parts: a cover term, included terms, and a semantic relationship. The *cover term* is simply the domain's name. *Included terms* are the subtypes or parts of the domain. A *semantic relationship* tells how the included terms fit logically within the domain. For

CHART 15.1   Forms of Relationships in Cultural Domains

SEMANTIC RELATIONSHIP	EXAMPLE OF USE
Is a type of	A bus *is a type of* motor vehicle [types of vehicles].
Is a part of/is a place in	A tire *is a part of* a car [parts of cars].
Is a way to	Cheating *is a way to* get high grades in school [ways students get high grades].
Is used for	A train *is used for* transporting goods [ways to transport goods].
Is a reason for	High unemployment *is a reason for* public unrest [reasons for public unrest].
Is a stage of	The charge *is a stage of* a battle [stages of battle].
Is a result of/is a cause of	A coal power plant *is a cause of* acid rain [causes of acid rain].
Is a place for	A town square *is a place for* a mob to gather [places where mobs gather].
Is a characteristic of	Wearing spiked, colored hair *is a characteristic of* punks [characteristics of punks].

example, in the domain of a witness in a judicial setting, the cover term is *witness.* Two subtypes or included terms are *defense witness* and *expert witness.* The semantic relationship is "is a kind of." Thus, an expert witness and a defense witness are both types of witnesses. Other semantic relationships are listed in Chart 15.1.

Spradley developed domain analysis by analyzing the argot of members in ethnographic field research, although we can extend it to other qualitative data. For example, Zelizer (1985) studied the changing social value of children by examining documents on attitudes and behaviors toward a child's death in the late nineteenth century. She could have used a domain analysis in which "attitude toward child's death" was a domain, and

the statements of various attitudes she discovered in documents were included terms. The attitudes could be organized by the semantic relationship "is a type of." Spradley identified three types of domains: folk domains, mixed domains, and analytic domains.

1. A **folk domain** contains terms from the argot of the members in a social setting. To use it, you pay close attention to language and usage. The domain uses the relationship among terms from a subculture's argot or in the language of historical actors to identify cultural meaning.
2. A **mixed domain** contains folk terms, but you add your own concepts. For example, types of runners are named by the terminology of runners (e.g., long-distance runner, track people), but you observe other types of people for whom no term exists in the argot and assign them labels (e.g., infrequent visitors, newcomers, amateurs).
3. An **analytic domain** contains terms from the researcher and social theory. They are most helpful when the meanings in a setting are tacit, implicit, or unrecognized by participants. You infer meaningful categories and identify patterns from observations and artifacts and then assign terms to them.

You can construct domains from data notes by proceeding as follows: read your notes and look for common semantic relationships (e.g., is a type of place, is a type of person, is a type of feeling) in order to find the organization of social relationships. Next, identify a list of cover terms. For example, a witness in a judicial setting could be a cover term. Once you have a list of cover terms, you next organize the information from the notes as included

Folk domain   A cultural area based on the argot and categories used by the people being studied in a field site.

Mixed domain   A cultural area that combines the argot and categories of members under study with categories developed by a researcher for analysis.

Analytic domain   A cultural area developed by a researcher using categories or terms that he or she developed to understand a social setting.

Example of Domain Analysis Worksheet

1. Semantic relationship: <u>Strict inclusion</u>
2. Form: <u>X (is a type of) Y</u>
3. Example: <u>An oak (is a type of) tree</u>

INCLUDED TERMS	SEMANTIC RELATIONSHIP	COVER TERM
laundromat, hotel lobby		
motor box, orchard	is a type of ⟶	flop
flophouse, under bridge		
box car, alley		
public toilet, steam grate		
Structural question: Would you call an alley a flop?		

INCLUDED TERMS	SEMANTIC RELATIONSHIP	COVER TERM
trusty, ranger		
bull cook, mopper	is a type of ⟶	jail inmate
head trusty, lockup		
bullet man, sweeper		
lawn man, inmate's barber		
Structural question: Would you call a trusty a type of jail inmate?		

terms. Prepare a worksheet for each domain relationship. The worksheet contains the cover term, the list of included terms, and the semantic relationship (see Example Box 15.1, Example of Domain Analysis Worksheet).

Next you locate your examples of the domain relationship from your notes. The analysis proceeds until all relevant domains have been identified. You then organize the domains by comparing their differences and similarities. Finally, reorganize domains into typologies or taxonomies and reexamine the domains to create new, broader ones that include other domains as included terms (see

Expansion Box 15.5, Summary of Steps in Domain Analysis). The process builds up from specifics in the notes to an overall set of logical relationships.[15]

Analytic Comparison

The British philosopher and theorist John Stuart Mill (1806–1873) developed a logic of comparison that is still widely used today. His method of agreement and method of difference form the basis for **analytic comparison**.[16] We can use the ideal type, successive approximation, the illustrative method, and domain analysis to examine qualitative data from a single case or from multiple cases; however, analytic comparison requires multiple cases. Analytic comparison uses a quasi-experimental approach that combines deductive with inductive theorizing. Basically, you identify many factors for a set of cases, sort through logical combinations of

Analytic comparison   Qualitative data analysis technique that uses the method of agreement and the method of difference to discover causal factors that affect an outcome among a set of cases.

Summary of Steps in Domain Analysis

Domain analysis formalizes six steps found in many types of qualitative data analysis:

1. Read and reread qualitative data notes that are full of details.
2. Mentally repackage the details into a few dozen organizing ideas.
3. Develop new ideas from the notes relying on subjective meanings or organizing ideas.
4. Look for relationships among the ideas and group them based on logical similarity.
5. Organize larger groups by comparing and contrasting the sets of ideas.
6. Reorganize and link the groups together into broader integrating themes.

factors, and compare them across cases. In certain ways, analytic comparison shares features with statistical reasoning more than with quantitative data analysis. It is even used with rational decision-making models, such that particular combinations of factors may make certain choices appear to be rational for people whereas other combinations do not.

Analytic comparison sometimes is called *nominal comparison* because the factors in the qualitative data are often at a nominal level of measurement but they can also be ordinal.[17] You organize data for a set of cases (often three to ten) into many mutually exclusive and exhaustive factors. When analytic comparison is formalized via a computer program (QCA for Qualitative Comparative Analysis, to be discussed later in this chapter), you construct what logicians and mathematicians call a *truth table*. A truth table contains all of the logically possible combinations of factors and outcomes among cases. This information is frequently organized as a chart (see Example Box 15.2, Example of Method of Agreement and Difference: Theda Skocpol's Theory of Revolution on page 524) that looks similar to a Guttman scale (discussed in Chapter 7). Analytic comparison helps you identify the combination of factors, often measured at the nominal level, that are associated with outcomes among a small number of cases.

Ragin (1994b) contrasted case-oriented, analytic comparison with traditional variable-oriented statistical analysis. He noted that case-oriented comparison "sees cases as meaningful but complex configurations of events and structures, and treats cases as singular, whole entities purposefully selected" (p. 300). Analytic comparison involves qualitative data from a small number of cases and adopts an intensive (i.e., a great many in-depth details about a few cases) rather than an extensive (i.e., a few details about a great many cases) data analysis strategy. Moreover, explanation in analytic comparison tends to be interpretative or structural rather than nomothetic. Analytic comparison emphasizes the effect of particular configurations of conditions in cases or context. It allows different causal factors to produce an outcome and considers highly complex outcomes that have qualitative differences.[18]

Method of Agreement. The **method of agreement** focuses attention on what is common across cases. You establish that cases have a common outcome and then try to locate a common cause, although other features of the cases may differ. The method proceeds by a process of elimination. You eliminate features as possible causes if they are not shared across cases that have a common outcome. For example, you look at four cases. All four share two common features, but they also differ in many respects. You look for one or more common causes to explain the common outcome in all cases. At the same time, you eliminate alternative possibilities and identify a few primary causal factors so that you can argue that, despite the differences, the critical similarities exist.

Method of Difference. You can use the **method of difference** alone or in conjunction with the

Method of agreement   A method of qualitative data analysis that compares characteristics that are similar across cases that share a significant outcome.

Method of difference   A method of qualitative data analysis that compares characteristics among cases in which some share a significant outcome but others do not; focuses on the differences among cases.

Example of Method of Agreement and Difference: Theda Skocpol's Theory of Revolution

	CAUSAL FACTOR		OUTCOME
CASE	*State Breakdown*	*Peasant Revolt*	*Revolution?*
France	Yes	Yes	Yes
Russia 1917	Yes	Yes	Yes
China	Yes	Yes	Yes
England	Yes	No	No
Russia 1905	No	Yes	No
Germany	No	No	No
Prussia	No	No	No
Japan	No	No	No

Source: Adapted from Mahoney 1999, Table 1.

method of agreement. The method of difference is usually stronger and is a "double application" of the method of agreement. First, locate cases that are similar in many respects but differ in a few crucial ways. Next pinpoint features in which a set of cases is similar with regard to an outcome and causal features and another set in which the cases differ on outcomes and causal features. The method of difference reinforces information from positive cases (e.g., cases that have common causal features and outcomes) by contrasting it with the negative cases (e.g., cases lacking the outcome and causal features). Thus, you look for cases that have many of the causal features of positive cases but lack a few key features and have a different outcome (see an example of analytic comparison in Example Box 15.3, Analytic Comparison to Study the Success and Failure of Homeless Organizations).

Narrative Analysis

Narrative, as well as the related idea of analyzing a sequence of events, has multiple meanings and is used in anthropology, archaeology, history, linguistics, literary criticism, political science, psychology, and sociology.[19] We encountered narrative in Chapter 14 regarding historical-comparative research in referring to a form of historical writing.

In addition, *narrative* refers to a type of qualitative data, a form of inquiry and data gathering, a way to discuss and present data, a set of qualitative data analysis techniques, and a kind of theoretical explanation. As Griffin (1992a:419) observed, "Narrative is both a rhetorical form and a generic, logical form of explanation that merges theorized description of an event with its explanation."

Narratives as a way to examine the world have several features: a connected relationship among parts, a causal sequence of episodes to form a "plot," a selection that emphasizes important versus less important parts, and a specific mix of time and place. We use narratives for several purposes. They can address the issue of "who are we" as individual people, or they can be public narratives that link us to larger groups, communities, or nations. Some narratives describe social forces that act on us. Finally, *metanarratives* are overall frameworks with master ideas. They organize the thinking of entire populations for generations (e.g., the ideas of progress, industrialization, or globalization (see Somers and Gibson, 1994), Despite its many uses, a narrative shares core elements (see Expansion Box 15.6, Six Features of a Narrative).[20]

Next we briefly consider several types of narrative, and then turn to examine narrative analysis, a type of qualitative data analysis.

EXAMPLE BOX **15.3**

Analytic Comparison to Study the Success and Failure of Homeless Organizations

Cress and Snow (1996) used analytic comparison to analyze field research data (1,500 pages of field notes) that they had gathered on fifteen social movement organizations to help homeless people in eight U.S. cities. They identified four general types of resources—moral, material, information, and human—that the movements could have. They measured a movement organization's resources by whether it had fourteen specific resources, at least two for each of the four types. For example, a specific moral resource was a public statement of support by an external organization, material support included supplies such as paper or telephone service, information support included people who were experienced at

running meetings, and human support included individuals who volunteered time on a regular basis and followed orders.

The researchers classified whether the movement organizations were *viable* (seven were and eight were not), meaning that the organization had survived for one year or more during which meetings were held at least twice a month. They found that nine specific resources were necessary or the organization would fail, as well as combinations of the five other resources. The development of the fifteen organizations followed one of three "paths" based on the combination of the nine necessary and the five "other" resources.

As raw data, a narrative refers to text and practice in social life. Narratives are how people organize their everyday practices and subjective understandings. Narratives appear in oral or written texts to express understandings and the quality of lived experience. They are a form by which people construct identities and locate themselves in what is happening around them at the micro and macro levels.[21]

Narrative text refers to data in a storylike format that people apply to organize and express meaning and understandings in social life. "Schooling, clinics, counseling centers, correctional facilities, hospitals, support groups, and self-help organizations, among many other sites for storing experience, provide narrative frameworks for conveying personal experience through time" (Gubrium and Holstein, 1998:164). We find narratives in stories in novels, poems, myths, epic tales, dramatic performances, film, newspaper or media reports, sermons, oral histories, interviews, and the telling of events of a person's life. More than a form of expression, narrative is also a practice.

Narrative practice is the storylike form through which people subjectively experience and give meaning to their daily lives and their actions. The narrative organizes information, events, and experiences that flow across time. It offers a story line or

plot from a particular point of view. The point of view is that of a motivated actor who expresses intentions. Because a narrative plot is embedded in a constellation of particular details, using it to make universal generalizations is difficult.

In a study of Caracas, Venezuela, Smilde (2003) emphasized the narrative he discovered in the beliefs of local Pentecostal churches. A local group of men used stories from the Pentecostal narrative to reinterpret their life experiences and it shaped their daily lives. The men adapted and used the narrative to reorganize their understandings of ongoing life events, and it gave a new coherence to

EXPANSION BOX **15.6**

Six Features of a Narrative

1. It tells a story or tale (i.e., presenting unfolding events from a point of view).
2. It has a sense of movement or process (i.e., a before and after condition).
3. It contains interrelations or connections within a complex, detailed context.
4. It involves individuals or groups that engage in action and make choices.
5. It has coherence, that is, the whole holds together.
6. It has a temporal sequencing of a chain of events.

events. Thus, the narrative offered by the Pentecostal churches blended a religious conversion with a new self-understanding. The local men used it to reinterpret their past actions and guide their current activities. More than the telling of a story, the church narrative helped them to construct identity and find meaning in life.

Narrative inquiry is a method of investigation and data collection that retains a narrativelike quality from social life (Chase, 2005). Using it as inquiry, we try to capture people's ordinary lived experience without disrupting, destroying, or reducing its narrative character. The inquiry is self-reflective; that is, you place yourself in a flow of events and self-consciously become part of the "plot." The inquiry itself—engaging participant-observers in a field setting or examining historical-comparative documents—appears in narrative terms; that is, as a tale with a sense of movement and a coherent sequence of events about an engaged social actor in a specific context.

Narrative presentation grows out of the interpretative social science approach. Often called *storytelling* (Berger and Quinney, 2004), this mode of presentation blends description, empathetic understanding, and interpretation. It dissolves the space between a researcher and the people being studied. This makes the researcher an integral aspect of description, discussion, and interpretation in a study. Together, researcher and the researched coparticipate in creating/gathering data, and both reflect on the data. Such a process interweaves a researcher's life with the lives of the people being studied. As an individual social actor, the researcher becomes inseparable from the research process and from data presentation. For this reason, a researcher's personal biography and life situation are often included in the story format and in data presentation, discussion, and interpretation. Besides "giving voice" to the people who are studied, the

researcher's voice, presence, and subjectivity appear. The storyteller-researcher is not a disembodied voice or detached observer; rather, he or she is a storyteller whose emotions, personal experiences, and life events become a part of the story that is told.

Narrative analysis, a method for analyzing data and providing an explanation, takes several forms. It is called *analytic narrative, narrative explanation, narrative structural analysis,* or *sequence analysis.*[22] Besides recognizing the core elements of a narrative (listed earlier), you may use narrative analysis techniques to map the narrative and give it a formalized grammar/structure. You can not only recognize the narrative character of social life but also analyze data in a manner that retains and unveils that character. The narrative is an outline or model for organizing data, but it also serves as a type of explanation.

Some researchers apply a few analytic concepts to qualitative data whereas others employ complex logical systems that outline the structure of a narrative, often with the aid of computer software. As you examine and analyze qualitative data for its narrative form and elements—whether it is an individual's life history, a particular historical event, the evolution of an organization over the years, or a macro-level historical process—you focus on events (rather than variables, individuals, or cases) and connections among them. You find that temporal features (e.g., order, pace, duration, frequency) are essential organizing concepts. You soon start to treat the sequence of events itself as an object of inquiry.

Franzosi (1998) argued that once we recognize narrative within data, we try to extract and preserve it without destroying its meaning-making ability or structure. We also look for what Abell (2004:293) called "action linkages"—that is, how a social actor engages in actions to transform one condition or situation into another or, simply put, makes things happen. As we map the structure of a narrative's sequence, the process operates as both a mode of data analysis and a type of explanation. It is an answer to this question: Why do events occur as they do? Some researchers believe that narrative explanations are not causal, but others believe nar-

Narrative analysis   Both a type of historical writing that tells a story and a type of qualitative data analysis that presents a chronologically linked chain of events in which individual or collective social actors have an important role.

rative analysis is a causal explanation although perhaps involving a different type of causality, from that common in a traditional positivist science approach.[23]

Tools of Narrative Analysis. We next examine three analytic tools: path dependency, periodization, and historical contingency.

1. *Path dependency.* The way that a unique beginning can trigger a sequence of events and create a deterministic path is called **path dependency**. The path is apparent in a chain of subsequent events, constraining or limiting the direction of the ongoing events that follow. The outcome explained using path dependency is sensitive to events that occurred very early in the process. Path dependency explanations emphasize how the choices of one period can limit future options, shape later choices, and even accelerate events toward future crises in which options may be restricted.[24]

When building a path dependency explanation, start with an outcome. You then show how the outcome follows from a sequence of prior events. As you trace and demonstrate each event's effect on another, you go backward in the process to initial events or conditions. The initial conditions you identify are a "historical fork in the road" (Haydu, 1998:352).

Explanations that use path dependency assume that the processes that generated initial events (a social relationship) or institution may differ from the processes that keep it going. There may be one explanation for the "starting event" and another for the path of subsequent events. Researchers often explain the starting event as the result of a contingent process (i.e., a specific and unique combination of factors in a particular time and place that may never repeat). In addition, causal processes in one historical period may not operate in another. "There is no good reason to assume that findings from one period support causal claims for another period" (Haydu, 1998:345).

Path dependency comes in two forms: self-reinforcing and reactive sequence.[25] If you use a *self-reinforcing* path dependency explanation, you examine how, once set into motion, events continue

to operate on their own or propel later events in a direction that resists external factors. An initial "trigger event" constrains, or places limits on, the direction of a process. Once a process begins, "inertia" comes into play to continue the process along the same path or track.

A classic example of inertia is the QWERTY pattern of letters on a keyboard. The pattern is inefficient. It takes longer for the fingers to hit keys than alternative patterns do, and it is difficult to learn. Engineers created QWERTY more than a century ago to work with early crude, slow, mechanical typewriters. They designed a keyboard pattern that would slow human typists to prevent the primitive machines from jamming. Later, mechanical typewriters improved and were replaced by electric typewriters and then by electronic keyboards. The old keyboard pattern was unnecessary and obsolete, but it continues to this day. The inertia to use an obsolete, inefficient system is strong. It overwhelms efforts to change existing machinery and people to a more rational, faster keyboard. Social institutions are similar. Once social relations and institutions are created in specific form (e.g., decentralized with many local offices), it is difficult to change them even if they are no longer efficient under current conditions.

The *reactive sequence* path dependency emphasizes a different process. It focuses on how each event responds to an immediately preceding one. Thus, instead of tracing a process back to its origins, it studies each step in the process to see how one influences the immediate next step. The interest is in whether the moving sequence of events transforms or reverses the flow of direction from the initial event. The path does not have to be unidirectional or linear; it can "bend" or even reverse course to negate its previous direction.

We can think of reactive sequence path dependency as a sequence of events that is like a pendulum; it swings back and forth. A single event may

Path dependency   An analytic idea used in narrative analysis to explain a process or chain of events as having a beginning that triggers a structured sequence so that the chain of events follows an identifiable trajectory over time.

set into motion a reaction that changes or reverses the direction of the events that preceded it. For example, as part of the long process of the U.S. civil rights movement, the assassination of Martin Luther King Jr. triggered more vigorous civil rights law enforcement and an expansion of welfare programs. Events had been moving in the direction of increased social equality, reduced discrimination, and expanded legal rights, yet vigorous civil rights enforcement and welfare expansion disrupted existing status and power relations. This created tensions and triggered a backlash by resentful Whites. The White backlash sought to restrict or reverse civil rights law enforcement and cut back social welfare programs. Thus, a reaction to events in the sequence reversed the direction of its path.

2. *Periodization.* In historical-comparative research, we know that historical reality flows as discontinuous stages. To recognize this, researchers may use **periodization** to divide the flow of time in social reality into segments or periods. For example, we may divide 100 years of history into several periods. We break continuous time into several discrete periods that we define theoretically through periodization. Theory helps us to identify what is significant and what is common within periods or between different periods. As Carr (1961:76) remarked, "The division of history into periods is not a fact, but a necessary hypothesis." The breaks between periods are artificial; they are not natural in history, but they are not arbitrary.

You cannot determine the number and size of periods and the breaks between them until you have examined the evidence. You may begin with a general idea of how many periods are necessary to create and what distinguishes them, but you should adjust the number and size of the periods and the location of breaks after you examine the evidence. You may then reexamine the evidence with added

data, adjust the periodization, and so forth. After several cycles of doing this, you get an approximate set of periods across 100 years based on successively theorizing and looking at evidence.

3. *Historical contingency.* **Historical contingency** refers to a unique combination of particular factors or specific circumstances that may not be repeated. The combination is idiosyncratic and unexpected from the flow of prior conditions. As Mahoney (2000a:513) explained, "Contingency refers to the inability of theory to predict or explain, either deterministically or probabilistically, the occurrence of a specific outcome. A contingent event is therefore an occurrence that was not expected to take place." A contingent situation may be unexpected, but once it occurs, it can profoundly influence subsequent events. Because many possible idiosyncratic combinations of events occur, we use theory to identify important contingent events for an explanation.

A *critical juncture* is often a part of historical contingency (see Example Box 15.4, Path Dependency, Critical Junctures, and Historical Contingency). We use it to explain how several viable options may exist at a specific point in time. After one option is selected, many idiosyncratic events converge, which often has a powerful continuing influence. We can combine historical contingency and path dependency.

Roy (1997) combined historical contingency and path dependency to explain the rise of the large corporation in the United States. He argued the preexisting power relations among investors and government officials in the mid-nineteenth century did not cause the large private corporation to rise to prominence. Instead, a unique set of factors at a particular time and place favored its appearance (i.e., historical contingency). Once the institution of the large modern corporation appeared, it encouraged the ascendance of certain groups and fostered new power arrangements. These groups and arrangements then operated to maintain the corporate form of organization. An elite of financiers, wealthy investors, and executives rose in power and benefited from the private corporation form of business organization. They actively supported it through new laws, government regulations, financial relations, and other conditions. The corporate form sustained the growing power and

Periodization Dividing the flow of time in social reality into segments or periods; a field researcher might discover parts or periods in an ongoing process (e.g., typical day, yearly cycle).

Historical contingency An analytic idea in narrative analysis that explains a process, event, or situation by referring to the specific combination of factors that came together in a particular time and place.

EXAMPLE BOX **15.4**
Path Dependency, Critical Junctures, and Historical Contingency

Researchers combine the concepts of path dependency and conjunction in narrative analysis to discover how a specific short-term combination of circumstances can set subsequent events off along a new trajectory, and they try to identify these "critical junctures" or historical turning points. Kiser and Linton (2002) used this idea in their study of France from 1515 to 1789, and noted, "Particular historical turning points change the relationships between variables" (p. 905). They focused on rebellions against taxation in France. Tax revolts occurred in about 20 percent of the years 1515 to 1789. The taxes were primarily gathered to pay for ongoing wars (wars took place in 65 percent of the time period). The Fronde was a set of large-scale revolts (1648 to 1653) that the king's army successfully suppressed. Prior to the Fronde, tax increases and offensive wars regularly generated local revolts, but after it they very rarely did. The theoretical implication is that researchers may find that one set of causal relations are stable and operate for a time period but find little evidence for them in another period. Moreover, researchers might identify a specific event or short-term period that operates as a critical juncture or tipping point after which important relations dramatically shift and then begin to operate differently. It is a pattern of continuity along a path that is interrupted at a juncture and then is redirected to a new trajectory.

privilege of the elites. Thus, the "chance" convergence of particular events at one time selected one form of business organization among alternatives; it was not inevitable. However, once established, this business form set into motion new dynamics that perpetuated it into the future and altered surrounding conditions. It made alternative business forms less viable because it reinforced sociopolitical arrangements and realigned economic power in ways that undermined the alternatives. Thus, the corporate form of organization created a path along which the events that followed in time depended.

The path dependency may be self-reinforcing to continue with inertia along one direction, or particular events might set off a reaction that alters

its direction. Along the flowing sequence of events across time, periodic critical junctures may occur. The process or conditions that were initially set into motion may resist change, or the contingent conditions may be powerful enough to trigger a major change in direction and initiate a new path of events.

Negative Case Method

We usually focus on what is evident in the data, yet we can also study what is *not* explicit in the data, or what did *not* happen. At first, studying what is not there may appear counterintuitive, but an alert observer who is aware of all clues notices what is missing as well as what is there. In the story "Silver Blaze," Sherlock Holmes solved a mystery when he noticed that a guard dog did not bark during the theft of an expensive racehorse, suggesting that the watchdog knew the thief. When what was expected did not occur, it was important information.

Negative evidence takes many forms (see Expansion Box 15.7, Types of Negative Evidence on page 530). It includes silences, absences, and omissions. For example, a field researcher notices that no one of a certain age, race, or gender is present in a social setting. This absence can be very revealing about the nature of the setting. Likewise, you notice some money lying on the floor, yet no one picks it up. The failure to pick it up can be an important clue. Perhaps in a historical-comparative study, you notice that there are no reports of a type of crime (e.g., hate crime, child abuse) in certain locations or times. You may find that the absence of reports or incidences can be equally important as their presence.

The **negative case method** is a way to systematically examine the absence of what is expected.[26] It combines the method of difference from analytic comparison with deviant case analysis. Deviant case analysis focuses attention on a few cases among a great many (including quantitative data sets) that do not conform to the general

> **Negative case method**   A qualitative data analysis that focuses on a case that does not conform to theoretical expectations and uses details from that case to refine theory.

Types of Negative Evidence

1. *Events that do not occur.* Some events are expected to occur on the basis of past experience, but do not. For example, research on the Progressive Era of U.S. history found that large corporations did not veto moderate labor reform legislation. Such a veto was expected after corporations had showed hostility toward labor for years. Instead, they actually encouraged the reform because it would quiet growing labor unrest.

    Likewise, nondecisions may occur when powerful groups do not participate directly in events because their powerful positions shape which issues arise. For example, a city has terrible air pollution, but there is no public action on the problem because "everyone" implicitly recognizes the power of polluting industry over jobs, tax revenue, and the community's economy. The polluting industry does not have to oppose local regulations over pollution because no such regulations are ever proposed.

2. *Events of which the population is unaware.* Some activities or events are not noticed by people in a setting or by researchers. For example, at one time the fact that employers considered a highly educated woman only for clerical jobs was not noticed as an issue. Until societal awareness of sexism and gender equality grew, few saw this practice as limiting the opportunities of women. Another example is that country-western song writers deny writing with a formula. Despite their lack of awareness, a formula is apparent through a content analysis of lyrics. The fact that members or participants in a setting are unaware of an issue does not mean that a researcher should ignore it or fail to look for its influence.

3. *Events the population wants to hide.* People may misrepresent events to protect themselves or others. For example, elites often refuse to discuss unethical behavior and may have documents destroyed or held from public access for a long period. Likewise, for many years, cases of incest went unreported in part because they violated such a serious taboo that incest was simply hushed up.

4. *Overlooked commonplace events.* Everyday, routine events set expectations and create a taken-for-granted attitude. For example, television programs appear so often in conversations that they are rarely noticed. Because most people have a television set and watch TV regularly, only someone who rarely watches television or who is a careful analyst may notice the topic. Or a researcher observes a historical period in which cigarette smoking is common. He or she may become aware only if he or she is a nonsmoker or lives in a period when smoking has become a public health issue.

5. *Effects of a researcher's preconceived notions.* Researchers must take care not to let their prior theoretical framework or preconceived notions blind them to contrary events in a social setting. Strong prior notions of where to look and what data are relevant may inhibit a researcher from noticing other relevant or disconfirming evidence. For example, a researcher expects violent conflict between drug addicts and their children and notices it immediately but fails to see that they also attempt to form a loving relationship.

6. *Unconscious nonreporting.* Some events appear to be insignificant and not worthy of being reported in the mind of a researcher, yet if detailed observations are recorded, a critical rereading of notes looking for negative cases may reveal overlooked events. For example, at first a researcher does not consider company picnics to be important. However, after rereading data notes and careful consideration, he or she realizes that they play an important symbolic role in building a sense of community.

7. *Conscious nonreporting.* Researchers may omit aspects of the setting or events to protect individuals or relations in the setting. For example, a researcher discovers an extramarital affair involving a prominent person but wishes to protect the person's good name and image. A more serious problem is a breach of ethics. This occurs when a researcher fails to present evidence that does not support his or her argument or interpretation of data. Researchers should present evidence that both supports and fails to confirm an interpretation. Readers can then weigh both types of evidence and judge the support for the researcher's interpretation.

Source: Lewis and Lewis (1980).

pattern. We use unusual cases to understand processes or generate new ideas.

Negative case methodology uses detailed knowledge of one particular case that does not conform to what would be expected based on a theory that has supporting evidence from many other cases. You use the single negative case to reexamine the theory, noticing lapses or problems in it. You can then apply insights from the negative case to revise the theory.

For example, Emigh (2003) observed that fifteenth century Tuscany, at the peak of the highly developed northern Italian Renaissance culture, had all preconditions predicted by major theories for producing a rapid "take off" to industrial capitalism: efficient agriculture, well-developed commercial manufacturing, no feudal nobility, a large urban economy, and a stable political organization. Yet it did not happen. Emigh asked why this was a negative case and gained an in-depth knowledge of the one such case. She then uncovered previously unknown factors (about local rural investment) that the major theories had failed to take into account. The types of analytic strategies used in qualitative analysis are summarized graphically in Figure 15.4 (page 532).

OTHER TECHNIQUES

Qualitative research involves using many analysis techniques. Here we briefly consider other techniques to illustrate the variety.

Network Analysis

The idea of social networks was discussed in Chapter 3 with network theory and in Chapter 8 with snowball sampling. In qualitative research, we often "map" the connections among a set of people, organizations, events, or places. Using sociograms and similar mapping techniques, we can discover, analyze, and display sets of relations. For example, in a company, Harry gives Sue orders; Sue and Sam consult and help one another. Sam gets materials from Sandra. Sandra socializes with Mary. We find that networks help us see and understand the structure of complex social relations.[27]

Time Allocation Analysis

Time is an important resource in research. We examine the way people or organizations spend or invest time to reveal implicit rules of conduct or priorities. We document the duration or amount of time devoted to various activities. Similar to the time budget survey discussed in Chapter 10, qualitative research examines the duration or amount of time devoted to activities. An analysis of how people, groups, or organizations allocate the valuable resources they control (such as time, space, money, prestige) can reveal much about their real, as contrasted with officially professed, priorities. Often people are unaware of or do not explicitly acknowledge the importance of an activity on which they spend time. For example, you notice that certain people are required to wait before seeing a manager, but others do not wait. You may analyze the amount of time, who waits, what they do while waiting, and whether they feel waiting is just. Or you document that people say that a certain celebration in a corporation is not important. Yet everyone attends and spends 2 hours at the event. The collective allocation of 2 hours for the celebration during a busy week signals its latent or implicit importance in the culture of the corporation.[28]

Flowchart and Time Sequence

In addition to the amount of time devoted to various activities, we analyze the order of events or decisions. Historical researchers have focused on documenting the sequence of events, but comparative and field researchers also look at their flow or sequence. In addition to when events occur, we can use a decision tree or flowchart to outline the order of decisions to understand how one event or decision is related to others. For example, we can outline an activity as simple as making a cake (see Figure 15.5 on page 533). Researchers applied the idea of mapping out steps, decisions, or events and investigating their interrelationship to many settings. For example, Brown and Canter (1985) developed a detailed flowchart for house-buying behavior. They divided it into fifty steps with a time line and many actors (e.g., involved buyer, financial official, surveyor, buyer's

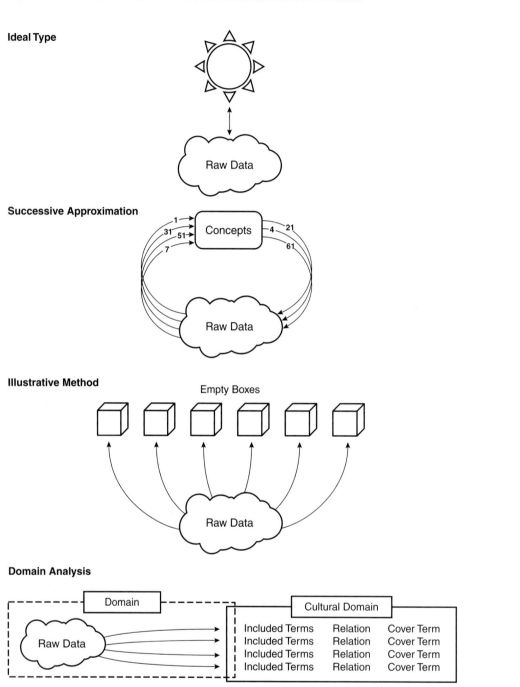

FIGURE 15.4 **Summary of Analytic Strategies Used in Qualitative Data Analysis**

Analytic Comparison

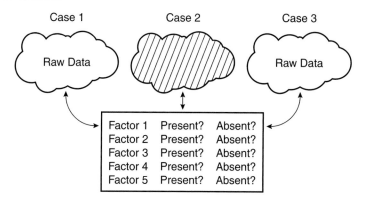

Narrative Analysis

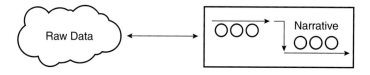

Negative Case Method

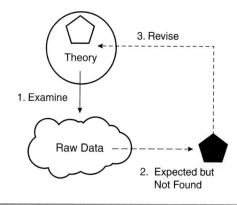

FIGURE 15.4   (Continued)

attorney, advertising firm/realtor, seller, seller's attorney).[29]

Multiple Sorting Procedure

Multiple sorting is a technique similar to domain analysis found in field research or oral history. Its purpose is to discover how people categorize their experiences or classify items into what is similar or different. Cognitive anthropologists and psychologists often use a multiple sorting procedure. You can use multiple sorting to collect, verify, or analyze data. Here is how it works. You give the people you are studying a list of terms, photos, places, names of people, and so on, and ask them to organize the lists into categories or piles. They use categories of their

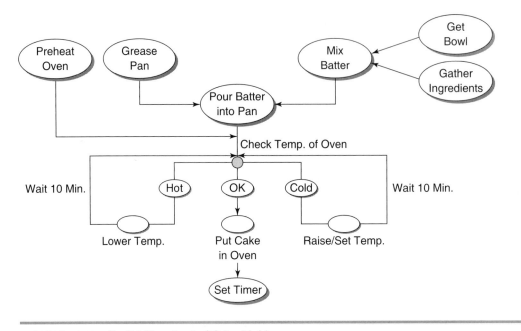

FIGURE 15.5   Partial Flowchart of Cake Making

own devising. Once sorted, you ask about the criteria used. You next give the people the items again and ask them to sort them in other ways that they may think of them. There is a similarity to Thurstone scaling (discussed in Chapter 7) in that people sort items, but here, the number of piles and types of items differ. The purpose of the sorting is not to create a uniform scale; rather, it is to discover how people understand the world. Canter et al. (1985:90) provide the example of a gambler who sorted a list of eight gambling establishments five times. Each sort had three to four categories. One of the sorts was organized based on "class of casino" (high to low). Other sorts were based on "frills," "size of stake," "make me money," and "personal preference." By examining the various sorts, you see how people organize their social reality.[30]

Diagrams

Qualitative research often presents data analysis as visual representations, such as diagrams and charts. Diagrams and charts help organize ideas and assist in systematically investigating data. They also communicate results to readers. We can use spatial or temporal maps (also see Chapter 13), typologies (see Chapter 3), and sociograms. Thus, in a study of Little League baseball, Fine (1987) used sociograms to show the social relations among players. In addition to taxonomies, maps, and lists, we use flowcharts, organizational charts, causal diagrams, and various lists and grids to advance analysis and illustrate findings (see Figure 15.6).

Maps

Both quantitative and qualitative researchers place data on maps to help them see spatial relations and to supplement or reinforce results from other data analyses. For example, Ballen and Richardson (2002) used maps of France and United States to examine data on geographic patterns in suicide rates and to support theories of social integration and imitation from Émile Durkheim. Kiser and Linton (2002) presented a map of France with sites of rebellions marked in their study (discussed in Example Box 15.4). Villarreal (2002, 2004) used a map of Mexico in his study of violence and social-political change. In their study of differences in local hate crime law enforcement, McVeigh and colleagues (2003) offered a map of

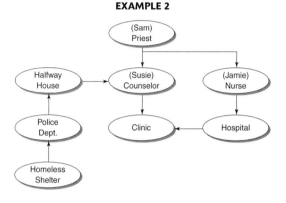

EXAMPLE 1

Person	Worked before College	Part-Time Job in College	Pregnant Now	Had Own Car
John	Yes	Yes	N/A	No
Mary	Yes	DK	No	Yes
Martin	No	Yes	N/A	Yes
Yoshi	Yes	No	Yes	Yes

DK = don't know, N/A = not applicable

EXAMPLE 2

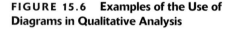

FIGURE 15.6   Examples of the Use of Diagrams in Qualitative Analysis

counties across the United States. Myers and Caniglia (2004) used a map of regions in the United States in a study of whether newspapers reported protest events. In their study of the endurance of distinct regional cultures, Griswold and Wright (2004) labeled areas of a U.S. map. Maps can be helpful in analyzing and presenting data to bolster an explanation; however, as a visual representation of information, they can also be misleading, so we should use them with care (see Monmonier, 1996).

Software for Qualitative Data

Since the mid-1960s, researchers have used computer technology to generate tables, graphs, statistical tests, and charts to analyze numerical data. By contrast, qualitative research has used computer technology only since the mid-1980s.[31] If you enter notes into a word processing program, you can quickly search for words and phrases. It is a small step to adapt such searching to data coding or linking codes to analytic

memos. Word processing can also help you revise and move codes and parts of field notes.

Software has been specifically created for qualitative data analysis and new computer programs are continuously being developed or modified. Most come with highly detailed and program-specific user manuals, so the review here does not go into detail about specific software. It covers only the major approaches to qualitative data analysis at this time.

Text Retrieval.   Some programs perform searches of text documents similar to the search function in word processing software. The specialized text retrieval programs are faster and have the capability of finding close matches, slight misspellings, similar sounding words, and synonyms. For example, if you look for the keyword *boat,* the program might also tell you whether any of the following appeared: *ship, battleship, frigate, rowboat, schooner, vessel, yacht, steamer, ocean liner, tug, canoe, skiff, cutter, aircraft carrier, dinghy, scow, galley, ark, cruiser, destroyer, flagship,* and *submarine.* In addition, some programs identify the combination of words or phases using logical terms (*and, or, not*) in what are called *Boolean searches* (named after George Boole, 1815–1864). For example, you may search long documents to identify where the keywords *college student, drinking,* and *smoking* occur within four sentences of one another and only when the word *fraternity* is not present in the block of text. This Boolean search uses *and* to seek the intersection of *college student* with either of the other two behaviors that are connected by the logical term *or,* whereas the logical search word *not* excludes situations in which the term *fraternity* appears.

Most programs show a keyword or phrase and the surrounding text. The programs may also permit you to write separate memos or add short notes to the text. Some programs count the keywords found and give their location. Most programs create a very specific index for the text based only on the terms of interest.

Textbase Managers.   Textbase managers are similar to text retrieval programs. The key difference is their ability to organize or sort information about search results. Many programs create subsets of text data that help you compare and sort notes by a key idea or to add factual information. For example, to detailed notes on interviews you can add the date and length of the interview, the gender of interviewee, the location of the interview, and so on. You can then sort and organize each interview or part of the interview notes using a combination of keywords and added information.

In addition, some programs have *hypertext* capability linking terms to other information, so when you click on one term it opens a new screen that has related information. You can identify keywords or topics and then link them to text. For example, in a field research study, you want to examine the person Susan and the topic of hair (including haircuts, hairstyles, hair coloring, and hats or hair coverings). You can use hypertext to connect all places that Susan's name appears to all discussions of hair. By clicking on Susan's name, one block of text quickly jumps to another in the notes, allowing you to see where Susan and the hair topic appear together.

Some text-based manager software creates cross-tabulation or scatterplot cross-classifications from information in text documents. For example, students keep journals on a course. They write their feelings about each day using one of four categories (boring, stimulating, challenging, or creative). The students also describe the major activities of each day (e.g., group work, discussion, videotape viewing, lecture, or demonstration). You can cross-classify student feelings by activity. By adding other information (e.g., male or female, academic major), you can learn whether students with different characteristics felt differently about the activities and see whether the feelings changed with the topic being presented in class.

Code-and-Retrieve Programs. We often assign codes or abstract terms to qualitative data (i.e., text field notes, interview records, and video or audiotape transcripts). Code-and-retrieve programs let us attach codes to lines, sentences, paragraphs, and blocks of text. The programs permit the use of multiple codes for the same data. In addition to attaching codes, most programs also help to organize the codes. For example, a program can help create outlines or "trees" of connections (e.g., trunks, branches, and twigs) among the codes, and among the data to which the codes refer. The program rearranges the text data based on the codes used and the relations among the indicated codes.

Code-Based Theory Builders. Researchers using qualitative research are often interested in the evaluation and generation of theory. To do this, code-based theory builders require first assigning codes to the data. The programs provide ways for manipulating or drawing contrasts and comparisons among the codes. The relationships among the codes then become the basis for testing or generating a theory. The types of relations created among the codes may vary by program. A program may permit "if-then" logical relations. For example, Corsaro and Heise (1990) described how they coded field research data on young children into separate events. They then examined the logical sequence and relations among the events to search for principles or a "grammar" of implicit rules. They looked for rules that guided the sequencing, combination, or disconnection among events. The computer software ETHNO asks for logical connections among the events (e.g., time order, necessary precondition, co-occurrence) and then shows the pattern among events.

In contrast to other qualitative programs, code-based theory builders have a powerful ability to manipulate codes to reveal patterns or show relations in data that are not immediately evident. It becomes easier for researchers to compare and classify categories of data.

Qualitative comparative analysis (QCA) is an analytic strategy and type of software that uses Boolean logic or algebra.[32] Charles Ragin created QCA in 1987. An entire system of logical, mathematic-like relations has become the basis for computer software and digital electronics. It includes set theory, binary relations, logic gates, Venn diagrams, and truth tables. The logic's principle lets you organize concepts into sets. For example, when you search a computer database, you often include a keyword and Boolean operators *or, and,* and *not.*

Qualitative comparative analysis (QCA) Qualitative data analysis and computer software based on Boolean logic that examines combinations of explanatory factors and various outcome measures to help a researcher identify complex, contingent causal relations.

QCA's strength is its ability to analyze multiple conjunctural causation. This implies that a combination of conditions produces the outcome, and different combinations of conditions may produce the same outcome. Depending on the context (conjuncture), a particular condition can have different impacts on the outcome. Together, QCA recognizes that different causal paths may yield the same outcome. QCA as a method of analysis and software works as an iterative process. It requires active engagement by the researcher. As Rihoux (2003: 354) describes it:

> In a nutshell, the researcher must first produce a raw data table in which each case displays a specific combination of conditions (with 0 or 1 values) and an outcome (with 0 or 1 values). The software then produces a truth table that displays the data as a list of configurations. A configuration is a given combination of some conditions (each one receiving a 1 or 0 value) and an outcome (receiving a 1 or 0 value). A specific configuration may correspond to several observed cases, and different cases may display the same configuration. Then the key step of the analysis is Boolean minimization—that is, reducing the long Boolean expression (the long description that is expressed by the truth table) to the shortest possible expression (the minimal equation) that unveils the causal regularities in the data. It is then up to the researcher to interpret this minimal equation.

QCA can help to analyze the characteristics of several cases and apply the method of difference and method of agreement. It performs the logical computations to identify common and unique characteristics among a set of cases. The algebra is not difficult, but it can be time consuming and subject to human error without the program (see Example Box 15.5, Example of QCA).

Conceptual Network Builders. This category of programs helps to build and test theory by presenting graphic displays or networks. The displays do more than diagram data; they help organize a researcher's concepts or thinking about the data. The programs use nodes, or key concepts, that the researcher identifies in data. They then show links or relationships among the nodes. Most programs give graphic presentations with boxes or circles that are connected by lines with arrows. The output looks similar to a flowchart diagram with a web or network of connections among concepts. For example, the data might be a family tree in which the relationships among several generations of family members are presented. Relations among family members (X is a sibling of Y, Z is married to Y, G is an offspring of X) can be used to discuss and analyze features of the network.

Event-Structure Analysis

Many qualitative researchers organize data chronologically in a narrative analysis. **Event-structure analysis (ESA)** is used to organize the sequence of events in ways that facilitate seeing causal relations. Researchers first used the method and ETHNO, a computer program used with it, to analyze field research data, but it can also be used for historical data. ESA first organizes the data into events and then places them into a temporal sequence.[33]

ESA facilitates narrative analysis. It helps to outline a set of links between events that happened. You separate what *had* to happen before other events from what *could* have happened. The computer program makes you answer questions about the logical relationships among events. For example, a situation has events A, B, C, X, and Y. You are asked: Must event A occur prior to X causing Y (i.e., is A a necessary precondition for the X:Y causal relationship?) or would X affect Y without A? If it is required, A must recur before X will again affect Y. This process forces you to explain whether the causal relation between two events is a unique and one-time relationship or a recurring relationship that can be repeated indefinitely or for a limited number of cycles.

Event-structure analysis has limitations. It does not provide the theory or causal logic; you must supply that. ESA creates only maps or diagrams (with the computer program) that make it easier for you to see relationships. When you decide about logically

---

Event-structure analysis (ESA) Qualitative data analysis often conducted with computer software that forces a researcher to specify the links among a sequence of many events; it clarifies causal relationships by asking whether one event logically had to follow another or just happened to follow it.

Example of QCA

Roscigno and Hodson (2004) used QCA to analyze qualitative data from workplaces. They were interested in worker resistance including the collective response in the form of union activity and strikes as well as individualized forms such as sabotage, theft, and work avoidance. They asked whether grievances and resistance unfold as a function of workplace organization or are caused by interpersonal mistreatment on the shop floor. The data (eighty-two workplace ethnographies) represented the population of available ethnographic evidence on organizations. As the authors noted (p. 18), "There is good reason to expect that organizational structure and social relations condition one another and, thus, have contingent effects on worker grievances and resistance strategies."

QCA forced Roscigno and Hodson to specify and focus on variables deemed theoretically important. QCA had theoretical rigor, a case-oriented logic, and specification of potentially complex, conditional configurations. It helped to identify typologies that denote unique combinations of attributes in the data. By coding the qualitative data, the authors identified six workplace conditions as explanatory factors: bureaucracy, good organization, conflict, abuse, union presence, and a history of strikes. They created a "truth table" with each possible confirmation of the factors, each coded 1 = present, or 0 = absent. The configurations denoted the minimum number of factors needed to cover all positive, negative, and contradictory cases in the data. The researchers also identified six possible outcomes or forms of worker resistance: strikes, social sabotage, work avoidance, play dumb, absenteeism, and theft. Based on the various combinations revealed in QCA, the authors identified three types of workplaces each with a type of worker resistance: contentious workplaces,

cohesive workplaces, and unorganized workplaces. Contentious workplaces had high levels of all forms of resistance, cohesive workplaces showed low levels of resistance, and unorganized workplaces largely had individual acts of resistance. See the following excerpt of the researchers' truth table. (Note that only the first three of thirty-six possible combinations are shown).

EXPLANATORY MEASURES

B = Bureaucracy. Workplace is bureaucratically organized with operational control of daily procedures in written rules.

G = Good Organization. There is coherence and integration of production practices.

C = Conflict. Ongoing conflict between workers and supervisors is common.

A = Abuse. Verbal, emotional, or physical abuse by supervisor of individual employees occurs.

U = Union Presence. Union representation exists in the particular workplace.

H = History of Strikes. Workplace has experienced strikes in the past.

RESISTANCE MEASURES

S = Strikes. There was a strike during the period of observation.

SS = Social Sabotage. There is undermining of superiors through mocking and ridicule.

AV = Work Avoidance. Avoiding work and/or work tasks occurs.

PD = Play Dumb. Workers pretend not to understand particular job tasks or organizational procedures.

AB = Absenteeism. Absenteeism is a response to workplace problems.

T = Theft. Stealing by workers while on the job takes place.

EXPLANATORY MEASURES (ALL POSSIBLE CONFIGURATIONS)						NUMBER OF CASES	RESISTANCE MEASURES WITHIN EACH CONFIGURATION					
B	G	C	A	U	H		S	SS	AV	PD	AB	T
0	0	1	1	0	0	2	0	2	2	1	2	0
1	0	0	1	1	0	4	1	2	3	1	3	1
1	1	1	1	1	0	1	0	0	0	0	0	0

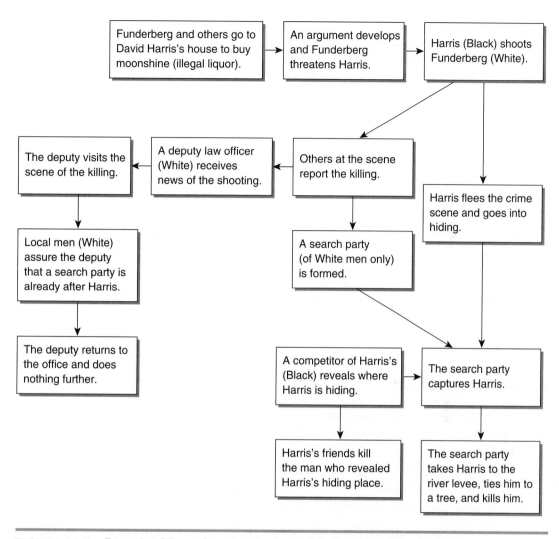

FIGURE 15.7 **Example of Event-Structure Analysis of the Lynching of David Harris**
Source: Adapted from Griffin (1993).

possible relations, ESA clarifies a chain of events and highlights those that might have been different. ESA does not have a place for enduring social structures that frame the action of event sequences.

Griffin's (1993) analysis of a lynching illustrates ESA. Based on many oral histories, a book, and newspaper reports, he reconstructed the sequence of events surrounding the lynching of David Harris in Bolivar County, Mississippi, in April 1930. After answering many yes/no questions about possible linkages among a series of events and analyzing the

linkages, Griffin was able to conclude that the critical factor was the inaction of the local deputy who could have stopped the process. An abbreviated summary of the ESA diagram is presented in Figure 15.7.

CONCLUSION

This chapter discussed how we analyze qualitative data. In many respects, qualitative data are more difficult to deal with than data in the form of numbers. Numbers have mathematical properties that allow us to use statistical procedures. Qualitative analysis requires more effort to read and reread data notes, reflect on what is read, and make comparisons based on logic and judgment.

Most forms of qualitative data analysis involve coding and writing analytic memos. Both are labor-intensive and time-intensive efforts. They require reading data carefully and thinking about them seriously. In addition, the chapter presented methods we used for the analysis of qualitative data. The

techniques presented in this chapter are only a sample of the full range of qualitative data analysis techniques. The chapter discussed also the importance of thinking about negative evidence and events that are not present in the data.

This chapter ends the section of the book on research design, data collection, and data analysis. Social research also involves preparing reports on a research project, which we examine in the next and final chapter.

KEY TERMS

analytic comparison
analytic domain
axial coding
cultural domain
domain analysis
empty boxes
event structure analysis (ESA)
folk domain

historical contingency
illustrative method
method of agreement
method of difference
mixed domain
narrative analysis
negative case method
open coding

outcropping
path dependency
periodization
qualitative comparative
   analysis (QCA)
selective coding
successive approximation

REVIEW QUESTIONS

1. Identify four differences between quantitative and qualitative data analysis.
2. How does the process of conceptualization differ for qualitative and quantitative research?
3. How does data coding differ in quantitative and qualitative research, and what are the three types of coding used by a qualitative researcher?
4. What is the purpose of analytic memo writing in qualitative data analysis?
5. Describe *successive approximation.*
6. What are the *empty boxes* in the illustrative method, and how are they used?
7. What is the difference between the method of agreement and the method of difference? Can a researcher use both together? Explain why or why not.
8. What are the parts of a domain, and how are they used in domain analysis?
9. What are the major features of a narrative?
10. Why is it important to look for negative evidence, or things that do not appear in the data, for a full analysis?

NOTES

1. See Miles and Huberman (1994) and Ragin (1987). These should not be confused with statistical techniques for "qualitative" data (see Haberman, 1978). These are sophisticated statistical techniques (e.g., logit and log

linear) for quantitative variables in which the data are at nominal or ordinal levels. They are better labeled as techniques for categorical data.

2. Sprague and Zimmerman (1989) discuss the importance of an explicit theory.

3. See Hammersley and Atkinson (1983:174–206) for a discussion of questions.

4. See Boyatzis (1998), Lofland and Lofland (1995: 192–193), Miles and Huberman (1994:57–71), Sanjek (1990:388–392), and Wolcott (1994) for additional discussions of coding.

5. See also Horan (1987) and Strauss (1987:25) for multiple indicator measurement models with qualitative data.

6. For more on memoing, see Lester and Hadden (1980), Lofland and Lofland (1995:193–197), Miles and Huberman (1994:72–77), and Strauss (1987:107–129).

7. Also see Barzun and Graff (1970:255–274), Bogdan and Taylor (1975), Lofland and Lofland (1984:131–140), Shafer (1980:171–200), Spradley (1979a, 1979b), and Schatzman and Strauss (1973:104–120) on notes and codes.

8. See Fetterman, 1989:68.

9. See Skocpol (1984) and Skocpol and Somers (1980).

10. For a discussion of analogies and models, see Barry (1975), Glucksmann (1974), Harré (1972), Hesse (1970), and Kaplan (1964).

11. For a discussion of the importance of analogies in social theory, see Lloyd (1986:127–132) and Stinchcombe (1978).

12. For more on successive approximation and a debate over it, see Applebaum (1978a), McQuaire (1978, 1979), P. Thompson (1978), Wardell (1979), and Young (1980).

13. For a discussion of empty boxes, see Bonnell (1980) and Smelser (1976).

14. For a discussion of the illustrative method, see Bonnell (1980) and Skocpol (1984). Bogdan and Taylor (1975:79) describe a similar method.

15. See Coffrey et al. (2002) for an example of domain analysis.

16. For a discussion of methods of difference and agreement, see Ragin (1987:36–42), Skocpol (1984), Skocpol and Somers (1980), and Stinchcombe (1978:25–29).

17. See Mahoney (1999) on a nominal comparison.

18. See Griffin (1993) and Mahoney (1999).

19. On various uses see Abbott (1995) and Franzosi (1998)

20. The six core elements are derived from the following: Abell (2001, 2004), Abbott (1995, 2001), Büthe (2002), Franzosi (1998), Griffin (1992, 1993), Gubrium and Holstein (1998), Haydu (1998), Mahoney (2000), Pedriana (2005), Sewell (1992, 1996), and Stryker (1996).

21. On narrative as a condition of social life, see Abbott (2001) and Somers (1994).

22. Abell (2004:288) remarked, "Although the term narrative and cognate concepts . . . are widely used . . . no settled definition is yet established." Some of the terms used include: analytic narrative (Pedriana, 2005), causal narrative (Sewell, 1996), comparative narrative (Abell, 2001), event structural analysis (Griffin, 1993), historical narrative (Mahoney, 2000b), narrative explanation (Abell, 2004), sequence analysis (Abbott, 1995), and structural analysis of narrative (Franzosi, 1998).

23. On debates about causality in narrative analysis and narrative as explanation, see Abbott (2001:290), Abell (2004), Büthe (2002), Griffin (1993), and Mahoney (2000b). For debate about the narrative, see Haydu (1998), Mahoney (1999), Sewell (1996), and Stryker (1996). Researchers such as Goldthrope (1991, 1997) and Lieberson (1991) question the narrative approach whereas Goldstone (1997) and Rueschemeyer and Stephens (1997) defend its utility.

24. See Haydu (1998:353).

25. Mahoney (2000a) gives a detailed description of the path dependency method and provides many examples of its use. Altman (2000) provides a discussion from the economics literature. Also see Blute (1997) and Pedriana (2005).

26. See Becker and Geer (1982) and Emigh (1997) on the negative case method. Blee and Billings (1986) discuss analyzing "silences" in ethnographic or historical text.

27. See Sanjek (1978) and Werner and Schoepfle (1987a).

28. See Gross (1984) and Miles and Huberman (1994:85, 119–126).

29. See Lofland and Lofland (1995:199–200) and Werner and Schoepfle (1987a:130–146).

30. See Canter et al. (1985) and Werner and Schoepfle (1987a:180–181).

31. See Dohan and Sanchez-Jankowski (1998) and Weitzman and Miles (1995) for a comprehensive review of software programs for qualitative data analysis. Also see Fielding and Lee (1991) and Richards and Richards (1994).

32. See http://www.u.arizona.edu/~cragin/fsQCA/software.shtml.

33. For a more in-depth discussion of event-structure analysis, see Abbott (1992), Griffin (1993), Griffin and Ragin (1994), Heise (1991), and Issac et al. (1994).

CHAPTER 16

Writing the Research Report and the Politics of Social Research

The Research Report	**Objectivity and Value Freedom**
The Politics of Social Research	**Conclusion**

> *But that's our business: to arrange ideas in so rational an order that another person can make sense of them. We have to deal with that problem on two levels. We have to arrange the ideas in a theory or narrative, to describe causes and conditions that lead to the effects that we want to explain, and do it in an order that is logically and empirically correct. . . . Finally, we want our prose to make the order we have constructed clear. We don't want imperfection in our prose to interfere with our readers' understanding. These two jobs converge and cannot be separated.*
>
> —Howard Becker, *Writing for Social Scientists*, p. 133

In the previous chapters, we have examined how to design studies, gather data, and analyze the data, yet a study is not complete until we share the results with others. Communicating results and describing in detail how you conducted a study are critical last steps in the research process. The form is usually a written report. Chapter 1 stressed how the norm of communalism emphasizes that we make public how we conducted research and its complete findings. Chapter 5 discussed how to locate previous studies in the scholarly literature. This chapter focuses on writing a research report.

Conducting a study and reporting its results can create controversy. As noted in Chapter 5, doing research can raise contentious ethical issues that largely involve protecting research participants, maintaining integrity while doing research, and dealing with pressure from research sponsors. Social research also involves political issues that can be even more contentious. The politics of social research can affect the possibility of conducting a study and disseminating findings from it as well as how others may try to misuse research findings.

This chapter combines two topics: writing a research report and the politics of social research. The writing requires mastering relatively straightforward, noncontroversial rules and skills. The issues in the politics of social research are not straightforward, however. They include issues such as the freedom to conduct a study and to prepare the report without interference from powerful social groups. There are rules for writing reports and codes of ethics, but there is no code or rules for research politics.

Social research may be imperfect, but its ultimate goal is to discover knowledge, expand understanding, and seek truth. We want to investigate all topics and fully share the method and findings of research with the scientific community and beyond without barriers. Political controversies develop when powerful groups or institutions try to block inquiry, prevent the free flow of new knowledge, place limits on the search for truth, or misuse and selectively ignore research findings. The groups or institutions usually do so to advance their own nonscientific goals and purposes.

The first part of this chapter examines how to write both quantitative and qualitative reports. Research reports require you to take the writing process very seriously. You must explain both how you conducted a study and its findings. The second part of the chapter focuses on the politics of social research. We consider attempts by powerful groups or governments to limit what researchers study, how they conduct a research study, and where they disseminate results. We end by considering the concepts of objectivity and value freedom.

THE RESEARCH REPORT

Reasons for Writing a Report

After you complete a study or a significant phase of a large project, it is time to communicate the findings to others through a research report. You can learn much about writing a research report by reading many published articles and taking a course in scientific and technical writing.

A research report is a written document (or oral presentation based on a written document) that communicates the methods and findings of a research project to others. It is more than a summary of findings; it is a detailed record of the research process.

Do not wait until the research is finished before thinking about the report; you must think ahead to the report and keep careful records while conducting research. In addition to findings, the report includes the reasons for initiating the project, a description of the project's steps, a presentation of data, and a discussion of how the data relate to the research question or topic.

The report tells others what you, the researcher, did and what you discovered. It is a way of disseminating knowledge. As noted in Chapter 1, the report plays a significant role in binding together the scientific community. Other reasons for writing a report are to fulfill a class or job assignment, to meet an obligation to an organization that paid for the study, to persuade a professional group to address specific aspects of a problem, or to tell the general public about findings. Communicating with the public is rarely the primary method for communi-

cation of scientific results; it is usually a second stage of dissemination that comes after communicating with other researchers.

The Writing Process

Your Audience. Professional writers say you must always know for whom you are writing. This is because communication is most effective when it is tailored to a specific audience. You should write a research report differently, depending on whether the primary audience is an instructor, students, professional social scientists, practitioners, or the general public. It goes without saying that the writing should be clear, accurate, and well organized.

Instructors assign a report for different reasons and may place requirements on how to write it. In general, instructors want to see the writing and the organization that reflect clear, logical thinking. Student reports should demonstrate a solid grasp of substantive and methodological concepts. A good way to do this is to use technical terms explicitly *when appropriate;* they should not be used excessively or incorrectly.

When writing for students, you need to define technical terms and label each part of the report. The discussion should proceed in a logical, step-by-step manner with many specific examples. Use straightforward language to explain how and why you conducted the various steps of the research project. One strategy is to begin with the research question and then structure the report as an answer.

Scholars do not need definitions of technical terms or explanations of why you used standard procedures (e.g., random sampling). They are most interested in how the research advances theory or previous findings in the literature. They want a condensed, detailed description of the research design. They pay close attention to how you gathered data, measured variables, and analyzed the data. Scholars desire a compact, tightly written but extensive section on data analysis with a meticulous discussion of results.

Practitioners prefer a short summary of how you conducted the study and the results presented in a few simple charts and graphs. They are less interested in details of the study design, measurement, data collection, or findings. They like to see an outline of alternative paths of action implied by results with the practical outcomes of pursuing each path. It is important for writers to caution practitioners not to overgeneralize from the results of one study. Although few practitioners demand it, you should place the details of research design and results in an appendix to the report.

When writing for the public, you want to use simple language, provide concrete examples, and focus on the practical implications of findings for current social problems. Do not include details of research design or results, and be careful not to make unsupported claims when writing for the public. Informing the public is an important service that can help nonspecialists make better judgments about public issues.

Style and Tone. We write research reports in a narrow range of styles with a distinct tone. The purpose of the report is to communicate the research method and findings clearly, directly, and honestly.

Style refers to the types of words the writer chooses and the length and form of sentences or paragraphs he/she uses. *Tone* is the writer's attitude or relation to the subject matter. For example, an informal, conversational style (e.g., colloquial words, idioms, clichés, and incomplete sentences) with a personal tone (e.g., these are my feelings) is appropriate for writing a letter to a close friend but not for research reports. The style for research reports is to be formal and succinct (saying a lot in few words). The tone expresses some distance from the subject matter; it is professional and serious. Field researchers sometimes use an informal style and a personal tone, but this is the exception. Moralizing and flowery language should be avoided; the primary goal is to inform, not to advocate a position, to moralize, or to entertain.

A research report should be objective, accurate, and clear. Check and recheck details (e.g., page references in citations) and fully disclose how you conducted the study. If readers detect carelessness in writing, they may question the research itself. The details of a research project can be complex, and such complexity means that confusion is always a danger so writing clearly is essential. The way to achieve clear writing is to have clear thinking, which means carefully rethinking the research problem and design, explicitly defining terms, writing with short declarative sentences, and limiting conclusions to what the evidence supports.

Organizing Thoughts. Writing does not happen magically or simply flow out of a person when he or she puts pen to paper (or fingers to keyboard) although some people have such an illusion. Rather, writing is hard work that requires diligence and involves following a sequence of steps that ultimately result in a final product. Writing a research report is not radically different from other types of writing. Although some steps differ and the level of complexity may be increased, most of what a good writer does when writing a long and complex letter, a poem, a set of instructions, or a short story applies to writing a research report.

First, a writer needs something about which to write. The "something" in the research report includes the topic, research question, design and measures, data collection techniques, results, and implications. With so many parts to write about, good organization is essential. The most basic tool for organizing writing is the outline. Outlines help a writer to ensure that all ideas are included and that the relationship among them is clear. Outlines are made up of topics (words or phrases) or sentences. Most of us are familiar with the basic form of an outline (see Figure 16.1).

Outlines can help the writer, but they can become a barrier if you use them improperly. An outline is simply a tool to help organize ideas. It helps (1) to put ideas in a sequence (e.g., what will be said first, second, and third), (2) to group related ideas together (e.g., these are similar to each other but differ from those), and (3) to separate the more general, or higher-level, ideas from more specific ideas, and the specific ideas from very specific details.

Some students believe that they need a complete outline before writing and that once an outline is prepared, deviations from it are impossible. Few good writers begin with a complete, detailed outline. The initial outline is often sketchy because until they write everything down, it is impossible to put all ideas in a

---

FIGURE 16.1   Form of Outline

I. First major topic	One of the most important
A. Subtopic of topic I	Second level of importance
1. Subtopic of A	Third level of importance
a. Subtopic of 1	Fourth level of importance
b. Subtopic of 1	"
(1) Subtopic of b	Fifth level of importance
(2) Subtopic of b	"
(a) Subtopic of (2)	Sixth level of importance
(b) Subtopic of (2)	"
i. Subtopic of (b)	Seventh level of importance
ii. Subtopic of (b)	"
2. Subtopic of A	Third level of importance
B. Subtopic of topic I	Second level of importance
II. Second major topic	One of the most important

---

sequence, group them together, or separate the general from the specific. For most writers, new ideas develop or become clearer during the process of writing.

A beginning outline may differ from the final outline by more than degree of completeness. The process of writing may not only reveal or clarify ideas for the writer but also stimulate new ideas, new connections between ideas, a different sequence, or new relations between the general and the specific. In addition, the process of writing may stimulate a reanalysis or reexamination of the literature or findings. This does not mean that beginning all over is necessary. Rather, it means the writer needs to keep an open mind to new insights and be candid about all aspects of the research project.

Back to the Library. You should be familiar with the literature before beginning a project, but most likely, you will need to return to the literature after completing data collection and analysis. This happens for several reasons. First, time has passed between the beginning and the end of a research project, and new studies may have been published. Second, after completing a research project, you will know better what is or is not central to the study and may have new questions in mind when rereading studies in the literature. Finally, when writing the report, you may find that your notes are not complete enough or a detail is missing in the citation of a reference

source. The visit to the library after data collection is less extensive and more selective or focused than the one you conducted at the beginning of research.

When writing a research report, most of us discard some of the notes and sources that we gathered prior to completing the research project. This does not mean that the initial library work and literature review were a waste of time and effort. We can expect that some of the notes (e.g., 25 percent) we took before completing the project will become irrelevant as the project gains focus. We do not include notes on the literature or references that are no longer relevant because they distract from the flow of ideas and reduce clarity.

Returning to the library to verify and expand references can focus your ideas. It also helps avoid plagiarism. **Plagiarism**, a serious form of cheating, is the use of another person's exact words without properly citing the original source. Many universities expel students who are caught engaging in it. If a professional ever plagiarizes in a scholarly journal, the entire scholarly scientific peer community treats the person as if he or she had committed a very serious offense.[1] Take careful notes and identify the

> **Plagiarism**   Theft of another person's ideas by using his or her exact words and the ideas without properly documenting the original source.

exact source of phrases or ideas to avoid unintentional plagiarism. Cite the sources of both directly quoted words and paraphrased ideas. For direct quotes, include the location of the quote with page numbers in the citation.

It is wrong to use another's written words and fail to give credit, but paraphrasing is less clear. **Paraphrasing** does not use another's exact words, but restates another's ideas in your own words while condensing. We regularly paraphrase, and good paraphrasing requires us to really understand what we are paraphrasing. This means that we do more than replace another's words with synonyms; paraphrasing is borrowing an idea, boiling it down to its essence, and giving credit to the source.[2]

The Writing Process

Writing is a process. The only way to learn to write is by writing.[3] It takes time and effort, and it improves with practice. There is no single correct way to write, but some methods are associated with good writing. The process has three steps:

1. *Prewriting.* Prepare to write by arranging notes on the literature, making lists of ideas, outlining, completing bibliographic citations, and organizing comments on data analysis.
2. *Composing.* Get your ideas onto paper as a first draft, a complete report from beginning to end, not a few rough notes or an outline, by freewriting, drawing up the bibliography and footnotes, preparing data for presentation, and forming an introduction and conclusion.
3. *Rewriting.* Evaluate and polish the report by improving coherence, proofreading for

Paraphrasing   Restating an author's ideas in one's own words and giving proper credit to the original source.

Prewriting   An early step in the writing process during which a writer organizes notes, makes lists of ideas, outlines thoughts, and makes certain that bibliographic citations are complete.

Freewriting   An initial step in the writing process in which the writer tries to get his or her ideas down on paper as quickly as possible, not worrying about grammar or spelling.

mechanical errors, checking citations, and reviewing voice and usage.

Many people find that getting started is difficult. Beginning writers often jump to the second step and end there, which results in poor-quality writing. **Prewriting** means that you begin with a file folder full of notes, outlines, and lists. You think about the form of the report and audience. Thinking time is important. It often occurs in spurts over a period of time before the bulk of composing begins.

Some people become afflicted with a strange ailment when they sit down to compose writing: a temporary inability to write known as *writer's block.* The mind goes blank, the fingers freeze, and panic sets in. Writers from beginners through experts occasionally experience it. If you do, calm down and work on overcoming it (see Expansion Box 16.1, Suggestions for Ending Writer's Block).

Numerous writers begin to compose by **freewriting,** a process of writing down everything you can as quickly as it enters into your mind. Freewriting establishes a link between a rapid flow of ideas in the mind and writing. When you freewrite, you do not stop to reread what you wrote, you do not ponder the best word, you do not worry about correct grammar, spelling, or punctuation. You just put ideas on paper as quickly as possible to get and keep the creative juices or ideas flowing. You can later clean up what you wrote.

Writing and thinking are so intertwined that it is impossible to know where one ends and the other begins. This means that if you plan to sit and stare at the wall, the computer output, the sky, or whatever until all thoughts become totally clear before beginning, you will rarely get anything written. The thinking process can be ignited during the writing itself.

Rewriting. Perhaps one in a million writers is a creative genius who can produce a first draft that communicates with astounding accuracy and clarity. For the rest of us mortals, writing means that rewriting—and rewriting again—is necessary. For example, Ernest Hemingway is reported to have rewritten the end of *Farewell to Arms* thirty-nine times.[4] It is not unusual for a professional researcher

EXPANSION BOX **16.1**
Suggestions for Ending Writer's Block

1. *Begin early.* Do not procrastinate or wait until the last minute. Beginning early not only gives you time to come back to the task but also reduces the tension because you have time to write a poor-quality first draft that can be improved upon. Shafer (1980:205) chided, "Writing is hard work, and the excuses authors find for postponing it are legendary." Set yourself a deadline for a first draft that is at least a week before the final deadline, and keep it!
2. *Take a break and then return.* Some writers find that if they take a walk, get a snack, read a newspaper, and come back to the task a half hour later, the block is gone. Small diversions, if they remain small and short term, can help on occasion.
3. *Begin in the middle.* You do not have to begin at the beginning. Begin in the middle and just start writing, even if does not seem to be directly relevant. It may be easier to get to your topic once the writing/thinking process is moving.
4. *Engage in personal magic rituals.* Some people have unusual habits or rituals that they engage in before writing (e.g., washing dishes, clearing a desk, sharpening pencils). These can serve as mental triggers to help you get started. Do what gets you started writing.
5. *Break the writing into small parts.* Do not feel that you have to sit down and complete the writing task as a whole. Begin with pieces that come easily to you and stitch together the pieces later.
6. *Do not expect perfection.* Write a draft, which means that you can throw away, revise, and change what you wrote. It is always easier to revise a rough draft than to create perfect writing the first time.

---

to rewrite a report a dozen times. Do not become discouraged. If anything, rewriting reduces the pressure; it means you can start writing soon and get out a rough draft that you can polish later. Plan to rewrite a draft at least three or four times.

Rewriting can help you express yourself with increased clarity, smoothness, and precision and an economy of words. When rewriting, the focus is on clear communication, not pompous or complicated language. As Leggett et al. (1965:330) stated, "Never be ashamed to express a simple idea in simple language. Remember that the use of complicated language is not in itself a sign of intelligence."

Rewriting means slowly reading what you have written and, if necessary, read it out loud to see whether it sounds right. It is a good idea to share your writing with others. Professional writers have others read and criticize their writing. New writers soon learn that friendly, constructive criticism is very valuable. Sharing your writing with others may be difficult at first. It means exposing your written thoughts and encouraging criticism of them, yet the purpose of the criticism is to clarify writing, and the critic is doing you a favor.

Rewriting involves two processes: revising and editing. **Revising** is inserting new ideas, adding supporting evidence, deleting or changing ideas, moving sentences around to clarify meaning, or strengthening transitions and links between ideas. **Editing** is cleaning up the more mechanical aspects of writing, such as spelling, grammar, usage, verb agreement and tense, sentence length, and paragraph organization. When you rewrite, go over a draft and revise it brutally to improve it. This is easier if some time passes between a writing draft and rewriting it. Phrases that seemed satisfactory in a draft may look fuzzy or poorly connected after a week or two (see Expansion Box 16.2, Suggestions for Rewriting on page 548).

Even if you have not acquired typing skills, it is a good idea to type, or print out if you use a word processor, at least one draft before the final draft

> **Revising** Correcting process that is part of rewriting, in which a writer adds ideas or evidence and deletes, rearranges, or changes ideas to improve clarity and better communicate meaning.
>
> **Editing** A step in the writing process, part of rewriting, in which a writer cleans up and tightens the language, checks grammar (e.g., verb agreement, usage), adjusts sentence length, and reorganizes paragraphs to improve communication and strengthen style.

EXPANSION BOX **16.2**
Suggestions for Rewriting

1. *Mechanics.* Check grammar, spelling, punctuation, verb agreement, verb tense, and verb/subject separation with each rewrite. Remember that each time new text is added, new errors can creep in. Mistakes are not only distracting but also weaken the confidence readers place in the ideas you express.

2. *Usage.* Reexamine terms, especially key terms, when rewriting to see whether you are using the exact word that expresses your intended meaning. Do not use technical terms or long words unnecessarily. Use the plain word that best expresses meaning. Get and use a thesaurus, an essential reference tool, like a dictionary, that contains words of similar meaning and can help you locate the exact word for a meaning you want to express. Precise thinking and expression require precise language. Do not say *average* if you use the *mean.* Do not say *mankind* or *policeman* when you intend *people* or *police officer.* Do not use *principal* for *principle.*

3. *Voice.* Writers of research reports often make the mistake of using the passive instead of the active voice. It may appear more authoritative, but passive voice obscures the actor or subject of action. For example, the passive, *The relationship between grade in school and more definite career plans was confirmed by the data,* is better stated as the active, *The data confirm the relationship between grade in school and more definite career plans.* The passive, *Respondent attitude toward abortion was recorded by an interviewer* reads easier in the active voice: *An interviewer recorded respondent attitude toward abortion.* Also avoid unnecessary qualifying language, such as *seems to* or *appears to.*

4. *Coherence.* Sequence, steps, and transitions should be logically tight. Try reading the entire report one paragraph at a time. Does the paragraph contain a unified idea? A topic sentence? Is there a transition between paragraphs within the report?

5. *Repetition.* Remove repeated ideas, wordiness, and unnecessary phrases. Ideas are best stated once, forcefully, instead of repeatedly in an unclear way. When revising, eliminate deadwood (words that add nothing) and circumlocution (the use of several words when one more precise word will do). Directness is preferable to wordiness. The wordy phrase, *To summarize the above, it is our conclusion in light of the data that X has a positive effect of considerable magnitude on the occurrence of Y, notwithstanding the fact that Y occurs only on rare occasions,* is better stated, *In sum, we conclude that X has a large positive effect on Y but Y occurs infrequently.* As Selvin and Wilson (1984) warned, verbose and excessive words or qualifiers make it difficult to understand what is written.

6. *Structure.* Research reports should have a transparent organization. Move sections around as necessary to fit the organization better, and use headings and subheadings. A reader should be able to follow the logical structure of a report.

7. *Abstraction.* A good research report mixes abstract ideas and concrete examples. A long string of abstractions without the specifics is difficult to read. Likewise, a mass of specific concrete details without periodic generalization also loses readers.

8. *Metaphors.* Many writers use metaphors to express ideas. Phrases such as *the cutting edge, the bottom line,* and *penetrating to the heart* are used to express ideas by borrowing images from other contexts. Metaphors can be an effective method of communication, but they need to be used sparingly and with care. A few well-chosen, fresh metaphors can communicate ideas quickly and effectively; however, their excessive use, especially overused metaphors (e.g., *the bottom line*), is a sloppy, unimaginative method of expression.

---

because it is easier to see errors and organization problems in a clean, typed draft. Feel free to cut and paste, cross out words, or move phrases on the printed copy.

Good typing skills and an ability to use a word processor are extremely valuable when writing reports and other documents. Serious professionals

find that the time they invest in building typing skills and learning to use a word processor pays huge dividends later. Word processing makes editing much easier. You can also check spelling, find synonyms in an attached thesaurus, and check grammar. You cannot rely on the computer program to do all the work, but it makes writing easier. The speed and ease that a word processor offers is so dramatic that few people who become skilled at using one ever go back to writing by hand or typing.

One last suggestion: Rewrite the introduction and title after you complete a draft so that they accurately reflect what you said.[5] Titles should be short and descriptive, communicating the topic and the major variables to readers. They can describe the type of research (e.g., "an experiment on . . .") but should not have unnecessary words or phrases (e.g., "an investigation into the . . .").

The Quantitative Research Report

The principles of good writing apply to all reports, but the parts of a report differ depending on whether the research is quantitative or qualitative. Before writing any report, read reports on the same type of research for models.

We begin with the quantitative research report. The sections of the report roughly follow the sequence of steps of a research project.[6]

Abstract or Executive Summary. Quantitative research reports begin with a short summary or abstract. The length of an abstract varies; it can be as few as fifty words (this paragraph has seventy-five words) or as long as a full page. Most scholarly journal articles place abstracts on the first page of the article. The abstract has information on the topic, the research problem, the basic findings, and any unusual research design or data collection features.

Reports of applied research that are written for practitioners have a longer summary called the **executive summary**. It contains more detail than an article abstract and includes the implications of research and major recommendations made in the report. Although it is longer than an abstract, an executive summary rarely exceeds four or five pages.

Abstracts and executive summaries serve several functions: For the less interested reader, they tell what is in a report; for readers looking for specific information, they help the reader determine whether the full report contains important information. Readers use the abstract or summary to screen information and decide whether they will read the entire report. It gives serious readers who intend to read the full report a quick mental picture of the

report, which makes reading the report easier and faster.

Presentation of the Problem. The first section of the report defines the research problem. It can be placed in one or more sections with titles such as "Introduction," "Problem Definition," "Literature Review," "Hypotheses," or "Background Assumptions." Although the subheadings vary, the first section should include a statement of the research problem and a rationale for what is being examined. It also provides an explanation of the significance of and a background to the research question. The first section explains the significance of the research by showing how different solutions to the problem lead to different applications or theoretical conclusions. Introductory sections frequently include a context literature review and link the problem to theory. Introductory sections also define key concepts and present conceptual hypotheses.

Description of the Methods. The next section of the report describes how you designed the study and collected the data. It goes by several names (e.g., "Methods," "Research Design," or "Data") and may be subdivided into other parts (e.g., "Measures," "Sampling," or "Manipulations"). It is the most important section for evaluating the methodology of the project. The section answers several questions for the reader:

1. What type of study (e.g., experiment, survey) was conducted?
2. Exactly how were data collected (e.g., study design, type of survey, time and location of data collection, experimental design used)?
3. How were variables measured? Are the measures reliable and valid?
4. What is the sample? How many participants or respondents are involved in the study? How were they selected?

Executive summary A synopsis of a research project's findings placed at the beginning of a report for an applied, nonspecialist audience; is usually a little longer than an abstract.

5. How were ethical issues and specific concerns of the design handled?

Results and Tables. After describing how data were collected, methods of sampling, and measurement, you then present the data. This section presents the data but does not discuss, analyze, or interpret them. Some researchers combine the "Results" section with the next section called "Discussion" or "Findings."

You must make choices in how to present the data.[7] When analyzing the data, you look at dozens of univariate, bivariate, and multivariate tables and statistics to get a feel for the data. This does not mean that you include every statistic or table in a final report. Instead, select the minimum number of charts or tables that fully inform the reader. Use data analysis techniques to summarize the data and test hypotheses (e.g., frequency distributions, tables with means and standard deviations, correlations, and other statistics).

You want to give a complete picture of the data without overwhelming the reader by providing data in excessive detail or presenting irrelevant data. Readers can make their own interpretations. Detailed summary statistics belong in appendixes.

Discussion. In the discussion section, give the reader a concise, unambiguous interpretation of its meaning. The discussion is not a selective emphasis or partisan interpretation; rather, it is a candid discussion of what is in the results section. The discussion section is separated from the results so that a reader can examine the data and arrive at different interpretations. Grosof and Sardy (1985:386) warned, "The arrangement of your presentation should reflect a strict separation between data (the record of your observations) and their summary and analysis on one hand, and your interpretations, conclusion, and comment on the other."

Beginning researchers often find it difficult to organize a discussion section. One approach is to organize the discussion according to hypotheses, discussing how the data relate to each hypothesis. In addition, you should discuss unanticipated findings, possible alternative explanations of results, and weaknesses or limitations.

Conclusions. You should restate the research question and summarize findings in the conclusion. Its purpose is to summarize the report, and it is sometimes titled "Summary." The only sections after the conclusion are the references and appendixes. The references section contain only sources that you referred to in the text or notes of the report. Appendixes, if used, usually contain additional information on methods of data collection (e.g., questionnaire wording) or results (e.g., descriptive statistics). The footnotes or endnotes in quantitative research reports expand or elaborate on information in the text. Use them sparingly to provide secondary information that clarifies the text. They should not distract from the flow of the reading.

The Qualitative Research Report

Compared to quantitative research, most people find writing a report on qualitative research more difficult. There are fewer rules and less structure. Nevertheless, the purpose is the same: to communicate the research process and the data collected through the process. Quantitative reports present hypotheses and evidence in a logically tight and condensed style. By contrast, qualitative reports tend to be longer, and book-length reports are common (see Expansion Box 16.3, Why Qualitative Research Reports Are Longer).

Field Research. Field research reports rarely follow a fixed format with standard sections, and theoretical generalizations and data are not separated into distinct sections.[8] Generalizations are intertwined with the evidence, which takes the form of detailed description with frequent quotes. Although there is no one way to write a field research report (see Expansion Box 16.4, Four Genres and Rhetorical Forms of Ethnographic Writing), most follow some general pattern.

Field research reports generally try to balance data presentation and analysis to avoid an excessive separation of the two, called the **error of segregation**. This occurs when we separate data

Error of segregation A mistake made when writing qualitative research in which a writer creates too large a separation between empirical details and abstract theorizing.

EXPANSION BOX **16.3**

Why Qualitative Research Reports Are Longer

1. The data in a qualitative report are more difficult to condense in comparison with a quantitative report. Data are in the form of words, pictures, or sentences and include many quotes and examples.
2. Qualitative researchers try to create a subjective sense of empathy and understanding among readers in addition to presenting factual evidence and analytic interpretations. Detailed descriptions of specific settings and situations help readers better understand or get a feel for settings. Researchers attempt to transport the reader into the subjective worldview and meaning system of a social setting.
3. Qualitative researchers use less standardized techniques of gathering data, creating analytic categories, and organizing evidence than quantitative researchers. The techniques applied may be particular to individual researchers or unique settings. Thus, researchers explain what they did and why because it has not been done before.
4. Exploring new settings or constructing new theory is a common goal in qualitative research. The development of new concepts and examination of relationships among them adds to the length of reports. Theory flows out of evidence, and detailed descriptions demonstrate how the researcher created interpretations.
5. Qualitative researchers may use more varied writing styles, which increases length. They have more freedom to employ literary devices to tell a story or recount a tale.

---

from analysis so much that readers cannot see the connection.[9]

The tone of field research reports tends to be less objective and formal and more personal than quantitative studies. Often, they are in the first person (i.e., using the pronoun *I*) because the researcher was directly involved in the setting, interacted with the people studied, and was the measurement "instrument." The researcher's decisions or indecisions, feelings, reactions, and personal experiences are essential features of the field research process.

Field research reports often face more skepticism than quantitative reports do. This makes assessing an audience's demands for evidence and establishing credibility essential. The key is to give readers enough evidence so that they believe the recounted events and accept the interpretations as plausible. In field research, readers expect a degree of selective observation, so the critical issue is whether other observers could reach the same conclusion had they been in the same field site and examined the same data.[10]

In presenting field research evidence, authors often have a data reduction dilemma. Most data are in the form of an enormous volume of field notes, but the authors cannot directly share all the observations or recorded conversations with the readers. For example, in their study of medical students, *Boys in White,* Becker et al. (1961) had about 5,000 pages of single-spaced field notes. Field researchers often include only about 5 percent of their field notes in a report as quotes. The remaining 95 percent is not wasted; there is just no room for it. Thus, writers select quotes and indirectly convey the rest of the data to readers. A field research report has no fixed organization to follow, although a literature review often appears near the beginning. There are many acceptable organizational forms. Lofland (1976) suggests the following:

1. Introduction
   a. Most general aspects of situation
   b. Main contours of the general situation
   c. How materials were collected
   d. Details about the setting
   e. How the report is organized
2. The situation
   a. Analytic categories
   b. Contrast between situation and other situations
   c. Development of situation over time
3. Strategies
4. Summary and implications

Devices for organizing evidence and analysis also vary a great deal.[11] For example, writers can organize the report in terms of a *natural history* (see Chapter 13), an unfolding of events as the writer discovered them, or as a chronology, following the developmental cycle or career of an aspect of the setting or people in it. Another possibility is to

Four Genres and Rhetorical Forms of Ethnographic Writing

Adler and Adler (2008) identified four genres and rhetorical forms used in field research-ethnographic writing: classical, mainstream, postmodern, and public ethnography.

The *classical* style is the oldest and is found in scholarly journals devoted to field research. It stresses readability and accessibility, to avoid overloading readers with a high-level vocabulary or long and complex sentences. Most often, the author will use an active rather than a passive voice and write simply to make the report accessible to an educated lay audience. The report starts with a topic or theoretical issue and a short literature review. The methods section is a personal story of the researcher's journey through the settings, the people met, and the relationships forged. Authors describe what they encountered in the field and how they gathered data in a specific time and place. Readers often get a subjective view and a sense that the researcher was "really there." Sometimes a discussion of data analysis is presented, but many classical works do not offer a detailed analysis. The data section frequently follows a progression: present a specific concept, next elaborate on it, and then offer data description. The data often are in a narrative form. The conclusions advance knowledge by adding to, going beyond, and/or modifying existing theory and often involve a shift to a more formal style. Writers often organize the report around building theory from the ground up.

Mainstream styles appear in mainstream scholarly journals. Because peer reviewers in these publications may be unfamiliar with the qualitative/interpretive sociology, they may push a positivist orientation onto ethnographic writers. As with the classical style, the author portrays a world accessed by gathering in-depth, firsthand, naturalistic data. However, the mainstream style frames the discussion differently than the classical style does. The mainstream style has more distance from readers and more of a tone of expert authority than the classical style. The introduction tends to be tighter, stiffer, and more formal than in the classical style. Instead of accessibility, the emphasis is conformity to standard social scientific rhetoric, often mimicking the positivist, quantitative research report. The introduction sections tend to be much longer than those in the classical style. In these sections,

authors define terms and provide a different type of literature review, which is longer and in more depth and often has multiple subsections. The extensive literature review implies that knowledge advances in a uniform, linear progression and builds on prior scholarly contributions that are consistent with a more positivist orientation. The methods section is also longer than in the classical style. It may elaborate to justify the use of qualitative methods and to explain their epistemological bases. Researchers rarely discuss personal connections to their topics, participants, and settings because mainstream audiences may interpret such statements as evidence of bias. Authors often present the research process as if it was preplanned rather than inductive and emergent. They use the passive voice with a tone of objectivity and neutrality. There is often a discussion of specific techniques or computer programs used instead of the vague, impressionistic discussion of method found in the classical style. The data or results section of mainstream style tends to have a subheading and often includes charts or tables of some form. The form of rhetoric removes the researcher and presents data in a detached form.

A *postmodern* style has been used only since the 1990s and tends to appear in a few scholarly journals that share a postmodern orientation. Compared to the classical style, it rejects attempts at objectivity, principles of validity and reliability, and notions of researcher authority. Instead, it rests on a belief that there is no fixed or single standard for doing or writing field research. To the extent the postmodern style has principles, they are ones of substantive empirical contribution, aesthetic merit, reflexivity, impact on the audience, and credibility of a person's lived experience. Writing leans toward a humanistic or artistic form. Often it is a story-telling narrative written in a colloquial manner with a plot, a moral, and a point to make. The subjective voice of the researcher-author is common with a high level of self-exposure and self-awareness or reflectivity. The postmodern style may have first-person accounts of the author's experiences interspersed with semi-detached discussions of those personal experiences. The primary or only source of data may be the author's personal experiences. Often the postmodern style flows in a nonlinear, unpredictable manner with frequent shifts in tone and direction and no

EXPANSION BOX **16.4**

(continued)

clearly outlined structure or organization to the over-all report.

The *public ethnography* style is the most recent form. It self-consciously tries to bring the social science findings to an educated lay audience. Its goal is to educate the public about social scientific knowledge. It usually relies on ethnographic or field research because this form of study is most easily accessible to the public. The style is found in book-length studies designed to be sold in the non-fiction sections of bookstores, appear as editorials in

op-ed pages of national newspapers, or as articles in more high-brow, intellectual magazines. In a book-length version, the author tries to draw in readers using visual maps, photographs, and rich descriptions. The discussions of methods are short and informal. There may not be a literature review. Authors relegate the methodology or literature citations to footnotes or appendices. The writing style is novelistic with very long quotes and very detailed descriptions. Theory is either absent or very limited in this style.

organize the report as a **zoom lens**, that is, to begin broadly and then increasingly focus narrowly on a specific topic. Statements can move from universal statements about all cultures, to general statements about a specific culture, to statements about a specific cultural scene, to specific statements about an aspect of culture, to specific statements about specific incidents.[12]

Researchers often organize the field research report around key concepts and themes. They may choose between using abstract analytic themes and themes taken from the people studied. The latter gives readers a vivid description of the setting and displays knowledge of the language, concepts, categories, and beliefs of the people being written about.[13]

Field researchers discuss their method in the report, but its location and form vary. One technique is to interweave a description of the setting, the means of gaining access, the role of the researcher, and the participant/researcher relationship into the discussion of evidence and analysis. This is intensified if the writer adopts what Van Maanen (1988:73) called a "confessional" style of writing. A chronological, zoom lens, or theme-based organization allows placing the data collection method near the beginning or the end. In book-length reports, writers usually put methodological issues in a separate appendix.

Many field research reports contain transcriptions of tape recordings, maps, photographs, or

charts illustrating analytic categories. To supplement the data, we usually place them near the data discussion that they complement. Photographs give a visual inventory of the settings described in the text and present their meanings in the terms of the people studied. For example, field research articles have appeared in the form of all photographs, a script for a play, and a documentary film.[14]

Direct, personal involvement in the intimate details of a social setting heightens ethical concerns. We write in a manner that protects the privacy of those we study and help prevent the publication of a report from harming the people we studied.[15] We usually change the names of members and exact locations in field reports. Personal involvement in field research leads many researchers to include a short autobiography. For example, in the appendix to *Street Corner Society* the author, William Foote Whyte (1955), gave a detailed account of the occupations of his father and grandfather, his own hobbies and interests, the jobs he had held, how he ended up going to graduate school, and how his research had been affected by his getting married.

Zoom lens   A method of organizing a field research report in which the author begins broadly with a topic and then increasingly focuses it more narrowly and specifically.

Historical-Comparative Research. There is no single way to write a report on historical-comparative research. Most frequently, researchers "tell a story" or describe details in general analytic categories. The writing usually goes beyond description and includes limited generalizations and abstract concepts.

Few historical-comparative (H-C) reports describe their methods in detail. Explicit sections of the report or an appendix describing methods are uncommon. Occasionally, a book-length report has a bibliographic essay that describes major sources used. More often, numerous detailed footnotes or endnotes identify sources and other evidence. For example, a twenty-page report on quantitative or field research typically has five to ten notes, whereas an H-C research report of equal length may have forty to sixty notes.

Historical-comparative reports can include photographs, maps, diagrams, charts, and tables of statistics throughout. They appear in the section that discusses the evidence to which they relate. The charts, tables, and so forth supplement a discussion and offer readers a feel for the places and people being described. These graphics can appear in conjunction with frequent quotes. Few H-C reports include tests of specific hypotheses as quantitative research does. Instead, authors try to build a web of meaning or descriptive detail and organize the evidence in a way to convey interpretations and generalizations.

Two basic modes of organizing historical-comparative research reports are by topic and chronological order. Most writers mix the two types. For example, they can organize information chronologically within topics or organized by topic within chronological periods. They occasionally use other forms of organization by place, individual person, or major events. If the report is truly comparative, the writer has additional options, such as making comparisons within topics (see Expansion Box 16.5, Features to Consider in the Historical-Comparative Research Report).[16]

Some H-C researchers mimic the quantitative research report and use quantitative research techniques in writing their studies. They extend quantitative research rather than adopt a distinct historical-comparative research method. Their reports follow the model of a quantitative research report.

You read about narrative analysis in Chapter 15. Researchers who use this strategy often adopt a narrative style of report writing. They organize data chronologically and try to "tell a story" around specific individuals and events.

The Research Proposal

What Is the Proposal? A research proposal is a document that presents a plan for a project to reviewers for evaluation. It can be a supervised project submitted to instructors as part of an educational degree (e.g., a master's thesis or a Ph.D. dissertation), or it can be a research project proposed to a funding agency. Its purpose is to convince reviewers that the researcher is capable of successfully conducting the proposed research project. Reviewers have more confidence that a planned project will be successfully completed if the proposal is well written and organized and demonstrates careful planning.

The proposal is similar to a research report, but is written before beginning research. A proposal describes the research question and its importance, offers a literature review, and provides a detailed account of the techniques and methods that will be used and why they are appropriate.

A quantitative research proposal has most of the parts of a research report: a title, an abstract, a problem statement, a literature review, a method or design section, and a bibliography. It lacks the results, discussion, and conclusion sections. The proposal includes a plan for data collection and analysis (e.g., types of statistics). It frequently includes a time schedule of the steps to be undertaken and an estimate of the time required for each step.

Proposals for qualitative research are more difficult to write because the research process itself is less structured and preplanned. You prepare a topic/problem statement, literature review, and bibliography. You can demonstrate your ability to complete a proposed qualitative project in two ways. First, you prepare a well-written proposal with an extensive discussion of the literature, significance of the problem, and sources. This shows reviewers your familiarity with qualitative research and the

EXPANSION BOX **16.5**

Features to Consider in the Historical-Comparative Research Report

1. *Sequence.* Historical-comparative researchers are sensitive to the temporal order of events and place them in a series to describe a process. For example, a researcher studying the passage of a law or the evolution of a social norm may break the process into a set of sequential steps.

2. *Comparison.* Comparing similarities and differences lies at the heart of historical-comparative research. Make comparisons explicit and identify both similarities and differences. For example, a researcher comparing the family in two historical periods or countries begins by listing shared and nonshared traits of the family in each setting.

3. *Contingency.* Researchers often discover that one event, action, or situation depends on or is conditioned by others. Outlining the linkages of how one event was contingent on others is critical. For example, a researcher examining the rise of local newspapers notes that it depended on the spread of literacy.

4. *Origins and consequences.* Historical-comparative researchers trace the origins of an event, action, organization, or social relationship back in time or follow its consequences into subsequent time periods. For example, a researcher explaining the end of slavery traces its origins to many movements, speeches, laws, and actions in the preceding 50 years.

5. *Sensitivity to incompatible meaning.* Meanings change over time and vary across cultures. Historical-comparative researchers ask themselves whether a word or social category had the same meaning in the past as in the present or whether a word in one culture has a direct translation in another culture. For example, a college degree had a different meaning in a historical era when it was extremely expensive and less than 1 percent of the 18- to 22-year-old population received a degree compared to the late twentieth century, when college became relatively accessible.

6. *Limited generalization.* Overgeneralization is always a potential problem in historical-comparative research. Few researchers seek rigid, fixed laws in historical, comparative explanation. They qualify statements or avoid strict determination. For

example, instead of a blanket statement that the destruction of the native cultures in areas settled by European Whites was the inevitable consequence of advanced technological culture, a researcher may list the specific factors that combined to explain the destruction in particular social-historical settings.

7. *Association.* The concept of association is used in all forms of social research. As in other areas, historical-comparative researchers identify factors that appear together in time and place. For example, a researcher examining a city's nineteenth century crime rate asks whether years of increased migration into the city are associated with high crime rates and whether those arrested tended to be recent immigrants.

8. *Part and whole.* Placing events in their context is important. Writers of historical-comparative research sketch linkages between parts of a process, organization, or event and the larger context in which it is found. For example, a researcher studying a particular political ritual in an eighteenth century setting describes how the ritual fit within the eighteenth century political system.

9. *Analogy.* Analogies can be useful, but their overuse or inappropriate use is dangerous. For example, a researcher examines feelings about divorce in country X and describes them as "like feelings about death" in country Y. This analogy requires a description of "feelings about death" in country Y.

10. *Synthesis.* Historical-comparative researchers often synthesize many specific events and details into a comprehensive whole. Synthesis results from weaving together many smaller generalizations and interpretations into coherent main themes. For example, a researcher studying the French Revolution synthesizes specific generalizations about changes in social structure, international pressures, agricultural dislocation, shifting popular beliefs, and problems with government finances into a compact, coherent explanation. Researchers using the narrative form summarize the argument in an introduction or conclusion. It is a motif or theme embedded within the description. Thus, theoretical generalizations are intertwined with the evidence and appear to flow inductively out of the detailed evidence.

appropriateness of the method for studying the problem. Second, you describe a qualitative pilot study. This demonstrates motivation, familiarity with research techniques, and ability to complete a report about unstructured research.

Proposals to Fund Research. A research grant provides the resources required to complete a worthy project. Researchers whose primary goal is to use funding for personal benefit or prestige, to escape from other activities, or to build an "empire" are less successful. The strategies of proposal writing and getting grants has become an industry called **grantsmanship**.

There are many sources of funding for research proposals. Colleges, private foundations, and government agencies have programs to award grants to researchers. Researchers use the funds to purchase equipment, to pay a salary or hire assistants, for research supplies, for travel to collect data, or for help with the publication of results. The degree of competition for a grant varies a great deal, depending on the source. Some sources fund more than three out of four proposals they receive, but others fund fewer than one in twenty.

Although many sources of funding for social research exist, there might be no source willing to fund a specific project. You need to investigate funding sources and ask questions: What types of projects do they fund: applied versus basic research, specific topics, or specific research techniques? What are the deadlines? What type of proposal (e.g., length, degree of detail) is necessary? How large are most grants? What aspects (e.g., equipment, personnel, travel) of a project are or are not funded? There are many sources of information on funding

sources. Librarians or officials responsible for research grants at a college are good resources. For example, private foundations are listed in the annual publication *The Foundation Directory. The Guide to Federal Funding for Social Scientists* lists sources in the U.S. government. In the United States, subscribers can search for funding sources in numerous newsletters on funding sources and national computerized databases. Some agencies periodically issue **requests for proposals (RFPs)** that ask for proposals to conduct research on a specific issue. Researchers need to learn about funding sources because it is essential to send the proposal to an appropriate source in order to be successful.[17]

You need to show a track record of past success in the proposal, especially if you are going to be in charge of the project. The person in charge of a research project is the **principal investigator (PI)**, sometimes called the *project director.* Proposals usually include the PI's curriculum vitae or academic résumé, letters of support from other researchers, and a record of past research. Reviewers feel safer investing funds in a project headed by someone with substantial research experience rather than an inexperienced novice. You can build a track record with small research projects and by assisting an experienced researcher before you seek funding as a PI.

The reviewers who evaluate a proposal judge whether a proposal project is appropriate for the funding source's goals. Most sources have guidelines that state the types of projects they will fund. For example, programs that fund basic research have the advancement of knowledge as a goal. Programs to fund applied research often have improvements in the delivery of services as a goal. Instructions for submission specify page length, number of copies, deadlines, and the like. Follow all instructions exactly. Why would reviewers give thousands of dollars to a researcher to carry out a complicated research project if he or she cannot even follow instructions on the page length of a proposal?

Proposals should be neat and professional looking. The instructions usually ask for a detailed plan for the use of time, services, and personnel. These should be clearly stated and realistic for the

Grantsmanship   The use of strategies and skills in locating appropriate funding sources and preparing quality proposals to fund research.

Request for proposals (RFP)   An announcement by a funding organization that it is soliciting written plans of research projects to fund.

Principal investigator (PI)   The person who is primarily in charge of research on a project that is sponsored or funded by an organization.

project. Excessively high or low estimates, unnecessary add-ons, or omitted essentials will lower reviewers' evaluation of a proposal. Creating a budget for a proposed project is complicated and usually requires technical assistance. For example, pay rates, fringe benefit rates, and so on may not be easy to obtain. It is best to consult a grants officer at a college or an experienced proposal writer. In addition, endorsements or clearances of regulations are often necessary (e.g., IRB approval; see Chapter 5). Proposals should also include specific plans for disseminating results (e.g., publications, presentations before professional groups) and a plan for evaluating whether the project met its objectives (see Chart 16.1).

The proposal is a type of contract between a researcher and the funding source. Funding agencies require a final report that must include details on what the funds were spent for, study findings, and an evaluation of whether the project met its objectives. Failure to spend funds properly, to complete

---

CHART 16.1   Factors Associated with a Successful Research Proposal

1. It addresses an important research question. It builds on prior knowledge and represents a substantial advance of knowledge for basic research. It documents a major social problem and holds promise for solutions for applied research.

2. It follows all instructions, is well written, and is easy to follow with clearly stated objectives.

3. It completely describes research procedures that include high standards of research methodology, and it applies research techniques that are appropriate to the research question.

4. It includes specific plans for disseminating the results and evaluating whether the project has met its objectives.

5. It indicates that the project is well designed and shows serious planning. It has realistic budgets and schedules.

6. It notes that the researcher has the necessary experience or background to complete the project successfully.

---

the project described in the proposal, or to file a final report may result in serious consequences. The researcher may be banned from receiving future funding or face legal action. A serious misuse of funds may result in the entire institution (e.g., university, business, hosptial) fined and banned from receiving future funding.

The process of reviewing proposals after they are submitted to a funding source takes anywhere from a few weeks to almost a year, depending on the funding source. In most cases, reviewers rank a large group of proposals and fund only highly ranked proposals. A proposal often undergoes a peer review in which the reviewers know the proposer from the vitae in the proposal, but the proposer does not know the reviewers. Sometimes nonspecialists or nonresearchers review the proposals. Instructions on preparing a proposal indicate whether to write for specialists in a field or for an educated general audience, or both. In general, proposals that ask for large amounts of money receive closer review.

If your proposal is funded, celebrate, but only for a short time. If it is rejected, which is more likely, do not despair. Most proposals are rejected the first or second time they are submitted. Many funding sources provide written reviewer evaluations of the proposal. Always request them if they are provided. Sometimes a courteous talk on the telephone with a person at the funding source will reveal the reasons for rejection. Strengthen and resubmit a proposal based on reviewer comments. Most funding sources accept resubmissions of revised proposals. Reviewed proposals are often stronger in subsequent competitions.

THE POLITICS OF SOCIAL RESEARCH

A naïve, innocent view of social research suggests that conducting and writing about research is a pure process that operates in a sociopolitical vacuum, totally insulated from the pressures or concerns of the larger society. A more realistic view is that we face an array of ethical and political concerns when doing social research. Ethical researchers protect research participants, conduct research honestly in accordance with codes of ethics, avoid interference from sponsors, and disseminate results in an open, clear manner. The politics of social research overlaps with many issues in sponsored research (discussed in Chapter 5). In addition, many social researchers face economically or politically powerful groups who attempt to limit what they study, how they conduct research, or how they disseminate the findings.

Limits on What Researchers Study

Direct Limits on Research. Governments or powerful groups in society may try to restrict free scientific inquiry. Some limits on research have always existed but in particular times or places they become very restrictive. In nondemocratic societies, control over or censorship of social research is the rule, not the exception. This is particularly the case with politically sensitive topics including public opinion surveys. Thus, during the late twentieth century in China, eastern Europe, South Africa, and Taiwan, for example, social researchers were suspect, limited to "safe" topics, or forced to support official government policy.[18] In a number of countries, the study of sociology itself was banned as subversive after a military coup. In an extreme case, 40 percent of German scientists were dismissed from their jobs for political reasons when the Nazis "purified" universities and research centers in 1937.[19] Hundreds of professors and researchers in the United States who did not publicly swear to anticommunism and cooperate with the McCarthy investigations of the 1950s were purged. At that time, people who objected to mandatory loyalty oaths, supported racial integration, or advocated the teaching of sex education were suspected of subversion and threatened with dismissal. For instance, at the University of California alone, twenty-five professors were fired for refusing to sign a loyalty oath.[20]

Two limitations on social research are (1) gatekeepers who control access to data or subjects and (2) controls over how official statistics are collected. Gatekeepers can limit what we study and may try to protect themselves or their organizations from criticism or embarrassment. They often limit access to subjects or areas with which they have concerns. For example, in 1997, the U.S. Army dropped several questions from a 153-item questionnaire on sexual harassment to be sent to 9,000 soldiers. The reason for eliminating the six questions was that "senior Army officials feared that the responses could be highly embarrassing to the Army" (Schmitt, 1997). A social anthropologist and a law professor who were consultants on the project were upset and noted that preliminary results from an early version of the questionnaire suggested that sexual harassment at military bases was correlated with questions that asked about certain soldier behaviors (e.g., going to strip clubs, watching X-rated movies). Gatekeeper army officials did not want such questions because the answers could prove embarrassing to widespread practices on military bases.

Another limitation involves official or existing statistics that government or other large organizations collect (this is discussed in Chapter 11). Whether agencies decide to collect information and how they collect it can affect research findings. Political factors often determine how phenomena (e.g., unemployment, income, educational success, poverty level) are defined in official statistics and whether such data are collected.[21]

Hundreds of social scientists regularly rely on the data collected by the U.S. Census Bureau for conducting demographic, economic, and other studies. The original purpose of a census was to allocate elected representatives among states and districts. Later the Census Bureau began to gather information for making policy decisions, providing social programs, and distributing government funds based on the population in an area. The Census Bureau has become a major source of social science information and a clearinghouse for official statistics on many topics. Serious distortions (e.g., systematic overcounts or undercounts of some people or areas) in Census Bureau statistics weaken research findings based on them, prevent full democratic representation, and undermine a fair distribution of social programs or funds (see discussion in Chapter 11).

Researchers who rely on existing statistics depend on the government to supply information or documents. In the United States, the Paperwork Reduction Act of 1980 created the Office of Information and Regulatory Affairs to determine whether collecting information and maintaining records were necessary. The act resulted in fewer publications from government-sponsored research. In addition, the law had been "used on occasion to restrict information not supportive of executive branch policy goals" (Shattuck and Spence, 1988:47). For example, in the health field, research projects with an environmental focus that indirectly criticized business or government policy had a higher chance of being rejected for publication under "paperwork reduction" justification than projects with a traditional disease focus that indirectly blamed the victim. In the name of cost cutting, government agencies stopped collecting information, removed information from public circulation, and shifted information collection to private businesses. Officials cut U.S. government publishing offices and raised prices of their documents. Bureaucratic decisions not to collect certain information can have research information and policy implications.

Limits Due to the Influence of Politicians. Unfortunately, some people outside the scientific community attack social research when it disagrees with their social or political values. A politician or journalist may hear about a research project in a controversial area, misinterpret it, and then use the occasion to attract publicity. For example, Professor Harris Rubin at the University of Southern Illinois intended to investigate the effects of THC (the active agent in marijuana) on sexual arousal. Only contradictory myths, and almost no scientific evidence, existed at the time. He very carefully followed all required procedures and obtained all clearances, and the National Institute of Mental Health decided to fund the research project after scientific peer review. However, a conservative member of Congress learned of the research topic from nearby newspapers and introduced an amendment to prohibit further funding. In addition, Dr. Rubin had to repay all funds for the project to the federal government. Despite arguments by the scientific community that politicians should not interfere with legitimate research, the funding was cut. Politicians might fear supporting social research if an opposing candidate could tell voters that the government was paying for students to "get stoned and watch porno

films."[22] In 1989, members of Congress blocked funding for a major national survey on sexual behavior to combat the AIDS epidemic because they did not believe that it was proper for social researchers to inquire into human sexual behavior (also see Example Box 16.1, U.S. Congressmen Question Research Funding).[23]

The U.S. Senate canceled a research project on teenage sex conducted by the National Institutes of Health (NIH). The study was to survey 24,000 teens about their social activities, family lives, and sexual behaviors to provide background for understanding AIDS and other sexually transmitted diseases. Many researchers said they did not want to speak out on the issue for fear that they would become the target of attacks by political groups. Some who

---

EXAMPLE BOX 16.1

U.S. Congressmen Question Research Funding

In 1998, Representative Marshall Sanford of South Carolina said he wanted to cut National Science Foundation (NSF) funding for studies of questionable "scientific value." Apparently believing he was a better judge of scientific value than the scientific community, he cited studies about automatic teller machines and billiards. NSF officials observed that the research to which the congressman referred, the abbreviated *ATM* for *asynchronous transfer modes,* a high-speech data technique, not *automatic teller machines,* and *billiards* is a term physicists use in atomic theory for a subatomic particle, not the game as the congressman had assumed. Representative Sanford, along with a representative from California, indicated a desire to punish the NSF for supporting what they deemed unnecessary, wasteful studies. These studies included those that investigated why people risk their resources to join social groups, differences between the social behavior of men and women, and why potential political candidates decide to run for office. Other Congress members defended the NSF and noted that such criticisms were the result of faulty, sloppy research by the politicians, not the type of research the NSF supports through its peer review process (Lederman, 1998).

spoke out said that the ability of a small minority with an extreme political ideology to kill important research was "a scandalous act" and "frightening." One researcher noted that the project was not canceled because of questions about its scientific quality or importance but because of an ideologically based decision that "we don't need to know this."[24]

Attacks on social research, even noncontroversial but misunderstood research, hurts all researchers. Politicians may try to stop research that the scientific community recognizes as legitimate, or they promote pet projects that have little scientific value. Researchers who apply for government funds will sometimes restate their project in terms that do not attract attention. The public ridicule of researchers or the denial of research funds also encourages self-censorship and fosters a negative public opinion about social research (see Example Box 16.2, Political Attacks Had "Chilling Effect" on Research).

National Security and Limits on Social Research. Military secrecy and national security became major issues in the United States during World War I and World War II. Most of the concern involved technology to create weapons, but some researchers have been limited in their study of foreign nations, issues of military interest, and research into government itself. U.S. security agencies such as the National Security Administration and the Central Intelligence Agency (CIA) influenced social and natural science research into the cold war period of the 1950s.

Government control over U.S. social science research about non-Western societies was strict during the cold war era, especially from the late 1940s to the mid-1960s. Intelligence and security agencies worked closely and clandestinely with most research centers and scholarly associations. During that period, security and military government agencies and a few politicized foundations provided most funds for social research about other societies, and officials

Project Camelot A controversial social research project in Chile funded by the U.S. Army in the 1960s that violated ethical principles and raised major political concerns.

EXAMPLE BOX **16.2**
Political Attacks Had "Chilling Effect" on Research

During the early years of the twenty-first century, U.S. Congressional representatives known as the Traditional Values Coalition targeted social and medical researchers who were to receive National Institutes of Health (NIH)-funded grants on a range of topics. As a result, the researchers report that they now engage in self-censorship. Kempner (2008) conducted two surveys in 2005 and 2006. One involved interviews with a random sample of thirty principal investigators (PIs) named in these controversies, and the other survey was a questionnaire sent to all PIs involved in these controversies (eighty-six responded). She found that a majority changed their research practices as a result of the political controversy. After the political attacks, the researchers avoided using certain terms in their research proposals or changed the focus of their research investigations to less politically sensitive topics.

monitored researchers' writings and statements for conformity with government policy. Scholars who secretly worked for or cooperated with the government agencies rapidly received research funding and see their careers advance. Independent researchers or those who asked questions about official policy rarely saw research funds and faced career limitations. Conducting research that contradicted official policy was almost impossible.[25]

One government research project in the 1960s created a great controversy. The U.S. Army funded **Project Camelot**, which involved respected social researchers who went to Chile to study political insurgency and mobilization. Several aspects of the project created controversy. First, the project's goal was to determine how to prevent peasants and disadvantaged groups in Third World countries from taking independent political action to oppose a dictator. The CIA usually conducted such counterinsurgency research. The researchers were accused of using their skills and knowledge to advance military interests against disadvantaged Third World people. Second, some researchers were unaware of the source of funds. Third, officials did not inform the research participants of the government of Chile about the project. Once Chileans discovered it, they asked that it end and that all researchers leave.[26]

By the late 1960s and 1970s, freedom to conduct research expanded, restrictions on cross-cultural researchers were relaxed, and the government classified fewer documents. The U.S. Congress passed the *Freedom of Information Act* (FOIA) in 1966 and strengthened it in 1974. The law opened many government documents to scholars and members of the public if they filed requests with the proper government agencies. The trend toward openness and freedom of research lasted for about fifteen years, then reversed in the 1980s.

By the late 1980s the U.S. federal government expanded the range of classified documents and reduced publicly available information.[27] The government broadened its definition of national security, expanded the system for classifying government documents, and imposed new limits on research into "sensitive areas" even if no government agency or funds were involved. New rules made classifying information and documents already in the public domain easier. In addition, military and security officials could restrict foreign researchers from attending scholarly meetings or visiting U.S. classrooms, libraries, and research centers.[28]

In the cold war era, CIA undercover agents often posed as social researchers to find information in foreign nations. Until 1986, the CIA had a blanket rule barring researchers from disclosing CIA sponsorship of their research. At that time, the rule was loosened to cover only cases about which the CIA believed such disclosure could harm the United States. For example, a Harvard professor had a contract with the CIA not to reveal that the agency paid for the research for a scholarly book on U.S. foreign policy.[29]

Cross-national research involves unique issues. The scientific community condemns the use of undercover agents in the guise of researchers and the practice of hiding the source of funding for such research. Ethical guidelines for conduct in other nations specify the cooperation with host officials, the protection of research participants, and the requirement to leave information in the host nation. Nevertheless, a researcher may find interference

from his-her own government, or protecting the basic human rights of the people being studied in a nondemocratic society may lead him or her to hide information from the host government involved.[30]

After the cold war, worldwide social researchers had increased independence and academic freedom to study various societies. However, political changes in the United States that have occurred since the September 11, 2001, terrorist attacks may produce more government monitoring and influence over cross-national research.

Indirect Limits through Control over Research Funding. The most common way that politics shapes social research is through control over funds for research. This is similar to the issues involved in sponsored research. Large-scale research projects can be expensive, costing as much as $1 million, and the funds often come from private sources or governments.

Most officials recognize that an open and autonomous social scientific community is the best path to unbiased, valid knowledge. The peer-review process promotes autonomous research. Researchers submit proposals to a government agency for funds to conduct research. Peer researchers evaluate the proposal on a proposal's scientific merit for the government agency. Although the government funds most basic research, researchers at many colleges, universities, and research centers across the nation conduct the research.

The sums for social research are tiny compared with the amounts that large corporations spend on research or with government funding of other activities. In the United States, most social research funding comes from the federal government, with university and private foundations funding projects that are limited in amount, scope, and number. Thus, for large projects, researchers go to the government for funds.

Prior to World War II in the United States, a few private foundations set up by wealthy families (Carnegie, Ford, Rockefeller, and Sage) funded most social research. The foundations sought information about the serious social problems that appeared with early industrialism. They also wanted to discourage links between radicals and social researchers and to protect established social institutions. After a number of years, "the production of social science research thus becomes regularized or routinized, and its connection with sponsoring organizations becomes obscured from the public's view" (Seybold, 1987:197). Private foundation funds redirected social research efforts away from its early applied, action-oriented, critical, neighborhood-centered focus that involved local participation and toward detached, professional, positivist, and academic research. After World War II, government research funding expanded. Private foundations maintained a role setting research priorities through the 1960s when federal government funds surpassed private funds.[31] Government research funds increased, but funding for the social sciences and sociology remained tiny. In the United States, research funding for sociology has been less than 1 percent of federal funding for basic research.

In the United States, social research funding is available from several federal agencies including the National Science Foundation; the Departments of Defense, Justice, Labor, Commerce, Housing and Urban Development, and Education; the National Endowment for the Humanities; Small Business Administration; and the many institutes under the Department of Health and Human Services. The federal government itself employs researchers, but most social research is conducted at colleges and universities or independent research institutes.

Early in their histories, the primary funding sources for social research in the United States (the National Science Foundation and National Institutes of Health) supported only basic positivist research for political reasons. Social scientists agreed to exclude nonpositivist social research and applied studies to win backing from natural scientists, to counter popular perceptions that social science was "fluff," and to repel charges by ideological conservatives that social science was "left-wing." In addition, the NSF avoided funding research on controversial topics (e.g., sex, political power) due to a fear in the political climate of the 1950s and 1960s that the study of such topics could jeopardize public support for social science research.

Political processes determine how much money goes to various agencies for social research

and the applied/basic split. Although the scientific review committees within agencies evaluate the scientific merit of submitted proposals, political officials decide the total amount of funds available. Politicians set the priorities based on political party or ideological interests. This affects the amount of research funding available (see Example Box 16.3, Political Influence on Crime Research in the United States).

Ideological criticisms of social research caused reduced funding for social science research in the National Science Foundation by 24 percent between 1976 and 1980 in constant dollars. Despite an outcry by researchers, funding dropped another 17 percent

EXAMPLE BOX 16.3

Political Influence on Crime Research in the United States

Savelsberg and colleagues (2002) asked whether political pressures in the United States altered the direction of social research on crime issues between 1951 and 1993. They looked at scholarly journal articles and asked whether shifts in politics affected research through providing funds for research and whether changing the organization of academic fields in colleges and universities influenced the theories used (i.e., individual problems versus social forces or inequalities), topics examined (e.g., street crime and illegal drugs versus white-collar crimes) and the crime perspectives applied (i.e., micro-level enforcement versus macro level or understanding criminal behavior). They found that funding by agencies that tried to advance a political agenda and new academic departments created to be better aligned and more responsive to political interests rather than acting as an independent research community both had an effect on the types of studies conducted. Nonetheless, while funding and new organizational units affected which topics researchers studied and which theories they tested, these factors did not affect whether data supported the theories. Thus, political forces did influence the theories, topics, and perspectives to which researchers devoted attention and efforts, but political factors did not influence how researchers designed or conducted the research studies or the results they determined.

between 1980 and 1983. Some political leaders believed that the research results supported the policies of their ideological opponents. Politicians also cut applied research funds. In response, the professional associations of several social science disciplines joined together to form a lobbying organization, the Consortium of Social Science Associations (COSSA).[32]

The overall level of funding for social research may have remained unchanged for 90 years. Funds from the private Social Science Research Council in the late 1920s, once adjusted for inflation and the size of the academic profession, probably totaled more than funding for social science research from the National Science Foundation given now.[33]

Political values can limit the questions researchers can examine and set research priorities. By focusing on some research questions and limiting alternatives, advocacy groups try to shape the research conducted, and the information that we have about society. For example, politicians may allocate funds for applied research to demonstrate how "burdensome" the costs of regulation are for large corporations but reject funding for research to investigate the benefits of regulation for consumers. Politicians can increase funds to study crime committed by drug addicts but eliminate funds to study crime committed by corporate executives. Politicians may provide funds for research on how to promote entrepreneurship while cutting funds to study the human consequences of social program cutbacks.[34]

Political-ideological interference into all scientific research increased between 2001 and 2008. A 2004 statement by the Union of Concerned Scientists and endorsed by 8,000 leading scientists said that the George W. Bush administration had politicized science to an egregious degree, sharply departing from the long-standing practices of presidents and administrators of both parties (Kevlevs, 2006:761).

Social researchers address issues that bear directly on social beliefs, values, and policies. The priorities of advocacy groups and ideologically committed politicians for these issues are distinct from the priorities of the scientific community. This has both positive and negative effects on the ability of social research to address societal needs and advance knowledge. It ensures that the concerns of politicians and vocal public groups are addressed and that issues defined as crucial to politically influential groups are researched. However, even if scientific research does not support a popular public myth (e.g., that capital punishment has a deterrent effect), politicians and advocacy groups press repeatedly to allocate funds to try to discover evidence that confirms their nonscientific, popular beliefs. At the same time, issues central to the scientific community may go unfunded.

The scientific community has some freedom to decide research questions, but issues affecting politically marginal social groups or issues for which there is no organized lobby receive limited research funding. This imbalance of funding creates an imbalance in knowledge across issues. Eventually, we have knowledge on the issues of most interest to powerful political groups but know little from the standpoint of the nonpowerful sectors of society.

In the United States, politicians can reject research proposals that have undergone rigorous peer review for scientific merit even if the politicians never read the proposal but dislike its research topic for political-ideological reasons.[35] For example, in 2005 the House of Representatives withheld funding from two peer-reviewed research projects at the National Institute of Mental Health (NIMH). One grant dealt with visual perception in pigeons; the other examined how psychological traits contribute to successful marriages. The request to block funds from these studies came from a congressman who was a real estate developer in Texas without scientific expertise. Such political interferences damage the peer-review process. In fact, the same congressman tried unsuccessfully to prohibit NIMH from funding two grants to study people's self-expression and value systems.[36]

Earmarked or "Pork Barrel" Funding for Research. Beginning in the 1990s, U.S. politicians increasingly circumvented the scientific peer-review process to allocate government financial support for research. The politicians "earmarked" or targeted money for specific projects at particular universities and research institutes. They allocated funds based on political favoritism rather than on competition among proposals based on research quality or merit as evaluated by informed members of the scientific community. It appears that "pork barrel" politics—the process by which a politician distributes money to major government projects not based on importance or high priority but because those projects bring money to the businesses and supporters in the politician's home district—had spread to the funding of research.

Increasingly, researchers in some states or electoral districts receive substantial funding while others get almost nothing, based on political connections rather than on scientific merit. For example, the State University of New York at Buffalo received $12 million to conduct research on traffic injuries as the result of a noncompetitive, political decision. The amount of research funds politically earmarked doubled between 1989 and 1993; it then remained stable for a few years. Since 1996 it has increased fivefold to roughly $2 billion per year.

The politicized allocation of government research funds pressures universities and research institutes to court favor with influential politicians. For example, in 1995, New Hampshire received no earmarked research funds. After New Hampshire Republican Senator Judd Gregg became the chairman of an appropriations subcommittee 4 years later, New Hampshire researchers benefited as their state became the seventh highest to receive government funds. When Senator John McCain tried to end pork barrel spending for research in 2001, the U.S. Senate defeated his measure 87 to 12. Many politicians are "proud of pork" and brag about the money they "bring home" based on political favoritism rather than scientific merit. To obtain research funds, universities and research institutes increasingly must devote efforts to courting political favor and lobbying rather than encouraging research proposals that will be competitive in the merit-based peer review process.[37]

As the April 29, 2010, issue of *Inside Higher Ed* reported, "The leading recipients of earmarks in academe resided, not surprisingly, in states represented by some of the most powerful people in Congress. Four Mississippi institutions . . . were among the top 25 recipients of academic earmarks, due in large part to the fact that Sen. Thad Cochran, the state's senior senator, is the top Republican on the Senate Appropriations Committee" (see Table 16.1). One study suggests that earmarks may increase research publications by people at universities that receive them but lower the overall quality of increased number of publications (Payne, 2002).

Many research institutes and universities have turned to private donors (wealthy individuals, corporations, or foundations) for research funds. Private funding often comes with strings attached. For example, a private donor withdrew $450,000 because a researcher at the university that received the money had publicly criticized a policy that the donor favored.[38] Some donors want to support independent research with no strings, but many others use the donated funds to create subtle pressure to advance a pet policy position, ideological stand, or political agenda. Universities and research institutes try to avoid limitations on research funding from private donators, but they must balance needed hard cash from a donor against abstract ideals, such as a researcher's freedom to conduct and publish any research that advances knowledge. Some universities and research institutes might resolve the difficulty of returning or rejecting a donor's funds by agreeing to limits on open, free inquiry.

Limits on the Dissemination of Knowledge. A major norm of the scientific community is to publicly distribute knowledge. Powerful groups or institutions can impinge on social research by limiting the flow of information, restricting publication, or silencing researchers.

A 1997 news report illustrates the suppression of research findings.[39] A pharmaceutical company that produced a widely used drug for thyroid problems prohibited a university research team from publishing its research results that showed the drug to be ineffective. In exchange for the research funds, the researchers had signed a contract giving the company a right to veto publications of the results. Other studies show that when drug companies fund research, 98 percent of the published findings show

TABLE 16.1   Fifteen Top Higher Education Recipients of Congressional Earmarks in 2010

HIGHER EDUCATION INSTITUTION	TOTAL EARMARK
1. University of Alabama at Tuscaloosa	$58,755,000
2. Mississippi State University	$47,919,000
3. Texas A&M University	$40,150,000
4. University of North Dakota	$39,660,000
5. North Dakota State University	$37,040,000
6. University of Mississippi	$33,655,000
7. University of Hawaii	$33,503,000
8. University of Massachusetts at Boston	$33,002,000
9. Utah State University	$27,190,000
10. New Mexico Institute of Mining and Technology	$27,000,000
11. Louisiana State University	$26,650,000
12. University of Southern Mississippi	$22,590,000
13. West Virginia University	$21,920,000
14. University of Louisville	$20,150,000
15. University of Kentucky	$19,709,000

Source: "The Academic Pork Barrel, 2010" from *Inside Higher Ed,* April 29, 2010; http://www.insidehighered.com/news/2010/04/29/earmark (accessed May 16, 2010).

that the drugs are effective. This number is far lower when the drug companies are not the funding source. Some people believe that negative findings about new products are suppressed when millions of dollars for a company are involved. Researchers may receive stock or financial incentives to show positive findings or to delay the release of negative findings. More than half of university researchers who received money from drug or biotechnology companies stated that private donors exerted influence on how they did their work.

Research on medicine or biotechnology is not the only area where profits and disseminating research findings conflict. In 1997, a Cornell University professor testified for 10 minutes at a town meeting about the labor practices of the largest nursing home corporation in the United States, Beverly Enterprises, which operates 700 nursing homes. The professor's testimony was backed up by years of research and documented by congressional reports, newspaper reports, court records, interviews, and other scholars. In 1998, the company sued the professor for $225,000 for defaming it and demanded years of research documents and notes. This is called a **Strategic Lawsuits against Public Participation** (SLAPP) suit; its purpose is to stop public testimony.

The practice began in the 1970s when companies issued "strategic lawsuits" to silence the opposition on controversial issues.

The threat of a lawsuit by managers interviewed in a study on corporate crime delayed publication and forced the researcher to change the results. A threatened lawsuit by school officials stopped publication of a study of a boarding school. School officials wanted to change what they had said in interviews and make other changes because they disagreed with the researcher's conclusions. In another example, a questionable researcher who had been charged with conflicts of interest threatened a lawsuit to force changes in an article conducted by a team of fellow researchers.[40]

SLAPP suit   Type of lawsuit that wealthy, powerful organizations use to intimidate researchers and stop them from publicly expressing ideas or revealing information.

Serious charges were made between 2002 and 2004 that the federal government of the United States restricted the release of scientific information that contradicted or failed to support the administration's policy positions. These changes included censoring data on the efficacy of condoms, blocking evidence that showed abstinence is not as effective as sex education, and directing the National Cancer Institute to post a claim on its Web site stating that abortion promotes breast cancer although a major study showed no connection. In addition, government officials had removed reports on global warming from distribution based on the objections from political advisers, not scientists. The Environmental Protection Agency said it would not analyze pollution studies that contradicted official administration policy. A U.S. Department of Agriculture researcher who studied how to decrease the odor of swine farms through diet developed related applications that also detected air contaminants. Unintentionally, the study also showed that large-scale hog confinements regularly violated federal pollution limits and produced antibiotic-resistant bacteria. A member of the hog industry learned of the research and contacted the researcher's supervisor, who in turn forbade him from presenting the findings at a research conference or submitting his study to scientific journals.[41] Such actions were not as drastic as Iran's government jailing survey researchers because their results showed that a large majority of the Iranian people wanted to improve relations with the United States, contrary to the Iranian government's policy (see Summary Review Box 16.1, A Summary of Political Issues).

SUMMARY REVIEW BOX **16.1**
A Summary of Political Issues

DIRECT LIMITS ON RESEARCH

1. The government (or vigilante groups) bans, fires, jails, or threatens professors and researchers who study unpopular topics, openly discuss "forbidden" ideas, or make statements that the government opposes.
2. Officials in government agencies or large organizations block access to official documents or statistical information or try to restrict how official data are gathered or made publicly available.
3. Politicians and those in high office criticize, attack, or put public pressure to block legitimate social research that they disagree with on personal, religious, or ideological grounds.
4. Officials try to block or censor research because they believe it might hinder national security or they clandestinely try to control social research for their own military or secret intelligence gathering purposes.

INDIRECT LIMITS ON RESEARCH THROUGH FUNDING

1. Limits or cuts in funding for research prevent the production of new knowledge that might challenge cherished ideological beliefs or political views.
2. Controls over the topics or issues receiving research funding redirect new knowledge so that it will provide support for certain policy positions.

3. Pork barrel spending by politicians circumvents the peer-review processes and allocates research funds based on political favoritism or on rewarding friends in one's home district instead of being based on competition by scientific merit.
4. Limits are placed on the techniques, tools, or services that researchers can use to fulfill political objectives and are unrelated to the scientific research process yet add costs, time, or complications to conducting research.

LIMITS ON OR BIAS IN THE DISSEMINATION OF RESEARCH RESULTS

1. Researchers are threatened with legal action or penalties if they speak freely in a public forum or openly publish the findings of their research.
2. Prior review or screening is required by nonscientists (i.e., corporate or political officials) before a researcher is allowed to share research findings with the scientific community or public.
3. Officials and other influential people promote research findings that the scientific community considers to be seriously defective, weak, or inadequate but that advance their political agenda.

EXPANSION BOX **16.6**
Models of Relevance

1. *No net effects.* Social science findings produce no greater social good. Several famous social scientists who argue this are William Graham Sumner, Vilfredo Pareto, Herbert Spencer, Edward Banfield, and James Q. Wilson. These conservative social scientists see the products of research as capable of being used for anyone's self-interest and believe that, in the long run, as much harm as good has come from the greater knowledge that social science yields.
2. *Direct and positive effects.* Social science knowledge results in an improvement for all. Liberal social scientists, such as Robert Merton, who adopt this stance see knowledge about social relations leading to a more rational world. Research results on social problems help us understand the social world much better, enabling us to know how we can modify it toward some greater good. For example, Lindblom and Cohen (1979) urged a redirection of social science toward what they see as social problem solving.
3. *Special constituency, the proletariat.* Social science should be used to advance the interests and position of the working class. This is the Marxist model of the appropriate use of social research. According to it, all social science falls into three categories: the trivial, that which helps the bourgeoisie, and that which aids the proletariat. Consistent with a critical science approach, research findings should be used to advocate and defend the interests of the working class and assist workers by exposing and combatting exploitation, oppression, injustice, and repression.
4. *Special constituency, the uncoopted.* Social science should be used to aid any disadvantaged or under-

privileged group in society. This model, associated with Karl Mannheim and C. Wright Mills, is more general than the Marxian position. It sees many social groups as lacking power in society (women, consumers, racial minorities, gays, the poor, etc.) and argues that these groups are oppressed by the powerful in society who have access to education, wealth, and knowledge. The social researcher should defend those who lack a voice in society and who are manipulated by those in power. The powerful can use or purchase social science research for their own ends. Because they have a unique role in society and are in a position to learn about all areas of society, social researchers have an obligation to help the weak and share knowledge with them.
5. *Special constituency, the government.* Social science's proper role is to aid the decision makers of society, especially public officials. This model has been expressed by Senator Daniel Patrick Moynihan and in official National Science Foundation policy reports and is common in nondemocratic societies. It is similar to the second model (direct and positive effects), but adds the assumption that government is in the best position to use social research findings and is fully committed to eradicating social problems. It is also similar to the first (no net effects) model but implies "selling" or providing findings to the highest bidder within the limits of national loyalty. It assumes that the government operates in the best interests of everyone and that researchers have a patriotic duty to give what they learn to officials holding political power.

The Dissemination of Findings

Positivist researchers recognize two areas in which values legitimately come into play. First, researchers can select a topic area or research question. Although there are "scientific frontier" areas of inquiry in topic areas, researchers can choose a research question based on personal preference.[42] Second, after a study is completed, researchers' values shape where they disseminate findings. The scientific community expects researchers to report findings, and funding agencies require a report, but beyond these requirements, the dissemination is up to the individual researcher.

Models of Relevance. After the research is completed an ethical-political concern may arise that Rule (1978a, 1978b) has called **models of relevance**. Rule reviewed the positions that social researchers took toward their research and its use and argued that the positions can be collapsed into five basic types (see Expansion Box 16.6, Models of Relevance).

The models of relevance are ideal types of the positions that social scientists take. Is the researcher

Models of relevance A set of ideal types of ways that social researchers understand the purposes of conducting research and the use of research results.

a technician who produces valid, reliable information about how society works that is be used by others? Or does the researcher belong to an independent community of professionals who have a say in what research questions are asked and how results are used? On a continuum, one extreme is the amoral researcher who lacks any concern or control over research or its use. He or she supplies the knowledge that others request and nothing more. This was the stance that many scientists in Nazi Germany took to justify collaborating with Nazi practices, which were later classified as "crimes against humanity." He or she "just follows orders" and "just does the job" but asks "no questions." At the other extreme are researchers who have total control over research and its use.

The approaches to social science discussed in Chapter 4 are associated with different models of relevance as are different political views.[43] Positivists tend to follow the "direct and positive effects" or "special constituency, the government" model. The interpretive researcher follows the "no net effects" or the "uncoopted" model. Critical social scientists follow the "special constituency, the proletariat" or "special constituency, the uncoopted" models.

Specific researchers or research projects cross between models. For example, Whyte (1986) described research on employee ownership as crossing between three constituencies (the proletariat, the uncoopted, and the government) and as having direct and positive effects.

Since Rule developed models of relevance, a new model has appeared with a large increase in the number and size of nongovernmental private **think tanks** in the United States. This sixth model is *special constituency, wealthy individuals, and corporations*. It states that social research can reflect a researcher's political values and advance the political goals of wealthy groups who seek to maintain or expand their power. The think tanks are research and public organizations funded by wealthy individuals, corporations, and political groups. For example, the Manhattan Institute, Cato Institute, Heritage Foundation, and American Enterprise Institute grew dramatically from the early 1980s to the 1990s. They have a particular political-ideological viewpoint and use social research or pseudoscience to advance their agenda. Think tanks pay researchers, sponsor research reports, and draw public attention to results supporting their views (see Example Box 16.4, Ethics, Politics, and the Misuse of Survey Research).

Think tank studies vary in quality. Their studies often lack peer review and are short on solid

EXAMPLE BOX **16.4**
Ethics, Politics, and the Misuse of Survey Research

In a highly unusual move, the leading professional public opinion organization, the American Association for Public Opinion Research (AAPOR), sharply criticized two organizations that engaged in blatantly unethical behavior with survey research to advance narrow political goals. In 1997, the Association found that Frank Luntz of Luntz Research Corporation "repeatedly refused to make public essential factors about his research." His surveys showed strong public support for a Republican Party proposal called "Contract with America" in November 1994 that other researchers did not find. Luntz widely publicized his findings but refused to disclose basic methodological information as is required in ethical surveys.

Three years later, the AAPOR criticized Campaign Tel, Ltd. for a gross violation of confidentiality. Campaign Tel used a list with names and telephone numbers of registered Wisconsin voters and claimed to be conducting a survey. In fact, the company turned over detailed information on survey responses and phone numbers to the Wisconsin Republican Party. The AAPOR stated that it "strongly condemns any practice that poses as a survey and elicits information from a respondent for any purpose other than legitimate survey research." Campaign Tel misrepresented its true nature. By the time the AAPOR had detected and documented the unethical behavior, Campaign Tel had ceased to exist.

Source: See AAPOR website, www.aapor.org/main1.html.

Think tank   An organization (usually nonprofit, nongovernmental) in which one or more researchers, writers, journalists, and others develop, refine, elaborate on, and publicize ideas about policy issues.

evidence but long on recommendations. Their audience is not the scientific community but politicians, journalists, and the public. Their primary goal is not to advance knowledge. They promote an ideological viewpoint to shape public thinking or influence political debate. They receive significant media publicity, fame, and fortune. At the same time, traditional social scientists who operate with meager funds and lack connections to the mass media find that the public and journalists overlook their more rigorous, careful studies of the same public issues because the publicity given to think tank results overwhelms the public and journalists.

After Findings Are Published. The communalism norm of the scientific community says to make findings public. Once findings are part of the public domain, the researcher loses control over them. This means that others can use the findings for their own purposes. Although the researcher may have chosen a topic based on his or her values, once the findings are published, others can use findings to advance opposing values.

Consider, for example, that you want to increase the political rights of a Native American tribe. You study the tribe's social practices including practices that become barriers to their achieving greater power in the community. Once you publish the findings, members of the tribe can use the results to break down barriers, yet opponents can use the same findings to restrict the power of the tribe and to reinforce the barriers.

Findings That Influence Future Behavior. Did you ever do something differently than you had before because of research findings that you read? If so, you are not alone. Sometimes the dissemination of findings affects social behavior. One example is the effect of political poll results. Public opinion polls affect the political preferences of voters; that is, parts of the population change their views to correspond to what opinion polls say they have found.[44]

Other social research findings can affect behavior. In fact, the dissemination of research findings may affect behavior in a way that negates or alters the original findings. For example, a study finds that professionals are likely to put a great deal

of stress on the academic achievement of their children. This creates highly anxious, unhappy children. If professionals read the findings, they may alter their child-rearing behavior. Then another study, years later, might find that professionals are not likely to rear their children to achieve in academic areas any more than other groups do.

Researchers have several responses to research findings that affect social behavior:

1. They ruin the predictability and regularity of human social behavior, undermining replication.
2. They change only trivial behaviors, so this is an issue only to researchers working in very narrow applied areas.
3. They change human behavior because there are few unalterable laws of human behavior, and people will use knowledge in the public domain to change their lives.

In any case, social research has not uncovered the full complexity of human relations and behavior. Even if it had and such knowledge were fully and accurately disseminated to the entire population, social researchers would still have to study which human behaviors change and how.

Academic Freedom. Most students have heard about academic freedom but few understand it. **Academic freedom** is the existence of an open and largely unrestricted atmosphere for the free exchange of ideas and information. In open democratic societies, many people value intellectual freedom and believe in providing scholars freedom from interference. This idea is based on the belief that fundamental democratic institutions, the advance of unbiased knowledge, and freedom of expression require a free flow of ideas and information. Academic freedom is related to the autonomy of research. New ideas for research topics, the interpretation of

---

Academic freedom The concept that researchers and/or teachers are free to examine all topics and discuss all ideas without any restrictions, threats, or interference from people or authorities outside the community of teachers, scholars, and scientists.

findings, the development of theories or hypotheses, and the open discussion of ideas require academic freedom.

Academic freedom in colleges, universities, and research institutes provides a context for the free discussion and open exchange of ideas that scientific research requires. For knowledge to advance, researchers, professors, and students need a setting in which they feel free to advance or debate diverse, and sometimes unpopular, opinions or positions—a setting in which people are not afraid to explore a full range of ideas in open discussion, in classrooms, in public talks, or in publications.

You can see the importance of academic freedom by the paucity of social research in places where it is nonexistent. Social-political advocacy groups and government officials that want to restrict discussion or impose a point of view can threaten academic freedom. Restrictions on academic freedom limit the growth of knowledge about society and undermine the integrity of the research process.

Academic freedom appeared as a significant issue in the late nineteenth century as the social sciences were being institutionalized in universities. In the early years, professors lost their jobs because political officials or economic elites disliked the views expressed in classrooms or publications. University officials forced famous scholars in the early U.S. social science, like Thorsten Veblen, out of jobs because of what they said in the classroom or ideas they wrote about. The development of tenure, the idea that faculty could not be fired after a long probationary period (typically six years) without a very good reason, advanced academic freedom but does not guarantee it totally. Tenure has greatly reduced the firing of professors and researchers by university officials merely for advocating unpopular ideas.[45]

Political attacks on social science are not new. They illustrate the conflict between the independent pursuit of knowledge and the views of political groups who want to impose their beliefs. These attacks raise the question: How autonomous should social science be from the values in the larger culture? The findings of social research frequently conflict with social beliefs based on nonscientific knowledge systems such as religion or political ideology. Galileo faced this issue about 400 years ago,

before natural science was accepted. His astronomical findings, based on free-thinking science, contradicted official Church doctrine. Galileo was forced to recant his findings publicly under threat of torture. Silencing him slowed the advance of knowledge for a generation. The challenges of evolutionary theory also illustrate how scientific knowledge and popular beliefs conflict with one another.

Academic freedom is integral to good research. Scientific research involves more than knowing technical information (e.g., how to draw a random sample); it requires a spirit of free and open discussion, criticism based on scientific merit regardless of values, and inquiry into all areas of social life. When academic freedom is restricted, these values are threatened.

OBJECTIVITY AND VALUE FREEDOM

Some argue that social science must be as objective and unbiased as the natural sciences; others maintain that value-free, objective social science is impossible. Part of the confusion is because each term has at least two alternative definitions. Sometimes, two different terms share the same definition (see Chart 16.2).

The positivist approach holds that science is value free, unbiased, and objective. It collapses the definitions together. Logical-deductive, formal theory, and the separation of facts from value-based concepts guarantee value neutrality. The scientific community is free of prejudice and governed by free and open discussion. With complete value freedom and objectivity, science reveals the one and only, unified, unambiguous truth.

Max Weber, Alvin Gouldner, and Karl Mannheim are three major nonpositivist social thinkers who discussed the role of the social scientist in society. Weber (1949) argued that the fact/value separation is not clear in the social sciences. He suggested that value-laden theories define social facts or socially meaningful action. Thus, social theories necessarily contain value-based concepts because members of specific cultures create all concepts about the social world. We cannot purge the cultural content of social concepts, and socially

---

CHART 16.2   Objective, Value Free, and Unbiased

1. *Objective:*
   a. Opposite of *subjective;* external, observable, factual, precise, quantitative
   b. Logical; created by an explicit rational procedure; absence of personal or arbitrary decisions; follows specific preestablished rules
2. *Value free:*
   a. Absence of any metaphysical values or assumptions; devoid of *a priori* philosophical elements; amoral
   b. Lack of influence from personal prejudice or cultural values; devoid of personal opinion; no room for unsupported views; neutral
3. *Unbiased:*
   a. Nonrandom error eliminated; absence of systematic error; technically correct
   b. Lack of influence from personal prejudice or cultural values; devoid of personal opinion; no room for unsupported views; neutral

---

meaningful action makes sense only in a cultural context. For example, when we study racial groups, the groups are not interested in the biological differences between races. Race is a social concept; we study it because the members of a culture have attached social meaning to racial appearance. Race would be meaningless if people did not attach significance to observable racial differences.

Other social researchers have built on Weber's ideas. For example, Moore (1973) asked whether majority-group (e.g., Anglo, White) researchers can accurately study racial minorities as "outsiders," because their questions, assumptions, and interests originate in a dominant, nonminority perspective. Are the culture, values, and belief system of the dominant White culture appropriate for asking important questions and really understanding the subculture of racial minorities? Similar concerns have been raised regarding gender.[46] Being from a different culture may not preclude researching a group, but it calls for extra care and sensitivity from a researcher.

Weber (1949) also argued that social scientists cannot avoid taking stands on the social issues they

study. Researchers *must* be unbiased (i.e., neutral and devoid of personal opinion and unsupported views) when applying accepted research techniques and focus on the means or mechanisms of how the social world works, not on ends, values, or normative goals. A researcher's values must be separate from the findings, and he or she should advocate positions on specific issues only when speaking as a private citizen.

Gouldner (1976) attacked the notion of value-free, objective social science. He argued that value freedom was used in the past to disguise specific value positions. In fact, value freedom is itself a value—one in favor of "value free." Gouldner said that complete value freedom was impossible and that scientists and other professionals use the term to hide their own values. He recommended making values explicit. A researcher can be motivated to do research by a desire to do more than study the world dispassionately. The researcher who is motivated by a strong moral desire to effect change need not invalidate good research practice.

Mannheim (1936) also questioned the ideas of *value neutrality* and *objectivity*. He saw the intellectuals of a society, especially those involved in social research, as occupying a unique social role. A person's social location in society shapes his or her ideas and viewpoints, yet social researchers are separate from most other people. Their social position influences them less because they make special efforts to learn the viewpoints of other people and empathize with all parts of society. Compared to most other people, they are less beholden to powerful elites and less subject to shifts in popular opinion, fads, and crazes. They can and should adopt a **relational position**—a position apart from any other specific social group yet in touch with all groups. They should be detached or marginal in society yet have connections with all parts of society, even those that are often overlooked or hidden.

Relational position   Karl Mannheim's idea that professional academic researchers and intellectuals occupy a unique social position and are detached from the major groups in society, which puts them in the best position to develop unbiased knowledge.

CONCLUSION

Communicating results is a central part of the larger scientific enterprise as are the ethics and politics of social research. "Solutions" to the political issues that you may face are threefold. First, you need to be aware of such issues, be aware of potential dangers, and adopt a realistic view of the sociopolitical environment instead of a naïve view of social research. Second, you should work with others to advocate for the independence of research from outside pressures. Third, you need to educate the public and leaders of major institutions about the value and importance of independent social research.

I want to end this chapter by urging you, as a consumer of social research or a new social researcher, to be self-aware. Be conscious of the place of the research in society and of the societal context of social research itself. Social researchers bring a unique perspective to the larger society. We have a responsibility to ourselves, the scientific community, and society, and we need to have an awareness of how the social sciences acquired our current place in society.

KEY TERMS

academic freedom
editing
error of segregation
executive summary
freewriting
grantsmanship

models of relevance
paraphrasing
plagiarism
prewriting
principal investigator (PI)
Project Camelot

relational position
request for proposals (RFP)
revising
SLAPP suit
think tank
zoom lens

REVIEW QUESTIONS

1. Discuss the relationship among prewriting, freewriting, rewriting, editing, and composing in the process of writing a research report.

2. What are the primary differences in the organization of a quantitative versus a qualitative research report?

3. How is a proposal to conduct research similar to and different from a final research report?

4. What types of limitations on social research come from the actions of politicians?

5. In what ways can control over funding influence the types of issues being researched?

6. How might the criteria used by government or private donors that provide funds for research differ from criteria used by peers in the scientific community?

7. What have been the trends in U.S. government funding for research over the past 20 years, and how might they be influencing the research that is being conducted now?

8. What is the source of Rule's models of relevance, and what is their usefulness?

9. How does academic freedom support or contradict a relational position?

10. What are the meanings of doing objective and value-free research?

NOTES

1. See "Plagiarism Case Documented," American Sociological Association *Footnotes,* 17(2), p. 2 or "Noted Harvard Psychiatrist Resigns Post after Faculty Group Finds He Plagiarized," *Chronicle of Higher Education,* 35(15), p. 1.

2. From Sociology Writing Group (1991).

3. For suggestions on writing, see Donald et al. (1983) and Leggett et al. (1965).

4. From Sociology Writing Group (1991:40).

5. See Fine (1988) for this and other suggestions on writing.

6. See Mullins (1977:11–30) for a discussion of outlines and the organization of quantitative research reports. Also see Williams and Wolfe (1979:85–116) for good hints on how to organize ideas in a paper.

7. Grosof and Sardy (1985:386–389) have provided suggestions on how to explain quantitative findings.

8. Lofland (1974) inductively discovered what he identifies as five major writing styles for reporting field research (generic, novel, elaborated, eventful, and interpenetrated) and discusses how they are evaluated.

9. The error of segregation is discussed in Lofland and Lofland (1984:146).

10. See Becker and Geer (1982:244) and Schatzman and Strauss (1973:130) for a discussion of this and related issues.

11. See Hammersley and Atkinson (1983) and Van Maanen (1988).

12. Discussed in Spradley (1970:162–167).

13. See Van Maanen (1988:13).

14. See Dabbs (1982) and Jackson (1978).

15. For a discussion of ethical concerns in writing field research reports, see Becker (1969), Punch (1986), and Wax (1971).

16. See Barzun and Graff (1970) and Shafer (1980) for excellent suggestions on writing about historical research.

17. For more on writing proposals to fund research projects, see Bauer (1988), Locke et al. (1987), and Quarles (1986). A somewhat dated but useful short introduction to proposal writing is found in Krathwohl (1965).

18. For Russian social science research, see Keller (1988, 1989) and Swafford (1987). Also see "Soviet Sociologist Calls Attention for Her Science," American Sociological Association *Footnotes* (April 1987), p. 2.

19. See Greenberg (1967:71).

20. For more on the decade of the 1950s and its effect on social reseachers, see Caute (1978:403–430), Goldstein (1978:360–369), and Schrecker (1986).

21. See Block and Burns (1986) and Starr (1987).

22. See Bermant (1982:138). Nelkin (1982a) provided a general discussion of "forbidden" topics in social science research.

23. "Sex Survey Is Dealt a Setback," *New York Times* (July 26, 1989), p. 7.

24. See Stephen Burd, "Scientists Fear Rise of Intrusion in Work Supported by NIH," *Chronicle of Higher Education* (October 2, 1991), p. Alff.

25. See Cumings (1997), Sanders (1979), and Simpson (1993) on U.S. government influence on area studies and internationally related academic research during the Cold War era.

26. Project Camelot is described in Horowitz (1965).

27. See Dickson (1984), Nelkin (1982b), and Shattuck and Spence (1988:2).

28. See Shattuck and Spence (1988) and Josephson (1988). Also see "Librarians Charge Plan Would Cut Flow of Data," *New York Times* (February 21, 1989).

29. For more on the CIA and social researchers, see Shattuck and Spence (1988:39–40) and Stephenson (1978).

30. For sensitive situations involving cross-national research, see Fuller (1988) and Van den Berge (1967).

31. For discussion, see Bannister (1987), Blumer (1991b), D'Antonio (1992), Hyman (1991), Ross (1991), and Seybold (1987).

32. See Dynes (1984) on COSSA.

33. The SSRC spent $20 million for the social sciences from 1924 to 1928 (Gieger, 1986:152) compared to $136 million allocated in 1989 by the NSF for the social sciences (D'Antonio, 1992). In the late 1920s, the number of academic social scientists was about one-tenth what it is today and a dollar had six times more purchasing power. The number of social science doctorates—including psychology, teaching, or conducting basic research—in 1986 was about 129,000 (Science and Engineering Personnel: A National Overview, Document NSF 90-310). The number of higher education faculty in all academic fields in 1930 was less than 83,000 (Historical Statistics of the United States, 1970, Table H696). The $20 million over 4 years in the 1920s, or $5 million per year, would be equivalent to roughly $300 million in 1990. The median family income before taxes in 1929 was $2,335 (Historical Statistics, Table G308).

34. For more on the effects of politics and funding cuts on social research in the 1980s, see Cummings (1984), Himmelstein and Zald (1984), and Zuiches (1984). For more general discussion of the effect of funding on research, see Galliher and McCartney (1973) and Dickson (1984).

35. See "NIH FY 1991 Budget Rescinded by $3.1 Million, Congress Objects to 31 Research Projects Funded by NSF," *The Blue Sheet* (F-D-C Reports, Inc.) (May 27, 1992), p. 3.

36. Nature Neuroscience Editorial (2005).

37. See Brainard and Borrego (2003), Brainard and Southwick (2001), Cordes (1998), Payne (2003a, 2003b), and Savage (2001) on rapidly increasing pork barrel academic spending.

38. See Golder (1996).

39. Lawrence Altman, "Experts See Bias in Drug Data," *New York Times* (April 29, 1997).

40. See Punch (1986:18–19; 49–69) and Sheryl Gay Stolberg, "Gifts to Science Researchers Have Strings, Study Finds," *New York Times* (April 1, 1998). On the nursing home "SLAPP suit," see Greenhouse, "Cornell Professor Fights a Slander Suit," *New York Times* (April 1, 1998), and news report of Morning Edition, National Public Radio (April 27, 1998).

41. See Block (2003), Clymer (2002), Krider (2004), Lee (2003), and Union of Concerned Scientists (2004).

42. For more discussion on how researchers select research questions or problems, see Gieryn (1978) and Zuckerman (1978).

43. See Brym (1980) on role of intellectuals in society.

44. Marsh (1984), Noelle-Neumann (1974, 1984), and Price (1989) discussed the effects of research results on subsequent public behavior and opinion.

45. Bartiz (1960), Schrecker (1986), Schwendinger and Schwendinger (1974), and Silva and Slaughter (1980) discuss the history of social researchers in society.

46. Committees on the Status of Women in Sociology (1986).

Table of Randomly Selected Five-Digit Numbers

10819	85717	64540	95692	44985	88504	50298	20830	67124	20557
28459	13687	50699	62110	49307	84465	66518	08290	96957	45050
19105	52686	51336	53101	81842	20323	71091	78598	60969	74898
35376	72734	13951	27528	36140	42195	25942	70835	45825	49277
93818	84972	66048	83361	56465	65449	87748	95405	98712	97183
35859	82675	87301	71211	78007	99316	25591	63995	40577	78894
66241	89679	04843	96407	01970	06913	19259	72929	82868	50457
44222	37633	85262	65308	03252	36770	51640	18333	33971	49352
54966	75662	80544	48943	87983	62759	55698	41068	35558	60870
43351	15285	38157	45261	50114	35934	05950	11735	51769	07389
11208	80818	78325	14807	19325	41500	01263	09211	56005	44250
71379	53517	15553	04774	63452	50294	06332	69926	20592	06305
63162	41154	78345	23645	74235	72054	84152	27889	76881	58652
17457	68490	19878	04981	83667	00053	12003	84614	14842	29462
28042	42748	55801	94527	21926	07901	89855	21070	80320	91153
32240	24201	24202	45025	07664	11503	97375	83178	26731	45568
87288	22996	67529	38344	29757	74161	16834	40238	48789	99995
39052	23696	42858	85695	50783	51790	80882	97015	81331	76819
71528	74553	32294	86652	15224	07119	45327	69072	64572	07658
76921	04502	78240	89519	02621	40829	88841	66178	01266	10906
45889	22839	77794	94068	85709	96902	19646	40614	03169	45434
10486	79308	75231	33615	42194	49397	91324	79553	66976	83861
42051	14719	80056	74811	58453	04526	90724	36151	09168	04291
47919	11314	80282	09297	02824	59530	31237	26311	62168	46591
19634	40589	28985	40577	33213	52852	17556	85342	66881	18944
10265	45549	38771	38740	48104	63990	73234	19398	33740	97345
74975	33526	36190	25201	19239	06254	02198	99109	01005	20983
37677	76778	15736	57675	81153	59651	69262	89250	75156	59164
18774	15979	26466	80236	65400	24272	02088	09307	33426	11230
93728	14965	85141	27821	53791	38728	66369	29415	55330	99228
34212	15590	41336	23614	26153	19466	44176	80885	00015	40077
81984	54478	45226	97338	14064	45768	13538	49093	05691	69720
72755	15743	00552	89374	85400	37392	26598	71917	64275	16125
13162	57044	75982	15819	23385	40860	51585	44542	39656	91139
64686	62224	34124	79171	73909	26196	54057	63264	72089	06658
00157	64594	03178	75774	32315	34443	37224	85593	55251	42666
84194	83591	82152	24311	22414	43244	81542	31491	42075	17275
05776	60399	65218	89299	20273	30071	53077	18853	56652	63896
33365	18314	81074	49433	10884	75467	56085	14731	98085	60895

67928	38976	38480	59980	23156	72335	33489	59420	67819	51874
64394	45154	81851	54228	73095	97217	16908	90242	92869	17311
73000	20948	57065	70195	87563	41590	85047	71743	94916	50534
63555	03388	96638	16591	13641	73342	59131	63144	63587	62084
84005	02035	08182	16395	44928	08897	44750	71378	67522	20180
42593	35102	14577	38102	60403	04540	53992	27069	69574	76682
49519	49517	88147	83375	87045	57466	91259	06680	45586	36257
42149	01579	83056	19423	28165	25620	68035	17919	09120	59078
66192	98427	10152	96970	89990	34604	49632	46533	63362	43151
16124	88620	87074	37851	77131	73855	03740	10306	63858	04349
35492	47334	57189	26465	70078	14477	00881	00929	86907	73764
54503	40155	94734	20689	32475	62851	13216	21419	95502	36783
88063	53451	15642	67345	06935	70644	68570	79176	31975	83082
83689	14426	40357	34906	56282	96104	83796	57663	88627	17521
40393	72810	00681	15351	28858	72086	99090	39741	17914	27385
76648	61322	06817	64674	50317	52373	78223	84222	14021	43432
42091	27088	37686	88033	68007	71009	24018	49568	64351	94130
78925	41509	14319	92389	85492	40880	01487	85509	48316	62618
61915	98081	87996	53798	51485	38912	85858	43392	64678	44458
29504	66960	42645	54547	20615	77035	79942	33972	46112	78290
90170	97643	46284	34591	42692	72933	66166	98389	37460	14545
96439	06806	76714	80084	57685	37447	44901	64699	89142	64657
98365	28725	84376	50634	79289	31106	71351	10533	57545	27399
74794	91013	89791	54236	02369	35317	31103	82481	52256	94510
37499	85907	16293	17673	13373	06599	50138	19860	46716	36928
77530	25960	33671	54383	25144	82627	99266	75134	96539	47242
67990	35106	05214	82928	39824	11128	31390	76293	52809	54881
07355	29187	09357	94498	69697	92515	89812	90794	44738	46806
40716	05787	68975	38937	44033	50064	25582	09428	10220	42455
97748	64395	13937	60406	99182	92720	80805	26242	81943	40341
83682	18775	60095	78600	03994	30313	21418	58563	47258	75582
73506	30672	18213	37887	26698	87700	75784	86878	74004	88636
36274	02333	43132	93725	87912	90341	74601	77001	30717	60002
73508	00852	94044	98474	12621	91655	55258	85551	76122	68052
06488	12362	60020	66902	90734	73689	22382	40896	09028	72925
20201	31560	98885	32275	46818	76114	07959	65639	33267	98595
49947	13114	06773	06454	95070	26564	08974	11640	76202	86105
79928	50600	06586	72129	37233	02564	83265	32579	21234	83535
76360	86412	36240	20210	17692	80482	67007	15474	23198	74250
54601	84643	66759	57661	16434	61708	93185	75957	61056	90678
23441	63863	95238	59665	55789	26180	12566	58645	15125	76707
47093	90509	48767	09874	23363	84954	09789	30178	28804	93294
93603	11580	94163	85561	71328	88735	69859	84563	25579	52858
68812	15299	99296	45906	37303	49507	70680	74412	96425	38134
69023	84343	36736	52659	90751	20115	89920	44995	17109	96613
76913	03158	83461	27842	03903	34683	89761	80564	45806	88009
99426	99643	00749	79376	44910	27490	59668	93907	73112	46365
59429	08121	06954	28120	17606	22482	91924	00401	16459	15570
38121	05358	01205	00662	73934	97834	56917	64058	05148	87599
97781	32170	99914	75565	79802	38905	17167	08196	46043	72094
79068	21760	78832	93795	67798	54968	87328	46494	74338	89805
46601	04015	00484	39366	56233	22622	90706	02327	60807	39009

Bibliography

Abell, Peter. (2001). Causality and low-frequency complex events. *Sociological Methods and Research,* 30:57–80.

Abell, Peter. (2004). Narrative explanation. *Annual Review of Sociology,* 30:287–310.

Abend, Gabriel. (2006). Styles of sociological thought: Sociologies, epistemologies, and the Mexican and U.S. quests for truth. *Sociological Theory,* 24(1):1–41.

Abend, Gabriel. (2008). The meaning of theory. *Sociological Theory,* 26(2): 173–199.

Abbott, Andrew. (1988). *The system of professions: An essay on the division of expert labor.* Chicago: University of Chicago Press.

Abbott, Andrew. (1992). From causes to events: Notes on narrative positivism. *Sociological Methods and Research,* 20:428–455.

Abbott, Andrew. (1995). Sequence analysis. *Annual Review of Sociology,* 21:93–113.

Abbott, Andrew. (2001). *Time matters: On theory and method.* Chicago: University of Chicago Press.

Abbott, Andrew. (2004). *Methods of discovery: Heuristics for the social sciences.* New York: W.W. Norton.

Abelson, Robert P., Elizabeth F. Loftus, and Anthony G. Greenwald. (1992). Attempts to improve the accuracy of self-reports of voting. In *Questions about questions: Inquiries into the cognitive bases of surveys,* edited by J. Turner, pp. 138–153. New York: Russell Sage Foundation.

Abrams, Philip. (1982). *Historical sociology.* Ithaca, NY: Cornell University Press.

Abt, Charles. (1979). Government constraints on evaluation quality. In *Improving evaluation,* edited by L. Datta and R. Perloff. Beverly Hills, CA: Sage.

Achen, Christopher H. (1982). *Interpreting and using regression.* Beverly Hills, CA: Sage.

Adams, Gerald R., and Jay D. Schvaneveldt. (1985). *Understanding research methods.* New York: Longman.

Adler, Patricia A. (1985). *Wheeling and dealing.* New York: Columbia University Press.

Adler, Patricia A., and Peter Adler. (1983). Shifts and oscillations in deviant careers: The case of upper-level drug dealers and smugglers. *Social Problems,* 31:195–207.

Adler, Patricia A., and Peter Adler. (1987). *Membership roles in field research.* Beverly Hills, CA: Sage.

Adler, Patricia A., and Peter Adler. (1993). Ethical issues in self-censorship: Ethnographic research on sensitive topics. In *Research on sensitive topics,* edited by C. Renzetti and R. Lee, pp. 249–266. Thousand Oaks, CA: Sage.

Adler, Patricia A., and Peter Adler. (1994). Observational techniques. In *Handbook of qualitative research,* edited by N. Denzin and Y. Lincoln, pp. 377–392. Thousand Oaks, CA: Sage.

Adler, Patricia A., and Peter Adler. (2008). Of rhetoric and representation: The four faces of ethnography. *Sociological Quarterly,* 49(1):1–30.

Adorno, Theodor W. (1976a). Sociology and empirical research. In *The positivist dispute in German sociology,* trans. Glyn Adey and David Frisby, edited by T. Adorno et al., pp. 68–86. New York: Harper & Row.

Adorno, Theodor W. (1976b). The logic of the social sciences. In *The positivist dispute in German sociology,* trans. Glyn Adey and David Frisby, edited by T. Adorno et al., pp. 87–104. New York: Harper & Row.

Agar, Michael. (1980). Getting better quality stuff: Methodological competition in an interdisciplinary niche. *Urban Life,* 9:34–50.

Agar, Michael. (1986). *Speaking of ethnography.* Beverly Hills, CA: Sage.

Agger, Ben. (1991). Critical theory, poststructuralism, postmodernism: Their sociological relevance. *Annual Review of Sociology,* 17:105–131.

Agnew, Neil McK., and Sandra W. Pyke. (1991). *The science game: An introduction to research in the social sciences,* 5th ed. Englewood Cliffs, NJ: Prentice-Hall.

Aiello, Lauren, and Jennifer Profitt. (2008). VNR usage: A matter of regulation or ethics? *Journal of Mass Media Ethics* 23(3):219–234.

Albrecht, Gary L. (1985). Videotape safaris: Entering the field with a camera. *Qualitative Sociology,* 8:325–344.

Aldenderfer, Mark S., and Roger K. Blashfield. (1984). *Cluster analysis.* Beverly Hills, CA: Sage.

Alford, Robert R. (1998). *The craft of inquiry: Theories, method, evidence.* New York: Oxford University Press.

Allison, Paul D. (2001). *Missing data.* Thousand Oaks, CA: Sage.

Almond, Gabriel A., and Sidney Verba. (1963). *The civic culture.* Princeton, NJ: Princeton University Press.

Altheide, David L. (1980). Leaving the newsroom. In *Fieldwork experience,* edited by W. B. Shaffir, R. Stebbins, and A. Turowetz, pp. 301–310. New York: St. Martin's Press.

Altman, Morris. (2000). A behavioral model of path dependency: The economics of profitable inefficiency and market failure. *Journal of Socio-Economics,* 29:127–145.

Alwin, Duane F. (1977). Making errors in surveys. *Sociological Methods and Research,* 6:131–150.

Alwin, Duane F. (1988). The general social survey: A national data resource for the social sciences. *PS: Political Science and Politics,* 21:90–94.

Alwin, Duane F., and David J. Jackson. (1980). Measurement models for response errors in surveys: Issues and applications. In *Sociological methodology, 1980,* edited by S. Leinhardt. San Francisco: Jossey-Bass.

Alwin, Duane F., and Jon A. Krosnick. (1985). The measurement of values in surveys: A comparison of ratings and rankings. *Public Opinion Quarterly,* 49:535–552.

American Sociological Association. (1997). *American Sociological Association style guide,* 2nd ed. Washington, DC: American Sociological Association.

Aminzade, Ronald. (1984). Capitalist industrialization and patterns of industrial protest: A comparative urban study of nineteenth century France. *American Sociological Review,* 49:437–453.

Anderson, Andy B., Alexander Basilevsky, and Derek P. J. Hum. (1983). Measurement: Theory and techniques. In *Handbook of survey research,* edited by P. Rossi, J. D. Wright, and A. Anderson, pp. 231–287. New York: Academic Press.

Anderson, Barbara A., Brian D. Silver, and Paul R. Abramson. (1988). The effects of the race of interviewer on race-related attitudes of black respondents in SRC/CPS national election studies. *Public Opinion Quarterly,* 52:289–324.

Anderson, Elijah. (1989). Jelly's place. In *In the field,* edited by C. Smith and W. Kornblum, pp. 9–20. New York: Praeger.

Anderson, N. (1923). *The hobo.* Chicago: University of Chicago Press.

Anderson, Perry. (1974a). *Linkages of the absolutist state.* London: New Left Books.

Anderson, Perry. (1974b). *Passages from antiquity to feudalism.* London: New Left Books.

Anderson, Robert, and Tina Fetner. (2008). Cohort differences in tolerance of homosexuality attitudinal change in Canada and the United States, 1981–2000. *Public Opinion Quarterly,* 72(2):311–330.

Anderson, R. Bruce W. (1973). On the comparability of meaningful stimuli in cross-cultural research. In *Comparative research methods,* edited by D. Warwick and S. Osherson, pp. 149–186. Englewood Cliffs, NJ: Prentice-Hall.

Andorka, Rudolf. (1987). Time budgets and their uses. *Annual Review of Sociology,* 13:149–164.

Andren, Gunnar. (1981). Reliability and content analysis. In *Advances in content analysis,* edited by K. Rosengren, pp. 43–67. Beverly Hills, CA: Sage.

Andrews, Frank M., Laura Klem, Terrence Davidson, Patrick O'Malley, and Willard Rodgers. (1981). *A guide for selecting statistical techniques for analyzing social science data.* Ann Arbor: Institute for Social Research, University of Michigan.

Applebaum, Richard. (1978a). Marxist method: Structural constraints and social praxis. *American Sociologist,* 13:73–81.

Applebaum, Richard. (1978b). Marx's theory of the falling rate of profit. *American Sociological Review,* 43:67–80.

Aquilino, William S. (1993). Effects of spouse presence during the interview on survey response concerning marriage. *Public Opinion Quarterly,* 57:358–376.

Aquilino, William S., and Leonard Losciuto. (1990). Effects of interview mode on self-reported drug use. *Public Opinion Quarterly,* 54:362–395.

Archer, Margaret, R. Bhaskar, A. Collier, T. Lawson, and A. Norrie, eds. (1998). *Critical realism: Essential readings.* New York: Routledge.

Ardener, Shirley. (1984). Gender orientations in fieldwork. In *Ethnographic research: A guide to general conduct,* edited by R. F. Ellen, pp. 118–129. Orlando: Academic Press.

Ariès, E. (1977). Male–female interpersonal styles in all male, all female, and mixed groups. In *Beyond sex roles,* edited by A. Sargent, pp. 292–299. Boulder, CO: West.

Armer, Michael. (1973). Methodological problems and possibilities in comparative research. In *Comparative social research,* edited by M. Armer and A. D. Grimshaw, pp. 49–79. New York: Wiley.

Aronson, Elliot, and J. Merrill Carlsmith. (1968). Experimentation in social psychology. In *The handbook of social psychology, Vol. 2: Research methods,* edited by G. Lindzey and E. Aronson, pp. 1–78. Reading, MA: Addison-Wesley.

Asch, Solomon E. (1955). Opinions and social pressure. *Scientific American,* 193(5):31–35.

Atkinson, Robert. (1998). *The life story interview.* Thousand Oaks, CA: Sage.

Auriat, Nadia. (1993). My wife knows best: A comparison of event dating accuracy between the wife, the husband, the couple, and the Belgium population register. *Public Opinion Quarterly,* 57:165–190.

Auster, Carol J. (1985). Manual for socialization: Examples from Girl Scout handbooks, 1913–1984. *Qualitative Sociology,* 8:359–367.

Ayella, Marybeth. (1993). "They must be crazy:" Some of the difficulties in researching cults. In *Research on sensitive topics,* edited by C. Renzetti and R. Lee, pp. 108–124. Thousand Oaks, CA: Sage.

Babbie, Earl. (1989). *The practice of social research,* 5th ed. Belmont, CA: Wadsworth.

Babbie, Earl. (1990). *Survey research methods,* 2nd ed. Belmont, CA: Wadsworth.

Babbie, Earl. (1998). *The practice of social research,* 8th ed. Belmont, CA: Wadsworth.

Backstrom, Charles H., and Gerald Hursh-Cesar. (1981). *Survey research,* 2nd ed. New York: Wiley.

Bailey, Kenneth D. (1983). Sociological classification and cluster analysis. *Quality and Quantity,* 17:251–268.

Bailey, Kenneth D. (1984). A three-level measurement model. *Quality and Quantity,* 18:225–245.

Bailey, Kenneth D. (1986). Philosophical foundations of sociological measurement: Notes on the three-level model. *Quality and Quantity,* 20:327–337.

Bailey, Kenneth D. (1987). *Methods of social research,* 3rd ed. New York: Free Press.

Bailey, Kenneth D. (1988). Ethical dilemmas in social problems research: A theoretical framework. *American Sociologist,* 19:121–137.

Bakanic, Von, Clark McPhail, and Rita Simon. (1987). The manuscript review and decision-making process. *American Sociological Review,* 52:631–642.

Bakanic, Von, Clark McPhail, and Rita Simon. (1989). Mixed messages: Referees' comments on the manuscripts they review. *Sociological Quarterly,* 30:639–654.

Ball, Michael, and Gregory W. H. Smith. (1992). *Analyzing visual data.* Thousand Oaks, CA: Sage.

Ballen, Robert D., and Kelly K. Richardson. (2002). Social integration, imitation and the geographic patterning of suicide. *American Sociological Review,* 873–888.

Banaka, William H. (1971). *Training in depth interviewing.* New York: Harper & Row.

Bannister, Robert C. (1987). *Sociology and scientism: The American quest for objectivity, 1880–1940.* Chapel Hill: University of North Carolina Press.

Baranik, Lisa E. et al. (2008). Examining the differential item functioning of the Rosenberg self-esteem scale across eight countries. *Journal of Applied Social Psychology,* 38(7):1867–1904.

Barber, Jennifer S., and William G. Axinn. (1998). Gender attitudes and marriage among young women. *Sociological Quarterly,* 39:11–31.

Barlow, Melissa Hickman, David E. Barlow, and Theodore G. Chiricos. (1995). Economic conditions and ideologies of crime in the media: A content analysis of crime news. *Crime and Delinquency,* 41:3–19.

Barnes, Barry. (1974). *Scientific knowledge and sociological theory.* Boston: Routledge and Kegan Paul.

Barnes, J. A. (1970). Some ethical problems in modern fieldwork. In *Qualitative methodology,* edited by W. J. Filstead, pp. 235–251. Chicago: Markham.

Barnes, J. A. (1979). *Who should know what? Social science, privacy and ethics.* New York: Cambridge University Press.

Barry, Brian. (1975). On analogy. *Political Studies,* 23:208–224.

Bart, Pauline. (1987). Seizing the means of reproduction: An illegal feminist abortion collective—How and why it worked. *Qualitative Sociology,* 10:339–357.

Bart, Pauline, and Linda Frankel. (1986). *The student sociologist's handbook,* 4th ed. New York: Random House.

Bartiz, Loren. (1960). *Servants of power: A history of the use of social science in American industry.* Middletown, CT: Wesleyan University Press.

Barton, Allen H. (1995). Asking why about social problems: Ideology and causal models in the public mind. *International Journal of Public Opinion Research,* 7:299–327.

Barzun, Jacques, and Henry F. Graff. (1970). *The modern researcher,* rev. ed. New York: Harcourt, Brace and World.

Bateson, Nicholas. (1984). *Data construction in social surveys.* Boston: George Allen and Unwin.

Bauer, David G. (1988). *The "how to" grants manual,* 2nd ed. New York: Macmillan.

Bauer, Raymond, ed. (1966). *Social indicators.* Cambridge, MA: MIT Press.

Bausell, R. Barker. (1994). *Conducting meaningful experiments: Forty steps to becoming a scientist.* Thousand Oaks, CA: Sage.

Bayless, David L. (1981). Twenty-two years of survey research at the Research Triangle: 1959–1980. In *Current topics in survey sampling,* edited by D. Krewski, R. Platek, and J. N. K. Rao, pp. 87–103. New York: Academic Press.

Beasley, David. (1988). *How to use a research library.* New York: Oxford University Press.

Beatty, Paul. (1995). Understanding the standardization/non-standardization controversy. *Journal of Official Statistics,* 11:147–160.

Beck, Bernard. (1970). Cooking welfare stew. In *Pathways to data,* edited by R. W. Habenstein, pp. 7–29. Chicago: Aldine.

Becker, Henk A., and Frank Vanclay. (2003). *The international handbook of social impact assessment: Conceptual and methodological advances.* Northampton, MA: Edward Elgar Publishing.

Becker, Howard. (1967). Whose side are we on? *Social Problems,* 14:239–247.

Becker, Howard S. (1969). Problems in the publication of field studies. In *Issues in participant observation,* edited by G. McCall and J. L. Simmons, pp. 260–275. Reading, MA: Addison-Wesley.

Becker, Howard S. (1970a). Practitioners of vice and crime. In *Pathways to data,* edited by R. W. Habenstein, pp. 30–49. Chicago: Aldine.

Becker, Howard S. (1970b). Problems of inference and proof in participant observation. In *Qualitative methodology: Firsthand involvement with the social world,* edited by W. J. Filstead, pp. 189–201. Chicago: Markham.

Becker, Howard S. (1970c). Whose side are we on? In *Qualitative methodology,* edited by W. J. Filstead, pp. 15–26. Chicago: Markham.

Becker, Howard S. (1986). *Writing for social scientists: How to start and finish your thesis, book or article.* Chicago: University of Chicago Press.

Becker, Howard S. (1993). How I learned what a crock was. *Journal of Contemporary Ethnography,* 22:28–35.

Becker, Howard S. (1998). *Tricks of the trade: How to think about your research while you're doing it.* Chicago: University of Chicago Press.

Becker, Howard S., and Blanche Geer. (1970). Participant observation and interviewing: A comparison. In *Qualitative methodology,* edited by W. J. Filstead, pp. 133–142. Chicago: Markham.

Becker, Howard S., and Blanche Geer. (1982). Participant observation: The analysis of qualitative field data. In *Field research: A sourcebook and field manual,* edited by R. G. Burgess, pp. 239–250. Boston: George Allen and Unwin.

Becker, Howard S., Blanche Geer, Everett C. Hughes, and Anselm Strauss. (1961). *Boys in white: Student culture in medical school.* Chicago: University of Chicago Press.

Becker, Howard S., Michal M. McCall, and Lori V. Morris. (1989). Theatres and communities: Three scenes. *Social Problems,* 36:93–116.

Beecher, H. K. (1970). *Research and the individual: Human studies.* Boston: Little, Brown.

Behm-Morawitz, Elizabeth, and Dana E. Mastro. (2008). Mean girls? The influence of gender portrayals in teen movies on emerging adults' gender-based attitudes and beliefs. *Journalism and Mass Communication Quarterly,* 85(1):131–146.

Belenky, Mary Field, Blythe McVicker Clinchy, Nancy Rule Goldberger, and Jill Mattuck Tarule. (1986). *Women's ways of knowing: The development of self, voice and mind.* New York: Basic Books.

Bellah, Robert N. (1957). *Tokugawa religion.* Glencoe, IL: Free Press.

Belli, Robert F., et al. (1999). Reducing vote overreporting in surveys: Social desirability, memory failure and source monitoring. *Public Opinion Quarterly,* 63:90–108.

Ben-David, Joseph. (1971). *The scientist's role in society.* Englewood Cliffs, NJ: Prentice-Hall.

Ben-Yehuda, Nachman. (1983). History, selection and randomness—Towards an analysis of social historical explanations. *Quality and Quantity,* 17: 347–367.

Bendix, Reinhard. (1956). *Work and authority in industry.* New York: Wiley.

Bendix, Reinhard. (1963). Concepts and generalizations in comparative sociological studies. *American Sociological Review,* 28:91–116.

Bendix, Reinhard. (1978). *Kings or people: Power and the mandate to rule.* Berkeley: University of California Press.

Benton, Ted. (1977). *Philosophical foundations of the three sociologies.* Boston: Routledge and Kegan Paul.

Berelson, B. (1952). *Content analysis in communication research.* Glencoe, IL: Free Press.

Berg, Bruce L. (1989). *Qualitative research methods.* Boston: Allyn and Bacon.

Berger, Peter. (1963). *An invitation to sociology: A humanistic perspective.* Garden City, NY: Anchor.

Berger, Peter, and Thomas Luckman. (1967). *The social construction of reality: A treatise in the sociology of knowledge.* Garden City, NY: Anchor.

Berger, Ronald, and Richard Quinney. (2004). *Storytelling sociology: Narrative as social inquiry.* Boulder, CO: Lynne Reinner.

Berinsky, Adam J. (1999). The two faces of public opinion. *American Journal of Political Science,* 43:1209–1230.

Berk, Richard A. (1983). An introduction to sample selection bias in sociological data. *American Sociological Review,* 48:386–397.

Berk, Richard A. (1995). Publishing evaluation research. *Contemporary Sociology,* 24:9–12.

Berland, Gretchen K., et al. (2001). Health information on the Internet. *JAMA: Journal of the American Medical Association,* 285:2612–2622.

Bermant, Gordon. (1982). Justifying social science research in terms of social benefit. In *Ethical issues in social science research,* edited by T. Beauchamp, R. Faden, R. J. Wallace, and L. Walters, pp. 125–142. Baltimore: Johns Hopkins University Press.

Bernard, H. Russell. (1988). *Research methods in cultural anthropology.* Newbury Park, CA: Sage.

Bernard, H. Russell, Peter Killworth, David Kronenfeld, and Lee Sailer. (1984). The problem of information accuracy: The validity of retrospective data. *Annual Review of Anthropology,* 13:495–517.

Bernstein, Robert, A. Chadha, and R. Montjoy. (2001). Overreporting voting: Why it happens and why it matters. *Public Opinion Quarterly,* 65:22–44.

Best, Joel. (2001). *Damned lies and statistics.* Berkeley: University of California Press.

Bhaskar, Roy. (1975). *A realist theory of science.* Atlantic Highlands, NJ: Humanities.

Bhaskar, Roy. (2003). *From science to emancipation: Alienation and enlightenment.* Thousand Oaks, CA: Sage.

Bian, Yanjie, Ronald Breiger, Deborah Davis, and Joseph Galaskiewicz. (2005). Occupation, class, and social networks in urban China. *Social Forces,* 83(4):1443–1468.

Biersack, Aletta. (1989). Local knowledge, local history: Geertz and beyond. In *The new cultural history,* edited by L. Hunt, pp. 72–96. Berkeley: University of California Press.

Billings, Dwight B., and Kathleen Blee. (2000). *The road to poverty.* Cambridge: Cambridge University Press.

Binson, Diane, and Joseph Catania. (1998). Respondents' understanding of the words in sexual behavior questions. *Public Opinion Quarterly,* 62:190–208.

Bischoping, Katherine, and Jennifer Dykema. (1999). Toward a social psychological programme for improving focus group methods of developing questionnaires. *Journal of Official Statistics,* 15:495–516.

Bishop, George F. (1987). Experiments with the middle response alternative in survey questions. *Public Opinion Quarterly,* 51:220–232.

Bishop, George. (1992). Qualitative analysis of question-order and context effects. In *Context effects in social and psychological research,* edited by N. Schwarz and S. Sudman, pp. 149–162. New York: Springer-Verlag.

Bishop, George F., R. W. Oldendick, and A. J. Tuchfarber. (1983). Effects of filter questions in public opinion surveys. *Public Opinion Quarterly,* 47:528–546.

Bishop, George F., R. W. Oldendick, and A. J. Tuchfarber. (1984). What must my interest in politics be if I just told you "I don't know"? *Public Opinion Quarterly,* 48:510–519.

Bishop, George F., R. W. Oldendick, and A. J. Tuchfarber. (1985). The importance of replicating a failure to replicate: Order effects on abortion items. *Public Opinion Quarterly,* 49:105–114.

Bishop, George F., A. J. Tuchfarber, and R. W. Oldendick. (1986). Opinions on fictitious issues: The pressure to answer survey questions. *Public Opinion Quarterly,* 50:240–251.

Bittman, Michael, and Judy Wajcman. (2000). The rush hour: The character of leisure time and gender equity. *Social Forces,* 79:165–190.

Blaikie, Norman. (1993). *Approaches to social enquiry.* Cambridge, MA: Polity.

Blalock, Hubert M., Jr. (1968). The measurement problem: A gap between the language of theory and research. In *Methodology in social research,* edited by H. Blalock and A. Blalock, pp. 5–27. New York: McGraw-Hill.

Blalock, Hubert M., Jr. (1969). *Theory construction: From verbal to mathematical formulations.* Englewood Cliffs, NJ: Prentice-Hall.

Blalock, Hubert M., Jr. (1979a). Measurement and conceptualization problems: The major obstacle to integrating theory and research. *American Sociological Review,* 44:881–894.

Blalock, Hubert M., Jr. (1979b). *Social statistics,* 2nd ed. New York: McGraw-Hill.

Blalock, Hubert M., Jr. (1982). *Conceptualization and measurement in the social sciences.* Beverly Hills, CA: Sage.

Blalock, Hubert M., Jr., and Ann B. Blalock, eds. (1968). *Methodology in social research.* New York: McGraw-Hill.

Blankenship, Albert B. (1977). *Professional telephone surveys.* New York: McGraw-Hill.

Blau, Judith R. (1978). Sociometric structure of a scientific discipline. *Research in sociology of knowledge, sciences and art,* 1:191–206.

Blee, Kathleen M. (1991). *Women of the Klan: Racism and gender in the 1920s.* Berkeley: University of California Press.

Blee, Kathleen M. (2002). *Inside organized racism: Women in the hate movement.* Berkeley: University of California Press.

Blee, Kathleen M., and Dwight B. Billings. (1986). Reconstructing daily life in the past: An hermeneutical approach to ethnographic data. *Sociological Quarterly,* 27:443–462.

Bleicher, Josef. (1980). *Contemporary hermeneutics.* Boston: Routledge and Kegan Paul.

Bloch, Marc. (1953). *The historian's craft,* trans. Peter Putnam. New York: Vintage.

Block, Fred. (1977). Beyond corporate liberalism. *Social Problems,* 24: 353–361.

Block, Fred, and Gene A. Burns. (1986). Productivity as a social problem: The uses and misuses of social indicators. *American Sociological Review,* 51:767–780.

Block, Jennifer. (2003). Science gets sacked. *Nation,* 277(6):5–7.

Bloemraad, Irene. (2006). Citizenship lessons from the past: The contours of immigrant naturalization in the early 20th century. *Social Science Quarterly,* 87(5):927–953.

Bloor, Michael J. (1983). Notes on member validation. In *Contemporary field research,* edited by R. M. Emerson, pp. 156–171. Boston: Little, Brown.

Blum, Debra E. (1989). A dean is charged with plagiarizing a dissertation for his book on Muzak. *Chronicle of Higher Education,* 35:A17.

Blumberg, Stephen, and Julian Luke. (2009). Wireless substitution: Early release of estimates from the National Health Interview Survey, July–December 2008. (report released by Centers for Disease Control May 5, 2009). Available at http://www.cdc.gov/nchs/data/nhis/earlyrelease/wireless200905.pdf. Accessed June 10, 2008.

Blume, Stuart S. (1974). *Toward a political sociology of science.* New York: Free Press.

Blumer, M. (1984). *The Chicago school of sociology.* Chicago: University of Chicago.

Blumer, Martin. (1991a). W. E. B. DuBois as a social investigator: The Philadelphia Negro 1889. In *The social survey in historical perspective, 1880–1940,* edited by M. Blumer, K. Bales, and K. Sklar, pp. 170–188. New York: Cambridge University Press.

Blumer, Martin. (1991b). The decline of the social survey movement and the rise of American empirical sociology. In *The social survey in historical perspective, 1880–1940,* edited by M. Blumer, K. Bales, and K. Sklar, pp. 271–315. New York: Cambridge University Press.

Blumer, Martin. (1992). The growth of applied sociology after 1945: The prewar establishment of the postwar infrastructure. In *Sociology and its publics: The forms and fates of disciplinary organization,* edited by T. C. Halliday and M. Janowitz,

pp. 317–346. Chicago: University of Chicago.

Blumer, Martin, K. Bales, and K. Sklar. (1991). The social survey in historical perspective. In *The social survey in historical perspective, 1880–1940,* edited by M. Blumer, K. Bales, and K. Sklar, pp. 1–48. New York: Cambridge University Press.

Blumstein, Alfred. (1974). Seriousness weights in an index of crime. *American Sociological Review,* 39: 854–864.

Blute, Marion. (1997). History versus science: The evolutionary solution. *Canadian Journal of Sociology,* 22: 345–364.

Bogardus, Emory S. (1959). *Social distance.* Yellow Springs, OH: Antioch Press.

Bogdan, Robert, and Steven J. Taylor. (1975). *Introduction to qualitative research methods: A phenomenological approach to the social sciences.* New York: Wiley.

Bohrnstedt, George. (1992a). Reliability. In *Encyclopedia of Sociology,* Vol. 3, edited by E. and M. Borgatta, pp. 1626–1632. New York: Macmillan.

Bohrnstedt, George. (1992b). Validity. In *Encyclopedia of Sociology,* Vol. 4, edited by E. and M. Borgatta, pp. 2217–2222. New York: Macmillan.

Bohrnstedt, George W., and Edgar F. Borgatta, eds. (1981). *Social measurement: Current issues.* Beverly Hills, CA: Sage.

Bohrnstedt, George, and David Knoke. (1994). *Statistics for social data analysis,* 3rd ed. Itasca, IL: Peacock.

Bollen, Kenneth A., Barbara Entwisle, and Arthur S. Alderson. (1993). Macrocomparative research methods. *Annual Review of Sociology,* 19:321–351.

Bolton, Ruth N., and Tina Bronkhorst. (1996). Questionnaire pretesting: Computer-assisting coding of concurrent protocols. In *Answering questions,* edited by N. Schwarz and S. Sudman, pp. 37–64. San Francisco: Jossey-Bass.

Bonnell, Victoria E. (1980). The uses of theory, concepts and comparison in historical sociology. *Comparative Studies in Society and History,* 22:156–173.

Borgatta, Edgar F., and George W. Bohrnstedt. (1980). Level of measurement: Once over again. *Sociological Methods and Research,* 9:147–160.

Boruch, Robert F. (1982). Methods for revolving privacy problems in social research. In *Ethical issues in social science research,* edited by T. Beauchamp, R. Faden, R. J. Wallace, and L. Walters, pp. 292–313. Baltimore: Johns Hopkins University Press.

Boswell, Terry, and Cliff Brown. (1999). The scope of general theory. *Sociological Methods and Research,* 28:154–185.

Bottomore, Thomas. (1984). *The Frankfurt School.* New York: Tavistock.

Bouchard, Thomas J., Jr. (1976). Unobtrusive measures: An inventory of uses. *Sociological Methods and Research,* 4:267–300.

Bourgeois, Philippe. (1996). *In search of respect: Selling crack in El Barrio.* New York: Cambridge University Press.

Bowker, Geoffrey C. and Susan Leigh-Star. (1999). *Sorting things out: Classification and its consequences.* Cambridge MA: MIT Press.

Boyatzis, Richard E. (1998). *Transforming qualitative information: Thematic analysis and code development.* Thousand Oaks, CA: Sage.

Bradburn, Norman M. (1983). Response effects. In *Handbook of survey research,* edited by P. Rossi, J. Wright, and A. Anderson, pp. 289–328. Orlando, FL: Academic.

Bradburn, Norman M., and Carrie Miles. (1979). Vague qualifiers. *Public Opinion Quarterly,* 43:92–101.

Bradburn, Norman M., and Seymour Sudman. (1980). *Improving interview method and questionnaire design.* San Francisco: Jossey-Bass.

Bradburn, Norman M., and Seymour Sudman. (1988). *Polls and surveys: Understanding what they tell us.* San Francisco: Jossey-Bass.

Bradshaw, York W., and Michael Wallace. (1996). *Global inequalities.* Thousand Oaks, CA: Pine Forge Press.

Bradsher, Keith. (2002). *High and mighty.* New York: Public Affairs.

Brainard, Jeffrey, and Ron Southwick. (August 10, 2001). A record year at the federal trough: Colleges feast on $1.67 billion in earmarks. *Chronicle of Higher Education.*

Brainard, Jeffrey, and Anne Borrego. (September 26, 2003). Academic pork barrel tops $2 billion for first time. *Chronicle of Higher Education.*

Brannigan, Augustine. (1992). Postmodernism. *Encyclopedia of Sociology,* Vol. 3, edited by E. and

M. Borgatta, pp. 1522–1525. New York: Macmillan.

Bratter, Jenifer L., and Rosalind B. King. (2008). "But will it last?": Marital instability among interracial and same-race couples. *Family Relations,* 57(2):160–171.

Braudel, Fernand. (1980). *On history,* trans. Sarah Matthews. Chicago: University of Chicago Press.

Braun, Michael. (2003). Communication and cognition. In *Cross-cultural survey methods,* edited by Janet Harkness, Fons Van de Vijver, and Peter Mohler, pp. 57–67. Hoboken NJ: Wiley.

Bredo, Eric, and Walter Feinberg, eds. (1982). *Knowledge and values in social and educational research.* Philadelphia: Temple University Press.

Brehm, John. (1994). Stubbing our toes for a foot in the door? Prior contact, incentives and survey response. *International Journal of Public Opinion Research,* 6:45–63.

Brenner, Michael. (1985). Survey interviewing. In *The research interview: Uses and approaches,* edited by M. Brenner, J. Brown, and D. Canter, pp. 9–36. New York: Academic Press.

Brenner, Michael, Jennifer Brown, and David Canter, eds. (1985). *The research interview: Uses and approaches.* Orlando, FL: Academic Press.

Brewer, Paul R., Sean Aday, and Kimberly Gross. (2005). Do Americans trust other nations? A panel study. *Social Science Quarterly,* 86(1):36–51.

Brick, J. Michael, Pat D. Brick, Sarah Dipko, Stanley Presser, Clyde Tucker, and Yuan Yangyang. (2007). Cell phone survey feasibility in the U.S.: Sampling and calling cell numbers versus landline numbers. *Public Opinion Quarterly,* 71(1):23–39.

Brickmayer, Johanna D. (2000). Theory-based evaluation in practice. *Evaluation Review,* 24:407–423.

Briggs, Charles L. (1986). *Learning now to ask: A sociolinguistic appraisal of the role of the interview in social science research.* New York: Cambridge University Press.

Brinberg, David, and Joseph E. McGrath. (1982). A network of validity concepts. In *Forms of validity in research,* edited by D. Brinberg and L. Kidder, pp. 5–21. San Francisco: Jossey-Bass.

Brint, Steven. (1994). *In an age of experts: The changing role of professionals in politics and public life.* Princeton, NJ: Princeton University Press.

Britton, Dana M. (1990). Homophobia and homosociality: An analysis of boundary maintenance. *Sociological Quarterly,* 31:423–440.

Broad, W. J., and N. Wade. (1982). *Betrayers of the truth.* New York: Simon and Schuster.

Brodsky, Stanley L., and H. O'Neal Smitherman. (1983). *Handbook of scales for research in crime and delinquency.* New York: Plenum.

Brody, Charles J. (1986). Things are rarely black or white: Admitting gray into the converse model of attitude stability. *American Journal of Sociology,* 92:657–677.

Brown, Jennifer, and David Canter. (1985). The uses of explanation in the research interview. In *The research interview: Uses and approaches,* edited by M. Brenner, J. Brown, and D. Canter, pp. 217–245. New York: Academic Press.

Brown, Richard Harvey. (1978). Symbolic realism and sociological thought. In *Structure, consciousness and history,* edited by R. H. Brown and S. M. Lyman, pp. 14–37. New York: Cambridge University Press.

Brown, Richard Harvey. (1989). *Social science as civic discourse: Essays on the invention, legitimation and uses of social theory.* Chicago: University of Chicago Press.

Brown, Steven R. (1980). *Political subjectivity: Applications of Q methodology in political science.* New Haven, CT: Yale University Press.

Brown, Steven R. (1986). Q technique and method: Principles and procedures. In *New tools for social scientists: Advances and applications in research methods,* edited by W. D. Berry and M. Lewis-Beck, pp. 57–76. Beverly Hills, CA: Sage.

Brym, Robert J. (1980). *Intellectuals and politics.* Boston: George Allen and Unwin.

Burawoy, Michael. (1977). Social structure, homogenization, and the process of status attainment in the United States and Great Britain. *American Journal of Sociology,* 82:1031–1042.

Burawoy, Michael. (1985). Karl Marx and the satanic mills: Factory politics under early capitalism in England, the United States, and Russia. *American Journal of Sociology,* 90:247–282.

Burawoy, Michael. (1989). Two methods in search of science: Skocpol versus Troksky. *Theory and Society,* 18: 759–806.

Burawoy, Michael. (1990). Marxism as science: Historical challenges and theoretical growth. *American Sociological Review,* 55:775–793.

Burawoy, Michael. (1991). The extended case method. In *Ethnography unbound: Power and resistance in the modern metropolis,* edited by M. Burawoy et al., pp. 271–287. Berkeley: University of California Press.

Burawoy, Michael. (1998). The extended case method. *Sociological Theory,* 16:4–33.

Burawoy, Michael, et al. (2004). Public sociologies. *Social Problems,* 51: 103–131.

Burgess, Robert G. (1982a). Approaches to field research. In *Field research,* edited by R. G. Burgess, pp. 1–11. Boston: George Allen and Unwin.

Burgess, Robert G. (1982b). Keeping field notes. In *Field research,* edited by R. G. Burgess, pp. 191–194. Boston: George Allen and Unwin.

Burgess, Robert G. (1982c). The unstructured interview as a conversation. In *Field research,* edited by R. G. Burgess, pp. 107–110. Boston: George Allen and Unwin.

Burke, Peter. (1980). *Sociology and history.* Boston: George Allen and Unwin.

Burke, Peter. (1992). *History and social theory.* Ithaca, NY: Cornell University Press.

Burnstein, Leigh, Howard E. Freeman, and Peter H. Rossi, eds. (1985). *Collecting evaluation data: Problems and solutions.* Beverly Hills, CA: Sage.

Burrage, Michael C., and David Corry. (1981). At sixes and sevens: Occupational status in the city of London from the 14th to the 17th century. *American Sociological Review,* 46:375–392.

Burton, Michael L., and Douglas R. White. (1987). Cross-cultural surveys today. *Annual Review of Anthropology,* 16:143–160.

Büthe, Tim. (2002). Taking temporality seriously: Modeling history and the use of narratives as evidence. *American Political Science Review,* 96:481–493.

Byrne, Noel. (1978). Sociotemporal considerations of everyday life suggested by an empirical study of the bar milieu. *Urban Life,* 6:417–438.

Calasanti, Toni. (2007). Bodacious berry, potency wood and the aging monster: Gender and age relations in anti-aging ads. *Social Forces,* 86(1):335–355.

Calhoun, Craig. (1996). The rise and domestication of historical sociology. In *The historical turn in the human sciences,* edited by T. J. McDonald, pp. 305–337. Ann Arbor: University of Michigan Press.

Camic, Charles. (1980). The institutionalization of the role of scientist: England in the seventeenth century and ancient Greece. *Comparative Social Research,* 3:271–285.

Camic, Charles, and Yu Xie. (1994). The statistical turn in American social science: Columbia University, 1890–1915. *American Sociological Review,* 59:773–805.

Campbell, Donald T., and D. W. Fiske. (1959). Convergent and discriminant validation by the multitrait-multimethod matrix. *Psychological Bulletin,* 56:81–105.

Campbell, Donald T., and Julian C. Stanley. (1963). *Experimental and quasi-experimental designs for research.* Chicago: Rand McNally.

Campbell, John P., Richard L. Daft, and Charles L. Hulin. (1982). *What to study: Generating and developing research questions.* Beverly Hills, CA: Sage.

Cancian, Francesca M., and Cathleen Armstead. (1992). Participatory research. In *Encyclopedia of Sociology,* Vol. 3, edited by E. and M. Borgatta, pp. 1427–1432. New York: Macmillan.

Cannell, Charles F., and Robert L. Kahn. (1968). Interviewing. In *Handbook of social psychology,* 2nd ed., Vol. 2, edited by G. Lindzey and E. Aronson, pp. 526–595. Reading, MA: Addison-Wesley.

Cannell, Charles F., Peter V. Miller, and Lois Oksenberg. (1981). Research on interviewing techniques. In *Sociological methodology, 1981,* edited by S. Leinhardt, pp. 389–436. San Francisco: Jossey-Bass.

Canter, David, Jennifer Brown, and Linda Goat. (1985). Multiple sorting procedure for studying conceptual systems. In *The research interview: Uses and approaches,* edited by M. Brenner, J. Brown, and D. Canter, pp. 79–114. New York: Academic Press.

Cantor, Norman F., and Richard I. Schneider. (1967). *How to study history.* New York: Thomas Y. Crowell.

Caplan, Arthur L. (1982). On privacy and confidentiality in social science research. In *Ethical issues in social science research,* edited by T. Beauchamp, R. Faden, R. J. Wallace, and L. Walters, pp. 315–327. Baltimore: Johns Hopkins University Press.

Cappell, Charles L., and Thomas M. Guterbock. (1992). Visible colleges: The social and conceptual structure of sociology specialties. *American Sociological Review,* 57:266–273.

Capron, Alexander Morgan. (1982). Is consent always necessary in social science research? In *Ethical issues in social science research,* edited by T. Beauchamp, R. Faden, R. J. Wallace, and L. Walters, pp. 215–231. Baltimore: Johns Hopkins University Press.

Carl, Jim. (1994). Parental choice as national policy in England and the United States. *Comparative Education Review,* 38:294–322.

Carley, Michael. (1981). *Social measurement and social indicators: Issues of policy and theory.* London: George Allen and Unwin.

Carmines, E., and R. Zeller. (1979). *Reliability and validity assessment.* Beverly Hills, CA: Sage.

Carney, Thomas F. (1972). *Content analysis: A technique for systematic inference from communications.* Winnipeg: University of Manitoba Press.

Carr, Edward Hallett. (1961). *What is history?* New York: Vintage.

Carr-Hill, Roy A. (1984a). The political choice of social indicators. *Quality and Quantity,* 18:173–191.

Carr-Hill, Roy A. (1984b). Radicalising survey methodology. *Quantity and Quality,* 18:275–292.

Cassell, Catherine, and Phil Johnson. (2006). Action research: Explaining the diversity. *Human Relations,* 59(6):783–814.

Catania, Joseph, D. Dinson, J. Canahola, L. Pollack, W. Hauck, and T. Coates. (1996). Effects of interviewer gender, interviewer choice and item wording on responses to questions concerning sexual behavior. *Public Opinion Quarterly,* 60:345–375.

Caute, David. (1978). *The great fear.* New York: Touchstone.

Chadwick, Bruce A., Howard M. Bahr, and Stan L. Albrecht. (1984). *Social science research methods.* Englewood Cliffs, NJ: Prentice-Hall.

Chafetz, Janet Saltzman. (1978). *A primer on the construction and testing of theories in sociology.* Itasca, IL: Peacock.

Chambers, Marcia. (October 22, 1986). Jesuit priest standing by the survey that Vatican attempted to suppress. *New York Times.*

Channels, Noreen L. (1993). Anticipating media coverage: Methodological decisions regarding criminal justice research. In *Research on sensitive topics,* edited by C. Renzetti and R. Lee, pp. 267–280. Thousand Oaks, CA: Sage.

Charmaz, Kathy. (2003). Grounded theory: Objectivist and constructionist methods. In *Strategies of qualitative inquiry,* 2nd ed., edited by N. Denzin and Y. Lincoln, pp. 249–291. Thousand Oaks CA: Sage.

Chase, Susan E. (2005). Narrative inquiry: Multiple lenses, approaches and voices. In *The Sage handbook of qualitative research,* 3rd edition, edited by Norman K. Denzin and Yvonna S. Lincoln, pp. 651–679. Thousand Oaks CA: Sage.

Chase-Dunn, Christopher. (1989). *Global formation: Structures of the world economy.* Cambridge, MA: Blackwell.

Chavez, Leo R. (2001). *Covering immigration: Popular images and politics of the nation.* Berkeley: University of California Press.

Cheng, Grand H. L., and Darius Chan. (2008). Who suffers more from job insecurity? A meta-analytic review. *Applied Psychology: An International Review* 57(2):272–303.

Chicago manual of style for authors, editors and copywriters, 13th ed., revised and expanded. (1982). Chicago: University of Chicago Press.

Christian, Leah Melani, and Don A. Dillman. (2004). The influence of graphic and symbolic language manipulations on response to self-administered questions. *Public Opinion Quarterly,* 68:57–80.

Christians, Clifford G. (2003). Ethics and politics in qualitative research. In *The Landscape of qualitative research,* 2nd ed., edited by N. Denzin and Y. Lincoln, pp. 208–244. Thousand Oaks, CA: Sage.

Church, Allan H. (1993). Estimating the effect of incentives on mail survey response rates: A meta analysis. *Public Opinion Quarterly,* 57:62–80.

Churchill, Gilbert A., Jr. (1983). *Marketing research: Methodological foundations,* 3rd ed. New York: Dryden.

Cicourel, Aaron. (1964). *Method and measurement in sociology.* Glencoe, IL: Free Press.

Cicourel, Aaron. (1973). *Cognitive sociology.* London: Macmillan.

Cicourel, Aaron. (1982). Interviews, surveys, and the problem of ecological validity. *American Sociologist,* 17:11–20.

Clammer, John. (1984). Approaches to ethnographic research. In *Ethnographic research: A guide to general conduct,* edited by R. F. Ellen, pp. 63–85. Orlando: Academic Press.

Clark, Herbert H., and Michael F. Schober. (1992). Asking questions and influencing answers. In *Questions about questions: Inquiries into the cognitive bases of surveys,* edited by J. Turner, pp. 15–48. New York: Russell Sage Foundation.

Clarke, Michael. (1975). Survival in the field: Implications of personal experience in field work. *Theory and Society,* 2:95–123.

Clemens, Elisabeth S., and Martin D. Hughes. (2002). Recovering past protest: Historical research on social movements. In *Methods of social movement research,* edited by Bert Klandermans and Suzanne Staggenborg, pp. 201–230. Minneapolis: University of Minnesota Press.

Clemens, Elizabeth S., and Walter Powell. (1995). Careers in print: Books, journals, and scholarly reputations. *American Journal of Sociology,* 101:433–497.

Clogg, Clifford C., and D. O. Sawyer. (1981). A comparison of alternative models for analyzing the scalability of response patterns. In *Sociological methodology 1981,* edited by S. Leinhardt, pp. 240–280. San Francisco: Jossey-Bass.

Clubb, Jerome M., E. Austin, C. Geda, and M. Traugott. (1985). Sharing research data in the social sciences. In *Sharing research data,* edited by S. Fineberg, M. Martin, and M. Straf, pp. 39–88. Washington, DC: National Academy Press.

Cogan, Johan, Judith Torney-Purta, and Douglas Anderson. (1988). Knowledge and attitudes toward global issues: Students in Japan and the United States. *Comparative Education Review,* 32:283–297.

Cohen, Patricia Cline. (1982). *A calculating people: The spread of numeracy in early America.* Chicago: University of Chicago Press.

Cohen, Stephen R. (1991). The Pittsburg survey and the social survey movement: A sociological road not taken. In *The social survey in historical perspective, 1880–1940,* edited by M. Blumer, K. Bales, and K. Sklar, pp. 245–268. New York: Cambridge University Press.

Cole, Jonathan R., and Stephen Cole. (1973). *Social stratification in science.* Chicago: University of Chicago Press.

Cole, Stephen. (1978). Scientific reward systems: A comparative analysis. *Research in the Sociology of Knowledge, Science and Art,* 1:167–190.

Cole, Stephen. (1983). The hierarchy of the sciences? *American Journal of Sociology,* 89:111–139.

Cole, Stephen. (1994). Why sociology doesn't make progress like the natural sciences. *Sociological Forum,* 9:133–154.

Cole, Stephen, Jonathan Cole, and Gary A. Simon. (1981). Chance and consensus in peer review. *Science,* 214:881–885.

Coleman, James, and Thomas Hoffer. (1987). *Public and private schools: The impact of community.* New York: Basic Books.

Collier, Andrew. (2005). Philosophical and critical realism. In *The politics of method in the human sciences: Positivism and its epistemological others,* edited by George Steinmetz, pp. 327–365. Durham, NC: Duke University Press.

Collins, H. M. (1983). The sociology of scientific knowledge: Studies of contemporary science. *American Review of Sociology,* 9:265–285.

Collins, Randall. (1984). Statistics versus words. *Sociological Theory,* 2:329–362.

Collins, Randall. (1986). Is 1980s sociology in the doldrums? *American Journal of Sociology,* 91:1336–1355.

Collins, Randall. (1988). *Theoretical sociology.* New York: Harcourt Brace Jovanovich.

Collins, Randall. (1989). Sociology: Proscience or anti-science? *American Sociological Review,* 54:124–139.

Collins, Randall. (1994). Why the social sciences won't become high-consensus, rapid-discovery science. *Sociological Forum,* 9:155–177.

Collins, Randall, and Sal Restivo. (1983). Development, diversity and conflict in the sociology of science. *Sociological Quarterly,* 24:185–200.

Comaroff, John, and Jean Comaroff. (1992). *Ethnography and the historical imagination.* Boulder, CO: Westview.

Committees on the Status of Women in Sociology. (1986). *The treatment of gender in research.* Washington, DC: American Sociological Association.

Connell, R. W. (1990). Notes on American sociology and American power. In *Sociology in America,* edited by H. Gans, pp. 265–271. Thousand Oaks, CA: Sage.

Conrad, Frederick G., and Johnny Blair. (2009). Sources of error in cognitive interviews. *Public Opinion Quarterly,* 73(1):32–55.

Conrad, Frederick G., and Michael Schober. (2000). Clarifying question meaning in a household telephone survey. *Public Opinion Quarterly,* 64:1–28.

Contrad, Peter, and Shulamit Reinharz. (1984). Computers and qualitative data: Editors' introductory essay. *Qualitative Sociology,* 7:3–15.

Converse, Jean M. (1984). Strong arguments and weak evidence: The open/closed questioning controversy of the 1940s. *Public Opinion Quarterly,* 48:267–282.

Converse, Jean M. (1987). *Survey research in the United States: Roots and emergence, 1890–1960.* Berkeley: University of California Press.

Converse, Jean M., and Stanley Presser. (1986). *Survey questions: Handcrafting the standardized questionnaire.* Beverly Hills, CA: Sage.

Cook, Judith A., and Mary Margaret Fonow. (1990). Knowledge and women's interests: Issues of epistemology and methodology in feminist sociological research. In *Feminist research methods,* edited by J. McCarl Nielsen, pp. 69–93. Boulder, CO: Westview.

Cook, Thomas D., and Donald T. Campbell. (1979). *Quasi-experimentation: Design and analysis issues for field settings.* Chicago: Rand McNally.

Cooper, Christopher A., and H. Gibbs Knotts. (2006). Region, race, and support for the South Carolina confederate flag. *Social Science Quarterly,* 87(1):142–154.

Cooper, Harris M. (1984). *The integrative research review: A systematic approach.* Beverly Hills, CA: Sage.

Cornelia, Dean. (August 30, 2005). Scientific savvy? In U.S., not much. *New York Times.*

Corra, Mamadi, and David Willer. (2002). The gatekeeper. *Sociological Theory,* 20(2):180–207.

Corsaro, William A. (1988). Routines in the peer culture of American and Italian nursery school children. *Sociology of Education,* 61:1–14.

Corsaro, William A. (1992). Cross-cultural analysis. In *Encyclopedia of Sociology,* Vol. 1, edited by E. and M. Borgatta, pp. 390–395. New York: Macmillan.

Corsaro, William. (1994). Discussion, debate, and friendship processes: Peer discourse in U.S. and Italian nursery schools. *Sociology of Education,* 67:1–26.

Corsaro, William A., and David Heise. (1990). Event structure models from ethnographic data. *Sociological Methodology,* 20:1–57.

Corsaro, William, and Luisa Molinari. (2000). Priming events and Italian children's transition from preschool to elementary school: Representations and action. *Social Psychology Quarterly,* 63:16–33.

Corsino, Louis. (1987). Fieldworkers blues: Emotional stress and research underinvolvement in fieldwork settings. *Social Science Journal,* 24: 275–285.

Coser, Lewis. (1981). The uses of classical sociological theory. In *The future of the sociological classics,* edited by Buford Rhea, pp. 170–182. Boston: George Allen and Unwin.

Costner, Herbert L. (1969). Theory, deduction and rules of correspondence. *American Journal of Sociology,* 75:245–263.

Costner, Herbert L. (1985). Theory, deduction and rules of correspondence. In *Causal models in the social sciences,* 2nd ed., edited by H. M. Blalock, Jr., pp. 229–250. New York: Aldine.

Cotter, Patrick R., Jeffrey Cohen, and Philip B. Coulter. (1982). Race of interview effects in telephone interviews. *Public Opinion Quarterly,* 46:278–286.

Couch, Carl J. (1987). Objectivity: A crutch and club for bureaucrats/ subjectivity: A haven for lost souls. *Sociological Quarterly,* 28:105–118.

Couper, Mick P. (1997). Survey introductions and data quality. *Public Opinion Quarterly,* 61:317–338.

Couper, Mick P. (2000). Review: Web surveys. *Public Opinion Quarterly,* 64:464–495.

Couper, Mick P. (2008). *Designing effective web surveys.* New York: Cambridge University Press.

Couper, Mick P., Frederick G. Conrad, and Roger Tourangeau. (2007). Visual context effects in web surveys. *Public Opinion Quarterly,* 71(4): 623–634.

Couper, Mick P., and Robert Groves. (2004). Introductory interactions in telephone surveys and nonresponse. In *Standardization and tacit knowledge,* edited by Douglas W. Maynard, et al., pp. 161–177. New York: Wiley.

Couper, Mick P., and Edith de Leeuw. (2003). Nonresponse in cross-cultural and cross-national surveys. In *Cross-cultural survey methods,* edited by J. Harkness, F. Van de Vijver, and P. Mohler, pp. 157–179. Hoboken NJ: Wiley.

Couper, Mick P., and Benjamin Rowe. (1996). Evaluation of a computer assisted self-interview component in a computer-assisted personal interview survey. *Public Opinion Quarterly,* 60:89–105.

Couper, Mick P., Eleanor Singer, et al. (1998). Participation in the 1990 decennial census. *American Politics Quarterly,* 26:59–81.

Couper, Mick P., Eleanor Singer, and Roger Tourangeau. (2003). Understanding the effects of audio-CASI on self-reports of sensitive behavior. *Public Opinion Quarterly,* 67: 385–395.

Couper, Mick P., Roger Tourangeau, and Kristin Kenyon. (2004). Picture this! Exploring visual effects on web surveys. *Public Opinion Quarterly,* 68:255–266.

Couper, Mick P., Michael Traugott, and Mark Lamias. (2001). Web survey design and administration. *Public Opinion Quarterly,* 65:230–253.

Cox, Stephen, and William Davidson. (1995). A meta-analysis of alternative education programs. *Crime and Delinquency,* 41:219–230.

Cozby, Paul C. (1984). *Using computers in the behavioral sciences.* Palo Alto, CA: Mayfield.

Craib, Ian. (1984). *Modern social theory: From Parsons to Habermas.* New York: St. Martin's Press.

Crane, Diana. (1967). The gatekeepers of science: Some factors affecting the selection of articles for scientific journals. *American Sociologist,* 2: 195–201.

Crane, Diana. (1972). *Invisible colleges.* Chicago: University of Chicago Press.

Crespi, Irving. (1987). Surveys as legal evidence. *Public Opinion Quarterly,* 51:84–91.

Cress, Daniel M., and David A. Snow. (1996). Mobilization at the margins: Resources, benefactors, and the viability of homeless social movement organizations. *American Sociological Review,* 61:1089–1109.

Creswell, John W. (1994). *Research design: Qualitative and quantitative approaches.* Thousand Oaks, CA: Sage.

Croyle, Robert T., and Elizabeth Loftus. (1992). Improving episodic memory performance of survey respondents. In *Questions about questions: Inquiries into the cognitive bases of surveys,* edited by J. Turner, pp. 95–101. New York: Russell Sage Foundation.

Crozat, Matthew. (1998). Are the times a-changin'? Assessing the acceptance of protest in Western democracies. In *The movement society,* edited by D. Meyer and S. Tarrow, pp. 59–81. Totowa, NJ: Rowman and Littlefield.

Cullen, Francis T., Bruce Link, and Craig Polanzi. (1982). The seriousness of crime revisited: Have attitudes toward white collar crime changed? *Criminology,* 20:83–102.

Cumings, Bruce. (1997). Boundary displacement: Area studies and international studies during and after the Cold War. *Bulletin of Concerns of Asian Scholars,* 29:6–26.

Cummings, Scott. (1984). The political economy of funding for social science research. *Sociological Inquiry,* 54:154–170.

Curran, Daniel J., and Sandra Cook. (1993). Doing research in post-Tiananmen China. In *Research on sensitive topics,* edited by C. Renzetti and R. Lee, pp. 71–81. Thousand Oaks, CA: Sage.

Czaja, Ronald, Johnny Blair, and Jutta P. Sebestik. (1982). Respondent selection in a telephone survey: A comparison of three techniques. *Journal of Marketing Research,* 19:381–385.

Czaja, Ronald, and Johnny Blair. (2005). *Designing surveys: a guide to decisions and procedures,* 2nd ed. Thousand Oaks, CA: Pine Forge Press.

Dabbs, James M., Jr. (1982). Making things visible. In *Varieties of qualitative research,* edited by J. Van Maanen, J. Dabbs, Jr., and R. R. Faulkner, pp. 31–64. Beverly Hills, CA: Sage.

Dale, Angela, S. Arber, and Michael Procter. (1988). *Doing secondary analysis.* Boston: Unwin Hyman.

Danermark, Berth, M. Ekström, L. Jakobsen, and J. Karlsson. (2002). *Explaining society.* New York: Routledge.

D'Antonio, William V. (August 1989). Executive office report: Sociology on the move. *ASA Footnotes,* 17, p. 2.

D'Antonio, William V. (1992). Recruiting sociologists in a time of changing opportunities. In *Sociology and its publics: The forms and fates of disciplinary organization,* edited by T. Halliday and M. Janowitz, pp. 99–136. Chicago: University of Chicago Press.

Danziger, Kurt. (1988). The question of identity: Who participated in psychological experiments? In *The rise of experimentation in American psychology,* edited by J. Morawski, pp. 35–52. New Haven, CT: Yale University Press.

Danziger, Sandra K. (1979). On doctor watching: Fieldwork in medical settings. *Urban Life,* 7:513–532.

Darnton, Robert. (1978). The history of mentalities. In *Structure, consciousness and history,* edited by R. H. Brown and S. M. Lyman, pp. 106–136. New York: Cambridge University Press.

Davis, Darren W. (1997). The direction of race of interviewer effects among African-Americans: Donning the black mask. *American Journal of Political Science,* 41:309–322.

Davis, Fred. (1959). The cabdriver and his fare: Facets of a fleeting relationship. *American Journal of Sociology,* 65:158–165.

Davis, Fred. (1973). The Martian and the convert: Ontological polarities in social research. *Urban Life,* 2:333–343.

Davis, James A. (1985). *The logic of causal order.* Beverly Hills, CA: Sage.

Davis, James A., and Tom W. Smith. (1986). *General social surveys 1972–1986 cumulative codebook.* Chicago: National Opinion Research Center, University of Chicago.

Davis, James A., and Tom W. Smith. (1992). *The NORC General Social Survey: A user's guide.* Newbury Park, CA: Sage.

Dawes, R. M., and T. W. Smith. (1985). Attitude and opinion measurement. In *Handbook of social psychology,* 3rd ed., Vol. 1, edited by G. Lindzey and E. Aronson, pp. 509–566. New York: Random House.

Dean, John P., Robert L. Eichhorn, and Lois R. Dean. (1969). Fruitful informants for intensive interviewing. In *Issues in participant observation,* edited by G. McCall and J. L. Simmons, pp. 142–144. Reading, MA: Addison-Wesley.

Dean, John P., and William Foote Whyte. (1969). How do you know if the informant is telling the truth? In *Issues in participant observation,* edited by G. McCall and J. L. Simmons, pp. 105–115. Reading, MA: Addison-Wesley.

Deegan, Mary Jo. (1988). *Jane Addams and the men of the Chicago School, 1892–1918.* New Brunswick: Transaction.

De Heer, Wim. (1999). International response trends: Results from an international survey. *Journal of Official Statistics,* 15:129–142.

DeLamater, John, and Pat MacCorquodale. (1975). The effects of interview schedule variations on reported sexual behavior. *Sociological Methods and Research,* 4:215–236.

DeLeeuw, Edith, Mario Callegaro, Joop Hox, Elly Korendijk, Gerty Lensvelt-Mulders. (2007). The influence of advance letters on response in telephone surveys: A meta-analysis. *Public Opinion Quarterly,* 71(3):413–143.

Della Porta, Donatella, and Michael Keating. (2008). Introduction. In *Approaches and methodologies in the social sciences.* Edited by D. Della Porta and M. Keating, pp. 1–15. New York: Cambridge University Press.

DeMaio, Theresa J. (1980). Refusals: Who, where and why? *Public Opinion Quarterly,* 44:223–233.

DeMaio, Theresa J. (1984). Social desirability and survey measurement: A review. In *Surveying subjective phenomena,* Vol. 2, edited by C. Turner and E. Martin, pp. 257–282. New York: Russell Sage Foundation.

Denzin, Norman K. (1970). Symbolic interactionism and ethnomethodology. In *Understanding everyday life,*

edited by J. Douglas, pp. 261–286. Chicago: Aldine.

Denzin, Norman K. (1989). *The research act: A theoretical introduction to sociological methods,* 3rd ed. Englewood Cliffs, NJ: Prentice-Hall.

Denzin, Norman K., and Kai Erikson. (1982). On the ethics of disguised observation: An exchange. In *Social research ethics,* edited by M. Blume. New York: Macmillan.

Denzin, Norman K., and Yvonna S. Lincoln, eds. (1994). Introduction: Entering the field of qualitative research. In *Handbook of qualitative research,* pp. 1–18. Thousand Oaks, CA: Sage.

Denzin, Norman K., and Yvonna S. Lincoln. (2003a). Introduction. In *Strategies of Qualitative Inquiry,* 2nd ed., edited by N. Denzin and Y. Lincoln, pp. 1–45. Thousand Oaks, CA: Sage.

Denzin, Norman K., and Yvonna S. Lincoln. (2003b). Introduction. In *The landscape of qualitative research,* 2nd ed., edited by N. Denzin and Y. Lincoln, pp. 1–45. Thousand Oaks, CA: Sage.

Derksen, Linda, and John Gartell. (1992). Scientific explanation. In *Encyclopedia of sociology,* Vol. 4, edited by E. and M. Borgatta, pp. 1711–1720. New York: Macmillan.

Desan, Susanne. (1989). Crowds, community and ritual in the work of E. P. Thompson and Natalie Davis. In *The new cultural history,* edited by L. Hunt, pp. 24–46. Berkeley: University of California Press.

Devault, Marjorie L. (1990). Talking and listening from women's standpoint: Feminist strategies for interviewing and analysis. *Social Problems,* 37:96–116.

deVaus, D. A. (1986). *Surveys in social research.* Boston: George Allen and Unwin.

Dexter, Lewis A. (1970). *Elite and specialized interviewing.* Evanston, IL: Northwestern University Press.

Diamond, Sigmund. (1988). Informed consent and survey research: The FBI and the University of Michigan Survey Research Center. In *Surveying social life: Papers in honor of Herbert H. Hyman,* edited by H. O'Gorman, pp. 72–99. Middletown, CT: Wesleyan University Press.

Dibble, Vernon K. (1963). Four types of inference from documents to events. *History and Theory,* 3:203–221.

Dickson, David. (1984). *The new politics of science.* Chicago: University of Chicago Press.

Diener, Edward, and Rick Crandall. (1978). *Ethics in social and behavioral research.* Chicago: University of Chicago Press.

Dijkstra, Wil, and Johannes van der Zouwen, eds. (1982). *Response behavior in the survey interview.* New York: Academic Press.

Dillman, Don A. (1978). *Mail and telephone surveys: The total design method.* New York: Wiley.

Dillman, Don A. (1983). Mail and other self-administered questionnaires. In *Handbook of survey research,* edited by P. Rossi, J. Wright, and A. Anderson, pp. 359–377. Orlando, FL: Academic Press.

Dillman, Don A. (1991). The design and administration of mail surveys. *Annual Review of Sociology,* 17: 225–249.

Dillman, Don A. (2000). *Mail and Internet surveys: The tailored design method,* 2nd ed. New York: Wiley.

Dillman, Don, and Cleo Redline. (2004). Testing paper self-administered questionnaires. In *Methods for testing and evaluating survey questionnaires,* edited by Stanley Presser et al., pp. 299–318. New York: Wiley.

Dillman, Don A., Eleanor Singer, Jon Clark, and James Treat. (1996). Effects of benefits, appeals, mandatory appeals and variations in statements of confidentiality on completion rates for census questionnaires. *Public Opinion Quarterly,* 60:376–389.

Dillman, Don A., and Leah Melani Christian. (2005). Survey mode as a source of instability in responses across surveys. *Field Methods* 17(1):30–52.

Dohan, Daniel, and Martin Sanchez-Jankowski. (1998). Using computers to analyze ethnographic field data. *Annual Review of Sociology,* 24:477–498.

Donald, Robert B., et al. (1983). *Writing clear paragraphs,* 2nd ed. Englewood Cliffs, NJ: Prentice-Hall.

Dooley, David. (1984). *Social research methods.* Englewood Cliffs, NJ: Prentice-Hall.

Douglas, Jack D. (1976). *Investigative social research.* Beverly Hills, CA: Sage.

Douglas, Jack D. (1985). *Creative interviewing.* Beverly Hills, CA: Sage.

Douglas, Jack D., and Paul K. Rasmussen. (1977). *The nude beach.* Beverly Hills, CA: Sage.

Drass, Kriss. (1980). The analysis of qualitative data: A computer program. *Urban Life,* 9:332–353.

Dressler, William H. (1991). *Stress and adaptation in the context of culture: Depression in a southern black community.* Albany: State University of New York Press.

DuBois, W. E. Burghardt. (1899). *The Philadelphia Negro.* New York: Benjamin Bloom.

Dunaway, David K., and Willa K. Baum, eds. (1984). *Oral history.* Nashville, TN: Association for State and Local History.

Duncan, Otis Dudley. (1975). *Introduction to structural equation models.* New York: Academic Press.

Duncan, Otis Dudley. (1984). *Notes on social measurement: Historical and critical.* New York: Russell Sage Foundation.

Duncan, Otis Dudley, and Magnus Stenbeck. (1988). No opinion or not sure? *Public Opinion Quarterly,* 52: 513–525.

Duneier, Mitchell. (1999). *Sidewalk.* New York: Farrar, Straus and Giroux.

Durkheim, Émile. (1938). *Rules of the sociological method,* trans. Sarah Solovay and John Mueller, edited by G. Catlin. Chicago: University of Chicago Press.

Dutka, Solomon. (1982). The use of survey research in legal proceedings. *American Bar Association Journal,* 68(11):1508–1511.

Dykema, Jennifer, and Nora Cate Schaeffer. (2000). Events, instruments, and reporting errors. *American Sociological Review,* 65:619–629.

Dynes, Russell R. (1984). The institutionalization of COSSA. *Sociological Inquiry,* 54:211–229.

Earl, Jennifer, Andres Martin, John McCarthy, and Sarah Soule. (2004). The use of newspaper data in the study of collective behavior. *Annual Review of Sociology,* 30:65–80.

Easterday, Lois, Diana Papademas, Laura Schorr, and Catherine Valentine. (1982). The making of a female researcher: Role problems in fieldwork. In *Field research,* edited by R. G. Burgess, pp. 62–67. Boston: George Allen and Unwin.

Eastrope, Gary. (1974). *History of social research methods.* London: Longman.

Eckberg, Douglas Lee, and Lester Hill, Jr. (1979). The paradigm concept and sociology. *American Sociological Review,* 44:937–947.

Economist. (2001) What's your poison? *The Economist,* March 31, 2001.

Eder, Donna. (1981). Ability grouping as a self-fulfilling prophecy: A microanalysis of teacher–student interaction. *Sociology of Education,* 54:151–162.

Eder, Donna. (1985). The cycle of popularity: Interpersonal relations among female adolescents. *Sociology of Education,* 58:154–165.

Eder, Donna. (1995). *School talk: Gender and adolescent culture.* New Brunswick, NJ: Rutgers University Press.

Eder, Donna, and David Kinney. (1995). The effect of middle school extracurricular activities on adolescents' popularity and peer status. *Youth and Society,* 26:298–325.

Edward, G. Franklin. (1974). E. Franklin Frazier. In *Black sociologists: Historical and contemporary perspectives,* edited by J. Blackwell and M. Janowitz, pp. 85–117. Chicago: University of Chicago Press.

Edwards, Allen L. (1957). *Techniques of attitude scale construction.* New York: Appleton-Century-Crofts.

Edwards, Rosalind. (1993). An education in interviewing: Placing the researcher and research. In *Research on sensitive topics,* edited by C. Renzetti and R. Lee, pp. 181–196. Thousand Oaks, CA: Sage.

Eichler, Margrit. (1988). *Nonsexist research methods: A practical guide.* Boston: George Allen and Unwin.

Einwohner, Rachel. (2003). Opportunity, honor, and action in the Warsaw Ghetto uprising of 1943. *American Journal of Sociology,* 109:650–675.

Elder, Glen H., Jr., Eliza Pavalko, and Elizabeth Clipp. (1993). *Working with archival data: Studying lives.* Thousand Oaks, CA: Sage.

Elder, Joseph W. (1973). Problems of cross-cultural methodology: Instrumentation and interviewing in India. In *Comparative social research,* edited by M. Armer and A. D. Grimshaw, pp. 119–144. New York: Wiley.

Eliasoph, Nina. (1998). *Avoiding politics: How Americans produce apathy in everyday life.* New York: Cambridge University Press.

Ellen, R. F., ed. (1984a). *Ethnographic research: A guide to general conduct.* Orlando: Academic Press.

Ellen, R. F. (1984b). Some other interactionist methods. In *Ethnographic research: A guide to general conduct,* edited by R. F. Ellen, pp. 273–293. Orlando: Academic Press.

Elster, Jon. (1998). A plea for mechanisms. In *Social mechanisms: An analytical approach to social theory,* edited by Peter Hedstrom and Richard Swedberg, pp. 45–73. New York: Cambridge University Press.

Ember, Carol R. (1977). Cross-cultural cognitive studies. *Annual Review of Anthropology,* 6:33–56.

Ember, Carol R., and Melvin Ember. (2001). *Cross-cultural research methods.* Lanham, MD: Altamira Press.

Emerson, Robert M. (1981). Observational field work. *Annual Review of Sociology,* 7:351–378.

Emerson, Robert M. (1983). Introduction. In *Contemporary field research,* edited by R. M. Emerson, pp. 1–16. Boston: Little, Brown.

Emerson, Robert M., Rachel Fretz, and Linda Shaw. (1995). *Writing ethnographic field notes.* Chicago: University of Chicago Press.

Emigh, Rebecca Jean. (1997). The power of negative thinking: The use of negative case methodology in the development of sociological theory. *Theory and Society,* 26:649–684.

Emigh, Rebecca Jean. (2003). Economic interests and structural relations: The underdevelopment of capitalism in fifteenth-century Tuscany. *American Journal of Sociology,* 108: 1075–1113.

Edgell, Penny, and Eric Tranby. (2007). Religious influences on understandings of racial inequality in the United States. *Social Problems,* 54(2): 263–288.

Ennis, James G. (1992). The social organization of sociological knowledge: Modeling the intersection of specialties. *American Sociological Review,* 57:259–265.

Entwisle, Barbara, Katherine Faust, Ronald Rindfuss, and Toshiko Kaneda. (2007). Networks and contexts: Variation in the structure of social ties. *American Journal of Sociology,* 112(5):1495–1533.

ERIC. (October 1, 1976). The faculty work week at the University of Connecticut. ERIC Database# ED142157.

Erikson, Kai T. (1970). A comment on disguised observation in sociology. In *Qualitative methodology,* edited by W. J. Filstead, pp. 252–260. Chicago: Markham.

Erikson, Kai T. (1978). *Everything in its path.* New York: Touchstone.

Evans, Peter, and John D. Stephens. (1989). Studying development since the sixties: The emergence of a new comparative political economy. *Theory and Society,* 17:713–746.

Fantasia, Rick. (1988). *Cultures of solidarity: Consciousness, action and contemporary American workers.* Berkeley: University of California Press.

Faris, R. E. L. (1967). *Chicago sociology, 1920–1932.* San Francisco: Chandler.

Fay, Brian. (1975). *Social theory and political practice.* London: George Allen and Unwin.

Fay, Brian. (1987). *Critical social science: Liberation and its limits.* Ithaca, NY: Cornell University Press.

Fazio, Russel, H. J. R. Jackson, B. C. Dunton, and C. J. Williams. (1995). Variability in automatic activation as an unobtrusive measure of racial attitudes: A bona fide pipeline? *Journal of Personality and Social Psychology,* 69(6):1013–1027.

Featherman, David L., and Richard C. Rockwell. (1992). Social science research council. In *Encyclopedia of sociology,* Vol. 4, edited by E. and M. Borgatta, pp. 1942–1945. New York: Macmillan.

Ferguson, Kristin M., Qiaobing Wu, Donna Sprjijt-Metz, and Grace Dyrness. (2007). Outcomes evaluation in faith-based social services: Are we evaluating faith accurately? *Research on Social Work Practice,* 17(2): 264–276.

Ferriss, Abbott L. (1988). The uses of social indicators. *Social Forces,* 66:601–617.

Fetterman, David M. (1989). *Ethnography: Step by step.* Newbury Park, CA: Sage.

Fetzer, Joel S. (2000). *Public attitudes toward immigration in the United States, France and Germany.* New York: Cambridge University Press.

Fichter, Joseph H., and William L. Kolb. (1970). Ethical limitations on sociological reporting. In *Qualitative methodology,* edited by W. J. Filstead, pp. 261–270. Chicago: Markham.

Field, Andy, and Graham Hole. (2003). *How to Design and Test Experiments.* Thousand Oaks, CA: Sage

Fielding, Nigel G., and Raymond M. Lee, eds. (1991). *Using computers in qualitative research.* Newbury Park, CA: Sage.

Fine, Gary Alan. (1979). Small groups and culture creation: The idioculture of Little League baseball teams. *American Sociological Review,* 44: 733–745.

Fine, Gary Alan. (1980). Cracking diamonds: Observer role in Little League baseball settings and the acquisition of social competence. In *Fieldwork experience,* edited by W. B. Shaffir, R. A. Stebbins, and A. Turowetz, pp. 117–132. New York: St. Martin's Press.

Fine, Gary Alan. (1987). *With the boys: Little League baseball and preadolescent culture.* Chicago: University of Chicago Press.

Fine, Gary Alan. (1988). The ten commandments of writing. *The American Sociologist,* 19:152–157.

Fine, Gary Alan. (1990). Organizational time: The temporal experience of restaurant kitchens. *Social Forces,* 69:95–114.

Fine, Gary Alan. (1992). The culture of production: Aesthetic choices and constraints in culinary work. *American Journal of Sociology,* 97: 1268–1294.

Fine, Gary Alan. (1996). *Kitchens: The culture of restaurant work.* Berkeley: University of California Press.

Fine, Gary Alan. (1999). Field labor and ethnographic reality. *Journal of Contemporary Ethnography,* 28:532–540.

Fine, Gary Alan, and Barry Glassner. (1979). Participant observation with children: Promise and problems. *Urban Life,* 8:153–174.

Finkel, Steven E., Thomas M. Guterbock, and Marian J. Borg. (1991). Race-of-interviewer effects in a pre-election poll: Virginia 1989. *Public Opinion Quarterly,* 55:313–330.

Finley, M. I. (Summer 1977). Progress in historiography. *Daedalus,* pp. 125–142.

Finsterbusch, Kurt, and Annabelle Bender Motz. (1980). *Social research for policy decisions.* Belmont, CA: Wadsworth.

Finsterbusch, Kurt, and C. P. Wolf. (1981). *Methodology of social impact assessment.* Stroudsburg, PA: Hutchinson Ross.

Firebaugh, Glenn. (1980). Cross-national versus historical regression models. *Comparative Social Research,* 3:333–344.

Firebaugh, Glenn. (2008). *Seven rules for social research.* Princeton, NJ: Princeton University Press.

Fischer, Claude S. (1992). *America calling: A social history of the telephone to 1940.* Berkeley: University of California Press.

Fischer, Claude S., et al. (1996). *Inequality by design: Cracking the bell curve myth.* Princeton, NJ: Princeton University Press.

Fischer, David H. (1970). *Historians' fallacies: Towards a logic of historical thought.* New York: Harper & Row.

Fischer, Frank. (1985). Critical evaluation of public policy: A methodological case study. In *Critical theory and public life,* edited by J. Forester, pp. 231–257. Cambridge, MA: MIT Press.

Fiske, Donald W. (1982). Convergent-discriminant validation in measurements and research strategies. In *Forms of validation in research,* edited by D. Brinberg and L. H. Kidder, pp. 72–92. San Francisco: Jossey-Bass.

Fiske, Edward B. (July 12, 1989). The misleading concept of "average" on reading tests changes, and more students fall below it. *New York Times.*

Fletcher, Colin. (1974). *Beneath the surface: An account of three styles of sociological research.* Boston: Routledge and Kegan Paul.

Flick, Uwe. (1998). *An introduction to qualitative research.* Thousand Oaks, CA: Sage.

Flora, Cornelia Butler. (1979). Changes in women's status in women's magazine fiction: Differences by social class. *Social Problems,* 26:558–569.

Foddy, William. (1993). *Constructing questions for interviews and questionnaires: Theory and practice in social research.* New York: Cambridge University Press.

Foddy, William. (1995). Probing: A dangerous practice in social surveys? *Quality and Quantity,* 29:73–86.

Fontana, Andrea, and James H. Frey. (1994). Interviewing: The art of science. In *Handbook of qualitative research,* edited by N. Denzin and Y. Lincoln, pp. 361–376. Thousand Oaks, CA: Sage.

Form, Willam H. (1973). Field problems in comparative research. In *Comparative social research,* edited by M. Armer and A. D. Grimshaw, pp. 83–117. New York: Wiley.

Foster, Gary S., Richard L. Hummel, and Donald J. Adamchak. (1998). Patterns of conception, natality and mortality from midwestern cemeteries: A sociological analysis of historical data. *Sociological Quarterly,* 39: 473–490.

Fowler, Edward. (1996). *San'ya blues: Laboring life in contemporary Tokyo.* Ithaca, NY: Cornell University Press.

Fowler, Floyd J., Jr. (1984). *Survey research methods.* Beverly Hills, CA: Sage.

Fowler, Floyd J., Jr. (1992). How unclear terms can affect survey data. *Public Opinion Quarterly,* 56:218–231.

Fowler, Floyd J. (2004). The case for more split-sample experiments in developing survey instruments. In *Methods for testing and evaluating survey questionnaires,* edited by Stanley Presser et al., pp. 173–188. New York: Wiley.

Fowler, Floyd Jackson, and Charles Cannell. (1996). Using behavioral coding to identify cognitive problems with survey questions. In *Answering Questions,* edited by N. Schwarz and S. Sudman, pp. 15–36. San Francisco: Jossey-Bass.

Fox, James Alan, and Paul E. Tracy. (1986). *Randomized response: A method for sensitive surveys.* Beverly Hills, CA: Sage.

Fox, John. (1992). Statistical graphics. In *Encyclopedia of Sociology,* Vol. 4, edited by E. and M. Borgatta, pp. 2054–2073. New York: Macmillan.

Fox, Richard, Melvin R. Crask, and Jonghoon Kim. (1988). Mail survey response rate: A meta-analysis of selected techniques for inducing response. *Public Opinion Quarterly,* 52:467–491.

Franke, Charles O. (1983). Ethnography. In *Contemporary field research,* edited by R. M. Emerson, pp. 60–67. Boston: Little, Brown.

Franke, Richard H., and James D. Kaul. (1978). The Hawthorne experiments: First statistical interpretation. *American Sociological Review,* 43: 623–643.

Frankel, Martin. (1983). Sampling theory. In *Handbook of survey research,* edited by P. Rossi, J. Wright, and A. Anderson, pp. 21–67. Orlando, FL: Academic Press.

Franzosi, Roberto. (1998). Narrative analysis—or why (and how) sociologists should be interested in narrative. *Annual Review of Sociology,* 24: 517–554.

Frazier, E. Franklin. (1957). *The black bourgeoisie.* Glencoe, IL: Free Press.

Frechette-Schrader, Kristin. (1994). *Ethics of scientific research.* Lanham, MD: Rowland and Littlefield.

Freeman, Howard. (1983). *Applied sociology.* San Francisco: Jossey-Bass.

Freeman, Howard. (1992). Evaluation research. In *Encyclopedia of Sociology,* Vol. 2, edited by E. and M. Borgatta, pp. 594–598. New York: Macmillan.

Freeman, Howard, and Merrill J. Shanks, eds. (1983). The emergence of computer assisted survey research. *Sociological Methods and Research,* 23:115–230.

Freidson, Eliot. (1986). *Professional powers: A study of the institutionalization of formal knowledge.* Chicago: University of Chicago Press.

Freidson, Eliot. (1994). *Professionalism reborn: Theory, prophecy and policy.* Chicago: University of Chicago Press.

Freire, Paulo. (1970). *Pedagogy of the oppressed,* trans. Myra Bergman Ramos. New York: Seabury.

Frey, Frederick W. (1970). Cross-cultural survey research in political science. In *The methodology of comparative research,* edited by R. Holt and J. Turner, pp. 173–294. New York: Free Press.

Frey, James H. (1983). *Survey research by telephone.* Beverly Hills, CA: Sage.

Friedrichs, Robert W. (1970). *A sociology of sociology.* New York: Free Press.

Frost, Peter, and Ralph Stablein, eds. (1992). *Doing exemplary research.* Newbury Park, CA: Sage.

Fuchs, Stephan, and Jonathan H. Turner. (1986). What makes a science "mature"? Patterns of organizational control in scientific production. *Sociological Theory,* 4:143–150.

Fuller, Linda. (1988). Fieldwork in forbidden terrain: The U.S. state and the case of Cuba. *American Sociologist,* 19:99–120.

Fuhse, Jan A. (2009). The Meaning Structure of Social Networks. *Sociological Theory,* 27(1):51–73.

Fulkerson, Gregory M., and Gretchen Thompson. (2008). The evolution of a contested concept: A meta analysis of social capital definitions and trends (1988–2006). *Sociological Inquiry,* 78(4):536–557.

Fumento, Michael. (August 1998). Road rage versus reality. *Atlantic Monthly,* 282:12–17.

Futrell, Robert, and Pete Simi. (2004). Free spaces, collective identity, and the persistence of U.S. White Power activism. *Social Problems,* 51:16–42.

Galaskiewicz, Joseph. (1985). Professional networks and the institutionalization of a single mind set. *American Sociological Review,* 50:639–658.

Galaskiewicz, Joseph. (1987). The study of a business elite and corporate philanthropy in a United States metropolitan area. In *Research methods for elite studies,* edited by G. Moyser and M. Wagstaffe, pp. 147–165. Boston: George Allen and Unwin.

Galaskiewicz, Joseph, and Stanley Wasserman. (1993). Social network analysis: Concepts, methodology and directions for the 1990s. *Sociological Methods and Research,* 22:3–22.

Gallie, W. B. (1963). The historical understanding. *History and Theory,* 3:149–202.

Galliher, John F., and James L. McCartney. (1973). The influence of funding agencies on juvenile delinquency research. *Social Problems,* 21:77–90.

Gamson, William A. (1992). *Talking politics.* Cambridge: Cambridge University Press.

Gangl, Markus. (2004). Welfare states and the scar effects of unemployment. *American Journal of Sociology,* 109:1319–1364.

Gans, Herbert J. (1982). The participant observer as a human being: Observations on the personal aspects of fieldwork. In *Field research,* edited by R. G. Burgess, pp. 53–61. Boston: George Allen and Unwin.

Garfinkel, Harold. (1967). *Studies in ethnomethodology.* Englewood Cliffs, NJ: Prentice-Hall.

Garfinkel, Harold. (1974a). The origins of the term "ethnomethodology." In *Ethnomethodology,* edited by R. Turner, pp. 15–18. Middlesex: Penguin.

Garfinkel, Harold. (1974b). The rational properties of scientific and common sense activities. In *Positivism and sociology,* edited by A. Giddens, pp. 53–74. London: Heinemann.

Gartell, C. David, and John W. Gartell. (1996). Positivism in sociological practice, 1967–1990. *Canadian Review of Sociology and Anthropology,* 33:143–159.

Gartell, C. David, and John W. Gartell. (2002). Positivism in sociological research: USA and UK (1966–1990). *British Journal of Sociology,* 53: 639–657.

Gaskell, George, Daniel Wright, and Colm O'Muircheartaigh. (2000). Telescoping landmark events. *Public Opinion Quarterly,* 64:77–89.

Gaston, Jerry. (1978). *The reward system in British and American science.* New York: Wiley.

Geer, John G. (1988). What do open-ended questions measure? *Public Opinion Quarterly,* 52:365–371.

Geertz, Clifford. (1973). *The interpretation of cultures.* New York: Basic Books.

Geertz, Clifford. (1979). From the native's point of view: On the nature of anthropological understanding. In *Interpretative social science: A reader,* edited by P. Rabinow and W. Sullivan, pp. 225–242. Berkeley: University of California Press.

Geiger, Roger L. (1986). *To advance knowledge: The growth of American research universities, 1900–1940.* New York: Oxford University Press.

Gentile, Douglas. (2008). Pathological video-game use among youth ages 8 to 18: A national study. *Psychological Science,* 20(5):594–602.

George, Alexander L., and Andrew Bennett. (2005). *Case studies and theory development in the social sciences.* Cambridge, MA: MIT Press.

Georges, Robert A., and Michael O. Jones. (1980). *People studying people.* Berkeley: University of California Press.

Gephart, Robert P., Jr. (1988). *Ethnostatistics: Qualitative foundations for quantitative research.* Newbury Park, CA: Sage.

Gerring, John. (2001). *Social science methodology: A critical framework.* New York: Cambridge University Press.

Gerring, John. (2007). *Case study research: Principles and practices.* New York: Cambridge University Press.

Gibbs, Jack. (1989). Conceptualization of terrorism. *American Sociological Review,* 54:329–340.

Giddens, Anthony. (1976). *New rules of sociological method: Positivist critique of interpretative sociologies.* New York: Basic Books.

Giddens, Anthony. (1978). Positivism and its critics. In *A history of sociological analysis,* edited by T. Bottomore and R. Nisbet. New York: Basic Books.

Giddens, Anthony. (1994). Elites and power. In *Social stratification: Class, race & gender in sociological perspective,* edited by D. Grusky, pp. 170–174. Boulder, CO: Westview.

Gieryn, Thomas F. (1978). Problem retention and problem change in science. In *The sociology of science,* edited by J. Gaston. San Francisco: Jossey-Bass.

Gieryn, Thomas F. (1999). *Cultural boundaries of science: Credibility on the line.* Chicago: University of Chicago Press.

Gilbert, Margaret. (1992). *On social facts.* Princeton, NJ: Princeton University Press.

Gilens, Martin. (1996). Race and poverty in America. *Public Opinion Quarterly,* 60(4):515–541.

Gillespie, Richard. (1988). The Hawthorne experiments and the politics of experimentation. In *The rise of experimentation in American psychology,* edited by J. Morawski, pp. 114–137. New Haven, CT: Yale University Press.

Gillespie, Richard. (1991). *Manufacturing knowledge: A history of the Hawthorne experiments.* New York: Cambridge University Press.

Gilljam, Mikael, and David Granberg. (1993). Should we take don't know for an answer? *Public Opinion Quarterly,* 57:348–357.

Glaser, Barney, and Anselm Strauss. (1967). *The discovery of grounded theory.* Chicago: Aldine.

Glaser, Barney, and Anselm Strauss. (1968). *A time for dying.* Chicago: Aldine.

Glasser, Gerald J., and Gale O. Metzger. (1972). Random digit dialing as a method of telephone sampling. *Journal of Marketing Research,* 9: 59–64.

Glucksmann, Miriam. (1974). *Structuralist analysis in contemporary social thought: A comparison of the theories of Claude Levi-Strauss and Louis Althusser.* Boston: Routledge and Kegan Paul.

Gold, Raymond L. (1969). Roles in sociological field observation. In *Issues in participant observation,* edited by

G. J. McCall and J. L. Simmons, pp. 30–38. Reading, MA: Addison-Wesley.

Golden, Tim. (December 9, 1996). Donations to universities sometimes carry a price. *New York Times.*

Goldstein, Kenneth M., and M. Kent Jennings. (2002). The effect of advance letters on cooperation in a list sample telephone survey. *Public Opinion Quarterly,* 66:608–617.

Goldstein, Robert Justin. (1978). *Political repression in modern America.* New York: Schenckman.

Goldstone, Jack A. (1997). Methodological issues in comparative macrosociology. *Comparative Social Research,* 16:107–120.

Goldthorpe, John. (1977). The relevance of history to sociology. In *Sociological research methods,* edited by M. Bulmer, pp. 178–191. London: Macmillan.

Goldthorpe, John. (1991). The uses of history in sociology: Reflections on some recent tendencies. *British Journal of Sociology,* 42:211–230.

Goldthorpe, John H. (1997). Current issues in comparative macrosociology: A debate on methodological issues. *Comparative Social Research,* 16: 1–26.

Gonor, George. (1977). "Situation" versus "frame": The "interactionist" and the "structuralist" analysis of everyday life. *American Sociological Review,* 42:854–867.

Goode, Erica. (February 5, 2002). A rare day: The movies get mental illness right. *New York Times.*

Goodwin, Jeff. (2006). A theory of categorical terrorism. *Social Forces,* 84(4):2027–2046.

Gorden, Raymond. (1980). *Interviewing: Strategy, techniques and tactics,* 3rd ed. Homewood, IL: Dorsey Press.

Gorden, Raymond. (1992). *Basic interviewing skills.* Itasca, IL: Peacock.

Gordon, David F. (1987). Getting close by staying distant: Fieldwork with proselytizing groups. *Qualitative Sociology,* 10:267–287.

Gordon, Randall A., T. A. Bindrim, M. L. McNicholas, and T. L. Walden. (1988). Perceptions of blue-collar and white-collar crime: The effect of defendant race on simulated juror decisions. *Journal of Social Psychology,* 128:191–197.

Gorelick, Sherry. (1991). Contradictions of feminist methodology. *Gender and Society,* 5:459–477.

Gotham, Kevin Fox, and William G. Staples. (1996). Narrative analysis and the new historical sociology. *Sociological Quarterly,* 37:481–502.

Gouldner, Alvin. (1970). *The coming crisis of Western sociology.* New York: Basic Books.

Gouldner, Alvin W. (1976). The dark side of the dialectic: Toward a new objectivity. *Sociological Inquiry,* 46:3–16.

Goward, Nicola. (1984a). Publications on fieldwork experiences. In *Ethnographic research: A guide to general conduct,* edited by R. F. Ellen, pp. 88–100. Orlando: Academic Press.

Goward, Nicola. (1984b). Personal interaction and adjustment. In *Ethnographic research: A guide to general conduct,* edited by R. F. Ellen, pp. 100–118. Orlando: Academic Press.

Gowda, Rajeev, and Jeffrey C. Fox, eds. (2002). *Judgments, decisions, and public policy.* New York: Cambridge University Press.

Goyder, John C. (1982). Factors affecting response rates to mailed questionnaires. *American Sociological Review,* 47:550–554.

Graham, Sandra. (1992). Most of the subjects were white and middle class: Trends in published research on African Americans in selected APA journals, 1970–1989. *American Psychologist,* 47:629–639.

Graneheim, U. H., and B. Lundman. (2004). Qualitative content analysis in nursing research: Concepts, procedures and measures to achieve trustworthiness. *Nurse Education Today,* 24:105–112.

Granovetter, Mark. (1976). Network sampling: Some first steps. *American Journal of Sociology,* 81:1287–1303.

Grant, Linda, Kathryn B. Ward, and Xue Lan Rong. (1987). Is there an association between gender and methods of sociological research? *American Sociological Review,* 52:856–862.

Gravlee, Clarence C. (2005). Ethnic classification in Southeastern Puerto Rico. *Social Forces,* 83:949–970.

Gray, Bradford H. (1982). The regulatory context of social and behavioral research. In *Ethical issues in social science research,* edited by T. Beauchamp, R. Faden, R. J. Wallace, and L. Walters, pp. 329–354. Baltimore: Johns Hopkins University Press.

Gray, Paul S. (1980). Exchange and access in field work. *Urban Life,* 9:309–331.

Greenberg, Daniel S. (1967). *The politics of pure science.* New York: New American Library.

Greenwald, Howard P. (1992). Ethics in social research. In *Encyclopedia of sociology,* Vol. 2, edited by E. and M. Borgatta, pp. 584–588. New York: Macmillan.

Greenwood, Davydd, and Marten Levin. (2003). Reconstructing the relationships between universities and society through action research. In *The landscape of qualitative research,* 2nd ed., edited by N. Denzin and Y. Lincoln, pp. 131–166. Thousand Oaks, CA: Sage.

Griffin, Larry J. (1992a). Temporality, events and explanation in historical sociology. *Sociological Methods and Research,* 20:403–427.

Griffin, Larry J. (1992b). Comparative-historical analysis. In *Encyclopedia of sociology,* Vol. 1, edited by E. and M. Borgatta, pp. 263–271. New York: Macmillan.

Griffin, Larry J. (1993). Narrative, event structure analysis and causal interpretation in historical sociology. *American Journal of Sociology,* 98:1094–1133.

Griffin, Larry J., and Charles Ragin. (1994). Some observations on formal methods of qualitative analysis. *Sociological Methods and Research,* 23:4–22.

Griffin, Larry J., Michael E. Wallace, and Beth A. Rubin. (1986). Capitalist resistance to the organization of labor before the New Deal: Why? How? Success? *American Sociological Review,* 51:147–167.

Grimshaw, Allen D. (1973). Comparative sociology. In *Comparative social research,* edited by M. Armer and A. Grimshaw, pp. 3–48. New York: Wiley.

Grinnell, Frederick. (1987). *The scientific attitude.* Boulder, CO: Westview.

Griswold, Wendy. (1983). The devil's techniques: Cultural legitimation and social change. *American Sociological Review,* 48:668–680.

Griswold, Wendy. (1987). A methodological framework for the sociology of culture. In *Sociological methodology, 1987,* edited by C. Clogg, pp. 1–35. San Francisco: Jossey-Bass.

Griswold, Wendy. (1994). *Cultures and societies in a changing world.* Thousand Oaks, CA: Pine Forge Press.

Griswold, Wendy, and Nathan Wright. (2004). Cowbirds, locals, and the dynamic endurance of regionalism. *American Journal of Sociology,* 109:1411–1451.

Groff, Ruth. (2004). *Critical realism, post-positivism, and the possibility of knowledge.* New York: Routledge.

Grosof, Miriam, and Hyman Sandy. (1985). *A research primer for the social and behavioral sciences.* Orlando: FL: Academic Press.

Gross, Daniel R. (1984). Time allocation: A tool for the study of cultural behavior. *Annual Review of Anthropology,* 13:519–558.

Groves, Robert M. (1996). How do we know what we think they think is really what they think? In *Answering Questions,* edited by N. Schwarz and S. Sudman, pp. 389–402. San Francisco: Jossey-Bass.

Groves, Robert M., and Mick Couper. (1996). Contact level uniqueness and cooperation in face-to-face surveys. *Journal of Official Statistics,* 12:63–83.

Groves, Robert M., and Mick Couper. (1998). *Nonresponse in household interview surveys.* New York: Wiley.

Groves, Robert M., Nancy H. Fultz, and Elizabeth Martin. (1992). Direct questioning about comprehension in a survey setting. In *Questions about questions: Inquiries into the cognitive bases of surveys,* edited by J. Turner, pp. 49–61. New York: Russell Sage Foundation.

Groves, Robert M., and Robert L. Kahn. (1979). *Surveys by telephone: A national comparison with personal interviews.* New York: Academic Press.

Groves, Robert M., and Nancy Mathiowetz. (1984). Computer assisted telephone interviewing: Effects on interviewers and respondents. *Public Opinion Quarterly,* 48: 356–369.

Groves, Robert M., Stanley Presser, and Sarah Dipko. (2004). The role of topic interest in survey participation decisions. *Public Opinion Quarterly,* 68:2–31.

Groves, Robert M., Eleanor Singer, and Amy Corning. (2000). Leverage saliency theory of survey participation. *Public Opinion Quarterly,* 64:299–308.

Guba, Egon G., and Yvonna S. Lincoln. (1994). Competing paradigms in qualitative research. In *Handbook of qualitative research,* edited by N. Denzin and Y. Lincoln, pp. 105–117. Thousand Oaks, CA: Sage.

Gubrium, Jaber F., and James A. Holstein. (1992). Qualitative methods. *Encyclopedia of sociology,* Vol. 3, edited by E. and M. Borgatta, pp. 1577–1582. New York: Macmillan.

Gubrium, Jaber F., and James A. Holstein. (1998). Narrative practice and the coherence of personal stories. *Sociological Quarterly,* 39: 163–187.

Gurevitch, Z. D. (1988). The other side of the dialogue: On making the other strange and the experience of otherness. *American Journal of Sociology,* 93:1179–1199.

Gurney, Joan Neff. (1985). Not one of the guys: The female researcher in a male-dominated setting. *Qualitative Sociology,* 8:42–62.

Gusfield, Joseph. (1976). The literary rhetoric of science: Comedy and pathos in drinking driver research. *American Sociological Review,* 41:16–34.

Gustavsen, Bjørn. (1986). Social research as participatory dialogue. In *The use and abuse of social science,* edited by F. Heller, pp. 143–156. Beverly Hills, CA: Sage.

Gustin, Bernard H. (1973). Charisma, recognition and the motivation of scientists. *American Journal of Sociology,* 86:1119–1134.

Gutterbock, Thomas M. (1997). Review: Why *Money* magazine's "Best Places" keep changing. *Public Opinion Quarterly,* 61:339–355.

Guttman, Louis. (1950). The basis for scalogram analysis. In *Measurement and prediction,* edited by S. A. Stouffer, L. Buttman, E. A. Suchman, P. F. Lazarfeld, S. A. Star, and J. A. Clausen, pp. 60–90. Princeton, NJ: Princeton University Press.

Guttman, Louis. (1970). A basis for scaling qualitative data. In *Attitude measurement,* edited by G. Summers, pp. 174–186. Chicago: Rand McNally.

Guy, Rebecca F., Charles E. Edgley, Ibtihaj Arafat, and Donald E. Allan. (1987). *Social research methods: Puzzles and solutions.* Boston: Allyn and Bacon.

Haberman, Shelby J. (1978). *Analysis of qualitative data.* New York: Academic Press.

Habermas, Jurgen. (1971). *Knowledge and human interests.* Boston: Beacon.

Habermas, Jurgen. (1973). *Theory and practice.* Boston: Beacon.

Habermas, Jurgen. (1976). *Legitimation crisis.* Boston: Beacon.

Habermas, Jurgen. (1979). *Communication and the evolution of society.* Boston: Beacon.

Habermas, Jurgen. (1988). *On the logic of the social sciences.* Oxford: Polity.

Hagan, John. (1990). The gender stratification of income inequality among lawyers. *Social Forces,* 63:835–855.

Hage, Jerald. (1972). *Techniques and problems of theory construction in sociology.* New York: Wiley.

Hagstrom, Warren. (1965). *The scientific community.* New York: Basic Books.

Hakim, Catherine. (1987). *Research design: Strategies and choices in the design of social research.* Boston: Allen and Unwin.

Halfpenny, Peter. (1979). The analysis of qualitative data. *Sociological Review,* 27:799–823.

Halfpenny, Peter. (1982). *Positivism and sociology: Explaining social life.* London: George Allen and Unwin.

Hallin, Daniel C. (1985). The American news media: A critical theory perspective. In *Critical theory and public life,* edited by J. Forester, pp. 121–146. Cambridge, MA: MIT Press.

Hallowell, Lyle. (August 26, 1985). *Ethical and legal problems of research: Professional workshop.* Presentation at the American Sociological Association annual meeting, Washington, DC.

Hammersley, Martyn. (1992). *What's wrong with ethnography? Methodological explorations.* New York: Routledge.

Hammersley, Martyn. (1995). Theory and evidence in qualitative research. *Quality and Quantity,* 29:55–66.

Hammersley, Martyn. (2000). Varieties of social research: A typology. *International Journal of Social Research Methodology,* 3:221–229.

Hammersley, Martyn, and Paul Atkinson. (1983). *Ethnography: Principles in practice.* London: Tavistock.

Hannan, Michael T. (1985). Problems of aggregation. In *Causal models in the social sciences,* 2nd ed., edited by H. Blalock, Jr., pp. 403–439. Chicago: Aldine.

Har, Janie. (June 29, 2008). "Stiffer ID requirements for Oregon driver's licenses kicking in. Applicants, even for renewals or replacements, need to prove they're in the U.S. legally." *The Oregonian.* http://www.oregonlive.com/politics/oregonian/index.ssf?/base/news/1214628912308650.xml&coll=7

Harding, Sandra. (1986). *The science question in feminism.* Ithaca, NY: Cornell University Press.

Hargens, Lowell L. (1988). Scholarly consensus and journal rejection rates. *American Sociological Review,* 53:139–151.

Hargens, Lowell L. (1991). Impressions and misimpressions about sociology journals. *Contemporary Sociology,* 20:343–349.

Harkens, Shirley, and Carol Warren. (1993). The social relations of intensive interviewing: Constellations of strangeness and science. *Sociological Methods and Research,* 21:317–339.

Harkness, Janet. (2003). Questionnaire in translation. In *Cross-cultural survey methods,* edited by J. Harkness, F. Van de Vijver, and P. Mohler, pp. 35–56. Hoboken, NJ: Wiley.

Harkness, Janet, Beth-Ellen Pennell, and Alisu Schoua-Glusberg. (2003). Survey questionnaire translation and assessment. In *Methods for testing and evaluating survey questionnaires,* edited by S. Presser et al., pp. 453–473. New York: Wiley.

Harkness, Janet, Fons van de Vijver, and Timothy Johnson. (2003). Questionnaire design in comparative research. In *Cross-cultural survey methods,* edited by J. Harkness, F. Van de Vijver, and P. Mohler, pp. 19–34. Hoboken, NJ: Wiley.

Harper, Douglas. (1982). *Good company.* Chicago: University of Chicago Press.

Harper, Douglas. (1987). *Working knowledge.* Chicago: University of Chicago Press.

Harper, Douglas. (1994). On the authority of the image: Visual methods at the crossroads. In *Handbook of qualitative research,* edited by N. Denzin and Y. Lincoln, pp. 403–412. Thousand Oaks, CA: Sage.

Harré, Rom. (1972). *The philosophies of science.* London: Oxford University Press.

Harré, R., and P. F. Secord. (1979). *The explanation of social behavior.* Totowa, NJ: Littlefield, Adams.

Harrington, Brooke. (2003). The social psychology of access in ethnographic research. *Journal of Contemporary Ethnography,* 32:592–625.

Harris, Benjamin. (1988). Key words: A history of debriefing in social psychology. In *The rise of experimentation in American psychology,* edited by J. Morawski, pp. 188–212. New Haven, CT: Yale University Press.

Harris, Marvin. (1976). History and significance of the emic/etic distinction. *Annual Review of Anthropology,* 5:329–350.

Harris Poll. (2003). Religious and other beliefs of Americans, 2003. http://www.harrisinteractive.com/vault/Harris-Interactive-Poll-Research-Religious-and-other-Beliefs-of-Americans-2003.pdf

Harris Poll. (2008). More Americans believe in the devil, hell, and angels than in Darwin's evolution. http://www.harrisinteractive.com/vault/Harris-Interactive-Poll-Research-Religious-Beliefs-2008.pdf

Harvey, Lee. (1990). *Critical social research.* London: Unwin Hyman.

Harwood, Jake. (2000). Sharp! Lurking incoherence in a television portrayal of an older adult. *Journal of Language and Social Psychology,* 19(1): 110–140.

Hastings, Philip K., and Dean R. Hodge. (1986). Religious and moral attitude trends among college students, 1948–84. *Social Forces,* 65:370–377.

Hauck, Matthew, and Michael Cox. (1974). Locating a sample by random digit dialing: Some hypotheses and a random sample. *Public Opinion Quarterly,* 38:253–260.

Hayano, David M. (1982). *Poker faces: The life and work of professional card players.* Berkeley: University of California Press.

Haydu, Jeffrey. (1998). Making use of the past: Time periods as cases to compare and as sequences of problem solving. *American Journal of Sociology,* 104:339–371.

Hayes, Andrew F., and Klaus Krippendorff. (2007). Answering the call for a standard reliability measure for coding data. *Communication Methods and Measures,* 1(1):77–89.

Hazelrigg, Lawrence E. (1973). Aspects of the measurement of class consciousness. In *Comparative social research,* edited by M. Armer and A. D. Grimshaw, pp. 219–246. New York: Wiley.

Headland, Thomas, Kenneth Pike, and Marvin Harris, eds. (1990). *Emics and etics: The insider/outsider debate.* Beverly Hills, CA: Sage.

Hearnshaw, L. S. (1979). *Cyril Burt: Psychologist.* London: Holder and Stoughten.

Heberlein, Thomas A., and Robert Baumgartner. (1978). Factors affecting response rates to mailed questionnaires: A quantitative analysis of the published literature. *American Sociological Review,* 43:447–462.

Heberlein, Thomas A., and Robert Baumgartner. (1981). Is a questionnaire necessary in a second mailing? *Public Opinion Quarterly,* 45: 102–107.

Heckathorn, Douglas D. (1997). Respondent-driven sampling: A new approach to the study of hidden populations. *Social Problems,* 44: 174–199.

Heckathorn, Douglas D. (2002). Respondent-driven sampling II: Deriving valid population estimates from chain-referral samples of hidden populations. *Social Problems,* 49:11–35.

Hector, Michael. (1975). *Internal colonialism.* Berkeley: University of California Press.

Hedstrom, Peter, and Richard Swedberg. (1998). Social mechanisms: An introductory essay. In *Social mechanisms: An analytical approach to social theory,* edited by P. Hedstrom and R. Swedberg, pp. 1–31. New York: Cambridge University Press.

Hegtvedt, Karen A. (1992). Replication. In *Encyclopedia of sociology,* Vol. 3, edited by E. and M. Borgatta, pp. 1661–1663. New York: Macmillan.

Hegtvedt, Karen A. (2007). Ethics and experiments. In *Laboratory experiments in the social sciences,* edited by Murray Webster, Jr. and Jane Sell, pp. 141–172 New York: Academic Press.

Heise, David. (1965). Semantic differential profiles for 1,000 most frequent English words. *Psychological Monographs,* 70 No. (8).

Heise, David. (1970). The semantic differential and attitude research. In *Attitude measurement,* edited by G. Summers, pp. 235–253. Chicago: Rand McNally.

Heise, David. (1974). Some issues in sociological measurement. In *Sociological methodology, 1973–74,* edited by H. L. Costner, pp. 1–16. San Francisco: Jossey-Bass.

Heise, David, ed. (1981). *Microcomputers in social research.* Beverly Hills, CA: Sage.

Heise, David. (1991). Event structure analysis. In *Using computers in qualitative research,* edited by N. Fielding and R. Lee, pp. 136–163. Newbury Park, CA: Sage.

Held, David. (1980). *Introduction to critical theory: Horkheimer to Habermas.*

Berkeley: University of California Press.

Heller, Nelson B., and J. Thomas McEwen. (1973). Applications of crime seriousness information in police departments. *Journal of Criminal Justice,* 1:241–253.

Hendry, Joy. (2003). *Understanding Japanese Society,* 3rd ed. New York: Routledge.

Henry, Gary T. (1990). *Practical sampling.* Newbury Park, CA: Sage.

Henry, Gary T. (1995). *Graphing data: Techniques for display and analysis.* Thousand Oaks, CA: Sage.

Herbert, Bob. (December 19, 2003). Change the channel. *New York Times.*

Herrera, C. D. (1999). Two arguments for "covert methods" in social research. *British Journal of Sociology,* 50: 331–343.

Herrnstein, Richard, and Charles Murray. (1994). *The bell curve: Intelligence and class structure in American life.* New York: Free Press.

Herting, Jerald R. (1985). Multiple indicator models using LISREL. In *Causal models in the social sciences,* 2nd ed., edited by H. Blalock, Jr., pp. 263–320. New York: Aldine.

Herting, Jerald R., and Herbert L. Costner. (1985). Re-specification in multiple indicator models. In *Causal models in the social sciences,* 2nd ed., edited by H. Blalock, Jr., pp. 321–394. Chicago: Aldine.

Herzberger, Sharon D. (1993). The cyclical pattern of child abuse: A study of research methodology. In *Research on sensitive topics,* edited by C. Renzetti and R. Lee, pp. 33–51. Thousand Oaks, CA: Sage.

Herzog, A. Regula, and Jerald G. Bachman. (1981). Effects of questionnaire length on response quality. *Public Opinion Quarterly,* 45: 549–559.

Hesse, Mary B. (1970). *Models and analogies in science.* Notre Dame, IN: Notre Dame Press.

Hicks, David. (1984). Getting into the field and establishing routines. In *Ethnographic research: A guide to general conduct,* edited by R. F. Ellen, pp. 192–199. Orlando: Academic Press.

Higher Education Research Institute. (2004). *Recent findings.* www.gseisucla .edu/heri/findings.html

Hill, Michael R. (1993). *Archival strategies and techniques.* Thousand Oaks, CA: Sage.

Hiller, Harry H. (1979). Universality of science and the question of national sociologies. *American Sociologist,* 14:124–135.

Himmelstein, Jerome L., and Mayer Zald. (1984). American conservatism and government funding of the social sciences and arts. *Sociological Inquiry,* 54:171–187.

Hindess, Barry. (1973). *The use of official statistics in sociology: A critique of positivism and ethnomethodology.* New York: Macmillan.

Hippler, Hans J., and Norbert Schwarz. (1986). Not forbidding isn't allowing: The cognitive basis of the forbid–allow asymmetry. *Public Opinion Quarterly,* 50:87–96.

Hirschman, Albert O. (1970). *Exit, voice, and loyalty: Response to decline in firms, organizations and states.* Cambridge, MA: Harvard University Press.

Hitlin, Steven, J. Scott Brown, and Glen Elder. (2007). Measuring Latinos: Racial vs. ethnic classification and self-understandings. *Social Forces,* 86(2):587–611.

Hochschild, Arlie. (1978). *The unexpected community: Portrait of an old age subculture.* Berkeley: University of California Press.

Hochschild, Arlie. (1983). *The managed heart.* Berkeley: University of California Press.

Hochschild, Jennifer L. (1981). *What's fair? American beliefs about distributive justice.* Cambridge, MA: Harvard University Press.

Hoffmann, Joan Eakin. (1980). Problems of access in the study of social elites and boards of directors. In *Fieldwork experience,* edited by W. B. Shaffir, R. A. Stebbins, and A. Turowetz, pp. 45–56. New York: St. Martin's Press.

Holbrook, Allyson, Young Ik Cho, and Timothy Johnson. (2006). The impact of question and respondent characteristics on comprehension and mapping difficulties. *Public Opinion Quarterly,* 70(4):565–595.

Holbrook, Allyson, Melanie Green, and Jon Krosnick. (2003). Telephone versus face-to-face interviewing of national probability samples with long questionnaires. *Public Opinion Quarterly,* 67:79–125.

Hollander, Jocelyn A. (2004). The social contexts of focus groups. *Journal of Contemporary Ethnography,* 33(5): 602–637.

Hollander, Myles, and Frank Proschan. (1984). *The statistical exorcist: Dispelling statistics anxiety.* New York: Marcel Decker.

Hollis, Martin. (1977). *Models of man: Philosophical thoughts on social action.* New York: Cambridge University Press.

Holstein, James A., and Jaber F. Gubrium. (1994). Phenomenology, ethnomethodology and interpretative practice. In *Handbook of qualitative research,* edited by N. Denzin and Y. Lincoln, pp. 262–272. Thousand Oaks, CA: Sage.

Holsti, Ole R. (1968a). Content analysis. In *Handbook of social psychology,* 2nd ed., Vol. 2, edited by G. Lindzey and E. Aronson, pp. 596–692. Reading, MA: Addison-Wesley.

Holsti, Ole R. (1968b). *Content analysis for the social sciences and humanities.* Reading, MA: Addison-Wesley.

Holt, Robert T., and John E. Turner. (1970). The methodology of comparative research. In *The methodology of comparative research,* edited by R. Holt and J. Turner, pp. 1–20. New York: Free Press.

Holub, Robert C. (1991). *Jürgen Habermas: Critic in the public sphere.* New York: Routledge.

Holy, Ladislav. (1984). Theory, methodology and the research process. In *Ethnographic research: A guide to general conduct,* edited by R. F. Ellen, pp. 13–34. Orlando: Academic Press.

Holyfield, Lori, Matthew R. Moltz, and Mindy Bradley. (2009). Race discourse and the US Confederate flag. *Race, Ethnicity & Education,* 12(4): 517–537.

Homan, Roger. (1980). The ethics of covert methods. *British Journal of Sociology,* 31:46–57.

Honan, William H. (January 22, 1997). Scholars attack public school TV program. *New York Times.*

Honigmann, John J. (1982). Sampling in ethnographic fieldwork. In *Field research,* edited by R. G. Burgess, pp. 79–90. Boston: Allen and Unwin.

Horan, Patrick. (1987). Theoretical models in social history research. *Social Science History,* 11:379–400.

Horn, Robert V. (1993). *Statistical indicators for the economic and social sciences.* Cambridge: Cambridge University Press.

Hornsby-Smith, M. P. (1974). The working life of the university lecturer. *Universities Quarterly,* 28:149–164.

Hornstein, Gail A. (1988). Quantifying psychological phenomena: Debates, dilemmas and implications. In *The rise of experimentation in American psychology,* edited by J. Morawski, pp. 1–34. New Haven, CT: Yale University Press.

Horowitz, Irving Louis. (1965). The life and death of Project Camelot. *Transaction,* 3:3–7, 44–47.

House, Ernest R. (1980). *Evaluating with validity.* Beverly Hills, CA: Sage.

Howell, Jayne. (2004). Turning out good ethnography, or talking out of turn? Gender, violence, and confidentiality in southeastern Mexico. *Journal of Contemporary Ethnography,* 33(3): 323–352.

Hoy, David Couzens. (1994). *Critical theory.* Cambridge, MA: Blackwell.

Hoynes, William. (May/June 1997). News for a captive audience extra. http://www.fair.org/extra/9705/ch1-hoynes.html. Accessed November 2, 1998.

Hubbard, Raymond, and Eldon Little. (1988). Promised contributions to charity and mail survey responses: Replication with extension. *Public Opinion Quarterly,* 52:223–230.

Huck, Schuyler W., and Howard M. Sandler. (1979). *Rival hypotheses: Alternative interpretations of data based conclusions.* New York: Harper & Row.

Humphreys, Laud. (1975). *Tearoom trade: Impersonal sex in public places,* enlarged ed. Chicago: Aldine.

Hunt, Lynn. (1989). Introduction. In *The new cultural history,* edited by L. Hunt, pp. 1–22. Berkeley: University of California Press.

Hunt, Morton. (1997). *How science takes stock: The story of meta-analysis.* New York: Russell Sage Foundation.

Hunter, Andrea G., et al. (2006). Loss, survival, and redemption: African American male youths' reflections on life without fathers, manhood, and coming of age. *Youth and Society,* 37(4):423–452.

Hunter, John E., Frank L. Schmidt, and Gregg B. Jackson. (1982). *Meta-analysis: Cumulating research findings across studies.* Beverly Hills, CA: Sage.

Hyman, Herbert H. (1975). *Interviewing in social research.* Chicago: University of Chicago Press.

Hyman, Herbert H. (1991). *Taking society's measure: A personal history of survey research.* New York: Russell Sage.

Hymes, Dell. (1970). Linguistic aspects of comparative political research. In *The methodology of comparative research,* edited by R. Holt and J. Turner, pp. 295–341. New York: Free Press.

Hymes, Dell. (1983). *Essays in the history of linguistic anthropology.* Philadelphia: John Benjamins Publishers.

Ingram, Paul, and Arik Lifschitz. (2006). Kinship in the shadow of the corporation: The interbuilder network in Clyde River shipbuilding, 1711–1990. *American Sociological Review,* 71(2): 344–352.

Inverarity, James M. (1976). Populism and lynching in Louisiana, 1889–1896: A test of Erikson's theory of the relationship between boundary crisis and repressive justice. *American Sociological Review,* 41:262–280.

Isaac, Larry W., and Larry J. Griffin. (1989). A historicism in time series analysis of historical process: Critique, redirection, and illustrations from U.S. labor history. *American Sociological Review,* 54:873–890.

Isaac, Larry W., Debra A. Street, and Stan J. Knapp. (1994). Analyzing historical contingency with formal methods: The case of the "relief explosion" and 1968. *Sociological Methods and Research,* 23: 114–141.

Jackson, Bruce. (1978). Killing time: Life in the Arkansas penitentiary. *Qualitative Sociology,* 1:21–32.

Jackson, Bruce. (1987). *Fieldwork.* Urbana: University of Illinois Press.

Jackson, David J., and Edgar F. Borgatta, eds. (1981). *Factor analysis and measurement in sociological research.* Beverly Hills, CA: Sage.

Jacob, Herbert. (1984). *Using published data: Errors and remedies.* Beverly Hills, CA: Sage.

Jaeger, Richard M. (1983). *Statistics as a spectator sport.* Beverly Hills, CA: Sage.

James, Franklin. (1991). Counting homeless persons with surveys of people using homeless services. *Urban Policy Debate,* 2(3):733–753.

Jasso, Guillermina. (2004). The tripartite structure of social science analysis. *Sociological Theory,* 22(3):401–431.

Jennings, M. Kent, and Vicki Zeitner. (2003). Internet use and civic engagement: A longitudinal analysis. *Public Opinion Quarterly,* 67:311–334.

Johnson, Bruce. (1982). Missionaries, tourists and traders. *Studies in Symbolic Interaction,* 4:115–150.

Johnson, David Richard, and James C. Creech. (1983). Ordinal measures in multiple indicator models: A simulation study of categorization error. *American Sociological Review,* 48:398–407.

Johnson, David W., and Roger T. Johnson. (1985). Relationships between black and white students in intergroup cooperation and competition. *Journal of Social Psychology,* 125: 421–428.

Johnson, John M. (1975). *Doing field research.* New York: Free Press.

Johnson, P. Timonty, James G. Hougland, Jr., and Richard R. Clayton. (1989). Obtaining reports of sensitive behavior: A comparison of substance-use reports from telephone and face-to-face interviews. *Social Science Quarterly,* 70:173–183.

Johnson, Timothy, and Fons van de Vijver. (2003). Social desirability in cross-cultural research. In *Cross-cultural survey methods,* edited by J. Harkness, F. Van de Vijver, and P. Mohler, pp. 195–206. Hoboken NJ: Wiley.

Jones, Gareth Stedman. (1976). From historical sociology to theoretical history. *British Journal of Sociology,* 27:295–305.

Jones, Gareth Stedman. (1983). *Languages of class.* New York: Cambridge University Press.

Jones, J. H. (1981). *Bad blood: The Tuskegee syphilis experiment.* New York: Free Press.

Jones, Wesley H. (1979). Generalizing mail survey inducement methods: Populations' interactions with anonymity and sponsorship. *Public Opinion Quarterly,* 43:102–111.

Jordan, Lawrence A., Alfred C. Marcus, and Leo G. Reeder. (1980). Response styles in telephone and household interviewing: A field experiment. *Public Opinion Quarterly,* 44: 210–222.

Jordan, Stephen M., and Daniel Layzell. (1992). A case study of faculty workload issues in Arizona: Implications for state higher education policy (policy paper). Denver, CO: Education Commission of the States.

Josephson, Paul R. (November 1, 1988). The FBI menaces academic freedom. *New York Times.*

Junker, Buford H. (1960). *Field work.* Chicago: University of Chicago Press.

Juster, F. Thomas, and Kenneth C. Land, eds. (1981). *Social accounting systems: Essays on the state of the art.* New York: Academic Press.

Kalberg, Stephen. (1994). *Max Weber's comparative-historical sociology.* Chicago: University of Chicago Press.

Kalmijn, Matthijus. (1991). Shifting boundaries: Trends in religious and educational homogamy. *American Sociological Review,* 56:786–801.

Kalton, Graham. (1983). *Introduction to survey sampling.* Beverly Hills, CA: Sage.

Kandel, Denise B. (1980). Drug and drinking behavior among youth. *Annual Review of Sociology,* 6: 235–265.

Kane, Danielle, and Jung Mee Park. (2009). The puzzle of Korean Christianity: Geopolitical networks and religious conversion in early twentieth century East Asia. *American Journal of Sociology,* 115(2):365–404.

Kane, Emily W., and Laura J. MacAulay. (1993). Interview gender and gender attitudes. *Public Opinion Quarterly,* 57:1–28.

Kaplan, Abraham. (1964). *The conduct of inquiry: Methodology for behavioral science.* New York: Harper & Row.

Kaplowitz, Michael, Timothy Hadlock, and Ralph Levine. (2004). A comparison of web and web survey response rates. *Public Opinion Quarterly,* 68:94–101.

Karp, David A. (1973). Hiding in pornographic bookstores: A reconsideration of the nature of urban anonymity. *Urban Life,* 1:427–452.

Karp, David A. (1980). Observing behavior in public places: Problems and strategies. In *Fieldwork experience,* edited by W. B. Shaffir, R. A. Stebbins, and A. Turowetz, pp. 82–97. New York: St. Martin's Press.

Karweit, Nancy, and Edmund D. Meyers, Jr. (1983). Computers in survey research. In *Handbook of survey research,* edited by P. Rossi, J. Wright, and A. Anderson, pp. 379–414. Orlando, FL: Academic Press.

Katovich, Michael A., and Ron L. Diamond. (1986). Selling time: Situated transactions in a noninstitutional setting. *Sociological Quarterly,* 27: 253–271.

Katz, Jay. (1972). *Experimentation with human beings.* New York: Russell Sage Foundation.

Kawakami, Kerry, Elizabeth Dunn, Francine Karmali, and John F. Dovidio. (January 9, 2009). Mispredicting affective and behavioral responses to racism. *Science* 323 (5911), 276–278.

Keat, Russell. (1981). *The politics of social theory: Habermas, Freud and the critique of positivism.* Chicago: University of Chicago Press.

Keat, Russell, and John Urry. (1975). *Social theory as science.* London: Routledge and Kegan Paul.

Keeter, Scott. (1995). Estimating telephone noncoverage bias with a telephone survey. *Public Opinion Quarterly,* 59:196–217.

Keeter, Scott, et al. (2000). Consequences of reducing non-response in a national telephone survey. *Public Opinion Quarterly,* 64:125–148.

Kelle, Helga. (2000). Gender and territoriality in games played by nine- to twelve-year-old schoolchildren. *Journal of Contemporary Ethnography,* 29:164–197.

Keller, Bill. (May 27, 1988). Ups and downs of conducting the poll. *New York Times.*

Keller, Bill. (January 19, 1989). Prying where it counts: Into census. *New York Times.*

Keller, Evelyn Fox. (1983). *A feeling for the organism: The life and work of Barbara McClintock.* New York: W. H. Freeman.

Keller, Evelyn Fox. (1985). *Reflections on gender and science.* New Haven, CT: Yale University Press.

Keller, Evelyn Fox. (1990). Gender and science. In *Feminist research methods,* edited by J. McCarl Nielsen, pp. 41–57. Boulder, CO: Westview.

Kelman, Herbert. (1982). Ethical issues in different social science methods. In *Ethical issues in social science research,* edited by T. Beauchamp, R. Faden, R. J. Wallace, and L. Walters, pp. 40–99. Baltimore: Johns Hopkins University Press.

Kemmis, Stephen, and Robin McTaggart. (2003). Participatory action research. In *Strategies of qualitative inquiry,* 2nd ed., edited by N. Denzin and Y. Lincoln, pp. 336–396. Thousand Oaks, CA: Sage.

Kemp, Jeremy, and R. F. Ellen. (1984). Informants. In *Ethnographic research: A guide to general conduct,* edited by R. F. Ellen, pp. 224–236. Orlando: Academic Press.

Kempner, Joanna. (2008). The chilling effect: How do researchers react to controversy? *PLoS MEDICINE,* 5(11):e222.

Kennedy, Courtney, Scott Keeter, and Michael Dimock. (2008). A "brute force" estimation of the residency

rate for undetermined telephone numbers in an RDD survey. *Public Opinion Quarterly,* 72(I):28–39.

Kent, Gardner. (July 2004). Rochester downtown casino: An economic & social impact assessment. Center for Governmental Research Inc. http://hdl.handle.net/10207/11037. Accessed March 10, 2010.

Kent, Stephen A. (1992). Historical sociology. In *Encyclopedia of sociology,* Vol. 2, edited by E. and M. Borgatta, pp. 837–843. New York: Macmillan.

Kercher, Kyle. (1992). Quasi-experimental research designs. In *Encyclopedia of sociology,* Vol. 3, edited by E. and M. Borgatta, pp. 1595–1613. New York: Macmillan.

Kerlinger, Fred N. (1979). *Behavioral research: A conceptual approach.* New York: Holt, Rinehart and Winston.

Kevles, Daniel J. (2006). What's new about the politics of science? *Social Research,* 73(3):761–778.

Kidder, Louise H. (1982). Face validity from multiple perspectives. In *Forms of validity in research,* edited by D. Brinberg and L. Kidder, pp. 41–57. San Francisco: Jossey-Bass.

Kidder, Louise H., and Charles M. Judd. (1986). *Research methods in social relations,* 5th ed. New York: Holt, Rinehart and Winston.

Kiecolt, K. Jill, and Laura E. Nathan. (1985). *Secondary analysis of survey data.* Beverly Hills, CA: Sage.

Kim, Jae-On, and Charles W. Mueller. (1978). *Introduction to factor analysis: What it is and how to do it.* Beverly Hills, CA: Sage.

Kimmel, Allan J. (1988). *Ethics and values in applied social research.* Newbury Park, CA: Sage.

Kincheloe, Joe L., and Peter L. McLaren. (1994). Rethinking critical theory and qualitative research. In *Handbook of qualitative research,* edited by N. Denzin and Y. Lincoln, pp. 138–157. Thousand Oaks, CA: Sage.

King, Desmond. (1998). The politics of social research: Institutionalizing public funding regimes in the United States and Britain. *British Journal of Political Science,* 28:415–444.

King, Gary, Robert O. Keohane, and Sidney Verba. (1994). *Designing social inquiry: Scientific inference in qualitative research.* Princeton, NJ: Princeton University Press.

King, Gary, C. Murray, J. Salomon, and A. Tandon. (2004). Enhancing the validity and cross-cultural comparability of measurement in survey research. *American Political Science Review,* 98:191–207.

Kirby, Douglas, Nancy Brener, Nancy Brown, Nancy Peterfreund, Pamela Hillard, and Ron Harrist. (1999). The impact of condom distribution in Seattle schools on sexual behavior and condom use. *American Journal of Public Health,* 89(2):182–187.

Kirk, Jerome, and Marc L. Miller. (1986). *Reliability and validity in qualitative research.* Beverly Hills, CA: Sage.

Kiser, Edgar, and April Linton. (2002). The hinges of history: State making and revolt in early modern France. *American Sociological Review,* 62:889–910.

Kish, L. (1965). *Survey sampling.* New York: Wiley.

Kleinman, Sherry. (1980). Learning the ropes as fieldwork analysis. In *Fieldwork experience,* edited by W. B. Shaffir, R. A. Stebbins, and A. Turowetz, pp. 171–183. New York: St. Martin's Press.

Kleinman, Sherry, and Martha A. Copp. (1993). *Emotions and field work.* Thousand Oaks, CA: Sage.

Klienenberg, Eric. (2002). *Heat wave: A social autopsy of disaster in Chicago.* Chicago: University of Chicago Press.

Knapp, Peter. (1990). The revival of macrosociology: Methodological issues of discontinuity in comparative-historical theory. *Sociological Forum,* 5:545–567.

Knäuper, Bärbel. (1999). The impact of age and education on response order effects in attitude measurement. *Public Opinion Quarterly,* 63: 347–370.

Koch, Nadine S., and Jolly A. Emrey. (2001). The Internet and opinion measurement: Surveying marginalized populations. *Social Science Quarterly,* 82:131–138.

Kohn, Melvin L. (1987). Cross-national research as an analytic strategy. *American Sociological Review,* 52: 713–731.

Kohn, Melvin L., ed. (1989). *Cross-national research in sociology.* Newbury Park, CA: Sage.

Koretz, Daniel. (Summer 1988). Arriving in Lake Wobegon: Are standardized tests exaggerating achievement and distorting instruction? *American Educator,* 12:8–15.

Kraeger, Derek A. (2008). Unnecessary roughness? School sports, peer networks and male adolescent violence.

American Sociological Review, 72:705–724.

Kraemer, Helena Chmura, and Sue Thiemann. (1987). *How many subjects? Statistical power analysis in research.* Newbury Park, CA: Sage.

Krathwohl, D. R. (1965). *How to prepare a research proposal.* Syracuse, NY: Syracuse University Bookstore.

Krider, Dylan Otto. (2004). Politicized science. *Dissent,* 51:45–48.

Krippendorff, Klaus. (2004). *Content analysis: An introduction to its methodology.* Thousand Oaks, CA: Sage.

Krosnick, Jon. (1992). The impact of cognitive sophistication and attitude importance on response-order and question-order effects. In *Context effects,* edited by N. Schwarz and Sudman, pp. 203–218. New York: Springer-Verlag.

Krosnick, Jon, and Robert P. Abelson. (1992). The case for measuring attitude strength in surveys. In *Questions about questions: Inquiries into the cognitive bases of surveys,* edited by J. Turner, pp. 177–203. New York: Russell Sage Foundation.

Krosnick, Jon, and Duane F. Alwin. (1988). A test of the form-resistant correlation hypothesis: Ratings, rankings and the measurement of values. *Public Opinion Quarterly,* 52:526–538.

Krosnick, Jon A., et al. (2002). The impact of "no opinion" response options on data quality. *Public Opinion Quarterly,* 66:371–403.

Krueger, Richard A. (1988). *Focus groups: A practical guide for applied research.* Beverly Hills, CA: Sage.

Krysan, Maria. (2008). Does race matter in the search for housing? An exploratory study of search strategies, experiences, and locations. *Social Science Research,* 37(2):581–603.

Krysan, Maria, Mick Couper, Reynolds Farley, and Tyrone Forman. (2009). Does race matter in neighborhood preferences? Results from a video experiment. *American Journal of Sociology,* 115(2):527–559.

Kuhn, Thomas S. (1970). *The structure of scientific revolutions,* 2nd ed. Chicago: University of Chicago Press.

Kuhn, Thomas S. (1979). The relations between history and the history of science. In *Interpretive social science: A reader,* edited by P. Rabinow and W. Sullivan. Berkeley: University of California Press.

Kusserow, Richard P. (March 1989). *Misconduct in scientific research.* Report of the Inspector General of

the U.S. Department of Health and Human Services. Washington, DC: Department of Health and Human Services.

Kviz, Frederick J. (1984). Bias in a directory sample for mail survey of rural households. *Public Opinion Quarterly,* 48:801–806.

Labaw, Patricia J. (1980). *Advanced questionnaire design.* Cambridge, MA: Abt Books.

Lachmann, Richard. (1988). Graffiti as career and ideology. *American Journal of Sociology,* 94:251–272.

Lachmann, Richard. (1989). Elite conflict and state formation in 16th and 17th century England and France. *American Sociological Review,* 54: 141–162.

Lachmann, Richard. (2003). Elite self-interest and economic decline in early modern Europe. *American Sociological Review,* 68:346–372.

Lacy, Dean. (2001). A theory of nonseparable preferences in survey responses. *American Journal of Political Science,* 45:239–258.

Lagemann, Ellen Condliffe. (1989). *The politics of knowledge: The Carnegie Corporation, philanthropy and public policy.* Chicago: University of Chicago.

Land, Kenneth. (1992). Social indicators. In *Encyclopedia of sociology,* Vol. 4, edited by E. and M. Borgatta, pp. 1844–1850. New York: Macmillan.

Lane, Michael. (1970). *Structuralism.* London: Jonathan Cape.

Lang, Eric. (1992). Hawthorne effect. In *Encyclopedia of sociology,* Vol. 2, edited by E. and M. Borgatta, pp. 793–794. New York: Macmillan.

Lankenau, Stephen E. (1999). Stronger than dirt. *Journal of Contemporary Ethnography,* 28:288–318.

Laslett, Barbara. (1980). Beyond methodology. *American Sociological Review,* 45:214–228.

Laslett, Barbara. (1992). Gender in/and social history. *Social Science History,* 16:177–196.

Lavrakas, Paul J., Charles Shuttles, Charlotte Steeh, and Howard Fienberg. (2007). The state of surveying cell phone numbers in the United States. *Public Opinion Quarterly,* 71(5): 840–854.

Layder, Derek. (1993). *New strategies in social research.* Cambridge, MA: Polity.

Lazarsfeld, Paul F., and Jeffrey G. Reitz. (1975). *An introduction to applied sociology.* Amsterdam: Elsevier.

Lazere, Donald, ed. (1987). *American media and mass culture: Left perspectives.* Berkeley: University of California Press.

Leal, David L., and Frederick Hess. (1999). Survey bias on the front porch: Are all subjects interviewed equally? *American Politics Quarterly,* 27: 468–487.

Lee, Alfred McClung. (1978). *Sociology for whom?* New York: Oxford University Press.

Lee, Harper. (1960). *To kill a mockingbird.* New York: Warner Books.

Lee, Jennifer, and Frank Bean. (2007). Reinventing the color line: Immigration and America's new racial/ethnic divide. *Social Forces,* 86(2):561–586.

Lee-Treweek, Geraldine, and Stephanie Linkogle, eds. (2000). *Danger in the field.* New York: Routledge.

Leggett, Glenn, C. David Mean, and William Charvat. (1965). *Prentice-Hall handbook for writers,* 4th ed. Englewood Cliffs, NJ: Prentice-Hall.

Leiter, Kenneth. (1980). *A primer on ethnomethodology.* New York: Oxford University Press.

LeMasters, E. E. (1975). *Blue collar aristocrats.* Madison: University of Wisconsin Press.

Lemert, Charles. (1979). Science, religion and secularization. *Sociological Quarterly,* 20:445–461.

Lemert, Charles, ed. (1981). *French sociology: Rupture and renewal since 1968.* New York: Columbia University Press.

Lenoir, Timothy. (1997). *Instituting science: The cultural production of scientific disciplines.* Stanford, CA: Stanford University Press.

Lenzer, Gertrud, ed. (1975). *Auguste Comte and positivism: Essential writings.* New York: Harper & Row.

Lester, Marilyn, and Stuart C. Hadden. (1980). Ethnomethodology and grounded theory methodology: An integration of perspective and method. *Urban Life,* 9:3–33.

Levine, Joel H. (1993). *Exceptions are the rule: An inquiry into methods in the social sciences.* Boulder, CO: Westview.

Lewis, George H., and Jonathan F. Lewis. (1980). The dog in the night-time: Negative evidence in social research. *British Journal of Sociology,* 31: 544–558.

Lieberson, Stanley. (1985). *Making it count: The improvement of social research and theory.* Berkeley: University of California Press.

Lieberson, Stanley. (1991). Small N's and big conclusions: An examination of the reasoning of comparative studies based on a small number of cases. *Social Forces,* 70:307–320.

Lieberson, Stanley, Susan Dumais, and Shyon Baumann. (2000). The instability of androgynous names: The symbolic maintenance of gender boundaries. *American Journal of Sociology,* 105:1249–1287.

Liebetrau, Albert M. (1983). *Measures of association.* Beverly Hills, CA: Sage.

Liebman, Robert, John R. Sutton, and Robert Wuthnow. (1988). Exploring social sources of denominationalism: Schisms in American Protestant denominations, 1890–1980. *American Sociological Review,* 53:343–352.

Liebow, Elliot. (1967). *Talley's corner.* Boston: Little, Brown.

Lifton, Robert J. (1986). *Nazi doctors.* New York: Basic Books.

Light, Richard J., and David B. Pillemer. (1984). *Summing up: The science of reviewing research.* Cambridge, MA: Harvard University Press.

Likert, Rensis. (1970). A technique for the measurement of attitudes. In *Attitude measurement,* edited by G. Summers, pp. 149–158. Chicago: Rand McNally.

Lindblom, Charles E., and David K. Cohen. (1979). *Usable knowledge: Social science and social problem solving.* New Haven, CT: Yale University Press.

Lindzey, Gardner, and Donn Byrne. (1968). Measurement of social choice and interpersonal attractiveness. In *The handbook of social psychology,* Vol. 2: Research methods, edited by G. Lindzey and E. Aronson, pp. 452–525. Reading, MA: Addison-Wesley.

Link, Michael W., Michael P. Battaglia, Martin R. Frankel, Larry Osborn, and Ali H. Mokdad. (2007). Reaching the U.S. cell phone generation: Comparison of cell phone survey results with an ongoing landline telephone survey. *Public Opinion Quarterly,* 71(5):814–839.

Link, Michael W., Michael Battaglia, Martin Frankel, Larry Osborn, and Ali Mokdad. (2008). A comparison of address-based sampling (ABS) versus random-digit dialing (RDD) for general population surveys. *Public Opinion Quarterly,* 72(1):6–27.

Link, Michael W., and Robert Oldendick. (1999). Call screening: Is it really a problem for survey research? *Public Opinion Quarterly,* 63:577–589.

Linton C. (2004). *The development of social network analysis: A study in the sociology of science.* Vancouver: Empirical Press.

Lipset, Seymour Martin. (1968). History and sociology: Some methodological considerations. In *Sociology and history: Methods,* edited by S. M. Lipset and R. Hofstadter, pp. 20–58. New York: Basic Books.

Little, Daniel. (1991). *Varieties of social explanation: An introduction to the philosophy of science.* Boulder, CO: Westview.

Lloyd, Christopher. (1986). *Explanation in social history.* New York: Basil Blackwell.

Locke, Lawrence F., Warren Wyrick Spirduso, and Stephen J. Silverman. (1987). *Proposals that work: A guide for planning dissertations and grant proposals,* 2nd ed. Beverly Hills, CA: Sage.

Loeb, Susanna, Margaret Bridges, Daphna Bassok, Bruce Fuller, and Russell Rumberger. (2007). How much is too much? The influence of preschool centers on children's social and cognitive development. *Economics of Education Review* 26(1):52–66.

Lofland, John. (1974). Styles of reporting qualitative field research. *American Sociologist,* 9:101–111.

Lofland, John, and Lyn H. Lofland. (1984). *Analyzing social settings,* 2nd ed. Belmont, CA: Wadsworth.

Lofland, John, and Lyn H. Lofland. (1995). *Analyzing social settings,* 3rd ed. Belmont, CA: Wadsworth.

Lofland, John, David Snow, Leon Anderson, and Lyn H. Lofland. (2006). *Analyzing social settings,* 4th edition. Belmont CA: Wadsworth.

Lofland, Lyn H. (1972). Self management in public settings: Parts I and II. *Urban Life,* 1:93–108, 217–231.

Loftus, Elizabeth, Mark Klinger, Kyle Smith, and Judith Fiedler. (1990). A tale of two questions: Benefit of asking more than one question. *Public Opinion Quarterly,* 54:330–345.

Loftus, Elizabeth, Kyle D. Smith, Mark R. Klinger, and Judith Fiedler. (1992). Memory and mismemory of health events. In *Questions about questions: Inquiries into the cognitive bases of surveys,* edited by J. Turner, pp. 102–137. New York: Russell Sage Foundation.

Long, J. Scott. (1976). Estimation and hypothesis testing in linear models containing measurement error: A review of Joreskog's model for the analysis of covariance structures. *Sociological Methods and Research,* 5:157–206.

Long, J. Scott. (1978). Productivity and academic positions in a scientific career. *American Sociological Review,* 43:889–908.

Longino, Helen E. (1990). *Science as social knowledge: Values and objectivity in scientific inquiry.* Princeton, NJ: Princeton University Press.

Lorr, Maurice. (1983). *Cluster analysis for social scientists: Techniques for analyzing and simplifying complex blocks of data.* San Francisco: Jossey-Bass.

Lovin-Smith, Lynn, and Charles Brody. (1989). Interruptions in group discussions: The effects of gender and group composition. *American Sociological Review,* 54:424–435.

Lowenthal, David. (1985). *The past is a foreign country.* New York: Cambridge University Press.

Lowery, Brian S., Naomi Eisenberger, Curtis Hardin, and Stacey Sinclair. (2007). Long-term effects of subliminal priming on academic performance. *Basic & Applied Social Psychology,* 29(2):151–157.

Lu, Shun, and Gary Alan Fine. (1995). The presentation of ethnic authenticity: Chinese food as a social accomplishment. *Sociological Quarterly,* 36:535–553.

Lucas, Jeffrey W. (2003). Theory-testing, generalization, and the problem of external validity. *Sociological Theory,* 21(3):236–253.

Luebke, Barbara F. (1989). Out of focus: Images of men and women in newspaper photographs. *Sex Roles,* 20: 121–133.

Luken, Paul C., and Suzanne Vaughan. (2006). Standardizing childrearing through housing. *Social Problems,* 53(3):299–331.

Lyberg, Lars, et al. (1997). *Survey measurement and process quality.* New York: Wiley.

Lynd, Robert S. (1964). *Knowledge for what? The place of social science in American culture.* New York: Grove. (Originally published in 1939 by Princeton University Press.)

MacFarlane, Alan. (1977). *Reconstructing historical communities.* New York: Cambridge University Press.

MacIver, A. M. (1968). Levels of explanation in history. In *Readings in the philosophy of the social sciences,* edited by M. Brodbeck, pp. 304–316. New York: Macmillan.

MacKeun, Michael B. (1984). Reality, the press and citizens' political agendas. In *Surveying subjective phenomena,* Vol. 2, edited by C. Turner and E. Martin, pp. 443–473. New York: Russell Sage Foundation.

Mahoney, James. (1999). Nominal, ordinal, and narrative appraisal in macrocausal analysis. *American Journal of Sociology,* 104:1154–1196.

Mahoney, James. (2000a). Path dependence in historical sociology. *Theory and Society,* 9:507–548.

Mahoney, James. (2000b). Strategies of causal inference in small-N analysis. *Sociological Methods and Research,* 28:387–424.

Mahoney, James. (2003). Long-run development and the legacy of colonialism in Spanish America. *American Journal of Sociology,* 109:50–106.

Mahoney, James. (2004a). Comparative-historical methodology. *Annual Review of Sociology,* 30:81–101.

Mahoney, James. (2004b). Revisiting general theory in historical sociology. *Social Forces,* 83:459–489.

Maier, Mark H. (1991). *The data game: Controversies in social science statistics.* Armonk, NY: M. E. Sharpe.

Maines, David R., William Shaffir, and Allan Turowetz. (1980). Leaving the field in ethnographic research. In *The fieldwork experience: Qualitative approaches to social research,* edited by W. B. Shaffir, R. Stebbins, and A. Turowetz, pp. 261–280. New York: St. Martin's Press.

Maloney, Dennis M. (1984). *Protection of human research subjects: A practical guide to federal laws and regulations.* New York: Plenum.

Mandel, Hadas, and Michael Shalev. (2009). How welfare states shape the gender pay gap: A theoretical and comparative analysis. *Social Forces,* 37(4):1873–1912.

Mann, Floyd C. (1970). Human relations skills in social research. In *Qualitative methodology,* edited by W. J. Filstead. Chicago: Markham.

Mannheim, Karl. (1936). *Ideology and utopia.* New York: Harcourt, Brace and World.

Mariampolski, Hyman, and Dana C. Hughes. (1978). The use of personal documents in historical sociology. *The American Sociologist,* 13: 104–113.

Marks, G., and Miller, N. (1987). Ten years of research on the false consensus effect: An empirical and theoretical review. *Psychological Bulletin* 102:72–90.

Marradi, Alberto. (1981). Factor analysis as an aid in the formation and refinement of empirically useful concepts. In *Factor analysis and measurement in social research: A multi-dimensional perspective,* edited by D. Jackson and E. Borgatta, pp. 11–50. Beverly Hills, CA: Sage.

Marsh, Catherine. (1982). *The survey method: The contribution of surveys to sociological explanation.* Boston: George Allen and Unwin.

Marsh, Catherine. (1984). Do polls affect what people think? In *Surveying subjective phenomena,* Vol. 2, edited by C. Turner and E. Martin, pp. 565–592. New York: Russell Sage Foundation.

Marshall, Catherine. (1985). Appropriate criteria of trustworthiness and goodness for qualitative research on educational organizations. *Quality and Quantity,* 19:353–373.

Marshall, Catherine, and Gretchen B. Rossman. (1989). *Designing qualitative research.* Beverly Hills, CA: Sage.

Marshall, Susan E. (1986). In defense of separate spheres: Class and politics in the antisuffrage movement. *Social Forces,* 65:327–351.

Marston, Cicely, and Eleanor King. (2006). Factors that shape young people's sexual behavior: A systematic review. *Lancet* 368(November 4, 2006):1581–1586.

Martin, Elizabeth. (1985). Surveys as social indicators: Problems of monitoring trends. In *Handbook of survey research,* edited by P. Rossi, J. Wright, and A. Anderson, pp. 677–743. Orlando, FL: Academic.

Martin, Elizabeth. (1999). Who knows who lives here? *Public Opinion Quarterly,* 63:200–236.

Martin, Elizabeth. (2004). Vignettes and respondent debriefing for questionnaire design. In *Methods for testing and evaluating survey questionnaires,* edited by Stanley Presser et al., pp. 149–172. New York: Wiley.

Martin, Jay. (1973). *The dialectical imagination.* Boston: Little, Brown.

Martin, John L., and Laura Dean. (1993). Developing a community sample of gay men for an epidemiological study of AIDS. In *Research on sensitive topics,* edited by C. Renzetti and R. Lee, pp. 82–100. Thousand Oaks, CA: Sage.

Martsolf, Donna, Tamra Courey, Terri Chapman, Clarie Draucker, and Barbara Mims. (2006). Adaptive sampling: Recruiting a diverse community sample of survivors of sexual violence. *Journal of Community Health Nursing,* 23(3):169–182.

Marvasti, Amir B. (2004). *Qualitative research in sociology.* Thousand Oaks, CA: Sage.

Marx, Anthony W. (1998). *Making race and nation: A comparison of the United States, South Africa and Brazil.* New York: Cambridge University Press.

Marx, Karl, and Friedrich Engels. (1947). *The German ideology, Parts I & III,* edited with introduction by R. Pascal. New York: International Publishers.

Masterman, Margaret. (1970). The nature of a paradigm. In *Criticism and the growth of knowledge,* edited by I. Lakatos and A. Musgrove, pp. 59–90. Cambridge: Cambridge University Press.

Mattingly, Marybeth, and Suzanne Bianchi. (2003). Gender differences in the quantity and quality of free time: The U.S. experience. *Social Forces,* 81(3):999–1030.

May, Reuben A. Buford. (2001). *Talking at Trena's.* New York: New York University Press.

Mayer, Charles S., and Cindy Piper. (1982). A note on the importance of layout in self-administered questionnaires. *Journal of Marketing Research,* 19:390–391.

Mayhew, Bruce H. (1980). Structuralism versus individualism, Part I: Shadowboxing in the dark. *Social Forces,* 59:335–375.

Mayhew, Bruce H. (1981). Structuralism versus individualism, Part II: Ideological and other obfuscations. *Social Forces,* 59:627–648.

Maynard, Douglas W., Hanneke Houtkoop-Steenstra, Nora Cate Schaeffer, and Johannes van der Zouwen (editors). (2002). *Standardization and tacit knowledge: Interaction and practice in the survey interview.* New York: Wiley-Interscience.

Maynard, Douglas W., and Nora Cate Schaeffer. (2004). Refusal conversion and tailoring. In *Standardization and tacit knowledge,* edited by Douglas W. Maynard et al., pp. 219–239. New York: Wiley.

McCall, George. (1969). Quality control in participant observation. In *Issues in participant observation,* edited by G. McCall and J. L. Simmons, pp. 128–141. Reading, MA: Addison-Wesley.

McCall, George. (1984). Systematic field observation. *Annual Review of Sociology,* 10:263–282.

McCall, Michael. (1980). Who and where are the artists? In *The fieldwork experience: Qualitative approaches to social research,* edited by William B. Shaffir, R. Stebbins, and A. Turowetz, pp. 145–158. New York: St. Martin's Press.

McCarthy, Thomas. (1978). *The critical theory of Jürgen Habermas.* Cambridge, MA: MIT Press.

McCartney, James L. (1984). Setting priorities for research: New politics for the social sciences. *Sociological Quarterly,* 25:437–455.

McCarty, John A., and L. J. Shrum. (2000). The measurement of personal values in survey research: A test of alternative rating procedures. *Public Opinion Quarterly,* 64:271–298.

McConaghy, Maureen. (1975). Maximum possible error in Guttman scales. *Public Opinion Quarterly,* 39:343–357.

McCracken, Grant. (1988). *The long interview.* Thousand Oaks, CA: Sage.

McDaniel, Timothy. (1978). Meaning and comparative concepts. *Theory and Society,* 6:93–118.

McDiarmid, Garnet. (1971). *Teaching prejudice: A content analysis of social studies textbooks authorized for use in Ontario.* Ontario: Ontario Institute for Studies in Education.

McDermott, Monica. (2006). *Working class white: The making and unmaking of race relations.* Berkeley: University of California Press.

McFarland, Daniel A. (2004). Resistance as a social drama. *American Journal of Sociology,* 109:1249–1318.

McFarland, Sam G. (1981). Effects of question order on survey responses. *Public Opinion Quarterly,* 45:208–215.

McGrath, Joseph, Joanne Martin, and Richard A. Kulka. (1982). *Judgment calls in research.* Beverly Hills, CA: Sage.

McIver, John P., and Edward G. Carmines. (1981). *Unidimensional scaling.* Beverly Hills, CA: Sage.

McCammon, Holly J., Soma Chaudhuri, Lyndi Hewitt, Courtney Sanders Muse, Harmony Newman, Carrie Lee Smith, and Teresa Terrell. (2008). Becoming full citizens: The U.S. women's jury rights campaigns, the pace of reform, and strategic adaptation. *American Journal of Sociology,* 113(4):1104–1147.

McKee, J. McClendon, and David J. O'Brien. (1988). Question order effects on the determinants of subjective well being. *Public Opinion Quarterly,* 52:351–364.

McKeown, Bruce. (1988). *Q methodology.* Thousand Oaks, CA: Sage.

McLennan, Gregor. (1981). *Marxism and the methodologies of history.* London: Verso.

McMahon, John, John McAlaney, and Fiona Edgar. (2007). Binge drinking behaviour, attitudes and beliefs in a UK community sample: An analysis by gender, age and deprivation. *Drugs: Education: Prevention And Policy* 14(4):289–303.

McMurtry, John. (1978). *The structure of Marx's world view.* Princeton, NJ: Princeton University Press.

McNall, Scott G. (1988). *The road to rebellion.* Chicago: University of Chicago Press.

McQuaire, Donald. (1978). Marx and the method of successive approximations. *Sociological Quarterly,* 20: 431–435.

McQuaire, Donald. (1979). Reply to Wardell. *Sociological Quarterly,* 20:431–435.

McVeigh, Rory. (2004). Structural ignorance and organized racism in the United States. *Social Forces,* 82: 895–936.

McVeigh, Rory, and Juliana M. Sobolewski. (2007). Red counties, blue counties, and occupational segregation by sex and race. *American Journal of Sociology,* 113(2):446–506.

Meadows, A. J. (1974). *Communication in science.* Toronto: Butterworths.

Mehan, Hugh. (1973). Assessing children's language using abilities (with discussion). In *Comparative social research,* edited by M. Armer and A. Grimshaw, pp. 309–345. New York: Wiley.

Mehan, Hugh, and Houston Wood. (1975). *The reality of ethnomethodology.* New York: Wiley.

Melbin, Murray. (1978). Night as frontier. *American Sociological Review,* 43:3–22.

Mendenhall, William, Lyman Ott, and Richard L. Scheaffer. (1971). *Elementary survey sampling.* Belmont, CA: Duxbury Press.

Merten, Don E. (1999). Enculturation into secrecy among junior high school girls. *Journal of Contemporary Ethnography,* 28:107–138.

Merton, Robert K. (1938). Social structure and anomie. *American Sociological Review* 3(5):672–682.

Merton, Robert K. (1957). *Social theory and social structure.* New York: Free Press.

Merton, Robert K. (1967). *On theoretical sociology: Five essays, old and new.* New York: Free Press.

Merton, Robert K. (1970). *Science, technology and society in seventeenth century England.* New York: Harper & Row.

Merton, Robert K. (1973). *The sociology of science.* Chicago: University of Chicago Press.

Meyer, Katrina A. (1998). Faculty workload studies: Perspectives, needs, and future directions. ASHE-ERIC Higher Education Report, Vol. 26, No. 1. Washington, DC: Office of Educational Research and Improvement.

Mihic, Sophia, Stephen Engelmann, and Elizabeth Rose Wingrove. (2005). Making sense in and of political science: Facts, values and "real" numbers. In *The politics of method in the human sciences: Positivism and its epistemological others,* edited by George Steinmetz, pp. 470–495. Durham, NC: Duke University Press.

Mikkelsen, Britha. (1995). *Methods for development work and research: A guide for practitioners.* Thousand Oaks, CA: Sage.

Milem, Jeffrey F., Joseph Berger, and Eric Dey. (2000). Faculty time allocation: A study of change over twenty years. *Journal of Higher Education,* 71:454–475.

Miles, Matthew B., and A. Michael Huberman. (1994). *Qualitative data analysis,* 2nd ed. Thousand Oaks, CA: Sage.

Milgram, Stanley. (1963). Behavioral study of obedience. *Journal of Abnormal and Social Psychology,* 6:371–378.

Milgram, Stanley. (1965). Some conditions of obedience and disobedience to authority. *Human Relations,* 18:57–76.

Milgram, Stanley. (1974). *Obedience to authority.* New York: Harper & Row.

Miller, Brian K., and Steve Werner. (2007). Predictors of helping behavior toward coworkers with disabilities. *Journal of Applied Social Psychology,* 37(11):2660–2687.

Miller, Delbert C. (1991). *Handbook of research design and social measurement,* 5th ed. Newbury Park, CA: Sage.

Miller, Gale. (1992). Case studies. In *Encyclopedia of sociology,* Vol. 1, edited by Edgar and Marie Borgatta, pp. 167–172. New York: Macmillan.

Miller, John D. (1998). The measurement of civic scientific literacy. *Public Understanding of Science* 7(3): 203–223.

Miller, John D., Eugenie C. Scott, and Shinji Okamoto. (2006). Public acceptance of evolution. *Science* 313 (5788):765–766 (August 11 2006).

Miller, J. Mitchell, and Richard Tewksbury, eds. (2000). *Extreme methods: Innovative approaches to social science research.* New York: Addison Wesley, Longman.

Miller, Richard. (1987). *Fact and method: Explanation, confirmation and reality in the natural and social sciences.* Princeton, NJ: Princeton University Press.

Miller, William L. (1983). *The survey method in the social and political sciences: Achievements, failures and prospects.* London: Frances Pinter.

Milligan, John D. (1979). The treatment of historical source. *History and Theory,* 18:177–196.

Mills, C. Wright. (1959). *The sociological imagination.* New York: Oxford University Press.

Miringoff, Marque-Luisa, and Sandra Opdycke. (2007). *America's social health: Putting social issues back on the public agenda.* New York. M.E. Sharpe.

Mishler, Elliot G. (1986). *Research interviewing: Context and narrative.* Cambridge, MA: Harvard University Press.

Mitchell, Alison. (May 17, 1997). Survivors of Tuskegee study get apology from Clinton. *New York Times.*

Mitchell, J. Clyde. (1984). Case studies. In *Ethnographic research: A guide to general conduct,* edited by R. F. Ellen, pp. 237–241. Orlando, FL: Academic Press.

Mitchell, Mark, and Janina Jolley. (1988). *Research design explained.* New York: Holt, Rinehart and Winston.

Mitchell, Richard G., Jr. (1993). *Secrecy and fieldwork.* Thousand Oaks, CA: Sage.

Mitroff, Ian. (1974). Norms and counternorms in a select group of the Apollo moon scientists: A case study of ambivalence of scientists. *American Sociology Review,* 39:579–595.

Molotch, Harvey, William Freudenburg, and Krista Paulsen. (2000). History repeats itself, but how? City character, urban tradition, and the accomplishment of place. *American Sociological Review,* 65:791–823.

Monaghan, Peter. (April 7, 1993a). Facing jail, a sociologist raises question about a scholar's right to protect sources. *Chronicle of Higher Education,* p. A10.

Monaghan, Peter. (May 26, 1993b). Sociologist is jailed for refusing to testify about research subject. *Chronicle of Higher Education,* p. A10.

Monaghan, Peter. (September 1, 1993c). Sociologist jailed because he "wouldn't snitch" ponders the way research ought to be done. *Chronicle of Higher Education,* pp. A8–A9.

Monmonier, Mark. (1996). *How to lie with maps,* 2nd ed. Chicago: University of Chicago Press.

Montemurro, Beth. (2005). Add men, don't stir: Reproducing traditional gender roles in modern wedding showers. *Journal of Contemporary Ethnography,* 34(1):6–35.

Mook, Douglas G. (1983). In defense of external invalidity. *American Psychologist,* 38:379–387.

Mooney, Chris. (2005). *The Republican war on science.* New York: Basic Books.

Moore, Barrington, Jr. (1966). *The social origins of dictatorship and democracy.* Boston: Beacon Press.

Moore, Joan. (1973). Social constraints on sociological knowledge: Academic and research concerning minorities. *Social Problems,* 21:65–77.

Moore, R. J. (2004). Managing troubles in answering survey questions: Respondents' uses of projective reporting. *Social Psychology Quarterly,* 67:50–69.

Moors, Guy. (2008). Exploring the effect of a middle response category on response style in attitude measurement. *Quality and Quantity,* 42:779–794.

Morgan, David L. (1996). Focus groups. *Annual Review of Sociology,* 22: 129–152.

Morgan, Kimberly J., and Monica Prasad. (2009). The origins of tax systems: A French-American comparison. *American Journal of Sociology,* 114(5):1350–1394.

Morning, Ann. (2009). Toward a sociology of racial conceptualization for the 21st century. *Social Forces,* 87(3):1167–1191.

Morrow, Raymond Allan. (1994). *Critical theory and methodology.* Thousand Oaks, CA: Sage.

Morse, Janice M. (1994). Designing funded qualitative research. In *Handbook of qualitative research,* edited by N. Denzin and Y. Lincoln, pp. 220–235. Thousand Oaks, CA: Sage.

Moser, C. A., and G. Kalton. (1972). *Survey methods in social investigation.* New York: Basic Books.

Mostyn, Barbara. (1985). The content analysis of qualitative research data: A dynamic approach. In *The research interview: Uses and approaches,* edited by M. Brenner, J. Brown, and D. Canter, pp. 115–145. New York: Academic Press.

Mouer, Ross, and Hirosuke Kawanishi. (2005). *A sociology of work in Japan.* New York: Cambridge University Press.

Mueller-Johnson, Katrin U., and Mandeep K. Dhami. (2010). Effects of offenders' age and health on sentencing decisions. *Journal of Social Psychology,* 150(1): 77–97.

Mulkay, Michael. (1979). *Science and the sociology of knowledge.* London: George Allen and Unwin.

Mullins, Carolyn J. (1977). *A guide to writing and publishing in the social and behavioral sciences.* New York: Wiley.

Mullins, Nicholas C. (1971). *The art of theory: Construction and use.* New York: Harper & Row.

Mullins, Nicholas C. (1973). *Theory and theory groups in American sociology.* New York: Harper & Row.

Munck, Gerardo L. (2004). Tools for qualitative research. In *Rethinking social inquiry: Diverse tools and shared standards,* edited by Henry E. Brady and David Collier, pp. 105–121. Baltimore: Rowman and Littlefield.

Murdock, George P. (1967). Ethnographic atlas. *Ethnology,* 6:109–236.

Murdock, George P. (1971). *Outline of cultural materials,* 4th ed. New Haven, CT: Human Relations Area Files.

Murphey, Murray G. (1973). *Our knowledge of the historical past.* Indianapolis: Bobbs-Merrill.

Musick, Marc A., John Wilson, and William Bynum. (2000). Race and formal volunteering: The differential effects of class and religion. *Social Forces,* 78:1539–1571.

Myerhoff, Barbara. (1989). So what do you want from us here? In *In the field,* edited by C. Smith and W. Kornblum, pp. 83–90. New York: Praeger.

Myers, Daniel J., and Beth S. Caniglia. (2004). All the rioting that's fit to print. *American Sociological Review,* 69:519–543.

Myers, Gloria, and A. V. Margavio. (1983). The black bourgeoisie and reference group change: A content analysis of *Ebony. Qualitative Sociology,* 6:291–307.

Myrdal, Gunnar. (1973). The beam in our eyes. In *Comparative research methods,* edited by D. Warwick and S. Osherson, pp. 89–99. Englewood Cliffs, NJ: Prentice-Hall.

Nadeau, Richard, Richard Miemi, and Jeffrey Levine. (1993). Innumeracy about minority population. *Public Opinion Quarterly,* 57:332–347.

Namenwirth, J. Z. (1970). Prestige newspapers and assessment of elite opinions. *Journalism Quarterly,* 47: 318–323.

Narayan, Sowmya, and John A. Krosnick. (1996). Education moderates some response effects in attitude measurement. *Public Opinion Quarterly,* 60:58–88.

Naroll, Raoul. (1968). Some thoughts on comparative method in cultural anthropology. In *Methodology in social research,* edited by H. Blalock and A. Blalock, pp. 236–277. New York: McGraw-Hill.

Nash, Jeffrey E., and David W. McCurdy. (1989). Cultural knowledge and systems of knowing. *Sociological Inquiry,* 59:117–126.

Nature Neuroscience Editorial. (2005). A political attack on peer review. *Nature Neuroscience,* 8(10):1273–1273.

Nederhof, Anton J. (1986). Effects of research experiences of respondents. *Quality and Quantity,* 20: 277–284.

Neild, Ruth Curran, Scott Stoner-Eby, and Frank Furstenberg. (2008). Connecting entrance and departure: The transition to ninth grade and high school dropout. *Education and Urban Society,* 40(5):543–569.

Nelkin, Dorothy. (1982a). Forbidden research: Limits on inquiry in the social sciences. In *Ethical issues in social science research,* edited by Tom L. Beauchamp, R. Faden, R. J. Wallace, and L. Walters, pp. 163–174. Baltimore: Johns Hopkins University Press.

Neuberg, Leland Gerson. (1988). Distorted transmission: A case study in the diffusion of "social scientific" research. *Theory and Society,* 17: 487–526.

Neuman, W. Lawrence. (1992). Gender, race and age differences in student definitions of sexual harassment. *Wisconsin Sociologist,* 29:63–75.

Neuman, W. Lawrence. (2000). *Social research methods: Qualitative and quantitative approaches,* 4th ed. Boston: Allyn and Bacon.

Neuman, W. Russell, Marion R. Just, and Ann N. Crigler. (1992). *Common knowledge: News and the construction of political meaning.* Chicago: University of Chicago Press.

Newman, Joshua. (2007). Old times there are not forgotten: Sport, identity, and the Confederate flag in the Dixie South. *Sociology of Sport Journal,* 24(3):261–282.

Niven, David. (2002). Bolstering an illusory majority: The effects of the media's portrayal of death penalty support. *Social Science Quarterly,* 83(3):672–689.

Noelle-Neumann, Elisabeth. (1974). Spiral of silence: A theory of public opinion. *Journal of Communication,* 24:43–51.

Noelle-Neumann, Elisabeth. (1984). *The spiral of silence: Public opinion— our social skin.* Chicago: University of Chicago Press.

Nolan III, James, Yoshio Akiyama, and Samuel Berhanu. (2002). The Hate Crime Statistics Act of 1990: Developing a method for measuring the occurrence of hate violence. *American Behavioral Scientist,* 46(1):136–153.

Norris, M. (1981). Problems in the analysis of soft data and some suggested solutions. *Sociology,* 15:337–351.

Norusis, Marija J. (1986). *The SPSS-X guide to data analysis.* Chicago: SPSS, Inc.

Novick, Peter. (1988). *That noble dream: The "objectivity question" and the American historical profession.* New York: Cambridge University Press.

Nowak, Stefan. (1989). Comparative studies and social theory. In

Cross-national research in sociology, edited by M. Kohn, pp. 34–56. Newbury Park, CA: Sage.

Nowotny, Helga, and Hilary Rose, eds. (1979). *Counter-movements in the sciences.* Boston: D. Reidel.

Nunnally, Jum C. (1978). *Psychometric theory.* New York: McGraw-Hill.

Oakley, Ann. (1981). Interviewing women: A contradiction in terms. In *Doing feminist research,* edited by H. Roberts, pp. 30–61. London: Routledge.

O'Brien, Robert M. (1992). Levels of analysis. In *Encyclopedia of sociology,* Vol. 3, edited by E. and M. Borgatta, pp. 1107–1112. New York: Macmillan.

Odette, Parry, and Natasha Mautner. (2004). Whose data are they anyway? *Sociology,* 38:139–152.

O'Donnell, John M. (1985). *The origins of behaviorism: American psychology, 1870–1920.* New York: New York University Press.

Oesterle, Sabrina, Monica Kirkpatrick Johnson, and Jeylan T. Mortimer. (2004). Volunteerism during the transition to adulthood: A life course perspective. *Social Forces,* 82:1123–1149.

Offe, Claus. (1981). The social sciences: Contract research or social movements? *Current Perspectives on Social Theory,* 2:31–37.

Oksenberg, Lois, Lerita Coleman, and Charles F. Cannell. (1986). Interviewers' voices and refusal rates in telephone surveys. *Public Opinion Quarterly,* 50:97–111.

Oliker, Stacey J. (1994). Does workfare work? Evaluation research and workfare policy. *Social Problems,* 41:195–211.

Olsen, Marvin E., and Michael Micklin, eds. (1981). *Handbook of applied sociology.* New York: Praeger.

Olsen, Virginia. (1994). Feminism and models of qualitative research. In *Handbook of qualitative research,* edited by N. Denzin and Y. Lincoln, pp. 158–174. Thousand Oaks, CA: Sage.

Olson, Kristen, and Andy Peytchev. (2007). Effect of interviewer experience on interview pace and interviewer attitudes. *Public Opinion Quarterly,* 71(2):273–286.

Orbuch, Terri, and Sandra L. Eyster. (1997). Division of labor among black couples and white couples. *Social Forces,* 76:301–332.

Orloff, Ann Shola. (1993). *The politics of pensions: A comparative analysis of Britain, Canada and the United States, 1880–1940.* Madison: University of Wisconsin Press.

Osgood, C. E., G. Suci, and H. Tannenbaum. (1957). *The measurement of meaning.* Urbana: University of Illinois Press.

Ostrom, Thomas M., and Katherine M. Gannon. (1996). Exemplar generation: Assessing how respondents give meaning to rating scales. In *Answering questions,* edited by N. Schwarz and S. Sudman, pp. 293–318. San Francisco: Jossey-Bass.

O'Sullivan, Katherine. (1986). *First world nationalisms.* Chicago: University of Chicago Press.

Overbye, Dennis. (January 2, 2007). Free will: Now you have it, now you don't. *New York Times.*

Øyen, Else. (1990). The imperfection of comparisons. In *Comparative methodology: Theory and practice in international social research,* edited by E. Øyen, pp. 1–18. Newbury Park, CA: Sage.

Pager, Devah. (2007). *Marked: Race, crime and finding work in an era of mass incarceration.* Chicago: University of Chicago Press.

Paige, Jeffrey M. (1975). *Agrarian revolution.* New York: Free Press.

Pampel, Fred C. (2006). Socioeconomic distinction, cultural tastes, and cigarette smoking. *Social Science Quarterly,* 87(1):19–35.

Parcel, Toby L. (1992). Secondary data analysis and data archives. In *Encyclopedia of sociology,* Vol. 4, edited by E. and M. Borgatta, pp. 1720–1728. New York: Macmillan.

Parker-Pope, Tara. (December 14, 2007). Wrinkle cream not working? Give me two more jars. *New York Times.*

Paulos, John Allen. (2001). *Innumeracy: Mathematical illiteracy and its consequences.* New York: Hill and Wang.

Payne, A. Abigail. (2002). Do US Congressional earmarks increase research output at universities? *Science and Public Policy,* 29(5):314–330.

Payne, A. Abigail. (2003a). The effects of congressional appropriation committee membership on the distribution of federal research funding to universities. *Economic Inquiry,* 41:325–345.

Payne, A. Abigail. (2003b). The role of politically motivated subsidies on university research activities. *Educational Policy,* 17:12–37.

Pearsall, Marion. (1970). Participant observation as role and method in behavioral research. In *Qualitative methodology,* edited by W. J. Filstead, pp. 340–352. Chicago: Markham.

Pearson, Michael Ross, and Robyn M. Dawes. (1992). Personal recall and the limits of retrospective questions in surveys. In *Questions about questions: Inquiries into the cognitive bases of surveys,* edited by J. Turner, pp. 65–94. New York: Russell Sage Foundation.

Pedriana, Nicholas. (2005). Rational choice, structural context, and increased return. *Sociological Methods and Research,* 33:349–382.

Peterson, Robert A. (1984). Asking the age question: A research note. *Public Opinion Quarterly,* 48:379–383.

Pettit, Becky, and Bruce Western. (2004). Mass imprisonment and the life course. *American Sociological Review,* 69:151–169.

Pew Center Forum on Religion and Public Life. (2005). Public divided on origins of life. http://pewforum.org/docs/?DocID=115. Accessed February 18, 2010.

Pew Center Research Center for the People and the Press. (2009). Public praises science; scientists fault public, media scientific achievements less prominent than a decade ago. July 9, 2009. http://people-press.org/report/528/. Accessed July 30, 2010.

Pfohl, Stephen. (1990). Welcome to the parasite cafe: Postmodernity as a social problem. *Social Problems,* 37:421–442.

Phillips, Bernard. (1985). *Sociological research methods: An introduction.* Homewood, IL: Dorsey.

Phillips, D. C. (1987). *Philosophy, science and social inquiry: Contemporary methodological controversies in social science and related applied fields of research.* New York: Pergamon.

Phillips, Derek. (1971). *Knowledge from what?* Chicago: Rand McNally.

Pierson, Paul. (2000). Increased return, path dependence, and the study of politics. *American Political Science Review,* 94:251–267.

Piliavin, Irving M., J. Rodin, and Jane A. Piliavin. (1969). Good samaritanism: An underground phenomenon?

Journal of Personality and Social Psychology, 13:289–299.

Platt, Jennifer. (1981). Evidence and proof in documentary research. *Sociological Review,* 29:31–66.

Poe, Gail S., et al. (1988). "Don't know" boxes in factual questions in a mail questionnaire: Effects on level and quality of response. *Public Opinion Quarterly,* 52:212–222.

Pollner, Melvin, and Richard Adams. (1997). The effect of spouse presence on appraisals of emotional support and household strain. *Public Opinion Quarterly,* 61:615–626.

Popovich, P. M., B. J. Licata, D. Nokovich, T. Martelli, and S. Zoloty. (1986). Assessing the incidence and perceptions of sexual harassment behaviors among American undergraduates. *Journal of Psychology,* 120:387–396.

Popper, Karl. (1959/1934). *The logic of scientific discovery.* New York: Basic Books.

Porter, Stephen, and Michael Whitcomb. (2003). The impact of contact type on web survey response rates. *Public Opinion Quarterly,* 67:579–588.

Porter, Theodore M. (1995). *Trust in numbers: The pursuit of objectivity in science and the public life.* Princeton, NJ: Princeton University Press.

Pottick, Kathleen, and Paul Lerman. (1991). Maximizing survey response rates for hard-to-reach inner-city populations. *Social Science Quarterly,* 72:172–180.

Presser, Stanley. (1984). Is inaccuracy on factual survey items item-specific or respondent-specific? *Public Opinion Quarterly,* 48:344–355.

Presser, Stanley. (1990). Measurement issues in the study of social change. *Social Forces,* 68:856–868.

Presser, Stanley, Johnny Blair, and Timothy Triplett. (1992). Survey sponsorship, response rates and response effects. *Social Science Quarterly,* 73: 699–702.

Prewitt, Kenneth. (1983). Management of survey organizations. In *Handbook of social research,* edited by P. Rossi, J. Wright, and A. Anderson, pp. 123–143. Orlando, FL: Academic Press.

Price, Vincent. (1989). Social identification and public opinion: Effects of communicating group conflict. *Public Opinion Quarterly,* 53:197–224.

Prior, Lindsay. (2003). *Using documents in social research.* Thousand Oaks, CA: Sage.

Prior, Markus. (2009a). The immensely inflated news audience: Assessing bias in self-reported news exposure. *Public Opinion Quarterly,* 73(1): 130–143.

Prior, Markus. (2009b). Improving media effects research through better measurement of news exposure. *The Journal of Politics,* 71(3):893–908.

Pronin, Emily, Daniel Wegner, Kimberly McCarthy, and Sylvia Rodriguez. (2006). Everyday magical powers: The role of apparent mental causation in the overestimation of personal influence. *Journal of Personality and Social Psychology,* 91(2):218–231.

Prucha, Francis Paul. (1987). *Handbook for research in American history: A guide to bibliographies and other reference works.* Lincoln: University of Nebraska Press.

Pruchno, Rachel, Jonathan Brill, Yvonne Shands, Judith Gordon, Maureen Wilson Genderson, Miriam Rose, and Francine Cartwright. (2008). Convenience samples and caregiving research: How generalizable are the findings? *The Gerontologist,* 48(6): 820–827.

Przeworski, Adam, and Henry Teune. (1970). *The logic of comparative inquiry.* New York: Wiley.

Przeworski, Adam, and Henry Teune. (1973). Equivalence in cross-national research. In *Comparative research methods,* edited by D. Warwick and S. Osherson, pp. 119–137. Englewood Cliffs, NJ: Prentice-Hall.

Punch, Maurice. (1986). *The politics and ethics of fieldwork.* Beverly Hills, CA: Sage.

Pusey, Michael. (1987). *Jürgen Habermas.* New York: Tavistock.

Pyke, Sandra W., and Neil McK. Agnew. (1991). *The science game,* 5th ed. Englewood Cliffs, NJ: Prentice-Hall.

Quach, Thu, Kim-Dung Nguyen, Phuon-An Doan Billings, Linda Okahara, Cathyn Fan, and Peggy Reynolds. (2008). A preliminary survey of Vietnamese nail salon workers in Alameda County. *California Journal of Community Health,* 33: 336–343.

Quadagno, Jill S. (1984). Welfare capitalism and the Social Security Act of 1935. *American Sociological Review,* 49:632–648.

Quadagno, Jill S. (1988). *The transformation of old age security.* Chicago: University of Chicago Press.

Quarles, Susan D., ed. (1986). *Guide to federal funding for social scientists.* New York: Russell Sage Foundation.

Raab, M. 1998. Condom availability in high school does not increase teenage sexual activity but does increase condom use. *Family Planning Perspectives,* 30(1):48–49.

Rabinow, Paul, and William M. Sullivan. (1979). The interpretative turn: Emergence of an approach. In *Interpretative social science: A reader,* edited by P. Rabinow and W. Sullivan, pp. 1–24. Berkeley: University of California Press.

Ragin, Charles C. (1987). *The comparative method.* Berkeley: University of California Press.

Ragin, Charles. (1989). New directions in comparative research. In *Cross-national research in sociology,* edited by M. Kohn, pp. 57–76. Newbury Park, CA: Sage.

Ragin, Charles C. (1992a). Introduction: Cases of "what is a case?" In *What is a case?: Exploring the foundations of social inquiry,* edited by C. Ragin and H. Becker, pp. 1–18. New York: Cambridge University Press.

Ragin, Charles C. (1992b). Casing and the process of social inquiry. In *What is a case?: Exploring the foundations of social inquiry,* edited by C. Ragin and H. Becker, pp. 217–226. New York: Cambridge University Press.

Ragin, Charles C. (1994a). *Constructing social research.* Thousand Oaks, CA: Pine Forge Press.

Ragin, Charles C. (1994b). Introduction to qualitative comparative analysis. In *The comparative political economy of the welfare state,* edited by Thomas Janoski and Alexander Hicks, pp. 299–319. New York: Cambridge University Press.

Ragin, Charles C. (2008). *Redesigning social inquiry: Fuzzy sets and beyond.* Chicago: University of Chicago Press.

Ragin, Charles C., and David Zaret. (1983). Theory and method in comparative research. *Social Forces,* 61:731–754.

Rampton, Sheldon, and John Stauber. (2001). *Trust us, we're experts.* New York: Putnam.

Rathje, W. L., and W. W. Hughes. (1976). The garbage project as nonreactive approach: Garbage in-garbage out.

In *Perspective on attitude assessment: Surveys and their alternatives,* edited by H. W. Sinaiko and L. A. Broeding. Champaign, IL: Pendleton Publications.

Rathje, William, and Cullen Murphy. (1992). *Rubbish: The archaeology of garbage.* New York: Vintage.

Ravo, Nick. (October 14, 1996). Index of social well-being is at the lowest in 25 years. *New York Times.*

Reason, Peter. (1994). Three approaches to participative inquiry. In *Handbook of qualitative research,* edited by N. Denzin and Y. Lincoln, pp. 324–339. Thousand Oaks, CA: Sage.

Reese, Stephen, W. Danielson, P. Shoemaker, T. Chang, and H. Hsu. (1986). Ethnicity of interview effects among Mexican Americans and Anglos. *Public Opinion Quarterly,* 50: 563–572.

Reingold, David A. (1999). The private sector as a sociological laboratory. *American Sociologist* 30(1):74–86.

Reingold, David A., Maureen Pirog, and David Brady. (2007). Empirical evidence on faith-based organizations in an era of welfare reform. *Social Service Review,* 81(2):245–283.

Reinharz, Shulamit. (1979). *On becoming a social scientist.* San Francisco: Jossey-Bass.

Reinharz, Shulamit. (1992). *Feminist methods in social research.* New York: Oxford University Press.

Reskin, Barbara. (1977). Scientific productivity and the reward structure of science. *American Sociological Review,* 42:491–504.

Reynolds, Paul Davidson. (1971). *A primer in theory construction.* Indianapolis: Bobbs-Merrill.

Reynolds, Paul Davidson. (1979). *Ethical dilemmas and social science research.* San Francisco: Jossey-Bass.

Reynolds, Paul Davidson. (1982). *Ethics and social science research.* Englewood Cliffs, NJ: Prentice-Hall.

Richards, Thomas J., and Lyn Richards. (1994). Using computers in qualitative research. In *Handbook of qualitative research,* edited by N. Denzin and Y. Lincoln, pp. 445–462. Thousand Oaks, CA: Sage.

Richardson, Jane, and Barry Godfrey. (2003). Towards ethical practice in the use of archived transcripted interviews. *International Journal of Social Research Methodology,* 6:347–355.

Ricoeur, Paul. (1970). The model of the text: Meaningful action considered as a text. In *Interpretative social science: A reader,* edited by P. Rabinow and W. Sullivan, pp. 73–102. Berkeley: University of California Press.

Ridgeway, Cecilia, and Kristan Glasgow Erickson. (2000). Creating and spreading status beliefs. *American Journal of Sociology,* 106:579–615.

Rihoux, Benoît. (2003). Bridging the gap between the qualitative and quantitative worlds? A retrospective and prospective view on Qualitative Comparative Analysis. *Field Methods,* 15(4):351–365.

Rind, Bruce, and David Strohmetz. (1999). Effect on restaurant tipping of a helpful message written on the back of customers' checks. *Journal of Applied Social Psychology,* 29: 139–144.

Risman, Barbara J. (2001). Calling the bluff of value-free science. *American Sociological Review,* 66:605–618.

Ritzer, George. (1975). *Sociology: A multi-paradigm science.* Boston: Allyn and Bacon.

Roadburg, Alan. (1980). Breaking relationships with field subjects: Some problems and suggestions. In *Fieldwork experience,* edited by W. B. Shaffir, R. Stebbins, and A. Turowetz, pp. 281–291. New York: St. Martin's Press.

Roberts, Carl W. (1989). Other than counting words: A linguistic approach to content analysis. *Social Forces,* 68:147–177.

Robertson, John A. (1982). The social scientist's right to research and the IRB system. In *Ethical issues in social science research,* edited by T. L. Beauchamp, R. Faden, R. J. Wallace, and L. Walters, pp. 356–372. Baltimore: Johns Hopkins University Press.

Robinson, John P., Jerrold G. Rusk, and Kendra B. Head. (1972). *Measures of political attitudes.* Ann Arbor: Center for Political Studies, Institute for Social Research, University of Michigan.

Robinson, John P., and Philip R. Shaver. (1969). *Measures of social psychological attitudes.* Ann Arbor: Survey Research Center, Institute for Social Research, University of Michigan.

Roderick, Rick. (1986). *Habermas and the foundations of critical theory.* New York: St. Martin's Press.

Roethlisberger, F. J., and W. J. Dickenson. (1939). *Management and the worker.* Cambridge, MA: Harvard University Press.

Roscigno, Vincent J., and Randy Hodson. (2004). The organizational and social foundations of worker resistance. *American Sociological Review,* 69 (2):14–39).

Rose, Gerry. (1982). *Deciphering social research.* Beverly Hills, CA: Sage.

Rosen, Lawrence. (1995). The creation of the Uniform Crime Report: The role of social science. *Social Science History,* 19:215–238.

Rosenau, Pauline Marie. (1992). *Postmodernism and the social sciences.* Princeton, NJ: Princeton University Press.

Rosenberg, Morris. (1968). *The logic of survey analysis.* New York: Basic Books.

Rosenbloom, Tova, Adar Ben-Eliyahu, Dan Nemrodov, Ariela Biegel, and Amotz Perlman. (2009). Committing driving violations: An observational study comparing city, town and village. *Journal of Safety Research,* 40(3):215–219.

Rosenthal, Robert. (1984). *Meta-analytic procedures for social research.* Beverly Hills, CA: Sage.

Rosnow, Ralph L. (1981). *Paradigms in transition: The methodology of social inquiry.* New York: Oxford University Press.

Ross, Dorothy. (1991). *The origins of American social science.* New York: Cambridge University Press.

Ross, James, S. Laston, P. Pelto, and L. Muna. (2002). Exploring explanatory models of women's reproductive health in rural Bangladesh. *Culture, Health and Sexuality,* 4:173–190.

Rossi, Peter H., ed. (1982). *Standards for evaluation practice.* San Francisco: Jossey-Bass.

Rossi, Peter H., and Howard E. Freeman. (1985). *Evaluation: A systematic approach,* 3rd ed. Beverly Hills, CA: Sage.

Rossi, Peter H., James D. Wright, and Eleanor Weber-Burdin. (1982). *Natural hazards and public choice.* New York: Academic Press.

Rossi, Robert J., and Kevin J. Gilmartin. (1980). *The handbook of social indicators: Sources, characteristics and analysis.* New York: Garland STPM Press.

Roth, Guenther, and Wolfgang Schluchter. (1979). *Max Weber's vision of history: Ethics and methods.* Berkeley: University of California Press.

Roth, Wendy D., and Jal D. Meta. (2002). The Rashomon effect: Combining positivist and interpretivist approaches in the analysis of contested events. *Sociological Methods and Research,* 31(2):131–173.

Roy, Donald. (1970). The study of southern labor union organizing campaigns. In *Pathways to data,* edited by R. W. Habenstein, pp. 216–244. Chicago: Aldine.

Roy, William. (2001). *Making societies.* Thousand Oaks, CA: Pine Forge Press.

Roy, William G. (1983). The unfolding of the interlocking directorate structure of the United States. *American Sociological Review,* 48:248–257.

Roy, William G. (1984). Class conflict and social change in historical perspective. *Annual Review of Sociology,* 10:483–506.

Roy, William G. (1997). *Socializing capital: The rise of the large industrial corporation in America.* Princeton, NJ: Princeton University Press.

Rubin, Herbert J. (1983). *Applied social research.* Columbus, OH: Charles E. Merrill.

Rueschemeyer, Dietrich, Evelyne Huber Stephens, and John D. Stephens. (1992). *Capitalist development and democracy.* Chicago: University of Chicago Press.

Rueschemeyer, Dietrich, and John Stephens. (1997). Comparing historical sequences: A powerful tool for causal analysis. *Comparative Social Research,* 16:55–72.

Ruggles, Steven. (2007). The decline of intergenerational coresidence in the United States, 1850 to 2000. *American Sociological Review,* 72(6):964–989.

Rule, James. (1978a). *Insight and social betterment: A preface to applied social science.* New York: Oxford University Press.

Rule, James. (1978b). Models of relevance: The social effects of sociology. *American Journal of Sociology,* 84:78–98.

Runciman, W. G. (1980). Comparative sociology or narrative history. *European Journal of Sociology,* 21:162–178.

Runyon, Richard P., and Audry Haber. (1980). *Fundamentals of behavioral statistics.* Reading, MA: Addison-Wesley.

Ryan, Mary. (1989). The American parade. In *The new cultural history,* edited by L. Hunt, pp. 131–153.

Berkeley: University of California Press.

Ryder, Norman B. (1992). Cohort analysis. In *Encyclopedia of sociology,* Vol. 1, edited by E. and M. Borgatta, pp. 227–231. New York: Macmillan.

Sabia, Daniel R., Jr., and Jerald T. Wallulis. (1983). *Changing social science: Changing theory and other critical perspectives.* Albany: State University of New York at Albany.

Sagarin, Edward. (1973). The research setting and the right not to be researched. *Social Problems,* 21: 52–64.

Sanday, Peggy Reeves. (1983). The ethnographic paradigm(s). In *Qualitative methodology,* edited by J. Van Maanen, pp. 19–36. Beverly Hills, CA: Sage.

Sanders, Jane. (1979). *Cold war on the campus: Academic freedom at the University of Washington, 1946–64.* Seattle: University of Washington Press.

Sanjek, Roger. (1978). A network method and its uses in urban anthropology. *Human Organization,* 37: 257–268.

Sanjek, Roger. (1990). On ethnographic validity. In *Field notes: The makings of anthropology,* edited by R. Sanjek, pp. 385–418. Ithaca, NY: Cornell University Press.

Savage, James. (2001). *Funding science in America: Congress, universities, and the politics of the academic pork barrel.* New York: Cambridge University Press.

Savelsberg, Joachim, Ryan King, and Lara Cleveland. (2002). Politicized scholarship? Science on crime and the state. *Social Problems,* 49: 327–48.

Sayer, Andrew. (1992). *Method in social science: A realist approach,* 2nd ed. New York: Routledge.

Schacter, Daniel L, ed. (1995). *Memory distortion: How minds, brains, and societies reconstruct the past.* Cambridge, MA: Harvard University Press.

Schacter, Daniel L. (2001). *The seven deadly sins of memory: How the mind forgets and remembers.* Boston: Houghton Mifflin.

Schaefer, David, and Don A. Dillman. (1998). Development of a standard e-mail methodology. *Public Opinion Quarterly,* 62:378–397.

Schaffer, Nora Cate. (1980). Evaluating race-of-interviewer effects in a national

survey. *Sociological Methods and Research,* 8:400–419.

Schaeffer, Nora Cate. (2004). Conversation with a purpose—or conversation? In *Standardization and tacit knowledge,* edited by Douglas W. Maynard et al., pp. 95–123. New York: Wiley.

Schaeffer, Nora Cate, and Stanley Presser. (2003). The science of asking questions. *Annual Review of Sociology,* 29:65–88.

Schatzman, Leonard, and Anselm L. Strauss. (1973). *Field research: Strategies for a natural sociology.* Englewood Cliffs, NJ: Prentice-Hall.

Scheibe, Karl E. (1988). Metamorphosis in the psychologist's advantage. In *The rise of experimentation in American psychology,* edited by J. Morawski, pp. 53–71. New Haven, CT: Yale University Press.

Scheuch, Erwin K. (1990). The development of comparative research: Towards causal explanations. In *Comparative methodology,* edited by E. Øyen, pp. 19–37. Newbury Park, CA: Sage.

Schmeling, Sharon L., and Mike Miller. (August 11, 1988). Whistleblower wins suit against UW. *Capital Times* (Madison, Wisconsin).

Schmitt, Eric. (June 27, 1997). Army criticized on survey on harrassment. *New York Times.*

Schneider, Mark A. (1987). Culture-as-text in the work of Clifford Geertz. *Theory and Society,* 16:809–883.

Schober, Michael, and Frederick G. Conrad. (1997). Does conversational interviewing reduce survey measurement error? *Public Opinion Quarterly,* 61:576–602.

Schober, Michael, and Frederick Conrad. (2004). A collaborative view of standardized survey interview. In *Standardization and tacit knowledge,* edited by Douglas W. Maynard et al., pp. 67–94. New York: Wiley.

Schofer, Evan. (2004). Cross-national differences in the expansion of science, 1970–1990. *Social Forces,* 83: 215–48.

Schrager, Laura, and James Short. (1980). How serious a crime? Perceptions of organizational and common crimes. In *White collar crime,* edited by G. Geis and E. Stotland, pp. 14–31. Beverly Hills, CA: Sage.

Schrecker, Ellen. (1986). *No ivory tower: McCarthyism and the university.* New York: Oxford University Press.

Schuessler, Karl. (1982). *Measuring social life feelings.* San Francisco: Jossey-Bass.

Schuman, Howard. (1992). Context effects: State of the past/state of the art. In *Context effects in social and psychological research,* edited by N. Schwarz and S. Sudman, pp. 5–20. New York: Springer-Verlag.

Schuman, Howard, and Lawrence Bobo. (1988). Survey-based experiments on white racial attitudes towards racial integration. *American Journal of Sociology,* 94:273–299.

Schuman, Howard, and Jean M. Converse. (1971). Effects of black and white interviewers on black response in 1968. *Public Opinion Quarterly,* 65:44–68.

Schuman, Howard, and Otis Dudley Duncan. (1974). Questions about attitude survey questions. In *Sociological methodology, 1973–1974,* edited by H. Costner, pp. 232–251. San Francisco: Jossey-Bass.

Schuman, Howard, and Jacob Ludwig. (1983). The norm of even-handedness in surveys in life. *American Sociological Review,* 48:112–120.

Schuman, Howard, and Stanley Presser. (1977). Question wording as an independent variable in survey analysis. *Sociological Methods and Research,* 6:151–170.

Schuman, Howard, and Stanley Presser. (1979). The open and closed question. *American Sociological Review,* 44:692–712.

Schuman, Howard, and Stanley Presser. (1981). *Questions and answers in attitude surveys: Experiments on question form, wording and content.* New York: Academic Press.

Schwandt, Thomas A. (1994). Constructivist, interpretivist approaches to human inquiry. In *Handbook of qualitative research,* edited by N. Denzin and Y. Lincoln, pp. 118–137. Thousand Oaks, CA: Sage.

Schwandt, Thomas A. (1997). *Qualitative inquiry: A dictionary of terms.* Thousand Oaks, CA: Sage.

Schwartz, Barry. (1997). Collective memory and history: How Abraham Lincoln became a symbol of racial equality. *Sociological Quarterly,* 38(3):469–496.

Schwartz, David. (1997). *Culture and power: The sociology of Pierre Bourdieu.* Chicago: University of Chicago Press.

Schwartz, Howard, and Jerry Jacobs. (1979). *Qualitative sociology: A method to the madness.* New York: Free Press.

Schwartz, Morris, and Charlotte Green Schwartz. (1969). Problems in field observation. In *Issues in participant observation,* edited by G. J. McCall and J. L. Simmons, pp. 89–105. Reading, MA: Addison-Wesley.

Schwarz, Norbert. (1996). *Cognition and communication: Judgmental biases, research methods, and the logic of conversation.* Mahwah, NJ: Lawrence Erlbaum Associates.

Schwarz, Norbert, and Hans-J. Hippler. (1995). Subsequent questions may influence answers to preceding questions in mail surveys. *Public Opinion Quarterly,* 59:93–97.

Schwarz, Norbert, Bäurbel Knäuper, Hans-J. Hippler, Elizabeth Noelle-Neumann, and Leslie Clark. (1991). Rating scales: Numeric values may change the meaning of scale labels. *Public Opinion Quarterly,* 55: 570–582.

Schwarz, Norbert, and Seymour Sudman. (1992). *Context effects in social and psychological research.* New York: Springer-Verlag.

Schwarz, Norbert, and Seymour Sudman. (1994). *Autobiographical memory and the validity of retrospective reports.* New York: Springer-Verlag.

Schweizer, Thomas. (1997). Embeddedness of ethnographic cases: A social networks perspective. *Current Anthropology,* 38(5):739–760.

Schwendinger, H., and J. Schwendinger. (1974). *Sociologists of the chair.* New York: Basic Books.

Scott, William A. (1968). Attitude measurement. In *The handbook of social psychology, Vol. 2: Research methods,* edited by G. Lindzey and E. Aronson, pp. 204–273. Reading, MA: Addison-Wesley.

Sears, David O. (1986). College sophomores in the laboratory: Influences of a narrow data base on social psychology's view of human nature. *Journal of Personality and Social Psychology,* 51:515–530.

Sellin, Thorsten, and Marvin E. Wolfgang. (1964). *The measurement of delinquency.* New York: Wiley.

Selvin, Hanan C., and Everett K. Wilson. (1984). On sharpening sociologists' prose. *Sociological Quarterly,* 25: 205–223.

Sepstrup, P. (1981). Methodological developments in content analysis. In *Advances in content analysis,* edited by K. Rosengren, pp. 133–158. Beverly Hills, CA: Sage.

Sewell, William H., Jr. (1980). *Work and revolution in France.* New York: Cambridge University Press.

Sewell, William H., Jr. (1987). Theory of action, dialectic, and history: Comment on Coleman. *American Journal of Sociology,* 93:166–171.

Sewell, William H., Jr. (1992). Introduction: Narratives and social identities. *Social Science History,* 16:479–488.

Sewell, William H., Jr. (1996). Three temporalities: Toward an eventful sociology. In *The historical turn in the human sciences,* edited by T. McDonald, pp. 245–280. Ann Arbor: University of Michigan Press.

Sewell, William H., Jr. (2005). The political unconscious of social and cultural history, or, confessions of a former quantitative historian. In *The politics of method in the human sciences: Positivism and its epistemological others,* edited by George Steinmetz, pp. 173–206. Durham, NC: Duke University Press.

Seybold, Peter. (1987). The Ford Foundation and the transformation of political science. In *The structure of power in America,* edited by M. Schwartz, pp. 185–198. New York: Holmes and Meier.

Shafer, Robert Jones. (1980). *A guide to historical method,* 3rd ed. Homewood, IL: Dorsey.

Shaffir, William B., Robert A. Stebbins, and Allan Turowetz. (1980). Introduction. In *Fieldwork experience,* edited by W. B. Shaffir, R. Stebbins, and A. Turowetz, pp. 3–22. New York: St. Martin's Press.

Shattuck, John, and Muriel Morisey Spence. (1988). *Government information controls: Implications for scholarship, science and technology.* Washington, DC: Association of American Universities.

Shaw, C. (1930). *The jack roller.* Chicago: University of Chicago Press.

Shearman, Sachiyo, and Rebecca Dumlao. (2008). A cross-cultural comparison of family communication patterns and conflict between young adults and parents. *Journal of Family Communication,* 8(3):186–211.

Sheatsley, Paul B. (1983). Questionnaire construction and item writing. In *Handbook of social research,* edited by P. Rossi, J. Wright, and A. Anderson, pp. 195–230. Orlando, FL: Academic Press.

Shih, Tse-Hua, and Xitao Fan. (2008). Comparing response rates from web and mail surveys: A meta-analysis. *Field Methods,* 20(3):249–271.

Shook, Natalie J., and Russel H. Fazio. (2008). Interracial roommate relationships: An experimental field test of the contact hypothesis. *Psychological Science,* 19(7):717–723.

Shupe, Anston D., Jr., and David G. Bromley. (1980). Walking a tightrope: Dilemmas of participation observation of groups in conflict. *Qualitative Sociology,* 2:3–21.

Sieber, Joan, ed. (1982). *The ethics of social research: Fieldwork, regulation, and publication.* New York: Springer-Verlag.

Sieber, Joan E. (1992). *Planning ethically responsible research: A guide for students and internal review boards.* Thousand Oaks, CA: Sage.

Sieber, Joan E. (1993). The ethics and politics of sensitive research. In *Research on sensitive topics,* edited by C. Renzetti and R. Lee, pp. 14–26. Thousand Oaks, CA: Sage.

Sieber, Sam D. (1973). The integration of fieldwork and survey methods. *American Journal of Sociology,* 78:1335–1359.

Sigelman, Lee. (1982). The uncooperative interviewee. *Quality and Quantity,* 16:345–353.

Sigelman, Lee, and Richard Niemi. (2001). Innumeracy about minority populations: African Americans and Whites compared. *Public Opinion Quarterly,* 65:86–94.

Silva, Edward T., and Sheila Slaughter. (1980). Prometheus bound: Limits of social science professionalization. *Theory and Society,* 9:781–819.

Silverman, David. (1972). Some neglected questions about social reality. In *New directions in sociological theory,* edited by P. Filmer et al. Cambridge, MA: MIT Press.

Silverman, David. (1993). *Interpreting qualitative data.* Thousand Oaks, CA: Sage.

Simpson, Christopher. (1993). U.S. mass communication research and counterinsurgency after 1945: An investigation of the construction of scientific "reality." In *Ruthless criticism: New perspectives in U.S. communication history,* edited by William Solomon and Robert McChesney. Minneapolis: University of Minnesota Press.

Singer, Benjamin D. (1989). The criterial crisis of the academic world. *Sociological Inquiry,* 59:127–143.

Singer, Eleanor. (1978). Informed consent: Consequences for response rate and response quality in social survey. *American Sociological Review,* 43:144–162.

Singer, Eleanor. (1988). Surveys in the mass media. In *Surveying social life: Papers in honor of Herbert H. Hyman,* edited by H. O'Gorman, pp. 413–436. Middletown, CT: Wesleyan University Press.

Singer, Eleanor. (1999). The effect of incentives. *Journal of Official Statistics,* 15:217–230.

Singer, Eleanor, and Martin R. Frankel. (1982). Informed consent procedures in telephone interviews. *American Sociological Review,* 47:416–426.

Singer, Eleanor, Robert Groves, and Amy Corning. (1999). Differential incentives: Beliefs about practices, perceptions of equity and effects on survey participation. *Public Opinion Quarterly,* 63:251–260.

Singer, Eleanor, and Luane Kohnke-Aguirre. (1979). Interviewer expectation effects: A replication and extension. *Public Opinion Quarterly,* 43:245–260.

Singer, Eleanor, John Van Hoewyk, and Mary Maher. (1998). Does the payment of incentives create expectation effects? *Public Opinion Quarterly,* 62:152–164.

Singer, Eleanor, John Van Hoewyk, and Mary Maher. (2000). Experiments with incentives in telephone surveys. *Public Opinion Quarterly,* 64:171–188.

Singer, Eleanor, Dawn R. Von Thurn, and Ester R. Miller. (1995). Confidentiality assurances and response: A quantitative review of the experimental literature. *Public Opinion Quarterly,* 59:66–77.

Singleton, Royce, Jr., B. Straits, Margaret Straits, and Ronald McAllister. (1988). *Approaches to social research.* New York: Oxford University Press.

Sitton, Thad, G. Mehaffy, and O. L. Davis, Jr. (1983). *Oral history.* Austin: University of Texas Press.

Skidmore, William. (1979). *Theoretical thinking in sociology,* 2nd ed. New York: Cambridge University Press.

Sklar, Kathryn Kish. (1991). Hull House maps and papers: Social science as women's work in the 1890s. In *The social survey in historical*

perspective, 1880–1940, edited by M. Blumer, K. Bales, and K. Sklar, pp. 111–147. New York: Cambridge University Press.

Skocpol, Theda. (1979). *States and social revolutions.* New York: Cambridge University Press.

Skocpol, Theda. (1984). Emerging agendas and recurrent strategies in historical sociology. In *Vision and method in historical sociology,* edited by T. Skocpol, pp. 356–392. Cambridge: Cambridge University Press.

Skocpol, Theda. (1988). The "uppity generation" and the revitalization of macroscopic sociology: Reflections at mid-career of a woman from the sixties. *Theory and Society,* 17:627–644.

Skocpol, Theda, and Margaret Somers. (1980). The uses of comparative history in macrosocial inquiry. *Comparative Studies in Society and History,* 22:174–197.

Slater, Phil. (1977). *Origin and significance of the Frankfurt School.* Boston: Routledge and Kegan Paul.

Smart, Barry. (1976). *Sociology, phenomenology, and Marxian analysis: A critical discussion of the theory and practice of a science of society.* Boston: Routledge and Kegan Paul.

Smelser, Neil J. (1959). *Social change in the industrial revolution.* Chicago: University of Chicago Press.

Smelser, Neil J. (1976). *Comparative methods in the social sciences.* Englewood Cliffs, NJ: Prentice-Hall.

Smelser, Neil J. (1991). Internationalization of social science knowledge. *American Behavioral Scientist,* 35:65–91.

Smilde, David. (2003). Skirting the instrumental paradox: Intentional belief through narrative in Latin American Pentecostalism. *Qualitative Sociology,* 26:313–329.

Smith, Christopher. (1995). Asian New York: The geography and politics of diversity. *International Migration Review,* 29:59–84.

Smith, Dennis. (1991). *The rise of historical sociology.* Philadelphia: Temple University Press.

Smith, George W., and Dorothy E. Smith. (1998). The ideology of "fag": The high school experience of gay students. *Sociological Quarterly,* 39:289–308.

Smith, James Allen. (1991). *The idea brokers: Think tanks and the new policy elite.* New York: Free Press.

Smith, Louis M. (1994). Biographical method. In *Handbook of qualitative* research, edited by N. Denzin and Y. Lincoln, pp. 286–305. Thousand Oaks, CA: Sage.

Smith, Mary Lee, and Gene V. Glass. (1987). *Research and evaluation in education and the social sciences.* Englewood Cliffs, NJ: Prentice-Hall.

Smith, Robert B. (1987). Linking quality and quantity. Part I: Understanding and explanation. *Quantity and Quality,* 21:291–311.

Smith, Robert B. (1988). Linking quality and quantity, Part II: Surveys as formalizations. *Quantity and Quality,* 22:3–30.

Smith, Rogers M. (1996). Science, non-science and politics. In *The historic turn in the human sciences,* edited by T. McDonald, pp. 119–159. Ann Arbor: University of Michigan Press.

Smith, Tom W. (1984). The subjectivity of ethnicity. In *Surveying subjective phenomena,* Vol. 2, edited by C. Turner and E. Martin, pp. 117–128. New York: Russell Sage Foundation.

Smith, Tom W. (1987). That which we call welfare by any other name would smell sweeter: An analysis of the impact of question wording on response patterns. *Public Opinion Quarterly,* 51:75–83.

Smith, Tom W. (1989). Random probes of GSS questions. *International Journal of Public Opinion Research,* 1:305–325.

Smith, Tom W. (1992). Thoughts on the nature of context effects. In *Context effects in social and psychological research,* edited by N. Schwarz and S. Sudman, pp. 163–184. New York: Springer-Verlag.

Smith, Tom W. (1995). Trends in non-response rates. *International Journal of Public Opinion Research,* 7: 156–171.

Smith, Tom W. (2002). The Muslim population of the United States. *Public Opinion Quarterly,* 66:404–417.

Smith, Tom W. (2003). Developing comparable questions in cross-national surveys. In *Cross-cultural survey methods,* edited by J. Harkness, F. Van de Vijver, and P. Mohler, pp. 69–91. Hoboken, NJ: Wiley.

Smith, Tom W. (2004). Developing and evaluating cross-national survey instruments. In *Methods for testing and evaluating survey questionnaires,* edited by S. Presser et al., pp. 431–452. New York: Wiley.

Smith, Tom W. (2009). *General social survey codebook, appendix A: Sampling design & weighting.* http://publicdata.norc.org:41000/gss/Documents/Codebook/A.pdf. Accessed July 30, 2010.

Smith, Wayne, Paul Mitchell, Karin Attebo, and Stephen Leeder. (1997). Selection bias from sampling frames: Telephone directory and electoral roll compared with door-to-door population census. *Australian and New Zealand Journal of Public Health,* 21(2):127–133.

Smyth, Jolene D., Don A. Dillman, Leah Melani Christian, and Mallory Mcbride. (2009). Open-ended questions in web surveys: Can increasing the size of answer boxes and providing extra verbal instructions improve response quality? *Public Opinion Quarterly,* 73(2):325–337.

Sniderman, Paul M., and Douglas Grob. (1996). Innovation in experimental design in attitude surveys. *Annual Review of Sociology,* 22:377–399.

Sniderman, Paul M., and Michael Gray Hagen. (1985). *Race and inequality: A study in American values.* Chatham, NJ: Chatham House.

Snow, David A., Susan G. Baker, Leon Anderson, and Michael Martin. (1986b). The myth of pervasive mental illness among the homeless. *Social Problems,* 33:407–423.

Snow, David A., E. Burke Bochford, Jr., Steven K. Worden, and Robert D. Benford. (1986a). Frame alignment process, micromobilization and movement participation. *American Sociological Review,* 51:464–481.

Sobal, Jeffery. (1984). The content of survey introductions and the provision of informed consent. *Public Opinion Quarterly,* 48:788–793.

Sociology Writing Group, UCLA. (1991). *A guide to writing sociology papers,* 2nd ed. New York: St. Martin's Press.

Sohn-Rethel, Alfred. (1978). *Intellectual and manual labor: A critique of epistemology.* New York: Macmillan.

Somers, Margaret R. (1994). Reclaiming the epistemological "other": Narrative and the social construction of identity. In *Social theory and the politics of identity,* edited by Craig Calhoun, pp. 37–99. Cambridge MA: Blackwell.

Sonquist, J. A., and C. Dunkelberg. (1977). *Survey and opinion research: Procedures for processing and analysis.* Englewood Cliffs, NJ: Prentice-Hall.

Sosinsky, Laura Stout, Heather Lord, and Edward Zigler. (2007). For-profit/nonprofit differences in center-based child care quality. *Journal of Applied Developmental Psychology,* 28(5/6): 390–410.

Spector, Paul E. (1981). *Research designs.* Beverly Hills, CA: Sage.

Spector, Paul E. (1992). *Summated rating scale construction.* Newbury Park, CA: Sage.

Spradley, James P. (1970). *You owe yourself a drunk.* Boston: Little, Brown.

Spradley, James P. (1979a). *The ethnographic interview.* New York: Holt, Rinehart and Winston.

Spradley, James P. (1979b). *Participant observation.* New York: Holt, Rinehart and Winston.

Spradley, James P., and B. J. Mann. (1975). *The cocktail waitress.* New York: Wiley.

Sprague, Joey, and Mary K. Zimmerman. (1989). Quality and quantity: Reconstructing feminist methodology. *American Sociologist,* 20:71–86.

Stack, Carol. (1989). Doing research in the flats. In *In the field,* edited by C. Smith and W. Kornblum, pp. 21–26. New York: Praeger.

Stack, Steven. (1987). Celebrities and suicide: A taxonomy and analysis, 1948–1983. *American Sociological Review,* 52:401–412.

Staggenborg, Susan. (1988). Hired hand research (revised). *American Sociologist,* 19:260–269.

Stake, Robert E. (1994). Case studies. In *Handbook of qualitative research,* edited by N. Denzin and Y. Lincoln, pp. 236–247. Thousand Oaks, CA: Sage.

Starr, Paul. (1982). *The social transformation of American medicine.* New York: Basic Books.

Starr, Paul. (1987). The sociology of official statistics. In *The politics of numbers,* edited by W. Alonso and P. Starr, pp. 7–58. New York: Russell Sage Foundation.

Stech, Charlotte G. (1981). Trends in nonresponse rates, 1952–1979. *Public Opinion Quarterly,* 45:40–57.

Steensland, Brian, J. Park, M. Regnerus, L. Robinson, W. Wilcox, and R. Woodberry. (2000). The measure of American religion: Toward improving the state-of-the-art. *Social Forces,* 79:291–318.

Steinmetz, George. (2005a). Positivism and its others in the social sciences. In *The politics of method in the human sciences: Positivism and its epistemological others,* edited by George Steinmetz, pp. 1–56. Durham, NC: Duke University Press.

Steinmetz, George (2005b). Scientific authority and the transition to post-Fordism: The plausibility of positivism in the U.S. sociology since 1945, in *The politics of method in the human sciences: Positivism and its epistemological others,* edited by George Steinmetz, pp. 275–323. Durham, NC: Duke Univeristy Press.

Stephens, John. (1989). Democratic transition and breakdown in western Europe, 1870–1939: A test of the Moore thesis. *American Journal of Sociology,* 94:1019–1077.

Stephenson, Richard M. (1978). The CIA and the professor: A personal account. *American Sociologist,* 13: 128–133.

Stern, Paul C. (1979). *Evaluating social science research.* New York: Oxford University Press.

Stevens, Carla, and Micah Dial, eds. (1994). Preventing the misuse of evaluation. *New Directions for Program Evaluation,* 64. San Francisco: Jossey-Bass.

Stevenson, Richard W. (October 16, 1996). U.S. to revise its estimate of layoffs. *New York Times.*

Stewart, David W. (1984). *Secondary research: Information sources and methods.* Beverly Hills, CA: Sage.

Stewart, Donald E. (1983). *The television family.* Melborne: Institute of Family Studies.

Stimson, Gerry B. (1986). Place and space in sociological fieldwork. *The Sociological Review,* 34:641–656.

Stinchcombe, Arthur L. (1968). *Constructing social theories.* New York: Harcourt, Brace and World.

Stinchcombe, Arthur L. (1973). Theoretical domains and measurement, Part 1. *Acta Sociologica,* 16:3–12.

Stinchcombe, Arthur L. (1978). *Theoretical methods in social history.* New York: Academic Press.

Stinchcombe, Arthur L. (2005). *The logic of social research.* Chicago: University of Chicago Press.

Stoecker, Randy. (1993). The federated frontstage structure and localized social movements: A case study of the Cedar-Riverside neighborhood movement. *Social Science Quarterly,* 74: 169–184.

Stoecker, Randy. (1999). Are academics irrelevant? Roles for scholars in participatory research. *American Behavioral Scientist,* 42:840–854.

Stoianovich, Traian. (1976). *French historical method.* Ithaca, NY: Cornell University Press.

Stone, Lawrence. (1987). *The past and present revisited.* Boston: Routledge and Kegan Paul.

Stone, Philip, et al. (1966). *The general inquirer: A computer approach to content analysis in the behavioral sciences.* Cambridge, MA: MIT Press.

Stone, Philip J., and Robert P. Weber. (1992). Content analysis. In *Encyclopedia of sociology,* Vol. 1, edited by E. and M. Borgatta, pp. 290–295. New York: Macmillan.

Stoner, Norman W. (1966). *The social system of science.* New York: Holt, Rinehart and Winston.

Strack, Fritz. (1992). "Order effects" in survey research. In *Context effects in social and psychological research,* edited by N. Schwarz and S. Sudman, pp. 23–24. New York: Springer-Verlag.

Strauss, Anselm. (1987). *Qualitative analysis for social scientists.* New York: Cambridge University Press.

Strauss, Anselm, and Juliet Corbin. (1990). *Basics of qualitative research: Grounded theory procedures and techniques.* Newbury Park, CA: Sage.

Strauss, Anselm, and Juliet Corbin. (1994). Grounding theory methodology: An overview. In *Handbook of qualitative research,* edited by N. Denzin and Y. Lincoln, pp. 273–285. Thousand Oaks, CA: Sage.

Streb, Matthew J., Barbara Burrell, Brian Frederick, and Michael A. Genovese. (2008). Social desirability effects and support for a female American president. *Public Opinion Quarterly,* 72(1):76–89.

Stryker, Robin. (1996). Beyond history versus theory: Strategic narrative and sociological explanation. *Sociological Methods and Research,* 24: 304–352.

Suchman, Luch, and Brigitte Jordan. (1992). Validity and the collaborative construction of meaning in face-to-face surveys. In *Questions about questions: Inquiries into the cognitive bases of surveys,* edited by J. Turner, pp. 241–267. New York: Russell Sage Foundation.

Sudman, Seymour. (1976a). *Applied sampling.* New York: Academic Press.

Sudman, Seymour. (1976b). Sample surveys. *Annual Review of Sociology,* 2:107–120.

Sudman, Seymour. (1983). Applied sampling. In *Handbook of survey research,* edited by P. Rossi, J. Wright, and A. Anderson, pp. 145–194. Orlando, FL: Academic Press.

Sudman, Seymour, and Norman M. Bradburn. (1983). *Asking questions: A practical guide to questionnaire design.* San Francisco: Jossey-Bass.

Sudman, Seymour, and Norman M. Bradburn. (1987). The organizational growth of public opinion research in the United States. *Public Opinion Quarterly,* 51:S67–S78.

Sudman, Seymour, Norman M. Bradburn, and Norbert Schwarz. (1996). *Thinking about answers: The application of cognitive processes to survey research.* San Francisco: Jossey-Bass.

Sullivan, John L., and Stanley Feldman. (1979). *Multiple indicators: An introduction.* Beverly Hills, CA: Sage.

Suls, Jerry M., and Ralph L. Rosnow. (1988). Concerns about artifacts in psychological experiments. In *The rise of experimentation in American psychology,* edited by J. Morawski, pp. 153–187. New Haven, CT: Yale University Press.

Sumner, Colin. (1979). *Reading ideologies.* New York: Academic Press.

Sung, Hung-En. (2003). Fairer sex of fairer system? Gender and corruption revisited. *Social Forces,* 82:703–723.

Suppe, Frederick, ed. (1977). *The structure of scientific theories,* 2nd ed. Urbana: University of Illinois Press.

Survey Research Center, Institute for Social Research. (1976). *Interviewer's manual,* rev. ed. Ann Arbor: University of Michigan.

Suskind, Ron. (2004). Without a doubt. *New York Times Magazine* 154 (53005):44–106, October 17, 2004.

Sutton, John R. (1991). The political economy of madness: The expansion of the asylum in progressive America. *American Sociological Review,* 56:665–678.

Sutton, John R. (2000). Imprisonment and social classification in five common-law democracies, 1955–1985. *American Journal of Sociology,* 106: 350–386.

Sutton, John R. (2004). The political economy of imprisonment in affluent Western democracies, 1960–1990. *American Sociological Review,* 69: 170–189.

Swanborn, Peter G. (1996). A common base for quality control criteria in quantitative and qualitative research. *Quality and Quantity,* 30:19–35.

Swanson, Guy E. (1971). Frameworks for comparative research. In *Comparative methods in sociology,* edited by I. Vallier, pp. 141–203. Berkeley: University of California Press.

Swartz, David. (1997). *Culture and power: The sociology of Pierre Bourdieu.* Chicago: University of Chicago Press.

Swidler, Ann. (1986). Culture in action: Symbols and strategies. *American Sociological Review,* 51: 273–286.

Tagg, Stephen K. (1985). Life story interviews and their interpretation. In *The research interview: Uses and approaches,* edited by M. Brenner, J. Brown, and D. Canter, pp. 163–199. New York: Academic Press.

Tanur, Judith M. (1983). Methods for large scale surveys and experiments. In *Sociological methodology, 1983–1984,* edited by S. Leinhardt, pp. 1–71. San Francisco: Jossey-Bass.

Tanur, Judith H., ed. (1992). *Questions about questions: Inquiries into the cognitive bases of surveys.* New York: Russell Sage Foundation.

Tarnai, John, and D. Dillman. (1992). Questionnaire context as a source of response differences in mail and telephone surveys. In *Context effects,* edited by N. Schwarz and S. Sudman, pp. 115–129. New York: Springer-Verlag.

Tarnai, John, and Danna L. Moore. (2004). Methods for testing and evaluating computer-assisted questionnaires. In *Methods for testing and evaluating survey questionnaires,* edited by S. Presser et al., pp. 319–335. New York: Wiley.

Tashakkori, Abbas, and Charles Teddlie. (1998). *Mixed methodology: Combining qualitative and quantitative approaches.* Thousand Oaks, CA: Sage.

Taylor, Charles. (1979). Interpretation and the sciences of man. In *Interpretive social science: A reader,* edited by P. Rabinow and W. Sullivan, pp. 25–72. Berkeley: University of California Press.

Taylor, Charles Lewis, ed. (1980). *Indicator systems for political, economic and social analysis.* Cambridge, MA: Oelgeschlager, Gunn and Hain.

Taylor, Marcia Freed. (1994). Ethical considerations in European cross-national research. *International Social Science Journal,* 46:523–532.

Taylor, Steven. (1987). Observing abuse: Professional ethics and personal morality in field research. *Qualitative Sociology,* 10:288–302.

Thompson, E. P. (1963). *The making of the English working class.* New York: Vintage.

Thompson, E. P. (1967). Time, work-discipline, and industrial capitalism. *Past and Present,* 38:56–97.

Thompson, E. P. (1978). *The poverty of theory and other essays.* New York: Monthly Review Press.

Thompson, Paul. (1978). *The voice of the past: Oral history.* New York: Oxford University Press.

Thompson, Steven K. (2002). *Sampling.* New York: Wiley.

Thompson, Steven K., and George A. Geber. (1996). *Adaptive sampling.* New York: Wiley.

Thompson, Steven K., and L. M. Collins. (2002). Adaptive sampling in research on risk-related behaviors. *Drug and Alcohol Dependence,* 68(Suppl 1):S57–67.

Thorne, Barrie, and Zella Luria. (1986). Sexuality and gender in children's daily world. *Social Problems,* 33:176–190.

Thrasher, F. M. (1927). *The gang.* Chicago: University of Chicago Press.

Thurstone, L. L. (1970). Attitudes can be measured. In *Attitude measurement,* edited by G. Summers, pp. 127–141. Chicago: Rand McNally.

Thye, Shane R. (2007). Logical and philosophical foundations of experimental research in the social sciences. *Laboratory experiments in the social sciences,* edited by Murray Webster, Jr. and Jane Sell, pp. 57–86. New York: Academic Press.

Tilly, Charles. (1964). *The vendee.* Cambridge, MA: Harvard University Press.

Tilly, Charles. (1981). *As sociology meets history.* New York: Academic Press.

Tilly, Charles, Louise Tilly, and Richard Tilly. (1975). *The rebellious century, 1830–1930.* Cambridge, MA: Harvard University Press.

Tjora, Aksel H. (2006). Writing small discoveries: An exploration of fresh observers' observations. *Qualitative Research,* 6(4):429–451.

Todorov, Alexander. (2000a). Context effects in national health surveys. *Public Opinion Quarterly,* 64:65–76.

Todorov, Alexander. (2000b). The accessibility and applicability of knowledge: Predicting context effects in national surveys. *Public Opinion Quarterly,* 64:429–451.

Topolski, Jerzy. (1976). *Methodology of history,* trans. Olgierd Wojtasiewicz. Boston: D. Reidel.

Toulmin, Stephen. (1953). *The philosophy of science: An introduction.* New York: Harper & Row.

Tourangeau, Roger. (1992). Context effects on responses to attitude questions. In *Context effects in social and psychological research,* edited by N. Schwarz and S. Sudman, pp. 35–47. New York: Springer-Verlag.

Tourangeau, Roger. (2004a). Survey research and societal change. *Annual Review of Psychology,* 55:775–801.

Tourangeau, Roger. (2004b). Experimental design considerations for testing and evaluating questionnaires. In *Methods for testing and evaluating survey questionnaires,* edited by Stanley Presser et al., pp. 209–224. New York: Wiley.

Tourangeau, Roger, Mick Couper, and Frederick Conrad. (2004). Spacing, position, and order. *Public Opinion Quarterly,* 68:368–393.

Tourangeau, Roger, and Tom Smith. (1996). Asking sensitive questions: The impact of data collection mode, question format and question context. *Public Opinion Quarterly,* 60: 275–304.

Tourangeau, Roger, et al. (1997). Who lives here? *Journal of Official Statistics,* 13:1–18.

Tourangeau, Roger, Darby Steiger, and David Wilson. (2002). Self-administered questions by telephone. *Public Opinion Quarterly,* 66:265–278.

Transue, John E. (2007). Identity salience, identity acceptance, and racial policy attitudes: American national identity as a uniting force. *American Journal of Political Science,* 51(1):78–91.

Traugott, Michael W. (1987). The importance of persistence in respondent selection for preelection surveys. *Public Opinion Quarterly,* 51:48–57.

Treiman, Michael. (1977). Towards methods for a quantitative comparative sociology: A reply to Burawoy. *American Journal of Sociology,* 82:1042–1056.

Trice, H. M. (1970). The "outsider's" role in field study. In *Qualitative methodology,* edited by W. J. Filstead, pp. 77–82. Chicago: Markham.

Tropp, Richard A. (1982). A regulatory perspective on social science research. In *Ethical issues in social science research,* edited by T. Beauchamp, R. Faden, R. J. Wallace, and L. Walters, pp. 391–415. Baltimore: Johns Hopkins University Press.

Troshynski, Emily I., and Jennifer K. Blank. (2008). Sex trafficking: An exploratory study interviewing traffickers. *Trends in Organized Crime* 11(1):30–41.

Trussell, Norm, and Paul Lavrakas. (2004). The influence of incremental increases in token cash. *Public Opinion Quarterly*, 68:368–393.

Tuchman, Gaye. (1994). Historical social science: Methodologies, methods and meanings. In *Handbook of qualitative research*, edited by N. Denzin and Y. Lincoln, pp. 306–323. Thousand Oaks, CA: Sage.

Tucker, Clyde. (1983). Interviewer effects in telephone interviewing. *Public Opinion Quarterly*, 47:84–95.

Tufte, Edward. (1983). *The visual display of quantitative information*. Cheshire, CT: Graphics Press.

Tufte, Edward. (1991). *Envisioning information*, rev. ed. Cheshire, CT: Graphics Press.

Tuma, Nancy B., and Andrew Grimes. (1981). A comparison of models of role orientations of professionals in a research oriented university. *Administrative Science Quarterly*, 21:187–206.

Turner, Charles. (1984). Why do surveys disagree? Some preliminary hypotheses and some disagreeable examples. In *Surveying subjective phenomena*, Vol. 2, edited by C. Turner and E. Martin, pp. 157–214. New York: Russell Sage Foundation.

Turner, Charles, and Elizabeth Martin, eds. (1984). *Surveying subjective phenomena*, Vol. 1. New York: Russell Sage Foundation.

Turner, Jonathan H. (1985). In defense of positivism. *Sociological Theory*, 3:24–30.

Turner, Jonathan H. (1992). Positivism. In *Encyclopedia of sociology*, Vol. 3, edited by E. and M. Borgatta, pp. 1509–1512. New York: Macmillan.

Turner, Roy. (1974). *Ethnomethodology*. Middlesex: Penguin.

Turner, Stephen P. (1980). *Sociological explanation as translation*. New York: Cambridge University Press.

Turner, Stephen P. (1991). The world of academic quantifiers: The Columbia University family and its connections. In *The social survey in historical perspective, 1880–1940*, edited by M. Blumer, K. Bales, and K. Sklar, pp. 269–290. New York: Cambridge University Press.

Turner, Stephen Park, and Jonathan H. Turner. (1991). *The impossible science: An institutional analysis of American sociology*. Newbury Park, CA: Sage.

Uecker, Jeremy E., Mark D. Regnerus, and Margaret L. Vaaler. (2007). Losing my religion: The social sources of religious decline in early adulthood. *Social Forces*, 85(4):1667–1692.

Union of Concerned Scientists. (2004). *Scientific integrity in policy making*. Cambridge MA: Union of Concerned Scientists.

United States Census Bureau. (2008). Linguistic isolation. *American Community Survey data 2007, Fact Finder*, Table 1602. http://factfinder.census.gov/servlet/STTable?_bm=y&-qr_name=ACS_2007_3YR_G00_S1602&-geo_id=01000US&-ds_name=ACS_2007_3YR_G00_&-_lang=en. Accessed July 30, 2010.

Unnever, James, and Francis T. Cullen. (2007). The racial divide in support for the death penalty: Does white racism matter? *Social Forces* 85(3):1281–1301.

Useem, Michael. (1976a). Government influence on the social science paradigm. *Sociological Quarterly*, 17:146–161.

Useem, Michael. (1976b). State production of social knowledge: Patterns of government financing of academic social research. *American Sociological Review*, 41:613–629.

Vallier, Ivan, ed. (1971a). *Comparative methods in sociology: Essays on trends and applications*. Berkeley: University of California Press.

Vallier, Ivan. (1971b). Empirical comparisons of social structure. In *Comparative methods in sociology*, edited by I. Vallier, pp. 203–263. Berkeley: University of California Press.

Van den Berg, Harry, and Cees Van der Veer. (1985). Measuring ideological frames of references. *Quality and Quantity*, 19:105–118.

Van den Berge, Pierre L. (1967). Research in South Africa: The story of my experiences with tyranny. In *Ethics, politics and social research*, edited by G. Sjøberg. New York: Schenckman.

Van der Zouwen, Johannes, and Johannes Smit. (2004). Evaluating survey questions by analyzing patterns of behavior codes and question-answer sequences. In *Methods for testing and evaluating survey questionnaires*, edited by Stanley Presser et al., pp. 109–130. New York: Wiley.

Van Maanen, John. (1973). Observations on the making of policemen. *Human Organization*, 32:407–418.

Van Maanen, John. (1982). Fieldwork on the beat. In *Varieties of qualitative research*, edited by J. Van Maanen, J. Dabbs, Jr., and R. Faulkner, pp. 103–151. Beverly Hills, CA: Sage.

Van Maanen, John. (1983a). Epilogue: Qualitative methods reclaimed. In *Qualitative methodology*, edited by J. Van Maanen, pp. 247–268. Beverly Hills, CA: Sage.

Van Maanen, John. (1983b). The moral fix: On the ethics of fieldwork. In *Contemporary field research*, edited by R. M. Emerson, pp. 269–287. Boston: Little, Brown.

Van Maanen, John. (1988). *Tales of the field: On writing ethnography*. Chicago: University of Chicago Press.

Van Poppel, Frans, and L. Day. (1996). A test of Durkheim's theory of suicide—Without committing the "ecological fallacy." *American Sociological Review*, 61:500–507.

Vaughan, Diane. (1992). Theory elaboration: The heuristics of case analysis. In *What is a case? Exploring the foundations of social inquiry*, edited by C. Ragin and H. Becker, pp. 173–202. Cambridge: Cambridge University Press.

Vaughan, Ted R. (1967). Government intervention in social research: Political and ethical dimensions of the Wichita jury recordings. In *Ethics, politics and social research*, edited by G. Sjøberg. New York: Schenckman.

Veltmeyer, Henry. (1978). Marx's two methods of sociological analysis. *Sociological Inquiry*, 48:101–112.

Venkatesh, Sudhir. (2008). *Gang leader for a day: A rogue sociologist takes to the streets*. New York: Penguin.

Verba, Sidney. (1971). Cross-national survey research. In *Comparative methods in sociology*, edited by I. Vallier, pp. 309–356. Berkeley: University of California Press.

Verba, Sidney, and Gary R. Orren. (1985). *Equality in America: The view from the top*. Cambridge, MA: Harvard University Press.

Vidich, Arthur Joseph, and Joseph Bensman. (1968). *Small town in mass society*, rev. ed. Princeton, NJ: Princeton University Press.

Villarreal, Andrés. (2002). Political competition and violence in Mexico. *American Sociological Review*, 67:477–498.

Villarreal, Andrés. (2004). The social ecology of rural violence. *American Journal of Sociology,* 110:349–399.

Vissersi, Geert, Gerton Heyne, Vincent Peters, and Jac Guerts. (2001). The validity of laboratory research in social and behavioral science. *Quality & Quantity,* 35:129–145.

Viterna, Jocelyn, and Kathleen M. Fallon. (2008). Democratization, women's movements, and gender-equitable states: A framework for comparison. *American Sociological Review,* 73(4): 668–689.

Wade, Nicholas. (1976). IQ and heredity: Suspicion of fraud beclouds classic experiment. *Science,* 194: 916–919.

Waksberg, J. (1978). Sampling methods for random digit dialing. *Journal of the American Statistical Association,* 73:40–46.

Wald, Matthew. (July 1, 2004). Any Saturday on highways ranks close to deadly holidays. *New York Times.*

Walder, Andrew G. (2003). Elite opportunity in transitional economies. *American Sociological Review,* 68: 899–916.

Wallace, Walter. (1971). *The logic of science in sociology.* Chicago: Aldine.

Wallerstein, Immanuel. (1974). *The modern world system.* New York: Academic Press.

Walsh, David. (1972). Varieties of positivism. In *New directions in sociological theory,* edited by P. Filmer et al. Cambridge, MA: MIT Press.

Walster, Elaine. (1965). The effect of self-esteem on romantic liking. *Journal of Experimental Social Psychology,* 1:194–197.

Walters, Ronald G. (1980). Signs of the times. *Social Research,* 47:537–556.

Walton, John. (1973). Standardized case comparison. In *Comparative social research,* edited by M. Armer and A. Grimshaw, pp. 173–191. New York: Wiley.

Walton, John. (1992a). *Western times and water wars: State, culture and rebellion in California.* Berkeley: University of California Press.

Walton, John. (1992b). Making the theoretical case. In *What is a case? Exploring the foundations of social inquiry,* edited by C. Ragin and H. Becker, pp. 121–138. Cambridge: Cambridge University Press.

Wang, Jichuan, Russel S. Falck, Linna Li, Ahmmed Rahman, and Robert G. Carlson. (2007). Respondent-driven sampling in the recruitment of illicit stimulant drug users in a rural setting: Findings and technical issues. *Addictive Behaviors,* 32(5):924–937.

Ward, Benjamin. (1972). *What's wrong with economics.* New York: Basic Books.

Ward, Kathryn B., and Linda Grant. (1985). The feminist critique and a decade of published research in sociology journals. *Sociological Quarterly,* 26:139–158.

Wardell, Mark L. (1979). Marx and his method: A commentary. *Sociological Quarterly,* 20:425–436.

Warner, R. Stephen. (1971). The methodology of Marx's comparative analysis of modes of production. In *Comparative methods in sociology,* edited by I. Vallier, pp. 49–74. Berkeley: University of California Press.

Warren, Carol A. B., and Paul K. Rasmussen. (1977). Sex and gender in field research. *Urban Life,* 6:349–369.

Warwick, Donald P. (1982). Types of harm in social science research. In *Ethical issues in social science research,* edited by T. Beauchamp, R. Faden, R. J. Wallace, and L. Walters, pp. 101–123. Baltimore: Johns Hopkins University Press.

Warwick, Donald P., and Charles A. Lininger. (1975). *The sample survey: Theory and practice.* New York: McGraw-Hill.

Warwick, Donald P., and Samuel Osherson. (1973). Comparative analysis in the social sciences. In *Comparative research methods,* edited by D. Warwick and S. Osherson, pp. 3–11. Englewood Cliffs, NJ: Prentice-Hall.

Wax, Rosalie H. (1971). *Doing fieldwork: Warnings and advice.* Chicago: University of Chicago Press.

Wax, Rosalie H. (1979). Gender and age in fieldwork and fieldwork education: No good thing is done by any man alone. *Social Problems,* 26:509–522.

Webb, Eugene J., Donald T. Campbell, Richard D. Schwartz, Lee Sechrest, and Janet Belew Grove. (1981). *Nonreactive measures in the social sciences,* 2nd ed. Boston: Houghton Mifflin.

Weber, Max. (1949). *The methodology of the social sciences,* trans. and edited by E. Shils and H. Finch. New York: Free Press.

Weber, Max. (1974). Subjectivity and determinism. In *Positivism and sociology,* edited by A. Giddens, pp. 23–32. London: Heinemann.

Weber, Max. (1978). *Economy and society,* Vol. 1, edited by G. Roth and C. Wittich. Berkeley: University of California Press.

Weber, Max. (1981). Some categories of interpretative sociology. *Sociological Quarterly,* 22:151–180.

Weber, Robert P. (1983). Measurement models for content analysis. *Quality and Quantity,* 17:127–149.

Weber, Robert P. (1984). Computer assisted content analysis: A short primer. *Qualitative Sociology,* 7:126–149.

Weber, Robert P. (1985). *Basic content analysis.* Beverly Hills, CA: Sage.

Webster, Murray, and Jane Sell. 2007. Why do experiments? In *Laboratory experiments in the social sciences,* edited by Murray Webster, Jr. and Jane Sell, pp. 1–24. New York: Academic Press.

Weeks, M. F., and R. P. Moore. (1981). Ethnicity of interviewer effects on ethnic respondents. *Public Opinion Quarterly,* 45:245–249.

Weil, Frederick D. (1985). The variable effects of education on liberal attitudes. *American Sociological Review,* 50:458–474.

Weinberg, Steven. (May 31, 2001). Can science explain everything? Anything? *New York Review of Books,* 48: 47–50.

Weinreb, Alexander A. (2006). The limitations of stranger-interviewers in rural Kenya. *American Sociological Review,* 71(6):1014–1039.

Weinstein, Deena. (1979). Fraud in science. *Social Science Quarterly,* 59:639–652.

Weisberg, Herbert F. (2005). *The total survey error approach: A guide to the new science of survey research.* Chicago: University of Chicago Press.

Weiss, Carol H. (1972). *Evaluation research: Methods of assessing program effectiveness.* Englewood Cliffs, NJ: Prentice-Hall.

Weiss, Janet A., and Judith E. Gruber. (1987). The managed irrelevance of educational statistics. In *The politics of numbers,* edited by W. Alonso and P. Starr, pp. 363–391. New York: Russell Sage Foundation.

Weiss, Robert S. (1994). *Learning from strangers: The arts and method of qualitative interview studies.* New York: Free Press.

Weitzman, Eben, and Matthew Miles. (1995). *Computer programs for qualitative data analysis.* Thousand Oaks, CA: Sage.

Wells, Gary L., and Elizabeth A. Olson. (2003). Eyewitness testimony. *Annual Review of Psychology,* 54: 277–295.

Wells, Gary L., Elizabeth Olson, and Steve Charman. (2003). Distorted retrospective eyewitness reports as functions of feedback and delay. *Journal of Experimental Psychology, Applied,* 9:42–52.

Wenger, G. Clare, ed. (1987). *The research relationship: Practice and politics in social policy research.* Boston: Allen and Unwin.

Wentworth, Ellen J. (1993). *Survey responses: An evaluation of their validity.* New York: Academic Press.

Werner, Oswald, and G. Mark Schoepfle. (1987a). *Systematic fieldwork, Vol. 1: Foundations of ethnography and interviewing.* Beverly Hills: Sage.

Werner, Oswald, and G. Mark Schoepfle. (1987b). *Systematic fieldwork, Vol. 2: Ethnographic analysis and data management.* Beverly Hills: Sage.

West, W. Gordon. (1980). Access to adolescent deviants and deviance. In *Fieldwork experience,* edited by W. B. Shaffir, R. A. Stebbins, and A. Turowetz, pp. 31–44. New York: St. Martin's Press.

Western, Bruce, and Becky Pettit. (2005). Black-white wage inequality, employment rates, and incarceration. *American Journal of Sociology,* 111 (2):553–578.

Westmarland, Louise. (2000). Taking the flak: Operational policing, fear, and violence. In *Danger in the field,* edited by G. Lee-Treweek and S. Linkogle, pp. 26–42. New York: Routledge.

Weston, Cynthia, T. Gandell, J. Beauchamp, L. McAlpine, C. Wiseman, and C. Beauchamp. (2001). Analyzing interview data: The development and evolution of a coding system. *Qualitative Sociology,* 24: 381–400.

Whalley, Peter. (1984). Deskilling engineers? The labor process, labor markets, and labor segmentation. *Social Problems,* 32:117–132.

Whiting, John W. M. (1968). Methods and problems in cross-cultural research. In *The handbook of social psychology,* 2nd ed., edited by G. Lindzey and E. Aronson, pp. 693–728. Reading, MA: Addison-Wesley.

Whyte, William F. (1989). Advancing scientific knowledge through participatory action research. *Sociological Forum,* 4:367–385.

Whyte, William Foote. (1955). *Street corner society: The social structure of an Italian slum,* 2nd ed. Chicago: University of Chicago Press.

Whyte, William Foote. (1982). Interviewing in field research. In *Field research,* edited by R. G. Burgess, pp. 111–122. Boston: George Allen and Unwin.

Whyte, William Foote. (1984). *Learning from the field: A guide from experience.* Beverly Hills: Sage.

Whyte, William Foote. (1986). On the uses of social science research. *American Sociological Review,* 51: 555–563.

Wibeck, Victoria, Madeleine Abrandt Dahlgren, and Gunilla Öberg. (2007). Learning in focus groups: An analytical dimension for enhancing focus group research. *Qualitative Research,* 7(2):249–267.

Wieder, D. Lawrence. (1977). Ethnomethodology and ethnosociology. *Mid-American Review of Sociology,* 2:1–18.

Wiedmer, Terry L. (1993). Perspectives on scholarship in education: Undergraduate and graduate students' views on faculty scholarship. Paper at the American Educational Research Association meeting, Atlanta, GA.

Wigginton, Eliot, ed. (1972). *Foxfire book.* New York: Doubleday.

Wilcox, Clyde, Lee Sigelman, and Elizabeth Cook. (1989). Some like it hot: Individual differences in responses to group feeling thermometers. *Public Opinion Quarterly,* 53:246–257.

Wilkins, Amy C. (2008). *Wannabes, Goths and Christians: The boundaries of sex, style and status.* Chicago: University of Chicago Press.

Wilkinson, Alec. (December 5, 2005). Man of letters. *The New Yorker,* 81(39):56–65.

Willer, David, and Henry A. Walker. (2007a). *Building experiments, testing theory.* Stanford, CA: Stanford University Press.

Willer, David, and Henry A. Walker. (2007b). Experiments and the science of sociology. In *Laboratory experiments in the social sciences,* edited by Murray Webster, Jr. and Jane Sell, pp. 25–54. New York: Academic Press.

Williams, Allison, Bill Holden, Peter Krebs, Nazeem Muhajarine, Kate Waygood, James Randall, and Cara Spence. (2007). Knowledge translation strategies in a community–

university partnership: Examining local quality of life. *Social Indicators Research,* 85:111–125.

Williams, Bill. (1978). *A sampler on sampling.* New York: Wiley.

Williams, Carol I., and Gary K. Wolfe. (1979). *Elements of research: A guide for writers.* Palo Alto, CA: Mayfield.

Williams, Christine L. (2006). *Inside Toyland: Working, shopping and social inequality.* Berkeley: University of California Press.

Williams, Terry, and E. Dunlap. (1992). Personal safety in dangerous places. *Journal of Contemporary Ethnography,* 21:343–375.

Williamson, John B., David Karp, John Dalphin, and Paul Gray. (1982). *The research craft.* Boston: Little and Brown.

Willimack, Diane K., Howard Schuman, Beth-Ellen Pennell, and James M. Lepkowski. (1995). Effects of prepaid non-monetary incentives on response rates and response quality in face-to-face survey. *Public Opinion Quarterly,* 59:78–92.

Willis, Gordon B. (2004). Cognitive interviewing revisited. In *Methods for testing and evaluating survey questionnaires,* edited by Stanley Presser et al., pp. 23–44. New York: Wiley.

Willis, Gordon B. (2005). *Cognitive interviewing: A tool for improving questionnaire design.* Thousand Oaks, CA: Sage.

Willis, Paul. (1977). *Learning to labor: How working class kids get working class jobs.* New York: Columbia University Press.

Wilson, John. (1982). Realist philosophy as a foundation for Marx's social theory. *Current Perspectives in Social Theory,* 3:243–263.

Wilson, Thomas P. (1970). Normative and interpretative paradigms in sociology. In *Understanding everyday life: Toward the reconstruction of sociological knowledge,* edited by J. Douglas, pp. 57–79. New York: Aldine.

Wilson, Timothy, Suzanne J. LaFleur, and D. Eric Anderson. (1996). The validity and consequence of verbal reports about attitudes. In *Answering questions,* edited by N. Schwarz and S. Sudman, pp. 91–114. San Francisco: Jossey-Bass.

Wilson, Timothy D., and Elizabeth W. Dunn. (2004). Self-knowledge: Its limits, value, and potential for improvement. *Annual Review of Psychology,* 55:493–518.

Wimberly, Dale W. (1990). Investment dependence and alternative explanations of third world mortality: A cross-national study. *American Sociological Review,* 55:75–91.

Wimmer, Andreas. (2008). The making and unmaking of ethnic boundaries: A multilevel process theory. *American Journal of Sociology,* 113(4):970–1022.

Winkler, Karen J. (January 11, 1989). Dispute over validity of historical approaches pits traditionalists against advocates of new methods. *Chronicle of Higher Education,* pp. A4ff.

Winston, Chester. (1974). *Theory and measurement in sociology.* New York: Wiley.

Wolcott, Harry F. (1994). *Transforming qualitative data: Description, analysis and interpretation.* Thousand Oaks, CA: Sage.

Wolf, Eric R. (1982). *Europe and the people without history.* Berkeley: University of California Press.

Wood, Elizabeth Anne. (2000). Working in the fantasy factory. *Journal of Contemporary Ethnography,* 29:5–32.

Woodrum, Eric. (1984). "Mainstreaming" content analysis in social science: Methodological advantages, obstacles, and solutions. *Social Science Research,* 13:1–19.

Wright, Debra L., William S. Aquilino, and Andrew J. Supple. (1998). A comparison of computer-assisted and paper-and-pencil administered questionnaires in a survey on smoking, alcohol and drug use. *Public Opinion Quarterly,* 62:311–353.

Wright, Erik O. (1978). *Class, crisis and state.* London: New Left Books.

Wright, James D., and Peter H. Rossi, eds. (1981). *Social science and natural hazards.* Cambridge, MA: Abt Books.

Wrigley, Julia, and Jonna Dreby. 2005. Fatalities and the organization of child care in the United States, 1985–2003. *American Sociological Review,* 70(5):729–757.

Wuthnow, Robert. (1979). The emergence of modern science and world system theory. *Theory and Society,* 8:215–243.

Wuthnow, Robert. (1987). *Meaning and moral order: Explorations in cultural analysis.* Berkeley: University of California Press.

Wysong, Earl, Richard Aniskiewicz, and David Wright. (1994). Truth and DARE: Tracking drug education from graduation and symbolic politics. *Social Problems,* 41:448–468.

Yammarino, Francis, Steven Skiner, and Terry Childers. (1991). Understanding mail survey response behavior: A meta-analysis. *Public Opinion Quarterly,* 55:613–640.

Yancey, William L., and Lee Rainwater. (1970). Problems in the ethnography of the urban underclasses. In *Pathways to data,* edited by R. W. Habenstein, pp. 245–269. Chicago: Aldine.

Yeo, Eileen James. (1991). The social survey in social perspective, 1830–1930. In *The social survey in historical perspective, 1880–1940,* edited by M. Blumer, K. Bales, and K. Sklar, pp. 49–65. New York: Cambridge University Press.

Yin, Robert K. (1988). *Case study research,* rev. ed. Newbury Park, CA: Sage.

Young, T. R. (1980). Comment on the McQuaire–Wardell debate. *Sociological Quarterly,* 21:459–462.

Yow, Valerie Raleigh. (1994). *Recording oral history: A practical guide for social scientists.* Thousand Oaks, CA: Sage.

Yu, J., and H. Cooper. (1983). A quantitative review of research design effects on response rates to questionnaires. *Journal of Marketing Research,* 20:36–44.

Zalcman, Rosely Flam, and Robert E. Mann. (2007). The effects of privatization of alcohol sales in Alberta on suicide mortality rates. *Contemporary Drug Problems,* 34(4):589–609.

Zaller, John, and Stanley Feldman. (1992). A simple theory of survey responses: Answering questions versus revealing preferences. *American Journal of Political Science,* 36:579–616.

Zane, Anne, and Euthemia Matsoukas. (1979). Different settings, different results? A comparison of school and home responses. *Public Opinion Quarterly,* 43:550–557.

Zaret, David. (1978). Sociological theory and historical scholarship. *The American Sociologist,* 13:114–121.

Zelditch, Morris. (2007). The external validity of experiments that test theories. In *Laboratory experiments*

in the social sciences, edited by Murray Webster, Jr. and Jane Sell, pp. 87–112. New York: Academic Press.

Zeisel, Hans. (1985). *Say it with figures,* 6th ed. New York: Harper & Row.

Zelizer, Viviana A. (1985). *Pricing the priceless child.* New York: Basic Books.

Zeller, Richard, and Edward G. Carmines. (1980). *Measurement in the social sciences: The link between theory and data.* New York: Cambridge University Press.

Zerubavel, Eviatar. (1981). *Hidden rhythms: Schedules and calendars in social life.* Chicago: University of Chicago Press.

Ziman, John. (1968). *Public knowledge: An essay concerning the social dimension of science.* New York: Cambridge University Press.

Ziman, John. (1976). *The force of knowledge: The scientific dimension of society.* New York: Cambridge University Press.

Zimbardo, Philip G. (1972). Pathology of imprisonment. *Society,* 9:4–6.

Zimbardo, Philip G. (1973). On the ethics of intervention in human psychological research. *Cognition,* 2:243–256.

Zimbardo, Philip G., et al. (April 8, 1973). The mind is a formidable jailer: A Pirandellian prison. *New York Times Magazine,* 122:38–60.

Zimbardo, Philip G., et al. (1974). The psychology of imprisonment: Privation, power and pathology. In *Doing unto others,* edited by Z. Rubin. Englewood Cliffs, NJ: Prentice-Hall.

Zipp, John F., and Joann Toth. (2002). She said, he said: The impact of spousal presence in survey research. *Public Opinion Quarterly,* 66: 209–234.

Zuckerman, Harriet. (1972). Interviewing an ultra-elite. *Public Opinion Quarterly,* 36:159–175.

Zuckerman, Harriet. (1978). Theory choice and problem choice in science. In *Sociology of science,* edited by J. Gaston, pp. 65–95. San Francisco: Jossey-Bass.

Zuiches, James J. (1984). The organization and funding of social science in the NSF. *Sociological Inquiry,* 54:188–210.

Name Index

Subject Index

Scholarly Journals in the Social Sciences in English

GENERAL SOCIAL SCIENCE

American Behavioral Scientist
Annals of the American Academy of Political and Social Science
Evaluation Practice (American Evaluation Association)
Evaluation Review
Human Relations
Public Opinion Quarterly (American Association for Public Opinion)
Rationality and Society
Social Science Journal (Western Social Science Association)
Social Science Quarterly (Southwestern Social Science Association)
Theory and Society

ANTHROPOLOGY

American Anthropologist (American Anthropological Association)
American Ethnologist (American Ethnological Society)
Critique of Anthropology
Ethnology
Human Organization (Society for Applied Anthropology)
Mankind Quarterly (Institute for the Study of Man)

CRIMINOLOGY/SOCIOLOGY OF LAW

Contemporary Crisis
Crime and Delinquency (National Council on Crime and Delinquency)
Crime, Law and Social Change
Criminal Justice and Behavior (American Association of Correctional Psychologists)
Criminology (American Society of Criminology)
Journal of Criminal Law and Criminology
Journal of Research in Crime and Delinquency (National Council on Crime and Delinquency)
Journal of Quantitative Criminology
Law and Social Inquiry (American Bar Association)
Law and Society Review (Law and Society Association)
Social Justice: A Journal of Crime, Conflict and World Order

RACE/ETHNIC RELATIONS

Ethnic Forum
Ethnic Groups
Ethnic and Racial Studies
Hispanic Journal of Behavioral Sciences
Journal of American Ethnic History
Journal of Black Studies
Negro Educational Review
Phylon: The Atlanta University Review of Race and Culture
Race and Class (Institute of Race Relations)
Review of Black Political Economy (National Economic Association)

COMPARATIVE-HISTORICAL RESEARCH

Comparative Political Studies
Comparative Studies in Society and History
Cross-Cultural Research
Development and Change
Economic Development and Cultural Change
International Journal of Comparative Sociology
International Journal of Contemporary Sociology
International Migration Review
Journal of Cross-Cultural Psychology
Review (Fernand Braudel Center)
Social Science History

POLITICAL SCIENCE/POLITICAL SOCIOLOGY

American Journal of Political Science (Midwest Political Science Association)
American Political Science Review (American Political Science Review)
American Politics Quarterly
British Journal of Political Science
Canadian Journal of Political Science (Canadian Political Science Association; also in French)
Journal of Conflict Resolution
Journal of Political and Military Sociology
Journal of Politics (Southern Political Science Association)
Political Methodology
Political Science Quarterly (Academy of Political Science)
Politics and Society
Review of Radical Political Economics (Union for Radical Political Economics)
Western Political Quarterly (Western Political Science Association)

SOCIOLOGY

Acta Sociologica (Scandinavian Sociological Association)
American Journal of Sociology
American Sociological Review (American Sociological Association)
Australian and New Zealand Journal of Sociology (Australian Sociological Association)
British Journal of Sociology
Canadian Journal of Sociology
Canadian Review of Sociology & Anthropology (Canadian Sociology & Anthropology Association)
Critical Sociology
Current Sociology (International Sociological Association)
European Sociological Review
Humanity and Society (Association for Humanist Sociology)
Rural Sociology (Rural Sociological Society)
Social Forces
Social Problems (Society for the Study of Social Problems)
Social Research
Sociological Focus (North Central Sociological Association)
Sociological Forum (Eastern Sociological Society)
Sociological Imagination (Wisconsin Sociological Association)
Sociological Inquiry (Alpha Kappa Delta, Sociology Honor Society)
Sociological Perspectives (Pacific Sociological Association)
Sociological Practice (Sociological Practice Association)
Sociological Practice Review (American Sociological Association)
Sociological Quarterly (Midwest Sociological Society)
Sociological Review
Sociological Spectrum (Mid-South Sociological Association)
Sociological Theory
Sociology (British Sociological Association)

SOCIAL WORK

Public Welfare (American Public Welfare Association)
Research on Social Work Practice
Scandinavian Journal of Social Welfare
Social Service Review

FIELD RESEARCH (see also ANTHROPOLOGY)

Journal of Contemporary Ethnography
Qualitative Inquiry
Qualitative Sociology

GENDER ISSUES

Feminist Issues
Feminist Review
Feminist Studies
Gender and Society
NWSA Journal (National Women's Studies Association)
Psychology of Women Quarterly (American Psychological Association)
Sex Roles
Women and Politics
Women's Studies Quarterly

QUANTITATIVE RESEARCH METHODS

Journal of Mathematical Sociology
Social Science Research
Sociological Methods and Research

SOCIOLOGY OF EDUCATION/YOUTH

Harvard Educational Review
Sociology of Education (American Sociological Association)
Urban Education

SOCIAL PSYCHOLOGY

Journal of Applied Social Psychology
Journal of Personality and Social Psychology (American Psychological Association)
Journal of Social Psychology
Social Psychology Quarterly (American Sociological Association)
Small Group Research

FAMILY AND YOUTH

Adolescence
Family Process
Journal of Adolescent Research
Journal of Comparative Family Studies
Journal of Marriage and Family (National Council on Family Relations)
Journal of Youth and Adolescence
Marriage and Family Review
Youth and Society